Young Adult Literature in the 21st Century

Pam B. Cole

Kennesaw State University

Mc Graw Hill **Higher Education**

Boston   Burr Ridge, IL   Dubuque, IA   New York   San Francisco   St. Louis
Bangkok   Bogotá   Caracas   Kuala Lumpur   Lisbon   London   Madrid   Mexico City
Milan   Montreal   New Delhi   Santiago   Seoul   Singapore   Sydney   Taipei   Toronto

The McGraw·Hill Companies

Mc Graw Hill Higher Education

This book is printed on acid-free paper.

1 2 3 4 5 6 7 8 9 0 DOC/DOC 0 9 8

ISBN 978-0-07-352593-8
MHID 0-07-352593-6

Editor in Chief: *Michael Ryan*
Editorial Director: *Beth Mejia*
Publisher: *David Patterson*
Sponsoring Editor: *Allison McNamara*
Marketing Manager: *James Headley*
Developmental Editor: *Emily Pecora*
Project Manager: *Amanda Peabody*
Cover Designer: *Margarite Reynolds*
Photo Research: *Natalia Peschiera*
Art Editor: *Sonia Brown*
Production Supervisor: *Louis Swaim*
Composition: *11/12 Bodoni Book by Laserwords*
Printing: *45# New Era Matte Plus, R. R. Donnelley*

Cover: *All photos courtesy of Pam Cole.*

Credits: *The credits section for this book begins on page 667 and is considered an extension of the copyright page.*

Library of Congress Cataloging-in-Publication Data

Cole, Pam.
    Young adult literature in the 21st century/Pam Cole. — 1st ed.

        p. cm.

    Includes bibliographical references and index.
    ISBN-13: 978-0-07-352593-8
    ISBN-10: 0-07-352593-6
    1. Reading (Middle school) 2. Young adult literature—Study and teaching (Middle school) I. Title.

LB1632.C565 2009
428.4071′2—dc22   2008023095

For my son,
Taylor

About the Author

Pam B. Cole is a Distinguished Professor of English Education and Literacy at Kennesaw State University in Kennesaw, Georgia. She is a former high school English teacher and middle school English/reading teacher from Virginia. Recipient of numerous awards for excellence in teaching, scholarship, and professional service, her work has been published widely in English language arts and reading journals and books, including *The ALAN Review, The Journal of Adolescent and Adult Literacy, Voices from the Middle,* and *SIGNAL Journal.* She is a past president of SIGNAL and former editor of *SIGNAL Journal.* She has served as vice president for the Georgia Council of Teachers of English and state conference coordinator. She currently teaches English language arts methods, young adult literature, reading methods and theory, and content area reading in the Clarice C. Bagwell College of Education at Kennesaw State University. She lives in Kennesaw, Georgia, with her son Taylor.

Brief Contents

Contents

Foreword by Chris Crutcher

When I was an adolescent, I made a personal, specific decision to stop reading. I can't be sure where that decision came from: from the fact that my parents loved books and I was a teenager so, well, what better way to say it, Up Yours? Or maybe it was because my teacher kept giving me books I didn't care about and then telling me what they meant. I came from a very small high school in a very small town, so I had the same English teacher all four years. She was quite literate and loved the classics. She had a list of those classics she thought we should read before graduation so we would have an opportunity to share her literacy. I think at least 99 percent of those books were published on Mars. They certainly had nothing to do with me.

My English teacher was a pretty good teacher, and I had no problem with her personally. She thought I was pretty funny—my strong suit at the time, had you asked me—though she did stop laughing way short of what I considered to be my best scatological humor. Although I couldn't have articulated it at the time, I think she didn't respect me academically. Like so many teachers and counselors and coaches—anyone who works with teenagers—she wanted me to hurry up and get where I was going, having little respect for where I *was*. With the exception of *To Kill a Mockingbird*, she didn't give me one book reflecting where I was.

What I love about *Young Adult Literature in the 21st Century* is that it respects its audience. It respects teachers and teachers of teachers and the teenagers about whom adolescent stories are written. And it respects the writers of those stories. This book will introduce you to a number of book titles, amazing in their number and in their diversity. It also will introduce you to a remarkable number of authors, providing not only basic background material but opening windows into their private thoughts and motives for writing what they write.

I have long thought that YA literature is considered the red-headed stepchild of "real" literature and that it is relegated to the same back corner in our culture that we also consign to teenagers. Yet, as a therapist (and as a guy with a good memory), I've seen what an important developmental time adolescence is, and I've seen the emotional and psychological damage done when we don't give it its due. I believe reading and celebrating stories is one of the best ways to explore *any* time, and I believe that within these pages lies a remarkable roadmap for teachers and teenagers and stories.

Young Adult Literature in the 21st Century is also utterly readable. I love the writing style, which is almost conversational and is nearly absent of the academic language that threatened to cause my early exit from higher education. So much of the information comes through story, proving we *can* learn from fiction. It also pays close attention to what teens read. While it focuses largely on traditional young adult literature, it also includes adult literature *and* many of the classics, breaking the barrier now present in schools and teacher education programs.

Preface

This book, like most, has been years in the making. I began my career teaching English in a rural school in the Appalachian Mountains of Virginia in the 1980s. What I enjoyed most, then and now, about teaching was learning from my students. They taught me how to use a computer. They taught me that it was okay to sit on the classroom floor and read a good book or sit on the baseball field and write or wander around in the graveyard behind the school building searching for some thread of inspiration for a poem or short story.

While I was passionate about learning from my students' experiences, I was also ardent about the classics. I realized in no time that many of my students couldn't comprehend the classics and, therefore, couldn't connect with them. That lack of connection created an "I could care less" attitude. Their I could care less attitude quickly became *my* I could care less attitude. If they couldn't read the literature and understand it, what was the point? What was I to do?

It was during this time that I began my own explorations into young adult literature. The first young adult novel I brought into the classroom was S. E. Hinton's *The Outsiders*. Magic occurred with that book. Few students in my class had ever read a complete novel; several read this book in one night. They wanted to discuss it, see the movie, and talk about the broken places in their own lives. The story spoke to the hearts and minds of every student in my 10th grade class. My students were outsiders. They were poor; some were repeating the 10th grade. All of them considered themselves to be on a fast track to nowhere; every single one felt marginalized. To this day, I have no doubt that every student in that class read *The Outsiders* from cover to cover. I also believe that one or two chose to "tough out" high school instead of dropping out as a result of reading and talking about that one story.

I didn't need a graduate degree to realize the power young adult literature had to elevate, excite, engage, and educate young minds. I knew I had found the right tool, so we finished the year out with Richard Peck's *The Pigman* and Robert Newton Peck's *A Day No Pigs Would Die*.

What's in Young Adult Literature in the 21st Century?

Young Adult Literature in the 21st Century places in the hands of teachers a wealth of up-to-date resources that will excite and motivate teens. Unlike other young adult literature texts I've read, this text recognizes a wide range of reading interests and abilities. Thus, titles presented include traditional young adult literature (both new titles and classics), adult books for mature readers, and traditional canonical texts. It also places an emphasis on young adult literature for the content area classroom and picture books appropriate for teens.

Comprehensive Genre Coverage Plus Sound Pedagogical Approaches

I've taught young adult literature for years and, while I've used a variety of textbooks, I've never found one that did what I needed it to do: cover the genres thoroughly *and* provide instructional strategies for teaching reading. I have written a book that bridges that divide, introducing teacher candidates to reading methods for building comprehension, fluency, and vocabulary strategies and introducing teachers to the world of young adult literature *without* sacrificing genre coverage. Through such an approach, English education majors can discuss, analyze, and write about the literature and authors in English class, and they can also explore and practice methods for teaching reading. A quick survey of the chapters will show that most are twofold: they begin by surveying and discussing the genre and close with strategies for teaching three dimensions of reading: comprehension skills, vocabulary, and fluency.[1]

Contributions from Rising and Established Voices in the Young Adult Literature Field

In much the same way that my students have taught me to be a better teacher, I believed I'd be a better author if I listened to the voices of other young adult authors and experts who have created this genre. I reached out to them and received a wonderful set of wise and insightful responses. Author essays provide factual information—describing the challenges of writing within particular genres, addressing the issues facing young adult literature (and young adults) today—and they provide stories that both inspire and teach. Chapter 1 consists entirely of these stories. In describing a defining moment in their own adolescence, 30 authors tell raw and poignant stories about their own life experiences, which mirror the experiences of today's teens. These brief vignettes are indicative of why teens connect with young adult literature.

Young adult novelist and family therapist Chris Crutcher provided a wealth of information and feedback throughout this book and gave generously of his time to write the foreword. His contributions on censorship in Chapter 3 are invaluable. James Blasingame from Arizona State University, co-editor of *The Alan Review,* contributed a chapter on young adult literature and writing (Chapter 13). This chapter demonstrates the interconnectedness of reading and writing and the power young adult literature has to motivate

---

[1]National Reading Panel identifies five dimensions of reading. Not covered in this text are phonics and phonemic awareness. Motivation is often identified as a sixth dimension.

students to think, feel, and write. It also illustrates links between in-school and out-of-school literacies.

In addition, several young adult experts contributed their voices to this effort: Marc Aronson, young adult expert and historian; Patty Campbell, noted young adult literature critic, author, teacher, and librarian; Don Gallo (professor emeritus), Central Connecticut University; Joan Kaywell, University of South Florida; Aaron Levy, Kennesaw State University; and Connie Zitlow (professor emerita), Ohio Wesleyan University.

Extensive Coverage of New and Emerging Genres

Today's young adult literature is evolving with ever-changing technologies and popular culture. Although much of this text covers traditional genres, discussing classic books and traditional text forms, the book also emphasizes emerging genres (e.g., verse novels, multigenre texts). Chapter 12, written by Faith H. Wallace from Kennesaw State University, is dedicated to the influence, and possibilities, of emerging new genres such as fanfiction, manga, graphic novels, and interactive books. Faith's research in environmental literacy, gaming, and out-of-school reading provided a strong framework for a chapter that speaks to the digital age and the influence technology has had on young adult literature. The chapter provides a wealth of resources for incorporating out-of-school reading interests into the traditional curriculum. Clearly, literature reflects an era and our classrooms should as well.

Up-to-Date Annotated Bibliographies

Once a limited genre, young adult literature has grown exponentially since the late 1960s. For the young adult literature novice, studying young adult literature can be akin to walking into a wallpaper store—choices and categories are endless. Teachers need and want guidance. What books work best for middle grades readers? Secondary readers? What are popular themes? Dozens of annotated bibliographies help direct readers to areas of interest. From Shakespeare in Young Adult Literature to Popular Culture and Content Area Learning, abundant bibliographies provide specific, current, and helpful suggestions for further readings.

Acknowledgments

I am indebted to dozens of people who helped bring this book full circle. They inspired, motivated, and challenged me when the work felt daunting. They aided me in collecting information, clarifying ideas, providing feedback and good advice, and preparing the text for publication.

From McGraw-Hill Publishers, I thank David Patterson for his commitment to young adult literature and for making this book possible, and Emily Pecora for her support, patience, and sound guidance. I also thank Kay Mikel, copyeditor, for her keen eye.

The reviewers of this manuscript offered dozens of constructive suggestions:

Jennifer Borek, *University of Memphis*
Carol Butterfield, *Central Washington University*
A. David Cappella, *Central Connecticut State University*
Mona Choucair, *Baylor University*
Leila Christenbury, *Virginia Commonwealth University*
Rebecca Compton, *East Central University*
Thomas Eaton, *Southeast Missouri State University*
Karen Foster, *University of Central Missouri*
Judith Hayn, *Loyola University–Chicago*
Goldie Johnson, *Winona State University*
Jeffrey Kaplan, *University of Central Florida*
Fern Kory, *Eastern Illinois University*
Jim Matthews, *Fairmont State University*
Laura Nicosia, *Montclair State University*
Robert Redmon, *Midwestern State University*
Linda Rice, *Ohio University*
Kia Jane Richmond, *Northern Michigan University*
Suzanna Rose, *Slippery Rock University*
Susan Swords Steffen, *Elmhurst College*
Sylvia Vardell, *Texas Women's University*
Connie Zitlow, *Ohio Wesleyan University*

Nearly 80 young adult authors wrote essays or contributed photos. I am grateful for their interest, candid and heartfelt responses, and passion for this project. Their stories and personal photos have elevated this book.

In addition to contributing a chapter on popular culture, Faith H. Wallace co-wrote Chapter 8, "Science Fiction and Fantasy," with me. She also helped write annotations for Chapter 5, "Romance, Humor, and Sports."

Several graduate and undergraduate KSU students aided in locating resources and writing annotations. I especially thank Julie Schunck, Shanna Carter, Katie Durham, Rebecca Coury, Jamie Strickland, and Mechele Dillard.

My mother, Daisy Burress, a reading specialist and former librarian, provided constructive criticism and helped develop the appendixes.

Finally, my son, Taylor Cole, an honor student at University of Georgia, spent hours locating resources and helping me write annotations.

Adolescence: Defining Moments

Introduction

In a world far removed from the childhood worlds of their parents, today's teens have grown up as our first *safety* generation: they were minivan-riding, car seat infants; kneepad-wearing, helmet-adorned tricycle riders; neon-colored, extra-padded, nonstick Band-Aid wearing champs; and bottled water drinkers—no drinking from the garden hose. They are our first Internet generation and cut their teeth on an explosion of new technologies: they are MySpace, Facebook addicts; ordained MP3 users, and cell-phone-packing kings and queens of text messaging. They IM from within the same room; and snap, load, and print photos in nanoseconds. New communication mediums have given rise to an entirely new way of social networking and a new variety of young adults.

But as much as today's adolescent *world* is different from that of their parents, adolescents themselves are pretty much the same in any time. Without going into dull statistical studies, there is general agreement that the adolescent mind isn't *done* yet. It isn't fully developed and may be incapable of processing information in a way we would like. And it is even clearer that adolescent *emotional* development is also in the process of evolving. It isn't *done* either. Teenagers live in a very selfish (in the nonpejorative sense of the word) phase of their lives. They are immediate and everything is *about* them. Egocentricism is necessary for them to develop into compassionate, empathic beings—the better you know yourself, the better you know yourself in relation to the world around you. Adolescence is a time of firsts: a period of rapid psychological, physical, and social change, a time of uncertainty, roller-coaster emotions, and conflict. It's a stage in which young people are separating from their parents, and trying out the identities they will carry into their adulthoods. That was true of us and it's true of them.

Times change; emotions remain constant. As an introduction to this text and to give you a deeper understanding of this confusing time, a number of young adult authors who are mentioned elsewhere in this text wrote about a defining moment, a life-altering time or experience, big or small, in their own adolescence. Their personal stories are accompanied by the title of one novel that in some way "defined" them as teen writers and Web site information where you can explore their work further. As you will note from the stories that follow, their memories are vivid. Collectively, their responses paint an absorbing portrait of the young adult years. They illustrate the understanding that young adult authors have about adolescent development and the connections they make with young people through story.

Years ago, in Fargo, North Dakota, a teen asked young adult writer Jerry Spinelli if he thought being a kid helped him become a writer. This chapter ends with his response to that question, an incredible lyrical narrative, that "sums up" the deep connection young adult writers have with their audience and the insight and reverence they have for these tender years.

Gary Paulsen
(*Hatchet*)

I'd been wandering the streets one bitter winter evening, waiting for the drunks in the bars to get juiced. I sold newspapers, trying to scrape together a little money and if I waited for the men who hung around in the bars to get a few drinks in them, I could hustle them for extra change.

I stopped in the library to warm up. The librarian noticed me, called me over, and asked if I wanted a library card. Then she handed me a card with my name on it and gave me a book.

Later that night, I took the book, a box of crackers, and a jar of grape jelly down to the basement, to a hideaway I'd created behind the furnace where someone had abandoned a creaky old armchair under a bare light bulb.

That first book must have taken me over a month to finish and I can't even remember the name of that first book. What I do remember about that evening at the library was that it marked the first of many nights the librarian would give me a book. "Here," she'd say,

handing me a few battered volumes, "I think you'll like these."

To learn more about Gary Paulsen, his writing, and contact information, visit Random House's Web site: www.randomhouse.com.

Susan Patron
(*The Higher Power of Lucky*)

It was my first date, and not with some smarmy 8th grader. Tomás was old enough to drive, and virile enough to make my parents say no for two months. My sister Patricia and I finally broke them down (she was 16 to my 13) through relentless pleading and by agreeing to these draconian restrictions:

1. We were to double-date and remain at all times with Patricia and her boyfriend.
2. We were to go *straight* to Olvera Street, a well-populated outdoor tourist attraction that seemed safe from any form of hanky-panky.
3. We were to drive *straight home* by 9:30.

It wasn't only his height and the fact that he shaved that drew me to Tomás. He also sang "Dedicated to the One I Love" and "Harbor Lights" into my ear as we slow-danced in the church basement

on Friday nights, harmonizing in his man's voice with the Shirelles and the Platters. And it was the way he ground his leg between my thighs as we danced, and

Continued

Susan Patron
(*The Higher Power of Lucky*)   *Continued*

then had to go outside for a while. Patricia explained that it was because he had a boner. I had a vague but thrilling idea what this meant: Although I was pathetically undeveloped, especially in comparison with my voluptuous sister, Tomás found me to be unbearably, even painfully sexy. I considered this a miracle.

They picked us up at our Spanish bungalow house in Hollywood. Tomás drove a 1955 powder-blue Cadillac convertible in cherry condition. With the top down. I prayed (in vain) that Jerry Sue or the Tyler twins would be out watering the lawn or washing their dad's car or something, so as to see me in my incredible, incomparable glory.

We drove downtown, where nobody ever went on dates. Olvera Street had long been considered by Patricia and me to be tacky beyond comment, a cheap tourist trap. But now it was transformed into an ultra-cool kind of tacky, which allowed us to view it with sophisticated detachment as we strolled along. For a date, it was original and even daring—not some cliché show-offy cruise down Hollywood Boulevard or a burger at Ship's. From one of the tiny vendor stalls, Tomás bought me a woven fringed shawl in muted brown tones; I slung it artfully over my shoulders and was sure I looked, not like some old granny, but hip. Quintessentially hip.

Then, as we wandered along the crowded cobblestone street, a great splat of something viscous and plentiful landed on my head. My fingers came away grayish-white.

"Oh, God!" Patricia said, utter horror on her face. We rushed into a nearby café and she pulled me to the bathroom in the back. "What is it?" I cried, unable to imagine what the stuff was in my hair.

"Pigeon shit," she said, and yes, she laughed. But she realized, too, how mortifying my situation was. She put my head under the faucet and let the water run a good long while before she would touch the mess. Then she got it all out, every globby bit. Pigeon shit is much more copious than you might think.

My hair was long and straight and Patricia said it looked pretty much the same either wet or dry. Nevertheless we used 900 paper towels for blotting. She inspected me carefully. I would have cried from humiliation when we re-emerged if the guys had pretended they hadn't known what happened. Instead they ground out their cigarettes and Tomás put an arm around me, laughing. "Life in L.A.," he said philosophically, which, it occurred to me, is probably how Sartre or e.e. cummings would have summed it up. "Exactly," I said, a woman-of-experience who now knew the difference between shat upon as a child and being shat upon as a worldly person on a date.

Tomás didn't last very long. But for the next two years, through epochs of other boyfriends (none of whom could touch Tomás's amazing pelvis-grinding slow-dance technique) I wore the shawl to junior high. It was my badge of separation from trite and juvenile clothing trends. It proclaimed that I was an existentialist and a poet, or maybe a novelist; someone, anyway, who could be sexy without trying.

To learn more about Susan Patron, her writing, and contact information, visit Simon & Schuster's Web site: www.simonsays.com.

Lois Lowry
(*The Giver*)

Thinking about it, I realize that a life-changing experience, for a young person, at least, so often involves a betrayal. I suppose that's part of growing up: realizing that things, and people, are not always what you thought, or wished, or hoped.

For me, the time came when I was 12, and a student at the American School in Tokyo, where I then lived. It was 4 years after the end of World War II but Tokyo was still a ruined place, its population very poor and struggling, under the U.S. occupation.

Continued

Lois Lowry
(*The Giver*) *Continued*

I rode to school each day on a bus filled with other American kids, most of them older than I, most of them high school students. I was in eighth grade, and young for eighth grade, at 12.

It was Christmas season, and school vacation would start soon. That December morning when we boarded the bus, its driver, a quiet middle-aged Japanese man, usually impassive, was smiling proudly. I took my usual seat near the front and looked around to see why. He had decorated the bus for the holiday. Garish ornaments, bright Christmas trees, Santa Clauses, candy canes, and long ropes of shiny red and green twisted paper were hanging from the window tops and draped festively down the length of the bus's ceiling.

It surprises me to remember my first two thoughts because I think they were unusual and perceptive for a 12-year-old. One was that the bus driver was very likely non-Christian. The maids in my family's household were Buddhist and Shinto. So, probably, was this man, whose name I didn't know. And yet he had hung celebratory decorations for our Christian holiday. I was touched by that.

I thought, too, that it had been a sacrifice for him. I knew that our school would not have paid for or supplied those silly, flimsy stars and Santas and snowmen. So the driver had used his own money, his hard-earned yen, to do this; no wonder the look on his face was one of pride. I could see his eyes in the rear-view mirror from where I sat. I found myself watching his face each time the bus stopped to take on new students, and I could see that he waited with delight for their reactions to his little surprise.

When all the passengers had been boarded, the bus continued on from Shibuya, where I lived, to Meguro and our school. A high school boy seated in the back, a loud-mouthed boy named Bob (and after 58 years I still remember his last name but I won't write it here) very suddenly tore down one of the hanging trinkets and, laughing, threw it at another boy. Then he did it again, throwing another ornament at someone else. And it became contagious. The high school boys tore and shredded all the Christmas

decorations, throwing them around the bus until the tatters covered the floor.

It couldn't have lasted a long time, though it seemed forever. It seemed forever that I sat mutely in my seat, and my eyes met the eyes of the driver in that mirror. We looked at each other, and I hoped then, and have hoped until this day, that he could see in my look the kind of shame and sympathy I felt. The loud shouts and wild merriment played itself out, and at the end of it all the decorations were destroyed and we had pulled up to our school. The driver opened the door and sat silently, ignored as always, as the students left the bus.

I was among them.

And that sentence is why this 30 minutes in 1949 remains as a life-changing incident in my memory. I spoke of betrayal in the first paragraph. Of course this was an ugly-American betrayal of courtesy and respect, and what those teenaged boys did was unspeakably awful. But I remember this as my own betrayal of my own self, my first remembered failure to act on my own beliefs, to stand up honorably and speak out for what would have been right.

I hope I learned from it.

To learn more about Lois Lowry, her writing, and contact information, visit her official Web site: www.loislowry.com.

David Klass
(You Don't Know Me)

When I was 13, my parents took us on a family trip to Mexico. Early one morning, when my whole family was still asleep at our beachside hotel, I walked down the dunes and went for a swim in the Pacific.

Dawn had broken but the sky was still dark. The surf roared in and broke hard on a sandy beach. I swam out through the breakers, and enjoyed the feeling of being alone on the vast ocean, a strong 13-year-old swimmer who had mastered the waves.

Then I tried to swim back. I fought my way close to shore, but a powerful riptide swept me back out to sea. I tried a second time, and then a third, with the same result. No one was on the beach. The hotel was a distant shadow atop the dunes. I could feel myself weakening.

For the first time in my life I thought I was going to die. Right there, within sight of the beach, and my body might never be found. My parents and sisters would wake up and search long and hard, but they would never find me. I would simply be gone.

Somehow, in the panic of the moment, I remembered reading that the worst thing a swimmer can do is keep fighting a riptide. The right thing to do is to swim parallel to shore for a while, till one finds a better spot to clamber out.

I swam for half-a-mile, rounded a point, and was at the last ebb of my strength when I found a sheltered cove and staggered out through the surf.

I never told my parents, because I thought they would be angry with me. But I also never looked at the world quite the same way again. The confidence and invulnerability of childhood had been shattered by the waves.

Oh, and one more thing. It's been 34 years and from that day to this I've never again gone swimming in the ocean alone.

To learn more about David Klass, his writing, and contact information, visit the Farrar, Straus & Giroux Web site: www.fsgkidsbooks.com.

Jerry Spinelli
(Maniac Magee)

When I was 12, I was on the small side, friendly, no troublemaker. I was the class "nice guy." I didn't push myself on anyone. I was happy to do things your way, not mine. But for reasons that still are not clear to me, something inside wanted to assert a different kind of me. Something inside wanted, if only for a minute, to get a taste of what it was like to be a bully, to be the one doing the pushing.

So one day as Joey Stackhouse and I were walking home after school, I decided to get my taste. Joey and I were pals. He was small like me. If anything, he weighed less than me. He was no threat. Somewhere along the 700 hundred block of George Street—the sidewalks were brick then—I argued with Joey. He didn't know it, but it was a setup. I just

Continued

Jerry Spinelli
(*Maniac Magee*)   *Continued*

wanted to create a context, a reason to ball my fist. And that's what I did. I acted as if something he said really ticked me off and I wound up and socked him in the jaw. I can still feel the surprising hardness of bone against my knuckles. In truth, I barely tapped him, only enough to once and for all find out what it felt like to hit someone. But you might have thought I had hit Joey with a sledgehammer. His eyes boggled in shock. This was the last thing he had ever expected his friend to do. And then he surprised me again—he cried. And cried out: "Wha'd ya do that for?" And he ran off.

And I just stood there, and that secret bully in me is still standing there more than 50 years later, knowing he is not welcome on the journey I have taken since that day.

To learn more about Jerry Spinelli, his writing, and contact information, visit his official Web site: www.jerryspinelli.com.

Lauren Myracle
(*ttyl*)

When I was 16, I would drive to Steve Curtis's house, park my car, and sit there for hours, wishing I had the nerve to walk up his driveway, knock on his door, and kiss him. But was it the kiss I was really after? No. I was a kissing wimp. In fact, I was a wimp in general. Steve, however, was not. Steve—at least to my eye—was full of guitar-playing passion and intense philosophical insights, and what I lusted for was his "aliveness." I wanted to know who I was. I wanted to radiate that self-knowledge from every pore.

When I think back about being a teenager, that's what comes to mind: that crazy-hungry drive to stretch beyond the limits of my awkward, confused, cramped little life. To get out of the car, for heaven's sake, and walk up the driveway. To knock on the door and announce to Steve, "There is more to me than you think. There is more to me than *I* think." And

then maybe I'd kiss him, or maybe I wouldn't. Maybe I'd simply turn and stride away, soul wide open to the world.

To learn more about Lauren Myracle, her writing, and contact information, visit her official Web site: www.laurenmyracle.com.

Walter Dean Myers
(*The Glory Field*)

The defining moment for me was when, at 14, I invited my best friend to my house and, while I was raiding the refrigerator for something to eat, he found my mother drunk on the floor. At that point I realized that what I had suspected for so long, that my parents were no longer to be the "safe shore" of my life, was now fact. I wasn't yet capable of supporting myself financially, but I knew that I had to find a way to support myself emotionally. It took all of my strength, all of my inner resources, to get through the next 2 years. I had nothing left over for study, nothing for social activity, nothing with which to plan my life. My grades plummeted, I withdrew from society, nearly from life, and dropped out of school. I plunged myself into books, and writing, and self-examination. On my 17th birthday I joined the army.

During my life I have recovered from chicken pox, scarlet fever, depression, and a plethora of male emergency room incidents. I have yet to recover from adolescence.

To learn more about Walter Dean Myers, his writing, and contact information, visit his official Web site: www.walterdeanmyers.net.

Anthony Horowitz
(*Stormbreaker*)

I had the great misfortune, when I was 8 years old, to be sent to a private boarding school called Orley Farm in North London. I was there until I was 13. This meant that, for the crucial years of my adolescence, I was in a completely weird, unnatural environment. For a start, there were no girls. But even worse than that, the head teacher was allowed to beat us with a cane (which he did, regularly) and many of the other teachers were real bullies who knew they had complete power over us and used it, mercilessly.

It's no exaggeration to say that a very large part of my adolescence was therefore spent in an atmosphere of fear and violence. And my parents actually paid for it! That was the weirdest thing of

Continued

Anthony Horowitz
(*Stormbreaker*)   *Continued*

all. Would you spend huge sums of money to send your kids to a place where they were obviously unhappy? Where the start of each term was greeted by tears and hysterics? My parents died when I was quite young so to this day I don't quite know what possessed them to send me to Orley Farm—and not to let me leave.

I have many memories about my time there and pretty much all of them are bad, but here's the worst one of all. I still have nightmares about it today.

I was not a good boy. According to my old school reports, I was lazy and uncooperative. "Able but idle" was how one teacher summed it up. The fact is that I was bottom in almost every class. I didn't show any aptitude for anything—except writing stories and for a long time nobody noticed that. More than that, I was always in trouble. I have a theory that just as some people catch the flu more easily than others, there are kids who attract trouble and it seems to stick to them whilst avoiding everybody else.

I'm not talking serious stuff. If a ball smashed a window, it would be discovered that I was the one who'd kicked it. If someone's homework got lost, it would inevitably be mine. Talking in class? Me again. Somehow, with me, the simplest mistake turned into a major crime. And gradually the punishments mounted up. Lines (having to write out the same sentence a hundred times). Early morning runs. Cold baths. Beatings.

And gradually, I got a reputation. That's another thing that happens in schools. There's this kid, like me, a magnet who attracts all this unwelcome attention until people actually *expect* him to do something bad. It's a bit like Bart Simpson but for me there was nothing to laugh about. Teachers scowled at me when they saw me coming. They expected me to misbehave and often, for that very reason, I did.

Anyway, the memory . . .

The school was divided into houses and each house had a league table. You earned stars for good behavior and black marks for bad behavior. At the end of the term, the house with the most stars and the least black marks got a prize.

It was three days before the end of the Christmas term and it hadn't escaped my attention that I had more black marks than anyone else at the school. But I hadn't expected what happened that day at breakfast. The assistant headmaster, a man called Mr. Priestman, asked me to stand up. I did. Suddenly all the eyes of the school were turned on me.

Mr. Priestman explained to me—and to the whole school—that I had the most bad marks and that, as a result, they were going to cancel Christmas for me. I would not come to the Christmas party that evening. I would not take part in Christmas games. That was it. Sit down again. Now pass the bacon . . .

I'm sorry if you were expecting something more vicious or bloody. There were plenty of those incidents too at Orley Farm. But I still remember that breakfast to this day. First, there was the humiliation. To be singled out like that, without any warning, in front of all my friends. Then there was the misery of being ostracized, particularly at a time designed to bring people together. But above all there was the sense of injustice. I knew that a great many of those black marks hadn't really been deserved. I knew that the school, the teachers, had an image of me that wasn't actually true. Inside me, even then, was the writer that I am now. But on that day, I think he came closest to being crushed.

To this day, I have one strong belief about adolescents and young people in general. You have to believe in them, trust them and do everything you can to encourage them. Because there is no such thing in the world as an entirely bad kid. That was what Orley Farm thought about me. They were wrong.

To learn more about Anthony Horowitz, his writing, and contact information, visit his official Web site: www.anthonyhorowitz.com.

Chris Crutcher
(Staying Fat for Sarah Byrnes)

In July of 1958, eight days after my 12th birthday, I pick up *The Saturday Evening Post* off the living room coffee table and open it to a picture that puts goose bumps on my goose bumps. I can't figure out why the picture freaks me out; it's just a head shot of a 6-year-old above a caption, "Have you seen this boy?"

Only I read a little farther and discover the picture is postmortem, a word soon-to-be, but not yet, branded into my vocabulary. The boy was wrapped in a blanket and placed in an appliance box, then left in a vacant lot in Philadelphia. It was Christmas time—cold—so no one knew how long the boy had been there, though the college kid who discovered him said he was pretty sure the box hadn't been there when he drove by a week earlier. The authorities doctored the picture to make the boy look closer to the way he looked when he was alive, but the eyes were *dead*. I read further to discover the Philadelphia police had sent that picture out with all the utility and telephone bills shortly after the body was found, with not a single viable response.

I can't take my eyes off that picture. First I pretend it doesn't bother me. Then I pretend it's funny. By the time I've been in bed a half hour I am sure the kid is in the cedar chest in my closet or creeping up the stairs, or floating in the air right outside my second story window. By ten o'clock I'm sneaking across the hall to my brother's room, begging him to let me sleep with him. He puts up with that for about 10 minutes before kicking me onto the floor. I spend the rest of the night in my parents' bed, embarrassed that, at 12, I need to sleep with them, but more than willing to sacrifice my dignity for the chance to be away from my room where that little bastard can haunt me, or where whoever did that to him could do it to me.

For the rest of the summer my morning ritual includes lying in bed until I hear my mother leave the house, rising to scour the far reaches for where she hid the magazine, then sitting on the couch maintaining constant eye contact with Mondo Horrifico until it is time for lunch.

Each night I crawl under the covers so far I'm lucky not to fall out at the foot of the bed and stay until I'm breathing coal miner's air then come up and sleep 10 minutes at a time for about six hours, praying the sun will come up. After about a week of that, I tell my parents I want to start preparing for my Boy Scout camping merit badge and will sleep on the lawn for the rest of the summer. Now if something sick and wrong wants to pull you out of bed and beat you to death it would be a lot easier to get you on your front lawn than in your second story bedroom, but something about the openness gives me hope. I can at least jump up and run. Plus that damned cedar chest in my closet, which looks exactly like a coffin in my imagination, is a lot further away.

The boy in the box leaks into everything. A girl in Boise named Charlene Zahn is kidnapped. Her picture in the Post Office joins the unknown boy's picture in my head to form a ghoulish duo that tracks me like zombies in a B-grade movie.

My mother notices each afternoon that I didn't put *The Saturday Evening Post* back exactly as I found it; knows I've been obsessing. She'd throw it away, but we have consecutive *Saturday Evening Posts* dating back before World War II. They will be valuable someday. My father shows me how far it is from Cascade, Idaho, to Philadelphia, Pennsylvania. We walk around the outside of the house so he can show me how difficult it would be to get into my room; window screens, inside locks. What he doesn't understand is, rational thought has no place here. I have seen a dead kid. He's younger than I am. He was there one day and then not. I am no longer safe. I'll never be safe again.

To learn more about Chris Crutcher, his writing, and contact information, visit his official Web site: www.chriscrutcher.com.

James Patterson
(*Maximum Ride: The Angel Experiment*)

When I was a boy, I lived in a small town on the Hudson River. During the summers, my grandfather would take me on his frozen food and ice cream delivery route once a week.

These trips were a treat for me. We'd be up at four in the morning packing his truck, and before five we'd be on our way.

Now, most of us know that driving a delivery truck isn't the most romantic job in the world. But every morning, my grandfather would drive over the Storm King mountain toward West Point, and he'd be **singing at the top of his voice.** His big, clumsy truck would be jouncing all over the road—and in a loud, terrible voice he'd sing "O Susannah, or Put Another Nickel in the Nickelodeon, or Coming 'Round the Mountain."

And my grandfather told me this: "Jim," he said, "when you grow up, I don't care if you're a truck driver or a famous surgeon—just remember that when you go over the mountain to work in the morning, **you've got to be singing.**"

It took me some time to find out my daily journey was going to involve writing books. In fact, I was working my way through college at a hospital outside Cambridge, Massachusetts—the nightshift.

I started reading everything I could get my hands on—Proust, Flaubert, Jean Genet, lots of theater. That's when I fell in love with books and writing.

And, ever since, even if my wife and son ask me not to do it so early—or so loudly—I've been singing every morning.

To learn more about James Patterson, his writing, and contact information, please visit his official Web site: www.jamespatterson.com.

Nancy Holder
(*Buffy the Vampire Slayer* Series)

When I was in middle school and high school, my father was chief of psychiatry at Yokosuka Naval Base in Japan. Every single chance I got, I went to the hospital movie theater to watch horror movies. It was an enormous Quonset hut. There we were, Captain Jones's kid and 300 men in dark blue pajamas, blue-and-white-striped seersucker bathrobes, and blue flip flops. The night before the first day of school, which was also my birthday, the guys and I watched *Hush, Hush, Sweet Charlotte,* starring Bette Davis. After it was over, I was so terrified I ran all the way home. I couldn't sleep at all, and as it was August, I listened to the mosquitoes buzzing over the thundering of my heart for hours. Then I had to get up for school and try to look like I hadn't spent the night in a clothes dryer with my

hair in a blender. It was the best birthday of my life so far.

To learn more about Nancy Holder, her writing, and contact information, visit her official Web site: www.nancyholder.com.

Will Weaver
(*Striking Out*)

I grew up in a divided house. My mother was deeply religious. My father, a farmer, believed in his own two hands and the work they could do: draw fence wires tight, build square corners, steer a tractor arrow-straightly down the field.

I tried to please them both, but my mother's manner, gentler and more accommodating, gradually won out. Along about 9 or 10 years old, I came to think that she might be right—that the Bible was stronger than any tractor. That life would be simpler and easier if I let go of my fears and accepted Jesus Christ.

One night she sensed I had a troubled, tender heart. Though I was far too old for bedtime stories, she came to my room and read me a couple of chapters from the New Testament. It was quite remarkable; I could feel the power of Jesus's life filling my little upstairs bed room.

When she was finished, she only smiled, tucked me in and said "Good Night." As she went down the steep stairs, I sat up as if to speak. I was going to say, "But is it true?"

Most certainly she would have replied, "Yes," and my life would have changed forever. But I couldn't say the words, and then she was gone downstairs, and the moment was lost.

In the morning, when I set about my chores, the sky felt lower, the dairy barn smaller, my fork and shovel heavier. I felt a sadness inside me, one that I knew would never go away.

To learn more about Will Weaver, his writing, and contact information, visit his official Web site: www.willweaverbooks.com.

Laurie Halse Anderson
(*Speak*)

My first three years of high school were hellish for a whole bunch of reasons. My father was unemployed, suicidal, and alcoholic. My mother was working constantly to keep a roof over our heads. We moved, and moved again, and moved again. I didn't know anyone in the new town and my new school was filled with stuck-up jerks. Overnight, it felt like my life and family had been stolen, and I was shoved into a nightmare. Oh, and people kept yelling at me because I wasn't "living up to my academic potential."

Pu-leeze.

So I decided to escape. Running away was an option, but the long-term consequences were icky. I didn't want to end up on a milk carton. I wasn't smart or motivated enough to graduate early. I wasn't allowed to get my driver's license because we

couldn't afford the insurance, so getting a job was a challenge. What was left?

Leaving the country, of course. So that's what I did.

Continued

Laurie Halse Anderson
(*Speak*)   *Continued*

I became a foreign exchange student with the American Field Service program. It took every dime I had saved for four years. Three weeks after my last final of my junior year of high school, my parents drove me to the airport. I was leaving for 13 months, flying to Denmark, a country I could barely find on a map. I was going to live on a pig farm with people who could not speak English. In addition to helping around the farm, I would be going to school. Yet another new school. I figured if people were mean to me there, at least I wouldn't be able to understand what they were saying.

I was completely terrified.

I spent the night before I left sobbing so much that my voice became ragged and raw. My parents cried all morning. (My little sister, it must be noted, was not unhappy at all.) We drove to the airport and checked in my luggage. Stood around watching the clock tick off the last minutes of my childhood. My boyfriend showed up, unexpectedly, which made me cry again. And finally, they announced that my plane was boarding.

I hugged everyone for the last time. My father held my face and looked into my eyes. "You can change your mind," he said. "If you want to stay, you can stay."

This was my father; my hero, the biggest person in my life. He was the world to me—a genius, a mountain climber, a storyteller, a sage. Yes, he drank too much, and he had made some huge mistakes that really hurt the family but he loved us, and I was ready to forgive him every single day.

"No, Daddy," I said. "It's time for me to go."

I wiped my eyes on his shirt, took a deep breath and walked to the door. I turned around once to wave good-bye, but I was crying so hard, I couldn't see them through my tears. And then I walked to the plane.

And then I started to grow up.

To learn more about Laurie Halse Anderson, her writing, and contact information, visit her official Web site: www.writerlady.com.

Will Hobbs
(*Bearstone*)

Every time I try to imagine a new young adult novel, I search for a way to spring the protagonist. Getting out on your own and trying out your wings is what adolescence is all about. My feelings and impressions from that age remain exceptionally vivid. Leaving home on my own, for example, for the entire summer when I was 15. Boarding the 'hound in sweltering San Antonio, waving good-bye to my family as the bus turns the corner and heads north. The plains of west Texas rolling by endlessly, my expectation rising by the mile, the uncertainty, the freedom, the sense of boundless possibility. There they are at last, looming on the horizon: the Sangre de Cristo Mountains of northern New Mexico. A job is waiting for me working in a remote camp at Philmont Scout Ranch. I'll be living outdoors all summer, actually earning a paycheck, with responsibilities to live up to and who knows what sort of adventures. I step off the bus and breathe deep of the dry, cool mountain air. I don't

know much, but I know these are the first steps along the path to the person I want to become.

To learn more about Will Hobbs, his writing, and contact information, visit his official Web site: www.willhobbsauthor.com.

Jack Gantos
(Joey Pigza Swallowed the Key)

When I turned 14, I wanted a job where I could make money because I already knew that money was the way in which I could separate myself from my parents. I desperately wanted not to be at their mercy and without money of my own I remained stuck in the needy role of a baby crying for milk every time I wanted something, rather than being a boy who could take on a man's job and get it himself. So I went down to the Winn-Dixie (in Plantation, Florida) and got a job as a bag-boy. The pay was next to nothing. Tips were ten cents if you were lucky. The manager was a redfaced drunk who passed out one night in the stock room with a lit cigar and caught the building on fire. By then I had worked there a year and had saved up a few bucks. I took a job at Publix Market—a bit more upscale—the pay was twenty cents more per hour and tips were averaging about a quarter. I kept saving. And saving. And finally the day came when my MONEY EQUALS POWER mantra cashed in. My parents moved from Florida to Puerto Rico. I had stayed down there for a while working construction with my dad's company, then moved back up to Florida on my own to finish my senior year in high school. After getting off to a rocky start living with some of my parents' friends, I decided to take a crack at living on my own. I was 16. I bought a car. I rented a cheap room in an old motel. I bought my own clothes, and food. I worked forty hours a week and kept my grades up as best I could. My life was not ideal. I worked long hours. There were times of great loneliness. I was not

a jock or a nerd or an artsy kid. I didn't play sports or fantasy board games or sing in musical theater. There were times when I made stupid mistakes—bad friends and bad behavior. But it was my life and I was living it my way and I figured—rightly—that eventually choosing to be independent was more than just about having the money to do so—it was the personal freedom that came with it. My time was my own. My thoughts were my own. I read what I wanted. I invented myself every which way I could. It was all about me figuring out how to take control of my own life. For me, adolescence was defined by the unrelenting effort to find myself. I'm not sure if I succeeded, but the quest was a brilliant ride and the experience has always enriched my adult life.

To learn more about Jack Gantos, his writing, and contact information, visit his official Web site: www.jackgantos.com.

Alex Sanchez
(Rainbow Boys)

When I was five, my family emigrated from Mexico to Texas. I started school speaking Spanish. For the first time in my life I experienced prejudice for my being different.

Fortunately, however, my teachers never made me feel inadequate or inferior. With their help, I worked hard to learn English. My school librarian and third-grade teacher especially inspired me by reading

aloud to us. And though none of the schoolbooks portrayed Mexican people like me, I developed a love of stories.

In order to fit in, I stopped speaking Spanish and learned to pass as white, hoping others would like and accept me. By the time I reached junior high, I had buried a core part of myself: my Mexican

Continued

Alex Sanchez
(*Rainbow Boys*) *Continued*

heritage. I was no longer different. Or so I thought. Then came the biggest challenge of my life.

I was 13 (in eighth grade) when I read an article in our local newspaper about being gay. Immediately, I knew that's what I was. Going through puberty, I'd kissed girls and also boys. I liked both but knew which my heart yearned for. And I hated myself for it.

I had learned to believe that being gay was the worst thing in the world a boy could be. One boy at my school who was obviously different in his appearance and mannerisms was labeled "queer" and consequently got beat up every day. I stood by, silently watching, wishing I had the courage to stand up for him. But I feared if I did say anything, people might suspect I was gay too.

After school, alone in my room, I would tell myself, "I'm not going to feel this way. I refuse to let this happen to me."

And just as I'd learned to hide I was Mexican, I learned to hide I was gay.

To learn more about Alex Sanchez, his writing, and contact information, visit his official Web site: www.alexsanchez.com.

Ruth White
(*Belle Prater's Boy*)

My first love and first heartbreak came to me when I was around 16. We will call him Sam. It was devastating. Most adults do not realize the depths of despair teenagers feel at times like these, but one wise old aunt did see my pain and counseled with me.

"You think because this boy has rejected you, you are worthless," she said to me. "You have given away your power to him. You have let him define who you are. Don't you know what Sam thinks of you is not important at all? It's what you think of yourself that counts. I know it doesn't feel that way now when you are so wounded, but please remember the most significant relationship you will ever have is with yourself."

I would like to say that it was a bright and shining moment in which everything changed and I wiped Sam from my mind. But it is not so. It was a softly lit and subtle moment in which I grew intellectually

without even realizing it. I still prayed for Sam to love me again, and I went through the whole grieving process before the healing came at last.

My aunt's words, however, stayed and paved the way for me as I grew up. They gave me comfort and

Continued

Ruth White
(*Belle Prater's Boy*)   *Continued*

hope, and I began to internalize their meaning—that there is nothing and no one outside myself to give my life meaning. Everything is within. That's why self-acceptance, self-respect and self-esteem are far more valuable than any kind of love from another.

These are ideas and ideals I would like to get across to young people in their most vulnerable years when they are inundated with romantic drivel on television, movies and especially in music, which encourages their feelings of inadequacy. Take for example these self-flagellating song lyrics that have brain-washed several generations:

> *How am I supposed to live without you?*
> *I have nothing if I don't have you.*
> *You're nothing 'til somebody loves you.*

> *It's the end of the world, it ended when you said*
> *goodbye.*
> *Can't live if living is without you.*

Many years and many relationships later I met Sam again quite by accident. We greeted each other warmly. Oh, yes, he had aged well. He was as handsome as I remembered him, and still had that winning smile. But he remained in the same place I had found him those many years ago—not physically, but spiritually. He had not changed. In other words he had not grown at all. He had stood still.

And what was I thinking at that moment? *Thank God for unanswered prayers!*

To learn more about Ruth White, her writing, and contact information, visit her official Web site: www.ruthwhite.net.

Paul Volponi
(*Black and White*)

I grew up in the shadow of Rikers Island in New York City. The jail is set behind an obscure avenue, hidden and hard to find. As a teen walking the streets with a basketball tucked under my arm, cars would come up to me constantly. The people inside would ask, "How do you get to Rikers Island?" This got to be so annoying to me and my friends that I came up with a smart mouth response. How do you get to Rikers? Rob a bank. My friends would howl over that response. But I couldn't do it to the real people who asked. They seemed so helpless, admitting to a stranger in the street that they were lost and needed to visit someone they loved in jail. I never noticed as a kid, but all the people who stopped and asked were either black or Hispanic. Maybe 10 years later, I took a job teaching teens to read and write on Rikers. That's when I saw it clearly. In a city that's fairly even along racial lines, some 95 percent of teens on Rikers are black or Hispanic. And that grew into the basis for my novel *Black and White*. What if two friends,

one black and one white, committed the same crime at the same time, giving them equal guilt? And what if the white teen was holding the gun? How would that story turn out?

To learn more about Paul Volponi, his writing, and contact information, visit his official Web site: www.paulvolponibooks.com.

Joan Bauer
(*Hope Was Here*)

It wasn't that I wasn't smart—I was.

It wasn't that I didn't want to succeed—I did.

But that long, awful sophomore year I felt like an overweight blob of defeat. I had problems at home, problems with my alcoholic dad who was on his fourth wife, problems with my grades, my emotions, my friends. I hated being 15.

My high school guidance counselor was a wise man—he took a nontraditional approach with me. He didn't say, "You need more time to study, Joan," he said, "You need a job." And he helped me get one—as a waitress at the local International House of Pancakes.

There is something powerful about a fresh beginning in the middle of a stale season. I'm not sure to this day I know how to fully explain what that job did for me. I'd felt like a failure as a sophomore, but as a waitress I felt like a star. Where I'd felt like a lumbering buffalo in gym class, at the IHOP I was good on my feet. I didn't brood on the weekends—I went to work. I made great money, dealt with a radical cook (he was a Black Panther; we became friends). I learned restaurant diplomacy and how to talk back to that old voice of discouragement:

"You're a loser, Joan; you can't do anything right; you're bad; you're an embarrassment."

"Oh yeah? Then how come I'm succeeding here? How come everyone seems to like me?"

I could feel good when I'd help an overwhelmed mom with her little children, smile at a lonely old man who needed to talk, keep up with my regulars who'd make a point to sit in my station.

That job didn't make my problems go away, but it did make something go away in me—I saw I was likable, competent, good with people, could earn real money and compete in the adult world.

You just never know what strengths you're developing when you don't give in to giving up. In case you've ever wondered if pancakes are good for you—trust me, they are.

To learn more about Joan Bauer, her writing, and contact information, visit her official Web site: www.joanbauer.com.

Naomi Shihab Nye
(*Habibi*)

From earth . . .

comes the bleeding berry, reaching arm of tomato, twisted vine. I promise you. First there will be dirt, then a shining line of corn tassels, neighborhood of grapes, burgeoning jewels. All from the ground up. *And who are you among them?* Reach in through prickly leaves to slice the stem. The boys I worked with lived across the black/white line in the borough that only grown-ups could see. First time we'd met. *May I use your knife?* We poured water over each other's hands. Years later, no line, not one house is missing. Oh! You can know what makes a plant easier than a person. To carry squash in a bucket. Human in relation to corn. Human in relation to empty bushel baskets stacked in barn.

Continued

Naomi Shihab Nye
(*Habibi*)   *Continued*

Human in relation to husk. *And what will you say years later when they keep asking you why you're attracted to "ordinary objects"?* Even before I worked on the farm, my mother pulled us down the hill in a wagon, tomatoes stacked in our laps. The seed of that early someone must travel in me now, flicker of light still shaping, tiny as an echo poured through a pipe—*what will you make make make of your lives?*

Reprinted with permission from *Mint Snowball.*

To learn more about Naomi Shihab Nye, her writing, and contact information, visit the HarperCollins Web site: www.harpercollinschildrens.com.

T.A. Barron
(*The Lost Years of Merlin* Epic)

The experience changed my life. It was warped, brutal, stressful, discouraging—and ultimately triumphant. It happened when I was 13 years old, just starting seventh grade. And it came in the form of a single word:

No.

For years, practically since I was old enough to hold a crayon, I'd played around with creative writing. I composed poetry, exploring rhymes, free verse, and haiku. I tried nature writing (a good excuse to spend a day outside under a ponderosa pine tree by the creek on my family's Colorado ranch). I wrote wacky, dreamlike stories, complete with equally wacky illustrations. I sprayed puns as constantly as a fountain sprays water. I wrote a few plays—one of them, a musical about the Beatles, was so screechy that any listeners cringed and grabbed their ear plugs. I crafted my first fantasy tales, often parodies of life at school. (And, bizarre as school was, I had plenty of material.) I even drew some pictures-only stories, what would now be called graphic novels.

Then, about to enter the trackless wilderness of middle school, I decided to create my own magazine.

Full of offbeat humor, silly satire, nutty news, and horrendously bad jokes—and, of course, the illustrations of an unknown graphic novelist—I decided to call it *The Idiot's Odyssey.* Purely for fun, I drafted a mock issue. For the cover story, I wrote a mock investigative report titled "Games Teachers Play: What Do Teachers Really Do In Their Free Time?" (I restrained

Continued

T.A. Barron
(*The Lost Years of Merlin* Epic)   *Continued*

my more blasphemous inklings . . . and just poked clean fun at some well-known characters.)

Even where my jokes flopped disastrously, one quality came through every page of this little magazine. Delight. In creating, in laughing at life, and in sharing that good humor with others.

And so I decided to publish *The Idiot's Odyssey*. I asked the school secretary if I could use the copy machine. She frowned at me, took a look at my sample copy, frowned more deeply, and spoke the word I'd hear many times.

"No." (Actually, her exact words were "No way." Accompanied by a glare that could freeze a pot of hot coffee.)

Undeterred, I asked the journalism teacher, who wore spectacles as big as saucers. She curled her nose, straightened her spectacles, and delivered her verdict. "No."

The gym teacher, who happened to live near my family's ranch, had access to a small printing press. Catching him after cross-country practice, I asked for permission to print my little project. "No."

My Boy Scout leader had a job at an office with a whole room of copy machines. Wouldn't he value the initiative and creativity behind this publication? After all, those qualities were deeply embedded in the moral code of scouting. He didn't even look up from whittling a walking stick as he answered "No."

"Remember how Tom Paine published those pamphlets for the Revolution?" I asked my social studies teacher, a serious history buff. "Well, I was hoping you'd let me use the school printer to make my—". He interrupted me with a word I'd come to loathe: "No."

I tried other people, too. Even, as a last resort, the local fundamentalist minister. Already suspicious of me because I didn't go to his church (or, for that matter, any church), he grew even more wary when I told him I'd gladly sell the magazine and donate all the proceeds to his church if only he'd allow me to use his printing press. With a wave of his hand, he sent me packing with yet another "No."

Finally, feeling both angry and desperate, I confided my troubles to my former English teacher,

a woman named Mary Dambman. Wearing her usual ironic grin, she listened patiently as I explained, "It's not great literature, I know. Not even close! But it is fun. And original. And maybe worth sharing."

To my utter astonishment, she asked to see my sample copy. More amazing, she burst out laughing at the portrait of one of her fellow teachers blowing enormous bubbles during his free time. More amazing yet, she looked up from the magazine, peered straight at me, and declared, "Let's do it."

She led me down several hallways to a nondescript door. Unlocking it, she ushered me into a storage room filled with old pieces of school equipment—including, at the back of the room, an old mimeograph machine. Purple ink stained its front, and a cobweb dangled from its knobs, but to me it looked exquisitely beautiful. Her grin expanding, Mrs. Dambman fired up the machine. Over the loud clatter and whining hum, she said something I couldn't hear. All I knew, and all that mattered, was that her words contained nothing resembling the word "No."

Because Mrs. Dambman suggested we pay the school something to cover the cost of paper and mimeograph fluid, I sold the first issue for five cents a copy. Seven copies were sold (and 2 more given away to the good-hearted English teacher and my parents). The second issue did slightly better, selling 9 copies. The third issue (featuring the heroic adventures of my St. Bernard dog with the unfortunate name Frecklepuss) took a dive and sold only six copies.

Then, seized by a sudden inspiration, I devoted the entire next issue to a single topic—a question that had nagged at me since the very first day of middle school, when I walked past a set of windowless doors. The sign above them announced: "Teachers' Lounge—No Students Allowed."

Hmmm . . . this called for a prize case of investigative reporting. And so I took an extra week to create the next issue of the magazine. Everything I had, I threw into one monumental story, an *Idiot's Odyssey* exclusive. Its title? "The Secret Truth Revealed at Last! What Really Goes on Behind the Locked Doors of the Teachers' Lounge."

Continued

T.A. Barron
(*The Lost Years of Merlin* Epic)   *Continued*

To my amazement, this issue sold an astounding 295 copies. (And would have surely sold more, if the old mimeograph machine hadn't suddenly died in a spasm of smoking gears.) This was, you could say, my first bestseller.

Everybody wanted to find out what secret doings transpired in the teachers' lounge. Students wanted to know. So did their parents. And most of all, so did the teachers. I even saw the school secretary, who had started me on this whole journey, sneaking a peek. When she turned to me and asked, "Did you really write this?"—I knew just what to say.

"No way."

To learn more about T. A. Barron, his writing, and contact information, visit his official Web site: www.tabarron.com.

Markus Zusak
(*The Book Thief*)

My brother was a grunter. He grunted to say hello. He grunted to say goodbye. There was a grunt for "You idiot," a grunt for "Not bad," . . . There was even a grunt for "That's pretty funny." It was a bit like the overused idea that Eskimos have numerous words for snow. My brother had a thousand grunts, each signifying something a normal person would actually say. He just couldn't be bothered. Nine hundred eighty of the grunts were derogatory, 15 were conversational, and a precious few were compliments.

He never really said much, even when he was young, but when he was a teenager, my brother barely said anything at all. My parents were frustrated at his lack of communication. My two sisters thought he was a complete bastard. I knew he was a complete bastard . . . but then there was one day when I was 12 and my brother was 14.

We were at Cronulla Beach, both with dinged up, third- or fourth-hand surfboards. My own was a twin-fin. No one rides twin-fins. Not even back then. Both boards were waxed and waxed, smeared, recoated, smeared again. Left in the sun. Smeared again. The wax on those boards was a perfect coat—buttons of tough, hard skin. Once you stood up, there was no slipping on either of those boards. The problem was standing up in the first place, until today.

Today, I had been in the water for an hour. It was an after-school surf—traditionally shorter than a normal one—and my brother was already out of

the water, standing with a towel across his shivering shoulders, and board shorts clamped to his legs. One moment I was sitting on my board and the next, over a small lump of swell, I saw a perfect set standing up in front of me. Immediately, I turned. I paddled. Without thinking I was picked up and was catching my first fully fledged wave. I was riding across it, shocked, amazed, exhilarated, all while trying not to bugger it up somehow and fall off. The wave was noise. The board at my feet shoved water out of its way. I could have sunk my hand into the wave still rising at my side.

Strangely, though, I could hear something else, and I could see it out of the corner of my eye.

My brother—the grunter, the non-communicator, the bastard—was cheering at me from the shore. The

Continued

Markus Zusak
(*The Book Thief*) *Continued*

towel had been dropped at his heels. His arms were held up, shaking at the air. His mouth was wide-open, grinning, fully toothed and alive.

On the way home in the car, he was in the front. I was in the back. That was the unwritten rule—Grunt #486—I'm in the front, you're in the back, Dipshit.

Our mother said, "That was some wave." I smiled with salt drying on my face. My brother just grunted, but I could tell he was smiling too. The bastard.

To learn more about Markus Zusak, his writing, and contact information, visit his official Web site: www.randomhouse .com/features/markuszusak.

An Na
(*A Step from Heaven*)

In eighth grade I tried out for a choral club called Bel Canto. At that point in middle school I was still very, very shy and putting myself on stage alone to audition for the group was my definition of nightmare. But my best friend was trying out, as was almost every other eighth grade girl and I wanted more than anything to belong or at least belong to that collective moment of nerves and stage fright and longing. I remember being on stage, the walk up there a total blank. It was me and the pianist and she began to play. I instantly forgot the words and began to mumble sing. The pianist gave me a kind smile and began to slow down. For a split-second, I thought I was going to lose it. Just start crying and carrying on, run off the stage, but for some reason, I opened my mouth and this incredibly pure note poured out. I stood there and held that note and I can still remember the stillness in the room pierced by that one high perfect note. I finished the rest of

the song and left the stage. I was accepted into Bel Canto and from that point on, I became a lot less shy and also started trying out for other clubs and student government.

To learn more about An Na, her writing, and contact information, visit her official Web site: www.anwriting.com.

Mike Lupica
(*Travel Team*)

It was December of 1958 and I was six years old and on the black-and-white television set the New York Giants and the Baltimore Colts were playing what is still considered by many to be the best pro football game ever played, and perhaps the most important, even more important than Joe Namath and the Jets upsetting the Colts in a Super Bowl more than a decade later.

The game would go into sudden death, and there is the feeling—and I believe a proper one—that this was the game that began to make pro football into the most popular sport in the history of television.

Johnny Unitas was on the field that day, and Lenny Moore, and Raymond Berry, and the opponent

Continued

Mike Lupica
(*Travel Team*)   *Continued*

was perhaps the most glamorous football team to ever play: the Giants of the 1950s, with Frank Gifford and Sam Huff and a quarterback with the wonderful name of Chuckin Charlie Conerly.

I was watching them from Earl Avenue in Oneida, New York, upstate New York, and so the Giants were my team.

No DirecTV in those days. No menu that allowed you to watch any game you wanted to. We got one game every Sunday. A Giants' game. So the Giants were my first team, the first one that mattered to me. I can remember, even now, carefully painting Mel Triplett's No. 33 on my blue replica Giants' helmet.

They were ahead until Gifford, the golden boy of the team, fumbled, and Unitas brought the Colts back. The Giants finally lost that sudden death game when Alan Ameche ran into the end zone.

But that wasn't the magic of the day.

The magic of the day was the feeling in the room with my father and my uncles. My Aunt Mary and my Aunt Theresa lived next door to us in those days, and we were watching on their television and more than any play that day, or the disappointment that I felt when it was over and my team had lost, was that this game had done something to the air in the room.

There was an excitement with my dad, and my Uncle Sam, and my Uncle Joe, a tension and a joy all at once, that I had never experienced before. There was a heightened sense of everything. Mostly, though, it was this football game changing the air, making you feel as if you were at a different altitude almost.

Sports was doing that.

More than Unitas or Gifford or Sam Huff, No. 70, it was sports in the room, the best of it, the living and dying with every play. And, best of all, not knowing how it would all come out.

I was six.

I remember that air.

My dear friend Pete Hamill said he had his day the first time he saw Jackie Robinson play at Ebbets Field in 1947. He says, "That was the day the template was cut." My day came in December of 1958. My father and I still watch games together, and now we watch them with my own sons. So there have been a lot of days. Giants vs. Colts, that was just the first one. It was a beauty.

Mike Lupica is a sports writer and a TV anchor for ESPN's *The Sports Reporters*. You can learn more about him on the Penguin Group Web site: www.us.penguingroup.com.

Jean Ferris
(*Once upon a Marigold*)

Because we moved so much when I was growing up, I was always the "new kid" at school. Each new place had its own customs—about dress, slang, play—and I didn't know any of them. Because I was shy and unsure about how to make the first move, for weeks I had no one to eat lunch with, or walk home with.

The ways I managed these situations are, I believe, the same things that made me a writer. First, I turned to books for companionship—and they never let me down. I could lose myself in a story and, for a while, forget how lonely I was. Stories also allowed me to imagine myself living lives completely

Continued

Jean Ferris
(*Once upon a Marigold*)　*Continued*

unlike my own—which seemed like a good idea at that time.

Second, I kept a journal. I had no one else to talk to (until I made some friends) so I wrote out my feelings—which meant I had to pay attention to them. I didn't ignore them or pretend I didn't have them—and sure, sometimes I positively wallowed in them!

Third, I eavesdropped at school, trying to learn the new slang expressions, to figure out who was nice and who wasn't, and what sorts of things were important there. It's amazing what you can learn when you let others do all the talking.

And last, I became an acute observer, again in an effort to catch on to how to dress in a new place, how to wear my hair and to carry my books, what to do after school and at recess. How to flirt with the boys.

I still do all four of these things, and every one of them still helps me with my writing. Eavesdropping teaches me how people really speak; observing teaches me how people really behave. Writing in my journal keeps me in touch with my varied emotions so I can use them in my work. And reading the books of other writers inspires me to improve my own work and entertains me as well.

I can't recommend moving a lot as preparation for becoming a writer, because I hated it, but I'll put money on reading, writing, eavesdropping, and observing.

To learn more about Jean Ferris, her writing, and contact information, visit her official Web site: www.jeanferris.com.

K.L. Going
(*Fat Kid Rules the World*)

I grew up in a small town in rural New York state. In fact, I graduated high school with many of the same kids with whom I'd gone to elementary school. I never liked school, although I did well. I always viewed myself as the same awkward misfit that I'd been in sixth grade—even long after my appearance had changed. It's hard to see yourself transform when your world stays the same.

Then in high school, I went to the National Young Leaders Conference in Washington, DC. I wouldn't have gone except a friend of mine who was two grades above me had attended and she raved about the experience. In order to go, I had to raise the money by finding local sponsors, and travel on a plane by myself—something I'd never done before.

Continued

K.L. Going
(*Fat Kid Rules the World*)   *Continued*

As the day of my departure approached, I regretted the decision big-time. What had I been thinking?! I was sure the trip would be a disaster.

You can probably guess that it turned out much better than all my worst-case scenarios. What I remember most when I look back on this experience is not the events, but the feelings: freedom and surprise.

Before the plane took off, I was terrified, but as soon as I was in the air, fear melted away until I felt as if, for the first time, my whole life was ahead of me. When I arrived and piece-by-piece, found my place in this new community, and when I realized that these strangers knew nothing of who I'd been, only who I was, I began to see myself through their eyes and was shocked to find that this version of me was confident, brave, made friends easily, and she was even *gasp* pretty!

For months after this experience, I was convinced I would go into politics and live my adult life in Washington, DC. But, of course, I didn't. It wasn't the place that changed me, but the eyes through which I was allowed to look. When I hear from kids today who hate school and feel rotten about themselves I think, "hold on." There will come a time when they will find out they're not the awkward misfit they used to be. Maybe that moment will come while they're still in high school. Maybe it won't come until college. Maybe they'll have to wait until they're adults. But it will happen and when it does, they'll feel the most magical surprise they've ever felt.

To learn more about K. L. Going, her writing, and contact information, visit her official Web site: www.klgoing.com.

Jean Thesman
(*The Rain Catchers*)

I am certain that every young adult author had an epiphany at an early age, and not a very pleasant one, either. One might even say that each of us walked into a nightmare and came out stuck with a hero's journey, whether we wanted it or not.

Mine came about in first grade, when I hit a boy. He was the class bully, and since he sat behind me, I was his regular target. He pulled out my hair, thudded blows on me, and broke the point of his pencil off in my shoulder, requiring painful surgery performed by my mother which left me with a small tattoo I hated.

Of course I tattled! Nothing happened. One day, when he had been called on to answer a question (even though the teacher must have known that he was no more likely to have a handy answer that time than any other), he pulled his flabby self to his feet, and began picking his nose and bumping against the back of my head. I was outraged. Without thinking, I jumped up, turned around, and hit his offending stomach with my fist so hard that he flew backward

into his seat. A few of the other students laughed. The wise ones remembered that he would not always be lying in his chair, wheezing and weeping.

I was sent to the office to speak to the principal, who told me that I should not hit boys. "He hits

Continued

Jean Thesman
(*The Rain Catchers*)   *Continued*

me all the time," I said. "Well, he shouldn't do that," the principal said. "But girls must never hit boys."

I was stunned. A boy should not hit me, but I must never hit him? I could not say another word in my own defense.

At home, my mother said, "Try to get along." My father said, "What possessed you to hit him in front of the teacher?" I got no sympathy. But I stored away the poison pellet the principal gave me, and it grew as time went by.

Girls couldn't wear pants in cold weather. Girls had to wear hats to church. In middle school, we had to take a class in cooking and sewing, even if we wanted woodshop. Girls grew up to teach school or marry. We didn't work at the zoo or dig for treasures in Egypt. And no matter how offensive boys were, we were expected to ignore them, not shout, argue, or (heaven help us) sock them, not even when we were told that we were lucky to be good looking, because otherwise nobody would take us out.

At university, we were denied access to some classes until all the men who wanted them had registered first, which left us preparing for work we didn't want to do.

So we seethed but obeyed (while our mothers watched us closely for signs of our becoming old maids), graduated, took tiresome jobs, and married the wrong men.

When the women's movement finally arrived, I leaped into it happily, rearranged my life, and wrote forty books for girls. Hidden inside the plots and subplots is this: Learn to take care of yourself, and then do it!

But I remember those minutes in the principal's office, and I still hope that his wife ran away with an explorer, leaving him with a large bill for her trunks, holes in his socks, and a sink full of unwashed dishes.

To learn more about Jean Thesman, her writing, and contact information, visit her official Web site: www.jeanthesman.com.

Deb Caletti
(*Honey, Baby, Sweetheart*)

I was very involved in drama while I was in junior high and high school, and when I was in the 11th grade, I was the lead in the play, "The Matchmaker." I played Dolly Levi, against Jeff Murray's Horace Vandergelder. Jeff was a big guy with a booming voice and humor that bordered on brilliant. He was a hurricane of depression and laughter who listened to Blue Oyster Cult and smoked pot in the costume room and with his friends did a Saturday Night Live-worthy song/dance rendition of "Only the Good Die Young." Which, I should quickly add, is not some cheap attempt at foreshadowing on my part, although I did hear that years later Jeff would permanently damage his brain in a drug overdose.

I, on the other hand, was the good girl who was only secretly spirited, with wrong-doing more along the lines of . . . Well, I get stuck here, because there really was no wrong doing. I was responsible to the point of

Continued

Deb Caletti
(*Honey, Baby, Sweetheart*) *Continued*

neurosis and was nice to people no one else was nice to, like Martha Parkinson, who was so fat she fell to the ground when a metal folding chair in the theater broke under her weight. Of course I cared about that play, really cared, and I studied my lines and attended every rehearsal with Ms. Rose, our director, whose gums descended halfway down her front teeth and who spent class time sitting in her glass office in the theater reading magazines, looking up every now and then to make sure nobody had set anything on fire.

In spite of our differences, though, Jeff Murray had decided he was in love with me, and it was love in the way that hurricanes of depression and laughter love—with wild-ride yearnings and desperate pleadings. With crises and bouts of dark sulking. With 15-page letters of impassioned longing and hit and run confessions. The night of the play came. We could hear the theater fill on the other side of the curtain—chatter, bodies shifting, coats removed and purses settled. I wore a long dress of shiny blue material, zipped suffocatingly tight around my waist. We wore our thick, exaggerated makeup. My family sat across one row. I felt the jazzed combination of nerves and excitement.

But Jeff wasn't there. The clock ticked, and still no Jeff. Phone calls, panic, nothing. It got later, the crowd antsy; the sense of panic turned to despair and then to anger. An announcement was made to the crowd. There was head-shaking and disgust and possessions gathered and cars starting up again in the parking lot. When I finally reached him, Jeff was awash in the despondency that big gestures of love denied bring. He was hurting too much to show up, he said. And if adolescence is a sort of rehearsal for the rest of your life, it was here that I further learned my own part, my future role as a woman in relation to a man. I forgave him. For a really lousy thing, for a selfish and hurtful thing, a meanly egocentric act. Adolescence, after all, is also a time when drama gets perhaps dangerously normalized. A time when people do bad things in the name of love and you forgive them in the name of love. It would be a long time before I would rewrite that script, prepared and practiced at 17. When I think about it now, I can still feel that dress, cinched too tight around the center of me.

To learn more about Deb Caletti her writing, and contact information, visit her official Web site: www.debcaletti.com.

Han Nolan
(*Dancing on the Edge*)

When I was in middle school I was a quiet and shy student. I always did my work and paid attention in class but I had a set of somewhat rowdy and fun-loving friends and when we got together we sometimes did some crazy but innocent (I thought) things. For example, one time we went backstage in the school auditorium and found a ladder leading up to an attic. So we climbed up the ladder and hung out there during study hall until the teacher found us and told us to come down.

One by one we climbed back down the ladder and I was the last one to come down. When I got to the bottom, the teacher turned to leave and I said, "Wait a minute, what about Nancy?"

Continued

Han Nolan
(*Dancing on the Edge*)   *Continued*

The teacher turned back around and called up the ladder to Nancy. When Nancy didn't answer she climbed up the ladder and went into the attic in search of her. Of course there was no Nancy and I said to the teacher, when she finally gave up and climbed back down to join the group of us snickering below, "Oops, she must have come down already." None of us got into any trouble.

Another time we decided that two of our teachers were spies and so during our lunch hour we would go around spying on them to see if we could catch them doing something "spy-like."

We finally got caught by one of the teacher spies and she turned us in to the guidance counselor saying that we had been playing hide and seek with her. The counselor told us to stop but we could tell she enjoyed the story when we told her what we had really been doing.

Well, I thought all of this was in good fun. We never meant any harm, we were basically good students who had too much imagination and a lot of free time to use it.

Then one afternoon in study hall the teacher had to leave the room for a while and my friends and I got the crazy idea of turning over some of the desks and using them for transportation. One person would climb on the upturned desk (with chair attached) and the other would push them around the room. We had a lot of fun until one of my friends pushed a desk out into the hallway with me on it, across the hall and into the next room where there happened to be a history class in session.

Imagine the look on the teacher's face when he saw me sail into his room on an upturned desk. We imagined it and thought it would be so funny. Strangely, he didn't.

Again, we got reported to the guidance counselor and this time, instead of dismissing us with a laugh as she had before, she sat us down and gave us a lecture. It was only then, as she spoke, that I realized how frightening our behavior must have seemed to the teachers. It was the early seventies and there were lots of student protests back then and bomb threats and so when the study hall teacher returned to the classroom to find all these desks turned over and a bunch of us riding around on them, she had become very frightened.

The counselor threatened to notify our parents and that too struck me, because she was talking to us and looking at us like we were bad kids—troublemakers. I had never thought of myself that way until that moment. I didn't want to be a bad kid and I didn't want to terrify my teachers. I vowed right then that I would clean up my act and never give someone cause to fear my actions. This change in my attitude and behavior cost me my friendships for a couple of years. I made new friends in the meantime and then when my other friends had also gotten tired of being the troublemakers, we all became friends again. That time in the guidance counselor's office was just one of those times where I was able to step back for a moment and see myself as someone else might see me and realize that I didn't like what I saw.

To learn more about Han Nolan, her writing, and contact information, visit her official Web site: www.hannolan.com.

Valerie Hobbs
(*Carolina Crow Girl*)

It was a Saturday morning, too hot to sleep in. Barefooted, I went downstairs to where the dining room floor was smooth and cool. It wouldn't be for long. By the time we flipped the SORRY WE'RE CLOSED sign to YES, WE'RE OPEN! the room would be cooking. All we had was the ceiling fan. It whirred like a brave little helicopter, but hardly made a difference. All the chairs upended on the tables looked like they were waving for help.

Mom was in the kitchen rolling out piecrusts. I kissed her cheek, reeling her back into our solar

Continued

Valerie Hobbs
(*Carolina Crow Girl*)   *Continued*

system. Where she really went was anybody's guess, any place but the Welsh Kitchen. Restaurants were never her thing. Still, I'd have been a fool not to watch her. She could smell deception like bad cheese. On weekdays, if I didn't look and act exactly like a normal girl on her way to school, she was going to catch me in the biggest lie of my life.

It blew my mind how easy it was to drop out. How you could get up in the morning, dress yourself like always, walk the same old route that took you to the yellow stucco box that was your school, and then not go in. Not join the swarm cramming through the double doors. Two months from graduation and nobody called to report you. All it took was a single call to the attendance office to say in my mother's feathery voice that we were moving back to New Jersey, and I was out of there. The sky didn't fall like it was supposed to, the earth didn't crack opened. I just slid off the map, easy as a fried egg from the griddle.

The kitchen was thick with heat, all the windows opened except for the one that wouldn't. Torn screens or no screens at all, which was what you got for the rent we paid. Mom was rolling six crusts in a line, her hands coated with flour, strands of brown hair stuck to the sweat on her forehead.

"You don't need to make so many pies," I said, pouring myself a cup of Dad's thick black coffee.

"Mmmmm."

"You only end up giving them away."

Her smile was as distant as Jupiter.

I took my coffee outside for the view of the gravel parking lot. Our back steps, worn smooth in the middle, were a good place to sit and get ready for the day.

Resting my head against the screen door, I watched my dad come crunching across the lot with bags from the farmer's market. His chef's whites dazzled in the glare of the sun, but before lunch began he would look like he'd been fingerpainted by a kindergarten class.

He was a great cook, though, world-famous for his Chicken Marengo.

Well, famous in the great big world of *Ojala*.

"Hot enough for you, lass?"

"Hot enough." I got up and held open the screen door.

"Got a kiss for the old man?"

I kissed his cheek as he passed. We were that kind of family. It got old, but then it didn't if you know what I mean.

"Come inside, I'll make you some scrambled eggs."

"No, thanks."

Up went his shaggy eyebrows. "Shirred eggs with thyme? Spinach frittata?"

"Nuh uh."

"Suit yourself."

On weekends, he'd let me go without breakfast. Weekdays I'd have to choke something down to "feed my brain." That morning I was choking on guilt. The night before, Mom had started talking about graduation, about finding a "pretty dress," which was what the girls wore under their robes, for all the sense it made. And, come to think about it, she said, wasn't it time to order my cap and gown? Her excitement swamped my heart so badly, all I could do was go along with it.

I would have finished the year if I could have. Lanie would have made me. After Will's accident, Lanie had been my first line of defense, batting away all the nosy questions before they could trip me up. She'd been my best friend, my only friend, but now she was in Texas, a housewife living a doublewide life.

And Will was dead.

Will was dead, and all the rules had flown right out the window. Life wasn't what you thought, and so you were free to change them. Somebody you loved could be standing on your porch one day, smiling that easy smile, and be dead the next. And so I figured if life was that kind of a crap shoot, why bother with it?

To learn more about Valerie Hobbs, her writing, and contact information, visit her official Web site: www.valeriehobbs.com.

Mrs. Seeton's Whistle[1]   by Jerry Spinelli

I was in Fargo, North Dakota, speaking at a school, and during the Q&A a boy stands up and says, "Do you think being a kid helped you to become a writer?"[1]

I don't think I've ever been asked a better question.

Did the midnight steam locomotive prowling up from the East End, roaring past my window at the back of the house, strum the fiddle strings of my bed with an early taste of terror?

Did six of us play Truth or Consequences one after-dinnertime in 1954? Did blonde-haired Kathy Heller stand before me on the sidewalk awaiting her Consequence with eyes closed behind her glasses, and did I deliver it by crashing my face into hers, *clacking* my teeth into hers—that is to say, consequentially kissing her—thereby acquiring an early taste of something else?

I wished I could take the kid from Fargo, North Dakota, back to summer nights in the West End of Norristown, Pennsylvania, and a game of OUTS. We would crouch behind the stone piles between the tracks and the creek, and I would whisper to him to listen for the crunchy footfall of Spider Sukoloski, searching the West End for us to make us OUTS—Spider Sukoloski, *who to this day still has not found me*—and crouching there I would look up at the blizzard of stars and the never-ending endlessness of the universe, and I would nudge the kid and he would look up too and we would swoon together in our sneakers.

If Fargo had had time enough I would have taken the kid back to Sunday School at First Presbyterian and pinned a ladder of attendance medals on his lapel and sat him down at the round oak table for the 13-to-15 age group, between Teddy Barrett and Douglas Nagy. And when the kid asked me the name of the teacher, I would say, "Garfield Shainline," and the kid would be impressed at such a tall name, and then he would ask me why Teddy and Douglas and the others were snickering and peeking under the table, and I would say, "Peek for yourself," and he would, and when his face came back up it would be different because he had discovered that the impressively

named Garfield Shainline was so tiny that his kid-size shoes did not even touch the floor.

Do I think being a kid helped me to become a writer?

Not if I could forget the sight of four-year-old Sharon Freilich sitting on the step of her parents' corner grocery, her knees dirty as always, two eyes and a nose running, so young, so little to be hated by the kids on George Street for no reason that I could see—and the feeling, the sour, too-fast-elevator-down feeling that I had no name for and still do not.

Not if I could forget Virginia Cory singing "They Try to Tell Us We're Too Young" at the bandshell amateur show on the Fourth of July and every other note a clunker. Not if I could forget Dr. Winters' brown, accommodating finger in my mouth because I was jealous of my mother getting all of the dentist's attention. Not if I could forget the day my dog Lucky ran clear out of it and into a car and died on Johnson Highway. Or the night I spelled myself out of the Montgomery County Spelling Bee by giving "lacquer" an "o" instead of an "e."

But I cannot forget.

The nasal honking of the rag man refuses to leave my ear; the taste of Bonomo's Turkish Taffy still sweetens my tongue; one accidental whiff in 1951 and my nose still recalls the unspeakable aroma of the oozing, crawling horrors that lurked under the galvanized lid of the garbage can at the farthest back of the back yard. Play "Pomp and Circumstance" around me today and my feet will fall to the measured cadence of right-left-pause-left-right-pause as I cross the gym floor of Stewart Junior High to the throne where I reign as King of the Ninth Grade Prom, the Queen my own girlfriend, what a country! I still hear Mrs. Seeton's whistle calling her kids home to dinner, and my heart still remembers the cream and green, whitewall-tired Roadmaster bicycle in the kitchen one Christmas morning, love leaning on a kickstand, and there are knots in my yo-yo string that I never did untie.

Cooling myself with a Popsicle stick fan . . . playing chew-the-peg . . . digging up grass between the front walk bricks (my most detested chore after taking out the garbage) . . . Mr. Freilich's long-handled

[1]First published in *SIGNAL* Journal. Reprinted with permission.

Continued

Mrs. Seeton's Whistle   *Continued*

grocery grippers reaching for Quaker Oats on the highest shelf . . . purple ribbons on a door saying, "We died here" . . . bathtubshaped Hudson cars . . . smoky dishwater marbles in the dirt . . . Bono's fruit and vegetable bus . . . the white plug of cream pushing up the cap of the milk bottle on our front step in January . . . the bread man . . . the egg man . . . the rag man . . . the rag man's horse, itself as gray and sagging as a sack of rags, as if every *clop* upon the street will be its last, the rag man's mournful cry, "Raaaaaaags!" . . . the sad slow syncopation passing George Street, heading for Kohn, Noble, Buttonwood, westward . . . "Raaaaaags!" *clop-clop,* "Raaaaaags!" *clop-clop* . . .

Do I think being a kid helped . . . ?

Yeah, it helped.

And then, to borrow a line from Dylan Thomas's "Fern Hill," green and golden I followed Time out of grace.

And in fact for some years there I did forget, was only too happy to forget, as my future, my prospects turned me to a new awakening in the world beyond school, and Mrs. Seeton's whistle faded like a dream I could not recall.

And then, years later, yet another awakening—I've never been able to pinpoint it. We're in our house on Darby Road, a square brick that we rent for $375 a month. There is Eileen now and there are kids, 6 of them, and somewhere in there, one evening, in a conversation with a visitor, a child was being described and quoted, and her answer to some question was a single word: "stuff."

At the sound of the word something inside me twitched, and some new sun peeked along the edges of a long-drawn shade and someone out of grace awoke in the house on Darby Road and those 6 kids became 7, were joined by this awakening somekid who dirtied the bathwater with them and abused the toothpaste tube and devoutly wished, just once, to share with them the aroma of the garbage can: a seventh sibling, their phantom brother, newly deforgotten, the re- and re- and re-remembered me.

The book that came then is called *Space Station Seventh Grade,* but its first title was *Stuff.*

And then I woke up again—yesterday, was it?—and all of a sudden the kid is not me or mine, but theirs, new kids so terrific that the word *kid* isn't

good enough, they've got to be "grand," 16 of them and counting. And mothers and fathers tell me not only that their kids read my books, but that *they* used to also.

Her name was Heidi Jo. Heidi Jo loved me. And my books. When I first heard from Heidi Jo, she was in fifth grade. She had just discovered me and simply could not let another minute go by without telling me how wonderful I was. (You understand, don't you, that's how it is between us authors and our fan letters. When a reader praises our book, we tend to transfer the praise to ourselves.) Heidi Jo acquired and read every book of mine and breathlessly awaited the next. I was her favorite author. I was her role model. I was her hero. She wanted to be a writer. She wanted to be just like me. She gave book talks. She did projects. One thing she never did was re-write one of my final chapters and send it to me, as some less-than-satisfied readers will do. My endings were always perfect in her eyes. When I imagined my readers in glorious warfare storming across the fields of indifference into the guns of video games and bad reviews, it was Heidi Jo I saw leading the charge, waving the flag.

She wrote to me in fifth grade and sixth grade and seventh grade and eighth grade. I ran out of new posters and bookmarks to send her. Through her letters I followed her year-by-year maturing—from medium kid to big kid to young adult—and in some sense I came to find some part of my own identity wrapped up in Heidi Jo.

And then one day it hit me like a ton of rejection slips: I hadn't heard from her in a year or more. I didn't fool myself. I knew she had dumped me, and for a moment or two it was 1956 all over again and I was hearing the Queen of the 9th Grade Prom say the words I couldn't believe. But between Heidi Jo and me one of us wasn't a kid anymore, and I understood. I understood it was her time to go, green and golden, so I took the high road and silently wished her well with Stephen King or Scott Fitzgerald or whoever my successor might be, and it pleased me to think that 10 or 20 years hence she might have an awakening of her own, and that she might then remember fondly and with some profit to herself the thing we had together.

Continued

Mrs. Seeton's Whistle   *Continued*

As for me, there will always be—hopefully—another letter to open, and the comforting notion that the kids who leave their favorite authors behind as they follow Time out of grace do not in fact leave us utterly abandoned, but in due time drive children of their own to the bookstore and the mailbox.

And so they come and go, each generation of readers so painfully brief—barely the lifespan of rabbits. Every second of every day, somewhere out there, a kid is turning into a former kid. And while one of the more popular characterizations of kids has them junking their kidhoods prematurely, thank goodness that isn't always or totally the case. Thank goodness there are plenty of kids out there content enough to let their kidhoods expire in their own good time.

It seems to me that's what we're hearing from Jonathan here: "I'm just a little kid in a little town in a little world and I'm not popular or famous so I don't expect any letter back from you."

And from Louis: "My teacher is a big fan of yours. I'm a little fan."

And from Victoria: "When I was reading, you said that you had a girlfriend in first grade, but let me give you some advice: You were too young to have a girlfriend!"

The persistence of childhood was in my mind when I wrote this poem. It's called "Dinosaur Hunter":

By the time I saw that Eden lies in the myth
*   that is each of us*
the Snake had already spoken to me and I was
*   cast out.*
Still, the fragrance of the memory recalls me
to that time, when Peter Orman shouted,
*   "There's a dinosaur down the street!"*
and I in marveling fear went to see.
And if I did not find it, it was only because
*   I got there too late,*
and if, armed with eyes,
*   I stalked the woods for giant footprints*
*   and found none,*
*   it was only because a dinosaur was too big*
*   to fit between the trees.*
And then a grown-up, smiling, informed me that
*   the last had died some sixty million years ago.*

What could I say?
I had not the means to quibble over dates
or to explain that the last dinosaur dies
*   only with each child.*

It's a kid's job to be a kid. Lightning bug bottler, cedar chest smeller, puppy holder, railroad car counter, tin can stomper, dandelion blower, snowball smoother, paper bag popper, wishbone puller, mixing bowl licker—such is a kid's resume, the original multi-tasker. And he won't sneak two-hour lunches and pack it in at 5 o'clock. And she'll work for peanuts—or Ju Ju Beads.

Which is not to say they never look ahead:

"I got my whole life planned out. First I'm gonna grow up. Then I'm going to go to college. Then off to the Air Force we go. Then I retire to Hawaii. Then I die. Does that sound good to you?"

Yeah, Timothy, it sounds good to me. You sound just like what you are, a kid taking a peek around Time's corner. You sound in many ways like a thousand other kids from a hundred other time zones. You sound like you could have been born anytime from the fifties to the nineties.

Yes, hairstyles and sneaker prices have changed along with other aspects of life in the world, but given themselves, kids continue to live out the same stories over and over:

Richard: "What I find amazing is that you can remember so well what it is like to be in the 7th grade."

Alan: "Most of those things that happened to Jason happened to me."

Will: "Who tipped you off to how real adolescent life is?"

These readers wrote to me in the nineties. Wouldn't they be surprised to know that my reference point for Jason in *Space Station Seventh Grade* was myself in 1954. Childhood is timeless. Stuff is still stuff. And a child's bedroom is as much a window to the universe as a scientist's lab or a philosopher's study.

Or, as Ben from San Rafael, California, writes, "I am an interesting person."

Or the lad from Manteno, Illinois: "My name is Corey. I have one eyebrow."

Continued

Mrs. Seeton's Whistle   *Continued*

Look around. Look in the mirror. Dinosaurs are dying everywhere. But don't despair—the last one will live forever. And who knows, maybe it will give all of us a lift in the dinnertime parade of my dreams. It's Mrs. Seeton I see, returning to her house on Elm Street. The neighborhood kids in their flying neon bubblesoled sneakers stare at the gray, slow-moving woman whom they do not know. She goes to the backyard, to the old spot by the fence, and she whistles. It's the old two-noter, sounds just the way it did in 1955. She doesn't need to whistle again—one is all it ever takes, because we're already on our way, returning from our homes and Hawaii retirements and cemeteries around the world—Spider Sukoloski and Virginia Cory and Teddy Barrett and Garfield Shainline in the shoes he never outgrew, and we're joined by Heidi Jo and Ben who is interesting and Corey and his one eyebrow—the whole parade of us across the creek and along the tracks and past the stone piles and down the streets and alleyways, all of us one more time heading home on Mrs. Seeton's whistle.

The Young Adult Reader

Introduction

There is in the state of Georgia the perfect teenage reader. In elementary school he chose to read—no, he *sought out,* Robert Louis Stevenson's *Treasure Island.* In middle school he devoured J. D. Salinger's *The Catcher in the Rye,* and Mark Twain's *Huckleberry Finn* and lamented when he closed the cover of *Tom Sawyer.* Reading Shakespeare, Chaucer, Wordsworth, and Shelley in high school prompted him to spend part of the summer following his junior year overseas studying English literature and history with other high school students at Oxford. In those same high school years, he devoured classic after classic and threw in *Harry Potter* and Ayn Rand for good measure. When he walked onto the University of Georgia's campus as a first-year honor student, he was *ready.*

There's a high school student just like him in every state, maybe a few; but there's not one in every class. This one student is of a special breed, a developmentally advanced being who, in his or her teenage years can "make the leap" back over time and culture to empathize with the characters in the story. He has a curiosity about history and culture so intense that the academic becomes emotional. He or she is *happy* to learn. He is a poster child for the rewards of reading, a teacher's favorite and a parent's dream; but he doesn't represent the majority of teen readers.

At the other end of the spectrum from Adam, our near-mythical Georgia student, are teenagers who won't read the back of a cereal box. A few don't read because of learning disabilities, but most don't read, or read poorly, because of their histories. Unlike the bouncing, wide-eyed kindergartner who is only beginning to negotiate school culture, teens have a long history of school successes and failures. By the time they enter high school, they have set beliefs about reading: they either like it or hate it; they either experience another kind of reading outside school reading, or they don't. They know they're successful readers or they know they have failed miserably at it. Thus, teachers of adolescents face a seemingly insurmountable challenge—reaching those teens with long histories of negative reading experiences, "undoing" negative attitudes and beliefs that have developed over time.

Adolescence is a developmental phase that includes conflict. Teens naturally push away from authority figures in order to discover their identities, or "who they are." Even for emotionally balanced kids, it makes sense that many naturally don't want to learn what we teach, or read what we assign. Kids living in domestic violence, who are neglected, or who live with overcontrolling parents or significant unresolved trauma are generally more reluctant—sometimes even combative—about "doing what they are told."

Despite national statistics and concerns about an increasingly under-literate teen population, adolescent literacy takes a backseat to the literacy needs in the earlier grades. This chapter addresses this inequity. It also addresses habits of teen readers and outlines five needs common to all. It gives a brief explanation of the reading process and concludes by identifying strategies readers use to comprehend text. These strategies are revisited in detail in subsequent chapters.

The Marginalization of Young Adult Literacy

Middle school and high school English teachers often teach as if all students were like Adam. Whether it is the fault of state or local standards, or those of No Child Left Behind, educators seem to pay more attention to whether high school students can identify authors and titles of the classics and give a short answer regarding the theme of each, than we do to whether or not students can actually *read*. This attitude has to do with the failure of our educational system to support reading instruction for teens.

For more than a decade, reading experts (e.g., Irvin, Buehl & Klemp, 2007) have lamented the lack of attention given to young adult literacy. Emphasis on reading instruction diminishes by the middle grades. By the middle years reading instruction is geared primarily toward *struggling readers;*[1] most other students move on to foreign language and college-prep classes. Another sign of neglect is the fact that middle and high school teachers receive minimum preparation in teaching reading. Pre-service teachers may have one or two reading courses (possibly none) before entering the field. Moreover, they seldom enter the classroom trained to diagnose reading difficulties, assess reading levels, and work with struggling readers.

Avid readers know how to find good books. Those who read very little don't.

As students move through the middle and secondary grades, they are required to read more complex texts. While that's to be expected, content area teachers (e.g., social studies, science, and math) are rarely prepared to help teens navigate complex expository material, the core of their curricula. This lack of preparation is grounded in a traditional belief that reading instruction belongs in the English classroom. Research (Bintz, 1997) shows that content area teachers are often unwilling or unable to teach content area reading. While they acknowledge the reading needs of their students, they are often unsure of their role as reading teachers. Content area teachers, without proper

---

[1]As Beers (2003) reminds us, anyone can be a struggling reader, depending on the complexity of the reading task. As used throughout this text, the term applies to those individuals who are lacking in comprehension strategies. Beers identifies several characteristics of struggling readers (e.g., they stop reading; they depend on someone else to explain or do the work; they read on through the text, failing to absorb meaning).

training in teaching students to read their content, can fall into the trap of teaching *around* reading; that is, they can lecture more, require less reading (because the textbook is too difficult), provide information through videos, handouts, and notes. Well intentioned, these practices translate into less time spent on reading and ensure that a struggling reader remains behind. Though some content area teachers do receive professional development in content area reading instruction and use reading strategies effectively, they're not the norm. In fact, training in content area reading is often ineffective because minimal training seldom transfers into actual practice.[2]

The marginalization of young adult literacy is further evident by the sheer number of state- and federal-funded programs that cater to preschool and elementary programs whose purpose is to get students "up to speed" in reading. The message being sent: learning to read is a skill achieved in the early grades. Irvin and colleagues (2007) point out this funding issue and argue further:

> The national mantra in literacy that "every child will learn to read by third grade," while it targets the crucial role of building a strong foundation in reading, unfortunately has communicated a misconception that learning to read is a short-term goal that can be accomplished during elementary school instruction. (p. 3)

In essence, young adult readers are cheated. Rather than being a time in which we pull back from reading instruction, the adolescent years should be a time in which we ratchet up reading support. In *NCTE Principles of Adolescent Literacy Reform* (2006), the National Council of Teachers of English cites six reports that speak to a desperate need for sound reading instruction for teens. Data from these reports suggest a growing under-literate class:

> The American Institutes for Research (AIR) reports that only 13 percent of American adults are capable of performing complex literacy tasks.
> The National Assessment of Educational Progress (NAEP) shows that secondary school students are reading significantly below expected levels.
> The National Assessment of Adult Literacy (NAAL) finds that literacy scores of high school graduates have dropped between 1992 and 2003.
> The National Center for Educational Statistics (NCES) reports a continuing and significant reading achievement gap between certain racial/ethnic/SES groups.
> The Alliance for Excellent Education (AEE) points to 8.7 million secondary students—that is one in four—who are unable to read and comprehend the material in their textbooks.
> The 2005 ACT College Readiness Benchmark for Reading found that only about half the students tested were ready for college-level reading, and the 2005 scores were the lowest in a decade. (p. 4)

---

[2]A number of factors influence how well a content area teacher transfers training in reading instruction into the classroom (e.g., quality of the training, amount of time spent in training, and support once they return to the classroom and teacher attitude).

Added to this neglect is the fact that literacy demands are increasing. Today's youth are growing up in a knowledge-based digital world, and jobs once needing limited reading and writing skills are fewer. Even so, many youth continue to graduate, believing literacy skills are "not necessary" for the kind of work they plan to do. The following story is based on a real person I know, a young man who began school behind, stayed behind, and survived by convincing himself education wasn't important. Though I've fictionalized J. T.'s experiences, the story, or one close to it, could belong to most any illiterate individual:

> J. T. never did that well in school. From first grade on he was behind in reading and was embarrassed to say when he didn't understand something because the other kids laughed. The further he progressed in school the worse it got, but the better he got at deception. He developed a long list of diversions he could employ to keep the teacher and the rest of the students off guard. By his first year in high school he could read third-grade material.
>
> But J. T. wasn't worried. He meant to follow in the tire treads of his father, a long-haul truck driver. "You don't need to read to drive a truck," he reasoned to himself. "Everybody knows what a stop sign looks like, and a yield sign and curve signs in either direction. And road words are easy." He traveled with his father when he could and worked on the truck with him when his dad was home.
>
> J. T. graduated from high school with under a C average, but he graduated. It took an extra year and some creative academic dancing, but he made it. After three attempts he obtained his commercial driver's license and got a job with a local long-haul trucking firm.
>
> For the first six months he drove tandem with another driver who taught him the ins and outs of driving through and delivering to some of our nation's largest cities. The senior driver navigated while J. T. drove, unaware of J. T.'s reading difficulties, and came away recommending that J. T. was ready to drive solo.
>
> It was a dream come true. He lived in his truck, showered, and sometimes slept in truck stops across the country. He saved his money and bought a great sound system and a portable Game Boy with an endless list of games. He made friends with other drivers and with waitpersons across the country.
>
> His third week driving solo he was nearly fired for arriving at a destination more than three hours late. J. T. had driven into the Nashville city limits more than an hour ahead of schedule, but the road signs were far more complicated than STOP and YIELD and many of the street names were maddeningly alike. He was afraid to call his dispatcher, believing if the company knew of his near illiteracy, they would fire him.
>
> He spent nine hundred dollars of his next paycheck on a GPS system.
>
> As many games as J. T. had for his Game Boy he began getting bored with them and looked for other distractions during his downtime. He walked past rack after rack of books and magazines and newspaper stands mentally checking those out as possibilities. The covers looked interesting, but he knew that once he opened the book he may as well be in a different country. He sat at the counter eavesdropping on other customers' conversations, picking up bits of local and national news which

would do until he could get to a television set. He hated being uninformed, so he spent five hundred dollars of his next paycheck on a satellite radio.

Credit card companies from near and far seemed to sense that J. T. was making a pretty good living. He was a single guy living in a low-rent studio apartment because fully three-quarters of his time was spent on the road. Before he knew it he was packing nearly a dozen credit cards, all of which had started out with low APRs. But J. T. had paid about as much attention in his high school Business Math class as he did in English and was unaware that those credit card companies *counted* on him paying late sometime in that first year and J. T. had been unable to read what that would plainly do to his low APR. In two years' time, the lowest APR on any of his credit cards was more than 25 percent. He just didn't get why he couldn't keep up. He was making a *good* living.

One of the waitpersons he liked worked at Great America, a *monster* truck stop in Wyoming, and J. T. began coercing his dispatcher into laying him over there as often as possible. He was a little embarrassed to ask her on a date, but he spent a lot of late-night/early morning coffee time in a booth near her station. She would sit and talk with him when breaks allowed, wondering why this polite man didn't ask her out. She knew he wasn't married; he'd told her that enough times that she knew he wanted her to know it. What she didn't know was that he watched her take some of her breaks, sitting in an empty booth reading a book. J. T. had long ago created radar for potentially embarrassing situations, and a relationship with a woman who loved to read as much as Madeline obviously did was fraught with obvious landmines.

J. T. finally worked up the courage to ask Madeline for a date the next time he went through Great America. She happily accepted. She'd been beginning to believe J. T. saw something wrong with her. On the night of the date when he didn't show up, her fears were confirmed.

However, they shouldn't have been. J. T. had a load to drop in Chicago but his GPS failed him. Major road construction was taking place on the way to his destination and GPS wasn't up to speed with the rerouting. J. T. became hopelessly lost in street signs and road directions he couldn't read. He was only an hour late, but his next scheduled load to Laramie was a rush and had been sent out with another driver. J. T. was rescheduled to Baltimore. Madeline sat waiting in her brand-new apartment, which had not yet been set up with phone service.

He was able to call her the next morning at work, but he could hear a bit of a rift developing in their relationship. He wanted to tell her, but years of embarrassment kept him from it.

J. T. kept on driving long haul. He became smarter and smarter, deceiving a reading world, but he never lost the vigilance that kept him afloat, which also kept him spending money on Pepcid.

In the end J. T. needed one thing: he needed to learn to read.

Reading Habits of Young Adults

Despite the marginalization of young adult literacy, a good number of teens do read and read a great deal. In fact, teens are buying books at a faster rate in decades. According to one industry analysis, sales are up a quarter between 1999 and 2005 (Goodnow, 2007). Multiple factors deserve credit: an exploding teen population, a robust cadre of talented teen writers, a growing sophistication of young adult literature, and possibly the *Harry Potter* series, as younger fans move into their teen years. When selecting books for pleasure reading, these voracious teen readers seldom choose school-approved novels. They read adult bestsellers, magazines, newspapers, and Internet text. They peruse the young adult section for chick lit, science fiction, fantasy, and horror titles. They read video-game manuals, self-help, and how-to books. They trade book suggestions like iTunes. Regardless of their reading interests, teen readers share a number of common traits.

Reading Is a Social Act

Reading is a social act. Teens enjoy talking about their reading and sharing their likes and dislikes.

I had a male student once who brought a different book to class each week. One week he would have *The Three Musketeers*, the next *War and Peace*. He wasn't a great reader, and others challenged whether he was reading what he claimed. He wasn't, but pretending he could read difficult books elevated him.

Teens measure themselves, their reading ability, and interest against their peers. They know they're "in" if they read *Harry Potter*; they know reading Tolstoy, Pushkin, or Hugo positions them among the elite. They believe, too, if they're reading below their peer group they're inferior, and unless they get ahead of the game by dismissing reading by becoming the class clown, a tough kid, and so on, they're in for a rough ride.

In any given school, you will find silent voracious readers—teens who develop intimate relationships with their own reading and share little with others. They're the minority. For the most part, reading is a social act (Zirinksy & Rau, 2001). Most teens share their reading experiences with peers and/or significant adults. They discuss the books they like; they make recommendations. They seek out reading suggestions from more experienced readers or from those they admire. They compare and contrast their likes and dislikes. They make "good guesses" as to whether they will like a book based on another's responses to it. There can be a competitive, or driven, element to their reading, especially among advanced readers. Reading, in short, is woven into relationships (Zirinsky & Rau, 2001).

Teen Readers, Just as Adults, Have Dry Spells

When Adam, our Georgia student, entered ninth grade, his reading came to a grinding halt. His mother became worried. Her once insatiable reader now hardly opened a book. Adam was spending too much time playing baseball; he was too social, he played on the Internet too much, and homework cut into time he could otherwise use for reading. His mother, a high school teacher, feared Adam was following a common pattern: Interest in reading tends to diminish as students move into high school. Understanding the conflict stage of adolescent development, she knew too much pressure could turn Adam against reading. She chose to "wait it out," but during that time, the home remained filled with reading materials; she subscribed to *Sports Illustrated, National Geographic, Time,* and *Newsweek,* playing upon his interest in sports, history, and current issues. She continued modeling reading for him and made time to talk with him about her own reading and about newsworthy events. Within a few months, Adam was on a slow train back.

It's important to remember as a teacher that all readers, especially teens, have dry reading spells—times when reading takes a backseat to other interests. A voracious reader one month may become a nonreader the next. Knowing when to push and when to back off is difficult. While Adam was preoccupied with baseball, he was also navigating the confusing waters of high school, but he was luckier than most. He had a mother who understood adolescent development, who modeled intellectual growth, and who also understood the importance of a print-rich environment. As teachers we can't go home with our students, but we can offer advice and encouragement to parents when reading bottoms out.

The Right Book Can Create a Lifelong Reader; the Wrong One a Nonreader

Herein lives the problem with reading the "class" novel. In our efforts to create readers, we can actually squelch desire by forcing students to read books they dislike. A certain number of teens will tolerate a class novel they don't like; they will participate in class discussion and activities even though they despise the book, but they have enough experiences with good books and they know where to find them that reading a class novel does them little harm. They see the ordeal as an educational hurdle. They develop boring book "tolerance." They're not, however, the majority. Many teens stop reading in middle school and never return to it because they develop a jaded view of reading. Reading equals teacher-assigned texts. Reading is work. The wrong class novel drives home their negative views.

Teens Tend to Read "a Little Up," . . . but Not Too Far

Whether male or female, 15-year-olds are more interested in reading about an 18-year-old than someone 13. Most have little interest in reading about mature adults. This only makes sense. They are on new ground and are curious, as they should be, about what's ahead: maturity, sexuality, relationships, social and political issues. They have hopes, dreams, and dreads. As mentioned in Chapter 1, they are immediate.

We sometimes forget the chasm between our experiences and theirs. As adults, we reflect on our lives, we've played out hopes and dreams and walked through fear; we look at life through a wider and more experienced spectrum. We have reverence for life and death that comes with age. We have regrets, missed opportunities, lost moments. We may find a story poignant, a life message powerful because we've experienced it at some level. Teens don't have that capability. Don't be surprised if some laugh at a text you find poignant. They're not being disrespectful; they're not sociopathic; they simply lack information and experience. And don't worry that they'll never "get it." That they'll never have empathy. They will. They just need some growing room.

Most teen readers, for instance, will connect better with a teen protagonist facing death (e.g., terminal cancer) than with an elderly protagonist reminiscing about his/her youth. A classic example that comes to mind is Katherine Anne Porter's (1969) "The Jilting of Granny Weatherall." In this short story, an elderly lady drifts in and out of consciousness on her deathbed. Readers enter her thoughts and learn about her life and the kind of woman she was: she was a hard worker, she loved, she was strong. It's difficult to find a more poignant story about those last moments of life. Adults find the story powerful; teens find it boring. What teens would value, though, is a story about a teen who has little time to live, such as the protagonist in Chris Crutcher's *Deadline* (2007). Eighteen-year-old Ben Wolf has to decide how he wants to spend the last few months of his life. Such a story can help teens make connections with their own mortality, which will give them the grounding they need to feel empathy for someone older.

Literary Quality Means Zilch

Teen readers, as do the majority of adults, seldom choose books based on literary quality. They choose books based on a connection they make with a character, or with the plot or theme; they make selections because they're hooked on a particular genre such as horror, fantasy, or history. Sometimes they choose a book because it's socially accepted (e.g., *Harry Potter*). It's a cool read, it's the "in" thing, it helps them belong. Literary merit has little to do with personal reading choices for most readers. This reading behavior speaks to the popularity of mass market serialized pop culture paperbacks.

Gender Influences Reading Preferences

I always hesitate when I hear individuals labeling books either boys' books or girls' books because labeling perpetuates stereotypes. My teaching experiences, however, have taught me that distinct patterns exist between boys and girls, granted exceptions exist. Below are a few I've observed over the years:

1. Boys prefer books with loads of action and multiple characters.
2. Girls forego the action and multiple characters for an intimate relationship with a single character.
3. With some encouragement, girls will read "boy books", whereas boys seldom cross over.
4. Boys pay more attention to a book's cover—it's a rare boy who will pack around a pink- or pastel-colored novel with pride.
5. Boys like lots of dialogue.
6. Girls choose books more often based on their friends' suggestions. They are more likely to read what a friend is reading or has read.
7. Boys are more likely to call themselves nonreaders—even though they may read auto repair manuals, video magazines, newspapers, etc.
8. More boys read nonfiction and historical texts.
9. More boys enjoy gross-out humor.
10. Girls can be uncomfortable with a great deal of violence.

Personal Culture Impacts Book Selection

Whether adult or teen, we're all likely to be drawn to stories that are about "us." When given the choice, teens generally choose to read about their own culture and will choose familiar settings and familiar times. While this is typically true for realistic fiction, teens who enjoy other genres (e.g., historical fiction, science fiction, fantasy, horror) make selections based on a specific interest. Readers with a passion for history, however, may be fascinated by a particular era and culture (e.g., the French Revolution, the American Civil War). When appropriate, students should be encouraged to choose books about other cultural experiences.

Teens Enjoy Being Read To

Christopher Paul Curtis shares a laugh with two high school fans at Kell High School in Georgia.

Contrary to popular thinking, teens do enjoy being read to, but only if the reader has an engaging reading voice. If you hear the thud of foreheads against wood when you read, you probably need to crank up your delivery. To find out how well you read, read aloud before a peer or friend who will

give you an honest assessment. Splattered throughout the chapters that
follow are a wealth of picture books, short novels, and short stories that
make excellent read-alouds.

What Teen Readers Need

My pre-service teachers always want to know what they can do to motivate
students to read. I ask them in turn to think about class experiences that
turned them off to reading. Together we brainstorm a list of turnoffs from
our collective pasts. Below is a typical list:

1. Being forced to read a book we didn't like or didn't understand.
2. Doing too many class activities with one book—that is, plodding
   through the book, chapter-by-chapter, and completing worksheet after
   worksheet.
3. Having read the assignment and failing the five-question pop quiz.
4. Writing book reports.
5. Having to choose books from the Accelerated Reading Program when
   we'd rather read something else.
6. Participating in round-robin reading.
7. Knowing a quiz or test is lurking around the corner.
8. Not having our responses and ideas validated. Being ridiculed for a
   belief.
9. Reading on a fixed schedule (i.e., read Chapters 1–3 by tomorrow and
   don't read ahead).
10. Reading a text but not having opportunities for deep conversation.

You probably connected with some of the points listed. Whether a proficient or struggling reader, we all perform better when our reading needs and
interests are met, when we're made to feel ownership, when we're validated,
and when reading is an invitation into a world of possibilities, learning, and
inquiry. Following are five common needs that go unattended in many classrooms. If you attend to these in your own classroom, you will be on the right
track to engaging young minds.

Literature They Can Relate To

Whether reading a classic text or young adult novel, young adults must
make connections with their reading. Most teens make that connection better
with young adult literature. Characters in young adult literature are "user
friendly"—they're openly accessible to a range of ability-level readers. They
often live in the same time and face the same dilemmas as today's teenagers.
Were they real they would be the friends and enemies of their readers. Conversations would be held, imaginations activated, relationships built. Can
the classics offer these kinds of relationships? Some can, but the success of
the relationship connection depends upon the teacher's ability and effort to
make the classics authentic and meaningful.

Support in Reading Difficult Texts

No one masters reading. Readers of all ability levels need support in reading difficult texts. However, needs are different. Struggling readers, for example, need to increase fluency, widen their vocabulary, and develop a stronger sense of text structure. Proficient readers need assistance in navigating difficult classics (e.g., the *Iliad*, *Paradise Lost*). Regardless of reading ability, all teens need instruction that moves them to deeper understanding of texts and increases their ability to generate questions and ideas.

Authentic Reading Opportunities

In an era of accountability teachers need to find time for authentic reading experiences, opportunities for teens to do real reading without fear of being quizzed or tested. Teens need opportunities to engage deeply with a wide range of texts and genres, both print and nonprint, and a range of multiple perspectives. In classrooms where teachers are overly concerned about covering the material, students often feel they do no real reading—they skim the surface of texts, read bits and pieces, and store details in memory in preparation for testing.

Literacy Communities

Teens need communities, or book clubs, in which they can engage in authentic and deep discussions about their reading. They need opportunities to explore their reactions, think critically, engage in multiple interpretations, and raise questions and issues free of ridicule or judgment. They need reading mentors—more experienced readers who serve as advocates and who model critical thinking and aid them in text selection.

An Understanding of the Politics of Literacy and Empowerment

In *Reading Reasons* (2003), Gallagher identifies nine reasons we should read:

1. Reading is rewarding.
2. Reading builds a mature vocabulary.
3. Reading makes you a better writer.
4. Reading is hard, and "hard" is necessary.
5. Reading makes you smarter.
6. Reading prepares you for the world of work.
7. Reading well is financially rewarding.
8. Reading opens the door to college and beyond.
9. Reading arms you against oppression. (p. 17)

While all are significant, readers should internalize the last, "Reading arms you against oppression." We need only examine people's lives in Afghanistan prior to September 11, 2001, North Korea today, female and child sex slavery worldwide, and think back on our own history with slavery to understand the value of literacy. We can look, too, to events in our own country such as the capture of Warren Jeffs, leader of a polygamist Mormon sect charged with arranging marriages between men and minors. Jeffs maintained control over his people, especially women, by keeping them ignorant, isolating them from the news and society. Literacy equals power. When we deny individuals access to information, keep them illiterate, we have the power to oppress them.

The Reading Process

Experts generally agree that reading is a dynamic, complex process. Over the years, dozens of theorists have posited theories of what happens when we read.[3] This book is grounded in a transactional, sociopsycholinguistic view of reading. Reading is a process of comprehending—of constructing meaning. Rather than absorbing meaning from the text, the reader, using his/her own experiences, creates meaning (Goodman, 1996). In doing so, transactions occur between the reader's mind and the language of the written text. Weaver (2002) records the following observations about reading, which illustrate this reader-text relationship:

1. In isolation, most words do not have a single meaning, but rather a range of possible meanings.
2. Words take on specific meanings as they transact with one another in sentence, text, social, and situational contexts.
3. Meaning is not in the text, nor will the meaning intended by the writer ever be perceived—or rather, constructed—exactly the same way by a reader.
4. Readers make sense of texts by drawing upon their schemas—their entire lifetime of knowledge, experiences, feelings, and beliefs.
5. Meaning emerges as readers transact with a text in a specific situational context.
6. Thus, the process of reading is to a considerable degree whole to part, top to bottom, deep to surface, and inside out (from the reader to the text). (p. 36)

A reader-text transaction doesn't occur in isolation, but rather, within situational and social contexts. While several kinds of contexts exist, below is one example (Weaver, 2002). Which sentence is easiest to follow and why?

1. Furry wildcats fight furious battles.
2. Furry jewelers create distressed stains.
3. Furry fight furious wildcats battles.
4. Furry create distressed jewelers stains.

Readers employ meaning-making strategies as they make transactions with the text that enable comprehension. In the above example, readers employ their knowledge of semantic context, that is, their understanding of the

---

[3] See recommended readings at the end of the chapter.

meaningful relationships among words. (For an extended discussion see Weaver, 2002.) A wonderful text to use in the classroom to discuss this type of context, as well as syntactic context, is nonsense poetry, of which Lewis Carroll's "Jabberwocky" (1871) is perhaps the most famous. As you read the opening two stanzas of the poem, think about your understanding of word order and how words function:

> *'Twas brillig, and the slithy toves*
> *Did gyre and gimble in the wabe:*
> *All mimsy were the borogoves,*
> *And the mome raths outgrabe.*
>
> *"Beware the Jabberwock, my son!*
> *The jaws that bite, the claws that catch!*
> *Beware the Jubjub bird, and shun*
> *The frumious Bandersnatch!"*

The examples illustrated are narrow conceptualizations of context. Context also includes the reader's purpose for reading and the expectations readers have of the text. It includes the situation in which the individual is reading and the individual's culture and time (Weaver, 2002). You will read more about the role of personal experiences and culture in Chapter 4.

Bartoli and Botel (1988) extend the transactional, sociopsycholinguistic theory of the reading process to define strategies readers use in the reading process:

> Reading comprehension is a process that involves the orchestration of the reader's prior experience and knowledge about the world and about language. It involves such interrelated strategies as predicting, questioning, summarizing, determining meanings of vocabulary in context, monitoring one's own comprehension, and reflecting. The process also involves such affective factors as motivation, ownership, purpose, and self-esteem. It takes place in and is governed by a specific context, and it is dependent on social interaction. It is the integration of all these processes that accounts for comprehension. They are not isolable, measurable subfactors. They are wholistic processes for constructing meaning. (p. 186)

In much the same way as we can drive mechanically from Point A to Point B and not remember a single mile of the trip, good readers use a range of these comprehension strategies, seemingly automatically, to make sense of text. In her seminal work, *When Kids Can't Read* (2003), Beers explains a number of "automatic" skills good readers use in making meaning of text:

1. They recognize the purpose of reading is to get meaning. Reading is a meaning-making process that requires active participation from the reader.
2. They use a variety of comprehension strategies (e.g., predicting, summarizing, questioning, and visualizing the text).
3. They make a range of inferences about the text such as providing their own concept examples and figuring out word meaning from context.

4. They use prior knowledge to inform their inferences, to connect ideas in the text to other texts and their own beliefs.

5. They monitor their understanding of the text. They recognize, for example, when reading is difficult; they know when their minds are wandering; they recognize which vocabulary is causing a problem, and they can identify parts of text that are confusing. Once they recognize a problem, they're able to use "fix-up" strategies to get back on track (e.g., rereading, changing their reading rate, consulting a dictionary).

6. They question the author's purpose and point of view.

7. They use text features (e.g., headings, boldfaced and italicized terms, visuals, and indexes) to aid in comprehension.

8. They evaluate their engagement and enjoyment of a text to determine if they liked it and whether or not they would recommend it to others.

9. They know the meaning of many words and, when they don't automatically recognize the meaning, they use context clues and word parts to discern meaning.

10. They recognize most words automatically, read fluently, vary their reading rate, and "hear" the text as they read. (pp. 34–35)

Though proficient readers use these strategies seemingly automatically, research (e.g., Wilhelm, 2001) suggests that explicit instruction can aid struggling readers in developing text comprehension skills. As you read this textbook, you will note that Chapters 4–11 are two-part chapters. The first part of each surveys a young adult literature genre; the latter illustrates ways the genre can be used to teach comprehension skills. Skills covered throughout the text include connecting to prior experiences, questioning, clarifying and monitoring for meaning, making predictions and inferences, summarizing, and visualizing text. In addition, activities are included that develop an awareness of text structure (e.g., comparison and contrast, cause and effect), that deepen and extend vocabulary, and that build fluency. Writing is an integral part of the reading process and an indispensable avenue for responding to literature. Chapter 13 addresses ways young adult literature can be used to teach writing. As you study the young adult genre and explore ways of teaching literature and reading with your students, keep in mind that all students can become better readers, but they're at different skill levels. Some will need more explicit (direct) instruction than others in the reading strategies presented here. Finally, as you read this book, you will become familiar with dozens of strategies. While it is important that you develop a wide repertoire of instructional strategies, it's also important that you concentrate on a select few at any give time with your students (e.g., focus on three or four questioning strategies as you read a class novel). Make sure students learn the strategies and use them effectively. Introducing a new strategy daily doesn't provide much opportunity for students to internalize or practice what you've shown them.

Final Thoughts

In the end some teens will be unreachable. There are kids who live outside our public schools' capacity to embrace; kids so damaged by their histories that we lack the power to create the intensity it would take to hold them. It is a mistake, however, to categorize these kids as such because we don't want to make the mistake of missing one we could have engaged. At the same time, when all is said and done, we need to give ourselves the benefit of the doubt. We take our best game into the classroom each day, bring our best materials, trade off students to other teachers better equipped to help under certain specific conditions, and walk away knowing we did our best.

Reading Resources

Allen, J. (1995). *It's never too late: Leading adolescents to lifelong literacy.* Portsmouth, NH: Heinemann.

Allen, J. (1999). *Words, words, words.* Portsmouth, ME: Stenhouse.

Allen, J. (2000). *Yellow brick roads: Shared and guided paths to independent reading 4–12.* Portsmouth, NH: Heinemann.

Allen, J. (2007). *Inside words: Tools for teaching academic vocabulary, Grades 4–12.* Portland, ME: Stenhouse.

Appleman, D. (2006). *Reading for themselves: How to transform adolescents into lifelong readers through out-of-class book clubs.* Portsmouth, NH: Heinemann.

Aronson, M. (2001). *Exploding the myths.* Lanham, MD: Scarecrow Press.

Beers, K., Probst, R., & Rief, L. (2007). *Adolescent literacy: Turning promise into practice.* Portsmouth, NH: Heinemann.

Berrill, D., Doucette, L., & Verhulst, D. (2006). *Tutoring adolescent readers.* Portland, ME: Pembroke.

Blachowicz, C., & Fisher, P. J. (2006). *Teaching vocabulary in all classrooms* (3rd ed.). Upper Saddle River, NJ: Pearson.

Booth, D. (2001). *Reading and writing in the middle years.* Portland, ME: Stenhouse.

Booth, D. (2002). *Even hockey players read.* Portland, ME: Pembroke.

Booth, D. (2006). *Reading doesn't matter anymore.* Portland, ME: Pembroke.

Brozo, W. G., & Simpson, M. L. (2007). *Content literacy for today's adolescents: Honoring diversity and building competence.* Upper Saddle River, NJ: Pearson.

Burke, J. (2000). *Reading reminders: Tools, tips, and techniques.* Portsmouth, NH: Boynton/Cook.

Burke, J. (2001). *Illuminating texts: How to teach students to read the world.* Portsmouth, NH: Heinemann.

Buss, K., & Karnowski, L. (2000). *Reading and writing literary genres.* Newark, DE: IRA.

Chambers, A. (1996). *The reading environment: How adults help children enjoy books.* Portland, ME: Stenhouse.

Chambers, A. (1996). *Tell me: Children, reading, and talk.* Portland, ME: Stenhouse.

Daniels, H., & Steineke, N. (2004). *Mini-lessons for literature circles.* Portsmouth, NH: Heinemann.

Daniels, H., & Zemelman, S. (2004). *Subjects matter.* Portsmouth, NH: Heinemann.

Dorn, L. J., & Soffos, C. (2005). *Teaching for deep comprehension.* Portland, ME: Stenhouse.

Ericson, B. O. (2001). *Teaching reading in high school English classes.* Urbana, IL: NCTE.

Fisher, D., & Frey, N. (2008). *Improving adolescent literacy: Content area strategies at work* (2nd ed.). Boston: Pearson.

Fountas, I. C., & Pinnell, G. S. (2006). *Teaching for comprehending and fluency: Thinking, talking, and writing about reading, K–8.* Portsmouth, NH: Heinemann.

Galda, L., & Graves, M. F. (2007). *Reading and responding in the middle grades: Approaches for all classrooms.* Boston: Allyn & Bacon.

Gallagher, K. (2004). *Deeper reading: Comprehending challenging texts, 4–12.* Portland, ME: Stenhouse.

Gallo, D. R. (1992). *Authors' insights: Turning teenagers into readers and writers.* Portsmouth, NH: Boynton/Cook.

Gunning, T. G. (2008). *Developing higher-level literacy in all students: Building reading, reasoning, and responding.* Boston: Pearson.

Harvey, S. (1998). *Nonfiction matters: Reading, writing, and research in Grades 3–8.* Portland, ME: Stenhouse.

Harvey, S., & Goudvis, A. (2007*). Strategies that work* (2nd ed.). Portland, ME: Stenhouse.

Hoyt, L. (1999). *Revisit, reflect, retell: Strategies for improving reading comprehension.* Portsmouth, NH: Heinemann.

Irvin, J. L., Buehl, D. R., & Radcliffe, B. J. (2007). *Strategies to enhance literacy and learning in middle school content area classrooms.* Boston: Allyn & Bacon.

Keene, E. O., & Zimmerman, S. (2007). *Mosaic of thought: The power of comprehension strategy instruction.* Portsmouth, NH: Heinemann.

Kendall, J., & Khuon, O. (2005). *Making sense: Small-group comprehension lessons for English language learners.* Portland, ME: Stenhouse.

Lapp, D., Flood, J., Brock, C., & Fisher, D. (2007). *Teaching reading to every child* (4th ed.). Mahwah, NJ: Lawrence Erlbaum.

Lesesne, T. S. (2003). *Making the match.* Portland, ME: Stenhouse.

Marshall, J. C. (2002). *Are they really reading? Expanding SSR in the middle grades.* Portland, ME: Stenhouse.

Mueller, P. N. (2001). *Lifers: Learning from at-risk adolescent readers.* Portsmouth, NH: Heinemann.

Newkirk, T. (2002). *Misreading masculinity: Boys, literacy, and popular culture.* Portsmouth, NH: Heinemann.

O'Donnell-Allen, C. (2006). *The book club companion: Fostering strategic readers in the secondary classroom.* Portsmouth, NH: Heinemann.

Olson, C. B. (2007). *The reading/writing connection: Strategies for teaching and learning in the secondary classroom.* Upper Saddle River, NJ: Pearson.

Opitz, M. F., Ford, M. P., & Zbaracki, M. D. (2006). *Books and beyond: New ways to reach readers.* Portsmouth, NH: Heinemann.

Pennac, D. (1999). *Better than life.* Portland, ME: Stenhouse.

Prescott-Griffin, M. L. (2004). *Fluency in focus: Comprehension strategies for all young readers.* Portsmouth, NH: Heinemann.

Reynolds, M. (2004). *I can't read and you can't make me.* Portsmouth, NH: Heinemann.

Santman, D. (2005). *Shades of meaning: Comprehension and interpretation in middle school.* Portsmouth, NH: Heinemann.

Schoenbach, R., Greenleaf, C., Cziko, C., & Hurwitz, L. (1999). *Reading for understanding: A guide to improving reading in middle and high school classrooms.* San Francisco: Jossey-Bass.

Shannon, P. (2007). *Reading against democracy: The broken promises of reading instruction.* Portsmouth, NH: Heinemann.

Shea, M. (2006). Where's the glitch? How to use running records with older readers, Grades 5–8. Portsmouth, NH: Heinemann.

Smith, F. (2003). *Unspeakable acts, unnatural practices: Flaws and fallacies in "scientific" reading instruction.* Portsmouth, NH: Heinemann.

Smith, F. (2006). *Reading without nonsense* (4th ed.). New York: Teachers College Press.

Smith, M. W., & Wilhelm, J. D. (2002). *Reading don't fix no Chevys.* Portsmouth, NH: Heinemann.

Strickland, D. S., Ganske, K., & Monroe, J. K. (2001). *Supporting struggling readers and writers: Strategies for classroom intervention 3–6.* Portland, ME: Stenhouse.

Sullivan, E. T. (2002). *Reaching reluctant young adult readers.* Lanham, MD: Scarecrow Press.

Tatum, A. W. (2005). *Teaching reading to black adolescent males.* Portland, ME: Stenhouse.

Tovani, C. (2000). *I read it, but I don't get it: Comprehension strategies for adolescent readers.* Portland, ME: Stenhouse.

Tovani, C. (2004). *Do I really have to teach reading? Content comprehension, Grades 6–12.* Portland, ME: Stenhouse.

Wilhelm, J. D. (2007). *Engaging readers and writers with inquiry: Promoting deep understandings in language arts and the content areas with guiding questions.* New York: Scholastic.

Wilhelm, J. D. (2008). *You gotta be the book: Teaching engaged and reflective reading with adolescents* (2nd ed.). New York: Teachers College Press.

Wilhelm, J. D., Baker, T. N., & Hackett, J. D. (2001). *Strategic reading: Guiding students to lifelong literacy, 6–12.* Portsmouth, NH: Heinemann.

Young, T. A., & Hadaway, N. (Ed.). (2006). *Supporting the literacy development of English learners: Increasing success in all classrooms.* Newark, DE: IRA.

References

Bartoli, J., & Botel, M. (1988). *Reading/learning disability: An ecological approach.* New York: Teachers College Press.

Beers, K. (2003). *When kids can't read: What teachers can do.* Portsmouth, NH: Heinemann.

Bintz, W. (1997). Exploring reading nightmares of middle and secondary school teachers. *Journal of Adolescent and Adult Literacy, 41*(1), 12–24.

Crutcher, C. (2007). *Deadline.* New York: HarperCollins.

Deshler, D. D., Palincsar, A. S., Biancarosa, G., & Nair, M. (2007). *Informed choices for struggling adolescent readers: A research-based guide to instructional programs and practices.* Newark, DE: IRA.

Gallagher, K. (2003). *Reading reasons: Motivational mini-lessons for middle and high school.* Portland, ME: Stenhouse.

Goodman, K. (1996). *On reading: A common-sense look at the nature of language and the science of reading.* Portsmouth, NH: Heinemann.

Goodnow, C. (2007, March 3). Teens buying books at fastest rate in decades. *Seattle-Post Intelligencer.* Retrieved May 14, 2007, from http://seattlepi.nwsource.com/books/306531_teenlit08.html

Irvin, J. L., Buehl, D. R., & Klemp, R. M. (2007). *Reading and the high school student: Strategies to enhance learning* (2nd ed.). Boston: Allyn & Bacon.

Muth, D. (1993). Reading mathematics: Middle school mathematics teachers' beliefs and practices. *Reading Research and Instruction, 32*(2), 76–83.

NCTE. (2006). *NCTE Principles of Adolescent Literacy Reform.* Urbana, IL: Author.

Porter, K. A. (1969). The jilting of Granny Weatherall. *The collected stories of Katherine Anne Porter.* Orlando, FL: Harvest/Harcourt.

Stewart, R. (1990). Factors influencing preservice teachers' resistance to content area reading instruction. *Reading Research and Instruction, 29*(4), 55–63.

Weaver, C. (2002). *Reading process and practice* (3rd ed.). Portsmouth, NH: Heinemann.

Wilhelm, J. (2001). *Improving comprehension with think-aloud strategies.* New York: Scholastic.

Zirinsky, D., & Rau, S. (2001). *A classroom of teenaged readers: Nurturing reading processes in senior high English.* New York: Addison Wesley Longman.

Trends and Issues in Young Adult Literature

Introduction

Over the last half century, experts have struggled to define young adult (YA) literature. *Young adult literature, adolescent literature, juvenile literature, junior books, children's literature, books for teens,* and *books for tweeners* describe texts that bridge the gap between children's literature and adult literature. Given the negative connotations of the words *adolescents* and *teens,* most experts today agree upon *young adult literature.* Following are characteristics that have historically defined the genre:

1. The protagonist is a teenager.
2. Events revolve around the protagonist and his/her struggle to resolve conflict.
3. The story is told from the viewpoint and in the voice of a young adult.
4. The genre is written by and for young adults.
5. The genre is marketed to the young adult audience.
6. Stories don't have "storybook" or "happily-ever-after" endings—a characteristic of children's books.
7. Parents are noticeably absent or at odds with young adults.
8. The genre addresses coming-of-age issues (e.g., maturity, sexuality, relationships, drugs).
9. Books contain under 300 pages, closer to 200.

Reliance upon a laundry list of characteristics, however, results in a narrow and misleading definition of young adult literature. Consider, for instance, the characteristics *parents are noticeably absent or at odds with young adults* and *the genre addresses coming-of-age issues.* These are characteristics of the earliest young adult novels, the problem novels discussed in Chapter 4 that laid the genre's foundation and that gave voice to the realistic struggles and issues of adolescence. While the problem novel holds an honored

YA books range from thin novellas to books with 800+ pages.

position in the young adult canon, young adult writers have branched out into every genre imaginable.

A better approach to defining young adult literature is to consider what teens *choose* to read as opposed to what they are *required* to read (i.e., classical texts). Most teens choose books that publishing companies market as YA literature, as well as books that are marketed for the adult audience. They choose books with teen protagonists and seldom choose to read the traditional canon. While this approach to defining the genre has merit, it's somewhat problematic. In latter years the young adult genre has evolved, become more sophisticated, more inclusive, and has gained more widespread popularity. In classrooms across the country, teachers have replaced classical texts with books marketed primarily for teens. The idea, therefore, that young adult literature is what young adults *choose* to read and not what they are *coerced* to read falls a bit short because sometimes teens are forced to read books traditionally labeled "young adult." That's not an optimistic thought, but you get my point. Perhaps the best definition an expert in the young adult literature field can give is "I know it when I see it."

In writing this book, I've focused on "all of the above." While the bulk of this textbook concentrates on quality literature written and marketed for teens, I've also included (in places) some poorly written texts, primarily because teens don't generally choose a book on literary merit, and as teachers we engage our students best when we know and respect what they enjoy. I've also included adult books and some classical works. As I argue in Chapter 11, the classics shouldn't be reserved for advanced readers, nor should young adult literature serve only less proficient readers. Some teens, however, are mature beyond their years and feel better engaged with classical texts. Also, because teens do read adult books, I've embedded a number of adult books throughout chapters.

In developing this chapter, I turned to several young adult experts for assistance. As I studied their work, I realized it made more sense to include their voices than it did to paraphrase or summarize their work. Including pieces written by them, I believe, makes for a more engaging read and also adds a rich layer of credibility to this chapter. You'll find, then, sections by three young adult experts interspersed throughout this chapter. In the section that follows, young adult expert Connie Zitlow provides brief analyses and descriptions of 20 time-tested young adult books and 20 forgotten titles worth knowing. Later in the chapter Patty Campbell provides an overview of how the genre has changed.[1] I am grateful for Chris Crutcher's thoughts on censorship that rounds out the chapter. Winner of the Intellectual Freedom Award, Crutcher is a prominent voice against censorship. My contributions deal primarily with the value of young adult literature, marketing and accessibility issues, and characteristics of quality literature.

---

[1]Campbell gives an overview of how the young adult genre has evolved. Individual genre chapters contain historical background on the development of that particular genre (e.g., short stories, romance).

Twenty Classic Young Adult Novels   by Connie Zitlow

Choosing 20 "classic" young adult novels is a subjective but pleasant exercise that makes it clear this relatively new genre of literature includes many works of notable literary merit. To be declared a classic work, it must be deemed an outstanding piece of literature, characterized by its originality, overall literary quality, and recognized worth. It must have a story with lasting significance, a piece of literature that rewards study because of its content and distinctive style, both its uniqueness and universality. The book must have proven itself with different readers who note its acknowledged artistry and use of literary elements: a believable and interesting plot, riveting dialogue, worthwhile theme, rich characterization, vivid setting, appropriate point of view, and carefully chosen language. It is a story that transports readers into the worlds of others and also helps them see their own lives in new ways. Many of the classic novels are award-winning books acknowledged for their emotional impact and lasting influence on subsequent works. In addition, although not originally published as young adult literature, many of the classics have become works that have been embraced by young readers.

thematic weight, depth of characterization, and striking symbolism. First-year student Jerry Renault "dares to disturb the universe" of Trinity High School by refusing to participate in the chocolate sale, and thereby defying the powerful Archie and his secret society, the Vigils, and the corrupt Brother Leon. With this book, Cormier makes vivid the real presence of evil in young people's lives and shows what happens when good people stand by and do nothing.

The Catcher in the Rye by J. D. Salinger. New York: Little, Brown, 1951.

This classic work, published before the young adult category existed, is the prototype of the genre. The story is told in the first-person voice of lonely, funny, cynical, and sometimes vulgar Holden Caulfield who wants to protect the innocent from what he sees as the phony adult world. Salinger's book, with Holden's choice of words and rite-of-passage incidents, stands as a vivid contrast to the "junior" books of the era that avoided taboo topics and forbidden language.

The Chocolate War by Robert Cormier. New York: Pantheon Books, 1974.

Not originally written for any particular audience, this seminal and enduring work set the standard for a new level of literary excellence in young adult literature. The story is noted for its exemplary plot structure,

The Chosen by Chaim Potok. New York: Simon & Schuster, 1967.

Another work, like *The Catcher in the Rye,* first published as an adult title. This classic story of fathers and sons is set in 1940s Brooklyn when news of the Holocaust began to emerge. Friends Danny, a Hasidic Jew, and Reuven, a secular Jew, agonize about abandoning their faith to pursue life in the society outside their ethnic group. This coming-of-age story with its universal themes is an example of the inner conflicts experienced by teens trying to understand themselves amid their crisis of faith.

The Contender by Robert Lipsyte. New York: HarperCollins, 1967.

Because of his curiosity about boxing, Alfred Brooks, a black teen and school dropout, climbs the stairs

Continued

Twenty Classic Young Adult Novels *Continued*

to Donatelli's gym and learns to be a contender in more than boxing. He refuses to help a gang rob the Jewish-owned grocery where he works. Published in a critical year for realistic YA literature, this landmark book helped break the myth that YA books were only about white middle-class families. More than a sports novel, it shows an adolescent searching for acceptance and reinventing himself.

Ender's Game by Orson Scott Card. New York: Tor, 1985.

In this crossover and complex novel, considered to be a significant work of science fiction, humans fear that they will again be attacked by aliens. Ender Wiggin, an adolescent and a genius, is trained to be part of an elite militia to protect the human race from further invasions.

Fallen Angels by Walter Dean Myers. New York: Scholastic, 1988.

Set in Vietnam and told by 17-year-old Richie Perry who wants to get out of Harlem, this highly acclaimed book conveys the horror and anguish of war. Perry becomes part of an integrated group of soldiers who bond together to survive. Dedicated to Myers's brother who died in Vietnam, the story is noted for its complex characters, genuine dialogue, vivid imagery and figurative language, including the extended metaphor that contrasts war's realities with romanticized portrayals in the media.

The Giver by Lois Lowry. Boston: Houghton Mifflin, 1993.

In this haunting and thought-provoking futuristic story, 12-year-old Jonas is chosen to become the next Receiver of Memory for his controlled community that is actually a dystopian society without sickness, poverty, or even color. In his sessions with the Giver, Jonas experiences pain and joy, love and sorrow. His decision to save the twin Gabriel inspires discussion about many social and political issues and affirms the power of the human spirit.

Hatchet by Gary Paulsen. New York: Bradbury Press, 1987.

Paulsen's convincing adventure begins when 13-year-old Brian Robeson must crash-land a small airplane into a Canadian lake. Readers are pulled into the story by his interior monologue, along with the third-person narrator and Paulsen's pacing and vivid descriptions of what it takes to survive alone for 54 days in the wilderness. Brian's physical and emotional struggle and his growth as a character resonate with teens who welcome the sequels to his story.

Holes by Louis Sachar. New York: Farrar, Straus & Giroux, 1998.

In this fanciful adventure, with its exaggerated images, humor, and mystery, there are actually two stories: Stanley Yelnats's contemporary story and that of his cursed ancestors. Mistakenly accused of theft, Stanley is sent to Camp Green Lake Juvenile Correction Facility, a desert setting with no lake, nothing green, and where he meets Zero. The cruel warden forces the boys to dig holes in the blistering Texas sand, supposedly to build character, but really to help her find a buried treasure.

The House on Mango Street by Sandra Cisneros. Houston, TX: Arte Publico, 1983.

Young readers have embraced this short, elegant book with its combination of harsh realities and poetic descriptions of Esperanza Cordero's life in the Latino quarter of Chicago. Originally written for her students, Cisneros's lyrical work is the story of young Mexican American women striving to create an identity that is more than the low expectations others have for them.

I Am the Cheese by Robert Cormier. New York: Knopf/Random House, 1977.

Adam Farmer, on a mysterious bicycle journey, searches for the truth about the death of his parents who were

Continued

Twenty Classic Young Adult Novels   *Continued*

under the witness relocation program. The three levels of this complex psychological plot—Adam's bike ride in first-person present tense, transcripts of tapes with a sinister interrogator named Brint, and third-person omniscient details about the past—come together at the end. This dark novel is noted for its hidden intrigue, masterful structure, and theme of innocence caught by corruption.

Ironman by Chris Crutcher. New York: Greenwillow/HarperCollins, 1995.

When high school senior Bo Brewster trains for a triathlon, he finds relief from the volatile relationship with his father. After losing his temper with his coach, he is assigned to an anger-management class led by the colorful Asian cowboy, Mr. Nak, and attended by teens caught in a variety of abusive situations. The story consists of Bo's letters to Larry King, omniscient entries, and the gripping present tense commentary of the triathlon.

Jacob Have I Loved by Katherine Paterson. New York: Crowell, 1980.

Twin Sara Louise, the firstborn, was soon cast aside when everyone's attention focused on her weaker sister, Caroline, the favored one. The setting, more than a background to the story, is the Chesapeake Bay island of Rass in the 1940s where Louise ("Wheeze"), the Esau character, loves working with her waterman father. Louise's strong first-person account is filled with beautiful figurative language, memorable characterization, literary and biblical allusions, and vivid water images.

Make Lemonade by Virginia Euwer Wolff. New York: Henry Holt, 1993.

To earn money for college, determined 14-year-old LaVaughn answers an ad for a babysitter. Her life is changed when she meets teen mother Jolly and her young children, Jeremy and Jilly. This highly acclaimed story in verse, written as 66 episodes of poetic stream-of-consciousness prose, is noted for its

rich character development, striking images of urban poverty, and blend of realism and hope.

Monster by Walter Dean Myers. New York: HarperCollins, 1999.

This multilayered and cinematic book was recognized for its literary excellence as the first winner of the Michael L. Printz Award. From the powerful first image, readers are immersed with Steve Harmon in the fear and desperation of being in prison. Is he guilty or innocent? Is he a monster? Steve tells his story with a handwritten memoir and typed screenplay. Drawings, photographs, mug shots, and video stills add to the complexity of this gripping story that raises many social and racial questions.

The Moves Make the Man by Bruce Brooks. New York: HarperCollins, 1984.

Jerome Foxworthy, the only black student in an all-white school, sets out to tell what really happened to his friend Bix Rivers, the talented baseball player who sees Jerome's fake-out basketball moves as a violation of truth. It is a story within a story revealing the quest of intelligent, talented Jerome whose authentic narrative voice is an example of Brooks's stylistic artistry. This book about friendship, racial prejudice, mental illness, family relationships, perception and truth, light and darkness, leaves readers with the vivid imagery of Jerome's spin light.

Out of the Dust by Karen Hesse. New York: Scholastic, 1997.

Fourteen-year-old Billie Jo lives in the Oklahoma panhandle in the 1930s, where there is dust everywhere, even on her beloved piano. Her strong, first-person voice is conveyed in diary-like entries filled with vivid imagery that fits the time and place, even details about how those who lived in the dust found ways to enjoy life. After a tragic fire that kills her mother and unborn baby brother, Billie Jo must learn to forgive her father, nature, and herself.

Continued

Twenty Classic Young Adult Novels   *Continued*

The Outsiders by S. E. Hinton. New York: Viking/Penguin, 1967.

Hinton editorializes through the voice of 14-year-old Ponyboy Curtis, who lives with his older brothers. Parents are missing in this story about the gang warfare between the Greasers and the "Socs" (Socials), teens in different social classes in 1960s Oklahoma. Written when Hinton was a teenager and a landmark work of young adult literature because of its subject matter, the book is widely read, although it is considered to be less realistic than when originally published.

The Pigman by Paul Zindel. New York: HarperCollins, 1968.

Two alienated adolescents, Lorraine and John, write what they call their "memorial epic" about their adventures with the Pigman, a lonely old man who can't admit his wife is dead. Their first-person voice

is reminiscent of *The Catcher in the Rye,* and like *The Contender,* the story is set in New York, although it lacks the realism of Lipsyte's story. Noted for its contrasting points of view and use of flashbacks, Zindel's book about friendship and caring is also a story about accepting responsibility.

Roll of Thunder, Hear My Cry by Mildred D. Taylor. New York: Dial/Penguin, 1976.

Taylor, noted for her poetic style and skill as a storyteller, used her own family history as the basis for her award-winning series about the Logans who are landowners in Mississippi in the 1930s. Narrator Cassie Logan, an adolescent in the sequel *Let the Circle Be Unbroken* (1981), finds it difficult to accept the racial prejudice, injustice, and fear that threatens her proud, loving family and other blacks in their community.

Copyright Connie Zitlow, 2008

Twenty Forgotten Young Adult Novels   by Connie Zitlow

Young adult novels that are the "forgotten" ones are either out of print or not readily available. Also among the forgotten books are those works that are available but are frequently overlooked. Although these stories made an impact when first published, they are now lost to the attention of many young readers and the adults who read and promote this literature as a worthy and enjoyable genre of literary works. The forgotten novels are not the ones chosen for whole class reading, small-group discussions, or as individual selections, and might even be missing from library shelves. Yet the books are too good to forget and have the potential to appeal to teens today. In these novels, readers can find a variety of compelling stories with relevant topics, interesting characters and settings, and worthwhile themes. The books on this list are examples of works that will once again become "found" for those readers who discover the value in their lost and forgotten stories.

Beyond the Divide by Kathryn Lasky. New York: Macmillan, 1983.

Fourteen-year-old Meribah Simon tells about the difficult journey she and her father take in 1849, when they head west after he is shunned from their Amish community for attending the funeral of a friend. Meribah, who has an artistic eye and lots of determination, faces many cruel and life-threatening situations, particularly when she must find a way to survive alone in the Nevada desert.

Blinded by the Light by Robin Brancato. New York: Knopf, 1978.

Gail Brower, a sophomore in college, is alarmed that her brother Jim has joined a religious cult. When she attempts to convince him to leave, she experiences the cult's powerful techniques. She realizes how easily young people, desperate to belong to a group and

Continued

Twenty Forgotten Young Adult Novels *Continued*

to have others make decisions for them, are drawn in by the cult's allure.

Celine by Brock Cole. New York: Farrar, Straus & Giroux, 1989.

Told by her father to show a little maturity, 16-year-old Celine is actually more adult than her divorced, self-absorbed parents, especially when she assumes responsibility for her young neighbor Jake. Beginning when her painting "Test Patterns" breaks into pieces as she walks home from school, Celine tells the story of her difficulties that continue as she struggles with an essay on Holden Caulfield and tries to figure out who she is.

Chernowitz by Fran Arrick. New York: Bradbury Press, 1981.

When Bob Cherno is 15, he looks back at what happened when he was bullied by the bigot Emmett Sundback, who ridicules Bob's Jewishness. The prejudice and hatred even take the form of a burning cross thrown in the yard and a swastika on the family car. Many of Bob's schoolmates are moved to tears when they see a film about the Holocaust, but Emmett does not change.

Drowning of Stephan Jones by Bette Greene. New York: Bantam, 1991.

In this fictionalized account of a real incident, the evil treatment of two peaceful gay men is encouraged by a homophobic minister and carried out by churchgoing boys whose hate and harassment lead to Stephan's death. The power of social conformity is portrayed by 16-year-old Carla as she struggles with her desire to belong and to face the truth about her popular boyfriend Andy.

The Eagle Kite by Paula Fox. New York: Orchard, 1995.

In this striking and sensitively told story, Fox does not soften the suffering and anguish of the whole family when one person is infected with AIDS. Liam is a first-year high school student when he learns about his father's illness. Liam not only grieves but

is angry, frustrated, and lonely until he goes to the seaside one Thanksgiving to see his father who has gone there to die.

Finding My Voice by Marie G. Lee. New York: HarperTrophy, 1992.

Ellen Sung feels that she cannot tell her strict immigrant parents about her classmates' racial slurs or about Tomper Sandel who wants to be her boyfriend. They expect her to focus on her studies and follow her older sister to Harvard. Ellen tells her story in first person in this book based on Lee's experiences of growing up Korean American on the Iron Range in Minnesota.

Friends by Rosa Guy. New York: Henry Holt, 1973.

This novel, significant as an early young adult book about immigrants treated as outsiders, deals realistically with issues of class, race, and poverty. Phyllisia Cathy, a black teen from the West Indies and living in Harlem, feels superior to the other blacks who reject her; however, when her mother's illness results in death, Phyllisia learns the value of her friendship with poor, indifferent Edith Jackson.

A Hero Ain't Nothin' but a Sandwich by Alice Childress. New York: Coward McCann, 1973.

Readers of this realistic problem novel set in Harlem must decide if 13-year-old Benjie Johnson can conquer his addiction to heroin. In this hard-edged story, Butler Craig, Benjie's would-be stepfather, is one who wants to help Benjie. The book's notable literary elements include the authentic black dialect and contrasting viewpoints of 12 different voices.

Home before Dark by Sue Ellen Bridgers. New York: Knopf, 1976.

Stella is 14, headstrong, proud, and tired of living with her family in the battered old station wagon as they travel to work the next crop. When they finally settle in a little tenant house on her father's family

Continued

Twenty Forgotten Young Adult Novels   *Continued*

farm in the tobacco fields of eastern North Carolina, Stella finds the place where she belongs and says she will never leave. This beautifully written story, with its vivid imagery and well-developed characters, explores complex family relationships.

In Summer Light by Zibby Oneal. New York: Viking, 1985.

Kate Brewer is an introspective 17-year-old who must come to terms with her demanding father, a famous artist who seems to dismiss her artistic talent. While on Martha's Vineyard recovering from mononucleosis and with the support of a graduate student who is cataloging her father's paintings, Kate completes a paper on Shakespeare's *Tempest* and finally sees her father in a different light.

Keeper of the Isis Light by Monica Hughes. New York: Atheneum, 1981.

This book is the first of a science fiction trilogy set in outer space (Isis) where Olwen is born to research scientists from Earth. When Olwen is orphaned, she is cared for by Guardian, a robot that must help her adjust to her physical and mental changes if she is to survive in the planet's hostile atmosphere. When colonizers from Earth arrive and Olwen meets 17-year-old Mark, she must face questions of identity and decide what it really means to be human.

Lizard by Dennis Covington. New York: Delacorte, 1991.

Told in first person by the boy called Lizard, this novel portrays the struggles that come with disfigurement. Because his face resembles a reptile, Lucius Sims is sent to Leesville Louisiana State School for Retarded Boys. He escapes with a traveling shoe salesman who claims to be his father and is rescued by an alcoholic actor who wants him to play the part of Caliban. This southern picaresque novel has a variety of richly drawn, offbeat characters.

The Magician by Sol Stein. New York: Delacorte, 1971.

Ed Japhet is 16 and an accomplished magician, but his intermission entertainment at a school dance arouses the jealousy of the bully Stanley Urek who tries to kill Ed. The theme, style, and characterization of this novel, which points to the problems of escalating violence and exposes injustices of the judicial system, is an appropriate choice for mature students.

Remembering the Good Times by Richard Peck. New York: Delacorte, 1985.

Travis, Kate, and Buck are friends who live in a suburban community where they enjoy being with Kate's great-grandmother, Polly, whose pear orchard is a symbol of the past and a place of refuge. In this important book, Peck artfully tells a story of change, violence, and friendship and points to the important issue of teen suicide.

Sex Education by Jenny Davis. New York: Orchard, 1988.

The title is somewhat misleading in this book about caring and healing, although the teacher does address the problems of teen pregnancy by adding a sex education unit to her biology curriculum. Livvie, who has had a mental breakdown, tells the story of her relationship with David, their caring for Maggie who is abused, and what led to David's death.

Sheila's Dying by Alden Carter. New York: Putnam, 1987.

Jerry Kincaid decides to break up with his girlfriend until he finds out she has terminal cancer and has only her alcoholic grandmother to care for her. The story is really about Jerry and his high school nemesis Bonnie who become partners as Sheila's caregivers. Carter conveys Jerry's fear, fatigue, anger, grief, growing respect, friendship, and love in this book that is not so much about death as about living on.

Summer Rules by Robert Lipsyte. 1981.

The story of Bobby Marks's 14th summer, when he is determined to change himself by losing 40 pounds, is told in *One Fat Summer* (Harper & Row, 1977). At the end of that summer, Bobby faces a future full of promise and challenge. But the continuation of

Continued

Twenty Forgotten Young Adult Novels   *Continued*

his coming-of-age adventures is lost to readers who cannot find the out-of-print novels, *Summer Rules* and *The Summerboy* (1982), books in which Lipsyte artfully conveys Bobby's development of social consciousness and self-transformation.

The Treasure of Plunderell Manor by Bruce Clements. New York: Farrar, Straus & Giroux, 1987.

Set in mid-Victorian England, this spoof of gothic thrillers is an example of the author's witty novels. Fourteen-year-old Laurel Bybank becomes the maid of Alice Plunderell, a young heiress whose life is in danger because she is to inherit a hidden treasure on her 18th birthday. Laurel must learn who is trustworthy, use her common sense, and keep her sense of humor if she and Alice are to survive.

Up in Seth's Room by Norma Fox Mazer. New York: Delacorte, 1979.

Finn is 15 and in love with 19-year-old Seth, but the conflict of whether to have intercourse creates tension between the two. Finn is a strong young woman who decides to come up with her own definition of pragmatic abstinence. Mazer portrays a teen who stands up to peer pressure and takes responsibility for making her own decisions.

Copyright Connie Zitlow, 2008

Marketing Issues, Accessibility, and the Value of Young Adult Literature

Just as with adult publishing, the young adult market is flooded with both quality and trash. Grounding their criticism in erroneous and misleading media coverage and in limited familiarity with young adult literature, some critics assert young adult literature is worthless and inferior to classical texts and adult literature. Those who study the young adult genre, however, understand multiple factors contribute to this negative pigeonholing. They also know that young adult literature offers some of the best in contemporary literature. It's almost impossible to read a book like John Green's *Looking for Alaska* (2005), for instance, and not develop huge respect for young adult literature and those who write for this audience. Deeply philosophical and richly textured, *Looking for Alaska* is an intense coming-of-age story about a group of teens, a boarding school, and one boy's search for the "Great Perhaps." First-time novelist Green depicts the intensity of adolescence seldom seen in contemporary literature. Dozens of authors pen equally well-crafted, deeply layered stories. Box 3.1 features a sampling of exceptional young adult novels that serves as a good introduction for skeptics who question young adult literature's literary merit.

A number of issues contribute to a stigmatic view of the genre. First, the location of young adult literature in bookstores is problematic. Some bookstores combine young adult literature with children's literature, and by doing so, send an unwritten message that young adult literature is not sophisticated enough for teens, especially older readers. Other bookstores place young adult literature in close proximity to children's literature,

Box 3.1   A Few Exceptional Reads in YA Literature

Apocalypse **by Tim Bowler. New York: McElderry/Simon & Schuster, 2004.**

Written by one of the best young adult thriller writers, this novel takes the reader on a startling journey into a malicious and terrifying world. Kit and his parents end up on a barren island after being shipwrecked in a storm, where they encounter an odd and brutal group of people who seem to hate Kit upon first encounter. Kit wanders off in search of a strange girl he believes can help them but upon returning discovers his parents are missing.

The Astonishing Life of Octavian Nothing, Traitor to the Nation: Volume 1. The Pox Party **by M. T. Anderson. Cambridge, MA: Candlewick Press, 2006.**

Given a classical education and growing up in a household of scholars, a young boy, Octavian, begins questioning the fanatical studies that take place around him. Upon opening a forbidden door, he discovers shocking experiments. A complex multigenre, multithemed tale that takes place in Boston during the American Revolution.

The Book Thief **by Markus Zusak. New York: Random House, 2006.**

A World War II setting is the backdrop for this coming-of-age story about Liesel Meminger, a foster girl living in Munich. Liesel loves books and steals them. Aided by her foster father, she learns to read and shares her books with her friends and the Jewish man hidden in their house.

The Center of the World **by Andreas Steinhöfel, Trans., Alisa Jaffa. New York: Delacorte/Random House, 2005.**

Seventeen-year-old Phil, a gay teen, lives with his mother and twin sister in a small German community. Phil's mother is promiscuous, and her sexual behavior causes negative fallout for Phil and his sister. A rich, multilayered story about family relationships and connection.

City of Bones: Book 1: The Mortal Instruments **by Cassandra Clare. New York: McElderry/Simon & Schuster, 2007.**

15-year-old Clary witnesses a murder. But does she? The body disappears into thin air and no one can see the murderers, three teenagers covered with bizarre tattoos. Clary becomes embroiled in the world of the Shadowhunters, warriors dedicated to ridding the earth of demons. A refreshing urban fantasy.

Gifts **by Ursula K. Le Guin. Orlando, FL: Harcourt, 2004.**

The Upland clans possess gifts, both wonderful and terrifying. They have the ability to create fire and move land, but they can also inflict illness and pain. Two young clan members refuse to use their powers. A cleverly crafted story about the cruelty of power.

The House of the Scorpion **by Nancy Farmer. New York: Simon & Schuster, 2002.**

An award-winning sci-fi thriller about a young clone. When Matt, cloned from an elderly drug lord, learns the real reason for his existence, he attempts a treacherous escape into an unknown world. A contemporary science fiction masterpiece, this book is a shocking examination of what might be scientifically possible in the near future. *The Sea of Trolls* (2004) is also an exceptional read.

Impulse **by Ellen Hopkins. New York: Simon & Schuster, 2007.**

Taking place within a psychiatric hospital, this massive verse novel traces the lives of three teens who each attempted suicide: one with a knife, another with a gun, and the last with a bottle. Together, can they chart a better course for their lives and battle the demons in their lives? Though this book reads fast, it includes more detail than usual in a young adult novel. *Crank* (2004) and *Burned* (2006) are similar in size and style.

Continued

Box 3.1   A Few Exceptional Reads in YA Literature *Continued*

Inexcusable **by Chris Lynch. New York: Simon & Schuster, 2005.**

This National Book Award Finalist is sure to provoke heated discussion. Keir is a good guy—a good son and brother, terrific athlete and friend. What happens between Keir and his long-term girlfriend, Gigi? Is it date rape? Or consensual sex? Keir doesn't think so. Masterfully crafted with an amazing voice and unforgettable male protagonist. A rare must read for all males.

Invisible **by Pete Hautman. New York: Simon & Schuster, 2005.**

Doug is a loner and misfit who builds trains in his basement. He does have one best friend: Andy, a superstar popular athlete. Doug retreats within himself and, as he does, the reader learns about what happened at the Tuttle place a long time ago. An exceptional book that illustrates Hautman's ability to build suspense and hook and surprise the reader.

Psyche in a Dress **by Francesca Lia Block. New York: HarperCollins, 2006.**

Like much of Block's work, *Psyche in a Dress* draws on Block's love of mythology. Psyche yearns to be transformed by true love. In her quest, she is challenged by demons and gods. Block's work is described as postmodern, magical realism. Her stories are generally otherworldly.

This Is All: The Pillow Book of Cordelia Kenn **by Aidan Chambers. New York: Harry Abrams, 2006.**

The sheer size of this volume sends a clear message that young adult literature isn't just for younger adolescents and at-risk readers. Nineteen-year-old Cordelia decides to narrate her life for her unborn child. In doing so, she paints a vivid portrait of a remarkable young woman, one who writes candidly about first love, sex, friendship, literature, faith, and one's place in the world. Amazing depth and complexity. The protagonist's age also attracts older readers.

Surrender **by Sonya Hartnett. Cambridge, MA: Candlewick Press, 2006.**

A young man recounts his past in this exquisitely written psychological thriller. Through flashbacks, the reader learns of a horrific mistake and a life filled with frustration and humiliation. A dark, brilliant, and tender story.

sending a similar message. Many older teens, boys especially, won't be caught dead perusing a young adult section for this reason. Also, bookstores seldom stock a wide range of quality young adult books. Formulaic serial books, chick lit, and mass market here-today-gone-tomorrow reads dominate shelves, many of which have cartoon and pop culture covers that degrade the book's integrity. While high school girls may carry around any number of pink- or pastel-colored books with cartoon-like figures and/or designs, few high school boys will take a cartoon cover seriously, much less a pastel-colored one.

Publishing houses have a huge impact on young adult literature. Editorial departments determine what is printed by accepting, rejecting, and editing manuscripts, and while writing quality sells manuscripts, editors have their likes and dislikes. And politics, for better or worse, plays a role (e.g., Jenna Bush's *Ana's Story*, 2007). By focusing on profits, marketing departments drive what sells and what the audience is exposed to by front listing[2] books they want to promote and developing expensive national marketing campaigns for books of their choice. A publisher, for instance, may develop a massive advertising campaign (e.g., pricey promotional materials, author tours, and colorful floor displays) for a young adult book written by a well-known adult writer[3] and push these titles to booksellers. Because the writer is a bestselling adult writer, the company has faith in his/her young adult title selling well, regardless of the book's quality. They will also do the same for celebrities. Such advertising campaigns—and there are many—distract from quality literature written by well-established, award-winning young adult authors. These latter authors, many who have been in the trenches for years and have received dozens of awards for their contributions to children's and young adult literature, seldom receive equal promotion. My point is not to devalue adult writers who decide to write a young adult novel, but to point out how name recognition gives authors a "leg up" in advertising. Simply stated: adult writers and celebrities move easily into the young adult market, and their first novels are upfront in bookstores. A young adult author does not cross over as easily.[4]

Don't leave this chapter believing publishers are totally missing the mark with older readers. In fact, in the last several years, an increasing number of books with multiple, complex themes have found their way onto young adult bookshelves. Many are well over the usual 200- to 300-page length. This trend may be the result of the *Harry Potter* phenomenon, which has hooked readers of all ages. While young adult literature has traditionally been a smaller sales market compared with children's and adult books, publishers also recognize that more teens today frequent bookstores, and publishers are making a bigger effort to capture them.

If you're reading this book, you're fortunate. Many colleges and universities do not require a course in young adult literature in teacher education programs. Some programs offer it as an elective, others attempt to integrate the literature into other courses, and still others do not value the genre enough to include it in teacher training. Thus, many teachers enter the teaching field with limited and/or skewed knowledge of the genre. Some teachers, however, learn to stay abreast of the field by subscribing to journals (e.g., *The ALAN Review, SIGNAL Journal, School Library Journal*) and professional organizations (ALAN/NCTE, SIGNAL/IRA, and ALA) through which they remain informed about new books, upcoming authors, and instructional strategies for teaching the literature.

---

[2]Several times a year publishers may send a "suggested" purchase list to bookstores and offer special deals on select titles.

[3]The general adult population chooses books in much the same way as teens—what they find interesting, not what they believe is written well. Thus, an adult writer may be popular but may not necessarily craft stories well.

[4]For example, Chris Crutcher's *King of the Mild Frontier* (2003) is comparable to David Sedaris's works such as *Dress Your Family in Corduroy and Denim* (2004) and *Me Talk Pretty One Day* (2000).

Young adult literature offers a window through which teens can examine their lives and the world in which they live. Unlike classical texts, young adult literature addresses modern-day issues—peer pressure, family relationships, sexuality, bigotry and racism, and it connects teens with the pop culture world in which they live. This connection with modern-day issues and culture peaks interest and hooks at-risk readers and nonreaders. While classical texts may share similar themes (emotions are timeless), young adult literature is not bound by archaic language; teens can more easily navigate the text and enjoy pop culture references, themes, and so on, resulting in more reading pleasure and ultimately enhancing reading comprehension.

Characteristics of Quality Young Adult Literature

So, what makes a good young adult novel? Much young adult literature prior to the 1970s has been criticized for being didactic, too focused on a message, and lacking character development and strong plot; however, a poorly written adult novel can be didactic too, but for a different reason. The difference lies in the message being hammered home: Older didactic works preach messages about morality and religion. The modern-day novel, however, if not well done, can browbeat the reader with a social issue. In a poorly written novel, the story can go over the top; that is, the writer works so hard to convince the reader of his/her point that the story is melodramatic or not plausible; for instance, the writer may make extreme use of violence and intrigue at the expense of realism. The trouble with evaluating the quality of a novel, however, lies in the fact that what one reader considers extreme, another may not; what one reader may consider real, another may not; what disturbs or offends one reader, may not disturb or offend another; and so on. There are, however, specific points that can aid readers in developing expertise in evaluating a novel's merit.

Multithemed Story
The reader walks away from the book with a lot to talk about. The reader thinks, "This isn't just about divorce. This book has other deep issues." On the surface, David Almond's *Kit's Wilderness* (2000) seems to be a story about a 13-year-old boy who moves to a moldering coal mining community to live with his grandfather and encounters ghosts; on a deeper level, it is a story about redemption.

Tension versus Shock Effect
The story creates tension as opposed to shock. A good way of examining tension is asking whether a book is a page turner. Can you not put it down? Are you constantly wanting to know what happens next? Or are you having a good time getting through it? The difficulty here has to do with interest. What engages one person may not engage another. Another

good question is, Do all scenes either advance the plot or deepen our understanding of the character? Any scenes that do neither are gratuitous. Sonya Hartnett's *Surrender* (2006) moves forward seamlessly with even tension.

Memorable Characters

Characters are neither all good nor all bad. A completely good or completely bad character leaves no room for tension. Characters can't possibly change or do anything that would surprise the reader and keep the reader turning pages; hence, a boring, flat, predictable storyline. Richard Peck, Christopher Paul Curtis, and Chris Lynch are known for developing rich, well-rounded, sometimes odd characters.

Accurate Facts and Details

If the story relies on a historical event, the writer has done some homework. If the story has a sports theme, game description, lingo, and game rules are believable and accurate. Kathryn Lasky and Ann Rinaldi are held in high regard for the meticulous research behind their historical fiction novels. No one hits the mark better than Robert Lipsyte and Mike Lupica with realistic depictions of sports.

No Unlikely Coincidences

If the protagonist in Chapter 5 wishes to see her alcoholic father who neglected her two years in the past, he doesn't show up on her doorstep in Chapter 6. You may find a rare exception to this point, but most good editors will give a book one coincidence, but not two.

Critic Pandering

The best stories are crafted by writers who avoid pandering to critics. That is, they think about the story, not the story's purpose, message, or the "sensitive" nature of their audience. The story is what it is.

Original Idea

The book wasn't written to ride a trend. After the Columbine shootings a host of books about school shootings hit the market. While some of these are exceptional (e.g., Walter Dean Myers's *Shooter*, 2004), others are tedious and predictable. The best writers write what they know, not what's popular.

Memorable Voice and Authentic Dialogue

Remember the stilted language in the basal readers such as *Dick and Jane?* A good novel captures the language of the characters, which includes dialect, word choice, and cultural expressions. It stands to reason that some characters may use profanity, racist language, or otherwise offensive expressions. A good test for voice is whether you can tell who is talking by the sound of the character's voice. For example, sometimes chapters alternate between narrators or points of view (e.g., Wendelin Van Draanen's *Flipped,* 2001; Angela Woodson's *First Part Last,* 2003; and Betty Hicks's *Out of Order,* 2005). If the reader has to work too hard to figure out who's talking in each chapter, the voices aren't strong or unique enough. Writers who have exceptional control of voice know how to break grammar rules for effect. Examine the following opening passage of Chris Lynch's *Gypsy Davey* (1994):

> My sister Joanne has a baby and sometimes after school I go over there and I help her with it and she lets me have a glass of wine and then I start to think of things.
>
> Things like that I'm really good with babies even though I'm only twelve and I can think of no reason why I should be after all good with babies since I don't have any of my own but I sure would like to. Better than my sister is with her own baby that's for sure though I don't actually mean to be mean because she's nice to me some of the time and it's hard for her and I fully understand that. She's only seventeen herself but her old man she calls him is thirty which is why there's always a glass of wine around although from what I can see the old man himself ain't. Around that is. (p. 3)

Effective, Clear Writing Style

Whatever stylistic devices a writer chooses, they are effective, purposeful, consistent, and clear. For instance, Meg Rosoff uses no quotation marks in her Michael L. Printz winner, *How I Live Now* (2004) and uses commas sparingly. While quotation marks help the reader know who's talking, and commas generally help with comprehension, Rosoff crafts her writing so well that readers never get confused. The result is a powerfully sweet, seamless, and memorable voice.

Sense of Humor

Comedian Mel Brooks once said, "Tragedy is when I cut my finger. Comedy is when you fall into an open sewer and die." Writers of the best problem novels understand this aphorism and use humor successfully. David Lubar illustrates this craft in many of his novels (e.g., *Sleeping Freshmen Never Lie* [2005]).

Lyrical/Poetic Language

A good novel mirrors a good poem—no wasted words to bore or slow down the reader. Markus Zusak's *Fighting Ruben Wolfe* (2001) reads like poetry, and the imagery in Paul Fleischman's *Whirligig* (1998) and Cynthia Rylant's *Missing May* (1992) are stellar.

No Superfluous Characters or Wasted Scenes

Everything has purpose. Events or minor characters are not left hanging. Any scenes that shock the reader but do not advance the plot or contribute to character development are unwarranted.

Widespread Appeal

The best novels will have universal appeal, much like a good picture book. Adults make personal connections with the text in much the same way as teens. The *Harry Potter* series is an obvious example. Laurie Halse Anderson's Michael L. Printz Honor book *Speak* (1999) is a second example. Melinda Sordino, ostracized by her peers for ratting out an end-of-summer party and raped by a schoolmate, stops talking. This book remains one of the top bestsellers in young adult fiction.

Openings

Young adult authors and publishers know that adolescents can be impatient readers. More so than adult books, good young adult novels will capture the reader's attention with the first few lines and/or first few pages. Robert Cormier's "They murdered him" from *The Chocolate War* (1974) is a classic opening; however, dozens of authors have written equally compelling opening lines. Consider the following:

> You wouldn't think we'd have to leave Chicago to see a dead body.
> (*A Long Way from Chicago* by Richard Peck. New York: Dial/Penguin, 1998.)

> Today I moved to a twelve-acre rock covered with cement, topped with bird turd and surrounded by water.
> (*Al Capone Does My Shirts* by Gennifer Choldenko. New York: Putnam, 2004.)

> Around 5:00 a.m. on a warm Sunday morning in October 1953, my Aunt Belle left her bed and vanished from the face of the earth.
> (*Belle Prater's Boy* by Ruth White. New York: Farrar, Straus & Giroux, 1996.)

> Maggot said we should go up to Times Square to watch the ball drop and pick some pockets, but we never got around to it.
> (*Can't Get There from Here* by Todd Strasser. New York: Simon & Schuster, 2004.)

> If you're planning on going out with a girl, take my advice: don't start over the summer holidays. Do it in term time, when there's loads of other distractions. Over the long summer holiday, keeping a girl happy on a day-to-day basis can really drain you. It's nonstop phone calls. Boring shopping trips into town. Coke and cappuccino consumption levels shooting sky high.
> (*Gotta Get Some Bish Bash Bosh* by M. E. Allen. New York: HarperCollins, 2005.)

I've been thinking about the undead.
(*Restless: A Ghost's Story* by Rich Wallace. New York: Viking/Penguin, 2003.)

Simon Glass was easy to hate. I never knew exactly why, there was too much to pick from. I guess, really, we each hated him for a different reason, but we didn't realize it until the day we killed him.
(*Shattering Glass* by Gail Giles. New Milford, CT: Roaring Brook Press, 2002.)

I grew up with my left hand tied behind my back.
(*Choosing Up Sides* by John H. Ritter. New York: Penguin, 1998.)

I grew up riding a rocket.
(*King of the Mild Frontier: An Ill-Advised Autobiography* by Chris Crutcher. New York: Greenwillow/HarperCollins, 2003.)

He did not want to be a wringer.
(*Wringer* by Jerry Spinelli. New York: HarperCollins, 1997.)

Closings

While young adult literature offers some of the best openings in literature, exceptional endings are fewer. Many novels are criticized for endings that wrap up too quickly or neatly. This problem exists for a couple of reasons. First, the societal belief that stories should have hope impacts the way some writers end their stories. While good writers shy away from the happily-ever-after endings, many still tend to "lighten" events by story's end. Second, the length of the story and story time frame (typically a few weeks in a character's life, a summer, or a school year) is not conducive to deep character development and, most importantly, it is not long enough realistically for characters to work through personal and family issues. The span of an academic school year, for example, is not an adequate amount of time to heal wounds between an abused child and a parent or for an adolescent to complete the grief cycle. Ron Koertge's *Arizona Kid* (2005) has an exceptional ending, as does Terry Trueman's *Stuck in Neutral* (2000).

Young Adult Literature and Censorship

Censorship, the willful removal or withholding of information, is done by individuals, religious groups, governments, businesses, and the media. In latter years, censors have become better organized and, though small in number, they have a collective voice that sometimes overrides the majority. When studying censorship or when caught in its throes, we should understand why censors want to control, remove, and/or withhold information: they operate out of fear, so they oppose any reading, viewing, or discussion that deviates from their world perceptions. A difficulty in dealing with censors is that they sincerely believe the material is so damaging and offensive that no one should believe it holds value, and when someone does, that

Trends in Young Adult Literature   by Patty Campbell

The river of young adult literature is overflowing its banks just now. From the trickle of a few books in the beginning almost 40 years ago, it has grown to a mighty flood of fine writing. Fed by tributaries of new forms, new subjects, and passing trends, it has survived the drought of the nineties to become a major part of the watercourse of world literature. What are the trends the genre has grown through, and how does it differ now from its early years?

From the start, the mainstream of young adult literature has been perceived as realism. (However, to belabor the metaphor to a ridiculous degree, the genre can also be seen as two parallel streams—realism and fantasy. More about this later.) Although the prototype for style and voice was J. D. Salinger's *The Catcher in the Rye* (1951), it was not until 16 years later that that book's promise began to be fulfilled. In the magic years of 1967–1968, S. E. Hinton's *The Outsiders,* Robert Lipsyte's *The Contender,* and Paul Zindel's *The Pigman* broke away from the saccharine formula of the junior novel to confront bold new subjects that soon earned such novels the name of "the new realism." Other new writers like Richard Peck, Norma Klein, M. E. Kerr, Norma Fox Mazer, and Harry Mazer took up the challenge of writing novels about serious adolescent realities without succumbing to didacticism.

Then in 1974 the publication of Robert Cormier's first YA novel, *The Chocolate War,* initiated a new level of literary excellence in the fledgling genre and also unleashed a storm of controversy about the darkness and hard truth-saying of his work, a type of controversy that became characteristic of the field in general in following years. For the first time, a YA novel had confronted the broader human condition beyond the problems of adolescence. Cormier had disturbed the universe of young adult literature with his dark vision and complex ambiguities, and the stunned critical reception of the book led to the realization that fiction for teens could be great literature. With the publication of *I Am the Cheese* in 1977 and *After the First Death* in 1979, it became apparent that *The Chocolate War* had been not a single anomaly, but the beginning of a body of work, and other writers were freed to follow their own vision, wherever it led. Cormier continued to up the ante throughout the

26 years and 14 novels of his career, and other writers were freed to rise to the challenge of honesty and excellence in their own ways.

However, changing trends in YA literature always come and usually go, both in the center and around the edges. In the early seventies a form arose that took books for teens in a less excellent direction. Emboldened by the new possibilities for writing about formerly taboo subjects, less skilled writers began to shape novels around social concerns, the more trendy the better. "The problem novel," as this variant came to be called, focused on the latest headlines for books about drugs, suicide, sexual molestation, prostitution, parents missing from death or divorce or desertion, runaways, anorexia. "The subject matter too often became the tail that wagged the dog of the novel," says Michael Cart in his history of the genre, *From Romance to Realism* (1996). The problem (or several problems), became the center, with all its statistics and possible outcomes, rather than a character or the writer's personal vision, and writers drew heavily on the possibilities for preachy moral instruction. These books were enormously popular with teens, but they grew sillier and sillier, until they were finally kidded to death by critics. The death knell was Daniel Pinkwater's delightful parody, *Young Adult Novel* (1982). The influence of the problem novel is often exaggerated. It lasted only a decade and was a mere digression, as the main body of the literature continued to grow in scope, relevance, and sophistication.

However, one type of problem novel preceded its heyday and continues with us to the present

Continued

Trends in Young Adult Literature *Continued*

time. Stories of teenage pregnancy and parenting, affectionately called "preggers novels," began in 1966 with *A Girl Like Me* by Jeannette Eyerly. Other early such books were *My Darling, My Hamburger* by Paul Zindel (1969), and *Mr. and Mrs. Bo Jo Jones* by Ann Head (1967). The pattern followed a formula: worry, discovery, revelation to boyfriend and parents, choice of three alternatives—abortion, keeping the baby, and adoption—with authorial approval of the last option. This pattern gradually loosened and was addressed with more literary skill in the nineties, to grow beyond its problem novel origins. Sometimes the point of view is even that of the young father, as in Angela Johnson's award-winning novel, *The First Part Last* (2003).

But what about that second river of YA fiction, fantasy? Today it seems as if it has become the predominant form in the genre, at least for this decade. However, fantasy (and science fiction) has always drawn enthusiastic young readers. Tolkien's trilogy *The Lord of the Rings,* of course, was the beginning, with the American edition published in 1966. However, it took several years until that mighty work trickled down to teen awareness from its first readership on the college level. Then it was an overwhelming phenomenon, bringing young people to the joy of reading as *Harry Potter* would 30 years later. Another seminal work that began publication in 1968 was Ursula Le Guin's *Earthsea* trilogy. In the next decade, a few writers like H. M. Hoover wrote science fiction aimed at YA readers, and most notably William Sleator with his behaviorist novel, *House of Stairs* (1974). But not until the publication of *The Sword of Shannara* by Terry Brooks in 1977 did American writers take up the more-or-less-medieval world in three volumes, the model set by Tolkien. The number of YA books based on this pattern, with its variant of the Arthurian novel, has grown steadily ever since, until legions of huge fantasy trilogies and series have come to dominate the YA market since 1993.

YA realism, meanwhile, has been enriched by a number of separate subject emphases that can, each in its own right, almost be thought of as subgenres. Most relevant to teens is sexuality, a subject that has been a major part of YA fiction since its beginning, and has often garnered YA literature the wrath of censors. The iconic book of sexual discovery is Judy Blume's *Forever,* appearing in 1975, just one year after *The Chocolate War* broke open the field to new challenges. Its frank celebration of human coupling has earned it a very long life and many readers. Although it is often said that *Forever* was unique in the reality of its portrayal of sexual activity, the truth is that during the sexual revolution of the seventies, there were many YA novels by Norma Klein and others that equaled its daring, if not its quality. Later, as AIDS made sexual intercourse a life-threatening practice, writers became leery of scenes of love-making. The sexual novel morphed into the AIDS novel, with M. E. Kerr's *Night Kites* (1986) and other books that showed us young people trying to make sense of the age of AIDS. Only recently, as the disease fades from the forefront of public consciousness in America, have YA authors begun to explore sexuality again in gritty novels like *Doing It* by Melvin Burgess (2004).

A related form is the novel of gay and lesbian awareness and identity. In his groundbreaking study of this literary type, *The Heart Has Its Reasons* (2004), Michael Cart traces the changes in the form. This theme has been a constant in YA fiction since John Donovan's *I'll Get There, It Better Be Worth the Trip* appeared in 1969. However, in the seventies the plot led inexorably to the death by automobile (or "death by gayness," as it jokingly came to be called) of the lead character or dog, presumably as a punishment. This trend came to be a running gag, and the form eventually grew beyond such naiveté. The first YA novel to deal with lesbian identity was *Ruby* by Rosa Guy (1976), but the icon has become *Annie on My Mind* by Nancy Garden (1982). Marion Dane Bauer's *Am I Blue: Coming Out from the Silence* (1994) was the first young adult anthology dealing with gay and lesbian issues. In later years, gay and lesbian characters have become a natural part of many YA novels without being seen as *the problem,* and in 2003 David Levithan's *Boy Meets Boy* showed us a beautiful world where nobody is upset that the homecoming queen is also the star quarterback.

For a long while YA fiction depicted an all-white mostly middle-class world. When multicultural awareness began to develop, the requirement was seen at first as a matter of making the history and presence of African Americans visible. A very early landmark

Continued

Trends in Young Adult Literature   *Continued*

book in this development was *I Know Why the Caged Bird Sings* by Maya Angelou (1969). In the seventies, publishers actively encouraged black writers, and new voices emerged like Alice Childress, Rosa Guy, Virginia Hamilton, Mildred Taylor, and the great Walter Dean Myers, whose first YA novel was *Fast Sam, Cool Clyde, and Stuff* (1975). As with gay characters, in later years African American characters have come to be seen as people with lives and issues beyond their racial identity. With the surge of immigration from Asia and Central America in the nineties, a need for books exploring those realities has arisen. YA novels reflecting the lives of contemporary American Asian teens have been especially scarce, despite the many Chinese historical or mythological novels of Laurence Yep. The Michael L. Printz winner, *American Born Chinese* (2006), by Gene Luen Yang is a step in this direction, but there is still a long way to go. Hispanic YA fiction of all kinds, however, is growing well, adding to the longtime examples of Gary Soto, Sandra Cisneros, and several others. YA fiction showing the lives of contemporary Muslim teens is still to come, regrettably. As the tide of immigration continues, more and more books focus on the problems of immigrants as outsiders, and the complex self-definition of teens who have more than one ethnic or racial identity.

For many years historical novels were said to be anathema to teens, and very few were written or published. Not until the unprecedented success of the *American Girls* series did publishers begin to change their minds. Ann Rinaldi and Kathryn Lasky have been the workhorses in historical fiction. In the 21st century the form has grown to new heights of creativity and originality, culminating in the two books of *The Astonishing Life of Octavian Nothing* by M. T. Anderson (2006) series.

Some current subjects in realistic YA fiction hark back to the problem novel, but without succumbing to the single-mindedness of that form. However, the repetition of these themes is beginning to be tiresome. Novels built around incidents of physical or sexual abuse have been around for two decades, and there have been excellent books, like Cynthia Voigt's *When She Hollers* (1994), Norma Fox Mazer's *When She Was Good* (1997), and Laurie Halse Anderson's *Speak* (1999). After the shootings at Columbine High School there were a number of books about a shootist who plans to bring a gun to school, but this theme, while important, is beginning to feel overdone. And surely it is time to give plots a rest that turn on alienation and overcoming bullies, either male or female.

Forms other than the novel have also become part of young adult fiction. The short story anthology, now a staple, began with the first collection by the now well-known anthologist Don Gallo, *Sixteen* (1984). The pattern, as set by Gallo, is to amass a group of original stories by familiar YA authors centering on a theme. These themes can range from quite specific, such as Gallo's recent *What Are You Afraid Of? Stories about Phobias* (2006), to quite amorphous, such as *All Sleek and Skimming* (2006), edited by Lisa Heggum. Sex, gay, and lesbian identity, and the supernatural have been popular themes. Sometimes these collections can be by one author, like Margo Lanagan's remarkable *Black Juice* (2005). An interesting experiment growing from this form was Michael Cart's *Rush Hour,* (2004), a quarterly literary journal encompassing not only short stories but poetry and art. Teachers are fond of these collections for their ability to snare short-attention-span readers and to fit neatly in a day's teaching plan.

The verse novel is a form peculiar to young adult literature, although narrative in verse is a very much older pattern, going back to the earliest literature. The young adult verse novel was inadvertently invented by Mel Glenn, in his collection titled *Class Dismissed! High School Poems* (1982). Characteristically the verse novel is a novel-length story told in a series of free verse poems written in first person. In the best of these books each separate poem is its own little jewel. Sometimes there is a single narrator, but there can also be multiple voices. The verse sometimes has a formal rhyme scheme, and sometimes just reflects the rhythms of natural speech, arranged in breath groups. There was a blossoming of this form in the late nineties and the first five years of the current century, but now they seem to have receded somewhat. A number of excellent books have been shaped as verse novels, some of the best being *Out of the Dust* by Karen Hesse (1997), *Make Lemonade* (1993) by Virginia Euwer Wolff, and its National Book Award–winning sequel *True Believer* (2001).

Continued

Trends in Young Adult Literature   *Continued*

Graphic novels were popular in Europe for many years before they were accepted in America, and I wrote about the appeal of this form in my "YA Perplex" column for Wilson Library Bulletin in the early eighties. But not until the last five years has this comics-inspired genre been enthusiastically embraced by teens and librarians. Now there are many guidebooks and Web sites to educate teachers and librarians who are latecomers to the form, and several mainstream YA publishers have moved into the field with graphic novel imprints, such as Roaring Brook's First Second. With the awarding of the Michael L. Printz Award to *American Born Chinese* by Gene Luen Yang in 2007, the graphic novel finally came to be respected as a valid literary form in America, even though Art Spiegelman's great Holocaust memoir *Maus* won a Pulitzer Prize in 1992. Manga is the Japanese form of the graphic novel, and is enormously popular currently with teens.

Audiobooks and other electronic forms look to the future, although they will probably continue to be supplements, rather than replacements for the print book. Many YA books are now published simultaneously as print and audiobooks, and the popularity of the electronic version with teens is high, especially with those who do not read well or who are English Language Learners.

Up to now, we have been looking only at hardcover YA fiction, but some of the most volatile YA publishing trends have been acted out in paperbacks. The tendency of librarians, teachers, and critics to deplore this popular subliterature is a very old one, going back to the example of the Stratemeyer Syndicate, a writing factory that churned out the *Nancy Drew* and *Hardy Boys* series, among others, in the first half of the 20th century. In the beginnings of young adult literature paperbacks were limited to reprints of previously published hardcover books. But in 1971, with the astounding success of *Go Ask Alice* by Beatrice Sparks, it began to dawn on publishers that teens would buy their own books, if they were the *right* books. Previous purchasers of YA books had been teachers, parents, and librarians, but now, with this new market, more hardcover YA titles were translated into paperback.

With the advent of the indoor shopping mall as a teen hangout, the stage was set for a wider marketing plan. Gambling that teens were tired of the gritty reality of the problem novel, and perhaps frightened by AIDS, publishers in the eighties began to bring out sweet, clean, and conventional paperback romance series, like *Wildfire, Sweet Dreams, Young Love, First Love, Wishing Star, Caprice,* and *Sweet Valley High*. They were an instant sensation with young girls, who bought them by the armload. The enormous significance of this move was that these were *original* paperbacks, not reprints. Librarians deplored; feminists wrung their hands. I wrote, "The books that are found in the chain bookstores are of far lower quality and aimed at much younger readers than those that are found on the similarly labeled shelves in public libraries. The whole field has become strangely bifurcated and we seem to be moving in the direction of two separate literatures."

The separatist trend continued as romance phased into horror paperbacks, beginning with Christopher Pike's *Slumber Party* in 1985, and continued on into the nineties. As the teen population declined to a new low in numbers, publishers desperate to keep this new market turned to ever more sensational and poor quality paperbacks, finally descending into the abyss with R. L. Stine's execrable *Goosebumps* and *Fear Street* series. At library conferences publishers and librarians moaned to each other that YA was dead.

Not hardly. Today, as we have said, the roaring mainstream of young adult literature is overflowing its banks. There is an all-time high of over 30 million teens in the United States, and that growth is not expected to peak until 2010. Teens account for a major part of bookstore sales, and they're not buying just popular paperbacks. Trends continue, yes, like the currently ubiquitous chick lit, but the best of YA literature now appears right alongside it on bookstore shelves. There are more literary and challenging books for older teens being written, often with strikingly original stylistic innovations and sophisticated themes. More formerly adult writers are moving into this fertile field of young adult literature, like Joyce Carol Oates, Alice Hoffman, James Patterson, Carl Hiassen, while the writers of the YA canon like Chris Lynch and M. T. Anderson get better with every book. The Michael L. Printz Award, the National Book Award, and the Los Angeles Times Book Prize have recognized the quality of young adult literature, and the day is not far off when YA masterworks will be seen not as "kids' books," but simply as great works of literature.

person is corrupt or misled; censors are incapable of recognizing or valuing that person's rights. Would-be censors genuinely believe they have a definitive take on "morality" and the world can benefit from their belief system. Others should believe as they do. Would-be censors criticize young adult authors for "corrupting the young," being evil," or "writing shocking, violent, and obscene stories to make a buck." What they fail to comprehend is if they succeed in suppressing information, they set a dangerous precedent. Sooner or later someone will use the same tactics and suppress what they like and value.

Censorship infringes upon freedom of speech and freedom of expression. It violates *intellectual freedom,* the individual right to access information from all viewpoints free of restriction, a defining characteristic of our democratic system. It violates the First Amendment to the United States Constitution, which protects our rights to read, view, listen to, and disseminate information, even if others are offended. Would-be censors argue, however, they are exercising their rights to free speech, but in doing so they suppress the rights of others. Ironically, they seek to deny rights to others by exercising "their rights." The problem with their stance, however, is that their rights to voice their opinion and to persuade others can only be protected if the rights of those being challenged are protected as well. As the American Library Association points out, unless the rights of both sides are protected, neither's rights will survive (ALA, 2007).

One way of understanding the dangers of censorship is to examine countries that have used it to control and suppress their populations (e.g., Afghanistan and Korea). We can turn to our own country, too, and reflect on the treatment of slaves and the efforts by slave owners to keep them illiterate—if they couldn't read, they couldn't "get ideas." Censors of young adult literature fail to see the parallels between their own desires to suppress information about such topics as sexuality, religion, violence, vulgarity, and the successful attempts by dictators, governments, and military groups to control and even brainwash their countries' population. They see their actions as "helpful" and "decent." They want adolescents to believe what they believe, see the world as they do. Thus, they should read and view what censors deem appropriate. Censors, or would-be censors, object to material with little regard or respect to others because it fails to fit into their own belief systems.

Censorship, of course, is as old as time. Throughout history people have been punished for standing up for their beliefs and/or writings. History tells us that people were forced to drink poison (Socrates), burned at the stake (John Hus), crucified (Jesus), exiled (the Dalai Lama), and forced into hiding (Salmon Rushdi) for what they believed or wrote. Literature for children and teens hasn't been an exception. Following is a list of challenged classical titles taken from "The Students' Right to Read" (NCTE, 1981), along with censors' objections.

- *Diary of a Young Girl* by Anne Frank ("Obscene and blasphemous.")
- *Moby Dick* by Herman Melville ("Contains homosexuality.")

- *The Catcher in the Rye* by J. D. Salinger ("A dreadful, dreary, recital of sickness, sordidness, and sadism.")
- *The Invisible Man* by Ralph Ellison ("The book is biased on the black question.")
- *The Republic* by Plato ("This book is un-Christian.")
- *The Scarlet Letter* by Nathaniel Hawthorne ("A filthy book.")
- *To Kill a Mockingbird* by Harper Lee ("The word *rape* is used several times. Children should not see this in any literature book.")
- *Slaughterhouse-Five* by Kurt Vonnegut ("Its repetitious obscenity and immorality merely degrade and defile, teaching nothing.")

While the classical canon continues to come under attack, contemporary young adult literature receives the most hits. Critics, uncomfortable with popular culture and changing societal trends, are more wary of new titles. They also tend to believe if *Macbeth* or *The Miller's Tale* didn't damage their own moral fiber, then they're not likely to damage young minds today.

Young adult literature became an easy target for censors because it emanated from the problem novel, realistic literature that focuses on teen coming-of-age issues such as sexuality, divorce, drugs, abuse. Judy Blume was among the first young adult authors to tackle controversial issues in her writing, and her novels were among the first to be challenged. *Are You There God, It's Me, Margaret* (1970) was attacked early on for menstruation, *Then Again, Maybe I Won't* (1971) for masturbation, and *Forever* (1975) for teen sex. More than three decades after its initial publication, *Forever* remains one of the most challenged young adult novels and is a young adult classic.

Dozens of young adult novels by some of the best writers in the field have been challenged (e.g., Lois Duncan's *Killing Mr. Griffin*, 1978; Katherine Paterson's *The Great Gilly Hopkins*, 1978; Caroline Cooney's *The Face on the Milk Carton*, 1990; and Jane Conly's *Crazy Lady!*, 1993). Over the years, challenges have grown exponentially. Following is a list of the 10 most challenged books of 2006 and a list of the most frequently challenged authors compiled by the American Library Association.

- *And Tango Makes Three* by Justin Richardson and Peter Parnell for homosexuality, anti-family, and unsuited to age group.
- *Gossip Girls* series by Cecily von Ziegesar for homosexuality, sexual content, drugs, unsuited to age group, and offensive language.
- *Alice* series by Phyllis Reynolds Naylor for sexual content and offensive language.
- *The Earth, My Butt, and Other Big Round Things* by Carolyn Mackler for sexual content, anti-family, offensive language, and unsuited to age group.
- *The Bluest Eye* by Toni Morrison for sexual content, offensive language, and unsuited to age group.
- *Scary Stories* series by Alvin Schwartz for occult/satanism, unsuited to age group, violence, and insensitivity.

Table 3.1

2003–2005 Most Challenged Authors

(Reported by ALA and listed in alphabetical order)

Judy Blume	Toni Morrison	Louise Rennison
Robert Cormier	Walter Dean Myers	Marilyn Reynolds
Chris Crutcher	Phyllis Reynolds Naylor	J. K. Rowling
Robie Harris	Barbara Park	J. D. Salinger
Stephen King	Katherine Paterson	Maurice Sendak
Lois Lowry	Gary Paulsen	Sonya Sones
Chris Lynch	Dav Pilkey	John Steinbeck

- *Athletic Shorts* by Chris Crutcher for homosexuality and offensive language.
- *The Perks of Being a Wallflower* by Stephen Chbosky for homosexuality, sexually explicit, offensive language, and unsuited to age group.
- *Beloved* by Toni Morrison for offensive language, sexual content, and unsuited to age group.
- *The Chocolate War* by Robert Cormier for sexual content, offensive language, and violence.

The American Library Association's Office of Intellectual Freedom (OIF) maintains a database of recorded challenges and related statistics (see www.ala.org). The overwhelming majority of challenges are initiated by parents. School libraries are attacked the most, followed by the school in general and the public library. OIF categorized 3,019 challenges between 2000 and 2005 within 20 categories. The categories and number of challenges are listed in Table 3.2.

"Offensive language" continues to top the list; however, complaints about books with sexual content, particularly those that "promote" sexuality, have increased. While support for books about homosexuality in libraries has risen from 55 percent to 73 percent over the last 30 years,[5] increased complaints against young adult literature with sexual and/or homosexual themes is due in part to an increase in young adult books that feature gay and lesbian characters, in part by the edgier nature of today's young adult literature, and in part by recent movies (e.g., *Brokeback Mountain,* 2005) and political platforms regarding marriage, civil unions, and gay rights.

It's not surprising that "offensive language" is the number one complaint. Many would-be censors don't read what they oppose; many boast they don't need to. Ludicrous? Most writers, teachers, and literary experts think so. When you encounter objectors who complain about "bad language," who generally read little or none of the story, they usually don't understand, or value, story craft and know little about characterization. One

---

[5]Office of Intellectual Freedom, ALA.

Table 3.2

OIF Challenges 2000–2005

Category	Challenges
Offensive Language	811
Sexually Explicit	714
Other	583
Unsuited to Age Group	504
Violence	405
Occult/Satanism	229
Homosexuality	164
Religious Viewpoint	155
Political Viewpoint	144
Drugs	122
Racism	108
Nudity	101
Sex Education	78
Anti-Family	57
Insensitivity	51
Inaccurate	36
Suicide	27
Anti-Ethnic	24
Abortion	19
Sexism	16

objector claimed to have found "128 curses" in Chris Crutcher's *Whale Talk*,[6] but couldn't connect with the real-world characters or the story's messages about bigotry and racism. Winner of numerous awards for fighting censorship, Crutcher is hands down the leading spokesperson against censorship in young adult literature. He is a recipient of NCTE's prestigious Intellectual Freedom Award and has been honored by the National Coalition Against Censorship. His work is excellent for talking about the importance of allowing characters to use their native language. In *Chinese Handcuffs* (1989) Dillon's brother, Preston, becomes involved with a motorcycle gang and loses his legs in a biking accident. Dillon witnesses his suicide. To get even, Dillon takes his brother's ashes to the gang hangout and sprinkles them on the pool table, floor, and bar. Dillon flees the hangout unharmed, but the bikers show up at his school to get even:

> "I'm sorry," Caldwell [the principal] said, "We don't have a student here by that name."
>
> "Then how did you know he was a student?" Wolf [biker] asked with a sneer, "Maybe he's a teacher or a janitor."
>
> Caldwell stood his ground. "We don't have anyone here by that name."
>
> One of the other bikers yelled, "He *told* us he goes to school here, asshole. Now get him out here before someone gets hurt."

---

[6]Chris Crutcher e-mail correspondence. April 29, 2007.

In a lapse of judgment even for him, John Caldwell flared. "You watch your mouth in front of these kids!"

The biker laughed. "Yes, *sir*. Try this: he told us he goes to school here, shithead. Now get him out here." (p. 111)

Not only are the bikers angry in this scene, but Crutcher portrays them early on as rough, uneducated, and mean. The language here is real, as it should be. The intent is to show their rage and disrespect. Their responses to the principal do just that, especially the come-back when the principal chides them for their "bad language."

Robert Cormier's *We All Fall Down* (1991) opens with the following passage:

They entered the house at 9:02 p.m. on the evening of April Fool's Day. In the next forty-nine minutes, they shit on the floors and pissed on the walls and trashed their way through the seven-room Cape Cod cottage. They overturned furniture, smashed the picture tubes in three television sets, tore two VCRs from their sockets and crashed them to the floor. They spray-painted the walls orange. They flooded the bathrooms, both upstairs, and down, and flushed face towels down the toilet bowls. They broke every mirror in the place and toppled a magnificent hutch to the floor, sending china cups and saucers and plates and assorted crystal through the air. In the second-floor bedrooms, they pulled out dresser drawers, spilled their contents on the floor, yanked clothing from the closets and slashed mattresses. In the downstairs den, they performed a special job on the spinet, smashing the keys with a hammer, the noise like a crazy soundtrack to the scenes of plunder.

There were four of them and although their vandalism was scattered and spontaneous, they managed to invade every room in the house damaging everything they touched. (pp. 3–4)

Critics of this book find it "disgusting" and "repulsive." The late Robert Cormier countered complaints by arguing that those emotional responses were exactly what he wanted to evoke. He wanted readers to feel the disgust and be sickened by the boys' destructive acts in the opening scene.

Further examples could illustrate the role "bad language" plays in young adult fiction; however, these two suffice. In the following essay, Chris Crutcher describes his censorship experiences. Because Crutcher writes honestly and candidly about adolescent development, his books appear regularly on the "100 Most Banned Books List" published by ALA. At the end of the chapter is an interview concerning his book *The Sledding Hill*. Frequently censored and banned for "bad language," Crutcher purposefully avoided "bad language" in this book in an effort to force critics to talk about real issues. Following the interview is a letter Crutcher wrote to students in the Limestone School District, an Alabama school system that banned *Whale Talk*.

Chris Crutcher receives the Intellectual Freedom Award from the National Coalition Against Censorship in 2005 in New York City. Pictured with Crutcher is Judy Blume.

Crutcher on Censorship

The most frequently debated issue regarding censorship revolves around the founding fathers' intent in writing the First Amendment. One side claims placing books with "bad" language or "offensive" issues in public schools is tantamount to yelling "Fire!" in a crowded theater. The other side says free expression is protected by the Constitution and if you want to keep your own children from reading those books, have at it, but don't try stopping *our* children from reading them. One side drags out kiddie porn and the other side drags out the *Bible*. When it's all said and done, there's a lot more said than done, as they say, and neither side brings in converts.

Certainly I'm a believer in the free expression/intellectual freedom side of this argument, but the second danger is a more personal one, in my opinion, and deserves a closer look. A few of my books sit near the top of challenged and banned books lists each year, and I have on a number of occasions, traveled to the places where they're challenged to get a more intimate look at the process and to stand with the librarians or teachers who are under fire. The challenger is most often someone from the Christian Right. Typically a member of a fundamental church will encounter one of my books on a reading list or as part of the curriculum and take his or her complaint to the school, then to the newspaper, then to a television station, not necessarily in that order. In Iowa a minister read the "offending" passages brought to him by a parent, called for a public apology by the teacher who had assigned the book, and for the book to be taken out of the curriculum. In his "Letter to the Editor," he quoted (using asterisks to block out certain letters of certain words) 19 lines of "proof" that the story was *filth,* as in "Do You Know What Filth Our Children Are Reading?" Like many censors he did not read the story and quoted the lines out of context. Because he was so public with his complaints, the school district halted students' reading of the book until the school board could come to a decision. That process took at least a week because an internal committee had to pass judgment before the school board could see it. The kids were two chapters from the end of the book when the challenge took place; the interruption lasted two weeks.

Of course the kids were disturbed. They signed petitions to retrieve their rights, sent letters to the editor on their own as well as scores of emails to me in support of the book. No sweat off my brow on that one, right? The book sold many more copies than it would have had the fuss not been made and my name became far more familiar than it had been. But look what happened in that school. When the administration stopped the class from reading the book while waiting for a resolution, the flow of the story, and indeed the flow of the class halted. An instant chasm between students and administration developed, with the teacher caught in the middle. By halting the reading, the administration put itself in the position of appearing ignorant of what was going on in its own classrooms, and of not trusting and backing its teachers. That's the educational equivalent of guilty until proven innocent, and it *invites* the censors. Even if they don't meet their ultimate objective, they wreak havoc.

A similar thing happened with the same book in a Michigan school a few years back. The school had an all-school read of *Whale Talk,* and taught it across disciplines; math teachers figured a math angle, science teachers a science angle and so on. I received some of the most remarkable mail and email during that time, that I have *ever* received. Teachers talked of a new connection with their students, students of new perspectives. Then a few *loud* fundamentalists (and make no mistake, they

Continued

Crutcher on Censorship   *Continued*

are *always* greater in decibels than they are in numbers) complained and the school interrupted the entire process until they could get it resolved. By the time they resumed teaching the book most of the momentum was lost, some teachers halted classroom discussions out of intimidation and simply had the kids finish, and it was taken out of the curriculum the following year. On my Web site I began seeing student backlash against the daughter of the woman who lodged the complaint (which I asked immediately to be stopped) and what seemed a unique educational experience was thwarted. I was in the area the following spring, and took a day to visit the school. The principal welcomed me but wanted assurance that I wasn't there to cause any more commotion. The teachers who had originally spearheaded the project, seemed snake bit. Again, an educational opportunity spoiled and a generational connection broken. And that's when it gets scary because as they say, the terrifying call comes from inside the house. Teachers and librarians become, unwittingly sometimes, conduits for the censors' intentions. They grow to be intimidated by adult sensibilities rather than remaining strong in their resolution to deal with tough issues and ideas, and the loud minority gathers power (see my response to teacher's listserv posting at the end of this chapter).

Forget that it was my book. Many authors "enjoy" this same experience, and we're not the ones who really suffer. The edict, "Any exposure is good exposure" is probably true. When one of my books is challenged and it hits the media, I can go right to amazon.com and see the spike in sales. People who would *never* know my name, know my name. It's teachers and librarians who suffer, having their expertise called into question by folks with nothing but an ax to grind, and very little sense of what education is really about; people who believe passing on a philosophy is more important than learning truths. It's the best argument I can find for the separation of church and state.

In my work as a therapist, I can't think of a situation when I didn't believe it was more advantageous to talk about an issue than to hide it or fail to address it out of fear, and it's no different in a therapist's office than it is in the so-called real world. In fact there's a great case to be made that if we talked about tough issues there would be need for fewer therapists. I always told kids *and* adults that the inside of my office was like the inside of their brains and their hearts. They could say anything they wanted in any language they wanted and there would be no judgment. It's amazing how much work got done when they came to believe that. While schools can't give kids quite that much leeway, they can operate on that same continuum. Life is tough. School is tough. We need all the help we can get.

There's another censorship issue that probably deserves discussion in this "post-Imus" era. You may remember Don Imus's notorious sexual/racial slur aimed at the Rutgers girl's basketball team which got him booted off both radio and television. His comments were hugely insensitive and brought outrage from the general population, though there's a pretty good case to be made that both networks' outrage came on the heels of lost sponsors. Such is the nature of greed over civility, but the issue deserves a close look because many observers called for the eradication of that kind of language from our public vocabulary.

Good luck.

Continued

Crutcher on Censorship   *Continued*

A few years ago a teacher in Michigan required a young African American girl to read aloud a passage from one of my short stories—"Telephone Man"—in class. It is a story about how racism and bigotry are passed down through innocence. Telephone Man's father is a racist at home, but quite civil in public. Telephone Man (so named because of his single-minded fascination with telephones) is an adolescent, borderline autistic boy with no internal editing function. If he thinks it, he says it. His father's racial slurs come out of his mouth fast and furious when he is angry, or sometimes when he is simply talking about any people of color. By the end of the story, with the help of a black classmate, he comes to some small recognition of his father's errant thinking. Because of the incendiary nature of that language, I wrote a preface to the story stating among other things that "racial slurs mean nothing about the people at whom they are directed, everything about the person using them."

The teacher made a big mistake; she required the young African American girl to read the first few pages of the story aloud, in which Telephone Man unleashes almost every racial slur he knows. She was uncomfortable reading those words aloud and went home and told her mother. By the end of the day the first couple pages of the story were all over the local news, the local head of the NAACP was calling for the ouster of the book, the teacher was relocated, my Web site was getting hits from David Duke followers and my e-mail in-box was overloaded. Most of the community believed the school was using an openly racist book. Over a period of days with the help of an African American talk-show host in the area and voices of people like Christopher Paul Curtis, we made clear the intent of the story, but the remaining question was whether or not there should be stories which included those slurs in our schools. As much as it would be nice to get those words out of our language, it's clear that's impossible. Realistic fiction writers of any ethnicity use that language to show the true colors of racists and of racism. It can't be done without the language. That isn't to say we shouldn't be careful when we go about working with those stories, but to deal with any problem, that problem has to be defined. Unfortunately that language is part of our shameful history. Take it out of the schools and *The Color Purple, To Kill a Mockingbird, I Know Why the Caged Bird Sings, Huckleberry Finn, The Autobiography of Malcolm X,* to name a very few, go with it.

Arguably a certain number of books are "censored" in our schools simply through selection. A school library doesn't have the capacity of a public library, and its purpose is to aid teachers in educating students, so books written to do that are rightly given priority. But there is no education without truth, and truth is sometimes harsh. A *truth* about "Telephone Man" is that it reflects one way bigotry flows down the generational turnpike through innocence. A *truth* about some rap music is that it reflects how some artists see the struggle between the sexes. A *truth* about *The Color Purple* is it speaks to the conquest of powerlessness. In each case I say *"a"* truth because there are so many. Those are truths as seen through *my* eyes. There are as many truths as there are eyes. It makes so much more sense to talk about these things than to pretend they don't exist.

Very often the censors come at teachers and librarians and writers with inflammatory language. We are *corrupting* children; exposing them to *filth.* We are either *evil* or are exposing kids to evil. We are insidious. Use of that language is a political

Continued

Crutcher on Censorship   *Continued*

trick. Get the listener to agree (or simply not disagree) to the terminology and you have secured the basic premise, forcing the other side onto the defense if they don't stop you in your tracks. The best counterstrategy is to refuse to accept that language, refuse to argue on those terms; refuse to accept that it's even *possible* for a word, or a real-world issue to be *evil,* or to *corrupt.* And you have to meet the censors with the same intensity with which they come at you. Call a spade a spade; call foolishness, foolishness with the same indignation the argument is thrown at you. Otherwise you give them credence. Often the *politics* of education outstrips true education—expressive education—forcing those of us who believe in intellectual freedom as behavior as well as philosophy, to get aggressive.

A little guy attending one of my school presentations recently highlighted my thoughts about whether or not words do the damage the censors claim. One of the books his class had read in preparation for my coming was my memoir, *King of the Mild Frontier: An Ill-Advised Autobiography.* There's a scene in the book where, as a frustrated 11-year-old, I call someone a "big fat shitburger." My father confines me to my room until I can produce a sheet of notebook paper with all the words I can find in that phrase. Before I began my presentation, in front of several hundred students in the school auditorium, this young man, who may have been borderline autistic, presented me with several pages of words, all under the heading BIG FAT SHITBURGER. He had found about five times more words than I could find *now.* The audience cheered him, and he walked away, seemingly satisfied, though because of his condition, he showed little emotion. His teacher told me that he had just presented the paper to her after reading the story. Imagine the damage she could have done scolding him, or humiliating him for his effort.

Those of us who stand against censorship are sometimes characterized as believing that anything in print is good for kids; that we think there should be no restraint in the making and selling of video games or that movies shouldn't be rated. The late (sigh) Kurt Vonnegut once said something close to, "One problem about standing against censorship is some of the shit we have to stand up *for.*" None of us believe that everything in print has merit. None of us doubt that media has influence. What we believe is that we live in a free country and as we have been told over and over, freedom comes at a price. Open-minded people know we can't shield our children from harm or tough ideas or tough language for very long. What we can do is deal with those things in a safe environment. Only we can create that environment.

Copyright Chris Crutcher, 2008

Upfront with Censorship

Most new teachers enter the field giving little thought to censorship and when confronted, sometimes feel desperate. Staying informed and being an advocate of intellectual freedom will give you additional confidence and information to confront censors. As a new teacher, you might spend time researching the history of censorship and procedures for dealing with complaints in your school system. Find out what books have been challenged in your system, what books are on the approved reading list, what, if any, have been removed. Learn the school and system's procedures for book selection. For example, many schools have an established committee that considers book selection procedures. Some committees include community members—a good idea because you have a support system if you are challenged. Whatever procedures are used to select books, they should clearly tie to course objectives, meet student needs, and you should be able to make a strong case for the book's overall curriculum value. Research, too, the procedures for dealing with a complaint. Many systems require would-be censors to submit a written complaint against a text before any discussion can occur (see Table 3.3). This procedure is advantageous, for it requires objectors to think through their complaints and encourages them to pay attention to other readers' viewpoints.

Table 3.3

Citizen's Request for Reconsideration of a Work

Author _____

Paperback _____ Hardback _____

Title _____

Publisher (if known) _____

Request initiated by _____

Telephone _____

Address _____

City _____

Zip Code _____

Complainant represents:

_____ Himself/Herself

_____ (Name of organization) _____

_____ (Identity of other group) _____

1. Have you been able to discuss this work with the teacher or librarian who ordered or used it? _____ Yes _____ No
2. What do you understand to be the general purpose for using this work?
   a. Provide support for a unit in the curriculum?
      _____ Yes _____ No
   b. Provide a learning experience for the reader in one kind of literature?
      _____ Yes _____ No
   c. Other _____
3. Did the general purpose for the use of the work, as described by the teacher or librarian, seem a suitable one to you?
   _____ Yes _____ No
   If no, please explain.

   _____
   _____

4. What do you think is the general purpose of the author in this book?

   _____
   _____

Continued

T a b l e 3 . 3   *Continued*

5. In what ways do you think a work of this nature is not suitable for the use the teacher or librarian wishes to carry out?

   _____

   _____

6. Have you been able to learn the students' response to this work?
   _____ Yes _____ No

7. What response did the students make?

   _____

   _____

8. Have you been able to learn from your school library what book reviewers or other students of literature have written about this work?
   _____ Yes _____ No

9. Would you like the teacher or librarian to give you a written summary of what reviewers and other students have written about this book or film?
   _____ Yes _____ No

10. Do you have negative reviews of this book?
    _____ Yes _____ No

11. Where were they published?

    _____

12. Would you be willing to provide summaries of the reviews you have collected?
    _____ Yes _____ No

13. What would you like your library/school to do about this work?
    _____ Do not assign/lend it to my child.
    _____ Return it to the staff selection committee/department for reevaluation.
    _____ Other—Please explain.

    _____

    _____

14. In its place, what work would you recommend that would convey as valuable a picture and perspective of the subject treated?

    _____

    _____

15. Have you read the book?
    _____ Yes, I've read all of it.
    _____ No.
    _____ I read the following parts:

    _____

    _____

    _____

Signature _____

Date _____

Source: Modified from "The Students' Right to Read," NCTE (1981).

Being familiar with organizations that support intellectual freedom is helpful (see Professional Resources). The American Library Association (ALA), for instance, has established an Intellectual Freedom homepage where it posts documents and resources such as "The Freedom to Read," "The Library Bill of Rights," and specific information on dealing with censorship issues. The National Council of Teachers of English makes available resources such as "The Students' Right to Read" and sample rationales for using specific titles in the classroom. Each fall the ALA encourages teens and adults to read challenged or banned books during Banned Book Week. Participate and encourage colleagues, friends, and the community to take part. Box 3.2 includes brief descriptions of high-quality, exceptional books that are good reads for Banned Book Week, and Box 3.3 features young adult novels with censorship themes. Below are additional suggestions (some are my ideas; others belong to the ALA) for taking a proactive stand against censorship:

- Study the issues.
- Network with others who support intellectual freedom.
- Establish yourself as a professional—parents listen to teachers whom they respect.
- Build a trusting, collegial, and respectful relationship with your school and system administration.
- Counter censorship in your community.
- Learn about the Freedom of Information Act.
- Learn how kids can help oppose censorship.
- Celebrate your freedom to read.
- Subscribe to various news and discussion e-lists.
- Contact elected officials about issues/legislation related to intellectual freedom.
- Stay abreast of both local and national censorship issues and offer your support.

What to Do When Censors Arrive

Predicting when a censor may arrive is like guessing when you'll be in a car wreck. If you know it's going to happen, you can prevent it. While as professionals we have some sense of what is acceptable in school culture, we cannot always predict or read parents, students, and the community. We can teach a piece of literature for years without confrontation; then someone lodges a complaint. The best piece of advice for the initial shock is *don't panic.* Don't allow yourself to be "cornered" (e.g., an unexpected meeting or phone call with the principal or other school officials and a parent) before you've had time to take a deep breath and gather your thoughts and the support you need. The objector has prepared for you; you deserve prep time, too. Let the objector know you respect his or her unease and work with school administrators to arrange a sensible meeting time for the objector to air concerns.

Box 3.2   Banned Book Reads

***The Buffalo Tree* by Adam Rapp. Arden, NC: Front Street, 1997.**

Thirteen-year-old Sura is pulling time in a harsh juvenile detention center. He and Coly Jo look out for each other. A realistic and dark story banned for sexual content.

***Daughters of Eve* by Lois Duncan. Boston: Little, Brown, 1979.**

A high school teacher, with evil intent, uses feminism to manipulate a group of girls into doing horrific deeds. Reminiscent of *Lord of the Flies*. Banded for profanity and sexual content.

***Doing It* by Melvin Burgess. New York: Henry Holt, 2004.**

A hilarious tale about boys and sexual maturation. Three British teens—Ben, Dino, and Jonathan—stumble through dating and sexual encounters. On-target portrayals of adolescence. Banded for profanity and sexual content, the book's cover is a sure magnet for censors.

***Don't You Dare Read This, Mrs. Dunphrey* by Margaret Peterson Haddix. New York: Simon & Schuster, 1996.**

An abused and neglected 16-year-old girl chronicles her life in a class-assigned journal. Banned for language and sexuality.

***The Drowning of Stephan Jones* by Bette Greene. New York: Bantam, 1991.**

Carla's mother wants to band all "anti-Christian" material from the library. When Carla's boyfriend participates in hate crimes against gays, Carla has to decide where she stands: with her mother and boyfriend or on the side of justice. Banned for promoting homosexuality.

***Geography Club* by Brent Hartinger. New York: HarperCollins, 2003.**

A group of gay and lesbian teens bond and create their own club at their high school. A funny and poignant read about love and friendship, but banned for promoting homosexuality.

***My Heartbeat* by Garret Freymann-Weyr. Boston: Houghton Mifflin, 2002.**

Fourteen-year-old Ellen is puzzled by the unusually close relationship between her brother and his best friend. She loves them both and enjoys their company. Banded for promoting homosexuality.

***Rainbow Boys* by Alex Sanchez. New York: Simon & Schuster, 2001.**

A group of high school boys, all seniors, with diverse backgrounds and experiences, struggle with family relationships, bullies, sexual encounters, and their own confused feelings about each other. Banned for profanity and promoting homosexuality.

***We All Fall Down* by Robert Cormier. New York: Delacorte/Random House, 1991.**

A group of boys vandalize a house and attack a young girl who arrives home early. Cormier's language is forceful and the story, told from alternating points of view, is richly layered. As with much of Cormier's work, the book explores humanity's darker side. Banned for language, violence, and its overall "disturbing" nature.

***Whale Talk* by Chris Crutcher. New York: Greenwillow/HarperCollins, 2001.**

A multiracial teen shuns high school athletics until he is challenged to organize a swimming team. Turned off by athletic elitism, he brings together a group of misfits to swim for Cutter High. Banned for profanity. Other banned books by Crutcher include *Stotan!* (1986), *Athletic Shorts* (1991), *Ironman* (1995), and *Staying Fat for Sarah Byrnes* (1993).

***When Jeff Comes Home* by Catherine Atkins. New York: Penguin/Putnam, 1999.**

Sixteen-year-old Jeff returns home after being kidnapped. What should be a happy reunion turns cold, for he must confront the issue of whether he had sex with his kidnapper.

Box 3.3   Censorship as a Theme in YA Novels

Curse of a Winter Moon by Mary Casanova. New York: Hyperion, 2000.

Dancing in Red Shoes Will Kill You by Dorian Cirrone. New York: HarperCollins, 2005.

The Day They Came to Arrest the Book by Nat Hentoff. New York: Dell, 1982.

Fahrenheit 451 by Ray Bradbury. New York: Ballantine, 1953.

A Hand Full of Stars by Rafik Schami. Trans. Rika Lesser. New York: Dutton/Penguin, 1990.

Heir Apparent by Vivian Vande Velde. Orlando, FL: Harcourt, 2002.

Hello, Groin by Beth Goobie. Custer, WA: Orca, 2006.

How to Get Suspended and Influence People by Adam Selzer. New York: Delacorte/Random House, 2007.

The Landry News by Andrew Clements. New York: Simon & Schuster, 1999.

The Last Book in the Universe by Rodman Philbrick. New York: Blue Sky/Scholastic, 2000.

The Last Safe Place on Earth by Richard Peck. New York: Delacorte/Random House, 1995.

Maudie and Me and the Dirty Book by Betty Miles. New York: Knopf/Random House, 1980.

Memoirs of a Bookbat by Kathryn Lasky. Orlando, FL: Harcourt, 1994.

Nothing but the Truth by Avi. New York: Orchard/Scholastic, 1991.

The Phantom Isles by Stephen Alter. New York: Bloomsbury, 2007.

Phoebe: A Novel by Marilyn Kaye. Orlando, FL: Harcourt, 1987.

The Siege by Kathryn Lasky. New York: Scholastic, 2004.

The Sledding Hill by Chris Crutcher. New York: HarperCollins, 2005.

A Small Civil War by John Neufeld. New York: Atheneum/Simon & Schuster, 1996.

Talk by Kathe Koja. New York: Farrar, Straus & Giroux, 2005.

The Trials of Molly Sheldon by Julian F. Thompson. New York: Henry Holt, 1995.

The Trouble with Mothers by Margery Facklam. New York: Clarion, 1989.

Water Shaper by Laura Williams McCaffrey. New York: Clarion, 2006.

Wizards of the Game by David Lubar. New York: Philomel/Penguin, 2003.

The Year They Burned the Books by Nancy Garden. New York: Farrar, Straus & Giroux, 1999.

When you do meet with the would-be censor, be friendly, remain calm, and listen more than you talk. Above all, you will be tempted to talk about the issue with other teachers and community members. Be judicious with whom you discuss the issue and in what you say and be extra thoughtful when talking with students and the media.

If after the initial meeting, the objector continues to oppose the book, he/she should be required to file a formal complaint, one that begins with completing a citizen's complaint form (see Table 3.3 on p. 79).

This procedure, as mentioned earlier, will encourage objectors to think through their complaints and will discourage "idle censors" (NCTE, 1981). Once the formal complaint has been filed, the complaint should move to a committee level, where it is reviewed and evaluated by a team of teachers/librarians, administrators, and possible community members and students. The teacher and school should also file a report with professional organizations such as NCTE and ALA. These organizations can provide additional support.

While there's no way of preventing a challenge, you can position yourself better by being proactive and remaining informed about local and national censorship issues. When you are confronted, remember to offer options for the objector's child (better yet, ask the objector to suggest titles that meet your course objectives); insist on the rights of other students and parents to choose for their own children. Stand strong and remember that censorship isn't about one book. It's about precedent. More importantly, Judy Blume reminds us it's about quelling thought[7]:

> It's not just the books under fire now that worry me. It is the books that will never be written. The books that will never be read. And all due to the fear of censorship. As always, young readers will be the real losers.

Final Thoughts

Young adult literature is no longer restricted to realistic fiction; it has transformed considerably since the birth of the problem novel. In the following chapters you will examine a wide range of genres; you will also notice a trend toward genre blending: realistic fiction may contain fantasy elements; fantasy may have historical settings; science fiction may take the form of a short story; and a poem may be classified as a novel, novella, or short story. Even though much of today's young adult literature crosses genres, it's necessary to organize the literature in some way in order to examine it. The categories I use are arbitrary, and some, such as sports, are more thematic than genre-specific. Each chapter includes historical overviews, key characteristics, issues and themes, landmark texts, and textboxes written by some of the best authors and experts in the field. Most chapters conclude with an instructional section that illustrates methods for teaching reading.

An Interview with Chris Crutcher: Censorship and *The Sledding Hill*[8]

Cole: I enjoyed your new book, *The Sledding Hill.* I was surprised with all the turns. Just what was the catalyst for this book?

Crutcher: Actually there were two catalysts I remember. One was remembering the power of an irrational fear of dying that comes in early adolescence (more powerful to wusses like me than to some others) and the other was my increasing exposure to inflexible censors trying to get my books out of classrooms and off school library shelves. The more I dealt

---

[7]Retrieved from www.judyblume.com, April 27, 2007.
[8]First published in *Voices from the Middle,* 2005.

with those censors, the more I became familiar with other writers' censorship problems. Censors, aka the Christian Right, have been wearing down teachers and librarians who stand up for intellectual freedom, and they've bullied a lot of school administrators.

Cole: This book comes out on the heels of a number of challenges to your other books. You're saying that's not a coincidence?

Crutcher: Actually, the bulk of this book was finished almost a year before publication, so I hadn't yet had my recent experiences in Michigan, Iowa, and South Carolina and Alabama and Kansas. Yet the language used by those censors is eerily similar to the language I gave to my fictional censors; and the sentiments also seem the same. I think we are, and have been for some time, in an atmosphere that is dangerous to our intellectual freedom in this country, so this book couldn't have come out at a better time for me. I'm feeling combative these days because I believe that good stories can lead to great discussions between adults and teenagers and because I believe that stories about hard times can make people in hard times feel less alone. It chafes me pretty good when people want to take those stories away, whether they're mine or some other author's.

Cole: The antagonists in the book, those who promote censorship, are members of the Red Brick Church, which can only be described as a "right-wing Christian" church. Much of what your protagonists say about censorship is that it promotes bigotry. Do you make a connection between the Conservative Right, the Christian Right, and bigotry?

Crutcher: Sometimes I do, and believe me I know what an inflammatory word that is. I don't call people bigots for being offended by rough language or being squeamish about certain issues, but if your beliefs and policies cause you to diminish or denigrate some specific portion of our society, you are a bigot. You may build houses for the homeless in Mexico, send money to Habitat, take food to the food bank, and give a tenth of your income to the church for good works. But if you treat a part of the population as if it is inferior, and I'm speaking specifically of the ten percent or so who are gay, you are a bigot. Much of my work—*Ironman* and *Athletic Shorts*, for example—gets challenged and/or censored because I place "gay characters in a positive light." The censors allow themselves that bigotry by declaring, without any credible evidence, that homosexuality is a "choice."

Cole: So you believe it's not a choice?

Crutcher: What right do bigots have to even ask that question? What answer would we give if asked when we made the "choice" to be heterosexual? Do you think 10 percent of the population would *choose* homosexuality, knowing it will make them reviled by their peers and treated as second-class citizens? Do you think the kids making up the three-times-the-normal-suicide-rate group would choose a lifestyle that makes them feel so desperate? I'm constantly accused of "promoting homosexuality" for simply writing about it. Forget that those characters are portrayed only in the light of humanity, and the Christian Right wants them censored simply because of their sexual persuasion. There will come a time when we are as ashamed of how our culture now treats the gay population as we are about how we treated blacks during and before the civil rights movement of the fifties and sixties. When we have this censorship discussion we should all leave our gurus at home—you leave Jesus and Mohammed and I'll leave Buddha and the Tao—and we'll talk about morality issues as they apply to humans. I miss the Christians I knew growing up; the Christians who preached inclusion and understanding, and understood that separation of church and state was as good for them as it was for the state. I know they still exist. I just wish they'd stand up and give Jesus his name back.

Cole: A lot of people would say you can't leave God out of a morality discussion.

Crutcher: And I would say you can't put him in. With God in the mix—anybody's God—morality becomes a list of things to do or not to do instead of a way to be. It then comes out of a fear rather than respect and is reduced to behaviors, at which time it has no meaning. I think your relationship with your God is entirely personal and you don't need it to be decent to other people.

Cole: You could have easily used one of your published books as the novel being attacked in *The Sledding Hill.* Why did you make up a book?

Crutcher: Because it let me separate the real Chris Crutcher from the fictional Chris Crutcher and it didn't hold me to the issues in *Whale Talk* or *Staying Fat for Sarah Byrnes* or any other single book. It also let me play with that line between fact and fiction. Chris Crutcher is a real guy, but his book in the story is fictional and to that degree he is fictional.

Cole: When I got to the end of the story I couldn't wait to hear Crutcher speak, yet he doesn't. Why doesn't he?

Crutcher: Because it wasn't his story. The fictional Chris Crutcher's presence in the book is to some degree a "bit" or a gag. I did it because I'm most familiar with the complaints people have about my work as opposed to other writers. This story is about the characters, about Billy and Eddie. The censorship issue in the story needs to be resolved by them. In many cases when my books have been challenged, it's the kids and the passionate teachers and librarians who fight the censors. It's too easy for the censors to write the author off as having a vested interest, which I suppose we do.

Cole: I've heard you say, "Censorship leaves kids behind." Can you explain how that's true?

Crutcher: The stories I write are inspired by real kids going through real hardships. That is true of many authors of adolescent fiction. Many of us write about kids who have come up through extremely difficult situations, and their behavior and language reflect those situations. When those kids' stories are censored, the kids are also censored. We leave them behind. They become an afterthought, or nothing. And they are the kids who have always been left behind. I'm waiting for the first politician with the guts to do what is needed to *really* leave no child behind.

Cole: *The Sledding Hill* isn't just about censorship. It's a story about loss as well. What were your thoughts about adolescence as you were writing the story?

Crutcher: My thoughts were that almost all humans suffer what seems like senseless and unfair losses. How we respond to those losses often influences our core mental health as we grow older. Most of us are told how we *should* feel and how we *should* believe as we're growing up, rather than being helped through the process of grief. What goes on with Eddie is pure grief.

Cole: You generally write about older kids; however, this book includes younger adolescents. Can you talk about that?

Crutcher: The protagonist is about three years younger than most of my main characters, and it's a shorter story. Part of that was in response to so many teachers and librarians over the years asking me to write something they could use in middle or upper elementary schools. I had written *King of the Mild Frontier* and come up with material I liked from my early adolescence, and that sparked ideas.

I did something else in this story I'd never done before. I purposely kept all the "bad" language out; because typically the censors attack the language because that's an easy target, when I think they're really offended by issues. So if they go after this one, they'll have to show their true colors.

Cole: It's true your books are often censored for "bad" language. Can you elaborate on that?

Crutcher: Censors love to take language out of context, purposely. On three different occasions, would-be censors have gone through *Whale Talk* and listed what they considered to be offensive words. One counted 128. I hope they were counting each usage. I don't know 128 offensive words. The point is, language out of context can be made to look pretty disgusting, when in fact, most kids don't even notice, or when they do, say it makes the story more authentic.

Cole: I've read reviews in wish critics say you load your books up with issues. What do you say to that kind of criticism?

Crutcher: It's always interesting to me when my books are criticized for being "loaded" with issues. Beginning back with *Chinese Handcuffs,* I heard that "Crutcher threw everything into this one but the kitchen sink." I remember thinking "I couldn't get the kitchen sink loose, or I'd have thrown that in too." I understand that as a therapist I've been privy to a lot of stories others don't often see or hear about. But that's the point. When a person is free to tell all, "all" is usually more than most of us expect. Certain kinds of critics seem to believe very differently from what I believe about young adult fiction. They think a "problem novel" should isolate a problem and address it all the way through; come to some conclusion, if you will. But in my view the "problem" in adolescence is adolescence. Very little occurs in a vacuum. Hard time kids are magnetic to hard time kids, and very few have one problem. For instance if there is sexual molestation in a family it often exists alongside intimidation, physical violence, complex and convoluted secrecy. Kids in trouble can find other kids in trouble with their eyes closed, and usually do.

It is no exaggeration to say it's hard to count the number of people I have known in other parts of my life who have written or emailed me to say my books mirror their lives. The surprising part of that to me is that so many of them were not clients, but people I grew up with or worked with in the fields of education and therapy. What I know is this, I have never written anything for shock value, and I have never written anything that didn't reflect something I knew about in real life. And I haven't even come close to writing all I know or have seen. When critics and/or censors come after my stories because they believe they are so much harsher than life, I can only laugh.

Cole: What parts of writing *The Sledding Hill* posed the greatest problem for you as a writer?

Crutcher: The voice of the deceased narrator. Once he was dead he became very smart because he automatically knew things living people don't, and I tended to give him an adult voice. He is funnier and cleverer with his young voice. I also struggled with the issue of censorship because it was close to home and I had to move away to do it justice. That's another reason for the "fictional" Crutcher book.

Cole: Why did you use a deceased narrator?

Crutcher: To take advantage of the vision of a third-person narrator along with the voice of a first-person narrator. You get "all seeing" along with intimacy with the narrator.

Cole: The reader doesn't learn much about the character in Warren Peece—a great name by the way. Are you thinking about using him as a character in a future book?

Crutcher: It's a pretty good pun, if I do say so myself, and the possibilities are inviting.

Cole: What do you want adolescents to take from this book?

Crutcher: I want them to read a good story, and I want them to have fun discussing censorship. I also want them to take a good look at who the censors are, their motives, and their world view.

Cole: What do you hope adults will take from it?

Crutcher: The same thing.

First published in *Voices from the Middle;* published in *The Sledding Hill,* 2006.

Letter to the Students of the Limestone School District: By Chris Crutcher

Recently my book, *Whale Talk,* was banned in your school district, and I thought I might address that. First, let it be known that I don't take it personally. None of the four school board members who voted to take the book out of your reach knows me and I have no reason to believe any of them bear me ill will. From all I have read, I believe the stated reason the book was banned was for "curses," which, where I come from are called "cuss words."

Arguably the two most offensive passages in the story occur when a four and a half year old bi-racial girl screams out the names she is called on a regular basis by her racist stepfather and later when that same racist stepfather is drunkenly threatening the foster family that is keeping her safe.

In the 1980s and early 1990s when I was working as a child abuse and neglect therapist in the Spokane (Washington) Community Mental Health

Center, I worked with a young bi-racial girl living in circumstances much like those depicted in the book. Her biological father didn't even know of her existence and her mother didn't have the emotional strength to keep her out of the eye of the hurricane of her stepfather's hatred. She couldn't eat at the table until her younger, white stepbrothers had finished, wasn't allowed to play with toys until they were broken and handed over to her. The first time I saw her she was standing over a sink, trying to wash the brown off her skin so her (step) daddy would love her. Time and time again in therapy she expressed the self contempt she had gained believing there was something fundamentally wrong with her because there was no way to find acceptance in his world. In play therapy she was allowed to work through her life trauma to ultimately better understand that it was not her fault she was treated as she was, and to come to a better understanding (in a four-year-old's way of understanding) of the world she lived in. The language that little girl used was even tougher than what my character used in *Whale Talk.*

When *Whale Talk* gets challenged or banned, it's often because a parent who hasn't read the book runs across that passage or one like it, sees the words (which in this case are in large font because the little girl is screaming) and decides they are a danger to you. They describe the story, more often than not without reading it, as obscene or insidious or evil or all three.

But what's truly obscene is that I know a real girl in the real world who has gone through this. What's obscene is that so do you, even if you're not aware of the specifics. What's obscene is that you know kids who have gone through, and are going through, worse. What's obscene is that kids who are mal-treated often grow up angry and depressed and anxious and desperate. They experience crippling difficulties in school, in social relations and in all matters of self-esteem. They use the language I use in the story and worse because it is all they have to try to match what is inside with the outside world. They need to be recognized, and brought into your fold. Often we adults can't help them, but you can. I write the stories I write to bring things like this to your attention because I believe if kids who are treated badly are to survive, they will survive through the acceptance of their peers, and that acceptance will come from understanding. It's true; I'm asking a lot from you.

Let me tell you something else I think is obscene. I think it is obscene that your school board doesn't trust you enough to know you can read harsh stories, told in their native tongue, and make decisions for yourself about what you think of the issues or the language. It is astonishing to me that grown men, in this case, don't believe you can think for yourselves. Some of you could have voted in the last election. Many more of you will be eligible in the next.

It is not a big deal that *Whale Talk* was removed from your school library shelves. There are plenty of good books out there that your school board hasn't had a chance to ban yet. But consider this. About a decade ago, a stellar author named Walter Dean Myers wrote *Fallen Angels,* a story about a young African American man fighting in Vietnam. Walter told his story, using the language of soldiers at war. It was pretty much the language I used to talk about this four-year-old girl, who was also at war. *Fallen Angels,* a critically acclaimed book, is constantly under the same attack that *Whale Talk* is under from your school board. Think about this a minute. In the not too distant future many of you will be soldiers also, asked to fight in the name of your country. Statistics say a few of your number will also be writers. Imagine risking your life in war, coming back to tell your story in as real a fashion as you can, only to have *your* children told they can't read your story in your school because the school board won't tolerate the realistic language in which you tell it. They not only tell *their* children it can't be part of their education, they tell *your* children it can't be part of their education.

I have no problem at all if any or all of you pick up *Whale Talk,* read a couple of chapters, or even a couple of pages, don't like it, slam it shut and never open it again. I don't even have a problem if you do that because you are offended by the situations or the language. I don't have a problem with that because it's *your* choice. I trust you to know what you like and what you don't, and what's good for you in terms of literature.

I can't change the minds of people who believe that the best way to keep kids safe is to keep you ignorant. What I can, and will do is this: Donate copies of *Whale Talk* to your public library, which is a lot less likely to try to think for you. I can urge you to take a look at it and decide for yourselves. I can encourage you to stand up for your own intellectual freedom; to choose what you want to read about and talk about and explore. I can encourage you to let those members of your school board who don't trust you with tough material, know you are a lot more savvy than they think you are, and that there is no way they can capture your intellectual freedom with the silliness of banning a book from the library shelves. There are plenty of places to get books.

I have to be honest. I don't think the only reason those four school board members wanted *Whale Talk* out of your schools was language. I could be wrong—it's certainly happened before—but I think there are other issues in the book that make them uncomfortable. But even on language alone, if you accept the banning of this book, you should demand that they also remove other books in which that language exists. Start with Alice Walker's Pulitzer Prize winning *The Color Purple,* then go to Maya Angelou's *I Know Why the Caged Bird Sings.* You certainly can't allow any of my other ten books there, nor any of Robert Cormier's, many of Walter Dean Myers's or Tim O'Brien's (*The Things They Carried* may well be one of the ten best written books of the twentieth century). Sherman Alexie, the great Native American writer is out, hands down and there is *no* way you can be allowed to cast your eyes upon Joseph Heller's *Catch-22.* If you accept this "protection" from your school board, demand that they step up and truly protect you.

I may seem somewhat *flip* here but I believe that adolescence is an extremely important time in any human's development. There are hundreds of questions about relationship and career and identity, and you are handcuffed to look at them when a group of men who believe that the depiction of true, rough language is a top-priority moral issue. I trust you to read my book, or any of the other far more familiar books mentioned above, and decide for yourselves what you think of them. It wouldn't be completely over the top for you to expect your school board to do the same. Remember this: your school board is there to make decisions to further your education, not keep themselves in their own comfort zones.

I do want to compliment those members and the superintendent who voted against the banning. It does my heart good to know there are many educators out there who understand that good education requires the opening rather than the closing of minds. Again, this isn't about *Whale Talk*, it really isn't. It's about you.

Sincerely,

Chris Crutcher

A Response to Teachers' Concerns about Sexually Explicit Material: By Chris Crutcher

I ran into a posting on a listserv talking about Sherman Alexie's *The Absolutely True Diary of a Part-Time Indian*. The author of that posting said she taught gifted kids in a Catholic middle school and had also been a YA librarian. Citing a scene in the story depicting the main character talking about masturbation, she said, "There is no way I can have that book in my room. The language, the passage about masturbation—I cannot have that book in my room. What age do you think that book would be for and who would you recommend it to? As librarians, can you recommend books with that kind of content in good conscience?" She went on to say she knows kids read on their own and that she had no problem with that, but, "My question is, why do authors do that when they know that kind of content eliminates a portion of their audience?" She talked about another book with sexual content, saying she knows her kids enjoyed reading it, but that, as an adult, she could not recommend it.

I felt an obligation to respond, to let her know why at least *some* of us "do that:"

This comment on your listserv was sent to me by a number of folks and I'm afraid I have to respond. It will give me something to do while procrastinating before deciding how to write my next masturbation scene.

Look, kids masturbate. They think about it. They talk about it. In graphic terms. When I started working as a child abuse and neglect family therapist back in the early eighties, one quick conclusion I came to was that until we are willing and able to talk openly about sex in this culture—healthy sex and sexual thought—we will never be capable of talking about sex abuse. I swear sometimes I'm embarrassed to live in a culture that can't talk about true things because someone might be offended. When that perspective comes from within *our educational culture, I'm even more embarrassed. A story like Sherman's mirrors a life; a whole life, not just the whitewashed parts of a life. A young reader doesn't come away from that story thinking about masturbation. He or she comes away thinking about loneliness and friendship and meanness; how to avoid meanness and how to be less mean. In that story a young man finds his way against all odds. And he whacks off while doing it. Big deal. Come on, people.*

Alex Flinn says she considers long and hard before putting a scene in a book that might be offensive. I love Alex's books. I think highly of her as a writer. But let it be known, if it isn't already, that I don't consider for a second whether someone will be offended by a given passage. I consider whether it's real, or if it seems real to me. This pandering to adult "sensibilities" is part of what keeps YA fiction from being considered real fiction. Someone gasps and grasps his or her chest at the mention of MASTURBATION and folks seem to think the rest of us need to recoil too.

For years kids—teenagers—came into my office to say how unheard they felt by the adults in their lives; parents and teachers. We're either able to hear about their lives in their native tongue, or we're not. When we're not, they stop talking to us. Who can blame them? There isn't a teacher out there who couldn't say, "There are scenes in this book that make me uneasy. They might make you uneasy too. Maybe we should talk about why we feel uneasy. Then we can talk about the book."

I wouldn't give Sherman's book to just any fifth grader, because it would be beyond many of them, but I'd sure as hell give it to any eighth grader. And I'd let any kid who wanted to read it, read it. If it's beyond them, they'll say so. Or they'll put it down.

And I have to tell you, I don't buy the Catholic argument. I've had some of the best discussions in my long string of school presentations in Catholic middle and high schools. There are a whole bunch of Catholic teachers and Jesuits who aren't one bit afraid of talking about real things in kids' lives. I was given the St. Katharine Drexel Award by the Catholic Library Association after writing about abortion and masturbation and sex abuse. There's no Catholic shroud to hide behind here.

This censorship thing has gotten out of hand because people who understand intellectual freedom are less willing to stand up for it, and because people who truly understand the nature of adolescence and pre-adolescence have become unwilling to speak up. The dis-ease we feel dealing with kids is exactly the reason to deal with the real stuff.

Professional Resources

Agee, J. (1999). "There it was, that one sex scene": English teachers on censorship. *English Journal, 89*(2), 61–69.

Anderson, J. (2002). When parents' rights are wrong. *School Library Journal, 48*(11), 43.

Barlow, D. (2002). Rationales for teaching young adult literature. *The Education Digest, 68*(2), 77–78.

Becker, B. C., & Stan, S. M. (2003). *Hit list for children 2: Frequently challenged books.* Chicago: ALA.

Brown J. E., (Ed.). (1994). *Preserving intellectual freedom: Fighting censorship in our schools.* Urbana, IL: NCTE.

Broz, W. J. (2001). Hope and irony: *Annie on My Mind. English Journal, 90*, 47–53.

Broz, W. J. (2002). Defending *I Am Blue. Journal of Adolescent and Adult Literacy, 45*(5), 340–350.

Church, S. M. (1997). When values clash: Learning from controversy. *Language Arts, 74*(7), 525–532.

Couvares, F. G. (2006). *Movie censorship and American culture.* Amherst: University of Massachusetts Press.

Crowe, C. (2001). The problem with YA literature. *English Journal, 90*(3), 146–150.

Crutcher, C. (2002). In defense of bad language. *Voices from the Middle, 9*(4), 5–6.

Curry, A. (2001). Where is Judy Blume? Controversial fiction for older children and young adults. *Journal of Youth Services in Libraries, 14*(3), 28–37.

Donelson, K. (1974). Censorship in the 1970s: Some ways to handle it when it comes (and it will). *English Journal, 63*(2), 47–51.

Dresang, E. T. (2003). Controversial books and contemporary children. *Journal of Children's Literature, 29*(1), 20–31.

Freedman, L., & Johnson, H. (2001). Who's protecting whom? I hadn't meant to tell you this, a case in point in confronting self-censorship in the choice of young adult literature. *Journal of Adolescent and Adult Literacy, 44*(4), 356–369.

Garden, N. (1996). Annie on trial: How it feels to be the author of a challenged book. *Voices of Youth Advocates, 19*(2), 79–84.

Glanzer, P. L. (2004). In defense of Harry. . . . But not his defenders: Beyond censorship to justice. *English Journal, 93*(4), 58–63.

Glick, A. (2002). Parents wage anti-porn campaign against schools. *School Library Journal, 48*(1), 26.

Goodson, F. T. (1998). Science fiction, fantasy, fundamentalist censors, and imaginative thinking: Motives of the censors, possible solutions for teachers. *SIGNAL Journal, 22*(1), 4–9.

Greenbaum, V. (1997). Censorship and the myth of appropriateness: Reflections on teaching reading in high school. *English Journal, 86*(2), 16–20.

Hipple, T. (2001). Somnolent bulls, red flags, dirty books, and censorship pedagogy. *English Journal, 90*(3), 18–19.

Howard, J. P. R. (2003). Tolerance in the school system: Should teachers be held to one standard and their teaching tools to another? *Education Canada, 43*(2), 42–43.

Isaacs, K. T. (2003). Reality check. *School Library Journal, 49*(10), 50–51.

Karolides, N., Bald, M., & Sova, D. B. (2005). *120 banned books: Censorship histories of world literature.* New York: Checkmark Books.

Kelly, P. (2003). *When I Was Puerto Rican* by Esmeralda Santiago: Responding to a censorship challenge. *Ohio Media Spectrum, 55*(1), 19–26.

Leporino, P., & Roessler, S. (1998). Trust your children: Voices against censorship in children's literature. *Language Arts, 76*(1), 78.

Lesesne, T. S. (2005). Censorship: The mind you close may be your own. *Voices from the Middle, 13*(1), 72–77.

Lesesne, T. S., & Chance, R. (2002). *List for young adults 2.* Chicago: ALA.

Marshall, J. M. (2003). Critically thinking about Harry Potter: A framework for discussing controversial works in the English classroom. *The ALAN Review, 30*(2), 16–19.

Mazer, N. F. (1997). Shhhh! *The ALAN Review, 24*(2), 46–48.

McCarthy, M. M. (2004). Filtering the Internet: The Children's Internet Protection Act. *Educational Horizons, 82*(2), 108–113.

Meyer, R. (2004). *Outlaw representation: Censorship and homosexuality in twentieth-century American art.* Boston: Beacon Press.

Mitoraj, S. O. (2000). Deliverance: The anatomy of a challenge. *English Journal, 89*(4), 105–111.

Mollineaux, B. (2001). Simply irresistible: Letting our reading inform theirs. *Voices from the Middle, 8*(4), 80–83.

Morris, D. M., & Ellis, L. (1996). Deep trouble in the heart of Texas. *Teaching and Learning Literature, 5*(5), 2–7.

Mossman, R. C. (2007). Literary magazines: To censor or not? *English Journal, (96)*5, 48–50.

Nakaya, A. (2005). *Censorship: Opposing viewpoints.* Farmington Hills, MI: Greenhaven Press.

O'Neal, S. (1990). Leadership in the language arts: Controversial books in the classroom. *Language Arts, 67*(7), 771–775.

Power, B. M., Wilhelm, J. D., & Chandler, K. (1997). *Reading Stephen King: Issues of censorship, student choice, and popular literature.* Urbana, IL: NCTE.

Reichman, H. (2001). *Censorship and selection: Issues and answers for schools.* Chicago: ALA.

Reid, L. (2000). To learn about promoting the freedom to read. *English Journal, 89*(6), 130–131.

Reid, L., & Neufield, J. H. (1999). *Rationales for teaching young adult literature.* Portland, ME: Calendar Islands.

Rossuck, J. (1997). Banned books: A study of censorship. *English Journal, 86*(2), 67–70.

Salvner, G. M. (1998). A war of words: Lessons from a censorship case. *The ALAN Review 25*(2), 45–49.

Scales, P. (2007). It takes three to tango. *School Library Journal, 53*(7), 24.

Schulten, K. (1999). Huck Finn: Born to trouble. *English Journal, 89*(2), 55–59.

Simmons, J. (1991). Censorship in the schools: No end in sight. *The ALAN Review, 18*(2), 6–8.

Small, R. C. (2000). Censorship as we enter 2000, or the millennium, or just new year: A personal look at where we are. *Journal of Youth Services in Libraries, 13*(2), 19–23.

Staples, S. F. (1996). What Johnny can't read: Censorship in American libraries. *The ALAN Review, 23*(2), 49–50.

Thompson, J. (1991). Defending YA literature against the Pharisees and censors: Is it worth the trouble? *The ALAN Review, 18*(2), 2–5.

Weiss, M. J. (2002). Rumbles! Bangs! Crashes! The road of censorship. *The ALAN Review, 29,* 54–57.

West, M. I. (1997). Speaking of censorship: An interview with Phyllis Reynolds Naylor. *Journal of Youth Services in Libraries, 10*(2), 177–182.

Winkler, L. K. (2005). Celebrate democracy! Teach about censorship. *English Journal, 94*(5), 48–51.

Wollman-Bonilla, J. E. (1998). Outrageous viewpoints: Teachers' criteria for rejecting works of children's literature. *Language Arts, 75*(4), 287–295.

ONLINE

American Booksellers Foundation for Free Expression: http://abffe.org

American Civil Liberties Union: http://aclu.org

American Library Association Office for Intellectual Freedom: http://www.ala.org/ala/oif/intellectual.htm

As If! Authors Support Intellectual Freedom: www.asifnews.blogspot.com

Center for First Amendment Rights, Inc.: www.cfarfreedom.org/index.shtml

Center for First Amendment Studies: www.csulb.edu/crsmith/1amendment.html

Electronic Frontier Foundation: www.eff.org/br

First Amendment Center: www.firstamendmentcenter.org/topicssummary.aspx

The First Amendment First Aid Kit by Random House: www.randomhouse.com/teens/firstamendment

First Amendment Schools: www.firstamendmentschools.org

The Free Expression Policy Project: http://fepproject.org

Freedom of Information & First Amendment Center: www.ire.org/foi

Freedom to Read: http://freedomtoread.ca

FREEMUSE: Freedom of Musical Expression: www.freemuse.org/sw305.asp

INDEX on Censorship for Free Expression: www.indexonline.org

International Federation of Library Associations and Institutions: www.ifla.org/faife/ifstat/ifstat.htm

Kidspeak: http://kidspeakonline.org

National Coalition Against Censorship: www.ncac.org

NCTE's Anti-Censorship Center: www.ncte.org/about/issues/censorship

PEN American Center: http://pen.org

People for the American Way: www.pfaw.org/pfaw/general

Project Censored Media: www.projectcensored.org

References

ALA. (2007). Intellectual freedom and censorship. Retrieved March 24, 2007, from http://www.ala.org

Almond, D. (2000). *Kit's wilderness.* New York: Delacorte/Random House.

Anderson, L. H. (1999). *Speak.* New York: Farrar, Straus & Giroux.

Anderson, M. T. (2006). *The astonishing life of Octavian Nothing, traitor to the nation: Volume 1. The pox party.* Cambridge, MA: Candlewick Press.

Angelou, M. (1969). *I know why the caged bird sings.* New York: Random House.

Bauer, M. D. (1994). *Am I blue? Coming out from the silence.* New York: HarperCollins.

Blume, J. (1970). *Are you there, God? It's me, Margaret.* Scarsdale, NY: Bradbury Press.

Blume, J. (1971). *Then again, maybe I won't.* Scarsdale, NY: Bradbury Press.

Blume, J. (1975). *Forever.* Scarsdale, NY: Bradbury Press.

Brooks, T. (1977). *The sword of Shannara.* New York: Random House.

Burgess, M. (2004). *Doing it.* New York: Henry Holt.

Bush, J. (2007). *Ana's story*. New York: HarperCollins.

Cart, M. (1996). *From romance to realism: Fifty years of growth and change in young adult literature*. New York: HarperCollins.

Cart, M. (2004). *Rush hour*. New York: Delacorte.

Cart, M., & Jenkins, C. A. (2004). *The heart has its reasons: Young adult literature with gay/lesbian/ queer content, 1969–2004*. Lanham, MD: Scarecrow Press.

Cole, P. (2005). Chris Crutcher on censorship and *The Sledding Hill:* An interview with Pam B. Cole. *Voices from the Middle, 13*(1), 74–77.

Conly, J. L. (1993). *Crazy lady!* New York: HarperCollins.

Cooney, C. B. (1990). *The face on the milk carton*. New York: Bantam/Random House.

Cormier, R. (1974). *The chocolate war*. New York: Pantheon Books.

Cormier, R. (1977). *I am the cheese*. New York: Pantheon Books.

Cormier, R. (1979). *After the first death*. New York: Pantheon Books.

Cormier, R. (1991). *We all fall down*. New York: Delacorte/Random House.

Crutcher, C. (1986). *Stotan!* New York: Greenwillow/HarperCollins.

Crutcher, C. (1989). *Chinese handcuffs*. New York: Greenwillow/HarperCollins.

Crutcher, C. (1991). *Athletic shorts: 6 short stories*. New York: Greenwillow/HarperCollins.

Crutcher, C. (1993). *Staying fat for Sarah Byrnes*. New York: Greenwillow/HarperCollins.

Crutcher, C. (1995). *Ironman*. New York: Greenwillow/HarperCollins.

Crutcher, C. (2001). *Whale talk*. New York: Greenwillow/HarperCollins.

Crutcher, C. (2003). *King of the mild frontier: An ill-advised autobiography*. New York: Greenwillow/HarperCollins.

Donovan, J. (1969). *I'll get there, it better be worth the trip*. New York: Harper & Row.

Duncan, L. (1978). *Killing Mr. Griffin*. New York: Little, Brown.

Eyerly, J. (1966). *A girl like me*. Philadelphia: Lippincott.

Fleischman, P. (1998). *Whirligig*. New York: Henry Holt.

Gallo, D. (1984). *Sixteen: Short stories by outstanding writers for young adults*. New York: Delacorte/ Random House.

Gallo, D. (2006). *What are you afraid of? Stories about phobias*. Cambridge, MA: Candlewick Press.

Garden, N. (1982). *Annie on my mind*. New York: Farrar, Straus & Giroux.

Glenn, M. (1982). *Class dismissed! High school poems*. New York: Clarion.

Green, J. (2005). *Looking for Alaska*. New York: Penguin.

Guy, R. (1976). *Ruby*. New York: Viking/Penguin.

Hartnett, S. (2006). *Surrender*. Cambridge, MA: Candlewick Press.

Head, A. (1967). *Mr. and Mrs. Bo Jo Jones*. New York: Putnam.

Heggum, L., (Ed.). (2006). *All sleek and skimming*. Custer, WA: Orca.

Hesse, K. (1997). *Out of the dust*. New York: Scholastic.

Hicks, B. (2005). *Out of order*. New Milford, CT: Roaring Brook Press.

Hinton, S. E. (1967). *The outsiders*. New York: Viking/Penguin.

Hopkins, E. (2004). *Crank*. New York: Simon & Schuster.

Hopkins, E. (2006). *Burned*. New York: Simon & Schuster.

Johnson, A. (2003). *The first part last*. New York: Simon & Schuster.

Kerr, M. E. (1986). *Night kites*. New York: Harper & Row.

Koertge, R. (2005). *Arizona kid*. Cambridge, MA: Candlewick Press. (Original work published 1988)

Lanagan, M. (2005). *Black juice*. New York: HarperCollins. (Original work published 2004)

Le Guin, U. (1968). A wizard of Earthsea. Berkeley, CA: Parnassus Press.

Levithan, D. (2003). *Boy meets boy*. New York: Knopf/Random House.

Lipsyte, R. (1967). *The contender*. New York: Harper & Row.

Lipsyte, R. (1977). *One fat summer*. New York: Harper & Row.

Lipsyte, R. (1981). *Summer rules*. New York: Harper & Row.

Lipsyte, R. (1982). *The summerboy*. New York: Harper & Row.

Lubar, D. (2005). *Sleeping freshmen never lie*. New York: Dutton/Penguin.

Lynch, C. (1994). *Gypsy Davey*. New York: HarperCollins.

Mazer, N. F. (1997). *When she was good*. New York: Levine/Scholastic.

Myers, W. D. (1975). *Fast Sam, cool Clyde, and stuff*. New York: Viking/Penguin.

Myers, W. D. (2004). *Shooter*. New York: Amistad/ HarperCollins.

NCTE. (1981). The students' right to read. Retrieved March 21, 2007, from http://www.ncte.org

Paterson, K. (1978). *The great Gilly Hopkins*. New York: Crowell.

Pike, C. (1985). *Slumber party*. New York: Scholastic.

Pinkwater, D. (1982). *Young adult novel*. New York: Crowell.

Rosoff, M. (2004). *How I live now*. New York: Random House.

Rylant, C. (1992). *Missing May*. New York: Orchard/Scholastic.

Salinger, J. D. (1951). *The catcher in the rye*. Boston: Little, Brown.

Sedaris, D. (2000). *Me talk pretty one day*. Boston: Little, Brown.

Sedaris, D. (2004). *Dress your family in corduroy and denim*. Boston: Little, Brown.

Sleator, W. (1974). *House of stairs*. New York: Dutton/Penguin.

Sparks, B. (1971). *Go ask Alice*. Upper Saddle River, NJ: Prentice Hall.

Spiegelman, A. (1991). *Maus II*. New York: Pantheon Books.

Taylor, M. D. (1981). *Let the circle be unbroken*. New York: Dial/Penguin.

Tolkien, J. R. R. (1966). *The lord of the rings*. Boston: Houghton Mifflin. (Original work published 1954–1955)

Trueman, T. (2000). *Stuck in neutral*. New York: HarperCollins.

Van Draanen, W. (2001). *Flipped*. New York: Knopf/ Random House.

Voigt, C. (1994). *When she hollers*. New York: Scholastic.

Wolff, V. E. (1993). *Make lemonade*. New York: Scholastic.

Wolff, V. E. (2001). *True believer*. New York: Atheneum/Simon & Schuster.

Woodson, A. (2003). *First part last*. New York: Simon & Schuster.

Yang, G. L. (2006). *American born Chinese*. New York: First Second.

Zindel, P. (1968). *The pigman*. New York: Harper & Row.

Zindel, P. (1969). *My darling, my hamburger*. New York: Harper & Row.

Zusak, M. (2001). *Fighting Ruben Wolfe*. New York: Arthur Levine/Scholastic. (Original work published 2000)

Realistic Fiction
Reading Skill: Making Connections

Introduction

The term *problem novel* developed in the latter part of the 20th century to identify realistic books such as S. E. Hinton's *The Outsiders* (1967) that spoke to personal and social issues. These stories often featured characters from lower socioeconomic backgrounds and broken homes who deal with gritty issues and who speak in their native language, which includes profanity and "poor grammar." Young adult experts, however, recognize that teens of all socioeconomic backgrounds, family structures, and education levels struggle with personal and social issues. In reality, a teen from a middle-class nuclear family, for example, may have a more difficult time navigating adolescence than a teen from a single-parent home. This view of the problem novel, therefore, is limiting.

The term also has been used loosely over time to define the entire young adult genre. The problem novel defined the young adult literature genre in the early years (late 20th century), but today it unduly stereotypes the entire body of literature. As you'll discover in this chapter, today's young adult literature includes a wide range of genres—many overlapping. As used in this chapter, *problem novel* refers to realistic fiction that addresses personal and social issues across socioeconomic boundaries and within both traditional and nontraditional family structures.

Realistic fiction is the backbone of the young adult literature genre, beginning with the inception of the problem novel in the second half of the 20th century. Other genres have developed over time, but realistic fiction remains a steady force in the classroom, the library, and the publishing market. This chapter examines the development of the problem novel, the mainstay of the realistic genre, and introduces readers to the "lighter" side of realistic fiction. It introduces reader-response theory and provides instructional strategies for helping students make connections with their reading.

The Problem Novel

J. D. Salinger's (1951) *The Catcher in the Rye* is considered a prototype of the problem novel, but young adult experts (e.g., Crowe, 2002; Gill, 1999; Wilder & Teasley, 1998) generally agree that the young adult problem novel came into its own in the late 1960s. The publication of S. E. Hinton's *The Outsiders* (1967), a multithemed story about class struggle, bigotry, and dysfunctional families; Ann Head's *Mr. and Mrs. Bo Jo Jones* (1967), a candid portrayal of teen pregnancy; Robert Lipsyte's *The Contender* (1967), a story in which a 17-year-old high school dropout struggles to become a boxer; and Paul Zindel's *The Pigman* (1968), a groundbreaking look at the lives of two troubled teens, carved out a separate genre for teen readers. Optimistic works of the early to mid-1900s that portrayed attractive, smart, carefree, and successful white teens with stable home lives (e.g., serial works such as *Nancy Drew*, *The Hardy Boys*, and *Cherry Ames*) were challenged by writers who wrote about harsh realities and moral dilemmas. The teens featured in these stories were navigating personal, family, and social struggles. Though the wholesome worlds of characters like Nancy Drew and the Hardy Boys remain with us, reinvented for today's pop culture world, they do not fit reality. The problems these protagonists face are impractical, and their lives are too perfect.

"In My Own Words" Richard Peck

When we consider that literature reflects an era, the development of the problem novel becomes clear. Twentieth-century child labor laws and mandatory secondary education changed young people's lives. No longer did teens enter the workforce straight out of grammar school; instead, they became *adolescents*. As Donna Gaines suggests in her ethnographic work *Teenage Wasteland: Surburbia's Dead End Kids* (1991), adolescence became a holding pen for teens. They were no longer children, but they were not adults; they were in limbo. In essence, mandatory secondary education and child labor laws created adolescence, a developmental stage accompanied by innumerable problems that previously had been ignored or invisible (e.g., bullying, alienation, dating and sex, substance abuse, tension between teens and adults).

A high school senior portrait of Richard Peck. Peck, one of the earliest writers of young adult realistic literature, is known for his well-developed, sometimes "quirky" characters.

The 1960s also brought about a dramatic shift in American social and cultural values. Previously, children's literature had reflected Victorian values: traditional families, obedient, happy children, and strict social rules for males and females, all characteristics of the 1950s traditional nuclear family. Stories were idealistic and didactic and promoted traditional values: interracial relations were wrong, divorce was taboo, sex before marriage was immoral, young people should be seen and not heard, and males and females had distinct and proper social roles. The unrest of the Vietnam conflict and the civil rights movement changed how young people viewed themselves, their families, and the world. High school boys went to war, families were torn apart, and schools were integrated. On college campuses across America, young people questioned authority. They believed, for instance, that they had been lied to about the war and about race relations (interracial dating and marriage) and about gender roles, and their attitudes and feelings filtered down into family units and high schools. Disillusioned by traditional values, young people began to believe they had alternatives. It was no longer okay to be seen and not heard or to accept ideas because you were told to. If young people were old enough to be killed in war, they were old enough to be heard and to choose their own values and beliefs. It became okay to ask "Why?" and to question realism and truth.

The nuclear family lifestyle portrayed by TV shows such as *Leave It to Beaver* and *Ozzie and Harriet* was viewed as trite, stereotypical, and narrow. In the face of racial tensions, for example, stories about an attractive, white, upper-middle-class female like Nancy Drew jetting across the country to solve a mystery seemed unimportant and idealistic. Animal stories for young teens that depicted warm and fuzzy relationships between animal and owner (e.g., Sheila Burnford's *The Incredible Journey,* 1961; Walter Farley's *The Black Stallion,* 1941; Jim Kjelgaard's *Big Red,* 1945) were wonderful stories, but they did not reflect the cultural climate. There were no stories about school problems, minorities, poverty, racial and family tensions, teen pregnancy and sex, and alternative family structures. These issues (and more) were direct spin-offs of the unrest of the '60s and the fact that teens, now required to attend high school, didn't immediately enter the workforce (the adult world).

A rare first edition of Robert Cormier's landmark title, *The Chocolate War.*

When Robert Cormier, one of the most influential young adult authors of the 20th century, penned his well-known classic, *The Chocolate War* (1974)—a multilayered and grim portrait of psychological warfare, fear, manipulation, and individualism (with no intention of marketing it for the young adult audience)—his timing could not have been better. Bullied by his peers in his Catholic school for refusing to sell chocolates, Jerry Renault ponders a question on a poster pinned inside his locker: "Do I dare disturb the universe?" (The question comes from T. S. Eliot's *The Love Song of J. Alfred Prufrock.*) The story and theme cut to the heart of the social unrest of the 1960s. Those who read and loved Robert Cormier hailed a fresh protagonist who questioned authority and stood up for what he believed.

Cormier's landmark novel was followed by other notable problem novels in the 1970s: *Z for Zachariah* (1975) by Robert C. O'Brien, *Are You in the House Alone?* (1976) by Richard Peck, *Ordinary People* (1976) by Judith Guest, and Mildred D. Taylor's *Roll of Thunder, Hear My Cry* (1976). The young adult market exploded thereafter with stories about orphans, dysfunctional families, alternative family structures, and teens struggling with peer relationships. Bullying, alienation, adolescent cruelty, mental and physical illness, disabilities, sexuality, divorce, bigotry, teen pregnancy, rape, incest, and suicide were all examined, and there has been no turning back the clock. In Marc Aronson's (1995) words, "the YA genre now engages the most profound, deepest, and richest issues that we face as a nation" (p. 36). Shelton L. Root (1977) used the term *new realism* to describe

> fiction for young readers which addresses itself to personal problems and social issues heretofore considered taboo for fictional treatment by the general public, as enunciated by its traditional spokesmen: librarians, teachers, ministers, and others. The new realism is often graphic in its language and always explicit in its treatment. (p. 19)

Because of their themes, problem novels are among the most censored books in the young adult literature field. While it is true that some young adult problem novels may be "graphic," *graphic* today and *graphic* in the mid-'70s and '80s are far from synonymous. Judy Blume's *Are You There, God? It's Me Margaret* (1970) pushed the envelope in the '70s with attention to "breasts" and "menstruation," as did Blume's *Forever* (1975) with sexual scenes. Chris Crutcher's *Running Loose* (1983) gave some adults nightmares with "Ole Norton," and Katherine Paterson's *The Great Gilly Hopkins* (1978) troubled some for its profanity. Ironically, despite being battered by critics, these novels have become young adult classics and are considered light fare when juxtaposed with today's edgy works.

You may wonder why controversial books become classics. History shows that works that push the envelope in one generation often become the benchmark or breakout books in the next. Harper Lee's *To Kill a Mockingbird* (1960), while controversial in the 1960s, is revered today by many as the greatest American novel. Ernest Hemingway called Mark Twain's *The Adventures of Huckleberry Finn* (1884) the basis for all American literature, but it was banned in 1885 on social grounds, even called "trash of the veriest sort" and "more profitable for the slums than . . . for respectable people" by the Concord Public Library ("Mark Twain's Last Book Excluded," 1885), and Robert Cormier's *The Chocolate War* (1974), a constant on the American Library Association's (ALA) top 100 most censored books for its bathroom stall masturbation scene, is an archetype in the young adult genre.

Controversial books raise uncomfortable questions about the human condition, which sometimes trouble those who believe edgy books can have a negative impact on readers. We need, however, to examine both sides of the coin: if we believe hard stories can negatively influence teens, we must also believe in the power of these same stories to have positive influences. The issue is relative.

Characteristics of Today's Problem Novels

Subject matter that deals with personal and social issues is a defining trait of the problem novel; however, other noteworthy characteristics also define these works. For one, *characters* are not perfect, and they come from all races, cultures, family structures, and socioeconomic backgrounds. In a 1995 interview, Ruth White, author of Newbery Honor book *Belle Prater's Boy*

(1996), addressed her concern over the lack of literature for black students and how that concern led to her first novel:

> When I taught seventh and eighth grade in Mt. Pleasant, North Carolina, I wrote *The City Rose*. The schools had just been integrated in North Carolina the year before I started teaching, and I had two black girls in one of my classes. When we would go to the library, I noticed that they didn't check any books out. I was trying to help them find books, and they finally told me that they couldn't find any books about black children—about themselves—so I decided that was something we would have to fix.
> I decided to write one. So that's how *The City Rose* was born. (Cole 1995, p. 4)

A second distinction of today's problem novel is *setting*. While Nancy Drew traveled the world solving crimes, today's problem novels take place closer to home: in schools, where teens struggle with racism, bigotry, violence, and adolescent cruelty; in less-than-perfect homes, where dysfunctional families struggle; and in impoverished communities subject to violence. In some cases, stories take place on the streets or on a journey or road trip or at home during summer vacation.

Third, is *atmosphere*, "the emotional tone pervading . . . a literary work" (Abrams, 2005, p. 15). Although problem novels may end with hope and may contain a good dose of humor, they have serious overtones and can have dark and tragic conclusions. Of course, this shift from "happily-ever-after" endings has long been an issue with critics who believe all children, regardless of age, should read "happy books." Robert Cormier, for example, is criticized for his bleak endings. His books breach an unwritten rule that teen books should have some glimmer of hope or send a positive message (MacLeod, as cited in Headley, 1994). Writers such as Cormier end books on a bleak note because, they argue, not all life events work out positively. As much as we want young people to believe in positive solutions to life's problems, we also need to honor reality—sometimes there is no happy ending.

When Ernest Hemingway called Mark Twain's *The Adventures of Huckleberry Finn* (1885) the basis of the American novel, he was referring to Twain's use of dialect, the native language of his characters. This use of *native language* is a fourth characteristic of problem novels, and is perhaps the most controversial, for it means allowing characters to use profanity and expressions that some readers consider offensive. Critics argue that exposing teens to such language encourages them to adopt the language, but writers argue that such language is prevalent in their everyday lives and, most important, a story wouldn't ring true, and may even sound silly, if some characters didn't use profanity, particularly in emotionally charged scenes. The character's personality should determine the character's language.

Finally, the problem novel, more than any other genre, has changed in *style*. Traditional chapter books, while still popular, are sometimes much shorter; chapters may have as little as one word, sentence, or paragraph per page. They may be written in verse, developed through alternating chapters with different voices, or framed in a collection of short stories. They may be multigenred texts, containing e-mails, text messages, journals, poetry, letters, news articles, and more. Any format goes for the problem novel.

Popularity and Importance of the Problem Novel

Problem novels dominate most any award that is not genre specific (e.g., the Michael L. Printz Award, the John Newbery Medal, and the California Young Reader's Medal), and they are identified more frequently than any other genre as best novels for teens. For example, in "The Best Young Adult Novels of All Time, or *The Chocolate War* One More Time" (2005), Hipple and Claiborne identify the 22 best teen books (Table 4.1). All 22 identified address serious personal or social issues. With the exception of Francesca Lia Block's *Weetzie Bat* (1989) and Jerry Spinelli's *Stargirl* (2000), which contain elements

Table 4.1
Best Young Adult Books of All Time, 2004 Survey

Title	Author	Number of Votes
The Chocolate War	Robert Cormier	28
The Giver	Lois Lowry	22
Speak	Laurie Halse Anderson	19
The Outsiders	S. E. Hinton	15
Hatchet	Gary Paulsen	13
Holes	Louis Sachar	13
Monster	Walter Dean Myers	13
Staying Fat for Sarah Byrnes	Chris Crutcher	13
Make Lemonade	Virginia Euwer Wolff	12
Out of the Dust	Karen Hesse	11
The Pigman	Paul Zindel	10
Fallen Angels	Walter Dean Myers	8
Weetzie Bat	Francesca Lia Block	8
Chinese Handcuffs	Chris Crutcher	7
The Watsons Go to Birmingham—1963	Christopher Paul Curtis	7
The Catcher in the Rye	J. D. Salinger	6
I Am the Cheese	Robert Cormier	6
Stargirl	Jerry Spinelli	6
After the First Death	Robert Cormier	5
Annie on My Mind	Nancy Garden	5
Ironman	Chris Crutcher	5
Roll of Thunder, Hear My Cry	Mildred D. Taylor	5

Source: Hipple & Claiborne (2005).

of fantasy; and Lois Lowry's *The Giver* (1993), a soft science fiction read, all are realistic fiction. Most fall within the category of *dark realism.* Earlier studies (Hipple, 1989, 1992) support this assertion as well.

The problem novel has incredible power to hook teens into reading. Because this genre deals with contemporary issues facing teens, teens make immediate and profound connections: they identify their own lives through the fictional characters and events. Once teens find stories that resonate with them, they typically want to read everything that author has written. In the following box, Chris Crutcher, author of three of Hipple and Claiborne's top 22 novels, shares his thoughts about the connection teens make with the problem novel and the power this genre has to help them understand their lives. Following his essay is a letter he received from a fan about *Deadline* (2007).

The Power of the Problem Novel   by Chris Crutcher

So-called problem novels are a staple in young adult literature, for good reason, I think. Though they are often seen by critics as novels that bring up issues kids don't need to know about or that emphasize the negative about being a teenager, the best of them perform a valuable service, both academically and emotionally.

A number of years ago an editor sent me a novel manuscript about a girl who cut on herself. The editor wanted me to blurb the book if I liked it, and I did like it, but I didn't have a comprehensive idea of its accuracy. So I gave it to a teenage cutter. She brought it back in a week and said, "This bitch knows what she's talking about." I asked how she knew, and soon we were talking about the heart and soul of my client's "problem": the *sources* of why she cut on herself; the *story* of why she cut on herself. My client made a connection with the character in the story (and therefore with the author). She was empowered, informing her therapist instead of the other way around, and she was able to reveal information about herself she wouldn't have revealed had she been asked to talk about herself straight out. It also gave me a chance to say some things about the character that she wouldn't have accepted had I said them about her. That's education in my book; education elevated above regurgitation and analysis.

We complain all the time about the fact that certain kids don't read. Boys don't read. Troubled kids don't read, or teens read material we think they shouldn't. Reading time is supplanted by video games and TV. Reading suffers from the rigors of a too fast-paced life. In truth, teens will read what captures their imagination, and if we paid more attention to that, the problem novel would be elevated in the pecking order of literature, and more teens would be reading.

Much academic content is arbitrary, particularly in social studies and English disciplines. In literature there seems to exist one school of thought that says the older and more obscure a work is, the more worthy of academic probing. But reading is a *meaning*-making process. If you could be a 20-year-old fly on the wall in my counseling office, you would have heard legions of kids yearning to be acknowledged; *longing* for recognition of their losses, the chaos of their lives, the desperation they sometimes feel. What might surprise you most is *who* those kids are.

Continued

The Power of the Problem Novel   *Continued*

Problem novels offer us a chance as educators to open lines of communication across the generations, to hook our lives to the lives of adolescents through character and story.

Copyright Chris Crutcher, 2008

Official Web site: www.chriscrutcher.com

Titles not mentioned in this chapter include *Stotan!* (1986), *Crazy Horse Electric Game* (1987), *King of the Mild Frontier* (2003), and *The Sledding Hill* (2005).

Hi Chris,

I don't expect you to remember this, but several years ago my mother (Lyla) emailed you. She asked if she could send you the book *Athletic Shorts* and have you sign it. It was a gift to me for my 19th birthday. My mother knew how much I loved (and related to in high school) the movie *Angus,* which lead me to discover you and your books. So she thought it would be the perfect gift, and it was.

I have the basic request of now asking you to sign a copy of *Deadline* so that I may give it to my mother for Christmas. If you have the time, please read on as to find out the reason behind the request. If not, I totally understand and you can skip to the end where you will find my contact information.

Since my 19th birthday, a lot has happened. I am married to the girl of my dreams whom I will gladly "**walk through a field of molten turds just to hear her fart over the phone.**" Being married has tempered my internal steel and allowed responsibility to somehow find this irresponsible kid. Hands down, best thing I have ever done.

I was lucky enough to know my best friend Jaye, for his entire 21 years of life, though early on I was not always aware that he was my best friend. I confess that I was the one who made him eat sand when he was 3. He fattened my lip in our last fight at the age of 13, with a flash of knuckled rage that to this day I still can't see. And when the sound of his drum cymbal crashing, came in the middle of the night two years later, it was I who found him in his room. He was convulsing while giving the audible clue of struggled breath and the visual cues of unoxygenated blood. When questioned by the medics on the way to the hospital about his potential drug use, Jaye wearily took the oxygen mask from his face, and uttered "Drugs are for losers." Jaye went from being

Used by permission of HarperCollins Publishers.

my sweet, **hey-soos** incarnate, talented bro, and over night became my sweet, **hey-soos** incarnate, talented, epileptic bro.

Even with meds, the electronic system which conducts the human body would sink up and discharge in unison. Thus, he would go through the ritual of a grand mal seizure. During one of these seizures, the seizing seemed to last forever. And once over, we could not get Jaye to come out of "the fog." He didn't know where he was and kept calling out for "daddy." My Dad, my Mother, and I huddled around him and I suddenly started singing our childhood lullaby "Jesus, Jesus, Jesus, there's just something about that name . . .." He not only settled down and appeared to feel safer; he even started to mumble/sing along.

Continued

The Power of the Problem Novel   *Continued*

I did my best to support him for the next couple of years as he warred against the betrayal of his body. You could see the denial, pain, and fear he carried if you knew where to look. The world had jumped him coming out of the gate and he battled to defeat the super villain inside. His resolve to deal with reality suddenly hit him senior year and he started to shine even brighter. He was a popular star soccer player, who hated the crowds. And he was amazing at loving the losers in his life. My bro found the needy kids in school and raised them up. Sacrificed for them, and made them stronger. He also had the ability to make you laugh till you cried, boy humor or PT (Parental Unit) appropriate, you laughed your head off (kur plop) with Jaye around.

I was ill prepared when 4 years later, I woke to find my father on my doorstep. He was 700 miles from my town of origin of which he and my mother still reside. He greeted me with the following words, which I will remember with clarity for the rest of my life "It's not your mom, it's Jaye."

I learned that Jaye had come home from a twelve hour shift at Micron. After hanging out with his roommate and a friend for a while, he headed off to take a shower. His roommate found Jaye 40 minutes later; face down in a tub full of water. We speculate that he seizured while showering, foot kicked the drain, and he drowned before he could come out of "the fog." Jaye died on June 28, 2005, 20 days after my 24th birthday.

I flew home and we waited a week for family to get into town before doing the memorial. During this time I spent 14–19 hour days compiling a memorial video out of all the old VHS tapes we had. I also went into the studio (did I mention that we are a crazy talented family and that Jaye and I rocked in a band for 3 years prior to my marriage and move to Oregon?) and recorded the last song (more of a lullaby really) that I had written. I had sung this song over the phone to Jaye on June 3, 2005. The lyrics are as follows:

> *"With Day to the left side, and Night to the right*
> *Dawn's taking Day's side and Dusk's taking Night's*
>
> *A star field audience's solar applause*
> *Filling the celestial coliseum*
>
> *Pulling passion from sinew and strength from old bones*
> *Aching from a want of a slumber unknown*
>
> *Clock wheel patterns in motion to end*
> *Sight of the death throws as they begin"*

Jaye asked me "Why the sad lyrics." I said. "Couldn't tell ya, guess I don't know I'm sad yet." I used this song with two others to compose a medley in C for the memorial video. I still grieve while listening.

Chris, I tell you this now, because much the same way *Angus* and your early books helped me cope with high school life. *Deadline* is helping me now (I still have 100 pages left). I stock pile the memories and the grief and bury the pain. But Ben, Cody, and yes, even that bastard Hey-soos are helping me remember.

If I don't hear back from you, I probably will try and send the book to the address on your site. And if you do sign this book and return it to me, please write some words of hope and strength to my mother. She is burdened and is in pain. But your book will help her remember her two boys. The one that is here, and the one who is gone.

Sincerely,
Jared

Pushing the Envelope

A discussion of the young adult problem novel is not complete without a discussion of books pushing the envelope today. There are plenty. In fact, publishers have created new imprints for these edgy books (e.g., PUSH by Scholastic, Pulse by Simon & Schuster, Razorbill by Penguin, and Tempest by

HarperCollins), and some bookstores (e.g., Borders in Kennesaw, Georgia) now label the young adult fiction section with parental warnings: "Titles may contain mature content. Parental supervision advised." Many of these books, despite opposition from critics, will set the standard for future generations of writers and readers.

Julie Anne Peters's *Luna* (2004), for example, breaks new ground in teen sexuality. Enter Liam, a transsexual teen who hates being a boy. By night, with the help of his younger sister's clothing and makeup, he transforms himself into Luna, the beautiful girl he wishes to be. Tired of keeping his secret, he reveals his true identity and faces repercussions and strained family relationships. Although transsexuality is an obvious theme, a deeper reading reveals an important statement about how relationships evolve and how we risk losing powerful connections.

Ellen Wittlinger explores the dangers of repressed emotions in *Sandpiper* (2005). Fifteen-year-old Sandpiper thrives off her sexuality and has had more boyfriends than anyone can count. Sex is power, so she meets up with boys for oral sex. Sandpiper's promiscuity may make some readers uncomfortable, but the book addresses a recent trend among teenagers to engage in oral sex under the pretense it is not "real" sex. Wittlinger's book is groundbreaking in that it helps readers understand teen promiscuity and speaks to the importance of human connection in intimate relationships.

The topic of R. A. Nelson's *Teach Me* (2005) strikes a fresh chord in young adult literature: sexual relations between teens and adults. When Carolina, a senior, learns that Mr. Mann, a teacher with whom she has been having an affair, is getting married, her obsession drives her toward unthinkable acts. Carolina's voice is authentic and frank; Nelson's language eloquent and metaphorical. Carolina's feelings are so powerful that Mr. Mann has become her world. Nelson's stunning depiction of a teacher-student relationship results in a universal novel that offers insight into the evolution of relationships between students and teachers. Is it possible that books like *Teach Me* can arm teens with information to protect them against precarious relationships? Or at least help teens understand the emotions that steer young adults into such relationships?

Numerous courageous authors in today's market tackle difficult topics. Kevin Brooks's work pushes him to the forefront of emerging voices in the field for its multilayered complexities, brilliant voice, imagery, and exceptional storylines. In *Candy* (2005), Brooks paints a disturbing account of a young boy drawn into a drug world of crime,

Reprinted by permission of Penguin Young Readers Group © 2007.

prostitution, and desperation. Unaware of Candy's real life, Joe falls in love and finds himself confronting real danger. In *The Road of the Dead* (Brooks, 2006), two teenage boys search for their sister's brutal rapist and killer. The author box features an essay by Brooks on writing the problem novel.

There are, of course, many serious issues confronting today's teens; most are disturbing and grim, but they are real stories about real issues that challenge our young people. Additional examples of edgy books are highlighted in Box 4.1, some of which will become the classics of this generation for breaking new ground for the teen problem novel.

Writing the Problem Novel   by Kevin Brooks

Stephen King once said that fiction writers don't understand very much about what they do—they don't understand why it works when it's good, and they don't understand why it doesn't work when it's bad. He also said that his books don't start with a plot, they start with a problem. He takes a character, or characters, puts them in some sort of predicament, and then watches them as they try to work themselves free. And I think that pretty much sums up my approach to writing novels too. I don't always know exactly what I'm doing when I'm writing, but I know that underneath it all I'm looking at people, seeing how they react to things, watching them as they try to work themselves free. It's a very simple idea, but like most simple ideas, it allows for an almost infinite variety of consequences. Problems create conflict. Conflict produces emotions. Emotions show us what we are, how we feel, what we want, why we do what we do. And once all that starts tumbling around on the page, you've got just about everything you need to take a story wherever you want.

So, yes, when I'm writing a book, I start with a problem. But that doesn't always mean that the problem is central to the story. In fact, by the end of the book it can often be almost forgotten. The problem is the catalyst, the spark that lights the fire. And once the fire gets going, there are far more interesting things to explore than the original spark—you've got the flames, the heat, the roar, the smoke, the chaos, the mystery, the ashes . . . all those infinite consequences.

The fascination for me lies not in the problem itself, but in the reactions it causes, and that's one of the reasons I don't try to solve any problems in my books. For me, that's not what novels are about,

especially novels for teenagers. So although I start with a problem, I don't go looking for solutions, and I certainly don't try to find any answers. Partly because I'm not particularly interested in answers, and partly because most of the big questions in life don't have any answers anyway. But the main reason I don't try to provide any answers is simply that I don't think it's my place. I'm a writer. I spend all my time sitting alone in a room, staring at a computer screen, making up stories. Don't get me wrong, it's a wonderful thing to do, and I love every second of it—but it's hardly the ideal qualification for solving the world's problems, is it?

Copyright Kevin Brooks, 2008

Official Web site: www.doublecluck.com

Works not mentioned in this chapter include *Martyn Pig*, (2002), *Being* (2007), and *Black Rabbit Summer* (2008).

Box 4.1   Edgy Reads—Old and New

***Bang!* by Sharon G. Flake. New York: Hyperion, 2006.**

Fourteen-year-old Mann lives in a violent inner-city community where young men die early. After witnessing the chance shooting of his baby brother, Jason, Mann suffers emotional turmoil and is convinced he, along with his friends, will die early too. His mother, who still holds birthday parties for her dead son, wants to move; his father, desperate to protect Mann, takes him on a camping trip where he concocts an African coming-of-age survival ritual and abandons Mann and his friend, Kee-lee. Mann makes it home, but Kee-lee's violent death once they return haunts him.

***Bee + Jacky* by Carolyn Coman. Asheville, NC: Front Street, 1998.**

One Labor Day weekend when their parents are away, siblings Bee and Jacky revisit childhood sexual war games in which they reenact the ambush that impaired their father during the Vietnam conflict.

***Before, After, and Somebody in Between* by Jeannine Garsee. New York: Bloomsbury, 2007.**

Martha is intelligent and musically talented but carries the weight of the world—she lives in a poverty-stricken neighborhood; her father is dead, and her alcoholic mother has sleazy boyfriends. Drive-by shootings, dangerous sex, and a bad foster home situation contribute to her struggles.

***Between Mom and Jo* by Julie Anne Peters. New York: Little, Brown, 2006.**

Fourteen-year-old Nick is sometimes taunted by his friends for having two mothers, Erin and Jo. When his mothers' relationship becomes strained due to Jo's inability to hold a job and her alcoholism, Nick faces the possibility of separation and losing Jo.

***Boy Kills Man* by Matt Whyman. New York: HarperTempest, 2005.**

Drawn into a world of drugs and violence, two 13-year-old poverty-stricken best friends are hired as killer assassins by drug lords on the city streets in Colombia.

***Chloe Doe* by Suzanne Phillips. New York: Little, Brown, 2007.**

This story narrates the life of a 17-year-old alienated girl—her tumultuous spiral downward into a life of prostitution and her struggle, through therapy, to build a normal life.

***Dark Angel* by David Klass. New York: Farrar, Straus & Giroux, 2005.**

Seventeen-year-old Jeff has a great deal to lose when his older brother Troy is released from a life sentence for premeditated murder. Jeff's family has begun a new life in a small New Jersey town, and Troy is a family secret. When Troy comes to live with the family, Jeff's lifestyle with his friends changes, and he is convinced something is seriously wrong with his brother.

***Doing It* by Melvin Burgess. New York: Henry Holt, 2004.**

An erotically charged novel about three teenage friends—Dino, Jonathon, and Ben—who explore, through alternating voices, their uncertainties, fears, joys, and feelings about adolescent sexuality. Both hilarious and painful, the book shows young males learning how to have healthy relationships.

***The Facts Speak for Themselves* by Brock Cole. Asheville, NC: Front Street, 1997.**

In a matter-of-fact voice, 13-year-old Linda narrates the events that led up to the murder of her middle-aged lover by her mother's boyfriend. As Linda unveils her story, the reader learns the horrifying facts of abuse and abandonment that define Linda's life.

Continued

Box 4.1   Edgy Reads—Old and New   *Continued*

Gingerbread by Rachel Cohn. New York: Simon & Schuster, 2002.

Kicked out of boarding school, 16-year-old Cyd Charisse is sexually active, brash, and coming to terms with a recent abortion. When her parents catch her spending the night with her new boyfriend Shrimp, they send her to New York to spend time with her biological father. Two follow-up sequels include *Shrimp* (2006) and *Cupcake* (2007).

Gone by Kathleen Jeffrie Johnson. New Milford, CT: Roaring Brook Press, 2007.

A raw look at a forbidden relationship—that between a 17-year-old boy and his former history teacher. Readers can connect with Connor's loneliness and the events and feelings that create the perfect storm for a student-teacher affair. Readers follow Connor down an abandoned path and struggle with him on his way back.

Johnny Hazzard by Eddie De Oliveira. New York: Scholastic, 2005.

Since his parents' divorce, 15-year-old Johnny Hazzard and his sister Lyda have spent summers with their father in England. This summer Johnny falls in love with an older girl and has his first sexual experiences. Skateboarding is a backdrop for this tender love story aimed directly at male young adult readers.

The Road of the Dead by Kevin Brooks. New York: Scholastic, 2006.

Fourteen-year-old Ruben Ford can read minds and see things others can't. When he "witnesses" his sister's brutal murder and rape, he and his brother, Cole, set out for Dartmoor, where Rachel was killed, to track down her killer. Ruben knows trouble awaits them. Powerful imagery allows readers to see, feel, hear and smell the ugly horror and brutality that Ruben himself experiences.

A Room on Lorelei Street by Mary E. Pearson. New York: Henry Holt, 2005.

Seventeen-year-old Zoe lives a miserable life caring for her depressed alcoholic mother. To escape being her mother's caregiver, Zoe rents a room from an elderly woman and works after school as a waiter. When money gets tight, Zoe chooses prostitution over returning to her wretched existence with her mother and mean-spirited grandmother.

Sisters in Sanity by Gayle Forman. New York: HarperCollins, 2007.

Brit's father enrolls her in an out-of-the way phony school for troubled teens, a school that dishes out punishment like candy and rewards girls for ratting out their friends. Brit joins forces with other troubled girls. Together, they devise a plan to bring the school down. Reminiscent of *Girl, Interrupted* (Kaysen 1993).

Target by Kathleen Jeffrie Johnson. New York: Roaring Brook Press, 2003.

After being attacked and brutally raped by two men, Grady transfers to a new high school, where he repeats the 11th grade. Grady isolates himself but makes new friends who help him deal with his shame and humiliation.

Under the Wolf, Under the Dog by Adam Rapp. Cambridge, MA: Candlewick Press, 2004.

Seventeen-year-old Steve Nugent carries a heavy load: his mother's death from cancer, his brother's suicide, and his father's depression. Required to keep a journal by his therapist, Steve describes his life in a group home, the series of events that put him there, his anger, and his emotional wounds and losses.

Lighter Fare

Teens are drawn to problem novels because they can find "themselves" in the story, but they go through periods in which they don't want to read about somber issues, particularly those close to home. During such times, teens will sometimes turn to other genres such as horror, mystery, historical fiction, science fiction, and fantasy because they provide an escape from immediate problems. Some teens, however, who dislike these other genres or who have limited exposure to them, may stop reading to avoid thinking about problems, or they dismiss problem novels because they're about "mushy stuff." Teens need not turn away from realistic fiction to find books they enjoy, nor do they need to stop reading. An abundance of realistic books deal with life issues in a more optimistic manner.

Lynne Rae Perkins's Newbery winner *Criss Cross* (2005) features a group of small town teens who spend their summer questioning their existence—do they control their destiny or does destiny control them—and trying to figure out what they want out of life. Perkins tells her story through a series of vignettes that merge toward a plot—the characters "criss cross" over the summer. Ron Carlson's *The Speed of Light* (2003) examines the friendship of three boys over the course of one summer. The boys spend the summer playing baseball, conducting science experiments, having sleepovers in the backyard, and raising questions about the existence of the universe.

Though the problem novel gets its label from "problem themes" associated with adolescence, in reality all novels have "problems." In order to have a story, a writer must create a plot, and a plot hinges on a problem or conflict that needs to be resolved. The problem need not be resolved in an uplifting manner, but the story does need a resolution. Conflict can be classified into four types: man versus self, man versus man, man versus society, and man versus nature. One might think of these in a hierarchal manner, the closer the conflict to self, the deeper the emotional response and vice versa:

Man versus nature

↑

Man versus society

↑

Man versus man

↑

Man versus self

Although a teen may have an intense emotional response to a story about a global disaster (nature), that response is most likely grounded in a deeply felt personal experience (self). Perhaps, for example, the reader of a global disaster event lost his/her family in an earthquake or tsunami. The response, you see, remains grounded in self (more on response theory later).

When viewed in a hierarchal manner, it's easy to see why teens wishing to escape "problem" literature may be drawn to stories that pit man against nature, such as books by Will Hobbs and Gary Paulsen. Reading about an external conflict—several layers removed from self—can be easier than addressing internal conflict. Although it's difficult to find stories that can be classified exclusively as one type of conflict, a plethora of books emphasize external conflict. Adventure and survival stories, for example, may feel more objective to readers who don't want to see themselves (man vs. self) in the story or who don't want to read about family-friend connections (man vs. man). The further readers are from self-examination and family-friend conflicts, the more they can escape their own issues. Adventure and survival stories are favorites among teens who like the challenge of overcoming seemingly insurmountable obstacles and who enjoy the outdoors.

Stories featuring animals as major characters provide another type of realistic story. Some of the all-time young adult classics include Fred Gipson's *Old Yeller* (1956), *The Incredible Journey* (1961) by Sheila Burnford, *Where the Red Fern Grows* (1961) by Wilson Rawls, and *The Yearling* (1938) by Marjorie Rawlings. Many of these stories have personal themes running throughout—often an animal dies and the protagonist "comes of age" in the process—but they lack the grittiness of tough problem novels. Some stories, such as Jean Craighead George's Newbery winner *Julie of the Wolves* (1972), feature young protagonists who run away from home to avoid a personal or family issue, only to find their biggest challenge is survival. While running away from an unwanted marriage, 13-year-old Julie, an Eskimo girl, becomes lost on the arctic tundra and is taken in by a wolf pack. The focus, thus, is on braving the weather, not on dealing with her family or her inner self. The third book in this series, *Julie's Wolf Pack* (1997), places people on the periphery of the story by shifting the point of view from Julie to the wolves. In *The Boy Who Spoke Dog* (2003) by Clay Morgan, a young orphan boy becomes marooned on an island with a group of dogs. Point of view alternates between Jack and a collie named Moxie, and although Jack is an orphan, the story centers around his efforts to survive. Some stories feature animals as the primary protagonist, which can remove the reader even further from personal issues; in many of these, the story is told from the animal's vantage point such as Cynthia Kadohata's *Cracker: The Best Dog in Vietnam* (2007). Though stories written from an animal's perspective are unrealistic in that animals can't think as humans, their experiences are realistic. Box 4.2 features a sampling of adventure, survival, and animal stories.

Box 4.2   Adventure, Survival, and Animal Stories

Black Beauty by Anna Sewell. New York: Signet, 2002 (Original work published 1877)

Though the language is somewhat archaic, this timeless story follows a colt from his early days with his mother through his years of abuse, being traded from one master to another. Written from the horse's point of view, the story, though filled with moral lessons, remains compelling. Sewell did not pen the story for children but rather for horse lovers of any age.

Death Mountain by Sherry Shahan. Atlanta: Peachtree, 2005.

Erin and her friend become lost on a trip to visit Erin's mother, whom she hasn't seen in a year. They struggle to survive in the rugged Sierra Nevada Mountains.

A Dog's Life: The Autobiography of a Stray by Ann M. Martin. New York: Scholastic, 2005.

A stray puppy tells her life story from leaving her mother to forging her way in the world, among humans who are both kind and brutal.

Far North by Will Hobbs. New York: William Morrow, 1996.

After their floatplane crashes, 15-year-old Gabe and his friend are stranded in the Canadian wilderness. When winter sets in, the two boys are trapped in Deadmen Valley.

A Girl Named Disaster by Nancy Farmer. New York: Orchard/Scholastic, 1996.

Nhamo flees her home in Mozambique to escape an unwanted marriage. On her way to Zimbabwe she confronts near drowning and starvation.

Hatchet by Gary Paulsen. New York: Bradbury Press, 1987.

When his plane crashes, Brian Robeson must put thoughts about his parents' divorce aside and concentrate on surviving in the Canadian wilderness with little more than a hatchet. A timeless classic and Newbery Medal Honor book. Brian's saga continues in *The River* (1991), *Brian's Winter* (1996), *Brian's Return* (1999), and *Brian's Hunt* (2003).

Ice Drift by Theodore Taylor. San Diego: Harcourt, 2004.

Two Inuits, 14-year-old Alika and his younger brother, are stranded on an ice floe for six months. The floe drifts south from Ellesmere Island toward the Greenland Strait.

Peak by Roland Smith. Orlando, FL: Harcourt, 2007.

A gripping adventure in which a 14-year-old boy attempts to be the youngest person to climb Mount Everest.

Rascal by Sterling North. New York: Dutton/Penguin, 1963.

Younger teens may warm to this story about a young boy and a pet raccoon. North based this story on his childhood growing up in a small midwestern town at the close of World War I.

Sheep by Valerie Hobbs. New York: Farrar, Straus & Giroux, 2006.

When a fire destroys a border collie's farm, he travels from owner to owner, hoping to find a home and become a sheep dog. Told from the collie's point of view.

Shiloh by Phyllis Reynolds Naylor. New York: Atheneum/Simon & Schuster, 1991.

Marty finds a neglected beagle near his West Virginia home and attempts to hide it from his family and the dog's real owner, who abuses the animal. There is a movie version and two follow-up sequels: *Shiloh Season* (1996) and *Saving Shiloh* (1997). Enjoyed primarily by younger teens.

Continued

Box 4.2   Adventure, Survival, and Animal Stories   *Continued*

***The Sign of the Beaver* by Elizabeth George Speare. Boston: Houghton Mifflin, 1983.**

A young boy is left alone in the wilderness to guard his family's log cabin. Without the aid of a Native American tribe, he would not survive.

***Straydog* by Kathe Koja. New York: Farrar, Straus & Giroux, 2002.**

A lonely girl volunteers at an animal shelter and finds connection with a feral collie. Both girl and dog must learn to trust.

***War Horse* by Michael Morpurgo. New York: Scholastic, 2007.**

Joey the horse describes his life growing up on an English farm and his experiences as a cavalry horse during World War I.

***Wild Man Island* by Will Hobbs. New York: HarperCollins, 2002.**

Fourteen-year-old Andy sneaks away from his kayaking trip to find the location where his father died. Along the way, a storm strands Andy. He battles the elements, wild animals, and strange people who inhabit the island.

***The Winter Road* by Terry Hokenson. Asheville, NC: Front Street, 2006.**

Having lost her brother and feeling abandoned by her father, a 17-year-old girl flies a small plane to get her mother in northern Ontario. The plane crashes, leaving Willa alone in the wintry wilderness.

Examining the Issues

In the following pages some of the best young adult problem novels, both classics and newer works that address personal and social issues, are analyzed. However, as mentioned previously, categorizing novels according to theme can minimize stories; salient themes, sometimes equally or more powerful, are lost. Categories are not mutually exclusive. Therefore, Box 4.3 includes problem novels that address multiple themes. The themes discussed are representative, not exhaustive, of themes found in young adult problem novels and other genres discussed in subsequent chapters such as historical fiction, short stories, poetry, science fiction, and fantasy.

Perfection in an Imperfect World

Almost daily we hear of a horrendous family ordeal in which domestic violence, a brutal murder, or an incestuous relationship rips apart a seemingly perfect family or community. Those who know the family are dumbfounded: "She was the perfect wife." "He was the perfect father." "He was a perfect student." "How could this happen?" Young adult author Chris Crutcher[1] asserts that when people speak of perfection, they are more often than not

---

[1]Chris Crutcher has spent more than 30 years as a child and family therapist.

Box 4.3   Multilayered Problem Novels

***33 Snowfish* by Adam Rapp. Cambridge, MA: Candlewick Press, 2003.**

Three troubled and lost runaway teens—a homeless boy, a 15-year-old drug-addicted prostitute with her baby brother, and a boy who has killed his parents— search for a better life but discover they can't leave their pasts behind.

***The Absolutely True Diary of a Part-Time Indian* by Sherman Alexie. New York: Little, Brown, 2007.**

Junior, a want-to-be cartoonist growing up on an Indian Reservation in Spokane, leaves the reservation to attend an all-white high school. A poignant and funny look at cultural tensions that arise when individuals cross cultural boundaries.

***Born Blue* by Han Nolan. San Diego: Harcourt, 2001.**

Daughter of a drug-addicted mother who abandoned her as a toddler, Janie has experienced abuse and neglect in foster homes and teen pregnancy. Despite a lifetime of abuse and feeling unwanted, Janie has a dream of becoming a famous singer.

***Breakout* by Paul Fleischman. Chicago: Cricket Books, 2003.**

A young woman presents a play based on her life as a 17-year-old runaway whose escape from her foster home in Los Angeles is thwarted by an all-day traffic jam, an event that provides time for her to explore her free-floating identity, hunger for her unknown mother, and yearn for human connection.

***Burned* by Ellen Hopkins. New York: Simon & Schuster, 2006.**

Patty Von Stratten is raised in a religious, but abusive, family. She has questions about sexuality, love, God, and a female's role in society. When her father finds her in a compromising position with a boy, she spirals out of control and is suspended from school. Sent to live with an unknown aunt in Nevada, she

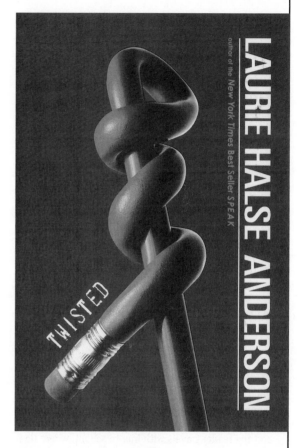

Reprinted by permission of Penguin Young Readers Group © 2007.

finds acceptance and love but discovers that old family demons hold fast, especially when she returns home. Other multilayered titles by Hopkins include *Crank* (2004), *Impulse* (2007b), and *Glass* (2007a).

***Catalyst* by Laurie Halse Anderson. New York: Viking/Penguin, 2002.**

Kate Malone is an exceptional student and has her future mapped out. Kate does not like Teri Litch, a "bad" kid in school, but when Teri's house burns down and Kate's father, a preacher, opens his doors

Continued

Box 4.3   Multilayered Problem Novels   *Continued*

to Teri and her younger brother, Kate must share her room. Both girls learn important lessons about life and relationships.

***Catch* by Will Leitch. New York: Razorbill/Penguin, 2005.**

During the summer before college, Tim Temples drinks, works hard, falls in love with an older girl, and begins questioning his small-town life.

***I Am the Messenger* by Markus Zusak. New York: Knopf/Random House, 2005.**

Nineteen-year-old Ed Kenney lives in a shack with Doorman, his dog, and drives a taxi and spends his spare time playing poker with his friends. Rejected as a boyfriend and constantly insulted by his mother, Ed feels like a loser. When he foils a bank robbery and begins receiving messages asking him to do good deeds (e.g., he helps a priest, buys Christmas lights for the poor), his life begins taking on meaning. A Michael L. Printz Honor book.

***Invisible* by Pete Hautman. New York: Simon & Schuster, 2005.**

Doug, a loner obsessed with model trains, and Andy, a popular football star, have grown up together and share an unbreakable bond. Doug is deeply disturbed, and the reader travels with him to school, where he is viciously bullied, and into the neighborhood, where he is a peeping Tom. The story takes some unusual turns, and the reader learns a truth about Andy.

***Ironman* by Chris Crutcher. New York: Greenwillow/HarperCollins, 1995.**

Bo Brewster is training for a triathlon, but an angry outburst, one of many, lands him in an anger management class at school, where he examines his relationship with his father.

***Just Like That* by Marsha Qualey. New York: Penguin, 2005.**

Eighteen-year-old Hanna is the last to see a teenage couple before they die in a tragic accident. Believing

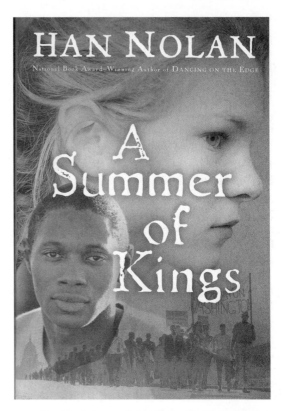

Copyright © 2006 by Han Nolan. Reproduced by permission of Harcourt, Inc.

she may have been able to save them, she returns, consumed by guilt, to the scene of the accident. She connects with Will, the young man who found the couple after their deaths, and the pair find comfort in each other's company; they are attracted to each other and engage in sex. Hanna is drawn into Will's eccentric family but becomes horrified to learn that Will, now her boyfriend, is only 14.

***Keeper of the Night* by Kimberly Willis Holt. New York: Henry Holt, 2003.**

Thirteen-year-old Isabel lives on the island of Guam. When her mother commits suicide, Isabel and her family must struggle through their loss. Isabel assumes

Continued

Box 4.3   Multilayered Problem Novels   *Continued*

the care of her younger siblings and searches for some understanding of her mother's death, her new family role, friendships, and her own developing questions about sexuality and womanhood.

Life Is Funny by E. R. Frank. New York: DK, 2000.

Eleven teens, each with a unique voice, narrate their individual struggles in this debut novel. Their stories, though separate, weave together to make a larger whole.

The Light Keeper's Daughter by Iain Lawrence. New York: Delacorte/Random House, 2002.

Seventeen-year-old Elizabeth "Squid" McCrae, with her three-year-old baby, returns to her childhood home on a remote British Columbia island after a four-year absence, where her father serves as the lightkeeper. Together with her parents, she unravels the family's painful past, which includes the accidental drowning of her brother, Alastair.

Looking for Alaska by John Green. New York: Dutton/Penguin, 2005.

Sixteen-year-old Miles Halter leaves Florida for an Alabama boarding school where he falls head over heels for his roommate's best friend—Alaska, a beautiful, smart, but reckless and self-destructive girl. Chip, Miles's roommate, and Alaska teach Miles to smoke pot, drink, and play pranks. As Alaska's unhappy life unfolds before her friends, they question what happens to her in the end.

Lucas by Kevin Brooks. New York: Chicken House/Scholastic, 2003.

The presence of a mysterious boy on an English island creates a troubling effect for island inhabitants. Fifteen-year-old Caitlin McCann is drawn to Lucas and a friendship develops. However, as disdain and fear for Lucas grow among islanders, most notably Caitlin's friends, Lucas is accused of a horrific crime, and Caitlin is forced to make choices.

Monster by Walter Dean Myers. New York: HarperCollins, 1999.

Sixteen-year-old Steve Harmon is being tried as an accomplice to murder. From his jail cell, Steve records his experiences and thoughts and raises ethical questions in the form of a movie script.

A Summer of Kings by Han Nolan. Orlando, FL: Harcourt, 2006.

Over the course of the summer of 1963, 14-year-old Esther Young discovers the passion within her when 18-year-old King-Roy Johnson, accused of murdering a white man in Alabama, comes to live with her family.

Twisted by Laurie Halse Anderson. New York: Viking/Penguin, 2007.

Tyler Miller is a school nerd until he is caught spray-painting graffiti on a school wall and is sentenced to perform summer work. After a summer of intense physical labor, Tyler returns buffed and toned to school and becomes part of the in-crowd. He attracts the attention of popular Bethany Milbury, the daughter of his father's boss. Tyler must balance his new position in school—that of a "bad boy"—with his personal views of self. He struggles with dysfunctional peers who disapprove of his "bad boy" reputation and bullying. His life becomes increasingly twisted as he searches for his true self.

The Weight of the Sky by Lisa Ann Sandell. New York: Viking/Penguin, 2006.

Sixteen-year-old Saran Green feels out of place in her small Pennsylvania high school where popular kids tease her about being Jewish. Her parents, understanding that Sarah feels lost, send her to Israel one summer, where she works on a kibbutz, finds friendship and love, and develops a new sense of her Jewish identity. A tender coming-of-age story told in fast-paced, lyrical verse.

speaking of self-contempt. Perfection is the thing we cannot achieve, and self-contempt is what we achieve instead:

> Kids who seem perfect often wear long sleeves so we cannot see cut scars or are rail thin because the only way to achieve their perception of perfection is to digest almost no calories. Kids who seem perfect may be idolized by other students; they may be captains of football teams, head cheerleaders, prom queens, or class valedictorians, but like kids who wear long sleeves, they mask incredible pain beneath their façades. We are a trial and error species that demands perfection (or, in the absence of it, the appearance of perfection), and that demand creates debilitating pressure in adolescence. (personal communication, June 2006)

Families who emphasize outward appearances, or raising perfect children, are volcanoes waiting to erupt. Teens who feel pressure to be perfect go to great lengths to be okay.

Research suggests that white girls struggle more with perfection than do girls in other racial groups (Buckley & Carter, 2005; Schooler, Ward, Merriwether, & Caruthers, 2004). This is due partly to the blonde, blue-eyed, perfect Barbie doll media images ever present in the pop culture glamour and glitz world. This problem for white girls plays out in a number of young adult novels. In *Perfect* (Friend, 2004), Isabelle Lee, who has just lost her father, believes she is fat and envies "perfect" girls from a distance. She is shocked to learn that Ashley, the most popular and beautiful girl at her school, is in her therapy group because she, too, has an eating disorder. The protagonist in Francesca Lia Block's *Echo* (2001) has a gorgeous and talented mother. Though her mother dotes on her, Echo can never equal her mother's beauty. Unable to cope with her mother's perfection, she battles depression and anorexia and validates herself through casual sex. Boys, too, struggle with outward appearances and the pressures to be perfect. A classic example is the narrator in Paul Fleischman's *Whirligig* (1998). The protagonist, a wealthy suburbanite, obsesses over being as rich as his peers, wearing the right clothes, knowing cool stuff, and saying the right things, but disaster befalls him. Jocks certainly are not immune from perfection worries. Popular football star Austin Reid in A. M. Jenkins's *Damage* (2001) dates the prettiest girl in school, yet suffers crippling depression.

There is no question that body shape and size concern teens, and the young adult market is saturated with a wide array of books addressing weight issues and eating disorders. In *The Earth, My Butt, and Other Big, Round Things* (2003) by Carolyn Mackler, Virginia Shreves is "oinked" at in the halls and called "pregnant" by her classmates. Though Colie Sparks in Sarah Dessen's *Keeping the Moon* (1999) has lost weight, she still struggles with low self-esteem. Of course, boys do not get a free pass. In *Kissing the Rain* (2004) by Kevin Brooks, overweight Michael "Moo" is constantly tormented by classmates and teachers. He calls the constant flow of abuse "the rain." Troy Billings, a 296-pound 17-year-old in *Fat Kid Rules the World* (2003) by K. L. Going, contemplates suicide when Curt MacCrae, a homeless high school dropout, walks into his life.

How quickly teens mature affects how they feel about themselves. Boys who mature slowly or are small in stature become the brunt of jokes (e.g., the protagonist in K. L. Going's *The Liberation of Gabriel King*, 2005), but fast maturation has a price too. Thirteen-year-old Earl Pryor in Chris Lynch's *Who the Man* (2002) shaves and towers over his peers. He feels clumsy and out of place and carries as much anger as weight. In *Stand Tall* (2002), Joan Bauer's protagonist, Tree, already 6'3" in seventh grade, struggles with expectations placed upon him to be a stellar athlete, though he is not athletic. Early-maturing girls often become ashamed of their bodies, as does the protagonist in Marlene Perez's *Unexpected Development* (2004) who contemplates breast reduction.

Kevin Brooks as a small child in Exeter, Devon.

No matter how we cut it, teens buy into cultural expectations about body type and will go to great lengths—including fad dieting, sexual promiscuity, and drug use, sometimes with dire consequences—to feel okay. A good problem novel can be a springboard for discussing perfection and societal demands. Box 4.4 features a number of books with stories ranging from pressures about physical appearance to pressures about academic and athletic performance. In some of these selections, pressure comes from home; in others, pressure comes from outside forces such as school. In all cases, the manner in which teens cope with the drive to succeed or perfection is closely tied to their family histories—how well they are accepted by loved ones, as opposed to how much they are criticized, neglected, or abused.

Sexuality

Any realistic novel about adolescent development that does not include sexuality is incomplete. When Bradbury Press published Judy Blume's *Forever* in 1975, a book that detailed sexual intercourse, teenage girls could not get enough of it. Finally, they had a story that spoke to the realities of teenage sex that did not preach a moral message about virginity or encourage guilt about their powerful sexual feelings. Girls read the book secretly and passed it around at school. Blume's book, however, caused such turmoil in the young adult market that relatively few writers dared write explicit sexual scenes for years to come.

Sexuality is a huge part of adolescence and drives a great deal of adolescent behavior. We can all recall bewildering and uncomfortable questions and situations. Most of us preferred walking barefoot across hot coals to asking our parents questions about sexuality. With no literature beyond the hygiene packets handed out in health class, information, faulty and incomplete, came from friends and experience. Silence and the social climate taught us that sex was "bad." Consumed with guilt feelings, most of us dealt with our first experiences and moral decisions alone.

Box 4.4   Image and Perfection

Alt Ed by Catherine Atkins. New York: Putnam/Penguin, 2003.

An overweight teen develops a better self-concept when she participates in an after-school counseling program for troubled teens.

Caught in the Act by Peter Moore. New York: Viking/Penguin, 2005.

Ethan keeps up a front before his smart and successful parents who believe that Ethan is a good kid and good student. He cannot tell them that he is having trouble in his honors class.

Crooked by Laura McNeal and Tom McNeal. New York: Random House, 1999.

Among the multiple themes in this novel is Clara Wilson's obsession with her crooked nose.

Dough Boy by Peter Marino. New York: Holiday House, 2005.

Fifteen-year-old Tristan is overweight, but happy. Criticism about his weight grows when the daughter of his mother's boyfriend, a popular weight-obsessed girl, moves in.

Golden by Jennifer Lynn Barnes. New York: Delacorte/Random House, 2006.

Lissy James struggles with the social group stratification at her new high school: the popular golden girls and the "nons" (short for non-golden). Lissy has extrasensory perception, which allows her to save classmates from pending disaster. Fans may also enjoy *Platinum* (2007).

Gotta Get Some Bish Bash Bosh by M. E. Allen. New York: HarperTempest, 2005.

The 14-year-old narrator tries changing his image after getting dumped by his girlfriend.

How to Be Popular by Meg Cabot. New York: HarperCollins, 2006.

Unpopular Steph Landry wants to be popular. She changes her wardrobe and becomes involved in school activities. As she gains popularity, her former relationships are strained.

I Was a Non-Blonde Cheerleader by Kieran Scott. New York: Penguin, 2005.

Dark-haired Annisa enters a new high school and learns that everyone there is blonde. Will the fact that she is a brunette keep her from making the cheerleading squad? Sequels include *Brunettes Strike Back* (2006) and *A Non-Blonde Cheerleader in Love* (2007).

Just Listen by Sarah Dessen. New York: Penguin, 2006.

Annabel's perfect life falls apart; her best friend drops her, leaving her friendless, and her family struggles with her sister's anorexia.

My Perfect Life by Dyan Sheldon. Cambridge, MA: Candlewick Press, 2002.

Ella Gerard's perfect life is shattered when her best friend nominates her to run against Carla Santana, a popular girl, for school president.

Pretty Is by Elizabeth Holmes. New York: Dutton/Penguin, 2007.

It's difficult being the new girl at school, but when your older sister is a dork, that's even worse. Snubbed by the popular crowd, Erin takes a desperate and vengeful step.

Pretty Things by Sarra Manning. New York: Dutton/Penguin, 2005.

Four friends in a summer drama group learn pretty exteriors are merely façades.

Continued

Box 4.4   Image and Perfection   *Continued*

***Quaking* by Kathryn Erskine. New York: Philomel/Penguin, 2007.**

Matilda's new foster parents are Quakers who oppose the war in the Middle East. Matilda, a tough girl who has shut out the world, softens to her new surroundings. When conflict arises in the town over the war, Matilda, her new family, and their friends are not safe.

***A Really Nice Prom Mess* by Brian Sloan. New York: Simon & Schuster, 2005.**

Cameron covers his gay identity by attending the prom with gorgeous Virginia McKinley, though he would rather be with Shane Wilson, his football star boyfriend. The night turns into a disaster.

***Sexy* by Joyce Carol Oates. New York: HarperTempest, HarperCollins, 2005.**

Darren Flynn seems to have everything. He is a good-looking athlete, but he is uncomfortable around girls and is self-conscious of his maturing body.

***The Skin I'm In* by Sharon G. Flake. New York: Hyperion, 1998.**

Meleeka Madison is teased at her inner-city school because of her dark skin. A new teacher with a white birthmark on her face helps Meleeka develop confidence.

***The Truth about Forever* by Sarah Dessen. New York: Viking/Penguin, 2004.**

On the outside Macy Queen seems fine: she maintains good grades and exhibits exemplary behavior. Inside, however, she drowns in grief over the loss of her father.

***Wait for Me* by An Na. New York: Penguin, 2006.**

Mina is an exceptional teen. She is a straight-A student bound for Harvard. She helps out in the family's dry cleaners and attends to her younger sister. She does everything right. Inside she is haunted by a personal secret.

***With Lots of Love from Georgia* by Brigid Lowry. New York: Holiday House, 2006.**

A depressed, overweight teen spends the summer eating and trying to make enough money to attend a rock concert.

Today's teens struggle in much the same way, but they are maturing in a nation that has become desensitized to sex. Pornography, some remarkably disturbing, is an Internet click away, and daily we delete pornographic spam from our e-mail. Cable TV bombards teens with sexual images and messages. (Parental controls on programming do little to prevent access—teens have an endless supply of peers from less restrictive environments.) The entertainment and business worlds exploit teen sexuality and send messages about what young people should look like and how they should behave. Teen magazines, too, focus on "being hot" and "how to please the opposite sex" as opposed to addressing the real issues and consequences of engaging in sex.

Despite today's sexually explicit world and changing social norms, adults can't reach consensus regarding teen sexuality and where, when, and how teens should have access to sexual information. We need only look at

Janet Jackson's 2004 "wardrobe malfunction" in Super Bowl XXXVIII to see that we remain a nation polarized and confused about sexuality. It is clear, too, that though some adults believe sexuality is best addressed at home, many teens do not come from environments in which parents provide straight talk about sexuality or teens feel safe asking questions.

One reason for exposing teens to problem novels that deal with teen sexuality is because so much incorrect information is available. A good problem novel with sexual content is about character development, not sex. Behaviors have results and consequences, and characters wrestle with the emotions associated with acts of sex and attraction. Books like these offer teens an honest examination of sexuality and provide valuable information. In a statement on *Real Time with Bill Maher* in 2006, Jason Alexander (George Costanza on *Seinfeld*) made a salient, but somber point about the Internet and teen sexuality, paraphrased here: *Teenage girls are expected to perform the first time out like porn stars.* His statement rings true when considering a chilling 2006 report by Allan Sherhoff on young adults and college partying and sexual exploitation of girls. Shown on *Paula Zahn Now,* Sherhoff exposed Internet pornographers and sexual predators who frequent frat parties and video, professionally or with cell phone cameras, drunken girls engaging in sexual activity, cheered on in ganglike fashion. Many of these images are then posted on Web sites frequented by teens. Such acts are disturbing and provide even more justification for arming girls with information to prepare them to enter the college climate. Boys, too, need this information, for date rape occurs far too frequently with today's youth. The Kobe Bryant case heightened our sensibilities to this problem and raised an important question, "How do we define consensual sex?" Chris Lynch examines this question brilliantly in *Inexcusable* (2005).

A recurring mistake our culture makes is *blaming* teens for engaging in sex instead of *examining* behavior so that we might understand it. What role, for instance, might family play in teen sexual behavior? How, for example, does the relationship between a girl and her father influence her sexual behavior? In *Story of a Girl* (Zarr, 2006), 13-year-old Deanna Lambert is caught by her detached father having sex in the backseat of a car with 17-year-old Tommy Webber. She does not love Tommy, does not even know if she likes him, but is looking for connection. In the following scene, she shows an awareness of her emptiness:

> Sometimes you might think you wanted to do it and then halfway through or afterwards realize no, you just wanted the company, really; you wanted someone to choose you, and the sex part itself was like a trade-off, something you felt like you had to give to get the other part. (p. 79)

Out of anger, Tommy spreads rumors about Deanna, and despite her heartfelt apologies, her father still cannot find a way to forgive her, even three years later. In response to her emptiness and longing, Deanna throws herself at her best friend, Jason, even though he goes steady with

Deanna's close friend Lee: "I could be your girlfriend. . . . I'd be a great girlfriend" (p. 145).

Zarr's book speaks to the detachment between a girl and her father and the emptiness a young girl feels when she grows up without that attachment. Deanna's heartbreaking story will resonate with girls and provides a wonderful opportunity for girls to reflect on their own relationships. Boys also can connect with this story—Tommy is genuinely surprised at the intensity of Deanna's emotional involvement. The story is a remarkably good one because it raises an important question, "When have we paid enough for our mistakes?" After three years, Deanna's father still feels anger and resentment toward his daughter.

In an era in which same-sex relationships defined a presidential campaign (Bush vs. Kerry, 2004), split political parties, and was a theme running through award-winning films in 2005 (*Brokeback Mountain, Capote,* and *Transamerica*), it would be a mistake not to address gay and transgender relationships. One of the most significant changes in the problem novel over the last few years has been the evolution of gay and lesbian characters, and the manner in which many writers have moved from "homophobic" to "homosexual" themes. In earlier works (e.g., Betty Greene's *The Drowning of Stephan Jones,* 1991) gay characters were victims of violence, or stories featured families (e.g., M. E. Kerr's *Deliver Us from Evie,* 1994) struggling with a teen coming out. Stories featuring gay characters as victims gives them voice and draws society's attention to bigotry; that recognition is vital, but gay teens, just like straight, also need to see themselves in powerful roles.

Though homophobia remains a theme, and rightfully so, gay and lesbian characters in today's problem novels are less victimized. Many new works feature sexually confused characters, protagonists who know they are attracted to the same sex but are not certain of their homosexuality; thus the conflict centers around protagonists struggling with themselves as opposed to struggling with outside forces (victimization). In Sara Ryan's *Empress of the World* (2001), Nicola Lancaster meets Katrina at summer camp and begins questioning her own sexual orientation; the protagonist in Kate Walker's *Peter* (1993) realizes his attraction to his brother's best friend and is devastated. The story ends with Peter still confused about his identity—a realistic ending.

In some problem novels, protagonists are not confused about their sexual orientation (though they may struggle with how to meet others like them). They and their friends take their "gayness" in stride. In *Geography Club* (2003) and its sequel *The Order of the Poison Oak* (2005) by Brent Hartinger, the protagonist Russel Middlebrook accepts his identity but struggles with finding ways of being with other guys. High schooler Paul, in laugh-out-loud *Boy Meets Boy* (Levithan, 2003), has always known he was gay. In fact, his kindergarten teacher wrote on his progress report: "Paul is definitely gay and has a very good sense of self" (p. 8). For the characters in *Boy Meets Boy,* being gay is not a "problem." When answering why she wrote *Gravel Queen* (2003), Tea Benduhn speaks to the need for literature of this kind:

> When I was growing up and discovering my identity, I read a lot about the tragic consequences of following desire lines, as well as negative stereotypes about the South, but did not see much evidence of either in my real, daily experience. (*Gravel Queen* book jacket, 2003)

In *Gravel Queen*, as in *Boy Meets Boy*, homosexuality is a fact of life. The plot revolves around the giddiness of first love, not the anguish that accompanies a gay teen coming to terms with his/her sexual orientation. In books like these, neither homosexuality nor homophobia is central to plot development. This change speaks to the maturity of the genre and to increased acceptance of gay teens by their peers.

Confusing and heartbreaking relationships between homosexual and heterosexual teens is another important sexual concern, and today's writers for teens honor these confusing relationships. The protagonist in Ellen Wittlinger's Printz Honor book, *Hard Love* (1999), falls for a lesbian, and the ending, though gut-wrenching, is honest. Julie Anne Peters repeats this theme in *Far from Xanadu* (2005). These books speak to changing societal attitudes. Although homophobia remains with us, and same-sex marriage has become a political issue, these books show that in some ways society has made progress toward acceptance of homosexuality.

In this confusing and changing time in which teens have free access to sexual information, the young adult market has broken open with books about teen sexuality. Young adult authors are writing courageous and realistic stories about sexual identity, sexual development; and teens, as well as adults, are devouring them. Box 4.5 features realistic books about teens falling in love, first sexual encounters, homosexuality, sexual encounters with adults, and teen pregnancy. These selections are about characters (not the act of sex) who are finding their way through sexuality.

Making and Maintaining Friends

Peer relationships are at the core of most problem novels, and with good reason. Adolescence is a time of discovering who we are, and we do that, in large part, through peer responses. As much as we like to give advice— Be your own man/woman; be a leader, do not fall under the influence of others—few of us forge our own way. The "Who am I?" question is answered in relationship to others. Stories about friendships are popular because teens evaluate their worthiness through friendships, or lack thereof, and test one another's friendship to determine their own worth.

Today's teens fear peer rejection and value being part of the in-group. Looking "right" and acting "right" determine peer acceptance. Teens ask, "Are we cool enough? Tough or pretty enough? Smart or athletic enough? Friendly enough?" Young people who feel excluded take desperate steps to belong. *Shopaholic* (Waite, 2003) and *Klepto* (Pollack, 2006) illustrate the extreme measures girls will take to have friends. In both stories two lonely girls develop friendships with girls they idolize. One girl uses her family's

Box 4.5   Sexual Identity, Dating, and Love

Absolute Brightness by James Lecesne. New York: HarperCollins, 2008.

Phoebe has problems of her own, but when her flamboyant gay cousin moves in, her life gets worse. Leonard wears weird clothes, works in a salon, and turns a blind eye to prejudice. When Leonard goes missing and Phoebe suspects foul play, she becomes obsessed with finding him.

Arizona Kid by Ron Koertge. Boston: Joy Street, 1988 (Candlewick Press, 2005).

Sixteen-year-old Billy spends his summer vacation in Arizona with his gay uncle, where he works on a ranch, meets new friends, and falls in love with Cara Mae, a horse exerciser. A funny, yet heartbreaking, coming-of-age story.

The Beet Fields: Memories of a Sixteenth Summer by Gary Paulsen. New York: Delacorte/Random House, 2000.

Running from what he believes are sexual advances by his drunken mother, a young boy takes a job one summer working in the beet fields of North Dakota, only to discover the farmer charges a fee for using his hoe, and he clears almost nothing. The boy then hooks up with a carnival, where he meets Ruby, a carnival stripper who teaches him about sex. The writing craft and complex sentences alone make this book a must read.

Blue Mirror by Kathe Koja. New York: Farrar, Straus & Giroux, 2004.

Maggy, an artistic loner who cares for her alcoholic mother, falls for charismatic Cole. Maggy learns that Cole has a dark and dangerous side and must find a way to break away. Written in a stream-of-consciousness style with gritty street scenes.

Bringing Up the Bones by Lara M. Zeises. New York: Random House, 2002.

Bridget sinks into severe depression, deferring her first year of college and working as a waitperson after the accidental death of her ex-boyfriend, Benji. When

Jasper enters her life, Bridget has to come to terms with herself and her relationship with Benji, who may or may not have loved her.

Darkness before Dawn by Sharon Draper. New York: Atheneum/Simon & Schuster, 2001.

Keisha has lost two people whom she loves: her ex-boyfriend has committed suicide and a best friend has died in a car accident. Keisha is vulnerable enough to fall for the high school track coach's smooth advances; however, he attempts to rape her on a romantic date.

The Dear One by Jacqueline Woodson. New York: Putnam, 2004.

Twelve-year-old Feni does not want to share her room with a tough, pregnant 15-year-old. But when the baby is born and Rebecca prepares to leave, Feni realizes she is about to lose a best friend.

Dreamland by Sarah Dessen. New York: Viking/Penguin, 2000.

Caitlin has always lived in her older sister's shadow. However, when her sister runs away, Caitlin is left to fill her void. Caitlin begins dating Rogerson Biscoe and withdraws from her friends. When Rogerson gets violent with Caitlin, her parents are too consumed by her sister's disappearance to notice.

First Part Last by Angela Johnson. New York: Simon & Schuster, 2003.

Mesmerizing and poetic, this novel details the life of a teenage father and his love for his infant daughter. In alternating chapters, the reader learns of Bobby's relationship with the mother of his child and how he came to raise her.

Freak Show by James St. James. New York: Dutton/Penguin, 2007.

Billy Bloom is a teenage drag queen who wants to be the school's homecoming queen. A funny read that

Continued

Box 4.5   Sexual Identity, Dating, and Love   *Continued*

tackles complicated issues such as bigotry, power, and self-acceptance.

Friction by E. R. Frank. New York: Simon & Schuster, 2003.

When Alex tells a new student that she believes the teacher has a crush on her, rumors about the teacher fly.

Getting the Girl by Markus Zusak. New York: Levine/Scholastic, 2003.

Cameron's older brother, Ruben, always gets the girl, but does not respect them. When Ruben dumps Octavia, a breathtaking girl, she turns to Cameron, and Cameron has a chance to explore his first romantic relationship.

The God Box by Alex Sanchez. New York: Simon & Schuster, 2007.

Paul dates Angie and likes her, but he struggles with being attracted to boys. When an outwardly gay boy, who professes to being a Christian, arrives in their small-town school, Paul is forced to reevaluate who he is. Can he love God if he can't love himself?

Hanging on to Max by Margaret Bechard. New Milford, CT: Roaring Brook Press, 2002.

A single dad, 17-year-old Sam struggles as a single parent. He lives with his father who has agreed to help him financially through high school but expects him to take a construction job when he finishes. Sam is overwhelmed with caring for Max and attending school and faces important decisions about his future.

Heavy Metal and You by Chris Krovatin. New York: Push/Scholastic, 2005.

Sam listens to heavy metal music, uses drugs, wears spiked jewelry, and cuts class with his friends. When he falls for Melissa, he tries to clean up his act. Does changing mean losing his identity?

Honey, Baby, Sweetheart by Deb Caletti. New York: Simon & Schuster, 2004.

Ruby McQueen falls in love with Travis, a rich boy who gives her gifts. She learns that he burglarizes houses and steals jewelry and is forced to rethink her relationship. She begins spending time with her mother, who is struggling with her own relationship issues. Together they work through their feelings by participating in a book group.

The House You Pass Along the Way by Jacqueline Woodson. New York: Delacorte/Random House, 1997.

Staggerlee Canan is shunned in her small, black southern community because she is biracial. Having kissed a girl in sixth grade and developing a new friendship in Trout, an adopted cousin visiting for the summer, Staggerlee also wonders if she is gay.

If You Come Softly by Jacqueline Woodson. New York: Penguin/Putnam, 1998.

Jeremiah, a 15-year-old black teen, meets Ellie, a white girl, at a private New York school. The two fall in love and have to cope with their families' and friends' reactions to their interracial relationship.

Inexcusable by Chris Lynch. New York: Atheneum/Simon & Schuster, 2005.

When Keir, a senior, date rapes a high school girl, he tries to persuade both himself and those around him that he is innocent.

Keeping You a Secret by Julie Anne Peters. New York: Little, Brown, 2003.

When straight Holland Jaeger meets admitted lesbian Cece Goddard, the two fall in love, but Holland loses friends and family in the process.

Continued

Box 4.5   Sexual Identity, Dating, and Love *Continued*

***Naomi and Ely's No Kiss List* by Rachel Cohn and David Levithan. New York: Knopf/Random House, 2007.**

Naomi and Ely are best friends, but when Ely kisses Naomi's boyfriend, their relationship is shattered. Is Naomi upset because her male friend, Ely, kisses her boyfriend? Or is there another reason?

***The Orpheus Obsession* by Dakota Lane. New York: HarperTempest, 2005.**

Anooshka Stargirl lives in New York City and becomes obsessed with a popular musician. She spends hours online reading his journal entries and plotting ways to meet him.

***Parrotfish* by Ellen Wittlinger. New York: Simon & Schuster, 2007.**

Angela has never felt comfortable being a girl and decides to come out as Grady, a transgendered boy. Grady isn't prepared for the responses he gets from his family and friends. A serious, yet funny, look at sexual identity.

***Peter* by Kate Walker. Boston: Houghton Mifflin, 1993.**

Fifteen-year-old Peter Dawson has no worries until he meets his brother's best friend David. Peter knows that David is gay, and he questions whether the admiration and powerful draw that he feels toward David means that he is gay too.

***Razzle* by Ellen Wittlinger. New York: Simon & Schuster, 2001.**

Kenyon Baker, a serious photographer, resents leaving his old school and moving with his elderly parents to Cape Cod, where they invest in beachfront rental property badly in need of repair. He captures stunning pictures of Razzle Penney, an inspiring, nonconforming, unique girl, but their relationship is jaded by beautiful, manipulative Harley, who convinces Kenyon to display her pictures instead in a local art show.

***Saints of Augustine* by P. E. Ryan. New York: HarperCollins, 2007.**

Told from alternating viewpoints, two former friends describe their struggles with personal problems. Charlie has an alcoholic father, smokes pot, and is in debt to a drug dealer. Sam lives with his father and his father's male lover and worries about his own sexual attraction. Their personal problems unite the former friends.

***What Mr. Mattero Did* by Priscilla Cummings. New York: Dutton/Penguin, 2005.**

Three seventh-grade girls accuse their teacher, Mr. Mattero, of touching them inappropriately. He is suspended and a formal investigation ensues.

food money to buy clothes for her friend to keep her happy; the other gets caught up in stealing clothes with her friend so they can both look good. Boys are no exception: Paul Richmond, a lonely outsider in *Breaking Point* (Flinn, 2002), is invited to join Charlie Good's elite inner circle, but at a price.

While friendships are about belonging, strong friendships move beyond image concerns and fitting in with the cool crowd. Deep-seated, lifelong meaningful relationships begin developing in the teen years. Those relationships are built on the athletic field, in other school-related events and extracurricular acitivities, during summer vacation, and in the neighborhood. More often than we may realize, the strongest friendships are established between boys and girls.

Alex Flinn on the first day of kindergarten. Her Disney School Bus lunchbox is the most popular lunchbox ever made.

It is difficult to find a better young adult novel about deep-seated, heart-felt friendships than *Staying Fat for Sarah Byrnes* (Crutcher, 1993). Sarah befriends Eric because he seems so weak. Being weak enrages Sarah because there are dire consequences when she shows weakness. Eric is delighted and relieved to have a friend, and Sarah teaches him to stand up for himself. But as Eric gets stronger and more popular, he lets Sarah slip away, and when she goes into a crisis he is not there for her, and she ends up in a psych ward. The shame of not returning all she has given him takes him over, and he goes back to get her, putting his life in peril. There is friendship of necessity, friendship of desperation, lost friendship, and true, hard-tested friendship.

A more recent book that resonates with the same deep, heartfelt friendship is Paul Volponi's *Black and White* (2005). Star basketball players with promising college careers, best friends Marcus (who is black) and Eddie (white) are not willing to be the only team members without Nike Marauders, nor are they willing to miss class trips by not paying senior dues. Together they commit a series of burglaries so they can buy the Nikes and fund school trips; only Eddie accidentally shoots a victim, and Marcus is the sole suspect. The story centers around who pays for their crime: who goes to jail, who loses his college scholarship. While hundreds of books have been written about friendship since *Staying Fat for Sarah Byrnes,* this book stands out for its depiction of pure, selfless friendship.

Adolescent Cruelty

Adolescent cruelty has been a constant theme in teen problem novels as far back as *The Outsiders* (Hinton, 1967) and *The Chocolate War* (Cormier, 1974). Adolescents are often called sociopathic narcissists (usually tongue in cheek) because of their attention to themselves and what often seems a lack of compassion. The belief that "everything is about me" is strong because adolescents are looking for their place to stand. Finding that position sometimes means putting others down in the belief that they can stand taller. Feelings of incompetence and fear of embarrassment are staples throughout this age, and cruelty, intended or not, becomes a constant. Cruelty tends to beget cruelty, whether through outright bullying or through more clandestine methods such as clique exclusion. We all want and need power, and the chaotic time of adolescence seems to bring out our worst treatment of each other.

Because the teenage years are a time of testing relationships and self-importance, teens, especially girls, are notorious for taking sides. When two girls fall out, everyone must choose sides, and whichever side friends come down on tells both girls how important they are. Friends usually align with the more popular girl, for being friends with her is a statement about their own worthiness. This behavior is superbly illustrated in Amy Goldman Koss's *The Girls* (2000). Popular and pretty Candace calls the shots about who is "in" and who is "out." When Maya is excluded from Darcy's sleepover party, the other girls make prank phone calls and ignore her at school. Nonfiction works such as Rachel Simmons's *Odd Girl Out* (2002) and Rosalind Wiseman's *Queen Bees and Wannabes: Helping Your Daughter Survive Cliques, Gossip, Boyfriends, and Other Realities of Adolescence* (2002), the basis for the 2004 movie *Mean Girls*, have drawn attention to this behavior, and the theme of mean girls is becoming prominent in problem novels. In *Poison Ivy* (Koss, 2006) Mrs. Gold, a teacher, learns that Ivy has been bullied and teased for years by Ann and her friends; she decides to hold a mock trial to teach students about the judicial system. In alternating voices, characters unveil what they know about Ann's treatment of Ivy. The characters' stories are all too familiar to teenagers, and the ending in which the "pretty" girl wins is chilling, but real. Readers are left pondering the meaning of "popularity." Is it about being likable? Or is it about having power? If there is a trend in the market for adolescent cruelty problem novels, it is this attention to the meanness of girls, perhaps captured best in early novels by Judy Blume (e.g., *Blubber*, 1974).

Anyone who spends a great deal of time around adolescents knows that boys do not generally test their worthiness in the same way. In fact, they are often bewildered by "girl behavior," but they do tend to torment weaker boys, sometimes quite violently, and test their maleness in athletics. In a speech given at the International Reading Association Convention in Orlando, Florida, David Klass (2003), critically acclaimed author of *You Don't Know Me* (2001), related a childhood experience that led him to write *Home of the Braves* (2002), a story set in a violent high school whose football players are bullies:

> On my first day in third grade, the biggest kid in the class—who had been held back—came up to me. He said, "We're gonna have a fight. Me and you. Today. After school. In the sandbox. Be there, or I'll come find you."
>
> The sandbox was in a corner of the schoolyard, sheltered by trees from any school windows. All that day I tried to figure out what to do. I was scared and didn't know exactly what a fight was. But I also sensed that if I didn't show up, this fear would go on. So when school ended I walked to the sandbox, where a dozen kids were waiting. The big kid and I started fighting, and the other kids ringed the sandbox shouting, "Hit him again, harder." Somehow I ended up on top of the big kid, and he said "Uncle" or whatever. From that day to when I graduated from high school, I was never picked on again.

> That experience encapsulates everything I know about school
> bullying. Boys who are new or weak or different are singled out and tested.
> Either you'll fight back or you won't. (p. 16)

Most of us are familiar with bullying and its effects. We've been bullied, or stood back, frightened and unsure of our own courage, and watched it happen, or we've bullied others. Problem novels with bullying themes are plentiful and are good choices for school programs designed to address teen relationships and violence. *Sleep Rough Tonight* (Bone, 2005), for example, is a disturbing portrait of teen bullying; *Shattering Glass* (Giles, 2002) and *What Happened to Lani Garver* (Plum-Ucci, 2002) show just how far teen bullying can go.

Boxes 4.6 and 4.7 include quality books that cover a wide range of peer-related issues. Included are stories about racial tensions, bigotry, loss, betrayal, commitment, crime, violence, adolescent cruelty, jealousy, and more. In all cases, these are stories about teens finding their way through peer relationships, either growing together or moving apart.

Box 4.6   Making, Maintaining, and Losing Friends

***All Alone in the Universe* by Lynne Rae Perkins. New York: Greenwillow/ HarperCollins, 1999.**

When Debbie's best friend, Maureen, forgoes their friendship for a new one, Debbie struggles with the loss, learns people change, and finds her way to new friendships.

***Autobiography of My Dead Brother* by Walter Dean Myers. New York: Amistad/ HarperCollins, 2005.**

Fifteen-year-old Jesse narrates the violence of his Harlem neighborhood, his best friend's involvement in drugs and gangs, and raises questions about his own future. Comic book sketches complement the text.

***Becoming Chloe* by Catherine Ryan Hyde. New York: Knopf/Random House, 2006.**

Jordy, a gay runaway teen from a wealthy family, tries to save an abused girl, Chloe, from a gang rape. They forge a sibling relationship and help each other survive on the streets. They decide to hitchhike and bike cross country, and along the way they search for hope and their place in the world.

***The Bermudez Triangle* by Maureen Johnson. New York: Razorbill/Penguin, 2004.**

Nina spends the summer before her senior year in a summer program at Stanford University, where she falls in love. Upon returning home to Saratoga Springs, she discovers that her best friends, Avery and Mel, have become lovers. Nina feels rejected and lonely, especially when her long-distance relationship begins to fall apart.

***Bridge to Terabithia* by Katherine Paterson. New York: Crowell, 1977.**

Jess practices running all summer so he can be the fastest boy in fifth grade; however, he is beaten by Leslie, a new girl. The two form a heartwarming relationship only to be torn apart by tragic circumstances.

Continued

Box 4.6   Making, Maintaining, and Losing Friends   *Continued*

A Corner of the Universe by Ann M. Martin. New York: Scholastic, 2002.

One summer 12-year-old Hattie makes two new friends: her mentally ill uncle Adam and Leila, a girl traveling with an itinerant carnival. A serious book about the power of friendship and loss.

Crunch Time by Mariah Fredericks. New York: Atheneum/Simon & Schuster, 2006.

A multilayered story that brings four unlikely teens together in an SAT study group: Daisy, a popular basketball star; Max, a promising writer attracted to Daisy; gorgeous Jane, daughter of a well-known actress; and bad boy Leo. When one of them cheats on the exam, their friendship is tested.

Emako Blue by Brenda Woods. New York: Penguin, 2004.

Emako Blue, killed in a drive-by shooting, was beautiful and had a singing voice like vanilla incense and was destined to be a star. She was Monterey's best friend, the girl Jamal loved, Eddie's confidant, and Savannah's rival. In alternating chapters, these four characters mourn her loss and detail the events that led up to her accidental death. A short, poignant story of friendship and love.

Girls Dinner Club by Jessie Elliot. New York: HarperCollins, 2005.

Junie, Celia, and Danielle, three racially diverse New York City girls, form a tight friendship while cooking dinners together and talking about their romantic relationships.

Hit the Road by Caroline B. Cooney. New York: Random House, 2006.

Sixteen-year-old Brittany reluctantly chauffeurs her grandmother and three elderly friends on a long road trip that involves deceit, robbery, and kidnapping. Brittany is inspired by their lifelong friendship.

Keeping the Moon by Sarah Dessen. New York: Viking/Penguin, 1999.

A former fat girl, Colie spends the summer at the beach with her eccentric aunt and works as a waitperson at a restaurant. She makes new friends who help her develop a strong sense of self, something she lost when she was overweight and picked on.

The Last Domino by Adam Meyer. New York: Penguin, 2005.

Lonely after his brother commits suicide and feeling alienated and bullied, Travis is drawn to Daniel, a dangerous, manipulative newcomer at his school, who convinces Travis that he has to take care of himself. Daniel stands up for Travis against the bullies, teaches him to use a gun, and convinces him to make a list of people who should be shot.

Lizzie Bright and the Buckminster Boy by Gary Schmidt. New York: Clarion Books, 2004.

Turner Buckminster, a minister's son who does not fit into his new community, meets Lizzie Bright Griffin, a poor black girl from a nearby island, and a close friendship develops. The good elders of Turner's town, Phippsburg, believe the island is an eyesore and want to dislocate the families living there. Rich in character. Both funny and sad.

The Moves Make the Man by Bruce Brooks. New York: Harper & Row, 1984.

Bix Rivers, a basketball player from a troubled home who believes in truth, develops a close friendship with Jerome Foxworthy, a gifted black athlete selected to

Continued

Box 4.6   Making, Maintaining, and Losing Friends   *Continued*

integrate Bix's all-white school. Jerome teaches Bix basketball moves, only Bix will not "fake."

Patiently Alice by Phyllis Reynolds Naylor. New York: Atheneum/Simon & Schuster, 2003.

Alice spends the summer after 9th grade as a camp counselor for poor children. This is the 15th book in a popular series in which Alice struggles with typical teen growing pains: friendships, family, boys, and more.

Peaches by Jodi Lynn Anderson. New York: HarperCollins, 2005.

The lives of three teenage girls, from different backgrounds, unfold over the course of one summer when they pick peaches together in a Georgia orchard. Fans may enjoy the sequel, *Secrets of Peaches* (2006).

The Rise and Fall of a 10th Grade Social Climber by Lauren Mechling and Laura Moser. Boston: Graphia/Houghton Mifflin, 2005.

When her parents separate, Mimi Shulman moves to New York to live with her dad and enrolls in an exclusive, upper-class school, where she makes a bet that she can get invited into the coolest clique. She is accepted, but trouble ensues when her private journal is leaked onto the Internet.

The Secret Language of Girls by Frances O'Roark Dowell. New York: Atheneum/Simon & Schuster, 2004.

Kate and Marylin's friendship is tested when scheming and know-it-all Flannery moves to town. Dowell raises coming-of-age questions about the meaning of friendship, fitting in versus individuality, peer pressure, and popularity.

Box 4.7   Adolescent Cruelty

Amy by Mary Hooper. New York: Bloomsbury, 2003.

Amy chats online with Zed, and the two decide to meet. Zed gives her a date rape drug and photographs her nude. When Amy realizes her shirt is on backward, she begins remembering what happened.

Blubber by Judy Blume. New York: Dell/Yearling, 1974.

A classic take on school bullying. Linda, an overweight, unpopular girl, is picked on by Wendy. Before long Wendy has elicited help from a group of classmates who are intent on making Linda's life miserable.

The Body of Christopher Creed by Carol Plum-Ucci. Orlando, FL: Harcourt, 2000.

When Chris Creed, the class misfit, disappears, no one knows why. Did he run away, commit suicide, or was he murdered? Sixteen-year-old Torey Adams and his friends reflect on their cruel pranks as facts about his disappearance come to light.

Breaking Point by Alex Flinn. New York: HarperCollins, 2002.

Paul Richmond can attend an elite private school because his mother works in the guidance office, but he is bullied unmercifully for that fact. Paul is invited

Continued

Box 4.7   Adolescent Cruelty *Continued*

into a social clique by popular Charlie Good at a steep price: He must hack into the school grading system and change Charlie's biology grade.

Breathing Underwater by Alex Flinn. New York: HarperCollins, 2001.

Nick does not understand why Caitlin, his girlfriend, and her family have taken out a restraining order against him. He only slapped her because she sang in the school talent school when he told her not to. She would get laughed at because she was fat and could not sing. Nick is required by the courts to keep a journal in which he reflects on his relationship with Caitlin.

Buddha Boy by Kathe Koja. New York: Farrar, Straus & Giroux, 2003.

Justin is paired with Jinsen, whom the kids call Buddha Boy, for a class project. At first he just wants to complete the project, but as he comes to know Jinsen's artistic talent, he begins questioning his own beliefs about what matters most: social status or extraordinary relationships.

Charlie's Story by Maeve Friel. Atlanta, GA: Peachtree, 1997.

Abandoned by her mother as a toddler and growing up with a distant father, Charlie could use some friends, but she is bullied relentlessly at school. Charlie becomes suicidal.

The Clique: A Novel by Lisi Harrison. New York: Little, Brown, 2004.

Claire, a middle-class teen, does not fit in with her wealthy classmates at an exclusive private school in New York. Massie schemes to exclude her, but Claire fights back.

The Confessional by J. L. Powers. New York: Knopf/Random House, 2007.

Racial tensions soar when a student is murdered at an all-boys Catholic school in El Paso, Texas.

Mackenzie Malone and his classmates are forced to examine their personal prejudices to save their school.

The Devil's Toenail by Sally Prue. New York: Scholastic, 2004.

Thirteen-year-old Stevie, covered with gasoline and set on fire at his old school, is determined to be accepted by the cool boys, a group of vandals and rogues. On a beach trip, Stevie finds a shellfish fossil that gives him the power to do the cruel things the gang leader, Daniel, asks him to do.

Indigo's Star by Hilary McKay. New York: Simon & Schuster, 2004.

Indigo is bullied at school; however, when a new boy enrolls, school bullies refocus their cruelty. Indigo stands up for himself and the boy who falls prey to their cruelty. This is one of five titles in the Casson Family series.

Inventing Elliot by Graham Gardner. New York: Penguin, 2004.

Fourteen-year-old Elliot, bullied at his former school, convinces himself he can start over at Holminster, his new high school; however, a school clique that terrorizes students at the school wants him to join.

Kissing the Rain by Kevin Brooks. New York: Scholastic, 2004.

Overweight, shy, and bullied by cruel classmates, 15-year-old Moo Nelson finds solace on a secluded bridge above a highway, where he witnesses a murder. The police, lawyers, the community, and even the cruel kids become interested in Moo.

Pretty Little Devils by Nancy Holder. New York: Razorbill/Penguin, 2006.

Hazel longs to be popular and envies the four-girl clique, the Pretty Little Devils. When she is invited

Continued

Box 4.7   Adolescent Cruelty   *Continued*

by the group's leader to become a member, she learns the group isn't what it seems.

Ricochet by Julie Gonzalez. New York: Delacorte/Random House, 2007.

Will bullies 15-year-old Conner into playing a game of Russian roulette. When Will turns the gun on Conner's friend, killing him, Connor must struggle with his role in his friend's death.

The Ruling Class by Francine Pascal. New York: Simon & Schuster, 2004.

In a wealthy suburban Dallas high school, a new girl seeks revenge on a popular and cruel clique. Realistic depiction of power games, manipulation, and peer struggles.

Schooled by Gordon Korman. New York: Scholastic, 2007.

Cap, an orphan, has lived his entire life with his grandmother in a community that shelters its people from the outside world. When his grandmother breaks her hip, Cap is forced to live with Mrs. Donnelly, a former community resident. He is, however, required to attend public school. Having been homeschooled, he is the "odd kid out" and struggles to find his way.

The Shadow Club by Neal Shusterman. New York: Speak/Penguin, 1988.

A group of boys who always come in second best establish a club for second-best kids. The mean-spirited pranks they play on their rivals escalate out of control.

The Shadow Club Rising by Neal Shusterman. New York: Dutton/Penguin, 2002.

In this sequel to *The Shadow Club,* 14-year-old Jared and his ex-club members are prime suspects when

pranks are played on a new kid, Alec Smaartz. Jared struggles to shake his bad reputation and prove his innocence, but consequences follow.

Shattering Glass by Gail Giles. New Milford, CT: Roaring Brook Press, 2002.

Popular, charismatic Rob sets out to turn nerdy Simon Glass into Prince Charming, but the plan has tragic consequences.

Sleep Rough Tonight by Ian Bone. New York: Penguin, 2005.

Alex is the class clown and a perfect target for bullies but is never afraid until the Jockey, an older boy that Alex betrayed to the police, returns from juvenile detention. The Jockey wants to rekindle a friendship with Alex and convinces Alex to "sleep rough" one night on the violent city streets. Alex accepts the challenge but learns the Jockey wants revenge.

Stargirl by Jerry Spinelli. New York: Knopf/Random House, 2000.

Stargirl, a new student at Mica High, stands out. She wears weird clothes, plays a ukulele in the school cafeteria, and brings a pet rat to school. Stargirl's originality makes her popular at first, but then a series of events turn students against her. Leo falls for her and convinces her to conform, but is that enough to save her from the cruelty? Fans will enjoy *Love, Stargirl* (2007).

The Tulip Touch by Anne Fine. New York: Little, Brown, 1997.

Natalie develops a dangerous relationship with Tulip, a farm girl who is abused by her father. Tulip is dishonest and manipulative, and Natalie is forced to make choices about their relationship.

Family Problems

Family issues have an interesting place in realistic problem novels. Teens are by nature pulling away from their parents, but they need their parents to be solid so they have something to push away *from*. Many family units break down, and teens are left to struggle through their adolescent years without guidance. Divorce, mental and physical illness, disabilities, death, child abuse, abandonment, and substance abuse place pressure on family relations, but relationships between teens and parents also can be strained by emotionally distant parents, absent parents, or parents with controlling behaviors. As mentioned earlier, teens in the most perfect appearing families can struggle from pressure to perform or to please their parents.

A rocky family relationship can be the catalyst for a very tough book because early family relationships are crucial to child development. Shaky family relationships set up problems later played out in all other teen relationships, including, and maybe most significantly, the relationship with self. The relationship teens have with their families can be their greatest strength or the cause of their most injurious wounds. Teens who do not feel emotionally connected to their parents engage in self-destructive behaviors; they look for that connection elsewhere, sometimes in gangs or sexual relationships, sometimes with drugs and/or alcohol. Girls may fall into depression, engage in self-mutilation, develop eating disorders, or engage in promiscuous sex to prove themselves or to find love. Boys are more likely to exhibit rage by engaging in violent acts and crime.

The young adult market is saturated with books—some great, others bad, and many in-between—that cover a wide range of family problems. One compelling 2006 title is Jennifer L. Holm's *Penny from Heaven*, a Newbery Honor book. Penny spends her summer moving back and forth between her mother's WASP family and her deceased father's Italian one. Penny wants to know about her father's death, but no one talks about him. A nearly devastating event leads to answers. Rich in period detail of the 1950s and loaded with offbeat characters, Holm's award-winning title speaks to the fragility of adolescence and the connection teens need with family. A second exceptional read is *Freaky Green Eyes* (2003) by Joyce Carol Oates. Franky Pierson's father is a former football star and current sportscaster who charms everyone around him, including his daughter. At home he is a controlling and abusive husband; Franky's mother, desperate to break free, moves out, leaving Franky and her younger sister feeling deserted and angry. When Franky's mother disappears for good, Franky faces some hard questions about her father and his possible role in her mother's disappearance. Box 4.8 features both old and new books that deal with family issues. These books give realistic and accurate portrayals of a variety of family dynamics. Some end with hope; others have dark, but real endings. Many mix humor with tragedy.

Box 4.8   Family Problems

***Al Capone Does My Shirts* by Gennifer Choldenko. New York: Putnam, 2004.**

Moose and his family move to Alcatraz Island in 1935, where his father is a prison guard, and Moose has to adjust to his unusual lifestyle and help out with his autistic sister.

***All Rivers Flow to the Sea* by Alison McGhee. Cambridge, MA: Candlewick Press, 2005.**

A car accident in the Adirondacks leaves Rose's sister, Ivy, brain dead. Rose, who was with her sister during the accident, struggles with her grief and guilt, and her mother refuses to admit Ivy will not get better. Rose turns to sex, desperate to feel something.

***Belle Prater's Boy* by Ruth White. New York: Farrar, Straus & Giroux, 1996.**

When Woodrow's mother mysteriously disappears, he goes to live with his cousin, Gypsy, and the two become close friends. Both struggle with family loss (Gypsy's father committed suicide). Set in the coal mining region of Virginia.

***Bottled Up* by Jaye Murray. New York: Penguin, 2003.**

Forced to attend counseling sessions, Pip must come to terms with his own drug addiction, as well as his father's violent alcoholic rages and his mother's neglect.

***Claws* by Will Weaver. New York: HarperTempest, 2003.**

Jed and Laura are two popular high school students whose lives are disrupted when they discover that Jed's father is having an affair with Laura's mother.

***Grace above All* by Jane St. Anthony. New York: Farrar, Straus & Giroux, 2007.**

Thirteen-year-old Grace spends the summer with her four siblings and mother at a lake cabin. Her mother is emotionally absent, forcing Grace to play the caregiver role for her siblings. A near-tragic accident and new friends give Grace the help she needs to stand up for herself.

***Indigo Blue* by Cathy Cassidy. New York: Penguin, 2005.**

Indigo, her mother, and baby sister move out of their comfortable apartment because of Mum's abusive boyfriend. The change is drastic: the new neighborhood is bad, the heat does not work, and there is no money for food. Indigo, already having friendship troubles, tries to keep her new life a secret.

***My Heartbeat* by Garret Freymann-Weyr. Boston: Houghton Mifflin, 2002.**

Ellen's brother, Link, and his best friend, James, are close, so much so that when they're teased for being a "couple" Ellen begins questioning whether both are gay. Ironically, Ellen is in love with James. James admits he may be gay, but he is not certain; Link breaks off the relationship under pressure from his father. As a relationship develops between Ellen and James, Ellen is aware that Link is falling apart.

***Olive's Ocean* by Kevin Henkes. New York: Greenwillow/HarperCollins, 2003.**

Martha spends one summer by the ocean with her grandmother, where she reflects on her desire to become a writer, deals with the death of a classmate, falls for an older boy, and comes to know her grandmother. A poignant coming-of-age story.

Continued

Box 4.8   Family Problems *Continued*

The One Left Behind by Willo Davis Roberts. New York: Atheneum/Simon & Schuster, 2006.

Mandy works through her grief and guilt over the death of her twin sister who died of *E. coli* poisoning.

One Whole and Perfect Day by Judith Clarke. Asheville, NC: Front Street, 2007.

Sixteen-year-old Lily lives with an eccentric, annoying family. As they plan for her grandfather's 80th birthday, she hopes for a perfect family day.

The Other Half of Me by Emily Franklin. New York: Delacorte/Random House, 2007.

Jenny is an outsider to her sports-obsessed family and doesn't know her biological father. Feeling alienated, she seeks comfort in painting. A new friend helps her search a donor sibling registry, and Jenny learns she has a half-sister. Jenny hopes she can build a relationship with Alexa.

The Same Stuff as Stars by Katherine Paterson. New York: Clarion Books, 2002.

Angel's father is in prison and her mother is a drunk. Abandoned by her mother, Angel lives with her great-grandmother and her younger brother. A strange man who lives in a broken-down trailer gives her hope.

Saving Francesca by Melina Marchetta. New York: Knopf/Random House, 2004.

Francesca's mother sends Francesca, against her wishes, to an all-boys' school that has started accepting girls. The year is a transitional one for Francesca: making new friends, getting along in an environment that does not accommodate girls, and dealing with a mother who falls into deep depression take their toll on her.

Scrambled Eggs at Midnight by Brad Barkley and Heather Hepler. New York: Penguin, 2006.

Cal and her mother travel across the country, sleeping in tents and owning nothing. When Cal meets Eliot, they develop an immediate connection, for both teens long for roots and stability. Eliot longs for the life he had before his obsessive father opened a religious camp for overweight teens; Cal wishes just to be normal.

Shadow of a Doubt by S. L. Rottman. Atlanta: Peachtree, 2003.

Fifteen-year-old Shadow has a lot on his mind—developing new friendships, making the forensics team, and coping with his runaway older brother who faces murder charges.

Summer's End by Audrey Couloumbis. New York: Putnam, 2005.

Three teenage cousins spend the summer on their grandparents' farm. The family is torn apart over the Vietnam conflict. Dolly's brother is in Vietnam; Theo's brother is a deserter; and Grace's brother has been disowned by his father because he does not believe in the war.

Touching Snow by M. Sindy Felin. New York: Atheneum/Simon & Schuster, 2007.

When Karina's stepfather is arrested for child abuse, her family begins to heal. New tensions arise when her family and a friend urge her to testify against him.

Undercover by Beth Kephart. New York: HarperCollins, 2007.

Elisa ghostwrites love letters for the boys in her school. Her letters—to pretty and popular girls—remind her

Continued

Box 4.8   Family Problems   *Continued*

she is neither. When her father leaves on an "extended" business trip, Elisa fears he won't return home.

Up Country by Alden Carter. New York: Putnam, 1989.

Carl wants to escape his alcoholic mother and her long list of boyfriends, so he fixes stolen car stereos to resell. Before he can save enough money to run away, his mother loses control and Carl is sent to live with distant relatives. Carl must decide to stay or set out on his own.

Vandal by Michael Simmons. New Milford, CT: Roaring Brook Press, 2006.

Younger brother Will, a gifted guitarist, is abused by his older brother Jason, who has spent time in a juvenile detention center. A tragic family accident involving Jason forces Will to examine his feelings for his brother.

The Whole Sky Full of Stars by René Saldaña Jr. New York: Delacorte/Random House, 2007.

Barry Esquivel must assume the role of the man in the family following his father's death. In an attempt to help his mother financially, he agrees to enter a shady boxing match.

You Don't Know Me by David Klass. New York: Farrar, Straus & Giroux, 2001.

John's life at school is like most boys'—he has friends and obsesses over a pretty girl. At home, he is abused by his mother's boyfriend. One of the most memorable voices in YA literature.

Mind, Body, and Spirit

Issues related to mental, physical, and spiritual, health are intertwined. Individuals born with disabilities or disease or injured in accidents struggle with emotional baggage, and individuals who are emotionally disturbed or imbalanced sometimes have physical limitations. Cynthia Voigt's *Izzy, Willy-Nilly* (1986) is a classic example. Fifteen-year-old Izzy has everything; she is rich, beautiful, popular, and the only sophomore cheerleader on her school's squad. When Izzy loses a leg in a car accident, she must build a new life.

A plethora of young adult literature features teens struggling with mental illness such as attention deficit disorder (ADD), bipolar disorder, depression, anxiety, mental retardation, and autism, or with physical limitations, including missing limbs, paralysis, blindness, and speech disorders. In Cynthia Lord's *Rules* (2006), a John Newbery Honor book, 12-year-old Catherine has an autistic brother and yearns for a normal life. Sometimes she's frustrated because David seems to dominate the family; other times she feels embarrassed by his presence. A new friendship with a boy who uses a wheelchair at David's clinic helps her work through her feelings about her family.

Stories of this nature serve two purposes: (1) they provide characters with whom teens with disabilities can identify, helping them understand that they are not alone, and (2) well-written, accurate stories help healthy teens understand teens who are disabled or sick and help all teens realize that other teens face similar obstacles. Teens with disabilities are frequent targets of bullies, and many teens live in homes with siblings, parents, or other family members who are disabled. These teens in some way feel responsible for their loved ones. Charlie Price's *Lizard People* (2007) is an honest portrayal of two young teens who meet in a psychiatric hospital, where both of their mothers are patients. When Marco tells Ben he isn't "from here," Ben's idea of reality is turned on its head, causing Ben to question his own sanity. Literature can provide a forum for conversations about how to treat those with differences and how to deal with the emotional and physical toll caused by disabilities.

Seventeen-year-old Pete Hautman rented a house in South Minneapolis. He is pictured here with his parents.

While there was a time when most teens accepted the religious beliefs of their parents, the unrest of the 1960s changed the way young people viewed authority. Add to that change the fact that today's teens are not as segregated as in the past: teens from all faiths sit together in classrooms, work together, and play sports together. They learn each other's customs and beliefs and do what all of us do with new information—they try to make sense of it. The results are religious or spiritual tension, for in juxtaposing our own family beliefs with those of others we start asking questions about what makes sense, what is right, and what is wrong. Given the pluralistic nature of today's world, this kind of questioning is inevitable. In *Godless* (2004), a National Book Award winner, Pete Hautman depicts how teens might play out religious and spiritual tensions with their friends. In "The Elusive Edge," Hautman (2005) describes how *Godless* grew out of his own diverse experiences as a teen:

> One summer day in 1967, I was hanging out with some friends beneath the local water tower. We were bored, of course, and our boredom led us to debate our respective religions. I was raised Catholic. My two friends were Jewish and Lutheran. Our discussion, as I recall it, was something of an irreverence competition, with each of us making the case for our own religion being the quirkiest. I argued that Catholicism was the most bizarre—church every Sunday, no meat on Friday, rosaries, holy water . . . *nuns.* My Jewish friend argued that matzah bread, lox, yarmulkes, and Hebrew school made his people the strangest of all. My Lutheran friend, a preacher's kid, had his stories from *Bible* camp and sang us a verse from "Onward Christian Soldiers."

> We decided, after some discussion, that the thing to do was bag our old religions and make up one of our own. But what to worship? We looked up at the belly of the million-gallon tank sixty feet above our heads. Our choice was clear.
>
> We stole bits and pieces from the great religions of the world. We wrote our own ten commandments, we bowed to the ten-legged one three times a day, and we provided functions for all the lesser gods—the svelte, single-stalked Edina water tower was our female deity, the scary-looking thirteen-legged Golden Valley water tower was our war god, and so forth. (p. 39)

A common religious theme in teen problem novels is the struggle between the adolescent and the "preacher father," usually a harsh, mean-spirited, and controlling figure. John Ritter's *Choosing Up Sides* (1998) opens with the classic line, "I grew up with one hand tied behind my back." Believing that being left-handed is the work of the devil, Luke Bledsoe's father, a fundamentalist preacher, ties Luke's hand behind his back as a small child, hoping to make him right-handed. Problems arise when Luke discovers he is a talented southpaw pitcher. Seventeen-year-old Lucy Peale's father is a fanatical fundamentalist preacher in Colby Rodowsky's *Lucy Peale* (1992). When Lucy becomes pregnant after being raped, her father insists that she confess to being a jezebel before the congregation. Lucy runs away instead. Han Nolan brilliantly portrays the struggle between fundamentalist father and daughter in *Send Me Down a Miracle* (1996). Charity Pittman befriends Adrienne Dabney, a New York artist who moves to Charity's small-town fundamentalist community in Alabama, but Charity's preacher father is suspicious of her eccentric ways, believing she is evil incarnate.

As society becomes increasingly diverse, more teens find themselves living in homes with parents of different religious faiths. In Ilene Cooper's *Sam I Am* (2004), Sam Goodman's mother is Christian, his father Jewish. Tension arises during the holidays, and Sam turns to God with his questions about faith. Sometimes parents feel challenged when their children question their religious beliefs, and power struggles result. When 17-year-old Mitch, the protagonist in *Singing Mountain* (1998) by Sonia Levitin, traveling one summer in Israel, chooses to pursue a Jewish Orthodox life, his California family is horrified. In *Walking on Air* (2004), Kelly Easton portrays the life of a traveling religious family. Twelve-year-old June is a tightrope walker who performs in her preacher father's carnival-like revival shows. June examines the lives of people around her and questions the life she might have.

Religious tension does not just occur when teens compare their faith with the faith of others. Sometimes teens whose religious experiences are different from their peers feel displaced. In *Full Service* (2005) by Will Weaver, Paul Sutton's family is a member of a closely knit rural religious community. His mother, believing Paul needs to break out from his sheltered life and meet the "public," pushes him to take a summer job in town, where he loses much of his innocence.

A discussion of teens exploring their spiritual identities is not complete without addressing the issue of religious worthiness. In Cynthia Rylant's *A Fine White Dust* (1986), Peter Cassidy has deep religious convictions and yearns for religious fulfillment. When Preacher Man comes to town, Peter gets caught up in religious fervor and must decide whether to follow Preacher Man or stay with his family. Archie, in Han Nolan's *When We Were Saints* (2003), feels responsible for his grandfather's death. When Archie hooks up with Claire shortly after his grandfather calls him a saint on his deathbed, Archie, feeling responsible for his grandfather's death, goes to extremes to *become* a saint, depriving himself of food and clothing and spending hours meditating.

Fanaticism is yet another theme running through problem novels and a timely one. In Judy Waite's *Forbidden* (2006), Elinor, brainwashed, lives in a cult. A friendship with an outsider to the True Cause provokes memories of her past life. Waite's work is a superb look at the inner workings of cults, brainwashing, and sexual abuse. In James Bennett's *Faith Wish* (2003), Anne-Marie is drawn to a cultlike Christian group and becomes attracted to its leader. When she becomes pregnant, she runs away. A lonely new girl is drawn into an evangelical Christian club, then disillusioned by its cultishness in Margaret Haddix's *Leaving Fishers* (1997). In *Armageddon Summer* (1998) by Jane Yolen and Bruce Coville, 14-year-old Marina and 16-year-old Jed accompany their parents' religious cult, the Believers, to await the end of the world atop a remote mountain, where they try to decide what they themselves believe in. Teens are spiritually curious, and the relationship they have with their families determines how well they move through spiritual development. Books such as these shed light on religious fanaticism and remind us of the power of manipulation and mind control.

The line between what is real and what is not becomes blurred when writers explore the issue of life after death. A number of young adult novels published from the late 1990s until now feature dead narrators exploring their past identities. The term *magical realism,* literature in which magical elements appear in otherwise realistic fiction, can be applied to these works. Of course, the problem with this definition is that calling religion and faith "magical" raises eyebrows.

After being murdered, Chuy observes the lives of his friends and family as a ghost in Gary Soto's *The Afterlife* (2003), and in *Elsewhere* (2005), Gabrielle Zevin addresses the questions, "Where do you go?" "What happens when you die?" Fifteen-year-old Miah, shot and killed, tries to make sense of his life in the afterlife, where he watches over all those whom he loves in Jacqueline Woodson's *Behind You* (2004). Frank, a teenage ghost unable to move on to a higher realm in the afterlife, tries to connect with his younger brother Herbie, a high school senior who was eight when Frank died in *Restless: A Ghost's Story* (2003) by Rich Wallace. Told in chapters with alternating voices, Adele Griffin's *Where I Want to Be* (2005) explores the relationship between two sisters: one living, the other in the afterlife. Although these books do not fit neatly within the lines of realistic fiction, they do treat the issue of life after death in an honest, plausible manner.

Books in Box 4.9 address mental and physical disabilities and present diverse perspectives about religion, death, and the afterlife.

Box 4.9   Mind, Body, and Spirit

Aimee by Mary Beth Miller. New York: Penguin, 2002.

Accused of helping her friend commit suicide, 17-year-old Zoe suffers loneliness and guilt and falls into depression.

America by E. R. Frank. New York: Simon & Schuster, 2002.

America, a boy who is emotionally disturbed, abused, and neglected, has spent years in mental institutions for antisocial behavior. America unveils his life story through conversations with a therapist.

The Beast by Walter Dean Myers. New York: Scholastic, 2003.

Having spent some time in an elite New York prep school, Spoon returns to his home in Harlem, only to discover his girlfriend has become a drug addict. He longs for his prep school friends and struggles with his feelings for his girlfriend.

Behind You by Jacqueline Woodson. New York: Putnam, 2004.

The police accidentally kill 15-year-old Jeremiah. As loved ones mourn his loss, they are unaware that he is watching them.

Blind Faith by Ellen Wittlinger. New York: Simon & Schuster, 2006.

Liz's mother spirals into depression after the death of Liz's grandmother and becomes fascinated with a church whose minister claims to communicate with the dead. Liz's father, an atheist, is driven away, and Liz turns to a new neighbor, Nathan, who is dealing with his own mother's terminal illness. Together they cope with their losses.

Blood Brothers by S. A. Harazin. New York: Delacorte/Random House, 2007.

Seventeen-year-old Clay works hard at the hospital, hoping one day to become a doctor. He wishes his life could be more like that of his best friend Joey, who seems to have everything—a great family, a future in a good college, and money. When a drug overdose lands Joey in the hospital where Clay works, Clay may be partly responsible.

Confessions of a Closet Catholic by Sarah Littman. New York: Dutton/Penguin, 2005.

Wanting to be like her best friend, Justine, a Jewish girl, converts to Catholicism, but when her grandmother passes away she rethinks her decision.

Crank by Ellen Hopkins. New York: Simon & Schuster, 2004.

On a trip to visit her father, 17-year-old Kristina Snow gets turned on to crank and cannot stop once she returns home. Once home the drug takes over, sending her spiraling into a black hole. Brilliant poetry. Horrific but powerful images.

Damage by A. M. Jenkins. New York: HarperCollins, 2001.

Suicidal and depressed, Austin Reid, a high school football star, is afraid to let anyone know how he feels. A realistic depiction of adolescent depression.

Dark Sons by Nikki Grimes. New York: Hyperion, 2005.

A unique novel that uses biblical references and a reflection on faith and father-son relationships.

Defiance by Valerie Hobbs. New York: Farrar, Straus & Giroux, 2005.

Not wanting to return to the cancer hospital, 11-year-old Toby keeps the new lump on his side a secret. He develops an unlikely relationship with an elderly lady who helps him discover meaning in life.

Continued

Box 4.9   Mind, Body, and Spirit   *Continued*

Evolution, Me and Other Freaks of Nature by Robin Brande. New York: Knopf/Random House, 2007.

Mena is kicked out of her church group for blowing the whistle on an attempt to "reform" a gay schoolmate. She distances herself further by befriending a classmate with an unconventional family and getting caught up in a class unit on evolution.

Feathers by Jacqueline Woodson. New York: Putnam/Penguin, 2007.

When a new white boy enrolls in Frannie's all-black school, everyone wonders why he doesn't attend the white school across the road. Frannie's friends start calling him "the Jesus boy" and begin wondering if he could be the savior.

Freak the Mighty by Rodman Philbrick. New York: Blue Sky Press, 1993.

Maxwell Kaner, who is overweight and has a learning disability, develops a friendship with Kevin, who is small, smart, and who has a physical disability. Together they take on the world. As Kevin's illness progresses, Maxwell faces the loss of a best friend.

Hard Hit by Ann Turner. New York: Scholastic, 2006.

Mark is the best baseball pitcher on his team and leads a good life; however, when his father is diagnosed with cancer, Mark's world is shattered. Written in verse, the story traces a young man's emotional journey through loss.

Helicopter Man by Elizabeth Fensham. New York: Bloomsbury, 2005.

Peter Sinclair's mother takes off, leaving 15-year-old Peter and his schizophrenic father to fend for themselves. Peter refuses to leave his father, and the two live an almost homeless existence, sleeping in sheds

and eating in soup kitchens. A powerful story of family loyalty.

In the Name of God by Paula Jolin. New Milford, CT: Roaring Brook Press, 2007.

A believer in the Qur'an, 17-year-old Nadia gets caught up in a violent movement that supports Muslim rule in Syria and opposes the Western world.

Life of Pi by Yann Martel. Orlando, FL: Harcourt, 2002.

The soul survivor of a shipwreck, Pi drifts in a lifeboat and mediates on religion, faith, and life. A spiritual adventure about the meaning of life.

Lizard People by Charlie Price. New Milford, CT: Roaring Brook Press, 2007.

Ben alone must care for his mentally ill mother who is admitted to a psychiatric hospital. He finds a friend in Marco, another teen whose mother has been admitted. When Marco begins talking about time travel to the year 4000 in which he claims to have learned a cure for mental illness, Ben begins questioning his own sanity.

Long Gone Daddy by Helen Hemphill. Asheville, NC: Front Street/Boyds Mills Press, 2006.

Harlan Stank has run away from his Bible-thumping preacher father to live with his grandfather. The death of Harlan's grandfather means Harlan has to reconnect with his father. Together, they take a road trip to collect the family inheritance.

Many Stones by Carolyn Coman. Asheville, NC: Boyds Mills Press, 2000.

Laura's sister is murdered in South Africa, and Laura and her father travel there to participate in

Continued

Box 4.9   Mind, Body, and Spirit   *Continued*

her sister's memorial. Once there, they move past their own grieving when they experience a country in turmoil.

Mercy, Unbound by Kim Antieau. New York: Simon Pulse/Simon & Schuster, 2006.

Mercy believes she is becoming an angel and does not need to eat; her parents believe she has a eating disorder and send her to a clinic.

Never Mind the Goldbergs by Matthue Roth. New York: Push/Scholastic, 2005.

Hava Aaronson, an Orthodox punk-rock Jew, leaves her New York community to star in a TV sitcom in Hollywood, where she struggles with her cultural identity.

Never So Green by Tim Johnston. New York: Farrar, Straus & Giroux, 2002.

Twelve-year-old Tex, born with a deformed hand, finds the courage to take baseball lessons from his new stepsister Jack and his stepfather. His life is brighter until he discovers dark family secrets.

Reaching for Sun by Tracie Vaughn Zimmer. New York: Bloomsbury, 2007.

Seventh-grader Josie has cerebral palsy and struggles with social isolation and a distant mother. Her life changes when she meets a new neighbor. Jordan, a science nerd, elicits Josie's help in conducting science experiments.

RX by Tracy Lynn. New York: SimonPulse/ Simon & Schuster, 2006.

Thyme becomes hooked on prescription drugs. To support her habit she steals from her friends' parents and sells to her peers. A timely issue.

The Silent Boy by Lois Lowry. Boston: Houghton Mifflin, 2003.

Katy Thatcher, daughter of the town doctor, develops a friendship with Jacob, a retarded boy.

Silent to the Bone by E. L. Konigsburg. New York: Simon & Schuster, 2004.

Branwell Zamborska stops speaking once he is accused of seriously injuring his infant sister Nikki.

Smack by Melvin Burgess. New York: Henry Holt, 1998.

Two runaway English teens search for ways of supporting their growing heroin addiction. A realistic, gritty depiction of the insidious nature of heroin addiction and the drug-dealing, prostitution world accompanying it.

Stained by Jennifer Richard Jacobson. New York: Atheneum/Simon & Schuster, 2005.

A multilayered story about teen sexuality, faith, abuse, betrayal, and belonging. Joss cares for two boys, both of whom have mysterious connections with the local priest, one of whom disappears.

Stoner & Spaz by Ron Koertge. Cambridge, MA: Candlewick Press, 2002.

A young boy with cerebal palsy and a young woman with a drug addition grow through an unlikely friendship.

Strange Relations by Sonia Levitin. New York: Knopf/Random House, 2007.

Fifteen-year-old Marne looks forward to spending the summer in Hawaii with her relatives. Still dealing with her younger sister's disappearance years earlier, Marne hopes to spend her days relaxing on the beach. She's not prepared for her Hasidic rabbi uncle, his wife, and a crowded home filled with children and visiting members of their Jewish community.

Stuck in Neutral by Terry Trueman. New York: HarperCollins, 2000.

Fourteen-year-old Shawn has cerebral palsy. Unbeknownst to his family, he is cognizant and keenly

Continued

Box 4.9   Mind, Body, and Spirit   *Continued*

aware of his surroundings. In a conversational tone, Shawn relates the events around him and his father's fascination with euthanasia.

Sweetblood by Pete Hautman. New York: Simon & Schuster, 2003.

Sixteen-year-old Lucy Szabo, a perfect student, joins an Internet chat room frequented by "vampires." Draco, a boy she agrees to meet, claims to be a real vampire. As she becomes more involved in the goth culture, her grades plummet, her relationship with her parents becomes strained, and her health falters.

Total Constant Order by Crissa-Jean Chappell. New York: HarperCollins, 2007.

Fin hears numbers in her head and can't stop counting. When she is diagnosed with depression and obsessive compulsive disorder, she begins taking medication that makes her worse.

Trigger by Susan Vaught. New York: Bloomsbury, 2006.

To those who knew him, Jersey had everything—looks, personality, athletic prowess—until the day he put a gun to his head. After a year in a rehabilitation center, Jersey returns home to find a depressed mother, stressed father, and former friends who feel he betrayed them. Jersey must deal with permanent brain damage and the effects his attempted suicide had on those around him.

The Very Ordered Existence of Merilee Marvelous by Suzanne Crowley. New York: Greenwillow/HarperCollins, 2007.

A well-crafted depiction of a young girl with Asperger's syndrome. Thirteen-year-old Marilee craves order but dislikes being touched. When young Biswick, a young boy with fetal alcohol syndrome, arrives in Marilee's small town, Marilee takes to him.

Where I Want to Be by Adele Griffin. New York: Penguin Putnam, 2005.

When tragedy claims the life of her sister, Jane, Lily tries to make sense of her loss. Chapters alternate between the two sisters' voices: one living, the other dead. Supernatural elements.

Making Connections with Realistic Fiction

Instructional strategies in this text are grounded in reader-response theory. Unlike other literary theories (see Table 4.2 for popular literary theories), reader-response theory does not describe or explain one particular critical theory but rather focuses on the *process* of reading a text. Unlike New Criticism theorists, who assert the meaning of the text resides in the words and structures of the text alone, reader-response theorists such as Louise Rosenblatt, Alan Purves, Richard Beach, and Robert Probst argue that the meaning of the text is *created* by the reader. While reader-response theorists differ in where they draw the line between what is subjective (experiences the reader brings to the text) and objective (information found in the written text), and take different stances on what constraints a text places on a reader, their underlying premise is the same: meaning doesn't reside solely in the text (Abrams, 2005).

Table 4.2

Popular Literary Theories

Historical Criticism	Focuses on the qualities of the language of literature relative to historical, social, economic, and cultural developments. Works are examined in light of what they reflect of a period.
New Criticism	Meaning of the text is seen to reside in the words and structures of the text alone. Personal experiences are "divorced" from meaning.
Feminism and Gender Studies	Concerned with the socially and culturally situated nature and function of women (and men) in the world as represented in literature. Focuses on how women (and men) write and read literary texts, how and why women resist male-gendered texts, and how they view traditional roles of women as a result of exploitation.
Marxism	Concerned with the relationship between literature and society. This theory situates texts politically and historically.
Gay and Lesbian Studies and Queer Theory	Concerned with the socially and culturally situated nature and function of gays and lesbians in the world as represented in literature. Focuses on how gays and lesbians write and read literary texts and how they view traditional gender roles.
Cultural Studies	Concerned with the socially and culturally situated nature and function of various cultural groups (e.g., blacks, Hispanics, Native Americans) in the world as represented in literature. Focuses on how these groups write and read literary texts, how they "resist" texts outside their culture, and how they view their traditional and often stereotypical roles.

Because reader-response is a theory about process, every analysis of a text, whether created from a Marxist perspective, feminist position, or New Criticism viewpoint, is a reader-response analysis. The reader, regardless of theoretical stance, creates the meaning based on his/her life experiences. A reader may read a text from a feminist perspective, but he/she creates the response.

Louise Rosenblatt's *Literature as Exploration* (1938) is often cited as the inaugural text in reader-response theory (Clifford, 1991), and her transactional view of reading is among the reader-response theories best known to English language arts teachers. Rosenblatt's work emphasizes the reader's experiences in text interpretation and asserts that readers construct a "personal text" as they read. Popularized in Rosenblatt's *The Reader, the Text, the Poem* (1978), the following key terms are helpful in understanding her transactional view of reading:

The Reader—the individual seeking to understand, or make meaning, by transacting (actively reading) a text (any kind of text—poem, short story, etc.).

The Text—the physical material being read. Rosenblatt refers to this material as word patterns and symbols.

The Poem—the "literary work" created in the reader's imagination when the reader transacts with the text. Her use of the word *poem* refers to any literary text—whether short story, play, poem, or novel—the reader creates as a result of having read the material.

As Rosenblatt asserts, the meaning we create is influenced by our prior experiences and our knowledge of the world. What we experience, both positive and negative, with our families, our friends, in our communities and travels, and what we witness in the media and in news headlines shape our perceptions of ourselves and our world *and* our perceptions of our reading. Our personal experiences help us construct meaning. Thus, when readers transact with the text, they create their own individual poem.

Realistic fiction is a "slice of life" or a "slice of experiences" from the world of today's teens. Teens may vary in their experiences, but none are excluded from coming-of-age issues; therefore, all can identify with characters in realistic fiction either directly or indirectly. Realistic fiction is a perfect tool for helping teens claim their own stories. It can help them explore and extend their connections with themselves, others, the world, and literature. Many activities can help teens make real-world connections with their reading, and these ideas are discussed next.

Opinion Surveys and Anticipation Guides

Walk into most any traditional reading or literature classroom and chances are you will witness the teacher preparing students to read a story by "telling" students something about the story or by introducing them to vocabulary words they will encounter in their reading. Although these techniques may provide background information for understanding the reading, they do not encourage meaningful text connections. Milner and Milner (2003) have found opinion surveys to be an effective means of engaging students in the text. They design several strong statements, taken from general observations or from an interpretation of the text, and ask students to respond to them. Easy to develop, these statements elicit quick, direct responses and provide rich opportunities for exploring text (p. 116) and can be used at any point in reading, depending on the type of question. Table 4.3 presents a sample after-reading opinion survey that can be used with what many claim is Robert Cormier's greatest work, *I Am the Cheese* (1977).

Anticipation guides differ from surveys in that they are used prior to reading (Tierney, Readence, & Dishner, 1995). They activate meaningful prior knowledge, engage students in reading, and are relatively easy to construct. The teacher reads the text and composes several controversial

Table 4.3

After-Reading Opinion Survey for *I Am the Cheese* by Robert Cormier, 1977

Adam Farmer is a brave person.	_____ Yes	_____ No
We are all alone in the universe.	_____ Yes	_____ No
Sometimes it is okay to keep secrets from those whom we love.	_____ Yes	_____ No
Individuals are helpless when pitted against powerful organizations.	_____ Yes	_____ No
Cormier writes of his fear of institutions manipulating/controlling individuals. But in this story, he manipulates the reader.	_____ Yes	_____ No

questions/statements (with no right or wrong answer) related to the reading and asks students either individually or in groups to agree or disagree. Table 4.4 contains an anticipation guide for Paul Fleischman's *Whirligig* (1998), a story about appearances and one boy's struggles to fit in with his rich, suburbanite friends. Think about the questions on the study guide, then read the first chapter of *Whirligig;* you will see how discussion of the anticipation guide facilitates thoughtful connections. Practice developing anticipation guides for some of the books you read for this course.

Table 4.4

Anticipation Guide for *Whirligig* by Paul Fleischman, 1998

Directions: Write YES if you agree with each statement in the before-reading column. When you finish the story, revise your responses using the after-reading column.

Before Reading	After Reading	
_____	_____	1. It is important to fit in with the cool crowd.
_____	_____	2. One should wear the "right" clothes to school and on weekends.
_____	_____	3. It is cool to have more money than your friends.
_____	_____	4. Extensive knowledge about cool things (e.g., music and bands, cars, designer clothes) helps you fit in.
_____	_____	5. Getting yelled at by someone on whom you have a crush is your worst nightmare.

Meaningful Questioning

Later you will read about teaching students to question texts. For now, let's examine questions that encourage personal interactions with reading. Myers (1988) developed the 20 questions in Table 4.5 to encourage students to connect personally with their reading. Note that these questions can be used for any story or poem. You may use them for discussion starters, freewriting, journaling, test questions, role-playing, and any number of activities. Post them in your room, give students a copy for their journals, and keep a copy handy for yourself. Avoid requiring students to respond to a large number of questions at any one time. As you perfect your ability to lead class discussions (something that takes time), you will find that these questions come in handy.

Do not be surprised, however, if some male students, particularly more mature boys, do not respond well to opening questions that ask for an emotional response. Some, too, may play the teacher-student game—responding with a personal connection, but not being genuine. What appears to the teacher as an *authentic* response (based on the nature of the question) can be, in actuality, an *expected* one. Crowe (2004) describes the attitude many boys have to opening questions that require emotional expression:

> When you're talking about a novel in class, start the discussion with what happens in the story. Let us get to know the characters and then help us unpack and figure out the plot before you lead us into that subtle and abstract stuff like motivation and emotion. We're not going to care much about what a character thinks or feels unless we first care about what a character is and does. If you can get us into the story, there's a decent chance you'll also be able to get us to talk about all the stuff that makes that story, including the thoughts and feelings of a character. Even if the character is a girl. (p. 4)

Crowe's thoughts seem to contradict the idea of facilitating personal connections with texts, but if we recognize that our purpose in facilitating meaningful connections is to actively engage students in literature, we need only look for additional questioning strategies that may feel more genuine to boys, questions that help them connect with the plot and action first, and move to questions requiring emotional expression as our discussions unfold. Questions like "What happened in the story?" "What happened to the protagonist and why?" and "How would you have responded if you were the central character and why?" are better entry points for some male students because they focus more on action and behavior. Consider, too, questions (Peck, 1978) such as "What would this story be like if the main character were the opposite sex?" and "If you were to film this story, what characters would you eliminate if you couldn't use them all?" (they will talk about why they like or do not like certain characters).

On a final note, you will be tempted during your early teaching experiences to supply answers to your own questions when you fail to get an immediate response. There is nothing wrong with an awkward silence; questions requiring more than a yes or no answer take some thought.

Table 4.5

Myers's 20 Reader-Response Questions

1. What character(s) was your favorite? Why?

2. What character(s) did you dislike? Why?

3. Does anyone in this work remind you of anyone you know? Explain.

4. Are you like any character in this work? Explain.

5. If you could be any character in this work, who would you be? Explain.

6. What quality(ies) of which character strike you as a good characteristic to develop within yourself over the years? Why? How does the character demonstrate this quality?

7. Overall, what kind of feeling did you have after reading a few paragraphs of this work? Midway? After finishing the work?

8. Do any incidents, ideas, or actions in this work remind you of your own life or something that happened to you? Explain.

9. Do you like this piece of work? Why or why not?

10. Are there any parts of this work that were confusing to you? If so, which parts? Why do you think you got confused?

11. Do you feel there is an opinion expressed by the author through this work? What is it? How do you know this? Do you agree? Why or why not?

12. Do you think the title of this work is appropriate? Is it significant? Explain. What do you think the title means?

13. Would you change the ending of this story in any way? If so, tell your ending. Why would you change it?

14. What kind of person do you feel the author is? What makes you feel this way?

15. How did this work make you feel? Explain.

16. Do you share any of the feelings of the characters in this work? Explain.

17. Sometimes works leave you with a feeling that there is more to tell. Did this work do this? What do you think might happen?

18. Would you like to read something else by this author? Why or why not?

19. What do you feel is the most important word, phrase, passage, or paragraph in this work? Explain why it is important.

20. If you were an English teacher, would you want to share this work with your students? Why or why not?

Source: Adapted from Myers (1988), p. 65.

Journaling

Journaling is a powerful venue for personal meaning-making and reflection and provides students with an opportunity to practice reading and writing skills (e.g., summarizing, making inferences and predictions, questioning and clarifying, evaluating, and generalizing). The success of journaling depends on good teacher guidance in developing, nurturing, and monitoring good journaling skills. Teachers who expect all students to write with minimum guidance may be disappointed when student comments are shallow, or even shocking (inappropriate comments). Structured journal assignments with writing topics work best for inexperienced (or less skilled) students. Students, for example, may keep single-entry journals in which they respond to a reader-response or open-ended question (see Table 4.5); double-entry journals in which they identify a passage or event in one column and respond to it in the second; two-column dialogical journals in which pairs of students discuss their reading; or teacher-directed online discussion boards. As students gain expertise in journaling, teachers can gradually release control over topics, allowing students to take ownership over their responses. The key is to provide a scaffold for immature writers and to release control gradually as students perfect their craft. Don't forget that journals are often overused—too much of a good thing can cause burnout.

Likert Scales

Likert scales are a good way to frontload meaning as students prepare to read (Beers, 2002). They involve having students indicate levels of agreement or disagreement with a topic they will encounter in their reading. The success of Likert scales, like surveys and anticipation guides, rests in the teacher's ability to identify thought-provoking statements. If you are preparing a Likert scale for Karen Hesse's *Out of the Dust* (1997), for example, a statement like "The Great Depression of the 1930s caused widespread poverty in the United States" is a "duh" statement and would evoke little class discussion. Good statements are ambiguous; they have no right, wrong, or popular answer, as shown in these Likert scale statements for Paul Volponi's *Black and White* (2005):

1. Marcus did the right thing by covering for Eddie. There was no reason both boys should go to jail. Marcus was already caught.

   strongly disagree   disagree   agree   strongly agree

2. The tragedy that befalls Marcus and Eddie is caused by their arrogance. They should not have gotten uptight because they were the only boys on the team without Marauders. They were the stud players. Wanting the "right" shoe was just dumb.

   strongly disagree   disagree   agree   strongly agree

3.   The friendship between Marcus and Eddie was more important to
     Marcus than to Eddie.

     strongly disagree   disagree   agree   strongly agree

4.   Eddie could not have saved Marcus. He did the right thing by taking
     care of himself.

     strongly disagree   disagree   agree   strongly agree

5.   When we get on airplanes, the flight attendant reminds us in case of
     an emergency to put an oxygen mask on ourselves prior to helping
     anyone around us, including small children. Putting an oxygen mask
     on ourselves first is a good metaphor for how we should live our lives.

     strongly disagree   disagree   agree   strongly agree

Contrast Charts

Contrast charts can be used to frontload meaning (Yopp & Yopp, 2001). They
are easy to develop, requiring only that the teacher identify a major theme
and develop contrasting categories. For example, a story in which protagonists are the new kids in town such as Joan Bauer's *Hope Was Here* (2000) and
Chris Lynch's *The Gravedigger's Cottage* (2004) can be introduced with the following contrast chart:

Good Things about Moving	Bad Things about Moving
1.	1.
2.	2.
3.	3.
4.	4.
5.	5.

Spotlight on Quotations, Phrases, and Words

To help students make connections either during or after reading, have them
identify passages, phrases, or words to share with the larger group. Students
may choose their favorite passage or word, an important passage or word,
a defining moment, or an important event and explain why they chose it. I
ask students to write their ideas on index cards, along with the page number
and their name, and hand them in; then we discuss them in numerical order.
Students often hit upon the same passage, phrase, or word, and I encourage
them to discuss why that happened.

Give-One, Get-One

To comprehend a text, a reader must first call up and make connections
with prior knowledge about a subject. Kagan's Give-One, Get-One is a

collaborative way for adolescents to tap into and build prior knowledge about a subject (Kagan, as cited in Zwiers, 2004). Here are the steps involved in this activity.

1. The teacher generates a topic idea based on the text and writes it on the overhead or board. Possible topics for Rodman Philbrick's *Freak the Mighty* (1993) include:

   - What I know about disabilities
   - Characteristics of friendship
   - Examples of bravery
   - What it means to be smart
   - What it means to be a hero

2. Have students fold a sheet of paper in half and on one side write GIVE ONE at the top and on the other side write GET ONE.
3. Refer to the topic you wrote on the board and ask students to brainstorm ideas about that topic and list them on the GIVE ONE side.
4. Have students circulate around the room "giving one idea" and "getting one" in return. You may have students list the person's name beside the "get one" idea he/she trades.
5. After 10 minutes or so ask students to return to their seats and discuss the ideas that developed from the activity.
6. Introduce the reading selection.

CATAPULT into Literature

CATAPULT is a prereading activity that is useful in helping students survey their reading (Zwiers, 2004). The idea is to help struggling readers develop some sense of the text before reading by asking them to consider a series of questions. The steps in the activity follow:

Step	Questions to Consider
Covers, front and back	What does the cover tell us about the story (both words and images)?
Author	What is the author's background?
	Has he/she written similar works? Different?
	What information do we know about him/her that may help us in understanding this book?
Title	What does the title tell us about the story?
	What could the story be about?
Audience	For whom was this text written? Teens, children, adults, boys, girls? People with disabilities? A person with a particular philosophical or political belief? Someone who likes to cook? Someone else?

Page 1	Read page 1 and discuss what the story might be about.
Underlying message or purpose	With what we know so far, what might be the author's intent or purpose or message?
Look at visuals, maps, charts, sketches, and so forth	Skim through the text. What do the visuals, maps, and so forth tell us about the text?
Time, place, characters	What can we tell about when the story takes place and where?
	What can we tell about the characters and what may happen to them?

Freewrites/Quick Writes

One of the easiest methods for tapping prior knowledge and helping students make connections with text is to give students a question that relates to the material being read and ask them to write for five minutes about the topic—not worrying about grammar, complete sentences, or organization (e.g., *Describe a situation in which . . .*). You may provide the question, ask students to think about it for a minute, and then proceed to write. The idea is for them to brainstorm as much information as they can about the topic. This is an effective method because it encourages students to think deeply about a question. It's a good idea to provide students with a choice between at least two questions—some prompts land "flat" on everyone, so a second one provides some flexibility.

Seeing Is Believing

If we can visualize a concept as opposed to reading a definition, we have some sense of its meaning. (In Chapter 8 you will read about the role of visualization in the comprehension process and examine visualization strategies.) Before reading a text in which setting plays an important role (e.g., a gothic setting, as in Edgar Allan Poe's work, or a lagoon, as in Scott O'Dell's Newbery Honor book *The Black Pearl*, 1967), have students close their eyes and envision a setting that you describe. Use words from the text in your description. You might also put together a brief PowerPoint visual display comprised of gothic images, lagoons, and so forth and preview it before students begin reading.

Final Thoughts

Some teens struggling with personal issues (e.g., divorced parents, family alcoholism) may not want to read about their problems because the connection is too close, the experience too raw. If you put Cynthia Voigt's *Izzy, Willy-Nilly* (1986) in the hands of a young girl who has lost a limb, she is as likely as not to slam the book down on your desk and say she is not reading it. Leave it on your shelf; let her find it. It may be that other forms of realistic fiction (e.g., adventure) or other genres such as historical fiction, fantasy, or science fiction are better choices for her just now. Other genres can provide avenues through which she, and other teens, can explore important life issues, but not quite so up close and personal.

Teachers can sabotage the problem novel and turn teens off to reading if they approach the problem novel as though they are teaching moral lessons or if instructional strategies become more important than *experiencing* literature (true for all genres). Meaningful connections occur when responses are *authentic* as opposed to *expected*. Louise Rosenblatt (1976) captures this concept in her seminal work *Literature as Exploration,* in which she reminds us to examine our methods:

> . . . to be sure that we are not in actuality substituting other aims—things to do *about* literature—for the experience *of* literature. We can ask of every assignment or method or text, no matter what its short-term effectiveness: Does it get in the way of the live sense of literature? Does it make literature something to be regurgitated, analyzed, categorized, or is it a means toward making literature a more personally meaningful and self-discipline activity? (p. 273)

Finally, to teach realistic fiction successfully, it is essential that you, the teacher, read widely and passionately with an open mind—and remember that your own prior experiences determine your reactions to the story and affect the way you respond in the classroom. The more you learn about your own responses, the better able you will be to line your shelves with a range of topics and experiences that cross cultural, gender, and ability levels, ensuring that all teens have a chance to identify themselves—claim their own lives—and make connections with those around them.

Professional Resources

Allen, J. (Ed.). (2002). *Using literature to help troubled teenagers cope with end-of-life issues.* Westport, CT: Greenwood Press.

Bauer, J. (2003). Speech given at the IRA convention in Orlando, Florida. *SIGNAL Journal, 26*(1), 2–5.

Beach, R. (1993). *A teacher's introduction to reader-response theories.* Urbana, IL: NCTE.

Beck, K. (1998). I believe it, I doubt it: Young adult fiction for questioning Christians. *Voice of Youth Advocates, 21*(2), 103–104.

Berger, L. R. (1996). Reader response journal: You make the meaning . . . and how. *Journal of Adolescent and Adult Literacy, 39*(5), 380–385.

Bodart, J. R. (2002). *Radical reads: 101 YA novels on the edge.* Lanham, MD: Scarecrow Press.

Bott, C. J. (2006). Why we must read young adult books that deal with sexual content. *The ALAN Review, 33*(3), 26–29.

Bowman, C. A. (Ed.). (2000). *Using literature to help troubled teenagers cope with health issues.* Westport, CT: Greenwood Press.

Brubaker, J. M. (1983). "Are You There, Margaret? It's Me, God." Religious contexts in recent adolescent fiction. *English Journal, 72*(5), 82–86.

Carroll, P. S. (1997). Today's teens, their problems, and their literature: Revisiting G. Robert Carlsen's *Books and the Teenage Reader* thirty years later. *English Journal, 86*, 25–34.

Carroll, P. S. (Ed.). (1999). *Using literature to help troubled teenagers cope with societal issues.* Westport, CT: Greenwood Press.

Carver, N. L. (1988). Stereotypes of American Indians in adolescent literature. *English Journal, 77*(5), 25–32.

Chatton, B. (1988). Apply with caution: Bibliotherapy in the library. *Journal of Youth Services in Libraries, 1*(3), 334–338.

Coffel, C. M. (2002). Strong portraits and stereotypes: Pregnant and mothering teens in YA fiction. *The ALAN Review, 30*(1), 15–21.

Crowe, C. (2001). The problem with YA literature. *English Journal, 90*(3), 146–150.

Crowley, S. (1989). *A teacher's introduction to deconstruction.* Urbana, IL: NCTE.

Darby, M. A., & Pryne, M. (2002). *Hearing all the voices: Multicultural books for adolescents.* Lanham, MD: Scarecrow Press.

Day, F. A. (2000). *Lesbian and gay voices: An annotated bibliography and guide to literature for children and young adults.* Westport, CT: Greenwood Press.

Doyle, M. (2002). Tough girls: Fiction for African American urban teens. *Voice of Youth Advocates, 25*(3), 174–175.

Endicott, A. (1992). Females also come of age. *English Journal, 81*(4), 42–47.

Franzak, J. (2003). Hopelessness and healing: Racial identity in young adult literature. *New Advocate, 16*(1), 43–56.

Franzak, J., & Noll, E. (2006). Monstrous acts: Problematizing violence in young adult literature. *Journal of Adolescent and Adult Literacy, 49*(8), 662–672.

Gallo, D. (2003). Tough books tackling tough issues. *SIGNAL Journal, 26*(1), 9–12.

Garner, A. (2004). *Families like mine: Children of gay parents tell it like it is.* New York: HarperCollins.

Gebhard, A. O. (1993). The emerging self: Young-adult and class novels of the black experience. *English Journal, 82*(5), 50–54.

Glasgow, J. N. (2001). Teaching social justice through young adult literature. *English Journal, 90*(6), 54–61.

Glenn, W. (2006). Boys finding first love: Soul-searching in *The Center of the World* and *Swimming in the Monsoon Sea. The ALAN Review, 33*(3), 70–75.

Gray, M. J. (1994). Characters in realistic fiction: Do they change with changing times? *Virginia English Bulletin, 44*(2), 70–72.

Hamilton, V. (1993). Everything of value: Moral realism in the literature of children. *Journal of Youth Services, 6*(4), 363–367.

Head, P. (1996). Robert Cormier and the postmodernist possibilities of young adult fiction. *Children's Literature Association Quarterly, 21*(1), 28–33.

Hillsberg, C., & Spak, H. (2006). Young adult literature as the centerpiece of an anti-bullying program in middle school. *Middle School Journal, 38*(2), 23–28.

Hughes-Hassell, S., & Guild, S. L. (2002). The urban experience in recent young adult novels. *The ALAN Review, 29*(3), 35–39.

Hunt, C. (1996). Young adult literature evades the theorists. *Children's Literature Association Quarterly, 21*(1), 4–11.

Jackett, M. (2007). Something to speak about: Addressing sensitive issues through literature. *English Journal, 96*(4), 102–1005.

Jones, J. B. (2003). *Helping teens cope: A guide to teen issues using YA fiction and other resources.* Worthington, OH: Linworth.

Jones, P. (1994). THIN books, BIG problems: Realism and the reluctant teen reader. *The ALAN Review, 20*(2), 18–28.

Jones, P. (2006). Stargirls, stray dogs, freaks, and nails: Person vs. society conflicts and nonconformist protagonists in young adult fiction. *The ALAN Review, 33*(3), 13–17.

Jordan, A. D. (1995). True-to-life: Realistic fiction. *Teaching and Learning Literature, 5*(1), 16–22.

Kaywell, J. F. (1997). Using young adult realistic literature to help troubled teenagers: Something new, tried and true, and recommended nonfiction. *English Journal, 86*(5), 91.

Kaywell, J. F., Kelly, P. P., Edge, C., McCoy, L., & Steinberg, N. (2006). Growing up female around the globe with young adult literature. *The ALAN Review, 33*(3), 62–69.

Kirby, D. L. (2003). What to read after Columbine: Issues of differentness, issues of caring. *SIGNAL Journal, 26*(1), 22–27.

Klass, D. (2003). Speech given at the IRA convention in Orlando, Florida. *SIGNAL Journal, 26*(1), 15–17.

Knafle, J. D. (2001). Religions in fiction for junior and senior high students. *Reading Improvement, 38*(1), 12–21.

Knickerbocker, J. L., & Rycik, J. (2002). Growing into literature: Adolescents' literary interpretation and appreciation. *Journal of Adolescent and Adult Literacy, 46*(3), 196–208.

Krapp, J. V. (2005). Building collections: The problem novel. *School Library Media Activities Monthly, 21*(5), 42–43.

LeMieux, A. C. (1998). The problem novel in a conservative age. *The ALAN Review, 25*(3), 4–6.

Lenz, M. (1980). Varieties of loneliness: Alienation in contemporary young people's fiction. *Journal of Popular Culture, 13*(4), 672–688.

Lovelace, J., & Smith, L. H. (2002). The motherless daughter: An evolving archetype of adolescent literature. *The ALAN Review, 29*(2), 16–20.

Manzo, K. K. (2007). Dark themes in books get students reading. *Education Weekly, 26*(31), 1.

Marler, M. D. (2002). The problem of poverty in three young adult novels: "A Hero Ain't Nothin' But a Sandwich," "Buried Onions," and "Make Lemonade." *The ALAN Review, 30*(1), 29–32.

McDiffett, D. (2001). Prejudice and pride: Japanese Americans in the young adult novels of Yoshiko Uchida. *English Journal, 90*(3), 60–65.

Miller, S. (2005). Shattering images of violence in young adult literature: Strategies for the classroom. *English Journal, 94*(5), 87–93.

Mitchell, D. (2005). Issues of faith in YA lit. *English Journal, 94*(5), 128–131.

Moore, J. N. (1997). *Interpreting young adult literature: Literary theory in the secondary classroom.* Portsmouth, NH: Heinemann.

Moore, J. N. (2001). Fathers and sons. *English Journal, 91*(2), 112–115.

Myracle, L. (1995). Molding the minds of the young: The history of bibliotherapy as applied to children and adolescents. *The ALAN Review, 22*(2), 36–40.

Nahmias, C. K. (2004). Reading boys, boys reading: Learning about male students through YA literature. *SIGNAL Journal, 27*(1), 27–32.

Noble, S. (1998). Why don't we ever read anything happy? YA literature and the optimistic ending. *The ALAN Review 26*(1), 46–50.

Norton, T. L., & Vare, J. W. (2004). Literature for today's gay and lesbian teens: Subverting the culture of silence. *English Journal, 94*(2), 65.

Poe, E. (1994). Gaining understanding and human relationships through young adult fiction. *Virginia English Bulletin, 44*(2), 57–64.

Probst, R. E. (1986). Mom, wolfman, and me: Adolescent literature, critical theory, and the English classroom. *English Journal, 75*(6), 33–39.

Probst, R. E. (1988). Transactional theory in the teaching of literature. *Journal of Reading, 31*(4), 378–381.

Probst, R. E. (1994). Reader-response theory and the English curriculum. *English Journal, 83*(3), 37–44.

Probst, R. E. (2000). Literature as invitation. *Voices from the Middle*, 8–15.

Probst, R. E. (2004). *Response and analysis: Teaching literature in secondary school* (2nd ed.). Portsmouth, NH: Heinemann.

Quinn, K. B., Barone, B., & Kearns, J. (2003). Using a novel unit to help understand and prevent bullying in schools. *Journal of Adolescent and Adult Literacy, 46*(7), 582–591.

Radley, G. (2001). Spiritual quest in young adult literature. *The ALAN Review, 28*(3), 40–43.

Reid, S., & Stringer, S. (1997). Ethical dilemmas in teaching problem novels: The psychological impact of troubling YA literature on adolescent readers in the classroom. *The ALAN Review, 24*(2), 16–18.

Ritter, J. (2003). Are YA novelists morally obligated to offer their readers hope? *The ALAN Review, 30*(3), 8–13.

Robertson, S. L. (1990). Text rendering: Beginning literary response. *English Journal, 79*(1), 80–84.

Rochman, H. (1993). *Against borders: Promoting books for a multiracial world.* Chicago: ALA.

Ross, C. S. (1985). Young adult realism: Conventions, narrators, and readers. *Library Quarterly, 55*(2), 174–191.

Ruggieri, C. (2007). Making connections with contemporary literature. *English Journal, 96*(4), 112–113.

Salvner, G. M. (2001). Lessons and lives: Why young adult literature matters. *The ALAN Review, 28*(3), 9–13.

Samuels, B. G. (1989). Young adults' choices: Why do students "really like" particular books? *Journal of Reading, 32*(8), 714–719.

Scherff, L., & Wright, C. L. (2007). Getting beyond the cuss words: Using Marxism and binary opposition to teach *Ironman* and *The Catcher in the Rye. The ALAN Review, 35*(1), 51–57.

Soter, A. (1999). *Young adult literature and new literary theory.* New York: Teachers College Press.

Stevens, S. (1994). A sense of balance: Realism in the characters of Chris Crutcher. *Virginia English Bulletin, 44*(2), 47–49.

Stoehr, S. (1997). Controversial issues in the lives of contemporary young adults. *The ALAN Review, 24*(2), 3–5.

Stringer, S. A. (1997). *Conflict and connection: The psychology of young adult literature.* Westport, CT: Heinemann.

Sutton, R. (1982). The critical myth: Realistic YA novels. *School Library Journal, 29*(3), 33–35.

Thacker, P. (2007). Growing beyond circumstance: Have we overemphasized hopelessness in young adult literature? *English Journal, 96*(3), 17–18.

Tighe, M. A. (2005). Reviving Ophelia with young adult literature. *The ALAN Review, 33*(1), 56–61.

Tillapaugh, M. (1993). AIDS: A problem for today's YA problem novel. *School Library Journal, 39*(5), 22–25.

Tribunella, E. L. (2007). Institutionalizing "The Outsiders": YA literature, social class, and the American faith in education. *Children's Literature in Education, 38*(2), 87–101.

Tyson, C. A. (1999). "Shut my mouth wide open": Realistic fiction and social action. *Theory into Practice, 38*(3), 155–159.

Van Horn, L. (2003). Trying on tough books: Tough books for tough times. *SIGNAL Journal, 26*(1), 40–44.

Vogel, M., & Creadick, A. (1993). Family values and the new adolescent novel. *English Journal, 82*(5), 37–42.

Yearwood, S. (2002). Popular postmodernism for young adult readers: "Walk Two Moons," "Holes," and "Monster." *The ALAN Review, 29*(3), 50–53.

York, S. (2002). The migrant experience in the works of Mexican American writers. *The ALAN Review, 30*(1), 22–25.

Zitlow, C. S. (2001). Young adult literature and the new literary theories: Developing critical readers in middle school. *English Journal, 90*(3), 135–137.

References

Abrams, M. H. (2005). *A glossary of literary terms* (8th ed.). Boston: Thomson Wadsworth.

Anderson, J. L. (2006). *Secrets of peaches.* New York: HarperCollins.

Anderson, L. H. (1999). *Speak.* New York: Farrar, Straus & Giroux.

Aronson, M. (1995, January). "The YA novel is dead," and other fairly stupid tales. *School Library Journal, 41*(1), 36–37.

Barnes, J. L. (2007). *Platinum.* New York: Delacorte/ Random House.

Bauer, J. (2000). *Hope was here.* New York: Putnam.

Bauer, J. (2002). *Stand tall.* New York: Putnam.

Beers, K. (2002). *When kids can't read.* Portsmouth, NH: Heinemann.

Benduhn, T. (2003). *Gravel queen.* New York: Simon & Schuster.

Bennett, J. (2003). *Faith wish.* New York: Holiday House.

Block, F. L. (1989). *Weetzie Bat.* New York: Harper & Row.

Block, F. L. (2001). *Echo.* New York: HarperCollins.

Blume, J. (1970). *Are you there, God? It's me, Margaret.* Scarsdale, NY: Bradbury Press.

Blume, J. (1974). *Blubber.* New York: Simon & Schuster.

Blume, J. (1975). *Forever.* Scarsdale, NY: Bradbury Press.

Bone, I. (2005). *Sleep rough tonight.* New York: Penguin.

Brooks, K. (2002). *Martyn Pig.* New York: Scholastic.

Brooks, K. (2004). *Kissing the rain.* New York: PUSH/Scholastic.

Brooks, K. (2005). *Candy.* New York: Scholastic.

Brooks, K. (2006). *The road of the dead.* New York: Scholastic.

Brooks, K. (2007). *Being.* New York: Scholastic.

Brooks, K. (2008). *Black rabbit summer.* New York: Penguin.

Buckley, T. R., & Carter, R. T. (2005, November). Black adolescent girls: Do gender role and racial identity impact their self-esteem? *Sex Roles, 53*(9–10), 647.

Burnford, S. (1961). *The incredible journey.* New York: Little, Brown.

Carlson, R. (2003). *The speed of light.* New York: HarperTempest.

Clifford, J. (Ed.). (1991). *The experience of reading: Louise Rosenblatt and reader-response theory.* Portsmouth, NH: Heinemann.

Cohn, R. (2006). *Shrimp.* New York: Simon & Schuster.

Cohn, R. (2007). *Cupcake.* New York: Simon & Schuster.

Cole, P. (1995, Winter). An interview with Ruth White. *The ALAN Review, 22*(2), 4–7.

Cooper, I. (2004). *Sam I am.* New York: Scholastic.

Cormier, R. (1974). *The chocolate war.* New York: Pantheon Books.

Cormier, R. (1977). *I am the cheese.* New York: Knopf/Random House.

Cormier, R. (1979). *After the first death.* New York: Pantheon Books.

Crowe, C. (2002, July). YA boundary breakers and makers. *English Journal, 91*(6), 116–118.

Crowe, C. (2004, Spring). Proud and prejudiced: Why boys don't like chick books. *SIGNAL Journal, 26*(2), 2–6.

Crutcher, C. (1983). *Running loose.* New York: Greenwillow/HarperCollins.

Crutcher, C. (1986). *Stotan!* New York: Greenwillow/HarperCollins.

Crutcher, C. (1987). *Crazy horse electric game.* New York: Greenwillow/HarperCollins.

Crutcher, C. (1989). *Chinese handcuffs.* New York: Greenwillow/HarperCollins.

Crutcher, C. (1993). *Staying fat for Sarah Byrnes.* New York: Greenwillow/HarperCollins.

Crutcher. C. (1995). *Ironman.* New York: Greenwillow/HarperCollins.

Crutcher, C. (2003). *King of the mild frontier.* New York: Greenwillow/HarperCollins.

Crutcher, C. (2005). *The sledding hill.* New York: Greenwillow/HarperCollins.

Crutcher, C. (2007). *Deadline.* New York: Greenwillow/HarperCollins.

Curtis, C. P. (1995). *The Watsons go to Birmingham—1963.* New York: Delacorte/Random House.

Dessen, S. (1999). *Keeping the moon.* New York: Viking/Penguin.

Easton, K. (2004). *Walking on air.* New York: Simon & Schuster.

Farley, W. (1941). *The black stallion.* New York: Random House.

Fleischman, P. (1998). *Whirligig.* New York: Henry Holt.

Flinn, A. (2002). *Breaking point.* New York: HarperCollins.

Friend, N. (2004). *Perfect.* Minneapolis, MN: Milkweed Editions.

Gaines, D. (1991). *Teenage wasteland: Suburbia's dead end kids.* New York: Pantheon Books.

Garden, N. (1982). *Annie on my mind.* New York: Farrar, Straus & Giroux.

George, J. C. (1972). *Julie of the wolves.* New York: Harper & Row.

George, J. C. (1997). *Julie's wolf pack.* New York: HarperCollins.

Gipson, F. (1956). *Old yeller.* New York: Harper.

Giles, G. (2002). *Shattering Glass.* New Milford, CT: Roaring Brook Press.

Gill, S. (1999, Winter). Young adult literature for young adult males. *The ALAN Review, 26*(2).

Going, K. L. (2003). *Fat kid rules the world.* New York: Putnam.

Going, K. L. (2005). *The liberation of Gabriel King.* New York: Putnam.

Greene, B. (1991). *The drowning of Stephan Jones.* New York: Bantam/Random House.

Griffin, A. (2005). *Where I want to be.* New York: Putnam.

Guest, J. (1976). *Ordinary people.* New York: Viking/Penguin.

Haddix, M. P. (1997). *Leaving Fishers.* New York: Simon & Schuster.

Hartinger, B. (2003). *Geography club.* New York: HarperCollins.

Hartinger, B. (2005). *The order of the poison oak.* New York: HarperCollins.

Hautman, P. (2004). *Godless.* New York: Simon & Schuster.

Hautman, P. (2005, Fall). The elusive edge. *SIGNAL Journal, 28*(1), 38–40.

Head, A. (1967). *Mr. and Mrs. Bo Jo Jones.* New York: Putnam.

Headley, K. N. (1994, Winter). Duel at high noon: A replay of Cormier's works. *The ALAN Review, 21*(2), 34–36.

Hesse, K. (1997). *Out of the dust.* New York: Scholastic.

Hinton, S. E. (1967). *The outsiders.* New York: Viking Press.

Hipple, T. (1989, December). Have you read . . . ? *English Journal, 78*(8), 79.

Hipple, T. (1992, November). Have you read . . . ? *English Journal, 81*(7), 91.

Hipple, T., & Claiborne, J. (2005, January). The best young adult novels of all time, or *The Chocolate War* one more time. *English Journal, 94*(3), 99–102.

Holm, J. L. (2006). Penny from heaven. New York: Random House.

Hopkins, E. (2004). *Crank.* New York: Simon & Schuster.

Hopkins, E. (2007a). *Glass.* New York: Simon & Schuster.

Hopkins, E. (2007b). *Impulse.* New York: Simon & Schuster.

Jenkins, A. M. (2001). *Damage.* New York: HarperCollins.

Kadohata, C. (2007). *Cracker: The best dog in Vietnam.* New York: Simon & Schuster.

Kaysen, S. (1993). *Girl, interrupted.* New York: Turtle Bay/Random House.

Kerr, M. E. (1994). *Deliver us from Evie.* New York: HarperCollins.

Kjelgaard, J. (1945). *Big Red.* New York: Holiday House.

Klass, D. (2001). *You don't know me.* New York: Farrar, Straus & Giroux.

Klass, D. (2002). *Home of the Braves.* New York: Farrar, Straus & Giroux.

Klass, D. (2003, Fall). Speech by David Klass at the IRA convention in Orlando, Florida. *SIGNAL Journal, 26*(1) 15–17.

Koss, A. G. (2000). *The girls.* New York: Dial/Penguin.

Koss, A. G. (2006). *Poison Ivy.* New Milford, CT: Roaring Brook Press.

Lee, H. (1960). *To kill a mockingbird.* New York: Lippincott.

Levithan, D. (2003). *Boy meets boy.* New York: Knopf/Random House.

Levitin, S. (1998). *Singing mountain.* New York: Simon & Schuster.

Lipsyte, R. (1967). *The contender.* New York: Harper & Row.

Lord, C. (2006). *Rules.* New York: Scholastic.

Lowry, L. (1993). *The giver.* Boston: Houghton Mifflin.

Lynch, C. (2002). *Who the man.* New York: HarperCollins.

Lynch, C. (2004). *The gravedigger's cottage.* New York: HarperCollins.

Lynch, C. (2005). *Inexcusable.* New York: Atheneum/Simon & Schuster.

Mackler, C. (2003). *The earth, my butt, and other big, round things.* Cambridge, MA: Candlewick Press.

Mark Twain's last book excluded from a public library. (1885, March 17). *St. Louis-Globe Democrat.*

Milner, J. O., & Milner, L. F. M. (2003). *Bridging English* (3rd ed.). Upper Saddle River, NJ: Merrill/Prentice Hall.

Morgan, C. (2003). *The boy who spoke dog.* New York: Dutton/Penguin.

Myers, M. (1988). Twenty (better) questions. *English Journal, 77*(1), 64–65.

Myers, W. D. (1988). *Fallen angels.* New York: HarperCollins.

Myers, W. D. (1999). *Monster.* New York: HarperCollins.

Naylor, P. R. (1996). *Shiloh season.* New York: Atheneum/Simon & Schuster.

Naylor, P. R. (1997). *Saving Shiloh.* New York: Atheneum/Simon & Schuster.

Nelson, R. A. (2005). *Teach me.* New York: Razorbill/Penguin.

Nolan, H. (1996). *Send me down a miracle.* San Diego: Harcourt.

Nolan, H. (2003). *When we were saints.* San Diego: Harcourt.

Oates, J. C. (2003). *Freaky green eyes.* New York: HarperCollins.

O'Brien, R. C. (1975). *Z for Zachariah.* New York: Atheneum/Simon & Schuster.

O'Dell, S. (1967). *The black pearl.* New York: Bantam/Doubleday/Dell.

Paterson, K. (1978). *The great Gilly Hopkins.* New York: Crowell.

Paulsen, G. (1991). *The river.* New York: Random House.

Paulsen, G. (1996). *Brian's winter.* New York: Random House.

Paulsen, G. (1999). *Brian's return.* New York: Random House.

Paulsen, G. (2000). *The beet fields: Memories of a sixteenth summer.* New York: Delacorte/Random House.

Paulsen, G. (2003). *Brian's hunt.* New York: Random House.

Peck, R. (1976). *Are you in the house alone?* New York: Viking/Penguin.

Peck, R. (1978, Spring). Ten questions to ask about a novel. *The ALAN Review, 5*(3), 17.

Perez, M. (2004). *Unexpected development.* New Milford, CT: Roaring Brook Press.

Perkins, L. R. (2005). *Criss cross.* New York: Greenwillow/HarperCollins.

Peters, J. A. (2004). *Luna.* New York: Little, Brown.

Peters, J. A. (2005). *Far from Xanadu.* New York: Little, Brown.

Philbrick, R. (1993). *Freak the mighty.* New York: Blue Sky Press.

Plum-Ucci, C. (2002). *What happened to Lani Garver.* San Diego: Harcourt.

Pollack, J. (2006). *Klepto.* New York: Viking/Penguin.

Price, C. (2007). *Lizard people.* New Milford, CT: Roaring Brook Press.

Qualey, M. (2005). *Just like that.* New York: Penguin.

Rawlings, M. (1938). *The yearling.* New York: Scribner.

Rawls, W. (1961). *Where the red fern grows.* New York: Doubleday.

Ritter, J. (1998). *Choosing up sides.* New York: Philomel/Penguin.

Rodowsky, C. (1992). *Lucy Peale.* New York: Farrar, Straus & Giroux.

Root, S. L. (1977). The new realism: Some personal reflections. *Language Arts, 54*(1), 19–24.

Rosenblatt, L. M. (1938). *Literature as exploration.* New York: Appleton-Century.

Rosenblatt, L. M. (1976). *Literature as exploration* (3rd ed.). New York: Noble & Noble.

Rosenblatt, L. M. (1978). *The reader, the text, the poem.* Carbondale: Southern Illinois University Press.

Rosenblatt, L. M. (1995). *Literature as exploration* (5th ed.). New York: MLA.

Ryan, S. (2001). *Empress of the world.* New York: Viking/Penguin.

Rylant, C. (1986). *A fine white dust.* New York: Bradbury Press.

Sachar, L. (1998). *Holes.* New York: Farrar, Straus & Giroux.

Salinger, J. D. (1951). *The catcher in the rye.* New York: Little, Brown.

Schooler, D., Ward, L. M., Merriwether, A., & Caruthers, A. (2004, March). Who's that girl: Television's role in the body image development of young white and black women. *Psychology of Women Quarterly, 28*(1), 38–47.

Scott, K. (2006). *Brunettes strike back.* New York: Penguin.

Scott, K. (2007). *A non-blonde cheerleader in love.* New York: Penguin.

Simmons, R. (2002). *Odd girl out.* Orlando, FL: Harcourt.

Soto, G. (2003). *The afterlife.* Orlando, FL: Harcourt.

Spinelli, J. (2000). *Stargirl.* New York: Knopf/Random House.

Spinelli, J. (2007). *Love, Stargirl.* New York: Knopf/Random House.

Taylor, M. (1976). *Roll of thunder, hear my cry.* New York: Dial/Penguin.

Tierney, R. J., Readence, J. E., & Dishner, E. K. (1995). *Reading strategies and practices: A compendium* (4th ed.). Boston: Allyn & Bacon.

Twain, M. (1884). *The adventures of Huckleberry Finn.* London: Chatto & Windus.

Voigt, C. (1986). *Izzy, willy-nilly.* New York: Atheneum/Simon & Schuster.

Volponi, P. (2005). *Black and white.* New York: Viking/Penguin.

Waite, J. (2003). *Shopaholic.* New York: Simon & Schuster.

Waite, J. (2006). *Forbidden.* New York: Atheneum/Simon & Schuster.

Walker, K. (1993). *Peter.* Boston: Houghton Mifflin.

Wallace, R. (2003). *Restless: A ghost's story*. New York: Viking/Penguin.

Weaver, W. (2005). *Full service*. New York: Farrar, Straus & Giroux.

White, R. (1996). *Belle Prater's boy*. New York: Farrar, Straus & Giroux.

White Miller, R. (1977). *The city rose*. New York: McGraw-Hill.

Wilder, A., & Teasley, A. B. (1998, Fall). Young adult literature in the high school. *The ALAN Review, 26*(1).

Wiseman, R. (2002). *Queen bees and wannabes: Helping your daughter survive cliques, gossip, boyfriends, and other realities of adolescence*. New York: Crown.

Wittlinger, E. (1999). *Hard love*. New York: Simon & Schuster.

Wittlinger, E. (2005). *Sandpiper*. New York: Simon & Schuster.

Woodson, J. (2004). *Behind you*. New York: Putnam.

Yolen, J., & Coville, B. (1998). *Armageddon summer*. San Diego: Harcourt.

Yopp, R. H., & Yopp, H. K. (2001). *Literature-based reading activities* (3rd ed.). Boston: Allyn & Bacon.

Zarr, S. (2006). *Story of a girl*. New York: Little, Brown.

Zevin, G. (2005). *Elsewhere*. New York: Farrar, Straus & Giroux.

Zindel, P. (1968). *The pigman*. New York: Harper & Row.

Zwiers, J. (2004). *Building reading comprehension in Grades 6–12: A toolkit of classroom activities*. Newark, DE: IRA.

C H A P T E R   **5**

Romance, Humor, and Sports
Reading Skill: Questioning

Introduction

Why do we always read about dead people? a senior asked, turning to James Joyce's *The Dead* in her anthology. The year was almost over, and we had covered a plethora of classics: *Beowulf, Le Morte D'Arthur, Macbeth, Paradise Lost, The Rime of the Ancient Mariner, In Memoriam, Lord Jim, Jude the Obscure,* and more. Not one was a light read. Not one was funny. Death and gloom prevailed. Her question was insightful and fair and caught me off guard—I mumbled some innocuous answer about "good literature."

There seems to be an unwritten rule in the literary world, and it holds true for both film and novels: for a story to have literary substance, it must be serious. Pit a comedy against a serious film for an Academy Award for best picture,[1] and you're pretty safe in betting your house the serious film will win. This chapter explores romance, humor, and sports books and addresses this attitude about "good literature." It concludes with a discussion on questioning and strategies for developing this skill.

Romance
Historical Development

When many hear "romance," they think fluff: bodice rippers,[2] formulaic writing, stereotypes, thin plotlines, sizzling hot sexual encounters, rakes, dukes, sheiks, princes, captains (or any guy in a uniform), and, of course, drop-dead, gorgeous, irresistible women. Intriguing maybe, but not classroom reading. Although some romance novels, particularly serial novels, lack substance, others have strong plots and well-drawn characters, defying formulaic style. Today's young adult romance genre features light, tender stories of young adult yearnings; heartbreaking, tough stories of loss; romantic comedies and satires; serious and not-so-serious same-sex relationships; and, of course, sizzling, hot formulaic reads.

Developed in 12th-century France, the term *romance* "originally signified a work written in the French language, which evolved from a dialect of the Roman language, Latin" (Abrams, 2005, p. 35). Unlike epics like the *Odyssey* and *Beowulf,* which represented an age of tribal wars,

---

[1]Between 2001 and 2006, winners have included *Gladiator, A Beautiful Mind, Chicago, The Lord of the Rings, Return of the King, Million Dollar Baby,* and *Crash.*
[2]Well-known romance novelist Elizabeth Mansfield (Paula Schwartz) once defined bodice rippers as "five parts sex to one part history . . . and terrible history at that" ("Why I Am Not Jane Austen: An Overview of Today's Romantic Fiction and How It Got That Way." Retrieved June 13, 2008, from www.deansmay.com/posts).

163

early romances like Malory's *Sir Gawain and the Green Knight* and Chaucer's *Troilus and Criseyde* celebrated "heroism, fealty to a lord or lady, and great deeds" (Bracket, 1999, p. xi), a chivalric age of highly developed manners, civility, courage, loyalty, and honor. Romantic heroes slew monsters (supernatural beings) and fought in tournaments for a damsel's sake or to win their lord's approval. These stories were told in verse, but as oral storytelling gave way to writing as a storytelling medium, the nature of romance also evolved. One major evolution was replacing the male hero with a female, possibly because of the rise of women writers.

The Victorian era, a defining time for the novel, was also a defining time for romance.[3] Female writers gained voice, and romance, though dark and brooding, permeated their work. Classic romances (e.g., Jane Austen's *Pride and Prejudice,* 1813; Charlotte Brontë's *Jane Eyre,* 1847; and Emily Brontë's *Wuthering Heights,* 1847) were popular reading and were not taken seriously. Sound familiar? These romances, though marketed as adult books, have long been read by teens. Romance took a lighter, more optimistic turn with Lucy Maud Montgomery's *Anne of Green Gables* series.[4] Teens who enjoy romance and who read classics are generally familiar with this enduring series.

Experts often cite a romance, Maureen Daly's *Seventeenth Summer* (1942), a quintessential love story, as the first young adult novel.[5] *Seventeenth Summer*'s success lies in the protagonist's fresh, honest, and poignant voice, a timeless narrative of the trials and tribulations of first love. As Cart (1996) points out, "innovation breeds imitation" (p. 19); therefore, a number of imitation romances followed *Seventeenth Summer*'s success (e.g., Betty Cavanna's *Going on Sixteen,*1946, and Rosamund du Jardin's *Practically Seventeen,*1949), and the novel may have catapulted *Seventeen* magazine in 1945. Reflecting on the light nature of 1940s romances, Cart (1996) says,

> These books [with the exception of *Seventeenth Summer*] were set in a *Saturday Evening Post* world of white faces and white picket fences surrounding small-town, middle-class lives where the worst thing that could happen would be a misunderstanding that threatened to leave someone dateless for the junior prom. (p. 20)

More original romances followed Daly's bestseller (e.g., Madeleine L'Engle's *And Both Were Young,* 1949; Beverly Cleary's *Fifteen,* 1956; and *Jean and Johnny,* 1959). Read mostly by younger teens, these were also light romances, unlike the edgier formula novels and problem novel romances that followed.

When the problem novel took root in the 1970s, the pure romance novel waned, probably because teens were intrigued by the realistic portrayals of love absent in most traditional romances. Romance generally played

---

[3]The first novel published, *Pamela* (1740), was a romance. Written by Samuel Johnson, *Pamela* was controversial and successful during its time and remains one of the most influential literary works today. In this story, Pamela, a servant, is pursued by her employer's son, a man of "loose" principles. Pamela is of lower class and unworthy of his attention.
[4]The first book in the series was published in 1908.
[5]Though cited by many as the "first" YA novel, the young adult genre didn't come into its own until 1967 with the publication of S. E. Hinton's *The Outsiders.*

a secondary role in problem novels, but it was depicted in real, down-to-earth ways. Problem novels spoke realistically to awakening sexuality, fears, heart-aches, and joys of first love (e.g., works by Judy Blume and Paul Zindel), and teens worried about more than prom dates (e.g., teen pregnancy, loss of a loved one). Though not pegged a young adult novel, Erich Segal's _Love Story_ (1970), in which a young man loses his new wife to a terminal illness, was undoubtedly the most influential love story of the 1970s.[6] Girls read it and passed it around; boys read it surreptitiously.

Even though the problem novel flourished during the 1980s, young adult romance rebounded and became a defining force, primarily in series form. Some researchers (e.g., Cart, 1996; Murray, 1998) credit this turnaround in part to the abundance of hard-hitting realistic fiction and the desire for escapism. Eighties romances were reminiscent of gentler midcentury love stories and provided an alternative to tough stories, allow-ing readers to retreat from social problems. However, we can't overlook the influence of the unprecedented marketing tactics that aimed to place romance series in every bookrack in the country.[7] In the 1980s, individuals couldn't enter a drugstore, grocery, discount, or chain store and *not* find mass-market paperback popular romance series. (Not true for the prob-lem novel, typically published in hardback a year before being released in paperback and sold almost exclusively in bookstores.) Scholastic's Teen-age Book Club, recognizing that light paperback romance titles sold well, developed a massive marketing strategy to sell a series (_Wildfire_) of romance novels in stores. Selling 1.8 million books the first year, Scholastic expanded with additional series such as _Wishing Star, Windswept,_ and the renowned _Sunfire_ historical series (Carpan, 2004, p. xix). Noting this "serial success," other publishers followed suit, most notably Bantam, who launched the infamous _Sweet Valley High_ soap opera series (1983)[8] portraying the lives of identical twins Jessica and Elizabeth Wakefield. The _Sweet Valley High_ series, created by Francine Pascal and written by various authors, domi-nated the decade. The series was so successful that Bantam published the Super Edition in 1985 titled _Perfect Summer,_ which became the first young adult novel to make the _New York Times_ bestseller list, remaining on the charts for four years (Huntwork, 1990, p. 138). Other _Sweet Valley_ series followed.[9] By the end of the 1980s, 34 million _Sweet Valley_ books were

---

[6]_Love Story_ became a Paramount picture in 1982, grossing more money than any previous movie. The movie's catchphrase "Love means never having to say you're sorry" became fodder for parody, much like "You had me at hello" (_Jerry Maguire,_ 1996) and "I wish I knew how to quit you" (_Brokeback Mountain,_ 2005).
[7]Ron Buehl, editorial director of Bantam's Books for Young Readers who launched the popular _Sweet Dreams_ series, announced the goal of mass-market paperback publishers to put serial romances "everywhere there's a rack in the country" (Pollack, 1981, p. 25).
[8]Francine Pascal first envisioned _Sweet Valley_ as a television soap opera. Carpan (2004) defines "soap opera series" as those with cliff-hanging endings and continuing characters—characters who reappear in the next serial installment.
[9]Research uncovered 16 spin-off series to the original _Sweet Valley High_ series: _Sweet Valley High Super Edition, Sweet Valley High Super Thriller, Sweet Valley High Super Star, Sweet Valley Magna Edition, Sweet Valley High Senior Year, Sweet Valley Twins, Sweet Valley Twins Super Chiller, Sweet Valley Twins Super Edition, Sweet Valley Twins Diaries, Sweet Valley Kids, Sweet Valley Junior High, Sweet Valley University, Sweet Valley University Thriller Edition, Sweet Valley Unicorn Club, Elizabeth,_ and _Secret Love Diaries._

in print (p. 138). To illustrate the popularity of the 1980s romance series, I have included a sampling of series (excluding the 16 or more *Sweet Valley* spin-offs) in Box 5.1, followed by the first book, that book's author (series often have several authors), and the year the series launched. One has to wonder what would have happened if similar marketing campaigns were used for other young adult genres.

Box 5.1   1980s Teen Series

Blossom Valley series (*Love at First Sight*) by Elaine Harper. New York: Silhouette (1981). [This is a series within the *First Love* series]

Caprice Romances series (*Jenny*) by Natalie Johnson. New York: Ace (1982).

Chrystal Falls series (*The Wrong Side of Love*) by Meredith Hill. New York: Scholastic (1985).

Class of '88 series (*Freshman*) by Linda A. Cooney.* New York: Scholastic (1987).

Class of '89 series (*Freshman*) by Linda A. Cooney. New York: Scholastic (1988).

Couples series (*Change of Hearts*) by Linda A. Cooney. New York: Scholastic (1985).

Couples: Special Editions series (*Summer Heat*) by M. E. Cooper.* New York: Scholastic (1986).

Cranberry Cousins series (*Rival Roommates*) by Christie Wells. Mahwah, NJ: Troll (1988).

First Kiss series (*Head Over Heels*) by Susan Blake. New York: Ballantine (1988).

Follow Your Heart Romances series (*Summer in the Sun!*) by Jan Gelman. New York: Archway (1983). [Interactive]†

Heart to Heart series (*Summer to Summer*) by Carol Ellis. New York: Ballantine (1985).

Magic Moments series (*The Love Vote*) by Jo Stewart. New York: Signet (1984).

Seniors series (*Too Much Too Soon*) by Eileen Goudge.* New York: Dell (1984).

Seniors: Super Seniors series (*Old Enough*) by Eileen Goudge. New York: Dell (1986).

Sisters series (*Three's a Crowd*) by Jennifer Cole. New York: Fawcett (1986).

Sorority Girls series (*Getting In*) by Anne Hunter Lowell.* New York: Fawcett (1986).

Sunfire series (*Amanda*) by Candice F. Ransom. New York: Scholastic (1984).

Sweet Dreams series (*P.S. I Love You*) by Barbara Conklin. New York: Bantam (1981).

Sweet Dream Specials series (*My Secret Love*) by Janet Quin-Harkin. New York: Bantam (1986).

Swept Away series (*Gone with the Wish*) by Eileen Goudge. New York: Avon (1986).

Texas Promises series (*Dreams at Dawn*) by Marie Lindquist. New York: Bantam (1987).

Turning Points series (*Friends Forever*) by Lisa Norby. New York: Signet (1984). [Interactive]

*According to the Crime Partners' Book List, Susan Wittig Albert has written young adult titles as Linda A. Cooney, M. E. Cooper, Ann Cole, Eileen Goudge, Rosemary Joyce, Anne Lowell, Susan Blake, Carolyn Keene, and Francine Pascal (www.mysterypartners.com/Books.html).

†For a more detailed discussion of interactive texts, see Chapter 12.

By the 1990s serial romances had peaked. These innocent and sweet romances, like 1940s romances, were ill-matched with the more knowledgeable and experienced teens growing up with Madonna, Janet Jackson, and MTV. The *Sweet Valley High* conservative images of Jessica and Elizabeth Wakefield may have been too wholesome when compared with Madonna's leather, stockings, and chains.[10] High school girls skipped *Sweet Valley High,* or spent minimum time with it, then moved on to adult romances. Also, other young adult genres began carving out a place in the young adult market (e.g., horror series by R. L. Stine and Christopher Pike) and dominated the 1990s in much the same way as romance did the 1980s. To maintain a stronghold in the young adult market, romance series had to change.

Today's romance series (e.g., *A-List, Gossip Girls, Seven Deadly Sins,* and *Fast Girls, Hot Guys*) are edgier than their predecessors and reflect current pop culture fixations—teen obsessions with lifestyles of the rich and famous, extravagant vacations, expensive cars, hot club scenes, and toned bodies and sex. These series are often joint efforts between the entertainment industry (e.g., MTV, Alloy Entertainment) and publishing houses, which speak to the series themes.[11] Although the traditional serial format remains popular, graphic novels and manga[12] are newer romance serial forms. Box 5.2 features a number of romance series today, along with the title of the first book in parentheses and its publication details. Many of these are light romance series, but others are sexually intense; a few graphic and manga series are included. (Graphic novels and manga are discussed in Chapter 12.)

Box 5.2 Teen Romance Series: Edgy and Light Reads

6X series (*The Uncensored Confessions*) by Nina Malkin. New York: Scholastic (2005).

The 310 series (*Life As a Poser*) by Beth Killian. New York: MTV/Simon & Schuster (2006).

Alice series (*The Agony of Alice*) by Phyllis Reynolds Naylor. New York: Atheneum/Simon & Schuster (1985).

The A-List series (*The A-List*) by Zoey Dean. New York: Little, Brown (2003).

The Au Pairs series (*The Au Pairs*) by Melissa de la Cruz. New York: Simon & Schuster (2004).

Bard Academy series (*Wuthering High*) by Cara Lockwood. New York: MTV/Simon & Schuster (2006).

Betsy Taylor series (*Undead and Unwed*) by MaryJanice Davidson. New York: Penguin (2004).

The Black Book (Diary of a Teenage Stud) series (*Girls, Girls, Girls*) by Jonah Black. New York: Avon/HarperCollins (2001).

Calypso Chronicles (*Pulling Princes*) by Tyne O'Connell. New York: Bloomsbury (2004).

College Life 101 series (*Cameron: The Sorority*) by Wendy Corsi Staub. New York: Penguin (1997).

The Dating Game series (*The Dating Game*) by Natalie Standiford. New York: Little, Brown (2005).

Continued

---

[10]Elizabeth Wakefield doesn't lose her virginity until *Max's Choice* (John, 2001).

[11]Advertisers present an idea for a series to publishing houses. If the publisher likes the idea, the series is written by "in-house" writers, quite different, of course, from the traditional novel. *The Sisterhood of the Traveling Pants* (Brashares, 2001) began this way.

[12]Manga are Japanese graphic novels characterized by sophisticated artwork. Originally written for adults, they are popular today with young adults (see Chapter 12 for more on this form).

Box 5.2   Teen Romance Series: Edgy and Light Reads   *Continued*

Diary of a Crush series (*French Kiss*) by Sarra Manning. New York: Speak/Penguin (2006).

Fast Girls, Hot Boys series (*Cruel Summer*) by Kylie Adams. New York: Simon Pulse/Simon & Schuster (2005).

Flirt series (*Write Here, Right Now*) by Nicole Clarke. New York: Grosset & Dunlap/Penguin (2006).

Girls Quartet series (*Girls in Love*) by Jacqueline Wilson. New York: Dell Laurel-Leaf/Random House (2002).

Gossip Girl series (*Gossip Girl*) by Cecily von Ziegesar. New York: Little, Brown (2002).

The Insiders series (*The Insiders*) by J. Minter. New York: Bloomsbury (2004).

The It Girl series (*The It Girl*) by Cecily von Ziegesar. New York: Little, Brown (2005).

Jessica Darling series (*Sloppy Firsts*) by Megan McCafferty. New York: Three Rivers Press (2001).

Love Hina series (*Love Hina*) by Ken Akamatsu. Los Angeles, CA: Tokyopop (2002).

Love Letters series (*Perfect Strangers*) by Jahnna N. Malcolm. New York: Simon & Schuster (2005).

Love Stories series (*My First Love*) by Callie West. New York: Bantam (1994).

Luna Bay series (*Peer Pressure*) by Francess Lantz. New York: HarperCollins (2003).

Making Out series (*Zoey Fools Around*) by Katherine Applegate. New York: Pan Macmillan (2001).

Mars series (*Mars*) by Fuyumi Soryo. Los Angeles, CA: Tokyopop (2002).

Mates and Dates series (*Mates, Dates, and Inflatable Bras*) by Cathy Hopkins. New York: Simon & Schuster (2002).

The Party Room series (*Get It Started*) by Morgan Burke. New York: Simon & Schuster (2005).

The Principles of Love series (*The Principles of Love*) by Emily Franklin. New York: Penguin (2005).

Private series (*Private*) by Kate Brian. New York: Simon Pulse/Simon & Schuster (2006).

Seven Deadly Sins series (*Lust*) by Robin Wasserman. New York: Simon Pulse/Simon & Schuster (2005).

Silver Beach series (*Summer Love*) by Diane Schwenn. New York: Bantam/Random House (2005).

The Sisterhood of the Traveling Pants series (*The Sisterhood of the Traveling Pants*) by Anne Brashares. New York: Delacorte/Random House (2001).

Summer Boys series (*Summer Boys*) by Hailey Abbott. New York: Point/Scholastic (2004).

Summer Share series (*LB Laguna Beach*) by Nola Thacker. New York: Simon & Schuster (2005).

Truth or Dare series (*White Lies and Barefaced Truths*) by Cathy Hopkins. New York: Simon & Schuster (2005).

Girls' Fascination with Romance

Romance literature is often called *escapist* or *wish-fulfilling literature* with little literary merit.[13] If we exam literary female images in history, we can deepen our understanding of this longing and female attraction to contemporary romances, stories in which female sexuality isn't oppressed and

[13]Romance advocates and theorists argue that historical gendering of romance is partly responsible for this criticism. That is, romance receives a bad "rap" because it has traditionally been "evaluated" by male-dominated cultures. Some supporters (e.g., Thompson, 2005) argue that romance critics seldom, if ever, cite novel specifics or analyze novels for content and style.

demoralized and in which characters fall head over heals in love. Consider the historical silencing of women's voices in literature and images of women in masculocentric literary works traditionally dominating English language arts classrooms (Hester Pryne is an adulteress; Tess Durbeyfield is raped; Mrs. Haversham is jilted; and Susan Henchard is sold by her husband). Some of the earliest romances written by female writers (e.g., the Brontë novels) also have depressing overtones. No wonder girls long for literature portraying women in happier circumstances and ending on a happy, yet predictable note—as poorly written as some of that literature may be. Equally important is their desire for literature portraying women with power.

Early homosexual-themed works portrayed gays and lesbians as victims, whereas today's homosexual literature includes portraits of happier characters, satisfied and confident with their identities (see Chapter 4). The same evolution is true for stories about women. The historical silencing of women led to stories that spoke to their suppression and victimization. As women gained a voice, stories began to depict women in happier, more powerful, and more positive roles. There was less need to show women's plight and a stronger need to show their increased power.

So why do girls digest romance novels so rapaciously?

Adolescent girls have a need to understand their own romantic relationships. They wish to be wanted, desirable, and important. Thus reading romance is a ritual of hope.[14] In allowing her female students to read romance novels as a course requirement, Ricker-Wilson (1999) gained a better understanding of female attraction to romances, perhaps summed up best by one student: "There was kissing and hugging in the book but no rough stuff, no pushing her into it. It showed love as something really nice. It was dreamy and beautiful . . . I liked this" (p. 58). This response speaks to girls' desires to navigate their own social and sexual relationships effectively. It also suggests girls' understanding of how badly some men treat women and the female wish to be valued. Because girls wish for happy relationships, they have a desire to play out their romantic involvements. Girls identify strongly with main characters and sometimes they become (pretend to be) the characters. Such imaginary role-playing helps them try out responses on males—and see possible results. They enjoy reading about what boys think and find pleasure in girls "speaking their minds" in arguments with boys (Moffitt, 1987).

During the summer of 2006, two upcoming high school female seniors read and discussed romances with me. They were glad, for once, to read something they didn't have to analyze. While they found the sizzling reads "disgusting" and "unrealistic," they couldn't help being fascinated by the characters' attitudes and lifestyles. It was difficult, they thought, to believe individuals could be so "singular-minded" (focused solely on looking "hot" and getting with the right person). However, they identified female celebrities who seemed to fit the mold. While they enjoyed romance novels,

---

[14]*Reading the Romance* (1984) by Janice A. Radway and *A Natural History of the Romance Novel* (2003) by Pamela Regis are wonderful research resources.

they were aware of negative portrayals of girls and wanted to talk about male-female social roles. They were also drawn more to realistic romances and romantic comedies than to series; this preference, they indicated, was because they wanted a deeper book. Serial romances, even Meg Cabot's best-selling *The Princess Diaries* series, seemed more like middle school reading to them. These older girls made the most meaningful connections in well-written, multithemed realistic fiction.

It's worth noting that these were college-bound, mature girls with strong academic backgrounds. It would be interesting to compare their responses to those of girls who do poorly academically and have no career aspirations. Would these latter girls be drawn more to the stereotypical, edgier reads? Would they accept the objectification of women more? Would they recognize and understand it?

Today's series remain almost exclusively about white girls. As mentioned in Chapter 4, white girls struggle more with image than do girls of other racial groups; this difference may speak to their fascination with series whose protagonists are gorgeous, rich, and irresistibly sexy. But what about black girls and other racial groups? Are they drawn to the same kind of characters and stories? What do they look for in romance? Why hasn't there been a rush on serial novels targeting black girls? Sharon G. Flake, author of *Who Am I without Him?* (2004), a Coretta Scott King Honor book, reflects on black girls, relationships, and these questions in the author box.

Black Girls, Romance, and Longing   by Sharon G. Flake

Boys always fascinated and scared me. I was the girl who ran to the opposite side of the street whenever I saw one. Never mind that I might have liked the boy, and thought he was cute. Inside I was all butterflies. So no wonder when I went to the library, I sought out books about the thing that excited and frightened me at the same time—romance. It was the 60s, and frankly there weren't many books about girls that looked like me and the boys that felt they couldn't live without me. So I read what the white girls read: books about suburban girls and the blue-eyed boys who chased after them.

Black girls today aren't that different than I was 35 years ago. They want romance, but they are typecast. People prefer to see them as video vixens and project freaks. It seems to strain the imaginations of publishers and producers to see our young black

Continued

Black Girls, Romance, and Longing   *Continued*

girls as heroines, or the positive love interests of admirable suitors.

In my short story collection *Who Am I without Him?* (2004), there are lots of different relationships between black girls and boys. There are three stories that especially excite black girls. One is about a girl who has a cheating, abusive boyfriend. Two others are about young black boys who simply exude romance. When I visit schools, girls often ask me, "Do you know Mooky?" They are talking about the character from "Mooky In Love." I tell them, "I made him up, but I'd love to meet him myself." Both boys and girls ask me about the boy in "Girl, Didn't I Tell You I Don't Write Letters?" The story takes an age-old format—letter writing between a boy and girl—and puts it in a modern day, urban classroom setting. Truth is the story shouldn't work. It does, however, because young black girls, like all girls, want their hearts and their heads sprinkled with a little fairy dust now and then, and they want to believe the boy next door just might be *the one*.

To write romance for black girls you have to believe that they can fly. That they dream. That they see themselves like other girls see themselves: loving, smart, beautiful, and ready for love. Add a dose of reality to that. If the characters live in the inner city, speak the way they speak. But keep in mind that not all inner-city people speak alike. Standard English is also spoken there. Add a dash of humor—you can't be in middle and high school without laughing a lot, so much of it is so ridiculously funny. Keep the tension high. No, that doesn't mean gun shots and exploding crack houses. It means keep the story moving. Pacing is everything to young black readers. They love the ride: the faster the better. Like other youth, they live in the digital age. They have cell phones and download music on iPods: speed might kill on the highway, but in young adult novels it's a sure winner.

All girls dream of being loved and treated like royalty. When our country sees young black girls this way, then romance novels featuring *them* will appear on store shelves as plentiful as ice cream in supermarket coolers. Until then, they will do what all girls do—sit back, close their eyes, and imagine a world where they are highly valued and much loved.

Copyright Sharon G. Flake, 2008
Official Web site: www.sharongflake.com
Titles by Sharon G. Flake not mentioned in this chapter include *The Skin I'm In* (1998), *Money Hungry* (2001), *Begging for Change* (2003), and *Bang!* (2005).

It would be a mistake not to mention nonserial romances by such writers as Catherine Clark, Kate Cann, Jan Coffey, and Rachel Hawthorne. Not all girls, of course, are drawn to serial romances; some are turned off by negative portrayals of girls, emphasis on A-listers[15] and lifestyles of the rich and famous, and poor writing quality, and some simply get bored reading about the same characters. They may not identify writing as an issue, but they may, for example, express boredom with plot—rightfully so, for serial plots are generally thin. It's likely better readers and girls who read more from a feminist perspective and who want to read meaningful stories that mirror their own lives comprise this lot. Romances written by the previously mentioned authors, though light reads, offer better and more original plots and stronger characters.

---
[15]*A-lister* comes from the term *a-list,* meaning the most desirable group of people. Directors, for example, have a-lists of Hollywood stars they want at their private parties.

Nonserial romances offer girls a less formulaic read, although plots can be predictable and circumstances contrived. They're not likely choices for the classroom; however, they are an alternative form of pleasure reading for girls turned off by romance novels with heavy pop culture influences or for girls who become bored with the same characters. These nonserial romances are characterized by girls on vacation (generally older girls so the absence of parents is more believable), many of whom take summer jobs at resorts such as the protagonist in Rachel Hawthorne's *Thrill Ride* (2006) or vacation in winter resorts (e.g., Kaz Delaney's *My Life As a Snow Bunny*, 2003), or on cruises (Rachel Hawthorne's *Caribbean Cruising*, 2004). Some of these romances feature little or no sexual contact; others have a great deal. Generally, the biggest problem girls deal with is "getting the guy." Nonetheless, some of these books make strong statements about being female in today's world and are good starting points for teaching students to examine texts from a feminist perspective.

Boys and Romance

The romance novel is considered a female genre, but that doesn't mean boys aren't interested in romance. Boys don't read traditional or serial romances, but they do read books with romantic themes. They have the same questions and issues about relationships, only they are socialized to withhold emotions and "check out" intimate relationships in indirect ways. In their reading, boys prefer novels in which romance is more subtle, or more sexually charged; romance is one of several threads in a novel they would choose. And, yes, sometimes it's difficult to distinguish between a boy's sexual interest and emotional connection in a young adult novel.

Unfortunately, little literature about romantic relationships appeals to males. How many high school boys, for instance, want to read the *Gossip Girl* series novel or a Louise Rennison novel? Boys need stories about relationships that are not feminine in nature: books about girls and dating must be realistic and gritty, not romantic or dreamy; they should contain action, suspense, or themes such as sports. Covers need to attract young men; they cannot be cartoonish nor resemble Harlequinn romances. Titles, too, must capture them.

Novels featuring these characteristics are rare; however, as the young adult literature genre matures, authors are beginning to write romantic stories that appeal to boys. Many of these titles fall within the problem novel genre. The problem novel was addressed in Chapter 4, but a few titles with heavy romantic themes are listed in Box 5.3. A narrative by Angela Johnson, author of *The First Part Last* (2003b),[16] that illustrates boys' concerns and questions about relationships and the hunger they have to understand themselves and girls is presented in the author box.

---

[16]*The First Part Last* won the Michael L. Printz Award in 2004.

Box 5.3   Romance for Boys

24 Girls in 7 Days by Alex Bradley. New York: Dutton/Penguin, 2005.

To find Jack a prom date, his friends place an ad on his behalf in the school newspaper. The result: over 100 responses. In this hilarious look at teen romance, Jack goes on 24 dates looking for the right girl to take to the prom.

An Abundance of Katherines by John Green. New York: Dutton/Penguin, 2006.

Colin Singleton has little luck with girls, especially ones named Katherine. In an attempt to get over his anguish, he takes a road trip with a friend. They end up in Tennessee, where they meet Lindsey Wells and her mother, Hollis. Hollis hires them to record oral histories. Colin spends the time devising a mathematical formula that he believes can predict the future of a romantic relationship.

After Summer by Nick Earls. Boston: Graphia/Houghton Mifflin, 2005.

While spending the Christmas break at his mother's beach house and waiting for news about his college applications, Alex Delaney falls for Fortuna, a tanned, muscular, exceptional girl. As their relationship intensifies, Alex realizes the end of summer means the end of their relationship.

Candy by Kevin Brooks. New York: Scholastic, 2005.

Joe discovers too late that he has fallen for a drug addict. He confronts danger as he tries helping Candy break away from a desperate world of drugs and violence. A heartaching tale of love and loyalty.

Nowhere Fast by Kevin Waltman. New York: Scholastic, 2002.

A summer coming-of-age story about 15-year-old Gary who works at a fast-food joint, hangs out with Wilson, his best friend, and struggles with his girlfriend, Lauryn. Lauryn disapproves of their reckless behavior.

Probably the World's Best Story about a Dog and the Girl Who Loved Me by D. James Smith. New York: Atheneum/Simon & Schuster, 2006.

When Paolo's dog is stolen, he sets out to find the dognappers, only Theresa has a huge crush on Paolo and won't leave him alone.

Storky: How I Lost My Nickname and Won the Girl by D. L. Garfinkle. New York: Putnam, 2005.

Storky chronicles his confused freshman year in a journal. The love of his life dates a football player, and Storky hopes to win her over. A comical and witty story of an average teen.

Stuff: The Life of a Cool Demented Dude by Jeremy Strong. New York: HarperCollins, 2007.

Fourteen-year-old Simon (a.k.a. Stuff) dreams of becoming an artist. His art teacher suggests he draw weekly cartoons for the school paper. His comics are influenced by his disagreeable stepmother, a girl he likes named Sky, other family members, and friends. Sky becomes the hero, and his stepmother becomes an evil galactic ruler. A book for boys by a British author reminiscent of Louise Rennison's *Georgia Nicolson* series.

Where the Kissing Never Stops by Ron Koertge. Cambridge, MA: Candlewick Press, 2005.

A young teen has more on his shoulders than he can handle. He's overweight, his father is dead, and his mother has taken a job as a stripper. When Walker meets a new girl, his life gets better.

Loving the Boy by Angela Johnson

As a teenager I was always a bit of a cynic about what I believed was the inability of boyfriends to truly see us for who we were. I believed like most of my group you never know what was on a boyfriend's mind once he was out of your sight. I never thought it was on us or our relationship. I had my teen prejudices, you see, about boys.

Did he really like you because you were smart and could outpace him in algebra and science? Did he really think you were fall-on-the-floor funny? Did he really think it was cool that you wore his jerseys and sweatshirts (and never gave them back)?

So what about now, 27 years later and a world away from what dating and loving the boy used to be?

I'd like to think boys have a little bit more to say than they used to. I'd like to see a few series out there in the young adult literature world where young men are talking about the pain, joy, and ridiculousness of it all loving the girl or boy (thank you Alex Sanchez!).

Very early on after the publication of *The First Part Last* I received much feedback from young women who loved the character of Bobby. What a boyfriend! They loved that he was warm, loyal, and even confused. They loved that even through tragedy and exhaustion he was still there.

I loved that about Bobby too. And many times I sat in large groups of young people with the teen boys saying nothing about the book or anything else for that matter. As usual the young women were very vocal and tuned in. The young men—silent they were. But about a year ago a young man spoke up as his class watched him in the library of a midwestern high school and said . . .

"It's hard out there."

"Out there" meaning the world with young men and women bumping into each other beginning the waltz of longing, love, relationships, and sex. And as none of his classmates laughed, he continued.

When did it get so hard to know what to do or say when it came to kicking it with a girl? The rules were all different from when they were little. You teased girls and grabbed their backpacks if you liked them in grade school. Sometimes, if people weren't looking, you might smile at her or give her your juice box. Sometimes she smiled at you and giggled with her friends. And sometimes you two could even walk together to school if there were other people around.

Now it was how long do you hang with her before you are considered a couple?

What about sex right now even before you are a couple? Safe sex 'cause his mother would kill him 12 times if he got somebody pregnant. What about your buddies and where she comes in on that? What about her friends? What about her mother who hates you and this person you know who likes her a little too much?

As the young man sat down I smiled. All of the other young men's heads were nodding. I now knew even though they hadn't been talking they'd been thinking. (I should have known it all along for I'm no longer 16.)

I've now rethought the old philosophy I had as a teen girl. Maybe it won't be so hard for girls now to understand while loving the boy.

Johnson writes for both children and teens. Popular teen titles include *Bird* (2004a), *Cool Moonlight* (2003a), *Looking for Red* (2002), *Heaven* (1998), *Humming Whispers* (1995), and *Toning the Sweep* (1993). Picture books appropriate for teens include *A Sweet Smell of Roses* (2005), *Just Like Josh Gibson* (2004b), and *When I Am Old with You* (1990).

Publishers are becoming increasingly aware of the power of visual images and titles. If a young adult novel looks like something a boy read in middle school or looks too feminine, high school boys won't read it. The cover (a girl's torso) and title of Markus Zusak's *Getting the Girl* (2003) is a sure winner with boys. Within the pages is a rugged, yet tender story about first love and brotherly solidarity. Cameron Wolfe lives in the shadow of his older, athletic brother, Ruben. While Cameron yearns for a girlfriend, he watches Ruben go through one relationship after another and cringes as Ruben talks trash about those he's dumped. Ruben wants each girl only because she is his next conquest; he has no feelings for girls and has never loved. Cameron disdains Ruben's behavior and vows he will treat girls better.

When Ruben and Octavia break up, Cameron's desire becomes a reality as he and Octavia develop a tender relationship. Though Ruben has moved on to another conquest, he is jealous of Cameron's sensitivity toward Octavia and beats him up. Octavia ends her relationship with Cameron because she refuses to come between two brothers. Cameron feels lost and hopeless; Ruben feels guilty for destroying the relationship.

Although a central theme of Zusak's novel is brotherly love, the novel has much to offer boys about boy-girl relationships. Ruben disrespects girls, whereas Cameron is affectionate and respectful. After fighting Cameron, Ruben feels shame and no longer boasts about conquering girls. Healthy relationships, he realizes, are not about winning girls, treating them like prizes, or even having sex. Getting all the "hot" girls does not make him a man; treating women with respect does. Cameron becomes his role model.

Zusak's novel raises the issue of respect. While some boys value girls, others emulate Ruben. Sometimes disrespect comes from family experiences; other times it may come from peer relations and other cultural forces. Because attitudes and behaviors are difficult to alter, it is unlikely that disrespectful boys will suddenly treat girls better after reading *Getting the Girl*; however, Zusak's novel can offer boys some insight into the nature of healthy relationships. Well-developed and realistic, Ruben and Cameron Wolfe are characters with whom boys can easily relate.

Boys often exploit girls, but boys also can be victimized. The male protagonist in Ellen Wittlinger's *Razzle* (2001) allows himself to be used despite numerous warnings. When 15-year-old Kenyon Baker moves with his retired parents to Cape Cod to restore and operate a dilapidated resort, he believes he will experience the worst summer ever; instead, he meets Razzle Penney, a tall, skinny eccentric girl, and the two become close friends. Their friendship is tested, however, when Kenyon falls for Harley, a gorgeous but dangerous girl, despite warnings from Razzle and Harley's castoffs.

With the aid of Frank, a gay plumber, Kenyon learns that beauty is truly skin deep, a hard but important lesson. When Harley tricks him into shooting photos of her and displaying them in an art show, hoping she will be discovered and can leave Cape Cod, Kenyon realizes Harley used him.

Though Razzle lacks Harley's sexual appeal and physical beauty, Kenyon realizes he cares for Razzle because she is real and true. Despite his revelation, Kenyon must leave Razzle when his aging parents admit repairing the rundown resort is too labor intensive.

Any boy who has ever felt used can relate to Kenyon's pain. Though teens place tremendous importance on physical attributes, Wittlinger's story illustrates that physical attractiveness means little unless it is accompanied by inner beauty. Though some boys, like Zusak's Ruben Wolfe, are callous and exploit girls, this book illustrates that boys can be used too. Kenyon is a wonderful role model for boys who find themselves in exploited situations. Unlike many boys who become resentful and angry, who lash out and develop negative attitudes toward girls, Kenyon works through his pain in grace. He walks away from Harley having learned an important lesson about intimacy and attraction.

Sharon Draper's *The Battle of Jericho* (2003), a story with a strong hazing theme, shows how far some boys will go for the girl of their dreams. When Jericho and his cousin, Josh, pledge for the Warriors of Distinction, an exclusive club in their school, Jericho believes life is perfect, especially when Arielle, a good-looking classmate, shows interest because he is a soon-to-be warrior. Believing Arielle is worth the price, Jericho endures brutal and dangerous initiation rituals. Only when a fatal accident occurs does Jericho realize the price he's paid.

Most boys will easily relate to Jericho's desire to impress Arielle. While girls may attract boys by wearing the right clothes and looking desirable, boys tend to impress girls through actions. Athletic boys attract girls through sports; other boys, such as Jericho, use organizations or activities that bestow manliness or social status.

First relationships are tough, and teens will go to extremes to maintain a relationship. Draper's work raises important questions: "What are you willing to sacrifice for the person of your dreams?" "What are you willing to do?" "What are the consequences?" We're not born knowing how to develop or respond to romantic relationships. Young adult literature with which boys can relate can be a safe portal through which boys can explore emotions without fear of ridicule; such literature can provide answers to questions boys may never ask.

Best in Romance: Realistic and Paranormal Love Stories

Chapter 2 addresses motivation and the importance of valuing teens' reading choices. While we want our young girls to grow into women who read more than Harlequinn romances (Does an occasional indulgence hurt?), romance novels can hook nonreaders into reading and can turn them on to other genres, themes, and more complex and better-written stories. Covered here are a number of well-written novels with strong romance themes (Chapter 4 addresses sexuality, love, and dating). As Charles, Mosley, and Bouricius (1999) remind us, romance novels are about love, not gratuitous sex, so the novels included here are ones in which teens are looking for intimate emotional connections. Some are better labeled "chick lit" because they focus on a single character's struggles to succeed in life, and romance plays only a part in those struggles. A *true* romance, whether realistic or paranormal,[17] is relationship driven, focusing on two characters as opposed to one, and ends happily-ever-after. Most of these would fail that test.

Melina Marchetta's *Looking for Alibrandi* (1999), for example, is a tender, smart, funny love story about Josephine Alibrandi, born into wedlock to an Italian mother. Josephine must confront the father she has never known and deal with her mother's need for love and her own adolescent yearnings. Annette Curtis Klause's *Blood and Chocolate* (1997), a major motion picture in 2007, is an example of a paranormal romance. Vivian, a young werewolf, is torn between keeping her family secret and her love for Aiden, a human. Ellen Schreiber's *Vampire Kisses* (2003), also a paranormal romance, is about 16-year-old Raven, a goth misfit, who dreams of becoming a vampire. When she falls in love with a mysterious new boy, she hopes he can make her wishes come true. Francesca Lia Block, who broke new ground in YA literature with her complex fairy-tale series about Weetzie Bat and her friends, is a master of the paranormal romance. Weetzie Bat, forty in *Necklace of Kisses* (2005), yearns for the romantic passion of youth. She checks into the Pink Hotel, where she received her first kiss. There she kisses and receives gifts from a series of characters—a sushi-eating mermaid, her father's ghost, an angel, a faun—who help her on her quest to inner healing.

Box 5.4 includes some of the best in romance for today's teens. Some are light reads (no hard-hitting problem that needs to be resolved); many contain a good dose of humor, strong female characters, and blur genre boundaries; all are crafted well, having interesting, well-rounded characters and strong plotlines and strong statements about male-female social roles. Excluded here are books with stereotypical characters and stories in which the only issue guys or girls care about is getting with the right person. (Same-sex relationships are discussed in Chapter 4.) In the author box, Joan Bauer, author of numerous acclaimed young adult novels, including the paranormal romantic comedy *Thwonk* (1995), discusses her desire to write honestly about teenage romance. Following her essay are reactions from high school girls about reading romance.

---

[17]Paranormal romances include elements of the fantastic (e.g., ghosts, vampires, witches), thus blending genres such as horror, fantasy, science fiction, and alternative history.

Box 5.4   Great Romance Reads

48 Shades of Brown by Nick Earls. New York: Penguin, 1999.

During his last year of high school, Dan lives with his 22-year-old Aunt Jacq and her college roommate Naomi. His feelings for Naomi instantly develop. Dan humorously learns tough coming-of-age lessons about love, relationships, and being yourself.

Accidental Love by Gary Soto. Orlando, FL: Harcourt, 2006.

Marisa, a street-smart girl, and Rene, a nerd from the nearby magnet school, unexpectedly meet and find romance. To be closer to Rene, Marisa finds a way to enroll at Rene's school, and their relationship sparks a change in Marisa's attitude and self-image. Can her transformation withstand being sent back to her old school?

Beating Heart: A Ghost Story by A. M. Jenkins. New York: HarperCollins, 2006.

This romantic mystery alternates voices between 17-year-old Evan and Cora, a ghost haunting his new home. As Evan works through his own relationship, he learns about Cora's romance and her tragic fate.

Boston Jane: An Adventure by Jennifer L. Holm. New York: HarperCollins, 2001.

Tomboy Jane is determined to attend Miss Hepple-white's Young Ladies' Academy to win the love of William, her father's apprentice. When William asks Jane to marry him, she follows him to the Oregon frontier. Once there, Jane learns that William has an ulterior motive. Jane ultimately learns to accept herself and find true love.

Boy Proof by Cecil Castellucci. Cambridge, MA: Candlewick Press, 2005.

High school student Victoria creates a "boy proof" identity: shaved head, white cloak, and colored

Seventeen-year-old Deb Caletti, author of *Honey, Baby, Sweetheart,* in front of her parents' western Washington beach house. *Honey, Baby, Sweetheart* is a National Book Award finalist.

eyebrows in honor of her science fiction heroine, Egg. This way she doesn't have to deal with the realities of relationships, but when she meets Max, the new boy at school, Victoria is ready to shed her boy-proof image. Fans may enjoy *The Queen of Cool* (2006) and *The Plain Janes* (2007), the latter written in graphic novel form.

Confessions of a Not It Girl by Melissa Kantor. New York: Hyperion, 2004.

While Jan pines for her crush, Josh, Rebecca's romance with a college law student steams up. Things don't go as planned as Josh focuses on his long-distance girl-friend, and Rebecca lies about her age. In-between romances, the girls focus on finishing high school and applying for college. Kantor fans may enjoy *The Breakup Bible* (2007), a story about heartache and healing following a romantic split.

Dancing with an Alien by Mary Logue. New York: HarperTempest/HarperCollins, 2000.

When Branko and Tonia meet, they immediately connect and quickly realize they were meant to be together. Branko and his people want the relation-ship, but can Branko take Tonia away from her family and her planet?

Continued

Box 5.4   Great Romance Reads *Continued*

Do-over by Rachel Vail. New York: Orchard/Scholastic, 1992.

Whitman Levy experiences first love, French kisses, and "stiffies" during eighth grade. At the same time, Whitman watches as his parents' marriage falls apart because of his father's affair with Whitman's drama teacher.

Flipped by Wendelin Van Draanen. New York: Knopf/Random House, 2001.

Told through alternating points of view, *Flipped* details the rocky relationship between Juli and Bryce. Juli has been enchanted with Bryce from age seven, but Bryce constantly avoided her until eighth grade. Will it be too late?

The Girl Who Invented Romance by Caroline B. Cooney. New York: Bantam, 1988.

Kelly, deeply interested in romance, watches the rocky romances of her parents and brother, reads about romance in magazines, and takes intimacy quizzes. To bide the time before her own romantic life begins, she develops a romance board game.

Honey, Baby, Sweetheart by Deb Caletti. New York: Simon & Schuster, 2004.

Ruby and her mother, Ann, are both nursing broken hearts from wild relationships. To ease their pain, they help a book club friend reunite with a lost love. Caletti fans may enjoy *Wild Roses* (2005) and *The Nature of Jade* (2007).

If We Kiss by Rachel Vail. New York: HarperCollins, 2005.

This romantic comedy follows Charlie as she tries to understand why Kevin, her best friend's boyfriend, kissed her and what she should do about it. In the meantime, Charlie's mom is dating Kevin's father, and he could become her stepbrother. Fans may also

enjoy *Megan Meade's Guide to the McGowan Boys* (Brian 2005).

Is Kissing a Girl Who Smokes Like Licking an Ashtray? by Randy Powell. New York: Farrar, Straus & Giroux, 1992.

Shy high school senior Biff has never had a girlfriend and has trouble even talking to girls until he meets Heidi, the wild and unpredictable teen staying with family friends. In an unlikely pairing, the teens find romance during spring break.

Jinx by Margaret Wild. New York: Simon & Schuster, 2002.

In a series of tragedies, Jinx loses both of her boyfriends—Charlie who commits suicide and Ben who dies in a freak accident. Jinx resorts to tormenting the boy she considers responsible for Ben's death until she unexpectedly falls in love with him.

Motown and Didi: A Love Story by Walter Dean Myers. New York: Dell, 1984.

In a fight against a drug dealer destroying Didi's brother's life, Motown and Didi fall in love.

Permanent Connections by Sue Ellen Bridgers. New York: HarperCollins, 1987.

Rob's family, determined to save him from self-destructive behavior, sends him to stay with family in rural North Carolina. There, Rob falls in love with Ellory, but when she ends the relationship, Rob finds the same trouble he found in the city and must take responsibility for his actions.

Send No Blessings by Phyllis Reynolds Naylor. New York: Atheneum/Simon & Schuster, 1990.

Beth deplores her life of poverty in West Virginia living in a trailer with eight siblings. She is determined to

Continued

Box 5.4   Great Romance Reads   *Continued*

make a better life for herself. But when she falls in love with high school dropout Harless, can she give up her dreams?

The Silver Kiss by Annette Curtis Klause. New York: Delacorte/Random House, 1990.

The unlikely romance of Zoe and Simon is centered around death. Zoe's mother is dying a painful death due to cancer. Simon is a 300-year-old vampire searching for revenge.

This Lullaby: A Novel by Sarah Dessen. New York: Viking/Penguin, 2002.

Remy has sworn off romance as her mother prepares for her fifth wedding. Then Remy meets Dexter, lead singer in a rock band, the summer after she graduates from high school, and she must face her intimacy fears.

Twilight by Stephenie Meyer. New York: Little, Brown, 2005.

When Bella moves to Washington, she is immediately drawn to beautiful and dangerous classmate Edward. When Bella learns Edward is a vampire, she is both disgusted and intrigued. Edward must save her from an evil vampire. Fans may enjoy other titles in the *Twilight Saga: New Moon* (2006), *Eclipse* (2007), and *Breaking Dawn* (2008).

The Unlikely Romance of Kate Bjorkman by Louise Plummer. New York: Delacorte/Random House, 1995.

In this romantic comedy, Kate's college brother, Bjorn, and his wife return for the Christmas holidays and bring Kate's long-time crush, Richard, Bjorn's friend. But Richard also brings Trish. Kate tells her story with the help of a romance writer's manual.

On Writing Romance   by Joan Bauer

Years ago my editor jokingly told me that the sure-fire way to have a YA hit was to put *boyfriend*, *chocolate*, or *horse* in the title. I briefly considered trying to write *My Boyfriend Has a Chocolate Horse*—thankfully, I didn't have it in me. It was, however, a crazy catalyst that got me contemplating teenage romance. It's a theme that conjures up all kinds of Hollywood images of gorgeous kids on the beach, or at the ski resort, or at private schools, or jetting around without cares or cellulite.

   Most of my novels have a romantic relationship tucked inside, and I always take care to think about the love interest quite seriously because I care deeply for my characters, and, like any good mother, I don't want them wasting their time (or mine) on shallow relationships. So I always have an important life interest that the boy and girl share—Ellie and Wes have agriculture in *Squashed* (1992); Ivy and Jack understand the need to push past fear on the wintry

mountain in *Backwater* (1999); Hope and Braverman know the depths of diner life in *Hope Was Here* (2000). They share each other's dreams because they

Continued

On Writing Romance *Continued*

understand them; they support each other's trials because they've had enough of their own.

I tend to write about responsible kids who've been through tough times, like Jenna Boller, ace shoe salesperson of *Rules of the Road* (1998) and *Best Foot Forward* (2005). In the second book, I wanted Jenna to have a boyfriend, but she was hardly mainstream romance material—too tall, sensible, not gorgeous, older than her years with a remarkable work ethic bordering on workaholism. She's dealing with both her dad's drinking and his abandonment, and she is staring down the very un-teenage issue of corporate corruption on the job. No beach boys for Jenna. Enter Charlie Duran—his family runs Chicago's premiere donut establishment. He works hard by day, goes to night school, and waxes eloquent about his grandpa's donut vision that gave the world the Duran raspberry cream. Jenna doesn't talk much about Charlie's looks, but she does declare the fullness of her heart when she dreamily declares, *"He understands retail!"*

But my novel *Thwonk* (1992) looks at the other side of relationships—the controlling and obsessive side. What would one girl do to get *the* guy? A. J. McCreary would do close to anything. She wants perfect love now that shows the world she's worthy of adoration. It takes a road-weary cupid to show her that "Love that embraces the entire person is a monumental gift that takes time to grow!" I wrote *Thwonk* for my daughter who was in middle school at the time, trying to navigate the murky waters of in crowds and out crowds.

There's a desperation sometimes in the affairs of the heart. Romance is a jungle; emotions are debilitating and misleading. But I have a simple rule for my characters who are about to step into romance: Be good friends first, girlfriend and boyfriend second. And, yes, I told my daughter that as well.

Copyright Joan Bauer, 2008
Official Web site: www.joanbauer.com
Titles by Joan Bauer not mentioned in this chapter include *Sticks* (1996), *Stand Tall* (2002), and *Peeled* (2008).

Girls Speak Out about Serial Romances

I've already gone through the phase in my life where situations fascinate me and emotions control actions, which is what those books [serial romances] were about. Now, I enjoy reading things that will make me think about a topic or inform me.

—*Sarah, senior*

These novels [serial romances] aren't bad at all. Some say they're brain junk food, polluting adolescent minds. But I say, who cares? They're reading, right? Which, these days, is a feat in itself. Where's the harm when a freshman stays up all night to finish *Cruel Summer?* As opposed to what? TV? The computer? At least they're reading. This way, when someone asks them what the last book they've read was, they can honestly answer, instead of saying "Ewww, books!" That sadly is the favored response of so many of my peers.

—*Sally, senior*

Final Thoughts on Romance

If you walk past the teen section in any bookstore, you will see an overwhelming number of pastel-colored books—mostly pink. Chick lit is a hot commodity in today's market. While not all chick lit is driven by a romantic theme, romance permeates most of it. Teens, especially girls, enjoy romance for its escapist value, and both sexes are drawn to it for the insight it provides about relationships.

We should remember that romance bias is gendered; criticism of romance dates back to the days when women were struggling to find their voice among men in society and in the publishing world. An undercurrent of that bias remains with us, and we can address it by reading widely in this genre. Whether we value romance or not, if we don't respect teens' interest, we can't expect them to respect ours. The romance genre, more than any other, gives women a voice and provides a statement about the historical subjugation and objectification of women.

Humor

Comedian Mel Brooks once said, "Tragedy is when I cut my finger. Comedy is when *you* fall into an open sewer and die" (Best Quotes, 2007). The ability to laugh, even when confronting tragedy, is uniquely human. Humor offers hope during times of sadness and provides constructive ways for dealing with difficult situations. Humor helps us overcome adversity and fears and provides a unique lens for examining human behavior and social problems. The ability to laugh at human behavior, including our own, enables us to grow beyond our struggles and fears.

Critics have voiced concern over the lack of humor in young adult literature, drawing attention to the heaviness and grittiness of the problem novel, the genre mainstay. For years, that criticism has been justified. Although many books are sprinkled with humor, it's difficult to find laugh-out-loud funny young adult literature prior to the 1990s. M. E. Kerr's brilliantly funny and poignant *Dinky Hocker Shoots Smack* (1972) is a notable exception. Still in print, this story follows Tucker Woolf as he finds a new home for Nader, his cat, a home belonging to Dinky Hocker, the weirdest girl Tucker has ever met.

Today, however, the young adult market has an abundance of humor; many are romantic spoofs or coming-of-age stories about sexual identity and family relations. The Society of Children's Book Writers and Illustrators, honoring this recent trend, developed the Sid Fleischman[18] Humor Award in 2002. David Larochelle's *Absolutely, Positively Not . . .* , the 2005 winner and unquestionably one of the best books of the year, features a protagonist who struggles with his sexual identity, minus gut-wrenching pain. The opening passage gives some insight into the book's hilarity:

> Everybody has at least one ugly secret, and mine is as ugly as they come.
>> I square-dance.
>> With my mother.
>> I'm not talking once-a-year square dancing. I'm talking *serious* square dancing, every week, where the women wear fluffy checkered skirts that stick out a yard on either side and the men wear matching cowboy shirts and everyone wears a big plastic name tag shaped like a music note.
>> And the ugliest part of this secret is . . . I actually like it. (p. 1).

It's refreshing to know teens can find books that address sexual identity with a touch of humor.

---

[18]Sid Fleischman, author of *The Whipping Boy* (1986), a Newbery winner, is known for his humorous stories for children and preadolescents.

Understanding and Appreciating Humor

Despite the human need for humor, many dismiss it as "fluffy" or "unsuitable classroom reading." In "The Straw Man Meets His Match: Six Arguments for Studying Humor in English Classes," Alleen Nilsen and Don Nilsen (1999) dispel these six assertions that contribute to our devaluing humor, thus excluding it from the classroom:

- Kids already get enough humor outside of school.
- Teaching humor will take away from the time I need to teach grammar, composition, literature, and public speaking.
- I'm supposed to be preparing kids to earn a living.
- If I bring humor into my class, I'll have censorship problems.
- Humor hurts people's feelings.
- I can't teach about humor when I can't even tell a joke or write a funny letter home.

Humor is ever present in our daily lives; to dismiss it from the classroom suggests that school is even less relevant than teens think. Studying humor helps students understand allusions and subtleties and aids teens in developing a repertoire of humorous forms (Nilsen & Nilsen, 1999, p. 34). Contrary to traditional thinking, well-written humor can provide excellent writing models and springboards for discussing personal, social, and political issues.

An additional faulty assertion about humor deals with text misinterpretation. As readers we set a purpose for reading. When we approach a book, we have some idea, some schema, about that book—the cover, the title, our knowledge about the author, and the genre all contribute to our reading expectations. Sometimes, however, a book fails our expectations. A book we perceived as realistic teen romance, for example, ends up being unrealistic or silly because of bizarre happenings, improbable, shallow characters, fabrications, coincidences, and absurdities. In actuality, these traits that threw the reader are often deliberate measures taken by the author; we need to adjust our schema and reread. The story could be a spoof, a satire, or a farce;[19] it could be an over-the-top look at human behavior or a social commentary. In cases like these, our value judgments are wrong because we fail to understand the author's intent.

A humorous debut novel that takes a look at a "popularity-challenged" boy's life.

Jacket cover from *Spanking Shakespeare* by Jake Wizner. Used by permission of Random House Children's Books, a division of Random House, Inc.

---

[19]Satire and farce are often used interchangeably; however, they are different. A satire generally makes fun of certain subjects, things, or people, usually with the purpose of ridicule, whereas a farce generally exaggerates characters, characteristics, and events for the purpose of humor and may include satire. Oscar Wilde's *The Importance of Being Earnest* (1895/1995) is a farce that makes fun of the elite English upper class.

On one level Kieran Scott's *I Was a Non-Blonde Cheerleader* (2005) may seem merely a light, nonsense read about cheerleading antics. Dark-haired Annisa Gobrowski, a New Jersey transplant, tries out for cheerleading in a Florida high school where all girls are either bleached, frosted, or natural blondes, including the black cheerleading coach. In fighting for a spot, Annisa confronts over-the-top crises: she breaks the nose of the most popular girl in school, and drama ensues when she becomes too friendly with a popular cheerleader's guitar-playing jock. If read as a satire, the book raises important questions about individuality, popularity, and fitting in with the cool crowd. The fact, as absurd and unreal as it is, that all girls, including the black coach, are varying shades of "blondeness" point to human follies about image, fitting in, and popularity. Blake Nelson's *Prom Anonymous* (2006), though a seemingly light read, can also be read as satire on school proms.

One of the best written and funniest young adult books ever, Susan Juby's *Alice, I Think* (2003), makes fun of overly protecting teenagers. Home-schooled by her hippie mother and somewhat distant father since first grade when she attended school dressed as a hobbit, Alice moves into the social landscape of high school on the advice of her inept therapist. Consider this scene when the family gets their first computer, thereby leaving the "Dark Ages" and entering the "Enlightenment":

> *Still later*
> Well, so far Internet culture sucks. I'm not even sure if I am on the Web or not. If this is it, all these stupid little boxes on the screen, then the Internet is the biggest fraud I've come across yet. I think there is supposed to be some kind of noise when the computer hooks up to the Net, but so far all I've gotten is these clanking sounds and squawks and beeps when I hit the keys.
> I can't take this anymore. I'm going to go wake up MacGregor.
> *Really late*
> It turns out I was in the Help menu. I don't know how a person is supposed to tell what's going on with these computers. (pp. 190–191)

Every page of *Alice, I Think* is filled with similar examples of smart, witty writing. In her author box Susan Juby explains why she writes humor.

Young adult authors also use comedy to satirize the romance novel. A popular structural device is the budding writer protagonist. Both Kathleen Jeffrie Johnson's *Dumb Love* (2005) and Carol Lynch Williams's *My Angelica* (1999) feature female protagonists searching for true love while writing their own romance novels.

It's easy to dismiss a good comedy by saying "this isn't realistic," but humor can cross the realism boundary. Good humor can be satirical, absurd, even sarcastic. Box 5.5 features some outstanding funny reads, outstanding for their humor but also exceptional for writing quality.

Humor includes puns and hyperbole like that used by Gary Paulsen in *Harris and Me: A Summer Remembered* (1993) or Paul Zindel in *The Undertaker's Gone Bananas* (1978). It contains quirky, zany characters such as those created by Richard Peck (e.g., *A Year Down Yonder*, 2000; *The Teacher's Funeral: A Comedy in Three Parts*, 2004; and *Here Lies the Librarian*, 2006). It can even be gross such as *Jack's Black Book* (1997) by Jack Gantos. In this book, everything is game: cafeteria workers cream chicken gizzards and a dog is buried twice. Humor can be *farce* such as Gary Schmidt's *First Boy* (2005), a story about an orphaned farm boy who learns he may be the

Why I Write Comedy   by Susan Juby

It has been said that "comedy deals with that portion of our suffering that is exempt from tragedy." That line goes a long way toward explaining why I write young adult comedies. Most of the world views all but the most utterly heinous types of adolescent suffering as not tragic but, well, sort of adolescent. If the issues don't involve social services agencies and hospitals, the run of the mill kinds of teen agony are not given the dignity they so desperately require. This is what makes adolescent life fertile ground for comedy. I know I still carry with me an aggrieved sense that NO ONE KNOWS MY PAIN and that when it comes to the multilayered and dynamic nature of my suffering, everyone is a bit thick.

At first I coped with my feeling of personal tragedy by reading compulsively. But when I became a teenager I got so gloomy that not even the tragedies of anthropomorphized animals could make me feel better. Fortunately, my mother understood my need to be depressed and depressing, and she also had her own techniques for snapping me out of it. She'd tempt me with funny books. If it hadn't been for those funny books, I might not have spoken to any members of my family from the time I was 13 to when I, to everyone's relief, turned 17. Those funny books allowed my mother and me to cross the River Kwaii of teenager-parent communication. She introduced me to books like the *Secret Diaries of Adrian Mole, Aged 13 ¾* and the works of Gerald Durrell, and, before I knew it, I was laughing. Comedies allowed me to deal with the tragedy of my adolescence and gave me models for when I started to write.

I set out wanting to write comedies that acknowledge there are some very painful things about being an adolescent. Humor often deals with that which isn't funny. Teenagers are handed countless disappointments as they emerge from childhood into

adulthood. Just ask Holden Caulfield, the most disappointed of them all. Loneliness, confusion, fitting in or not fitting in, trouble at school, finding out who you are and maybe being a bit disappointed or worried at the discovery. These are all things teens have to cope with.

As we grow, I think the most interesting among us discover one effective way to cope with tragedy is through comedy, and those of us who learn to laugh are the fortunate ones. The eminently quotable Peter De Vries wrote that "We all have to climb out of the pit of desolation, or, what is more likely, manage to live in it, planting our flowers in the ashes and squirting them with our gaiety."

That's what I'm trying to do when I write.

Copyright Susan Juby, 2008

Official Web site: www.susanjuby.com

Other titles by Juby include two sequels to *Alice, I Think: Miss Smithers* (2004) and *Alice MacLeod, Realist at Last* (2005), and *Another Kind of Cowboy* (2007).

Box 5.5   Outstanding Funny Reads

***Airball: My Life in Briefs* by L. D. Harkrader. New Milford, CT: Roaring Brook Press, 2005.**

Klutzy Kirby Nickel goes out for the seventh-grade basketball team in order to meet basketball superstar Brett McGrew, whom Kirby believes is his father. This is an amusing look at small-town obsession with sports and will appeal mostly to middle school readers.

***Born to Rock* by Gordon Korman. New York: Hyperion, 2006.**

Leo Caraway, a high school self-proclaimed republican, is on his way to Wall Street success with an early acceptance to Harvard until he discovers his father is really King Maggot, the lead singer of the 1980s punk band Purge—and the band is working on a comeback.

***Burger Wuss* by M. T. Anderson. Cambridge, MA: Candlewick Press, 1999.**

Anthony has vowed revenge on Turner, who stole his girlfriend and makes his life miserable working at O'Dermotts. But Anthony's scheme to spark a bitter war between the O'Dermotts and Burger Queen at Turner's expense doesn't work as planned.

***Frogs and French Kisses* by Sarah Mlynowski. New York: Delacorte/Random House, 2006.**

Rachel's mother and sister are witches and use their gifts to solve everyday problems with unexpected consequences: cows end up in the school gym before the prom and a love spell affects the wrong brother. Fans will enjoy other titles in the series: *Bras and Broomsticks* (2005) and *Spells and Sleeping Bags* (2007).

***King of the Creeps* by Steven Banks. New York: Knopf/Random House, 2006.**

Tommy Johnson has never had a girlfriend, and he blames his looks: big nose, frizzy hair, and glasses. When he's about to do something drastic, he sees a photo of Bob Dylan and realizes he can get the girl by being a folk singer!

***The Manny Files* by Christian Burch. New York: Atheneum/Simon & Schuster, 2006.**

The Dalinger family finally finds the right nanny for their children, but the nanny turns out to be a man, Matthew, and is dubbed the *manny*. Lulu is skeptical of the manny's strange outfits and plans, but Keats thinks he's great, and so does Uncle Max, which leads to a surprising revelation.

***Me, Dead Dad, and Alcatraz* by Chris Lynch. New York: HarperCollins, 2005.**

Elvin's mother has always told him that Uncle Alex was dead. Then Uncle Alex shows up on the doorstep. He has been in prison and wants to redeem himself by helping awkward and overweight Elvin through life. This is the third book in the *Elvin* series.

***Millicent Min, Girl Genius* by Lisa Yee. New York: Levine/Scholastic, 2003.**

Millie, 11, has just finished her junior year of high school. This girl genius struggles with balancing her intelligence with an underdeveloped social prowess. Trying to fit in and find her first friend, Millie pretends she's just average. In the sequel *Stanford Wong Flunks Big-Time*, Millie's enemy Stanford Wong needs her help to pass English class.

***No More Dead Dogs* by Gordon Korman. New York: Hyperion, 2000.**

Eighth-grader Wallace Wallace is tired of classic literature with dying dog themes and tells his teacher so. He finds himself in detention and involved in the dramatic production of the book he panned. Can he liven up the production and save the dog?

***Notes from the Midnight Driver* by Jordan Sonnenblick. New York: Scholastic, 2006.**

Sixteen-year-old Alex wants revenge. His parents are separated, and his father is dating Alex's third-grade

Continued

Box 5.5   Outstanding Funny Reads   *Continued*

teacher. Alex gets in trouble and must do community service at a senior center, where he is assigned to care for an elderly, but feisty patient, Solomon Lewis. The two become friends.

Sleeping Freshmen Never Lie by David Lubar. New York: Dutton/Penguin, 2005.

Scott Hudson humorously chronicles the tumultuous life of a first-year student from having lunch money stolen to joining clubs to impressing a beautiful girl. With the help of an insightful English teacher, Scott learns he is a talented writer and joins the school newspaper.

Son of the Mob by Gordon Korman. New York: Hyperion, 2002.

Vince and Kendra are meant for each other, except Vince's father is a mafia boss and Kendra's father is the FBI agent on his tail in this hilarious Romeo and Juliet–style romance. Follow Vince's adventures in *Son of the Mob: Hollywood Hustle* (2004).

They Wear What under Their Kilts? by Katie Maxwell. New York: Dorchester, 2004.

In this sequel to *The Year My Life Went Down the Loo* (2003), Em has moved to a Scottish sheep farm to complete a work study program. Louise Rennison and Susan Juby fans will enjoy this series.

Tofu and T. Rex by Greg Leitich Smith. New York: Little, Brown, 2005.

Cousins Freddie and Hans-Peter have little in common. Freddie is a militant vegan championing the rights of animals everywhere. Hans-Peter is an archeologist in training; his passion is dinosaurs. When Freddie moves in with Hans-Peter, adventures begin.

Totally Joe by James Howe. New York: Atheneum/Simon & Schuster, 2005.

Joe, a character from Howe's *The Misfits* (2001), is given an assignment by his seventh-grade teacher to write an alphabiography throughout the school year.

What Would Joey Do? by Jack Gantos. New York: Farrar, Straus & Giroux, 2002.

Joey's father is in town trying to win back the love of Joey's mother, but he is unemployed and sports a new motorcycle, and Joey's mother has a boyfriend. In the meantime, Joey is homeschooled by the religious Mrs. Lapp with her bully daughter, Olivia. This is the third book in the *Joey* series.

---

president's son. Exaggerated calamity ensues upon the death of Cooper's grandfather, his caregiver. The political world, symbolized by ominous black sedans, invades Cooper's rural community, catapulting Cooper into a world of sleazy politicians, thugs, and stolen cars. Read as a farce, the story contrasts traditional country values with the worldly ambitions of politicians and their friends. Paul Fleischman's *A Fate Totally Worse Than Death* (1995), a farce on teen horror, features three vain girls who begin aging rapidly when a beautiful Norwegian exchange student, whom they believe is the ghost of a girl they murdered, moves to their school and draws a bead on a popular boy.

Another form of humor, *dark humor* or *black comedy,* satirizes serious topics such as death, murder, drug abuse, sickness, rape, and war. This type of humor is one of the most misunderstood comic forms, mostly because

Bruce Brooks (left) and Chris Crutcher (right) having some fun at the Youngstown State University's English Festival.

some readers have difficulty applying humor to serious circumstances. A superb picture book for teaching and learning about black comedy is *Once Upon a Tomb: Gravely Humorous Verses* (Lewis, 2006). More than 20 comic poems make fun of such topics as death and murder (e.g., a teacher has his head cut off with a paper airplane). In Andrew Auseon's *Funny Little Monkey* (2005), Artsy, barely over four feet tall and bullied by his six-foot, hulking hormonal monster twin, Kurt, elicits help from a group of kids in seeking revenge. Darkly comic events ensue.

Comic fantasies and comic science fiction by fantasy and science fiction writers (e.g., Terry Brooks, Diana Wynne Jones, Terry Pratchett, and William Sleator) are also popular with teens. In these books, authors use standard genre conventions such as alien invasion, time travel, and mythical creatures for comic effect—much like the movies *Ghostbusters* (1984), *Spaceballs* (1987), and *Galaxy Quest* (1999). Well-known comic science fiction writer Douglas Adams is famous for his series *The Hitchhiker's Guide to the Galaxy* (1979), which begins with the planned destruction of Earth in order to create an interstellar highway.[20] Author Dent survives his planet's destruction, only to be embroiled in various escapades with an unlikely band of comrades, including Marvin the Paranoid Android.

Romantic Comedies

In 1987 Brenda Daly raised the question, "Why do young adult literature romance heroines take themselves so seriously?" Her question was a response to the somber-minded heroines common in 1980s romance serial novels (e.g., the *Starfire* series), heroines so serious that readers scoffed at young adult romance. Almost two decades later, we can ask the opposite: "Why are heroines so funny?" Why do teens and adults alike find much romance brilliantly written, engaging, and refreshing? Romantic comedy has become one of the most well-liked forms of young adult humor.

Romantic comedy was popularized in the Elizabethan era by Shakespeare in plays such as *Much Ado About Nothing*.[21] Today it has found

---

[20]*The Hitchhiker's Guide to the Galaxy* started as a radio series in the late 1970s. It was later novelized with five books in the series, made into a television show, computer game, and then a movie.
[21]A play about two headstrong individuals who are more like opponents than partners. Shakespeare employed skillful use of verbal puns, metaphor, and carefully thought out insults to create comic effect. It first appeared in a quarto in 1599.

its way into bestselling adult novels (e.g., Fielding's *Bridget Jones's Diary*, 1998) and numerous award-winning films (e.g., *Tootsie*, 1982; *When Harry Met Sally*, 1989; *There's Something about Mary*, 1998; and *The Forty-Year-Old Virgin*, 2005). Despite its immense popularity, romantic comedy has only lately taken a strong hold in the young adult genre. *Angus, Thongs and Full-Frontal Snogging* (2000), a Printz Honor book and the first in the Georgia Nicolson series by British author Louise Rennison,[22] has popularized the romantic teen comedy. Fourteen-year-old Georgia Nicolson describes her emotional, angst-ridden, whirlpool life in diary format. From whether to pluck her eyebrows to taking kissing lessons and coloring her hair, Georgia is the consummate drama queen, but hysterically funny and likeable. Notice Georgia's comic voice in the opening passage:

> Dad had Uncle Eddie around, so naturally they had to come and see what I was up to. If Uncle Eddie (who is bald as a coot) says to me one more time, "Should bald heads be buttered?" I may kill myself. He doesn't seem to realize that I no longer wear romper suits. I feel like yelling at him, "I am fourteen years old, Uncle Eddie! I am bursting with womanhood, I wear a bra! OK, it's a bit on the loose side and does ride up round my neck if I run for the bus . . . but the womanly potential is there, you bald coot!" (p. 1)

Since Rennison's bestselling series, numerous authors have delved into the romantic comedy genre, producing a number of wildly entertaining, well-crafted, fun reads. In the author box, Louise Rennison discusses the origins of humor in her work and the popularity of her work with American readers.

A young adult romantic comedy is often written in diary format and generally features two well-matched likeable characters unable to unite because of dramatic internal or external obstacles. One character may feel unworthy, not ready to commit, or may not "like" the other (internal), or the relationship may be hampered by another relationship, parental interference, and so on (external). Love rules in the end, nonetheless, and the two usually come together in an almost fairy-tale style.

When evaluating a book, it pays to remember that a good work doesn't need to tear at our heart strings; a cleverly written, side-splitter can hold merit. Authors such as Louise Rennison, Meg Cabot, and Megan McCafferty have crafted some of the best young adult romantic comedies. Many can be used as models of good writing. A number of well-written and popular romantic comedies, many award-winning and several featuring male protagonists laughing at their own romantic follies, are included in Box 5.6.

---

[22]Published in the UK by Piccadilly Press (1999); first U.S. printing by HarperCollins (2000). Sue Townsend's *Adrian Moles* series (1982) chronicles the soap opera life of a young male's life in diary format. A satire, *The Secret Life of Adrian Mole, Aged 13 ¾* was read by teens and became an international bestseller almost 20 years prior to Rennison's series.

An Interview with Louise Rennison

Cole: In past interviews, you've mentioned that your stories are based on your actual life experiences. How is it that you find humor in situations most girls would consider disastrous? Where does your humor come from, and did you have it when you were a teen?

Rennison: I was doing a reading in Yorkshire, and the hall was full of teenage girls (and some brave boys) queuing up to have their books signed. It was the one that in the United States (or Hamburgeragogoland) is called *Away Laughing on a Fast Camel* but in England (Billy Shakespeareland) it is titled *And That Is When It Fell Off in My Hand*. I had been telling the girls about how it had been retitled and the fight I had had over it with my American publishers who said that *And That's When It Fell Off in My Hand* was too rude. I said "In what way?" and they said "Well, it implies, you know, that well . . . it is something to do with a boy's . . . well . . . manly parts." And I said, "How could that be? If a boy's manly parts fell off in your hand that would not be a comedy book, that would be a medical book." And the audience and I laughed together. And I think that is in a way the essence of how I take events that might be difficult to swallow and make peace with them. I find the humor in whatever has happened, but more essentially I share it with people and thereby make myself feel less alienated. At school instead of hugging a hurt or a slight or an injustice to myself, I would redescribe it to my mates (the Ace Gang) highlighting the comedy value. Often even physically acting it out.

I've always done it, and I think it might be a bit culturally influenced. I came from a rather chaotic household. (My mum's family were poor Irish Catholics and my dad's poor Yorkshire Jews. Imagine the weddings and funerals! Fighting and laughing mostly!) Both cultures are storytellers and like the craic. Additionally, English humor is as we are always observing in an ironic way, ironic! And it also tends towards the self-deprecating, which essentially is another way of making yourself part of the crowd.

Cole: What reaction do you have when you hear someone say comedy is good for laughs, but it has no real educational value, therefore, no real place in the classroom?

Rennison: I say, save me from those classrooms. I always found the teachers I valued most were the ones who "got it" and who were confident enough in themselves and their subject to have a joke or a witty observation when it popped up. I even had a math teacher who made up jokes about Pythagoras, which is not easy. Also, it is a fact that developing humans practice communication skills by joking and telling little stories. Only yesterday one of my little mates (he's 6) told me his first funny story. It happened at Christmas in his class's nativity play. When they got in front of the audience, one of the smaller boys, who was playing the innkeeper, was hysterical with excitement at seeing his parents watching him. And when Mary and Joseph came and knocked on his inn door for the obligatory being turned away part of the story, the innkeeper beamed at them and said, "Of course I've got room, come in come in, I've got loads of room, bring your donkey in!" And my little friend was proud that he had genuinely had the skill to make me laugh.

Cole: British writers seem to have a corner on the young adult romantic comedy market in the United States. In responses you've received from American girls, do you have any thoughts as to why British romantic comedies are so popular.

Continued

An Interview with Louise Rennison   *Continued*

Rennison: Hmmmm. Tricky, isn't it. Because the popular generalization is that British men are a bit tongue-tied and stiff upper-lipped (not an easy combination mouthwise!), but I think although a temperate climate will certainly not breed so much of the hot Latin lover type, but there is a deep, almost poetic longing, for a "courtly" love. The idea of wooing and chivalry appeals to both men and women. Also, language plays a tremendously important part in our culture; it's significant that the most popular programs recently have been to do with the meaning of words, and the preservation of old buildings. One of my mates compiles dictionaries, and his latest one is on slang. It is absolutely enormous and lists both old slang words (*slattern, prat, tosspot,* even and I know you probably won't be able to print this, but . . . *cunt*— which is an Anglo Saxon word) and new ones. The point being that we love words and always have, and the combination of romance and humor can be a very sexy thing.

I would also just add that humor can and does link and reconcile all kinds of differences in race, age, and sex. We have just had the World Cup beamed to us every day for the last month (joy unbounded as I am a footie fan), and I sincerely believe that the comedy value of the chanting and commentaries and shared jokes has brought nations together. In particular, the host nation, Germany, instead of overreacting with political correctness when some English fans dressed up as Hitler in shorts and England scarves, the police backed off and let the German fans find their own ways of responding with some of their own chants and dressing up. I did laugh when the English fans, toward the end, were dressing up in chain mail, especially as it was about a zillion degrees.

Just as a final PS about the durability of humor and its part in life's rich tapestry. At the same gig I was doing the signings, a mum came up to me to have her book signed and she said, "OOOoohh Louise, I did laugh about you going to a party dressed as a stuffed olive, because I went to a fancy dress party dressed as a fried egg." I laughed and said, "Blimey what were we like?" And she said; "No, Louise, you don't understand, this was last week!" Rave on!

Official Web site: www.georgianicolson.com

Additional books in the Georgia Nicolson series: *On the Bright Side, I'm Now the Girlfriend of a Sex God* (2001), *Dancing in My Nuddy-Pants* (2002a), *Knocked Out by My Nunga-Nungas: Further, Further Confessions of Georgia Nicolson* (2002b), *Away Laughing on a Fast Camel: Even More Confessions by Georgia Nicolson* (2004), *Then He Ate My Boy Entrancers* (2005), *Startled by His Furry Shorts* (2006), *Love Is a Many Trousered Thing: Confessions of Georgia Nicolson* (2007), and *Stop in the Name of Pants* (2008).

Box 5.6   Romantic Comedies

***30 Guys in 30 Days* by Micol Ostow. New York: Simon Pulse/Simon & Schuster, 2005.**

Claudia Clarkston cuts ties with her high school boyfriend her first year in college. Having dated Drew for so long, Claudia doesn't know how to flirt. Her roommate suggests she meet one guy every day for 30 days for practice.

***All-American Girl* by Meg Cabot. New York: HarperCollins, 2002.**

In an unlikely turn of events, the unpopular Samantha Madison soars to "it" girl status when she saves the life of the president of the United States. Saving the president was easy, but can she survive dating the president's son, David?

Continued

Box 5.6   Romantic Comedies   *Continued*

The Bridesmaid by Hailey Abbott. New York: Delacorte/Random House, 2005.

Abby and Carol vow never to get married after watching their parents work with too many bridezillas. Much to Abby's dismay, Carol breaks this vow and *becomes* a dreaded bridezilla herself. At the same time, Abby's own love life picks up and threatens her soccer scholarship.

Girl, 15: Charming but Insane by Sue Limb. New York: Delacorte/Random House, 2004.

Jess Jordan covets Flora's body and the love of Ben Johnson. She doesn't give a second romantic thought to her nerdy friend Fred until Flora expresses interest in him. Jess, who wants to be a comedian, humorously learns about relationships, including friendship. Fans can read more about Jess Jordan in *Girl, (Nearly) 16: Absolute Torture* (2005), *Girl, Going on 17: Pants on Fire* (2006), and *Girl, Barely 15: Flirting for England* (2008).

Lily B. on the Brink of Love by Elizabeth Cody Kimmel. New York: HarperCollins, 2005.

Lily wants to be a professional writer and starts her career as an advice columnist for her school newspaper and an assistant to a real writer. But Lily starts to lose her cool when she falls in love with *the* boy, and all of their encounters are embarrassing and strained. Other titles in the series include *Lily B. on the Brink of Cool* (2005) and *Lily B. on the Brink of Paris* (2006).

M or F? by Lisa Papademetriou and Chris Tebbetts. New York: Razorbill/Penguin, 2005.

Best friends Marcus and Frannie are looking for romance. Marcus crosses the line by pretending to be Frannie and chatting online with Jeff, Frannie's crush. Marcus falls head over heels in love with Jeff. Creative, funny, and sophisticated.

Planet Janet by Dyan Sheldon. Cambridge, MA: Candlewick Press, 2003.

Janet's diary entries follow the turmoil at her home, falling in love with a teen filmmaker, and the journey into her "Dark Phase." As she humorously tries to win the love of Elvin, she realizes he is only interested in becoming friends with her brother.

The Princess Diaries by Meg Cabot. New York: HarperCollins, 2000.

In the bestselling *Princess Diary* series, Mia Thermopolis, a New York City teenager, learns that she is heir to a throne in a European country. Cabot's writing is wacky, silly, and entertaining. Fans are sure to enjoy other titles in this series.

Scary Beautiful by Niki Burnham. New York: Simon Pulse/Simon & Schuster, 2006.

Beautiful Chloe thinks everything in her life is just right until her boyfriend moves away. Now girls mistrust her, boys are interested in her, and she doesn't know what she wants. This romantic comedy focuses on Chloe learning to be comfortable with herself.

Shrimp by Rachel Cohn. New York: Simon & Schuster, 2005.

After returning home from her New York summer vacation, the heroine of *Gingerbread* (2002), Cyd Charisse, vows to reclaim her boyfriend, Shrimp, and maintain peace with her mother. Cohn continues Cyd's story in *Cupcake* (2008).

Stealing Princes by Tyne O'Connell. New York: Bloomsbury, 2005.

In the sequel to *Pulling Princes* (2004), Calypso Kelly returns to boarding school, looking forward to a good year with Prince Freddie, but something is drastically wrong when she seems on the outs with her circle of friends. Fans will enjoy other titles in the Calypso Chronicles: *Pulling Princes* (2004), *Dueling Princes* (2005), and *Dumping Princes* (2006).

Continued

Box 5.6   Romantic Comedies   *Continued*

***Truth or Dairy* by Catherine Clark. New York: HarperTempest/HarperCollins, 2000.**

Courtney is furious after her boyfriend breaks up with her and vows her senior year in high school will be boyfriend-free. Then she meets Grant. Find out what happens when Courtney heads to college in the sequel, *Wurst Case Scenario* (2001).

***The Year My Life Went Down the Loo* by Katie Maxwell. New York: Smooch/ Dorchester, 2003.**

Emily is transplanted from Seattle, Washington, to Piddlington-on-the-Weld, England, much to her dismay. The move isn't all bad despite the ghost in her panty drawer and school uniforms. Emily falls for Aidan.

Humor and the Problem Novel

Humor plays an instrumental role in problem novels, for it prevents stories from being too hopeless and depressing. The foremost young adult novelists understand the fine line between humor and tragedy and balance the two effectively. Doing so is no easy feat: the writer runs the risk of creating inconsistent characters and unrealistic scenes. Effective humor reduces melodrama and the likelihood of a singularly driven plot; it also draws readers to the protagonist, as opposed to pushing them away. We admire a character who can laugh much more than a character who constantly laments. As Hogan (2005) points out, the quality of realistic fiction is strengthened, not trivialized, by humor. Authors known for including a good dose of humor in serious reads include Joan Bauer, Chris Crutcher, Rodman Philbrick, Randy Powell, and Jerry Spinelli.

Ron Koertge masterfully uses humor in *The Arizona Kid* (2005), a stirring coming-of-age story about 16-year-old Billy who spends the summer living with his gay uncle, falling in love, and working on a ranch. The ending chapter is one of the best-ever endings in young adult literature, made so partly by Koertge's skillful use of humor. The reader aches for Billy, but smiles too. In the following passage, Billy tells his summer love, Cara Mae, good-bye, knowing he'll never see her again:

> She smiled, leaning over to kiss me.
> For the last time I took off my hat so I wouldn't put her eye out. That was something else I wouldn't have to do anymore, wouldn't *get* to do anymore.
> "I think I'm gonna die," I said into her shoulder.
> "No, you're not," she replied softly.
> "If I do, will you take my body to Phoenix with you?"
> "You're great," she said, pulling away and grinning bravely. "It was a great summer."
> She touched the brim of her hat politely, then slid out of the van, ran up the three concrete blocks that served as steps, and closed the door behind her. (p. 278)

Mary Hogan's *The Serious Kiss* (2004) is a heartrending story about a family ripped apart by the father's alcoholism. Leaving her best friend behind, Libby moves with her family to a trailer park because her family can't pay their bills. Despite the heavy theme, *The Serious Kiss* is a memorable and zany read, made so by the light tone of the writing and the character's witty voice:

> My dad drinks too much and my mom eats too much, which pretty much sums up why I am the way I am: a knotted mass of anxiety, a walking cold sweat. Three weeks ago, when I entered my fourteenth year of existence, I realized the only stable, solid truth in my universe: Being me isn't easy. (p. 1)

Christopher Paul Curtis broke into the young adult market with his award-winning *The Watsons Go to Birmingham—1963* (1995), a story blending realism and humor so effectively that readers don't see tragedy coming. In *Bud, Not Buddy* (1999), *Bucking the Surge* (2004), and *Elijah of Buxton* (2007), his funniest book to date, Curtis uses humor in a similar manner. In the author box, Curtis addresses the complexities of humor and the fine line between comedy and tragedy. Box 5.7 provides a sampling of additional authors and problem novels that effectively balance tragic events with humor.

Understanding Humor   by Christopher Paul Curtis

There is nothing I can think of that is more difficult to understand than humor. And that includes the game cricket. Most experts agree that to "get" humor a certain keen intelligence is required, which is easy to agree with. But if that's the case, why do many people, young and old, find the simple words *fart* or *boogers* so amusing? Seems to me if you had to be really smart to enjoy humor, those two words would be nothing but words, they wouldn't produce chuckles and guffaws. It also seems to me if humor were a function of a superior intelligence, certain very bright animals would appreciate humorous situations too, but trust me, they don't. I can't tell you how many great jokes I've told my cat Suki, and he's never once laughed. The only reaction I've ever gotten from him is that same old expression that seems to be saying, "Fifty pounds, you jerk, if I only had fifty more pounds, we'd see who was funny then." Or, "Yeah, yeah, yeah, now where's dinner, you idiot."

Speaking of very bright animals, humor is also unusual in that it is so often closely tied to tragedy. Don't believe me? Think of any joke you know,

something about it is truly tragic. Take one of my favorite cartoons for example, *The Far Side* by Gary Larson. Very funny, but also horrible. The one I like best shows a dog standing on his rear legs at the back

Continued

Understanding Humor *Continued*

door of a porch, hovering behind him is a giant space-ship with two other dogs at the controls. The dog has knocked on the door, and his owner has answered. The dog tells the woman, "Well, they finally got here. But before I go why don't you roll over a couple of times?" Hilarious! But think of the sadness in there. Imagine the years of humiliation the dog underwent while his owner treated him, well . . . like a dog. Imagine the humiliation the woman's about to experience as she's forced to roll over at Fido's command. And who knows where Fido's going to stop? I don't see anything particularly pleasant in the woman's future.

Humor appears to be the type of thing that fades as we grow older, a young person who gets jokes and sees the humorous in many situations is so lucky. Oh, how I long for the days when the simplest of things

seemed funny, when, under the right circumstances, another person being terrified by something would send me into spasms of laughter. Why am I jealous of young folks who can laugh so freely and easily? Because there is no feeling quite so good as a good, rib-ripping, choking, lose-your-mind laugh. And, sad to say, as we age, laughs become fewer and fewer. One place I can still find these laughs, though, is in the pages of a really good book. As my daughter would say on her instant messaging, a good funny book can leave me lol over and over.

Official Web site: www.nobodybutcurtis.com
Other titles by Curtis included *Mr. Chickee's Funny Money* (2005), *Mr. Chickee's Messy Mission* (2007b), and *Elijah of Buxton* (2007a).

Box 5.7   Problem Novels That Balance Tragedy with Humor

The Agony of Alice by Phyllis Reynolds Naylor. New York: Atheneum/Simon & Schuster, 1985.

This ongoing series chronicles the growing pains of Alice McKinley from elementary through high school. The series is often frank and candid, controversial and funny. The *Alice* series is one of the longest running series in young adult history. Naylor introduced the protagonist, Alice McKinley, in 1985. *Almost Alice* (2008) takes place during the protagonist's junior year in high school.

Boy Girl Boy by Ron Koertge. Orlando, FL: Harcourt, 2005.

Teresa, Elliot, and Larry are long-time friends. As graduation nears, they plan to escape their small town and controlling parents by running away to California. Each teen begins doubting the plan. Poignant, yet laced with humor.

Crazy Weekend by Gary Soto. New York: Scholastic, 1994.

Best friends Mando and Hector spend a weekend with Hector's uncle in Fresno. Uncle Julio, an aerial photographer, takes the boys with him on a shoot. When he captures an armored car robbery on camera and the boys are featured in a local paper regarding the holdup, the thieves set out to teach them a lesson. A comic thriller.

Deliver Us from Normal by Kate Klise. New York: Scholastic, 2005.

When a cruel school clique defaces campaign posters belonging to Charles Harrisong's sister, the family decides to move. They sink their savings into a houseboat, an over-the-phone purchase that ends up being a catastrophe. Some characters are funny; others will make readers cry. Readers can

Continued

Box 5.7   Problem Novels That Balance Tragedy with Humor   *Continued*

continue the family saga with the sequel, *Far from Normal* (2006).

Drums, Girls & Dangerous Pie by Jordan Sonnenblick. New York: Scholastic, 2004.

Steven, a drummer, writer, and overall good student, confronts the pressures of living with a younger brother diagnosed with leukemia. A serious theme interspersed with humor. Sonnenblick fans will want to read *Zen and the Art of Faking It* (2007), a blend of romance, comedy, and tragedy.

Freak the Mighty by Rodman Philbrick. New York: Scholastic, 1993.

Two misfits, one with a learning disability and the other physically impaired, develop a friendship. Both sad and funny with memorable characters. Released in movie format, *The Mighty,* in 1998.

It's Kind of a Funny Story: A Novel by Ned Vizzini. New York: Miramax/ Hyperion, 2006.

Craig Gilner, accepted into an elite private school, can't handle the pressure and slips into depression. He becomes suicidal and ends up in a psych ward. Suspend a little belief about reality and Craig's voice becomes funny and ironic.

Rats Saw God by Rob Thomas. New York: Simon & Schuster, 1996.

Eighteen-year-old Steve York, failing English class, agrees to write a 100-page essay about his life. The writing allows Steve to reflect on his four years of high school—his relationship with his astronaut father, his ex-girlfriend, and more. A realistic depiction of adolescence with a dose of humor.

Three Clams and an Oyster by Randy Powell. New York: Farrar, Straus & Giroux, 2002.

Three high school juniors, Flint, Rick, and Dwight, need a fourth member for their flag football team. They want to go to Nationals, and the best prospect is girl jock, Rachel Summerfield, who doesn't shave her legs. Funny conversations.

The Unthinkable Thoughts of Jacob Green by Joshua Braff. New York: Algonquin, 2004.

Jacob Green finds himself constantly disappointing his father. In the fourth grade, a forgotten prayer shawl for Hebrew school somehow results in an assault on a Rabbi. Jacob's humiliation from fourth grade until high school is hysterical, but then the reader begins to realize the emotional abuse he suffers at the hands of his father.

Humor and Older Teens

Tastes in humor evolve as young people mature. During the preschool years children enjoy incongruities—events or things that are out of harmony or that don't fit into our expectation schema—such as animals talking, carpets flying, and objects falling from the sky. They enjoy plays on language such as Dr. Seuss and nursery rhymes. Early elementary children enjoy wacky characters such as Peggy Parish's Amelia Bedelia, who takes everything literally. Dusting the furniture means covering them with dusting powder; drawing the drapes means sketching a picture. As children move through the upper elementary grades, they enjoy riddles, jokes, and puns (Klesius, Laframboise, & Gaier, 1998). In their article "Humor and the Reading

Program," Gentile and McMillan (1978) outline the stages of cognitive development from 10 through 16 and relate those developmental years to interest in humor:

- Age 10: Humor is of the literal or obvious type and quite often not funny to adults. Some of it is slapstick,[23] but much of it is a reaction to anything unexpected.
- Age 11: Humor is "corny" and often smutty, with much laughing at misbehavior and minor accidents. The child can understand a little adult humor, but his/her own humor is of a different type and still based at a general, concrete level.
- Age 12: This stage is marked by many practical jokes of an obvious kind, teasing, and some exchange of banter with adults.
- Age 13: Humor is rather less obvious and more reserved than at earlier or later stages; the beginnings of sarcasm mark this stage of development.
- Age 14: Humor is used against parents or others in authority; smutty jokes among members of one's own sex and dislike of parents' jokes are characteristic of this age group.
- Age 15: Evident at this stage are the beginnings of the ability to laugh at oneself and to see something funny when teased or "kidded." Also emerging at this time is the understanding of irony as a form of humor.
- Age 16 and above: Ability to understand more subtle forms of humor, such as satire, for example, participation in adult jokes, and the beginnings of spontaneous humor on an adult level mark this stage of development.

As a former teacher, I've seen these stages play out in the classroom. One behavior I've noticed about older teens is that they seldom choose to read traditional young adult comedy. Young adult comedy typically focuses on the angst and antics of being a teenager; it's often slapstick or gross humor, and mature teens view books like these as middle school fare. Furthermore, many have cartoonlike covers, a turnoff for older teens, especially males.

Today's older teens enjoy political satire and tune in to Comedy Central's *The Daily Show* and *The Colbert Report* and *Real Time with Bill Maher* on HBO. They check out stand-up routines by Robin Williams, Sarah Silverman, and Chris Rock. They read funny Web sites and humorist magazine and newspaper columns and enjoy political cartoons such as *South Park.* Box 5.8 includes a number of comedians and humorist essayists, columnists, and novelists popular with older readers. Humorists such as these can be used to discuss politics and current events and are wonderful reads for encouraging teens to look beyond their own ethnocentrism.

---

[23]Slapstick comedy involves horseplay, collisions, falling down or bumping into things, and crude practical jokes. Early slapstick comedians include Groucho Marx, Laurel and Hardy, and Jerry Lewis. Jim Carrey is popular with today's teens (*Dumb and Dumber*, 1994).

Box 5.8   Humor for Mature Teens

Bill Maher is a political humorist who has hosted the cable television shows *Politically Incorrect* (1993) and *Real Time with Bill Maher* (2003). In addition to myriad editorials, Maher has written several books including *New Rules: Polite Musings from a Timid Observer* (2005) and *Does Anybody Have a Problem with That? The Best of Politically Incorrect* (1996).

Christopher Buckley is a political satirist and editor for *Forbes* magazine. His experience as chief speechwriter for Vice President George H. W. Bush was the basis for his satire on White House office politics, *The White House Mess* (lunchroom) published in 1986. His book *Thank You for Smoking* (1994), a satire on tobacco lobbyists, was adapted for a movie in 2005.

Christopher Moore, author of almost a dozen laugh-out-loud funny novels, has been called the greatest satirist since Jonathan Swift. Reminiscent of Kurt Vonnegut, Moore is known for putting a comic spin on universal issues. His popular work includes *A Dirty Job* (2006) and *The Stupidest Angel* (2005).

Dave Barry has been with *The Miami Herald* since 1983. He is a renowned humor columnist and, for 25 years, wrote a syndicated column that appeared in over 500 newspapers around the world. In 1988 Barry won the Pulitzer Prize for Commentary. His works include *Dave Barry Slept Here: A Sort of History of the United States* (1989) and *Dave Barry's Money Secrets: Like: Why Is There a Giant Eyeball on the Dollar?* (2006).

David Sedaris, National Public Radio humorist and essayist, is regarded as one of the best modern-day satirists. Frequently challenging cultural euphemisms and the hypocrisy of a politically correct society, Sedaris has written bestsellers such as *Barrel Fever* (1994), *Holidays on Ice* (1997), *Naked* (1997), *Me Talk Pretty One Day* (2000), and *Dress Your Family in Corduroy and Denim* (2004). Sedaris became the third recipient of the Thurber Prize for American Humor and was named Humorist of the Year by *Time* magazine.

James Thurber (1894–1961), cartoonist, short story writer, and namesake for the Thurber Prize for American Humor, is regarded as one of the most outstanding 20th-century humorists. Thurber is recognized for his short story and cartoon contributions to *The New Yorker*. His work includes approximately 40 books, essays, short stories, fables, and children's stories.

Jon Stewart is an actor, comedian, and has been host of cable TV's fake news show, *The Daily Show,* since 1999. Stewart published *The Daily Show with Jon Stewart Presents America (The Book): A Citizen's Guide to Democracy Inaction* in 2004, a satirical look at the history of our country written in textbook style. Stewart's earlier book, *Naked Pictures of Famous People* (1998), is a compilation of comic essays.

Jean Shepherd (1921–1999) spent more than 5,000 hours on the radio, was inducted into the Radio Hall of Fame, and wrote for numerous magazines, including *Playboy*. He won the *Playboy* Satire Award for his work. His short story collection *In God We Trust, All Others Pay Cash* (1966) was the basis for the classic movie *A Christmas Story*.

Patrick F. McManus is a humor essayist and an outdoor writer; his essays have appeared in *Field and Stream*. He has written numerous books over the years, including *A Fine and Pleasant Misery* (1978), which addresses the impact modern technology has had on outdoor activity.

Rick Reilly is a senior writer for *Sports Illustrated* and author of the weekly *Sports Illustrated* column, "Life of Reilly." The column is known for its placement in the magazine: the last page. Frequently humorous, his columns provide superb essay models for the classroom. Reilly's first novel, *Missing Links,* a humorous golf romance, was released in 1996 and has been called the *Bull Durham* of its genre. Its sequel, *Shanks for Nothing: A Novel,* was released in 2006.

Final Thoughts on Humor

French novelist, playwright, and filmmaker Marcel Pagnol once said, "Tell me what you laugh at, and I will tell you who you are" (quoted in Lewis, 1995, p.11). Our attitudes toward humor are influenced by our identity— our personal tastes and experiences, our maturity level, and our level of detachment. While one teen may laugh out loud at Chris Lynch's *Slot Machine* (1995), another reader who can relate to Elvin Bishop, an overweight teen trying to find his athletic "slot," may feel offended—the story may be too close to a teen struggling with similar physical challenges. Our role as teachers is to help students find the right match and to help them develop critical thinking skills that allow them to understand sophisticated humorous forms such as farce and satire.

This section concludes with . . . well . . . a bit of humor: an excerpt from Chris Crutcher's *King of the Mild Frontier: An Ill-Advised Autobiography* (2003), an amusing recollection of the author's childhood years.

Brotherly Love   by Chris Crutcher

"Wanna do something neat?" are four words that strike terror in my heart to this day. My answer was always yes when the question came from my brother. Then he'd tell me what the neat thing was, and it would always seem not so neat until he explained how what seemed like something that could really get you in trouble was, in fact, neat. Then I'd get in trouble.

I'm around six years old and I'm playing cowboys outside with my friend Ron Boyd and some other kids from the neighborhood. I have to pee so bad I'm about to turn into a hurled water balloon, but Ron's older brother, Joe, is not around and we younger kids have sworn that no one will tell him we're playing Roy Rogers, lest we pay dearly, and for the last half hour or so, I've been Roy. If I go inside to pee, I stand to lose my exalted spot atop the yellow broomstick that is Roy's mighty palomino, Trigger, and I'm working my sphincter muscles like a bodybuilder, prolonging those last precious minutes. Finally agony wins out and I drop my cap pistol to get a better grip on my penis and streak for my house. My brother John, sitting in a chair reading a book, observes the obvious as I burst through the door and says, "Wanna do something neat?"

"Yeah, but just a sec. I gotta go to the bathroom."

"That's the neat thing," he says. "Go there." He points to the four-by-five heat-register grate in the middle of the living-room floor.

"Huh-uh," I say. "You'll tell."

"Promise I won't," he says. "Wait till you see what happens. It's really neat."

By now I have to go so bad I'm dizzy, and only my death grip is stopping me from peeing into the wall like a strip miner.

"Just take down your pants and pee down the grate," he says. "I promise I won't tell. I'd do it myself, but I don't have to go."

"Have you ever done it before?"

"Lots of times," he says. "And see? I never got in trouble for it."

"No sir . . ."

"You'll be sorry if you don't. It's really neat."

"Okay, but you promise you won't tell."

He crosses his black heart.

In the same nanosecond my pee hits that hot furnace, the yellow steam rolls up around me like I'm Mandrake the Magician in the middle of a disappearing act, which I'm not but really wish I was. I know instantly from the sssssssss and the horrific stench that I better not be making plans to play Roy Rogers again soon. I best be rehearsing my role as a jailbird, because it is going to be a long time before I leave my room.

This is a job for bawlbaby. My eyes squint and my lips roll back over my buckteeth and not one tear comes out because every drop of water in me is shooting out like I'm trying to arc it across the Grand Canyon.

My brother calmly closes all the windows.

When the last drop sizzles off the top of the hot oil furnace, I stand, gazing dazed through the yellow mist. "You said you wouldn't tell."

"I won't, he says, "but what are you going to tell Jewell and Crutch when they come home and smell

Continued

Brotherly Love   *Continued*

this?" (We called our parents by their first names for some unexplained reason.)

"You better open those windows."

"And let the whole neighborhood smell it? Then you'd really be in trouble."

John could always get me to help him pound those last few nails into my coffin for him. He not only got me, he got me to get me. I'm running around closing the rest of the windows for him so the neighbors won't form a mob to run my parents out of town for having me as a kid.

True to what I now know my brother already knew, he didn't have to tell on me. When Jewell walks through the door carrying my baby sister, the aroma fills Candy's tiny nostrils and sets her off like a siren. Besides, if you're from Mars, there's no mistaking that smell. The good news is that Jewell is so mad she doesn't know exactly how she wants to kill me, so I get a short reprieve "until your father gets home."

I can truthfully say I don't ever remember my father hitting me, but somewhere I got the idea he could hit really hard, and I always put that idea together with this particular incident. So if my dad ever did warm my butt, it was in response to my doing something neat onto the oil-furnace fire through the living-room grate. But make no mistake about it: Whether or not my father hit me, that didn't change my behavior one bit. The claustrophobic horror of those first few seconds, and the telling and retelling of the tale, are far more natural consequence than I need to never again pee down the heater. It is good that my grandmother and grandfather live just across the street, because our house is uninhabitable for at least four days and we have to wait two days after that for the curtains to get back from the dry cleaners. But I don't go down totally alone. It is widely believed I am telling the truth when I say John told me to do it ("I was just teasing. Geez, I didn't think he'd really do it") but his is a misdemeanor and mine a felony that spawns another of those unanswerable questions I will hear throughout my elementary-school years: "If your brother told you to jump off a bridge, would you do it?"

Of course I would, if he made it seem neat.

There are plenty of wanna-do-something neat? stories, each more embarrassing than the last, but my brother's real coup had to be the time he shot me in the head with a BB gun and didn't spend one second behind bars for it.

My father would never let us kids have a BB gun. "I'll let you have a twenty-two when it's time," he'd say, "but a BB gun is a toy and that makes it dangerous." We would be allowed to own and shoot a real weapon when we were of age for a hunting license and when he was convinced he had taught us the gravity of holding in our hands, a weapon that can kill. So how badly do you think each of us longed for a BB gun? Of course John knew how to get his hands on one.

We had moved into the big house near the beginning of my second-grade year and found new friends in the Young brothers, Eddie and Richie. Their dad, along with his brother, owned Cascade Auto. Eddie and Richie Young could unerringly identify any car made within the last fifteen years that drove down Main Street; and they could have shot the windows out of any one of them because they had a Daisy Red Ryder BB gun.

One of many grievous errors I could never convince my parents they were making was that of appointing my brother baby-sitter whenever they left home. Cascade, Idaho is a small town, and in those days so safe no one even locked the doors to their houses and cars. Nine- and ten-year-olds were routinely left to baby-sit younger siblings, and I am lucky to have lived long enough to say it was a bad idea, at least in the case of John Morris Crutcher. They must have known it wasn't a great idea because they left my sister with our grandparents. "You don't know what he's like," I'd tell my parents when they were getting in the car.

"Oh, it can't be that bad, Chris," my mother would say. "You always overdo it."

Oh yeah?

I'm seven and John is two years and nine months older. No sooner than the dust clears our driveway, he asks, "Wanna do something neat?"

"What?"

"This is something really neat."

The yellow steam rolling out of the heat register, forever staining my T-shirt and my reputation, is little more than a distant memory.

"Tell me what it is?"

Continued

Brotherly Love *Continued*

"Wait here."

He returns, Eddie Young in tow, packing Eddie's brand-new BB gun.

I've got him now. "You're gonna get in trouble. We're not supposed to have those."

"We're not having it. It's Eddie's."

"Yeah, but we're not supposed to even have it around."

"Shut up. Now do you want to do something neat?"

I eye the gun. So forbidden. So neat. "I guess. What?"

"You go down and hide behind the tree, then whenever you're ready, run as fast as you can along the ditch and we'll shoot at you."

Our front lawn sprawls over a gently sloping hill clear down to Main Street, the only paved street in town. Thick pine trees stand on the north and south ends of the lawn and a shallow gravel ditch runs its length, next to the highway.

"No sir. I'm not doing that. What if you hit me in the head?"

He points to the sky. "Look, dummy, it's almost dark. We'll barely be able to see you, much less hit you in the head. It's like the shooting gallery at Zim's. Come on, it'll be neat."

The image of the shooting gallery does it. About forty miles north of Cascade, six miles outside an even smaller town called New Meadows, is Zim's Plunge, a swimming pool fed by natural hot springs. It is open year round, even on the coldest days of a snowy winter, and going there is a truly special treat. No one leaves Zim's without spending a few dimes in its shooting gallery, which consists of a primitive electronic rifle holstered about twenty feet from a small plastic bear behind glass on runners. The bear has an electronic target on both sides and on his stomach, and if the light from the gun hits that target, the bear rises to its hind legs and roars, turns a one-eighty, and heads the other way. Once you get him on his hind legs, you can keep him there by firing into the target on his stomach. He roars and kind of jerks one way and then the other until you miss. No matter how many times you hit him, nothing happens more than a roar and a reversal of direction. He does not drop to the ground like a rock the way I do when the first BB my brother fires hits me square in

the temple. Porch lights switch on in all three houses on adjacent blocks as I lie on the ground holding my head, screaming what I know are probably the last sounds I will make. Eddie Young snatches his BB gun and runs for home as my brother races down the hill to my side.

"What's going on over there?" a neighbor hollers. "Chris Crutcher, is that you making all that noise?"

"It's okay!" my brother yells back. "He just fell down. I'll take him in the house."

I scream louder, my temple pulsating. John takes my hand away from my head and feels the spot where the BB hit. There is a small bump. I scream louder. "Shut up!" he says. "I'll get you in the house." The pain isn't all that bad, really. The thud of the BB scared me more than it hurt me, but I have him on the ropes, because he has shot me in the head with a BB gun we weren't supposed to have and he is in big trouble now and I can even imagine my parents will from now on make me the baby-sitter, should I pull through. I scream louder.

"You better shut up," he warns. "The BB is in your head and if you keep screaming, it will work its way to your brain."

I suck back my next scream like a black hole.

"Fastest way to get anything to go to your brain," he says, "is loud noise." He picks me up and helps me up the hill.

"Maybe so," I tell him, "but you're really in trouble now. You're gonna get it. I'm tellin'."

"You can if you want," John says, "but if Jewell and Crutch ever find out you have a BB in your head, you're really in trouble, way more than me."

"No sir . . ."

John shrugs. "Don't believe me."

"How am I in trouble?"

"They'll want to get it out," he says. "If you just leave it alone it will come out by itself, but you know grown-ups. You'll have to go to the doctor. He'll put you to sleep and cut it out with a knife. A lot of guys don't make it."

Man, this is no fair. "Don't worry," he says. "I won't tell."

"Promise?"

"Yeah, well, you know, if you don't make me."

"I won't make you . . . How would I make you?"

Continued

Brotherly Love *Continued*

"You know, like being a jerk, or not doin' me favors."

I promise I won't be a jerk and I'll do all the favors he wants if he will please, oh, please not tell Jewell and Crutch I have a BB in my head, so they won't take me to the doctor to have my head knifed open.

My brother extorted late-night glasses of water, extra desserts, and cover-ups until I was nearly in junior high school, all because I had a BB in my head. Instead of a brain. In fact, I didn't have either.

I didn't have the heart to gun down my four-year-old sister in that same ruthless fashion, but a few months later I did talk her into swallowing a BB, then coerced favors from her with an altered version of what happens when a BB works its way from your stomach to your heart. My ploy worked until just after breakfast of the next day when Candy, famous for rifling through her stools looking for corn, found the BB.

I told that story to my parents sometime in my late thirties, at one of our annual Christmas get-togethers, and John, by then a respected Seattle accountant, listened carefully, even smiled in places, and denied it like the older brother he is. He said, "He's a fiction writer, for crying out loud."

Both my parents are gone now; they died without knowing for certain.

. . .

My brother was responsible not only for much of my gullibility, but also for a certain sense of spiritual confusion.

Most of the kids I knew growing up, besides the Catholics and Mormons, attended the Red Brick Church because it had the best Sunday school; for all I know, the only one. You could get your kid Bible lessons and get him or her out of there before they got to the incomprehensible adult Bible lessons delivered later in church. It was a kind of come-one-come-all place with, I now see, a decided fundamentalist flair and about a fifty percent casualty rate on preachers who got involved with other people's wives and teenagers.

My parents weren't avid churchgoers, but they were more than willing to get rid of us for a couple of hours on any given Sunday, and my mother had a good enough alto voice to be a standout in the choir on special occasions. They always gave us a choice whether or not to attend, but for many of my early years I was consistent.

In fact, between my fifth and sixth year, my shiny face showed up exactly fifty-two times. I wanted the Prize; the mysterious, oft-alluded-to, never described reward for perfect attendance. It was very special, they said. You couldn't buy it in stores, they said. Be the first and only kid on your block to have one, they said. Only those who showed up every Sunday, for better or worse, in green-slime nose-running, projectile-vomiting queasiness and in health, would walk away with the mysterious, coveted Prize. Out of probably twenty-five or thirty kids, three of us made it. On Sunday of that fifty-second week, we stayed after Sunday school for grown-up church, to be celebrated and embraced for righteous tenacity before the entire congregation. The Reverend Pardee told the rapt parishioners that from among us might spring the next Billy Graham.

The perfect attendance award was laid in soft cotton inside a small, white, expensive-looking box. Inside, mounted on a brown plastic base, were thick greenish white plastic letters reading JESUS SAVES.

I had hoped for one of those little plastic frogmen you could send away for from Kellogg's Frosted Flakes. You filled a little compartment on his foot with baking soda and when the baking soda soaked up water, he would actually dive deep into your bathtub.

JESUS SAVES.

My disappointment was brief. The Reverend Pardee instructed the three of us to hold our trophies high for the rest of the congregation to see, then made the entire fifty-two weeks worth it. "These children, these lambs of God, will never be without this message," he said. "Spring or winter. Summer or fall." His intensity built. "Good times and bad. Sickness and health." We fidgeted now, swaying from foot to foot. And then he sprung the Good News, pointing at a church deacon to douse the lights. "Day or night." There was a slight gasp from the audience, and we looked up. JESUS SAVES, JESUS SAVES, JESUS SAVES was glowing in the dark.

I couldn't wait to get it home, flashing it briefly to my parents and brother on my lightning trip from

Continued

Brotherly Love   *Continued*

the front door to the downstairs bedroom I shared with John. I pulled the curtains on the one small high window and turned out the lights.

The dim greenish glow of that same plastic they use to make glow-in-the-dark vampire teeth said it all. JESUS SAVES.

My brother came down to tell me Sunday breakfast was ready. Sunday morning meant link sausage and waffles. My favorite.

I said I wasn't hungry.

"How come you're sitting in the dark?"

I nodded toward the shelf from which glowed the message of the lifeguard Jesus.

"You gonna sit here all day and look at that thing?"

"Yeah. You can come down if you want, too. We could put on our pajamas."

He picked it up to take a closer look and I yelled and jumped up, snatching it from his grasp and knocking it to the hardwood floor. I snatched it up. ESUS SAVES. The J glowed back at me from the floor.

Stunned, I stepped into my imaginary telephone booth, whipped off my imaginary glasses and suit jacket, and out stepped . . . bawlbaby. Fifty-two weeks of coloring the bearded, robed men and veiled women of Nazareth. Fifty-two weeks memorizing the names of the disciples, never understanding whether or not they were the same guys as the apostles. Fifty-two weeks of singing "Jesus loves me, this I know . . ."

There was much wailing and gnashing of teeth. "I'm tellin'!" I convulsed. "You're really in trouble now."

"I didn't mean to break it," he said.

"You're s'posed to keep your hands off my stuff. You never let me touch your stuff."

He looked around the room. "You can touch anything you want."

"No sir. Too late."

He reached into his toy box. "Here," he said. "You can break some Tinkertoys."

Those Tinkertoys belonged to both of us. Plus, I was not about to even this up so easily. I had been wronged in a serious and spiritual way.

"No sir, I'm not breakin' anything. I'm tellin'."

"I'm not the one who broke it," he said. "I just picked it up to look at it. You're the one who grabbed

it out of my hand. What a stingy guts anyway. God probably had you break it because you're a stingy guts."

I shook my head hard. "Huh-uh. You're not s'posed to put your hands on my stuff."

"Stingy guts."

"I'm tellin'."

"Did you know Jesus had a big brother?"

"No, sir, Jesus did not have a big brother. And even if He did, I bet He made him keep his hands off His stuff."

"I'm not kidding. He had a big brother. That's where He got most of His big ideas. I even know what his name was."

Don't even try it, John. I'd been going to church for fifty-two weeks straight, and there had been not one mention of Jesus' big brother.

"Nobody knows about him, at least not very many people. But he was actually smarter than Jesus. He wrote some of the stuff in the Bible for Him."

"Okay, if you're so smart, what was his name?"

"I'm not tellin'," he said. "You wouldn't believe me anyway." He picked up the Tinkertoys he had given me to break and put them back in the toy box.

Man, I had one short attention span. "I might believe you. What was his name?"

Even this early in life, this many years before I would be brutally gunned down with a Daisy Red Ryder BB gun, this should have had a familiar ring; but if this was true, I could take it back and be the smartest kid in my Sunday school class. "Okay, I said reluctantly. "I promise. I'll believe you. Tell me what was his name."

"Esus. And you're the only kid who has a glow-in-the-dark sign of him."

Jesus had a big brother named Esus? He did not. You're a liar."

"You promised you'd believe me."

"That's no fair," I said. "There's nobody named Esus."

"Cross my heart," my brother said. "But he wasn't famous like Jesus, even though he was smarter. One of his eyes was poked out, I think. That's why nobody talks about him. He wasn't famous."

"I'm still tellin'."

Continued

Brotherly Love   *Continued*

"I know," he said. "But if you do, they'll take your ESUS SAVES away from you because nobody's supposed to know about him. You're probably the only kid in the world with a sign about him. Too bad you'll have to give it away."

"How come I have to give it away?"

"I told you, dummy, nobody knows about him. When you tell that I broke it, they're going to take it away. Nobody's supposed to know about Esus, even though he had most of the best ideas."

In order to maintain its glow, the plastic trinket needed to be held up to the light intermittently, so I plucked it off the shelf again and reached as high as I could toward the bulb now burning in the middle of the ceiling. My brother, relieved that he may have just avoided the need to explain to my parents why he was touching my stuff, took it gingerly from me and held it the difference between our heights closer.

I don't know why I always felt the need to educate my friends when I learned some new bit of information most of the rest of the world didn't know, such as the secret existence of Jesus' older, smarter brother. But I did, and ended up on the wooden bench outside Mr. Mautz's Sunday school classroom the very next Sunday for what would become the first in a long string of blasphemous statements. John had his internal distant early warning system turned on high that morning, with which he intercepted me coming into the house, my lower lip quivering like an eggbeater, ready to tell my parents how I'd been wrongly banished from my Sunday school classroom. John reminded me that if I told them I got put out of the room I'd also have to tell them why, which would mark the last day of my special relationship with Esus.

That night before I got under the covers, I knelt next to my bed and prayed to Esus that Mautz would not remember to tell my parents about our Sunday school difficulties when he saw them on the street during the week. Esus answered my prayers.

Sports

I was riding a London tube when sudden pandemonium broke out—people began running, screaming, and yelling obscenities, convincing me the British subway was experiencing another terrorist attack. I had entered at King's Cross and was on the circle line headed toward Aldgate, a terrorist's path a year earlier. When a teenage boy spit Wayne Rooney's name like venom, I realized there was no terrorist but that England had fallen to Portugal in the quarter-finals of the World Cup, crushing England's hopes of yet another victory. Wayne Rooney's red-card exit for stomping another player infuriated die-hard British fans. That, and the referees' "dodgy calls."

There's no getting around it, whether American, British, Portuguese—name the culture—humans are obsessed with sports and have an unquench-able, love-hate fascination with athletic superstars, on field and off. Our attraction is due in part to the wish-fulfilling nature of sports. (Notice a similarity with romance?) What boy hasn't dreamed about going one-on-one with LeBron James? Sticking Terrell Owens as he catches a pass? Sending a Greg Maddux laser-precise pitch over the centerfield wall? Or owning Lance Armstrong in the Tour de France? And while girls aren't typically as captivated by sports, female tennis enthusiasts envy the Williams sisters' strength; soccer girls dream of outscoring American's soccer legend Mia Hamm, or scoring a quadruple double in the WNBL. The love of competition cuts to our core, and winning defines how good we are. Sports themes pull die-hard sports fans into the reading world.

As with any young adult genre, it's difficult to identify starting points and first books as genres generally develop gradually.[24] We do know that sports novels originate from the dime novel (Crowe, 2004). Popular during the 1800s and early 1900s, dime novels were generally sensational adventure and thrill-seeking stories despised by moralists for their lack of principles and for violent themes, criticized by literary critics for poor writing quality, and devoured by the working class. Today they are synonymous with quickly written mass-market paperbacks and series. By the early 1900s, many adults were concerned about the moral impact dime novels had on young people and wanted a different kind of read.

Often called the father of American sports fiction, Gilbert Patten, writing as Burt L. Standish in the early 1900s, penned a new kind of book that used sports as a vehicle for preaching morality (Crowe, 2004). His books, though formulaic, were hugely successful because they offered a moral alternative to the dime novel. Athletes were good sportsmen and model students; they followed the coach's orders, wore blazers to ball games, never swore or smoked or drank, and didn't date girls who did.[25] Moral depictions of character came first, plot secondary. Dozens of sports fiction writers followed his lead.

By the late 1940s sports series were in vogue. Clair Bee (1998), former college basketball coach turned writer, is perhaps the most remembered serial writer; his *Chip Hilton* stories are still in print, reissued with updated covers. Matt Christopher, popular with younger teens, published more than 120 series and single titles from 1954 to 1997; his books, too, remain in print (Crowe, 2004). Today's series also include nontraditional sports, sports not generally included in school athletic programs, such as Todd Strasser's *Impact Zone* series (2004) (surfing) and Pam Withers's *Extreme* series (2003) (e.g., rock climbing, skateboarding, snowboarding, whitewater rafting); some of today's series are written in manga form such as the *Shaolin Soccer* series (2003) by Andy Seto and the *Rebound* series (2003) by Yuriko Nishiyama.

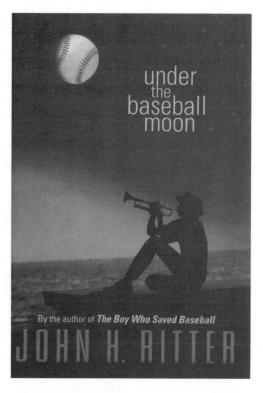

Reprinted by permission of Penguin Young Readers Group © 2006.

---

[24]Chris Crowe's *More Than a Game: Sports Literature for Young Adults* (2004) provides a superb historical account of young adult sports literature.
[25]While today's athletes don't fit this moralist picture, they do hold "jock" status, which is probably a carryover from the Patten/Clair Bee generation of athletes.

John R. Tunis had an unquestionable influence on young adult sport fiction as the author of more than 30 sports novels, many still in print. Literary critics, who dismissed sports books as being mere play-by-play game descriptions, took notice with the publication of *Iron Duke* in 1938. Unlike his predecessors, Tunis didn't preach, and play-by-play accounts were balanced with character development and plot. Tunis lay the groundwork for today's writers who write quality sports stories with depth. *The Kid from Tomkinsville* (1940), *Keystone Kids* (1943), and *Rookie of the Year* (1944) remain three of his most widely read books. Until Tunis's work, play-by-play sports scenes and an emphasis on the game as opposed to character and plot defined sports as a genre. As Tunis's style took hold, writers relied less on these elements, blurring the line between the problem novel and sports and raising the question of whether sports was a true genre. Today, most critics consider sports a theme.

Crowe (2000) uses the term *sportlerroman* to describe work by today's most noted sports fiction writers for teens (see the A-list of young adult sports fiction writers in Box 5.9). These authors hold true to the sports theme, develop strong plotlines, and give characters emotional depth. It's worth noting that of the A-listers, three have won the prestigious Margaret A. Edwards Award for contributions to young adult literature. Having three of these award winners in such a list speaks to today's availability of quality sports literature for young adults. Among these authors, Chris Crutcher is often considered the standard by which all new sports fiction writers are judged. Crutcher, as do our other A-listers, writes against the grain of those early simple moralistic stories, placing his characters in realistic situations that don't always turn out the way they might have in a Clair Bee novel. In the author box, Rich Wallace, author of *Wrestling Sturbridge* (1996) and one of the foremost sports fiction writers today, explains why he writes more than play-by-play action stories. His words may easily be echoed by other sports writers.

Box 5.9   Young Adult Sports Fiction Writers A-List

Bruce Brooks. Won two Newbery Awards for problem novels with sports themes: *The Moves Make the Man* (1984), a 1985 Honor book, and *What Hearts* (1992), a 1993 Newbery Honor book. Brooks is also author of the *Wolfbay Wings* series (1997), a well-known ice hockey series. His sports themes include basketball, baseball, and ice hockey.

Carl Deuker. An award-winning writer who began his YA sports fiction writing career with *On the Devil's Court* in 1988. Like other A-listers, Dueker's books move beyond a simple sports theme. *Heart of*

a Champion (1993) deals with alcohol abuse; *Painting the Black* (1997) with sexual assault; and *Night Hoops* (2000) with violence and neglect.

Chris Crutcher. The standard by which most other YA sports fiction writers are measured. A two-time California Young Reader's Medalist, Crutcher published his first book, *Running Loose,* in 1983 and remains one of the most popular teen sports fiction writers today. *The Crazy Horse Electric Game* (1987), *Staying Fat for Sarah Byrnes* (1993), *Ironman* (1995),

Continued

Box 5.9   Young Adult Sports Fiction Writers A-List   *Continued*

Whale Talk (2001), and *Deadline* (2007) are among his most popular sports books. Winner of the 2000 Margaret A. Edwards Award for lifetime contributions to young adult literature.

Chris Lynch. Prolific and diverse award-winning writer known for excellence in style, voice, and overall writing craft. Some of his works include *Shadow Boxer* (1993), *Iceman* (1994), *The Slot Machine* (1995), and *Gold Dust* (2000).

Dan Gutnam. One of the most prolific YA sports fiction writers today. He is known for his *Baseball Card Adventure* series (1997), *Tales from the Sandlot* series (1999), and *Million Dollar* series (2003). He is primarily a middle school sports fiction writer.

John Feinstein. Began his writing career as an adult sports writer. He is a political and sports reporter for *The Washington Post* and a commentator for NPR. He broke into the young adult world with *Last Shot: A Final Four Mystery* (2005), which won an Edgar Allan Poe Award for Best Young Adult Mystery. Other titles include *Vanishing Act: Mystery at the U.S. Open* (2006) and *Cover Up: Mystery at the Super Bowl* (2007).

John H. Ritter. Broke into the YA market with *Choosing Up Sides* (1998), winner of the 1999 International Reading Association's Children's Book Award. Additional award-winning books include *Over the Wall* (2000), *The Boy Who Saved Baseball* (2003), and *Under the Baseball Moon* (2006).

Mike Lupica. A syndicated sports columnist, bestselling novelist, and regular on ESPN's The Sports Reporters. His first teen book, *Travel Team* (2004), became a national bestseller. Follow-up teen titles include *Heat* (2006a), *Miracle on 49th Street* (2006b), and *Summer Ball* (2007b). His *Comeback Kids* (2007a) series is for younger readers.

Rich Wallace. Former sports fiction writer and newspaper editor who gained recognition with *Wrestling Sturbridge* in 1996, a moving coming-of-age story of growing up in a small town. Wallace has become one of the most prolific YA sports fiction writers today. He is the author of the *Winning Season* series (2004).

Robert Lipsyte. An award-winning writer for *The New York Times* and *USA Today*. He published *The Contender* in 1967, the year often identified as a defining year for the young adult genre. Other award-winning books include *The Brave* (1991), *The Chief* (1993), and *Warrior Angel* (2003). Winner of the 2001 Margaret A. Edwards Award for lifetime contributions to young adult literature.

Sue Macy. One of the few female sports fiction writers. Macy is known best for her nonfiction accounts of women in sports (e.g., *Winning Ways: A Photohistory of a Winning Season,* 1996; *Girls Got Game,* 2001).

Thomas J. Dygard. Wrote in the spirit of John Tunis and penned more than a dozen sports books for teens. Among the most popular are *Forward Pass* (1989), *Backfield Package* (1992), *Game Plan* (1993), and *Infield Hit* (1995). His primary sports themes include basketball, football, and baseball.

Walter Dean Myers. Known in young adult sports literature for writing about Harlem and basketball. Notable works include *Hoops* (1981), *The Outside Shot* (1984), and *Slam!* (1996). Myers also writes nonfiction sports material (e.g., *Malcolm X: By Any Means Necessary,* 1993; *The Greatest: Muhammad Ali,* 2001). Winner of the 1994 Margaret A. Edwards Award for lifetime contributions to young adult literature.

Will Hobbs. A prolific writer of outdoor sports/adventure stories. Hobbs makes frequent use of the man versus nature conflict. Many of his works are good reads for the science classroom. Themes include hiking, canoeing, kayaking, and rafting. Hobbs's novels offer an alternative to a body of work that focuses primarily on organized team sports. Notable titles include *Downriver* (1991), *Ghost Canoe* (1997), and *Leaving Protection* (2004).

Will Weaver. Known for his Billy Baggs baseball stories. *Striking Out* (1993), a story about a farm boy who yearns to play baseball with the town kids, has one of the most remarkable opening chapters in YA literature. *Striking Out* and its two sequels (*Farm Team,* 1995; *Hard Ball: A Billy Baggs Novel,* 1998) have won numerous YA literature awards.

On Writing Sports Stories   by Rich Wallace

Like a lot of boys, I took a long hiatus from reading anything significant around the time I became a teenager. I still read comic books and *Sports Illustrated,* but a novel? Forget it. I had basketball practice.

So I understood what I was up against when I decided, years later, that I'd start writing for that very audience. Teenage boys who were interested in sports. I could just hear the librarians trying to push my first novel on "reluctant" readers. "It's about an athlete, just like you."

"That's nice. Maybe later. I've got wrestling practice."

Why read about a sport when you could spend time playing it?

But I knew I was going to write about much more than *sports.* The sports novels I'd read in elementary school mostly followed a basic, superficial formula: the hard-working team gunning for the league title but thwarted by the selfish efforts of one antagonist among them. The narrative was anchored by the perspective of the team hero. There was at least one rather blatant moral lesson in every chapter, it seemed.

I have a shelf full of novels like that, written over the past 100 years or so. I find them at flea markets and antique shops. Books by writers like Harold Sherman and Matt Christopher and Clair Bee. (In general, the books became less moralistic and more exciting as the past century progressed.)

What was missing from my experience of reading such books when I was a kid was a protagonist who really seemed to be like me. A kid with more depth to his life, much more going on inside than being the best shortstop in the league. What about real conflicts with parents; real, gut-wrenching longings for a connection with the opposite sex; real soul-searching interior monologue about the character's past, his present, and his future?

So I started writing about kids like that. Novels about the whole person, not just the *Winning Pitcher* or the *Left-footed Halfback* or the *Strikeout King.* (Those are all titles on my shelf of sports books, by the way.)

Don't get me wrong; I loved reading sports novels when I was young, and I still enjoy them now. But I always felt that they were a step or two removed from what went on in the heads of the athletes I knew, and especially of what was going on in my life. I set out to write books that hone much closer to the edge, closer to real life, that demonstrate that even jocks can have a significant interior life.

The kinds of books I might have wanted to read as a teenager.

Copyright Rich Wallace, 2008

Official Web site: www.randomhouse.com

Wallace's *Winning Season* series (*The Roar of the Crowd* #1, 2004) is popular with early teens. Sports reads by Rich Wallace not mentioned in this chapter include *Shots on Goal* (1997), *Playing without the Ball* (2000), and *Losing Is Not an Option* (2003).

Conflict, Pressure, and Sports

John H. Ritter's *Choosing Up Sides* (1998) has one of the most memorable opening lines in young adult literature: "I grew up with my left hand tied behind my back." The protagonist struggles with a fundamentalist preacher father so dogmatic that he tied his son's left hand behind his back as a child in an effort to prevent him from being left-handed.[26] Imagine the conflict Luke Bledsoe has with his father when Luke, a gifted left-handed pitcher, wants to play baseball. In *Choosing Up Sides,* sports is a catalyst for addressing intolerance and conflict between a father and son. Sports themes can, of course, serve as backdrops to any number of family-peer relationships and social issues. In the author box, Ritter explains how his novels use baseball as a backdrop for more important issues.

Whether Little League player, Olympic gymnast, or NBL superstar, athletes have always known pressure to excel. No sports book illustrates this weight any better than *Friday Night Lights* (1990) by Pulitzer Prize–winning journalist H. G. Bissinger. Bissinger spent 1988 in Odessa, Texas, a small town obsessed with its high school football team, the Permian Panthers, a team with the winningest record in state history. In his classic, he paints

It's Always More Than Baseball   by John H. Ritter

The role of the storyteller, I've always believed, is to make the invisible visible. To tell the untold story, to shine a light on hidden truths.

Just as important, however, is making the story widely appealing—that is, "more than baseball." My first novel, *Choosing Up Sides* (1998), was a metaphorical baseball tale exposing the prejudice and intolerance embedded in right wing fundamentalism. I wrote my follow-up book, *Over the Wall* (2000), an anti-war novel about anger and vengeance, in anticipation of America's inevitable war with Iraq. But after publishing these two books, my style as a writer changed dramatically.

I still take my characters on journeys—actual, developmental, and historical—and deal with age-old questions: Who am I? Where do I fit in? And, What are my values and beliefs? But I now fill my books with a tenderness, an understanding of humanity, children will never glean from our leaders or the nightly news.

Hope burns eternal inside Tom Gallagher in *The Boy Who Saved Baseball* (2003), even against great odds. Tom reflects my belief that *no* human being is beyond hope or redemption. It takes only love and a storyteller's light to see the potential. In *Under the Baseball Moon* (2006), I spotlight characters who've decided to drop out of society, to live parallel to it,

by rejecting the values of a materialistic culture and searching for a deeper joy in life. Both books celebrate cultural fusion, not division. Are they more than baseball novels? Sure. That's always been part of the fun. What better backdrop for me to use than that age-old crucible of Americana, a baseball diamond? After all, a good story should be more than its sums; and good writing more than it seems.

Copyright John H. Ritter, 2008
Official Web site: www.johnhritter.com

---

[26]In folklore, superstitions, and some religions, the devil is associated with the left hand. He is often drawn as being left-handed.

a disquieting portrait of a town and its people whose identity, for better or worse, is tied up in the success of its players. Through superstar football player Boobie Miles, a likely future NFL player, readers live the heartbreak of broken dreams.

In dealing with pressures to run faster, hit harder, lift more, and break records, athletes of all ages have turned to supplements and steroids, and the side effects are enormous. John Coy's *Crackback* (2005) provides readers with a glimpse into the high school steroid world and the pressures teens feel to use them. Miles Manning doesn't take steroids but his friends do, and his coach benches him because he isn't muscular enough. In *Raider's Night* (2006), renowned young adult author Robert Lipsyte takes the reader inside the chilling psyche of a high school football player on steroids. He addresses the pressures placed on young athletes to perform in the author box.

Books in Box 5.10 feature both male and female protagonists who struggle with athletic pressure. These books, like those by the A-listers, use sports as a backdrop for exploring coming-of-age and relationship issues. Nonfiction sports books comprise a good corner of the nonfiction market. Box 5.11 features a sampling. Many are biographies; others are how-to or skill-building books. Additional ones can be found with nonfiction in Chapter 10.

Reading Jock Culture   by Robert Lipsyte

Sports should be the most fun you can have legally with your body in public, a chance to make friends, learn skills, and grow strong. Instead, it's become a place where kids are too often marked for life as heroes or zeroes, and those with early promise are channeled into vocational training for superstardom. No wonder they're taking performance enhancers in high school when it's books they need.

I wish there had been more positive changes in the youth sports experience during the four decades between my first YA novel, *The Contender,* in 1967 and my tenth, *Raiders Night,* in 2006. For the most part, a kid is under even more pressure now from peers, coaches, and parents to make the team and win the big game, to make the school proud, and to authenticate oneself as a real man (even if you are 10 and a girl!).

The customs and values of sports, what I call Jock Culture, can have enormous constructive impact on growth and socialization. Alfred Brooks

in *The Contender* never became much of a boxer, but because of the dedication, the work ethic, and self-esteem that are some of Jock Culture's greatest

Continued

Reading Jock Culture   *Continued*

gifts, he became someone who could take care of himself and others.

But Jock Culture swings a two-faced bat. Some of its lessons may be among the most destructive for teenagers, bordering on child abuse. Matt Rydek, the gifted football hero of *Raiders Night,* needs to struggle for his soul against Jock Culture's selfishness, its insularity, its bigotry, the blind obedience it demands. He's dealing with hazing, drugs, and the entitled behavior of athletes who have been conditioned to respond only to coach and team.

ESPN and 24-hour sports talk radio bombard kids, all the more reason to get them to read liberating books, books that acknowledge their fears about getting hurt, more importantly about being humiliated, and find out that most other people, even professional stars, share those feelings. They need to read books in which, as in life, nice guys do finish last and their world doesn't end, books in which, as in life,

making the team and even winning the championship don't solve your problems.

Truthful books about sports might encourage kids to relax and enjoy their lives, to challenge themselves for the pleasure of it, without self-doubt and without fear, and give themselves the room to make their own choices.

Books can give kids the moral courage to absorb the best of Jock Culture, its optimism and discipline, and stand up to the worst, its bullying and authoritarianism. And this is for the rest of us, too, in the grandstand and on the couch. Jock Culture is learned early and influences our work and our politics, relations between men and women, and, completing the cycle, how we raise our children.

Copyright Robert Lipsyte, 2008

Official Web site: www.robertlipsyte.com

Additional sports titles not mentioned elsewhere in this chapter include *Jock and Jill* (1982) and *Yellow Flag* (2007).

Box 5.10   Going Deep with Sports

Ball Don't Lie by Matt de la Peña. New York: Delacorte/Random House, 2005.

A boy thrust into foster care dreams of a basketball scholarship and one day playing for the NBA. Poor, alone, and often alienated, Sticky makes poor choices that may prevent his dreams from coming true. Fans may also enjoy *Mexican White Boy* (2008).

Fighting Ruben Wolfe by Markus Zusak. New York: Levine/Scholastic, 2001.

Two teenage brothers, Cameron and Ruben, take work as underground fighters to help support their family and earn respect. Ultimately, the boys must face each other in the ring.

Getting in the Game by Dawn FitzGerald. New Milford, CT: Roaring Brook Press, 2005.

Thirteen-year-old Joanna is the first and only girl on her school's hockey team, but she finds no support for this endeavor, not even from her best friend, Ben. Amidst harsh cruelty for wanting to play this sport, Jo must also deal with an ailing grandparent. FitzGerald fans will also want to read *Soccer Chick Rules* (2006).

Head above Water by S. L. Rottman. Atlanta: Peachtree, 1999.

High school junior Skye juggles responsibility for her sick brother, her competitive swimming, and new

Continued

Box 5.10   Going Deep with Sports   *Continued*

boyfriend Mike. When she becomes overwhelmed, the lies begin and Mike betrays her.

The Hoopster by Alan Lawrence Sitomer. New York: Jump at the Sun/Hyperion, 2005.

Andre Anderson demonstrates that ballplayers can be more than the sum of their court moves. An excellent basketball player, he is also a talented writer taking on a difficult assignment for a prestigious magazine.

Keeper by Mal Peet. Cambridge, MA: Candlewick Press, 2007.

This story is an unusual blend of soccer and the supernatural. El Gato, a world renown goalkeeper, narrates a tale (told to a reporter) about a ghostly mentor who emerges from the South American rainforest to teach a poor, awkward boy to play soccer. Magical realism at its best. Soccer fans may also enjoy *The Penalty* (2007), part sports novel, part mystery/thriller.

Knights of the Hill Country by Tim Tharp. New York: Knopf/Random House, 2006.

Friday night football defines a small Oklahoma town. On the surface Hampton Green's life seems perfect. On the field, he is the team's star; but off, his world is a disaster. His father has walked out, his mother has a new boyfriend every few days, and competition builds between Hampton and his best friend.

Last Shot: A Final Four Mystery by John Feinstein. New York: Knopf/Random House, 2005.

Two eighth-grade students win a national writing contest and are sent as reporters to cover the Final Four championship game, where they discover that a player is being blackmailed into throwing the game.

Learning the Game by Kevin Waltman. New York: Scholastic, 2005.

Nate has a lot going for him: good grades, great girlfriend, and he plays on a fabulous basketball team. Everything begins to change when Nate confesses his part in a burglary.

My Thirteenth Season by Kristi Roberts. New York: Henry Holt, 2005.

Life is hard for Franny Culler. After her mother died, her father became depressed, and they live with her aunt. What's worse is that no one wants a girl on the baseball team.

One Good Punch by Rich Wallace. New York: Random House, 2007.

Michael Kerrigan is the perfect student. He is captain of the track team and editorial assistant for the *Scranton Observer*. He takes his schoolwork seriously and avoids trouble. When authorities find joints in his school locker, Michael's world turns upside down.

One-handed Catch by M. J. Auch. New York: Henry Holt, 2006.

Despite losing his hand in an accident at his father's butcher shop, Norman works hard to learn the game of baseball.

Open Ice by Pat Hughes. New York: Lamb/Random House, 2005.

Nick defines his life through hockey, so how will that definition change when he suffers a brutal concussion and is unable to play?

The Perfect Distance by Kim Ablon Whitney. New York: Knopf/Random House, 2005.

Francie Martinez dreams of victory at the equestrian finals, but she doesn't come from the privileged background of her peers at the prestigious stables. Francie's father works as a barn manager, and she is the only Mexican rider.

Continued

Box 5.10   Going Deep with Sports   *Continued*

Pinned by Alfred C. Martino. Orlando, FL: Harcourt, 2005.

Two high school students work their way through the wrestling season and meet at the state championship. Both have worked hard on and off the mat, one dealing with the death of his mother, and the other working through his parents' break up and his girlfriend's possible pregnancy.

Rat by Jan Cheripko. Honesdale, PA: Boyds Mills Press, 2002.

When the school's basketball coach sexually assaults a cheerleader, Jeremy testifies against him and deals with the rebuke of the team.

Rebound by Bob Krech. Tarrytown, NY: Marshall Cavendish, 2006.

Everybody in Raymond Wisniewski's school knows that Polish boys wrestle and black kids play basketball. Wisniewski makes the basketball team and tensions rise. As the story progresses, Raymond learns both the subtleties and overtness of racism and that prejudice occurs in different ways.

The Rhyming Season by Edward Averett. New York: Clarion, 2005.

It's hard enough that Brenda is struggling with playing in the shadow of her brother, the star of the school team who was killed the previous year, and the separation of her parents. Now the coach of the girls' basketball team takes another job, and their eccentric English teacher, their new coach, makes them recite poetry as they play.

Safe at Second by Scott Johnson. New York: Philomel/Penguin, 1999.

Todd Bannister, a good-looking star pitching prospect sought after by scouts and agents, is hit in the face by a line drive and loses an eye. Todd must work through his tragedy. A compelling work with complex characters and universal themes.

Shakespeare Bats Cleanup by Ron Koertge. Cambridge, MA: Candlewick Press, 2003.

While recovering from mono, 14-year-old Kevin takes a break from playing baseball and discovers it is not only okay for boys to write poetry, poetry writing is almost as much fun.

Sliding into Home by Dori Hillestad Butler. Atlanta: Peachtree, 2003.

Thirteen-year-old Joelle moves to a new town with her family and refuses to accept their rule that she cannot play baseball because she is a girl.

Swollen by Melissa Lion. New York: Lamb/Random House, 2004.

Samantha is a gifted runner, but will she devastate her future because she is unable to deal positively with her low self-esteem?

Tangerine by Edward Bloor. San Diego: Harcourt, 1997.

Twelve-year-old soccer-playing Paul is legally blind, but he has decided to make some changes when he and his family move to Tangerine, Florida. He soon finds that trying to keep up with his athletic older brother awakens painful memories.

Throwing Like a Girl by Weezie Kerr Mackey. Tarrytown, NY: Marshall Cavendish, 2007.

Ella has just moved from Chicago to Dallas. Though nervous about her unfamiliar surroundings, Ella joins a softball team. She learns the value of teamwork and learns to believe in herself.

Travel Team by Mike Lupica. New York: Penguin, 2004.

When 12-year-old Danny Walker, small for his age, is cut from the travel team, he and his father put together their own team.

Box 5.11   Nonfiction Sports Books

Babe Didrikson Zaharias: Driven to Win by Nancy Wakeman. Minneapolis, MN: Lerner, 2000.

Babe excelled in many areas of athletics: swimming, track and field, and baseball. This biography highlights her accomplishments, particularly her part in creating the first women's professional golf circuit.

Bicycle Stunt Riding!: Catch Air by Chris Hayhurst. New York: Rosen, 2000.

This informational book describes bicycle stunt riding, including how to start and how to enter competitions.

Black Hoops: The History of African Americans in Basketball by Fredrick McKissack Jr. New York: Scholastic, 1999.

Young basketball fans might be surprised to learn that a sport so dominated by black athletes once struggled to provide equal opportunity to black athletes. McKissack traces the early history of black athletes' struggles.

Eagle Blue: A Team, a Tribe and a High School Basketball Team in Arctic Alaska by Michael D'Orso. New York: Bloomsbury, 2006.

The story of a 2005 Yukon basketball team and the struggles they overcome to win a championship. Most high school teams board a bus and ride to the next town to play, but this group must use a small plane to fly to their games. In addition to the basketball angle, the book explores ethnic issues of Alaskan tribes and their way of life.

Extreme Sports by Chris McNab. Broomall, PA: Mason Crest, 2004.

This is an extreme sports encyclopedia that provides a history of extreme sports, details about physical and mental preparation, and highlights of professional athletes.

Figure Skating Now: Olympic and World Champions by Gérard Châtaigneau and Steve Milton. New York: Firefly, 2001.

This nonfiction book includes essays, photographs, and bibliographic information about Olympic and world champion figure skaters.

Fitness Stars of Pro Baseball: Featuring Profiles of Ivan Rodriguez, Mark McGwire, Brady Anderson, and Ken Griffey Jr. by Ann Graham Gaines. Hockessin, DE: Mitchell Lane, 1999.

This book highlights the fitness regimens of four sports stars. Each section begins with an overview of the sport and a player profile. This is one book in the *Legends of Health and Fitness* series.

Football by John Wright. Broomall, PA: Mason Crest, 2004.

Part of the *Sports Injuries* series, this book gives a brief history of football, explains warm-up activities, equipment, and career opportunities.

Girl Power on the Playing Field: A Book about Girls, Their Goals, and Their Struggles by Andy Steiner. Minneapolis, MN: Lerner, 1999.

Information about girls in sports, the positive side of competition, and health and sports issues are covered in this engaging book. The author provides resources for students and teachers, including Web sites and magazines.

Heroes of Baseball: The Men Who Made It America's Favorite Game by Robert Lipsyte. New York: Simon & Schuster, 2006.

This is a beautiful history of baseball superstars written by one of the best sports fiction writers of all time. Features such greats as Babe Ruth, Ty Cobb, Shoeless Joe Jackson, Ted Williams, Lou Gehrig, Hank Aaron, Mickey Mantle, and Willie Mays. Remarkable photos.

Continued

Box 5.11   Nonfiction Sports Books   *Continued*

A History of Basketball for Girls and Women: From Bloomers to Big Leagues by Joanne Lannin. Minneapolis, MN: Lerner, 2000.

Lannin details the history of women's basketball, from its beginning at Smith College in 1891 to the creation of the WNBA.

Ladies First: Women Athletes Who Made a Difference by Ken Rappoport. Atlanta: Peachtree, 2005.

Outlines the history of women in sports—women who broke barriers in a variety of sports. Sled racing and gymnastics are highlighted.

NASCAR Pole Position Adventure series (Rolling Thunder) by T. B. Calhoun. New York: HarperCollins, 1998.

This series takes a look at each of the crew members of a NASCAR racing team. Each book explores the skills needed in a crew member while telling the story of a heroic driver and the risks he takes to win.

NASCAR Racer series (Fast Lane) by J. E. Bright. New York: HarperCollins, 2002.

This series is about team Fastex and the ultimate in high tech cars that race at unheard-of speeds, perform incredible stunts, and take on dangerous off-road courses. The four crew members are part of a group called Unlimited Division Drivers who believe no action is too fast or too scary.

The Nazi Olympics: Berlin 1936 by Susan D. Bachrach. Boston: Little, Brown, 2000.

This is a historical look at the 1936 Olympics that details the political atmosphere of both the United States and Germany and the treatment of Jewish and black athletes. Written in a serious, accurate tone.

Science Projects about the Physics of Sports by Robert Gardner. Springfield, NJ: Enslow, 2000.

Real-life science abounds in sports (e.g., speed and gravity). This book details numerous science experiments dealing with sports with detailed and easy-to-follow directions.

Skateboarding in the X-Games by Suzanne J. Murdico. New York: Rosen, 2003.

This is one book in the *World of Skateboarding* series. History, highlights, and heroes of the X-Games are detailed with plenty of color.

Soccer Skills: For Young Players by Ted Buxton. Tonawanda, NY: Firefly, 2000.

This is an instructional guide for honing soccer skills. Interspersed throughout the book are famous player updates.

Surf Diva: A Girls' Guide to Getting Good Waves by Izzy Tihanyi and Coco Tihanyi. Orlando, FL: Harcourt, 2005.

This surf guide for girls provides information about how to become a successful surfer. It includes tips on posture, workouts, brands of boards, surf destinations, skill level required, and popular surf competitions.

Within Reach: My Everest Story by Mark Pfetzer and Jack Galvin. New York: Penguin/Puffin, 1998.

Mark Pfetzer chronicles his mountain climbing expeditions; many peaks have only been reached by men twice his size. He describes being the youngest climber to scale Mount Pisco and Cotopaxi at age 14 and his attempts to reach the top of Mount Everest.

Final Thoughts on Sports

Despite the immense popularity of sports, sports novels have long been absent from award lists and, like romances, have been considered lesser fare. In researching this section and reflecting on that absence, I question whether sports books have been treated fairly. As gendering of romance has relegated the entire genre to an inferior status, is it possible that award committees have operated in the same manner toward sports? Since the field of education is dominated by women, do they have stronger voice in the selection of award winners? Although the pure sports novel seems to have had its heyday, today's well-developed sports novels featuring strong plots and round characters contain doses of play-by-play sports action scenes. Do these turn off nonathletes? Particularly women? If so, do sports novels hold an inferior position due to sports gendering? What do you think?

Teaching Questioning with YA Romance, Humor, and Sports Fiction

One of my greatest fears as a beginning teacher was leading class discussions. The night before class I agonized over a list of questions I would use to discuss a piece of literature; I would jot notes in the margin indicating how long I thought it would take students to respond to each question. No matter how many questions I developed, or what kind, I feared students would not talk, or they'd give brief responses and I'd run out of questions. I feared dead silence. Even more, I feared the possibility of being asked a question I couldn't answer. Not having an answer made me feel incompetent. As a beginning teacher, I felt safest if I could control the classroom—if I could be the questioner and students the responders.

While maintaining control in the classroom is important, too much control, or the wrong kind, reaps hazard on classroom conversation, as well as on student-teacher relationships. Many teachers, both novice and experienced, operate out of fear when they lead class discussions. They fear not knowing enough or being challenged by a student or learning that a student may know more than they do. Insecure teachers can come across as threatening or challenging, even condescending.

Maybe you're asking, What does all this have to do with teaching questioning strategies?

Learning how to lead a class discussion and teaching students how to question texts is a common concern among new teachers. Insecure teachers create high-risk environments in which students give teacher-pleasing responses and ask few relevant questions. Student thinking and questioning in such an environment are stifled. As Christenbury (1994) points out, "it is virtually impossible to move into real, productive conversation[s] in a controlled classroom" (p. 212). In such an environment, it's impossible to move students into deep levels of thinking about texts.

Before examining a number of techniques for teaching questioning, reflect on the following points:

1. Tell yourself right now you can't know everything, but you can be a lifelong learner.

2. Accept the fact that you will stumble some early on and that you may feel awkward at times.

3. Enter class discussions expecting (and wanting) to learn from your students.

4. When asked a question you can't answer, admit you don't know the answer. Don't fudge. Students figure out that tactic rather quickly.

5. Recognize when a student's intelligence intimidates you and learn to embrace and celebrate his/her aptitude.

6. Let students know you value learning from them.

7. Know that you will have a few rare students who make comments and ask certain questions for "shock effect." Don't give these kinds of responses power. If you do, you will show them an Achilles' heel, and they will stab it more often.

8. Remind yourself that an awkward silence is a good thing. Students need time to formulate their thoughts. Don't rush to answer your own question. If you wait long enough, someone will respond, and most often the response will push the conversation forward.

9. Know that some of the best questions have no answers, but multiple possibilities. Rather than having answers, good questions may raise additional questions.

10. Learn to close all your classes with, *"What* questions do you have?" as opposed to *"Do* you have any questions?" The former invites and expects questions; the latter sets an awkward tone.

11. Your central role should be as a facilitator. Enter some class discussions with the mind-set that you aren't "offering" any information; rather, you are there to guide their interpretations. Students are often eager to know what "you" think. At times you may want to be an active participant, but measure your role carefully. Because you are the teacher, your opinion carries incredible power, sometimes more than it should. You can, in essence, keep your students from thinking.

12. Spread the conversation around. Make sure a select number of students do not dominate the conversation. A few students will be engaged more than others, and you'll need to work around their eagerness without crushing their enthusiasm.

13. *Listen* to their answers. I had a student teacher once who asked her students how the bombing of the World Trade Center made them feel. One boy answered, "It made me feel like I wanted to go over there

and blow them up." My student teacher didn't recognize that he had answered with an action rather than an emotion. Also, listen to all answers, not just the one you expect. Students will offer viewpoints that you hadn't previously considered.

14. Remain aware of adolescent development. Teens can use classroom discussions as put-down opportunities.

15. Scaffold students' questions. Although you should enter class with specific questions in mind, you cannot dictate the course of a natural conversation. Rather than working through a laundry list of questions, use student responses as springboards for additional questions. Go off on relevant tangents, but stay conscious of the time and when the conversation should be "pulled back" to a more specific place.

If you internalize these ideas, they can ease your fears and help you become an effective facilitator of classroom discussions.

An environment in which students can ask and answer questions engages readers and deepens comprehension. Questions stimulate thought and help clarify meaning. Questions propel readers forward, peaking curiosity and encouraging readers to explore texts for deeper meaning and to pursue outside research. The ability to question is at the heart of thoughtful reading (Harvey & Goudvis, 2000). Students need to know that questions are important; they need to understand and be able to ask and respond to different question types. Several activities for helping students develop questioning skills are discussed next.

Question-Answer Relationships (QAR)

QAR is a reading strategy that helps students understand four basic *question-answer relationships*.[27] Understanding these types of relationships aids students in monitoring and assessing comprehension and encourages critical thinking. A clear understanding also helps students respond to teacher-directed questions. (Readers learn, for example, to look farther down the page and deeper—past the text—for answers posed by the teacher.) As students develop an understanding of the last two question types listed, they begin to dispell the common misconception that all answers are found *in* the text:

Right There: The answer is found in the text. Words in the question and in the answer are usually in the same sentence. A reader can point to the answer.

Think and Search: The answer is found in the text. However, the answer will not be found in one place. The reader will have to search through the selection and piece together an answer.

---

[27] An expanded model was introduced by Pearson and Johnson (1978) and Raphael (1982).

Author and Reader: The answer is *not* found in the text. The reader has to use information (details) in the text and information in his/her head (prior knowledge).

On Your Own: The reader does not need to read the text at all to answer the question. The text may simply be a springboard for discussing an issue.

In using young adult sports fiction to teach these question types, I locate a passage from a book the class will be reading. As a teaser, I develop four questions that fit the preceding categories. I choose an engaging passage and give students the passage, along with the four questions, and we work through the answers together. To reinforce the activity, I may give a follow-up passage students can do individually, or I may ask students to develop question types from other class reading. Table 5.1 presents an example based on Scott Johnson's sports novel, *Safe at Second* (2001), a story in which a superstar baseball player loses an eye in a horrific accident. Read the passage and the questions; then look for the answers in the passage. You'll see how the questions fit the definitions outlined previously. Finding a good passage takes a little time, so don't get discouraged when you begin designing your own.

Table 5.1

Question-Answer Relationships

Out of the corner of my eye I saw it, and heard the two sounds almost together. The solid *ping* of a line drive off the bat. Then the ugly *clunk,* as the ball smacked into Todd's face and jerked his whole head backward.

From all around the field I heard one loud, sharp gasp.

I stampeded over with everyone else. Todd had landed hard on his right shoulder, and now, sprawling halfway off the mound, he looked as still and lumpy as an old duffel bag full of bats. Some of the guys on the field got to him first, and as I came up, one of them, Wayne Linder, turned away, his face white and sickly. I eased past him to get closer.

"Get back," somebody said. "Don't crowd him."

I saw from the slight rise of his chest that at least he was breathing. He must have been knocked out, and now was coming to. A couple of guys reached for his legs to try to straighten him out. Somebody else yelled, "Don't move him, don't move him."

"He's okay," I heard myself whisper, and kneeled down behind him to put my hand half around his left shoulder. "He's all right." (Johnson, 2001, p. 54)

Question Type	Sample Question	Answer
Right There	Where does the ball hit Todd?	Face
Think and Search	What two sounds does the narrator hear?	Ping, clunk
	(or this harder question)	

Continued

T a b l e 5 . 1 *Continued*		
Question Type	**Sample Question**	**Answer**
	What orders did the boys scream?	"Get back." "Don't crowd him." "Don't move him, don't move him." (This second question is particularly good because some will stop reading and not get the last statement.)
Author and Me	What position does Todd play?	Pitcher (This is a great one. Notice how the word *pitcher* appears nowhere. Sports fans will pick up on the words *mound* and *line drive*.)
On Your Own	Should aluminum bats be banned in high school?	(Students can argue either way. Todd's tragedy provides a springboard for discussing this issue. The reader doesn't know the kind of bat being used—the ping suggests aluminum. But baseball fans will be eager to inform the rest of the class about the dangers of aluminum bats—the ball travels faster and farther— over wooden bats. Again, you don't have to have read the passage to discuss this issue.)

Schoenbach, Greenleaf, Cziko, and Hurwitz (1999) suggest two variations of the QAR strategy Question Around and Categorizing Questions. Both can be used after you introduce students to the four question types to reinforce learning.

Question Around

- Have students (possibly for homework) generate several questions based on a common text.
- After students have created their individual questions, have a volunteer read a question.
- Ask students to raise their hand if they can answer the question *and* if they can identify the question type.

- Have the student who posed the question call on someone to answer.
- After the student answers both parts of the question, he/she poses the next question and so forth. (p. 82)

This activity requires close monitoring. You will want to make sure that all students have a chance to respond and that a few don't dominate the activity.

Categorizing Questions

- Have students (possibly for homework) generate two or three questions of *each* type based on a common text.
- Have students share their questions in small groups.
- Have each group create four posters (one for each question type). For each question type, they are to choose four questions from their group and write them on the corresponding poster.
- Once students agree on the categorized questions on each poster, ask them to sign the poster indicating their agreement.
- Display all the posters and ask students to go around the room (in their groups) and examine all the posters.
- Ask students to put a star beside any question that seems to be incorrectly categorized.
- Once students have examined all the posters, guide the class in analyzing each starred question and deciding where it belongs. (p. 84)

This QAR activity helps students recognize that categorizing questions can be challenging. It's an easy—and efficient—activity for providing students with repeated practice in developing question types.

Question the Author (QtA)

QtA encourages students to think past the written word and consider the author's purpose (Beck, McKeown, Hamilton, & Kucan, 1997). It was designed for guiding students through difficult nonfiction texts and helping them see that sometimes their confusion is justified—sometimes we don't fail at reading; the author fails at writing.[28] This technique, the authors point out, is invaluable, for it teaches readers that texts are human creations and, therefore, susceptible to error and bias. McKeown et al. use the term *queries* to differentiate between traditional short answer questions and questions that promote big understandings—ones that focus on connections, or relations, deep principles, and structure. Consider the following paragraph provided by Buehl (2001):

> Position the factory-applied nailing fin drip cap upright for installation. Ensure drip cap lip hangs over the head jamb extrustion. Note: Clad Safe-T-Plus model lacks drip cap attachment to head jamb nailing fin. Do not apply the nailing fin corner gaskets at this time. (p. 112)

This paragraph is a "how-to" explanation for installing a window. Students can think through such an impossible text and come to the conclusion that

---

[28]See Chapter 10 for dozens of nonfiction materials for teaching this strategy.

Used by permission of Little, Brown and Company, a division of Hachette Book Group USA, Inc.

the author failed to consider the audience. Students could be guided through such a text with the following questions:

1. What is the author trying to say?
2. What is the author's message?
3. What is the author talking about?
4. Did the author explain clearly?
5. What does the author assume that we already know?
6. How could the author have said things more clearly?
7. What would you say instead?[29]

Finding nonfiction texts to introduce query-led discussions is relatively easy—have students and friends help gather instructions for how-to home projects (installing a doorknob, putting together a treadmill, replacing a part on an automobile—even directions for preparing tax returns work well). Teaching students this type of questioning process helps them understand that authors are accountable for conveying their message clearly.

Though designed for guiding students through difficult nonfiction material, this strategy can also aid readers in thinking through multilayered fictional texts and arriving at deeper text-author understandings.[30] This idea works beautifully to help students understand satire and social commentary. The following queries work well when delving into rich story layers:

1. What is the author trying to tell you?
2. Why is the author telling you that?
3. What attitude does the author have? How do you know? (This question helps them analyze tone.)
4. What message do you think he/she is conveying? (Is there an underlying theme—social commentary perhaps in a romance novel?)
5. What might be the author's purpose in writing this story (poem, text, etc.)?
6. How does the author want you to feel?
7. What does he/she want you to know or pay attention to?
8. What is the author's motive or agenda? How do you know?
9. How persuasive is the author? That is, how effectively does he/she convince you to believe certain things?
10. How do his/her ideas connect with your own?

---

[29]Questions are synthesized from Buehl (2001) and Beck et al. (1997).
[30]Try this approach with poetry; see Chapter 9.

Table 5.2

YA Satire and Social Commentary

Adam Canfield of the Slash by Michael Winerip. Cambridge, MA: Candlewick
  Press, 2005.
American Born Chinese by Gene Yang. New York: First Second, 2006.
The Astonishing Life of Octavian Nothing, Traitor to the Nation: Volume One.
  The Pox Party by M. T. Anderson. Cambridge, MA: Candlewick Press, 2006.
A Great and Terrible Beauty by Libba Bray. New York: Delacorte/Random
  House, 2003.
Hoot by Carl Hiaasen. New York: Random House, 2002.
Jennifer Government by Max Barry. New York: Doubleday, 2003.
King Dork by Frank Portman. New York: Delacorte/Random House, 2006.
Larklight by Philip Reeve. New York: Bloomsbury, 2006.
The Murder of Bindy MacKenzie by Jaclyn Moriarty. New York: Scholastic, 2006.
Parent Swap by Terence Blacker. New York: Farrar, Straus & Giroux, 2006.
Prom Anonymous by Blake Nelson. New York: Viking/Penguin, 2006.
Rash by Pete Hautman. New York: Simon & Schuster, 2006.
Rat Boys: A Dating Experiment by Thom Eberhardt. New York: Hyperion, 2001.
Story Time by Edward Bloor. Orlando, FL: Harcourt, 2004.
Wide Awake by David Levithan. New York: Knopf/Random House, 2006.
The Wish List by Eoin Colfer. New York: Hyperion, 2003.

Romantic satires and humor are wonderful choices for teaching this technique. Because romance and humor are often dismissed in favor of more "serious" texts, this particular strategy teaches readers to delve beneath the story surface in search of deeper ideas. Table 5.2 lists 16 titles that use satire and social commentary to convey deeper meanings. While most are romance and humor, I've added a few political satires because boys will favor these.

Thick and Thin Questions

Most teachers are familiar with Bloom's cognitive taxonomy[31] and know that modeling higher-level questions is vital to critical thinking and intellectual growth. However, research has shown that teachers engage students in ways that give rise to a disproportionate number of fact-level, copy-the-answer-from-the-text questions, identify *this,* list *that,* and procedural questions (e.g., When is this paper due?). Students spend too much time looking for knowledge-level answers. Explicit instruction in question types can aid students in developing higher-level thinking skills such as analyzing, synthesizing, and evaluating.

---

[31]A method of categorizing questions by level of abstract thought: knowledge, comprehension, application, analysis, synthesis, and evaluation.

Harvey and Goudvis (2000) use the terms *thick* and *thin* to differentiate between large global questions and smaller questions that clarify text. Thick questions help us explore universal ideas and can take us beyond the text. We may make predictions, compare, analyze, or evaluate ideas. Thick questions are deeper and require longer answers and discussions. *Why?* and *How?* are examples of thick questions. Thin questions help us clarify confusion, understand words or phrases, or help us discover basic information. They can be answered with few words. Questions that begin with *who, when, where,* and *how many* usually elicit short responses.

You can model thick and thin questions by reading aloud a passage from a young adult novel. As you read aloud, stop and ask students thin questions that come to mind. For example, you might read the second chapter of Ritter's *Under the Baseball Moon* (2006) and come to this passage:

> "Well, first I have to make Kayla's travelball team. That's why we're here. And I knew something *extraordinaire* was going to happen today."
> "Why?" I still couldn't believe I was talking to her.
> "Because there's a baseball moon."
> "A what?" I asked. (p. 16)

The thin question you might pose is, *What* is a baseball moon? An answer to this question helps you clarify meaning. Ritter's novel offers plenty of opportunities to pose thick questions. Consider the following passage:

> Sometimes I'd skateboard under the Sunset Cliffs Boulevard Bridge, near Robb Field, where the San Diego River empties into the ocean. I'd sit up on the riprap and play to the girders and water pipes above, letting the concrete echo rain down on me. Lines of cars would rumble by, just over my head, their tires drumming the metal bridge joints—*tha-dump, tha-dump*—giving me my beat, and I'd blow like a jazzman under a blue light, keeping it tight, keeping it raspy, maybe stir up a few tourists from Nebraska. (p. 9)

After reading this passage, you may remind the class that the narrator plays a trumpet and that there seems to be a lot of sound in this passage: "concrete echo rain down on me," "cars would rumble by," "tires drumming," "tha-dump, tha-dump," and more. You may ask a thick question like, "What connection can you make between the protagonist's music and Ritter's writing style?" This passage, too, offers opportunities for thin questions: What is *riprap*? What are *girders*?

Ranking Questions

I learned this technique from Patricia P. Kelly, my doctoral mentor at Virginia Tech University. Each student develops three to four questions based on a text read by the class and shares his/her questions in a small-group setting comprised of four to five students. The group chooses six to ten of the most important questions. They set the other questions aside and begin discussing their choices. They rank them from the most important to the least important and prepare to justify their rankings. This simple activity creates rich conversations. In justifying questions and rank ordering them, students must delve into deep conversations about the text. They develop an understanding of simple, "right there" kinds of questions and questions that move readers deep into the text.

Hillocks's Questioning Hierarchy

Hillocks (1980) proposed a seven-tiered hierarchy that begins with literal questions and moves to what he calls structural generalizations. His model is based on the premise that before we can engage in abstractions we have to understand literal meaning. Students don't always approach discussions with a level-one question. In fact, their conversations can be quite circular—moving back and forth from one level to another as they make sense of their reading. Hillocks's hierarchy is a good tool for determining how deep a student can go with a given text and can also aid students in understanding and developing their own deep questions. Table 5.3 lists Hillocks's seven levels and a proposed question based on John Green's Printz Honor book, *An Abundance of Katherines* (2006). This interpretation of Hillocks's model is based on an example developed by Jeff Wilhelm (Wilhelm, Baker, & Dube, 2001) for Steinbeck's *Of Mice and Men*. After reading the examples, develop your own questions based on a favorite romance, humor, or sports novel you've discovered in this chapter.

Reprinted by permission of Penguin Young Readers Group © 2006.

Questioning Circles

Questioning circles support students in combining their personal experiences with textual reading and world experiences (Christenbury, 1994; Christenbury & Kelly, 1983). This model suggests that students need not go through a range of hierarchal questions to engage in deep thinking. The model consists of three overlapping areas. As illustrated in Figure 5.1, these three areas come together in the center, an area representing the highest-order thinking and referred to by Christenbury and Kelly (1983) as *dense*.

One way of working through Christenbury's (1994) model is to have students develop a series of eight questions that get increasingly difficult (the idea here isn't to lead a hierarchal discussion but to help students understand different levels of questioning). Questions fit eight overlapping categories, which require students to think about (1) the text, (2) the reader (self),

Table 5.3

Hillocks's Seven-Tiered Hierarchy

Level 1: Basic Stated Information	**Example:** What is Colin Singleton doing in the opening passage? **Purpose:** To determine whether students can read and comprehend repeated information.
Level 2: Key Detail	**Example:** Why does Colin believe Katherine has dumped him? **Purpose:** References an important element in the plot. Used to determine whether readers can notice a detail that will be important later in the reading.
Level 3: Stated Relationships	**Example:** Why does Colin's dad disagree with Colin about the road trip? **Purpose:** Determines whether readers can ascertain the relationship between and among several stated pieces of information close together in the text. In this case it is a relationship between two people.
Level 4: Simple Implied Relationships	**Example:** Why does Hassan take Colin on a road trip? **Purpose:** Similar to Level 3. Needed information is close together in the text; however, the information is implied, not stated.
Level 5: Complex Implied Relationships	**Example:** There seems to be more than one reason Hassan wants to take Colin on a road trip. Identify at least three and explain which is most important. **Purpose:** Determines whether the reader can make inferences from a large number of details located throughout the text. To do so, the reader must be able to identify essential pieces of information.
Level 6: Author's Generalization	**Example:** What might John Green say to teenage boys who have been dumped? Use supporting evidence to support your idea. **Purpose:** Determines whether the reader can generalize to the world.
Level 7: Structural Generalizations	**Example:** How does Green use the road trip to reinforce the story's themes? **Purpose:** Readers must explain how the story structure works to create meaning.

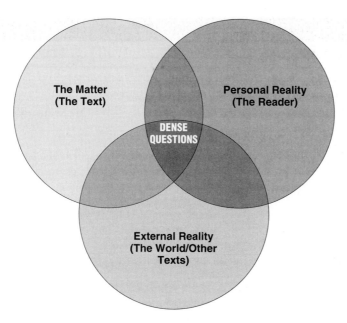

Figure 5.1 *Questioning Circles*

From *Questioning: A Path to Critical Thinking* by Lelia Christenbury and Partricia P. Kelly. Urbana, IL: NCTE, 1983.

and (3) the world or other literature. Table 5.4 shows sample questions based on the author's model for Markus Zusak's *Fighting Ruben Wolfe* (2001), a story about boxing and brotherly love. The beauty of this activity is that it works well for most any book. With practice, students begin developing deeper questions and more thoughtful text responses.

Socratic Circles/Seminars

In its simplest form, a Socratic circle/seminar provides an opportunity for students to raise questions and share their thoughts about a piece of litera- ture or an important issue. It is a method that deposes the teacher's role: the teacher is required to remain silent throughout the discussion. Prior to class, students should read, analyze, and develop questions about a text. On the day of discussion, the teacher arranges seats in two concentric circles. Stu- dents taking seats within the circle participate in questioning and discuss- ing the text; those on the outside serve as listeners and take notes and write responses to what they hear. Two or three empty chairs are placed within the circle and are used to invite an outer member into the group when the conversation lags, someone makes a put-down remark, the conversation veers off topic, or any member of the inner circle doesn't move the discus- sion forward. The teacher may develop questions for the group (in the form of a handout), but the group decides how to conduct the conversation. They may choose to go around the circle until everyone has spoken, appoint a discussion leader, or let speakers choose when to speak. Once students have

Table 5.4

Dense Questioning for *Fighting Ruben Wolfe* by Markus Zusak, 2001

Type of Question	Question Description	Student Question
Text	Information found in text	Who is the narrator of the story?
Reader	Reader's experiences and beliefs	Have you ever felt like you were living in someone else's shadow, such as a sibling or a classmate?
World or Other Literature	Knowledge of history, other cultures, and other literature	What other character does Ruben remind you of?
Text-to-Reader	Combine knowledge of text with knowledge of history, other cultures	In what ways are you either like or different from Ruben?
Text-to-Other Literature	Combine knowledge of text with knowledge of other literature	How does Ruben's relationship with his brother, Cameron, resemble that of George and Lennie's from *Of Mice and Men?*
Reader-to-World	Combine knowledge of reader's own experiences with knowledge of other culture and peoples	How are American boys' attitudes toward sports similar to those of boys in third world countries? How are they different?
Reader-to-Other Literature	Combine knowledge of reader's own experiences with other literature	In what ways are you like George or Lennie from *Of Mice and Men?*
Dense Question	Combine knowledge of all three areas into one "dense" question	For what reason(s) do(es) Cameron feel he has to beat Ruben, and are those reasons similar to what your friends would feel? Include reasons you either share or don't share these feelings.

learned how to develop deep questions, they can design their own. A superb resource for an in-depth discussion on conducting Socratic seminars is Matt Copeland's *Socratic Circles* (2005).

Final Thoughts on Questioning

Questions matter. When we model good questioning strategies with literature teens enjoy, they are more likely to be engaged and, thus, more likely to develop better critical thinking skills. Construction of meaning requires that students have the ability to ask and respond to good questions about their reading. The ability to ask questions helps us monitor our reading, clarify meaning, move deeper into a text, and make better connections. Chapter 10 explores questioning activities for reading informational texts.

Professional Resources

Allen, J. S. (1997). Do you really think that's funny? *English Journal, 86*(3), 102–103.

Baker, W. D. (2007). When English language arts, basketball, and poetry collide. *English Journal, 96*(5), 37–41.

Barell, J. (2003). *Developing more curious minds.* Alexandria, VA: ASCD.

Beck, I. L., & McKeown, M. G. (2006). *Improving comprehension with questioning the author: A fresh and expanded view of a powerful approach.* New York: Scholastic.

Bennion, J. (2002). Austen's granddaughter: Louise Plummer re(de)fines romance. *English Journal, 91*(6), 44–50.

Brackett, V. (1999). *Classic love and romance literature: An encyclopedia of works, characters, authors and themes.* Santa Barbara, CA: ABC-CLIO.

Charles, J., & Mosley, S. (2002). Getting serious about romance: Adult series romances for teens. *Voice of Youth Advocates, 25*(2), 87–93.

Crutcher, C. (1998). From Chip Hilton to Bo Brewster: Some little truths about heroes. *Voices from the Middle, 5*(2), 3–6.

DeBlase, G. (2003). Acknowledging agency while accommodating romance: Girls negotiating meaning in literacy transactions. *Journal of Adolescent and Adult Literacy, 46*(8), 624–635.

Dickson, C. L. (2001). A psychological perspective of teen romances in young adult literature. *The ALAN Review, 28*(3), 44–48.

Karnes, F. A. (2005). *Questioning strategies for teaching the gifted.* Austin, TX: Prufrock Press.

Kelly, P. P. (1991). Transitional novels for readers of teen romances. *The ALAN Review, 19*(1), 19–21.

Lewis, J. (1992). *The road to romance and ruin: Teen films and youth culture.* New York: Routledge.

Loomans, D., & Kolberg, K. (2002). *The laughing classroom: Everyone's guide to teaching with humor and play.* Novato, CA: New World Library.

McKenney, C. S. (1989). A natural high: YA books about sports, horses, music. *English Journal, 78*(4), 27–30.

McMahon, M. (1999). Are we having fun yet? Humor in the English class. *English Journal, 88*(4), 70–72.

Mitchell, D. (1995). If you can't beat 'em, Join 'em: Using the romance series to confront gender stereotypes. *The ALAN Review, 22*(2), 8–9.

Morris, B. S. (1999). Why is George so funny? Television comedy, trickster heroism, and cultural studies. *English Journal, 88*(4), 47–52.

Oriard, M. V. (1982). *Dreaming of heroes: American sports fiction, 1868–1980.* Chicago: Nelson-Hall.

Raphael, T. E., Highfield, K., & Au, K. H. (2006). *QAR now: A powerful and practical framework that develops comprehension and higher-level thinking in all students.* New York: Scholastic.

Roberts, P. L. (1997). *Taking humor seriously in children's literature: Literature-based mini-units and humorous books for children ages 5–12.* Lanham, MD: Scarecrow Press.

Ruggieri, C. A. (1999). Laugh and learn: Using humor to teach tragedy. *English Journal, 88*(4), 53–58.

Seventeen. (2007). *Seventeen real girls, real-life stories: True love.* New York: Hearst Books.

Simmons, J. S. (2001). John R. Tunis and the sports novels for adolescents: A little ahead of his time. *The ALAN Review, 29*(1), 67–72.

Skretta, J. (1997). Beavis and Butt-head: Two more white males for the canon. *English Journal, 86*(8), 24–28.

Smith, S. A. (2000). Talking about "real stuff": Explorations of agency and romance in an all-girls' book club. *Language Arts, 78*(1), 30–38.

Thacker, P. (2007). Growing beyond circumstance: Have we overemphasized hopelessness in young adult literature? *English Journal, 96*(3), 17–18.

Walsh, J. A., & Sattes, B. D. (2004). *Quality questioning: Research-based practice to engage every learner.* Thousand Oaks, CA: Corwin Press.

ONLINE

English Teachers Network: www.etni.org.il/ farside/humorme.htm

Historical Romance Writers: www .historicalromancewriters.com

The History of Humorous Teen Romances: www.ccb.lis.uiuc.edu/Projects/yalit/ female_funnybones/404hist.html

Reach Every Child: www.reacheverychild.com/ feature/humor.html

Romance Authors Page: www. romanceauthorspage.com

Romance Fiction for Teens: www.beavertonlibrary .org/teens/romance.html

Romance Novels for Older Teens: www.library. loganutah.org/books/YA/RomanceOlder.cfm

Romance Writers of America: www.rwanational.org

Sports Classroom: www.sportsclassroom.org

Sports Writers: www.sportswriters.net

Teen Web: www.sjlibrary.org

Young Adult Romance Writers: www.youngadultromancewriters.com

References

Abrams, M. H. (with Geoffrey Galt Harpham). (2005). *A glossary of literary terms* (8th ed.). Boston: Thomson Wadsworth.

Adams, D. (1979). *The hitchhiker's guide to the galaxy.* New York: Ballantine.

Auseon, A. (2005). *Funny little monkey.* Orlando, FL: Harcourt.

Austen, J. (1983). *Pride and prejudice.* New York: Bantam. (Original work published 1813)

Barry, D. (1989). *Dave Barry slept here: A sort of history of the United States.* New York: Random House.

Barry, D. (2006). *Dave Barry's money secrets: Like: Why is there a giant eyeball on the dollar?* New York: Crown.

Bauer, J. (1992). *Squashed.* New York: Delacorte/ Random House.

Bauer, J. (1995). *Thwonk.* New York: Delacorte/ Random House.

Bauer, J. (1996). *Sticks.* New York: Delacorte/ Random House.

Bauer, J. (1998). *Rules of the road.* New York: Penguin/Putnam.

Bauer, J. (1999). *Backwater.* New York: Penguin/ Putnam.

Bauer, J. (2000). *Hope was here.* New York: Penguin/ Putnam.

Bauer, J. (2002). *Stand tall.* New York: Penguin/ Putnam.

Bauer, J. (2005). *Best foot forward.* New York: Penguin/Putnam.

Bauer, J. (2008). *Peeled.* New York: Penguin/ Putnam.

Beck, I. L., McKeown, M. G., Hamilton, R. L., & Kucan, L. (1997). *Questioning the author: An approach for enhancing student engagement with text.* Newark, DE: International Reading Association.

Bee, C. (1998). *Chip Hilton* series. (*Touchdown pass.* #1). Nashville, TN: Broadman & Holman. (Original work published 1948)

Best Quotes-Poems. Retrieved October 14, 2007, from http://www.best-quotes-poems.com/ Mel-Brooks.html

Bissinger, H. G. (1990). *Friday night lights.* New York: Addison-Wesley.

Block, F. L. (2005). *Necklace of kisses.* New York: HarperCollins.

Brackett, V. (1999). *Classic love and romance literature: An encyclopedia of works, characters, authors and themes.* Santa Barbara, CA: ABC-CLIO.

Brashares, A. (2001). *The sisterhood of the traveling pants.* New York: Delacorte/ Random House.

Brian, K. (2005). *Megan Meade's guide to the McGowan boys.* New York: Simon & Schuster.

Brontë, C. (2003). *Jane Eyre.* New York: Penguin. (Original work published 1847)

Brontë, E. (2002). *Wuthering heights.* New York: Penguin. (Original work published 1847)

Brooks, B. (1984). *The moves make the man.* New York: Harper & Row.

Brooks, B. (1992). *What hearts.* New York: HarperCollins.

Brooks, B. (1997). *Wolfbay Wings* series (*Woodsie #1*). New York: HarperCollins.

Buckley, C. (1986). *The White House mess.* New York: Knopf/Random House.

Buckley, C. (1994). *Thank you for smoking: A novel.* New York: Random House.

Buehl, D. (2001). *Classroom strategies for interactive learning.* Newark, DE: IRA.

Caletti, D. (2005). *Wild roses.* New York: Simon & Schuster.

Caletti, D. (2007). *The nature of Jade.* New York: Simon & Schuster.

Carpan, C. (2004). *Rocked by romance.* Westport, CT: Libraries Unlimited/Greenwood Publishing Group.

Cart, M. (1996). *From romance to realism: 50 years of growth and change in young adult literature.* New York: HarperCollins.

Castellucci, C. (2006). *The queen of cool.* Cambridge, MA: Candlewick Press.

Castellucci, C. (2007). *The plain Janes.* Illus. Jim Rugg. New York: Minx.

Cavanna, B. (1946). *Going on sixteen.* Philadelphia: Westminster Press.

Charles, J., Mosley, S., & Bouricius, A. (1999). *Romancing the YA reader. Voice of Youth Advocates, 21*(6), 414–419.

Christenbury, L. (1994). *Making the journey: Being and becoming a teacher of English Language Arts.* Portsmouth, NH: Heinemann.

Christenbury, L., & Kelly, P. P. (1983). *Questioning: A path to critical thinking.* Urbana, IL: NCTE.

Clark, C. (2001). *Wurst case scenario.* New York: HarperCollins.

Cleary, B. (1956). *Fifteen.* New York: William Morrow.

Cleary, B. (1959). *Jean and Johnny.* New York: William Morrow.

Cohn, R. (2002). *Gingerbread.* New York: Simon & Schuster.

Cohn, R. (2008). *Cupcake.* New York: Simon & Schuster.

Copeland, M. (2005). *Socratic circles.* Portland, ME: Stenhouse.

Coy, J. (2005). *Crackback.* New York: Scholastic.

Crime Partners' Book List. (n.d.). Retrieved July 13, 2006, from http://www.mysterypartners .com

Crowe, C. (2000). An interview with John H. Ritter. *The ALAN Review, 27*(3), 5–9.

Crowe, C. (2004). *More than a game: Sports literature for young adults.* Lanham, MD: Scarecrow Press.

Crutcher, C. (1983). *Running loose.* New York: Greenwillow/HarperCollins.

Crutcher, C. (1987). *The Crazy Horse Electric game.* New York: Greenwillow/HarperCollins.

Crutcher, C. (1993). *Staying fat for Sarah Byrnes.* New York: Greenwillow/HarperCollins.

Crutcher, C. (1995). *Ironman.* New York: Greenwillow/HarperCollins.

Crutcher, C. (2001). *Whale talk.* New York: Greenwillow/HarperCollins.

Crutcher, C. (2003). *King of the mild frontier: A ill-advised autobiography.* New York: Greenwillow/HarperCollins.

Crutcher, C. (2007). *Deadline.* New York: Greenwillow/HarperCollins.

Curtis, C. P. (1995). *The Watsons go to Birmingham— 1963.* New York: Random House.

Curtis, C. P. (1999). *Bud, not Buddy.* New York: Random House.

Curtis, C. P. (2004). *Bucking the sarge.* New York: Random House.

Curtis, C. P. (2005). *Mr. Chickee's funny money.* New York: Random House.

Curtis, C. P. (2007a). *Elijah of Buxton.* New York: Scholastic.

Curtis, C. P. (2007b). *Mr. Chickee's messy mission.* New York: Random House.

Daly, B. (1987). Laughing *with,* or laughing *at* the young-adult romance. *English Journal, 78*(6), 50–60.

Daly, M. (1942). *Seventeenth summer.* New York: Dodd, Mead.

de la Peña, M. (2008). *Mexican white boy.* New York: Random House.

Delaney, K. (2003). *My life as a snow bunny.* New York: Smooch/Dorchester.

Deuker, C. (1988). *On the devil's court.* Boston: Joy Street.

Deuker, C. (1993). *Heart of a champion.* Boston: Joy Street.

Deuker, C. (1997). *Painting the black.* Boston: Houghton Mifflin.

Deuker, C. (2000). *Night hoops.* Boston: Houghton Mifflin.

Draper, S. (2003). *The battle of Jericho.* New York: Simon & Simon.

du Jardin, R. (1949). *Practically seventeen.* Philadelphia: Lippincott.

Dygard, T. J. (1989). *Forward pass.* New York: William Morrow.

Dygard, T. J. (1992). *Backfield package.* New York: William Morrow.

Dygard, T. J. (1993). *Game plan.* New York: William Morrow.

Dygard, T. J. (1995). *Infield hit.* New York: William Morrow.

Feinstein, J. (2005). *Last shot: A final four mystery.* New York: Knopf/Random House.

Feinstein, J. (2006). *Vanishing act: Mystery at the U.S. Open.* New York: Knopf/Random House.

Feinstein, J. (2007). *Cover up: Mystery at the Super Bowl.* New York: Knopf/Random House.

Fielding, H. (1998). *Bridget Jones's diary.* New York: Viking/Penguin.

FitzGerald, D. (2006). *Soccer chick rules.* New Milford, CT: Roaring Brook Press.

Flake, S. G. (1998). *The skin I'm in.* New York: Hyperion.

Flake, S. G. (2001). *Money hungry.* New York: Hyperion.

Flake, S. G. (2003). *Begging for change.* New York: Hyperion.

Flake, S. G. (2005). *Bang!* New York: Hyperion.

Flake, S. G. (2004). *Who am I without him? Short stories about girls and the boys in their lives.* New York: Jump at the Sun/Hyperion.

Fleischman, P. (1995). *A fate totally worse than death.* Cambridge, MA: Candlewick Press.

Fleischman, S. (1986). *The whipping boy.* New York: Greenwillow/HarperCollins.

Gantos, J. (1997). *Jack's black book.* New York: Farrar, Straus & Giroux.

Gentile, L. M., & McMillan, M. M. (1978). Humor and the reading program. *Journal of Reading, 21*(4) 343–349.

Greece Central School District. (n. d.). Retrieved July 15, 2006, from http://www.greece .k12.ny.us/instruction/ela/6-12/Reading/ Reading%20Strategies/dense%20questioning .htm

Green, J. (2006). *An abundance of Katherines.* New York: Dutton/Penguin.

Gutnam. D. (1997). *Baseball card adventure* series (*Honus and me* #1). New York: Auon Books.

Gutnam. D. (1999). *Tales from the sandlot* series (*Shortstop who knew too much* #1). New York: Scholastic.

Gutnam. D. (2003). *Million dollar* series (*Million dollar kick* #1). New York: Hyperion.

Harvey, S., & Goudvis, A. (2000). *Strategies that work.* York, ME: Stenhouse.

Hawthorne, R. (2004). *Caribbean cruising.* New York: Avon/HarperCollins.

Hawthorne, R. (2006). *Thrill ride.* New York: Avon/ HarperCollins.

Hillocks, G. (1980). Toward a hierarchy of skills in the comprehension of literature. *English Journal, 69*(3), 54–59.

Hinton, S. E. (1967). *The outsiders.* New York: Viking Press.

Hobbs, W. (1991). *Downriver.* New York: Atheneum/Simon & Schuster.

Hobbs, W. (1997). *Ghost canoe.* New York: HarperCollins.

Hobbs, W. (2004). *Leaving protection.* New York: HarperCollins.

Hogan, M. (2004). *The serious kiss.* New York: HarperCollins.

Hogan, W. (2005). *Humor in young adult literature: A time to laugh.* Lanham, MD: Scarecrow Press.

Howe, J. (2001). *The misfits.* New York: Simon & Schuster.

Huntwork, M. (1990). Why girls flock to *Sweet Valley High. School Library Journal, 36*(3), 137–140.

John, L. (2001). *Max's choice.* New York: Bantam.

Johnson, A. (1990). *When I am old with you.* Illus. David Soman. New York: Orchard/ Scholastic.

Johnson, A. (1993). *Toning the sweep.* New York: Orchard/Scholastic.

Johnson, A. (1995). *Humming whispers.* New York: Orchard/Scholastic.

Johnson, A. (1998). *Heaven.* New York: Simon & Schuster.

Johnson, A. (2002). *Looking for Red.* New York: Simon & Schuster.

Johnson, A. (2003a). *Cool moonlight.* New York: Dial/Penguin.

Johnson, A. (2003b). *The first part last.* New York: Simon & Schuster.

Johnson, A. (2004a). *Bird.* New York: Dial/Penguin.

Johnson, A. (2004b). *Just like Josh Gibson.* Illus. Beth Peck. New York: Simon & Schuster.

Johnson, A. (2005). *A sweet smell of roses.* Illus. Eric Velasquez. New York: Simon & Schuster.

Johnson, K. J. (2005). *Dumb love.* New York: Roaring Brook Press.

Johnson, S. (2001). *Safe at second.* New York: Penguin/Puffin.

Juby, S. (2003). *Alice, I think.* New York: HarperTempest/HarperCollins.

Juby, S. (2004). *Miss Smithers.* New York: HarperTempest/HarperCollins.

Juby, S. (2005). *Alice MacLeod, realist at last.* New York: HarperTempest/HarperCollins.

Juby, S. (2007). *Another kind of cowboy.* New York: HarperCollins.

Kantor, M. (2007). *The breakup bible.* New York: Hyperion.

Kerr, M. E. (1972). *Dinky Hocker shoots smack.* New York: Harper & Row.

Kimmel, E. C. (2005). *Lily B. on the brink of cool.* New York: HarperCollins.

Kimmel, E. C. (2006). *Lily B. on the brink of Paris.* New York: HarperCollins.

Klause, A. C. (1997). *Blood and chocolate.* New York: Delacorte/Random House.

Klesius, J., Laframboise, K. L., & Gaier, M. (1998). Humorous literature: Motivation for reluctant readers. *Reading Research and Instruction, 37*(4), 253–261.

Klise, K. (2006). *Far from normal.* New York: Scholastic.

Koertge, R. (2005). *The Arizona kid.* Cambridge, MA: Candlewick Press. (Original work published 1988)

Korman, G. (2004). *Son of the mob: Hollywood hustle.* New York: Hyperion.

Larochelle, D. (2005). *Absolutely, positively not . . .* New York: Levine/Scholastic.

L'Engle, M. (1949). *And both were young.* New York: Lothrop, Lee & Shepard.

Lewis, J. (2006). *Once upon a tomb: Gravely humorous verses.* Illus. Simon Bartram. Cambridge, MA: Candlewick Press.

Lewis, P. (1995). Why humor? *Voices from the Middle, 2*(3), 10–16.

Limb, S. (2005). *Girl, nearly 16: Absolute torture.* New York: Delacorte/Random House.

Limb, S. (2006). *Girl, going on 17: Pants on fire.* New York: Delacorte/Random House.

Limb, S. (2008). *Girl, barely 15: Flirting for England.* New York: Delacorte/Random House.

Lipsyte, R. (1967). *The contender.* New York: Harper & Row.

Lipsyte, R. (1982). *Jock and Jill.* New York: Harper & Row.

Lipsyte, R. (1991). *The brave.* New York: HarperCollins.

Lipsyte, R. (1993). *The chief.* New York: HarperCollins.

Lipsyte, R. (2003). *Warrior angel.* New York: HarperCollins.

Lipsyte, R. (2006). *Raider's night.* New York: HarperTempest/HarperCollins.

Lipsyte, R. (2007). *Yellow flag.* New York: HarperCollins.

Lupica, M. (2004). *Travel team.* New York: Philomel/Penguin.

Lupica, M. (2006a). *Heat.* New York: Philomel/ Penguin.

Lupica, M. (2006b). *Miracle on 49th Street.* New York: Philomel/Penguin.

Lupica, M. (2007a). *Comeback Kids* series (*Two-minute drill* #1). New York: Penguin.

Lupica, M. (2007b). *Summer ball.* New York: Philomel/Penguin.

Lynch, C. (1993). *Shadow boxer.* New York: HarperCollins.

Lynch, C. (1994). *Iceman.* New York: HarperCollins.

Lynch, C. (1995). *Slot machine.* New York: HarperCollins.

Lynch, C. (2000). *Gold dust.* New York: HarperCollins.

Macy, S. (1996). *Winning ways: A photohistory of a winning season.* New York: Henry Holt.

Macy, S. (Ed.). (2001). *Girls got game.* New York: Henry Holt.

Maher, B. (1996). *Does anybody have a problem with that? The best of* Politically Incorrect. New York: Villard.

Maher, B. (2005). *New rules: Polite musings from a timid observer.* Emmaus, PA: Rodale Press.

Marchetta, M. (1999). *Looking for Alibrandi.* New York: Orchard.

Maxwell, K. (2003). *The year my life went down the 100.* New York: Dorchester.

McManus, P. F. (1978) *A fine and pleasant misery.* New York: Holt, Rinehart and Winston.

Myer, S. (2006). *New moon.* New York: Little, Brown.

Myer, S. (2007). *Eclipse.* New York: Little, Brown.

Myer, S. (2008). *Breaking dawn.* New York: Little, Brown.

Mlynowski, S. (2005). *Bras and broomsticks.* New York: Random House.

Mlynowski, S. (2007). *Spells and sleeping bags.* New York: Random House.

Moffitt, M. A. (1987). *Understanding the appeal of the romance novel for the adolescent girl: A reader-response approach.* Presentation to the International Communication Association Conference, Montreal. (ERIC Document Reproduction Service No. ED284190)

Montgomery, L. M. (1992). *Anne of Green Gables.* New York: Random House. (Original work published 1908)

Moore, C. (2005). *The stupidest angel: A heartwarming tale of Christmas terror.* New York: William Morrow.

Moore, C. (2006). *A dirty job.* New York: William Morrow.

Murray, G. S. (1998). *American children's literature and the construction of childhood.* New York: Twayne/Simon & Schuster.

Myers, W. D. (1981). *Hoops.* New York: Delecorte/Random House.

Myers, W. D. (1984). *The outside shot.* New York: Delacorte/Randon House.

Myers, W. D. (1993). *Malcolm X: By any means necessary.* New York: Scholastic.

Myers, W. D. (1996). *Slam!* New York: Scholastic.

Myers, W. D. (2001). *The Greatest: Muhammad Ali.* New York: Scholastic.

Naylor, P. R. (2008). *Almost Alice.* New York: Atheneum/Simond & Schuster.

Nelson, B. (2006). *Prom anonymous.* New York: Viking/Penguin.

Nilsen, A. P., & Nilsen, D. (1999). The straw man meets his match: Six arguments for studying humor in English classes. *English Journal, 88*(4), 34–42.

Nishiyama, Y. (2003). *Rebound* series (*Rebound #1*). Los Angeles: Tokyopop.

O'Connell, T. (2004). *Pulling princes.* New York: Bloomsbury.

O'Connell, T. (2005). *Dueling princes.* New York: Bloomsbury.

O'Connell, T. (2006). *Dumping princes.* New York: Bloomsbury.

Pascal, F. (1985). *Perfect summer.* New York: Bantam.

Paulsen, G. (1993). *Harris and me: A summer remembered.* Orlando, FL: Harcourt.

Pearson, P. D., & Johnson, D. (1978). *Teaching reading comprehension.* New York: Holt, Rinehart and Winston.

Peck, R. (2000). *A year down yonder.* New York: Dial/Penguin.

Peck, R. (2004). *The teacher's funeral: A comedy in three parts.* New York: Dial/Penguin.

Peck, R. (2006). *Here lies the librarian.* New York: Dial/Penguin.

Peet, M. (2007). *The penalty.* Cambridge, MA: Candlewick Press.

Pollack, P. D. (1981). The business of popularity. *School Library Journal, 28*(3), 25–28.

Radway, J. A. (1984). *Reading the romance: Women, patriarchy, and popular literature.* Chapel Hill, NC: UNC Press.

Raphael, T. (1982). Question-answering strategies for children. *The Reading Teacher, 36*(2), 186–197.

Regis, P. (2003). *A natural history of the romance novel.* Philadelphia: University of Pennsylvania Press.

Reilly, R. (1996). *Missing links.* New York: Doubleday.

Reilly, R. (2006). *Shanks for nothing: A novel.* New York: Doubleday.

Rennison, L. (2000). *Angus, thongs and full-frontal snogging.* New York: HarperTempest/HarperCollins.

Rennison, L. (2001). *On the bright side, I'm now the girlfriend of a sex god.* New York: HarperTempest/HarperCollins.

Rennison, L. (2002a). *Dancing in my nuddy-pants.* New York: HarperTempest/HarperCollins.

Rennison, L. (2002b). *Knocked out by my nunga-nungas: Further, further confessions of Georgia Nicolson.* New York: HarperTempest/HarperCollins.

Rennison, L. (2004). *Away laughing on a fast camel: Even more confessions by Georgia Nicolson.* New York: HarperTempest/HarperCollins.

Rennison, L. (2005). *Then he ate my boy entrancers.* New York: HarperTempest/HarperCollins.

Rennison, L. (2006). *Startled by his furry shorts.* New York: HarperTempest/HarperCollins.

Rennison, L. (2007). *Love is a many trousered thing: Confessions of Georgia Nicolson.* New York: HarperTempest/HarperCollins.

Rennison, L. (2008). *Stop in the name of parts.* New York: HarperCollins.

Ricker-Wilson, C. (1999). Busting textual bodices: Gender, reading, and the popular romance. *English Journal, 88*(3), 57–63.

Ritter, J. (1998). *Choosing up sides.* New York: Penguin.

Ritter, J. (2000). *Over the wall.* New York: Penguin.

Ritter, J. (2003). *The boy who saved baseball.* New York: Penguin.

Ritter, J. (2006). *Under the baseball moon.* New York: Penguin.

Schmidt, G. (2005). *First boy.* New York: Henry Holt.

Schoenbach, R., Greenleaf, C., Cziko, C., & Hurwitz, L. (1999). *Reading for understanding.* San Francisco: Jossey-Bass.

Schreiber, E. (2003). *Vampire kisses.* New York: HarperTrophy/HarperCollins.

Scott, K. (2005). *I was a non-blonde cheerleader.* New York: Putnam.

Sedaris, D. (1994). *Barrel fever.* New York: Little, Brown.

Sedaris, D. (1997). *Holidays on ice.* New York: Little, Brown.

Sedaris, D. (1997). *Naked.* New York: Little, Brown.

Sedaris, D. (2000). *Me talk pretty one day.* New York: Little, Brown.

Sedaris, D. (2004). *Dress your family in corduroy and denim.* New York: Little, Brown.

Segal, E. (1970). *Love story.* New York: Harper & Row.

Seto, A. (2003). *Shaolin soccer* series (*Shaolin* #1). Los Angeles: Tokyopop.

Shepherd, J. (1966). *In God we trust, all others pay cash.* New York: Doubleday.

Sonnenblick, J. (2007). *Zen and the art of faking it.* New York: Scholastic.

Stewart, J. (1998). *Naked pictures of famous people.* New York: William Morrow.

Stewart, J. (2004). The Daily Show with Jon Stewart *presents America (The book): A citizen's guide to democracy inaction.* New York: Warner.

Strasser, T. (2004). *Impact zone* series (*Take off* #1). New York: SimonPulse.

Thompson, A. E. (2005). Rereading fifties teen romance: Reflections on Janet Lambert. *The Lion and the Unicorn, 29*(3), 373–396.

Townsend, S. (1982). *The secret life of Adrian Mole, aged 13 ¾.* London: Methuen.

Tunis, J. R. (1938). *Iron duke.* Orlando, FL: Harcourt.

Tunis, J. R. (1940). *The kid from Tomkinsville.* Orlando, FL: Harcourt.

Tunis, J. R. (1943). *Keystone kids.* Orlando, FL: Harcourt.

Tunis, J. R. (1944). *Rookie of the year.* Orlando, FL: Harcourt.

Wallace, R. (1996). *Wrestling Sturbridge.* New York: Knopf/Random House.

Wallace, R. (1997). *Shots on goal.* New York: Knopf/Random House.

Wallace, R. (2000). *Playing without the ball.* New York: Knopf/Random House.

Wallace, R. (2003). *Losing is not an option.* New York: Knopf/Random House.

Wallace, R. (2004). *Winning season: The roar of the crowd*. New York: Viking/Penguin.

Wallace, R. (2004). *Winning Season* series (*The roar of the crowd* #1). New York: Penguin.

Weaver, W. (1993). *Striking out*. New York: HarperCollins.

Weaver, W. (1995). *Farm team*. New York: HarperCollins.

Weaver, W. (1998). *Hard ball: A Billy Baggs novel*. New York: HarperCollins.

Wilde, O. (1995). *The importance of being earnest*. New York: Penguin. (Original work published 1895)

Wilhelm, J., Baker, T. N., & Dube, J. (2001). *Strategic reading: Guiding students to lifelong literacy 6–12*. Portsmouth, NH: Heinemann.

Williams, C. L. (1999). *My Angelica*. New York: Delacorte/Random House.

Withers, P. (2003). *Take it to the Xtreme* series (*Raging river* #1). Ontario: Walrus.

Wittlinger, E. (2001). *Razzle*. New York: Simon & Schuster.

Yee, L. (2005). *Stanford Wong flunks big-time*. New York: Levine/Scholastic.

Zindel, P. (1978). *The undertaker's gone bananas*. New York: Harper & Row.

Zusak, M. (2001). *Fighting Ruben Wolfe*. New York: Scholastic.

Zusak, M. (2003). *Getting the girl*. New York: Scholastic.

Historical Fiction
Reading Skills: Monitoring and Clarifying

Introduction

Historical fiction is a window to the past through which we can view events and people that shaped the world, discover universal truths, and empathize with those who have gone before us and those currently living in similar circumstances. Through reading historical fiction, we make emotional connections between the past and present that aid us in understanding and valuing our own heritage and the world in which we live. Historical fiction is a vehicle through which we can experience the past vicariously and understand human folly, greed, and aggression.

This chapter surveys the genre, discusses its value, summarizes trends, and outlines differences between hard and soft historical fiction. It also identifies quality characteristics. Historical fiction provides a springboard for discussions about social issues. Four broad categories are covered: war, the black experience, women and history, and immigration. History is vast, and it's impossible to discuss every historical topic imaginable; therefore, additional annotated bibliographies addressing specific events, times, and social issues are included, along with a list of picture books appropriate for teens. The last third of the chapter is devoted to monitoring and clarifying essential comprehension skills.

Value of Historical Fiction

Stated simply, historical fiction puts humanity back into history. Social studies textbooks focus on coverage rather than depth, reducing historical events and historical figures to a few brief sentences; human emotions, motives, and behavior are absent. One way to illustrate this point is to have a group reflect on the emotional turmoil surrounding 9/11, speculate about the similarities between 9/11 and the attack on Pearl Harbor, then examine a description of Pearl Harbor in most any high school textbook. Readers easily see that decades from now the emotional impact of 9/11 will be lost.

Historical figures and events in history texts become one dimensional, making history appear either black or white. Historical fiction situates people among history-making events, coupling history with human responses, revealing neither completely good or bad people, or right or wrong situations, but rather the complexity of human behavior. Because historical fiction concentrates on depth, not coverage, history unfolds multidimensionally.

One argument against the value of historical fiction is the blending of fact with fiction: Is a work historical fiction or fictionalized history? Critics contend that readers unfamiliar with historical facts learn misconceptions. While that can happen, the benefits of reading historical fiction are immeasurable. Historical fiction exposes readers to multiple perspectives and multiple text interpretations. Readers approach history from varying viewpoints, an experience that encourages critical reading and creates proficiencies needed to identify and correct misconceptions. Even textbooks are biased and contain erroneous information, and historical fiction helps raise questions about real-life events and people. The more discrepancies students identify, the more wary they become; hence the more critically they read.

Reading historical fiction can be a valuable lesson in critical thinking. Historical fiction provides an opportunity for readers to question texts—if it's in print, does that make it true? If students study a historical novel in tandem with a corresponding history unit, they can identify inaccuracies in the novel and discuss whether the discrepancies were deliberate deviations for the sake of the story or errors on the part of the writer. Such an exercise is valuable, for it encourages critical reading skills they will need in their adult lives.

Viewing history from multiple perspectives enables readers to evaluate history more clearly and creates a better understanding of humanity. What young adult wouldn't have a better understanding of World War II after reading Markus Zusak's *The Book Thief* (2006), a story in which a young foster girl, Liesel Meminger, scratches out a meager existence by stealing? What reader doesn't understand the cruelty and brutality of slavery and the effects on both blacks and whites after reading Julius Lester's *Time's Memory* (2006), a historical account of the slave trade mixed with magical realism? An African spirit, Ekundayo, inhabits the body of a young slave named Nathaniel in an attempt to bring peace to his people. When Nathaniel falls in love with the slave master's white daughter, disaster awaits. Craig Crist-Evans's *Amaryllis* (2003) is set during the Vietnam conflict. One brother goes to war, and from his perspective we see the horrors on the battlefield; the other brother remains home and through him we experience the pain of family suffering and repercussions on the homefront. These two pitch-perfect voices resonate with readers and illustrate what the Vietnam era was really like. No textbook or peer-reviewed article can create these human responses and experiences.

By reading historical fiction, teens can learn truths of their heritage, come to understand themselves and their families, and, it is hoped, avoid the mistakes of their predecessors. In reflecting on historical fiction's value, young adult author Alden R. Carter comments that historical fiction explains "how we and our kind became what we are"; he uses his novel *Crescent Moon* (1999) as an example of how adolescents can come to understand and value their past:

> I set my novel *Crescent Moon* in 1912 at the close of the great logging era in Wisconsin. My adolescent protagonist, Jeremy, senses not only the changes coming in his own physical and emotional life, but the changing nature of his town and his times. A lover of airplanes, automobiles, and every new convenience, he is thoroughly a boy of the new century. But his great-uncle, a carver of traditional wooden advertising figures, and an aging Indian, Two-Horse, seek to hold Jeremy back, if only for a brief time, to show him what is lost when traditions die. So it is that over the course of

a summer Jeremy is caught not only between childhood and adulthood but between the old and the new as he helps the two elderly gentlemen plan and carve an Indian maiden as a tribute to Two-Horse's people. (personal communication, March 2007)

In an era in which pop culture attracts more media coverage than the Iraq War and genocide in Darfur, historical fiction reminds young adults of global issues and worldwide atrocities. Linda Sue Park's *When My Name Was Keoko* (2002) addresses the impact of World War II on a brother and sister living under the Japanese occupation of Korea. In our high schools, teens typically study the effects of World War II on our own country. Reading about the struggles of others during this time reminds us of our interconnectedness, shared humanity, and global responsibilities.

Much like quality films (e.g., *Saving Private Ryan,* 1998), historical fiction creates a sense of place noticeably absent from other text forms. Readers are drawn into the setting, the landscape, the architecture, the language, clothing, and material objects of the era. Historical fiction provides situational clues and visuals of how people lived and how events unfolded that capture the imagination of disinterested and at-risk readers. More important, it encourages a shared sense of humanity.

Defining Historical Fiction

Historical fiction is not easily defined. As Brown and St. Clair point out in *The Distant Mirror: Reflections on Young Adult Historical Fiction* (2006), an exhaustive study of the rise and development of young adult historical fiction, no agreed-upon time frame separates historical fiction from other fiction. It's easy to classify a story set during the Civil War as historical fiction, but it's more difficult to classify more recent events. How much time must pass before an event becomes history? A decade? Five years? One day? What about an event like 9/11? When does that become history?

In her work *Sublime Desire: History and Post-1960s Fiction,* Amy Elias offers a workable definition of historical fiction composed of three distinguishing characteristics and excluding a specific time factor:

1. Specific historical detail, featured prominently, is crucial to plot or character development or some experimental representation of these narrative attributes;
2. A *sense* of history informs all facets of the fictional construct (from authorial perspective to character development to selection of place);
3. This sense of history emerges from and is constructed by the text itself (cited in Brown & St. Clair, 2006).

These characteristics are useful, for as Brown and St. Clair (2006) point out, they help categorize novels that are set in the present but that focus on the past (e.g., historical detail may be provided through letters, flashback scenes, altering chapters between a real world and the past). Novels, as such, may be viewed as historical fiction. By *not* arguing that a specific amount of time must pass between the author's life and the story setting for a work to be historical, we can include works with a setting contemporary with the lives of their authors. A classic example is John Steinbeck's *The Grapes of Wrath* (1939). Penned during the height of the Great Depression and the Dust Bowl, the novel reflects the social issues of Steinbeck's time. Today, it offers a historical perspective on a deplorable era in American history.

Brown and St. Clair (2006) argue that there is a difference between books whose history is contemporary with the author's life and those set in an earlier time. Therefore, they suggest a fourth characteristic: a clash between opposing sociopolitical powers, which helps distinguish between fiction deliberately set in the past and fiction that gains historical status over time. They illustrate the significance of this point with Louisa May Alcott's *Little Women* (1868) in which the Civil War is peripheral to the conflict of the story—the sisters' efforts to overcome obstacles preventing them from maturity into "virtuous" young ladies. Although some novels with a contemporary setting that becomes historical over time may feature characters engaged in social or political issues, their struggles, for the most part, and involvement in those issues are less intense (Brown & St. Clair, 2006).

Brown and St. Clair's assertion holds true for many contemporary novels that become historical with the passage of time. An event that we deem historically significant today may have provided only a backdrop, or have been mentioned only in passing, by the author who penned the contemporary story. This isn't always true, however. A notable exception is *The Grapes of Wrath* (1939) in which Steinbeck's political views and portrayal of the dastardly side of capitalism are evident. The Dust Bowl and the Great Depression are central to the story. One might argue that *The Grapes of Wrath* is a response to a current affair. Current affairs, of course, become history. A young adult example is Walter Dean Myers's *Sunrise over Fallujah* (2008), a story about the early stages of Operation Iraqi Freedom told through the eyes of a young American soldier.

Historical fiction typically precedes an author's own lifetime, but authors may reconstruct historical events that happened earlier in their own lives. Plots and dialogue are generally imaginary; however, the overall story reconstructs history. Historical fiction may re-create a historical event, give life to a historical figure, and/or paint a portrait of a historical time. Because young adult literature is a relatively new genre and hasn't had time to become historical, this chapter primarily examines historical fiction set at some time in the past, preceding an author's lifetime.

Trends in Historical Fiction

Historical fiction hasn't always been popular with young adults; however, the recent emphasis in content area reading has energized the genre. In addition to young adult historical fiction single titles, publishing houses have capitalized on historical series such as *The Orphan Train Adventures* (1987) and *The Ellis Island* series (1992) by Joan Lowery Nixon,

Carolyn Meyer's *Young Royals* series (1999), and the *Golden Mountain Chronicles* (1984) by Laurence Yep. The *Young Heroes of History* series (2001) by Alan N. Kay is published by White Mane, a publishing house specializing in historical fiction. Although older adolescents may read these series, most historical series (e.g., *Dear America, My America, My Name Is America,* and *Royal Diaries*) are geared toward younger audiences, primarily girls.

Great for stimulating class discussion and for introducing multiple perspectives, historical fiction picture books suited for middle grades and secondary classrooms have increased significantly over the last decade. Many focus on historical figures such as Carole Weatherford's *Moses: When Harriet Tubman Led Her People to Freedom* (2006), dramatically illustrated by Kadir Nelson. Readers take a spiritual journey with Tubman as she contemplates her escape from a Maryland plantation via the Underground Railroad. Others focus on historical settings. J. Patrick Lewis and Rebecca Kai Dotlich's *Castles: Old Stone Poems* (2006), illustrated by Dan Burr, is steeped in architectural history and includes historical notes. The visual element of this work provides an understanding of antiquity unparalleled by written text. Still others emphasize events such as Ken Mochizuki's *Baseball Saved Us* (1993), a story about a Japanese American boy's life in a World War II internment camp.

Whereas most young adult historical literature falls within the 19th and 20th centuries, and older young adult historical fiction works typically focused on great men (e.g., Martin Luther King Jr., Abraham Lincoln) and world-changing events (e.g., American and European wars, Western Expansion, the Great Depression), an abundance of newer historical fiction concentrates on the impact historical events have on the lives of ordinary people. The setting of Audrey Couloumbis's *Summer's End* (2005) is a family farm during the Vietnam conflict. The family worries about a missing uncle in Vietnam and deals with the agitated political climate characteristic of the 1960s. Gretchen Moran Laskas's *The Miner's Daughter* (2007) is set in a West Virginia coal mining community during the height of the Great Depression. Sixteen-year-old Willa Lowell longs for a better life: she knows backbreaking work, hunger, coal dust, and threadbare clothes. For most, the Great Depression conjures images of the Dust Bowl, immigration issues, Hoovervilles, and soup lines. Laskas's work sheds light on the hardships of coal mining families during this austere time. Rather than looking at the larger picture of historical events and key figures, some of today's stories illuminate the impact historical events have on smaller, lesser known segments of society.

In addition to examining the impact world-changing events have on everyday lives, today's historical fiction writers search for unique pieces of history. Sometimes these are forgotten heroes or little known events such as New York City's Triangle Shirtwaist Factory Fire in 1991. Mary Jane Auch illuminates the impact this fire had on the lives of the immigrant factory workers through the eyes of Margaret Rosen Nolan, a 16-year-old girl in *Ashes of Roses* (2002). Meticulously researched, Carolyn Meyer's *Marie, Dancing* (2005) depicts the life of Marie van Goethem, the real-life model for the French artist, Edgar Degas, and an otherwise unknown historical figure. This search for unique stories has broadened the genre, provided a wider range of subjects, and captured more interest in young adult historical fiction.

This broadening of theme has included an emphasis on global events and has educated young adults to worldwide atrocities. In an era in which many believe our country could better support humanitarian efforts, these stories are priceless. Patricia McCormick's *Sold* (2006), for example, reveals the horrific story of young Nepali girls being sold by their families to brothels in India. In writing her book, McCormick interviewed prostitutes and girls sold into sex slavery in India and Nepal.

In writing historical fiction, a writer must choose a point of view, a lens through which the story can be told. Sometimes writers present history through the eyes of real-life characters, either friends, family, or foe; other times they create individuals who didn't exist or weren't involved in the events. Raymond Wemmlinger's *Booth's Daughter* (2007) tells the story of Edwina Booth, the real-life niece to Lincoln's assassin, John Wilkes Booth. Branded by her uncle's crime, she wrestles with her identity and place in society. Though details such as dialogue are fictional, this novel illustrates the horrific impact such a crime has on a family.

Lynn Cullen's *I Am Rembrandt's Daughter* (2007) illustrates the manner in which many authors take poetic license with characters—or deviate from the truth—when writing historical fiction. Thirteen-year-old Cornelia, with her mother dead and her brother recently married, is left alone with her famous father. They live in poverty. Rembrandt, showing signs of madness, is no longer a revered artist and, despite financial hardship, refuses to alter his artistic style. Those familiar with the artist's life may know he had two daughters named Cornelia; both died in infancy. By using a "fictional daughter," Cullen is able to take readers closer to the real man. Despite this discursion from truth, Cullen's book provides remarkable period detail and history about one of the most famous artists of all times. It is a well-written story and, if read through a critical lens, can encourage teens to find out more about the extraordinary artist.

Historical fiction has changed dramatically over the years. As the genre continues to evolve, the much argued question about when an event becomes history may become less important, worldwide events will remain prominent, and authors will continue to search for smaller, less known pieces of lost history.

Types of Historical Fiction

Hard historical fiction typically weaves together the lives of fictional characters and real people and places them amid a significant turning point in history, an event that plays an instrumental role in their lives. Ronald Kidd's *Monkey Town: The Summer of the Scopes Trial* (2006) is an excellent example. In re-creating the infamous 1925 Scopes Monkey Trial that challenged the teaching of evolution, Kidd stays close to history. Key historical figures appear in the story: John Thomas Scopes, the 24-year-old first-year high school teacher; F. E. Robinson, the drugstore owner who organized and led the challenge; lawyers William Jennings Bryan and Clarence Seward Darrow, the latter of whom represented Scopes. The setting rings true: Kidd details the small-town community, Rhea County High School, the courthouse, and the drugstore where citizens met to organize the challenge. Kidd includes an author's note in which he explains historical deviations: F. E. Robinson's daughter, 9 at the time of the trial, is 15 in the story. It is through her eyes that the story unfolds. He also adds credibility to his novel by explaining the research behind *Monkey Town* in an author's note.

Kidd's work is a good example of hard historical fiction, and dozens of authors spend countless hours meticulously researching historical events, places, and people. Ann Rinaldi (see the author box and her books in Box 6.1) is among the most noted and admired. Winner of countless historical fiction awards, Rinaldi has researched dozens of historical events, uncovering forgotten and suppressed pieces of history. Her research and resulting historical novels have added much needed perspectives to history, most notably the female viewpoint. In *The Secret of Sarah Revere* (1995), Rinaldi brings to life the character of Paul Revere, his famous ride, and the Boston Tea Party through the eyes of his daughter, Sarah Revere. *A Break with Charity: A Story about the Salem Witch Trials* (1992), told from a female perspective by Susanna English, describes the terror experienced by many during the witch hunts. The character of Tituba, a real-life slave accused of conjuring spells, is particularly well drawn.

Writing Historical Fiction   by Ann Rinaldi

Back in 1982 when I wrote my first historical fiction novel, *Time Enough for Drums,* 10 publishers turned it down with the reasoning "we can't give children history." I was too much of a neophyte at publishing then to know that things in New York went in trends. After the manuscript spent four years brewing in a drawer like a good wine, my own publisher (Holiday House) decided to publish it. They asked me for another historical when it won an ALA "best book" award.

Publishers have been asking me for historicals ever since. And in the interim years they have become so popular that almost every publisher had an imprint out, at least for girls.

Lately, of course, the trend has been fantasy. More recently chick lit and super realistic problem novels. Historicals are out of favor again, but I continue to write them. Mostly because I have discovered that the story of this country is the best that ever was and

Continued

Writing Historical Fiction   *Continued*

because of the letters I get from all over the country from young people.

They run the gamut from "I always hated historicals until my teacher made me read one of yours, and now I want to know—when is your next one coming out?" to "I have a very unhappy life, but your books make me know that others, in more crucial times, have suffered as much as I and survived."

Then there are the verbal responses I get when I visit classrooms. "You know, I didn't realize I was learning when I read your book. I was enjoying it too much." Did I mention the letters from mothers? "Thank you for inspiring my 15-year-old daughter to read. She has read three of your novels already and can't wait for her fourth."

These are the responses every writer looks for. But I know full well that to keep them coming, I must continue doing the things I've been doing over the last 20 years.

I must continue being in competition with others, even though they're writing those fabulous sci-fi's and fantasies, those popular chick lits and well-written problem novels. But I must also be in competition with myself, with each book sharper, more powerful, and page-turning than the last.

After all, why should young adults pick up an Ann Rinaldi book, when they can pick up any award-winning novel out there? First, because I honor my parallel obligation to them. To always give them a good story. To remember that the story is as important and *almost* as significant as the history. There is nothing more page-turning than a good story. If I don't have one, all the history in the world won't do it.

Second, the history that I do have must be *accurate*. Which is why I am surrounded by research books as I write. I must never mislead them in the history, so they stand up in the classroom and say that so-and-so said such-and-such on Bunker Hill because Ann Rinaldi said so.

If I honor these obligations, as I've been doing, let's hope that when the next trend comes out in New York, I'll still be writing historical novels.

Box 6.1   Ann Rinaldi's Historical Fiction   *by Alice Terry*

***An Acquaintance with Darkness*. San Diego: Harcourt, 1997.**

Emily Pigbush is dealing with more than the normal struggles of a 14-year-old. Her mother has just died, and because her father is also dead, she is forced to live with her evil, law-breaking uncle. As the nation is struggling because of the assassination of President Lincoln, Emily struggles with the knowledge that the mother of her best friend was an accomplice of John Wilkes Booth.

***Amelia's War*. New York: Scholastic, 1999.**

Growing up during the Civil War isn't easy for adolescent Amelia Grafton from Hagerstown, Maryland, who thinks of herself as a Southerner for the Union. Amelia finds herself going beyond the traditional women's duties during war of aiding the wounded and preparing food. By tricking a Confederate officer, she ends up saving her town from being burned down.

***The Blue Door*. New York: Scholastic, 1996.**

The third volume of the *Quilt Trilogy*, a patchwork of three generations of one family, this saga starts at a South Carolina plantation and ends up—after a shipwreck—at a textile mill in Massachusetts. Amanda is sent to Maryland to make amends with her great-grandfather and represent the family's

Continued

Box 6.1   Ann Rinaldi's Historical Fiction   *Continued*

cotton interests, but when her ship is sabotaged and because she can identify the culprit, she establishes a new identity. She ends up working at her great-grandfather's large textile mill and becomes a pro-tester against grim labor conditions.

A Break with Charity: A Story about the Salem Witch Trials. San Diego: Harcourt, 1992.

Susanna is like any other young adolescent who wants to be accepted into a social circle. What is different is that the girls she wants to accept her are about to begin a series of false accusations, accusations that will lead to the imprisonment and execution of many innocent people in Salem, Maryland. What should she do? If she says nothing, the witch hunt will continue; if she *breaks charity* with the group, she risks having her own family members accused of practicing witchcraft.

Broken Days. New York: Scholastic, 1995.

The second volume in the *Quilt Trilogy,* this book is woven around 14-year-old Walking Breeze, whose dying mother directs her to find her family in Salem. Ebie Clemsford sets out to discredit her half-Shawnee cousin, Walking Breeze. Her jealousy causes danger-ous pulls in the Chelmsford family quilt.

Brooklyn Rose. Orlando, FL: Harcourt, 2005.

As the 20th century ushers in, 15-year-old Rose Frampton is uprooted from her Southern plantation and follows her new husband to Brooklyn, New York, to manage a large Victorian estate. Rose relates this scary and enticing experience through her diary, and readers follow her life as a frightened young girl maturing into a loving, capable, and strong woman.

Cast Two Shadows: The American Revolution in the South. San Diego: Harcourt, 1998.

Rinaldi portrays how families were torn apart in the Revolutionary War through the character of

14-year-old Caroline Whitaker, who lived on a Southern plantation in 1780. Her personal struggle with discovering her biological mother is a slave reflects the complexity of the difficulties she faced living through such turbulent times.

The Coffin Quilt: The Feud between the Hatfields and the McCoys. San Diego: Harcourt, 1999.

Following the historical feud between the Hatfields and the McCoys, this book offers a deeper view of what occurred when men returned home to the moun-tains from the Civil War with deep psychological wounds that caused them to overreact to any per-ceived violation, especially against their kin. With Roseanna McCoy fanning these flames by running off with a Hatfield, Fanny, her youngest sister, relates this tragic tale of love and vengeance.

The Color of Fire: A Novel. New York: Hyperion, 2005.

When 18th-century New York City is gripped by burning homes and warehouses, fingers point to disgruntled slaves. Indentured white servants flame the accusations, and fear prevails. Fourteen-year-old Phoebe faces emotional and ethical issues as she watches her fellow slave and friend indicted.

Come Juneteenth. Orlando, FL: Harcourt, 2007.

The Emancipation Proclamation was the best-kept secret in Texas for two years. Imagine discovering that your freedom has been kept from you for two years by those you trusted! Thirteen-year-old Luli, a Texas slave, brings up moral and ethical questions relating to Reconstruction from her experience.

The Education of Mary: A Little Miss of Color, 1832. New York: Jump at the Sun/ Hyperion, 2000.

Against the backdrop of the abolitionist movement, the Industrial Revolution, prejudice, and lack of

Continued

Box 6.1   Ann Rinaldi's Historical Fiction   *Continued*

justice during the early part of the 19th century, 13-year-old Mary Harris is growing up. As the white community tries to close the new, controversial school for young black women she attends, Mary helps with the Underground Railroad movement and examines issues and people in her world.

The Ever-After Bird. Orlando, FL: Harcourt, 2007.

CeCe accompanies her uncle to Georgia in search of a rare bird, the scarlet ibis. Unbeknowst to CeCe, her uncle's expedition is a cover for his involvement in the Underground Railroad. CeCe learns firsthand the horrors of slavery.

The Fifth of March: A Story of the Boston Massacre. San Diego: Harcourt, 1993.

Rachel, 14, is a servant of John and Abigail Adams in colonial Boston. She becomes emotionally involved with a Royalist sent to guard the home of John Adams. He goes on trial for the death of five colonists during a riot on March 5, 1770, and Rachel's social conscious and self-awareness is awakened.

Finishing Becca: A Story about Peggy Shippen and Benedict Arnold. San Diego: Harcourt, 1994.

At 14, Becca becomes a maid to Peggy Shippen, the betrothed of General Benedict Arnold, whereupon she becomes a witness to unfolding history. Becca examines her loyalty to her country, her family, and herself.

Girl in Blue. New York: Scholastic, 2001.

Weary of her father's abuse, young Sarah Wheelock joins the Union forces in 1861 as Neddy Compton. When her secret is later discovered, she is forced to become a Pinkerton spy and goes undercover as a maid for a well-known Confederate socialite and spy.

Hang a Thousand Trees with Ribbons: The Story of Phillis Wheatley. San Diego: Harcourt, 1996.

This view of pre-Revolutionary War life in Boston is told through the voice of young Phillis Wheatley, the first renown black poet. Phillis relates an early crush she has on Nathaniel Wheatley, the son of Phillis's owners who is also her tutor. It concludes with her interviewing George Washington.

In My Father's House. New York: Scholastic, 1993.

Imagine being a young, Southern girl living between 1852 and 1865 with the Civil War starting on your family's Manassas farm and ending in Appomattox, the place where your family moves by the end of war. This happens to young Oscie McLain, who grows up under the cloud of turmoil both in her world and in her mind as she questions the status quo.

The Journal of Jasper Jonathan Pierce, a Pilgrim Boy. New York: Scholastic, 2000.

Fourteen-year-old Jasper, an indentured servant, relates his first 15 months in America in his journal after arriving on the *Mayflower*. The hardships faced by the Pilgrims on the *Mayflower* and in the new world are realistically portrayed. Everyday details bring this period to life.

Keep Smiling Through. San Diego: Harcourt, 1996.

What was the World War II homefront in New Jersey like in 1943? Ten-year-old Kay Hennings, a young heroine caught in an unloving home situation, shares the hardships of her life. Details of rationing, the importance of radio, having to quit school to work, and pressures of being 10 years old in difficult times bring this era to life.

Continued

Box 6.1   Ann Rinaldi's Historical Fiction   *Continued*

The Last Silk Dress. New York: Holiday House, 1988.

Starting out supporting the Confederacy during the Civil War by collecting silk dresses from the ladies of Richmond to create a balloon to spy on the Yankees, Susan Chilmark, 14, begins to question her loyalty. She discovers secrets that force her to reexamine and challenge the Southern cause she has always defended.

Mine Eyes Have Seen. New York: Scholastic, 1998.

Viewing events surrounding the Harper's Ferry attack in 1859 through John Brown's 15-year-old daughter's eyes offers a new angle on this historic event. Brown's daughter, Annie, both loves and resents a charismatic and mysterious leader. She relates a period of American history full of social change and political upheaval.

Mutiny's Daughter. New York: HarperCollins, 2004.

In 1787 William Bligh set sail on the *HMS Bounty* for Tahiti to get breadfruit plants, but a great mutiny took place led by Fletcher Christian. What really happened to Christian after the mutiny? It is rumored that he survived a massacre and returned to England. This tale involves his 14-year-old daughter, Mary, who is determined not to reveal her real identity while searching for her loving, disgraced father.

My Heart Is on the Ground: The Diary of Nannie Little Rose, a Sioux Girl. New York: Scholastic, 1999.

In 1879, 12-year-old Nannie Little Rose begins her diary in order to improve her English skills at the Carlisle Indian School in Pennsylvania. Details of her earlier life and her present life reveal a remarkable girl uprooted from her home and heritage and trying to fit into a new world while struggling to maintain her Sioux identity.

Nine Days a Queen: The Short Life and Reign of Lady Jane Grey. New York: HarperCollins, 2004.

Who says growing up is easier when you are royal? Certainly not Lady Jane Grey who at 15 was executed for treason after reigning as Queen of England for only nine days. Caught in a tempest, sensitive Lady Jane became a pawn in a power struggle in which she wanted no part.

Numbering All the Bones. New York: Jump at the Sun/Hyperion, 2002.

While Andersonville Prison, a place where 13,000 Union soldiers died, remains in our collective memory, it meant more to 13-year-old Eulinda whose slave brother met his demise at Andersonville. Eulinda, the daughter of a slave and slave owner, connected with Clara Barton after the Civil War ended and worked with her to give the soldiers who died in Andersonville Prison proper burials.

Or Give Me Death: A Novel of Patrick Henry's Family. Orlando, FL: Harcourt, 2003.

Most young students have heard Patrick Henry's famous quote, "Give me liberty or give me death," but how many know anything about young Patrick Henry and his family? Through the eyes of two of Patrick Henry's sisters, this book addresses three primary themes: mental illness, precognition or second sight, and complex social relationships.

The Redheaded Princess: A Novel. New York: HarperCollins, 2008.

A carefully researched account of Queen Elizabeth I's years as a young girl. Steeped in period history, the novel depicts young Elizabeth as strong willed, yet accepting. Though she is the King's daughter, Elizabeth fears she can never be queen because she is a female. After all, her mother was executed for

Continued

Box 6.1   Ann Rinaldi's Historical Fiction   *Continued*

treason. At times Elizabeth is accepted by the royal court; at other times she is shunned and sent to the country to live. Elizabeth's youth is one of fear and uncertainty.

A Ride into Morning: The Story of Tempe Wick. San Diego: Harcourt, 1991.

In the creases of the Revolutionary War, a beautiful young girl, Tempe Wick, struggles to help her family survive. Confused and overwhelmed by war as well as family and farm responsibilities, Tempe is faced with the hardest decision of her life—whether to join the revolt or not.

Sarah's Ground. New York: Simon & Schuster, 2004.

With the Civil War casting its shadow, 18-year-old Sarah Tracy leaves New York to become caretaker at Mount Vernon. Sarah, young and inexperienced, faces down threats to Mount Vernon, to Washington's tomb, as well as to her own reputation and safety.

The Second Bend in the River. New York: Scholastic, 1997.

Rebecca Galloway is a young pioneer girl living in the wilds of 18th-century Ohio, who ultimately rejects the visionary Shawnee leader Tecumseh's offer of marriage because their worlds are so different. Rebecca's pioneer life is portrayed as both difficult and rewarding; the plight and frustrations of Native Americans is also addressed.

The Secret of Sarah Revere. San Diego: Harcourt, 1995.

We are all aware of the famous deed of Paul Revere. In this book, Revere's life is shared through the voice of his 13-year-old daughter, Sarah. She portrays her father as a caring family man and a dedicated patriot. Very aware of political events, she relates this period of history with sensitivity and finesse.

The Staircase. San Diego: Harcourt, 2000.

Thirteen-year-old Lizzy Enders is dropped off at a Santa Fe convent school in the 1870s by her father days after losing her mother to the fever. Born a Methodist, Lizzy has difficulty understanding Catholicism. When a chapel stairway needs building, she engages an elderly unemployed carpenter, while the other girls at the convent school pray for a miracle. The real-life, enduring mystery of the chapel staircase makes this book even more intriguing.

A Stitch in Time. New York: Scholastic, 1994.

This is the first in the *Quilt Trilogy* about a Salem shipping merchant family during the years following the American Revolution. Hannah, the older sister, stays in Salem creating a quilt from fabric taken from close friends and family, while other family members make dangerous and exciting journeys, some to the Western territory. The concept of the quilt is integral to the entire trilogy, representing the woven patchwork of this family's journey over three generations.

Taking Liberty: The Story of Oney Judge, George Washington's Runaway Slave. New York: Simon & Schuster, 2002.

Born a Mount Vernon slave, Oney Judge is referred to as a servant. Personal servant and close confidante to Martha Washington, she feels like a family member. Once she realizes she is still a slave, she is faced with a choice: Does she continue where she is as a slave, or does she take her liberty like her father before her?

Time Enough for Drums. New York: Holiday House, 1986.

Jemima Emerson relates the events of the Revolutionary War through the lens of her family and hometown of Trenton, New Jersey. Jemima's family represents many families of the period having divided loyalties.

Continued

Box 6.1   Ann Rinaldi's Historical Fiction   *Continued*

An Unlikely Friendship: A Novel of Mary Todd Lincoln and Elizabeth Keckley. Orlando, FL: Harcourt, 2007.

Though seemingly unlikely, First Lady Mary Todd Lincoln and freed slave Lizzy Keckley share a close friendship during the turbulent days of the Lincoln administration. Both women are tracked through very different childhoods and their path to friendship. The book sheds light on the social conditions of the period and slavery.

Wolf by the Ears. New York: Scholastic, 1991.

Harriet Hemings, one of Thomas Jefferson's slaves and considered by some to be his daughter by Sally Hemings, must decide whether to remain a slave at Monticello or take her freedom when she turns 21. A tragic incident convinces her to leave Monticello, and she moves to Washington D.C., passing as white. This historical novel addresses significant moral issues, many that are front-page news even today.

Soft historical fiction contains historical elements, but may lack historical figures and/or significant historical events. It focuses instead on the general social, cultural, physical, and political landscape, painting a canvas of a different time, place, and people. Patricia Reilly Giff's *Water Street* (2006), for example, takes place in 19th-century Brooklyn during the construction of the Brooklyn Bridge towers. The story revolves around the lives of everyday people: Bird, who wants to be like her mother and yearns for a best friend, and Thomas, who journals about his bar-hopping Pop and the mother he doesn't have. Nonetheless, the historical backdrop of the story is so rich that readers are transported to another time and place.

In recent years, historical fiction has blended with other genres, creating an abundance of historical fantasies filled with magic and time travel, romance, horror, and mystery. In *London Calling* (2006), Edward Bloor uses magical realism to transport Martin Conway to an earlier time and place. While at home working on an independent study project, Martin connects with Jimmy, a young boy growing up in London during World War II, through his grandmother's radio. Martin travels with Jimmy through London during the Blitz, the sustained bombing of the United Kingdom by Germany between 1940 and 1941.

Matthew Skelton paints an exquisite canvas of the University of Oxford and the town of Oxford, England, during the Middle Ages in *Endymion Spring* (2006). A disgruntled Blake Winters accompanies his academic mother and annoying sister to the University of Oxford, where he stumbles across an ancient, magical book in the Bodleian Library, a book brought there by Gutenberg's apprentice to protect it from evil forces.[1] While these

---

[1]Johannes Gutenberg, printer and European inventor, created movable type and printed the Gutenberg Bible around 1455.

are not pure historical fiction novels, settings, descriptive lifestyle details, and historical references offer readers an authentic sense of time and place. Chapter 8 includes examples of historical fantasies, and Chapter 5 includes historical romance titles.

Quality historical fiction presents a well-developed story with realistic characters congruent with historical records (see Chapter 3 for additional characteristics). Although dialogue may be contrived, events, setting, and time lines remain historically true. The work paints a clear and accurate picture of social customs, beliefs, values, and physical surroundings. Settings may not be exact replicas, but they are, at least, genuine. Character actions, values, and beliefs are congruent with the time, and dialect is a close approximation, without being burdensome. While some anachronisms[2] may appear, they don't distract the reader or minimize the story's authenticity.

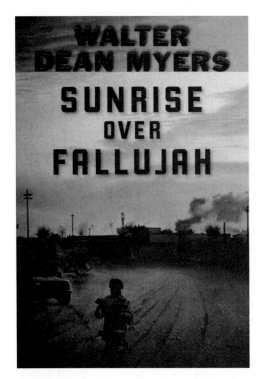

A thought-provoking perspective on the war in Iraq.

Illustration © 2008 by Scholastic, Inc. Used by permission.

Young Adult Historical Fiction and Social Issues

Historical fiction is a wonderful vehicle for examining social issues because it allows readers to examine social issues and individual responses from a comfortable distance. A multitude of social themes, many overlapping, run through historical fiction: war, peace, adversity, survival, marginalized and suppressed people, greed, diversity, and immigration. Discussions on four themes that occur routinely in middle school and secondary classrooms follow. Each theme is accompanied by an annotated list of books. Additional themes and books follow these discussions.

War

Tim O'Brien has taught us much about writing war stories and history. Based on his personal experiences in Vietnam, *If I Die in a Combat Zone, Box Me Up and Ship Me Home* (1973), and *Going after Cacciato* (1978) helped pave the way for what's called creative nonfiction.[3] His works are used widely in classrooms across the country. Much like Tim O'Brien's *The Things They Carried* (1990) and Stephen Crane's *The Red Badge of Courage* (1895), Walter Dean Myers's young

---

[2]A person, thing, event, or idea that is out of its time. (An obvious example: a machine gun during the Civil War era.)
[3]Creative nonfiction, or the nonfiction novel, is discussed in Chapter 10 with other forms of nonfiction.

adult novel *Fallen Angels* (1988) is a classic study of soldiers at war. Told from the viewpoint of a 17-year-old black soldier who enlists in the summer of 1967, *Fall Angels* is a riveting depiction of fear and hatred and the horrors and gruesomeness of the Vietnam conflict. Readers know Richie and his comrades intimately and understand the strength that helps them survive—the desire to leave Vietnam alive. Readers also experience the living conditions of Vietnamese citizens, an experience that aids them in recognizing their humanity. In Michael Morpurgo's *Private Peaceful* (2003), readers meet 17-year-old Thomas, a young man who lies about his age and follows his older brother, Charlie, into war.[4] As Thomas stands nightwatch over the battlefields in France during World War I, he reminisces about his life: his childhood growing up in the countryside, his brothers, his mother, and Molly, the love of his life. Though he's lived through gas attacks, watched best friends get killed, and battled mud, lice, and rats, he knows this is the longest night of his life: if he falls asleep, he'll get shot. When morning comes, a court martial of a comrade will change his life forever. It's impossible to read *Private Peaceful* and not understand or vicariously experience the human cost of war.

There's no question that war has both a psychological and physical effect on soldiers and their families. It also takes a devastating toll on innocent civilians. In *War Comes to Willy Freeman* (1987), a Newbery Honor book by James Lincoln Collier and Christopher Collier, readers encounter war through the eyes of a 13-year-old free black girl growing up in Connecticut. Willy witnesses the killing of her father and the kidnapping of her mother. Fearing she will be returned to slavery, she disguises herself as a boy and searches for her mother who has disappeared. Willy faces unlikely odds: she is black and female.

When we think of war, we tend to think of human casualties and human heroes. Unbeknownst to many are the experiences and contributions of animals during conflict. The use of dogs in war, for example, goes back to antiquity. In every modern war since World War I, dogs have been trained to frighten soldiers, distract and locate the enemy, defend camps, and sniff out bombs, booby traps, mines, illegal drugs, and weapons. War dogs have saved thousands of lives while sometimes sacrificing their own. In *Cracker! The Best Dog in Vietnam* (2007), a meticulously researched story about

Seventeen-year-old
Graham Salisbury.

---

[4]Michael Morpurgo, author of numerous books for children and adults, served as the Children's Laureate of Britain from 2003 to 2005.

the role of dogs in Vietnam, Cynthia Kadohata traces the experiences of war dogs. Alternating between two points of view, that of Hanski, a 17-year-old dog handler, and Cracker, a Vietnam war dog trained to locate enemy troops and sniff out bombs, *Cracker* relates the heroic efforts of a German shepherd and the unbreakable bond that develops between war dog and handler.

One of today's most respected young adult authors of war stories is Graham Salisbury. Winner of the prestigious Scott O'Dell Award for Historical Fiction, Salisbury grew up in Hawaii after World War II and saw firsthand the effects of the war on the Hawaiian Islands. Through *Under the Blood-Red Sun* (1994), *Eyes of the Emperor* (2005), and *House of the Red Fish* (2006), award-winning historical fiction accounts of World War II set in Hawaii, Salisbury re-creates one of the most challenging times in our history. Cross-generational and cross-cultural studies of ordinary people, Salisbury's novels chronicle the racism and hatred held against Japanese Americans, many who joined the U.S. Army, only to be abused and given menial jobs. In the author box Salisbury addresses the impact his books are having on a new generation of readers.

Box 6.2 lists war stories grouped together by the wars they address.

Americans   by Graham Salisbury

At first with *Eyes of the Emperor,* I didn't set out to do anything but build a story around a piece of WW II military history that captured me—the story of 25 of Hawaii's Americans of Japanese ancestry involved in military war dog training on Cat Island, Mississippi. I'd discovered this well-hidden story through my continuing research following the publication of my novel, *Under the Blood-Red Sun.*

The more I researched it, the more fascinating it became. The wiry little story hunter in my head was ecstatic. This *has* to be your next novel!

Amazingly, I found 8 of the 25 men who participated in this piece of history, men who were actually *there*. I found them by way of . . . well, more research. They agreed to a face-to-face interview, and we set up a meeting at the 100th Infantry Battalion veteran's clubhouse in Honolulu. They were humble, happy, and deeply thoughtful men, all hovering around 90. Without question, meeting them and hearing their story firsthand was one of the greatest occasions of my writerly life.

Some time later I flew down to Gulfport, Mississippi, and took a boat out to walk around on

Cat and Ship Islands, where in the early 1940s this secret dog training happened. It was there that my quest became more than a story project to me—it became a mission. And that mission was to in some way honor the men who made this never-told piece of history, men from my home state, men from my neighborhood. Men nobody knew about, and should.

Continued

Americans *Continued*

And I guess I wanted to spend some time considering the virtues of honor, loyalty, friendship, and courage—parts of being human that are not enough talked about in today's USA.

Based on the true events and real men of that time, I created my cast of characters and started writing.

Once I felt the heartbeat of this story I could not turn my back on it, nor did I want to. These Japanese men from Hawaii were Americans in the finest sense of what that means. They put duty to country and fellow citizens above themselves, which in a time of war is what brave men do. We ought to know about them, and know of their sacrifice and courage.

So in this work I have been doing, exploring Hawaii's involvement in WW II, I have had two loyalties: one, to the Americans of Japanese ancestry who gave everything they had in WW II to help liberate the people of Europe, even in the face of gross prejudicial treatment; and two, to the United States military, which continues to assure us the freedoms that we hold so dear. To those who serve, thank you.

Copyright Graham Salisbury, 2008

Official Web site: www.grahamsalisbury.com

Titles not mentioned in this chapter include *Blue Skin of the Sea* (1992), *Shark Bait* (1997), *Jungle Dogs* (1998), *Lord of the Deep* (2001), *Island Boyz* (2002), and *Night of the Howling Dogs* (2007).

 ## Box 6.2   War

The Revolutionary War

1776: Son of Liberty by Elizabeth Massie. New York: Tor, 2000.

April Morning: A Novel by Howard Fast. New York: Crown, 1961.

The Arrow over the Door by Joseph Bruchac. Illus. James Watling. New York: Dial/Penguin, 1998.

Carry on, Mr. Bowditch by Jean Lee. Illus. John O'Hara Cosgrave II. Boston: Houghton Mifflin, 1995.

Early Thunder by Jean Fritz. Illus. Lynd Ward. New York: Coward-McCann, 1967.

Fever 1793 by Laurie Halse Anderson. New York: Simon & Schuster, 2000.

The Fighting Ground by Avi. New York: Lippincott, 1984.

Give Me Liberty by L. M. Elliott. New York: Tegen/HarperCollins, 2006.

Hope's Crossing by Joan Elizabeth Goodman. Boston: Houghton Mifflin, 1998.

Kings Mountain by G. Clifton Wisler. New York: HarperCollins, 2002.

Midnight Rider by Joan Hiatt Harlow. New York: Simon & Schuster, 2005.

The Rifle by Gary Paulsen. Orlando, FL: Harcourt, 1995.

Where the Great Hawk Flies by Liza Ketchum. New York: Clarion, 2005.

The Year of the Hangman by Gary Blackwood. New York: Dutton/Penguin, 2002.

The Civil War

1863: A House Divided: A Novel of the Civil War by Elizabeth Massie. New York: Tor, 2000.

Assassin by Anna Myers. New York: Walker, 2005.

Booth's Daughter by Raymond Wemmlinger. Honesdale, PA: Calkins Creek/Boyds Mills Press, 2007.

Bull Run by Paul Fleischman. New York: Geringer/HarperCollins, 1993.

Continued

Box 6.2   War   *Continued*

The Deep Cut by Susan Rosson Spain. New York: Marshall Cavendish, 2006.

Hearts of Stone by Kathleen Ernst. New York: Dutton/Penguin, 2006.

Iron Thunder by Avi. New York: Clarion, 2007.

The Judas Field: A Novel of the Civil War by Howard Bahr. New York: Henry Holt, 2006.

The Passage by James Killgore. Atlanta: Peachtree, 2006.

Red Moon at Sharpsburg by Rosemary Wells. New York: Penguin, 2007.

The River Between Us by Richard Peck. New York: Penguin, 2003.

Second Sight by Gary Blackwood. New York: Dutton/Penguin, 2005.

Soldier's Heart: Being the Story of the Enlistment and Due Service of the Boy Charley Goodard in the First Minnesota Volunteers by Gary Paulsen. New York: Bantam Doubleday Dell/Random House, 1998.

Trembling Earth by Kim L. Siegelson. New York: Penguin, 2004.

A Voice from the Border by Pamela Smith Hill. New York: Holiday House, 1998.

World War I

B for Buster by Iain Lawrence. New York: Delacorte/Random House, 2004.

The Foreshadowing by Marcus Sedgwick. New York: Lamb/Random House, 2006.

Hattie Big Sky by Kirby Larson. New York: Delacorte/Random House, 2006.

Littlejim by Gloria Houston. New York: Philomel/Penguin, 1990.

Lord of the Nutcracker Men by Iain Lawrence. New York: Delacorte/Random House, 2001.

Megiddo's Shadow by Arthur Slade. New York: Lamb/Random House, 2006.

The Night of the Burning: Devorah's Story by Linda Press Wulf. New York: Farrar, Straus & Giroux, 2006.

Pictures, 1918 by Jeanette Ingold. Orlando, FL: Harcourt, 1998.

Remembrance by Theresa Breslin. New York: Delacorte/Random House, 2002.

The Silver Donkey by Sonya Hartnett. Cambridge, MA: Candlewick Press, 2006.

Tree by Leaf by Cynthia Voigt. New York: Atheneum/Simon & Schuster, 1988.

War Horse by Michael Morpurgo. New York: Scholastic, 2007.

Without Warning: Ellen's Story, 1914–1918 by Dennis Hamley. Cambridge, MA: Candlewick Press, 2007.

World War II

The Amazing Story of Adolphus Tips by Michael Morpurgo. New York: Scholastic, 2006.

The Bomb by Theodore Taylor. New York: Avon Books, 1995.

Code Talker: A Novel about the Navajo Marines of World War II by Joseph Bruchac. New York: Dial/Penguin, 2005.

Emil and Karl by Yankev Glatshteyn. Trans. Jeffrey Shandler. New Milford, CT: Roaring Brook Press, 2006.

Escaping into the Night by D. Dina Friedman. New York: Simon & Schuster, 2006.

Fire in the Hills by Donna Jo Napoli. New York: Penguin, 2006.

Heroes Don't Run: A Novel of the Pacific War by Harry Mazer. New York: Simon & Schuster, 2005.

I Had Seen Castles by Cynthia Rylant. Orlando, FL: Harcourt, 1993.

Milkweed by Jerry Spinelli. New York: Knopf/Random House, 2003.

Continued

Box 6.2   War   *Continued*

Postcards from No Man's Land by Aidan
Chambers. New York: Dutton/Penguin,
2002.

Room in the Heart by Sonia Levitin. New York:
Dutton/Penguin, 2002.

Someone Named Eva by Joan M. Wolf. New York:
Clarion, 2007.

Stones in Water by Donna Jo Napoli. New York:
Dutton/Penguin, 1997.

Summer of My German Soldier by Bette Greene.
New York: Dial/Penguin, 1973.

Summer of the War by Gloria Whelan. New York:
HarperCollins, 2006.

Weedflower by Cynthia Kadohata. New York:
Atheneum/Simon & Schuster, 2006.

The Vietnam Conflict

Almost Forever by Maria Testa. Cambridge, MA:
Candlewick Press, 2003.

Georgie's Moon by Chris Woodworth. New York:
Farrar, Straus & Giroux, 2006.

Going after Cacciato by Tim O'Brien. New York:
Delacorte/Random House, 1978.

Greetings from Planet Earth by Barbara Kerley.
New York: Scholastic, 2007.

Letters from Wolfie by Patti Sherlock. New York:
Viking/Penguin, 2004.

Park's Quest by Katherine Paterson. New York:
Lodestar, 1988.

Patrol: An American Soldier in Vietnam by Walter
Dean Myers. Illus. Ann Grifalconi. New York:
HarperCollins, 2002.

Sammy and Julianna in Hollywood by Benjamin
Alire Sáenz. El Paso, TX: Cinco Puntos Press,
2006.

Search and Destroy by Dean Hughes. New York:
Atheneum/Simon & Schuster, 2005.

Sonny's War by Valerie Hobbs. New York: Farrar,
Straus & Giroux, 2002.

The Things They Carried by Tim O'Brien. Boston:
Houghton Mifflin, 1990.

Too Big a Storm by Marsha Qualey. New York:
Dial/Penguin, 2004.

Other Perspectives/Other Wars and Conflicts

Blood Red Horse by K. M. Grant. New York:
Walker, 2005.

*Brothers in Hope: The Story of the Lost Boys of
Sudan* by Mary Williams. Illus. R. Gregory
Christie. New York: Lee & Low, 2005.

Dawn and Dusk by Alice Mead. New York: Farrar,
Straus & Giroux, 2007.

Escape to West Berlin by Maurine Dahlberg.
New York: Farrar, Straus & Giroux, 2004.

Habibi by Naomi Shihab Nye. New York: Simon
& Schuster, 1997.

In the Name of Gold by Paula Jolin.
New Milford, CT: Roaring Brook Press, 2007.

An Innocent Soldier by Josef Holub. New York:
Scholastic, 2005.

Karoo Boy by Troy Blacklaws. Orlando, FL:
Harcourt, 2005.

Parvana's Journey by Deborah Ellis. Toronto, ON:
Groundwood Books, 2002.

Refugee Boy by Benjamin Zephaniah. New York:
Bloomsbury, 2001.

Secrets in the Fire by Henning Mankell.
New York: Annick, 2003.

A Stone in My Hand by Cathryn Clinton.
Cambridge, MA: Candlewick Press, 2002.

Under the Persimmon Tree by Suzanne Fisher
Staples. New York: Farrar, Straus & Giroux,
2005.

Whey My Name Was Keoko by Linda Sue Park.
New York: Clarion, 2002.

Year of No Rain by Alice Mead. New York: Farrar,
Straus & Giroux, 2003.

Christopher Paul Curtis (left) as a teen. His novel *Elijah of Buxton* won the 2008 Scott O'Dell Award for Historical Fiction and the Coretta Scott King Award. It is also a Newbery Honor title.

The Black Experience

For as long as cultures have existed, people have been marginalized and suppressed and used for personal gain by those more powerful. Evidence of slavery predates writing and exists in virtually all cultures, and it is a defining experience in the history of our country and in the lives of black Americans. By reading young adult historical fiction that speaks to the cruelty of slavery, teens increase their understanding of this age-old atrocity. Black teens gain a better understanding of their heritage and the events, behaviors, and actions that both suppressed and elevated their lives. Other cultural groups, whites especially, can examine their own roles. All cultural groups can gain an understanding of the residue and fallout that occurs when one group suppresses another.

In *Day of Tears: A Novel in Dialogue* (2005), Julius Lester re-creates a merciless time in U.S. history. In 1859 the largest slave auction on record in the United States, known as *The Weeping Time,* occurred in Savannah, Georgia. Despite inheriting two plantations, Pierce M. Butler lost a great deal of money—some in the stock market, the rest gambling. To pay his debts, he sold 436 slaves.[5] The slaves were held in horse stalls at a Savannah racetrack, where prospective buyers could examine them (Lester, 2005). Lester's provocative novel, written in dialogue form, reads like a play[6] and recounts the events and emotions surrounding that dreadful day in which families were ripped apart. Lester discusses why he writes historical fiction in the author box.

Gary Paulsen traces the life of a young slave girl in *Nightjohn* (1993). Nightjohn, a runaway slave, returns to the plantation to teach reading, even though he knows getting caught means dismemberment. Through the voice of 12-year-old Sarny, Paulsen addresses misconceptions about slavery—that slaves were well cared for, happy, and content with their lives.

An excellent companion to Paula Fox's classic *The Slave Dancer* (1973), a story about a kidnapped flute player who witnesses life aboard a slave ship, is *Copper Sun* (2006), by National Teacher of the Year Sharon Draper. *Copper Sun* provides an unparalleled examination of American slavery and the slave trade. Her story begins in a village in Africa where

---

[5]Lester points out that some records indicate 429 were sold (*Day of Tears,* 2005, p. 172).
[6]This work is perfect for Reader's Theater. See the section on fluency in Chapter 9.

"pale-faced" men capture the fittest and murder the rest. Amari and others are taken aboard a slave ship and transported to America, where Amari is sold into slavery in the Carolinas and given to a 16-year-old plantation owner's son as a birthday present. Although many consider slavery a past atrocity, it isn't. Trafficking, particularly of women and children, occurs today on almost every continent, including North America: most are sold for sexual favors; others for domestic labor. Reading historical fiction with slavery themes can be a springboard for discussing current problems.

While slavery is perhaps the most chronicled black experience in American history, the civil rights movement is another milestone. Chris Crowe's book, *Mississippi Trial, 1955* (2002), portrays the wretched treatment of blacks in the South prior to the civil rights movement. In the author box, Crowe talks about the research behind this book and his companion nonfiction book, *Getting Away with Murder: The True Story of the Emmett Till Case* (2003). Han Nolan's *A Summer of Kings* (2006) takes place during 1963, the height of the civil rights movement. Esther Young, a rich white girl, feels upstaged by her talented younger siblings and abandoned by her friends. In search of acceptance, she becomes obsessed with King-Roy Johnson, a young black man accused of murder, and sets out to develop a romantic relationship. As their relationship develops, the two have philosophical discussions about Martin Luther King Jr. and Malcolm X. King-Roy becomes a supporter of the Nation of Islam and a radical follower of Malcolm X. Esther, changed by their relationship, persuades her family to join her in the famous 1963 march in Washington, D.C., with Martin Luther King Jr. In the end, King-Roy teaches Esther not only about racial injustice but also about her own power to effect change.

There's no question that slavery and the civil rights movement are two juggernauts in our nation's history. Their weight, however, over-shadows other consequential black experiences in the high school curricula. What, for example, was city life like for blacks in the 19th century? What about frontier life? Historical fiction provides an outlet for exploring those experiences. Diane Lee Wilson narrates the experiences of a biracial boy who takes a job riding for the Pony Express in 1860 in *Black Storm Comin'* (2005). Abandoned by his father on a California-bound wagon train, Colton delivers secret government information during the years preceding the Civil War. Based on historical facts, *Black Storm Comin'* provides a provocative picture of racial issues across the country, an exceptional addition to a genre that situates most historical racial issues in the South.

Prior to the 1980s little literature focused on black history; today that is no longer true. A great number of authors give voice to the black experience (see Box 6.3 for additional YA titles and Box 6.4 for picture books appropriate for teens). You will find additional black history resources—nonfiction books, autobiographies, biographies, and diaries—in Chapter 10.

Why Write Historical Fiction   by Julius Lester

I believe in the named and nameless dead. I believe in the past, not as something completed and forever pinioned to memory but as the accretion of known and unknown lives from whom I came and to whom I am indebted and for whom I am responsible.

For me, literature is the faithful psychic record of who and what was. It is a record not of great events but of the ordinary ones in ordinary lives. Literature is the means through which I share my knowledge of past as present, of past as presence, of past as evermore.

The past is not something that is "behind us." We are affected by the past whether we know it or not. History is not something found in a textbook. History is who we are. All our lives are history. The root meaning of the word *history* is "to see." History enables us to see, and in seeing we hope to learn how or how not to live. That is why it is interesting that another of the root meanings of history is "guide." In history we seek a guide to our own lives and times.

I write about the past because I do not want it to be forgotten. I write about the past because one day I will be someone else's past, and I, like all of us, will want to be remembered. I write about the past because it is one way to understand the present.

Copyright Julius Lester, 2008

Official Web site: www.members.authorsguild.net/juliuslester

Titles not mentioned elsewhere in this chapter include *Pharaoh's Daughter* (2000), *Cupid* (2007), and Guardian (2008).

History Is Hard Work   by Chris Crowe

Though I'd like to claim that it was strategic and forward-looking, my nonfiction book, *Getting Away with Murder: The True Story of the Emmett Till Case,* followed my historical novel, *Mississippi Trial, 1955,* because of laziness.

At least that was the initial idea.

Writing *Mississippi Trial, 1955* required lots of historical and field research, more than a year's worth of digging, searching, and reading. When I felt that I knew as much as there was to know about the 1950s, Emmett Till, his murder, and the sham trial of his killers, my work slammed to a stop.

I had a brain brimming with information, but I had no story, no fictional yarn to wrap about the post of historical fact. Part of my problem was that I hadn't gone to the source. I couldn't set the story in Mississippi if I didn't *know* Mississippi. So I booked a trip to

Continued

History Is Hard Work   *Continued*

Greenwood, Mississippi, a small town on the edge of the Mississippi Delta that was just a few miles from the village where Emmett was kidnapped and not much farther from Sumner, site of the famous trial.

I arrived in Greenwood on August 21, the same day Emmett Till had arrived almost 50 years earlier. My headquarters was a nostalgic bed and breakfast on the banks of the Yazoo River, and I spent my days walking around town, talking to people, taking photos, and exploring back streets. I made notes on dialect and attitudes and spent many hours—usually midday hours when the brutal August heat and humidity made the air-conditioned public library the only smart place to be—reading microfilm of the local newspaper's coverage of the kidnapping, murder, and trial. I drove up to Money, then on to Sumner, with my sensory radar on full: I documented sights, sounds, and smells, picked up maps, and explored historic buildings.

Every night and every morning, I wrote in my journal about what I had seen, experienced, and thought, all the while searching for the first thread of a yarn that I could spin into a novel.

When I finally finished *Mississippi Trial, 1955,* an idea popped into my head, an idea that came from my years of being a lazy student: "Hey, why not use the same paper for two different classes?" It would be easy, I figured, to recast my research from the novel as a nonfiction book.

As I thought more carefully about it, I came up with an even better reason to tell the Emmett Till story as nonfiction: I worried that some teens reading *Mississippi Trial, 1955* might believe that it was much more *fiction* than it was *history.* Some might even think that this Crowe guy made up the entire story, that there never really was a kid named Emmett Till.

To my great disappointment, the nonfiction writing was devilishly difficult. I suffered from information overload—I knew so much about the case and the history surrounding it that I had no idea how to condense it into something readable for teens. I had no idea how to acquire photographs. I had no idea how to blend the details of the case with the necessary historical context, or even what historical context was necessary.

I thought and scribbled, outlined and researched, even interviewed Emmett's mother twice. Gradually, slowly, painfully, the book began to come together. It turned out to be a great companion to *Mississippi Trial, 1955,* but if I had known at the outset how difficult it would be to nonfictionalize historical fiction, I probably wouldn't have attempted it in the first place.

You see, I'm still a lazy student at heart.

Box 6.3   The Black Experience

47 by Walter Mosley. New York: Little, Brown, 2005.

Part historical fiction, part fantasy, this title is a thought-provoking account of slave life on a Georgia plantation in 1832. The narrator, called 47, picks cotton and lives under the watchful eye of a cruel landowner. 47's life changes when he meets a runaway slave named Tall John, who tells him he is from another world.

The Baptism by Shelia P. Moses. New York: McElderry/Simon & Schuster, 2007.

A poignant story about a young boy growing up in the Occoneechee Neck of North Carolina. In the week leading up to his baptism, Leon Curry questions whether he wants to give up lying and sinning. Leon's story is set against a backdrop of historical details and racial conflict.

Continued

Box 6.3   The Black Experience   *Continued*

The Big Burn by Jeanette Ingold. San Diego: Harcourt, 2002.

The lives of three teens intertwine as they fight one of the biggest fires in our nation's history. Based on the 1910 Montana and Idaho wildfire that scorched millions of acres and changed the way firefighters fought them.

Black Angels by Rita Murphy. New York: Delacorte/Random House, 2001.

When Celli's mother goes to Atlanta for a month-long vacation, Celli stays behind with Sophie, their maid. Sophie becomes a civil rights advocate and Celli is embarrassed by her behaviors until Celli's grandmother visits from Ohio and shares a secret.

The Legend of Buddy Bush by Shelia P. Moses. New York: McElderry/Simon & Schuster, 2004.

Taking place during the 1940s in North Carolina, this is the story of Pattie Mae, whose life changes forever when Uncle Goodwin "Buddy" Bush returns from Harlem. Uncle Goodwin is accused of raping a white girl, and Pattie Mae's family fights to save his life. Fans may enjoy the sequel, *The Return of Buddy Bush* (2006).

Lizzie Bright and the Buckminster Boy by Gary D. Schmidt. New York: Clarion, 2004.

Son of the new town minister, Turner Buckminster is shunned by local boys and befriends Lizzie Bright, a girl living on the Malaga Island, a poor slave community. Their friendship develops as they play and dig for clams along the shore. When the town attempts to drive the families from the island in order to build a tourist attraction, Turner tries to help Lizzie save her community.

New Boy by Julian Houston. Boston: Houghton Mifflin, 2005.

Fifteen-year-old Rob Garrett, a young black boy growing up in Virginia in the 1950s, leaves the segregated South for a Connecticut boarding school. As trouble brews at home, Rob searches his soul about the issues that divide the South.

Sarny: A Life Remembered by Gary Paulsen. New York: Delacorte/Random House, 1997.

In this sequel to *Nightjohn* (1993), Sarny narrates the terrific events of her slave life: the death of her husband and selling of her children, the violence and atrocities surrounding her as a slave, and her search for her children once she becomes free.

Stumptown Kid by Carol Gorman and Ron J. Findley. Atlanta: Peachtree, 2005.

Growing up in a small Iowa town, Charlie Nebraska loves baseball, only he is cut from the team. When a former Negro League player, Luther Peale, moves to town, Charlie befriends him and learns the meaning of racism.

A True and Faithful Narrative by Katherine Sturtevant. New York: Farrar, Straus & Giroux, 2006.

Sixteen-year-old Meg Moore is the ultimate bookworm and writer. She spends hours with books and talking with famous authors who visit her father's bookstore. When pirates capture a friend, she is determined to use her writing skills to secure his release. A detailed description of life in Restoration London when writing was "unladylike."

Trouble Don't Last by Shelley Pearsall. New York: Random House, 2002.

Two slaves, one young and the other elderly, escape via the Underground Railroad to Canada. On their way they are helped by real-life figures. Pearsall brings to life this dangerous freedom journey.

White Lilacs by Carolyn Meyer. San Diego: Harcourt, 1993.

Inspired by real-life events in Texas in the 1920s when the white residents of Denton forcibly replaced a black community with a park.

Box 6.4   Black History Picture-Book Titles for Older Readers

Almost to Freedom by Vaunda Micheaux Nelson. Illus. Colin Bootman. Minneapolis, MN: Carolrhoda, 2003.

Blues Journey by Walter Dean Myers. Illus. Christopher Myers. New York: Holiday House, 2003.

Circle Unbroken: The Story of a Basket and Its People by Margot Theis Raven. Illus. E. B. Lewis. New York: Farrar, Straus & Giroux, 2004.

Coming on Home Soon by Jacqueline Woodson. Illus. E. B. Lewis. New York: Putnam, 2004.

Duke Ellington: The Piano Prince and His Orchestra by Andrea Davis Pinkney. Illus. Brian Pinkney. New York: Hyperion, 1998.

The Escape of Oney Judge: Martha Washington's Slave Finds Freedom by Emily Arnold McCully. New York: Farrar, Straus & Giroux, 2007.

Going North by Janice N. Harrington. Illus. Jerome Lagarrigue. New York: Melanie Kroupa/Farrar, Straus & Giroux, 2004.

Henry's Freedom Box by Ellen Levine. Illus. Kadir A. Nelson. New York: Scholastic, 2007.

He's Got the Whole World in His Hands by Kadir A. Nelson. New York: Dial/Penguin, 2005.

I've Seen the Promised Land: The Life of Dr. Martin Luther King, Jr. by Walter Dean Myers. Illus. Leonard Jenkins. New York: HarperCollins, 2003.

Jazz by Walter Dean Myers. Illus. Christopher Myers. New York: Holiday House, 2008.

John Henry by Julius Lester. Illus. Jerry Pinkney. New York: Dial/Penguin, 1994.

Just Like Josh Gibson by Angela Johnson. Illus. Beth Peck. New York: Simon & Schuster, 2004.

Mr. Williams by Karen Barbour. New York: Henry Holt, 2005.

The Old African by Julius Lester. Illus. Jerry Pinkney. New York: Dial/Penguin, 2005.

People Could Fly: The Picture Book by Virginia Hamilton. Illus. Leo Dillon and Diane Dillon. New York: Random House, 2004.

Rosa by Nikki Giovanni. Illus. Bryan Collier. New York: Henry Holt, 2005.

Show Way by Jacqueline Woodson. Illus. Hudson Talbott. New York: Putnam, 2005.

Sweet Music in Harlem by Debbie A. Taylor. Illus. Frank Morrison. New York: Lew & Low, 2004.

A Sweet Smell of Roses by Angela Johnson. Illus. Eric Velasquez. New York: Simon & Schuster, 2005.

Uptown by Bryan Collier. New York: Henry Holt, 2000.

Women and History

Since antiquity, women have left their mark on the world, sometimes dramatically influencing the course of history and at other times playing less consequential, but marked roles. They sometimes made positive changes; other times not. Throughout history, women have held inferior positions: they weren't allowed to own property, to vote, to choose their mates, to have careers, and until the 20th century history silenced their voices and contributions. Little was known about how women contributed to history—to their countries, their communities, and their families, and even less was known about how they viewed their lives.

Historical fiction has been instrumental in recognizing women's roles, contributions, and struggles throughout history; moreover, it has given voice to how women viewed themselves and their social positions. Sadly, famous women have seldom played roles in young adult historical

Eighteen-year-old Ruth Compton (Ruth C. White) near the Levisa River in Grundy, Virginia. White's novels are rich portraits of life in the Appalachian coalfields of the 1950s.

Book cover from *A Northern Light*, © 2003 by Jennifer Donnelly, reproduced by permission of Harcourt, Inc.

fiction; for the most part, fictional women are situated within historical events and times. A notable exception is Pauline Chandler's *Warrior Girl: A Novel of Joan of Arc* (2006), a story re-creating the life of Joan of Arc, a young woman who believed she was driven spiritually to liberate France and who was burned at the stake for treason in 1431. Chandler chooses a mute cousin and companion, Mariane, to convey the life and times in which Joan lived. *Warrior Girl* illustrates the heroic roles that women have played in times of war.

Female resiliency and ingenuity are strong themes in young adult historical fiction. In Sarah L. Thomson's *The Secret of the Rose* (2006), set in 16th-century England, a time of religious persecution, 14-year-old Rosalind's father is imprisoned for being Catholic. Fearing for her life, Rosalind disguises herself as a boy and flees the countryside with her younger brother. They find haven in London, where playwright Christopher Marlowe hires them as his servants. William Shakespeare has a cameo appearance. *Parvana's Journey* (2002) by Deborah Ellis shows a young girl facing similar odds. Parvana lives in worn-torn Afghanistan. Her city, Kabul, has been destroyed and her father dies. Parvana, disguised as a boy, leaves Kabul in search of her mother whom she lost in the chaos. She bands together with other children, and they survive amidst the ruin of war.

We cannot study the roles of women in history without examining the ways in which women have been oppressed and abused. Donna Jo Napoli's *Bound* (2004), based on the Cinderella fairy tale, is set in northern China during the Ming Dynasty, a time in which girls' feet were bound at an early age. Xing Xing's stepsister is of marriageable age; however, her mother cuts off her toes and binds them, hoping she will attract more desirable suitors. Xing-Xing, the family servant, is sent to find a medicine man. In this historical context, Napoli introduces readers to social norms and beliefs about the value and roles of women.

Perhaps the most significant contribution young adult historical fiction has made has been enabling us to examine female emotions as women struggled to overcome oppression. Jennifer Donnelly's Printz Honor book, *A Northern Light* (2003), is a superb example. Set at the turn of the 20th century in the Adirondack Mountains, *A Northern Light* takes readers into the heart and mind of 16-year-old Mattie Gokey, a young girl determined to attend college and become a writer despite her father's opposition and her fiancé's wishes. Mattie takes a job at a tourist hotel. While there, she reads letters given to her by Grace, a young woman who asks that they be destroyed. When Grace is killed in an apparent boating accident, Mattie reads the letters and learns Grace was pregnant by the man who planned the accident. Grace's anguish comes through in her letters and helps Mattie see she must leave the mountains. Realizing her own happiness is more important than her duty, she leaves for New York. *A Northern Light* is an exceptional story, one that pulls readers in to the female psyche and illuminates the female sense of self-worth, female desires, and dreams.

Women play more prominent roles in historical fiction than ever before; however, real-life figures are noticeably absent from young adult fiction. Fortunately, they are present in informational books, autobiographies, and biographies. Chapter 10 contains a plethora of these kinds of books about famous women (see Box 6.5 for additional historical fiction titles).

Box 6.5   Women, History, and Culture

Annie, between the States by L. M. Elliott. New York: HarperCollins, 2004.

Annie and her mother nurse wounded soldiers for both the Union and the Confederate during the Civil War. Even though her brothers have enlisted for the South, Annie wrestles with slavery.

Bowery Girl by Kim Taylor. New York: Viking/Penguin, 2006.

Pickpocket Mollie Flynn and prostitute Annabelle Lee live together in a windowless tenement apartment in the Fourth Ward, a poverty-stricken, rat-infested part of New York City known for gambling, crime, and prostitution. When Emmeline DuPre opens the Cherry Street Settlement House, both girls have a chance at a better life. Set in 1883.

Eleanor Hill by Lisa Williams Kline. Asheville, NC: Front Street, 1999.

Determined not to get married and live out her life in a small North Carolina fishing town, Eleanor has a chance at a different life, a chance for an education, when she leaves home to live with her aunt and uncle in a nearby community. Takes place during the early part of the 20th century.

For Freedom: The Story of a French Spy by Kimberly Brubaker Bradley. New York: Delacorte/Random House, 2002.

A young French girl dreams of becoming an opera singer and travels throughout France, where she performs in opera houses and is recruited as a spy to carry messages for the resistance. Based on a true story of a teenage World War II spy.

A Girl Named Disaster by Nancy Farmer. New York: Orchard/Scholastic, 1996.

Nhamo, an 11-year-old village girl, travels from Mozambique to Zimbabwe to avoid an unwanted marriage. Along the way, she endures starvation. Both humorous and poignant.

Haveli by Suzanne Fisher Staples. New York: Random House, 1993.

This sequel to *Shabanu* (1989) picks up with Shabanu having married an older man against her will. Shabanu is caught amidst the family's feuding and the cruelty of the other wives. A wonderful book for discussing tyranny and ancient customs.

Continued

Box 6.5   Women, History, and Culture   *Continued*

Marie, Dancing by Carolyn Meyer. Orlando, FL: Gulliver/Harcourt, 2005.

This story is based on the life of the model for Edgar Degas's famous sculpture, *Little Dancer Aged Fourteen*. Marie van Goethem, a young ballet dancer in Paris, lives a life of hardship. When the famous artist chooses her as his model, she believes her life will change for the better.

My Lady Pocahontas by Kathleen V. Kudlinski. New York: Marshall Cavendish, 2006.

Inspired by the real-life experiences of the daughter of Chief Powhatan, this story traces her coming-of-age as a daughter of a famous leader and her divided loyalties between the Algonkians and Captain John Smith.

My Last Skirt: The Story of Jennie Hodgers, Union Soldier by Lynda Durrant. New York: Clarion, 2006.

Believing that men have better opportunities than women, Jennie Hodgers dressed as a boy and pretended to be Albert Cashier, a grocery store clerk in Queens, New York. She also worked on an Ohio farm and served in the 95th Illinois Infantry during the Civil War. It wasn't until the latter years of her life that her true sexuality became known.

The Ornament Tree by Jean Thesman. Boston: Houghton Mifflin, 1996.

Fourteen-year-old Bonnie, an orphan, moves to a Seattle boardinghouse in 1918 to live with her cousin. She learns about life from a group of progressive women who work at the boardinghouse.

Shabanu: Daughter of the Wind by Suzanne Fisher Staples. New York: Random House, 1989.

Eleven-year-old Shabanu, daughter of a Pakistan nomad, is promised in marriage to a wealthy older man whom she doesn't love. She must accept the custom or defy her father and face dire consequences. A rich and colorful depiction of desert life. A Newbery Honor book.

Star-Crossed by Linda Collison. New York: Knopf/Random House, 2006.

Though raised a proper British lady, Patricia Kelley becomes a stowaway after her father's death. Eighteenth-century English law forbade women to travel aboard ships. To claim her inheritance, she travels to Barbados hidden in the bowels of a merchant ship. At times, she disguises herself as a young man.

The Voyage of the Continental by Katherine Kirkpatrick. New York: Holiday House, 2002.

Emeline McCullough, an orphan, abandons her mill job in Lowell, Massachusetts, and sets sail aboard the steamship *Continental* for Seattle, Washington. Along the way she narrates her experiences aboard the ship in her diary. Based on the true story of the Mercer Girls, a plan by Asa Mercer to "import" women to the Pacific Northwest.

Immigration

We are a nation of immigrants. From the early settlers who carved out the beginnings of the new world to the thousands of immigrants who annually enter our country hoping for a better life, the United States has historically dealt with immigration issues: To what degree should new arrivals merge into the existing American culture? What is our country's role and responsibility? How do we educate immigrants, and how do we address the prejudice they encounter? How do we help others understand the cultural tensions immigrants experience? Historical fiction is the perfect source for informing readers about these issues and the emotional responses raised by them.

Much young adult historical fiction depicts the Italian and Jewish immigration experiences in the 19th and 20th centuries. *The King of Mulberry Street* (2005), by Donna Jo Napoli, chronicles the growth of Benjamino, a young Italian boy smuggled aboard an American-bound ship by his mother. Benjamino is swept into the turbulent Five Points community of Manhattan, an area overrun by homeless children, many of whom become victims of the padrone system.[7] While the protagonist is only 9, Napoli paints a stark picture of the unspeakable cruelties experienced by poor immigrants. For older adolescents, *Lost in America* (2005), by Marilyn Sachs, explores the life of 14-year-old Nicole, a Jewish holocaust survivor who makes her way to the United States to live with distant relatives shortly after World War II. Nicole faces seemingly insurmountable challenges: she must mourn the loss of her family, accept that her American-born cousins do not like her, and struggle with a new language and culture. Laced with historical detail, *Lost in America* is a fabulous snapshot of one individual adjusting to a new life.

There could be no better description of a family searching for the American Dream in young adult literature than Francisco Jiménez's *The Circuit: Stories from the Life of a Migrant Child* (1997). Reminiscent of Steinbeck's *The Grapes of Wrath* (1939), *The Circuit* is an inside look at the life of a Mexican migrant family hoping to find a better life in California. Impermanence and poverty, sorrow and sweetness, and generosity and greed define their lives. Ardent about an education, the narrator struggles with teachers who refuse to integrate Spanish into the classroom. Jiménez continues his childhood saga in *Breaking Through* (2001).

Immigration is one of America's most hotly contested issues of this decade. Proponents on one side argue immigrants (primarily those here illegally) weaken the social, economic, and political fabric of our country: they don't pay taxes and they exploit (and burden) our health care and educational systems. Others say they do work Americans won't do and that we should support global citizenship; if we reach beyond our own egocentric borders, we gain global respect and become stronger. It's easy, amid these arguments, to lose sight of the people—individuals who give up their lives, who leave their homes, their families, and, in many ways, their culture to live in a foreign world. Young adult literature with immigration themes provides a portal for addressing crucial questions such as, "Why do people choose to leave their homes for another country?" Although reasons vary, most leave because of hardship and/or danger. In *Crossing the Wire* (2006), Will Hobbs describes the plight of a Mexican family. Fifteen-year-old Victor Flores lives in the mountains of central Mexico, where he and his family carve out a meager living by farming. Fearing he cannot sell his crop, he heads north on a harrowing journey, hoping to cross the U.S.

---

[7]Impoverished Italian immigrants were treated like slaves by Italian Americans who paid their passage to America for labor.

Will Hobbs's love of the outdoors began at an early age. He is pictured here hiking in the High Sierras of California along the John Muir Trail as a teen.

border and find work. Grounded in 19th-century Russian history, Kathryn Lasky's classic, *The Night Journey*[8] (1981), relates the story of Nana Sashie, a young girl who flees czarist Russia at a time when Jews either served in the Czar's army or were murdered in pogroms. Its companion book, *Broken Song* (Lasky, 2005), tells what happens to a young boy who helps Nana Sashie. Young adult literature is certainly no panacea for solving social issues, but works such as these can provide a foundation for discussing the human element of immigration and will help teens develop an understanding of global issues.

Of course, immigrants from all ethnic groups have found their way to the United States. Though separated by their heritage, they shared similar dreams and hopes and confronted similar obstacles. They experienced backbreaking work, betrayal and injustice, and the anguish of leaving their homes and culture. They shared dreams of riches and dreams of returning to their home countries or being reunited with their loved ones in America. Box 6.6 includes a sampling of titles steeped in history and covering a range of ethic experiences. A few are more recent occurrences and may be better defined as current event stories. Boxes 6.7 through 6.13 contain lists of historical fiction on a variety of topics.

Box 6.6   Immigration and Assimilation

Behind the Mountains by Edwidge Danticat. New York: Orchard/Scholastic, 2002.

In a journal given to her by her teacher, Celiane chronicles her life experiences moving from her rural home in Haiti to Brooklyn. Celiane journals about her love for her island life, her family's struggles during the political unrest, and the adjustment process she experiences living in a concrete and asphalt city.

Call Me Henri by Lorraine M. López. Willimantic, CT: Curbstone, 2006.

Confronted with family problems and gang wars in his ghetto, Enrique has enough challenges. When he wants to study French instead of English, however, the curriculum mandates that he take an ESL class. Support from two teachers, Monsieur Nassour who encourages him to join the French Club and Ms. Byers who gives him additional support, helps Enrique navigate his difficult life.

Continued

---

[8]*The Night Journey* earned a National Jewish Book Award.

Box 6.6   Immigration and Assimilation   *Continued*

Cecilia's Year by Susan Abraham and Denise Gonzales Abraham. El Paso, TX: Cinco Puntos, 2004.

Growing up in a poverty-stricken part of New Mexico, 14-year-old Cecilia yearns to become a teacher, but her mother's traditional Hispanic beliefs about a woman's role threaten her dreams. A wonderful tribute to young girls throughout the world who must choose between their own desires and family beliefs. Told against the backdrop of the Great Depression. Fans may enjoy the sequel, *Surprising Cecilia* (2006).

Child of Dandelions by Shenaaz Nanji. Asheville, NC: Front Street, 2008.

In 1972 Idi Amin required all people of Indian descent to leave Uganda. Nanji's historical work tells the story of 15-year-old Sabine and her wealthy Indian family who try to find a degree of normalcy amid a time of terror.

Downtown Boy by Juan Felipe Herrera. New York: Scholastic, 2005.

After years of migrant work in California, Juanito and his parents move to San Francisco to live with relatives. What Juanito wants most is to settle in one place forever; however, his father continues to move them from one place to another. Juanito is torn between his mother's teachings and the street life around him.

Macaroni Boy by Katherine Ayres. New York: Delacorte/Random House, 2003.

Mike Costa's Italian family runs a wholesale business in the Strip, Pittsburgh's warehouse district, during the Great Depression. Mike is bullied at school and on the streets.

A Step from Heaven by An Na. Asheville, NC: Front Street, 2001.

Winner of the Michael L. Printz Award, this title chronicles the story of a Korean immigrant family living in California. Hoping for a slice of the American Dream, the family confronts cultural differences and hardships. Though the family struggles, Young Ju adjusts well and excels in school.

Tangled Threads: A Hmong Girl's Story: A Novel by Pegi Deitz Shea. New York: Clarion, 2003.

Mai Yang has lived with her grandmother in a Thailand refugee camp for 10 years. When she and her grandmother are allowed to leave the camp, they travel to Providence, Rhode Island, to join their family. Mai can't wait to live like an American. Adjusting to her new life, however, isn't easy. She is teased about being a refugee and feels detached from her Americanized family.

The Traitor by Laurence Yep. New York: HarperCollins, 2003.

In 1885 an unlikely friendship develops between two boys in a tough Wyoming coal mining town. One boy is a social outcast, the other Chinese American. Chinese miners earn slave wages and mine in dangerous conditions. Racial tensions escalate and fuel race riots. Inspired by actual race riots of that century.

Truth and Salsa by Linda Lowery. Atlanta: Peachtree, 2006.

Hayley Flynn moves to Mexico to live with her grandmother when her parents separate; she makes a new friend and enjoys her new life. She learns about poverty and the desperate measures people will take to support loved ones through her new friendship.

Under the Same Sky by Cynthia DeFelice. New York: Farrar, Straus & Giroux, 2003.

Joe Pedersen wants a motorbike. To earn it, his father makes him work alongside Mexican migrant workers on the family's upstate New York farm. Told from Joe's point of view, the narrative humanizes illegal immigrants and their hardships.

Web of Lies by Beverley Naidoo. New York: Amistad/HarperCollins, 2007.

Nigerian refugees, Sade and Femi, adjust to a new life in London. Femi is sucked into a drug-dealing, pot-smoking street gang. Sade keeps Femi's actions a secret for fear of worrying her family.

Box 6.7   Historical Fiction YA Classics   by Michael Ross

Catherine, Called Birdy by Karen Cushman. New York: Clarion, 1994.

Birdy has been promised in marriage but finds her future husband is much older and much to her disliking. As we explore Birdy's life, we learn a great deal about life in a manor house in 11th-century England. A Newbery Honor book.

The Glory Field by Walter Dean Myers. New York: Scholastic, 1994.

A five-generation family saga that traces a family's history from the capture of an African youth in the 18th century to the lives of his descendents in South Carolina. Recounts their hardships and determination through the Civil War, segregation, and beyond.

Heroes by Robert Cormier. New York: Delacorte/Random House, 1998.

After having his face blown off by a grenade in World War II, 18-year-old Francis Cassavant returns home. Though he can return as a hero, he hides his identity with the hopes he can find, and kill, a childhood enemy.

Island of the Blue Dolphins by Scott O'Dell. Boston: Houghton Mifflin, 1960.

A young, beautiful girl living on an isolated island with her brother struggles to survive. More important, Karana discovers her strength from living on the island. Readers may also enjoy the sequel, *Zia* (1976). A Newbery Medal book.

Johnny Tremain by Esther Forbes. Boston: Houghton Mifflin, 1943.

A silversmith apprentice, Johnny's future takes a turn when he injures his hand. He becomes a messenger for the Sons of Liberty in the days before the American Revolution.

The Midwife's Apprentice by Karen Cushman. New York: Clarion, 1995.

Brat has no family, no home, and no future until a midwife known as Jane takes her as an apprentice. Set in medieval England, Brat changes her name to Alyce and gains knowledge, confidence, and the courage to dream. A Newbery Medal book.

My Brother Sam Is Dead by James Lincoln Collier and Christopher Collier. New York: Four Winds Press, 1974.

Torn between the older brother he worships and his father's expectations, Tim Meeker struggles to love and respect both men. After his father dies, Tim is faced with his biggest challenge: saving his brother's life. A Newbery Honor book.

Nightjohn by Gary Paulsen. New York: Delacorte/Random House, 1993.

Well-researched, this short novella tells the story of a female slave named Sarny. Nightjohn, a captured slave, arrives on the plantation, his body scared and a rope around his neck. He plans to teach reading and Sarny is willing to learn. The penalty if caught is dismemberment.

Number the Stars by Lois Lowry. Boston: Houghton Mifflin, 1989.

As a 10-year-old girl living in Nazi-occupied Sweden, Annemarie discovers how brave and courageous she is when she must help shelter her Jewish friend from the Nazis. A Newbery Medal book.

Rifles for Watie by Harold Keith. New York: Crowell, 1957.

Set during the American Civil War, the plot revolves around Jefferson Davis Bussey, who is caught up in the events of history. Jefferson provides

Continued

Box 6.7   Historical Fiction YA Classics   *Continued*

the viewpoint of an ordinary soldier. A Newbery Medal book.

Roll of Thunder, Hear My Cry by Mildred D. Taylor. New York: Dial/Scholastic, 1976.

Taylor chronicles the story of a black family struggling with the legacy of racism during the Great Depression in Mississippi. In addition, they deal with illness, poverty, and betrayal. A Newbery Medal book.

Sing Down the Moon by Scott O'Dell. Boston: Houghton Mifflin, 1970.

A young Navaho girl fights for her home. After being taken away twice, she makes her way back, each time demonstrating her incredible will power and ingenuity. A Newbery Honor book.

The True Confessions of Charlotte Doyle by Avi. New York: Orchard/Scholastic, 1990.

Thirteen-year-old Charlotte, the only female passenger on a transatlantic voyage, becomes caught between a villainous captain and a mutinous crew. She is charged with murder. Set in the 19th century. A Newbery Honor book.

The Witch of Blackbird Pond by Elizabeth George Speare. Boston: Houghton Mifflin, 1958.

Kit Tyler has been orphaned and has to relocate from her home in the Caribbean to the cold, bleak shores of Connecticut. Her loneliness and feelings of isolation are eased by her friendship with an old Quaker woman. This unlikely friendship results in Kit being accused of practicing witchcraft. A Newbery Medal book.

Box 6.8   Nobility, Warriors, Peasants, and Ancient Times   by Julie Schunck

Blue Fingers: A Ninja's Tale by Cheryl Aylward Whitesel. New York: Clarion, 2004.

When Koji, a 12-year-old boy living in 16th-century Japan, attempts to run away from his shame, he is captured by ninjas and forced to attend a ninja training camp. His life changes as he learns about himself and his world as a ninja.

Breath by Donna Jo Napoli. New York: Atheneum/Simon & Schuster, 2003.

Salz does not yield to the same illness in which the whole medieval town of Hameln is afflicted. The townspeople assume the plague of rats is causing the fits of madness; therefore, Salz convinces the townspeople to free him so he can find the Piper to charm the rats out of Hameln.

By These Ten Bones by Clare B. Dunkle. New York: Henry Holt, 2005.

Maddie befriends a traveling woodcarver when he comes to a village set in the Highlands of Scotland during the Middle Ages. Soon evil surrounds the village and only Maddie knows why. Maddie must choose whether to make the ultimate sacrifice for those around her.

Crispin: The Cross of Lead by Avi. New York: Hyperion, 2002.

Accused of a crime he didn't commit, a 13-year-old boy flees his home for fear of being captured by

Continued

Box 6.8   Nobility, Warriors, Peasants, and Ancient Times   *Continued*

bounty hunters, but not before the village priest shares a family secret. Filled with 13th-century historical detail (e.g., feudal system injustices). Fans may enjoy *Crispin at the Edge of the World* (2006).

The Dark Flight Down by Marcus Sedgwick. New York: Lamb/Random House, 2005.

Boy is still on the run after the death of his master, magician Valerian. He faces a cruel emperor who wants to live forever and believes the answers to immortality lie within one of Valerian's books. Boy also wants the book to learn the secrets of his past.

Duchessina: A Novel of Catherine de' Medici by Carolyn Meyer. Orlando, FL: Harcourt, 2007.

Though sole heir to the Medici family fortune, Catherine's childhood was void of luxury. After spending years in a convent, she enters public life and is promised in marriage to Henry, the second son of King Frances I of France. When dauphin François dies, Henry becomes the new dauphin and Catherine, his future wife, the new dauphine. Meticulous historical detail. Rich in setting.

Girl in a Cage by Jane Yolen and Robert J. Harris. New York: Philomel/Penguin, 2002.

After the new king of Scotland is crowned in 1306, his 11-year-old daughter, Marjorie, is captured by England's King Edward Longshanks. She is held captive in a cage on public display in an English village, where she finds the will to survive.

Jackaroo by Cynthia Voigt. New York: Atheneum/Simon & Schuster, 1985.

Gwyn, an innkeeper's daughter, finds a way to right the wrongs of a feudal system by dressing as the legendary Jackaroo and becoming a female Robin Hood.

Leonardo's Shadow: Or, My Astonishing Life as Leonardo da Vinci's Servant by Christopher Grey. New York: Atheneum/Simon & Schuster, 2006.

Leonardo da Vinci's servant, 15-year-old Giacomo, must find a way to help da Vinci complete his painting of *The Last Supper* before the Duke of 15th-century Milan asks Michelangelo to complete it. Young Giacomo hopes that da Vinci can help him find the secrets of his past and teach him to paint.

The Midwife's Apprentice by Karen Cushman. New York: Clarion, 1995.

Homeless and nameless, Alyce is taken in by Jane Sharp as a midwife's apprentice in medieval England. When failure strikes, she runs away but returns to find independence, strength, and beauty within herself. Younger adolescents may also enjoy *Matilda Bone* (2000).

Pagan's Scribe by Catherine Jinks. Cambridge, MA: Candlewick Press, 2005. (Originally published 1997)

Father Pagan, the Archdeacon of Carcassonne in 1209 France, hires Isidore, a 15-year-old boy beset with epilepsy, as his scribe. Together they find themselves in the middle of a war between the North and the South as the crusades siege Carcassonne.

Viking Warrior: The Strongbow Saga by Judson Roberts. New York: HarperCollins, 2006.

When Halfdan Hroriksson, a 15-year-old slave in the ninth-century Viking world, is freed because of his mother's sacrifice, he strives to become accepted as a great Viking warrior. Halfdan must prove to the clan and his half-brother that a former slave can become a free warrior. Readers may also enjoy *Dragons of the Sea* (2007) and *The Road to Vengeance* (2008).

Box 6.9   Native Americans and Western Expansion

The Beaded Moccasins: The Story of Mary Campbell by Lynda Durrant. New York: Clarion, 1998.

Twelve-year-old Mary is captured by Delaware Lenape on the morning of her birthday. Ordered by the British government to abandon their homeland, the Lenape travel on foot into the Ohio wilderness. Well-researched, this novel recounts Mary's physical and emotional adjustments to a new home and family. Includes a glossary, bibliography, and author comments.

Billy the Kid by Theodore Taylor. Orlando, FL: Harcourt, 2005.

An action-packed adventure based on the life of William H. Bonney Jr. (Billy the Kid). Billy heads to Arizona, where he meets up with a band of train robbers. Though fiction, the tale is a colorful canvas of gunslinging outlaws and the West.

Blood Gold by Michael Cadnum. New York: Viking/Penguin, 2004.

Will Dwinelle and his friend Ben travel from Philadelphia to California in search of the man who disgraced Elizabeth, Willie's friend. Will survives cholera, bandits, snakes, and rough terrain on his quest but is lured by gold fever. Fictional characters are set within a credible historical setting.

Cabin on Trouble Creek by Jean Van Leeuwen. New York: Dial/Penguin, 2004.

In 1803 Daniel and Will travel with their father to rich farmland in Ohio, where they clear enough land and build a log cabin. When their father returns to Pennsylvania for the rest of the family, Daniel and Will are left to guard their cabin. When their father doesn't return, they must survive the winter. Based on an actual incident.

Crooked River by Shelley Pearsall. New York: Knopf/Random House, 2005.

A young Chippewa is accused of murdering a white trapper in 1812. Shackled in leg irons, he awaits his trial in a family's loft. Thirteen-year-old Rebecca believes in Amik's innocence and defies her family and the community to help him. Inspired by a true story, this novel probes injustices bestowed upon Native Americans.

Daniel's Walk by Michael Spooner. New York: Henry Holt, 2001.

It's 1844. Daniel LeBlanc's father, an experienced trapper, has disappeared, and Daniel knows he is in danger. Daniel sets out from his Missouri home with only a bedroll and Bible to walk the Oregon Trail, hoping to find his father.

Geronimo by Joseph Bruchac. New York: Scholastic, 2006.

Meticulously researched, this novel chronicles the heroic life of Geronimo, the great Apache warrior and leader, through the eyes of a fictional grandson. Readers are pulled into events surrounding the deportation of the Apache from Arizona, their incarceration to camps throughout the Southwest, and Geronimo's capture by federal troops in 1886.

Grasslands by Debra Seely. New York: Holiday House, 2002.

Thirteen-year-old Thomas lives an aristocratic life in Virginia with his grandparents. When his father, who lives on a Kansas farm, sends for him, Thomas envisions living the life of a real cowboy. The laborious farm life isn't what he expected. Portrays a vivid picture of rural America in the 1880s. Fans will enjoy the sequel, *The Last of the Roundup Boys* (2004).

Hearts of Iron: A Novel by Kathleen Benner Duble. New York: McElderry/ Simon & Schuster, 2006.

Best friends Jesse and Lucy have their futures planned for them. Lucy's father wants a better life for her and expects her to marry a sophisticated man outside the community. Jesse's family expects him to follow in his father's footsteps and work in the forge, but

Continued

Box 6.9   Native Americans and Western Expansion   *Continued*

he wants to join the Navy. Both teens struggle with their own desires and family loyalties. Set in the New England mountains in 1820.

Last Child by Michael Spooner. New York: Henry Holt, 2005.

Rosalie (Last Child) considers herself white, though she is half Native American. She splits her time between living at the fort with her father and living in the village with her mother. When a steamboat carries smallpox into Rosaline's world, Rosaline's life is changed forever.

Last Dance on Holladay Street by Elisa Carbone. New York: Knopf/Random House, 2005.

Having lost her family, 13-year-old Eva sets out for Denver in search of her birth mother. Denver holds two surprises: Eva's mother is white, while Eva is black, and her mother works as a prostitute in a brothel. A unique look at the exploitation of frontier women.

Prairie Whispers by Frances Arrington. New York: Philomel/Penguin Putnam, 2003.

On the banks of the Missouri River and far removed from the raging Civil War, Colleen McCall delivers her

mother's premature baby when her father is away. When the baby dies shortly after birth, Colleen sets out for help, only to encounter a covered wagon, a dying woman, and a newborn. When the dying woman begs Colleen to care for the baby, Colleen switches it with her dead baby sister.

The Sign of the Beaver by Elizabeth George Speare. Boston: Houghton Mifflin, 1983.

A Newbery Honor and Scott O'Dell Award book, this title tells the story of a young boy left to protect his family's wilderness home while his father returns South for the remainder of the family. Matt becomes friends with the Native Americans who teach him how to survive. Set in Maine during the 1700s.

Streams to the River, River to the Sea: A Novel of Sacagawea by Scott O'Dell. Boston: Houghton Mifflin, 1986.

Renown historical writer Scott O'Dell brings to life the story of Sacagawea, the young Shoshone girl who served as an interpreter and guide for the Lewis and Clark Expedition. Hired by Lewis and Clark for her knowledge of Shoshone language and territory, Sacagawea survives her French husband's cruelty and earns the respect of the white explorers.

Box 6.10   High Seas Adventures and Survival

Bloody Jack: Being an Account of the Curious Adventures of Mary "Jacky" Faber, Desperate Journey by Jim Murphy. New York: Scholastic, 2006.

After losing her family to the plague, Mary Faber survives by joining a band of beggars and thieves. To escape the cold and hunger, Mary disguises herself as a boy and becomes a ship's captain aboard a British warship that sets sail in search of pirates.

The Cannibals by Iain Lawrence. New York: Delacorte/Random House, 2005.

In this sequel to *The Convicts* (2005) Tom Tin, accompanied by other young criminals, travels aboard a prison ship to Australia, where they will serve their prison term. Falsely accused of murder, Tom and some others escape the ship and head for a Pacific island, home of headhunters and cannibals.

Continued

Box 6.10   High Seas Adventures and Survival   *Continued*

The Cay by Theodore Taylor. New York: Doubleday, 1969.

When their freighter is torpedoed by a German submarine, a white boy and an old black man are marooned on a Caribbean island. Blinded by the explosion, Phillip relies on the old West Indian man, Timothy, to survive. Set during World War II, Phillip overcomes racial prejudice as his and Timothy's friendship develops.

The Convicts by Iain Lawrence. New York: Delacorte/Random House, 2005.

After his father is jailed in debtor's prison, 13-year-old Tom Tin sets out to avenge his imprisonment. Tom Tin encounters ruffians on the foggy London streets and is accused of murder. He is dragged onboard a prison ship to serve a 7-year term in Australia. A dark and disturbing tale based on actual events in 19th-century England.

The House of Windjammer by V. A. Richardson. New York: Bloomsbury, 2003.

After tulip fever claims his father's life, Adam, heir to the House of Windjammer, must keep his family's shipping business afloat. Takes place in Amsterdam in 1636. Fans will also enjoy *The Moneylender's Daughter* (2006).

Ice Drift by Theodore Taylor. Orlando, FL: Harcourt, 2004.

Stranded on an ice floe while seal hunting, two Inuit brothers face starvation and bitter cold as they travel for months down the Greenland Strait. Steeped in Inuit culture and traditions.

The Lost Voyage of John Cabot by Henry Garfield. New York: Atheneum/Simon & Schuster, 2004.

A fictional tale about John Cabot, the famous explorer who journeyed to the new world in 1498 with his two sons and never returned home.

Maata's Journal: A Novel by Paul Sullivan. New York: Atheneum/Simon & Schuster, 2003.

Maata grew up in the Arctic tundra, living a nomadic life. When her parents die, she attends a boarding school and learns to read and write. She goes on an expedition with a team researching the geology and weather in her native home and becomes stranded on an island.

Pirates! The True and Remarkable Adventures of Minerva Sharpe and Nancy Kington, Female Pirates by Celia Rees. New York: Bloomsbury, 2003.

After her father's death, Nancy Kington, a wealthy young girl, is sent to Jamaica, where her brother plans to marry her off. Unwilling to be married and unhappy with the treatment of slaves, Nancy flees with Minerva, a young slave girl. Together they become pirates and sail the high seas.

Prison Ship: Adventures of a Young Sailor by Paul Dowswell. New York: Bloomsbury, 2006.

Falsely accused of a crime, Sam Witchall is sent to Australia aboard a prison ship. Once there, he escapes into the Bush, only to be captured by a cannibal. Sailing life is vividly portrayed in this sequel to *Powder Monkey* (2005).

Ship of Fire by Michael Cadnum. New York: Viking/Penguin, 2003.

Thomas Spyre, a surgeon's apprentice sailing aboard Sir Francis Drake's ship in 1587, must assume responsibilities as the ship's surgeon when his master dies. Based on Sir Francis Drake's raid on the Spanish port of Cadiz.

Continued

Box 6.10   High Seas Adventures and Survival   *Continued*

***Trapped in Ice!: An Amazing True Whaling Adventure* by Martin W. Sandler. New York: Scholastic, 2006.**

Inspired by the largest disaster in whaling history. Thirty-nine whaling vessels left New Bedford, Massachusetts, and other American ports in spring of 1871. Most neglected Eskimo warnings that winter was setting in and found themselves trapped in ice. This story re-creates the men's struggle to survive.

***The Wreckers* by Iain Lawrence. New York: Delacorte/Random House, 1998.**

Book one in the *High Seas Trilogy* begins with 14-year-old John Spencer shipwrecked on the coast of Cornwall. John learns the local villagers are pirates, wreckers, who lure ships ashore to steal their cargo. A fast-paced, harrowing story filled with murder, mystery, and treachery in the style of Robert Louis Stevenson. Fans may want to read the other two volumes: *The Smugglers* (1992) and *The Buccaneers* (2001).

Box 6.11   The Holocaust   by Taylor Cole

***The Boy in the Striped Pajamas* by John Boyne. New York: Fickling/Random House, 2006.**

Bruno's family moves away to a new house where there is nothing to do. Bruno believes there must be more to his new surroundings than meets the eye and sets out to explore his environment. His explorations lead him to a friendship with disastrous consequences.

***Daniel Half Human and the Good Nazi* by David Chotjewitz and Doris Orgel. New York: Atheneum/Simon & Schuster, 2004.**

Daniel and Armin admire Hitler, but as the Nazis adopt anti-Semitic policies, Daniel learns that he is half Jewish. The revelation threatens his friendship with Armin as their beloved city of Hamburg becomes a hotbed of Nazi activity.

***The Devil's Arithmetic* by Jane Yolen. New York: Viking, 1988.**

Hannah Stern is 12 years old and tired of remembering the atrocities of the Holocaust. While celebrating Passover at her grandparent's house, she is chosen to welcome the Prophet Elijah (by opening the front door). When she does, she is transported back to Poland in 1941 and lives under Nazi oppression.

***Emil and Karl* by Yankev Glatshteyn. Trans. Jeffrey Shandler. New Milford, CT: Roaring Brook Press, 2006.**

A translation from Yiddish of a book originally published in 1940, *Emil and Karl* tells of the dilemmas faced by two boys—one Jewish, one not—who live in Vienna on the eve of World War II.

***Escaping into the Night* by D. Dina Friedman. New York: Simon & Schuster, 2006.**

When her mother is killed in the evacuation of a Polish ghetto, Halina Rudowski flees by entering a secret Jewish encampment in the woods. She survives as the group attempts to protect themselves from advancing Germans.

***The Fighter* by Jean-Jacques Greif. New York: Bloomsbury, 2006.**

Maurice, a Polish emigrant, takes up boxing at a Jewish sports club in Paris. As the Blitz rolls through Paris, Maurice is sent to Auschwitz, where he is coerced by the SS to fight a dying prisoner. He faces a moral dilemma: kill the prisoner or face certain death.

Continued

Box 6.11   The Holocaust   *Continued*

Hidden Child by Isaac Millman. New York: Farrar, Straus & Giroux, 2005.

As a Jewish child living in German-occupied France, Isaac witnesses the arrest of his father before being arrested with his mother. In an attempt to elude the Germans, Isaac is shuttled from city to countryside and encounters random acts of kindness and cruelty.

Lisa's War by Carol Matas. New York: Scribner, 1987.

Lisa, a young Jewish girl living in Denmark, fights back against the Nazi persecution of her Jewish allies by distributing pamphlets and leading hundreds of Danish Jews to safety in Sweden.

Room in the Heart by Sonia Levitin. New York: Dutton/Penguin, 2003.

Julie Weinstein and her friends cope with the German occupation of Denmark by finding ways to avoid the Nazis.

The Thought of High Windows by Lynne Kositsky. Tonawanda, NY: Kids Can Press, 2004.

Esther, a 16-year-old German girl, registers with the Red Cross and is removed to France to escape the Nazis. When France surrenders, Esther is captured but escapes by jumping from a window.

Torn Thread by Anne Isaacs. New York: Scholastic, 2000.

Eva and her sister are imprisoned in a Nazi labor camp, where they are forced to spin thread for German military uniforms. She makes a home for herself among the Nazi savagery and brutality and tries to save her sister from sickness.

Yellow Star by Jennifer Roy. New York: Marshall Cavendish, 2006.

A Jewish girl and her mother struggle to survive in a Polish ghetto during the climax of World War II.

Box 6.12   The Great Depression   by Shanna Carter

The Barn Burner by Patricia Willis. New York: Clarion, 2000.

Ross, a homeless but honest young boy, wakes up one fateful evening to a raging fire in a barn in which he is sleeping. Though he risks his own life to save the animals, he is accused of arson.

Dark Water Rising by Marian Hale. New York: Henry Holt, 2006.

Seth's life is booming along at a pace matching that of the city around him, until one unsuspected storm devastates his new hometown. His struggle to reach safety and to help others do the same amidst danger provides a perspective shift like none he has ever experienced.

The Darkest Evening by William Durbin. New York: Orchard/Scholastic, 2004.

Jake's dad sees socialism as a welcome political shift, so much so that he moves his unwilling family to Karelia, a Soviet-run communist state. When socialist theory proves better on paper than in action, Jake and his family must find a way to escape a place that controls their every move.

Esperanza Rising by Pam Muñoz Ryan. New York: Scholastic, 2000.

Along with her mother, Esperanza is torn from her lavish life in Mexico by necessity and forced to work in Southern California labor camps. Her struggle to

Continued

Box 6.12   The Great Depression   *Continued*

assimilate to a culture that denigrates her own and to the lifestyle of an illegal immigrant laborer teaches her a great deal about her culture, her true friends, and herself.

Ghost Girl: A Blue Ridge Mountain Story by Delia Ray. New York: Clarion, 2003.

April's family is poverty-stricken and grief-fractured after the sudden loss of her younger brother. When the Hoover White House announces the possibility of a school to be built near her home, April's inability to communicate with her sorrowful mother nearly destroys her chance at ever learning to read.

Hitch by Jeanette Ingold. Orlando, FL: Harcourt, 2005.

Moss Trawnley is just a kid, but poverty motivates, and he has to survive in a country destroyed by debt. Joining a work camp, he is determined to make an honest living, proving to the doubtful world that he would not be a no-good alcoholic criminal.

Poor Is Just a Starting Place by Leslie J. Wyatt. New York: Holiday House, 2005.

Poor won't keep Artie down. She has dreams of higher education, of a more plentiful life beyond the familiar, impoverished Kentucky hills. A $25 scholarship for winning an essay contest about heritage seems the perfect opportunity. And if that doesn't work, there's always the hidden treasure.

Red Palms by Cara Haycak. New York: Lamb/Random House, 2004.

Depression hits the hardest where there is much to hit, a reality Benita and her well-off family experience. The family hopes such a drastic lifestyle change is only temporary.

Thursday's Child by Sonya Hartnett. Cambridge, MA: Candlewick Press, 2002.

One person stands out in Harper's mind: her little brother Tin, fatefully born on a regular Thursday with

no way to rise above his family's poverty. So, why not tunnel out from under it? Through his unnatural knack for digging, Tin experiences his difficult life from the safety of a hole in the ground.

The Truth about Sparrows by Marian Hale. New York: Henry Holt, 2004.

Ripped by necessity from her best friend and familiar, but destitute Missouri hometown, Sadie must come to terms with her new home, with new, unwelcoming people. She soon finds that the familiar elements of life are not defining elements and sets out to create a new identity and life.

Walking on Air by Kelly Easton. New York: McElderry/Simon & Schuster, 2004.

If there's one thing the world always needs, it's a tightrope walker, someone adept at balancing fear of the fall with agility and skill. June doesn't mind being this for other people, but who is she for herself? June's is a tale of finding her own truths in a culture falling apart around her.

A Year Down Yonder by Richard Peck. New York: Dial/Penguin, 2000.

Grandma Dowdel is scary. It's that simple. And now Mary Alice has to spend an entire year in her company, away from her Chicago home. She soon finds herself an outcast from the farmin' and shootin' locals and comes to understand her grandma's enigmatic, cunning schemes. Sequel to *A Long Way to Chicago* (1998).

Your Eyes in Stars by M. E. Kerr. New York: HarperCollins, 2006.

Jessie and Elisa are best friends. They share everything, even criminals like the newly imprisoned murderer who plays so beautifully in the prison band. All too soon, Elisa moves home to Germany and the good-looking prisoner escapes. The girls' innocent fantasies give way to inescapable social and political crises.

Box 6.13   Inhumanity

Ask Me No Questions by Marina Budhos. New York: Atheneum/Simon & Schuster, 2006.

Nadira and her family are living in New York City during 9/11. In the wake of the tragedy and with expired visas, Nadir and her family start out for Canada, hoping to escape harassment from the U.S. government.

Chandra's Secrets by Allan Straton. Toronto: Annick, 2004.

Chandra's father is killed in an African diamond mine and her mother disappears, leaving Chandra to care for her siblings. When Chandra's younger sister dies, Chandra learns the awful truth that her family members have AIDS. Readers may enjoy the sequel, Chandra's Wars (2008).

Coram Boy by Jamila Gavin. New York: Farrar, Straus & Giroux, 2001.

In the style of Charles Dickens, Gavin creates a dark and riveting account of orphan life in 18th-century England. Otis Gardner peddles pots and pans and acquires and disposes of babies. Sometimes he takes them to orphanages; other times he buries them alive.

Dawn and Dusk by Alice Mead. New York: Farrar, Straus & Giroux, 2007.

Thirteen-year-old Azad has always known war. He lives in a Kurdish town in Iran, and the Kurds are at war with Saddam Hussein's regime. Azad tries living a normal life, but when Saddam threatens his town with weapons of mass destruction, he is torn between staying in the town he loves or fleeing.

Diamonds in the Shadow by Caroline B. Cooney. New York: Delacorte/Random House, 2007.

As part of a church-sponsored program, the Finch family welcome an African refugee family into their home. Jared learns that things are not always as they appear, and he must make a decision that will change the lives of both families.

Forgotten Fire by Adam Bagdasarian. New York: DK, 2000.

A disturbing account of Armenian genocide based on the experiences of Bagdasarian's great uncle. In 1915 Vahan Kenderian, son of a wealthy Armenian family, lives a privileged life. His world is shattered when some of his family are murdered and others are kidnapped. A National Book Award finalist.

Girl of Kosovo by Alice Mead. New York: Farrar, Straus & Giroux, 2001.

In 1998 Albanians are expelled from Kosovo by Serbian forces. Escaping ethnic cleansing, families flee to the mountains where the Kosovo Liberation Army wards off the Serbs in guerrilla warfare fashion. Zanak's father and brothers are killed, and her leg is shattered in the conflict.

Karoo Boy by Troy Blacklaws. Orlando, FL: Harcourt, 2005.

Against the backdrop of the violence and growing racial tensions in South Africa during the 1970s, a young boy and his mother leave their Cape Town home and begin a new life in the desert region of Karoo. A lyrical and spiritual look at South Africa during this nightmarish time.

Krik? Krak! by Edwidge Danticat. New York: Soho Press, 1995.

Nine powerful stories recounting the lives of families living under Haitian dictatorship. Some fled to America for a better life; others remained behind in villages where their days were filled with terror. A National Book Award finalist.

No Laughter Here by Rita Williams-Garcia. New York: HarperCollins, 2003.

Best friends Akilah and Victoria spend their summer apart. When Victoria returns with her family from visiting their family in Nigeria, she seems withdrawn and disturbed. Through a series of events, the reader learns that she has been circumcised, a

Continued

Box 6.13   Inhumanity *Continued*

ritual still practiced in many countries. A realistic portrayal of the emotional pain endured by many young Nigerian girls.

***Over a Thousand Hills I Walk with You* by Hanna Jansen. Trans. Elizabeth D. Crawford. Minneapolis, MN: Carolrhoda, 2006.**

A terrifying and haunting account of the 1994 Rwandan genocide, ethnic cleansing that took the lives of more than a million people. Jeanne, a Rwandan girl, lived a normal life until the genocide. The only surviving member of her family, Jeanne witnesses horrific acts of violence. Descriptions of brutal murders are horrifying, but real and needed.

***Red Midnight* by Ben Mikaelsen. New York: HarperCollins, 2002.**

Santiago flees Guatemala with his four-year-old sister after guerrilla soldiers murder his family and destroy his village. They set sail in shark-infested waters for the United States in a kayak, hoping to build a new life.

***Tree Girl* by Ben Mikaelsen. New York: HarperCollins, 2004.**

Hidden within the branches of a tree, Gabriela watches in horror as her Mayan village is destroyed and her family and friends massacred. She joins bands of refugees fleeing to the Mexican border.

***Under the Persimmon Tree* by Suzanne Fisher Staples. New York: Farrar, Straus & Giroux, 2005.**

Najmah's mother and infant brother are killed in an air raid and their father conscripted by the Taliban to fight in the Afghan War. Alone, Najmah finds a friend in Elaine, wife of an Afghan doctor, who teaches refugee children while waiting for her husband's safe return.

Monitoring and Clarifying Reading

As discussed in Chapter 2, proficient readers use a wide range of cognitive strategies to make meaning. They recognize when they're making sense of their reading and when they're lost. They *monitor* and *clarify* their reading: they detect confusing parts, identify when they're lost or when meaning-making breaks down, and plot a course of action to "repair" comprehension.

We have all been stumped by a character in our reading, someone introduced some time earlier. Inside our heads we ask, "Who is this?" If we really want to know, we turn back through the book, scanning for the passage where the character first entered the story. Of course, there are times when we are stumped, but we continue to read. We may miss some information about the character, but we make a conscious decision to read on. We *monitor* our reading when we realize we don't know the character. If we look back through the book for the character, we choose to *clarify*.

We use a similar process when we encounter unknown vocabulary words. We stop when we're confused and search for meaning. We use context clues—information before and after the word—to help determine meaning. If that doesn't help, we may consult another reader, look up the word, or continue to read without understanding the word, sometimes hoping we will encounter it later in a different context that will provide clarification. Good readers ask questions and comment inside their heads as they read:

"What does that mean?"
"This is hard."
"I need to concentrate. I should go back (reread)."
"I'm lost. I don't understand this."

As we monitor, we determine what clarifying actions or "fix-up" strategies we need. Our ability to use a wide array of fix-up strategies improves as we become more proficient readers. As proficient readers, we may do any of the following to repair comprehension:

1. *Ignore the confusion and continue to read.* A proficient reader may choose to read because he/she comprehends enough to understand the text or simply because he/she doesn't want/need to determine meaning.

2. *Continue to read, hoping the meaning will become clearer.* Think of the times an instructor has used a vocabulary word or expression you didn't know, but you didn't ask for clarification, mostly out of embarrassment. You hoped, though, that the instructor would use the term again in a different context. Of course, despite the instructor repeatedly using the word, sometimes you still didn't get it and were more embarrassed.

3. *Reread the confusing part.* Proficient readers may reread the section silently or aloud. Reading aloud allows us to hear the passage, especially when we're alone and not worried about performing for an audience. When rereading the confusing part, we sometimes use our understanding of text structure to clear up confusion (see Chapter 10). Good readers understand text structure and know to *read over* text to capture the basic gist of the sentence. They might, for example, "read around" a long appositive or information set off in parentheses to get to the gist of the sentence, then reread, adding the information previously skipped.

4. *Reread the passage immediately before.* Because proficient readers can identify the point where comprehension breaks down, they often backtrack to the last point of understanding and reread. Well-written texts flow smoothly and are held together by words and phrases that connect ideas and explain relationships.

5. *Make connections with information you already know.* In their groundbreaking text, *Mosaic of Thought* (1997), Keene and Zimmerman

conclude that readers make three kinds of connections that aid in comprehension:

Text-to-self: Connecting your own life to what you're reading by reflecting on your prior knowledge and past experiences.

Text-to-text: Connecting what you're reading with another text you have read such as a book, short story, poem, essay, article, movie, or song.

Text-to-world: Connecting what you're reading to another person, place, event, or issue outside the text.

These types of connections aid readers in developing clearer images as they read; setting the purpose for reading; understanding character emotions, behaviors, and motivations; and asking questions that facilitate understanding.

6. *Use additional resources.* Proficient readers also take advantage of dictionaries (e.g., dictionary.com), thesauruses, and other expert readers.

Proficient readers have metacognitive knowledge about their own thinking processes; that is, they have an understanding of how they *think* about their *thinking.* As a result, they have internal metacognitive conversations as they read that aid in monitoring and clarifying text. These conversations signal when they need to "fix" comprehension. Baker (1985) identified several monitoring strategies, or questions, that proficient readers use:

1. Do I understand all the words in the text?
2. Do my knowledge of the topic and my understanding of the text harmonize?
3. Does anything I comprehend from the text contradict other parts?
4. Are individual words or word groups correct grammatically?
5. Does each proposition or sentence hold together within itself?
6. Do propositions or sentences fit together?
7. Is the information I understand in this text clear and complete?

Proficient readers use these standards of evaluation more frequently and effectively than do struggling readers (Baker, 1985). Struggling readers need help developing metacognitive awareness and assistance in developing a repertoire of clarifying strategies. Schoenbach, Greenleaf, Cziko, and Hurwitz (1999) suggest readers can increase their metacognitive awareness by using the following strategies:

- noticing what is happening in their minds in a variety of everyday situations
- identifying various thinking processes they engage in in a variety of everyday situations
- noticing where their attention is when reading
- identifying the different processes going on during reading (p. 29)

Understanding External and Internal Distractions with TOR

Understanding external and internal distractions that affect reading comprehension is a crucial step in developing metacognitive awareness. One activity that encourages students to think about external and internal distractions while reading is tune-out reading (TOR). I place the following settings on an overhead and ask students to speculate about the kinds of distractions they would encounter when reading in each: cafeteria, gym, TV or game room, outside, and car. We discuss obvious distractions, most of which are visual or auditory (e.g., movements, objects, talking, car horns, and birds singing). I then add these settings: library, classroom, quiet place at home. At first students believe these are distraction-free settings, but I probe with questions like this: "There may not be any *obvious* distractions, but are there times you're not thinking about what you're reading? Even in a quiet place?" They begin talking about internal distractions, times when their mind wanders from the text: the prom, homecoming, weekend plans, family problems, friends, things they need to do, and/or issues that are causing stress and anxiety. We then discuss fix-up strategies that can help us focus. Students come up with ideas like the following:

1. Move to another setting.
2. Modify my environment—close the door, turn off the iPod, and so on.
3. Decide to read later when I'm better able to focus.
4. Reread what I missed.
5. Decide to read a small piece, then reward myself with a break.
6. Ask myself if the piece is too difficult.
7. Address the thought that prevents me from concentrating (e.g., the argument with my friend, finishing my other homework, or studying for an important test).

Students then read (a poem, a short story, textbook chapter) in several different environments (both highly stimulating and less) for 10 to 15 minutes and record the distractions around them and the thoughts that swept through their mind as they read. They chart their distractions after each reading exercise and record what they did to get back on track. To prevent the activity from becoming monotonous, I generally ask them to respond to a set number of distractions per setting (e.g., three). A beginning distraction log might resemble Table 6.1.

I model this assignment (with my preservice teachers) right before they complete a Web quest on topics such as researching a young adult author, exploring a reading issue or skill, or an issue or theme in young adult literature. After they've completed their Web quests, I ask them to think about the computer distractions that pulled them off task: the obsession to check e-mail and the news, to IM a friend, to visit MySpace, Facebook, and YouTube, and cluttered Web pages with alluring ads.

Table 6.1

Sample Distraction Log

Setting	Distraction	Fix-Up Strategy
Library	The librarian talking with another student.	I waited until they finished.
	I found myself thinking about what I'm doing after school.	I kept reminding myself to put the thought in the back of my mind. I reread and underlined important ideas.
	I was thinking about the chapter being boring.	I read a little at a time and did some other homework in between.

Clarifying Meaning with Graphic Organizers

In addition to developing strategies for responding to distractions, struggling readers need practice using fix-up strategies that aid them in clearing up confusing texts. I use a modified graphic organized proposed by Schoenbach et al. (1999) to help students think about how they monitor and clarify confusing texts. To get a feel for how this activity will work with your students, finish the following chart as you read the accompanying passage in Table 6.2; I've provide one example. Note this is a difficult text. I want you to *experience* this activity; thus, it's important that you be confused so that you use fix-up strategies.

Clarifying Meaning with Text-to-Self, Text-to-Text, and Text-to-World Connections

Activities that encourage students to make text connections (text-to-self, text-to-text, and text-to-world) can also help readers develop necessary skills for monitoring and clarifying read. Struggling readers sometimes don't activate prior knowledge and at other times may lack appropriate prior knowledge to make text connections. (In the latter case, appropriate prereading strategies can be helpful.) Once you've discussed these three types of connections, students can practice using them by keeping a connection log as they read. Note the sample log in Table 6.3 based on Jennifer Donnelly's *A Northern Light* (2003). Of course, you don't want to require that they make all three connections with everything they read. The idea is to give them some initial practice so they become familiar with the three types of connections. As they develop as readers, they will develop the habit of applying whichever strategy helps them make sense of the text.

Table 6.2

Sample Graphic Organizer to Clarify Text

Passage or word that confused me	Question or confusion it raised	Strategy I used to "fix-up" my confusion 1 = Ignore and read on 2 = Read on, looking for clarification 3 = Reread the confusing part 4 = Reread the passage before 5 = Make connections with prior knowledge 6 = Consult additional resources	Clarification
1. . . . *what some of them would do for a little ink.*	What does that mean? What is ink in this context?	I reread the confusing part then reread some of the text before it.	The author means what some people would do to get their names in a paper. The narrator is a war correspondent.
2.			
3.			
4.			

"Hey, what're you guys, with the USO? Aw, we thought you was with the USO 'cause your hair's so long." Page took the kid's picture, I got the words down and Flynn laughed and told him we were the Rolling Stones. The three of us traveled around together for about a month that summer. At one lz the brigade chopper came in with a real foxtail hanging off the aerial, when the commander walked by us he almost took an infarction.

"Don't you men salute officers?"

"We're not men," Page said. "We're correspondents."

When the commander heard that, he wanted to throw a spontaneous operation for us, crank up his whole brigade and get some people killed. We had to get out on the next chopper to keep him from going ahead with it, amazing **what some of them would do for a little ink.** Page liked to augment his field gear with freak paraphernalia, scarves and beads, plus he was English, guys would stare at him like he'd just come down off a wall on Mars. Sean Flynn could look more incredibly beautiful than even his father, Errol, had thirty years before as Captain Blood, but sometimes he looked more like Artaud coming out of some heavy heart-of-darkness trip, overloaded on the information, the input! The input! He'd give off a bad sweat and sit for hours, combing his mustache through with the saw blade of his Swiss Army knife. We packed grass and tape: Have You Seen Your Mother Baby Standing in the Shadows, Best of the Animals, Strange Days, Purple Haze, Archie Bell and the Drells, "C'mon now everybody, do the Tighten Up. . . ." Once in a while we'd catch a chopper straight into one of the lower hells, but it was a quiet time in the war, mostly it was lz's and camps, grunts hanging around, faces, stories. (Herr, 1977, p. 8)

T a b l e   6 . 3

Text Connections for *A Northern Light* by Jennifer Donnelly, 2003

Passage/Event	Text-to-Self	Text-to-Text	Text-to-World
Mattie's work at the boardinghouse	Makes me think of stories told to me about my great-grandmother working in a boarding-house owned by her mother. I keep visualizing the family house that served as a boardinghouse in the early 1900s.		
Character of Mattie		She reminds me of Erzebet in *The Blood Confession* because both girls question and defy female norms of their times.	
Drowning of Grace Brown by Chester Gillette			Reminds me of Lacy Peterson and how her husband drowned her in a marina in the San Francisco area. Both women were pregnant.

Reciprocal Teaching

Developed by Brown, Palincsar, and Armbruster (1984), reciprocal teaching (RT) aids students in clarifying text. Sometimes described as a dialogue between teachers and students in which participants take turns assuming the teacher role, the method requires that readers stop at regular intervals to ask questions, clarify text, make predictions, and summarize. The teacher starts by asking a question, then the student reciprocates with her/his own question. The teacher initiates the strategy but gradually releases responsibility to a small group in which one student assumes the lead teacher role. In the beginning, the teacher familiarizes students with question stems like those that follow and gives students a copy to reference as they participate:

1. Summarizing

    What is the most important information?
    This is about . . .
    What should you remember about this passage?
    What would a teacher ask about this passage?

2.   Questioning

   One question I had while reading was . . .
   What were you thinking as you read?
   What question(s) can you ask about your reading?

3.   Clarifying

   I wasn't sure about the word . . .
   What word(s) or phrase(s) do you not understand?
   What words can we use in place of . . .
   I'm stuck here. I need to . . . (what fix-up strategy is needed?)

4.   Predicting

   What do you think might happen?
   I predict . . .

One historical fiction title that works well for teaching reciprocal teaching is Kirby Larson's *Hattie Big Sky* (2006), a 2007 Newbery Honor book. The teacher, or student trained in reciprocal teaching, might begin the process by reading this opening passage:

> *December 19, 1917*
> *Arlington, Iowa*
> *Dear Charlie,*
>
> *Miss Simpson starts every day with a reminder to pray for you—and all the other boys who enlisted. Well, I say we should pray for the Kaiser—he's going to need those prayers once he meets you!*
> *I ran into your mother today at Uncle Holt's store. She said word is you are heading for England soon, France after that. I won't hardly be able to look at the map behind Miss Simpson's desk now; it will only remind me of how far you are from Arlington.* (p. 1)

After reading the above passage, the teacher might model:

1. *From what I've read I can tell someone has written a letter to a friend or loved one. Can someone help me with my* **summary?** (Students add details)

2. *The teacher may then ask* **questions,** being careful to ask both knowledge-level questions and higher-level questions.

   Where does the narrative say her friend is headed? (knowledge-level question).

   Why is her friend headed to England, then France? (higher-level question requiring inferential thinking).

   (Students provide answers, then reciprocate with their own questions. If they figure out the friend is going to war, they might ask, Which war? How do you know?)

3. *I need some help with the word* Kaiser. *I believe this is a person, but I'm still confused. Can anyone help me* **clarify** *that word or tell me what fix-up strategy I should use?* (Some students may know *Kaiser* can mean *emperor* and predict this is Hitler, if they have some prior knowledge about World War I or World War II. A history fanatic may nail the correct response: Kaiser Wilhelm II ruled Germany during World War I, the setting for this

story. Students might suggest the teacher continue to read and look for the meaning later in the text.)

4. *Based on what I've read so far (and the title and cover), I* **predict** *this story is going to be about a young person left at home, while her friend or loved one goes off to fight in World War I. Who agrees and who has a different prediction?* (Some students will agree and extend the teacher's reasoning; others may suggest alternatives.)

The sequence of questions doesn't have to follow the summarizing, questioning, clarifying, predicting pattern above, but it makes sense that prediction is the last question. It also makes sense that teachers not use this process all the way through a chapter, short story, or novel. It's obviously slow and tedious. Research has shown, however, that regular RT practice improves reading comprehension (Brown et al., 1984).

Think-Alouds

The think-aloud is a strategy that "slows down the reading process," allowing struggling readers to see how proficient readers make meaning from text (Davey, 1983). As outlined in Chapter 2, proficient readers perform a number of implicit cognitive processes as they read:

- Activate prior knowledge
- Set a purpose or goal for reading
- Make connections
- Decode words
- Make inferences
- Make predictions
- Visualize
- Summarize
- Ask questions
- Compare and contrast
- Understand causal relationships
- Generalize and draw conclusions
- Monitor and clarify meaning

Struggling readers don't use these strategies effectively and need explicit and direct instruction in developing these skills. Expert readers can model how they use these strategies by thinking aloud a text (Beers, 2003, p. 41). As students read, they pause at intervals to "think aloud" about the text. Much like reciprocal teaching, students comment or raise questions about connections they are making, comprehension problems, and ways of repairing comprehension. When students engage in think-alouds, they construct text knowledge, but they also develop a better understanding of the cognitive processes used in constructing that knowledge. A good resource for exploring think-alouds in depth is Jeffrey Wilhelm's *Improving Comprehension with Think-Aloud Strategies* (2001). Wilhelm illustrates a variety of ways to conduct think-alouds (e.g., teacher performs the think-aloud while students listen; students do think-alouds in large groups while the teacher monitors; students do written think-alouds).

Final Thoughts

The historical fiction titles shared in this chapter cover a wide range of events, people and places, time periods, and social and political issues. They can easily be used to teach students to monitor and clarify their reading. For most of us, *monitoring our reading* and *clarifying texts* are natural processes. When comprehension fails, we use fix-up strategies automatically with little thought given to our metacognitive processes. Many of the students we teach lack these skills. They stop reading or read through without comprehending. The reading strategies presented in this chapter, coupled with the professional resources that follow, will aid you in working with readers who can't—or don't—monitor what they read.

Professional Resources

Adamson, L. G. (1994). *Recreating the past: A guide to American and world historical fiction for children and young adults.* Westport, CT: Greenwood Press.

Adamson, L. G. (1999). *American historical fiction: An annotated guide to novels for adults and young adults.* Phoenix: Oryx.

Adamson, L. G. (1999). *World historical fiction.* Phoenix: Oryx.

Ammon, R., & Tunnell, M. O. (1992). *The story of ourselves: Teaching history through children's literature.* Portsmouth, NH: Heinemann.

Avi. (1999, Summer). Writing backwards but looking forward. *SIGNAL Journal, 22*(2), 17–23.

Barnhouse, R. (2000). *Recasting the past: The Middle Ages in young adult literature.* Portsmouth, NH: Heinemann.

Brown, J. (1998). Historical fiction or fictionalized history? Problems for writers of historical novels for young adults. *The ALAN Review, 26*(1), 7–11.

Burt, D. S. (Ed.). (1997). *What historical fiction do I read next?* Detroit: Gale.

Cole, P. (1997, Spring). Ann Rinaldi's great episodes: A clearer window to the past. *SIGNAL Journal, 21*(2), 16–18.

Elkassabany, A., Johnston, C., Lucas, T., Conway, J., Lyle, R., Budd, J. S., et al. (2000). How do you incorporate history into the English classroom? *English Journal, 89*(3), 26–30.

Erickson, J. (1994, February). The truth of historical fiction: Researching Osseo Senior High. *English Journal, 83*(2), 36–39.

Garfield, L. (1988, December). Historical fiction for our global times. *The Horn Book, 64*(6), 737–743.

Gauch, P. L. (1993, Fall). Why writers write of war: Looking into the eye of historical fiction. *The ALAN Review, 21*(1), 12–16.

Harmon, J. (1998). *Lyddie and Oliver:* Instructional framework for linking historical fiction to the classics. *The ALAN Review, 25*(2), 16–20.

Herald, D. T. (2000). *Genreflecting: A guide to reading interests in genre fiction* (5th ed.). Westport, CT: Libraries Unlimited.

Herald, D. T. (2003). *Teen genreflecting* (2nd ed.). Westport, CT: Libraries Unlimited.

Johnson, S. (2005). *Historical fiction: A guide to the genre.* Westport, CT: Greenwood Press.

Lasky, K. (1990, Summer). The fiction of history: What did Miss Kitty really do? *The New Advocate, 3*(3), 157–166.

Lasky, K. (1997, Spring). Keyhole history. *SIGNAL Journal, 21*(3), 5–10.

Loewen, J. W. (1996). *Lies my teacher told me: Everything your American history textbook got wrong.* New York: Simon & Schuster.

MacLeod, A. S. (1998, January/February). Writing backward: Modern models in historical fiction. *The Horn Book, 74*(1), 26–33.

Pavonetti, L. M. (2001, December). Historical fiction—new and old. *Voices from the Middle, 9*(2), 78–82.

Sipes, L. R. (1997, Summer). In their own words: Authors' views on issues in historical fiction. *The New Advocate, 10*(3), 243–258.

Zarian, B. B. (2004). *Around the world with historical fiction and folktales.* Lanham, MD: Scarecrow Press.

ONLINE

Gander Academy & Classroom Connect: www.cdli .ca/CITE/lang_historical_fiction.htm

Historical Fiction: www.historicalfiction.org

Historical Fiction Review: www .historicalfictionreview.com

Historical Novel Society: www .historicalnovelsociety.org

Paradox: www.paradoxmag.com

Reader's Club: www.readersclub.org

Red Inkworks: www.redinkworks.com/ historical_fiction.htm

Soon's Historical Fiction: www.histfiction.net

Western Writers of America: www .westernwriters.com

References

Abraham, S. G., & Abraham, D. G. (2006). *Surprising Cecilia.* El Paso, TX: Cinco Puntos Press.

Alcott, L. (1868). *Little women.* Boston: Roberts Brothers.

Auch, M. J. (2002). *Ashes of roses.* New York: Henry Holt.

Avi. (2006). *Crispin at the edge of the world.* New York: Hyperion.

Baker, L. (1985). Differences in the standards used by college students to evaluate their comprehension of expository prose. *Reading Research Quarterly, 20*(3), 297–313.

Beers, K. (2003). *When kids can't read: What teachers can do.* Portsmouth, NH: Heinemann.

Bloor, E. (2006). *London calling.* New York: Knopf/ Random House.

Brown, A. L., Palincsar, A. S., & Armbruster, B. B. (1984). Instructing comprehension-fostering activities in interactive learning situations. In H. Mandl, N. Stein, & T. Trabasso (Eds.), *Learning and comprehension of text* (pp. 255–285). Hillsdale, NJ: Erlbaum.

Brown, J., & St. Clair, N. (2006). *The distant mirror: Reflections on young adult historical fiction.* Lanham, MD: Scarecrow, Press.

Carter, A. R. (1999). *Crescent moon.* New York: Holiday House.

Chandler, J. (2006). *Warrior girl: A novel of Joan of Arc.* New York: Greenwillow/HarperCollins.

Collier, J. L., & Collier, C. (1983). *War comes to Willy Freeman.* New York: Delacorte/Random House.

Couloumbis, A. (2005). *Summer's end.* New York: Putnam.

Crane, S. (1991). *The red badge of courage.* New York: Bantam Doubleday Dell/Random House (Original work published 1895)

Crist-Evans, C. (2003). *Amaryllis.* Cambridge, MA: Candlewick Press.

Crowe, C. (2002). *Mississippi trial, 1955.* New York: Dial/Penguin.

Crowe, C. (2003). *Getting away with murder: The true story of the Emmett Till case.* New York: Dial/ Penguin.

Cullen, L. (2007). *I am Rembrandt's daughter.* New York: Bloomsbury.

Cushman, K. (2000). *Matilda Bone.* Boston: Houghton Mifflin.

Davey, B. (1983). Think-aloud: Modeling the cognitive processes of reading comprehension. *Journal of Reading, 27*(1), 44–47.

Donnelly, J. (2003). *A northern light.* Orlando, FL: Harcourt.

Dowswell, P. (2005). *Powder monkey: Adventures of a young sailor.* New York: Bloomsbury.

Draper, S. (2006). *Copper sun.* New York: Atheneum/Simon & Schuster.

Ellis, D. (2002). *Parvana's journey.* Toronto: Groundwood Books.

Fox, P. (1973). *The slave dancer.* Scarsdale, NY: Bradbury Press.

Giff, P. R. (2006). *Water street.* New York: Lamb/Random House.

Hobbs, W. (2006). *Crossing the wire.* New York: HarperCollins.

Jiménez, F. (1997). *The circuit: Stories from the life of a migrant child.* Albuquerque: University of New Mexico Press.

Jiménez, F. (2001). *Breaking through.* Boston: Houghton Mifflin.

Kadohata, C. (2007). *Cracker! The best dog in Vietnam.* New York: Simon & Schuster.

Kay, A. N. (2001). *Young heroes of history* series (*Send 'em south* #1). Shippensburg, PA: White Mane.

Keene, E., & Zimmerman, S. (1997). *Mosaic of thought.* Portsmouth, NH: Heinemann.

Kidd, R. (2006). *Monkey town: The summer of the Scopes trial.* New York: Simon & Schuster.

Larson, K. (2006). *Hattie big sky.* New York: Delacorte/Random House.

Laskas, G. M. (2007). *The miner's daughter.* New York: Simon & Schuster.

Lasky, K. (1981). *The night journey.* New York: Frederick Warne & Co.

Lasky, K. (2005). *Broken song.* New York: Viking/Penguin.

Lawrence, I. (1999). *The smugglers.* New York: Delacorte/Random House.

Lawrence, I. (2001). *The buccaneers.* New York: Delacorte/Random House.

Lawrence, I. (2005). *The convicts.* New York: Delacorte/Random House.

Lester, J. (2000). *Pharaoh's daughter.* Orlando, FL: Harcourt.

Lester, J. (2005). *Day of tears: A novel in dialogue.* New York: Jump at the Sun/Hyperion.

Lester, J. (2006). *Time's memory.* New York: Farrar, Straus & Giroux.

Lester, J. (2007). *Cupid.* Orlando, FL: Harcourt.

Lester, J. (2008). *Guardian.* New York: Amistad.

Lewis, J. P., & Dotlich, R. K. (2006). *Castles: Old stone poems.* Illus. Dan Burr. Honesdale, PA: Wordsong/Boyds Mills Press.

McCormick, P. (2006). *Sold.* New York: Hyperion.

Meyer, C. (1999). *Young royals* series (*Mary, Bloody Mary* #1). Orlando, FL: Harcourt.

Meyer, C. (2005). *Marie, dancing.* Orlando, FL: Harcourt.

Mochizuki, K. (1993). *Baseball saved us.* Illus. Dom Lee. New York: Lew & Low.

Morpurgo, M. (2003). *Private Peaceful.* New York: Scholastic.

Moses, S. P. (2005). *The return of Buddy Bush.* New York: McElderry/Simon & Schuster.

Myers, W. D. (1988). *Fallen angels.* New York: Scholastic.

Myers, W. D. (2008). *Sunrise over Fallujah.* New York: Scholastic.

Napoli, D. J. (2004). *Bound.* New York: Atheneum/Simon & Schuster.

Napoli, D. J. (2005). *The king of Mulberry Street.* New York: Lamb/Random House.

Nixon, J. L. (1987). *The orphan train adventures* (*A family apart* #1). New York: Bantam.

Nixon, J. L. (1992). *Ellis Island* series (*Land of hope* #1). New York: Bantam.

Nolan, H. (2006). *A summer of kings.* Orlando, FL: Harcourt.

O'Brien, T. (1973). *If I die in a combat zone, box me up and ship me home.* New York: Delacorte/Random House.

O'Brien, T. (1978). *Going after Cacciato.* New York: Random House.

O'Brien, T. (1990). *The things they carried.* Boston: Houghton Mifflin.

O'Dell, S. (1976). *Zia.* Boston: Houghton Mifflin.

Park, L. S. (2002). *When my name was Keoko.* Boston: Houghton Mifflin.

Paulsen, G. (1993). *Nightjohn.* New York: Bantam Doubleday Dell/Random House.

Peck, R. (1998). *A long way from Chicago.* New York: Dial/Penguin.

Richardson, V. A. (2006). *The moneylender's daughter.* New York: Bloomsbury.

Rinaldi, A. (1992). *A break with charity: A story about the Salem Witch Trials.* San Diego: Harcourt.

Rinaldi, A. (1995). *The secret of Sarah Revere.* San Diego: Harcourt.

Roberts, J. (2007). *Dragons of the sea: The strongbow saga.* New York: HarperCollins.

Roberts, J. (2008). *The road to vengeance: The strongbow saga.* New York: HarperCollins.

Sachs, M. (2005). *Lost in America.* New Milford, CT: Roaring Brook Press.

Salisbury, G. (1992). *Blue skin of the sea.* New York: Random House.

Salisbury, G. (1994). *Under the blood-red sun.* New York: Random House.

Salisbury, G. (1997). *Shark bait.* New York: Random House.

Salisbury, G. (1998). *Jungle dogs.* New York: Random House.

Salisbury, G. (2001). *Lord of the deep.* New York: Random House.

Salisbury, G. (2002). *Island boyz.* New York: Random House.

Salisbury, G. (2005). *Eyes of the emperor.* New York: Random House.

Salisbury, G. (2006). *House of the red fish.* New York: Random House.

Salisbury, G. (2007). *Night of the howling dogs.* New York: Lamb/Random House.

Schoenbach, R., Greenleaf, C., Cziko, C., & Hurwitz, L. (1999). *Reading for understanding: A guide to improving reading in middle and high school classrooms.* San Francisco: Jossey-Bass.

Seely, D. (2004). *The last of the roundup boys.* New York: Holiday House.

Skelton, M. (2006). *Endymion Spring.* New York: Delacorte/Random House.

Stoples, S. F. (1989). *Shabanu: Daughter of the wind.* New York: Random House.

Steinbeck, J. (1939). *The grapes of wrath.* New York: Viking/Penguin.

Stratton, A. (2008). *Chandra's wars.* New York: HarperCollins.

Thomson, S. L. (2006). *The secret of the rose.* New York: Greenwillow/HarperCollins.

Weatherford, C. B. (2006). *Moses: When Harriet Tubman led her people to freedom.* Illus. Kadir Nelson. New York: Jump at the Son/Hyperion.

Wemmlinger, R. (2007). *Booth's daughter.* Honesdale, PA: Calkins Creek/Boyds Mills Press.

Wilhelm, J. D. (2001). *Improving comprehension with think-aloud strategies.* New York: Scholastic.

Wilson, D. L. (2005). *Black storm comin'.* New York: McElderry/Simon & Schuster.

Yep, L. (1984). *Golden Mountain chronicles (The serpent's children* #1). New York: Harper & Row.

Zusak, M. (2006). *The book thief.* New York: Knopf/Random House.

Mysteries, Thrillers, and Horror
Reading Skills: Inferential Thinking and Predicting

Introduction

Aunt Mavis is forevermore on the lookout for car wrecks. When an ambulance, fire truck, or rescue squad passes her house, she grabs her car keys and races to the accident scene—curious to know what happened, how it occurred, and whether someone was hurt. She attends funerals of people she hardly knows, especially funerals for suicide or accident victims, and she spends hours in front of CNN watching the media frenzy over kidnapped girls, sociopath serial killers, school/community shootings, and mass murders. She reads books like *Salem's Lot* (King, 1975), *The Vampire Lestat* (Rice, 1985), and *The Last Juror* (Grisham, 2004) and watches Alfred Hitchcock reruns. Although she doesn't wish anyone ill will, relaying horrific news elevates her, and solving mysteries before anyone else is empowering.

We are a nation intrigued by mystery and titillated by the grotesque. Murderers become celebrities, victims martyrs. We remember O. J. Simpson for his murder trial, not for being one of the greatest running backs in the game of football. Every Christmas the media reminds us of Laci Peterson, the young pregnant wife murdered by her husband, who dominated the 2003 news. World issues, even the war in Iraq, were tabled when John Carr claimed to have murdered JonBenet Ramsey. For unexplainable reasons we are drawn to the unknown, to fear, to violence, to danger, to celebrities entangled in scandalous crimes, to victimized, beautiful kids. Some call such attraction blatant escapism, but if escapism is the sole reason for enjoying mystery and the grotesque, why do we escape into terrifying worlds? Why not safe places? An interesting question. Perhaps we enjoy the adrenaline rush—that rollercoaster-like feeling we get when we're scared. Perhaps, too, thinking about bigger problems minimizes our own. Whatever the reason, mysteries, thrillers, and horror novels sell.

This chapter explores young adult mysteries, thrillers, and horror and examines defining characteristics. It introduces leading young adult authors in these areas and includes a section on adult writers for advanced readers. Themed boxes provide a wide range of titles conducive to the needs of all students. Rounding out the chapter is a reading strand that illustrates ways young adult literature can be used to teach inferential skills and prediction. The chapter closes with a brief introduction to several literary elements that work well with this genre and a list of additional professional resources that can aid in lesson development and further research.

Characteristics of Good Mysteries

Many novels have a sense of mystery and leave readers guessing about the ending, but classic mysteries (or whodunits) have rules or conventions. Numerous authors have attempted to define rules for writing the mystery genre; however, most rules mimic S. S. Van Dine's "Twenty Rules for Writing Detective Stories," first published in 1928. According to Van Dine, detective stories (predecessor to the wider mystery genre) are intellectual games: "It [a detective story] is a sporting event. And for the writing of detective stories there are very definite laws—unwritten, perhaps, but none the less binding; and every respectable and self-respecting concocter of literary mysteries lives up to them."[1]

A classic young adult mystery follows many of Van Dine's rules. A teen assumes the role of amateur sleuth, private eye, investigator, special agent, or detective who uncovers a family or community secret or investigates a murder, organized crime, espionage, or missing person. *Nancy Drew*, the *Hardy Boys*, and *Trixie Beldon* are classic young adult examples. In a well-constructed mystery, the criminal, or villain, is introduced early. (A story that introduces the villain toward the end falls flat.) Readers need to know the person, otherwise they can't care about the ending. *Red herrings*, or teasers, in the form of clues, events, multiple motives, or characters that distract readers from the real culprit are essential. If readers solve the mystery too early, the book fails. Clues are carefully placed so the reader is challenged, and the outcome is not predictable. Quality mysteries include several motives, alibis, and plot twists, and the crime is significant. In *The Creek* (2003), for instance, unsolved malicious acts terrorize an entire town. Young adult author Jennifer Holm makes such skillful use of red herrings, clues, and plot twists that predicting the ending is impossible. The red herring is an in-your-face, well-rounded, likely villain; readers can hardly fathom his/her innocence.

Though not required, a mystery may be a suspense thriller; that is, in solving the mystery,

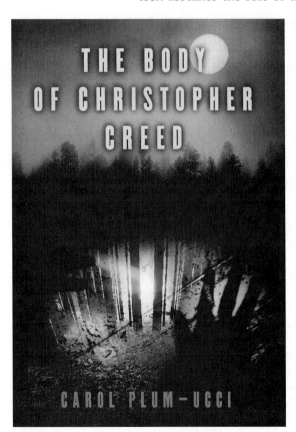

[1]Originally published in the *American Magazine*, September 1928. Retrieved June 20, 2008, from http://gaslight.mtroyal.ab.ca/gaslight. S. S. Van Dine is a pseudonym for Willard Huntington Wright.

the protagonist places himself in peril. *Edenville Owls* (2007), by adult crime fiction icon Robert B. Parker, features a group of teens, members of the school's JV basketball team, who witness their attractive female teacher being threatened and abused by a malicious, strange man. They intend to protect her—at any cost. They confront danger at every turn as they learn the man's identity: he is a military deserter, a crazed racist, and their pretty teacher's former husband.

Settings are important to mood. Spooky settings such as graveyards or abandoned old houses or mansions can add suspense or tension, but such settings are not necessary. Finally, the mystery should be solved, and the story often ends with a reconstruction of the crime. Generally two or more characters "talk through" the story's events, piecing together the puzzle, helping the reader fill in gaps, and bringing closure to the story. The book may end with a hint of a possible sequel.

Amateur Sleuths, Detectives, Special Agents, and Spies

Edgar Allan Poe is often credited with creating the first literary detective: C. Auguste Dupin in "The Murders in the Rue Morgue" (*Graham's Magazine*, 1841). Dupin investigates a brutal double murder that takes place in an inaccessible room. Probably the most famous literary detective, however, is Sherlock Holmes, created by Sir Arthur Conan Doyle in 1887. Doyle penned four novels featuring Holmes and 56 short stories, most of which were narrated by Dr. John H. Watson, biographer and friend of Holmes. Holmes first appeared in serialization form, a popular 19th-century publication style.

Early detective stories featured adult detectives (generally males), but today's young adult mysteries typically feature a teenage amateur sleuth or detective. (Of course, readers must suspend belief to enjoy stories in which teens actually work in or have access to crime labs, crime scenes, and so forth.) These protagonists notice clues to mysteries the average teen doesn't. Also, some solve crimes for financial rewards such as the Baker Street Irregulars, a group of homeless kids who do detective work for the infamous Sherlock Holmes in *Sherlock Holmes and the Baker Street Irregulars: The Fall of the Amazing Zalindas* (2006) by Tracy Mack and Michael Citrin. In another Sherlock Holmes spin-off, *The Case of the Missing Marquess: An Enola Holmes Mystery* (2006) by Nancy Springer, the younger sister of Sherlock Holmes is an amateur sleuth searching for her missing mother. She, of course, is driven by a personal need. *Gilda Joyce: Psychic Investigator* (2005) by Jennifer Allison features ninth-grader Gilda Joyce, an inspiring psychic crime solver. Gilda spends the summer with her uncle in his Victorian mansion and uses her psychic powers and investigative skills to solve the mystery of a locked tower. Gilda's adventures continue in *The Ladies of the Lake* (2006) and *The Ghost Sonata* (2007).

The publication of *Casino Royale* (1954), first in the *James Bond* series by British writer Ian Fleming, laid the groundwork for a new young adult genre: special agents, secret agents, and spies.[2] More than 20 movies have been made based on the James Bond character, along with innumerable video games, comics, parodies, and television spin-offs (e.g., *I Spy,* 1965–1968; *Get Smart,* 1965–1970). Bond has become a household name. With its Bond-like themes and gadgets, Anthony Horowitz's *Alex Rider* series (first book *Stormbreaker,* 2001) are young adult national bestsellers. When Alex Rider's guardian uncle, Ian Rider, is killed in a suspicious car accident, Alex learns his uncle was an M16 spy for British Special Operations. He realizes, too, that his uncle was grooming him for a similar career. Alex is coerced into replacing his uncle and sets out with Bond-like gadgets on his first mission. Subsequent books follow Alex on action-packed, cliff-hanging missions.

Of course, where would readers be without the adventures of James Bond himself as an adolescent? Recruited by the Ian Fleming estate to write a young adult *James Bond* series, Charlie Higson published the first in the *Young Bond* series, *SilverFin,* in 2005. In this series, Bond fans, both young and old, read about the young boy who became the world's most infamous spy. Higson's meticulous research into the Bond character and Ian Fleming's novels make this series ring true. The books have plenty of action and horrifying villains, and true to the adult novels, there's always a pretty girl.

With today's emphasis on strong female characters, young adult spy novels featuring female protagonists are a part of today's young adult market. *Live and Let Shop* (2005), the first installment of Michael Spradlin's *Spy Goddess* series, features Beverly Hills teenager Rachel Buchanan, a troubled teen who lands in a private Pennsylvania academy where she becomes mixed up in a case of espionage. Mark Delaney's *Misfits, Inc.* series (first installment *The Vanishing Chip,* 1998) features four high school misfits, one of whom is a smart, inquisitive girl. Byte and her three male companions solve impossible mysteries.

Fantasy Mysteries

Mystery and fantasy genres blend easily. Fantasy may rely upon a central character who must solve a riddle or problem so good can overcome evil. The *Harry Potter* series, for example, could be classified as a mystery series. A better example, however, of a fantasy mystery is Matthew Skelton's *Endymion Spring* (2006). This story, taking place in the university setting of Oxford, England, and alternating between the past and present, features Blake Winters, a young adolescent who has unwillingly accompanied his academic mother to Oxford. Wiling away time in the Bodleian Library, Blake

---

[2]Published first in Britain in 1953. Before his death in 1964, Fleming penned 13 additional James Bond books. For over 30 years various authors, including John Gardner who wrote 16, continued the series.

runs his hands across an ancient book that strikes him back. Blake opens the book, only to find blank pages that quiver as though they are alive. Unbeknownst to Blake, the ancient magical book was brought to Oxford by Gutenberg's apprentice[3] to save it from the dark forces of evil. Upon opening the book, Blake is drawn into a perilous magical quest to prevent evil from taking over the world.

Blake is a classic detective: he's determined, despite impending danger, to unravel the ancient book's mystery. This story, too, has a classic spooky setting, common to mysteries. Dark, ancient tunnels run beneath the Bodleian Library; gargoyles, with chiseled claws, grip the ledges of ancient stone buildings; and shadows lurk on the dark cobblestone Oxford streets.

River Secrets (2006) by Newbery Honor winner Shannon Hale is a second example of fantasy mystery. Razo, a confidante of Queen Isi of the kingdom of Bayern, is chosen to become a spy. A mystery unfolds as Razo discovers charred bodies, left behind by the Tiran army in an effort to reignite a war with the Kingdom of Bayern, and Razo must find the people responsible for the deaths. While *Endymion Spring* contains realistic elements (e.g., a real and familiar setting), *River Secrets* is an example of high-fantasy mystery. The story takes place in a completely imaginable and impossible world. Mystery/fantasy blends abound in young adult literature. Although these two stories have very different plots, both contain a puzzle or problem that needs solving and magical elements. (Chapter 8 includes a detailed discussion of fantasy characteristics and elements.)

Reprinted by permission of Penguin Young Readers Group © 2006.

Forensic Science and Crime Mysteries

The mystery genre offers something for everyone. Some teens prefer light, humorous mysteries or fantasy mysteries; others prefer darker, more realistic stories about corruption, brutal slayings, kidnappings, serial killers, and bizarre human behavior. The term *hardboiled*[4] refers to hardedge crime stories like these. Most hardboiled mysteries have a street-smart

---

[3]The Gutenberg character is the creator of the Gutenberg Bible.
[4]*Hardboiled* is a slang expression meaning *tough;* it originated from the idea of a hardboiled egg. Dashiell Hammett and Raymond Chandler pioneered the style in the 1920s and 1930s.

detective or professional investigator; a familiar archetype is Mickey Spillane's Mike Hammer. Callous and cynical of the law, Hammer takes the law into his own hands. *Noir*[5] mysteries, a subgenre of hardboiled mysteries, differ in that the protagonist is not a detective but a victim or suspect. Few young adult authors, however, target teens with these themes and hard-edge books.

Anthony Horowitz's *Gatekeeper* series is a *noir fantasy mystery.* Matt Freeman, a troubled teen falsely accused of murder, is sent to live with a sinister foster mother, Mrs. Deverill, in the opening book (*Raven's Gate,* 2005). Upon finding a photo of his parents' funeral in Mrs. Deverill's house, he tries to escape. Violent deaths await those who try to help him escape. Matt is pursued by witches, dinosaurs, hellhounds, and vile bogs; he learns he possesses magical powers and must turn from victim to hero and stop evil monsters from overtaking the world.

CSI and *Law & Order* fans will enjoy the Christopher Golden's *Body of Evidence* series, classic noir material.[6] In *Thief of Hearts* (Golden, 1999), college student Jenna Blake works as a pathology assistant and becomes embroiled in a case in which a serial killer removes human hearts. In *Throat Culture* (Golden & Hautala, 2005), Jenna races against time to solve a case in which party attendees at her father's wedding consume food tainted with a deadly virus.

Alane Ferguson's *Forensic Mystery* series is based on Ferguson's real-life forensics experiences and provides forensic fans with gruesome crime scene details. In this series, 17-year-old Cameryn Mahoney is her coroner father's assistant. Though realistically a teenager would not have access to crime scenes and crime labs, Ferguson's descriptions of forensics procedures are not for the faint of heart. Prior to taking Cameryn with him on her first crime scene (*The Christopher Killer,* 2005), her father warns:

> "We're going to need a trap, just in case," her father said, flipping down the backseat of their station wagon to make room for the body they'd be picking up. His voice sounded muffled as he added, "We'll need a sheet, too. And heavy gloves. The guy's skin might have come off in the water and we'll have to fish it out of the drain, which is a job you'll want the long gloves for. You okay?" (p. 18)

In this series, Ferguson builds an even stronger chill/ugh factor with such details as Cameryn's grandmother washing the corpse sheets in the family machine, the family car serving as the coroner's hearse, Cameryn working in a restaurant and bleaching her hands before work, and Cameryn being reminded it's a good idea to have autopsy shoes that stay at the "office" and shoes that go home.[7] In the author box Ferguson explains the real-life events that led to her *Forensic Mystery* series.

---

[5]*Noir* means *black* in French. *Roman noir* in French means *black novel.*
[6]Some books in the series are co-written with Rick Hautala.
[7]Examples taken from *The Christopher Killer,* 2005, and *The Angel of Death,* 2006.

On Writing Forensic Mysteries   by Alane Ferguson

Murder. It's a powerful word, a catalyst for thousands of books that entertain from beginning to end, carefully crafted puzzles that dare the reader to solve their mysteries. But in my life, my personal interest in homicide and the study of forensics was sparked by something much more infinitely and painfully real. My best friend, Savannah Leigh Anderson, lost her life at the hands of a serial killer on Mother's Day, 1979. An only child, she was slaughtered in her own apartment just moments after she finished a long and loving two-hour Mother's Day call. When she walked into her bedroom she found a man hovering in her closet, a man named Robert Lloyd Sellers, the security guard at her complex. They didn't find her for two days, but when her remains were finally discovered, I got a call I can still remember so vividly it feels branded into my memory. "Savannah's dead," the voice told me. "Someone broke into her apartment and strangled her. Whoever did it left a pillow over her face."

That was the day everything changed in my life.

An obvious question is why would I choose to write about the very thing that brought me so much pain. Why forensics? Why murder mysteries? The answer is as complex as the question, but I think, after so many years, that I finally understand: Writing is cathartic in a way that real life cannot be. I couldn't save my friend, but the characters I create can defeat the evil that threatens them. In my work, those who are weak become strong, and the victim becomes the victor. I create my own reality on those blank pages. My protagonist lives. In the shadow of my imagination, I save Savannah again and again.

I began writing a four-part forensic series for Penguin Putnam because I wanted to show the slow, laborious process that is actually involved in finding and catching human monsters. Television makes the process look easy, but the real world of forensics is messy and time-consuming, as much art as science. The first step of my journey was trying to understand the *why*. Why would someone choose to selfishly take another's life? I read every book I could get my hands on that attempted to explain the twisting of the human psyche. I discovered some markers that

pointed the way (abuse, mental illness), but the precise answer is still unfathomable. The next step dealt with the science of catching those who wreak havoc on the innocent. How do the police find them? What clues do killers leave behind, and how can detectives interpret them to prevent others from suffering the same fate?

The third step took me to the autopsy table, where I discovered that the body is, in and of itself, a crime scene—in many ways the final and most important of all. Refracting a scalp and pulling it over a face, removing a brain from a skull, cutting away ribs or searching stomach contents isn't done for voyeuristic pleasure. These procedures are performed because every bullet hole, every petechial hemorrhage, even the last meal are clues that lead to the killer. And catching the killer is the reason I write.

It is my hope that my protagonist, 17-year-old Cameryn Mahoney, a character who uses her wit, intelligence, and guts to save others, will resonate with readers everywhere. It is she who reads the clues and finds the killers. May there be a fresh crop of actual, flesh-and-blood Cameryns ready to tackle the tragedy of murder in the real world.

Official Web site: www.alaneferguson.com

Titles in her *Forensic Mystery* series include *The Christopher Killer* (2005), *The Angel of Death* (2006), and *The Circle of Blood* (2008).

Seventeen-year-old Kathryn Reiss with her dog Embers. Photo taken in 1975 at her home in Brecksville, Ohio.

Historical Mysteries

Some writers situate mysteries in historical settings, transporting readers to a different time and place. An enduring classic is *The House of Dies Drear* (1968) by Virginia Hamilton, which provides rich descriptions of the Underground Railroad and African American culture during the 1800s.[8] The setting in Philip Pullman's *Sally Lockhart Mystery* trilogy is reminiscent of that found in Victorian English novels such as those written by Charles Dickens and Thomas Hardy. *The Ruby in the Smoke* (Pullman, 1985) and its sequels are set in Victorian London and paint a detailed and colorful picture of the seedy side of 18th-century London. Sixteen-year-old Sally Lockhart, in searching for clues to unravel her father's murder in book one, encounters scoundrels and rogues and becomes embroiled in the opium trade.[9] Dorothy Hoobler and Thomas Hoobler's *The Ghost in the Tokaido Inn* (1999) and its sequels are set in 18th-century Japan and provide a historical account of samurai soldiers, shoguns, and the military government of that time.[10]

Humorous Mysteries

While funny mysteries may be enjoyed by all ages, young adult humorous mysteries typically target the middle school audience, probably because publishers and writers are uncomfortable providing more serious and realistic mysteries to this age group, such as forensic science mysteries and crimes featuring serial killers and rapists and those containing drugs, promiscuous sex, and violence. Anthony Horowitz is one of the better known mystery writers who employs humor in his story lines. *Three of Diamonds: A Diamond Brothers Mystery* (2005) features three mystery novellas about the Diamond Brothers and their hilarious escapades. Vicki Grant does a superb job with humor in her award-winning *Quid Pro*

---

[8]Hamilton published a sequel: *The Mystery of Drear House* (1987).
[9]*The Shadow in the North* (1988) and *The Tiger in the Well* (1990) complete the trilogy. *The Tin Princess* (1994) features characters from the original trilogy.
[10]Sequels include *The Demon in the Teahouse* (2001), *In Darkness, Death* (2004), *The Sword That Cut the Burning Grass* (2005), and *A Samurai Never Fears Death* (2007).

Quo (2005). In this story Cyril MacIntyre's lawyer mother goes missing, and Cyril searches for clues to her disappearance.

Puzzle Mysteries

Puzzle mysteries are appealing to many adolescents, particularly younger ones. In these mysteries the author provides numerous clues, puzzle pieces that engage and challenge readers to solve a mystery. *The Westing Game* (1978) by Ellen Raskin is a young adult archetype. In this story a group of heirs must piece together clues concerning the mysterious death of an eccentric millionaire before they can receive their inheritance. Blue Balliett's national bestseller *Chasing Vermeer* (2004) and its sequels, *The Wright 3* (2006) and *The Calder Game* (2008), are excellent examples. In *Chasing Vermeer*, both Calder and Petra love art. The story revolves around their efforts to recover a stolen Vermeer painting. Mathematical puzzle pieces, a mysterious book, and hidden codes in the book's illustrations challenge readers to make predictions and use their imagination and problem-solving skills to catch the villain. In Kathryn Reiss's *PaperQuake* (1998), for older readers, Violet discovers a mysterious letter. As she and her triplet sisters try to understand the letter, more clues reveal themselves, creating a mysterious puzzle and a race against time to determine the link between the infamous San Francisco 1906 earthquake and a possible modern-day earthquake that could collapse the Golden Gate Bridge.

Time Travel Mysteries

Time travel is a common structural device in mysteries. A central character might journey into the future or the past to gather clues that aid in solving a real-life problem or to change a historical event affecting the future. Sometimes the protagonist need not actually travel. The protagonist may come in contact with a troubled spirit. For instance, Kathryn Reiss, one of the foremost young adult mystery writers today, connects protagonists with spirits through an antique dollhouse in multiple novels. In her award-winning *Time Windows* (1991), 13-year-old Miranda Browne moves from New York City with her parents to a historical house in a small Massachusetts town. To her delight, she discovers a dollhouse (a replica of her family's house) built by runaway slaves during the mid-1800s. Miranda's enthusiasm soon wanes as she learns the house holds secrets to the lives of its former occupants, secrets that affect her own family's well-being. Miranda races to discover the secrets before her own family experiences tragedy. In the author box, Reiss, a creative writing instructor, discusses her fascination with time travel, history, and the supernatural.

Box 7.1 provides a list of mystery titles for young teens, and Box 7.2 lists mystery titles for older teens.

Prickles at the Back of the Neck: Writing Suspense Fiction   by Kathryn Reiss

I do not associate with murderers, imposters, or kidnappers, and my life so far has been blessedly free of danger. I've never stumbled through a time portal, however much I've hoped to find one, nor have I chanced upon a magic talisman, though I keep close watch. Ghostly sightings, likewise, have been disappointingly few and far between. I think I'm probably like most of my readers in that I get my thrills by communing with fictional characters in books who have all the adventures that continue to elude me.

My books are not based on personal experiences but on my interests. I write the same sort of thing I love to read: murder mysteries and time travel tales and creepy stories of the supernatural—and especially about kids and teens who stumble upon magic and then have to deal with the consequences.

Often the magic discovered in my stories leads my characters—modern teens—into the past. I have a keen interest in history and how the past affects our present. One of my favorite quotes comes from William Faulkner: "The past is not dead. In fact, it is not even past." I've used his idea in most of my books.

A story from the past figures importantly in each novel's plot and has bearing on characters' lives. In *Paint by Magic,* a tragic event from decades past needs to be investigated and understood before peace and safety in Connor's life are possible; ghosts from long ago in *Sweet Miss Honeywell's Revenge* need Zibby's and Jude's help before they can rest; and secrets from another era have bearing on the here and now in *Pale Phoenix,* leading my intrepid characters, Miranda and Dan, to travel centuries backward before they can save the day.

But connection to the past comes not only through physical time travel or contact with ghosts. In *PaperQuake,* past meets present via a paper trail of letters and diaries, in *Dreadful Sorry* via dreams and visions, in *Time Windows* via an antique dollhouse, and in both *The Glass House People* and *Blackthorn Winter* via the route most common to us in real life: memories.

The best suspense fiction pulls readers in fast and keeps them riveted to the characters' struggles. Yet too often for my liking, creepy stories tend to be violent, offering graphic descriptions of blood and gore to capture and hold the readers' attention. To my mind, that device seems too easy—a cheap ploy. I'm trying, instead, to write stories that make readers burrow under their covers, holding their breath as they follow my characters into unexpected places, exploring the dangerous, uncharted territory of magic. I'm hoping they'll refuse to turn out their bedside lights until the last page. I can feel I've done my job as a writer if I leave my readers with two things at the end of a book: first, a new sense that all sorts of things they never thought of before just *might* be possible, seen and unseen, past and present—much as Shakespeare wrote in *Hamlet*: "There are more things in heaven and earth, Horatio / Than are dreamt of in your philosophy"; and second—a delicious prickle at the back of their necks!

Box 7.1   Mystery and Detective Stories for Younger Teens

***Chasing the Jaguar* by Michele Dominguez Greene. New York: HarperCollins, 2006.**

After dreaming about the kidnapping of her mother's employer's daughter, 15-year-old Martika learns she is a descendant of Mayan women who have magical powers.

***Danger in the Dark: A Houdini & Nate Mystery* by Tom Lalicki. New York: Farrar, Straus & Giroux, 2006.**

Thirteen-year-old Nathaniel befriends the famous Harry Houdini, who helps Nathaniel unveil a plot to steal his great-aunt's fortune. An intriguing blend of fact and fiction. First in the *Houdini and Nate Mystery* series.

***Do You Know the Monkey Man?* by Dori Hillestad Butler. Atlanta: Peachtree, 2005.**

Samantha's twin sister drowned in a quarry when the girls were three. Over the years Samantha's mother refuses to talk about the incident and their father's leaving. Wanting to know more, Samantha, along with her friend, Angela, search the Internet for clues, challenge authority, and cross state lines, determined to discover some truths. A light mystery that moves quickly.

***From Charlie's Point of View: A Mystery* by Richard Scrimger. New York: Dutton/Penguin, 2005.**

When Charlie Fairmile's father is accused of bank robbery by the police, Charlie, his best friends, and guardian angel set out to prove Charlie's father is not the Stocking Bandit. Fast-paced and funny.

***Ghost Canoe* by Will Hobbs. New York: HarperCollins, 1997.**

After a ship crashes into the rocks off Cape Flattery, Nathan MacAllister, son of a lighthouse keeper, refuses to believe everyone perished. Sightings of a "wild man," unexplained footprints in the sand, and other clues cause Nathan and his friend, Lighthouse George,

to set out in dangerous waters in search of answers. Grounded in Native American heritage.

***The Ghost Children* by Eve Bunting. New York: Clarion, 1989.**

Matt's Aunt Gerda cares for and talks to life-sized wooden dolls. When two dolls are stolen, Matt and his friend Kristin set out to find the thief. Of course, they're not alive. Or are they?

***Grooves: A Kind of Mystery* by Kevin Brockmeier. New York: HarperCollins, 2006.**

Dwayne Ruggles is an average teen living in an average town. When wealthy entrepreneur Howard Thigpen visits the school, Dwayne begins noticing strange occurrences: a cloud of tiny sparks follows Thigpen around, and Thigpen brand jeans and potato chips are encoded with secret messages. Dwayne sets out to solve the mystery. A light and humorous read.

***Kiki Strike: Inside the Shadow City* by Kirsten Miller. New York: Bloomsbury, 2006.**

Ananka Fishbein discovers an underground room leading to an underground city in a New York City park. Teaming up with mysterious Kiki Strike and a group called the Irregulars, they explore the city and learn that the city may be in danger of attack by terrorists. Reviewed as a hardboiled mystery for teens, chapters end with topics such as "how to be a master of disguise" and "how to foil a kidnapping." Fans will enjoy the sequel, *Kiki Strike: The Empress's Tomb* (2007).

***The Last Treasure* by Janet S. Anderson. New York: Dutton/Penguin, 2003.**

Thirteen-year-old Ellsworth Smith lives alone with his dad. When he accepts an invitation to visit his father's family in Smith Mills, New York, he learns he must search for a hidden family treasure that only

Continued

Box 7.1   Mystery and Detective Stories for Younger Teens   *Continued*

a child related to John Matthew Smith, the family's patriarch, can find.

Lulu Dark Can See through Walls by Bennett Madison. New York: Razorbill/Penguin, 2005.

After losing her purse with Alfy Romero's phone number inside, Lulu and her friends set out to find it and become embroiled in a homicide case. Lulu's adventures continue in *Lulu Dark and the Summer of the Fox* (2006).

Spy Goddess: Live and Let Shop by Michael P. Spradlin. New York: HarperCollins, 2005.

Rachel Buchanan is a Beverly Hills teen. When she gets in trouble with the law, the judge sends her to Blackthorn Academy, a boarding school in Pennsylvania. When Rachel learns the school has secrets, she sets out to uncover them, only to become embroiled in an international espionage case. Fans will enjoy the sequel, *To Hawaii, with Love* (2006).

Three of Diamonds: Three Diamond Brothers Mysteries by Anthony Horowitz. New York: Philomel/Penguin, 2005.

In these three humorous short stories, Tim and Nick search for a missing philanthropist, get put in a Parisian prison, and are stranded on an island with a murderer.

A Tour of Evil by Suzi Wizowaty. New York: Penguin, 2005.

One by one children begin missing. An 11-year-old runaway, a foster mother, and an old man with a dreadful past must solve the mystery and save the children from an evil tour guide in a cathedral in France. Delightful, yet creepy.

Vanishing Act by John Feinstein. New York: Knopf/Random, 2006.

The second book in Feinstein's *Final Four Mystery* series, *Vanishing Act* follows Susan Carol and Stevie as they reunite at the U.S. Open as junior sports writers. There, they investigate the disappearance of a top Russian player.

The Wright 3 by Blue Balliett. New York: Scholastic, 2006.

Supersleuths Petra, Calder, and Tommy are drawn into an art mystery. Responding to a series of mysterious coincidences and accidents, the trio lead their classmates in an effort to save Frank Lloyd Wright's famous Robie House from being destroyed. This sequel to *Chasing Vermeer* (2004), an international bestseller, doesn't disappoint.

Box 7.2   Mystery Reads for Older Teens

Acceleration by Graham McNamee. New York: Random House, 2003.

Seventeen-year-old Duncan works in Lost and Found in a subway station. When he discovers a diary belonging to a serial killer, he sets out to find the man before it is too late.

Bad Kitty by Michele Jaffe. New York: HarperCollins, 2006.

Jasmine Callihan is vacationing with her father and stepmother at a posh hotel. She and her best friends, who come from Los Angeles to join her, become involved

Continued

Box 7.2   Mystery Reads for Older Teens   *Continued*

in a high-profile murder investigation. Readers need to suspend a great deal of belief to enjoy the plot twists. Hilarious dialogue and appealing characters.

Black Taxi by James Moloney. New York: HarperCollins, 2003.

When Rosie Sinclair's grandfather is jailed for a "little bit" of crime, he leaves his precious black Mercedes and cell phone in Rosie's care. Rosie is thrilled to have her own wheels and phone, but she isn't prepared for the mysterious phone calls. For readers who enjoy suspense blended with humor.

The Boy in the Burning House by Tim Wynne-Jones. New York: Farrar, Straus & Giroux, 2000.

Two years after Tim's father disappears, Tim meets Ruth Rose, stepdaughter of Father Fisher, the town pastor. When Ruth tells Tim her stepfather murdered his dad, Tim sets out to solve the mystery of his father's disappearance.

Finding Lubchenko by Michael Simmons. New York: Razorbill/Penguin, 2005.

Evan Macalister's millionaire father gives him little money, so Evan steals equipment from his dad's business and sells it over the Internet. When a man is murdered at his father's business, Evan holds the key to the murderer's identity on a stolen computer. Evan must either admit his own crime or solve the mystery himself.

Haunted by Judith St. George. New York: Penguin/Putnam, 1980.

Sixteen-year-old Alex is hired to house-sit the Von Dursts' estate following the murder-suicide of the house's owners. Alex looks forward to lying by the pool and inviting friends to parties. The house, however, is haunted by two forces: one wants to help him, the other wants him dead.

The Highest Form of Killing by Malcolm Rose. Orlando, FL: Harcourt, 1992.

Chemist Derek Thorn, his student Sylvia Cooper, and her former boyfriend Mark Little investigate the murder of Derek's sister. In searching for answers to her murder, the trio stumble upon secret chemical weapons and learn that a vial of deadly T42 has passed through security.

The Invisible by Mats Wahl. New York: Farrar, Straus & Giroux, 2007.

One Monday morning Hilmer Eriksson walks into school, only to discover that he has become invisible. That same morning, a police officer arrives to investigate his disappearance. Through shifting points of view between the officer and Hilmer, Wahl unfolds the events of a missing person's report that ends tragically.

King Dork by Frank Portman. New York: Delacorte/Random House, 2006.

Fourteen-year-old Tom Henderson is an outsider who finds solace in music and songwriting. He finds a copy of *The Catcher in the Rye,* owned by his father, a detective who died mysteriously, and his life changes forever. The book includes secret codes written by his father, and Tom sets out to solve the mystery.

Phoning a Dead Man by Gillian Cross. New York: Holiday House, 2002.

Told that her fiancé, a demolition expert, has been killed in an accident in Russia, Annie Glasgow, confined to a wheelchair, doesn't believe authorities are honest about John's death. She and John's sister, Hayley, travel to Russia in search of the truth. Meanwhile John, lost in the Siberian wilderness, is running for his life.

The She by Carol Plum-Ucci. Orlando, FL: Harcourt, 2003.

Eight years ago, Evan Barrett's parents were lost at sea, and Evan listened in terror to his parents' frenzied Mayday radio calls. Now 17, Evan returns to his former seaside home, where he relives that frightening night and investigates serious allegations against his parents. Could his parents still be alive, or were his parents devoured by a legendary sea creature?

Continued

Box 7.2   Mystery Reads for Older Teens   *Continued*

***So Yesterday* by Scott Westerfeld. New York: Razorbill/Penguin, 2004.**

Corporations pay Hunter Braque, a New York City teenager, to spot the newest cool trends. When Hunter's boss goes missing, he teams up with Jen James, a fashion innovator, to solve Mandy's disappearance. Reads also as a satire on hip-hop and pop culture.

***Things Hoped For* by Andrew Clements. New York: Philomel/Penguin, 2006.**

Seventeen-year-old Gwen lives with her grandfather in Manhattan, where she attends music school. When her grandfather disappears, she teams up with another music student to solve the mystery of his disappearance. A multilayered novel about friendship, family, and love and a follow-up to *Things Not Seen* (2002).

***Tightrope* by Gillian Cross. New York: Holiday House, 1999.**

Ashley, who cares for her invalid mother, is a graffiti tagger in her grungy English neighborhood. When someone starts leaving her threatening notes, she can't turn to the police—in her neighborhood police are not popular. Ashley searches for the culprit on her own. A spine-tingling mystery thriller.

***Wolf Rider* by Avi. New York: Simon Pulse/Simon & Schuster, 1986.**

Andy Zadinski receives a phone call from an unidentified man who claims to have murdered a college student at the college where Andy's father works as a professor. No one, not even the police, takes him seriously. Andy investigates and learns the girl isn't dead, not yet at least. He believes with time the caller will kill his victim.

Suspense Thrillers

A book may be classified as mystery and thriller, thriller and horror, or even mystery/thriller/horror, but each genre has distinguishing characteristics. Mysteries are challenges; they usually have readers piecing together bits of evidence to solve whodunit puzzles. Edge-of-the-seat, nail-biting suspense may or may not be present; they emphasize character development. A thriller on the other hand, thrills; it is action packed, suspenseful, fast moving, and contains scary scenes and may or may not contain a mystery. *Secret Window* (2004) starring Johnny Depp, the film based on Stephen King's novella "Secret Window, Secret Garden," is a familiar example of the thriller genre.[11]

The most differentiating characteristic between mysteries and thrillers is the thriller's stronger plot and action emphasis compared with the mystery's focus on character development. Unlike the mystery protagonist concerned with solving or uncovering a crime, the thriller protagonist is more concerned with escaping from danger, saving someone, or thwarting the plans of an evil pursuer or perpetrator. Although thrillers may contain horror elements, they may go light on gore, slasher scenes, and may or may not

---

[11]"Secret Window, Secret Garden" appears in *Four Past Midnight* (1990), a collection of four King novellas.

contain ghosts, shapeshifters, the supernatural, and other defining horror elements. In most thrillers the protagonist is placed in a dangerous situation and must race against time to escape, save someone, or carry out a difficult task or assignment. The protagonist usually knows, or learns early on, the enemy. In Neal Shusterman's *Full Tilt* (2003), for instance, 16-year-old Blake meets a strange female who invites him to an invitation-only carnival. Once Blake enters the bizarre and eerie grounds, he can't turn back; to his horror, he must survive seven treacherous carnival rides before dawn in order to save himself and his brother, Quinn. Blake doesn't solve a mystery. He fights for survival, for a way out of the bizarre carnival world.

Lois Duncan, one of the best-known young adult thriller writers, is a master at writing cliff-hanging chapters and creating realistic situations. In *Don't Look Behind You* (1989), for example, April's father, an FBI informant, testifies against a notorious drug dealer, and the family must relocate under a federal witness protection program to flee a hired killer. April, naïve and lonely, tries contacting her former boyfriend, placing the family in jeopardy. The book becomes difficult to put down once April and her grandmother become involved in a high-speed chase. In the author box, Duncan describes her development as a writer of suspense and outlines elements in good suspense/thriller stories.

Teaching the Young Adult Suspense/ Thriller Novel   by Lois Duncan

I can't remember a time when I didn't think of myself as a writer. When I was 3 years old, I was dictating stories to my parents; and, as soon as I learned to print, I was setting them on paper. I started submitting manuscripts to magazines when I was 10 and became published at 13. Seeing that first story in print was the most thrilling experience of my life.

Nobody taught me how to write. I learned from rejection—figuring out why editors sent a story back to me, rewriting it to make it better, and resubmitting it. As with most beginning writers, my main problem was structure. That's a hard concept for kids, who generally assume that words flow out of the author's fingertips like water from a faucet. With certain types of writing, like poetry and slice-of-life essays, that occasionally may be true. But in the type of writing I'm best known for—mystery and suspense—structure is essential. The plot is the skeleton beneath the story's flesh, holding it up and giving it a shape. All the pretty words in the world won't make a mystery story work unless it is structurally sound.

If I were teaching young readers about suspense novels, I would ask them, first, to read the book for pleasure, without any attempt to analyze it. Then, once they've read it and either liked or disliked it,

Continued

Teaching the Young Adult Suspense/ Thriller Novel   *Continued*

I would ask them to compare their personal reaction to the story to the three elements of plot: (1) having a character the reader likes, (2) reaching an important goal, (3) overcoming increasingly difficult obstacles. Each of those elements is crucial. If readers don't relate to the character, they won't be emotionally invested in what happens to him/her. If the goal isn't important, there won't be any tension because it won't matter if the hero reaches that goal or not.

With those two elements in place—the hero and the goal—you have a situation, but you don't have a plot. That only occurs when the author inserts the third element and places obstacles between the hero and the goal. The *process* of the hero surmounting those obstacles is what makes a *story*.

The reason that mystery/suspense is such a popular genre is that the goal is the strongest one possible—survival. Between the hero and survival lie frightening dangers for the hero to confront. The closer together the author places those obstacles, the "faster paced" the story becomes, until, toward the end, the hero is racing toward his destiny, leaping over boulders as he runs. When the peril becomes so great that the reader fears the hero will not come through alive, we have the moment of "dark before the dawn." Then the hero overcomes that final obstacle and survives.

Of course, interesting characters, vivid descriptions, and realistic dialogue are important as well. But, for a suspense novel, the plot is what carries the story.

Copyright Lois Duncan, 2008

Official Web site: www.loisduncan.arquettes.com

Lois Duncan has written more than a dozen thriller novels and earned the Margaret A. Edwards Award for a distinguished body of literature for young adults in 1992. Popular titles not mentioned in this chapter include *Summer of Fear* (1976), *Killing Mr. Griffin* (1978), *Stranger with My Face* (1981), *The Third Eye* (1984), *Locked in Time* (1985), and *The Twisted Window* (1987).

We often lump mysteries and thrillers together, mostly because a good thriller keeps readers on the edge, much like a mystery, by withholding key information. For example, Nancy Werlin's *The Killer's Cousin* (1998), a suspense thriller, has a tense plot but no mystery: David Yaffe, acquitted of murdering his girlfriend, moves to Massachusetts to live with his aunt and uncle and finish his senior year. David immediately knows his young cousin, Lily, has emotional problems; as no one listens to his concerns, Lily's behavior escalates, endangering her family's life, David's, and her own. The story is a definite page-turner; however, both the reader and David are keenly award of Lily's alarming and dangerous behavior. What the reader doesn't know is what Lily will do next.

Thrillers can be divided into numerous, but arbitrary, categories (e.g., mystery thrillers, murder thrillers, psychological thrillers, forensic thrillers, legal thrillers, spy thrillers, romance thrillers, suspense thrillers, science fiction and fantasy thrillers, serial killer thrillers, and supernatural thrillers). *Twisted Summer* (1996) by Willo Davis Roberts may be classified as both mystery and murder thriller. This fast-paced and short murder mystery engages readers to the riveting end. Cici Linden's summer vacation at her grandparents' lake house takes an unexpected turn when she learns the brother of the boy she likes has been convicted of murder. Believing Brody is innocent, she searches for the real killer, only someone doesn't want her uncovering the truth.

Shusterman's *Full Tilt* (2003) may best be described as psychological thriller. Each of the seven rides that Blake endures is based on seven of his personal fears and demons. To save himself and his brother, the narrator must face his fears in *Paranoid Park* (Nelson, 2006), a more recent psychological thriller. In this work, the unnamed narrator accidentally kills a security guard with his skateboard. Consumed by guilt and fear, he agonizes over whether he should tell. Internal dialogue takes readers into the teen's psyche. Master of the supernatural thriller, Joan Lowery Nixon uses elements of the supernatural in many of her thriller novels, most of which contain elements of mystery. The protagonist in *Whispers from the Dead* (1989) makes contact with the spirit world after a near-death experience, then feels haunted when her family moves to a new home. Immediately upon entering the house for the first time, Sarah feels a cold presence. In addition to these selections, titles in Box 7.3 provide a good starting point for readers eager for a good page-turner.

Lois Duncan's father, Joseph Janney Steinmetz, an internationally acclaimed photographer, captured this photo of Lois around age 14.

Box 7.3   Thrillers and Chillers for Teens

***All Hallows' Eve: 13 Stories* by Vivian Vande Velde. Orlando, FL: Harcourt, 2006.**

A collection of bloodcurdling horror short stories about Halloween—ghosts, vampires, and nasty pranks.

***The Book of Dead Days* by Marcus Sedgwick. New York: Lamb/Random House, 2004.**

Valerian, a magician, must save his own life during the dead days, the time between Christmas and New Year's Eve, or pay the consequences for an agreement he made with evil years ago. With the help of his servant, known as Boy, and Willow, a smart orphan girl, Valerian digs in cemeteries and journeys to a dark city in an effort to save his life.

***The Creek* by Jennifer L. Holm. New York: HarperCollins, 2003.**

Penny's suburban neighborhood believes a young man recently released from a juvenile home is the psychopath terrorizing their neighborhood. When a child is murdered, the community is forced to look inside themselves for the perpetrator. A suspense thriller, well plotted, with even tension (suspense) throughout.

Continued

Box 7.3   Thrillers and Chillers for Teens   *Continued*

Diamonds in the Shadow by Caroline B. Cooney. New York: Random House, 2007.

Working through their church, a Connecticut family shelters an African refugee family. Despite mounting evidence, they don't realize the Amabos have a dangerous past and aren't a family.

Echo by Kate Morgenroth. New York: Simon & Schuster, 2007.

Justin witnesses the horrific death of his younger brother Mark. Deeply affected by Mark's death, Justin isolates himself and begins hearing unrelenting voices in his head. As the dark story unfolds, Justin struggles to distinguish between reality and illusion. What will Justin do? What does he know about Mark's death? A fast-paced psychological thriller.

First Shot by Walter Sorrells. New York: Penguin, 2007.

David Crandall's mother was murdered, and the crime remains unsolved. David, a high school senior, can't rest without knowing who killed her. In his search for clues, he uncovers a family secret involving embezzlement and observes his father burying a rifle. Could his father be the killer?

Gothic! Ten Original Dark Tales edited by Deborah Noyes. Cambridge, MA: Candlewick Press, 2004.

A collection of horror stories by some of the best in the genre: Vivian Velde, M. T. Anderson, Celia Rees, Neil Gaiman, and more. Stories evolve around a wide array of characters and spirits: a lovesick count, a serial killer, a possessed house, witches, and vampires.

Horowitz Horror: Stories You'll Wish You'd Never Read by Anthony Horowitz. New York: Philomel/Penguin, 2006.

A collection of nine macabre tales set in England in which everything appears normal. Each tale focuses on an everyday item with creepy qualities: a bathtub, camera, a bus, and more.

The Intruders by E. E. Richardson. New York: Delacorte/Random House, 2006.

Joel Demetrius and his sister, Cassie, move into a new house with their new stepbrothers, Tim and Damon. Cassie, who resents her stepbrothers, is blamed for strange occurrences; however, when Joel and Tim begin having the same bizarre dreams, the four stepsiblings begin searching for the intruder who is wrecking their house and lives.

Jude by Kate Morgenroth. New York: Simon & Schuster, 2004.

When Jude's drug-dealing father is murdered, Jude is sent to live with his mother, a DA running for mayor, to attend an elite private school. A schoolmate dies of a drug overdose and Jude is implicated in his death. Harry, his mother's deputy police commissioner's boyfriend, promises to clear Jude if Jude will help in an elaborate scheme to win his mother the election. Jude confesses to a crime he didn't commit, only to learn that Harry had no intention of proving his innocence. Fast-placed plot with well-developed characters.

Premonitions by Jude Watson. New York: Scholastic, 2004.

Gracie is haunted by premonitions that have disturbed her since before her mother's death. She knows how to deal with them, but when Emily, her best friend, disappears, Gracie must use the premonitions to help save her friend. Fans will also enjoy *Disappearance* (2005), the second book in this series.

Shock Point by April Henry. New York: Penguin/Putnam, 2006.

Cassie Streng's stepfather gives dangerous experimental drugs to his psychiatric patients. Cassie plans to expose him, but Cassie is thrown into the back of a van and taken to a boot camp for troubled teens in Mexico. Boot camp is a horrific place where teens

Continued

Box 7.3   Thrillers and Chillers for Teens   *Continued*

die. Can Cassie find a way out and expose the truth about the camp?

The Silent Room by Walter Sorrells. New York: Dutton/Penguin, 2006.

Oz's stepfather, a vicious man, sends Oz to Briarwood School, a prisonlike boarding school deep in a southern Georgia swamp. Isolated from the world with no method of escape, Oz experiences and witnesses the evilness of the boarding school staff. Oz must escape before he and his friends end up dead.

Storm Catchers by Tim Bowler. New York: McElderry Books/Simon & Schuster, 2001.

Fin and his family live on the stormy English coast. When Fin's younger sister is kidnapped in the middle of a storm, Fin feels guilty for leaving her alone. Fin's younger brother is lured to the cliff's edge by the voice of a spectral ghost, and Fin sets out to stop him and rescue their sister from the teenage boy who is hiding her in a cave. The story moves fast, and tension builds evenly and rapidly.

Horror and the Supernatural

Why would anyone enjoy reading about a cannibal freak like Hannibal Lecter who opens a victim's skull, removes part of the brain, sautés then eats it? (Harris, 1999). To non–horror lovers, horror fans seem sick, perverted, or twisted. We watch horrific movies, hands over faces, eyes peeking through, like *Psycho* (1960), *The Texas Chainsaw Massacre* (1974), and *The Silence of the Lambs* (1991).[12] We read books that keep us awake at night, fodder for nightmares, such as Stephen King's *Cell* (2006) and *The Shining* (1977) and Jeffery Deaver's *The Bone Collector* (1997). We don't sharpen axes or oil chainsaws in our basements. Yet we read books like these, along with outlandish stories about giant mutant Easter bunnies, enormous cockroaches, silk-spinning, paralyzing spiders, and bloodsucking mosquitoes. We're not alone in our delight; teens comprise a good portion of the horror fan base.

Over the years, horror (much as fantasy and science fiction) has been viewed as poor literature. "Real literature" has been serious works such as problem novels and historical fiction—stories with messages and morals. This attitude is easy to understand when we reflect on the history of education, the moral obligations our forefathers believed in. Though we've shifted somewhat from didactic, moralistic, virtuous stories of the early 1900s, teaching realistic, serious fiction about human experiences and human responses remains with us.[13] School shootings, psycho killings, abuse, and war make us nervous about what students read and view on TV and computers. Horror

---

[12]All three movies were loosely based on the real-life murderer, Ed Gein—perhaps the most infamous but least remembered serial killer of all time. Hannibal Lecter is possibly the most famous all-time fictitious character.

[13]Any genre has the possibility of teaching us about humanity. Chapter 8 features a section on fantasy literature and social commentary.

scares us. Those of us who aren't horror fans walk away from a blood, guts, and gore movie asking:

- What kind of person *likes* this stuff? *Weirdoes.*
- What's the purpose? *No point.*
- What's the value? *None.*
- Why do people like this? *I don't know.*

However, horror fans know. In *Presenting Young Adult Horror Fiction* (1992), Kies makes a case for the horror fan base:

> As lovers of horror know, the answer is easy. Horror scares us, and the relief following the realization that the horror is not real brings pleasure. Horror is fun just because it is scary and shocking. Not only does it scare and shock those of us who read [and view] horror, but it has the added value of scaring and shocking those who wonder how anyone could read [and view] the stuff in the first place. It is especially fun, of course, to shock those in authority, such as parents, teachers, and librarians. (p. 2)

And it's the latter statement that scares many adults.

Mention horror and one writer comes to the minds of all readers: Stephen King. Author of more than 50 horror/fantasy novels (most making the bestseller list) and innumerable short stories, King is synonymous with horror.[14] King identifies three levels of horror: terror, fear, and revulsion (cited in Kies, 1992). Terror is the finest, most intense emotion the writer of horror fiction can evoke, followed by fear, a somewhat less emotive response. We can fear something but still not be terrorized by it. Revulsion is the "gag" factor—a human head bursts open and worms crawl out. It creates the least level of intensity. The selections discussed in this chapter span all levels and examine three broad, overlapping young adult horror subgenres: gothic horror, extreme horror, and creatures (shapeshifters, demons, and ghosts).

Gothic Horror

The word *gothic* originates from an early Germanic tribe, the Goths, who participated in the destruction of Rome. With time, the term came to mean "Germanic," then "medieval" (Abrams, 2005, p. 117). The *gothic novel*, also called *gothic romance,* is commonly believed to have begun with Horace Walpole's *The Castle of Otranto: A Gothic Story* (1764). This work heavily influenced literature for decades. Even today's horror writers for both young and old remain heavily influenced by the gothic tradition.[15]

Gothic literature has discernible characteristics. Setting, for instance, plays a fundamental role in gothic fiction. Gothic writers may situate their stories in medieval times, such as young adult author Clare B. Dunkle in her work *By These Ten Bones* (2005). In this story, set in the medieval Scottish

---

[14]King has penned one novel marketed to the young adult audience, *The Girl Who Loved Tom Gordon* (1999).
[15]The gothic tradition has influenced such writers as Bram Stoker, Mary Shelley, Ann Radcliffe (credited with creating today's standard gothic form), Edgar Allan Poe, Nathaniel Hawthorne, Charles Dickens, Robert Louis Stevenson, Charlotte and Emily Brontë, Oscar Wilde, and even writers today such as Stephen King and Anne Rice.

Highlands, a mysterious woodcarver with a terrifying secret falls in love with young Maddie. Maddie must search for a way to protect her community and save the woodcarver from an ancient evil spell. Others set them in European countries such as Spain and Italy. Whether taking place during medieval times or later, stories typically take place in buildings with gothic architecture[16]—eerie castles, mansions, monasteries, and cathedrals with secret passageways and winding stairways, dungeons, torture chambers— all of which are by and large remote and falling into ruin and decay. Much of the story takes place in darkness, dreary, damp, and foggy weather, and many are set in the United Kingdom, most in England.

Libba Bray's national bestseller, *A Great and Terrible Beauty* (2003), and its sequels, *Rebel Angels* (2005) and *Sweet Far Thing* (2007), are set in an eerie and mysterious 19th-century English boarding school. After her mother's horrific death in India, 16-year-old Gemma is sent to the Spence Academy in London, where she discovers her connection with the supernatural and an obscure cult called the Order.

Chris Wooding's *The Haunting of Alaizabel Cray* (2001) has a Jack-the-Ripper-like Victorian London setting. Note the effect created by word choice in this dark, descriptive passage:

> There was a chill in the air . . . a cold nip that had crept in from the Thames and settled into the bones of London. And of course there was the fog, which laid itself over everything like a gossamer blanket and softened the glow of the black lamp-posts to a haze. The fog came almost every night in autumn, as much a part of London as the hansom cabs that rattled around Piccadilly Circus or the stout peelers that walked their beats north of the great river. Not to the south, though; not in the Old Quarter. That was the domain of the mad and the crooked and the things best left unthought of. (p. 1)

Dangerous supernatural "wych-kin" and macabre humans loiter around corners and in alleyways, waiting to prey on humans. Seventeen-year-old Thaniel Fox, a wych-hunter, stumbles upon Alaizabel Cray, a crazed young woman possessed by a demon. Thaniel sets out to rescue Alaizabel from Thatch (the demon) and the menacing faction who placed the evil spirit in Alaizabel's body.

Gothic novels typically evoke both physical and psychological terror. They usually contain mystery, ghosts, phantoms, demons, necromancers, or the supernatural; curses, madness, death and blood-curling scenes; and youthful handsome heroes and heroines who play both victim and hero (Cuddon, 2000). Traditionally, females fall victim to villainous, malevolent males or vampires, werewolves, demons, ghosts, or monsters; however, females may also be *femmes fatales*,[17] female protagonists who deliberately mislead and ensnare hapless males, usually by using their beauty and charm. They also oppose the traditional subservient female role.

A superb example of a young adult gothic novel employing most, if not all, of these characteristics is Alisa M. Libby's *The Blood Confession* (2006),

---

[16]Gothic architecture includes pointed arches and vaults, stained glass, nooks and crannies, gargoyles, and grotesques.
[17]*Femme fatale* is French for "deadly woman."

Reprinted by permission of Penguin Young Readers Group © 2006.

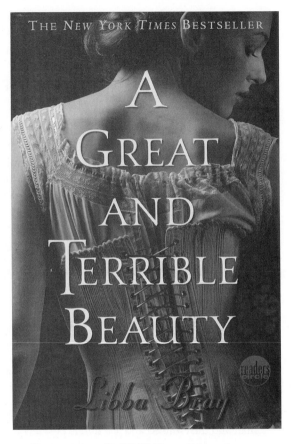

Used by permission of Dell Publishing, a division of Random House, Inc.

set in 16th-century Hungary. Countess Erzebet Bizecka, a femme fatale, lives in a remote castle with her insane mother, who is confined to one wing; her disapproving father is absent for months and/or years at a time. Erzebet has no desire to marry and lives a solitary life. When she learns of the mythic power of blood to create eternal youth and beauty, with the encouragement of Sinestra, her ghostlike lover, she weaves a deceptive web to ensnare virgin servants. Drawing a group of girls to her through coercion and material bribery, Erzebet bleeds them so she may cleanse herself with their blood. As Erzebet becomes more obsessed with the immortality of the blood ritual and the addictive power of Sinestra, the servants—blood girls—help brutally butcher girls so Erzebet may bathe in their blood. The murders take place in the darkness of the castle dungeon:

> The pulley system had been reconstructed in the dungeon chamber, just as it had been set up to bleed the deer dry [Erzebet understood her attraction to blood by watching servants slaughter a deer]. The tub was placed beneath the pulley, and the grate was removed. While Dariah was

dying, the girls bound her feet with rope. She was strung up by the pulley, suspended over the tub. I administered the fatal wound, slipping the blade easily between her ribs.

Sarah moved forward to help me quickly undress. I lay down in the tub beneath the dying girl, her blood flowing directly from her body onto my skin. The sight of it mesmerized me: this was my greatest triumph, drawing one life directly into my own. (p. 354)

Libby's grisly story is based on real-life Hungarian Countess Bathory, who lived during the 16th century. In the author box, Libby addresses the creation of *The Blood Confession.*

On Writing *The Blood Confession*   by Alisa M. Libby

When I was a teenager, I borrowed an anthology of vampire stories from the Natick Public Library and read the legend of Countess Bathory, a 16th-century Hungarian countess who believed that bathing in the blood of virgin girls would preserve her youth and beauty. According to that book, the countess murdered as many as 650 virgins in her quest for eternal youth. Since many of the victims were poor women from the surrounding countryside, and because Countess Bathory was part of the wealthy nobility, her crimes were overlooked.

The countess's crimes both horrified and fascinated me. The story stuck with me, and years later I began to write about the countess. But how would I tell her story? Inspiration aside, many questions will arise as you decide how to handle your subject matter. The more you write, the more you will discover the story you want to tell.

An essential part of writing any novel is getting to know your character, and historical research can be a valuable part of this process. Your character is greatly influenced by her daily life and ritual, where she lives, what she eats, what she reads, and what images surround her on a daily basis. Beyond making your writing historically accurate, these details can shape your character and establish the setting and mood of the book.

Next, investigate your character's motivation for her actions. I find that engendering some form of empathy for my main character helps me learn more about her and understand her actions, if not condone them. In the case of *The Blood Confession,* I wanted to figure out how someone would be driven not only to kill, but to bathe in her victim's blood. What was she thinking? How could she justify her actions? She

would have to be crazy, wouldn't she? While this is probably the most accurate explanation, it didn't answer my question in a satisfying way. I wanted to figure out her motive, her thoughts, which would be more complex and interesting than a purely psychiatric evaluation.

So how could I empathize with a murderess? With writing and revising, I discovered two important friendships at the center of Erzebet's story. One is her close friendship with Marianna, a young girl who lives in the village of Novoe Mesto. The other is her romantic relationship with a mysterious stranger named Sinestra. I learned a lot about Erzebet by seeing her respond to those around her, particularly to Marianna. This made Erzebet's character more human, more real. Before she became a murderess, she was merely a young girl full of complex insecurities. From here, I could follow along with her on the path to her madness.

Extreme Horror

David J. Schow, co-writer of the *Texas Chainsaw Massacre* screenplay, coined the word *splatterpunk* in 1986 to describe a realistic modern horror subgenre distinguished by disturbing blood and guts scenes (Carroll, 1995). Splatterpunk, cousin to science fiction cyperpunk, comprises much of the extreme horror genre. Unlike other horror subgenres, extreme horror is realistic, usually jettisoning supernatural and fantastic elements for serial killers and psychopaths. We're all familiar with classic films like John Carpenter's *Halloween* (1978) and Wes Craven's *Scream* (1996), and we're familiar with bestselling adult authors who enthrall and/or sicken us with grisly psychopathic serial killings (e.g., Thomas Harris, Patricia Cornwell, Jeffery Deaver, and James Patterson).

Extreme horror is sparse in the traditional young adult genre for several reasons. Obviously, issues surrounding violent content raise censorship concerns (see the censorship discussion in Chapter 3). Some parents allow their teens to read and view extreme horror, but schools are more leery. Teen writers seldom delve into the topic; they, too, see a boundary issue. Also, extreme horror is considered by many to be the antithesis of "quality writing." In an effort to create the extreme, to create as much gore as possible, most movies and novels sacrifice plot, dialogue, and character development. Nonetheless, many teens do read and view extreme horror, and a few quality works less extreme than traditional splatterpunk exist.

Richard Peck's *Are You in the House Alone?* (1976),[18] a quality work minus the gore factor, is likely the first novel targeting the young adult audience that features a psychotic character. In this chiller, a 16-year-old girl receives threatening phone calls while babysitting and anonymous threatening notes in her school locker; ultimately, she is a crime victim. The novel is important because it raises the question, Should a victim be blamed for a crime?

In 1991, Scholastic published Patricia Windsor's *The Christmas Killer*, one of the first young adult novels featuring a serial killer. Rose Potter has disturbing dreams and visions when a local girl, Nancy Emerson, is murdered. After realizing her psychic powers are warnings of other murders, Rose shares her information with the police. Though skeptical at first, they eventually seek Rose's help in solving the crimes, and Rose becomes the next target. Windsor doesn't shy away from realistic, extreme horror. In her most recent book, *Nightwood* (2006), Casey and her two friends, Maryann and Gena, skip their senior trip to spend the weekend in Casey's parents' Georgia cabin. Unbeknownst to MaryAnn and Gena, Casey plans to surprise her boyfriend and his buddies, who are vacationing at the resort. Mutilated animals, a brutal murder, cannibalism, and the disappearance of Gena and Jeff turn the vacation into a nightmare. Hannibal Lecter fans—and there are many among our high school students—will enjoy this creepy, ghastly, and suspenseful story, though classroom teachers may shy away from its gruesomeness.

---

[18]*Are You in the House Alone?* was made into a movie in 1978.

One of the edgiest young adult horror novels in today's market is Dean Vincent Carter's *The Hand of the Devil* (2006). Ashley Reeves, a writer for a science magazine, receives an unusual letter about the Ganges Red mosquito,[19] penned by Dr. Mather who lives on a secluded island. Lured by the uniqueness of the mosquito, Reeves visits Dr. Mather. Reeves wrecks his boat and is stranded on the island. He discovers that the doctor conducts gruesome experiments on human beings, and he is the next victim. In the following passage, Reeves tumbles into a pit of decomposing bodies:

> I plunged headfirst into the mound of corpses. Luckily, I had my arms in front of me to soften the impact, but I was still left dazed. In my fall I had kicked over the lamps by the doorway, in addition to the lamp in the pit, so that I was in darkness. As I pushed myself onto my elbows, I felt something soft and wet yield beneath me. I slowly turned and sat up, not wanting the pile to collapse. The smell was nauseating now, and each breath brought me closer to madness. . . . The smell was in my lungs, my throat, my sinuses, everywhere. I tried slowing my breathing, but the only result was an oxygen deficit, which I had to compensate for by gulping down huge mouthfuls of the detestable air.
>
> My right foot started to slip between two bodies, so I shifted my position to avoid being sucked down. (p. 119)

You may be saying, "I can't teach these books." Every title introduced in this text, however, isn't introduced with the intent that it be taught. A role of any good teacher is to instill in students the desire to be lifelong readers. Therefore, we shouldn't simply examine young literature through the lens of what we can or cannot teach in the classroom. We should become familiar with what teens read, or will be willing to read, on their own time. We should know the young adult genre inside and out: books we approve of and some we don't, books we know we can teach, those that can be on classroom and library shelves, and those better read outside school. The more we know about the reading interests and habits of teens, whether we approve or not, the more opportunities we have to connect with them and possibly encourage them to read what we value. The more we know about the genre, the better able we become to make wise choices. Most important, when we honor (and I don't mean agree with) teens' reading choices, we stand a better chance that they will respect our choices in turn.

One argument against using young adult literature in the classroom is the belief that teens should be protected from the "horrors" of the world (see Chapter 3). In the author box, nationally acclaimed horror and mystery writer Christopher Golden—author of the *Body of Evidence* series (1999) and the *Prowlers* series (2001), co-author of *The Hollow* series (2005), and regular writer for the *Buffy the Vampire* series (1997)—addresses why and how he began writing realistic stories for teens devoid of sugarcoating. His award-winning *Prowlers* series features 19-year-old Jack Dwyer whose best friend Artie is murdered. Artie appears as a ghost and warns jack about the Prowlers, evil creatures who disguise themselves as humans in order to prey on them.

---

[19]The Ganges Red mosquito drains victims' entire bodies—a "touch" of magical realism.

Writing for Teens   by Christopher Golden

When the publishing industry first developed the category *Young Adult,* or YA, the books in that category were supposed to appeal to readers in their mid to late teens. Over the years, the average age of the YA reader slid until, by the time R. L. Stine came along, YA as a segment of the marketplace was supposed to include kids aged 9 to 13.

A vacuum was created in bookstores, one that left a vital part of the reading public without anything targeted at their demographic. Older teens had very little reason to go into a bookstore, unless they had a school assignment or if they were passionate enough about reading to have jumped ahead and begun reading books written for a more mature audience.

Though publishing has been slow to catch on, some editors and publishing houses did notice this gap and have been working to address it. Fortunately, my editor at Pocket Books was one of them. She and her colleagues there had been thinking about the problem for quite some time, and Pocket had considered a number of initiatives directed at that segment of the industry.

My editor had an idea.

Fortunately for me, I had been working with her on the Buffy the Vampire Slayer license, and she approached me with this idea in the hope that we could develop it together. It was a simple, but brilliant concept—a book series about a teenage girl just entering college who takes a job working for a medical examiner.

It was an unusual way to work, to have an editor come to me with the germ of an idea. But I loved the concept, and I ran with it immediately. From that first conversation, I began to weave the story of Jenna Blake, a girl from Natick, Massachusetts, whose mother is a surgeon and whose father—whom she has rarely seen in the past 15 years—is a criminology professor at the very same university she will attend. (This became the *Body of Evidence* series.)

Jenna likes puzzles, and she likes helping people; she's very interested in medicine, and yet she is profoundly bothered by the sight of someone's blood and terrified at the thought of having someone's life in her hands. It is her father who first suggests that, perhaps, she ought to get a job as a pathology assistant working for the medical examiner. Fortunately, the university she attends also has a medical school and a teaching hospital attached. Then, of course, weird things start to happen—Hey, it's what I do.

As an assistant to the medical examiner, Jenna finds a mentor in Dr. Walter Slikowski, who admires her intuition and incisive mind. Though it never occurred to me until this very moment, it is not unlike the relationship that Mary Russell shares with Sherlock Holmes in the works of Laurie King.

So the mysteries . . . people bleeding from their ears and going into homicidal rages . . . performing bizarre rituals in order to attempt to force their soul into someone else's body . . . ripping out human hearts and eating them . . . real zombies . . . manipulating brain chemistry to create murderers . . . pyrokinetic serial killers . . .

Horror, but not the supernatural. Weird science mysteries.

And yet there's more to it than that. The real surprise for me was how much pleasure I took from exploring the attitudes of a first-year college student, returning to those days I had enjoyed so much. If that's the epicenter of my audience for this series, and for my horror series, *Prowlers,* then how fortunate for me. It is an age, and a moment, when minds are at their most adventurous.

Continued

Writing for Teens   *Continued*

I have found that if you write for those minds, the result is often a story that can easily be embraced by older readers as well. So, while *Body of Evidence* and *Prowlers* require different skills and a different focus from me than such other novels as *Strangewood, Straight on 'til Morning* and *The Ferryman*, it's my hope that in the end they all accomplish the same goal. In my adult novels, I do my best to capture ordinary people, with ordinary problems, and explore how they respond when their lives are touched by extraordinary events. And in that respect, writing for teens is no different.

Copyright Christopher Golden, 2008

Official Web site: www.christophergolden.com

Thriller fans will enjoy Golden's *The Veil* series (2006).

Creatures: Shapeshifters, Demons, and Ghosts

Horror fiction uses a wide array of nonhuman characters to create chills and humor and set mood. Creatures can be categorized into four types: the vampire (e.g., Dracula), any Jekyll/Hyde creature that shapeshifts (e.g., werewolves), human-made monsters (e.g., Frankenstein), supernatural beings (ghosts), and the unexplainable nonshapeshifting monster (e.g., aliens). Most common among these is the vampire.

Vampires, mythological creatures often believed to be undead human corpses, gain power and energy through drinking human blood. Young adult literature is filled with vampirelike creatures: some fit Bram Stoker's Dracula archetype, others break this mold. Some are frightening creatures, such as James in Stephenie Meyer's *Twilight* (2005).[20] Bella falls in love with Edward, a handsome vampire who returns her love; however, when James encounters her with Edward's vampire family, he begins stalking her, determined to make her his prey. This book and its three sequels, *New Moon* (2006), *Eclipse* (2007), and *Breaking Dawn* (2008), are lengthy. With strong character development and tight plots, they are excellent choices for advanced readers. Because of the popularity of vampire themes, vampire stories make good serializations. In the author box, Ellen Schreiber discusses the creation of her bestselling *Vampire Kisses* series (2003) and the allure of vampires.

M. T. Anderson gives readers a likeable and funny vampire in *Thirsty* (1997). Chris learns that he is destined to be a vampire and begins thirsting for human blood. He struggles to remain normal and find a cure for his vampirism. While light and funny, *Thirsty* can also be read as a morality tale: Chris struggles with his own evil nature and with doing what's right.

Young adult vampire stories are often steeped in history. Melissa de la Cruz's *Blue Bloods* (2006), for instance, is grounded in the 1600s when Miles Standish, Constance Hopkins, and others set sail to America aboard the *Mayflower*. Some passengers aboard were not escaping religious persecution: they

---

[20]See Chapter 5 for a discussion of paranormal romances.

On Writing *Vampire Kisses*   by Ellen Schreiber

I was drawn to write about vampires via the character I was writing about—Raven Madison—a lone goth girl living in a conservative town she refers to as "Dullsville." Raven's dull world as an outsider suddenly comes to life when a family moves into an abandoned mansion atop Benson Hill, and rumors begin circulating throughout her small town that they are vampires. It occurred to me that Raven would be fascinated with vampires—and dream of becoming one.

Even as a little girl, Raven is charmed by the lure of the bloodsuckers she sees on TV. Raven bonds with her father as a child when they watch scary movies together. When her younger brother is born, parental focus shifts to her younger sibling. Raven then watches the B movies alone and is comforted and kept company by screen versions of Dracula.

In writing *Vampire Kisses,* I wanted to explore the romantic vampire—with the focus being on eternal love, bonding, and allure and mystery, as opposed to blood and gore. Many things make vampires appealing—they're dangerous, seductive, and almost always sexy. Raven was attracted to that aspect of vampires, and she wanted to belong in that world.

Originally, the ending of *Vampire Kisses* was upbeat and the reader, like Raven, didn't know whether Alexander was a vampire. My HarperCollins editor, Katherine Tegen, wanted a different ending—one that wasn't tied up so neatly. I decided to make it clear that Alexander was indeed a vampire and the novel's tone became darker, but it retained comedy and sarcasm.

With the new ending, I was able to write a series and further explore Raven and Alexander's unusual relationship. I began to examine other issues such as the price of becoming a vampire, Alexander's own feeling of alienation from the violent vampire world, and the struggle of mortal and immortal love thriving together in one world. With the addition of Jagger, Luna, and Valentine, nefarious vampires from Alexander's past, the couple must keep the town safe, while also keeping themselves out of danger.

Vampires are mysterious, dangerous, dark, and sexy and can leave their mates, along with the reader, breathless. I think that is why they appeal so much to young adult readers as well as adults.

Official Web site: www.ellenschreiber.com

Ellen Schreiber is also the author of *Vampire Kisses 2: Kissing Coffins* (2005), *Vampire Kisses 3: Vampireville* (2006), *Vampire Kisses 4: Dance with a Vampire* (2007), *Teenage Mermaid* (2003a), *Comedy Girl* (2004), *Vampire Kisses: Blood Relatives,* Vol. 1 (2007a), and *Vampire Kisses 5: The Coffin Club* (2008).

were vampires who gathered in the New World and rose to prominent levels of power and wealth. Readers move forward in time to a prestigious New York City private high school. Fifteen-year-old Schuyler notices unusual blue veins on her arms, craves raw meat, and is haunted by the mysterious death of a female schoolmate.

Werewolves, mythological individuals who crave human flesh and shapeshift into wolves usually during a full moon, are common in young adult fiction.[21] Werewolf fans are familiar with the film *The Howling* (1981), its sequels, and *Teen Wolf* (1987), featuring Michael J. Fox. Werewolves

---

[21]The concept of shapeshifting during a full moon is a modern werewolf trait.

appear in numerous young adult classic series: C. S. Lewis's *Chronicles of Narnia* (1950), Terry Pratchett's *Discworld* (1983), and J. K. Rowling's *Harry Potter* series (1997). Stephen Cole's *The Wereling: Wounded* (2003) is the first book in a later series containing strong werewolf themes.

In *The Wolving Time* (2003) by Patrick Jennings, Laszlo Emberek is torn between tending his family's sheep and the werewolf life of his parents. As a 13-year-old, Laszlo knows his "change" nears. Can he maintain human traits of kindness and compassion? Or is he destined to become a beast? Though Laszlo lives during the medieval era, teens can relate to his internal struggle. A more recent story with a werewolf theme is Cynthia Leitich Smith's *Tantalize* (2007). Werewolves and vampires exist in 17-year-old Quincie Morris's world; however, when multiple murders occur, Quincie worries that her friend Keiren could be the killer.

David Stahler Jr. creates an interesting shapeshifting character in *Doppleganger* (2006)[22] and raises an interesting question about what it means to be a monster. The narrator, the doppelganger, is raised by a non-loving mother. Once he leaves home, he must kill to assume human form, only the doppelganger doesn't like violence or hurting people. He does, though, kill a teenage boy (Chris) and assumes his role as superstar athlete and boyfriend. Ironically, Chris's father, abusive to his children and wife, is the real monster. In the author box, Stahler addresses what it means to be a monster and illustrates how a seemingly easy read can be fodder for good discussion.

What It Means to Be a Monster: Grendelescence   by David Stahler Jr.

In the high school course I teach on English literature, monsters abound. Not in the classroom itself (though in my darker moments, I wonder). Rather, they dot the literary landscape, appearing—to the delight of my adolescent students—in all different shapes and sizes. In fact, the very first character we encounter is a monster of the highest order, one of the oldest kinds around: the boogeyman.

The Anglo-Saxon Grendel is a nasty creature. Brooding and bitter, he chafes at the harpers' songs, the drunken, joyful echoes trickling down into his swamp from Herot and—like a demonic extrapolation of Dr. Seuss's Grinch (at least that old grouch never showed a penchant for Who-flesh)—creeps up in the dark, bursts into the great hall, and proceeds to wolf down as many sleepy Danes as he can get his scaly

Continued

---

[22]Dopplegangers are creatures, sometimes ghosts, who are "doubles" for living people.

What It Means to be a Monster: Grendelescence   *Continued*

paws on. And then he comes back, night after night, until a young Geatish warrior finally shows up and puts an end to the nonsense. That's about as monstrous as it gets.

The kids love Grendel. They love that—beyond the fact that he's big, walks upright, and hates harp music—he's never described in any concrete way. Though they would probably never admit it, and who can blame them, I think they also love him because he's a bit of a rebel, an irritable sulker who is clearly annoyed by anyone else's good mood. (*Grendelescence*—how's that for a neologism?) More than a few of them, even the ones who haven't read John Gardner, feel sorry for him when he drags himself, minus an arm, back to the swamps to die; they're indifferent to the notion of what would happen to them if a *real* Grendel showed up at their house in the middle of the night. Beowulf is a meany. A bully. Grendel is just doing his thing.

And that's what fascinates me: the fact that it's this side of Grendel, the animal in defeat—wounded, vulnerable, afraid—that makes him seem most human, that brings out the humanity in my students. Beowulf is too perfect, too confident. I try to tell them that Beowulf and Grendel are symbols, that they embody both what we hope for and what we fear. They're okay with that. I tell them that we all have a Grendel lurking inside us, just as we have a Beowulf waiting there to grapple with him. They question their capacity for heroism. But they have no doubts about the Grendel part.

Some of the scariest monsters—rampaging dragons, mutant sharks, gut-sucking aliens—lack a human shape. Others may have a human form but lack any sort of humanity. (Anything to do with zombies terrifies me.) But the best monsters, the ones that stay with us, that engage both our intellect and our emotions, are the ones with at least some bit of soul. And the more soul they have—in other words, the closer they get to reminding us of ourselves—the more we respond. That's why, for me, Shakespeare has the best monsters. Richard III, as shriveled and twisted as he is, as rotten and destructive as he is, never fails to seduce me with his misanthropic charm and self-pity, even as everything is crumbling around him. Macbeth is about as close as you can get to watching a man become a monster without having him grow fangs or sprout horns before your eyes. And then, at the end, he becomes a man again, shattered and alone.

In the end, most monsters suffer, deservedly so, for the suffering they inflict upon others. But the monsters I like the best are the ones who surprise me with their humanity and cause me to wonder about my own. How far away are we from the monsters within? How far away are our monsters from defeat, or even redemption? These are the questions writers must wrestle with when they creep into the dark layers of the soul.

Copyright David Stahler Jr., 2008

For more information visit the HarperCollins Web site: www.harpercollins.com

Fans might enjoy *Truesight* (2004) and *The Seer* (2007).

Some horror nonhuman characters are demonic, such as the Scourge in Sam Enthoven's *The Black Tattoo* (2006). In this richly layered story, Jack's best friend Charlie becomes obsessed with the Scourge, evident by a moving black tattoo on his back. Jack must decide whether to follow Charlie into hell in an effort to save him. The *Demonata* series (2005) by bestselling author Darren Shan loses none of the gruesomeness of the *Cirque Du Freak* series (2005–2007). The *Demonata* series opens with Grubbs Grady putting rat guts in his sister's bath towel; shortly thereafter Grubbs witnesses the chilling and brutal deaths of his family at the hands of Lord Loss, a demon who thrives on human pain.

Of course, where would horror be without apparitions—ghosts, specters, phantoms, zombies, or spirits of troubled souls? A young adult favorite is *Sweet Miss Honeywell's Revenge: A Ghost Story* (2004) by Kathryn Reiss, a story about a dollhouse with voodoo-like powers: the house seems haunted, dolls move around on their own, and strange things happen to Zibby's family that parallel events inside the dollhouse.

William Sleator writes both science fiction and horror, often blending the two. Most of his works, whether science fiction or horror, contain supernatural beings, occurrences, and beasts. In *Fingers* (1983), 15-year-old Humphrey is a pianist prodigy. When his fame wanes, his mother devises a scheme to convince people Humphrey communicates with a dead composer. Ghostly happenings suggest the dead composer has taken over Humphrey's fingers. One of Sleator's creepiest works is *The Boy Who Couldn't Die* (2004) in which 16-year-old Ken yearns for immortality. Once he has a ritual performed, Ken can't die, but he can kill. He learns he is a zombie, and the psychic who performed the ritual is using his body to do evil.

Ghosts are not always dead souls. A prime example can be found in Nina Kiriki Hoffman's *A Stir of Bones* (2003) in which a haunted house is a living, breathing thing. In Dietlof Reiche's *Ghost Ship* (2005), the bay dries up and an ancient ship appears out of nowhere. Vicki and her friend Peter set out to unravel the mystery surrounding the Storm Goddess.

Writers often create characters with psychic abilities to connect the living with the dead. For example, in *The Unseen: It Begins* (2005) by Richie Tankersley Cusick, Lucy, fearing she is being stalked, seeks shelter in a graveyard one night, only she stumbles into an open grave where a dead girl gives her psychic powers. When Marco's psychic sister sees lights in the basement in Sleator's *Marco's Millions* (2001), they discover an extraordinary tunnel. The tunnel is a passageway to bizarre creatures and spine-chilling adventures. Box 7.4 includes a sampling of books that contain shapeshifters, demons, and ghostlike beings. (Additional titles can be found in Chapter 5 under paranormal romance.) Traditional mysteries, thrillers, and grisly horror novels have a common element: they keep readers on the edge of their seats. Thus they are good selections for motivating reluctant readers. Box 7.5 lists mystery, thriller, and horror writers of young adult literature. Box 7.6 lists adult mystery, thriller, and horror writers.

Many adult writers of mystery, thriller, and horror novels have crossed over into the young adult market (e.g., Kate Morgenroth, Walter Sorrells, Kathe Koja, John Feinstein, Carl Hiaasen, and James Patterson). Readers often question the difficulty of the transition: What does the writer have to do differently to write for a younger audience? How does he/she rethink the protagonist? Do they alter their writing style—vocabulary, sentence structure, the amount of dialogue and description? What about length? Adult crime novelist Peter Abrahams shares his thoughts and experiences in the author box.

As you read some of the horror selections in this chapter, no doubt they will shape your beliefs about horror.

Box 7.4   Vampires, Shapeshifters, Demons, and Ghosts

***Being Dead* by Vivian Vande Velde. Orlando, FL: Harcourt, 2001.**

A collection of seven chilling short stories about haunted souls who make contact with the living. The dead sleep under beds, follow teens from school, and dance with the living.

***Bloodline* by Kate Cary. New York: Razorbill/Penguin, 2005.**

A World War I British soldier returns from the trenches haunted by nightmares; he learns that his regiment commander is descended from Count Dracula. Written in journal and letter form. Readers may enjoy the sequel, *The Reckoning* (2007).

***Creepy Creatures* by R. L. Stine. Adapted & Illus. by Gabriel Hernandez, Greg Ruth, & Scott Morse. New York: Graphix/ Scholastic, 2006.**

This graphic story collection, first book in the *Goosebumps Graphix* series, features three stories based on R. L. Stine horror novels: *The Werewolf of Fever Swamp, The Scarecrow Walks at Midnight,* and *The Abominable Snowman of Pasadena.*

***Dangerous Girls* by R. L. Stine. New York: HarperCollins, 2003.**

Sixteen-year-old Destiny and her twin sister are turned into vampires at a summer camp. When they return home, they set out to find the Restorer, someone who can make them normal.

***Demon in My View* by Amelia Atwater-Rhodes. New York: Dell Laurel-Leaf/ Random House, 2000.**

High school senior Jessica Allodola, an outcast in her school, writes vampire tales; however, when a character in her story appears as a student in her school, Jessica doesn't know his intentions toward her. Does he want to harm her? Seduce her? As she searches for an answer in her writing, she encounters vampires, witches, and other supernatural beings.

***Dreadful Sorry* by Kathryn Reiss. Orlando, FL: Harcourt, 1993.**

Seventeen-year-old Molly has recurring nightmares after she almost drowns. Shortly afterward she begins witnessing events through the eyes of a girl who lived in her father's house more than a century earlier.

***The Ghost behind the Wall* by Melvin Burgess. New York: Henry Holt, 2003.**

David sneaks through ventilation shafts in his apartment and pulls pranks on other tenants. His antics awaken the ghost of a boy who holds a grudge against an elderly tenant in David's London apartment.

***Masquerade: A Blue Bloods Novel* by Melissa de la Cruz. New York: Simon & Schuster, 2007.**

Blue Bloods are mysteriously dying, and Schuyler Van Alen wants to know why. She travels to Italy in search of answers, only the real danger remains at home where Blue Bloods are preparing for the Four Hundred Ball, a fashionable gala for rich, powerful, nonhumans. A sequel to *Blue Bloods* (2006).

***Monster Blood Tattoo Book 1: Foundling* by D. M. Cornish. New York: Penguin/ Putnam, 2006.**

A foundling boy leaves the orphanage that has been his home and plunges into a world where humans battle monsters and beast slayers are given a tattoo mark. A complex story reminiscent of J. R. R. Tolkien. Fans may enjoy the sequel, *Lamplighter* (2008).

***My Father the Werewolf* by Henry Garfield. New York: Atheneum/Simon & Schuster, 2005.**

After Miranda and Danny's father is bitten by a werewolf, the family moves to Maine so their father can isolate himself on a nearby desert island during the full moon. The ocean freezes, connecting the island with the mainland, and the brother and sister pair must save the mainland from their father.

Continued

Box 7.4   Vampires, Shapeshifters, Demons, and Ghosts   *Continued*

The Old Willis Place: A Ghost Story by Mary Downing Hahn. New York: Clarion, 2004.

Diana befriends the daughter of the caretaker of a haunted house. Her newfound friendship leads to releasing the demonic spirit of a crazy woman who once lived in the old house. Ghost fans may enjoy *All the Lovely Bad Ones* (2008).

Poison by Chris Wooding. New York: Scholastic, 2005.

Poison, a stubborn, quarrelsome, and difficult girl, searches for the Phaerie Lord after evil faeries kidnap her sister. Her journey takes Poison into a dangerous world of murder and intrigue.

Vampirates: Demons of the Ocean by Justin Somper. New York: Little, Brown, 2006.

Twins Connor and Grace are shipwrecked and separated. Connor is saved by a pirate ship, Grace by mystifying vampire pirates. The two long to find each other, and danger lurks around the corner. The twins continue their adventures in *Vampirates: Tide of Terror* (2007) and *Vampirates: Blood Captain* (2008).

Water Shaper by Laura Williams McCaffrey. New York: Clarion, 2006.

An outsider in her father's court, Princess Margot goes to live with her mother's people in the Western Isles. King Orrin, a holy man, takes Margot in; however, when he demands the magical book belonging to her dead mother, Margot finds herself in danger. Margot discovers she has developing powers that allow her to visit a kingdom beneath the sea.

The Wereling series (*Wounded* #1) by Stephen Cole. New York: Razorbill/Penguin, 2005.

Teenagers Tom Anderson and Kate Folan flee from Kate's werewolf family. They take a cross-country journey in hopes of finding a mysterious man whom they think can prevent them from becoming werewolves. Sequels include *Prey* (2005a) and *Resurrection* (2005b).

Box 7.5   Mystery, Thriller, and Horror Writers Who Have Made a Significant Impact on YA Literature

Amelia Atwater-Rhodes. The teen queen of horror fiction, Atwater-Rhodes published her first novel, *In the Forest of the Night* (1999), when she was 15. Since that time, she has published one book each subsequent year. Among her works is *The Kiesha'ra* series, a five-book series about shapeshifters beginning with *Hawksong* (2003). She has been called the Stephen King and Anne Rice of young adult horror.

Anthony Horowitz. Horowitz is known for the comic edge he brings to writing. His *Diamond Brothers* series (2005) features the world's worst detectives: Tim and Nick Diamond. His blockbuster *Alex Rider* series (Book 1: *Stormbreaker*, 2001) and his follow-up *The Gatekeepers* series (Book 1: *Raven's Gate*, 2005) have catapulted him to the top of the thriller genre. For older teens, these series contain less humor, but plenty of crime, gun fights, mayhem, and tension that keep readers returning for more. *Stormbreaker* has also been made into a graphic novel by Antony Johnston, Kanako Damerum, and Yuzuru Takasaki for Philomel/Penguin (2006).

Caroline B. Cooney. *The Face on the Milk Carton* was published in 1990. Two decades later it remains widely read and has earned its place among young adult classics. When 15-year-old Janie Johnson sees a picture of a 3-year-old missing child on a milk carton, she instantly knows she is that person and sets

Continued

Box 7.5   Mystery, Thriller, and Horror Writers Who Have Made a Significant Impact on YA Literature   *Continued*

out to learn her true identity. Fans, unsatisfied with the ending of the book, encouraged Cooney to write three sequels: *Whatever Happened to Janie?* (1993), *Voice on the Radio* (1996), and *What Janie Found* (2000). Cooney penned the first title, and several others, in the popular vampire-themed *Cheerleaders* series of the 1980s.

Cate Tiernan. Tiernan is known for her *Sweep* series, which includes more than a dozen books. In the first title, *Book of Shadows* (2001), 16-year-old Morgan falls for a gorgeous new boy and is pulled into the world of witchery. Her series, *Balefire,* begins with *A Chalice of Wind* (2005) and illustrates Tiernan's superb talent for blending genres.

Christopher Golden. Golden is an award-winning author of both adult and teen fiction. He is lead author of the *Body of Evidence* teen thriller series, co-author with Ford Lytle Gilmore of *The Hollow* teen horror series, author of the award-winning *Prowlers* teen horror series, and a regular writer for the *Buffy the Vampire Slayer* series. He has also written for comic books—he may be best known for *Hellboy.*

Christopher Pike. Kevin MacFadden took his pen name from a character in the first *Star Trek* series. His first thriller novel for teens, *Slumber Party* (1985), became an instant hit. He has written dozens of books for teens, among them *The Last Vampire* series (1994) and the *Remember Me* series (1989). Mostly thrillers, his books contain elements of science fiction, spirituality, mystery, horror, and mythology. *Falling* (2007) has been compared to Thomas Harris's Hannibal Lecter novels.

Darren Shan. Ask any young adult to name a horror writer and you'll undoubtedly hear Darren Shan. Darren's *A Living Nightmare* (2001) spawned his bestselling *Cirque Du Freak* horror series. Darren (Shan named the protagonist after himself) visits a freak show and journeys into a dark and bloody vampire world. His follow-up series, *The Demonata,* thus far includes *Lord Loss* (2005), *Demon Thief* (2006), *Slawter* (2006), *Bec* (2007), *Blood Beast* (2007), and *Demon Apocalypse* (2008), and appeals to older readers.

Joan Lowery Nixon. Before her death, Nixon had written more than 130 books for young readers. She is the only four-time winner of the Edgar Allan Poe Award for Best Young Adult Mystery. Her winning novels include *The Kidnapping of Christina Lattimore* (1979), *The Séance* (1980), *The Other Side of Dark* (1986), and *The Name of the Game Was Murder* (1993). Her novels are set in a variety of locations, and her mystery stories are high suspense.

Kathryn Reiss. One the most prolific mystery/suspense writers for young adults of this decade, having written more than a dozen books for children and teens, her young adult novels *Pale Phoenix* (1994) and *PaperQuake* (1998) are Edgar Award nominees. *Time Windows* (1991), her first novel, was chosen as an ALA Best Book for Young Adults. *Blackthorn Winter* (2006) is her first young adult murder mystery.

Lois Duncan. Duncan is known for creating edge-of-the-seat thriller novels. She is perhaps best known for *I Know What You Did Last Summer* (1973), a story in which a group of friends are involved in a hit-and-run that became a major motion picture. In addition to writing thriller novels, Duncan has published several children's books (e.g., *I Walk at Night,* 2000) and has edited several short story anthologies. Duncan's youngest daughter, Kaitlyn Arquette, was murdered in Albuquerque, New Mexico, in 1989; the case remains unsolved.

Marcus Sedgwick. *The Book of Dead Days* (2004) cemented Sedgwick as a talented mystery/horror writer for teens. Sedgwick's books are steeped in myth and history and have a strong sense of place and time. His work has been honored for its historical accuracy by the National Council for the Social Studies.

Nancy Werlin. Werlin is known for her well-developed characters, unexpected plot twists, and creating edge-of-the seat suspense in thriller mysteries such as *Locked Inside* (2000), an Edgar Allan Poe Nominee for Best Young Adult Mystery, and *The Killer's Cousin* (1998), an Edgar Allan Poe Award winner for

Continued

Box 7.5 Mystery, Thriller, and Horror Writers Who Have Made a Significant Impact on YA Literature *Continued*

Best Young Adult Mystery. Thriller/Suspense fans will also enjoy *The Rules of Survival* (2006).

Neal Shusterman. Shusterman has the creep factor down. He is known for writing fantasy thrillers pitting good against evil. His *Star Shard* trilogy (Book 1: *Scorpion Shards,* 1995) begins with a group of outcast teens; each has a deformity that is turning him/her into a freak. An evil power enters their bodies, and it is hungry to destroy. His *Dark Fusion* series (Book 1: *Dread Locks,* 2005), modern-day fractured fairy tales, have earned Shusterman wide acclaim. His work explores morality themes without preaching.

Philip Pullman. Pullman, a British writer, illustrates his ability to effect mood in his celebrated *Sally Lockhart Mysteries: The Ruby in the Smoke* (1985), *The Shadow in the North* (1988), *The Tiger in the Well* (1990), and *The Tin Princess* (1994). The stories take place in the seedy, scoundrel-infested side of London. Pullman's award-winning *His Dark Materials* trilogy, beginning with *The Golden Compass* (1996), defies genre.

R. L. Stine. Where would middle school readers be without R. L. Stine's *Goosebumps* series? Or high schoolers without *Fear Street*? One of the bestselling children's and young adult writers of all time, Stine has sold over 300 million books. His first teen horror

novel, *Blind Date* (1986), was an instant bestseller, and in 1989 he created the well-known *Fear Street* series, often touted as the bestselling young adult series in history. *Goosebumps* began in 1992, became an instant world hit, and so far has been translated into 32 languages.

Stephenie Meyer. Few writers burst into the publishing market with the fury of Stephenie Meyer. Since its 2005 debut, *Twilight* remains a blockbuster national bestseller. Fans of romance and vampire lore waited eagerly for sequels, and *New Moon* (2006), *Eclipse* (2007), and *Breaking Dawn* (2008) have delivered the same mesmerizing and thrilling blend of fantastic mystery, vampire lore, and romance.

William Sleator. Sleator is conceivably a king of young adult science fiction horror. Having authored dozens of science fiction and horror novels for teens, Sleator is known for well-developed characters and for creating tight plots with surprising twists and turns. Each book is unique; he doesn't write series.

Willo Davis Roberts. Before her death in 2004, Roberts had written more than a dozen young adult mystery and suspense novels. In her lifetime she earned three Edgar Allan Poe Awards for Best Young Adult Mystery: *The Absolutely True Story . . . How I Visited Yellowstone Park with the Terrible Rupes* (1994), *Megan's Island* (1988), and *Twisted Summer* (1996).

Box 7.6 Adult Mystery, Thriller, and Horror Writers for Mature Readers

Agatha Christie. Christie's 66 mystery crime novels have earned her the title Queen of Crime and singled her out as one of the most innovative writers in the development of the mystery novel. She is considered by many to be the greatest mystery writer of all time. *Murder on the Orient Express* (1935) is her most famous mystery. Her novels typically lack

the hard edge characteristic of some contemporary mystery, thriller, and horror writers.

Dan Brown. By 2004 Brown had written four novels, and all were on the *New York Times* bestseller list at the same time in that year. He is known best for *The Da Vinci Code* (2003), one of the most widely

Continued

Box 7.6   Adult Mystery, Thriller, and Horror Writers for Mature Readers   *Continued*

read books in history. Other books include *Angels and Demons* (2000), *Digital Fortress* (1998), and *Deception Point* (2001). He was named by *Time* magazine as one of the world's 100 most influential people. His novels have been translated into more than 40 languages.

David Baldacci. Known for penning legal thrillers, Baldacci has published more than a dozen novels, most of which have been national and international bestsellers. Advanced young adult readers will enjoy his first novel and now major motion picture, *Absolute Power* (1996). Also, *The Camel Club* (2005), *The Collectors* (2006), and *Stone Cold* (2007) are good bets.

Dean Koontz. One of the most prolific contemporary mystery detective writers, Koontz rarely writes multiple books featuring the same character. His *Odd Thomas* (2003) series is a notable exception. He is known for writing suspenseful page-turners and blending genres (e.g., horror, science fiction, and mystery). He makes frequent use of satire.

Elizabeth Peters. Peters creates strong female characters and makes many archaeological connections. She is known best for her *Amelia Peabody* series, featuring more than a dozen novels. Many of her books are historical mysteries. *Lion in the Valley* (1986) is one of her most popular Amelia Peabody novels. In *The Mummy Case* (2007), Amelia encounters a murder suspect at an archaeological dig and follows his trail, a harrowing experience that takes her inside an ancient tomb.

James Patterson. His books featuring Alex Cross, a black forensic psychologist, are his most popular (e.g., *Mary, Mary*, 2005a; *Cross*, 2006a). In later years, Patterson has explored the young adult genre with his *Maximum Ride* series: *The Angel Experiment* (2005b), *School's Out—Forever* (2006b), *Saving the World and Other Extreme Sports* (2007), and *The Final Warning* (2008).

Janet Evanovich. Evanovich's books generally contain a romance theme. She is known for her series featuring Stephanie Plum, a lingerie buyer turned bounty hunter. The series, which began with *One for the Money* (1994), has a comic edge. Her *Alex Barnaby* series (2005) has a NASCAR theme.

John Grisham. Grisham, known for writing legal thrillers, spent much of his earlier life as a small-town criminal and civil law attorney. He based his first novel (now a movie), *A Time to Kill* (1989), on a real-life courtroom experience. Numerous publishers rejected *A Time to Kill* before Wynwood Press purchased it. Since his first book, Grisham has published approximately one novel a year, most national bestsellers. His most popular works include *The Firm* (1991), *The Pelican Brief* (1992), and *The Runaway Jury* (1996), and most recently *The Last Juror* (2004), *The Broker* (2005), and *The Appeal* (2008). *Publisher's Weekly* named Grisham the bestselling novelist of the 1990s.

Michael Connelly. Known for his detective stories featuring Harry Bosch, Connelly is known for *Blood Work* (1998), made into a 2002 film featuring Clint Eastwood. *The Black Echo* earned an Edgar Award for Best First Novel of 1992. *Echo Park* (2006) is a recent bestseller.

Patricia Cornwell. Known for her best-selling series (beginning with *Postmortem,* 1990) of forensic mystery/crime novels featuring Dr. Kay Scarpetta, a medical examiner. Other notable books in the series include *The Body Farm* (1994), *Trace* (2004), *Predator* (2005), and *Book of the Dead* (2007).

Stephen King. With more than three dozen bestselling horror novels (many of which are now movies), King is the "king" of contemporary horror novels. *Salem's Lot* (1975), *Carrie* (1974), *The Shining* (1977), and *Cujo* (1981) are among his most notable. He has also published outside the horror genre: *The Green Mile* (1997), and *Rita Hayworth and Shawshank Redemption* (1982)—movie version *The Shawshank Redemption*. He is widely read by high school students, especially boys.

Tony Hillerman. An award-winning author of detective novels, most of which are set in New Mexico or Arizona, *Dance Hall of the Dead* (1973) won an Edgar Award for best novel. His books are rich in Navajo and Hopi culture; they often entail witchcraft and elements of the supernatural and explore social class issues. *The Dark Wind* (1982) and *The Shape Shifter* (2006) are among his bestsellers.

On Writing the *Echo Falls* Series   by Peter Abrahams

I'd written 15 crime fiction novels before tackling my first young adult novel, *Down the Rabbit Hole,* book one in the *Echo Falls* series. People always ask what I did to adjust to the younger readership. The answer is nothing. The *Echo Falls* series is written in the third person, but not of the omniscient kind. Instead it's a tightly focused third person, and that focus is on the main character, 13-year-old Ingrid Levin-Hill. The effect is close to first person in some ways, but at the same time, it can reveal things that Ingrid sees but does not understand, a useful technique for writing suspense. The main point, though, is that the vocabulary, syntax, thought patterns and attitude are those of a young teenager, and thus no adjustment on my part was necessary. Had I been writing for an adult audience the books would have been exactly the same.

Not to say this hasn't been an adventure for me. That freshness that I hope is characteristic of Ingrid is shared by the readership. Recently I got an e-mail from a kid in the Midwest. "I have to do a report on your book *Down the Rabbit Hole.* Please tell me the story in your own words." A bit of dialogue that could have come right from the books themselves: I knew I was on the right track.

The *Echo Falls* books are mysteries. Teasing apart all the strands of crime fiction is probably tedious, but I'd actually written only one book before that could be called a pure mystery (*Oblivion,* 2005). *Oblivion* fits in the sub-category of private-eye novel. Ingrid, of course, is an amateur sleuth. But as a bookstore owner pointed out to me, she never self-identifies as such. She's in many ways an ordinary kid. And Echo Falls is in many ways an ordinary corner of America.

Mystery, danger, suspense: they're all more believable if they're not just surrounded by but also actually arise from the everyday. The series is an opportunity for me to explore this bit of America in a sneaky way that's painless for the reader; you don't even have to know I'm doing it. By the end, Ingrid will solve a lot of mysteries, yes; but she will also know her little town like no one has before.

Titles in the *Echo Falls Mystery* series include *Down the Rabbit Hole* (2005a), *Behind the Curtain* (2006), and *Into the Dark* (2008). Adult books include *The Fury of Rachel Monette* (1980), *Hard Rain* (1988), *The Fan* (1995), *Crying Wolf* (2000), *The Tutor* (2002), *Last of the Dixie Heroes* (2001), *Oblivion* (2005b), and *Lights Out* (1994)—an Edgar Award Best Novel nominee.

Teaching Inferential Thinking and Prediction with YA Mystery, Thriller, and Horror Literature

As we read, we construct meaning, or what Judith Langer (1995) calls an envisionment—a personal text-world inclusive of all we understand or imagine. In essence, we create a text in our minds. As we continue reading, our mind text changes and deepens; as we tap into our own prior knowledge and experiences, we begin automatically to ask questions, make *inferences* and *predictions* (Olson, 2007)—terms we interchange loosely. Harvey and Goudvis (2000), however, make clear distinctions between the two:

> We predict outcomes, events, or actions that are confirmed or contradicted by the end of the story. Inferences are often more open-ended and may remain unresolved when the story draws to a close. (p. 108)

Predictions come from inferences; inferences help us predict, or anticipate, what will happen next.

Mysteries and thrillers make frequent use of foreshadowing, red herrings, and cliff-hangers, thereby making them perfect genres for providing practice in making inferences and predictions. Activities that encourage inferential thinking and prediction are discussed in the following sections.

Inferential Thinking and Metacognition

Many students who can respond to questions based on explicit facts may struggle with inferential thinking—the cognitive process necessary for constructing implicit meanings from written texts. Unlike *literal* understanding, in which readers recognize and understand explicitly stated information, inferential or "interpretive" thinking requires an ability to read between the lines, an ability to make assumptions (Roe, Stoodt, & Burns, 1995). This ability is at the heart of literary interpretation. To identify literary themes or an author's tone or stance, to make predictions, draw conclusions, make hypotheses, clarify meaning, and to raise important questions and/ or issues, readers must be skilled inferential thinkers. Students who have poor inferential skills do poorly in literature classes. In addition, inferential thinking is a key reading skill on standardized reading/verbal tests such as the SAT, and these same students generally test badly. In Table 7.1, you will find a sample reading passage taken from an SAT literature subject test and three of the accompanying test questions, which demand inferential thinking.

Involving students in reading activities that encourage them to think about how readers naturally use prior knowledge to make inferences and to comprehend implied or interpretive meanings can help them understand the role of prior knowledge in comprehension, thus making them better readers. To explore with readers our natural tendencies to make inferences, share the following passage (or any passage in which answers to your questions are implicit):

> Scott jumped out of bed and sprinted to the bathroom for a shower. Three minutes later he raked a comb through his hair and then ran to the dryer in search of his favorite T-shirt. Downstairs he gulped down milk from the jug, grabbed a Pop-Tart, and searched frantically for his history book and literature notebook. Stuffing everything into his backpack in record speed, Scott raced down the steps and out the door to the bus stop.

Table 7.1

Sample SAT Test Questions

A Divine Mistress

In Nature's pieces still I see
Some error that might mended be;
Something my wish could still remove,
Alter or add; but my fair love
Was framed by hands far more divine,
For she hath every beauteous line.
Yet I had been far happier
Had Nature, that made me, made her.
Then likeness might (that love creates)
Have made her love what now she hates;
Yet, I confess, I cannot spare
From her just shape the smallest hair;
Nor need I beg from all the store
Of heaven for her one beauty more.
She hath too much divinity for me:
You gods, teach her some more humanity.

5. Which of the following best states the wish of the speaker in lines 7–14?
   (A) He wants the woman to be even more beautiful than she is.
   (B) He wants the woman to ignore other men.
   (C) He wants the woman to be both beautiful and accessible.
   (D) He does not want the woman to love him in the same way he loves her.
   (E) He does not want the woman to be so vain.

6. The speaker's tone in lines 15–16 is best described as
   (A) bitter sarcasm
   (B) amused indifference
   (C) dignified solemnity
   (D) playful exasperation
   (E) cold rationality

7. The unannounced intention of the speaker in this poem is to
   (A) commend a woman for her impeccable virtue
   (B) praise a woman for her unequaled beauty
   (C) make a woman more receptive to his passion
   (D) delude a woman into thinking that he loves her
   (E) flatter a woman so that she will have a better opinion of herself.

Source: The Official Study Guide for All SAT Subject Tests (2006), p. 24.

Answers: 5 (C), 6 (D), 7(C)

After students have read the selection, have them respond to the following questions: (1) Where is Scott going? (2) What mood is he in? Students will guess Scott is going to school. Though a simple question-response, the purpose here is to reflect on *how* they knew the answer—there's no mention of school in the paragraph. The paragraph does offer explicit clues: backpack, his books, and bus stop; these clues aid in inferring the answer. Students will also predict he is panicked, and possibly frustrated, though these emotions are not stated. Once students work through a simple exercise such as this, they are better prepared to understand the importance of inferential thinking and can move on to more complicated texts and questions.

Stop and Question: A Modified Think-Aloud

Good readers question texts. Struggling readers do not. In fact, some students will read well orally, but when questioned about their reading, they are clueless. They read words or sound out words, but they do not *think* about what they are reading. They don't focus on meaning when reading; instead, they think about what they're doing after class, after school, or when they get home. Think-aloud strategies require that students stop and question, which can teach students to focus on meaning, thus improving their comprehension. Think-aloud strategies can help students monitor their reading, identify problems, visualize text, make inferences and predictions, and draw comparisons. In a typical think-aloud, students may read a sentence or two and then stop and ask questions or comment on what they have read. Sometimes they may ask the teacher or a peer questions; the teacher participates in an effort to model good questioning techniques.

It's not realistic, nor beneficial, to ask students to read an entire novel, stopping after every two or three sentences to question or comment; therefore, think-alouds are best done with short texts. In reading longer texts, I use a modified think-aloud strategy. I have students read large chunks, log their experiences, and then discuss their reading. Ursula K. Le Guin's short story, "The Wife's Story," makes an excellent think-aloud piece for illustrating the complexities of inferential thinking.

I begin by asking students to make a three-column chart with the following headings: (1) Predict What Will Happen Next, (2) Inferences, and (3) Clues. I then divide the story into six segments and ask students to read and record their thoughts in each column. I begin by showing them only the title.

Work through the activity that begins on the next page*. Be careful not to jump to the ending. If you do, you will "spoil" the activity. (Understanding that it works is one thing, experiencing its effect is another.) To prevent students from spoiling the activity, I give them one story piece at a time.

---

*Dera Weaver, a former KSU colleague, shared this activity at KSU.

Modified Think-Aloud Strategy for Longer Texts

Story Segment 1—only the title

"The Wife's Story" by Ursula K. Le Guin

STOP READING

What can you infer from the title? Record your thoughts.

Predict What Will Happen	Inferences	Clues

Share ideas.

Story Segment 2

BEGIN READING

He was a good husband, a good father. I don't understand it. I don't believe in it. I don't believe that it happened. I saw it happen but it isn't true. It can't be. He was always gentle. If you'd have seen him playing with the children, anybody who saw him with the children would have known that there wasn't any bad in him, not one mean bone. When I first met him he was still living with his mother, over near Spring Lake, and I used to see them together, the mother and the sons, and think that any young fellow that was that nice with his family must be one worth knowing. Then one time when I was walking in the woods I met him by himself coming back from a hunting trip. He hadn't got any game at all, not so much as a field mouse, but he wasn't cast down about it. He was just larking along enjoying the morning air. That's one of the things I first loved about him. He didn't take things hard, he didn't grouch and whine when things didn't go his way. So we got to talking that day. And I guess things moved right along after that, because pretty soon he was over here pretty near all the time. And my sister said—see, my parents had moved out the year before and gone south, leaving us the place—my sister said, kind of teasing but serious, "Well! If he's going to be here every day and half the night, I guess there isn't room for me!" And she moved out—just down the way. We've always been real close, her and me. That's the sort of thing doesn't ever change. I couldn't ever have got through this bad time without my sis.

STOP READING

What can you infer from segment 2? How are your previous ideas reinforced and/or altered? Record your thoughts.

Predict What Will Happen	Inferences	Clues

Share ideas.

Continued

Modified Think-Aloud Strategy for Longer Texts   *Continued*

Story Segment 3

BEGIN READING

Well, so he come to live here. And all I can say is, it was the happy year of my life. He was just purely good to me. A hard worker and never lazy, and so big and fine-looking. Everybody looked up to him, you know, young as he was. Lodge Meeting nights, more and more often they had him to lead the singing. He had such a beautiful voice, and he'd lead off strong, and the others following and joining in, high voices and low. It brings the shivers on me now to think of it, hearing it, nights when I'd stayed home from meeting when the children was babies—the singing coming up through the trees there, and the moonlight, summer nights, the full moon shining. I'll never hear anything so beautiful. I'll never know a joy like that again.

It was the moon, that's what they say. It's the moon's fault, and the blood. It was in his father's blood. I never knew his father, and now I wonder what become of him. He was from up Whitewater way, and had no kin around here. I always thought he went back there, but now I don't know. There was some talk about him, tales, that come out after what happened to my husband. It's something runs in the blood, they say, and it may never come out, but if it does, it's the change of the moon that does it. Always it happens in the dark of the moon. When everybody's home and asleep. Something comes over the one that's got the curse in his blood, they say, and he gets up because he can't sleep, and goes out into the glaring sun, and goes off all alone—drawn to find those like him.

STOP READING

What can you infer from segment 3? How are your previous ideas reinforced and/or altered? Record your thoughts.

Predict What Will Happen	Inferences	Clues

Share ideas.

Continued

Modified Think-Aloud Strategy for Longer Texts *Continued*

Story Segment 4

BEGIN READING

And it may be so, because my husband would do that. I'd half rouse and say, "Where you going to?" and he'd say, "Oh, hunting, be back this evening," and it wasn't like him, even his voice was different. But I'd be so sleepy, and not wanting to wake the kids, and he was so good and responsible, it was no call of mine to go asking "Why?" and "Where?" and all like that.

So it happened that way maybe three times or four. He'd come back late, and worn out, and pretty near cross for one so sweet-tempered—not wanting to talk about it. I figured everybody got to bust out now and then, and nagging never helped anything. But it did begin to worry me. Not so much that he went, but that he come back so tired and strange. Even he smelled strange. It made my hair stand up on end. I could not endure it and I said, "What is that—those smells on you? All over you!" And he said, "I don't know," real short, and made like he was sleeping. But he went down when he thought I wasn't noticing, and washed and washed himself. But those smells stayed in his hair, and in our bed, for days.

STOP READING

What can you infer from segment 4? How are your previous ideas reinforced and/or altered? Record your thoughts.

Predict What Will Happen	Inferences	Clues

Share ideas.

Continued

Modified Think-Aloud Strategy for Longer Texts   *Continued*

Story Segment 5

BEGIN READING

And then the awful thing. I don't find it easy to tell about this. I want to cry when I have to bring it to my mind. Our youngest, the little one, my baby, she turned from her father. Just overnight. He come in and she got scared-looking, stiff, with her eyes wide, and then she begun to cry and try to hide behind me. She didn't yet talk plain but she was saying over and over, "Make it go away! Make it go away!"

The look in his eyes, just for one moment, when he heard that. That's what I don't want ever to remember. That what I can't forget. The look in his eyes looking at his own child.

I said to the child, "Shame on you, what's got into you!"—scolding, but keeping her right up close to me at the same time, because I was frightened too. Frightened to shaking.

He looked away then and said something like, "Guess she just waked up dreaming," and passed it off that way. Or tried to. And so did I. And I got real mad with my baby when she kept on acting crazy scared of her own dad. But she couldn't help it and I couldn't manage it.

He kept away that whole day. Because he knew, I guess. It was just beginning dark of the moon.

It was hot and close inside, and dark, and we'd all been asleep some while, when something woke me up. He wasn't there beside me. I heard a little stir in the passage, when I listened. So I got up, because I could bear it no longer. I went out into the passage, and it was light there, hard sunlight coming in from the door. And I saw him standing just outside, in the tall grass by the entrance. His head was hanging. Presently he sat down, like he felt weary, and looked down at his feet. I held still, inside, and watched, I didn't know what for.

STOP READING

What can you infer from segment 5? How are your previous ideas reinforced and/or altered? Record your thoughts.

Predict What Will Happen	Inferences	Clues

Share ideas.

Continued

Modified Think-Aloud Strategy for Longer Texts *Continued*

Story Segment 6

BEGIN READING

And I saw what he saw. I saw the changing. In his feet, it was, first. They got long, each foot got longer, stretching out, the toes stretching out and the foot getting long, and fleshy, and white. And no hair on them.

The hair begun to come away all over his body. It was like his hair fried away in the sunlight and was gone. He was white all over then, like a worm's skin. And he turned his face. It was changing while I looked. It got flatter and flatter, the mouth flat and wide, and the teeth grinning flat and dull, and the nose just a knob of flesh with nostril holes, and the ears gone, and the eyes gone blue—blue, with white rims around the blue—staring at me out of that flat, soft, white face.

He stood up then on two legs.

I saw him, I had to see him, my own dear love, turned into the hateful one.

I couldn't move, but as I crouched there in the passage staring out into the day I was trembling and shaking with a growl that burst out into a crazy, awful howling. A brief howl and a terror howl and a calling howl. And the others heard it, even sleeping and woke up.

It stared and peered, that thing my husband had turned into, and shoved its face up to the entrance of our house. I was still bound by mortal fear, but behind me the children had waked up, and the baby was whimpering. The mother anger come into me then, and I snarled and crept forward.

The man thing looked around. It had no gun, like the ones from the man places do. But it picked up a heavy fallen tree branch in its long white foot, and shoved the end of that down into our house, at me. I snapped the end of it in my teeth and started to force my way out, because I knew the man would kill our children if it could. But my sister was already coming. I saw her running at the man with her head low and her mane high and her eyes yellow as the winter sun. It turned on her and raised up that branch to hit her. But I come out of the doorway, mad with the mother anger, and the others all were coming answering my call, the whole pack gathering, there in that blind glare and heat of the sun at noon.

The man looked round at us and yelled out loud, and brandished the branch it held. Then it broke and ran, heading for the cleared fields and lowlands, down the mountainside. It ran, on two legs, leaping and weaving, and we followed it.

I was last, because love still bound the anger and the fear in me. I was running when I saw them pull it down. My sister's teeth were in its throat. I got there and it was dead. The others were drawing back from the kill, because of the taste of the blood, and the smell. The younger ones were cowering and some crying, and my sister rubbed her mouth against her forelegs over and over to get rid of the taste. I went up close because I thought if the thing was dead the spell, the curse must be done, and my husband could come back—alive, or even dead, if I could only see him, my true love, in his true form, beautiful. But only the dead man lay there white and bloody. We drew back and back from it, and turned and ran, back up into the hills, back to the woods of the shadows and the twilight and the blessed dark.

STOP READING

Continued

Modified Think-Aloud Strategy for Longer Texts   *Continued*

What can you infer from segment 6? How are your previous ideas reinforced and/or altered? How do your initial and final thoughts differ? Record your thoughts.

Predict What Will Happen	Inferences	Clues

Share ideas.

If you worked through the above activity, you realized Le Guin reverses the werewolf idea—that is, a werewolf turns into a man, terrifying his wolf family. This story is excellent for teaching inference and prediction because Le Guin "tricks" us into believing the characters are human. Our prior experiences, of course, "deceive" us beginning with the title. At some point, someone will guess that a werewolf is involved; however, seldom, if ever, does anyone get the idea that the werewolf is changing into a man, frightening his wolf family until the end. When students begin "getting it," your role is to facilitate their ideas. Refrain from giving any hints or agreeing with their ideas. Because students are conditioned to look to us for answers, they will be expecting you to validate or deny their responses.

Read, Infer, Share

We base inferences and predictions on our prior knowledge about a reading topic. One technique I have used to build inferential thinking skills is Read, Infer, Share, which is based on the Tea Party developed by Sue Perona (Beers, 2003). Mel Glenn's *Who Killed Mr. Chippendale? A Mystery in Poems* (1996) is a perfect selection. In this mystery and detective story told in free verse, students and faculty reveal their innermost thoughts and feelings about the murder of a popular English teacher. One morning, Mr. Chippendale is shot and killed by an unknown attacker as he prepares for his morning run on the school track. In alternating poems, readers learn who admired him, who hated him, and the one person who loved him. Ultimately, as police investigate the murder, the killer is revealed.

Approximately 100 short, one-page poems comprise this thin, quick read. I first assign reading partners or place students in reading groups and then divide the text into four sections and give each student four index cards. Detailed instructions follow:

1. Silently read the first 25 poems. (This reading can be done in minutes.)
2. Make a prediction about "whodunit" and write that character's name on one side of your index card.
3. Below the name, list clues from the text that support your prediction.
4. Share your prediction and clues with your partner. On the back of your card, list additional details that support your prediction or list details that refute your initial prediction.

5. Class discussion/predictions.
6. Repeat the above steps until the assignment is complete.

Word Scramble Prediction

Kelly Gallagher (2004) uses Word Scramble Prediction to encourage students to predict what will happen next in a story and to pique curiosity. The teacher provides students with a list of words they will encounter in a chapter. Based on the words alone, students make predictions about their planned reading.

Elise Broach's *Desert Crossing* (2006), a mystery involving four teens on a road trip from Kansas City to Phoenix, can illustrate this technique. While driving across New Mexico in a blinding rainstorm, their car hits a bump. Backtracking to see if they killed an animal, they discover a dead girl on the roadside. Did they kill her? Or was she already dead? Chapters 1 and 2 set up the story. I created the following word list from these initial chapters:

driving	gushing	blurred	skidded
six-pack	rain	bump	ballerina
thunking	coyote	gravel	crunch

Notice the words *coyote* and *ballerina*; I used them purposefully to create dissonance. We want students to think deeply about possibilities, not merely jump at the obvious. You may put these words on the overhead, whiteboard, index cards, or a one-page handout, and then ask students to make predictions individually, in pairs, or in small groups.

External-Internal Story Line Prediction

Psychological thrillers work well for teaching students to make external *and* internal predictions. Because external events are generally explicit, predicting what will happen is natural. Internal conflicts (psychological character changes resulting from story events) are more implicit, and readers may not think a great deal about character growth and change and why characters behave as they do. Zwiers (2004) uses a modified story map to encourage students to make predictions about external events *and* to make predictions about character behavior and changes. In Table 7.3, I have developed a modified version of Zwiers's story line procedure. As students read, they stop after key events (the chart allows for five) and make predictions. Young adult psychological thrillers that work well with this activity include *Paranoid Park* (Nelson, 2006), *Full Tilt* (Shusterman, 2003), and *Surrender* (Hartnett, 2006).

Final Thoughts

Mysteries, thrillers, and horror stories are powerful genres for hooking unmotivated readers. Cliff-hanger endings, unsuspected plot twists, and red herrings pique interest and grab readers' attention. Moreover, the whodunit factor provides opportunities for students to examine the roles prior knowledge, inferences, and predictions play in comprehension. As teachers,

Table 7.3

Modified Story Map

External Changes (Events)

Event 1:	Event 2:	Event 3:	Event 4:	Event 5:
Prediction:	Prediction:	Prediction:	Prediction:	Prediction:

Internal Changes (Character Responses to Events)

Event 1:	Event 2:	Event 3:	Event 4:	Event 5:
Prediction:	Prediction:	Prediction:	Prediction:	Prediction:

Source: Based on Zwiers's (2004) story line procedure.

we need to understand these roles because they are an essential thinking process for successful reading. If students do not develop strong inferencing skills, no amount of vocabulary instruction (vocabulary instruction can be overemphasized) will prepare them for complex reading in high school and college classrooms and on standardized tests, which play a significant role in college admissions decisions and scholarship opportunities. Chapter 10 examines prediction from a different angle: how words move texts; that is, how key words help us predict upcoming information.

Professional Resources

Beinhart, L. (1996). *How to write a mystery*. New York: Ballantine/Random House.

Bell, A. C. (1998). The rise and fall of the detective novel. *Contemporary Review, 272,* 197–201.

Bentley, N., & Guthrie, D. (2001). *Writing mysteries, movies, monster stories, and more.* Illus. Jeremy Tugeau, Brookfield, CT: Millbrook Press.

Billman, C. (1984, Spring). The child reader as sleuth. *Children's Literature in Education, 15*(1), 30–41.

Castle, M. (Ed.). (2007). *On writing horror.* Cincinnati, OH: Writer's Digest.

Cruz, M. C., & Duff, O. B. (1996, October). Witches, ghosts, and other apparitions. *English Journal, 85*(6), 100–102.

Dickson, R. (1998, November). Horror: To gratify, not edify. *Language Arts, 76*(2), 115–122.

Evans, V. (1972, April). The mystery as mind stretcher. *English Journal, 61*(4), 495–503.

Flack, J. D. (1990). *Mystery and detection: Thinking and problem solving with the sleuths.* Englewood, CO: Teacher Ideas.

Flack, J. D. (1991, November/December). Put some mystery in your classroom. *Teaching K–8, 22*(3), 62–65.

Grafton, S. (Ed.). (2002). *Writing mysteries: A handbook.* Cincinnati, OH: Writer's Digest.

Greenwald, M. S. (2004). *The secret of the Hardy boys: Leslie McFarlane and the Stratemeyer Syndicate.* Athens: Ohio University Press.

Herbert, R. (2003). *Whodunit?: A who's who in crime and mystery writing.* New York: Oxford University Press.

Horsley, L. (2005). *Twentieth-century crime fiction.* New York: Oxford University Press.

Howe, J. (1995). Mirth & mayhem: Humor and mystery in children's books. *Voices from the Middle, 2*(3), 4–9.

Huang, J. (2000). *100 favorite mysteries of the century.* Carmel, IN: Crum Creek Press.

Jones, P. (1998). *What's so scary about R. L. Stine?* Lanham, MD: Scarecrow Press.

Jones, S., & Carson, D. (2004). *The world's greatest horror stories.* London: Magpie Books.

Kies, C. (1992). *Presenting young adult horror fiction.* New York: Twayne.

Larson, J. (2000). Mysteries for young detectives. *Book Links, 10*(1), 57–61.

Mitchell, D. (1997, October). Ghosts and fear in language arts. *English Journal, 86*(6), 96–99.

Moore, L. D. (2006). *Cracking the hard-boiled detective: A critical history from the 1920s to the present.* Jefferson, NC: McFarland.

Murphy, B. F. (1999). *The encyclopedia of murder and mystery.* New York: St. Martin's Press.

Priestman, M. (2003). *The Cambridge companion to crime fiction.* New York: Oxford University Press.

Rehak, M. (2006). *Girl sleuth: Nancy Drew and the women who created her.* Orlando, FL: Harvest/ Harcourt.

Roberts, W. D. (1996). Writing mysteries for young readers. *The Writer,* 21–23.

Rzepka, C. J. (2005). *Detective fiction: Cultural history of literature.* Cambridge, England: Polity Press.

Scaggs, J. (2005). *Crime fiction.* London: Routledge.

Smith, L. A. (2006, May). Think-aloud mysteries: Using structured, sentence-by-sentence text passages to teach comprehension strategies. *The Reading Teacher, 59*(8), 764–773.

Spiegel, D. L. (1982, April). The clip sheet: Clues to good mystery books for young readers. *The Reading Teacher, 35*(7), 852–854.

Stilwell, S. A. (1999). *What mystery do I read next? A reader's guide to recent mystery fiction* (2nd ed.). Detroit: Gale.

Swanson, J., & James, D. (1998). *Killer books: A reader's guide to exploring the popular world of mystery and suspense.* New York: Penguin.

Perry, L. A., & Butler, R. P. (1997, October). Are *Goosebumps* books real literature? *Language Arts, 74*(6), 454–456.

Twitchell, J. B. (1985). *Dreadful pleasures: An anatomy of modern horror.* New York: Oxford University Press.

Vardell, S. M. (1983, December). Reading, writing, and mystery stories. *English Journal, 72*(8), 47–51.

Zanarini, A. (2001, December). Who dun it? Mysteries. *Voices from the Middle, 9*(2), 85–87.

ONLINE

Explore: www.42explore.com

GeoMysteries: www.childrensmuseum.org

History Mysteries: www.teacher.scholastic.com/ histmyst

Historical Mystery Fiction: www.members.tripod .com

Horror Writers Association: www.horror.org

Kids Love a Mystery: www.kidsloveamystery .com

Life's Little Mysteries: www.livescience.com/ mysteries

Masterpiece Theatre and Mystery: www.pbs.org

Mysteries Magazine: www.mysteriesmagazine .com

Mystery Ink: www.mysteryinkonline.com

Mystery Nets Kids Mysteries: www .kids.mysterynet.com

Mystery Scene: www.mysteryscenemag.com

The Mystery Spot: www.accessexcellence.org/ AE/mspot

Mystery ThinkQuest: www.library.thinkquest.org

Mystery Writers of America: www.mysterywriters .org

MysteryNet.Com: www.mysterynet.com

Red InkWorks: www.redinkworks.com/ horror_resources.htm

Red InkWorks: www.redinkworks.com/ mystery_writers.htm

Sisters in Crime: www.sistersincrime.org

References

Abrahams, P. (1980). *The fury of Rachel Monette.* New York: Macmillan.

Abrahams, P. (1988). *Hard rain.* New York: Dutton/Penguin.

Abrahams, P. (1994). *Lights out.* New York: Warner.

Abrahams, P. (1995). *The fan.* New York: Warner.

Abrahams, P. (2000). *Crying wolf.* New York: Ballantine/Random House.

Abrahams, P. (2001). *Last of the Dixie heroes.* New York: Ballantine/Random House.

Abrahams, P. (2002). *The tutor.* New York: Ballantine/Random House.

Abrahams, P. (2005a). *Down the rabbit hole.* New York: HarperCollins.

Abrahams, P. (2005b). *Oblivion.* New York: William Morrow/HarperCollins.

Abrahams, P. (2006). *Behind the curtain.* New York: HarperCollins.

Abrahams, P. (2008). *Into the dark.* New York: HarperCollins.

Abrams, M. H. (2005). *A glossary of literary terms* (8th ed.). Boston: Thomson Wadsworth.

Allison, J. (2005). *Gilda Joyce: Psychic investigator.* New York: Philomel/Penguin.

Allison, J. (2006). *Gilda Joyce: The ladies of the lake.* New York: Philomel/Penguin.

Allison, J. (2007). *Gilda Joyce: The ghost sonata.* New York: Philomel/Penguin.

Anderson, M. T. (1997). *Thirsty.* Cambridge, MA: Candlewick Press.

Atwater-Rhodes, A. (1999). *In the forest of the night.* New York: Delacorte/Random House.

Atwater-Rhodes, A. (2003). *Hawksong.* New York: Delacorte/Random House.

Baldacci, D. (1996). *Absolute power.* New York: Warner.

Baldacci, D. (2005). *The camel club.* New York: Warner.

Baldacci, D. (2006). *The collectors.* New York: Warner.

Baldacci, D. (2007). *Stone cold.* New York: Grand Central.

Balliett, B. (2004). *Chasing Vermeer.* Illus. Brett Helquist, New York: Scholastic.

Balliett, B. (2006). *The Wright 3.* Illus. Brett Helquist, New York: Scholastic.

Balliett, B. (2008). *The Calder game.* New York: Scholastic.

Beers, K. (2003). *When kids can't read: What teachers can do.* Portsmouth, NH: Heinemann.

Bray, L. (2003). *A great and terrible beauty.* New York: Delacorte/Random House.

Bray, L. (2005). *Rebel angels.* New York: Delacorte/Random House.

Bray, L. (2007). *Sweet far thing.* New York: Delacorte/Random House.

Brewer, H. (2007). *The chronicles of Vladimir Tod.* New York: Dutton/Penguin.

Broach, E. (2006). *Desert crossing.* New York: Henry Holt.

Brockmeier, K. (2006). *Grooves: A kind of mystery.* New York: HarperCollins.

Brown, D. (1998). *Digital fortress.* Boston: St. Martin's Press.

Brown, D. (2000). *Angels and demons.* New York: Pocket/Simon & Schuster.

Brown, D. (2001). *Deception point.* New York: Pocket/Simon & Schuster.

Brown, D. (2003). *The Da Vinci code.* New York: Doubleday/Random House.

Carroll, D. (1995) *Splatterpunk: The grossery list.* Tabula Rasa. Retrieved November 26, 2006, from http://www.tabula-rasa.info/Horror/Splatterpunk.html

Carter, D. V. (2006). *The hand of the devil.* New York: Delacorte/Random House.

Cary, K. (2007). *The reckoning.* New York: Penguin.

Christie, A. (1934). *Murder on the Orient Express.* London: Collins.

Clements, A. (2002). *Things not seen.* New York: Philomel/Penguin.

Cole, S. (2003). *Wereling* series (*Wounded #1*). New York: Razorbill/Penguin.

Cole, S. (2005a). *Prey.* New York: Razorbill/Penguin.

Cole, S. (2005b). *Resurrection.* New York: Razorbill/Penguin.

Cooney, C. B. (1985). *Cheerleaders.* New York: Scholastic.

Cooney, C. B. (1990). *The face on the milk carton.* New York: Bantam Doubleday/Random House.

Cooney, C. B. (1993). *Whatever happened to Janie?* New York: Delacorte/Random House.

Cooney, C. B. (1996). *The voice on the radio.* New York: Delacorte/Random House.

Cooney, C. B. (2000). *What Janie found.* New York: Delacorte/Random House.

Connelly, M. (1992). *The black echo.* New York: Little, Brown.

Connelly, M. (1998). *Blood work.* New York: Little, Brown.

Connelly, M. (2006). *Echo Park.* New York: Little, Brown.

Cornish, D. M. (2006). *Monster blood tattoo* series (*Foundling* #1). New York: Penguin/Putnam.

Cornish, D. M. (2008). *Monster blood tattoo* series (*Lamplighter* #2). New York: Penguin/Putnam.

Cornwell, P. (1990). *Postmortem.* New York: Scribner/Simon & Schuster.

Cornwell, P. (1994). *The body farm.* New York: Scribner/Simon & Schuster.

Cornwell, P. (2004). *Trace.* New York: Penguin.

Cornwell, P. (2005). *Predator.* New York: Penguin.

Cornwell, P. (2007). *Book of the dead.* New York: Penguin.

Cuddon, J. A. (2000). *The Penguin dictionary of literary terms and literary theory* (4th ed.). New York: Penguin.

Cusick, R. T. (2005). *The unseen: It begins.* New York: Speak/Penguin.

de la Cruz, M. (2006). *Blue bloods.* New York: Hyperion.

de la Cruz, M. (2007). *Masquerade: A blue bloods novel.* New York: Hyperion.

Deaver, J. (1997). *The bone collection.* New York: Viking/Penguin.

Delaney, M. (1998). *The misfits, inc.* series (*The vanishing chip* #1). Atlanta: Peachtree.

Duncan, L. (1973). *I know what you did last summer.* New York: Little, Brown.

Duncan, L. (1974). *Down a dark hall.* New York: Little, Brown.

Duncan, L. (1976). *Summer of fear.* New York: Little, Brown.

Duncan, L. (1978). *Killing Mr. Griffin.* New York: Little, Brown.

Duncan, L. (1981). *Stranger with my face.* New York: Little, Brown.

Duncan, L. (1984). *The third eye.* New York: Little, Brown.

Duncan, L. (1985). *Locked in time.* New York: Little, Brown.

Duncan, L. (1987). *The twisted window.* New York: Delacorte/Random House.

Duncan, L. (1989). *Don't look behind you.* New York: Delacorte/Random House.

Duncan, L. (2000). *I walk at night.* New York: Viking/Penguin.

Dunkle, C. B. (2005). *By these ten bones.* New York: Henry Holt.

Enthoven, S. (2006). *The black tattoo.* New York: Razorbill/Penguin.

Evanovich, J. (1994). *One for the money.* New York: Scribner/Simon & Schuster.

Evanovich, J. (2005). *Alex Barnaby* series (*Metro girl* #1). New York: HarperCollins.

Ferguson, A. (2005). *The Christopher killer.* New York: Viking/Penguin.

Ferguson, A. (2006). *The angel of death.* New York: Viking/Penguin.

Ferguson, A. (2008). *The circle of blood.* New York: Viking/Penguin.

Fleming, I. (1954). *Casino royale.* New York: Macmillan.

Gallagher, K. (2004). *Deeper reading: Comprehending challenging texts, 4–12.* Portland, ME: Stenhouse.

Glenn, M. (1996). *Who killed Mr. Chippendale? A mystery in poems.* New York: Lodestar.

Golden, C. (1999). *Body of evidence* series (*Body bags* #1). New York: Pocket Books.

Golden, C. (1999). *Thief of hearts.* New York: Pocket/Simon & Schuster.

Golden, C. (2001). *Prowlers* series (*Prowlers* #1). New York: Pocket Books.

Golden, C. (2006). *The veil* series (*The myth hunters* #1). New York: Spectra/Random House.

Golden, C., & Gilmore, F. L. (2005). *The hollow* series (*Horseman* #1). New York: Pocket Books.

Golden, C., & Hautala, R. (2005). *Throat culture.* New York: Simon Pulse/Simon & Schuster.

Golden, C., & Holder, N. (1997). *Buffy the vampire: Halloween rain.* New York: Pocket Books.

Grant, V. (2005). *Quid pro quo.* Custer, WA: Orca.

Grisham, J. (1989). *A time to kill.* New York: Wynwood Press.

Grisham, J. (1991). *The firm.* New York: Bantam Doubleday Dell/Random House.

Grisham, J. (1992). *The pelican brief.* New York: Bantam Doubleday Dell/Random House.

Grisham, J. (1996). *The runaway jury.* New York: Bantam Doubleday Dell/Random House.

Grisham, J. (2004). *The last juror.* New York: Bantam Doubleday Dell/Random House.

Grisham, J. (2005). *The broker.* New York: Bantam Doubleday Dell/Random House.

Grisham, J. (2008) *The appeal.* New York: Doubleday/Random House.

Hahn, M. D. (2008). *All the lovely bad ones.* New York: Clarion.

Hale, S. (2006). *River secrets.* New York: Bloomsbury.

Hamilton, V. (1968). *The house of Dies Drear.* New York: Macmillan.

Hamilton, V. (1987). *The mystery of Drear house.* New York: Greenwillow/HarperCollins.

Harris, T. (1999). *Hannibal.* New York: Dell/Random House.

Hartnett, S. (2006). *Surrender.* Cambridge, MA: Candlewick Press.

Harvey, S., & Goudvis, A. (2000). *Strategies that work.* York, ME: Stenhouse.

Higson, C. (2005). *Young Bond* series (*SilverFin: A James Bond adventure* #1). New York: Hyperion.

Hillerman, T. (1973). *Dance hall of the dead.* New York: Harper & Row.

Hillerman, T. (1982). *The dark wind.* New York: Harper & Row.

Hillerman, T. (2006). *The shape shifter.* New York: Harper & Row.

Hoffman, N. K. (2003). *A stir of bones.* New York: Penguin.

Holm, J. L. (2003). *The creek.* New York: HarperCollins.

Hoobler, D., & Hoobler, T. (1999). *The ghost in the Tokaido Inn.* New York: Penguin Putnam.

Hoobler, D., & Hoobler, T. (2001). *The demon in the teahouse.* New York: Penguin Putnam.

Hoobler, D., & Hoobler, T. (2004). *In darkness, death.* New York: Penguin Putnam.

Hoobler, D., & Hoobler, T. (2005). *The sword that cut the burning grass.* New York: Penguin Putnam.

Hoobler, D., & Hoobler, T. (2007). *A samurai never fears death.* New York: Penguin Putnam.

Horowitz, A. (2001). *Alex Rider adventures series* (*Stormbreaker* #1). New York: Philomel/Penguin.

Horowitz, A. (2005). *The gatekeepers* series (*Raven's gate* #1). New York: Scholastic.

Horowitz, A. (2005). *Three of Diamonds: A Diamond brothers mystery.* New York: Philomel/Penguin.

Jennings, P. (2003). *The wolving time.* New York: Scholastic.

Kies, C. (1992). *Presenting young adult horror fiction.* Lanham, MD: Scarecrow Press.

King, S. (1974). *Carrie.* New York: Bantam Doubleday Dell/Random House.

King, S. (1975). *Salem's lot.* New York: Bantam Doubleday Dell/Random House.

King, S. (1977). *The shining.* New York: Bantam Doubleday Dell/Random House.

King, S. (1981). *Cujo.* New York: Viking/Penguin.

King, S. (1982). Rita Hayworth and Shawshank redemption. In *Different seasons.* New York: Viking/Penguin.

King, S. (1990). *Four past midnight.* New York: Viking/Penguin.

King, S. (1997). *The green mile: A novel in six parts.* New York: Plume/Penguin.

King, S. (1999). *The girl who loved Tom Gordon.* New York: Scribner/Simon & Schuster.

King, S. (2006). *Cell.* New York: Scribner/Simon & Schuster.

Koontz, D. (2003). *Odd Thomas.* New York: Bantam Doubleday Dell/Random House.

Landon, D. (2005). *Shapeshifter's quest.* New York: Dutton/Penguin.

Langer, J. A. (1995). *Envisioning literature: Literary understanding and literature instruction.* New York: Teachers College Press.

Larson, J. (2004). *Bringing mysteries alive for children and young adults.* Worthington, OH: Linworth.

Libby, A. M. (2006). *The blood confession.* New York: Dutton/Penguin.

Le Guin, U. K. (2005). The wife's story. In *The compass rose* (pp. 327–333). New York: Perennial/HarperCollins. (Original work published 1982)

Lewis, C. S. (1950). *The chronicles of Narnia* (*The lion, the witch, and the wardrobe* #1). Illus. Pauline Baynes. New York: Macmillan.

Mack, T., & Citrin, M. (2006). *Sherlock Holmes and the Baker Street irregulars: The falling of the amazing Zalindas.* New York: Orchard/Scholastic.

Madison, B. (2006). *Lulu Dark and the summer of the fox.* New York: Penguin.

Meyer, S. (2005). *Twilight.* New York: Little, Brown.

Meyer, S. (2006). *New moon.* New York: Little, Brown.

Meyer, S. (2007). *Eclipse.* New York: Little, Brown.

Meyer, S. (2008). *Breaking dawn.* New York: Little, Brown.

Miller, K. (2007). *The empress's tomb.* New York: Bloomsbury.

Nelson, B. (2006). *Paranoid park.* New York: Penguin.

Nixon, J. L. (1979). *The kidnapping of Christina Lattimore.* Orlando, FL: Harcourt.

Nixon, J. L. (1980). *The séance.* Orlando, FL: Harcourt.

Nixon, J. L. (1986). *The other side of dark.* New York: Delacorte/Random House.

Nixon, J. L. (1989). *Whispers from the dead.* New York: Delacorte/Random House.

Nixon, J. L. (1993). *The name of the game was murder.* New York: Delacorte/Random House.

The official study guide for all SAT Subject Tests. (2006). Plano, TX: College Board.

Olson, C. B. (2007). *The reading/writing connection: Strategies for teaching and learning in the secondary classroom.* Boston: Allyn & Bacon.

Parker, R. B. (2007). *Edenville Owls.* New York: Penguin.

Patterson, J. (2005a). *Mary, Mary.* New York: Little, Brown.

Patterson, J. (2005b). *Maximum ride: The angel experiment.* New York: Little, Brown.

Patterson, J. (2006a). *Cross.* New York: Little, Brown.

Patterson, J. (2006b). *Maximum ride: School's out—forever.* New York: Little, Brown.

Patterson, J. (2007). *Maximum ride: Saving the world and other extreme sports.* New York: Little, Brown.

Patterson, J. (2008). *Maximum ride: The final warning.* New York: Little, Brown.

Peck, R. (1976). *Are you in the house alone?* New York: Viking/Penguin.

Peters, E. (1986). *Lion in the valley.* New York: Atheneum/Simon & Schuster.

Peters, E. (2007). *The mummy case.* New York: HarperCollins.

Pike, C. (1985). *Slumber party.* New York: Scholastic.

Pike, C. (1989). *Remember me* series (*Remember me* #1). New York: Simon & Schuster.

Pike, C. (1994). *The last vampire* series (*The last vampire* #1). New York: Simon & Schuster.

Pike, C. (2007). *Falling.* New York: Forge/Tom Doherty.

Pratchett, T. (1983). *Discworld* series (*The colour of magic* #1). New York: St. Martin's Press.

Pullman, P. (1985). *The ruby in the smoke.* New York: Knopf/Random House.

Pullman, P. (1988). *The shadow in the north.* New York: Knopf/Random House.

Pullman, P. (1990). *The tiger in the well.* New York: Knopf/Random House.

Pullman, P. (1994). *The tin princess.* New York: Knopf/Random House.

Pullman, P. (1996). *The golden compass.* New York: Knopf/Random House.

Raskin, E. (1978). *The Westing game.* New York: Dutton/Penguin.

Reiche. D. (2005). *Ghost ship: A novel* (John Brownjohn, Trans.). New York: Scholastic.

Reiss, K. (1991). *Time windows.* Orlando, FL: Harcourt.

Reiss, K. (1992). *The glass house people.* Orlando, FL: Harcourt.

Reiss, K. (1994). *Pale phoenix.* Orlando, FL: Harcourt.

Reiss, K. (1998). *PaperQuake: A puzzle.* Orlando, FL: Harcourt.

Reiss, K. (2002). *Paint by magic.* Orlando, FL: Harcourt.

Reiss, K. (2004a). *Dreadfully sorry.* Orlando, FL: Harcourt.

Reiss, K. (2004b). *Sweet Miss Honeywell's revenge: A ghost story.* Orlando, FL: Harcourt.

Reiss, K. (2006). *Blackthorn winter.* Orlando, FL: Harcourt.

Rice, A. (1985). *The vampire lestat.* New York: Knopf/Random House.

Roberts, W. D. (1988). *Megan's island.* New York: Atheneum/Simon & Schuster.

Roberts, W. D. (1994). *The absolutely true story . . . How I visited Yellowstone Park with the terrible Rupes.* New York: Atheneum/Simon & Schuster.

Roberts, W. D. (1996). *Twisted summer.* New York: Atheneum/Simon & Schuster.

Roe, B. D., Stoodt, B. D., & Burns, P. C. (1995). *The content reading areas: Secondary school reading instruction.* Boston: Houghton Mifflin.

Rowling, J. K. (1997). *Harry Potter* series (*Harry Potter and the sorcerer's stone* #1). New York: Scholastic.

Schreiber, E. (2003a). *Teenage mermaid.* New York: HarperCollins.

Schreiber, E. (2003b). *Vampire kisses.* New York: HarperCollins.

Schreiber, E. (2004). *Comedy girl*. New York: HarperCollins.

Schreiber, E. (2005). *Vampire kisses 2: Kissing coffins*. New York: HarperCollins.

Schreiber, E. (2006). *Vampire kisses 3: Vampireville*. New York: HarperCollins.

Schreiber, E. (2007a). *Vampire kisses: Blood relatives (Vol. 1.)*. Los Angeles: Tokyopop.

Schreiber, E. (2007b). *Vampire kisses 4: Dance with a vampire*. New York: HarperCollins.

Schreiber, E. (2008). *Vampire kisses 5: The coffin club*. New York: HarperCollins.

Sedgwick, M. (2004). *The book of dead days*. New York: Random House.

Shan, D. (2001). *Cirque du freak* series (*A living nightmare* #1). New York: Little, Brown.

Shan, D. (2005). *The Demonata* series (*Lord loss* #1). New York: Little, Brown.

Shan, D. (2006a). *Demon thief*. New York: Little, Brown.

Shan, D. (2006b). *Slawter*. New York: Little, Brown.

Shan, D. (2007a). *Bec*. New York: Little, Brown.

Shan, D. (2007b). *Blood beast*. New York: Little, Brown.

Shan, D. (2008). *Demon apocalypse*. New York: Little, Brown.

Shusterman, N. (1995). *Scorpion shards*. New York: Tor.

Shusterman, N. (2003). *Full tilt*. New York: Simon & Schuster.

Shusterman, N. (2005). *Dread locks*. New York: Dutton/Penguin.

Skelton, M. (2006). *Endymion spring*. New York: Delacorte/Random House.

Sleator, W. (1083). *Fingers*. New York: Atheneum/Simon & Schuster.

Sleator, W. (2001). *Marco's millions*. New York: Dutton/Penguin.

Sleator, W. (2004). *The boy who couldn't die*. New York: Harry N. Abrams.

Smith, C. L. (2007). *Tantalize*. Cambridge, MA: Candlewick Press.

Somper, J. (2007). *Vampirates: Tide of terror*. New York: Little, Brown.

Somper, J. (2008). *Vampirates: Blood captain*. New York: Little, Brown.

Sorrells, W. (2005). *Fake ID*. New York: Puffin/Penguin.

Sorrells, W. (2006). *Club dread*. New York: Puffin/Penguin.

Spradlin, M. (2005). *Spy goddess* series, (*Live and let shop* #1). New York: HarperCollins.

Spradlin, M. P. (2006). *Spy goddess: To Hawaii, with love*. New York: HarperCollins.

Springer, N. (2006). *The case of the missing marquess: An Enola Holmes mystery*. New York: Philomel/Penguin.

Stahler, D., Jr. (2004). *Truesight*. New York: HarperCollins.

Stahler, D., Jr. (2006). *Doppleganger*. New York: EOS/HarperCollins.

Stahler, D., Jr. (2007). *The seer*. New York: HarperCollins.

Stine, R. L. (1986). *Blind date*. New York: Scholastic.

Stine, R. L. (1989). *Fear street* series (*The new girl* #1). New York: SimonPluse/Simon & Schuster.

Stine, R. L. (1992). *Goosebumps* series (*Welcome to dead house* #1). New York: Scholastic.

Thomas, H. (1999). *Hannibal*. New York: Dell/Random House.

Tiernan, C. (2001). *Sweep* series (*Book of shadows* #1). New York: Penguin.

Tiernan, C. (2005). *Balefire* series (*A chalice of wind* #1). New York: Penguin.

Watson, J. (2005). *Disappearance: A premonitions mystery*. New York: Scholastic.

Werlin, N. (1998). *The killer's cousin*. New York: Delacorte/Random House.

Werlin, N. (2000). *Locked inside*. New York: Delacorte/Random House.

Werlin, N. (2006). *The rules of survival*. New York: Dial/Penguin.

Windsor, P. (1991). *The Christmas killer*. New York: Scholastic.

Windsor, P. (2006). *Nightwood*. New York: Delacorte/Random House.

Wooding, C. (2001). *The haunting of Alaizabel Cray*. New York: Scholastic.

Zwiers, J. (2004). *Building reading comprehension habits in Grades 6–12: A toolkit of classroom activities*. Newark, DE: International Reading Association.

Science Fiction and Fantasy
Reading Skills: Visualizing and Vocabulary

Introduction

We are inquisitive and imaginative beings. Young and old alike speculate and ask questions about the past, present, and future: Is there life on other planets? How will the world end? Can we perfect the human species and find a way to live forever? What if Hitler won World War II or the South won the Civil War? We dream of altered worlds and worlds unlike our own—magical and fantastical places and frightening and violent realms inhabited by otherworldly creatures such as faeries, gnomes, unicorns, and hobbits. Science fiction and fantasy, two separate and distinct genres, have long satisfied our curiosity and imagination.[1]

In some works, science fiction and fantasy create a blended genre. Within the *Star Wars* series, for instance, magic and technology work hand-in-hand. In Eoin Colfer's *Artemis Fowl* series (2001) fairy magic is part magic, part technology. Kenneth Oppel's Michael L. Printz Honor book, *Airborn* (2004), and its sequel, *Skybreaker* (2006), reminiscent of Jules Verne's work, blend both genres. So does the young adult classic *A Wrinkle in Time* (1962) by Madeleine L'Engle. Examples of blended genres are endless.

In an effort to identify the unique characteristics of each, this chapter addresses each genre separately. For each genre a historical context is provided, the distinct and overlapping qualities of both genres are discussed, and popular themes, titles, and authors are highlighted. In much the same way as serial romance novels dominated the 1980s, today's YA market is saturated with fantasy sequels, trilogies, and series. The fantasy titles highlighted here are a mere slice of the young adult market. Because of the vastness of the science fiction and fantasy genres (primarily fantasy) and the fact that many young adult fairy tales are reinventions of classics, folklore and fairy tales are examined in Chapter 11. This chapter concludes with instructional strategies for using science fiction and fantasy to teach visualization and vocabulary.

Science Fiction
What Is Science Fiction?

Alien encounters and space exploration are hallmarks of science fiction—think of classic stories and films such as *The War of the Worlds* (1898), *2001: A Space Odyssey* (1968), various *Star Trek* creations, and *Independence Day* (1996). However, the use of aliens is only one of many plot devices

---

[1]"Science Fiction" primary author Faith H. Wallace; "Fantasy" co-authors Pam B. Cole and Faith H. Wallace; "Visualizing" and "Vocabulary" by Pam B. Cole.

(e.g., time travel, mad scientists, genetic manipulations). Disagreement centers on the nature and use of science and technology within the story structure (del Rey, 1980; Mann, 2001). In fact, Isaac Asimov (1981) once defined science fiction as "that branch of literature that deals with human responses to changes in the level of science and technology" (p. 21). This definition constrains the genre and may exclude works that emphasize alternative history and social sciences (e.g., political science, sociology). While a succinct definition may be elusive, three core elements set quality science fiction apart from other genres: (1) stories present alternate perspectives of reality, (2) authors ground the work in elements of science, and (3) the work maintains internal consistency.

Alternate Perspectives

Science fiction is the ultimate "What if?" Authors use "what if" questions to generate stories that present alternate perspectives of reality. That is, science fiction imagines a possible future (e.g., colonization of another planet, the development of new technologies) or reconceptualizes the past (e.g., the South wins the Civil War). The plot can involve a mystery, romance, comedy, adventure, and so forth; the construction of the alternate time or place is critical. At the heart of the story is the element of speculation:

> Science fiction, to a noticeable extent, rejects the unchanging order of
> things. It states implicitly, if not explicitly, that the world of the story
> is different from the accepted present or past of the reader. The change
> may be in science, environment, attitude, morality, or the basic nature of
> humanity. But it must have this change in the story. (del Rey, 1980, p. 9)

As such, many authors prefer the term *speculative fiction*[2] to *science fiction* because they are creating speculations of alternate possibilities. How alternate is alternate? Classic science fiction speculates on new discoveries and scientific advancement (e.g., Jules Verne's *Twenty Thousand Leagues under the Sea*, 1870; and H. G. Wells's *The Invisible Man*, 1897). Asimov has been speculating on the artificial intelligence of robotics since the 1940s with *I, Robot* (1950).[3] Among the best in alternative history, *The Man in the High Castle* (1962) by Philip K. Dick speculates on life after Hitler wins World War II.

Young adult science fiction began in the early 1900 serials in which young adult inventors, mostly boys, constructed elaborate contraptions, taking them on innumerable adventures.[4] Molson (1999) notes that these

---

[2]There is much debate about use of the term *speculative fiction*. Renowned science fiction author Isaac Asimov publicly opposed its use, believing that science fiction, by definition, should deal with changes in science and technology. He conjectured that the term *speculative fiction* was conceived in order to keep the SF abbreviation.

[3]Asimov wrote a series of short stories dealing with robotics published in magazines in the 1940s. In 1950, Gnome Press published the series in a book titled *I, Robot*. In 2004 the movie adaptation was released starring Will Smith.

[4]This early science fiction was called technological fiction and was often serialized.

early works focused on inventions in three main areas: radio, auto, and air—appropriate technological speculations for the time. Perhaps the most recognized are the *Tom Swift*[5] books (Sullivan, 2006), tackling inventions in airplanes, warships, and moving pictures. Young adult science fiction was transformed when Robert Heinlein published *Rocket Ship Galileo* (1947) in which a group of young adults, with the help of a scientist, create a rocket to take them to the moon. While the genre was being taken seriously, it hadn't lost its fascination with technological and scientific speculation.

Speculations, however, aren't necessarily linked to inventions. For example, *Z for Zachariah* (O'Brien, 1974), considered classic young adult science fiction, depicts the results of a nuclear war with only a few survivors, including 15-year-old Ann Burden. O'Brien's book set a new standard for young adult fiction in a time when most writers were writing problem novels. So, too, did William Sleator (e.g., *House of Stairs*, 1974). One of today's foremost "what if" writers is Terry Pratchett. In *Johnny and the Bomb* (2007), a 12-year-old protagonist knows exactly when the Germans will bomb London during World War II. Johnny has the ability to time travel. What will happen if he stops the bomb and changes the course of history? This kind of speculation appeals to the young adult audience.

Speculation topics are as limitless as our ability to ask *what if*, and asking *what if* demands possibilities. Authors have to posit answers to their questions and challenge characters to deal with the consequences. This idea leads to the second core quality of science fiction: authors ground their work in elements of science.

Grounding Reality

Despite the fact that science fiction authors create, in essence, alternate realities, quality science fiction *must* be rooted in scientific principles, which generally sets it apart from fantasy. That is why magic doesn't work in science fiction—unless it can be explained scientifically or technologically. If the author asks readers to speculate on a technological invention, possible future, or alternative past, readers must have a sense of rationality that the speculations are *possible* (not necessarily *plausible*) given the story framework (e.g., space travel, life on other planets). Authors ground science fiction in existing science, math, technology, and even history. Instead of magic, science fiction includes genetic engineering or manipulations. Classics include Aldous Huxley's *Brave New World* (1932) and Michael Crichton's *Jurassic Park* (1990). A recent young adult example is Joe Craig's *Jimmy Coates* series (2005) in which the protagonist is genetically engineered and created to kill by the government.

---

[5]The original *Tom Swift* books were written by Edward Stratemeyer under the house name Victor Appleton starting in 1910 and included close to 40 titles. The series continued with *Tom Swift Jr.* in the 1950s, thus the inventions changed with times. *Tom Jr.* dealt with the ocean, earth, moon, and solar system. A third series began in the '80s focusing on space travel and aliens, and a fourth series in the '90s expanded to include technology such as lasers.

When writing alternative history, authors must couch their speculations in historical events. Harry Turtledove, for instance, is famous for alternative history showcasing differing outcomes to the Civil War, World War I, and World War II. His more recent work explores an alternative history in which Japan bombs, invades, and occupies Pearl Harbor (*Days of Infamy*, 2004, and *End of the Beginning*, 2005). The success of an alternative history work hinges on the historical accuracy until the author diverges from real to alternate.

Young adult science fiction is often criticized for not being rooted in science principles (Mendlesohn, 2004), for relying too much on loose explanations and plot gimmicks. Grounding in real science and technology, however, can be traced back to some of the earliest works. In the *Airship Boys* series (Salyer, 1909), for instance, two teen inventors actually create a working airplane. Molson (1999) notes,

> The youths work out the elements of an innovative propulsion system employing liquefied hydrogen and install it in the Cibola, a dirigible balloon they have constructed in their workroom. . . . What is even more startling is the author's laying out in an illustrated two-page spread the details of the youths' invention. (p. 10)

At the time of the *Airship Boys* series the Wright brothers were experimenting with flight. What appear to be "loose" scientific explanations in one generation may be highly probable later.

Current names in young adult science fiction such as William Sleator ground their work in complex science: chaos theory (e.g., *Strange Attractors*, 1990) and quantum physics (e.g., *The Last Universe*, 2005). Sleator addresses the appeal of science fiction to young adults in the author box. Malcolm Rose, a scientist and young adult author, discusses the natural link between science and science fiction in his author box.

Interestingly, Robert W. Bly (2005) notes, "Many of the most fascinating ideas in science originated not in the laboratory, but in the minds of imaginative science fiction writers" (p. 1). He cites submarines, satellites, and cloning as examples. While young adult science fiction authors like Sleator and Rose deal with complex scientific concepts in the "hard" sciences, other authors focus on social (or "soft") sciences. *Jennifer Government* (Barry, 2003) explores economics and consumerism in a future in which corporations are more powerful than governments. Whether authors emphasize science, technology, math, or history, science fiction can be an entry point for discussing important content area topics. Box 8.1 showcases some examples.

A general misconception is that science fiction is escapist and simplistic because of its imaginative story lines. What is often overlooked is the complexity of rooting the stories in *real* principles. The reader has work to do imagining the author's world, understanding the science and technology involved, and considering prior historical knowledge. The more the author asks readers to speculate, the more the author must create boundaries for the story line and maintain internal consistency.

Writing Science Fiction for Young Adults   by William Sleator

In an unexpected way, young adults are a very satisfying audience. They are not polite. They don't read something because it received good reviews or is part of the current "culture." Picking up a book does *not* mean they feel obliged to finish it, as it does for many adults. In fact, given the barrage of TV shows, movies, games, and instant messages constantly vying for teenagers' attention, it is pretty amazing if they read an entire book at all.

What this means to a writer is that if young adults do read a book and actually finish it they really like it. And if they are then moved to write to the author about it (of their own volition, *not* by a class assignment), then you know for a fact you've reached them. At the risk of bragging, I have to admit to often receiving letters that essentially say, "I don't like to read. I never read a whole book before. Then my teacher (or librarian, or friend, or sibling) gave me your book, and I started reading it and couldn't stop, and I read the whole thing! Now I want to read all your books." A letter like this is proof that you've won. You have *shown* them that reading is the best entertainment there is. You can't just tell them this: they have to experience it; they have to be carried off into the world of books.

From my perspective, science fiction is a wonderful way to create this experience for teenagers. Of course, you also have to do all the obvious things that hook readers and keep them involved: starting out at an exciting moment that pulls them in, keeping the excitement going with techniques such as cliff-hanging chapter endings, writing about believable characters they can identify with (not paragons of virtue) in situations that most readers can relate to. If you then add to this mix some of the characteristics of science fiction, you can come up with a real winning package.

Of course, I don't deny the pervasive popularity of fantasy. But from what I have observed, fantasy is embraced more by younger, middle grade readers. By the time they are teenagers, they have become more skeptical. That's why I think science fiction can have such great appeal to older teens—especially reluctant readers. They (and I) don't believe in elves, fairies, or wizards who can wave their wands and make anything happen; such beings have no parallel in the real world as we experience it. But we all know that other planets are real, and spaceships—we can see them both. Even those scientists who are absolutely grounded in

reality can't deny that it's more likely than not that intelligent aliens really do exist—the universe is so huge that they have to be there somewhere. For this reason, with science fiction you can have all sorts of wondrous, unearthly events taking place, and at the same time, *you can really believe they're happening*. This takes teenagers' skepticism and demolishes it. It can give them something wonderful, even magical, to read that is also as real as a true crime story.

One quick example. It has been a demonstrable fact for almost a century that gravity slows down time. Although we perceive time as clicking along unchangingly forever, this just isn't the way it is. Once readers are made aware of this fact, you can then give them a story about a shed in which time goes more slowly: an hour passes inside, while outside only one second goes by. Think how great this would be for teenagers! You could go inside and stay as long as you wanted, and your parents would never even know you were gone. The possibilities are endless. Once readers accept this fact, you can create scenarios as enchanting and scary as any fantasy, but, once again, they have the unbeatable advantage that they could really happen. What could be better than that?

Official Web site: www.cs.cmu.edu/~sleator

Sleator's works include *Run* (1973), *House of Stairs* (1974), *Among the Dolls* (1975), *Into the Dream* (1979), *Green Futures of Tycho* (1981), *Fingers* (1983), *Interstellar Pig* (1984), *Singularity* (1985), *The Boy Who Reversed Himself* (1986), *Duplicate* (1988), *Strange Attractions* (1990), *Spirit House* (1991), *Oddballs* (1993), *Others See Us* (1993), *Dangerous Wishes* (1995), *The Night the Heads Came* (1996), *Beasties* (1997), *The Boxes* (1998), *Boltzmon!* (1999), *Rewind* (1999), *Marco's Millions* (2001), *Parasite Pig* (2002), *The Boy Who Couldn't Die* (2004), *The Last Universe* (2005), and *Hell Phone* (2006).

Science in Young Adult Science Fiction by Malcolm Rose

Toward the end of 2004, newspapers in the UK reported that a man had been jailed for an armed robbery he'd committed more than a decade earlier. An itchy scalp and modern forensic science put him behind bars. Years after the crime, he was identified through DNA profiling of dandruff flakes left inside a stocking after he'd pulled it over his head to hide his identity during the robbery.

What does this tell us? We love reading about crime. We like it when clever science gets the bad guys. It also tells us that forensic science has advanced a lot in the last few years, and new techniques can solve cases that would otherwise remain a mystery. What does it tell authors? Writers looking for original ideas for contemporary stories should look to science because something new is always emerging from laboratories. And it's not just forensic science. Some topics that have recently made the leap from labs to news bulletins are face transplants, cloning, attempts to make simple life-forms from scratch (synthetic biology), virtual reality, chemical and biological warfare, the bird flu virus, sophisticated weaponry, surveillance techniques, and embryo screening. It's a gold mine of new ideas and ethical dilemmas for thrillers and crime fiction.

A writer may opt to put some science in a work of fiction, but it remains a novel and not a textbook. That may seem to be a weakness when it comes to educating readers in science, but the fact that a novel is entertainment is actually a strength. The frilly wrapping makes the concepts inside far more digestible, especially for a young audience.

In my teenage thriller, *Plague* (2000), I let loose a hemorrhagic fever on a mixed community in the UK. That allowed me to explore how the alien virus would bring out the best and worst in the different social groups, and how modern biological science would deal with the threat. I interspersed the text with a biologist's lecture notes on viruses. These passages dealt with history:

> In the winter of 1918–19, swine flu made half the world's population ill and annihilated one fifth of humanity in six months. It caused over 20 million deaths.

They covered some basic biology and chemistry:

> A ten millionth of an inch across, a virus is a package of genetic material wrapped in a jacket of protein, sometimes with a greasy overcoat, sometimes sugar-coated. Inside a cell, a virus pirates the host's chemical machinery and churns out more copies of itself. That is its sole purpose: to reproduce itself as many times as possible. Viruses do not eat, grow or have sex; they just multiply.

And the greater the yuck factor, the more readers are engaged to it.

> The skin around the mouth is home to many microbes and the mouth teems with different bacteria. When people kiss, the outer layers of bacteria are ripped away from their moorings on the teeth. Grease from the corners of the mouth is torn away, along with spurts of acne bacteria. A passionate kiss generates a wind tunnel effect, a howling gale to bacteria and viruses, which stream from one person to the other with

Continued

Science in Young Adult Science Fiction *Continued*

the sloshing saliva. After, if the kissing couple rests their foreheads together, the invisible families of demodex mites living on their eyelashes interchange, hunting for food like mascara or acne cream.

Synthetic biology is the theme of a new thriller for young people, *The Death Gene* (2006). Attempting to create a new bacterium from nonliving substances is an audacious aim that will illuminate what life is and what it means to be alive. Religious believers may be uncomfortable with scientists taking the role of creators; entrepreneurs may like to develop synthetic organisms for cleaning up pollution or treating ill health, and environmentalists may fear designer bacteria escaping from the laboratory and causing havoc in the community. In the book, I've represented all these viewpoints, and one other. It's a thriller because terrorists and military groups may wish to use emerging technology to tailor-make a living weapon for biological warfare.

I strongly believe that young people can and do absorb the latest—and even complex—science as long as language is appropriate. In *The Death Gene*, there is a key passage on bacterial quorum-sensing,

a full understanding of which may lead to the next generation of antibiotics:

> Bacteria are like school bullies. They only turn nasty if they're convinced they've got the numbers to swamp their victim's immune system. So they must be able to estimate their own numbers. How do they do that? They send out a chemical signal to each other. They all detect this signal and gauge its concentration. The more of them there are, the greater the concentration. It's almost as good as counting. It's called quorum-sensing, like a committee that only makes decisions when it's got a quorum.

The solution to the bioterrorism in the novel lies with this intricate aspect of biology. If I had omitted it, the story would have had a very different and devastating conclusion.

Copyright Malcolm Rose, 2008

Official Web site: www.malcolmrose.co.uk

Science fiction fans will want to check out Rose's the *Lawless and Tilley* series (1997) and the *Traces* series (2005d).

Box 8.1   Science Fiction for Content Area Classrooms

The Aquanauts by John Lunn. Plattsburg, NY: Tundra, 2005.

Greta's father is a renowned scientist working on space-time theories. When she accompanies him to his deep-sea research center, she has no idea that his team created a black hole that serves as a time travel device. Greta and the other children of researchers must control time traveling and destroy the lab experiment before disaster ensues.

Code Orange by Caroline B. Cooney. New York: Delacorte/Random House, 2005.

Variola major is a severe form of smallpox, taking over cells in the body and spreading until no healthy cells remain. When Mitty Blake discovers two scabs between the pages of an old medical book, will he unleash a dangerous disease previously eradicated?

Continued

Box 8.1   Science Fiction for Content Area Classrooms   *Continued*

Darwinia by Robert Charles Wilson. New York: Tor, 1998.

In 1912 Europe was changed overnight—cities, forests, and people all disappeared and were replaced with a primeval landscape complete with otherworldly trees, plants, and animals. In this alternate version of the early 20th century, President Woodrow Wilson did not declare war on Germany—there was no Germany. Instead, he introduced the Wilson Doctrine, which declared Europe a wilderness open for resettlement.

Hurricane Force by Malcolm Rose. New York: Simon & Schuster, 2005.

Can the weather be used as a weapon? That is exactly the scenario teenager Jake Patmore fears if the wrong people gain access to his late father's groundbreaking scientific weather discoveries.

The Last Universe by William Sleator. New York: Amulet/Harry N. Abrams, 2005.

Susan cares for her sick older brother Gary, who believes a garden maze may allow them to travel to a parallel universe, where he will not be sick. Uncle Arthur, a quantum physicist, plays an important role.

Murphy's Gambit by Syne Mitchell. New York: ROC/Penguin, 2000.

Thiadora Murphy, an outcast and Floater, joins the space academy despite harsh treatment from peers. Floaters believe physics is a religion. When Thiadora is unjustly framed for a crime, she must work on a ship that can fold space and time. Throughout are scientific explanations.

ReVisions edited by Julie E. Czerneda and Isaac Szpindel. New York: DAW/Penguin, 2004.

In this collection of alternative history short stories, the speculations center on scientific and mathematical discoveries: Could laser technologies have affected World War I? What if dogs had not been domesticated? How would Victorian England have dealt with the AIDS virus?

The Supernaturalist by Eoin Colfer. New York: Miramax/Hyperion, 2004.

Orphans are used as lab rats in a futuristic society run by corporations. A group of vigilante orphans fight a deadly parasite that only they can see. Colfer mixes science and technology in this science fiction thriller.

Surviving Antarctica: Reality TV 2083 by Andrea White. New York: EOS/HarperCollins, 2005.

In a future where education is viewed as entertainment, a group of teenagers embark on a new reality television show: *Antarctic Historical Survivor*. The teens plan to re-create the doomed first journey to the Antarctic in 1912 by Robert F. Scott to the last detail.

Traces series (Framed #1) by Malcolm Rose. Boston: Kingfisher, 2005.

Luke Harding is only 16, but he is the youngest forensic investigator working for the authorities. His first assignment: clear his name of triple murder. Harding uses sound scientific practices to uncover the truth. His adventures continue in *Lost Bullet* (2005b), *Roll Call* (2005c), *Double Check* (2007a), and *Final Lap* (2007b).

Turnabout by Margaret Peterson Haddix. New York: Simon & Schuster, 2000.

Project Turnabout was created to stop the aging process by preventing genetic material from shrinking. The research has unforeseen effects: the genetic material not only shrinks, but grows. During an experiment, two elderly women begin to un-age—they grow younger and younger. Will they reach zero age?

Useful Idiots by Jan Mark. New York: Fickling/Random House, 2004.

When a violent storm crosses the North Sea and uncovers a human skull on a beach, Merrick, a graduate archaeology student, finds himself in a politically explosive environment. Merrick and his supervising professor do not expect the riots that follow the exhumation of the skeleton. A futuristic social commentary in which a society tries to forget its past.

Internal Consistency

Science fiction writers cannot create a free-for-all universe where anything can happen at any time (well, they can, but it wouldn't be of great quality). Orson Scott Card (1990), master science fiction author, explains, "Because speculative fiction always differs from the knowable world, the reader is uncertain about what can and can't happen in the story *until* the writer has spelled out the rules" (p. 36). Writers have to create boundaries, and sometimes even cultures and languages. Doing so may be easier said than done. For example, the character Data in *Star Trek: The Next Generation* is the rational, analytical android; part of his programming limits his ability to use contractions when speaking. While it appears to be a minor boundary for the character, it requires that anyone writing thoughts or dialogue for Data[6] refrain at all times from using contractions (unless, of course, Data's programming has been changed or the character is really Data's evil brother, but that's another story).

Internal consistency is paramount to quality science fiction, so authors must never break their own rules—rule breaking undermines the story. Good writers are well versed in their story world parameters. As del Rey (1980) notes, "A good story requires that the writer try to discover every ramification of his original idea and build a world, society, or situation as completely as possible without violating the limits of his original assumption or dragging in conflicting ones" (p. 7).

The depth and complexity of the boundaries are, in a way, determined by the nature of the story: how alternate is the alternate world and how intricate is the science or social science of the plot? Time travel is a classic science fiction and fantasy plot device (e.g., *The Time Machine* by H. G. Wells, 1895) that exemplifies the need for boundaries and internal consistency: will traveling back in time affect history (e.g., *A Sound of Thunder* by Ray Bradbury, 1952), will characters continue to exist if they change history, namely their own past (e.g., *Back to the Future*, 1985), and can characters travel outside their own time lines (e.g., *Quantum Leap* television series[7])? Of course, we don't want the plot interrupted with extraneous details about cultures, customs, languages, and technologies, but authors should be adept at weaving in details when necessary and remaining consistent in language and story structure.

Science Fiction Formats and Subgenres

Some argue that the first science fiction novel was Mary Shelley's *Frankenstein* (1818), but science fiction as a genre gained momentum in the mid- and late 1800s with works from authors like Jules Verne, Robert Louis Stevenson, and H. G. Wells (Clute, 1995). Despite the complexity of these early works, science fiction wasn't always taken seriously and that, perhaps, has to do

---

[6]A number of novelized extensions by various authors exist for the *Star Trek* franchise. For more information about novelized extensions, see Chapter 12.
[7]*Quantum Leap,* created by Donald P. Bellisario, aired from 1989 to 1993 on NBC.

with the emergence of the *pulps* (magazines) in the 1920s[8] featuring science fiction short stories (Mann, 2001) This format was cheap, easy to publish, and some of science fiction's greatest writers[9] got their start in these. Robert Heinlein and Isaac Asimov wrote for *Astounding Science Fiction* (1938–1960),[10] and Ray Bradbury wrote for *Planet Stories* (1939–1955). Thus, science fiction has a rich history in the short story.

Many contemporary young adult science fiction short stories have been turned into novels. Orson Scott Card's *Ender's Game* (1977) first appeared as a short story in *Analog* magazine in 1977. It was later expanded into a novel as the first novel in the *Ender Wiggin* series. *The Last Book in the Universe* (2000) by young adult author Rodman Philbrick became a novel after appearing in the short story collection *Tomorrowland* (1999) by Michael Cart. Other short stories are listed later in the chapter.

Regardless of format, science fiction is either *hard* or *soft*. Hard science fiction emphasizes scientific accuracy or technical detail. It's generally grounded in quantitative sciences such as physics, chemistry, and geology. Hard science fiction is deeply rooted in the scientific background that allows for the possibilities created in the author's world, and the author spends a great deal of time explaining the science of the story. For example, Hal Clement's *Mission of Gravity* (1954) explores another planet with very different atmospheric properties than Earth, which poses exploration problems. Issues of gravitational pull, temperature, and other planetary features are discussed in detail and are critical to the plotline. Soft science fiction is grounded in the social sciences such as philosophy, political science, psychology, sociology, and anthropology, which are qualitative disciplines. It is character-driven and presents commentary on societal issues.[11] Pete Hautman's *Rash* (2006), for instance, takes a satirical look at a futuristic society in which freedom and individual rights are sacrificed for safety.

Mann (2001) cautions, however, that hard and soft science fiction are not polar opposites. Soft science fiction may contain elements of the hard sciences, and hard science fiction may emphasize character and story over scientific underpinnings of the story line. For instance, young adult authors such as Sleator (e.g., *The Last Universe,* 2005) and Rose (e.g., *Hurricane Force,* 2005) use hard sciences in their novels, but the real emphasis is on the characters and storytelling, which push their books more toward soft science fiction.

Because young adults are drawn to science fiction primarily because of speculation, adventure, and suspense *and* because publishers and some authors fear science can "go over teens' heads," most young adult science fiction leans toward soft science fiction,[12] using just enough "hard" science to ground their stories and help readers make connections and predictions and

---

[8]*Amazing Stories* was considered the first pulp to successfully focus exclusively on science fiction.
[9]Isaac Asimov, Arthur C. Clake, Robert Heinlein, and Ray Bradbury are often considered the fathers of modern science fiction.
[10]*Astounding Science Fiction* started publishing in the 1930s and changed its name to *Analog* in the 1960s. *Analog* continues to be published today.
[11]Because of the emphasis on characters and style, soft science fiction is sometimes called literary science fiction.
[12]One of the debates in the young adult literature world is the idea of what teens can and cannot handle. Many believe the genre is sometimes "dummied" down.

to fuel their sense of wonder. Character-driven social commentaries are the heart of young adult science fiction. In *Firestorm* (2006), the first book of the *Caretaker Trilogy,* Klass warns of the impending destruction of Earth's ecology because of our current behaviors. In *Spacer and Rat* (2005), Bechard presents sharp commentary about blind bigotry in a futuristic society where humans and robots coexist in space. In the author box, young author Sonia Levitin discusses social commentary in two of her works: *The Cure* (1999) and *The Goodness Gene* (2005).

Hard science fiction, soft science fiction, or social commentary: the core elements of science fiction do not limit the storytelling structure. Science fiction can embody elements from other genres, such as mystery (*The Red Thread* by Roderick Townley, 2007), romance (*Journey between Worlds* by Sylvia Louise Engdahl, 2006), and comedy (*Princess from Another Planet* by Mindy Schanback, 2005). Two science fiction categories are important to note: *space operas* and *cyberpunk.*

The easiest way to understand the space opera is to call to mind a classic: *Star Wars.* Space operas get their name from their soap opera counterparts on daytime television. The emphasis is on action-packed adventure with complex relationships, deceit, and disaster

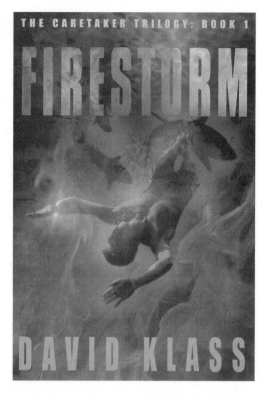

Reprinted by permission of Farrar, Straus and Giroux, LLC.

far away from Earth. It doesn't hurt to include a variety of alien races, technological wonders, an evil enemy, and plenty of cliff-hangers. Space operas move quickly, relying more on adventure than science. Scott Westerfeld's *Succession* series (2003) is a classic space opera. It takes place in an interstellar empire with tension among humans, the resurrected (humans that cheat death), and cyborgs (humans aided by mechanical or electronic devices). Kidnapping, escape plots, and war make for an action-packed, fast-paced read.

While cyberpunk may include advanced technology and gripping action sequences, it is darker and presents frightening versions of a future in which humans are enslaved or overrun by technology. This science fiction subgenre developed in the 1980s[13] when major advances in technology were being realized, including virtual reality and cyberspace. Cyberpunk offers a message of caution: technology cannot and should not be trusted—think of movies like *The Matrix* (1999) and *Minority Report* (2002). M. T. Anderson's *Feed* (2002) is a harrowing piece of cyberpunk for young adults. All beings in this futuristic society have computer chip implants monitoring and controlling their environments. Anderson's commentary on consumerism makes this piece particularly relevant today. Young adults relish adventure in science fiction. Box 8.2 presents a sampling of space operas, cyperpunk, and other adventures to quell voracious science fiction appetites.

---

[13]William Gibson's *Neuromancer* (1984) is often credited with launching the cyberpunk subgenre.

Social Commentary   by Sonia Levitin

Few literary forms lend themselves to social commentary as well as science fiction, especially for the young adult reader. Why is science fiction such a powerful tool for promoting independent thinking and influencing teens to grapple with difficult decisions? Because, let's face it, being a teen means being constantly nagged, admonished, and corrected. The teen years are an awkward, self-conscious time, filled with personal and existential doubt and longings. Some of these are expressed in popular music or in long night talks with peers. Rarely, however, are serious, deeper thoughts of social concern allowed to rise to the surface: It, just isn't "cool."

Enter the science fiction tale, with a compelling hero who is willing to confront the world, not the recognizable world of today, with its complications and problems, its fads and political extremes. No, the science fiction world is even *more* extreme in its evils, the hero more passionate about his aspirations, because often his success or failure determines not only his own fate but the fate of the entire planet and beyond. What an astounding premise! Everybody, especially young people just on the verge of adulthood, wants to feel that their actions can make a difference. In the science fiction novel the stakes are the highest possible: total annihilation or rebirth. Science fiction poses more sharply than any other literature the contrast between privilege and democracy, slavery versus freedom, war versus peace, destruction versus genesis. Science fiction offers the greatest possible reward for courage and wise action.

Science fiction gives the writer a wonderful opportunity for social criticism. Here we can zero in on the foibles and fallacies of our time, without insulting anyone. In *The Goodness Gene,* for example, sexual pleasure comes from "sym-sex," a vaguely described electronic simulator that provides satisfaction without guilt or responsibility. Sounds like some of today's activities, doesn't it? But the novel offers no critique, only a model for the reader to examine. Similarly, in *The Cure,* characters are treated almost interchangeably; if one disappears, another shows up. There is no real intimacy, with its attendant challenges and emotional risks. Without emotion, without love and risk, there is no creativity, only a kind of bland extremism, where rules and strange ideologies take the place of individual choice. The reader must wonder: How much choice do I really have? What can be changed? How, and to what effect?

In both novels we see euphemisms and distortions. Things are not what they seem. We must be wary. In both novels, blind obedience to power maintains the bitter status quo, and characters caught in this dilemma must strike out to proclaim their own uniqueness and their ability to solve even the most horrific problems. Science fiction shows that we are all united on this planet. Each small action can have a universal effect. Our choices matter. Science fiction proclaims that it isn't too late: We still have the power to change the world for the better.

Official Web site: www.sonialevitin.com

Levitin writes in a wide array of genres. Additional works, primarily historical fiction (WW II) and problem novels, include *Journey to America* (1970), *Beyond Another Door* (1977), *Return* (1987), *Silver Days* (1989), *Annie's Promise* (1993), *The Golem and the Dragon Girl* (1993), *Escape from Egypt* (1994), *Evil Encounter* (1996), *Yesterday's Child* (1997), *Singing Mountain* (1998), *Dream Freedom* (2000), *Room in the Heart* (2003), and *Strange Relations* (2007).

Box 8.2   Space Operas, Cyberpunk, and Other Science Fiction Adventures

2099 (Doomsday #1) by John Peel. New York: Scholastic 1999.

America is completely computerized. Tristan, the 14-year-old hero, has an evil clone who has generated a computer virus that, if unleashed, could take down the entire social system—virtual and real. Can Tristan stop him?

Be More Chill by Ned Vizzini. New York: Miramax/Hyperion, 2004.

In this light cyberpunk, Jeremy Heere, needing help navigating his social world, purchases and swallows a squip, a computer chip that takes over his thoughts and actions. Jeremy's squip tells him what to wear, what to say, and how to move. Just when Jeremy seems to have made social club status, the squip malfunctions.

Dervish Is Digital by Pat Cadigan. New York: Tor, 2000.

Detective Lieutenant Konstantin works in the Artificial Reality section of TechnoCrime. In her latest case, a cyberstalker has traded places with an Artificial Intelligence, so he is completely digital—something believed to be impossible.

Dragon and Thief by Timothy Zahn. New York: Tor, 2003.

Orphaned teen Jack Morgan must make it on his own with just the holographic image of his uncle and Draycos, an alien warrior. Jack and Draycos bond after Draycos's host dies in a space battle, and the two set out to clear Jack's name of a crime he did not commit.

The Foreigner series (Destroyer #7) by C. J. Cherryh. New York: DAW/Penguin, 2005.

Interpreter Bren Cameron has returned from a two-year rescue mission in outer space to find that the life he and his cohorts left has disintegrated into chaos. As with the previous books in this series, much of the

trouble arises from the cultural misunderstandings between the humans on space station Alpha and the alien races with which they must coexist in order to survive outside Earth's safety zone.

The Hungry City Chronicles (Mortal Engines #1) by Philip Reeve. New York: Scholastic, 2001.

In a technologically advanced future, cities move about and devour towns for spare parts. An orphaned teenager working as a historian is tossed off the moving city, and he must learn to survive. In the meantime, a weapon on the moving city is designed to take over the planet.

The Jazz by Melissa Scott. New York: Tor, 2001.

Tin Lizzy and Keyz, a teenage hacker, team up against corporate executive Gardner Gerretty. Gardner has created new technology that spreads false information under the guise of entertainment.

The Outpost by Mike Resnick. New York: Tor, 2001.

The Outpost is a bar in neutral territory where aliens of a distant galaxy share their stories of adventure and sorrow. While some alien races are battling across the galaxy, no fighting is allowed in The Outpost.

The Princess of Neptune by Quentin Dodd. New York: Farrar, Straus & Giroux, 2004.

When Theora, a middle school student, is recruited to represent Earth in an intergalactic beauty pageant (the Cavalcade of Loveliness), she must battle the beast of the mall, a giant fern from the Crab Nebula. This is a comic science fiction adventure with a strong heroine.

Realware by Rudy Rucker. New York: EOS/HarperCollins, 2000.

When Phil Gottner's father is swallowed by a hyperspatial anomaly, Phil travels to another dimension, falls in

Continued

Box 8.2   Space Operas, Cyberpunk, and Other Science Fiction Adventures   *Continued*

love with a young woman visiting from the Moon, and meets a race of aliens living at the bottom of the sea.

The Secret under My Skin by Janet McNaughton. New York: EOS/HarperCollins, 2000.

A complete backlash against technology has overtaken life in the year 2368. The world has suffered traumatic biological degradation; humans cannot walk outside without protection lest they risk severe damage from the sun's rays. Blay Raytee, trying to survive on the street, discovers that a tiny chip embedded under her skin may hold the key to a bright future.

Singing the Dogstar Blues by Alison Goodman. New York: Firebird/Penguin, 2002.

Seventeen-year-old Joss Aaronson, the daughter of a famous newscaster and an unknown sperm donor,

feels like an outsider. When Joss teams up with a hermaphrodite from the planet Choria, they take a trip in time that could change both their lives.

The Xenocide Mission by Ben Jeapes. New York: Fickling/Random House, 2002.

In a distant solar system, Lieutenant Joel Gilmore and his crew are attacked by aliens whom they were sent to observe. Their rescue becomes a race against time.

The Zenith Angle by Bruce Sterling. New York: Del Rey/Random House, 2004.

Derek Vandeveer, computer wizard and information-age security expert, works as a successful VP of research for a growing Internet company. When 9/11 happens, he must decide if he wants to use his skills to defend the world.

Popular Themes in Young Adult Science Fiction

Material for science fiction changes with time, especially when science catches up to science fiction (e.g., Mars is no longer an origin for aliens invading Earth). Despite changes, several themes have established histories in science fiction: aliens and other worlds frequent story pages. This is the ultimate speculation: do alien races exist? What do they look like? How will we interact with them? Orson Scott Card's classic, *Ender's Game* (1977), examines the ultimate alien interaction and near destruction of an entire race. Other works explore first contact with aliens, alien attacks, and alien occupation such as Sleator's *Interstellar Pig* (1984), *Parasite Pig* (2002), *Survival* (2004) by Julie E. Czerneda, and Shusterman's *The Dark Side of Nowhere* (1999).

According to many science fiction plotlines, humans shouldn't solely fear the destruction of Earth by aliens. Postapocalyptic themes run rampant through young adult science fiction as authors speculate about Earth's future. These futuristic societies are often classified as *dystopias*—oppressed societies with a controlling and authoritarian government as in Lois Lowry's young adult classic, *The Giver* (1993). These works, like cyberpunk, send a warning about our possible futures. James DeVita explores this theme in the author box. Sambell (2004) notes that the message is particularly powerful in young adult science fiction as corrupt adults control, exploit, and manipulate children: "child victims (although rarely the main child protagonist) actually die in order to highlight the negligence and corruption of the adult-created world they have inherited" (p. 250). In Philbrick's future (*The Last Book in the Universe,* 2000), the Big Shake further segments the populations of Earth, where only the Proovs (genetically improved humans) living in Eden are healthy and have food and proper shelter. Those that live in the Urb barely survive the filth and famine. In Tom Pow's *The Pack* (2004) children live in dog packs in order to survive in a frightening futuristic society. Additional examples of postapocalyptic stories are listed in Box 8.3. Some of these blend fantasy and science; a few are adult titles for better readers and diehard science fiction fans.

The Silenced   by James DeVita

*T*he Silenced (2007) was inspired by Sophie Scholl and the real resistance group called the White Rose. Although fictionalized, many of the characters and events in the book are based on real people and incidents that actually occurred.

In the summer of 1942, leaflets calling for resistance against the Nazi regime began appearing around the city of Munich. The group responsible for these treasonous acts called themselves the White Rose. Their primary form of resistance was the printing of leaflets, by the tens of thousands, which they ran off one sheet at a time on an old mimeograph machine and secretly distributed.

Sophie Scholl, her brother Hans, Christoph Probst, Alexander Schmorell, Willie Graf, and Professor Kurt Huber were the driving forces behind the White Rose. Their acts of resistance have been described as "heroism unsurpassed in European history."

I first read about Sophie Scholl in a newspaper clipping. The article had said something about college students being arrested for passing out leaflets. That image haunted me. How could someone be arrested for writing what they thought on a piece of paper? How could one of the most terrifying regimes in history be so threatened by these writings that they would mobilize their forces, frantically trying to put a stop to them? I was struck, of course, by the power of the written word and by those brave enough to use it.

I was also struck by the fact that Sophie and her friends did not have to do what they did. They were ethnically acceptable to the regime. They could have remained silent and survived. But they did not. They saw students and teachers disappearing; they saw the marches in the streets and the book burnings; Hans and his friends brought back news from the front of atrocities being committed against civilians and prisoners and ethnic populations; and, with the full knowledge of the risks involved, Sophie and her friends would not be silent. Here were young people who refused to blindly follow, who fought against one of the most powerful regimes on earth with no greater weapon than their words.

There is a line Sophie wrote: "The world has widened for me." This book, while working on it, also widened for me. The early drafts were merely

Continued

The Silenced   *Continued*

retellings of Sophie's life and times, slightly veiled, but still much too overt. With each new revision, though, the story became more and more fictionalized. Marena seemed to be demanding a story of her own. In my mind, she transformed into more of a fictional daughter of the White Rose, silenced under yet another totalitarian regime; the horrible nightmare was happening again. This freed me to be influenced by other sources and contemporary events. Unfortunately, they were all too plentiful. Intolerance and oppression abound in every corner of the globe. Every time I opened a newspaper, I found present-day words, phrases, and ideas from all over the world that made their way into the book.

On February 22, 1943, Sophie Scholl, aged 21, Hans Scholl, 24, and Christoph Probst, 23, were sentenced to death and executed. Alexander Schmorell, Willie Graf, and Professor Kurt Huber were executed on July 13, 1943. Many others involved were subsequently executed or imprisoned. They were triumphant in their deaths. The leaflets of the White Rose were eventually copied and smuggled out of the country, and near the end of the war Allied planes dropped them by the millions over Germany and occupied countries. It is said that people wept when they read them.

Box 8.3   Apocalyptic Themes in Young Adult Science Fiction

The Big Empty by J. B. Stephens. New York: Razorbill/Penguin, 2004.

Half to three-quarters of the world's population is destroyed by a plague called Strain 7. Infrastructures collapse and the surviving U.S. population is relocated to the coastline. The heartland is a wasteland—the Big Empty. Seven teens attempt to piece together their lives. Fans may enjoy the sequels *Paradise City* (2004b) and *Desolation Angels* (2004a).

Cat's Cradle by Kurt Vonnegut. New York: Delacorte/Random House, 1963.

A satirical and funny commentary about the end of life on Earth and human madness. Considered one of Vonnegut's greatest works and a literary achievement that has left a lasting impression on generations of readers.

Cell by Stephen King. New York: Simon & Schuster, 2006.

A burst of energy known as the Pulse turns everyone holding a cell phone to their heads into zombies, killing machines. Those not using phones at the time must deal with the monsters and living hell left behind.

The City of Ember by Jeanne DuPrau. New York: Doubleday/Random House, 2003.

The City of Ember is the last refuge for the human race. When the lamps that light the city begin to dim and flicker, citizens fear the city's destruction. Lina and her friend find an ancient message and must decipher it before the lights go out forever. More fantasy than science fiction. Sequels include *The People of Sparks* (2004) and *The Prophet of Yonwood* (2006).

Fearless by Tim Lott. Cambridge, MA: Candlewick Press, 2007.

A dystopian world in which city streets are clean and safe from terrorists. Hidden behind the walls of a community faith school are enslaved girls whose

Continued

Box 8.3   Apocalyptic Themes in Young Adult Science Fiction   *Continued*

birth names are replaced by letters and numbers. The bravest girl in the school, Little Fearless, sets out on a quest that will free the girls.

Green Angel by Alice Hoffman. New York: Scholastic, 2003.

When a cataclysmic fire destroys 15-year-old Green's home, community, and her family, she must survive on her own. Magical realism. A postapocalyptic fairy tale.

Hole in the Sky by Pete Hautman. New York: Simon & Schuster, 2001.

Sixteen-year-old Ceej Kane lives in a futuristic world devastated by a mutant virus. Few people populate the planet, and those who have been infected but survived are damaged. Ceej, his sister Harryette, and their uncle live in an abandoned hotel near the Grand Canyon, away from bands of renegade survivors. Their uncle's disappearance changes their lives.

The Last Days by Scott Westerfeld. New York: Razorbill/Penguin, 2006.

An uncontrollable epidemic holds New York City in its throes: rats are everywhere, black oil spews from fire hydrants; giant worms live underground. Can five teens save the world from an apocalypse? A sequel to *Peeps* (2005).

Longlight Legacy trilogy *(The Dirt Eaters #1)* by Dennis Foon. Toronto, ON: Annick Press, 2003.

The world has been destroyed by wars, and 16-year-old Roan's family and people have perished. Roan joins a group of warriors to fight the enemy, only he is horrified when he commits his first act of violence. A provocative look at a wasted world.

Predator's Gold by Philip Reeve. New York: EOS/HarperCollins, 2004.

Cities travel on wheels around Earth. Two years have passed since the destruction of London, and Tom and Hester, now lovers, make an emergency landing of their airship in the frozen city of Anchorage. Hester is outraged when Tom kisses the Margravine of Anchorage and flies to Arkangel, where she reveals the location of Anchorage, making it possible for the city of Arkangel to consume Anchorage and enslave its people.

The Tomorrow series *(Tomorrow, When the War Began #1)* by John Marsden. Boston: Houghton Mifflin, 1995.

Seven Australian teens return home from a camping trip, only to discover their country has been invaded and residents of their town have been taken as prisoners. The series follows their struggle to survive, fight, and to find loved ones.

Genetic research currently captures newspaper headlines and provides fodder for political commentaries. Not surprisingly, it is a dominant theme in young adult science fiction. At the heart of much of this fiction is the search for identity and the struggle of adolescence, particularly when adolescents must question their humanity (Ostry, 2004). Nancy Farmer's award-winning book, *The House of the Scorpion* (2002), deals with cloning but also with the ethical and emotional dilemmas involved. Matteo is cloned in order to prolong his grandfather's life. El Patron, Matteo's grandfather, plans to harvest Matteo's organs to replace his dying ones. In Sonia Levitin's *The Goodness Gene* (2005), Will and Berk, clones of a 20th-century military leader, are poised to take over as leaders of a future dystopian Earth. When Will learns of his origins, he must fight to overcome his genetic hardwiring.

Rather than being cloned, young adults in science fiction are sometimes genetically "improved," a result of our human drive for perfection. Scott Westerfeld's latest series, *Uglies* (2005), tackles the issues of radical cosmetic surgery: 16-year-old teens undergo operations to become supermodel beautiful—except for those few radicals, the Uglies. Westerfeld talks about the reception of his work with girls in the author box. Box 8.4 presents more titles dealing with genetics, DNA, and cloning.

Science fiction plots can take on anything from mad scientists and scientific experiments (William Sleator's *House of Stairs*, 1974, and Peter Dickinson's *Eva*, 1988) to discovering new—and old—creatures (Roland Smith's *Cryptid Hunters*, 2005). Perhaps this vastness is the appeal of science fiction for young adults. Fans are bound to find a story that intrigues them, and they may learn some science and technology during the process.

Girls, Social Technologies, and Science Fiction   by Scott Westerfeld

The term *science fiction* on the spine of a novel brings to mind the iconic images of the space age: rocket ships, robots, and colonies on other planets. But within the lifetime of today's teenagers, real-world technological innovation has come at a more personal scale. We hold laptops, cell phones, and music players in our hands, carry them in our pockets and purses, even wear them around our necks. They are intimate accessories, half mood ring and half secret diary. They've become part of our daily lives in a way that Saturn V rockets and electron microscopes never could.

Though domesticated, these technologies really are science fiction; they move at lightning speed, transforming the world around them as they go. Weblogs, social networking software, and text messaging create whole new categories of social space. They change the way teens interact with peers, parents, teachers, and corporations, and thus, how they define themselves. These days, choosing a Livejournal icon can be more important than knowing which trendy label to wear.

When I started *Uglies*, I figured it would be crazy to write about the future without these technologies, so I included a host of personal communication systems (and their attendant violations of privacy). What I didn't expect was the effect doing so would have on readers. A surprising amount of my mail about the series begins with the words, "I always hated science

fiction, but . . ." And almost all the readers who feel this way are girls. Of course, the key technology in *Uglies* is cosmetic surgery, which probably gets a lot of female readers onto the first page. But they seem to be just as fascinated by my "interface rings" and clique-shared "skintennas," the logical offspring of cell phones and MySpace.

The obvious point to make about these technologies is that they're social. They don't involve going faster or farther, they involve finding and nurturing relationships—the obsessions we traditionally associate with teenage girls. Mind you, *Uglies* also has hoverboards and bungee jackets, futuristic weaponry and survival gear, and girls have responded positively to those as well. But the social technologies seem to round out the experience for many girls, providing a kind of pleasure that they don't associate with science fiction and making all the futuristic elements more relevant and intriguing.

Very possibly (and hopefully) the assumption that technology and science fiction are "guy things" is a notion whose days are numbered.

Official Web site: www.scottwesterfeld.com

Other works not mentioned in this chapter include *Midnighters* series (*The Secret Hour*, 2004b; *Touching Darkness*, 2004d, and *Blue Noon*, 2004a) and *So Yesterday* (2004c), *Peeps* (2005a), and *The Last Days* (2006a).

Box 8.4   Genetics, DNA, and Cloning

Blueprint **by Charlotte Kerner. Trans. Charlotte Kerner. Minneapolis, MN: Lerner, 2000.**

Siri, a clone, owes her entire physical existence to her mother/sister, Iris, and accepts that she was created to prolong Iris's life, who suffers from multiple sclerosis. As Siri matures, she resists her mother/sister's dominance.

Clone **by Malcolm Rose. New York: Scholastic, 2002.**

Jordan isn't sure how he feels about cloning, and his beliefs are complicated by the fact his dad is a leading scientist in clone research. Jordan has seen what can happen when cloning goes wrong in monkeys—the physical trauma, even death. His dad wants to use cloning to perfect the human race.

Cloning Miranda **by Carol Matas. New York: Scholastic, 1999.**

Is cloning a "spare" self for extra parts ethical? That is the question with which Miranda is forced to grapple. Miranda discovers that she has a younger sister, whom her parents cultivated for spare body parts in case Miranda got sick. She learns, too, that she herself was cultivated from a deceased older sister.

The Diary of Pelly D **by L. J. Adlington. New York: Greenwillow/HarperCollins, 2005.**

DNA testing and the power of prejudice are central to this novel. Many years after the Holocaust, Tony V finds the diary of a young girl, Pelly D, and learns about the horrors inflicted on her through DNA testing.

Double Helix **by Nancy Werlin. New York: Penguin, 2004.**

Eli Samuels gets the job of his dreams at Wyatt Transgenics as a laboratory technician. When Eli meets someone who looks remarkably like his mother, he wonders how far Dr. Wyatt is going with his genetics research, especially since his mother is suffering from a deadly disease.

Dr. Franklin's Island **by Ann Halam. New York: Lamb/Random House, 2002.**

Inspired by H. G. Wells's creepy *Island of Dr. Moreau*, three stranded teens are subjected to genetic manipulations on a remote island. Will they get off the island? Will they regain their human form after having been turned into animals?

Dusk **by Susan Gates. New York: Putnam/Penguin, 2005.**

Dusk is a creation of the military, a genetic blending of humanity and the animal kingdom. While she is human in form, she has the genes of a hawk imprinted within her DNA, giving her hawklike vision. When a fire occurs in the laboratory, she escapes, along with a super-intelligent rat and a guard dog.

Maximum Ride: The Angel Experiment **by James Patterson. New York: Little, Brown, 2005.**

The six children of this adventure are 98 percent human DNA, 2 percent bird DNA, which enables them to fly. Sounds exciting, but they are experiments living in cages. When they devise an escape plan, their evil creators have no plans of releasing them.

Mergers **by Steven L. Layne. Gretna, LA: Pelican, 2006.**

Four teens have unique powers that an evil leader wishes to harvest: one is psychic, one is an empathic, one can morph, and one can time travel. These teens, who bear the now-archaic distinguishing features of race, could undo all of Senator Broogue's work assimilating all races into one homogenized genetic group.

Continued

Box 8.4   Genetics, DNA, and Cloning   *Continued*

***The Missing Link* trilogy *(Fourth World #1)* by Kate Thompson. New York: Random House, 2005.**

Christie and his "differently-abled" brother, Danny, take off in search of Danny's mother, only to discover her working in a genetic research lab. Along the way, moral questions are raised about genetic manipulation.

***Regeneration* series *(Regeneration #1)* by L. J. Singleton. New York: Berkley, 2000.**

Five humans have been cloned on a yacht in a secret experiment gone awry. Fifteen years later, one of the doctors wants to hide the evidence by killing the teens, who have no idea that they are clones.

***Replica* series *(Amy, Number Seven #1)* by Marilyn Kaye. New York: Bantam/Skylark, 1998.**

While doing a school project, Amy discovers her birth certificate is fake and wants to dig deeper into the strange happenings that have plagued her life: enhanced vision and hearing, sudden increased ability in gymnastics, and an odd birthmark on her back.

***Sharp North* by Patrick Cave. New York: Atheneum/Simon & Schuster, 2006.**

In a dystopian future, reproduction is restricted, so wealthy families create clones for spare parts. Cave deals with issues of science ethics, class, and privilege.

***Star Split* by Kathryn Lasky. New York: Hyperion, 1999.**

In the year 3038, genetic enhancement is commonplace. Unauthorized genetic cloning, however, is rare and forbidden. So how was Darci cloned?

***Taylor Five* by Ann Halam. New York: Lamb/Random House, 2004.**

Taylor lives with her brilliant scientist mother on a remote island. Taylor is unique in many ways: she knows how to survive in the jungle, she has an orangutan as a relative, and she is a clone—one of only five worldwide.

***This Side of Paradise* by Steven L. Layne. St. Charles, IL: North Star, 2001.**

Jack's father moves the family into Eden, a village owned and controlled by the CEO of Jack's father's employer. Everything in Eden, including the people, are too perfect. Could they have been genetically enhanced in order to live in this modern-day paradise?

***Transplant* by Malcolm Rose. New York: Scholastic, 2003.**

When Cassie's face is damaged in an acid attack, doctors use new genetic technology to repair it. However, something is suspicious about the clinic, and the revolutionary techniques used to save Cassie from disfigurement may lead to her demise.

***Uglies* trilogy *(Uglies #1)* by Scott Westerfeld. New York: Simon Pulse, 2005.**

Tally cannot wait to turn 16 because she can then leave her life as an "Ugly" behind and, like all those who went before her, have the surgery her culture demands to make her perfect and "Pretty." Fans will enjoy *Pretties* (2005b), *Specials* (2006b), and a companion book, *Extras* (2007).

***Violet Eyes: A Novel* by Nicole Luiken. New York: Simon & Schuster, 2001.**

Angel thinks she is a student living in Canada in 1987, but she discovers she is part of the Canadian government project, Renaissance, and it is really the year 2089. She is a genetically enhanced experiment.

Fantasy
What Is Fantasy?

Science fiction and fantasy have much in common. In fact, the short story and the pulps that helped launch the science fiction genre did the same for fantasy. In early magazines around the world, fantasy was popular as early as the 1600s. The first magazine devoted to fantasy, *The Thrill Book,* was published in 1919. As the pulps became more popular in the United States in the 1930s, magazines such as *Strange Stories* and *Fantastic Adventures* were launched.

Science fiction is grounded in science and technology; fantasy employs magic and enchantments. Science fiction authors use scientists and mathematicians as characters; fantasy authors invent wizards, witches, and sorcerers. These two imaginative genres diverge in this fundamental principle: fantasy includes any plot that cannot be explained rationally (now or in the future) through science and technology. Author Orson Scott Card (1990) explains this perfectly: "Science fiction is about what *could* be but isn't; fantasy is about what *couldn't* be" (p. 22). Magic, a familiar plot device in fantasy, does not easily exist in science fiction because magic can't be explained rationally. Enchantments, talking animals, and toys that come to life all go without scientific explanation in fantasy. Rational scientific explanation isn't necessary to appreciate how the enchantment *affects* plot and characters. Although this difference is significant, the two genres share core elements: the creation of new or different worlds and the need for internal consistency.

High Fantasy

In fantasy, authors create new worlds—worlds that do not exist although they sometimes feel familiar. No matter how advanced science becomes, we will never be able to walk through a wardrobe and get to Narnia.[14] Ursula K. Le Guin's Earthsea will never be found on a map, and no rabbit hole will take us to Wonderland.[15] New worlds can be far different from our own with unique landscapes and inhabitants. In addition to humans, familiar characters like dragons and elves frequent these other worlds along with not-so-familiar creatures—sometimes friends, sometimes foes. For example, in Suzanne Collins's *The Underland Chronicles,* humans deal with killer plants, bartering giant spiders, and rats that wage war (see her discussion on creating animal characters in the author box).

When a new world has been created, the work is high fantasy (Clute & Grant, 1999). J. R. R. Tolkein is considered the first author to make a work of high fantasy accessible to mainstream readers (Gates, Steffel, & Molson, 2003). The first work of young adult high fantasy is considered to be Lewis

---

[14]*The Chronicles of Narnia* (1950) is a series of seven books written by C. S. Lewis between 1949 and 1954.
[15]*Alice's Adventures in Wonderland* was first published in 1865 by Macmillan.

Carroll's *Alice's Adventures in Wonderland*. A widely read high fantasy among young adults is the *Redwall* series (1986) by Brian Jacques. High fantasy is characterized by a unique new world *and* a heroic quest "which deal[s] with matters affecting the destiny of those worlds" (Clute & Grant, 1999, p. 466).

Three prominent and long-standing prolific writers of young adult high fantasy are T. A. Barron, Tamora Pierce, and Diana Wynne Jones. Barron is known best for *The Lost Years of Merlin* epic (1996) and *The Great Tree of Avalon* series (2005); Pierce established herself as a master of the genre with *The Song of the Lioness Quartet* (1983) and has gone on to write numerous series, including her most recent series, *Beka Cooper* (2006), and Jones is known for her *Chrestomanci* (2001) books. Kai Meyer, a newer young adult high fantasy writer, has written one of the best young adult trilogies in recent years, the *Dark Reflections Trilogy*. *The Water Mirror* (2005) tells the story of two orphan girls serving as apprentices to a magic mirror craftsman in a mythical city of Venice, ruled by the Flowing Queen whose spirit is held captive in a tiny vial. When the two young apprentices learn the Egyptians plan to overthrow the city, they struggle to protect the city from its foes. Mythical creatures abound (e.g., winged lions, mummy warriors, and mermaids). Light, shadow, stone, and water imagery make this tale set within the canals and buildings of a fantastical medieval Venice an exceptional, sophisticated read.

T. A. Barron as a teenager standing on the summit of a Colorado mountain peak. He's still happiest in hiking boots!

Regardless of how the reader arrives in other worlds, the more *unfamiliar* the world, the harder the author must work to make the world believable. Internal consistency is critical. Readers have to believe that this other world exists and that it makes sense. Any inconsistencies in the story elements (e.g., magic, movement between worlds, curses) will lessen the work, and readers will have little enticement to read further (Wadham & Wadham, 1999). Card (1990) explains that when creating new worlds, good authors must "also establish a whole new set of laws, explain them right up front, and then faithfully abide by them throughout" (p. 23). He reminds us of the popular three wishes plot device: if a character has only three wishes, he shouldn't miraculously have a fourth at a crucial moment in the plot. Renowned fantasy writer Terry Brooks (1998) notes that when fantasy authors fail to create story boundaries, the result is "invariably disastrous" (p. 1). In high fantasy, authors may provide intricate maps of these other worlds as a guide for readers. Other authors have detailed accounts of the histories, language, and customs distinct to the story, sometimes published in companion books.[16] Box 8.5 presents examples of high fantasy.

Animal Characters in High Fantasy   by Suzanne Collins

Fantasy worlds abound, with eccentric characters and settings that spark the imagination and defy human experience as we know it. A well-conceived fantasy world is quite meticulously constructed, providing an internal consistency and integral dimension of story serving the characters who inhabit it, as well as establishing a framework in which readers may comfortably suspend their "disbelief," embrace all things extraordinary and, ultimately, reflect on aspects of their real worlds.

—*Rosemary Stimola, Children's Literary Agent*

In *The Underland Chronicles,* Gregor, an 11-year-old boy, and his 2-year-old sister, Boots, accidentally fall through a grate in their laundry room and plummet miles beneath New York City to a sunless, dangerous place called the Underland. Unlike Alice's fall to a world beneath the bucolic English countryside where she meets rabbits and turtles and the like, the Underland, in keeping with the New York City environs above, is inhabited by giant, intelligent urban animals and a pale, violet-eyed race of humans.

From Book I, *Gregor the Overlander,* the primary role of the Underland and the characters that inhabit it was to serve the story. While the series happily fits into the fantasy genre, it was always first and foremost a war saga in my mind. That meant, from the beginning, I needed distinctive species that would be in conflict.

Continued

---

[16]Companion books are discussed thoroughly in Chapter 12.

Animal Characters in High Fantasy   *Continued*

While researching the animals who play key roles—rats, bats, spiders, and cockroaches—I found that each had biological traits that suggested their global position in the Underland.

Militarily, the humans and rats became the two superpowers. As on the earth's surface, they naturally compete for territory and resources. Both are deadly fighters. But if you place a human on the ground against a 6-foot rat with razor sharp claws and teeth, they're at a disadvantage. Arming the humans with swords helped, but to really level the playing field I needed something additional to counter the rats' size, strength, and ability to operate in total darkness.

That's where the bats came in. Put humans on bats and now they have speed, echolocation, and an aerial advantage. So the human-bat alliance, their practice of "bonding" until death, came from a desire to create a worthy opponent for the rats. The bats are aided in their alliance with the humans as well. Less aggressive than the rats, they become stronger by bonding with a species with opposable thumbs. Humans can create lethal weapons, plant food, heal wounds, and build a fortress city like Regalia.

The cockroaches are objects of fun to some when the story opens because they aren't built for fighting the likes of the superpowers. Cockroaches tend to flee their enemies. But because they have a stellar track record in survival, a heightened sensitivity to danger, and great numbers, they are a force to be reckoned with. When push comes to shove, they will defend themselves, and several dramatic moments hinge on their choices. Also, the cockroaches, who become completely enamored with Boots, demonstrate an extraordinary ability for loyalty.

The spiders are isolationists at heart, wishing only to be left alone, but doomed to be dragged into warfare. With their venomous fangs and fancy web tricks, spiders are better built for fighting than cockroaches. However, they join into battle only when it's forced upon them and, if possible, aid both sides to guarantee favor with the victors.

Throughout the series other creatures make appearances: mercenary fireflies who sell their light for food, ants who protect their queen and colony with no concern for personal survival, a lizard who fights only after camouflage, bluffing, and flight have failed. But each was required to have a military role. Ultimately, any species that didn't have a direct impact on the ongoing war or Gregor's fate as the warrior didn't make it into *The Underland Chronicles*. Those who did make it are players in a war where "good and evil" are not always clear, where initial choices and first impressions are not always correct, and where friendship, loyalty, and "humanity" are called upon to achieve victories both personal and global.

Official Web site: www.suzannecollins.com

Titles in *The Underland Chronicles* include *Gregor the Overlander* (2003), *Gregor and the Prophecy of Bane* (2004), *Gregor and the Curse of the Warmbloods* (2005), *Gregor and the Marks of Secret* (2006), and *Gregor and the Code of Claw* (2007).

Box 8.5   High Fantasy for Young Adults

Anatopsis by Chris Abouzeid. New York: Dutton/Penguin, 2006.

Fourteen-year-old Princess Anatopsis is an immortal in a world where mortals are considered a lower class and are condemned to live in the ghetto.

The Bartimaeus trilogy *(The Amulet of Samarkand #1)* by Jonathan Stroud. New York: Miramax/Hyperion, 2003.

Twelve-year-old Nathaniel is a magician's apprentice. Because he is constantly overlooked and humiliated, he

Continued

Box 8.5   High Fantasy for Young Adults   *Continued*

develops a desire for revenge and summons up the djinni Bartimaeus to help him steal the Amulet of Samarkand, with which he intends to extract his revenge.

Castaways of the Flying Dutchman series *(Castaways of the Flying Dutchman #1)* by Brian Jacques. New York: Philomel/Penguin, 2001.

In the 17th century, Neb and his dog are stowaways on the infamous *Flying Dutchman*. Neb is the cook's assistant and is treated cruelly until he and his dog are cast ashore and given the gift of eternal youth.

Darkest Age series *(The Coming of Dragons #1)* by A. J. Lake. New York: Bloomsbury, 2006.

Edmund and Elspeth, both 11, have unwanted gifts: Edmund can read minds, and Elspeth is bonded to a magical sword. The two are the only survivors of a shipwreck and, upon receiving their gifts, must fend off the wicked sorcerer, Orgrim.

Dragon Rider by Cornelia Funke. New York: Chicken House/Scholastic, 2004.

Dragonkind is facing extinction unless the cruel artificial golden dragon, Nettlebrand, can be stopped from achieving its goal: the death of all silver dragons. Firedrake decides he must try to find the mythical Rim of Heaven, the place where dragons can live in peace and harmony, if he and his kind are to survive.

Dreamhunter Duet (Dreamhunter #1) by Elizabeth Knox. New York: Frances Foster/Farrar, Straus & Giroux, 2006.

When 15-year-old Laura discovers she has the ability of the dreamhunter—she can cross from the real world into the world of dreams—her life changes forever.

The Farsala trilogy *(Fall of a Kingdom #1)* by Hilari Bell. New York: Simon & Schuster, 2004.

The land of Farsala has experienced peace and prosperity for thousands of years. When a new enemy

approaches, three youth are determined to save Farsala from the Flames of Destruction. Social commentary and a tale of self-exploration.

The Hagwood trilogy *(Thorn Ogres of Hagwood #1)* by Robin Jarvis. San Diego: Silver Whistle/Harcourt, 2002.

The Werlings of Hagwood are shapeshifters, existing peacefully in the woods, basically forgotten. One night as they are teaching young Gamaliel and his fellow students shapeshifting, the evil High Lady is alerted to their presence and decides that Gamaliel can help her find her missing heart.

His Dark Materials trilogy *(The Golden Compass #1)* by Philip Pullman. New York: Knopf/Random House, 1996.

Lyra and her daemon, an animal paired with a human for life, are on a quest to rescue kidnapped children being used in scientific experiments. A unique perspective on politics and science.

The Icemark Chronicles (The Cry of the Icemark #1) by Stuart Hill. New York: Scholastic, 2005.

After her father's death, 14-year-old Thirrin Freer Strong-in-the-Arm Lindenshield, Wild Cat of the North, must lead her people into battle. She enlists the nearby werewolves, vampires, giant snow leopards, and forest people in her quest and proves herself a worthy successor.

Inheritance trilogy *(Eragon #1)* by Christopher Paolini. New York: Knopf/Random House, 2003.

When 15-year-old Eragon finds an intriguing blue stone, he never dreams that it is actually a dragon's egg! The egg hatches, and Eragon learns that he is to become a Dragonrider. King Galbatorix is threatened by the emergence of this potential challenger to his throne and kills Eragon's entire family, sending Eragon and his dragon, Saphira, on a quest for vengeance.

Continued

Box 8.5   High Fantasy for Young Adults   *Continued*

***Inkheart* by Cornelia Funke. New York: Chicken House/Scholastic 2003.**

Twelve-year-old Meggie learns that her father, Mo, has the ability to read characters in and out of books. Some of the characters are evil.

***The Keys to the Kingdom* series (*Mister Monday #1*) by Garth Nix. New York: Scholastic, 2003.**

Eleven-year-old Arthur Penhaligon receives a book and a key during a near-fatal asthma attack. This key, the minute hand of a clock, allows him to breathe easily, but it also puts him in grave danger.

***The Old Kingdom* trilogy (*Sabriel #1*) by Garth Nix. New York: HarperCollins, 1995.**

Eighteen-year-old Sabriel is the daughter of the kingdom's necromancer, whose duty it is to put the dead back to rest. A necromancer-in-training, Sabriel is devastated when she receives her father's sword and tools, a symbol her father is either dead or trapped in the Realm of Death.

***The Oracle Prophecies (The Oracle Betrayed #1)* by Catherine Fisher. New York: Greenwillow/HarperCollins, 2004.**

Mirany is the youngest and shyest of the Nine who serve Archon. She uncovers a plot to install a false god and realizes she must find the strength to overcome her own shy nature and reveal the true Archon to the world, regardless of personal consequences.

***The Pellinor* series (*The Naming #1*) by Alison Croggon. Cambridge, MA: Candlewick Press, 2006.**

Sixteen-year-old Maerad, a slave, is freed by Cadvan, Bard of the Light. After her escape, she learns that she, too, is one of the magical bards, and she and Cadvan travel to a school where Maerad can begin magical training.

***The Princetta* by Anne-Laure Bondoux. New York: Bloomsbury, 2006.**

Fifteen-year-old Malva escapes her arranged marriage by hiding in a wine barrel and being smuggled out of the palace where she reigns as Princetta of Galnicia. Freedom is sweet for Malva and her maid, and the two confront fascinating and dangerous adventures outside the safety of the palace walls.

***The Secret History of Tom Trueheart* by Ian Beck. New York: Greenwillow/HarperCollins, 2007.**

Twelve-year-old Tom Trueheart is the youngest of seven brothers, who have been assigned fantastic adventures as heroes in the Land of Stories. Tom fears he will never get his chance. When his brothers go missing before completing their quests, Tom is assigned the task of finding out what happened to his brothers.

***Septimus Heap* series (*Magyk #1*) by Angie Sage. New York: HarperCollins, 2005.**

Septimus Heap, the seventh son of a seventh son of a family of magyk, was stillborn—or was he? A young girl, a princess, was found in the snow the night Septimus was presumed dead and raised as the Heaps's daughter. Was it just a coincidence that the Heaps's child died and a baby princess was abandoned nearby? Is Septimus really dead?

***The Shamer Chronicles (The Shamer's Daughter #1)* by Lene Kaaberbol. New York: Henry Holt, 2004.**

Ten-year-old Dina is the daughter of a Shamer and has inherited the ability to look into people's eyes and force them to face their most secret, shameful actions. Her gift makes her a target for rulers of the kingdom.

***Storm Thief* by Chris Wooding. New York: Scholastic, 2006.**

Moa and Rail are two teenage thieves in the city of Orokos, a city surrounded by ocean and plagued

Continued

Box 8.5   High Fantasy for Young Adults   *Continued*

by probability storms that can change reality (e.g., making an entire town disappear).

Treasure at the Heart of the Tanglewood by Meredith Ann Pierce. New York: Viking/Penguin, 2001.

Brown Hannah is a magical healer with no memory of how she arrived in Tanglewood. She has been serving as a healer as long as she can remember; once a month she creates a much-needed medicine for the evil sorcerer.

Wolfblade trilogy (*Wolfblade #1*) by Jennifer Fallon. New York: Tor, 2006.

Marla Wolfblade is intent on returning her royal family to its former power, but in the patriarchal world of Hythria, succession is only legitimate through a male heir. She marries a warlord and gives birth to a son, thinking her son's birth will restore her family's power, but dark forces are determined to keep the Wolfblade family from reclaiming power.

Low Fantasy and Urban Fantasy

Not all fantasy takes place in a completely imagined world. Much fantasy takes place in realistic settings, and the author weaves fantastical elements into the story. The realistic setting helps ground the work and avoids complicated laws and rules. This kind of story is considered *low fantasy* or *magical realism.* Such fantasy "has the appearance of a work of realism, but gradually introduces the fantastic as an integral, and necessary, part of the story" (Tomlinson & Lynch-Brown, 2007, p. 65). Clute and Grant (1999) note that a work of low fantasy may include "dream imagery, dislocations in time and space, haunting juxtapositions, etc., but reality is the frame within which the narration, whether visual or textual, proceeds" (p. 618). For example, Cornelia Funke's *The Thief Lord* (2002) paints a realistic story of orphans on the streets of Italy, but she weaves in a subtle plotline about a magical merry-go-round. In *Hidden Talents* (Lubar, 1999), a group of misfits in an alternative school find out that they are actually gifted with a variety of abilities. Additional examples can be found in Box 8.6. Among these titles are selections by David Almond, Alice Hoffman, and Francesca Lia Block, three masters of magical realism.

Urban fantasy is edgier magical realism, taking place in urban areas and dealing with contemporary issues. In the author box, urban fantasy author Adam Stemple explores this provocative genre.

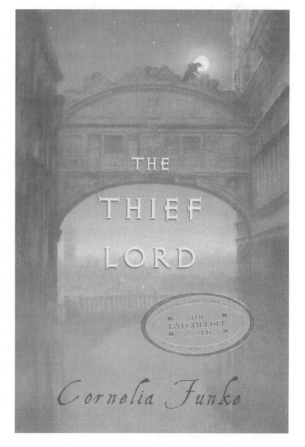

Illustration © 2002 by Scholastic Inc. Used by permission.

Box 8.6   Low Fantasy and Urban Fantasy

***Apocalypse* by Tim Bowler. New York: McElderry/Simon & Schuster, 2005.**

When their sailboat begins sinking, Kit and his family ground it on an island inhabited by an unusual and hostile people who believe they were sent there by God. Compasses and watches don't work, and ghostly sounds come from the sea.

***The Blue Girl* by Charles de Lint. New York: Viking/Penguin, 2004.**

Seventeen-year-old Imogene is attempting to leave her gang life behind at her new school. She finds herself in the midst of faeries and the school's ghost, Adrian, a victim of bullying.

***Children of the Red King* series (*Midnight for Charlie Bone #1*) by Jenny Nimmo. New York: Orchard/Scholastic, 2003.**

After discovering he can hear the thoughts of people in photographs, Charlie Bone reluctantly enters Bloor's Academy, a school for those with special gifts.

***Clay* by David Almond. New York: Random House, 2006.**

Davie and his best friend are altar boys and, at the request of Father O'Mahoney, the two befriend a new boy, Stephen. Stephen is a sculptor, and one day brings a clay figure to life before Davie's eyes. What will the live sculpture do?

***Hanged Man* by Francesca Lia Block. New York: HarperCollins, 1994.**

Seventeen-year-old Laurel stops eating after the death of her father and is haunted by family secrets. Laurel tries losing herself in the magical city life of L.A.

***Heaven Eyes* by David Almond. New York: Random House, 2001.**

Erin, Mouse, and January live in an orphanage and long for freedom. They escape from the orphanage on a raft and travel downstream, passing warehouses and factories. Along the way, they meet an odd old man and an unusual girl with webbed hands.

***Incantation* by Alice Hoffman. New York: Little, Brown, 2006.**

A mystic tale set in medieval Spain about a young girl, Estrella, and her family, Spanish Jews, who pretend they are of Catholic faith during the Spanish Inquisition.

***Kit's Wilderness* by David Almond. New York: Delacorte/Random House, 2000.**

Thirteen-year-old Kit Watson moves with his family to a coal mining town to care for his Grandpa Watson. Kit struggles to belong, but finds two friends. When the friends play a game of "Death" in an abandoned coal mine, Kit has an otherworldly experience.

***The Onion Girl* by Charles de Lint. New York: Tor, 2001.**

Two plots crash into one when Jilly, severely wounded in a hit-and-run accident, and two abused sisters meet in an alternate world.

***Poison* by Chris Wooding. New York: Orchard/Scholastic, 2005.**

Sixteen-year-old Poison searches for her kidnapped baby sister. On her quest, the rebellious teen confronts hostile creatures: phaeries, witches, and talking animals.

***River Boy* by Tim Bowler. New York: Simon & Schuster, 2000.**

Jess travels with her ailing grandfather to his boyhood home, where he hopes to finish a painting he calls the *River Boy*, only it doesn't appear to have a boy in it. Jess becomes interested in the painting and, at the

Continued

Box 8.6   Low Fantasy and Urban Fantasy   *Continued*

same time, notices a presence in the river, a young boy. Is he real, or magical, and what role does he play in her grandfather's life and in the painting?

Singer of Souls by Adam Stemple. New York: Tor, 2005.

Minnesota resident Douglas "Doc" Stewart plays his guitar and writes songs for a living. When a young woman offers him a vial of white powder, Doc shoots up, but this trip is different: He sees phaeries and evil creatures. His gift of sight puts him in danger—evil beings attempt to draw him into their war and have him fight to the death.

Skellig by David Almond. New York: Bantam Doubleday Dell/Random House, 1999.

Michael moves with his family into a new neighborhood. One day he goes into an old garage and encounters a mysterious being who eats insects. Is he a homeless man or something else?

Spirits in the Wires by Charles de Lint. New York: Tor, 2003.

Spirits invade technology and become part of a virus crashing computers of visitors to the Woodward Web site, and people begin to disappear. One of the virus victims is Saskia, a young woman who believes she was born in the realm of a Web site.

Stormwitch by Susan Vaught. New York: Bloomsbury, 2005.

Sixteen-year-old Ruba lives in Haiti. When her grandmother is killed, Ruba moves to America to live with Grandmother Jones, who wants her to abandon her Haitian culture. When Hurricane Camille batters the coastline, Ruba knows the hurricane is actually Zashar, a stormwitch, and she must embrace her heritage to battle this ancient enemy.

Tithe: A Modern Faerie Tale by Holly Black. New York: Simon & Schuster, 2002.

Sixteen-year-old Kaye has no real prospects in life. She remembers seeing faeries when she was young and yearns to see them again. She gets her wish when she saves the life of a dark faerie knight, learns she is a changeling, and winds up in the middle of an ongoing faerie war. An urban fantasy continued in sequels *Valiant: A Modern Tale of Faerie* (2005) and *Ironside: A Modern Faery's Tale* (2007).

Wasteland by Francesca Lia Block. New York: HarperCollins, 2003.

A challenging look at teen suicide, loss, and incest. Block uses first-person viewpoints of both Marina and her brother, Lex (who commits suicide). Lex's narration comes from beyond the grave.

Way Down Deep by Ruth White. New York: Farrar, Straus & Giroux, 2007.

A toddler is found on the courthouse steps and is taken in by the owner of a boardinghouse. Ruby thrives and is well liked by the townspeople. When a new family arrives in town with information about her past, Ruby must leave her town. Is there something, possibly magic, that binds her to her hometown?

The Wrong Hands by Nigel Richardson. New York: Knopf/Random House, 2005.

Teenager Graham Sinclair is a misfit and yearns for a true friend. He has oversized, oddly shaped hands and hides a personal secret: his hands allow him to fly.

On Writing Urban Fantasy   by Adam Stemple

Urban fantasy is to the fantasy genre what urban crime is to the mystery genre: a gritty, realistic take on a field that is sometimes too polite and refined for its own good. Bursting into existence in the 1980s with books like Megan Lindholm's *Wizard of the Pigeons* (1986) and Charles de Lint's *Moonheart* (1986), it told readers that the world they lived in might not be quite as simple as they'd thought. That maybe magic hadn't died out with the industrial revolution, but had survived, adapting and adjusting, living now in the cement, steel, and circuitry of our modern landscape.

As opposed to traditional fantasy, which takes readers to entirely new worlds built from the ground up, urban fantasy begins in our own, very real world, before stepping seamlessly into the fantastic. This subtle shift often lends the fantasy elements a frighteningly real aspect. Instead of forcing readers to accept a whole new reality, an urban fantasy story only has to alter their perceptions slightly to accept that the fantastic exists. But in doing so, the details of the magical and mythical elements must be as—or even more—convincing than the mundane ones. With its feet rooted so firmly in the world we live in, it takes a special kind of writer to lift a rational tale up and away into the fantastic unknown.

Urban fantasies are rawer and more violent than traditional fantasy. There are certainly savage sections in many traditional fantasies (getting killed by a sword certainly can't be the cleanest way to go), but the reader is afforded a sense of distance due to the mythical settings. Any relation to the real world is usually allegorical—*The Lord of the Rings* (1955) may really have been about the dangers of the industrial revolution and the horrors J. R. R. Tolkien experienced in WW II, but there isn't a tank, trench, or assembly line in all of Middle-Earth. There's no such distance in urban fantasy. The characters move through the exact same world as we do—the same except for the often terrifying creatures that sneak out of the author's mind and onto the page.

I say "often terrifying" because urban fantasy owes a great deal to classic horror, those old stories where the protagonist's normal existence is cruelly upset by supernatural terrors. Many of H. P. Lovecraft's tales could almost be urban fantasy. But the difference between fantasy horror and urban fantasy is that in the latter, the fantastic is rarely completely malevolent. Horror stories like *The Exorcist* (1973) or *The Omen* (1976) share traits with urban fantasy by taking place in the real world and containing supernatural elements, but the antagonists in them are inarguably pure evil. In Emma Bull's urban fantasy novel, *War for the Oaks* (1987), the protagonist comes into contact with the Seelie and Unseelie courts, good and evil respectively. One aims to help her, the other to harm. In horror, it is unlikely that the Seelie Court would ever reach the stage.

But even basic concepts like morality can be twisted in an urban fantasy—much like the characters' sense of reality. A fey creature's concept of good and evil is likely to be markedly different from a human's. So, too, their sense of truth, fairness, honesty, and many other moral precepts that we would hold unalterable. In urban fantasy, the good are rarely all good, the bad rarely all bad. Much like the real world, a locale is almost always more complex than its fictional counterpart. Which is more real? Ming the Merciless, bent on universal domination for no discernible reason other than his creator's whim? Or a minor politician who believes he can save his beloved country by wiping out those races he believes have brought it low? And which is more terrifying?

Urban fantasy tries to bridge the gap between realism and fantasy. To meld real characters and settings with the mythic and the fabled. And do something that all fiction aims to: create something even more true than the truth.

Adam Stemple is co-author with Jane Yolen of *Pay the Piper* (2005) and *Troll Bridge* (2006), and the author of *Singer of Souls* (2005).

Popular Fantasy Elements

No matter what type of fantasy, certain plot elements remain constant. First and foremost is magic. Magic is bound by different rules in each author's work, but magic principles are often linked to folklore (e.g., the wand or the wizard hat). Skilled authors weave this folklore throughout the story. Magic, as a plot device, has three common features: "to produce, protect, or destroy" (Maurer & Wright, 2001, p. 71). Characters who use magic or other forces for either good or evil are often foes within the same story. In the *Harry Potter* series (1998), Harry and other teens attend Hogwarts School of Witchcraft and Wizardry and align with either good (Albus Dumbledore) or evil (Lord Voldemort). Not all fantasy employs such overt magic. In low fantasy or urban fantasy, magic may be an enchantment on just one object—a handsome prince is turned to a frog, a beautiful princess or maiden falls into a deep sleep. Of course witches, wizards, warlocks, and sorcerers are needed to cast spells. The Wicked Witch of the West, the Good Witch of the East, Merlin, and Gandalf are iconic characters. Young adult fantasy fans are familiar with Tiffany Aching, the witch-in-training of the *Discworld* series (Pratchett, 2000). In *Wintersmith* (Pratchett, 2006), Tiffany attracts romantic interest from the element of winter and needs the help of the Wee Free Men to restore the cycle of seasons. Whether spell, enchantment, or incantation, magic permeates contemporary young adult fantasy.

Jane Yolen played basketball in high school. YA author Adam Stemple is her son.

Much young adult fantasy includes animals that communicate between and among themselves or with humans. For example, in Garth Nix's *Keys to the Kingdom* series (2005) teen characters converse with a frog and a carp. Younger fantasy fans are familiar with Erin Hunter's *Warrior* series (2003),[17] which follows the adventures of housecats, warrior cats, as they set out to protect and save their world; Kathryn Lasky's *Guardians of Ga'Hoole* series (2003), an "owl" adventure; and Kenneth Oppel's *Silverwing* series (1997) about bats. The personality and characteristics of the animal characters are usually true to the nature of the animal. Mythical creatures like dragons, griffins, goblins, miniature people, fairies, elves, dwarves, trolls, and unicorns also abound. Dragons appear in Jason Hightman's *Samurai* (2006), miniature people in Terry Pratchett's *The Wee*

---

[17]"Erin Hunter is a pen name for Kate Carey and Cherith Baldry and their editor, Victoria Holmes.

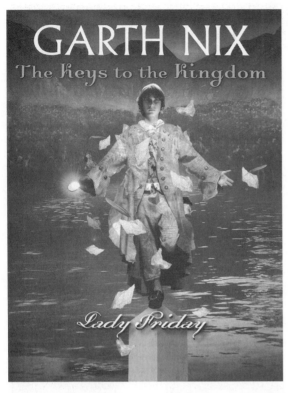

Illustration © 2007 by Scholastic, Inc. Used by permission.

Free Men (2003), unicorns in Hilari Bell's *The Prophecy* (2006), and faeries in Holly Black's *Ironside* (2007).

Miller and Clark (2001) explain that for a creature to be considered a "race" in fantasy literature, several characteristics are necessary such as having a specific, unique culture, the ability to procreate, and a system for caring for offspring. Elves are the most common race in fantasy and are often portrayed as magical and beautiful. Perhaps the most famous elves are those of J. R. R. Tolkien's *The Lord of the Rings* (1995).[18] These elves, magical and beautiful, are artisans and scholars.

A final fantasy element is that of an unlikely hero who goes through a transformation. Wadham and Wadham (1999) explain, "At its core, the hero journey pattern is about growth and the risks involved in growing" (p. 27). Unlikely heroes have a disability or weakness they must overcome at the same time as the hero joins the quest. For example, the hero of the Nix's *Keys to the Kingdom* series (2005) is a teenager with severe asthma. Box 8.7 highlights additional young adult fantasy with magic, real and mythical creatures, and unlikely heroes. Box 8.8 lists short story collections.

Box 8.7   Magic, Real/Mythical Creatures, and Unlikely Heroes

***Avielle of Rhia* by Dia Calhoun. Tarrytown, NY: Marshall Cavendish, 2006.**

Fifteen-year-old Princess Avielle of Rhia hates her silver skin, pointed ears, and forehead ridges, all of which mark her as a descendent of the magical Dredonians and, more specifically, of her infamous great-great-grandmother, who used her powers to curse the kingdom.

***The Book of Story Beginnings* by Kristin Kladstrup. Cambridge, MA: Candlewick Press, 2006.**

Twelve-year-old Lucy moves to a farmhouse with her family and discovers a magical book that helps her unravel the mystery of her great-uncle Oscar's disappearance. Actual adventures come to life as Lucy reads the story.

Continued

---

[18]*The Lord of the Rings* began with *The Hobbit* in 1937. Tolkien wrote the complete work over a period of 12 years. The complete work was published for the first time in 1955.

Box 8.7   Magic, Real/Mythical Creatures, and Unlikely Heroes   *Continued*

Circle of Magic series (*Sandry's Book #1*) by Tamora Pierce. New York: Scholastic, 1997.

Four orphans are rescued and brought to a school of magic, where they learn to control their individual powers, trust each other, and form a team.

The Circle Opens series (*Magic Steps #1*) by Tamora Pierce. New York: Scholastic, 2000.

Fourteen-year-old Sandry is a "stitch witch," which means she has the ability to weave magic as one would cloth. She reluctantly becomes the teacher of Pasco, a 12-year-old boy who can dance magic.

Darkhenge by Catherine Fisher. New York: Greenwillow/HarperCollins, 2006.

Rob takes a job drawing an archeological dig to pay for his comatose sister's mounting medical expenses. What he discovers, however, is a portal to the Underworld, which turns out to be where his sister is residing as her body awaits above. Will she remain in the Underworld or return to her former life?

David Rain's Dragon series (*The Fire Within #1*) by Chris d'Lacey. New York: Orchard/Scholastic, 2001.

David answers a rental ad in the newspaper for an extra room in Liz Pennykettle's home. Although he thinks the condition that the renter "must love dragons" is strange, he soon discovers oddities don't end there. Liz, a sculptor, is known for her portrayal of dragons, many of which reside in her home. Liz's sculptures are not normal. The dragons have "a fire within," which must be nurtured to keep the sculptures alive.

Discworld series (*The Colour of Magic #1*) by Terry Pratchett. New York: HarperCollins, 2000.

Rincewind, a wizard college dropout, is assigned to protect Twoflower, a visitor to Discworld. The two attract attention because Twoflower is from the gold

city of Ankh-Morpork, and the hefty amount of gold she brings attracts the less scrupulous.

Faerie Wars by Herbie Brennan. New York: Bloomsbury, 2003.

Henry is in the midst of his own personal trauma—the separation of his parents—when he meets Prince Pyrgus, a parallel universe faerie whose life is currently in danger because he has found the secret ingredient for glue: kittens. Together, the two work to defeat the dark forces threatening the prince and to prevent war from erupting in the faerie realm.

Flora Segunda by Ysabeau S. Wilce. Orlando, FL: Harcourt, 2007.

Flora knows she should stick with the same route in Crackpot Hall because it is easy to get lost in an 11,000-room house. Still, when she finds herself running late for school one morning, Flora cannot resist taking a shortcut and becomes lost. She stumbles upon Valefor, the butler her mother banished, and naively believes him when he claims he was punished improperly.

The Gateway trilogy (*Night Gate #1*) by Isobelle Carmody. New York: Random House, 2005.

Courage "Rage" Winnoway holds two things dear: her mother and her beloved dogs. When her guardians forbid her from seeing her comatose mother, Rage steps through a magic gate, leading to another world, and she and her dogs search for the wizard who has the power to awaken her mother.

Gifts by Ursula K. Le Guin. Orlando, FL: Harcourt, 2004.

Both Orrec and Gry, childhood friends, have received gifts, as is customary in the Uplands. Orrec can destroy someone with just a look, and Gry can communicate with animals. Both agree that the gifts people have received over the years have been abused and refuse to use their gifts. Their refusal causes great duress.

Continued

Box 8.7   Magic, Real/Mythical Creatures, and Unlikely Heroes   *Continued*

***The Grey Griffins* series (*The Revenge of the Shadow King #1*) by Derek Benz and J. S. Lewis. New York: Orchard/ Scholastic, 2005.**

The Grey Griffins are a foursome of friends who enjoy playing *The Round Table,* a magical card game. They do not realize the game's power, but they learn playing the game opens portals to another world.

***The Healer's Keep* by Victoria Hanley. New York: Holiday House, 2002.**

In this sequel to *The Seer and the Sword* (2000), four teens of different backgrounds and philosophies must work together to keep the Shadow King from taking over the world and destroying the Healer's Keep, a school for healers.

***The Kate and Cecilia* series (*Sorcery and Cecelia or The Enchanted Chocolate Pot #1*) by Patricia C. Wrede and Caroline Stevermer. Orlando, FL: Harcourt, 2003.**

Written as an epistolary novel, this story begins with the two cousins, living in an alternate 19th-century England. Adventure and romance intertwine with magic as the girls correspond through letters. The influence of Jane Austen will thrill many readers, and the fantastical twist is just enough to renew a classic style.

***Magic or Madness* trilogy (*Magic or Madness #1*) by Justine Larbalestier. New York: Razorbill/Penguin, 2005.**

Fifteen-year-old Reason isn't sure what to believe. Her mother has raised her to think magic doesn't exist. But when she opens a locked door, she is transported from the Outback of Australia to the wintry streets of New York City. How does she return home?

***Pendragon* series (*The Merchant of Death #1*) by D. J. MacHale. New York: Aladdin, 2002.**

Fourteen-year-old Bobby Pendragon's perfect teenage world begins falling apart when his Uncle Press arrives.

Bobby is swept through a wormhole to Denduron, an alternate reality teetering on the edge of civil war.

***Pure Dead Magic* series (*Pure Dead Magic #1*) by Debi Gliori. New York: Knopf/Random House, 2001.**

Pandora, Titus, and Damp do not want a nanny, but they have no choice. Their mother is a witch-in-training, and their father has disappeared. Little do they know he has been kidnapped by his evil brother and needs their help, and their new, unwanted nanny can help them travel to Italy to rescue their father.

***The Saint of Dragons* by Jason Hightman. New York: EOS/HarperCollins, 2004.**

Thirteen-year-old Simon has lived his entire life in boarding school, knowing nothing about his family, his roots, or the fact that dragons exist worldwide. Then his father, a legendary dragonslayer, arrives and informs Simon he is about to become a dragonslayer himself.

***The Sea of Trolls* by Nancy Farmer. New York: Atheneum/Simon & Schuster, 2004.**

Jack is apprenticed to a Druid Bard. When Jack and his younger sister, Lucy, are captured by Viking Berserkers and enslaved, Jack must reach Jotunheim, home of the trolls. Threats include giant spiders, a dragon, and a troll-boar.

***The Tiger's Apprentice* series (*The Tiger's Apprentice #1*) by Laurence Yep. New York: HarperCollins, 2003.**

Tom Lee's life turns upside down when he meets a talking tiger on the way home from school. Tom grew up learning his grandmother's magic and will get the chance to use it when he becomes the apprentice for this talking tiger, the guardian of the phoenix egg.

***The Valley of the Wolves* by Laura Gallego García. Trans. Margaret Sayers Peden. New York: Levine/Scholastic, 2006.**

Ten-year-old Dana and her invisible best friend, Kai, travel to the Valley of the Wolves so Dana can study

Continued

Box 8.7   Magic, Real/Mythical Creatures, and Unlikely Heroes   *Continued*

to become a sorceress. Her study reveals her gift to see the dead, her invisible friend's identity, and her mentor's evil past.

The Wall and the Wing by Laura Ruby. New York: EOS/HarperCollins, 2006.

Most people can fly in the future, and the few who cannot, like Gurl, usually find themselves abandoned at Hope House for the Homeless and Hopeless. One night Gurl discovers she can fade and become invisible.

The Warrior Heir by Cinda Williams Chima. New York: Hyperion, 2006.

Sixteen-year-old Jack is in training to fight wizards. After forgetting his morning doses of "heart medication," his warrior powers appear. Wizards, both good and evil, begin recruiting him.

The Wizard Test by Hilari Bell. New York: EOS/HarperCollins, 2005.

Dayven has been told his entire life that wizards are bad, evil people. Now he has discovered he is one of them.

The Wizard's Hall by Jane Yolen. Orlando, FL: Harcourt, 1991.

Henry, student #113, is a new student at Wizard Hall and something special is going to happen. Although he struggles, his belief in himself will provide the skills he needs to save the school from the clutches of an evil wizard.

Box 8.8   Short Story Collections

Science Fiction

2041: Twelve Short Stories about the Future by Top Science Fiction Writers edited by Jane Yolen. New York: Delacorte/Random House, 1991.

The Engine of Recall by Karl Schroeder. Calgary, AB, Canada: Red Deer Press, 2005.

Future Sports edited by Jack Dann and Gardner Dozois. New York: Penguin, 2002.

Genometry edited by Jack Dann and Gardner Dozois. New York: Ace/Penguin, 2001.

Masterpieces: The Best Science Fiction of the Century edited by Orson Scott Card. New York: Ace/Penguin, 2001.

New Skies: An Anthology of Today's Science Fiction edited by Patrick Nielsen Hayden. New York: Tor, 2003.

NextWorld: Super Science Fiction Stories by John Whitman. Los Angeles, CA: Roxbury Park/Lowell House, 2000.

Packing Fraction & Other Tales of Science & Imagination edited by Julie E. Czerneda. Toronto, ON: Trifolium, 1999.

Sol's Children edited by Jean Rabe and Martin H. Greenberg. New York: DAW/Penguin, 2002.

A Woman's Liberation: A Choice of Futures by and about Women edited by Connie Willis and Sheila Williams. New York: Warner, 2001.

The Year's Best Science Fiction: Twenty-third Annual Collection edited by Gardner Dozois. New York: St. Martin's/Griffin, 2006.

Fantasy

Across the Wall: A Tale of the Abhorsen and Other Stories by Garth Nix. New York: EOS/HarperCollins, 2005.

The Faery Reel: Tales from the Twilight Realm edited by Ellen Datlow and Terri Windling. New York: Viking/Penguin, 2004.

Continued

Box 8.8   Short Story Collections   *Continued*

Familiars edited by Denise Little. New York: DAW/Penguin, 2002.

A Gift of Dragons by Anne McCaffrey. New York: Ballantine, 2002.

The Green Man: Tales from the Mythic Forest edited by Ellen Datlow and Terri Windling. New York: Viking/Penguin, 2001.

Half-Human compiled by Bruce Coville. New York: Scholastic, 2001.

New Magics: An Anthology of Today's Fantasy edited by Patrick Nielsen Hayden. New York: Tor, 2004.

Oceans of Magic edited by Brian M. Thomsen and Martin H. Greenberg. New York: DAW/Penguin, 2001.

Oceans of Space edited by Brian M. Thomsen and Martin H. Greenberg. New York: DAW/Penguin, 2002.

Unexpected Magic: Collected Stories by Diana Wynne Jones. New York: Greenwillow/HarperCollins, 2004.

Waifs and Strays by Charles de Lint. New York: Viking/Penguin, 2002.

Water: Tales of Elemental Spirits by Robin McKinley and Peter Dickinson. New York: Putnam, 2002.

Waters Luminous and Deep: Shorter Fictions by Meredith Ann Pierce. New York: Viking/Penguin, 2004.

A Wolf at the Door and Other Retold Fairy Tales edited by Ellen Datlow and Terri Windling. New York: Simon & Schuster, 2000.

Young Warriors: Stories of Strength edited by Tamora Pierce and Josepha Sherman. New York: Random House, 2005.

Science Fiction and Fantasy

A Constellation of Cats edited by Denise Little. New York: DAW/Penguin, 2001.

Dogs of Truth: New and Uncollected Stories by Kit Reed. New York: Tor, 2005.

Firebirds: An Anthology of Original Fantasy and Science Fiction edited by Sharyn November. New York: Firebird/Penguin, 2003.

Firebirds Rising: An Anthology of Original Science Fiction and Fantasy edited by Sharyn November. New York: Firebird/Penguin, 2006.

Futureshocks edited by Lou Anders. New York: ROC/Penguin, 2006.

ReVisions edited by Julie E. Czerneda and Isaac Szpindel. New York: Daw, 2004.

What if . . . ?: Amazing Stories compiled by Monica Hughes. Plattsburgh, NY: Tundra, 1998.

The Year's Best Science Fiction and Fantasy for Teens edited by Jane Yolen and Patrick Nielsen Hayden. New York: Tor, 2005.

Final Thoughts on Science Fiction and Fantasy

Science fiction and fantasy share another element: complexity. Authors use science fiction and fantasy "to comment on social ills, to predict the future, and to express the most basic human emotions" (Wadham & Wadham, 1999, p. 3). To accomplish these goals with new and different worlds, authors use metaphor, symbolism, and satire. Readers, too, have to visualize a new and different world, one they've never known or one that is significantly altered. They have to synthesize information, much of it unfamiliar, about setting, creatures, and cultures; they learn unfamiliar names and sometimes a customized language, and they make inferences about the rules of the world as they read. The more unfamiliar the setting, the more the reader has to work. Science fiction and fantasy require a great deal of mental energy for understanding. It is precisely these issues that make science fiction and fantasy excellent mediums for helping students develop strategies for visualizing text and understanding new vocabulary.

Visualizing

Most of us can recall reading and viewing the same story and experiencing a level of disappointment—our mental images of characters and place didn't match our next encounter. A recent experience for me was *Brokeback Mountain* (2005). I viewed the movie version of Annie Proulx's short story first—starring heartthrobs Jake Gyllenhaal and Heath Ledger. I liked it so much I simply had to read the short story, but I couldn't help feeling let down by the physical appearance of Proulx's characters. Unlike Hollywood's Jack Twist (Gyllenhaal) and Ennis del Mar (Ledger), Proulx's characters are coarse, dirty, and unattractive. The original Jack is a "small man" with buckteeth, who carries "some weight in the haunch" (p. 7). Ennis resembles a horse: "Ennis, high-arched nose and narrow face, was scruffy and a little cave-chested, balanced a small torso on long, caliper legs" (pp. 7–8).

The setting disappointed me too. Those who have viewed Ang Lee's adaptation know the cinematography is spectacular. Much of the movie contains sweeping pastoral scenes of the Canadian wilderness.[19] After viewing the movie, I had difficulty conjuring those romanticized images from Proulx's short story. In fact, Proulx repelled me with her story's opening paragraph:

> Ennis del Mar wakes before five, wind rocking the trailer, hissing in around the aluminum door and window frames. The shirts hanging on a nail shudder slightly in the draft. He gets up, scratching the grey wedge of belly and pubic hair, shuffles to the gas burner, pours leftover coffee in a chipped enamel pan; the flame swathes it in blue. He turns on the tap and urinates in the sink, pulls on his shirt and jeans, his worn boots, stamping the heels against the floor to get them full on. (p. 3)

I'm not suggesting the movie is better, and I'd be hard pressed to choose one over the other. They're both classics, but Annie Proulx and Ang Lee were working toward different effects. My point is to draw attention to the power of visualization and its role in comprehension. No doubt viewers and readers leave the two texts with different visualizations, and those visualizations affect their emotional responses *and* the manner in which they comprehend and relate to the two stories.

Visualizing is a reading skill in which we formulate mental images from text that aid in comprehension. Beers (2003) defines it as "seeing the action of the text." Harvey and Goudvis (2000) assert that visualizing supports other comprehension skills:

> Visualizing strengthens our inferential thinking. When we visualize, we are in fact inferring, but with mental images rather than words and thoughts. Visualizing and inferring are first cousins, the offspring of connecting and questioning. Hand in hand, they enhance understanding. (p. 96)

---

[19]While much of the original story takes place in Wyoming, much of the movie was filmed in Canada.

Proficient readers create a multiplicity of mental images as they read, and what they visualize, and how well, is tied to prior knowledge. To understand the role prior knowledge plays in visualization, consider doing this class activity: Ask a class (the more diverse the better) to draw a picture of a *home,* something they would have drawn in elementary school.[20] Give them ample time to embellish their drawings—to add window curtains, chimneys, smoke, flowers, cars, stick people, and so forth. Don't offer suggestions or tell them why they're doing the drawings. If room permits (floors work), have them lay out their drawings and talk among themselves about what they drew and why. They will discover their houses differ considerably. Some will have the traditional box with the A-shaped roof; others will have more elaborate designs. Some will include apartment buildings, and if your class is diverse enough, you will find a hut or home with a thatched roof. You may also note gender differences (frilly curtains and flowers are more common among girls). Mental images of "home" and "sense of place" are based on life experiences.

The more detailed our images, the easier and more memorable the text. Images aid us in creating meaning and help us organize information in our heads. Research proves, too, that students who are given explicit visualization instruction have better recall (Gambrell & Bales, 1986).

While we form personal images from all texts and all genres, science fiction and fantasy are fun genres for providing students with explicit instruction in visualization. The new worlds that are often created provide an added challenge for visualization. Several activities that will aid students in developing and using visualization skills are discussed in the following sections.

The Movie versus the Book

Having students read a book, view the movie, then write a paper comparing/contrasting the two is a mundane practice in classrooms across the country and takes little creative imagination. It's also easy to view the movie-watching as a reward for reading the book. Students without a good grasp of signal words (see Chapter 10) need guided practice in constructing and organizing their ideas. Simply telling them to write a comparison/contrast doesn't teach anything. Using books and films to teach visual literacy in conjunction with comparison/contrast skills rejuvenates and improves this common practice. While reading a *Harry Potter* novel and then viewing the accompanying movie, students may maintain a four-column journal based on guiding questions in which they describe, compare, and contrast their visual perceptions. A four-column journal on any *Harry Potter* movie might look like Table 8.1.

---

[20]If they ask if you want a "house," tell them the activity is about a "home" and that they are to make their own interpretations.

Table 8.1

Harry Potter Journal Entries

Describe Harry's physical appearance (or that of any favorite character).

Harry Potter, Book #1	*Harry Potter, Film #1*	*Similarities/Differences*	*Personal Reaction* What did you comprehend differently? What did you "miss"? What do you understand "better"?

What mental images do you have of Quidditch?

Harry Potter, Book #1	*Harry Potter, Film #1*	*Similarities/Differences*	*Personal Reaction* What did you comprehend differently? What did you "miss"? What do you understand "better"?

How do you visualize the Great Dining Hall at Hogarts School of Witchcraft and Wizardy?

Harry Potter, Book #1	*Harry Potter, Film #1*	*Similarities/Differences*	*Personal Reaction* What did you comprehend differently? What did you "miss"? What do you understand "better"?

What mental images do you have of either Platform 9 ¾ or the Sorting Hat tradition?

Harry Potter, Book #1	*Harry Potter, Film #1*	*Similarities/Differences*	*Personal Reaction* What did you comprehend differently? What did you "miss"? What do you understand "better"?

Depending on the class, you may need to provide writing parameters; that is, let them know how many images or points you want them to mention per question. The four-column journal may serve as a springboard for class discussion or a structural device for writing a comparison/contrast paper on visual images in a *Harry Potter* book. Chapter 9 includes a list of young adult novels that have been made into films. Also, Teasley and Wilder (1994) suggest great films for teaching visual literacy. Given the popularity of film, resources are endless.

Visualizing Imagery-Loaded Texts

The most common form of visualizing teachers employ with students is visualizing from an imagery-loaded text, one like the paragraph taken from *Brokeback Mountain*. A good way of having students concentrate on visual images is to read an imagery-loaded piece out loud. Have students then draw what they envisioned, "paint" a picture of it with words, and/or complete a graphic organizer. Ask students to share their responses, discuss the differences, and talk about reasons for the differences (prior knowledge). Keep three points in mind: (1) use a short 3–5 minutes selection; (2) practice reading beforehand and use a good reading voice—if your oral reading skills are lacking, you'll put them to sleep; (3) choose passages with vivid descriptions, such as this one from Catherine Fisher's *Snow Walker* (2004):

> The door was the last one in the corridor.
> As the flames flickered over it they showed it was barred; a hefty iron chain hung across it, and the mud floor beneath was red with rust that had flaked off in the long years of locking and unlocking.
> The keeper hung his lantern on a nail, took the key from a dirty string around his neck, and fitted it into the keyhole. Then he looked behind him.
> "Get on with it!" the big man growled. "Let me see what she keeps in there!"
> The keeper grinned; he knew fear when he heard it. With both hands he turned the key, then tugged out the red chain in a shower of rust and pushed the door. It opened, just a fraction. Darkness and a damp smell oozed through the black slit. (p. 3)

Or, the opening from Holly Black's *Valiant: A Modern Tale of Faerie* (2005):

> The tree woman choked on poison, the slow sap of her blood burning. Most of her leaves had already fallen, but those remaining blackened and shriveled along her back. She pulled her roots up from the deep soil, long hairy tendrils that flinched in the chill late autumn air.
> An iron fence had surrounded her trunk for years, the stink of the metal as familiar as any small ache. The iron scorched her as she dragged her roots over it. She tumbled onto the concrete sidewalk, her slow tree thoughts filling with pain.
> A human walking two little dogs stumbled against the brick wall of a building. A taxi screeched to a halt and blared its horn. (p. 1)

Good selections will be loaded with nouns, strong verbs, and precise adjectives. Not all imagery-loaded texts are easily visualized. Science fiction and fantasy can create an added burden for readers because authors create new worlds with unique rules (e.g., magic) of which readers have no real prior knowledge. They also use uncommon vocabulary and create their own, which may or may not be understood through context clues. Compare the following passage from Christopher Paolini's *Eldest* (2005) with the previous excerpts, paying attention to the underlined words. All five are real words, and they're in close proximity within the passage, but readers unfamiliar with medieval weaponry will struggle with the image. Some will break comprehension on the last few lines, given the sheer number of unusual words:

> On the grass by the road was a camp of soldiers. Thirty helmets gleamed in a shaft of morning light as their owners devoured fowl and stew cooked over several fires. The men were mud splattered and travel stained, but Galbatorix's symbol was still visible on their red tunics, a twisting flame outlined in gold thread. Underneath the tunics, they wore leather brigandines—heavy with riveted squares of steel—mail shirts, and then padded gambesons. Most of the soldiers bore broadswords, though half a dozen were archers and another half-dozen carried wicked-looking halberds. (p. 41)

Sometimes an author's word choice and sentence structure are deliberately vague, and to understand the passage we must reread until we create an acceptable mental image. Read the opening of T. A. Barron's *The Great Tree of Avalon: Shadows on the Stars* (2005). Note his use of the words *something* and *it*. Stay with the passage until you have the complete image.

> Deep underground, in a cavern of dark shadows, **something** even darker hovered in the air.
> Slowly **it** spun—a venomous snake of smoke. As **it** twirled, the air around **it** crackled with black sparks. And wherever **its** tail brushed against the cavern floor, stones burst apart like trees shattered by lightning, leaving only heaps of smoldering ash.
> The dark spiral floated menacingly toward a small, radiant crystal on a stone pedestal. The crystal's light, frail but still defiant, glowed white with ribbons of blue and green. As the shadowy **being** approached, **it** swelled a bit brighter. (p. 1)

Barron makes the reader work to figure out this creature. Readers must use visual images to make inferences about the "being." Good readers hone in on words such as *snake of smoke, tail, spiral,* and *floated* to formulate an image and idea about the creature. The more practice students have with a variety of imagery-laden texts—some easy, others more difficult—the better they become at visualizing and recognizing where comprehension breaks down.

Visualizing Graphic Novels

You may look at this suggestion and say, "Wait, that makes no sense. Graphic novels *have* visuals!" True, but graphic novel fans will say reading a graphic novel takes tremendous mental energy and focus. To comprehend a graphic novel, or a comic strip, readers rely heavily on inferential thinking. The artist leaves gaps between images, and the reader must visualize to fill in missing information. Gene Luen Yang's *American Born Chinese* (2006), winner of the 2007 Michael L. Printz Award, is a perfect text for illustrating the visualization process needed for comprehending graphic novels. A complex story, *American Born Chinese* weaves together three seemingly unrelated tales with a surprising twist: the ancient fable of the Monkey King, proud ruler of the monkeys punished for being an uninvited guest at the god's dinner party; the story of Jim Wang, an immigrant struggling with his Chinese heritage in an American school; and Cousin Chin-Kee, a Chinese stereotype. A good activity for drawing attention to the visualization process required for comprehending graphic novels (or comics) is to ask readers to place sticky notes alongside images for which they had to create their own mental images. To prevent this activity from being a monotonous, endless task, limit students to three or four images. Either in whole groups, small groups, or with partners, have students share their personal images. An additional activity that can be quite engaging is having students collect newspaper and magazine comics and talk about the visualization process needed for comprehension. How are their visualizations similar? How are they different? (See Chapter 12 for more graphic novels.)

Visualizing Wordless Picture Books

Harvey and Goudvis (2000) suggest using wordless picture books to teach and reinforce visualizing skills. Wordless picture books may seem "too elementary" for teens; however, many are multilayered and exceptional visualization resources. David Wiesner, the only author to hold three Caldecott Medals[21] and arguably the most inventive and talented visual storyteller, has created numerous fantasy stories excellent for teaching visualization. *Flotsam* (2006), his recent Caldecott winner, is extraordinary. A young boy finds an antique camera washed up on the beach and develops the film. The pictures are detailed images of a surreal underworld (octopi reading in armchairs and cities built of seashells). Images decrease in size. There is, for example, a portrait of a girl holding a portrait of a boy who is holding a portrait of another boy, and so on. Readers make meaning from the visuals. They read the visuals like text; that is, they "combine them with the missing pictures we create in our minds to make meaning"

---

[21]The Caldecott Medal is awarded to an artist of the most distinguished picture book for children. The award is given by the American Library Association.

(Harvey & Goudvis, 2000, p. 97). Here is a list of wordless picture books that work well with teens:

Anno's Journey by Mitsumasa Anno. Cleveland, OH: Collins-World, 1978.
The Arrival by Shaun Tan. New York: Scholastic, 2007.
A Day, A Dog by Gabrielle Vincent. Asheville, NC: Front Street, 1999.
Free Fall by David Wiesner. New York: Lothrop, Lee, & Shepard, 1988.
Hurricane by David Wiesner. New York: Clarion, 1990.
June 29, 1999 by David Wiesner. New York: Clarion, 1992.
Rainstorm by Barbara Lehman. Boston: Houghton Mifflin, 2007.
The Red Book by Barbara Lehman. Boston: Houghton Mifflin, 2004.
The Secret of Love by Sarah Emmanuelle Burg. New York: Penguin, 2006.
Sector 7 by David Wiesner. New York: Clarion, 1999.
The Three Pigs by David Wiesner. New York: Clarion, 2001.
Time Flies by Eric Rohmann. New York: Crown, 1994.
Tuesday by David Wiesner. New York: Clarion, 2001.
The Yellow Balloon by Charlotte Dematons. Asheville, NC: Front
     Street, 2003.

Visualizing Nonfiction

Although nonfiction isn't a topic of this chapter, this is a good place to talk about visualizing as it applies to nonfiction. We tend to relate visualizing to story, and teachers tend to teach it that way. We do, however, visualize nonfiction, and because these texts are the primary reading genre in other subject disciplines, students need support. Because reading expository is generally more difficult than reading narrative, visualizing exercises with nonfiction can help students understand text and recognize when comprehension breaks down.

In reading about genetics, a student might visualize DNA, a double-stranded molecule coiled into the shape of a double-helix. The quality of this image will depend upon the reader's understanding of "molecule" and "double-helix." To understand unfamiliar information, a reader may make visual comparisons such as visualizing DNA as a twisted ladder. A student reading about the earth's layers might conjure an image of an onion, the outer layer being the crust, the inner most being the core. Of course, readers who comprehend the text make these analogies. Table 8.2 illustrates a reader's process in visualizing nonfiction. Read the passages in the left column, and then the reader's response in the right. Note how the reader "sees" things that aren't really there (a product of prior knowledge), has emotional responses, and recognizes an unfamiliar concept.

The two-column journal can help students concentrate on visualization, but another idea is to have them maintain a two-column journal in which they list an unclear concept and/or passage on the left, then on the right they indicate what part they can't "see." Note the reference to carbon-14 in Table 8.2.

T a b l e   8 . 2

Nonfiction Visualization

Nonfiction Passage	My Visualizations
Bats aren't really blind, but they do fly safely in some very dark places. They have sharp hearing and emit high-pitched squeaks that bounce off objects in their way. (*Earth's Core and Mantle*, Vogt, 2007a, p. 23)	Several bats flying around, shrieking, in a cave.
Before the coming of white people, antelope, elk, bison, wolves, and grizzly bears were animals of the plains. As the prairie was settled, the big game retreated westward to the mountains. The bison were slaughtered—as many as sixty to eighty million of them! (*On the Trail of Lewis & Clark*, Lourie, 2002, p. 15)	A dry, hot prairie littered with bison carcasses.
Volcanic eruptions will create lots of ash that covers up forests. The age of the forest can be estimated by measuring the amount of carbon-14 present in the wood. (*The Lithosphere*, Vogt, 2007b, p. 25)	A dense stand of trees, whose leaves are coated with black dust. I have some trouble with carbon-14. I can't "see" it. I don't know what it is.
Modern embalming techniques are themselves a public health hazard. For example, body fluids go into the common sewer, followed by a splash of Clorox. (*Corpses, Coffins, and Crypts*, Colman, 1997, p. 58)	I do NOT like what this makes me see! Dead bodies, lying on slabs, blood draining down the sink. Into the "common" sewer? Oh, my.
Insects detect the odor of a newly dead body long before people do. Flies, especially flesh flies and blowflies, arrive first from as far away as two miles and lay thousands of eggs that soon hatch maggots. Then come beetles, spiders, mites, and millipedes. (*Corpses, Coffins, and Crypts*, Colman, 1997, p. 49)	Not going here.

Choose several nonfiction selections and create your own visualization chart based on your own reading (or experiment with another graphic organizer). Use your results to illustrate to students how we visualize expository material, then ask them to create their own visual. Don't be afraid to have some fun with your responses. Also, remember that as we continue to read our visual images change. Consider the first passage in Table 8.2. The reader sees bats in a cave, but that image may change depending on what he/she sees next in the text.

Vocabulary

Cole: What do you do when you encounter an unfamiliar word?

Student: I look it up. (*what the teacher wants to hear*)

Cole: Really?

Student: Well, no. Most of the time I skip it. (*hesitation*)

Cole: What if you really *need* to know it?

Student: Then I look it up.

Cole: Are you sure? The reason I ask is when I don't know a word and I finally decide I need to, I call my mom.

The point of this exchange in my content area reading classroom is to begin a conversation about how proficient readers approach vocabulary. The truth is, until I discovered www.dictionary.com, I *did* call my mom. If she didn't know the word, she did the motherly thing and looked it up for me. Funny, I know. But it proves a point: Like many readers, my last strategy for figuring out words has always been consulting the dictionary.

Proficient readers employ several strategies before referencing a dictionary or before logging onto the computer. First, we'll ignore the word and read on. We'll either watch for it to occur again, hoping the next context will be helpful, or we'll decide it doesn't affect comprehension and forget it. We'll also use context clues. We'll study words and phrases surrounding the troublesome word, hoping for some clue or hint as to the word's meaning. We'll also look beyond the immediate sentence. We'll recognize the meaning could be paragraphs and pages before or after the word. We hunt for other words *and* punctuation that may add some clarity. If we can't clear up confusion on our own, we may ask someone—that's much easier (and quicker) than looking up a word. If all else fails and we care about knowing, we use other resources. We'll consult either an online dictionary or hard copy, a glossary, or another resource. (A small percentage of people do use dictionaries often and may consult those early on.)

Before delving into vocabulary activities, let's consider the following question: How do you know *when* you know a word? Do we know a word, for instance, when

- we can pronounce it?
- we recognize it when we hear it?
- we can recite the definition?
- we can use it in a sentence?
- we can give examples?
- we know how it functions? (e.g., noun, verb, adjective)
- we can relate it to other words?

Knowing a word actually means all of these, but common vocabulary assessment techniques (e.g., match the word with the definition, fill in the blank, write the definition, use the word in a sentence) don't provide deep understanding. Bronzo and Simpson (2003) use the term *definitional knowledge* to define word understanding limited to dictionary definitions and *contextual understanding* to represent sophisticated word schema that lead to rich and varied interpretations in a variety of contexts. Whatever vocabulary activities you use, and there are no end to them, your goal should be the latter.

Teaching Syntactic and Semantic Context Clues

To understand the importance of teaching and understanding words in context, envision a common word like *light* on a note card, then try to define it. While you will think of the most obvious definitions, you won't know the exact meaning unless you see or hear the word in context. You may turn on a *light, light* a candle, eat a *light* dinner, wear *light* clothes, and so forth. Proficient readers automatically use context clues within the sentence to determine the meaning of an unfamiliar word. They use syntactic context, information either before or after the word, to determine meaning (e.g., Is the confusing word a noun? Verb?). If that doesn't work, they know information in preceding or following paragraphs (semantic context) may help them. Consider the word *Urgal* in the opening passage of Paolini's *Eldest* (2005):

> The songs of the dead are the lamentations of the living.
>
> So thought Eragon as he stepped over a twisted and hacked *Urgal,* listening to the keening of women who removed loved ones from the blood-muddied ground of Farthen Dûr. Behind him Saphira delicately skirted the corpse, her glittering blue scales the only color in the gloom that filled the hollow mountain.
>
> It was three days since the Varden and dwarves had fought the *Urgals* for possession of Tronjheim, the mile-high, conical city nestled in the center of Farthen Dûr, but the battlefield was still strewn with carnage. (p. 1)

Unless you are familiar with Paolini's work, your first encounter with *Urgal* triggers confusion.[22] You may recognize it as a "thing" because of *syntax*—it operates as a noun. As a proficient reader, you then begin relying on *semantic* context: *Twisted and hacked* may or may not be helpful, so you file that in your mind and continue reading. Women are *keening,* but that may trigger further confusion because it's an uncommon expression. You may guess women are lamenting; you may remain confused. You read on and encounter *blood-muddied ground;* you determine violence has occurred. *Farthen Dûr* is odd too. Is it a place? It must be, because of *blood-muddied ground.* You see an unusual name, *Saphira,* and it seems like a female name (provided English is your primary language), only she/it has blue scales. Possibly a dragon but not helpful in figuring out *Urgal.* Beyond that you encounter a strange

---

[22]Fantasy fans are familiar with the creation of "new worlds." They expect, and even relish, unfamiliar vocabulary and odd names. The creation of a new world with its own language is part of fantasy's allure. If you're a fantasy fan, and this passage is "easy," find a more challenging one in a favorite book and share it with peers.

proper noun: *Varden*. Okay, you probably get it now. The Varden and the Urgals have been at war over a city (Tronjheim). Weird names. You don't know if they're humans, beasts, or magical creatures. But you'll figure that out later through additional context clues.

This is a typical process of a proficient reader, and struggling readers need to see this process at work. To give students practice using syntactic and semantic clues, choose a short paragraph similar to the one just discussed, give students copies so they can follow along, and read aloud, pausing to talk through confusing words and clues. Then have students work with partners to do the same. Your modeling the process is important; so is repeated practice. They may feel awkward the first go-around. You may too.

Teaching Punctuation Clues and Signal Word Clues

Readers who understand how punctuation works have an additional tool for determining word meaning. Commas, parentheses, and dashes may set off a definition. Note the examples below—the same sentence with different punctuation:

- Ostracods, tiny creatures related to shrimp, have clamlike shells.
- Ostracods (tiny creatures related to shrimp) have clamlike shells.
- Ostracods—tiny creatures related to shrimp—have clamlike shells.

Dashes may introduce an explanation:

The afternoon was catching up with him—the violence, the shallowness and cruelty of the teens, the indifference of this man—all of it crashing down in a wave that threatened to wash him away. (*The Seer* by David Stahler Jr., 2007, p. 46)

Colons may also:

Then the pain of warming began: the burns on my ankles and wrists, my swollen tongue, my cramped limbs. (*Bloodtide* by Melvin Burgess, 2001, p. 162)

Punctuation clues make excellent mini-lessons. Place several examples on an overhead, discuss how they work, and ask students to record the samples in a writing notebook. Draw their attention to these kinds of word clues in their reading and encourage them to model them in their own writing.

Word (Morphemic) Analysis

When context clues aren't enough to determine meaning, proficient readers may use structural analysis to determine word meaning; that is, they use their knowledge of word parts (roots, prefixes, and suffixes). To recognize how knowledge of *morphemes*, the smallest unit of meaning in a word, aids in determining meaning, ask students to see how many words they can create on their own using a common root word. A good one is *phon*. In a manner of minutes, most students will identify more than a dozen. Here are some possibilities:

cacophony	gramophone	phone
chordophone	homophone	phoneme
dictaphone	iPhone	phonemic
euphony	megaphone	phonetics
phonics	speakerphone	videophone
phonogram	symphony	waterphone
phonograph	telephone	xylophone
phonological	vibraphone	

Have students share their lists and ask them what most, if not all, the words have in common. Students will have no trouble coming up with *sound*. This activity is powerful for helping students recognize how knowledge of word parts aids in understanding vocabulary. Students see that once they know a single meaning-bearing unit, they can transfer that meaning to a larger number of words. This approach works better than memorizing and being quizzed on the meanings of roots, prefixes, and suffixes. One final note: make sure students know how to break words apart. Some adolescents will not break longer words into meaningful parts. Select high-utility prefixes and roots. The more frequently used the word part, the more words students will learn. Word sorts are superb activities for teaching students word analysis. An excellent resource is *Words Their Way: Word Sorts for Derivational Relations Spellers* (Johnston, Bear, & Invernizzi, 2006).

Possible Sentences

Moore and Arthur (1981) suggest having students make predictions about word meanings based on what they know or can anticipate. The strategy is easy to implement. Students should know the selection they are going to read; that is, is it a poem? A fantasy short story? A geology textbook chapter? What does the book cover look like? Are there illustrations? Having an idea about the reading selection provides "context." Identify 10 or 12 words students will be reading, and write them on the board. Ask students to choose 3 to 4 words and write sentences about how they think the words might be used. Students then share their predictions, and you write one sentence per word on the board. Students read the selection, checking the use of the words as they read. Does reading back up their definition? Refute it? Or can they not tell from the context? Have them make note of their findings. Table 8.3 is an example based on Chapter 1 of Philip Pullman's *The Golden Compass* (1996).

This activity is particularly difficult with fantasy and science fiction because of writers' tendencies to create their own language (of which readers have no prior knowledge). Don't choose many "odd" words created by the author; stick with what's more familiar.[23] No matter the genre, always include some common words such as *patronize*. Students need "some"

---

[23]You may want to use this activity first with realistic fiction or nonfiction.

Table 8.3

**Predicting Word Meanings Chapter 1, *The Golden Compass*
(1996) by Philip Pullman**

Word	Possible Sentence	Prediction Key
		Correct = √ Incorrect = **X** Can't Tell = ?
Daemon	The evil magician released a daemon bent on destroying the keepers of the underworld.	?
decanted	The sorcerer decanted the evil spell cast by the dark force.	?
dais	The queen reclined on the brocade-covered dais, while her lap dog slept at her heels.	**X**
Retiring Room	After dinner, the twin brothers joined their father in the Retiring Room.	√
patronize	My uncle seems to patronize me mostly in front of my father.	√

---

success with this activity. If all their answers are wrong, they can feel the activity is pointless. So will you. Don't be afraid to give this idea a second try if the first try fails.

Knowledge Rating Activity

Blachowicz (1986) suggests introducing key words by asking students to evaluate their level of knowledge about each word. Such an activity invites active participation on the reader's part. An activity based on the first chapter in Kai Meyer's *The Stone Light* (2007) might resemble Table 8.4.

Knowledge rating activities are efficient and quick, and they help both student and teacher recognize what the student already knows. To encourage active involvement further, students might take turns choosing five words from each reading assignment for their class. If you have difficulty finding "tough enough" words, your reading selection might not be conducive to vocabulary instruction.

Table 8.4

Vocabulary Knowledge Rating

Chapter 1, *The Stone Light* (2007) by Kai Meyer

Word	Very Familiar	Somewhat Familiar	Not Familiar
obsidian			
succulent			
scarab			
suboceanic			
lagoon			
irrevocably			
sphinx			
submissiveness			
crenellated			
filaments			

Shades of Meaning

We've all had those moments when we used a word that wasn't quite right; it was a close approximation of what we intended. That's because synonyms have variations, or subtle differences, in meaning. Think of *pompous* and *majestic*. Which would you likely use to describe someone you disliked? Which for someone you admired? Fisher and Frey (2008) suggest an activity by Cathy Blanchfield (Table 8.5). Give each student a sample paint card from a local home improvement store. One student may have a card with

Table 8.5

Shades of Meaning Chart

Shades of Meaning	Definitions and Sentences
fear	a feeling of anxiety because danger is near I have a *fear* of getting a shot at the doctor.
dread	a great fear mixed with awe or respect The girl *dreaded* moving to a new school.
terror	an intense fear and shock I saw *terror* in the driver's eyes right before he crashed.
panic	a sudden fear that might cause the person to collapse My mother *panicked* when she saw the cut on my face.
phobia	a fear that doesn't make sense My friend has a phobia about rollercoasters.

Source: Fisher & Frey (2008), p. 63.

shades of blue, another yellow, and so on. Students identify synonyms for a vocabulary word. They clip the card to notebook paper and assign a shade for each word. Across from each word, students write a definition for that particular word, along with a sentence that illustrates the word's meaning. You may have some disagreements over definitions (e.g., I'd argue *dread* isn't always mixed with *awe* or *respect*), but the process creates conversations about word meanings, and that's an essential point.

Final Thoughts

Science fiction and fantasy allow us to explore worlds in which we could conceivably live and worlds we can only imagine. They're complex and imaginative genres that allow us to dream, to envision, and to ask "what if?" Many are packed with dense vocabulary, complex sentence structure, detailed descriptions, and alternate worlds and cultures, making them challenging but good reads. They're perfect for reinforcing visualization and fun books for vocabulary development. Whatever vocabulary activities you use, remember the importance of teaching in context, provide ample opportunity for students to use new words, and to connect new vocabulary to prior experiences. Above all, emphasize students' active involvement in vocabulary acquisition and teach deeper meanings; help students know the different ways of knowing words.

Professional Resources

Beers, K. (1998). Fantasy and realism: Two topics, one author: a talk with T. A. Barron. *Journal of Adolescent and Adult Literacy, 41*(7), 588–592.

Card, O. S. (2001). *Writing science fiction and fantasy.* Cincinnati, OH: Writer's Digest.

Cavanaugh, T., & Cavanaugh, C. (2004). *Teaching science with science fiction films: A guide for teachers and media specialists.* Columbus, OH: Linworth.

Donawerth, J. (1990). Teaching science fiction by women. *English Journal, 79*(3), 39–46.

Dozois, G. (1991). *Writing science fiction and fantasy.* New York: St. Martin's Press.

Fantasy and Science Fiction. Hoboken, NJ: Spilogale, Inc.

Gallo, D. (2007). Speculative fiction: Classroom must-reads. *English Journal, 97*(1), 118–122.

Garner, J. (2006). *Wings of fantasy: Using readers theatre to study fantasy genre.* Portsmouth, NH: Teacher Ideas Press.

Gillett, S. (2001). *World-building: A writer's guide to constructing star systems and life-supporting planets.* Cincinnati, OH: Writer's Digest.

Gunn, J. (2003). *The science of science-fiction writing.* Lanham, MD: Scarecrow Press.

Hampton, G. J., & Brooks, W. M. (2003). Octavia Butler and Virginia Hamilton: Black women writers and science fiction. *English Journal, 92*(6), 70–74.

Herald, D. T. (1999). *Fluent in fantasy: A guide to reading interests.* Portsmouth, NH: Libraries Unlimited.

Johnson, W. H., Silberling, S. J., Watts, L. S., & Mollineaux, B. (2003). What work of fantasy literature do you recommend for the high school or middle school classroom? *English Journal, 92*(5), 23–24.

Louden, W., Cowan, E., & Louden, G. (2001). Reality and Harry Potter. *Journal of Adolescent and Adult Literacy, 44*(7), 668–669.

MacRae, C. D. (1998). *Presenting young adult fantasy.* Woodbridge, CT: Twayne.

MacRae, C. D. (2000). Harry Potter update: Is it for YAs? *English Journal, 89*(4), 137–138.

Moore, J. N. (2001). Fathers and fantasy. *English Journal, 91*(2), 114–115.

New York Review of Science Fiction. Bloomington, IN: Dragon Press.

Perry, P. J. (2003). *Teaching fantasy novels: From* The Hobbit *to* Harry Potter and the Goblet of Fire. Portsmouth, NH: Teacher Ideas Press.

Pierce, E. (2001). Science fiction and fantasy. *Voices from the Middle, 9*(2), 74–77.

Polette, N. (2005). *Teaching thinking skills with fairy tales and fantasy.* Portsmouth, NH: Teacher Ideas Press.

Raham, R. G. (2004). *Teaching science fact with science fiction.* Portsmouth, NH: Teacher Ideas Press.

Reid, S. (1998). *Presenting young adult science fiction.* Woodbridge, CT: Twayne.

Science Fiction and Horror Digest. Lexington, KY: Apex.

Scott, M. (1997). *Conceiving the heavens: Creating the science fiction novel.* Portsmouth, NH: Heinemann.

Thomas, M. (2003). Teaching fantasy: Overcoming the stigma of fluff. *English Journal, 92*(5), 60–64.

Wadham, T., & Wadham, R. (1999). *Bringing fantasy alive for children and young adults.* Columbus, OH: Linworth.

Wild, J. (1998). Learning from fantasy. *Voices from the Middle, 59*(2), 40–42.

Yep, L. (2005). The outsider in fiction and fantasy. *English Journal, 94*(3), 52–54.

Zigo, D., & Moore, M. T. (2004). Science fiction: Serious reading, critical reading. *English Journal, 94*(2), 85.

ONLINE

Analog Science Fiction and Fact: www.analogsf.com/0712/issue_12.shtml

Asimov's Science Fiction: www.asimovs.com

Association of Science Fiction & Fantasy Artists: www.asfa-art.org

Best on the Web for Teachers: www.teachers.teach-nology.com

Center for the Study of Science Fiction: www2.ku.edu/~sfcenter

Dictionary: www.dictionary.com

Ed Helper: www.edhelper.com

English Club: www.englishclub.com/vocabulary/index.htm

Fantasy and Science Fiction: www.sfsite.com/fsf

Fantasy Factor: www.fantasy.fictionfactor.com

Fantasy Magazine: www.fantasymagazine.blogspot.com

Fantasy Readers: www.fantasyreaders.com

Fantasy Realms: www.fantasyrealmsonline.com

Fantasy Writers: www.fantasy-writers.org

Free Speculative Fiction: www.freesfonline.de/Home2.html

Interactive Games-Matching Words: www.teflgames.com/interactive.html

Locus Online: www.locusmag.com

The Los Angeles Science Fantasy Society: www.lasfs.info

Odyssey: www.sff.net/odyssey

Proteacher Directory: www.proteacher.com/070169.shtml

Reading Comprehension: www.literacy.uconn.edu/compre.htm

Science Fiction & Fantasy Writers of America: www.sfwa.org

Science Fiction Museum: www.sciencefictionmuseum.com

Science Fiction Studies: www.depauw.edu/sfs/backissues/19/teaching19forum.htm

Scifidimensions: www.scifidimensions.com

SFRT: www.sfrt.com

Sites for Teachers: www.sitesforteachers.com

Speculative Vision: www.speculativevision.com/network

Teaching Science Fiction Writing: www.teachersnetwork.org/dcs/cyberenglish/scifi.htm

ThinkMap Visual Thesaurus: www.visualthesaurus.com

University of Michigan Fantasy & Science Fiction: www.umich.edu/~umfandsf

Vocabulary Lesson Plans: www.vocabulary-lesson-plans.com/vocabulary-websites.html

Your Dictionary: www.yourdictionary.com

References

Anderson, M. T. (2002). *Feed.* Cambridge, MA: Candlewick Press.

Asimov, I. (1950). *I, robot.* New York: Gnome Press.

Asimov, I. (1981). *Asimov on science fiction.* New York: Doubleday.

Barron, T. A. (1996). *The lost years of Merlin* epic (*The lost years of Merlin* #1). New York: Philomel/Penguin.

Barron, T. A. (2005). *The great tree of Avalon: Shadows on the stars.* New York: Philomel/Penguin.

Barry, M. (2003). *Jennifer government.* New York: Vintage/Random House.

Bechard, M. (2005). *Spacer and rat.* Milford, CT: Roaring Brook Press.

Beers, K. (2003). *When kids can't read: What teachers can do.* Portsmouth, NH: Heinemann.

Bell, H. (2006). *The prophecy.* New York: EOS/HarperCollins.

Blachowicz, C. L. (1986). Making connections: Alternatives to the vocabulary notebook. *Journal of Reading, 29*(7), 643–649.

Black, H. (2005). *Valiant: A modern tale of faerie.* New York: Simon & Schuster.

Black, H. (2007). *Ironside: A modern faery's tale.* New York: Simon & Schuster.

Bly, R. W. (2005). *The science in science fiction: 83 SF predictions that became scientific reality.* Dallas, TX: Benbella Books.

Bradbury, R. (2005). *A sound of thunder and other stories.* New York: HarperCollins. (Original work published 1952)

Bronzo, W. G., & Simpson, M. L. (2003). *Readers, teachers, learners.* Upper Saddle River, NJ: Merrill/Prentice Hall.

Brooks, T. (1998). Introduction. In Writer's Digest (Ed.), *The writer's complete fantasy reference.* Cincinnati, OH: Writer's Digest.

Brooks, T. (2006). *Wintersmith.* New York: HarperCollins.

Burgess, M. (2001). *Bloodtide.* New York: Tor.

Card, O. S. (1977). *Ender's game.* New York: Tor.

Card, O. S. (1990). *How to write science fiction and fantasy.* Cincinnati, OH: Writer's Digest.

Carroll, L. (1865). *Alice's adventures in Wonderland.* New York: Macmillan.

Cart, M. (Ed.). (1999). *Tomorrowland: 10 stories about the future.* New York: Scholastic.

Clement, H. (1954). *Mission of gravity.* New York: Doubleday.

Clute, J. (1995). *Science fiction: The illustrated encyclopedia.* London: Dorling Kindersley.

Clute, J., & Grant, J. (1999). *The encyclopedia of fantasy.* New York: St. Martin's Griffin.

Colfer, E. (2001). *Artemis Fowl.* New York: Scholastic.

Collins, S. (2003). *Gregor the overlander.* New York: Scholastic.

Collins, S. (2004). *Gregor and the prophecy of bane.* New York: Scholastic.

Collins, S. (2005). *Gregor and the curse of the warmbloods.* New York: Scholastic.

Collins, S. (2006). *Gregor and the marks of secret.* New York: Scholastic.

Collins, S. (2007). *Gregor and the code of claw.* New York: Scholastic.

Colman, P. (1997). *Corpses, coffins, and crypts: A history of burial.* New York: Henry Holt.

Craig, J. (2005). *Jimmy Coates: Assassin?* New York: HarperCollins.

Crichton, M. (1990). *Jurassic Park.* New York: Knopf/Random House.

Czerneda, J. E. (2004). *Survival.* New York: DAW/Penguin.

del Rey, L. (1980). *The world of science fiction: 1926–1978.* New York: Garland.

DeVita, J. (2007). *The silenced.* New York: EOS/HarperCollins.

Dick, P. K. (1962). *The man in the high castle.* New York: Penguin.

Dickinson, P. (1988). *Eva.* New York: Delacorte/Random House.

DuPrau, J. (2006a). *The people of sparks.* New York: Random House.

DuPrau, J. (2006b). *The prophet of Yonwood.* New York: Random House.

Engdahl, S. L. (2006). *Journey between worlds.* New York: Penguin.

Farmer, N. (2002). *The house of the scorpion.* New York: Atheneum/Simon & Schuster.

Fisher, C. (2004). *Snow walker.* New York: HarperCollins.

Fisher, D., & Frey, N. (2008*). Improving adolescent literacy: Content area strategies at work.* Upper Saddle River, NJ: Pearson.

Funke, C. (2002). *The thief lord.* New York: Chicken House/Scholastic.

Gambrell, L. B., & Bales, R. J. (1986). Mental imagery and the comprehension-monitoring performance of fourth- and fifth-grade poor readers. *Reading Research Quarterly, 21*(4), 454–464.

Gates, P. S., Steffel, S. B., & Molson, F. J. (2003). *Fantasy literature for children and young adults.* Lanham, MD: Scarecrow Press.

Gibson, W. (1984). *Neuromancer.* New York: Ace.

Hanley, V. (2000). *The seer and the sword.* New York: Holiday House.

Harvey, S., & Goudvis, A. (2000). *Strategies that work.* York, ME: Stenhouse.

Hautman, P. (2006). *Rash.* New York: Simon & Schuster.

Heinlein, R. A. (1947). *Rocket Ship Galileo.* Chicago: Scribner.

Hightman, J. (2006). *Samurai.* New York: EOS/HarperCollins.

Hunter, E. (2003). *Warrior* series (*Into the wild* #1). New York: HarperCollins.

Huxley, A. (1932). *Brave new world.* London: Chatto & Windus.

Jacques, B. (1986). *Redwall: The legend begins.* New York: Firebird/Penguin.

Johnston, F., Bear, D. R., & Invernizzi, M. (2006). *Words their way: Word sorts for derivational relations spellers.* Upper Saddle River, NJ: Pearson.

Jones, D. W. (2001). *The chronicles of Chrestomanci.* New York: HarperCollins.

Klass, D. (2006). *Firestorm.* New York: Farrar, Straus & Giroux.

Lasky, K. (2003). *Guardians of the Ga'Hoole* series (*The capture* #1). New York: Scholastic.

L'Engle, M. (1962). *A wrinkle in time.* New York: Farrar, Straus & Giroux.

Levitin, S. (1970). *Journey to America.* New York: Simon & Schuster.

Levitin, S. (1977). *Beyond another door.* New York: Simon & Schuster.

Levitin, S. (1987). *Return.* New York: Simon & Schuster.

Levitin, S. (1989). *Silver days.* New York: Simon & Schuster.

Levitin, S. (1993a). *Annie's promise.* New York: Simon & Schuster.

Levitin, S. (1993b). *The golem and the dragon girl.* New York: Dial/Penguin.

Levitin, S. (1994). *Escape from Egypt.* New York: Little, Brown.

Levitin, S. (1996). *Evil encounter.* Topeka, KS: Sagebrush.

Levitin, S. (1997). *Yesterday's child.* New York: Simon & Schuster.

Levitin, S. (1998). *Singing mountain.* New York: Simon & Schuster.

Levitin, S. (1999). *The cure.* Orlando, FL: Harcourt.

Levitin, S. (2000). *Dream freedom.* Orlando, FL: Harcourt.

Levitin, S. (2003). *Room in the heart.* New York: Dutton/Penguin.

Levitin, S. (2005). *The goodness gene.* New York: Penguin.

Levitin, S. (2007). *Strange relations.* New York: Random House.

Lewis, C. S. (1950). *The chronicles of Narnia* series (*The lion, the witch and the wardrobe* #1). London: Geoffrey Bles.

Lourie, P. (2002). *On the trail of Lewis and Clark: A journey up the Missouri River.* Honesdale, PA: Boyds Mills Press.

Lowry, L. (1993). *The giver.* Boston: Houghton Mifflin.

Lubar, D. (1999). *Hidden talents.* New York: Starscape/Tor.

Mann, G. (Ed.). (2001). *The mammoth encyclopedia of science fiction.* New York: Carroll & Graf.

Maurer, A., & Wright, R. (2001). Magic. In *The writer's complete fantasy reference.* Cincinnati, OH: Writer's Digest.

Mendlesohn, F. (2004). Is there any such thing as children's science fiction? A position piece. *The Lion and the Unicorn, 28*(2), 284–313.

Meyer, K. (2005). *Dark reflections* trilogy (*The water mirror* #1). Trans. Elizabeth D. Crawford. New York: McElderry/Simon & Schuster.

Meyer, K. (2007). *The stone light.* New York: McElderry/Simon & Schuster.

Miller, A. P., & Clark, D. (2001). Fantasy races. In *The writer's complete fantasy reference.* Cincinnati, OH: Writer's Digest.

Molson, F. J. (1999). American technological fiction for youth: 1900–1940. In C. W. Sullivan (Ed.), *Young adult science fiction* (pp. 7–20). Westport, CT: Greenwood Press.

Moore, D., & Arthur, S. V. (1981). Possible sentences. In E. K. Dishner, T. W. Bean, & J. E. Readence

(Eds.), *Reading in the content areas: Improving classroom instruction*. Dubuque, IA: Kendall/Hunt.

Nix, G. (2005). *The keys to the kingdom* series (*Mister Monday* #1). New York: Scholastic.

O'Brien, R. C. (1974). *Z for Zachariah*. New York: Simon & Schuster.

Oppel, K. (1997). *Silverwing*. New York: Simon & Schuster.

Oppel, K. (2004). *Airborn*. New York: HarperCollins.

Oppel, K. (2006). *Skybreaker*. New York: HarperCollins.

Ostry, E. (2004). "Is he still human? Are you?": Young adult science fiction in the posthuman age. *The Lion and the Unicorn, 28*(2), 222–246.

Paolini, C. (2005). *Eldest*. New York: Knopf/Random House.

Philbrick, R. (2000). *The last book in the universe*. New York: Scholastic.

Pierce, T. (1983). *The song of the lioness quartet* (*Alanna: The first adventure* #1). New York: Atheneum/Simon & Schuster.

Pierce, T. (2006). *Beka Cooper* series (*Terrier* #1). New York: Random House.

Pow, T. (2004). *The pack*. New York: Random House.

Pratchett, T. (2000). *Discworld* series (*The colour of magic* #1). New York: HarperCollins.

Pratchett, T. (2003). *The wee free men*. New York: HarperCollins.

Pratchett, T. (2006). *Wintersmith*. New York: HarperCollins.

Pratchett, T. (2007). *Johnny and the bomb*. New York: HarperCollins.

Proulx, A. (2005). *Brokeback Mountain*. New York: Scribner.

Pullman, P. (1996). *The golden compass*. New York: Knopf/Random House.

Rose, M. (1997). *Lawless and Tilley* series (*The secrets of the dead* #1). New York: Scholastic.

Rose, M. (2000). *Plague*. New York: Scholastic.

Rose, M. (2005a). *Hurricane force*. New York: Simon & Schuster.

Rose, M. (2005b). *Lost bullet*. Boston: Kingfisher.

Rose, M. (2005c). *Roll call*. Boston: Kingfisher.

Rose, M. (2005d). *Traces* series. (*Framed* #1). Boston: Kingfisher.

Rose, M. (2006). *The death gene*. New York: Simon & Schuster.

Rose, M. (2007a). *Double check*. Boston: Kingfisher.

Rose, M. (2007b). *Final lap*. Boston: Kingfisher.

Rowling, J. K. (1998). *Harry Potter* series (*Harry Potter and the scorcerer's stone* #1). New York: Levine/Scholastic.

Sambell, K. (2004). Carnivalizing the future: A new approach to theorizing childhood and adulthood in science fiction for young adults. *The Lion and the Unicorn, 28*(2), 247–267.

Sayler, H. L. (1909). *The quest of the Axtec treasure*. Chicago: Reilly & Britton.

Schanback, M. (2005). *Princess from another planet*. New York: Holiday House.

Shelley, M. (1818). *Frankenstein: Or, the modern Prometheus*. London: Lackington, Huges, Harding, Mavor & Jones.

Shusterman, N. (1999). *The dark side of nowhere*. New York: Tor.

Sleator, W. (1973). *Run*. New York: Dutton/Penguin.

Sleator, W. (1974). *House of stairs*. New York: Dutton/Penguin.

Sleator, W. (1975). *Among the dolls*. New York: Dutton/Penguin.

Sleator, W. (1981). *Green futures of Tycho*. New York: Dutton/Penguin.

Sleator, W. (1983). *Fingers*. New York: Dutton/Penguin.

Sleator, W. (1984). *Interstellar pig*. New York: Dutton/Penguin.

Sleator, W. (1985). *Singularity*. New York: Dutton/Penguin.

Sleator, W. (1986). *The boy who reversed himself*. New York: Dutton/Penguin.

Sleator, W. (1988). *Duplicate*. New York: Dutton/Penguin.

Sleator, W. (1990). *Strange attractors*. New York: Dutton/Penguin.

Sleator, W. (1991). *Spirit house*. New York: Dutton/Penguin.

Sleator, W. (1993a). *Oddballs*. New York: Dutton/Penguin.

Sleator, W. (1993b). *Others see us*. New York: Dutton/Penguin.

Sleator, W. (1995). *Dangerous wishes*. New York: Dutton/Penguin.

Sleator, W. (1996). *The night the heads came*. New York: Dutton/Penguin.

Sleator, W. (1997). *The beasties*. New York: Dutton/Penguin.

Sleator, W. (1998). *The boxes*. New York: Dutton/Penguin.

Sleator, W. (1999a). *Boltzmon!* New York: Dutton/Penguin.

Sleator, W. (1999b). *Rewind.* New York: Dutton/Penguin.

Sleator, W. (2001). *Marco's millions.* New York: Dutton/Penguin.

Sleator, W. (2002). *Parasite pig.* New York: Dutton/Penguin.

Sleator, W. (2004). *The boy who couldn't die.* New York: Amulet/Harry N. Abrams.

Sleator, W. (2005). *The last universe.* New York: Amulet/Harry N. Abrams.

Sleator, W. (2006). *Hell phone.* New York: Amulet/Harry N. Abrams.

Smith, R. (2005). *Cryptid hunters.* New York: Hyperion.

Stahler,D., Jr. (2007). *The seer.* New York: EOS/HarperCollins.

Stemple, A. (2005). *Singer of souls.* New York: Tor.

Stephens, J. B. (2004a). *Desolation angels.* New York: Razorbill/Penguin.

Stephens, J. B. (2004b). *Paradise City.* New York: Razorbill/Penguin.

Stevenson, R. L. (1886). *The strange case of Dr. Jekyll and Mr. Hyde.* New York: Scribner.

Sullivan, C. W. (2006). Robert A Heinlein: Reinventing series SF in the 1950s. *Extrapolation, 47*(1), 66–76.

Teasley, A., & Wilder, A. (1994).Teaching for visual literacy: 50 great young adult films. *The ALAN Review, 21*(3), 18–23.

Tolkien, J. R. R. (1937). *The hobbit.* London: Allen & Unwin.

Tolkien, J. R. R. (2004). *The lord of the rings.* Boston: Houghton. (Original work published 1955)

Tomlinson, C. M., & Lynch-Brown, C. (2007). *Essentials of young adult literature.* Boston: Pearson.

Townley, R. (2007). *The red thread.* New York: Atheneum/Simon & Schuster.

Turtledove, H. (2004). *Days of infamy: A novel of alternative history.* New York: New American Library/Penguin.

Turtledove, H. (2005). *End of the beginning.* New York: ROC/Penguin.

Verne, J. (1865). *From the earth to the moon.* Paris: Pierre-Jules Hetzel.

Verne, J. (2003). *Twenty thousand leagues under the sea.* New York: Scholastic. (Original work published 1879)

Vogt, G. L. (2007a). *Earth's core and mantle.* Minneapolis, MN: Lerner.

Vogt, G. L. (2007b). *The lithosphere.* Minneapolis, MN: Lerner.

Wadham, T., & Wadham, R. L. (1999). *Bringing fantasy alive for children and young adults.* Worthington, OH: Linworth.

Wells, H. G. (1999). *The time machine.* New York: Bantam Doubleday Dell. (Original work published 1895)

Wells, H. G. (2002). *The invisible man.* New York: Penguin. (Original work published 1897)

Westerfeld, S. (2003). *Succession* series (*The risen empire #1*). New York: Tor.

Westerfeld, S. (2004a). *Blue noon.* New York: HarperCollins.

Westerfeld, S. (2004b). *The secret hour.* New York: HarperCollins.

Westerfeld, S. (2004c). *So yesterday.* New York: Penguin.

Westerfeld, S. (2004d). *Touching darkness.* New York: HarperCollins.

Westerfeld, S. (2005a). *Peeps.* New York: Penguin.

Westerfeld, S. (2005b). *Pretties.* New York: Simon & Schuster.

Westerfeld, S. (2005c). *Uglies.* New York: Simon & Schuster.

Westerfeld, S. (2006a). *The last days.* New York: Penguin.

Westerfeld, S. (2006b). *Peeps.* New York: Penguin.

Westerfeld, S. (2006c). *Specials.* New York: Simon & Schuster.

Westerfeld, S. (2007). *Extras.* New York: Simon & Schuster.

Wiesner, D. (2006). *Flotsam.* Boston: Houghton Mifflin.

Yang, G. L. (2006). *American born Chinese.* New Milford, CT: Roaring Brook Press.

Yolen, J., & Stemple, A. (2005). *Pay the piper: A rock 'n' roll fairy tale.* New York: Tor.

Yolen, J., & Stemple, A. (2006). *Troll bridge: A rock 'n' roll fairy tale.* New York: Tor.

Short Stories, Poetry, and Drama
Reading Skill: Fluency

Introduction

As mentioned earlier, young adult literature is generally more accessible to teenage readers than classical literature. No where is this accessibility issue more true than with short stories, poetry, and plays, the backbone of the high school literature anthology. High school students are expected to read sonnets, metaphysical poetry, epics, satires, and Shakespearean plays, all of which threaten both struggling and disinterested readers. Many students hate poetry and plays because they lack the necessary prior knowledge and inferential skills to extract meaning. Nikki Giovanni (1999c), anthologized in most high school texts and recipient of more than 20 honorary doctorate degrees, maintains that poetry doesn't need to be complicated to hold value. As you explore this area, you may agree.

The first author box contains part of an essay written by a high school senior for admission to a college honors program. The brief passage reminds us that some students do relate to the classics. My point is not to dismiss the classics—they hold a priceless place in the curriculum—but to provide some alternatives. Whether we're teaching classical or contemporary short stories, poetry, or plays, connection is the key to understanding, appreciation, enjoyment, and lifelong reading. This chapter introduces you to a plethora of short stories, both edited collections by multiple authors and single-author collections, an abundance of poetry, a variety of poetry styles, verse novels, and illustrated poetry, and drama. The last section in the chapter addresses fluency, the one skill with which most struggling readers need practice. Short stories, poetry, and drama are superb genres for developing fluency skills.

Short Stories

The short story lies somewhere between the novel and the novella.[1] The classification, however, is arbitrary, for the question arises, how *long* is "short"? Short stories may range from a few pages to under a hundred, making it synonymous with the novella. One can argue that the short story originated from myths, legends, parables, fairy tales, fables, essays, and anecdotes, many of which were embedded in classical literature such as Chaucer's *Canterbury Tales* and Boccaccio's *Decameron*. Biblical stories, too, may be considered forerunners of the short story such as the story of Cain and Abel and that of the Prodigal Son (Cuddon, 1999, p. 816).

---

[1]The novella is a short, fictional narrative restricted to a single event, situation, or conflict. Suspense is evident and the ending generally has a twist.

Reflections upon a Knoll   by R. Taylor Cole, freshman honor student

History will not remember me as a great poet. In fact, I have only experienced the thrill of poetic inspiration twice in my life, once while baking in the summer heat at Pembroke College in Oxford, England, and again while reclining in the shade of an ancient oak tree later that summer. Upon reaching the peak of a knoll overlooking the English countryside on that latter day, I was awestruck by the grandeur and power of the pastoral landscape. My companion on this journey was a battered copy of William Wordsworth's greatest verses, and as I sat, cradled in that tree's gnarled roots, I contemplated the Romantic notion of the sublime. Despite valiant efforts by teachers in my Georgia hometown, I had failed to comprehend this powerful force.

Upon reading Wordsworth's "I Wandered Lonely as a Cloud," I understood why Wordsworth was moved to euphoria by his tiny daffodils, why Shelley hailed the magnitude of Mont Blanc—I understood because sitting under that tree overlooking the rustic English countryside, I *experienced* the sublime; believed I shared Wordsworth's experiences. I put pen to paper and witnessed a literary miracle: the birth of my first decent poem. I knew in that moment that college for me would not be a career training ground, but an intellectual exploration, a place that fed my rabid curiosity.

R. Taylor Cole is currently an honor student at the University of Georgia.

During the 18th century, the short story developed quickly due to the British interest in horror and gothic novels. By the 19th century, the short story format was highly formed; especially developed were stories featuring horror, supernatural, and ghost themes (p. 816). Today's young adults read works by 19th-century short story writers, founders of the modern-day short story. Many are American: Washington Irving, Nathaniel Hawthorne, Edgar Allan Poe, Ambrose Bierce, Herman Melville, O. Henry, Mark Twain, Stephen Crane, and Jack London. Others are British: Thomas Hardy, Sir Arthur Conan Doyle, Rudyard Kipling, W. W. Jacobs, Joseph Conrad, and Robert Louis Stevenson. These writers explored varying approaches to the short story and structured their stories around a single event, a single day, a character trait/flaw, a dream/wish/fantasy, an experience, or an action (p. 817).

Young adult short story collections, either compiled by editors or written by single authors, began appearing in the 1980s. Pantheon Books published Robert Cormier's *8 Plus 1* in 1980, a collection of Cormier's stories that had appeared in publications such as *The Saturday Evening Post* and *Red-book*. Almost 30 years later, the collection remains popular. Bradbury Press published Cynthia Rylant's *Every Living Thing* in 1985, a collection of "short"

short stories. Dozens of short story collections exist today, but early collections like *Baseball in April and Other Stories* (Soto, 1990) and *Athletic Shorts: 6 Short Stories* (Crutcher, 1991) remain the all-time bestselling single-author collections. Since his classic *Baseball in April and Other Stories*, Soto has published six additional short story collections in addition to a plethora of essays, poetry collections, novels, and two plays. No other young adult author has produced as many short story collections. In the author box Soto presents a poignant, yet funny narrative about the sources of his poetic inspiration and his love of reading. Whether short story or poem, Soto's writing is lyrical and imagery laden.

In 1984, Random House published the first ever edited anthology of short stories written by various young adult authors: Don Gallo's *Sixteen: Short Stories by Outstanding Writers for Young Adults.* Undeniably the leading young adult short story expert, Gallo has edited a dozen young adult short story anthologies since his groundbreaking 1984 anthology (see Box 9.1). Most collections center around a contemporary young adult theme, and most are realistic problem themes (see Gallo's author box). Gallo's idea was original, and publishing houses and editors responded. HarperCollins published *A Gathering of Flowers: Stories about Being Young in America* edited by Joyce Carol Thomas in 1990. Now a young adult short story classic, *Am I Blue? Coming Out of the Silence* (1994) by Marion Bauer became the first collection of young adult short stories dealing with homosexuality. This volume features 16 short stories by prominent young adult authors (e.g., Bruce Coville, Nancy Garden, M. E. Kerr, Lois Lowry, Jacqueline Woodson). Some are funny, others serious. Young adult experts Hazel Rochman and Darlene McCampbell published *Leaving Home* in 1997, an award-winning collection. By the turn of the century, a number of authors and editors were publishing short story anthologies. In addition to Gallo, today's most noted editors of short story anthologies include Michael Cart, M. Jerry Weiss, Helen Weiss, and Marilyn Singer.

Over the years, short story collections have covered a variety of topics, most paralleling contemporary issues: homosexuality, guns and violence, gender issues, race relations, and diversity. While early collections were primarily problem short stories, today's stories span every genre. Horror short stories are among the most plentiful. Deborah Noyes has compiled some of the best (e.g., *Gothic! Ten Original Dark Tales*, 2004; *The Restless Dead*, 2007). The latter is a collection of 10 short stories about the supernatural

A Young Adult short story classic. Copyright © 1990 by Gary Soto. Reproduced by permission of Harcourt, Inc.

Why Read, or My Time with Samuel Pepys　by Gary Soto

Aristotle, the bearded sage in a toga, came up with the notion that we operate by our five senses—taste, touch, smell, sight, and hearing. Of course, every man and woman employed these senses all along, but it wasn't until Aristotle said something to the effect of, "Hey, wait a minute, I just realized something" that one more discovery was made about the human species.

Just a few hours ago I employed one—no, make that two, possibly three—of my senses when I lifted my fork and plied my mouth with a steamy bite of an enchilada. It was a marvelous experience. And so were the salsa, my overly sugared tea, and the beans and rice. While I employed these senses, I also enjoyed a few pages of the biography *Samuel Pepys* by Claire Tomalin. It's not important that you know too much about Mr. Pepys (pronounced "Peeps") except that he was a civil servant (worked for the government) who lived from 1633 to 1703, observed the Plague, the Great Fire of London, and some more of the Plague, and wrote one of the world's greatest diaries—five volumes of it.

When I finished my lunch at the restaurant, I took my Samuel Pepys biography to a park in the Diamond District in Oakland. I sat on a bench with the book in my lap. I thought of Pepys and his City of London, the most populous city in the world around 1630—120,000 folks. Triple that for the number of rats foraging in brick-lined sewers during the day and surfacing at night to steal grub from kitchens.

But my mental visit to old London was interrupted when a pigeon settled in front of me. He was a well-fed pigeon, almost Buddha-like in shape. The poor feathered creature warbled when I said, "You don't know what this is, do you?" I asked the bird a second time as I held up Tomalin's biography. No, he didn't know what it was and, in fact, shuffled back a few steps because of my arm movement. The large scholarly book cast a shadow across the pebbly ground before us.

The pigeon, sensing that I offered no handouts, lifted his Buddha-body into the air and went to pester a nanny at another bench. His departure allowed me to close my eyes, sigh at my good luck to have a Saturday to myself, and reflect, "Now where was I? Oh, yes, old London." I imagined the Thames River, the sun filtered by clouds over this river, and moored ships anchored at wharves. Sniffing, I employed one of my more acute senses. Yes, I inhaled and imagined the funky-smelling river—"funky" had yet to be part of our language but I'm sure the Londoners of the time used a similarly descriptive word for the Thames.

At my age, 54, I'm acutely aware of my position in life. I'm doomed to sit on park benches, doomed to observe others play volleyball on a muddy lawn, doomed to wince with worry at the tiny children parachuting from swings. Why they don't get hurt, I don't know. Moreover, I can't join the teenagers in pick-up football. For one, I am slow and, two, I fear resembling that pigeon: a pest.

But have no pity for me. I have a book in hand and I have lots of others at home. I can at any time whip open a novel, book of poems, biography, or play and enjoy the highest form of gossip, namely, literature. What's wrong with thinking of, say, *Madame Bovary*, my favorite novel of all time, as a sort of gossip? Without much exertion, I get it all: the cheats, the pompous, the inept, the wise, the unwise, the holy, and the sinner. I read novels, one after another, some out of print, some neglected classics, and some translated from French, Spanish, Italian, Japanese, or mighty Russian. I find none of the characters from the novels follow me home.

But I take that back. I have had several characters follow me home. I recall Mary Shelley's *Frankenstein*, which sort of scared me when I read an abridged, illustrated version when I was 10. Inspired by the narrative, I assumed my own Frankenstein role. With my arms outstretched in front of me, I walked

Continued

Why Read, or My Time with Samuel Pepys   *Continued*

stiffly into our house as if my legs were encased in cardboard. This role-playing lasted no more than an hour before I grew bored and leafed through a comic book in search of an action hero to imitate.

In turn, in my teens, I read *To Sir with Love,* a novel set in a poor part of 1950s London. The kids—juvenile delinquents—had no money, their neighborhood was rundown, and their parents were gruff; it sounded remarkably like my own life. After I read the book I assumed the surly attitude of the 1950 London kids—sneering lips, hair hanging over one eye, a stalk of grass in the corner of my mouth. I tucked my hands in my jeans and went about muttering like Bob Dylan. I assumed their moodiness for a few days until my parents told me to knock it off and go mow the lawn.

I don't have to read in order to become smart, as I already own a tweed jacket with patches on the elbows, a stylish indication that I belong to the intellectual crowd. I don't read to educate others. I don't read to take a test. I don't read to enlarge my soul like a balloon. I don't read to carry on the tradition we call Western Civilization. At parties, I don't name drop the great writers to elevate my self-worth as I nibble on finger food. For instance, I don't say, "The symbol of a whale suggests the wondering complexities of man in search of a moral harbor in order to anchor his soul," but will utter, "Wow, Moby Dick is one big daddy fish. And, hey, did you try this killer dip?" I don't read to kill time as the people in airplanes do. What else would they do strapped in their seats? Look straight ahead?

Why, then, do I read? It's the pleasure of a story, and the intimacy of getting to know the characters well enough to exercise tenderness (or dislike) toward them. It's to weigh but not judge the behavior of characters, who are like ourselves except that they are in print and possibly immortal while we humans are flesh, thus very much mortal. Moreover, I look for fresh language and not the repeated gibberish we get daily. Just as some search for a daily jolt of a good joke, the latest clothing styles, a fresh sound in music, or the renewed experience on a basketball court—a fake to the left, then a cut to the right for a sweet lay-up—I'm looking for phrasing that excites me.

Yet another observation about reading: it doesn't make me sweat. I mean, I play tennis and basketball three or four times a week and love it, and then over dinner embellish my triumphs. However, while reading, I don't involve much of my body. I bat my eyelashes and lick my thumb to turn the page. I raise a hand to my mouth to stifle an occasional yawn. I bite a fingernail, I bite my lower lip. Once, I stopped reading to observe my stomach rise and fall, and the movement perturbed me when I realized that my stomach was a little ball on my 5'8" frame. Feeling horrible, feeling that my physical fitness was at stake, I blamed reading for that little paunch, and immediately got into my sweats: the courts beckoned.

But reading beckons too. It's a worthwhile activity, as it gives pleasure, it makes us observant, it offers fresh uses of language, and it offers us vistas into people's lives. Surprisingly, however, I have never seen myself in the novels that I have read. The cheat? No, I can't see that's me. The romantic hero cast about on the High Seas. No, I'm just in a recliner. The rebellious youth? No, I tried that, but it wasn't me. The money-grubbing captain of industry found center stage in Sinclair Lewis's *Dodsworth?* No, I have no great interest in money or position. But here's something confounding to me: I have read probably 800 novels, great ones and minor ones, plus a bunch of awful ones. During my reading life, which didn't begin until I was in my teens, I have not encountered a novel in which a character marched the page and *he* was me. It's always someone else, someone more troubled or noble or handsome! I have not made the grade to main character, I guess. I don't have that archetypal resonance that would make a novelist conjure up a plot and place someone like me at the center, or even at the fringes.

When is someone going to write a novel about a man who takes a large scholarly book first to a restaurant and then to a park? It will be a Saturday, a fall day, and children will be on the swings or roughing it up on the lawn. This character will be middle-aged, content with a little ball on his belly, but suddenly in shock when he looks down and sees that one sock is blue, the other black. A horrible mixup! Who will write the novel about a myopic gentleman reading a biography of Samuel Pepys on a fall day?

Soto's short story collections include *Baseball in April and Other Stories* (1990), *Local News: A Collection of Stories* (1993), *Petty Crimes* (1998), *Nickel and Dime* (2004), *Help Wanted: Stories* (2005), *A Fire in My Hands* (2006), and *Facts of Life: Stories* (2008).

Box 9.1   Don Gallo's Young Adult Short Story Anthologies

***Connections: Short Stories by Outstanding Writers for Young Adults*. New York: Delacorte/Random House, 1989.**

This collection includes Chris Crutcher's first short story, "A Brief Moment in the Life of Angus Bethune." This short story was made into a movie (*Angus*) in 1995.

***Destination Unexpected: Short Stories*. Cambridge, MA: Candlewick Press, 2003.**

Ten stories about teenagers who go on some kind of journey where they learn something about themselves as well as about a part of the wider world.

***First Crossing: Stories about Teen Immigrants*. Cambridge, MA: Candlewick Press, 2004.**

Stories about teen immigrants from Mexico, China, Romania, Haiti, Korea, Kazakhstan, Sweden, Venezuela, Cambodia, and Palestine, and their experiences adjusting to American life.

***Join In: Multiethnic Short Stories by Outstanding Writers for Young Adults*. New York: Delacorte/Random House, 1993.**

Seventeen multiethnic short stories about the lives of contemporary American teenagers whose ethnic backgrounds are Vietnamese, Chinese, Puerto Rican, Cuban, Mexican, Pueblo Indian, Japanese, Lebanese, Laotian, and African American.

***No Easy Answers: Short Stories about Teenagers Making Tough Choices*. New York: Delacorte/Random House, 1997.**

These 16 short stories about character development show teenagers facing situations that test their moral strength as they deal with such issues as computer blackmail, drug use, pregnancy, gang violence, and peer pressure.

***On the Fringe*. New York: Dial/Penguin, 2001.**

Eleven stories focus on the experiences of teenage outsiders struggling with peer pressure, conformity, personal identity, popularity, and harassment.

***Owning It: Stories about Teens with Disabilities*. Cambridge, MA: Candlewick Press, 2008.**

Ten stories about teens with physical or psychological disabilities facing the normal pressures of school, friends, and parents. Authors are Chris Crutcher, Alex Flinn, Gail Giles, Kathleen Jeffrie Johnson, Ron Koertge, Robert Lipyste, David Lubar, Julie Anne Peters, Rene Saldaña Jr., and Brenda Woods.

***Short Circuits: Thirteen Shocking Stories by Outstanding Writers for Young Adults*. New York: Delacorte/Random House, 1992.**

Ghost and thriller stories by Joan Aiken, Frances A. Miller, Joan Lowery Nixon, and others.

***Sixteen: Short Stories by Outstanding Writers for Young Adults*. New York: Delacorte/Random House, 1984.**

The first ever anthology of original short stories for teenagers written by a variety of authors who write for young adults. One of YALSA's 100 Best of the Best Books published between 1966 and 1999.

***Time Capsule: Short Stories about Teenagers throughout the Twentieth Century*. New York: Delacorte/Random House, 1999.**

Ten different authors each explore a major aspect of each decade of the 20th century through the point of view of teenage characters whose feelings and concerns are similar to those of contemporary teens.

***Ultimate Sports: Short Stories by Outstanding Writers for Young Adults*. New York: Delacorte/Random House, 1995.**

In this knockout collection of 16 stories, both male and female teens engage in a variety of sports, including basketball, football, track, cross-country, sailing, scuba diving, boxing, wrestling, racquetball, triathlon, and the ultimate sport of the future.

Continued

Box 9.1   Don Gallo's Young Adult Short Story Anthologies   *Continued*

Visions: Nineteen Short Stories by Outstanding Writers for Young Adults. New York: Delacorte/Random House, 1987.

The second ever collection of new short stories for teens. Includes stories by Sandy Asher, Sue Ellen Bridgers, Norma Fox Mazer, Colby Rodowsky, and Ouida Sebestyen.

What Are You Afraid Of? Stories about Phobias. Cambridge, MA: Candlewick Press, 2006.

Ten stories about teens with various fears—of small spaces, clowns, string, crossing the street, and so forth by such notable authors as Joan Bauer, Angela Johnson, David Lubar, Neal Shusterman, and Jane Yolen.

On Short Story Collections   by Don Gallo

Few people in the publishing world have been as fortunate as I. Although I have never published a short story of my own (I've never even written a publishable story), I have been responsible for the publication of some of the best and most popular short stories ever written for teenagers. (Among them are Richard Peck's now famous "Priscilla and the Wimps," Lensey Namioka's "The All-American Slurp," Todd Strasser's "On the Bridge," and Chris Crutcher's "A Brief Moment in the Life of Angus Bethune.")

This all started in the early 1980s when I realized that there were no anthologies of contemporary short stories about teens that were written by a variety of authors whose novels were popular with young people and their teachers. I asked several authors whom I had met at national and state English conferences if they might be interested in writing something for such a collection, and then I approached the editor-in-chief at two publishing houses, whom I had also met. One of those two—George Nicholson at Delacorte—supported the idea enthusiastically, and a new branch of literature sprouted in the young adult field.

The publisher and I agreed that we should start by inviting the very best authors we knew, and I have continued to do that for more than 20 years. As a result, I've gotten to work with many of the stars in this business, including Joan Bauer, Alden Carter, Chris Crutcher, M. E. Kerr, Ron Koertge, Angela Johnson, Robert Lipsyte, David Lubar, Walter Dean Myers, Richard Peck, Neal Shusterman, and Jane Yolen.

The first three anthologies were not themed—that is, I simply asked authors to write a story about some aspect of teen life where the main character was a teenager. But then it seemed easier to categorize—and promote—an anthology if it had a clear focus, and so every one of my books since then has had a theme. For example, my newest anthology is about teens with disabilities. So authors were asked to write a story in which a teenager had a disability or dealt with someone with a disability; authors chose which disability they wanted to feature in their story. Whether the topic is disabilities or moral dilemmas, historical events of the 20th century or phobias, the essential characteristic is that each story be interesting and readable on its own.

Continued

On Short Story Collections   *Continued*

The issue/topic/theme is secondary. In other words, I want an excellent story first, one that teen readers will love and teachers will value.

Because all these stories are written in response to my invitation, I'm usually the first person on Earth to read them. It's a thrilling experience to read something no one else has read before. I also am responsible for editing each story, to be sure it's the most effective story it can be, and that means I get to tell those famous writers what in their story doesn't work as well as it should. That, I must say, is a heavy burden, because I'm responsible for noticing any weakness in the story, but I must always be sure that any changes I recommend are in keeping with the author's intent and style and that I am tactful in how I suggest such changes.

Remembering editors who in the past have changed my words and writing style without my permission, I never make substantive changes without consulting the author; in fact, I don't make changes; I recommend them and always try to suggest an alternative. I do correct verb tenses and grammatical errors without permission, and before everyone had spell-checkers on their computers, I fixed spelling errors as well. (It's great fun to know which famous authors are not good spellers, who has trouble keeping his or her tenses consistent, and who doesn't know the difference between *its* and *it's*—there are two of the latter, actually, but I can't name names.) There is also always a backup to my judgments, because there is an in-house editor and an executive editor at the publishing company who approve my recommendations and occasionally make additional ones. Of course, every revised manuscript is also gone over thoroughly by a copy editor who makes additional recommendations for clarity and accuracy before the final manuscript is sent to the printer. (Though their highly trained judgments are invaluable, copy editors sometimes get a bit overzealous. More than once I've had a copy editor "fix" the grammar of a character who is supposed to be only semi-literate!)

How do famous authors react to my telling them what's wrong with their stories? Almost without exception they thank me for my suggestions, just as I am thankful to copy editors for their keen eyes and ears—all of us get much too close to our own work to see its flaws. Of the dozens of stories I have edited over the years, only one author refused to change a line I felt was not needed in her story. I still feel that line contributed nothing to the story, but she wanted it there and it stayed there.

Because I start by inviting the best writers I know, I have seldom had to reject a story because it hasn't been good enough or because it didn't fit the theme well enough. I believe that's happened only five or six times in more than a dozen anthologies, and only two of those stories were just awful (and wouldn't you love to know who wrote them?). The quality and variety of those I've accepted for publication has been truly amazing. As I said at the start, I've been incredibly fortunate. And the world of young adult books has been richer for that.

Copyright Don Gallo, 2008

Gallo created Authors4Teens: www.authors4teens.com.

---

written by some of today's best horror writers (e.g., Holly Black, Libba Bray, Herbie Brennan, Annette Curtis Klause, Marcus Sedgwick, Chris Wooding). One of the most talked about collections in recent years, an example of blended genres, is Margo Lanagan's *Black Juice* (2005), winner of a Best Collection World Fantasy Award in 2005 and the first short story collection to receive a Printz Honor Award.[2] Remarkably unique, *Black Juice* explores human behavior and consequences, providing a glimpse into the darker side of human nature and the frailty of the human spirit. Lanagan's short stories

---

[2]Some may consider Helen Frost's *Keesha's House* (2003), a Printz Honor book, a short story collection; however, because it is written in traditional poetic forms, it is better classified as a verse novel.

are complex and fall short of being breezy reads. She has written equally riveting short story collections: *White Time* (2006) and *Red Spikes* (2007). See her comments about her collections in the author box.

Traditionally, short story collections are held together by a theme, as illustrated by Don Gallo's collections or many collections listed in Boxes 9.2 and 9.3.[3] A current trend, however, is the interconnected short story novel— a short story collection that works together to tell one story, often through alternating voices. For instance, reminiscent of the story structure used by the screenwriters for *Crash* (2005), 10 characters narrate their experiences in Laurie Stolarz's *Bleed* (2006). Over the course of one day, the lives of 10 teens intersect. Nicole, for instance, has a crush on her best friend's boyfriend; Robby would kill for true love—he has before; Joy is bullied; Derik thinks he's a girl magnet; Kelly has two boyfriends, one in jail. While the interconnected short story novel is part of a new trend in young adult fiction, poetry is another area in which writers are exploring different storytelling and poetic structures. Interconnected poems work in much the same way as interconnected short stories.

The Weird and the Wondrous   by Margo Lanagan

I've now written three collections of short stories: *White Time* (2006), *Black Juice* (2005), and *Red Spikes* (2007). Each collection contains 10 stories, all of which have some element of science fiction, fantasy, or horror.

White Time includes the six stories I wrote at Clarion West writing workshop in 1999 and is perhaps the most varied of the three because I was having a good play around with different genre ideas: fabulous beasts, unexplained phenomena, time travel, space travel, animal stories. The story "The Queen's Notice," about a colony of naked mole rats, was the award winner in that collection, although the title story and "The Boy Who Didn't Yearn" did well too. My own favorite, I think, is "The Night Lily," because even now, I couldn't tell you where it comes from and what it means, although I know it has to do with grief and consolation. And I think it is a good indicator of where my writing went from there, following a more instinctive method.

Black Juice was less consciously driven and the stories in that collection coughed up from my subconscious. "Singing My Sister Down," which is the hit single of the collection, was inspired by a documentary about a village built next to a tar pit (I think it may have been the one shown on this site: www.richard-seaman.com/Travel/TrinidadAndTobago/Trinidad/PitchLake/index.html—if not, it was very much like it). As soon as I saw people walking out onto the tar and slowly beginning to sink, I knew I was

Continued

---

[3]Most annotations in these two boxes were compiled by Don Gallo.

The Weird and the Wondrous   *Continued*

going to write a story about someone being executed by being made to stand still on the tar. Other stories take place in medieval fantasy lands; a European city that's a mixture of Paris and Berlin; an India–Africa mixture; a made-over, landlocked Mont-Saint-Michel, and post-apocalyptic Australia. In this book I was just trying to escape the real world (I'd recently returned to full-time work, and I wrote the first drafts on the train to and from work), so I created vivid other worlds and as intense situations as I could.

Red Spikes has two animal stories—a monkey story (not gentle at all!) and a reincarnated-budgerigar story. It also has stronger references to existing fables, including the nursery rhyme "Wee Willy Winkie" (brrr!), the *Narnia Chronicles*, Fairyland, and Roman Catholic beliefs about Limbo. But as with the other two books, all these things are background scenery for stories about relationships being established or developing in

unexpected ways, about crises of responsibility in the lives of people of all ages, about sad times and times when wondrous things happen in ordinary lives. It's the characters I care about, and what they're going through.

I'm also trying for particular storytelling rhythms, so that the reader is carried through the story in a way that feels inevitable, but that contains surprises, both beautiful ones and horrible ones. I love beautiful and ugly imagery when they are well done, but I can't stand prettiness or sentimentality, or an author telling me how I should interpret something. I assume that my readers are the same sort of readers as I am.

Copyright Margo Lanagan, 2008

For more information visit HarperCollins's Web site: www.harpercollins.com.

Box 9.2   Edited Short Story Collections

13: Thirteen Stories That Capture the Agony and Ecstasy of Being Thirteen edited by James Howe. New York: Atheneum/Simon & Schuster, 2003.

The title says it all—by writers such as Meg Cabot, Bruce Coville, Ron Koertge, Alex Sanchez, Rachel Vail, and Lori Aurelia Williams.

The Color of Absence: 12 Stories about Loss and Hope edited by James Howe. New York: Atheneum/Simon & Schuster, 2001.

Annette Curtis Klause, Norma Fox Mazer, Walter Dean Myers, Naomi Shihab Nye, and others portray various kinds of losses in the lives of an interesting array of fictional teenagers.

Dirty Laundry: Stories about Family Secrets edited by Lisa Rowe Fraustino. New York: Viking/Penguin, 1998.

Excellent variety of stories about plagiarism, abortion, child abuse, mental illness, and transgender acceptance by authors such as Bruce Coville, Chris Crutcher, M. E. Kerr, Richard Peck, and Rita Williams-Garcia.

Dreams and Visions: Fourteen Flights of Fantasy edited by M. Jerry Weiss and Helen S. Weiss. New York: Tor, 2006.

A collection of science fiction and fantasy short stories by award-winning young adult authors: Joan Bauer, David Lubar, John Ritter, S. L. Rottman, Neal

Continued

Box 9.2   Edited Short Story Collections   *Continued*

Shusterman, Nancy Springer, and Rich Wallace. (See also *From One Experience to Another,* 1997; *Lost and Found,* 2000; and *Big City Cool,* 2002.)

Every Man for Himself: Ten Short Stories about Being a Guy edited by Nancy E. Mercado. New York: Dial/Penguin, 2005.

A variety of life lessons from the pens of Ron Koertge, David Levithan, David Lubar, Walter Dean Myers, Rene-Saldaña Jr., Terry Trueman, and others.

Face Relations: 11 Stories about Seeing beyond Color edited by Marilyn Singer. New York: Simon & Schuster, 2004.

Race relation stories by Rita Williams-Garcia, Ron Koertge, Ellen Wittlinger, and others. (See also *Stay True: Short Stories for Strong Girls,* 1998; and *Make Me Over: 11 Original Stories about Transforming Ourselves,* 2005.)

Firebirds: An Anthology of Original Fantasy and Science Fiction edited by Sharyn November. Firebird/Penguin Putnam, 2003.

A hefty collection of 16 stories by Lloyd Alexander, Michael Cadnum, Nancy Farmer, Diana Wynne Jones, Garth Nix, Meredith Ann Pierce, Nancy Springer, and other stellar fantasy and science fiction writers.

Girls Got Game: Sports Stories and Poems edited by Sue Macy. New York: Henry Holt, 2001.

Finally, a collection of original stories just about female athletes playing baseball, softball, basketball, soccer, stickball, football, tetherball, and so on.

Half-Human edited by Bruce Coville. New York: Scholastic, 2001.

Ten engaging stories about creatures that are half human, half animal of some kind, by Gregory

Maguire, Tamora Pierce, Nancy Springer, Jane Yolen, and others.

Necessary Noise: Stories about Our Families as They Really Are edited by Michael Cart. New York: Cotler/HarperCollins, 2003.

Packed with award-winning authors: Joan Bauer, Nikki Grimes, Lois Lowry, Walter Dean Myers, Sonya Sones, and Rita Williams-Garcia. (See also Cart's earlier collection, *Love and Sex: Ten Stories of Truth,* 2001.)

Night Terrors: Stories of Shadow and Substance edited by Lois Duncan. New York: Simon Pulse/Simon & Schuster, 1996.

Chilling and horrifying tales by 11 of the best: Joan Aiken, Alane Ferguson, Madge Harrah, Annette Curtis Klause, Chris Lynch, Harry Mazer, Norma Fox Mazer, Joan Lowery Nixon, Richard Peck, Theodore Taylor, and Patricia Windsor.

On the Edge: Stories at the Brink edited by Lois Duncan. New York: Simon & Schuster, 2000.

A dozen new stories from writers such as Alden R. Carter, Terry Davis, Margaret Peterson Haddix, and Ellen Wittlinger about teenagers on various edges: the edge of sanity, the edge of a family, the edge of a ravine, the edge of annihilation.

Outside Rules: Short Stories about Noncomformist Youth edited by Claire Robson. New York: Persea, 2007.

A compelling collection of stories focusing on teen outsiders and their efforts to belong. Brainy, geeky, poor, emotionally disturbed, anorexic teens and more have a place in this volume. Contributors include Sandra Cisneros, Rand Cooper, Chris Fisher, and Wally Lamb.

Continued

Box 9.2   Edited Short Story Collections   *Continued*

***Rush Hour: Sin* edited by Michael Cart. New York: Random House, 2004.**

With stories and poems by Joan Bauer, Alex Flinn, Nikki Grimes, Ron Koertge, Chris Lynch, Sonya Sones, and many others. (See also *Rush Hour: Bad Boys,* 2004; *Rush Hour: Face,* 2005; and *Rush Hour: Reckless,* 2006.)

***Shattered: Stories of Children and War* edited by Jennifer Armstrong. New York: Knopf/Random House, 2002.**

Joseph Bruchac, David Lubar, Marilyn Singer, Suzanne Fisher Staples, and eight other authors describe how different young people are affected by and deal with war in various forms and times, including the American Civil War, WW II, the Six-Day War in the Middle East, and Afghanistan.

***Shelf Life: Stories by the Book* edited by Gary Paulsen. New York: Simon & Schuster, 2003.**

Paulsen has long been a supporter of literacy programs. Stories in this collection illustrate the positive impact of reading on our lives. Paulsen has donated all proceeds from this book to ProLiteracy Worldwide. Some authors in this collection include M. T. Anderson, Joan Bauer, Marion Bauer, Jennifer L. Holm, Margaret Peterson Haddix, and Ellen Wittlinger.

***Soul Searching: Thirteen Stories about Faith and Belief* edited by Lisa Rowe Fraustino. New York: Simon & Schuster, 2002.**

Shonto Begay, Minfong Ho, David Lubar, William Sleator, and others write about a variety of teen religious experiences, including Christianity, Judaism, Islam, Hinduism, Buddhism, Confucianism, Taoism, and Navajo.

***Tomorrowland: Ten Stories about the Future* edited by Michael Cart. New York: Scholastic, 1999.**

Two of these imaginative stories are set in the past, a few in the present, and the rest in the future—all

looking at future problems and possibilities concerning the environment, alienation, responsibility, and family relationships.

***Trapped: Cages of Mind and Body* edited by Lois Duncan. New York: Simon & Schuster, 1998.**

Eleven stories by people such as Francesca Lia Block, Gary Crew, and Rob Thomas, along with a play by Rita Williams-Garcia, and a series of poems by Lois Lowry reveal teenagers trapped in a variety of situations—some physical, others emotional—from which only some escape.

***Twelve Shots: Outstanding Short Stories about Guns* edited by Harry Mazer. New York: Delacorte/Random House, 1997.**

In addition to stories about violence and the threat of violence, there are also stories of personal discovery, friendship, and even humor in this powerful collection written by Chris Lynch, Walter Dean Myers, Richard Peck, and others.

***Twice Told: Original Stories Inspired by Original Art* edited by Scott Hunt. New York: Dutton/Penguin, 2006.**

These 18 stories are the result of nine pairs of authors being given a different charcoal drawing for which they were asked to write a story. Among the authors are Jaime Adoff, M. T. Anderson, Bruce Coville, Sarah Dessen, Alex Flinn, Neal Shusterman, and Nancy Werlin.

***What a Song Can Do: 12 Riffs on the Power of Music* edited by Jennifer Armstrong. New York: Knopf/Random House, 2004.**

An engaging assemblage of short stories by Joseph Brushac, Gail Giles, Ron Koertge, Dian Curtis Regan, and eight others in which music plays a key role.

Box 9.3   Author Short Story Collections

145th Street: Short Stories **by Walter Dean Myers. New York: Delacorte/ Random House, 2000.**

Interconnecting stories about the lives of a variety people in a New York City neighborhood.

Athletic Shorts: 6 Short Stories **by Chris Crutcher. New York: Greenwillow/ HarperCollins, 1989.**

May be the best set of short stories about teenagers ever written. Most are based on characters from Crutcher's novels.

Crazy Loco **by David Rice. New York: Dial/Penguin, 2001.**

Nine short stories about Mexican American kids growing up in the Rio Grande Valley. The stories are funny, the characters complex. An ALA Best Book for Young Readers.

Ghost Town: Seven Ghostly Stories **by Joan Lowery Nixon. New York: Delacorte/ Random House, 2000.**

Eerie stories set in real ghost towns across the United States. An afterword describes the actual towns on which the stories are based.

Graven Images: Three Stories **by Paul Fleischman. Cambridge, MA: Candlewick Press, 2006. (Original work published 1982).**

A trilogy of tales about statues that communicate secrets and desires. A 1982 Newbery Honor book and young adult classic.

The Human Fly and Other Stories **by T. C. Boyle. New York: Speak/Penguin, 2005.**

Boyle has written over a dozen adult novels and numerous adult short stories. This volume is a collection of previously published adult short stories, including

the O. Henry Award–winning "The Love of My Life." A superb collection for older, mature young adults.

Island Boyz: Short Stories **by Graham Salisbury. New York: Random House, 2002.**

Eleven stories, five previously published, all set in Hawaii, about a variety of topics, including fishing, bullying, and romance.

Kissing Tennessee and Other Stories from the Stardust Dance **by Kathi Appelt. Orlando, FL: Harcourt, 2000.**

Touching stories about the lives and dreams of several junior high students in one school before and during the eighth-grade Stardust Dance.

Losing Is Not an Option **by Rich Wallace. New York: Knopf/Random House, 2003.**

Nine short stories take readers through the highlights of Ron's teenage years, from sneaking into a football game in sixth grade and playing basketball in a fierce summer league to making the wrong moves on a girl he's attracted to, all the while developing his ability as a long-distance runner with his eye on the state championship.

Love, Football, and Other Contact Sports **by Alden R. Carter. New York: Holiday House, 2006.**

Carter has combined several previously published stories with a number of new ones to create a readable and entertaining look at high school football and the guys who play it. Loosely interconnected stories.

Odder Than Ever **by Bruce Coville. Orlando, FL: Harcourt, 1999.**

A ghost who bakes biscuits, a Japanese mirror that urges a teenage viewer to change places with his image, and a princess who smells bad are just three of the bizarre situations that greet readers in these engrossing (sometimes just gross) and entertaining stories.

Continued

Box 9.3   Author Short Story Collections   *Continued*

***Odds Are Good: An Oddly Enough and Odder Than Ever Omnibus* by Bruce Coville. Orlando, FL: Harcourt, 2006.**

A combination of previously published stories and new ones, this collection is one of Coville's best works. Many stories can be used to teach and reinforce literary elements.

***Out of Bounds: Seven Stories of Conflict and Hope* by Beverley Naidoo. New York: HarperCollins, 2003.**

These previously published stories illustrate the effects of apartheid on various South African children from 1948 through 2000.

***Past, Perfect, Present Tense: New and Collected Stories* by Richard Peck. New York: Dial/Penguin, 2004.**

A compilation of 13 previously published stories and 2 new ones from this contemporary master of the short story, with insightful introductions and advice on writing short stories.

***Twelve Impossible Things before Breakfast* by Jane Yolen. Orlando, FL: Harcourt, 1997.**

Jane Yolen assembles nine previously published stories and three new ones into an appealing collection of fantasy stories that are fanciful and chilling, delightful and gross.

Elements of Short Stories

Short stories may be faster to write than novels, but they are not easier. Authors must be true masters at combining the five key elements that go into any good piece of fiction: character, setting, conflict, plot, and theme. Unlike the novel, in which these elements can develop slowly, the brevity of the short story requires that these elements be compact and advance quickly. Economy of words, precise scenes, and single plots characterize good short stories. Because of its brevity, the short story is used extensively in high school classes to teach literary elements. All stories contain these five essential elements, but one element or more may stand out as exceptional in any given story. Table 9.1 features several literary elements and a classical text frequently used to teach the element. The third column features young adult short stories that also capture the element well.

Poetry

When young adult novels emerged at the end of the 20th century, little young adult poetry existed. *Reflections on a Gift of Watermelon Pickle . . . and Other Modern Verse* (1966), edited by Steve Dunning, Edward Lueders, and Hugh Smith, was one of the first collections used by classroom teachers of adolescents. After the success of this initial collection, Dunning, Lueders, and Smith published additional volumes. Of course, *Where the Sidewalk Ends: The Poems and Drawings of Shel Silverstein* (Silverstein, 1974) is an enduring classic for young and old alike.

Table 9.1

Literary Elements in Classic and YA Short Stories

Literary Element	Classical Short Story	Young Adult Short Story
Allegory	"The Pearl" by John Steinbeck	"Teenage Chimps" by Gary Soto in *Help Wanted: Stories* (2005)
Characterization	"The Legend of Sleepy Hollow" by Washington Irving	"The Electric Summer" by Richard Peck in *Past Perfect, Present Tense: New and Collected Stories* (2004)
Dialect	"The Ghost in the Mill" by Harriet Beecher Stowe	"Big Joe's Funeral" by Walter Dean Myers in *145th Street:Short Stories* (2000)
Imagery	"The Open Boat" by Stephen Crane	"Because My Father Always Said He Was the Only Indian Who Saw Jimi Hendrix Play 'The Star-Spangled Banner' at Woodstock" by Sherman Alexie in *Moccasin Thunder: American Indian Stories Today* (2005a) edited by Lori Marie Carlson
Magical realism	"A Horseman in the Sky" by Ambrose Bierce	"Jameel and the House of Djinn" by Suzanne Fisher Staples in *Dreams and Visions* (2006) edited by M. Jerry Weiss and Helen Weiss
Plot	"The Pit and the Pendulum" by Edgar Allan Poe	"The Swede" by Alden R. Carter in *First Crossing: Stories about Teen Immigrants* (2004) edited by Don Gallo
Point of view	"To Build a Fire" by Jack London	"Ryan and Angel in the Green Room, A Heavenly Fantasy; or, The Ultimate in High-Stakes Testing" by Mel Glenn in *Dreams and Visions* (2006) edited by M. Jerry Weiss and Helen Weiss
Setting	"The Lottery" by Shirley Jackson	"Hat of Clouds" by Graham Salisbury in *Island Boyz: Short Stories* (2002)
Style	"The Ransom of Red Chief" by O. Henry	"Bearing Paul" by Chris Lynch in *Night Terrors: Stories of Shadow and Substance* (1996) edited by Lois Duncan
Symbolism	"The Scarlett Ibis" by James Hurst	"The Box" by Bruce Coville in *Odds Are Good* (2006)
Theme	"The Minister's Black Veil" by Nathaniel Hawthorne	"You're Not a Winner Unless Your Picture's in the Paper" by Avi in *The Color of Absence* (2001) edited by James Howe
Voice	"The Jilting of Granny Weatherall" by Katherine Anne Porter	"Way Too Cool" by Chris Crutcher in *Owning It: Stories about Teens with Disabilities* (2008) edited by Don Gallo

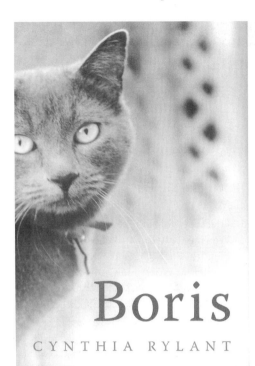

Boris

CYNTHIA RYLANT

A poignant story about love, loss, and connection told through interconnected poems. Book cover from *Boris*, © 2005 by Cynthia Rylant, reproduced by permission of Harcourt, Inc.

Several early poetry collections won the coveted John Newbery Medal.[4] Nancy Willard's *A Visit to William Blake's Inn: Poems for Innocent and Experienced Travelers* (1981) is a collection of poems describing a menagerie of travelers who arrive at William Blake's Inn. Willard was inspired to write this collection based on William Blake's *Songs of Innocence and Songs of Experience.* The collection consists of 16 poems describing an unusual group of travelers—a dragon, a cow, an angel, a tiger, and a cat, many of whom appear in Blake's darker works. Although Willard's work lacks the pessimism of Blake's writing, her work resembles his lyrical style, and she references some of his characters. This Newbery winner makes an excellent companion to Blake's poetry (for more on companion works see Chapter 11).

Paul Fleischman's *Joyful Noise: Poems for Two Voices* (1988), a Newbery winner, and its earlier companion, *I Am Phoenix: Poems for Two Voices* (1985), are additional examples of earlier poetry collections. These latter collections, designed to be read aloud by two voices, sometimes simultaneously, sometimes alternating, are excellent for developing fluency skills as is Fleischman's *Big Talk: Poems for Four Voices* (2000). (I discuss methods for building fluency at the end of this chapter.) *Heart to Heart: New Poems Inspired by Twentieth-Century American Art* (Greenberg, 2001), a 2002 Michael L. Printz Honor book, is a unique collection of poetry by today's award-winning young adult poets. Angela Johnson, Naomi Shihab Nye, Nancy Willard, Jane Yolen, and others create heartfelt poetic responses to paintings by well-known artists (e.g., Thomas Hart Benton, Jacob Lawrence, and Georgia O'Keeffe). Over the years, young adult poetry has assumed a stronger position in the young adult genre thanks to an increasing number of talented young adult poets (poetry collections are listed in Box 9.4).

Poetry comprises a good part of the classical canon, and teachers are hesitant to replace this tradition with contemporary literature. Many argue students need the classics for SATs and AP exams; others assert young adult poetry lacks the complexity and depth of works by poets such as Shelley, Keats, Shakespeare, Donne, Poe, Tennyson, and T. S. Eliot. Acclaimed poet Nikki Giovanni wrote the poem in the author box to illustrate her belief that good poetry need not be difficult.

Cynthia Rylant's work has the same poignant simplicity. The poems in *God Went to Beauty School* (2003) are held together by a unifying question, "What if God were human?" Each poem poses a new possibility: What if he got a dog? Went to a movie? Wrote a book? Climbed a mountain?

---

[4]These collections have primarily been used with younger audiences.

Box 9.4   A Sampling of YA Poetry

***Behind the Wheel: Poems about Driving* by Janet S. Wong. New York: McElderry/ Simon & Schuster, 1999.**

Driving is the metaphor for life in this unconventional collection of 36 free verse poems. From car crashes to backseat romance, Wong covers everything and relates these universal experiences to the highs and heartbreaks of teens' lives.

***Blue Lipstick: Concrete Poems* by John Grandits. New York: Clarion, 2007.**

With a cover sure to attract girls, this collection addresses girl issues such as hairstyles, makeup, and clothing. Told through the voice of 15-year-old Jessie, an opinionated girl who writes poetry to her cat. Funny and sarcastic. The poems have inventive forms and patterns.

***Cool Salsa: Bilingual Poems on Growing Up Latino in the United States* compiled by Lori M. Carlson. New York: Henry Holt, 1994.**

This vibrant collection of poems explores the experience of growing up Latino in an English-speaking culture and suggests that the ultimate solution to cultural clashes is the intermingling of the two languages. Poems in this collection are presented in both English and Spanish, except for six poems that mix the two languages. Readers may also enjoy *Red Hot Salsa: Bilingual Poems on Being Young and Latino in the United States* (2005), a follow-up collection.

***Dead on Town Line* by Leslie Connor. New York: Dial/Penguin, 2005.**

Using poetic verse, 16-year-old Cassie Devlin narrates from beyond the grave the account of her murder by a classmate. The story is presented as a mystery and confirms the idea that, eventually, justice will prevail.

***Foreign Exchange: A Mystery in Poems* by Mel Glenn. New York: Morrow/ HarperCollins, 1999.**

Hudson Landing seems like a passive little town, but when a young white girl is murdered, the town's hidden hatred and prejudice bubble to the surface. This collection of free verse poetry tells the town's story through the eyes of various townspeople, both adults and teens.

***Hoofprints: Horse Poems* by Jessie Haas. New York: Greenwillow/HarperCollins, 2004.**

More than 100 poems chronicle the development of the relationship between horses and humans from 5000 BC to present day.

***How to Cross a Pond: Poems about Water* by Marilyn Singer. Illus. Meilo So. New York: Knopf/Random House, 2003.**

These 19 poems celebrate the power and wonder of nature by capturing, through both word and illustrations, the various manifestations of water and encourage readers to become more involved with and aware of the beauty around them.

***I Feel a Little Jumpy around You: A Book of Her Poems & His Poems Collected in Pairs* compiled by Naomi Shihab Nye and Paul Janeczko. New York: Simon & Schuster, 1996.**

How do males and females look at the world? This collection explores that very question, pairing poems—one with a male author, one with a female author—to demonstrate where gender ideas merge and where they take separate paths.

***I Hit the Ball!: Baseball Poems for the Young* by Gene Fehler. Illus. Mike Schacht. Jefferson, NC: McFarland 1996.**

Baseball is the all-American pastime, and this book of poetry celebrates the glory of the game, highlighting not only the dreams of youngsters but the memories of old-timers. One of two collections of baseball poems, the other is titled *Center Field Grasses: Poems from Baseball* (1991).

Continued

Box 9.4   A Sampling of YA Poetry *Continued*

***If I Had a Million Onions* by Sheree Fitch. Illus. Yayo. Custer, WA: Tradewind Books, 2005.**

This collection of 25 poems draws on everyday themes and items in an attempt to demonstrate how the beauty and excitement of life can be found in the seemingly ordinary.

***Jazz ABZ: A Collection of Jazz Portraits from A to Z* by Wynton Marsalis. Illus. Paul Rogers. Cambridge, MA: Candlewick Press, 2005.**

Jazz fans and lovers of modern art will enjoy this poetry collection. Features poetry about famous artists such as Louis Armstrong and Dizzy Gillespie.

***Jump Ball: A Basketball Season in Poems* by Mel Glenn. New York: Lodestar/ Dutton, 1997.**

Could it be that an inner-city high school basketball team will finally be the "dream team" the players have worked so hard to become? Or, will Tower High's season—not to mention individual lives—be shattered by a series of tragic events? This series of poems, expressing the thoughts and feelings of the adults and teens of the high school and the community, weaves a series of events and narrates a life experience from which all readers, not just basketball fans, will learn.

***A Lion's Hunger: Poems of First Love* by Ann Warren Turner. Tarrytown, NY: Marshall Canvendish, 1998.**

Unifying poems that chronicle one girl's experiences dating, falling in love, and experiencing heartbreak.

***A Maze Me: Poems for Girls* by Naomi Shihab Nye. Illus. Terre Maher. New York: Greenwillow/HarperCollins, 2005.**

Adolescent girls face a number of challenges, the most daunting being understanding themselves and discovering how they fit into the world. These 72 poems dare young women to discard the trappings of the digital world and find the beauty that exists around them naturally. Also, Shihab encourages girls to journal, assuring them that what they will learn about themselves will be worth the effort.

***Neighborhood Odes* by Gary Soto. Illus. David Díaz. San Diego: Harcourt, 1992.**

Twenty-one unrhymed poems celebrate the blended Latino American culture. The poems are written in English and feature many items and incidents commonly experienced in Latino American neighborhoods. An appendix is included for those unfamiliar with words, expressions, and phrases used in the verses.

***A Nest Full of Stars* by James Berry. Illus. Ashley Bryan. New York: Greenwillow/ HarperCollins, 2004.**

Growing up can be fun, boring, exciting, joyous, thrilling, painful, and bewildering. This collection takes the reader on a trip of growing up.

***The Place My Words Are Looking For: What Poets Say about and through Their Work* compiled by Paul Janeczko. New York: Bradbury Press, 1990.**

Sixty-three poems and essays from various contemporary artists. Readers learn about growing up, as well as the importance of inspiration, determination, and heart.

***Poetry from A to Z: A Guide for Young Writers* compiled by Paul Janeczko. Illus. Cathy Bobak. New York: Bradbury Press, 1994.**

Sixty-one poems serve as examples for budding poets. Included are writing exercises, tips, tools, and advice from a number of contemporary children's poets.

Continued

Box 9.4   A Sampling of YA Poetry   *Continued*

***Salting the Ocean: 100 Poems by Young Poets* compiled by Naomi Shihab Nye. Illus. Ashley Bryan. New York: Greenwillow/HarperCollins, 2000.**

The four sections of this collection—The Self and the Inner World, Where We Live, Anybody's Family, and the Wide Imagination—contain poems by students from Grades 1 to 12.

***She's All That!: Poems about Girls* compiled by Belinda Hollyer. Illus. Susan Hellard. Boston: Kingfisher/Houghton Mifflin, 2006.**

This collection is a celebration of girls. Poets such as Maya Angelou and Alice Walker make each milestone in a girl's life memorable.

***Short Takes: Fast-Break Basketball Poetry* by Charles R. Smith. New York: Dutton/Penguin, 2001.**

Basketball poems inspired by hip-hop, jazz, movies, and music videos. Beautifully illustrated. A wonderful picture book for older readers.

***Soda Jerk* by Cynthia Rylant. New York: Scholastic, 1990.**

Intended for older adolescents, a young small-town soda jerk reflects on the people and places around him.

***Soft Hay Will Catch You: Poems by Young People* compiled by Sandford Lyne. Illus. Julie Monks. New York: Simon & Schuster, 2004.**

Middle schoolers and teens explore their lives through poetry. Topics include finding one's self, overcoming loneliness, and the raging hormones that accompany the change from child to teen.

***Something Permanent* by Cynthia Rylant. Orlando, FL: Harcourt, 1994.**

A collection of short, lyrical poems documenting the lives of ordinary people. Poems are paired with photographs taken by Walker Evans of southern families during the Great Depression. Both poetic and visual images are of survival, love, hope, despair, and loss. Evans's photographs resulted in the infamous book *Let Us Now Praise Famous Men* (1941), a legendary account of the Great Depression.

***The Taking of Room 114: A Hostage Drama in Poems* by Mel Glenn. New York: Penguin, 1997.**

A high school history teacher cracks under the weight of the world and takes his students hostage. The story is told through a series of poems, exploring the thoughts and fears of other teachers, students, emergency workers, parents, and other onlookers.

***Technically, It's Not My Fault: Concrete Poems* by John Grandits. New York: Clarion, 2004.**

Grandits structures a series of poems in inventive shapes and typefaces. Each poem connects with teen concerns: boring homework, sports, failure, and so forth. A funny, terrific book for exploring form.

***This Place I Know: Poems of Comfort* compiled by Georgia Heard. Cambridge, MA: Candlewick Press, 2002.**

This collection of poetry was compiled as a source of comfort and strength for young adults after the tragedy of 9/11. Eighteen well-known artists such as Chris Raschka and William Steig add an edge of color and emotion.

***Tough Boy Sonatas* by Curtis L. Crisler. Illus. Floyd Cooper. Honesdale, PA: Wordsong/Boyds Mills Press, 2007.**

Crisler creates powerful voices of young black men growing up amidst the poverty of Gary, Indiana. Images of holdups, violence, and drug addiction mingle with images of family and childhood play. Depicts both the dark and good sides of young men growing up in Gary.

Continued

Box 9.4   A Sampling of YA Poetry   *Continued*

***What Is Goodbye?* by Nikki Grimes. Illus. Raúl Colón. New York: Jump at the Sun/ Hyperion, 2004.**

Jerilyn and her younger brother Jared express their emotions dealing with the loss of their older brother, Jaron. The 52 poems are divided between Jerilyn's free verse and Jared's rhymed verse, showcasing how differently two people can grieve in the same situation.

***Worlds Afire: The Hartford Circus Fire of 1944* by Paul Janeczko. Cambridge, MA: Candlewick Press, 2004.**

On July 6, 1944, 167 were killed in a fire that engulfed a circus tent during a performance. Through

poetry, Janezcko gives a fictional account of what it must have been like for those killed, those injured, and those who watched as fire consumed the big tent in minutes.

***Worlds Apart: Traveling with Fernie and Me: Poems* by Gary Soto. Illus. Greg Clarke. New York: Putnam/Penguin, 2005.**

This poem collection is a take-off on Robert Frost's "The Road Not Taken." Fernie and his friend want to travel around the world, so they do—in their imaginations.

Good Poetry and Simplicity   by Nikki Giovanni

Everything Good Is Simple
Everything good is simple: a soft boiled egg . . .
    toast fresh from the oven with a pat of butter
    swimming in the center . . . steam off a cup
    of black coffee . . . John Coltrane bringing me
    Violets for My Furs
Most simple things are good: Lines on a yellow
    legal pad . . . dimples defining a smile . . . a
    square of grey cashmere that can be a scarf
    . . . Miles Davis *Kind of Blue*
Some things clear are complicated: believing in
    a religion . . . trying to be a good person . . .
    getting rid of folk who depress you . . . Horace
    Sliver Blowing the Blues Away
Complicated things can be clear: Dvorak's New
    World Symphony . . . Alvin Ailey's Resurrection
    . . . Mae Jemison's ride in space . . . Mingus
    Live at Carnegie Hall
All things good are good: poetry . . . patience . . .
    a ripe tomato on the vine . . . a bat in flight
    . . . the new moon . . . me in your arms . . .
    things like that

Copyright Nikki Giovanni, 2008
Official Web site: www.nikki-giovanni.com

Poetry collections: *Ego-tripping and Other Poems for Young People* (1993), *Grand Mothers: Poems, Reminiscences and Short Stories about the Keepers of Our Traditions* (1994), *Selected Poems of Nikki Giovanni* (1996), *Love Poems* (1997), *Blues for All the Changes: New Poems* (1999), *Grand Fathers: Reminiscences, Poems, Recipes, and Photos of the Keepers of Our Tradition* (1999), *Quilting the Black-eyed Pea: Poems and Not Quite Poems* (2002), *The Collected Poetry of Nikki Giovanni: 1968–1998* (2003), *Acolytes: Poems* (2007), and *On My Journey Now: Looking at African-American History through the Spirituals* (2007).

Though easy to read, the poems are deeply reflective, sometimes funny, often spiritual. Collectively they provide glimpses of everyday life, forcing readers to examine what it means to be human. What more could we ask of good poetry?

Rylant's more recent works strike a similar cord. In *Boris* (2005), a gray cat teaches his owner unconditional love, and an Appalachian woman lives a simple but rich life in *Ludie's Life* (2006). Some readers may call these latter two works verse novels because the poems are more dependent upon each other. All three works are exceptional and can be enjoyed by young and old alike, and their slim size makes them excellent choices for at-risk readers and superb choices for the fluency activities at the end of this chapter.

A current trend in poetry for teens is the illustrated rendition of a classic poem. Illustrations add an aesthetic element that makes traditional classics more engaging. Kids Can Press, for example, has developed an entire illustrated classic series (e.g., *The Lady of Shalott, Casey at the Bat, The Raven,* and *The Highwayman*). Sterling Publishers has a similar series, *Poetry for Young People.* Other beautifully illustrated classics abound such as Henry Wadsworth Longfellow's *Paul Revere's Ride,* illustrated by Monica Vachula (2003),[5] Robert Louis Stevenson's *The Moon,* illustrated by Tracey Campbell Pearson (2006), and Robert Frost's *Stopping by Woods on a Snowy Evening,* illustrated by Susan Jeffers (1978). Additional titles are listed later in the chapter.

Poetry is also a good resource for reading in the content areas. J. Patrick Lewis, for example, has published more than 50 poetry picture books, many of which can be used in content area reading. While some are more appropriate for upper elementary and middle grades (e.g., *Arithmetickle: An Even Number of Odd Riddle-Rhymes,* 2002a; *Scien-trickery: Riddles in Science,* 2004a), others are more sophisticated and work well in high school classrooms. *Castles: Cold Stone Poems* (2006c) works beautifully in a social studies classroom, and *Once Upon a Tomb: Gravely Humorous Verses* (2006d) is a superb collection for teaching dark humor in English language arts classes. Lewis has also co-authored *Poems for Teaching in the Content Areas* (Lewis & Robb, 2007) and has published dozens of poems in journals and magazines such as *Cricket, Cicada, Highlights for Children,* and *Journal of Children's Literature.* In the author box, Lewis outlines his views about poetry.

Poetry-Novel Hybrids

The line between young adult poetry and young adult novels has blurred in recent years, and today's market includes an abundance of novels containing elements of poetry: verse novels, novels-in-verse, poetic prose, proetry, blank verse, and free verse are all terms for these poetry-novel hybrids. Reviewers tend to use these terms loosely, resulting in widespread disagreement and

---

[5]Ted Rand illustrated *Paul Revere's Ride* in 1990, and Christopher Bing did so in 2001.

Twenty-Five Poems (An Introduction/Preface)   by J. Patrick Lewis

Much of children's poetry today is not splendid but Splenda-ed.

Children's verse cannot be concocted by dripping honey over clouds.

When stuck together, the two worst words in the English language are "poetry" and "unit."

A poem is to a video game what a painting is to a graffito.

The eternal question: Where does a poet get his ideas? I believe they rise, after several hours, through the bottom of a chair.

The idea for a poem does not begin with an idea: it begins with a word, a phrase.

Keep a poem in your pocket? Yes, all right. But keep a pocket in your poem, and let the pocket have a hole in it, a Swiss Army knife, blue taffeta fringe, six aggies, a hawk feather, and a lottery ticket. Poetry, like life, is in the details.

Hearing at least one poem should be part of every child's everyday experience.

Rhyming is too important to be left to children. Forcing young writers inside the box of rhymes is like telling them to color between the lines.

The stuff of poetry is not the daily news but daily clues to the ordinary. Your purse is a country; your garden, a continent.

If you are writing poems to "educate" the young, you are in the wrong room.

A great poet, as Clive James said of Emily Dickinson, is someone "who could enamel the inside of a raindrop."

Telling children that writing poetry is easy does them a disservice by setting them up for even more disappointment than they are likely to encounter.

In writing children's verse, nothing succeeds like failure: Fail as much, as often as you can. How else to get it right?

The finest free verse poets know that you must learn the rules . . . before you break them.

Adjectives are fat; verbs are muscles. (Adverbs are cholesterol.)

To quote the postman who was befriended by the great Chilean poet Pablo Neruda in the movie Il Postino: "Poetry does not belong to those who write it, but to those who need it."

The poem is always more important than the poet. Poets biodegrade long before poems do.

Verse novels unable to justify their line breaks may qualify as novels, but they are not novels in verse and should not be confused with poetry.

To get started, a would-be poet should buy two things: a dictionary and a large wastebasket, and use them in equal measure.

It is no criticism of the great pioneer Dr. Seuss that he learned well the first rule of creative writing: Find your own voice. Which is why you can tell a Seuss poem coming from a mile away.

The muse takes far too many days off. So consider a spider weaving a web, take in a ball game, talk to your loquacious uncle. Substitute muses roam the world.

Poetry predates books, predates the alphabet. Let it boom into the silence of a room. Always read it aloud, even if you are reading it all alone.

Poets are born, not made, but they are usually not born until sometime after their 30th birthday.

Stop carping that no one reads poetry. Just write.

Copyright J. Patrick Lewis, 2008

Official Web site: www.jpatricklewis.com

Poetry collections by J. Patrick Lewis for content area reading:

History: *Freedom Like Sunlight: Praisesongs for Black Americans* (2000), *A World of Wonders: Geographic Travels in Verse and Rhyme* (2002b), *The Stolen Smile* (2004b), *Heroes and She-Roes: Poems of Amazing and Everyday Heroes* (2005b), *Monumental Verses* (2005c) *Black Cat Bone: The Life of Blues Legend Robert Johnson* (2006a), *Blackbeard the Pirate King* (2006b), *Vherses: A Celebration of Outstanding Women* (2006e), and *The Brothers' War: Civil War Voices in Verse* (2007).

English/Language Arts: *Doodle Dandies: Poems That Take Shape* (1998), *The Bookworm's Feast: A Potluck of Poems* (1999), *Please Bury Me in the Library* (2005d), and *Wing Nuts: Screwy Haiku* (2006f).

Science: *Earth Verses and Water Rhymes* (1991), *The Snowflake Sisters* (2003a), *Swan Song* (2003b), *Scien-trickery: Riddles in Science* (2004a), and *Galileo's Universe* (2005a).

Mathematics: *Arithme-tickle: An Even Number of Odd Riddle-Rhymes* (2002a).

confusion over labels and categories. The verse novel[6] has a long-standing history in adult literature. The success of the prose novel during the Romantic period may have given rise to the verse novel. Poets may have envied the larger canvas available to novelists (Cuddon, 1999, p. 166).

Cuddon defines verse novels as narrative poems, often in chapters or cantos, dealing "with the substance of everyday modern life in much the same way as a work of prose fiction" (p. 966). Most have realistic, contemporary settings, credible dialogue, and readers can "feel" prose novel conventions. Most verse novelists acknowledge the need to retain the emotional power, imagery, and music of poetry (Cuddon, 1999, p. 966). Common to all is the interconnectedness of the poems/chapters. Together they create a plotline; thus readers need information in earlier poems/chapters to fully understand the story.

Winner of numerous book awards, *Make Lemonade: A Novel* (1993) by Virginia Euwer Wolff drew attention to this new writing style. Fourteen-year-old LaVaughn, wanting to attend college and have a better life, takes a babysitting job for Jolly, a 17-year-old single mom living in a squalid apartment. LaVaughn, feeling sorry for Jolly, begins babysitting for free and her grades drop.

Sonya Sones is one of today's most recognized verse novelists. In the author box she writes about the development of her awarding-winning first novel, *Stop Pretending: What Happened When My Big Sister Went Crazy* (1999), a story in which 13-year-old Cookie's older sister is hospitalized for emotional problems. Winner of innumerable awards for her verse novels, Sones writes realistically about girls growing up and teenage rites of passages.

On Becoming a Verse Novelist   by Sonya Sones

When I was a little girl, my friends used to spend the summers at their country homes or at camp. But *my* family couldn't afford such luxuries. So I traveled to the library instead and let books take me places I wished I could go. When I hit my teens, I began reading the diaries of Anais Nin and became an avid journal writer. My journal was a tireless writing coach, teaching me many of the techniques I'd need later in life, when I'd finally decide to become a writer. Though I still had no idea that that's what I would choose to do. Not even when I turned 16 and discovered the poetry of Richard Brautigan. Brautigan made poetry look so easy that I sat down and began writing reams of it myself. Of course, it was all deeply personal stuff, intended for my eyes only, but it sure felt great when it was gushing out of me onto those clean white pages.

Continued

---

[6]I'll use the term *verse novels* throughout our discussion.

On Becoming a Verse Novelist   *Continued*

Who knows? Maybe if I hadn't enrolled in an animation class the summer I turned 17, I'd have become a writer sooner. But the minute I learned how to make animated films, I was off and running. *That's what I'd do with my life: I'd become a filmmaker!*

So, how did I end up living in Hollywood? What did Robin Williams have to do with how I met my husband? What was it like to be kissed by John Travolta? Why did I quit show business to write books for teens? I love answering questions like these when people invite me to speak at schools and libraries. In fact, the only thing that I enjoy as much as writing, is *speaking* about writing, and teaching people how to write poetry.

The woman who taught *me* how to write poetry was the great Myra Cohn Livingston. It was Myra who set me on the path to writing *Stop Pretending*, my first novel-in-verse. When I was writing those poems about my sister, I didn't even realize I was writing a novel. I just thought it was a themed collection of poems. It wasn't until my editor wrote me a letter full of poem-provoking questions, that the collection morphed into a novel-in-verse. And once I began using poetry to tell my stories, I was hooked.

I hadn't set out to write books for teens, but that turned out to be the voice that came most naturally to me. Lots of people talk about having an inner child, but *I've* got an inner teen. And she's right there with me, whispering in my ear whenever I sit down to write. In fact, she'd probably argue that *she* was the one who wrote my books, without any help from me at all. And you might even believe her. She can be very persuasive. Last week she almost had me convinced I should get my bellybutton pierced. Which is *not* a good look for someone my age.

Copyright Sonya Sones, 2008

Official Web site: www.sonyasones.com

Her other verse novels include *What My Mother Doesn't Know* (2001), *One of Those Hideous Books Where the Mother Dies* (2004), and *What My Girlfriend Doesn't Know* (2007).

Verse novels have earned a respectable place in the young adult literature genre, winning numerous awards and often addressing historical and social issues (see titles in Box 9.5). Karen Hesse's *Out of the Dust* (1997), a story set in the Oklahoma Dust Bowl during the Great Depression about a young girl overcoming the loss of her mother, was the first verse novel to win the Newbery Medal. Hesse paints a gripping portrait of poverty and farm life. Marilyn Nelson's *Carver: A Life in Poems* (2001), a Newbery Honor and Coretta Scott King Honor book, is a biography in poems depicting the life of George Washington Carver. Nelson paints a spellbinding portrait of Carver's life, beginning with his kidnapping in infancy by night raiders and being sold as a slave in Arkansas and ending with his death in 1943. Jaime Adoff's *Jimi and Me* (2005), winner of a Coretta Scott King Award for New Talent, is a deeply moving story about a young man whose father dies unexpectedly. While his father's loss is overwhelming, Keith's life is thrown into further turmoil when he learns his father had a secret family.

Most verse novelists take great care in story structure. Two stories, told in parallel first-person voices, are framed within one in *Dark Sons* (2005) by Nikki Grimes, another Coretta Scott King Honor book. The first is a retelling of the biblical story about Abraham, Sarah, and Hagar. When Sarah, Abraham's elderly first wife, gives birth to their firstborn, Abraham banishes his younger wife and their son Ishmael to wander in the desert. A modern story of betrayal parallels this biblical retelling: Sam's father leaves Sam and his

Box 9.5   Poetry-Novel Hybrids

***Aleutian Sparrow* by Karen Hesse. New York: McElderry/Simon & Schuster, 2003.**

After the attack on Pearl Harbor in 1942, the Japanese navy invaded Alaska's Aleutian Islands. This story chronicles a family's and a community's struggle to survive during that time. Fans will also enjoy *Witness: A Novel* (2001), a poetic tale about fanaticism and racism set in a small Vermont town in 1924.

***A Bad Boy Can Be Good for a Girl* by Tanya Lee Stone. New York: Random House, 2006.**

Three girls—Josie, Nicolette, and Aviva—become involved with the same boy, a slick and sexy senior who can talk them into doing whatever he wants. Each girl struggles with self-doubt, the boy's magnetism, what to give up, and what to keep.

***Bronx Masquerade* by Nikki Grimes. New York: Dial/Penguin, 2002.**

A high school teacher hosts open-mike poetry on Fridays. His students, teens living in the Bronx, find an avenue for exploring their emotions, their identities, and their connection with those around them. A blend of short narrative vignettes and poetry.

***By the River* by Steven Herrick. Asheville, NC: Front Street/Boyds Mills Press, 2006.**

Life in a small Australian river town in 1962 isn't easy for a 14-year-old boy. His mother is dead and his friend is swept away by a flood. Harry longs to leave the small town, even though he knows he may never come back. Fans will also enjoy *The Simple Gift* (2004b), *A Place Like This* (2004c), *Love, Ghosts & Facial Hair* (2004a), and *The Wolf* (2007).

***Cloud Busting* by Malorie Blackman. New York: Doubleday/Random House, 2004.**

Told in first-person verse, this story chronicles a friendship between two boys. Sam befriends Davey at his mother's insistence. At first he is embarrassed to be seen with Davey, but their relationship deepens until a tragic event happens.

***Escaping Tornado Season: A Story in Poems* by Julie Williams. New York: HarperCollins, 2004.**

Thirteen-year-old Allie lives in a small Minnesota town with her grandparents. Writing helps her cope with the loss of her father, abandonment from her mother, and the challenges of a new school.

***Frenchtown Summer* by Robert Cormier. New York: Bantam Doubleday Dell/ Random House, 1999.**

A series of vignettes in which Cormier reminisces about his life as a 12-year-old boy growing up in a small Massachusetts town. Though other Cormier novels have bits of verse (e.g., *I Am the Cheese,* 1977), this is the only novel he wrote completely in verse. As with his prose, his language is elegant, his themes complex.

***The Geography of Girlhood* by Kirsten Smith. New York: Little, Brown, 2006.**

Abandoned by her mother when she was six, Penny adjusts to a blended family and navigates the hurdles of adolescence—boyfriends, friendships, self-consciousness, and belonging. Memorable voice.

***Girl Coming in for a Landing: A Novel in Poems* by April Halprin Wayland. New York: Knopf/Random House, 2002.**

Covers the life of a teenage girl over the course of one school year. Typical adolescent themes—kissing, first love, and friendships. The central character is a poet. The story ends with suggestions for writing and submitting poetry for publication.

***Hard Hit* by Ann Turner. New York: Scholastic, 2006.**

Mark is a baseball superstar, but when his father is diagnosed with cancer, Mark's world changes. Turner hits a home run with her baseball metaphor. A multi-layered, complex, tough, and rich story about a boy's love for his father. Give this one to nonreaders.

Continued

Box 9.5   Poetry-Novel Hybrids   *Continued*

***Heartbeat* by Sharon Creech. New York: HarperCollins, 2004.**

Twelve-year-old Annie loves to run. While running barefoot and listening to her heart beating, she ponders her mother's pregnancy, her grandfather's health, and her friendship with her best friend. Fans will also enjoy *Love That Dog* (2001), a story in which a young boy hates poetry—at least he thinks he does until he falls in love with the structure of poetry: poems laid out in specific shapes, sharp phrasing, and crisp images.

***Hold Me Tight* by Lorie Ann Grover. New York: Simon & Schuster, 2005.**

Essie's father walks out on her and her pregnant mother. Twelve-year-old Essie deals with a series of crises: the kidnapping of a classmate, her mother's depression, and sexual abuse. Grover has written additional verse novels, *Loose Threads* (2002) and *On Pointe* (2004).

***I Don't Want to Be Crazy* by Samantha Schutz. New York: PUSH/Scholastic, 2006.**

A hard, raw, and honest examination of panic disorder. Schutz bases her story on her own experiences as a college student struggling with the illness.

***Impulse* by Ellen Hopkins. New York: Simon & Schuster, 2007.**

In short free verse chapters, Hopkins chronicles the lives of three teenagers—Vanessa, Conner, and Tony—who have attempted suicide and are living in a residential treatment center. Readers may enjoy *Crank* (2004), *Burned* (2006), and *Glass* (2007).

***Learning to Swim: A Memoir* by Ann Warren Turner. New York: Scholastic, 2000.**

A series of verses conveying the emotions of a young girl who is sexually abused at her family's summer house.

***Locomotion* by Jacqueline Woodson. New York: Penguin, 2003.**

Locomotion is an 11-year-old orphan, living it up with his foster mom and his baby sister Lili. When his new teacher, Mrs. Marcus, opens his eyes to a completely new world—the world of poetry—Locomotion discovers that his own voice has more power than he ever knew possible.

***North of Everything* by Craig Crist-Evans. Cambridge, MA: Candlewick Press, 2004.**

The narrator's family moves to a Vermont farm. Soon after settling, the father is diagnosed with cancer and dies. The narrator, his mother, and new baby sister adjust to a new life by themselves. Evocative and eloquent language.

***One Night* by Margaret Wild. New York: Random House, 2004.**

Gabe is the best-looking guy in school, and Helen is not much to look at—that's why her friends keep her around. But Helen gets under Gabe's skin in a way no other girl has. Fans will also enjoy *Jinx* (2004), a story in which a teenage girl feels cursed when two boyfriends die.

***The Realm of Possibility* by David Levithan. New York: Knopf/Random House, 2004.**

Through a series of interconnected poems, a diverse group of high school students share their experiences, beliefs, emotions, and friendships. This interconnected collection mirrors the hopes, dreams, angst, and fears of being a teenager. A must for every classroom.

***Rubber Houses* by Ellen Yeomans. New York: Little, Brown, 2007.**

Relates 17-year-old Kit's emotions and experiences when her younger brother is diagnosed with cancer. A quick read.

Continued

Box 9.5   Poetry-Novel Hybrids   *Continued*

***Running Back to Ludie* by Angela Johnson. New York: Orchard/Scholastic, 2001.**

The narrator of this verse novel lives with her father and aunt and has never known her mother, except through old photos and vague memories. Now she is going to meet her, and as she waits, she explores her feelings about her mother, her aching heart, and her family.

***The Secret of Me* by Meg Kearney. New York: Persea, 2005.**

Fourteen-year-old Lizzie has always known she, her older brother, and sister were adopted as infants. She struggles with her inner feelings about being adopted and can't talk with her loving parents. What will her boyfriend think if he knows her parents adopted her?

***Shakespeare Bats Cleanup* by Ron Koertge. Cambridge, MA: Candlewick Press, 2003.**

When Kevin Boland, a 14-year-old star baseball player, catches mononucleosis, he experiments with writing in a journal to pass the time; with time, the journal helps him deal with life and loss. Koertge's *The Brimstone Journals* (2001) is one of today's most talked about interconnected YA poetry collections. A group of teens narrate the violence in their schools and lives. The emotional impact is chilling.

***Sister Slam and the Poetic Motormouth Road Trip* by Linda Oatman High. New York: Bloomsbury, 2004.**

A combat-boot-wearing 17-year-old, Laura Crapper, renames herself Sister Slam and takes a road trip with her best friend, Twig. When Laura's father experiences a heart attack, Laura must face her fears about her home and the loss of her mother.

***Sold* by Patricia McCormick. New York: Hyperion, 2006.**

Unbeknownst to 13-year-old Lakshmi, her stepfather has sold her into prostitution in Calcutta. She is held prisoner, beaten, drugged, and raped. Told in first-person short vignettes.

***Splintering* by Eireann Corrigan. New York: Scholastic, 2004.**

Alternating brother and sister voices tell the story of a family torn apart by a random act of violence. Corrigan's first verse novel, *You Remind Me of You: A Poetry Memoir* (2002), recounts her personal experiences with eating disorders—an anorexic girl recovers when her boyfriend tries to kill himself.

***Talking in the Dark: A Poetry Memoir* by Billy Merrell. New York: PUSH/Scholastic, 2003.**

Pieces of Merrell's own life appear in this work, divided in five parts and spanning several years. The narrator struggles with his parents' divorce, his sexual identity, unrequited love, and his own immortality when his friend is diagnosed with HIV. Superb companion to Corrigan's *You Remind Me of You* (2002).

***The Weight of the Sky* by Lisa Ann Sandell. New York: Viking/Penguin, 2006.**

Sixteen-year-old Sarah, a geek and the only Jewish student in her class, never fits in. Sarah travels overseas to spend the summer in Israel on a kibbutz, where she examines her past and reflects on her future.

***Who Will Tell My Brother?* by Marlene Carvell. New York: Hyperion, 2002.**

A mixed race high school student tries to rid the school of an offensive mascot. He encounters opposition but learns about his heritage and his place in the world.

***Yellow Star* by Jennifer Roy. Tarrytown, NY: Marshall Cavendish, 2006.**

The Germans invaded Lodz, Poland, in 1939. They horded all Jews into a ghetto barbed-wire area. Two hundred and seventy thousand people were held prisoners; in 1945, 800 walked out when the town was liberated. This is the story of one survivor as told to her niece. Raw but poignant.

A poignant verse novel—rich in metaphor—about family, loss, and love. Photo illustration © 2006 by March Tauss from *Hard Hit* by Ann Turner. Scholastic Press-Scholastic, Inc. Used by permission.

mother for another woman, and Sam and his mother are left to pick up their shattered lives. When Sam's father remarries, Sam comes to terms with a new half-brother.

Helen Frost, author of the Printz Honor book *Keesha's House* (2003), weaves together the lives of seven teens with traditional poetic forms: sestinas and sonnets. Sestinas, complex verses, consist of six stanzas of six lines each and three concluding lines. The six end words in the first stanza must appear again in subsequent stanzas, creating a distinct pattern, as in "Questions about Joe" spoken by Keesha below. The first end word is in bold. Notice its repetition in subsequent stanzas, and then trace the additional five end words from the first stanza through the poem.

When Katie came, she kept asking **questions**
about Joe. Since he owns the house, she thought
he'd tell us what to do. She kept saying, I can pay
rent. I can buy my own food. I'll work
for what I need. *There was one room upstairs with a bed*
and a window, but she said she'd rather stay

in the basement room. We all stay
out of there unless she asks us in. No one asks **questions**
about why she keeps her door locked. The bed
in there is just a foam pad on the floor, but Katie said she
thought

the room was heaven. We hardly see her, she's at work
so much. I think she's worried Joe might make her pay

some other way if she runs out of money. He says we can pay
him if we want to, but not much. Me, I want to stay
in school. I want good grades. So I just work
twelve hours a week, enough for food. I hate the **questions**
people ask though. Even my ex-boyfriend thought
the girls here must be going to bed

with Joe, or someone else. Not me—I won't go to bed
with anyone unless I want to. And I don't pay
for *nothin' with my* body! *At first I thought*
we should do something nice for Joe—he lets us stay
here and he doesn't ask too many **questions.**
So if he was tired when he got home from work

I used to cook or do some kind of work
like clean up the house. Once I made his bed
for him, like Mama used to do. That raised some **questions**
in his mind, I guess. He said, Keesha, don't you pay
me no mind. Everyone deserves a place to stay.
So now I don't give Joe much thought.

I appreciate him though. If I thought
I had to find a place to rent, I'd have to work
full-time. I know I wouldn't stay
in school. This one thing—a free bed—
makes all the difference. I can stay awake in school and pay
attention to the teachers, answer almost all their **questions.**

I go to school, I work, I eat okay and get to bed
on time. I thought Child Welfare might ask **questions,**
But as long as they don't pay attention, I can stay. (pp. 22–23)

Italian sonnets, English sonnets[7] and English-Italian hybrids all appear in *Keesha's House.* Sonnets are 14-line poems with a given meter, usually iambic pentameter, and rhyme patterns. Italian sonnets are typically *abbaabba, cdcdcd,* or *abbaabba, cdecde;* English sonnets usually follow an *abab, cdcd, efef, gg* rhyme scheme. Consider "She's Doing Okay" spoken by Keesha's father:

Tobias knows the place where Keesha stays,
that house on Jackson Street with a blue door.
She's prob'ly better off there. Still, some days
I wonder—if I went over there and swore
I'd stay sober: first, would she come home?
and second, could I keep my word?
Sounds like she's doing okay on her own,
and why should she believe me now? Third
time I've been through this. The other two
I lasted a few weeks, then let someone talk
me into just one drink. Twelve steps. That shoe
fits some people, but it's not the way I walk.
Love holds up an angry fist to pride;
they beat each other down till I'm half dead inside. (p. 81)

In most English sonnets each quatrain, or four-line stanza, addresses an aspect of the theme. In the first four lines, Keesha's father identifies where his daughter lives; in the second quatrain, he questions whether he should go to her; and in the last he addresses his alcohol addiction. Note how the last two lines, a couplet, resolve the argument of the poem—the father's struggle with his relationship with his daughter. English sonnets typically close with a "resolution."

Frost invented a formal structure for *The Braid* (2006) based on her admiration of Celtic knots. The structure contains three elements: (1) narrative poems told in two alternating voices; (2) praise poems that commend something named in the narrative poems, and (3) line lengths based

Helen Frost (center) and classmates working on their school literary magazine.

---

[7]English sonnets are also called Elizabethan or Shakespearean sonnets. Italian sonnets are synonymous with Petrachan sonnets.

on syllabic count (p. 91). In the author box, Frost takes us deeper into the formal structures behind her poetry.

As illustrated by Frost's work, verse novels are excellent resources for helping students understand poetic forms, elements, and other creative structures. They also provide excellent writing models and, as illustrated later in this chapter, they are excellent resources for building fluency.

Poetry—Attentive Language   by Helen Frost

Through language we inherit intelligence; thought comes to us through generations of speakers, over thousands of years, in the form of words shaped into sentences, novels, speeches, textbooks, recipes—and poems. Each word carries its own linguistic history as it moves through time and space. Whenever words are written or spoken, and understood, that history is remembered and brought into the present. Such history is monumental, yet language often flows through our pens and conversations with such lightness we barely notice.

Poetry is a particularly attentive form of language. When I write poetry, I often focus on a formal structure as a way of shaping language. It helps me turn my gaze aside in order to allow language to work in its mysterious ways. Later, I can look back more analytically to see how it did its heavy lifting.

Look, for example, at the word *run* in its seven manifestations in Dontay's first sestina, "How I See It," in *Keesha's House:*

> They'll be sayin' I **ran**
> off, but that ain't how I see it. To me—
> I went to Carmen's house
> where all my friends chill out,
> and when I called home for a ride,
> my foster dad said, You got there on your
>   own, son;
>
> you should be able to get home. *They call
>   me* son
> like that. But if I was, they'd **run**
> out in that fancy car and give me a ride
> when I need one. It ain't no home to me.
> It look like one, sittin' on that green lawn, out
> in the suburbs. *My caseworker say,* This house

> has everything. Four bedrooms, three baths, the
>   house
> of your dreams. *Sound like she sellin' it. Their
>   real son*
> has a bathroom to hisself, and a sign that says
>   KEEP OUT
> on his door. He got the whole crib on lock, **runnin'**
> the whole show. But me—
> I feel like I'm beggin' if I ask for a ride.
>
> I hafta ask if I can eat! I got a ride
> home last Thursday, and when I went in, the house
> was quiet. They was all done eatin', nothin' left
>   for me.
> *My foster mom said,* Sorry son,
> you need to learn, if you want to **run**
> around with those kids, and stay out
>
> past suppertime, you can't expect us to go out
> of our way to feed you. *Where they live, you need
>   a ride*
> to go get food. You can't just **run**

Continued

Poetry—Attentive Language   *Continued*

to the corner for a sandwich or go to a friend's
    house
and eat with them. Carmen's grandmamma call
    me son
too, sometimes, but if I'm hungry a their house,
    she'll feed me.

So now I don't know what to do. It's gonna look
    like me
messin' up again. But to me—they locked me out!
If I had my own key like their son,
I coulda got in last night when I finally got a ride
from Carmen. It was midnight, and the house
was dark. Carmen thought I'd gone inside. I tried
    to **run**

and catch her, but she didn't see me standin' out
    there in the dark street—no house, no food,
    no ride.
I didn't **run** *off. I shivered in the backyard, waitin'*
    for the sun.

Even if you don't know the whole story, it's clear that Dontay is struggling with issues of power and privilege: Between the first accusation and the final denial of it, are all those idioms of running that express ease for others and urgency for him. Because others are running things, he is running to escape their power. As the author, I don't need to say that directly—I describe the situation through my character's voice, and the language of the poem carries nuances that the reader will absorb.

In *The Braid*, the echoes between repeated words are more widely spaced, and so their effect may be more subtle. But again, idioms and metaphors reach greater depths when they are braided together through the formal structure of the poetry than they would without that structure. Here is an example from the first two narrative poems:

> Sarah: But I know better than to speak such thoughts. I hold my **tongue** (p. 3).
> Jeannie: Then we dipped our hands into the sea and touched our / **tongues** to the sea-water, each of us swallowing a bit (p. 6).

Sarah's idiom, *I hold my tongue*, describes her thoughts and feelings, as defined by her language. Jeannie picks up the word *tongue* in her poem, and gives it a literal meaning, but the echo from Sarah's poem lets the reader know that they each have the "sea" of their shared history, language, and childhood conversations between them. This becomes a central metaphor as the story unfolds.

As I have worked intensely with language in poetry, I have found it to be almost infinitely powerful and flexible. Whether it is, in fact, infinite is something for future generations to discover.

Copyright Helen Frost, 2008
Official Web site: www.helenfrost.net
Frost has also written *Spinning through the Universe* (2004) and *Diamond Willow* (2008).

Selecting Poetry

Mention the word *poetry* before a group of high school seniors and be prepared for a collective groan—*and* increased anxiety. Most have histories dissecting and explicating difficult poems: searching for and explaining poetic conventions, struggling "to get" the meaning, and ultimately feeling as though they're the only dumb ones in the room. Most everyone reading this text (myself included) remembers tense situations with poetry, if not in high school, somewhere in college: images were confusing, lines too complex, language too archaic, the meaning elusive. Everyone else in the room seemed smarter.

Poetry has the ability to delight and also the ability to destroy interest and confidence. Emphasis on poetic elements can prevent teens from enjoying poetry because their attention is drawn away from the emotion and music of poetry. It can also reinforce the idea the poem has only one meaning and the teacher owns it. Teaching poetry with which teens do not connect also curtails interest. While many classics are truly masterpieces and many argue teens should be taught to navigate such texts, the fact remains that when read in modern times, many metaphors, nuances, and historical, social, and cultural references are lost on readers—adults and teens alike. Added to this problem is a diversity concern. English language learners (ELLs) struggle even more with metaphor, language nuances, and so forth that are unique to the English language. If we truly want to foster a love for poetry, the right poem makes all the difference.

So how do we find the right poem?

Foremost is remembering the nature and developmental stages of adolescence and choosing poems with themes, settings, and emotions that interest them. For teens who haven't found a pleasure in poetry, contemporary poetry works best. Worthwhile poetry contains rich sensory imagery and/or evokes a deep emotional response. Language resonates. Ideally, the poem represents a young person's perspective on the world. For teens already turned off by poetry, free verse is a good starting point. Teens aren't threatened by complex meter and rhyme scheme, and the teacher doesn't feel pressured to teach those conventions. Instead, with free verse the emphasis is easily placed on the vibrancy of the language, imagery, and the poem's lyrical sound. Fortunately, as you will discover in this chapter, free verse is a common form in young adult poetry. Humorous poetry such as limericks also are good starters for disinterested teens. A study by Kutiper and Wilson (1993) determined that the humorous poetry by Jack Prelutsky and Shel Silverstein are teen favorites.

Teaching Poetry

Most likely, however, if you poll your peers teaching young adult literature, a high percentage would say they are uncomfortable with poetry and dread teaching it. Such fears come from negative poetry experiences. In *The Literature Workshop: Teaching Texts and Their Readers* (2003), Blau tells an engaging story about visiting an English language arts classroom. Blau awaits eagerly for the teacher to cover a section of a poem which he himself never understood. When the teacher reaches that point, he skips it. When asked why, the teacher responds he/she doesn't understand it.

While this scenario is a bit humorous, it's realistic and reminds us that even experienced teachers can fear poetry, and as much as we'd like to understand every line we read, we find some poems confusing. It suggests, too, the likelihood that high school English teachers may rely heavily on answers found in English anthologies—at least until they have them memorized.

It is with poetry that the value of reader-response is the greatest (see Chapter 4). One way I help beginning teachers overcome their fear of teaching poetry is by having them teach poetry they haven't read using a reader-response approach. Sound contradictory? Try the following exercise with your peers:

1. We have ready access to laptops in my class, but printed copies of poems could be handed out. I put my preservice teachers in groups of four and send them to www.readprint.com, where they find a wealth of online classic poems, short stories, and novels. (I don't use young adult poetry because I want a really difficult poem that will challenge preservice teachers.)
2. I instruct them to find a poem, one they have never read or with which they have minimal experience.
3. Next, I tell them they will *teach* the poem at this moment in their groups. I do get a few gasps and disgruntled stares; however, we launch into a discussion on reader-response and the idea that the least baggage we bring to a poem, the more willing we are to consider other possibilities and the harder we work to determine meaning. I also reinforce the idea of releasing the all-knowing, authoritarian approach we've seen modeled. We don't have to *know* it. Let's consider *discovering* it with our students. Let's enter the reading of the poem on a level playing field.
4. From a list of reader-response questions (see Chapter 4), I ask them to choose three to four questions to initiate a class discussion. One of these must be asking them to identify a confusing word or passage. Once they've chosen their questions, they're ready to engage their peers.
5. Preservice teachers facilitate their discussions, and by the end of the session they acknowledge the comfort they feel when they relinquish the idea that they have to know everything.

Although this activity might fit better in an article geared toward teacher educators on preparing preservice teachers, I place it here because it illustrates a method for overcoming our fear of poetry. I used the word *facilitate* in Step 5. It is an important word, for preservice teachers learn at this point not to interject their own thoughts, feelings, or beliefs into class literature discussions; otherwise, student discussion is more prone to teacher-pleasing responses. Preservice teachers understand they guide the discussion by scaffolding questions and responses, reiterating and summarizing what students have said, to take the conversation to another point. By the end of the discussion, preservice students—or teens—have not absorbed the teacher's beliefs about the poem but have developed their own. The peer discussion sometimes reinforces and deepens their original thoughts; other times it alters their responses completely. The bottom line is that students learn that the teacher isn't going to tell them the poem's meaning—indeed, she/he may not know it in the first place—so they're more active in figuring it out. Such approaches illustrate the power and possibilities of reader-response and foster a sense of community in the classroom.

You're probably wondering, though, about poetic conventions. The AP literature test makes good use of them. First-year college composition professors require students not only to identify poetic elements but also to write essays explaining how these conventions contribute to a poem's meaning. A specific question might be, "How do poetic conventions such as *caesura* contribute to a poem's mood?" It's rather clear that explicating a poem to death spells disaster for most, yet some understanding of poetry conventions can elevate a student's appreciation of both poem and craft.

So what's the answer? Where's the balance?

Look for windows of opportunity to teach poetic conventions from the bottom up. Depending on the grade and ability level, you will have some sense of what poetic elements you need to cover each semester. Choose poetry containing these elements, and watch for places in class conversations where you can *raise questions* about those elements. (Never begin a class by defining a literary element.) A student may, for example, comment that a stanza is funny. You may ask, "What makes that line seem funny?" Allow students time to consider your question and guide them to a possible answer—maybe *alliteration*. At this moment, a definition is needed.

Basically, practice developing a good ear for student responses. Watch for those comments, or teachable moments, to interject a literary element. You don't have to do this in a random or arbitrary way. You can strategically build in a literary element (no more than one or two) in any class discussion. If the teachable moment isn't there, or if you miss it, you can interject the literary element at the end, but pose it in the form of a question. Here is a possible question for Walt Whitman's "O Captain! My Captain!"

> We didn't talk about the historical context of this poem. Some critics suggest this poem is an extended metaphor. The captain represents Abraham Lincoln? What do you think of that?

This isn't an easy approach to teaching poetry—it takes practice, skill, and commitment, and the belief that our students are capable—but the payoff is immeasurable.

Table 9.2 lists 20 ideas for teaching poetry to your students. Specific reading activities are explained in the fluency section.

Poetry Forms for Young Adult Readers

The following sections describe 15 poetry forms commonly read and written by young adults.

Acrostic Poems

These are short poems in which words are formed by either the first, middle, or last letters of each poetry line when read downward. Acrostics were possibly first used as mnemonic devices, and ancient ones may have religious

Table 9.2

Ideas for Teaching Poetry in the Classroom

1. Have students practice genre switching. They can turn a narrative poem into an essay, a brief news article, or a short story. They may also do the reverse.

2. Have students maintain a poetry notebook. Half is devoted to a collection of their favorite poems, and half includes their own creations.

3. Avoid teaching poetry "units." Instead, integrate poetry throughout the curriculum. Teach poetry that enhances other genres alongside a novel, short story, or play.

4. Have students model, imitate, or modify a poem written by a professional poet.

5. Participate in poetry slams (www.poetryslam.com) and other oral presentation forums.

6. Have students create "found" poetry. They locate a prose passage (in a magazine, textbook, or elsewhere) that has strong images or "poetic possibilities." They then copy it into lines of poetry, emphasizing important words by placing them at the end of lines. Then they delete any unnecessary or dead words. They can repeat words and rearrange words and phrases anyway they wish. They can't, however, add words (Milner & Milner, 2003).

7. Have students examine some of their favorite music for poetic elements.

8. Have students read Lewis Carroll's *Jabberwocky* and create their own nonsense poem.

9. Have students visit a magnetic poetry Web site (www.magneticpoetry.com) and create their own magnetic poem.

10. Have students create a poem based on a favorite photo or painting.

11. Integrate poetry across content areas. Haikus, for example, are wonderful forms for defining mathematical and scientific terms and concepts. For dozens of poetry exercises for the mathematics, science, and social studies classroom, see Sara Holbrook's *Practical Poetry: A Nonstandard Approach to Meeting Content-Area Standards* (2005).

12. Help students publish their work on bulletin boards, in online poetry journals, local and school papers, literary magazines, and poetry contests.

13. Have students write brief research papers in the form of narrative poetry.

14. Play off teens' sense of humor by challenging them with topics such as "What would you cook your teacher for dinner?"

15. Provide appropriate structural guidance. If you ask students to write a poem without providing a poem structure (e.g., write a *cinquain*), many will submit a piece that resembles a prose paragraph. Some students need more instruction on poetry forms than others.

16. Have students discover the extraordinary in the ordinary. Have them identify five everyday objects and list details and crisp words to describe them. They will construct a poem about one object (e.g., an ode to socks).

17. Write poetry with your students. Share your enthusiasm and writing struggles.

Continued

T a b l e 9 . 2   *Continued*
18.   Collect enough poetry anthologies that you can pass one out to each student. Give them 20 minutes to find a poem they like (reasonable short ones). Each day have one student lead a discussion on her/his poem. The conversation begins with why the student liked the poem. Students may write a poem in response to their selection.
19.   Introduce students to online poetry blogs.
20.   When having students write poems, provide some choice, either by way of poetry form or theme. Restrictions limit imagination.

meanings. They are fun poems to write and often considered easy, but a number of well-known poets used the form (e.g., Chaucer, Ben Johnson). The Cirencester word square, also known as the Sator Square, is one of the most famous. It is both an acrostic and a palindrome:[8]

R O T A S
O P E R A
T E N E T
A R E P O
S A T O R

Historians have long speculated on its meaning. "Ode of Welcome," a salute to soldiers returning from duty, by Oliver St. John Gogarty is a famous acrostic.

Allegories

Whether short story, novel, or poem, an allegorical text has a meaning beneath the surface. Nathaniel Hawthorne's short story "Young Goodman Brown," a classic example, is an allegory about Everyman's journey down the road of faith. Edmund Spenser's *The Faerie Queene* is a classic allegorical poem.

Ballads

Ballads are songs that tell stories. The story is told through simple language by an impersonal narrator and includes dialogue and action. Ballads usually relate a dramatic event, and little attention is given to detail and setting—imagery is sparse. Two forms of ballads exist: folk or traditional ballads and literary ballads. The former comes out of an oral tradition and has been passed down from generation to generation. The author is unknown. You

---

[8]A palindrome is a word, verse, line, sentence, or number that reads the same backward or forward, up or down.

may be familiar with *Bonny Barbara Allan;* it's a common ballad read in high school. Below are the opening four lines:

> *It was in and about the Martinmas time,*
> *When the green leaves were a falling,*
> *That Sir John Graeme, in the West Country,*
> *Fell in love with Barbara Allan*

Folk ballads have thrived in rural areas and among cultures lacking formal education. Literary ballads, on the other hand, are penned and created by poets.

Blank Verse

This verse form is the most commonly used form in English verse. Blank verse most closely resembles the rhythms of everyday language, which explains its frequent use. It consists of unrhymed iambic pentameter lines (five-stress iambic verse). Popular classic poets who used the form include Milton; Wordsworth; Alfred, Lord Tennyson; and T. S. Eliot. It's often confused with free verse.

Cinquains

The American poet Adelaide Crapsey is credited with developing the cinquain. These are five-line poems with each line having a set number of syllables. A common form consists of lines with the following number of syllables: two, four, six, eight, and two, respectively. Cinquains are commonly taught across all grade levels because of their brevity. They offer students a chance to explore and play with words that create strong sensory images. Carl Sandburg popularized the form.

Concrete Poems

Also know as pattern or shape poetry, concrete poetry creates a picture or visual image. The visual shape contributes to the poem's meaning. *Technically, It's Not My Fault: Concrete Poems* (2004) by John Grandits is a collection of young adult concrete poems.

Diamonte Poems

These verse forms create a visual diamond shape. Traditionally, the seven-line poem addresses two opposites (e.g., autumn and spring). The pattern is as follows:

Line 1: Single word (subject)
Line 2: Two adjectives that describe the subject
Line 3: Three words that describe the subject and end in *–ing*
Line 4: Four words—the first two describe the subject in the first line; the last two describe the subject's opposite
Line 5: Three words that describe the subject's opposite and end in *–ing*

Line 6: Two adjectives that describe the subject's opposite
Line 7: One word (subject's opposite)

This form gives students practice with crisp language and antonyms. The form can also be used to teach synonyms (use two similar subjects as opposed to opposites). It is excellent for teaching cause and effect relationships. Note the cause and effect relationship in this example:[9]

The Spelling Test
Study
Challenge, Dedication
Repeating, Memorizing, Writing
Practice, Analysis, Success, Victory
Cheering, Smiling, Celebrating
Excellent, Masterful
100%

This form is easily used in content area writing. For example, compose a poem about the effect of global warming on polar ice caps.

Dramatic Monologues

Dramatic monologues are typically written in free verse and are conversational in tone. They are voiced by a single character and, while the speaker addresses a specific topic, she/he unwittingly reveals a great deal about her- or himself. Alfred, Lord Tennyson's *Ulysses* is an early dramatic monologue. T. S. Eliot's *The Love Song of J. Alfred Prufrock* (1915) is a modern one.

Epics

Epics are long, somber poems that tell stories about heroic figures. They are written on a grand scale and usually have historical significance. Homer's *Iliad* and the *Odyssey* are classic examples, so is Henry Wadsworth Longfellow's *The Song of Hiawatha*. There are two kinds: those originating from the oral tradition and those penned as literary pieces; that is, they are written down from the start.

Free Verse

This verse form has few boundaries, doesn't rhyme, and establishes its own rules. In the hands of a good poet, the free style can be quiet lyrical. It is commonly used in today's young adult poetry-novel hybrids and is sometimes confused with blank verse because both forms have unrhymed lines. Unlike blank verse, it does not include iambic pentameter.

Haiku

The haiku is a 17-syllable Japanese poetic form consisting of three lines: the first contains five syllables, the second seven, and the last five. Traditional haiku refer to nature or the seasons.

---

[9]This example is from the IRA's Web site: www.readwritethink.org.

Limericks

These verse forms are generally humorous, five-line poems with an *aabba* rhyme scheme. They are often bawdy. Rudyard Kipling, Mark Twain, and Robert Louis Stevenson experimented with the form. Edward Lear's *A Book of Nonsense* (1846) is one of the best-known limerick collections. Limericks are wonderful writing forms in content area classes. Students can write lyrics about current affairs or scientific topics.

Odes

Odes honor a special person, object, or occasion. In antiquity, they were sung in a celebratory manner. They are elaborate in form and elevated in tone. Many of us are familiar with John Keats's "Ode on a Grecian Urn" and "Ode to a Nightingale."

Sestina

These poems are elaborate and difficult to master. They consist of six, six-line stanzas and a three-line envoy, the shorter, final stanza of a poem. The last words of the first stanza are repeated in varying order as end words in the other stanzas and recur in the envoy. T. S. Eliot and Rudyard Kipling mastered it; so have young adult poets (see the author box by Helen Frost).

Sonnets

Complex and elegant verse forms, sonnets consist of 14 iambic pentameter lines with an elaborate rhyme scheme. The most familiar, the Shakespearean sonnet, consists of three quatrains, ending with a couplet.

Drama

The word *drama* comes from the Greek wording meaning "action" or "to do." Greek tragedies, comedies, and satyrs are early drama types and were performed in the Dionysos theatre in Athens. The drama masks—the smiling and sad faces—are symbols of comedy and tragedy muses, Thalia and Melpomene.

Most dramas, with the exception of *closet dramas*,[10] are meant to be performed, either live, through film and/or television, or via radio. Drama can include music and dance, resulting in operas and/or musicals. *Improv,* an ad-libbed performance, is also a drama form. Plays, of course, are dramatic works—living, breathing art forms designed for the stage.

Unlike novels, poems, or short stories, plays provide participants an opportunity to interact or role-play. Role-playing requires that we examine

---

[10]Closet dramas are written in play format but are meant to be read, not staged (e.g., Percy Bysshe Shelley's *Prometheus Unbound,* 1819).

Students in Aaron Levy's class develop readers' theatre scripts for the play, *Pizza with Shrimp on Top*. (Aaron Levy, center standing)

human feelings, behavior, and responses from alternative perspectives. Assuming the role of a teenager in wartorn Baghdad, for example, can give students emotional intelligence about war, hatred, loss, and the struggle to survive that they can't gain from reading. Assuming the role of Romeo in Shakespeare's *Romeo and Juliet* can help students understand times change but emotions are timeless.

Unfortunately, high school students traditionally *read* plays as opposed to *performing* them. However, most great playwrights, including Shakespeare, wrote plays to be performed, not read. (I've often wondered what Shakespeare's reaction would be to students reading as opposed to viewing his plays.) During Shakespeare's time, actors spent limited time rehearsing lines; they did not, therefore, adhere tightly to the script. Ironically, high school students, when reading a Shakespearean play, tend to envision the play being delivered line by line. Few are aware that actors deviated from the lines and that parts of Shakespeare's plays have been altered through time. Box 9.6 includes a listing of commonly read high school plays; I have excluded Shakespeare because we're most acquainted with his work.

Few contemporary writers pen original plays targeting the young adult audience, perhaps because teens, on average, spend more time viewing movies and films than they do watching live performances; perhaps also because most students don't choose to read plays. Don Gallo's *Center Stage: One-Act Plays for Teenage Readers and Actors* (1990) is the first and possibly

Box 9.6   Classic High School Plays   by Shanna Carter

The Crucible by Arthur Miller, 1953.

This play offers readers/viewers a comprehensive view of the historical, political, and religious landscape surrounding the Salem Witch Trials.

Death of a Salesman by Arthur Miller, 1951.

This notorious tale of the American Dream gone awry laments the life of a failed traveling salesman, who, unable to provide for his family, relies on his sons to succeed in his place.

The Diary of Anne Frank by Frances Goodrich and Albert Hackett, 1958.

Anne Frank, an adolescent girl hidden away in an attic with seven other people, records with vivid detail her thoughts and emotions about the Holocaust atrocities going on around her.

A Doll's House by Henrik Ibsen, 1932.

Nora lives the life of a doll, appreciated by her husband only aesthetically. An excellent selection for a unit on gender studies.

The Glass Menagerie by Tennessee Williams, 1945.

Dying of the dullness and monotony of his thankless job, Tom invites an acquaintance to dinner to woo his agonizingly timid sister, but glass is weak and apt to break. This play screams and shows the fragility of life unappreciated.

The Importance of Being Earnest by Oscar Wilde, 1895.

A Jekyll and Hyde tale of deception and alter egos, this play presents the life of a devoted public servant who always complains about his evil-doing, rarely seen brother, Ernest. A great play for discussing morality, hypocrisy, and deception.

Inherit the Wind by Jerome Lawrence and Robert E. Lee, 1955.

A teacher imprisoned struggles to support his right to teach evolutionism in a small Christian town led by an overzealous minister, who is quick to damn anyone to an eternity in hell.

A Man for All Seasons by Robert Bolt, 1962.

Sir Thomas More remains faithful to his king but refuses to betray God and Catholic doctrine at the command of King Henry VIII.

The Miracle Worker by William Gibson, 1957.

This play recounts Anne Sullivan's life as Helen Keller's teacher and examines the effects of her teaching on the entire Keller family.

The Night Thoreau Spent in Jail: A Play by Jerome Lawrence and Robert E. Lee, 1971.

Speaking out against the Vietnam War, Lawrence and Lee conjure Thoreau's spirited refusal to pay taxes that would fund a baseless war.

Our Town by Thornton Wilder, 1938.

Wilder ponders the nature of life and death, stressing the importance of building relationships and making every day count. With the help of the "Stage Manager," the audience watches the trifold progression of life, from birth to marriage and love to death.

Pygmalion by George Bernard Shaw, 1916.

The play that inspired *My Fair Lady*, *Pygmalion* is a beloved story of rags to riches and a study of the complexity of human relationships.

Gary Soto as a young boy (front) in 1963. From left to right: sister, Debbie; mother, Angie; and older brother, Rick.

only collection of original plays written by young adult authors. Gary Soto has written two one-act plays for teens. His one-act play, *Novio Boy: A Play* (1997), is a humorous, yet heart-wrenching account of a young boy preparing for a date with an attractive older girl. *Nerdlandia: A Play* (1999) strikes a similar cord. In this brief and humorous one-act play, Martin, a Chicano nerd, undergoes a transformation and falls in love. Some authors include drama and screen-writing themes and/or screenwriting structural elements in their novels (e.g., Paul Fleischman's *Breakout*, 2003; Sharon Creech's *Replay*, 2005).

James DeVita is an award-winning play-wright for young adults. His play *A Midnight Cry* (2004) is a historical work based on the true story of Caroline Quarrels, a runaway slave who, with the help of the Underground Railroad, eventually made her way to free-dom in Canada. DeVita developed the play after researching hundreds of slave narratives that detailed accounts of a slave's life, family, and living conditions.

Some publishers who specialize in producing plays for teens include Dramatic Publishing, Baker's Plays, and Eldredge Publishing. Play adapta-tions from young adult novels are common. In Box 9.7, Aaron Levy, author of the play *Pizza with Shrimp on Top* (2006) and expert on young adult plays, shares an annotated bibliography of young adult plays that have been proven successful with teens.

Box 9.7   A Bibliography of YA Plays   by Aaron Levy

Anne Frank and Me by Cherie Bennett. Woodstock, IL: Dramatic Publishing, 1997.

Nicole Burns, a modern-day hip-hop dancing, MTV watching teenager, who just happens to be a Holocaust denier, suddenly finds herself transported back to Nazi-occupied Paris circa 1942. This multiple national award-winning new American classic is about the awakening of a modern teen as she eventually meets Anne Frank on a cattle car and finds herself in the middle of one of the worst tragedies in the history of humankind.

The Bully Show! By Brian Guehring. Woodstock, IL: Dramatic Publishing, 2006.

This is an interactive play within a play for young people. *The Bully Show!* opens with the audience arriving at the live taping of the pilot episode of a new game show. The audience members, who are chosen to become contestants, actually partici-pate in games in which they have to pick out who could be a bully or which scenario features bullying behaviors.

Continued

Box 9.7   A Bibliography of YA Plays *Continued*

***Deadly Weapons* by Laurie Brooks. Woodstock, IL: Dramatic Publishing 2002.**

A young adult play that explores the hazards and consequences of reckless behavior. This mystery thriller finds three friends on a harmless dare to uncover a murder, but an accident in the plan leads to discoveries about themselves that none of them could ever have imagined.

***The Emerald Circle* by Max Bush. Woodstock, IL: Dramatic Publishing, 1998.**

Fourteen-year-old Dave has taken to shooting hoops in his driveway to avoid thinking about the trauma that occurred with his girlfriend in the Emerald Circle, a secluded, romantic section of an old cemetery surrounded by large pine trees. Maggie, Dave's mother, presses him to retell the incident, which he relives in front of the audience.

***Eric and Elliot* by Dwayne Hartford. Woodstock, IL: Dramatic Publishing, 2004.**

This is a lyrical, beautiful, unfolding story of a family's journey toward healing following a devastating suicide. The title characters are brothers who must find help for their severely depressed mother. Two young brothers find themselves on a journey in a strange new place, seemingly to save their mother, where they encounter a woman obsessed with the past, a man focused on the future, and another woman trying desperately to ignore both.

***Everyday Heroes* by Laurie Brooks. Woodstock, IL: Dramatic Publishing, 2006.**

Two brothers spend their young lives taking care of their alcoholic mother. When a devastating fire destroys their home, the younger brother, Win, becomes a reluctant media hero, but the brothers harbor a terrible secret.

***Everything Is Not Enough* by Sandra Fenichel Asher. Woodstock, IL: Dramatic Publishing, 2006 (Adapted from her novel).**

It's the summer before Michael's senior year and Michael's father has planned out his life for him. Michael, eager to discover the real world beyond his parents' protection, lands a job as busboy at the Jolly Mackerel restaurant in Braden's Port, a resort town where he, his family, and his friends have long been summer people—well-to-do vacationers.

***A Heart Divided* by Cherie Bennett and Jeff Gottesfeld. Woodstock, IL: Dramatic Publishing, 2004 (Adapted from their novel).**

Is the Confederate flag a racist symbol or a historical icon? This gripping and thought-provoking story shines new light on a controversy that continues to divide our national heart.

***John Lennon & Me* by Cherie Bennett. Woodstock, IL: Dramatic Publishing, 1996.**

Star, 13, and the ultimate Beatles fan, is destined to be a Hollywood star but is hampered by cystic fibrosis, an inherited disease that spells a young death for most. Her new hospital roommate, who isn't very ill, helps Star obtain a new perspective on life.

***Love, Death and the Prom* by Jon Jory. Woodstock, IL: Dramatic Publishing, 1991.**

These are related mini-plays that connect and create a fascinating full evening of theatre. They are real, hard-hitting, poignant, and funny episodes that take the audience through an amazing journey of love and death. While extremely humorous throughout, some young people have to cope with the devastating and unexpected news of a suicide.

Continued

Box 9.7   A Bibliography of YA Plays   *Continued*

Seek **by Paul Fleischman. Woodstock, IL: Dramatic Publishing, 2006 (Adapted from his novel).**

When high school senior Rob Radkovitz is assigned to write his own autobiography, he decides to "listen" back on his life. He hears his grandmother's mystery novels, Mexican soap operas, shortwave announcers, his multilingual mother, his rabble-rousing grandfather, but most cherished of all, he hears the voice of his absent DJ father from a single tape of one of his radio shows.

Uncool **by Vin Morreale Jr. Woodstock, IL: Dramatic Publishing, 1998.**

As the first play in the innovative *River Ridge High* series, this one-act teen comedy combines all the fast-paced hilarity of the movie *Clueless* with social issues familiar to anyone who has ever experienced the unique trauma of growing up and going to school.

A Woman Called Truth **by Sandra Fenichel Asher. Woodstock, IL: Dramatic Publishing, 1993.**

This remarkable play chronicles the life of one amazing woman from the day she is sold away from her family as a young girl, through her struggle to free herself and her son, to her eventual emergence as a popular and respected figure advocating abolition and women's rights.

The Wrestling Season **by Laurie Brooks. Woodstock, IL: Dramatic Publishing, 2000.**

Using only the unique setting of a wrestling mat, a referee facilitates eight teenagers' struggles to find and own their true identities amongst dangerous peer pressure. Uncovered are subject matter vital to young adults and their families.

Zen Junior High **by Kirk Lynn. Woodstock, IL: Dramatic Publishing, 2006.**

Zen Junior High follows a new pack of students who leave home to embark on a special journey where each student must take a vow "not to talk to strangers and not to talk to friends; the only ones to talk to are fellow students of Zen." This strange vow of silence causes trouble but challenges each student to make a spiritual leap to overcome difficulty.

Film plays an important role in the lives of today's teens, and teens are especially drawn to stories that feature young men and women coming of age. It may be difficult to use *American Pie* (1999) in the classroom, but plenty of alternatives exist. Box 9.8 features a number of contemporary films popular with today's teens that feature young adult actors and teen concerns. Some work better than others in the classroom; all are young adult favorites. In *Reel Conversations: Reading Films with Young Adults,* Tesley and Wilder (1997) discuss the literary merit of film and demonstrate its powerful role in the classroom. They also include teaching strategies.

The American Film Institute (AFI) recognizes excellence in the art of film, television, and digital media. Their list of the 100 greatest movies of all time is a good starting point for selecting films for classroom use. Criteria used in identifying the best films include historical significance, critical recognition and awards, and box-office popularity (go to www.afi.com).

Box 9.8   Contemporary Young Adult Films

American Graffiti, 1973

Angus, 1999 (short story by Chris Crutcher)

Back to the Future, 1985

Because of Winn-Dixie, 2005 (book by Kate DiCamillo)

Blood and Chocolate, 2007 (book by Annette Curtis Klause)

The Breakfast Club, 1984

Bridge to Terabitha, 2007 (book by Katherine Paterson)

The Bumblebee Flies Anyway, 1999 (book by Robert Cormier)

The Chocolate War, 1988 (book by Robert Cormier)

Clueless, 1995

Dead Poets Society, 1989

The Emperor's Club, 2002

Eragon, 2006 (book by Christopher Paolini)

Fast Times at Ridgemont High, 1982 (book by Cameron Crowe)

Ferris Bueller's Day Off, 1986

Footloose, 1984

Freaky Friday, 1976

Friday Night Lights, 2004 (book by H. G. Bissinger)

From the Mixed Up Files of Mrs. Basil E. Frankweiler, 1995 (book by E. L. Konigsburg)

Girl, Interrupted, 1999 (book by Susanna Kaysen)

The Golden Compass, 2007 (book by Philip Pullman

Grease, 1978

The Great Santini, 1979 (book by Pat Conroy)

Harry Potter film series (books by J. K. Rowling)

Harry Potter and the Sorcerer's Stone, 2001

Harry Potter and the Chamber of Secrets, 2002

Harry Potter and the Prisoner of Azkaban, 2004

Harry Potter and the Goblet of Fire, 2005

Harry Potter and the Order of the Phoenix, 2007

Harry Potter and the Half-Blood Prince, 2008

Holes, 2003 (book by Louis Sachar)

I Am the Cheese, 1983 (book by Robert Cormier)

I Know What You Did Last Summer, 1997 (book by Lois Duncan)

Ice Castles, 1979

The Karate Kid, 1984

Looking for Alibrandi, 2008 (book by Melina Marchetta)

Lord of the Flies, 1990 (book by William Golding)

The Lord of the Rings film trilogy (books by J. R. R. Tolkien)

The Fellowship of the Ring, 2001

The Two Towers, 2002

The Return of the King, 2003

Mean Girls, 2004 (book by Rosalind Wiseman)

The Mighty, 1998 (book by Rodman Philbrick)

The Outsiders, 1983 (book by S. E. Hinton)

The Princess Diaries, 2001 (book by Meg Cabot)

Rebel without a Cause, 1955

Remember the Titans, 2000

Risky Business, 1983

Rumble Fish, 1983 (book by S. E. Hinton)

Saved!, 2004

A Separate Peace, 2004 (book by John Knowles)

Shiloh, 1996 (book by Phyllis Reynolds Naylor)

Sisterhood of the Traveling Pants, 2005 (book by Anne Brashares)

Sixteen Candles, 1984

Speak, 2005 (book by Laurie Halse Anderson)

Stand by Me, 1986 (book by Stephen King)

Stormbreaker, 2006 (book by Anthony Horowitz)

Taps, 1981

Tex, 1982 (book by S. E. Hinton)

Vision Quest, 1985 (book by Terry Davis)

Whale Rider, 2002 (book by Witi Ihimaera)

Final Thoughts

All three genres discussed in this chapter—the short story, poetry, and drama—are wonderful selections for encouraging students to read and interact with texts. (See Box 9.9 for a list of illustrated poetry, short story, and play classics.) They work especially well with struggling readers

Box 9.9   Illustrated Poetry, Short Story, and Play Classics

Beowulf retold by Michael Morpurgo. Illus. Michael Foreman. Cambridge, MA: Candlewick Press, 2006.

Call of the Wild by Jack London. Illus. Barry Moser. New York: Simon & Schuster, 1994.

The Canterbury Tales by Geoffrey Chaucer. Illus. Trina Schart Hyman. New York: HarperCollins, 1988.

Casey at the Bat by Ernest L. Thayer. Illus. Joe Morse. Tonawanda, NY: Kids Can Press, 2006.

Chaucer's Canterbury Tales retold and illustrated by Marcia Williams. Cambridge, MA: Candlewick Press, 2007.

A Christmas Carol by Charles Dickens. Illus. P. J. Lynch. Cambridge, MA: Candlewick Press, 2006.

Christmas Day in the Morning by Pearl S. Buck. Illus. Mark Buehner. New York: HarperCollins, 2002.

The Gift of the Magi by O. Henry. Illus. Lisbeth Zwerger. New York: Simon & Schuster, 2006.

The Great Stone Face: A Tale by Nathaniel Hawthorne. Retold by Gary D. Schmidt. Illus. Bill Farnsworth. Grand Rapids, MI: Eerdmans Books, 2002.

Hamlet by William Shakespeare. Retold by Bruce Coville. Illus. Dennis Nolan. New York: Dial/Penguin, 1999.

The Highwayman by Alfred Noyes. Illus. Murray Kimber. Tonawanda, NY: Kids Can Press, 2005.

Jabberwocky by Lewis Carroll. Illus. Joel Stewart. Cambridge, MA: Candlewick Press, 2003.

Jabberwocky by Lewis Carroll. Illus. Stéphane Jorisch. Tonawanda, NY: Kids Can Press, 2004.

Knoxville, Tennessee by Nikki Giovanni. Illus. Larry Johnson. New York: Scholastic, 1994.

The Lady of Shalott by Alfred, Lord Tennyson. Illus. Geneviève Côté. Tonawanda, NY: Kids Can Press, 2005.

The Legend of Sleepy Hollow by Washington Irving. Illus. Will Moses. New York: Penguin, 1995.

The Odyssey by Homer. Retold by Robin Lister. Illus. Alan Baker. Boston: Kingfisher/Houghton Mifflin, 2004.

Othello by William Shakespeare. Retold by Adam McKeown. Illus. Sterling Hundley. New York: Sterling, 2005.

Poetry for Young People: Alfred, Lord Tennyson edited by John Maynard. Illus. Allen Garns. New York: Sterling, 2003.

Poetry for Young People: Carl Sandburg edited by Frances Shoonmaker Bolin. Illus. Steven Arcella. New York: Sterling, 1995.

Poetry for Young People: Edgar Allan Poe edited by Brod Bagert. Illus. Carolynn Cobleigh. New York: Sterling, 1995.

Poetry for Young People: Edna St. Vincent Millay edited by Frances Shoonmaker. Illus. Mike Bryce. New York: Sterling, 1999.

Poetry for Young People: Edward Lear edited by Edward Mendelson. Illus. Laura Huliska-Beith. New York: Sterling, 2001.

Poetry for Young People: Emily Dickinson edited by Frances Shoonmaker Bolin. Illus. Chi Chung. New York: Sterling, 1994.

Poetry for Young People: Henry Wadsworth Longfellow edited by Frances Schoonmaker. Illus. Chad Wallace. New York: Sterling, 1998.

Poetry for Young People: Langston Hughes edited by David Roessel and Arnold Rampersad. Illus. Benny Andrews. New York: Sterling, 2006.

The Raven by Edgar Allan Poe. Illus. Ryan Price. Tonawanda, NY: Kids Can Press, 2006.

Romeo and Juliet by William Shakespeare. Retold by Bruce Coville. Illus. Dennis Nolan. New York: Dial/Penguin, 1999.

Sir Gawain and the Green Knight retold by Michael Morpurgo. Illus. Michael Foreman. Cambridge, MA: Candlewick Press, 2004.

Tales from Shakespeare by Tina Packer. Illus. Diane Dillon, K. Nelson, B. Moser, and Gail De Marcken. New York: Scholastic, 2004.

Tales of Terror by Edgar Allan Poe. Illus. Michael McCurdy. New York: Random House, 2005.

because they are shorter than novels, faster to read and, thus, create a sense of accomplishment—struggling readers know they have a better chance of finishing a short piece than a longer one. One skill struggling readers may need to develop is oral fluency. The last part of this chapter demonstrates ways these genres can be used to teach this skill.

Building Fluency with Young Adult Short Stories, Poetry, and Drama

Fluency is one of five critical components needed for proficient reading identified in *The Report of the National Reading Panel* (NICHD, 2000). The report defines fluency as "the ability to read text quickly, accurately, and with proper expression" (pp. 3–5), but some reading experts argue that this definition is limited because it doesn't take into account the reflective reader who pauses, rereads, and questions text (e.g., Pikulski, 2006). Neither does it take into account *word callers* who read smoothly, free from word identification problems that could hinder comprehension—yet, when asked to explain their reading, they can't. Word callers *sound* proficient but fail to comprehend text. Pikulski presents a more comprehensive definition of fluency:

> Reading fluency is a developmental process that refers to efficient,
> effective decoding skills that permit a reader to comprehend text. There is
> a reciprocal relationship between decoding and comprehension. Fluency
> is manifested in accurate, rapid, expressive oral reading and is applied
> during, and makes possible, silent-reading comprehension. (p. 73)

Clearly, a give-and-take relationship exists between fluency and comprehension. When readers invest considerable effort in "surface-level aspects of reading"—that is, when reading is too slow and laborious and when decoding takes too much effort—readers deplete or exhaust cognitive resources that could otherwise be invested in meaning-making.

To understand why teens struggle with fluency, we have to examine their preschool and elementary years. Children who have had limited exposure to adult readers and reading experiences in which they listened to, recited, and/or memorized childhood stories, rhymes, and books tend to struggle with fluency. Those whose past reading experiences emphasized letters, word parts, and words, and de-emphasized reading whole texts may not have developed an acceptable level of fluency (if readers don't actually *read*, fluency can't develop). While a number of factors, some hidden, account for why some children read fluently and others don't, it seems reasonable that successful readers whose primary school reading experiences are part-to-whole instruction receive a balanced diet by reading independently, living in a language and book-rich home environment, and having additional school experiences that supplement decontextualized instruction.

Though silent reading plays a role in fluency development, oral reading is essential. If students haven't become fluent by the time they reach middle school, they are at risk of remaining poor readers because from that point on they have little opportunity in most classrooms to participate in activities that support fluency development. Reading aloud in middle school and high school classrooms consists primarily of round robin and popcorn reading, insufficient methods for developing fluency. In addition, these methods heighten reading anxiety and fail to promote comprehension.

Most of us have experienced round robin. The teacher calls on the first student in the first row to read, then the next, and next, until all students have read. Our experiences tell us why this strategy is ineffective: rather than reading along and paying attention to the story, students are searching for and trying to guess what they will be reading, and worrying about whether they will pronounce a word incorrectly. Also, those who read first are finished and have no motivation to continue.

Popcorn reading is an ineffective round robin alternative. The teacher starts the reading process by calling on one student. That student reads; then he/she randomly calls on a classmate, hence students never know when they will be called upon. Reading bounces from one student to another, much like corn kernels popping. This "I don't know when I'll be called upon" experience is intended to keep students glued to the text; the tradeoff is an increase in anxiety. Other negatives are clear: students call on friends, excluding others less able readers. Those who need the practice most are left out, so are those who aren't part of the "in" crowd. Adolescents can be cruel; they may also call upon struggling readers to read a difficult section.

The complexity of reading material affects a reader's ability to read fluently. Once students enter the middle grades, they begin encountering more expository texts and are expected to read more independently. This trend deepens in high school, and nonfluent readers have difficulty keeping up. If material is above students' reading levels, readers can't read automatically, evenly, or with expression; they concentrate on word accuracy and not making mistakes. Frustration-level material also destroys the desire to read and, consequently, the desire to learn. Moreover, teachers play an unknowing role in inhibiting fluency development when they call upon faster, better readers to read aloud, sometimes because they need to "get through the material" and other times for fear of embarrassing less able readers.

To create successful readers, middle grades and secondary teachers must engage adolescents in authentic oral reading experiences. Middle school and high school teachers need to model fluent reading and create situations in which students can practice and perform. When students can read at a good rate, with automaticity and little energy devoted to decoding, they have more cognitive resources for comprehension.

The oral reading methods that follow will help students read faster, more accurately, and with appropriate expression.[11] As you experiment with these selections, remember text selection is paramount. No high school student wants to read an elementary story or feel like he/she is sitting in an elementary reading class. Remember, too, that speed, expression, and accuracy alone don't create proficient readers.

---

[11]Many of these fluency methods are summarized in Samuels (2006).

Before beginning these methods, you'll want to evaluate students' abilities to work collaboratively in small groups. Don't make the mistake of assigning group work activities without assessing students' abilities to work collaboratively in small group settings and end up blaming the student when the class gets out of control and/or the activity falls apart. Some students need to be taught to work in groups. Simply telling students to talk in low voices, to be respectful, and to stay on task doesn't work. Many need practice and support in learning appropriate group interaction skills.

Oral Reading Methods and Books for Developing Fluency

Audiobooks

Students may follow along with a recorded version of a young adult novel. A word of caution, however. Some commercial recordings may be read too quickly, and teachers may have difficulty knowing when students are actually reading along. Teachers may find assisted reading a good approach for using audiobooks: students read aloud with the recording, stopping and reading difficult passages. Box 9.10 includes a sampling of young adult books on CDs. Others can be readily found by googling "young adult audiobooks" or "young adult books on tape." Another Web site that can be helpful is audiobookstand.com.

 Box 9.10   YA Audiobooks

47 by Walter Mosley (Read by Ossie Davis). New York: Little, Brown, 2005.

An Abundance of Katherines by John Green (Read by Jeff Woodman). New York: Penguin, 2006.

Becoming Naomi León by Pam Muñoz Ryan (Read by Annie Kozuch). New York: Scholastic, 2004.

Belle Prater's Boy by Ruth White (Read by Alison Elliott). New York: Farrar, Straus & Giroux, 1996.

The Book of Dead Days by Marcus Sedgwick (Read by Roger Rees). New York: Lamb/Random House, 2004.

The Book Thief by Markus Zusak (Read by Allan Corduner). New York: Random House, 2006.

Brian's Hunt by Gary Paulsen (Read by Ron McLarty). New York: Scholastic, 2004.

The Cay by Theodore Taylor (Read by Michael Boatman). New York: Doubleday, 1969.

The Death Collector by Justin Richards (Read by Steven Pacey). New York: Bloomsbury, 2005.

The Dragon Rider by Cornelia Funke (Read by Brendan Fraser). New York: Scholastic, 2004.

Dragonwings by Laurence Yep (Read by Bo Wong). New York: Harper & Row, 1975.

Elsewhere by Gabrielle Zevin (Read by Cassandra Morris). New York: Farrar, Straus & Giroux, 2005.

Endymion Spring by Matthew Skelton (Read by Richard Easton). New York: Random House, 2006.

Everything on a Waffle by Polly Horvath (Read by Kathleen McInerney). New York: Farrar, Straus & Giroux, 2001.

First Boy by Gary D. Schmidt (Read by Jesse Berns). New York: Henry Holt, 2005.

Flush by Carl Hiaasen (Read by Michael Welch). New York: Knopf/Random House, 2005.

Continued

Box 9.10   YA Audiobooks   *Continued*

Girl Nearly 16: Absolute Torture by Sue Limb (Read by Katherine Kellgren). New York: Random House, 2005.

Graven Images: Three Stories by Paul Fleischman (Read by Paul Michael, Susan Denaker, and Lincoln Hoppe). Cambridge, MA: Candlewick Press, 2006.

Gregor the Overlander: Book 1 by Suzanne Collins (Read by Paul Boehmer). New York: Scholastic, 2003.

Hatchet by Gary Paulsen (Read by Peter Coyote). Orlando, FL: Harcourt, 1975.

Here Lies the Librarian by Richard Peck (Read by Laura Everly). New York: Penguin, 2006.

The Higher Power of Lucky by Susan Patron (Read by Cassandra Campbell). New York: Simon & Schuster, 2006.

Holes by Louis Sachar (Read by Kerry Beyer). New York: Farrar, Straus & Giroux, 1998.

How I Live Now by Meg Rosoff (Read by Kim Mai Guest). New York: Random House, 2004.

I Am the Messenger by Markus Zusak (Read by Marc Aden Gray). New York: Random House, 2005.

Incantation by Alice Hoffman (Read by Jenna Lamia). New York: Little, Brown, 2006.

The Incredible Journey by Sheila Burnford (Read by Megan Follows). New York: Little, Brown, 1961.

Inkheart by Cornelia Funke (Read by Lynn Redgrave). New York: Scholastic, 2003.

Inkspell by Cornelia Funke (Read by Brendan Fraser). New York: Scholastic, 2005.

King Dork by Frank Portman (Read by Lincoln Hoppe). New York: Bantam Doubleday Dell/ Random House, 2006.

King of the Mild Frontier: An Ill-Advised Autobiography by Chris Crutcher (Read by the author). New York: Greenwillow/ HarperCollins, 2003.

Kira-Kira by Cynthia Kadohata. (Read by Elaina Erika Davis). New York: Simon & Schuster, 2004.

The Last Apprentice: The Revenge of the Witch by Joseph Delaney (Read by Christopher Evan Welch). New York: HarperCollins, 2005.

The Liberation of Gabriel King by K. L. Going (Read by Robert Keefe). New York: Penguin, 2005.

Lizzie Bright and the Buckminster Boy by Gary D. Schmidt (Read by Sam Freed). Boston: Houghton Mifflin, 2004.

London Calling by Edward Bloor (Read by Robertson Dean). New York: Knopf/Random House, 2006.

Looking for Alaska by John Green (Read by Jeff Woodman). New York: Penguin, 2005.

Maximum Ride: Book 1: The Angel Experiment by James Patterson (Read by Evan Rachel Wood). New York: Little, Brown, 2005.

Maximum Ride: Book 2: School's Out—Forever by James Patterson (Read by Valentina De Angelis). New York: Little, Brown, 2006.

Messenger by Lois Lowry (Read by David Morse). Boston: Houghton, 2004.

Milkweed by Jerry Spinelli (Read by Ron Rifkin). New York: Random House, 2003.

Millicent Min, Girl Genius by Lisa Yee (Read by Keiko Agena). New York: Scholastic, 2003.

Mister Monday: Book 1 by Garth Nix (Read by Allan Corduner). New York: Scholastic, 2005.

New Moon by Stephenie Meyer (Read by Ilyanna Kadushin). New York: Little, Brown, 2006.

The Outsiders by S. E. Hinton (Read by Jim Fyfe). New York: Viking, 1967.

Penny from Heaven by Jennifer L. Holm (Read by Amber Sealey). New York: Random House, 2006.

Rebel Angels by Libba Bray (Read by Josephine Bailey). New York: Bantam Doubleday Dell/ Random House, 2005.

River between Us by Richard Peck (Read by Lina Patel). New York: Penguin, 2003.

Roll of Thunder, Hear My Cry by Mildred D. Taylor (Read by Lynne Thigpen). New York: Dial, 1976.

Continued

Box 9.10   YA Audiobooks   *Continued*

The Sea of Trolls by Nancy Farmer (Read by Gerard Doyle). New York: Simon & Schuster, 2004.

The Thief Lord by Cornelia Funke (Read by Simon Jones). New York: Scholastic, 2002.

Twilight by Stephenie Meyer (Read by Ilyanna Kadushin). New York: Little, Brown, 2005.

Twisted by Laurie Halse Anderson (Read by Mike Chamberlain). New York: Penguin, 2007.

The Watsons Go to Birmingham—1963 by Christopher Paul Curtis (Read by LeVar Burton). New York: Random House, 1995.

When Zachary Beaver Came to Town by Kimberly Willis Holt (Read by Will Patton). New York: Henry Holt, 1999.

Where the Red Fern Grows by Wilson Rawls (Read by Anthony Heald). New York: Doubleday, 1961.

The Wish House by Celia Rees (Read by Christopher Cazenove). Cambridge, MA: Candlewick Press.

The Witch's Boy by Michael Gruber (Read by Denise O'Hare). New York: HarperCollins, 2005.

Wormwood by G. P. Taylor (Read by Davina Porter). New York: Penguin, 2004.

The Wright 3 by Blue Balliett (Read by Ellen Reilly). New York: Scholastic, 2006.

A Wrinkle in Time by Madeleine L'Engle (Read by the author). New York: Ariel, 1962.

Choral Readings

Teachers and students may read material aloud in unison. They may also split the reading, alternating lines or passages. Poetry works well with choral reading; music lyrics are huge hits with high school students. Begin with short, simple texts.

Echo Reading

The reader "echoes" or imitates a proficient reader. A proficient reader reads a line or brief passage with good rate and expression. The learner repeats the passage or line, imitating the proficient reader's tone and speed. This method works well with poetry and verse novels.

Guided Pairs

A more skilled reader (parent, teacher, older peer) reads the selection solo as the less skilled reader follows along. Then both read the selection in unison several times over. At some point, the less skilled reader reads solo.

Partner Readings

Students take turns reading aloud to partners. Students may reread the same passage; they may alternate back and forth in reading a short story together. Poetry (e.g., Paul Fleischman's materials) works well with this activity. Paired poems (e.g., *I Feel a Little Jumpy around You: A Book of Her Poems & His Poems Collected in Pairs*, 1996, by Nye and Janeczko) work especially well.

Radio Reading

The reader assumes the reading stance of a reporter and reads a selection aloud. This method works best with nonfiction sources such as newspaper or magazines articles.

Read-Alouds

If you're uncomfortable reading aloud to students, know you're not alone. Most of us have limited experience with oral reading. When reading to students, *always* practice reading aloud to yourself beforehand and *always* model good expression, appropriate pausing, and emphasis—many teachers read too fast and in a monotone. Use punctuation as a guide (e.g., pause at commas and show appropriate expression with exclamation points and question marks). Avoid feeling silly for expressing yourself. Also, a good tip to remember is to emphasize every fourth or fifth word. If you do so, you will avoid reading in monotone fashion.

Wilder and Teasley (1998) point out that books we choose for reading aloud are generally not the classics. Successful read-alouds move fast, and classics typically read slow because of description and longer, more complex, sentence structures. Wilder and Teasley ask two questions when choosing read-aloud selections: (1) Does the story have a strong narrative voice? (2) Does the plot move quickly? Young adult novels with minimum description, lots of dialogue, and quirky, unique characters are good read-alouds. An authentic, unique voice such as that found in Meg Rosoff's *How I Live Now* (2004) and Gary Paulsen's *Harris and Me* (1993) capture and hold audiences. Short stories and verse novels also make great read-alouds: short stories for their brevity, verse novels for their rhythm and short chapters. Mysteries and thrillers with cliff-hanger endings are good too. Box 9.11 features good read-aloud choices.

Readers' Theatre

This reading method is an oral presentation of a text read expressively and dramatically. There are many variants of readers' theatre; however, they share common characteristics. They use minimum props, costumes, and sets, and emphasize visualization and use of the imagination. Scripts are read, not memorized. Readers' theatre is usually performed with plays and poems; however, short stories, novels, and content area material can be modified. Readers do repeated readings alone or in groups in preparation for a staged performance. The practice provides students with real-life reasons to practice oral reading. In addition to improving fluency, readers' theatre aids in developing comprehension and vocabulary.

Readers' theatre scripts may be made from most any text, expository or narrative. Scripts written from young adult novels are plentiful. *Scholastic Scope,* for instance, publishes scripts regularly (e.g., Christopher Paolini's *Eragon,* William Shakespeare's *Twelfth Night,* and Bram Stoker's *Dracula*). In creating a readers' theatre script, you cut to the core of the story

Box 9.11   YA Books for Read-Alouds

Because of Winn-Dixie by Kate DiCamillo.
Cambridge, MA: Candlewick Press, 2000.

The Boy in the Burning House by Tim Wynne-Jones. New York: Farrar, Straus & Giroux, 2001.

Bronx Masquerade by Nikki Grimes. New York: Dial/Penguin, 2002.

Daisy Fay and the Miracle Man by Fannie Flagg. New York: Warner, 1992.

A Day No Pigs Would Die by Robert Peck. New York: Knopf/Random House, 1972.

Far North by Will Hobbs. New York: Morrow/HarperCollins, 1996.

Freak the Mighty by Rodman Philbrick. New York: Blue Sky Press, 1993.

The Girl Who Loved Tom Gordon by Stephen King. New York: Simon & Schuster, 1999.

The Great Gilly Hopkins by Katherine Paterson. New York: HarperCollins, 1978.

Guys Write for Guys Read: Boys' Favorite Authors Write about Being Boys edited by Jon Scieszka. New York: Viking/Penguin, 2005.

Harris and Me by Gary Paulsen. Orlando, FL: Harcourt, 1993.

Hidden Talents by David Lubar. New York: Doherty Tor, 1999.

Hoops by Walter Dean Myers. New York: Delacorte/Random House, 1981.

How Angel Peterson Got His Name and Other Outrageous Tales about Extreme Sports by Gary Paulsen. New York: Lamb/Random House, 2003.

Killing Mr. Griffin by Lois Duncan. New York: Little, Brown, 1978.

Knots in My Yo-Yo String: The Autobiography of a Kid by Jerry Spinelli. New York: Knopf/Random House, 1998.

The Last Book in the Universe by Rodman Philbrick. New York: Blue Sky Press, 2000.

The Lightning Thief by Rick Riordan. New York: Hyperion, 2005.

A Long Way from Chicago by Richard Peck. New York: Dial, 1998.

The Martian Chronicles by Ray Bradbury. New York: Doubleday, 1950.

No More Dead Dogs by Gordon Korman. New York: Hyperion, 2000.

Remember Me by Christopher Pike. New York: Pocket/Simon & Schuster, 1989.

Running Loose by Chris Crutcher. New York: Greenwillow/HarperCollins, 1983.

The Secret Life of Bees by Sue Monk Kidd. New York: Viking Penguin, 2002.

Spellbound by Janet McDonald. New York: Farrar, Straus & Giroux, 2001.

Stargirl by Jerry Spinelli. New York: Knopf/Random House, 2000.

Tuesdays with Morrie: An Old Man, a Young Man, & Life's Greatest Lesson by Mitch Albom. New York: Doubleday, 1997.

Up Country by Alden R. Carter. New York: Putnam, 1989.

Walk Two Moons by Sharon Creech. New York: HarperCollins, 1994.

Wringer by Jerry Spinelli. New York: HarperCollins, 1997.

A Year Down Yonder by Richard Peck. New York: Scholastic, 2001.

by eliminating descriptive passages and scenes that slow the story down. Readence, Bean, and Baldwin (2004) provide the following strategies for preparing scripts:

1. Select passages from a novel that move the story forward.
2. Reproduce those sections.
3. Delete noncritical lines and divide these parts for each student to deliver.

4. Label sections with students' names.
5. Model the process of reading aloud in dramatic fashion. (p. 130)

Rehearsal Readings

Students preread a passage several times to themselves and to a small group prior to reading it aloud in class. An attractive alternative to round robin, rehearsal reading allows repeated practice in a low-risk environment. I model the following strategies:

1. Select appropriate age and ability level reading material and reproduce one copy.
2. Divide the section equally by the number of students in class. I do this by boxing passages with a pen and numbering them consecutively: 1, 2, 3, and so on.
3. Reproduce copies for each student and assign each student a numbered section.
4. Place students in groups of four and have them read their sections several times to the other group members. Encourage students to work with one another to ensure they know all the words. Have dictionaries available as an additional resource.
5. Once students feel comfortable reading in their groups, come together as a class and read the selection together. Discussion should follow.

Repeated Readings

Students reread a short, meaningful passage several times. With each reading, the reader sets a goal: to read faster, to read with fewer errors, or to read with more meaningful expression. Short stories and poetry work well.

Dramatic Monologues

Teens can write dramatic monologues based on a short story or novel character and then perform them. Unlike readers' theatre, which involves student groups, dramatic monologues can be performed—and practiced—individually.

Final Thoughts

Fluency is indeed an important reading skill. However, as Weaver (2002, p. 215) reminds us, fluency does not ensure comprehension, and comprehension doesn't demand pitch-perfect fluency. A thoughtful reader often pauses. A word caller may read with a good, even rate. Teens have fewer opportunities to practice oral reading. The more opportunities we provide them in the classroom, the better their chances become of developing into fluent, articulate, confident readers. The responsibility lies with the teacher to ensure that fluency exercises do not replace meaning-making. Fluency activities in this chapter combined with activities in other chapters will provide a good balance for developing readers.

Professional Resources

Abrahamson, R. F. (2002). Poetry preference research: What young adults tell us they enjoy. *Voices from the Middle, 10*(2), 20–22.

Allen, J. (2002). Painting word pictures: The language of poetry. *Voices from the Middle, 10*(2), 52–53.

Anderson, A. P. (1998). Doing poetry. *Voices from the Middle, 6*(2), 28–36.

Athanases, S. Z. (2005). Performing the drama of the poem: Workshop, rehearsal, and reflection. *English Journal, 95*(1), 88–96.

Atwell, N. (2005). *Naming the world: A year of poems and lessons.* Portsmouth, NH: Heinemann.

Barchers, S. I. (2005). *In short: How to teach the young adult short story.* Portsmouth, NH: Heinemann.

Beck, G. (1994). *No peeping under the curtain: Tips and scripts for school drama productions.* Lanham, MD: Scarecrow Press.

Beers, K. (2002). Like who can grade a poem?: Thoughts on poetry instruction. *Voices from the Middle, 10*(2), 4–5.

Bernal, P. (2007). Acting out: Using drama with English learners. *English Journal, 96*(3), 26–28.

Bloland, D. (1998). O taste and see: Poetry with eighth graders. *Voices from the Middle, 5*(1), 12–16.

Bolton, G. (1999). *Acting in classroom drama.* Portsmouth, NH: Heinemann.

Boynton, R. W., & Mack, M. (1992). *Introduction to the short story.* Portsmouth, NH: Heinemann.

Caruso, S., & Kosoff, S. (1998). *The young actor's book of improvisation: Dramatic situations from Shakespeare to Spielberg.* Portsmouth, NH: Heinemann.

Chance, R. (2001). Beyond Silverstein: Poetry for middle schoolers. *Voices from the Middle, 9*(2), 88–90.

Coencas, J. (2007). How movies work for secondary school students with special needs. *English Journal, 96*(4), 67–72.

Daw, K., & Matthews, J. (1998). *A guide to scenes and monologues from Shakespeare and his contemporaries.* Portsmouth, NH: Heinemann.

Dias, P. X. (1995). *Reading and responding to poetry: Patterns in the process.* Portsmouth, NH: Heinemann.

Dupre, B. (2004). Defusing difference through drama. *Voices from the Middle, 12*(1), 32–38.

Felske, C. K. (2005). Beyond the page: Students as actor-readers. *English Journal, 95*(1), 58–63.

Fisher, B., & Medvic, E. F. (2003). *For reading out loud: Planning and practice.* Portsmouth, NH: Heinemann.

Foster, M., & Shiras, A. (1998). *The play behind the play: Hamlet and Quarto One.* Portsmouth, NH: Heinemann.

Frazier, C. H., & Wellen, C. (1998). The way in is the way out: Poetry writing in the classroom. *Voices from the Middle, 5*(1), 3–9.

Goodson, F. T., & Goodson, L. A. (2005). You oughta use the periods and stuff to slow down: Reading fluency through oral interpretation of YA lit. *Voices from the Middle, 13*(2), 24–29.

Graves, D. (1992). *Explore poetry.* Portsmouth, NH: Heinemann.

Gustafson, C. (1999). *Acting out: Reader's theatre across the curriculum.* Cincinnati, OH: Linworth.

Holbrook, S., & Salinger, M. (2006). *Outspoken! How to improve writing and speaking skills through poetry performance.* Portsmouth, NH: Heinemann.

Jewell, V. M. (2004). Poetry made easy: Of swag and sense. *English Journal, 93*(5), 31–35.

Kozlowski, R. (2002). *The art of Chicago improv: Short cuts to long-form improvisation.* Portsmouth, NH: Heinemann.

Kuroly, N. T. (2004). The power(point) of poetry. *Voices from the Middle, 11*(3), 30–33.

Laminack, L. L., & Wadsworth, R. M. (2006). *Learning under the influence of language and literature: Making the most of read-alouds across the day.* Portsmouth, NH: Heinemann.

Lane, S. F. (2007). *Let's put on a show: Theatre production for novices.* Portsmouth, NH: Heinemann.

Leeper, A. (2006). *Poetry in literature for youth.* Lanham, MD: Scarecrow Press.

Lesesne, T. S. (2006). Reading aloud: A worthwhile investment? *Voices from the Middle, 13*(4), 50–54.

Maher, J. (2006). *Most dangerous women: Bringing history to life through readers' theater.* Portsmouth, NH: Heinemann.

Mahoney, J., & Matovcik, J. (2005). *Power and poetry.* Portsmouth, NH: Heinemann.

Miles, J., & Greene, A. (2003). *A theatre for women's voices: Plays and history from The Women's Project at 25.* Portsmouth, NH: Heinemann.

Miller, S. (2006). *Strike up the band: A new history of musical theatre.* Portsmouth, NH: Heinemann.

Muller, V. (2006). Film as film: Using movies to help students visualize literary theory. *English Journal, 95*(3), 32–38.

Pagnucci, G. (2004). *Living the narrative life: Stories as a tool for meaning making.* Portsmouth, NH: Heinemann.

Perry, T. (2005). Beyond memorization: Using drama to promote thinking. *English Journal, 95*(1), 120–123.

Probst, R. E. (2002). We did fourteen lines . . . *Voices from the Middle, 10*(2), 48–49.

Quintero, K., & Cooks, J. (2002). Hip-hop as authentic poetry. *Voices from the Middle, 10*(2), 56–57.

Rasinski, T., & Padak, N. D. (2005). Fluency beyond the primary grades: Helping adolescent struggling readers. *Voices from the Middle, 13*(1), 34–41.

Rodh, M. (1998). *Theatre for community conflict and dialogue.* Portsmouth, NH: Heinemann.

Ruggieri, C. A. (2005). Demystifying drama. *English Journal, 95*(1), 124–128.

Schwalb, N. (2006). East of the river: Crossing borders through poetry in middle schools. *English Journal, 96*(1), 40–45.

Shosh, J. M., & Wescoe, J. A. (2007). Making meaningful theater in the empty space. *English Journal, 96*(5), 42–47.

Smith, J. L., & Herring, J. D. (2001). *Dramatic literacy: Using drama and literature to teach middle-level content.* Portsmouth, NH: Heinemann.

Timmerman, D. (2004). *Spare scenes: 60 skeletal scenes for acting and directing.* Portsmouth, NH: Heinemann.

Vetrie, M. (2004). Using film to increase literacy skills. *English Journal, 93*(3), 39–45.

Watts, I. (1990). *Just a minute: Ten short plays and activities for your classroom.* Portsmouth, NH: Heinemann.

Wilhelm, J. D. (1998). Learning by being: Drama as total immerson. *Voices from the Middle, 6*(2), 3–10.

Wilhelm, J. D. (2002). Poetry doing hard and healthy work: A poetpourri of ideas from the Maine Writing Project. *Voices from the Middle, 10*(2), 15–19.

Wormser, B., & Cappella, D. (2004). *A surge of language: Teaching poetry day by day.* Portsmouth, NH: Heinemann.

ONLINE

Academy of American Poets: www.poets.org

The Acting Company: www.theactingcompany.org

American Poems: www.americanpoems.com

The Atlantic Online Poetry Pages: www.theatlantic.com/index/fiction

Classic Short Stories: www.classicshorts.com

Drama Kids International: www.dramakids.com

East of the Web: www.eastoftheweb.com/short-stories

The English Room: www.msrogers.com

Famous Poetry Online: www.poetryoutloud.org

Find poetry: www.findpoetry.com

ISLMC Poetry for Children: www.falcon.jmu.edu/~ramseyil/poechild.htm

Magnetic Poetry: www.magneticpoetry.com

Mathematical Poetry: www.mathematicalpoetry.blogspot.com

Playing around with Poetry: www.english.unitecnology.ac.nz/resources/units/poetry/home.html

Poem Hunter: www.poemhunter.com

Poet's Corner: www.galegroup.com

Poetry: www.poetrymagazine.org

Poetry Archives: www.emule.com/poetry

Poetry and Mathematics: www.mathforum.org

Poetry Can: www.poetrycan.co.uk

Poetry Class: www.poetryclass.net

Poetry Express: www.poetryexpress.com

Poetry4Kids: www.poetry4kids.com

Poetry Foundation: www.poetryfoundation.org

Poetry Index of Canonical Verse: www.poetry.eserver.org

Poetry Out Loud: www.poetryoutloud.org

Poetry Slam: www.poetryslam.org

The Poetry Society: www.poetrysociety.org

Poetry Teachers: www.poetryteachers.com
Read, Write, Think: www.readwritething.org
Readers Theatre Institute: www
  .readerstheatreinstitute.com
Science and Nature Poems: www.firstscience.com

Shadow Poetry: www.shadowpoetry.com
Shambles: www.shambles.net
Teen Ink: www.teenink.com
The War Poetry Web site: www.warpoetry.co.uk
Zoetrope All-Story: www.all-story.com

References

Adoff, J. (2005). *Jimi and me.* New York: Jump at the Sun/Hyperion.

Agee, J., & Evans, W. (1941). *Let us now praise famous men.* Boston: Houghton Mifflin.

Bauer, M. D. (Ed.). (1994). *Am I blue? Coming out of the silence.* New York: HarperCollins.

Blau, S. D. (2003). *The literature workshop: Teaching texts and their readers.* Portsmouth, NH: Heinemann.

Carlson, L. M. (Ed.). (2005a). *Moccasin thunder: American Indian stories today.* New York: HarperCollins.

Carlson, L. M. (Ed.). (2005b). *Red hot salsa: Bilingual poems on being young and Latino in the United States.* New York: Henry Holt.

Cart. M. (Ed.). (2001). *Love and sex: Ten stories of truth.* New York: Simon & Schuster.

Cart, M. (Ed.). (2004). *Rush hour: Bad boys.* New York: Random House.

Cart, M. (Ed.). (2005). *Rush hour: Face.* New York: Random House.

Cart, M. (Ed.). (2006). *Rush hour: Reckless.* New York: Random House.

Cormier, R. (1977). *I am the cheese.* New York: Knopf/Random House.

Cormier, R. (1980). *8 plus 1.* New York: Pantheon/Random House.

Corrigan, E. (2002). *You remind me of you: A poetry memoir.* New York: PUSH/Scholastic.

Coville, B. (2006). *Odds are good: An oddly enough and odder than ever omnibus.* Orlando, FL: Harcourt.

Creech, S. (2001). *Love that dog.* New York: HarperCollins.

Creech, S. (2005). *Replay.* New York: HarperCollins.

Crutcher, C. (1991). *Athletic shorts: 6 short stories.* New York: Greenwillow/HarperCollins.

Cuddon, J. A. (1999). *Dictionary of literary terms and literary theory* (4th ed.). Rev. C. E. Preston. New York: Penguin/Putnam.

DeVita, J. (2004). A *midnight cry: The underground railroad to freedom.* Woodstock, IL: Dramatic Publishing.

Duncan, L. (Ed.). (1996). *Night terrors: Stories of shadow and substance.* New York: Simon Pulse/Simon & Schuster.

Dunning, S., Lueders, E., & Smith, H. L. (1966). *Reflections on a gift of watermelon pickle . . . and other modern verse.* New York: Scott, Foresman.

Eliot, T. S. (1976). *The love song of J. Alfred Prufrock.* Mattituck, NY: Amereon, Ltd. (Original work published 1915)

Fehler, G. (1991). *Center field grasses: Poems from baseball.* Jefferson, NC: McFarland.

Fleischman, P. (1985). *I am phoenix: Poems for two voices.* New York: Harper & Row.

Fleischman, P. (1988). *Joyful noise: Poems for two voices.* New York: Harper & Row.

Fleischman, P. (2000). *Big talk: Poems for four voices.* Cambridge, MA: Candlewick Press.

Fleischman, P. (2003). *Breakout.* Chicago: Cricket.

Frost, H. (2003). *Keesha's house.* New York: Farrar, Straus & Giroux.

Frost, H. (2004). *Spinning through the universe.* New York: Farrar, Straus & Giroux.

Frost, H. (2006). *The braid.* New York: Farrar, Straus & Giroux.

Frost, H. (2008). *Diamond willow.* New York: Farrar, Straus & Giroux.

Frost, R. (2001). *Stopping by woods on a snowy evening* (Susan Jeffers, Illus.). New York: Dutton/Penguin. (Original poem published 1928; Original illustrated version published 1978)

Gallo, D. (Ed.). (1984). *Sixteen: Short stories by outstanding writers for going adults.* New York: Delacorte/Random House.

Gallo, D. (Ed.). (1990). *Center stage: One-act plays for teenage readers and actors.* New York: HarperTrophy.

Gallo, D. (Ed.). (2004). *First crossing: Stories about teen immigrants.* Cambridge, MA: Candlewick Press.

Gallo, D. (Ed.). (2008). *Owning it: Stories about teens with disabilities.* Cambridge, MA: Candlewick Press.

Giovanni, N. (1993). *Ego-tripping and other poems for young people* (George Ford, Illus.). Chicago: Chicago Review Press. (Original work published 1973)

Giovanni, N. (Ed.). (1994). *Grand mothers: Poems, reminiscences and short stories about the keepers of our traditions.* New York: Henry Holt.

Giovanni, N. (1996). *Selected poems of Nikki Giovanni* (Virginia Fowler, Illus.). New York: HarperCollins.

Giovanni, N. (1997). *Love poems.* New York: HarperCollins.

Giovanni, N. (1999a). *Blues for all the changes: New poems.* New York: HarperCollins.

Giovanni, N. (Ed.). (1999b). *Grand fathers: Reminiscences, poems, recipes, and photos of the keepers of our tradition.* New York: Henry Holt.

Giovanni, N. (1999c). Speech given at GCTE. Savannah, GA.

Giovanni, N. (2002). *Quilting the black-eyed pea: Poems and not quite poems.* New York: HarperCollins.

Giovanni, N. (2003). *The collected poetry of Nikki Giovanni: 1968–1998* (Virginia Fowler, Illus.). New York: HarperCollins.

Giovanni, N. (2007a). *Acolytes: Poems.* New York: Morrow/HarperCollins.

Giovanni, N. (2007b). *On my journey now: Looking at African-American history through the spirituals.* Cambridge, MA: Candlewick Press.

Grandits, J. (2004). *Technically, it's not my fault: Concrete poems.* New York: Clarion.

Greenberg, J. (2001). *Heart to heart: New poems inspired by twentieth-century American art.* New York: Harry N. Abrams.

Grimes, N. (2005). *Dark sons.* New York: Jump at the Sun/Hyperion.

Grover, L. (2002). *Loose threads.* New York: Simon & Schuster.

Grover, L. (2004). *On pointe.* New York: Simon & Schuster.

Hawthorne, N. (2005). *Young Goodman Brown.* Rockville, MD: Wildside Press. (Original work published 1835)

Herrick, S. (2004a). *Love, ghosts & facial hair.* New York: Simon Pulse/Simon & Schuster.

Herrick, S. (2004b). *The simple gift.* New York: Simon Pulse/Simon & Schuster.

Herrick, S. (2004c). *A place like this.* New York: Simon Pulse/Simon & Schuster.

Herrick, S. (2007). *The wolf.* Hondesdale, PA: Front Street/Boyds Mills Press.

Hesse, K. (1997). *Out of the dust.* New York: Scholastic.

Hesse, K. (2001). *Witness.* New York: Hyperion.

Holbrook, S. (2005). *Practical poetry: A nonstandard approach to meeting content-area standards.* Portsmouth, NH: Heinemann.

Hopkins, E. (2004). *Crank.* New York: Simon Pulse/Simon & Schuster.

Hopkins, E. (2006). *Burned.* New York: Simon & Schuster.

Hopkins, E. (2007). *Glass.* New York: Simon & Schuster.

Howe, J. (Ed.). (2001). *The color of absence: 12 stories about loss and hope.* New York: Atheneum/Simon & Schuster.

Koertge, R. (2001). *The Brimstone journals.* Cambridge, MA: Candlewick Press.

Kutiper, K., & Wilson, P. (1993). Updating poetry preferences: A look at the poetry children really like. *The Reading Teacher, 47*(1), 28–35.

Lanagan, M. (2005). *Black juice.* New York: HarperCollins.

Lanagan, M. (2006). *White time.* New York: EOS/HarperCollins.

Lanagan, M. (2007). *Red spikes.* New York: Knopf/Random House.

Lear, E. (2002). *A book of nonsense.* London: Taylor and Francis. (Original work published 1846)

Levy, A. (2006). *Pizza with shrimp on top.* Woodstock, IL: Dramatic Publishing.

Lewis, J. P. (1991). *Earth verses and water rhymes.* Illus. Robert Sabuda. New York: Atheneum/Simon & Schuster.

Lewis, J. P. (1998). *Doodle dandies: Poems that take shape.* Illus. Lisa Desimini. New York: Atheneum/Simon & Schuster.

Lewis, J. P. (1999). *The Bookworm's feast: A potluck of poems.* Illus. John O'Brien. New York: Dial/Penguin.

Lewis, J. P. (2000). *Freedom like sunlight: Praisesongs for black Americans.* Mankato, MN: Creative Editions.

Lewis, J. P. (2002a). *Arithme-tickle: An even number of odd riddle-rhymes.* Illus. Frank Remkiewicz. Orlando, FL: Harcourt.

Lewis, J. P. (2002b). *A world of wonders: Geographic travels in verse and rhyme.* Illus. Alison Jay. New York: Dial/Penguin.

Lewis, J. P. (2003a). *The snowflake sisters.* Illus. Lisa Desimini. New York. Atheneum/Simon & Schuster.

Lewis, J. P. (2003b). *Swan song.* Illus. Christopher Wormell. Mankato, MN: Creative Editions.

Lewis, J. P. (2004a). *Scien-trickery: Riddles in science.* Illus. Frank Remkiewicz. Orlando, FL: Harcourt.

Lewis, J. P. (2004b). *The stolen smile.* Illus. Gary Kelley. Mankato, MN: Creative Editions.

Lewis, J. P. (2005a). *Galileo's universe.* Illus. Tom Curry. Mankato, MN: Creative Editions.

Lewis, J. P. (2005b). *Heroes and she-roes: Poems of amazing and everyday heroes.* Illus. Jim Cooke. New York: Dial/Penguin.

Lewis, J. P. (2005c). *Monumental verses.* Washington, DC: National Geographic Society.

Lewis, J. P. (2005d). *Please bury me in the library.* Illus. Kyle M. Stone. Orlando, FL: Gulliver/Harcourt.

Lewis, J. P. (2006a). *Black cat bone: The life of blues legend Robert Johnson.* Illus. Gary Kelley. Mankato, MN: Creative Editions.

Lewis, J. P. (2006b). *Blackbeard the pirate king.* Illus. Jeffrey Thompson. Washington, DC: National Geographic Society.

Lewis, J. P. (2006c). *Castles: Cold stone poems* (with Rebecca Kai Dotlich). Illus. Dan Burr. Honesdale, PA: Boyds Mills Press.

Lewis, J. P. (2006d). *Once up a tomb: Gravely humorous verses.* Illus. Simon Bartram. Cambridge, MA: Candlewick Press.

Lewis, J. P. (2006e). *Vherses: A celebration of outstanding women.* Illus. Mark Summers. Mankato, MN: Creative Editions.

Lewis, J. P. (2006f). *Wing nuts: Screwy haiku.* Illus. Tricia Tusa. New York: Little, Brown.

Lewis, J. P. (2007). *The brothers' war: Civil War voices in verse.* Washington, DC: National Geographic Society.

Lewis, J. P., & Robb, L. (2007). *Poems for teaching in the content areas.* New York: Scholastic.

Longfellow, H. W. (1990). *Paul Revere's ride.* Illus. Ted Rand. New York: Dutton/Penguin. (Original work published 1861)

Longfellow, H. W. (2001). *The midnight ride of Paul Revere.* Illus. Christopher Bing. New York: Handprint.

Longfellow, H. W. (2003). *Paul Revere's ride.* Illus. Monica Vachula. Honesdale, PA: Boyds Mills Press.

Milner, J.O., & Milner, L. F. (2003). *Bridging English* (3rd ed.). Upper Saddle River, NJ: Merrill/Prentice Hall.

Myers, W. D. (2000). *145th Street: Short Street.* New York: Delacorte/Random House.

National Institute of Child Health and Human Development (NICHD). (2000). *Report of the National Reading Panel. Teaching children to read: An evidence-based assessment of the scientific research literature on reading and its implications for reading instruction* (NIH Publication No. 00–4769). Washington, DC: U.S. Government Printing Office.

Nelson, M. (2001). *Carver: A life in poems.* Asheville, NC: Front Street/Boyds Mills Press.

Noyes, D. (Ed.). (2004). *Gothic! Ten original dark tales.* Cambridge, MA: Candlewick Press.

Noyes, D. (Ed.). (2007). *The restless dead: Ten original stories of the supernatural.* Cambridge, MA: Candlewick Press.

Nye, N. S., & Janeczko, P. (1996). *I feel a little jumpy around you: A book of her poems & his poems collected in pairs.* New York: Simon & Schuster.

Paulsen, G. (1993). *Harris and me.* Orlando, FL: Harcourt.

Peck, R. (2004). *Past, perfect, present tense: New and collected stories.* New York: Dial/Penguin.

Pikulski, J. J. (2006). Fluency: A developmental and language perspective. In S. J. Samuels & A. E. Farstrup (Eds.), *What research has to say about fluency instruction* (3rd ed., pp. 70–93). Newark, DE: International Reading Association.

Readence, J., Bean, T. W., & Baldwin, R. S. (2004). *Content area reading: An integrated approach.* Dubuque, IA: Kendall/Hunt.

Rochman, H., & McCampbell, D. Z. (1997). *Leaving home.* New York: Cotler/HarperCollins.

Rosoff, M. (2004). *How I live now.* New York: Lamb/Random House.

Rylant, C. (1985). *Every living thing.* New York: Simon & Schuster.

Rylant, C. (2003). *God went to beauty school.* Orlando, FL: Harcourt.

Rylant, C. (2005). *Boris.* Orlando, FL: Harcourt.

Rylant, C. (2006). *Ludie's life.* Orlando, FL: Harcourt.

Salisbury, G. (2002). *Island boyz: Short stories.* New York: Random House.

Samuels, S. J. (2006). Toward a model of reading fluency. In S. J. Samuels, & A. E. Farstrup (Eds.), *What research has to say about fluency instruction* (3rd ed., pp. 24–46). Newark, DE: International Reading Association.

Silverstein, S. (1974). *Where the sidewalk ends: The poems and drawings of Shel Silverstein.* New York: Harper & Row.

Singer, M. (Ed.). (1998). *Stay true: Short stories for strong girls.* New York: Scholastic.

Singer, M. (Ed.). (2005). *Make me over: 11 original stories about transforming ourselves.* New York: Dutton/Penguin.

Sones, S. (1999). *Stop pretending: What happened when my big sister went crazy.* New York: HarperCollins.

Sones, S. (2001). *What my mother doesn't know.* New York: Simon & Schuster.

Sones, S. (2004). *One of those hideous books where the mother dies.* New York: Simon & Schuster.

Sones, S. (2007). *What my girlfriend doesn't know.* New York: Simon & Schuster.

Soto, G. (1990). *Baseball in April and other stories.* Orlando, FL: Harcourt.

Soto, G. (1993). *Local news: A collection of stories.* Orlando, FL: Harcourt.

Soto, G. (1997). *Novio boy: A play.* San Diego: Harcourt.

Soto, G. (1998). *Petty crimes.* Orlando, FL: Harcourt.

Soto, G. (1999). *Nerdlandia: A play.* New York: Penguin.

Soto, G. (2004). *Nickel and dime.* Albuquerque: University of New Mexico Press.

Soto, G. (2005). *Help wanted: Stories.* Orlando, FL: Harcourt.

Soto, G. (2006). *A fire in my hands.* Orlando, FL: Harcourt.

Soto, G. (2008). *Facts of life: Stories.* Orlando, FL: Harcourt.

Spenser, E. (1979). *The faerie queen.* New York: Penguin. (Original work published 1590)

Stevenson, R. L. (2006). *The moon.* Illus. Tracey Campbell Pearson. New York: Farrar, Straus & Giroux.

Stolarz, L. F. (2006). *Bleed.* New York: Hyperion.

Teasley, A. B., & Wilder, A. (1997). *Reel conversations: Reading films with young adults.* Portsmouth, NH: Boynton/Cook.

Thomas, J. C. (Ed.). (1990). *A gathering of flowers: Stories about being young in America.* New York: Harper & Row.

Weaver, C. (2002). *Reading process and practice* (3rd ed.). Portsmouth, NH: Heinemann.

Weiss, M. J. (Ed.). (2006). *Dreams and visions: Fourteen flights of fantasy.* New York: Tor.

Weiss, M. J., & Weiss, H. S. (1997). *From one experience to another: Award-winning authors share real-life experiences through fiction.* New York: Tor.

Weiss, M. J., & Weiss, H. S. (2000). *Lost and found: Award-winning authors sharing real-life experiences through fiction.* New York: Forge.

Weiss, M. J., & Weiss, H. S. (2002). *Big city cool: Short stories about urban youth.* New York: Persea.

Wild, M. (2004). *Jinx.* New York: Simon Pulse/Simon & Schuster.

Wilder, A., & Teasley, A. B. (1998). The high school connection: Young adult literature in the high school. *The ALAN Review, 26*(1), 42–45.

Willard, N. (1981). *A visit to William Blake's Inn: Poems for innocent and experienced travelers.* Illus. Beppe Giacobbe. Orlando, FL: Harcourt.

Wolff, V. E. (1993). *Make lemonade: A novel.* New York: Henry Holt.

Nonfiction, Autobiographies, Biographies, Diaries, and Memoirs

Reading Skills: Text Structure and Summarizing

Introduction

The Internet hurled us head first into an unprecedented age of exploding information. Less than three decades after its creation, we face *knowledge economy*—how do we manage, organize, store, and learn an overwhelming amount of new information? According to Lyman and Varian (2003), researchers at UC Berkeley's School of Information Management and Systems, new information is stored in four physical media: film, print, optical, and magnetic. These four forms produced about five exabytes of new information in 2002.

What's an exabyte?

The Library of Congress's 19 million books and other print collections, if digitized, would be 10 terabytes of information. Five exabytes could store the collections of half a million libraries the size of the Library of Congress. Staggering?

Today information is easily accessed through the telephone, radio, TV, the Internet, or the written page. We have conversations in our homes, at school, in social settings, and in the workplace. When a question arises, we google, we text message, we telephone, we turn to print. Accessibility to information has altered the way we think and what we believe. We're no longer a society satisfied with simplistic answers or content with what others tell us. We're more educated and more curious. We demand information.

What does this change mean for teen readers and the classroom? Educators have long acknowledged the shallow nature of textbooks, and publishers have an even harder time today making decisions about what to include and how much to say about any given topic. Even the best textbooks become outdated before going to press. Fortunately, publishing houses continually flood the market with a wide range of nonfiction texts, subject specific, for all content areas. Information on any imaginable topic is readily available, and new printing technologies have made nonfiction more visually appealing.

Numerous factors have contributed to the growth of young adult nonfiction over the last decade: an increased focus on content area reading, the Information Age, a more educated community, an interest in global issues, and new technologies that make for better, more beautiful texts. A noticeable concern, however, is the lack of quality nonfiction for older teens. A plethora of books for middle schoolers and series after series of nonfiction titles are produced for at-risk readers, but fewer in-depth and challenging books are marketed specifically for older, more accomplished readers. As you read through the titles in this chapter that can support, deepen, and extend course content, you will find a sampling of adult nonfiction appropriate for mature readers. I've also included a sampling of nonfiction picture books for all ages. The last section of this chapter discusses how to use young adult literature to introduce various text structures and provides activities for teaching students how to summarize.

Nonfiction

Nonfiction texts deliver factual material on any imaginable topic. Illustrations, graphs, charts, tables, and photographs generally accompany text, and format and length vary considerably. Nonfiction employs more difficult text structures (e.g., compare/contrast, cause/effect, and problem/solution) and introduces complex vocabulary with few context clues to aid comprehension. Though complex text structures are predominant in nonfiction, lines separating nonfiction and fiction are not sharply defined. Many of today's nonfiction writers borrow literary structure and form from their fiction counterparts. This tendency can be traced back to the latter part of the 20th century when news reporters and journalists began testing the boundaries between fiction and nonfiction.

When Truman Capote learned of the brutal 1959 slayings of a wealthy Kansas farmer, his wife, and two children, he traveled to Kansas (accompanied by his childhood friend, author Harper Lee) to investigate and write about the murders. The pair spent years pouring over the case, taking notes, and talking with residents and investigators. The result was *In Cold Blood* (1965).[1] Described by Capote as a *nonfiction novel*,[2] the book spawned a new nonfiction genre. *In Cold Blood* read like a novel, not a news account of a tragic event. By the 1970s and 1980s critics were using the term *new journalism* to describe nonfiction writing that contained fictional elements. An edited collection of journalist articles by Tom Wolfe and E. W. Johnson (1973) served as a manifesto for this new literary form. Nonfiction writers began relating factual information through scene-by-scene construction. That is, rather than relying on historical narrative or secondhand accounts, the writer re-creates the events for the reader. New journalism also adopted dialogue. Traditionally, nonfiction writers used quotations and public "statements" to support their ideas; as a result of the new journalism movement, they began re-creating actual conversations in an effort to define and establish character. Everyday details about surroundings became important. Considered irrelevant in the past, new journalism proponents believed everyday details helped readers envision people as they actually are. Finally, advocates believed readers should get inside a person's head, to know what people are thinking or believing, to understand their motivation. They believed instead of simply reporting facts, journalists should create for readers a *feeling*. Third-person point of view gave way to first-person narrative. Despite these borrowings from literary

---

[1] *In Cold Blood* was released first in a four-part series by *The New Yorker* prior to its publication by Random House.
[2] Also known as creative nonfiction. See the discussion in Chapter 6, "Historical Fiction."

fiction, nonfiction writers maintained credibility by strict adherence to facts and accuracy and by the writer being the primary researcher/reporter.

This trend has continued today and has altered the way in which nonfiction texts are written. Some writers today are pushing the literary form further by experimenting with nonfiction poetry (e.g., Marilyn Nelson). Nonfiction writers present their story in much the same way as fiction writers (e.g., scene construction, dialogue). Lines between fiction and nonfiction blur to the point that sometimes it's difficult to determine whether a work is a historical fiction novel or a nonfiction account of a historical event—a decisive factor remains the invention of fictional people and events. Books lie somewhere on the continuum between the two. In the discussions that follow, I've attempted to stay more closely aligned with the nonfiction side of the continuum.

The Missing Genre

Students are exposed daily to nonfiction in content area classrooms (science, history, mathematics, art, psychology), but they experience it minimally in English language arts classrooms. English language arts reading assignments are almost exclusively fiction: novels, short stories, poetry, and drama. Even the term *novel* is the standard term for *books* in curricula planning and class assignments. Reading programs (e.g., Accelerated Reader) and summer reading lists rarely contain nonfiction reads, and class book sets are almost always fiction (with the exception of an occasional biography or autobiography). Literary awards are given primarily for fiction. Whether intentional or not, nonfiction is noticeably absent from the English language arts curriculum. The message sent: nonfiction isn't important.

Why is nonfiction held with so little regard? Why do teachers and librarians support what Sullivan (2001) calls a *fictioncentric* curriculum?

One reason is simply habit. We've always taught fiction in the English language arts classroom; therefore, we will continue to teach fiction. This inclination is deeply grounded. During silent reading, for instance, some teachers insist that students read novels—no magazines, newspapers, and so forth—a practice that sends the message that reading anything other than a novel isn't *real* reading. Influenced by teacher and librarian attitudes, teens don't view their recreational reading as *real* reading. When asked about what they read, teens typically name novels or say they don't read. They fail to mention their Internet reading, their favorite magazines, game books, manuals, almanacs, newspapers, and so forth. If they do mention these, they may offer up an apology for reading "junk."

Another reason nonfiction isn't valued is our romantic notion of fiction—the long-standing belief that fiction gives us insight into humanity, helping us understand ourselves, our fellow human beings, and the world in which we live. Much of this belief is grounded in Louise Rosenblatt's transactional theory of reading, known by most teachers as reader-response theory (see Chapter 2). The problem is most teachers concentrate on only part of the theory. In her seminal work, *The Reader, the Text, the Poem* (1978), Rosenblatt asserts we read for two purposes: aesthetic (pleasure) and efferent (information).

Teachers tend to focus on the power of the personal connection and approach reader-response with the belief that we only read fiction aesthetically; however, a teen who loves to cook can read a cookbook for both aesthetic and efferent purposes. A mature teen reader who is fascinated by Vietnam can read *Dispatches* (1977) from an aesthetic and efferent stance.

Teachers also lack skill in knowing *how* to teach for information. Just as they do with fiction, teens can make deep and meaningful connections with nonfiction. Teachers, however, tend to approach nonfiction as though they're on a "fact-finding" mission. Rarely are students encouraged to make connections with self, other texts, and the world when reading nonfiction. Abrahamson and Carter (1991) offer guidelines for encouraging meaningful responses to nonfiction texts. Though two decades old, their suggestions remain relevant:

1. How would this book be different if it had been written 10 years earlier? Ten years later?
2. Which illustrations do you wish you had taken or drawn yourself? Why?
3. Compare this nonfiction book with another one written on the same topic. How do they differ? How are they alike? Which one do you like better (or believe more)? Why?
4. What segment, portion, or focus of this book would make a good documentary? Why?
5. What steps do you think the author followed to research and write this book?
6. How would this book be different if it had been written for a fourth grader?
7. What kind of teacher do you think the author would make?
8. If you had a chance to interview the authors of this book, what would you ask them?
9. Tell me three facts, theories, or incidents that you found particularly interesting. Now, assume you haven't read the book. Can you find this information? Why or why not?
10. Look at the title and the jacket of this book. What do they indicate the book will be about? Do they give a fair representation of the book's contents? (pp. 185–187)

Another reason nonfiction plays an insignificant role in the English language arts classroom is teacher exposure to the genre. Most education majors have little opportunity to develop and implement instructional plans for nonfiction. They spend their energies on reading, studying, and preparing to teach the classics (novel units), writing, and grammar. Little emphasis is given to instructional plans based on essays, letters, articles, documentaries, and so forth. A question that arises, too, is what kind of reading do English language arts teachers choose for leisure? Do they choose nonfiction? Are they familiar with nonfiction works written in the new journalism style? Or do they have misconceptions about nonfiction being dry, boring, and factual? It might be that preservice and in-field teachers themselves have an erroneous view of nonfiction. A related factor that comes into play is gender. Nonfiction is more popular with males; female educators are the majority. Do male teachers read more nonfiction and know it better than their female counterparts?

A crucial issue in the marginalization of nonfiction is the myth that teens don't like it. However, Abrahamson and Carter (1991) cite several studies that show a strong interest in nonfiction emerges in fourth grade and continues through the teen years; and while statistics vary, studies indicate that nonfiction makes up a third to half of teen's leisure reading. In fact, research shows an increasing gap between what students want to read and what schools provide (Worthy, Moorman, & Turner, 1999).

Negative perceptions of nonfiction young adult books arise from an abundance of poorly written nonfiction, which are money makers for publishing houses but do little to support the value of nonfiction. Many turn out "dummied" down titles written in short, choppy, simplistic sentences and a condescending, elementary, and nonengaging tone. A large percentage are carelessly written, biased, and inaccurate. (See Table 10.1 for guiding questions for evaluating nonfiction.) The fact that nonfiction is marketed

Table 10.1

Questions for Evaluating and Selecting Nonfiction

- Is the author an authority in his/her field?
- Can you find evidence of slanted or biased writing?
- Does the author make sweeping generalizations or are points well documented?
- Is this an area of expertise for the publisher and editor?
- Is information accurate and up to date?
- Is it documented well? Are references made to primary or secondary sources?
- Is the book organized and structured in a clear manner? Are headings and subheadings laid out plainly?
- What role does diversity play in the text?
- Are the table of contents, glossary, index, and appendixes complementary to the text? Are they easy to use and helpful?
- Do illustrations and other visuals (e.g., charts, diagrams, graphs, photos, sketches, maps) support the text? Are they easy to follow or confusing? Are they supported by useful captions?
- Is there a clear distinction between fact and opinion?
- Are there elements of fiction? If so, is the work nonfiction or historical fiction?
- Is the text appropriate for the age group? What about tone? Does sentence structure vary or are sentences short, choppy, and primarily structured in subject/verb order? When read out loud, does the text sound condescending? (Does it sound as though it were written for elementary students?)
- Is the writing style engaging?
- Are directions in how-to books complete and easy to follow? Are step-by-step illustrations clear?
- If a common topic, what does this book offer that others do not? Is it better? Is it worth the cost?

and talked about in educational circles as "informational texts," a term suggesting "resource materials," adds another negative mark. Resource materials are thought of as being factual and dry and are primarily used for report writing.

How can we make a case for incorporating nonfiction in the English language arts classroom? Nonfiction texts can function as resource tools *and* as aesthetic reading experiences. In much the same way that fiction ignites the imagination and satisfies the curiosity of fiction fans, nonfiction is the kindling for many adolescents. It is their preferred reading choice. As they mature, teens develop the need to understand things about themselves and the world in which they live; they develop a need to explore, to discover truths, make connections, and find answers to questions they're uncomfortable asking. When we don't make nonfiction available, we turn our backs on their real reading interests and needs. Nonfiction can be the fuel that turns teens into lifelong readers and learners. By excluding it, we throw away possibilities for engagement and learning; we throw water on a glowing coal.

Ironically, in classrooms that exclude nonfiction, students are required to *write* nonfiction. They write essays, news briefs, research papers, lab reports, and more—all writing genres that increase in complexity, yet they have little chance to examine the models they are trying to create. It stands to reason that well-written nonfiction texts can and should serve as writing models. Nonfiction texts provide opportunities for teens to critically examine text structure, evaluate "truth," and differentiate between fact and opinion. Through reading nonfiction, students can learn to evaluate slanted or biased writing, and they gain a better understanding of rhetoric and how good writers compose arguments. Nonfiction can also help readers understand style, subtle arguments, irony, and sarcasm. By excluding nonfiction we fail to expose students to the forms of writing we expect them to do.

A further argument for reading nonfiction in the English language arts class is that doing so can eradicate the disconnect between the kind of reading teens do in English and what they experience in other content areas. Nonfiction is the primary text form teens read in other course work and becomes a chief stumbling block for adolescents as they move from elementary to the middle grades and then from middle to secondary schools where they are required to read increasingly longer, more complex texts. Incorporating nonfiction into the English language arts curriculum prepares teens to tackle the complex text structures they encounter in other subjects.

Teachers who set out to make nonfiction an integral part of the curriculum find their lessons richer and their students more engaged. Box 10.1 contains annotations for books that can alter negative beliefs about nonfiction. These are excellent books for mature high school students, but they also are a superb introduction for teachers who want to explore the adult world of nonfiction for personal and professional enrichment.

Box 10.1 Adult Nonfiction for Mature Readers

***All the President's Men* by Carl Bernstein and Bob Woodward. New York: Simon & Schuster, 1974.**

The story that broke open the Watergate scandal. Pulitzer Prize–winning investigators Bernstein and Woodward narrate the behind-the-scenes events the way they occurred.

***The Assassins' Gate: America in Iraq* by George Packer. New York: Farrar, Straus & Giroux, 2005.**

Journalist George Packer describes in detail how we became involved in the Iraq War and provides a history of neo-conservatism and its role in America's political fabric.

***Blink: The Power of Thinking without Thinking* by Malcolm Gladwell. New York: Little, Brown, 2005.**

This national bestseller shows that the difference between making good choices and bad ones has little to do with how much information we have and more to do with gut reactions.

***Dispatches from the Edge* by Anderson Cooper. New York: HarperCollins, 2006.**

Cooper narrates his experiences as a journalist covering the tragic events of 2005: the tsunami in Asia, increased violence in Iraq, Katrina, and famine in Africa.

***Fates Worse Than Death: An Autobiographical Collage of the 1980s* by Kurt Vonnegut. New York: Putnam, 1991.**

A collection of essays that examines the issues and events of the 1980s. A combination of personal recollections and political commentary.

***Freakonomics: A Rogue Economist Explores the Hidden Side of Everything* by Steven D. Levitt and Stephen J. Dubner. New York: HarperCollins, 2005.**

Levitt and Dubner use economics to address questions that seem removed from the discipline (e.g., how to determine if teachers help students on standardized testing).

***If I Die in a Combat Zone, Box Me Up and Ship Me Home* by Tim O'Brien. New York: Delacorte/Random House, 1973.**

A personal account of one year in O'Brien's life as a foot soldier in the Vietnam conflict.

***Lies My Teacher Told Me: Everything Your American History Textbook Got Wrong* by James W. Loewen. New York: W. W. Norton, 1995.**

Loewen meticulously researched American history books at the Smithsonian Institution. This book details the omissions, untruths, and misrepresentations he found.

***A Short History of Nearly Everything* by Bill Bryson. New York: Broadway Books, 2003.**

An informative account of the world of science. In this bestseller, Bryson addresses some of the oldest questions about the universe and humanity. How did we come to be; how has civilization evolved?

***Stiff: The Curious Lives of Human Cadavers* by Mary Roach. New York: W. W. Norton, 2003.**

A humorous, yet factual look at what happens to humans after they die. Based on Roach's travels

Continued

Box 10.1 Adult Nonfiction for Mature Readers *Continued*

around the globe and her work in forensic science investigations. Readers may also enjoy *Spook: Science Tackles the Afterlife* (2005).

Voices from the Future edited by Susan Goodwillie. New York: Crown, 1993.

A collection of interviews in which teens talk about the violence in their lives.

The World Is Flat: A Brief History of the Twenty-first Century by Thomas L. Friedman. New York: Farrar, Straus & Giroux, 2005.

Based on Friedman's worldwide travels, this is an account of the challenges and changes taking place in our time as we become a more technologically connected global society.

Historical Perspective

The first book written specifically for a younger audience was *Orbis Pictus* by John Amos Comenius, a nonfiction work. First published in Latin and German in 1658 and in English in 1659, *Orbis Pictus* was a children's encyclopedia, illustrated with woodcuts and covering topics such as botany, zoology, human activities, and religion. The first recipient of the John Newbery Medal was *The Story of Mankind* (1921), a "history of the world" written especially for children by Hendrik van Loon. Though obviously outdated and not factual by today's standards, the work illustrates an early effort to create nonfiction for young readers.

Interestingly, early on women made substantial contributions to nonfiction for children and teens. Elizabeth Seeger's *Pageant of Chinese History* (1934) earned a Newbery Honor, and Katherine Shippen penned two Newbery Honor books, *New Found World* (1945) and *Men, Microscopes, and Living Things* (1954). Genevieve Foster also earned a Newbery Honor for *Birthdays of Freedom* (1952). Although young adult nonfiction is a male-dominated authors' market, it's by no means exclusive. A number of notable women do write young adult nonfiction. Susan Bartoletti, for instance, has written several distinguished nonfiction titles. *Black Potatoes: The Story of the Great Irish Famine, 1845–1850* (2001a), a 2004 Robert Sibert Medalist, explains the horrific effects the infamous potato blight had on 6 million people who scavenged fields for snippets of vegetables and edible weeds. Many died of starvation and disease, others fled their homes. Some committed deliberate crimes, hoping to be jailed where they would be fed. *Hitler Youth: Growing Up in Hitler's Shadow* (2005), a Sibert Medal Honor book, explores the Hitler Youth program (Hitlerjugend) and Hitler's efforts to draw German youth into his folds through camping trips, parades, and other alluring activities. See Bartoletti's comments in the author box about writing *Hitler Youth*.

Gerald W. Johnson penned one of the first nonfiction series for youth. *America Is Born: A History for Peter* (1959), *America Grows Up: A History for Peter* (1960a), and *America Moves On: A History for Peter* (1960b) trace the historical roots and growth of our nation. Since Johnson's series, dozens of publishing

Hitler Youth   by Susan Bartoletti

I have long been interested in the power and potential power of children and teenagers. In my other books, I have often explored the agency of young people who banded together to improve their working and living conditions. I have also explored the lives of young people as they struggled to survive during dire times.

From teaching, I recognize the idealism of young people. I admire their energy and drive. I see their need to belong and to seek out role models and heroes. I also see young people who have a strong sense of right and wrong. Many are rebellious: They want the opportunity to access and transform the political systems in their lives.

Adolf Hitler had similar feelings. "I begin with the young," he once said. "We older ones are used up. . . . But my magnificent youngsters! Are there finer ones anywhere in the world? Look at all these men and boys! What material! With them I can make a new world."

Those words are chilling. They sound like words a teacher might say.

For me, a book doesn't begin with fact; it begins with the feeling I get about a fact. I was researching World War II when I stumbled across a 1944 magazine article in which the author claimed that the Nazi Party "rode to power on the shoulders of politically active youth."

Those words, that possibility, made my heart turn over.

Those words made me wonder. Was it true? What role did young people serve in Hitler's Third Reich? Did they help Adolf Hitler and his rising Nazi Party seize power in Germany? If so, were they willing monsters in his machinery of oppression and murder? Or were they brainwashed victims? Or something in-between?

When I get a feeling like that, when my heart turns over, there's only one place to go. The library. I hurried to the library to find out more. To find out if it was true.

I began to read all I could about Hitler Youth. I began to trace the lives of young people who lived in Germany and German-occupied territory during the years that we call the Third Reich. I researched the lives of the boys and girls who donned uniforms and who called themselves the Hitler Youth.

As I researched, as I pored over newspapers and magazines published in the 1930s, I was aghast at the volume of material that had warned us about Hitler and the Nazi Party and the threat they posed to world peace and the Jews.

By nature, human beings search to make sense and meaning out of their lives and their world. One way that we make meaning is through telling our stories. No matter our age, stories connect us, teach us, and warn us never to forget. That's the power of stories.

Kids want to know: Can it happen again? And at the end of my book, I ask them, "What are you willing to do to prevent such a shadow from falling over you and others?"

So when readers want to know if this could happen again, when they want to know what I think, I tell them this: take a generation of young people, teach them conformity, complete obeisance to authority, prohibit outlets for freedom of expression, suppress opinion and individual thought, teach them that brute strength matters more than intellect, suppress their imagination and creativity, ban books, teach them to hate and to enjoy power over others, teach them that they are entitled and privileged, and you will find your answer to that question.

The lessons of the Third Reich are lessons we must never forget and continue to learn. The issues that led and continue to lead to genocide—issues

Continued

Hitler Youth   *Continued*

such as racism, bullying, stereotyping, intellectual superiority, and arrogance, to name a few—are issues that we must continue to fight and confront.

Do I dare? Do we dare disturb the universe?

We want young readers to become capable meaning-makers. We want them to question and think critically about their education and institutions. (More hideous crimes have been committed in the name of obedience than rebellion.) We want them to formulate their own opinions, to decide for themselves, to think for themselves.

We want them to stand up. We want to give them the courage and the resources to do these things, so that they can stand up, so that they can make a difference, so that they will disturb the universe.

Each of us has a responsibility to disturb the universe. I am blessed to have work that my hands, my head, and my heart love, work that I hope helps to make this world a better place.

Other books by Bartoletti: *Growing Up in Coal Country* (1996), *Kids on Strike!* (1999a), *No Man's Land* (1999b), *A Coal Miner's Bride: The Diary of Annetka Kaminski* (2000), *The Christmas Promise* (2001b), *The Flag Maker* (2004), and *The Boy Who Dared* (2008).

houses and authors have created nonfiction series (both nonfiction and biographical). Today, National Geographic is an industry leader in the sheer number of series it produces. Other publishers who produce series include Chelsea House, Greenhaven Press, Lucent Books, Sterling Publishing, Twenty-First Century Books/Lerner, Heinemann, and Kingfisher Publications. Many of these companies (e.g., Twenty-First Century Books/Lerner), recognizing how easily nonfiction becomes outdated, construct Web sites to accompany their texts (e.g., www.inamericanbooks.com accompanies Lerner's *In America* series). Some series are exceptional, but many are "dummied down" texts for struggling readers.

Most early nonfiction focused on historical events and a smaller number on science, but few nonfiction books addressed the arts. Janet Gaylord Moore's Newbery Honor book, *The Many Ways of Seeing: An Introduction to the Pleasures of Art* (1968), is a notable exception. This work introduces readers to line, form, and color, teaching them to "read" and understand art. Today dozens of books take advantage of new technologies that produce and reproduce captivating images. *Vincent's Colors: Words and Pictures by Vincent van Gogh* (2005) is an example. Created by the Metropolitan Museum of Art, this work captures the essence of van Gogh's masterpieces. Rhyming stanzas, based on van Gogh's correspondence with his brother, accompany full-color reproductions of his famous paintings. Advanced technology underscores the color and vibrant detail of the brush strokes characteristic of van Gogh. Although marketed to younger readers, this book can be appreciated by all.

Russell Freedman, author of nearly 50 nonfiction titles, took teen nonfiction to a new level with his Newbery winner, *Lincoln: A Photobiography* (1987). Biographies are covered later in this chapter, but the impact Freedman's work had on the nonfiction field warrants mentioning this book now. In this meticulously researched account of Lincoln's life, Freedman provides a well-articulated and thoughtful account of Lincoln's childhood, his self-education, early business efforts, his rise to political fame, and his untimely death in the Ford Theatre. Placed throughout the text are dozens of complementary photos—some familiar, others rarely seen. Books on historical figures are plentiful, but Freedman's account of Lincoln's life exemplifies quality teen nonfiction. Since its publication, numerous other individuals have established themselves as authors of well-written, well-researched, and entertaining works suitable for older teens.

To honor quality nonfiction, the National Council of Teachers of English (NCTE) established the Orbis Pictus Nonfiction Award in 1990, named after van Loon's work, *The Story of Mankind* (1921). The award excludes works of fiction and historical fiction, but biographies are included. The first award, given in 1990, was to Jean Fritz's biography, *The Great Little Madison* (1989). Subsequent titles and honor books can be found on NCTE's Web site (www.ncte.org). The preponderance of winners suit elementary and lower middle grades; however, many of the picture books work well in content area classes as discussion prompts and mini-lessons.

In 1995 Scholastic published Jim Murphy's *The Great Fire* (1995), a nonfiction account of the infamous Chicago disaster of 1871 that debunks the popular myth that Mrs. O'Leary and her cow started the fire. Murphy's work illustrated to parents and educators worldwide that history need not be boring. Since publishing *The Great Fire,* Murphy has written over a dozen nonfiction and historical fiction works. In the author box he takes us behind the scenes with the creation of his award-winning *An American Plague: The True and Terrifying Story of the Yellow Fever Epidemic of 1793* (2003a).

From an Innocent Beginning   by Jim Murphy

My books often have very innocent beginnings. Take *An American Plague*. Sometime in the early 1990s I was unpacking boxes from a recent move when I came across one of my wife's books that I'd never seen before. It had an ominous black cover and was clearly very old.

Ordinarily, I would have put it aside and forgotten about it (we have around 4,000 books between us and many of them are very old), but the title stopped me. *Bring Out Your Dead* was emblazoned on the jacket in faded gold letters.

The thing is, I love reading about the Black Death, and I knew this phrase was used by carters when gathering up victims of bubonic plague. So I started reading the book. Only it wasn't about the Black Plague at all; it was about the yellow fever epidemic that hit Philadelphia in 1793.

Continued

From an Innocent Beginning   *Continued*

I might have stopped reading right there. I mean, yellow fever was a disease of the distant past that no one cared about, right? But I didn't stop reading. The author—J. H. Powell—mentions in the opening pages that yellow fever also had a nickname: the Black Vomit. That's almost as good as the Black Death, gooier and more disgusting really, so I had to see what this epidemic was all about. And when I finished his book, which is about how a disease brought the nation's largest, most powerful city, and temporary capital of the nation, to its knees, I remember thinking, "Now, I never knew about that."

And it was that little phrase that started me doing serious research on the epidemic.

For me, research is like detective work. I begin with a general objective—to know more about the subject. But as I gather in more and more of the details, I begin asking myself specific questions. What was Philadelphia like before the epidemic struck? Who was in the city at the time, and how did they react when they heard about the disease? Who ran to the safety of the countryside (half the city, it turned out, including George Washington, Thomas Jefferson, James Madison, and James Monroe, as well as every other elected or appointed official from the federal, state, and local government, except for the mayor of Philadelphia)? What did the few doctors brave enough to stay do to help fever victims? Were there any real heroes of the epidemic?

Each question prompted independent lines of investigation. For instance, I learned that doctors back in 1793 had virtually no real knowledge about the disease. They could chart its progress in a patient in great detail, but in the end they had no idea where it came from, how it spread, or how to treat it. The confusing nature of the illness prompted a great deal of experimentation, some of it ludicrous (such as one doctor's recommendation that spreading two inches of fresh dirt on the floor of every room every day would prevent the disease), some of it downright dangerous (such as Benjamin Rush's belief that bleeding patients until they fainted was the best form of treatment).

In addition to this, I investigated various theories of medicine that prevailed at the time, the doctor-patient relationship and how this factored into treatment, what sort of medicines were actually available and to whom, and the role that myth and legend played in people's day-to-day health care. And, of course, I had to understand the history of yellow fever after 1793 and our modern approach to the disease.

Powell's book provided some clues as to the route of his research, but his book was really aimed at a general readership and didn't include detailed notes on his sources. The good news was that Philadelphia is only two hours from my home, so I was able to make frequent visits over the next few years.

Preparation for my first trip there was simple. I bought a Fodor's guide to Philadelphia, which listed a wide variety of museums, libraries, and historical associations, and I called, then visited most of them. The Pennsylvania Historical Society was particularly important in helping me re-create what the city was like in 1793, and the College of Physicians of Philadelphia gave me insight into medical practices and individual doctors. The one institution that proved to be a treasure trove of yellow fever information was The Library Company. It has original firsthand accounts from the time, published books about the epidemic written by doctors, ministers, and ordinary citizens who survived that terrible summer, editions of the newspapers put out while the fever raged in the city, plus a wide variety of other material. Probably even more important was the help I received from The Library Company's Chief of Reference, Philip Lapsansky. He guided me to various important books (and pointed out changes in editions), answered my questions patiently, and had keen insights into the role played by the African American community during the illness, a subject I wanted to explore in detail in my book.

As you can imagine, all of this research took a good deal of time (somewhere between six and eight years), but it was well worth the effort. It not only let me get to know the subject in depth, it allowed me time to think about the topic and plan my approach to the book. If I remember correctly, there were two keys to the latter. The first was a line I found in printer Mathew Carey's history of the epidemic that went: "About this time, this destroying scourge, the malignant fever, crept in among us." I realized that this wasn't just an impersonal disease to the people

Continued

From an Innocent Beginning   *Continued*

of Philadelphia; it was a living thing come to stalk them. I decided to infuse the text with as much of this emotional aspect of the disease as possible, mostly through the use of quotes.

The other important element was how the doctors reacted to the illness, which was with fear and desperate remedies. They were completely baffled by the disease and so upset that they soon started squabbling among themselves and calling each other nasty names in the newspapers. It was, in short, a medical mystery to them, one they never solved. This led me to write the book so that today's readers would hear only what people in 1793 knew or assumed about yellow fever (holding back our current scientific knowledge of it until the very last chapter). In this way, I

hoped to let readers experience the epidemic just as someone would have over 200 years ago.

That's pretty much how the research helped shape the book, and how opening a box of old books led me on a long, interesting journey of discovery.

Copyright Jim Murphy, 2008

Official Web site: www.jimmurphybooks.com

Additional nonfiction titles include *The Boys' War: Confederate and Union Soldiers Talk about the Civil War* (1990), *The Long Road to Gettysburg* (1992), *Across America on an Emigrant Train* (1993), *The Great Fire* (1995), *A Young Patriot: The American Revolution as Experienced by One Boy* (1996), *Gone A-Whaling: The Lure of the Sea and the Hunt for the Great Whale* (1998), *Blizzard! The Storm That Changed America* (2000), *Pick & Shovel Poet: The Journeys of Pascal D'Angelo* (2000), *Inside the Alamo* (2003), and *The Real Benedict Arnold* (2007).

In 2001 the American Library Association established the Robert F. Sibert Informational Book Award, given annually to the most distinguished nonfiction book published the preceding year. Named in honor of Robert F. Sibert, former president of Bound To Stay Bound Books, the award has elevated the young adult nonfiction genre and is the most prestigious award for teen nonfiction. Winners are chosen based on accuracy, organization, design, and writing style. Marc Aronson, critically acclaimed nonfiction writer, editor, and historian, earned the first award for *Sir Walter Ralegh and the Quest for El Dorado* (2000), an accurate and lively account of the multifaceted life of Walter Ralegh, the famous Elizabethan explorer, poet, and soldier (historians now agree on the spelling of his name), and his quest for El Dorado, the mythical South American city of gold. Aronson has gone on to publish numerous award-winning works. See his discussion about researching *Witch-Hunt: Mysteries of the Salem Witch Trials* (2003b) in the author box.

Team Moon: How 400,000 People Landed Apollo 11 *on the Moon* (2006) by Catherine Thimmesh, a recent Sibert Medalist, demonstrates today's emphasis on quality nonfiction in science, mathematics, and technology classrooms. Dramatic NASA photographs accompany Thimmesh's unfolding narrative about the events that threatened the *Apollo 11* mission. Oral histories and personal interviews add a sense of urgency to the dramatic story. Because textbooks in the science, mathematics, and technology fields quickly become outdated, young adult nonfiction is an excellent supplemental resource. Nonfiction resources also keep readers abreast of current events. Al Gore has written two movie tie-ins to *An Inconvenient Truth,* his 2006 documentary film on the effects of global warning (see Box 10.2 for more documentaries). The first tie-in, *An Inconvenient Truth: The Planetary Emergency of Global Warming and What We Can Do about It* (2006), though not marketed to teen audiences, is chocked full of valuable information for the high school classroom. The scaled-down version, *An Inconvenient Truth: The Crisis of Global Warming* (2007), works better for younger readers. Beautiful images accompany both texts.

On Writing *Witch-Hunt: Mysteries of the Salem Witch Trials*   by Marc Aronson

When I set out to write a book on the Salem Witch Trials, I thought it would be easy. I started out in grad school as a medieval history major—focused on the history of heresy. I later switched to turn of the 20th century American history, but I also found myself taking one class after another about the colonial period. I was fascinated by the experiences of the devout Puritans as they interacted with a changing world.

I'd studied Salem in grad school, and it seemed to fit perfectly with my interests. When I told my mother I was writing about the trials, she reminded me that she and my father had designed the original sets for *The Crucible*. So I had family history to call on for *The Crucible* connection, and I also knew how to move past the Miller play. In grad school I read Paul Boyer and Stephen Nissenbaum's fine *Salem Possessed*, which carefully traced the financial and social tensions in Salem. I had also learned that the Puritans of 1692 were not the sexually repressed rigid characters of Miller's play. Indeed, in books like David Hall's wonderful *World of Wonders*, close reading of Puritan diaries showed that belief in portents, magic, astrology was common in New England. I knew that Tituba was not black, and that she did not bring any Caribbean island rituals to Salem. I set out to read the transcripts of the actual pretrial hearings in Salem (which are the records we have; we don't have the actual trial records) keeping all I had learned in graduate school in mind. I thought my book would update Miller by taking readers into the world as people experienced it in 1692—a world where people really did believe in witches.

And then I read *Salem Story* by Bernard Rosenthal. Rosenthal is a professor of English, and a very close reader. He read through the trial records as I was doing, but he came to a very different conclusion. Rosenthal was certain that the accusers lied, and knew they were lying. Salem was not a portrait

of medieval beliefs in America but of a consciously created plot. His best evidence was the fact that, often enough, accusers claimed that evil forces were sticking them with pins in court—and they produced the pins to prove it. He argued that if the accusers had props, they must have brought them. In fact in one case they were actually caught doing just that. If you bring props to court you have to plan. If you plan, you must have a reason, a calculated strategy.

Rosenthal stopped me in my tracks. I still think the anthropological understanding of New England beliefs is important. But he made a very good case that the accusers planned out their actions. He is less convincing about why. So I was faced with two distinct forms of explanation. And even as I started to write, I learned that the historian Mary Beth Norton had found new evidence, and had a new theory. She focused not on beliefs or accusers, but the judges. She found evidence that there had recently been clashes with Indians near Salem, and that many of the judges were either thought to have handled them poorly, or even to have sold guns to the Indians. She

Continued

On Writing *Witch-Hunt: Mysteries of the Salem Witch Trials*   *Continued*

did a good job of explaining the judges, but I found her analysis of the accusers less convincing.

As I wrote my book I had six approaches to Salem: Miller's, Boyer and Nissenbaum's, Hall's, Rosenthal's, Norton's, and my own reactions as I read the transcripts. I decided, then, that my book would be as much about the ways we put history together as it would be about Salem. I did not know, for sure, what happened there. I found parts of each explanation convincing. So I thought it best to let readers in on that conversation among scholars, equip them with information about what took place in Salem, and turn them loose.

I decided that my book would offer questions, not just answers. We may never know exactly why 19 people were hanged as witches in Salem. But I hope my book makes it easier for young people to use their interest in Salem to become thinkers, investigators, people who ask questions and form new theories. I want young people to read about Salem not just to explain that witch-hunt, but to sharpen their ability to think about anything in the past. That is certainly what studying Salem taught me.

Copyright Marc Aronson, 2008

Official Web site: www.marcarnson.com

Other works include *Art Attack: A Brief Cultural History of the Avant-Garde* (1998), *Exploding the Myths: The Truth about Teenagers and Reading* (2001), *Beyond the Pale: New Essays for a New Era* (2003a), *John Winthrop, Oliver Cromwell, and the Land of Promise* (2004), *The Real Revolution: The Global Story of American Independence* (2005), *Race: A History beyond Black and White* (2007a), *Up Close: Robert F. Kennedy* (2007b), *The World Made New: Why the Age of Exploration Happened and How It Changed the World* (with John W. Glenn) (2007c), *War Is . . . Soldiers, Survivors, and Story-tellers Talk about War* (co-editor Patty Campbell) (2008).

Box 10.2   Documentaries for Teens

American Experience: Ansel Adams by PBS, Paramount (2002).

Andy Warhol by PBS, Paramount (2006).

Auschwitz: Inside the Nazi State by BBC, Warner (2005).

Berkeley in the Sixties by First Run Features (1990).

Bowling for Columbine by MGM (2002).

Dalai Lama: The Soul of Tibet by A & E (2005).

Enron: The Smartest Guys in the Room by Magnolia (2004).

Fahrenheit 9/11 by Sony Pictures (2004).

The Fog of War by Sony Pictures (2003).

Hoop Dreams by Criterion (1994).

An Inconvenient Truth by PBS, Paramount (2006).

Jesus Camp by Magnolia (2006).

March of the Penguins by Warner (2005).

Murderball by Velocity/Thinkfilm (2005).

Outfoxed: Rupert Murdoch's War on Journalism by Disinformation (2004).

Roger & Me by Warner (1989).

Stephen Hawking's Universe by PBS, Paramount (2004).

Super Size Me by Hart Sharp Videos (2004).

The Thin Blue Line by MGM (1988).

Wetback by National Geographic (2004).

The interactive nonfiction book is a current trend in nonfiction. (See Chapter 12 for more interactive texts.) Once boring and drab, nonfiction now includes pages of glossy photos, some black and white and some with spectacular color. John Matthews, for instance, has created two outstanding interactive nonfiction books about pirates: *Pirates* (2006) and *Pirates Most Wanted:*

Thirteen of the Most Bloodthirsty Pirates Ever to Sail the High Seas (2007). Both books have stunning foldout illustrated pages, removable notes, letters, and cards that add pleasure and curiosity to nonfiction reading for young and old alike. Simon and Schuster and Candlewick Press specialize in interactive texts, both fiction and nonfiction.

Many youth gravitate toward nonfiction about the entertainment world because they dream of becoming superstar athletes and entertainers; they are enthralled by the stardom, money, and glamour of the entertainment industry. Quality nonfiction takes readers behind the scenes of the glamour and glitz of being a high-profile celebrity to the realities of the entertainment world: intense training and practice, sacrifice, and restraint. The fame surrounding a celebrity is obvious, but the drawbacks of stardom are often overlooked. Responsible nonfiction can help dispel myths teens have about the entertainment business. Although the preponderance of sports and celebrity nonfiction are biographical in nature, examples of nonfiction that speak authentically about fame, that address the history of sports, game rules, current issues, and historical events (e.g., the Olympics) exist, along with almanacs and fact books. A sampling of sports nonfiction can be found in Box 10.3.

Self-help and how-to books exist for teens. Some of the more recognized ones are books that cover emotional and spiritual topics for teens. Two best-sellers include *Chicken Soup for the Teen Soul* (Canfield, Hansen, Meyer, & Meyer, 2007) and *Don't Sweat the Small Stuff for Teens* (Carlson, 2000). Some of the most valuable self-help books address emotional issues and disorders (e.g., anxiety, depression, bipolar, obsessive compulsive behavior). Many teens are hesitant to share their emotional selves; some have emotional problems and don't recognize they have real health issues. Responsible and reliable

Box 10.3   Notable Sports Nonfiction

***Ballpark: The Story of America's Baseball Fields* by Lynn Curlee. New York: Simon & Schuster, 2005.**

Explores the history, culture, and changing climate of America's baseball parks. Beautiful illustrations and engaging anecdotes.

***Eagle Blue: A Team, a Tribe, and a High School Basketball Season in Arctic Alaska* by Michael D'Orso. New York: Bloomsbury, 2006.**

D'Orso follows an Alaskan basketball team, the Fort Yukon Eagles, six-time regional champions, through

an entire season. Set against the Arctic winter, 50-below-zero temperatures.

***Heroes of Baseball: The Men Who Made It America's Favorite Game* by Robert Lipsyte. New York: Simon & Schuster, 2006.**

Details the lives and achievements of baseball's greatest players: Ty Cobb, Christy Mathewson, Babe Ruth, Joe DiMaggio, Lou Gehrig, Mickey Mantle, Ted Williams, Hank Aaron, Shoeless Joe Jackson, Jackie Robinson, Willie Mays, and more.

Continued

Box 10.3   Notable Sports Nonfiction   *Continued*

Ice Time: The Story of Hockey by Michael McKinley. Plattsburg, NY: Tundra, 2006.

Presents the history of hockey—its beginnings and rise to popularity, legends, and major events. Beautifully illustrated.

John Madden's Heroes of Football by John Madden with Bill Gutnam. New York: Dutton/Penguin, 2006.

Traces the development of pro football from its 19th-century origins as a college pastime to one of the most popular and profitable sports in American history. Identifies key players, teams, and significant historical events.

Ladies First: Women Athletes Who Made a Difference by Ken Rappoport. Atlanta: Peachtree, 2005.

Celebrates the lives and experiences of courageous and determined female athletes in a wide range of sports: golf, track and field, horse racing, swimming, hockey, figure skating, gymnastics, and more.

Shades of Glory: The Negro Leagues and the Story of African-American Baseball by Lawrence D. Hogan. Washington, DC: National Geographic, 2006.

Summarizes the remarkable achievements and contributions of African Americans to professional baseball. Amazing photos and other artifacts.

Sports by Tim Hammond. New York: DK, 2005.

Explains the development, rules, and equipment in a variety of sports (e.g., softball, cricket, ice hockey, table tennis, soccer, and archery).

Sports Illustrated: Almanac 2007 by Sports Illustrated. New York: Time, 2007.

Almost two decades in the making, this is American's most recognized almanac. Includes stats, records, essays, and more.

Twelve Rounds to Glory: The Story of Muhammad Ali by Charles R. Smith Jr. Illus. Bryan Collier. Cambridge, MA: Candlewick Press, 2007.

Chronicles Ali's childhood, his Olympic gold medal, his fights in the professional ring with boxers such as Sonny Liston and Joe Frazier, his fight against Parkinson's disease, and lighting the Olympic torch. Also highlights his humanitarian efforts to fight prejudice and poverty.

Winning Ways: A Photohistory of American Women in Sports by Sue Macy. New York: Henry Holt, 1996.

Women athletes have struggled to earn an equal place in the sports world. This carefully researched book explores the social backdrop for girls eager to compete in basketball, swimming, baseball, and soccer.

self-help books can be invaluable. Books about safe dieting and developing relationships are also plentiful. In today's pop culture world, these books are much needed. Teen craft how-to books are plentiful (e.g., how to knit or crochet, how to cook, how to build things, how to garden). Self-help and how-to books are extremely specific and generally not big sellers, but they do cover a broad range of topics. For a sampling of titles, see Box 10.4.

The National Council for Social Studies (NCSS) and the National Science Teachers Association (NSTA) recognize exceptional trade books yearly. Their top choices are easily found on their Web sites. The American Library Association (ALA) is an outstanding go-to Web site for new titles,

Box 10.4   Self-Help and How-To for Teens

***Amazing Leonardo da Vinci Inventions You Can Build Yourself* by Maxine Anderson. Norwich, VT: Nomad Press, 2006.**

Readers examine some of da Vinci's most famous inventions and then can follow step-by-step directions for building some of their own projects. Contains historical and scientific facts and anecdotes.

***Chew on This: Everything You Don't Want to Know about Fast Food* by Eric Schlosser and Charles Wilson. Boston: Houghton Mifflin, 2006.**

Provides interesting and frightening facts about popular fast foods consumed by today's teens. A must-read for today's youth.

***Crack and Cocaine* by Karla Fitzhugh. Portsmouth, NH: Heinemann, 2005.**

Explains where these drugs originated and the nature of the illegal drug trade. Also examines why people use drugs, these drugs' effects, and their dangers.

***Drawing: The Only Drawing Book You'll Ever Need to Be the Artist You've Always Wanted to Be* by Kathryn Temple. New York: Sterling, 2007.**

A brief introduction to drawing instruments, followed by how-to lessons on drawing techniques (e.g., elements of shape, shading techniques, drawing landscapes).

***How to Write a Children's Book and Get It Published* by Barbara Seuling. Hoboken, NJ: Wiley, 2004.**

Helpful information on writing fiction, nonfiction, plays, and poetry. Also provides tips on developing writing topics and selling your work.

***Mean Chicks, Cliques, and Dirty Tricks: A Real Girl's Guide to Getting through the Day with Smarts and Style* by Erika V. Shearin Karres. Avon, MA: Adams Media, 2004.**

Practical suggestions and support for dealing with mean girls. Discusses what makes girls mean and how they operate.

***Not Another Teen Knitting Book* by Vickie Howell. New York: Sterling, 2006.**

Explains in simple terms how to knit cool teen items (e.g., athletic socks, theater mask hats, seat belt cozies).

***The Real Freshman Handbook: A Totally Honest Guide to Life on Campus* by Jennifer Hanson. Boston: Houghton Mifflin, 2002.**

Provides much-needed advice on dealing with roommates, living on your own, and adjusting to the college academic environment. Thoughtful and useful.

***Weight Loss Confidential: How Teens Lose Weight and Keep It Off—and What They Wish Parents Knew* by Anne M. Fletcher. Boston: Houghton Mifflin, 2006.**

Teens and parents describe teen weight problems and strategies teens used to lose weight. Based on surveys and interviews.

***Whatcha Mean, What's a Zine?: The Art of Making Zines and Mini Comics* by Mark Todd and Esther Pearl Watkins. Boston: Houghton Mifflin, 2006.**

Handmade magazines and comics containing personal stories, diary entries, poetry, interviews, and so forth

Continued

Box 10.4   Self-Help and How-To for Teens   *Continued*

are part of the teen pop culture. A good resource for teens wanting to create their own zines.

When Nothing Matters Anymore: A Guide for Depressed Teens by Bev Cobain. Minneapolis, MN: Free Spirit, 2007.

Teen depression is an often untreated health issue. Includes information on symptoms, causes, nutrition, medication, and additional resources.

Who Moved My Cheese? for Teens by Spencer Johnson. New York: Putnam, 2002.

Many teens have read the adult version. This one addresses teen-related issues: dealing with parents, dating, school challenges, and college decisions.

You Are Not Alone: Teens Talk about Life after the Loss of a Parent by Lynne Hughes. New York: Scholastic, 2005.

Testimonials of teens who have experienced loss and helpful advice for others.

---

award-winners, and series. National journals such as *Voice of Youth Advocates (VOYA)* and ALA's *Booklist* publish yearly updates on new releases and annual lists of top choices. See Box 10.5 for a sampling of notable YA nonfiction titles and Boxes 10.6 through 10.8 for nonfiction texts for content area Classrooms.

Box 10.5   Notable YA Nonfiction

Adventurous Women: Eight True Stories about Women Who Made a Difference by Penny Colman. New York: Henry Holt, 2006.

Colman outlines the contributions of eight courageous women who took risks and overcame obstacles to achieve their goals.

Children of the Great Depression by Russell Freedman. New York: Clarion, 2005.

Using diaries, memoirs, oral history, and letters, Freedman captures the hardscrabble lives of children growing up during the Great Depression. Illustrated with photographs by well-known photographers Dorothea Lange and Walker Evans.

Corpses, Coffins, and Crypts: A History of Burial by Penny Colman. New York: Henry Holt, 1997.

Chapters cover varying aspects of death with a touch of humor: funeral rituals across cultures, cremation, and burials. Engaging photos. Well researched.

Escape!: The Story of the Great Houdini by Sid Fleischman. New York: Greenwillow/HarperCollins, 2006.

Newbery Medalist and former magician, Fleischman has penned a fascinating account of the life of Harry Houdini, the greatest escape artist of all time. Could Houdini actually dematerialize? Could he really walk through brick walls? Make elephants disappear?

Continued

Box 10.5   Notable YA Nonfiction   *Continued*

***Freedom Walkers: The Story of the Montgomery Bus Boycott* by Russell Freedman. New York: Holiday House, 2006.**

A well-researched account of the Montgomery, Alabama, bus boycott and a rich portrait of growing up black in the South in the 1950s. Freedman draws on personal accounts, including experiences by Rosa Parks and Martin Luther King Jr. Illustrated with memorable black and white photos.

***Freedom Writers Diary: How a Teacher and 150 Teens Used Writing to Change Themselves and the World around Them* by the Freedom Writers with Erin Gruwell. New York: Doubleday, 1999.**

Now a major motion picture, a powerful look at urban schooling and a teacher who made a difference.

***Friday Night Lights: A Town, a Team, and a Dream* by H. G. Bissinger. Reading, MA: Addison-Wesley, 1990.**

A riveting account of small-town obsession with football and the impact sports craziness has on athletes, families, and communities.

***The Good Fight: How World War II Was Won* by Stephen E. Ambrose. New York: Simon & Schuster, 2001.**

Written by one of the most acclaimed historians of all time, this young adult work traces the origins of the war and discusses the major battles and events. Includes maps and stunning photos of soldiers, the Pearl Harbor attack, and the dropping of the atomic bomb.

***Hear Us Out!: Lesbian and Gay Stories of Struggle, Progress, and Hope, 1950 to the Present* by Nancy Garden. New York: Farrar, Straus & Giroux, 2007.**

Nancy Garden, an early trailblazer in gay and lesbian young adult literature, writes an account of what it meant to grow up gay in the mid-20th century. She traces a number of themes from mid-century on: the beginnings of the gay rights movement, the HIV and AIDS outbreak, and more.

***Kids at Work: Lewis Hine and the Crusade against Child Labor* by Russell Freedman. New York: Clarion, 1994.**

A photobiography of Lewis Hine, an early 20th-century photographer whose images of working children created an outcry for child labor laws.

***Ladies First: 40 Daring Women Who Were Second to None* by Elizabeth Cody Kimmel. Washington, DC: National Geographic, 2006.**

Profiles women who paved the way for females in their respective fields. Contains photos, biographical information, and important facts.

***Quest for the Tree Kangaroo: An Expedition to the Cloud Forest of New Guinea* by Sy Montgomery and Nic Bishop. Boston: Houghton Mifflin, 2006.**

Montgomery and Bishop provide an account of journeying through the remote cloud forest of Papua New Guinea in search of the Matschie tree kangaroo. Stunning close-up photos of plants and animals.

***Up before Daybreak: Cotton and People in America* by Deborah Hopkinson. New York: Scholastic, 2006.**

Using oral histories and photos, Hopkinson gives voice to the men, women, and children who labored in cotton fields, both sharecropper and slave, and the girls who worked in the New England mills.

***The Voice That Challenged a Nation: Marian Anderson and the Struggle for Equal Rights* by Russell Freedman. New York: Clarion, 2004.**

Acclaimed young adult historian Russell Freedman captures the social and political climate of the civil rights movement and the voice of the great African American vocalist, Marian Anderson, who left an enduring mark on the music industry.

Box 10.6   Nonfiction for the Arts

Acting for Young Actors: The Ultimate Teen Guide by Mary Lou Belli and Dinah Lenney. New York: Back Stage Books, 2006.

Provides exercises on character development, details on auditioning, rehearsal, and improvisation, and suggestions for breaking into film, theater, and television.

Andy Warhol: Pop Art Painter by Susan Goldman Rubin. New York: Harry N. Abrams, 2006.

An examination of Warhol's pop culture paintings, his rise from poverty, and examples of his early drawings.

Artist to Artist: 23 Major Illustrators Talk to Children about Their Art by the Eric Carle Museum of Picture Book Art. New York: Penguin, 2007.

Award-winning children's authors such as Eric Carle and Maurice Sendak talk about their art and how they began their careers. Includes photos of their early work.

Faces, Places, and Inner Spaces: A Guide to Looking at Art by Jean Sousa. New York: Harry N. Abrams, 2006.

Discusses how artists express themselves through their art. Works discussed include African masks, sculptures, screens, and paintings.

Footnotes: Dancing the World's Best-Loved Ballets by Frank Augustyn and Shelley Tanaka. Minneapolis, MN: Lerner, 2002.

An engaging look into the world of ballet. Explains the grueling work hours, commitment, and pain necessary to be a world-class performer.

In Real Life: Six Women Photographers by Leslie Sills. New York: Holiday House, 2000.

Sills profiles famous female photographers, their rise to recognition, the nature of their work, their struggles, and their sacrifices.

Shakespeare: His Work and His World by Michael Rosen. Illus. Robert Ingpen. Cambridge, MA: Candlewick Press, 2001.

Provides a political and social backdrop for Shakespeare's life and information on his early life, his marriage, and his acting and writing career.

Take-off: American All-Girl Bands during WWII by Tonya Bolden. New York: Knopf/Random House, 2007.

Historical approach to female jazz and swing musicians during World War II. Discusses what was appropriate for women during this time and how women gained voice in the musical world. Wonderful photos, source lists, suggested videos, discography, and recommended readings.

Walker Evans: Photographer of America by Thomas Nau. New York: Roaring Brook Press, 2007.

One of the greatest photographers of the 20th-century, Evans is most remembered for his photographs of farmers and rural families during the Great Depression. Nau's narrative of Evans's life is accompanied by reproductions of his work.

Box 10.7   Nonfiction for the Social Studies Classroom

Come Back to Afghanistan: A California Teenager's Story by Said Hyder Akbar and Susan Burton. New York: Bloomsbury, 2005.

Hyder Akbar, an Afghanie teen living in California during 9/11, describes the impact the incident had on his life and family. Hyder Akbar travels to Afghanistan with his father, who became a part of the political climate.

Darkness over Denmark: The Danish Resistance and the Rescue of the Jews by Ellen Levine. New York: Holiday House, 2000.

A narrative about the heroism of the Danish people who protected and rescued Jewish neighbors during World War II. Accompanied by archival photos.

Dust to Eat: Drought and Depression in the 1930s by Michael L. Cooper. Boston: Houghton Mifflin, 2004.

A well-presented account of the 1929 stock market crash and the Midwest drought that created double disasters: the Great Depression and the Dust Bowl.

Fields of Fury: The American Civil War by James M. McPherson. New York: Simon & Schuster, 2002.

Pulitzer Prize–winning author and renowned historian James M. McPherson provides an engaging account of the facts and events of the Civil War. The text is accompanied by a glossary, timeline, Web sites, index, and bibliography. Fabulous resource for the history classroom and the Civil War enthusiast.

Flags of Our Fathers: Heroes of Iwo Jima by James Bradley. New York: Random House, 2000.

Son of one of the Iwo Jima flag raisers, James Bradley gives a well-researched account of the lives of the six soldiers who became a symbol of hope, courage, and victory for our country.

Good Brother, Bad Brother: The Story of Edwin Booth and John Wilkes Booth by James Cross Giblin. New York: Clarion, 2005.

Describes the lives and relationships between John Wilkes Booth, Lincoln's assassin, and Booth's brother Edwin, who was a Lincoln supporter. John was a Confederacy advocate.

Hidden on the Mountain: Stories of Children Sheltered from the Nazis in Le Chambon by Deborah Durland DeSaix and Karen Gray Ruelle. New York: Holiday House, 2006.

The story of thousands of children hidden in the mountains of Le Chambon, a French village. Contains photos and first-person accounts of individuals who hid there.

Into the West: From Reconstruction to the Final Days of the American Frontier by James M. McPherson. New York: Simon & Schuster, 2006.

A stimulating account of westward expansion and the nation's attempt to heal its wounds during Reconstruction and the exploration and settlement of the American frontier. Accompanied by maps, photos, and anecdotes.

Our Eleanor: A Scrapbook Look at Eleanor Roosevelt's Remarkable Life by Candace Fleming. New York: Atheneum/Simon & Schuster, 2005.

Narrates the amazing life of Eleanor Roosevelt, first lady, political leader, and human rights advocate. Provides examples of her life contributions from her efforts to help the poor to her role as the first female delegate to the United Nations.

Continued

Box 10.7   Nonfiction for the Social Studies Classroom   *Continued*

Photo by Brady: A Picture of the Civil War by Jennifer Armstrong. New York: Simon & Schuster, 2005.

Photographer Matthew Brady captured devastating and unforgettable images of the Civil War. In this book, a photoessay, his pictures add life and texture to Armstrong's narrative about major war events.

Undaunted Courage: Meriwether Lewis, Thomas Jefferson, and the Opening of the American West by Stephen E. Ambrose. New York: Simon & Schuster, 1996.

Stephen E. Ambrose, one of the most distinguished historians of all time, chronicles the hardships and extraordinary adventures of the most famous pioneering expedition in the history of our country. For advanced readers.

War, Women, and the News: How Female Journalists Won the Battle to Cover World War II by Catherine Gourley. New York: Atheneum/Simon & Schuster, 2007.

Prior to World War II, the work of women journalists was rarely valued. Columns written by female reporters seldom made the front page, and female reporters were assigned to the social pages. At the outbreak of World War II, female journalists demanded the chance to report from the battlefields. This book chronicles their efforts.

Warriors by James Harpur. New York: Simon & Schuster, 2007.

Harpur describes more than a dozen different premodern warrior groups including Alexander the Great and Richard the Lionheart (e.g., their roles in the social fabric of the time and their experiences). Beautiful and informative images accompany the text.

Box 10.8   Nonfiction for Math, Science, and Technology Classrooms

Count Down: The Race for Beautiful Solutions at the International Mathematical Olympiad by Steve Olson. Boston: Mariner, 2005.

What makes some students great problem solvers? Why do some fear geometry? Olson addresses these questions and more as he describes a national mathematics olympiad in which hundreds of high school students compete to find mathematical solutions.

Guinea Pig Scientists: Bold Self-Experimenters in Science and Medicine by Leslie Dendy and Mel Boring. Illus. C. B. Mordan. New York: Henry Holt, 2005.

Discusses scientists who used themselves as guinea pigs in efforts to pursue scientific research (e.g., Lazzaro

Spallanzani, an 18th-century scientist swallowed food in wooden tubes in an effort to study the digestive system). Includes sketches and archival photos.

Hurricane Force by Joseph B. Treaster. Boston: Kingfisher, 2007.

New York Times journalist Joseph Treaster watched the destruction of Hurricane Katrina from the New Orleans police headquarters. A behind-the-scenes account of one of the greatest natural disasters in U.S. history.

Invisible Allies: Microbes That Shape Our Lives by Jeanette Farrell. New York: Farrar, Straus & Giroux, 2005.

Microbes are normally associated with disease; however, Farrell outlines the healthy role microbes play in our daily lives (e.g., preserving food).

Continued

Box 10.8   Nonfiction for Math, Science, and Technology Classrooms   *Continued*

***Longitude Prize: The Race between the Moon and the Watch-Machine* by Joan Dash. Illus. Dusan Petricic. New York: Farrar, Straus & Giroux, 2000.**

Describes the efforts of John Harrison, an 18th-century clockmaker, to invent a clock that could survive the high seas and compute longitude accurately.

***Meltdown: A Race against Nuclear Disaster at Three Mile Island: A Reporter's Story* by Wilborn Hampton. Cambridge, MA: Candlewick Press, 2001.**

A step-by-step account of the worst nuclear power accident in U.S. history. Hampton details the human error and mechanical/technical failure that triggered the Three Mile Island disaster in 1979.

***Problem Solving and Word Problems* by Rebecca Wingard-Nelson. Berkeley Heights, NJ: Enslow, 2004.**

An easy-to-understand overview of common problem-solving strategies, both algebraic expressions and word problems.

***The Race to Save the Lord God Bird* by Phillip Hoose. New York: Farrar, Straus & Giroux, 2004.**

What role did humans play in the extinction of the ivory-billed woodpecker? What have we learned about our environment and protecting endangered species?

***Secrets of a Civil War Submarine: Solving the Mysteries of the H. L. Hunley* by Sally M. Walker. Minneapolis, MN: Carolrhoda/Lerner, 2005.**

A fascinating narrative about the development of the Civil War submarine. Complete with diagrams, maps, and photos. Addresses a wide variety of scientific fields.

***Six Days in October: The Stock Market Crash of 1929* by Karen Blumenthal. New York: Atheneum/Simon & Schuster, 2002.**

An account of the events and people behind the 1929 stock market crash. Includes newspaper articles, photos, even cartoons of the six-day event.

***The Tarantula Scientist* by Sy Montgomery. Boston: Houghton Mifflin, 2004.**

A Robert F. Sibert Honor book that takes readers through the French Guiana rainforest in search of tarantulas. Captivating pictures by Nic Bishop are sure to grab readers. Readers should also check out *The Snake Scientist* (Montgomery & Bishop, 1999).

Autobiographies, Biographies, Diaries, and Memoirs

Biographies, autobiographies, diaries, and memoirs are based on people's lives. *Biographies* are written about other people, generally famous individuals, whereas *autobiographies* are written by the individual whose story is being told. *Diaries* and *memoirs* are similar to autobiographies but generally cover a specific period of time in a person's life (e.g., a politician's time in office) rather than his/her life span. An *unauthorized biography* is a biography written about an individual without that person's permission or input. Some writers (e.g., Lemony Snicket and Chris Crutcher) toy with this term, or similar terms, in writing about their own lives: *Lemony*

Snicket: The Unauthorized Autobiography (Snicket, 2002) and *King of the Mild Frontier: An Ill-Advised Autobiography* (Crutcher, 2003). Much like an unauthorized biography, which may not be a close account of someone's life, Snicket and Crutcher suggest the same about their autobiographies.

Point of view is an important consideration when studying these literary forms. When individuals write their own stories, they have the liberty to censor or alter history, an often cited criticism of autobiographies and memoirs. Critics argue they are too close to their experiences and sometimes paint skewed pictures of truth. Biographers, though, can do the same and often are criticized for exploiting lives. Biographers don't have the advantage of having lived in their subject's shoes, but credible biographers research thoroughly and do their best to write fairly balanced life stories.

Quality biographies and autobiographies can be measured in part by the characteristics outlined in Chapter 4, and well-written and responsible ones have a few additional characteristics. First, they are true to history. If the writer takes liberties with truth, he/she informs the reader, and the biography is positioned on the continuum between biography and *fictionalized biography* depending on the story's level of truth. The quality of the writing need not be questioned as long as the author represents the work honestly. A recent example of a questionable life story is James Frey's *A Million Little Pieces* (2003). Sold and marketed as a memoir, the book incited outrage when

Jack Gantos as an eighth grader (left) and his prison mugshot (right). His autobiography *Hole in My Life* is a Robert F. Sibert Honor book, a Parents' Choice Award title, and a Michael L. Printz Honor book.

readers learned the memoir was mostly fabricated. Quality biographies also move beyond being factual profiles of an individual's life: facts about an individual's birth, schooling, career, family/relationships, and death. Well-written biographies and autobiographies probe the emotional growth and experiences of the subject.

Biographies can be traced to antiquity when scribes wrote on stone tablets. The modern English biography and autobiography took hold in the late 1700s with such works as James Boswell's *Life of Johnson* (1791) and Samuel Johnson's *Critical Lives of the Poets* (1779–1781). Such works became popular as the masses became more educated and people believed studying the lives of great individuals contributed to our understanding of humanity and the world. Many early works were formulaic; however, as the genre matured, the biography developed into a much respected literary form. The Pulitzer Prize for Biography or Autobiography (first given in 1917) recognizes a distinguished biography or autobiography annually. *The Most Famous Man in America: The Biography of Henry Ward Beecher* (2006) by Debby Applegate is a recent winner and is suitable for teens. Historian David McCullough is a two-time recipient of the Pulitzer Prize for Biography or Autobiography with *John Adams* (2001) and *Truman* (1992). Both books are superb choices for advanced readers.

Early notable biographies for young readers include *Invincible Louisa: The Story of the Author of Little Women* (1933) by Cornelia Meigs and James Daugherty's *Daniel Boone* (1939), both Newbery Medal winners. One of the most notable early biographers for young readers was Clara Ingram Judson, recipient of numerous awards for her biographies. Judson penned more than 70 works for young readers, most being biographies or historical accounts of famous people (e.g., *Abraham Lincoln, Friend of the People*, 1950; *Theodore Roosevelt, Fighting Patriot*, 1953).

Most early biographies for young readers were more suitable for elementary and lower middle school, and the tone was patronizing and moralistic. Biographies for older readers have been slow developing, and most marketed for teens lack sufficient depth. Walter Dean Myers's *Malcolm X: By Any Means Necessary* (1993) is outstanding. Milton Meltzer's work is also noteworthy. As a literary biographer, Meltzer has written several outstanding literary figure biographies suitable for older teens. (e.g., *Edgar Allan Poe*, 2003; *Emily Dickinson*, 2005; *Nathaniel Hawthorne*, 2006; and *Henry David Thoreau*, 2007). All have depth, are interesting, and are enjoyable to read. They are also wonderful research resources. Because few biographies marketed especially for teens have enough depth for older adolescents, I have included some adult selections in Boxes 10.9 and 10.10 for more mature readers.

Early biographers, driven to write biographies to teach youth about the impact history makers have had on the world, focused on politicians, world leaders, scientists, and explorers. While some of today's biographers do the same, others write stories about Hollywood celebrities and super-star athletes. Many of these are mediocre. There are, however, a few good career biographies about successful musicians, entertainers, and athletes. Elizabeth Partridge's *John Lennon: All I Want Is the Truth* (2005), a Michael

Box 10.9   Notable Adult Autobiographies/Memoirs

Angela's Ashes: A Memoir by Frank McCourt. New York: Scribner, 1996.

The Autobiography of Alice B. Toklas by Gertrude Stein. Orlando, FL: Harcourt, 1933.

The Autobiography of Malcolm X by Malcolm X with Alex Haley. New York: Grove Press, 1965.

Barrio Boy by Ernesto Galarza. Notre Dame, IN: University of Notre Dame Press, 1971.

Black Boy by Richard Wright. New York: Harper & Brothers, 1945.

The Circuit by Francisco Jiménez. Albuquerque: University of New Mexico Press, 1997.

Girl, Interrupted by Susanna Kaysen. New York: Turtle Bay, 1993.

I Know Why the Caged Bird Sings by Maya Angelou. New York: Random House, 1969.

Kaffir Boy: An Autobiography: The True Story of a Black Youth's Coming of Age in Apartheid South Africa by Mark Mathabane. New York: Macmillan, 1986.

Of Beetles and Angels by Mawi Asgedom. Chicago: Magadee Books, 2001.

Rocket Boys: A Memoir by Homer H. Hickam Jr. New York: Delacorte/Random House, 1998.

Running with Scissors: A Memoir by Augusten Burroughs. New York: St. Martin's Press, 2002.

Warriors Don't Cry by Melba P. Beals. New York: Pocket/Simon & Schuster, 1994.

When I Was Puerto Rican by Esmeralda Santiago. Reading, MA: Addison-Wesley, 1993.

Box 10.10   Notable Young Adult Biographies

Ben Franklin's Almanac: Being a True Account of the Good Gentleman's Life by Candace Fleming. New York: Simon & Schuster, 2003.

e. e. cummings: A Poet's Life by Catherine Reef. New York: Clarion, 2006.

Einstein: His Life and Universe by Walter Isaacson. New York: Simon & Schuster, 2007.

Genius: A Photobiography of Albert Einstein by Marfe Ferguson Delano. Washington, DC: National Geographic, 2005.

George Washington Carver by Tonya Bolden. New York: Harry N. Abrams, 2008.

Isaac Newton: Giants of Science by Kathleen Krull. Illus. Boris Kulikov. New York: Viking/Penguin, 2006.

Johnny Cash by Anne E. Neimark. New York: Penguin, 2007.

The Louis Armstrong You Never Knew by James Lincoln Collier. New York: Scholastic, 2004.

Mockingbird: A Portrait of Harper Lee by Charles J. Shields. New York: Henry Holt, 2006.

Out of Darkness: The Story of Louis Braille by Russell Freedman. Illus. Kate Kiesler. New York: Clarion, 1997.

The Poet Slave of Cuba: A Biography of Juan Francisco Manzano by Margarita Engle. New York: Henry Holt, 2006.

Portraits of African-American Heroes by Tonya Bolden. Illus. Ansel Pitcairn. New York: Dutton/Penguin, 2003.

Robert E. Lee: Virginia Soldier, American Citizen by James I. Robertson Jr. New York: Simon & Schuster, 2005.

Something Out of Nothing: Marie Curie and Radium by Carla Killough McClafferty. New York: Farrar, Straus & Giroux, 2006.

Up Close: Bill Gates by Marc Aronson. New York: Penguin, 2008.

Continued

Box 10.10   Notable Young Adult Biographies   *Continued*

Up Close: Ellen Fitzgerald by Tanya Stone. New York: Penguin, 2008.

Up Close: Elvis Presley by Wilborn Hampton. New York: Penguin, 2007.

Up Close: Frank Lloyd Wright by Jan Adkins. New York: Penguin, 2007.

Up Close: Jane Goodall by Sudipta Bardhan-Quallen. New York: Penguin, 2008.

Up Close: John Steinbeck by Milton Meltzer. New York: Penguin, 2008.

Up Close: Johnny Cash by Annie E. Neimark. New York: Penguin, 2007.

Up Close: Oprah Winfrey by Ilene Cooper. New York: Penguin, 2007.

Up Close: Rachel Carson by Ellen Levine. New York: Penguin, 2007.

Up Close: Robert F. Kennedy by Marc Aronson. New York: Penguin, 2007b.

Up Close: Ronald Reagan by James Sutherland. New York: Penguin, 2008.

Up Close: Thurgood Marshall by Chris Crowe. New York: Penguin, 2008.

Up Close: W. E. B. Du Bois by Tonya Bolden. New York: Penguin, 2008.

Vincent van Gogh: Portrait of an Artist by Jan Greenberg and Sandra Jordon. New York: Delacorte/Random House, 2001.

Yeah! Yeah! Yeah!: The Beatles, Beatlemania, and the Music That Changed the World by Bob Spitz. New York: Little, Brown, 2007.

Reprinted by permission of Penguin Young Readers Group © 2005.

L. Printz Honor book, is a marvelous portrait of the former Beatle's life and musical contributions. Pop culture has had an astounding impact on the biography genre.

Numerous young adult authors have written autobiographies: some are true life stories, others contain varying doses of fiction. Many write specifically about their lives as writers, how they came to be writers, and how they have developed as writers (e.g., Lois Lowry). Still others have written memoirs about particular times in their lives. Gary Paulsen, for instance, has penned a number of memoirs. In *Caught by the Sea: My Life on Boats* (2001), he recounts his life living on a boat in the Pacific Ocean. Dozens of biographies also have been written by young adult literature experts about young adult writers, and these are exceptional research resources for young and old alike. Most contain biographical information and an analysis of their work. Scarecrow Press, Rosen Publishing, and Twayne specialize in young adult author biographies. See Boxes 10.11 and 10.12 for young adult author autobiographies and biographies.

Box 10.11   Young Adult Author Autobiographies/ Memoirs

Ann Turner. *Learning to Swim: A Memoir*. New York: Scholastic, 2000.

Chris Crutcher. *King of the Mild Frontier: An Ill-Advised Autobiography*. New York: Greenwillow/HarperCollins, 2003.

Cynthia Rylant. *But I'll Be Back Again: An Album*. New York: Beech Tree/HarperCollins, 1993.

Gail Carson Levine. *Writing Magic: Creating Stories That Fly*. New York: HarperCollins, 2006.

Gary Paulsen. *The Beet Fields: Memories of a Sixteenth Summer*. New York: Delacorte/ Random House, 2000.

Gary Paulsen. *Caught by the Sea: My Life on Boats*. New York: Bantam Doubleday Dell, 2001.

Gary Paulsen. *Father Water, Mother Woods: Essays on Fishing and Hunting in the North Woods*. New York: Delacorte/Random House, 1994.

Gary Paulsen. *Guts: The True Stories behind Hatchet and the Brian Books*. New York: Delacorte/Random House, 2001.

Gary Paulsen. *My Life in Dog Years*. New York: Bantam Doubleday Dell, 1998.

Gary Paulsen. *Woodsong*. New York: Bradbury Press, 1990.

Gary Paulsen. *Zero to Sixty: The Motorcycle Journey of a Lifetime*. Orlando, FL: Harvest/ Harcourt, 1999.

Gary Soto. *Living Up the Street: Narrative Recollections*. San Francisco, CA: Strawberry Hill Press, 1985.

Gary Soto. *A Summer Life*. Hanover, NH: University Press of New England, 1990.

Jack Gantos. *Hole in My Life*. New York: Farrar, Straus & Giroux, 2002.

Jean Craighead George. *The Tarantula in My Purse: And 172 Other Wild Pets*. New York: HarperCollins, 1996.

Jean Fritz. *Homesick: My Own Story*. New York: Penguin, 1982.

Jerry Spinelli. *Knots in My Yo-Yo String: The Autobiography of a Kid*. New York: Knopf/ Random House, 1998.

Joan Lowery Nixon. *The Making of a Writer*. New York: Delacorte/Random House, 2002.

Joseph Bruchac. *Bowman's Store: A Journey to Myself*. New York: Dial/Penguin, 1997.

Judith Ortiz Cofer. *Silent Dancing: A Partial Remembrance of a Puerto Rican Childhood*. Houston, TX: Arte Público, 1990.

Julius Lester. *On Writing for Children and Other People*. New York: Dial/Penguin, 2004.

Laurence Yep. *The Lost Garden*. Englewood Cliffs, NJ: Messner, 1991.

Lemony Snicket. *Lemony Snicket: The Unauthorized Autobiography*. New York: HarperCollins, 2002.

Lois Duncan. *Chapters: My Growth as a Writer*. New York: Little, Brown, 1982.

Lois Lowry. *Looking Back: A Book of Memories*. Boston: Houghton Mifflin, 1998.

M. E. Kerr. *Blood on the Forehead: What I Know about Writing*. New York: HarperCollins, 1998.

M. E. Kerr. *Me, Me, Me, Me, Me: Not a Novel*. New York: Harper & Row, 1983.

Milton Meltzer. *Milton Meltzer: Writing Matters*. New York: Franklin Watts, 2004.

Milton Meltzer. *Starting from Home: A Writer's Beginnings*. New York: Viking, 1988.

Ned Vizzini. *Teen Angst? Naaah . . . A Quasi-Autobiography*. Minneapolis, MN: Free Spirit, 2000.

Patricia Reilly Giff. *Don't Tell the Girls: A Family Memoir*. New York: Holiday House, 2005.

Paul Zindel. *The Pigman and Me*. New York: HarperCollins, 1992.

Peg Kehret. *Five Pages a Day: A Writer's Journey*. Morton Grove, IL: Albert Whitman, 2002.

Phyllis Reynolds Naylor. *How I Came to Be a Writer*. New York: Atheneum/Simon & Schuster, 1978.

Richard Peck. *Anonymously Yours*. New York: Beech Tree/HarperCollins, 1991.

Roald Dahl. *Boy: Tales of Childhood*. New York: Farrar, Straus & Giroux, 1984.

Roald Dahl. *Going Solo*. New York: Farrar, Straus & Giroux, 1986.

Continued

Box 10.11   Young Adult Author Autobiographies/ Memoirs   *Continued*

Robert Cormier. *I Have Words to Spend: Reflections of a Small-Town Editor.* New York: Delacorte/Random House, 1991.

Ruth C. White. *Little Audrey,* New York: Farrar, Straus & Giroux, 2008.

Sid Fleischman. *The Abracadabra Kid: A Writer's Life.* New York: Greenwillow, 1996.

Terry Brooks. *Sometimes the Magic Works: Lessons from a Writing Life.* New York: Del Rey/Random House, 2003.

Walter Dean Myers. *Bad Boy: A Memoir.* New York: HarperCollins, 2001.

Yoshiko Uchida. *The Invisible Thread.* New York: Silver Burdett, 1991.

Box 10.12   Young Adult Author Biographies

Library of Authors' Biographies by Rosen Publishing

Avi by Michael A. Sommers (2004)

Chris Crutcher by Michael A. Sommers (2005)

Christopher Paul Curtis by Judy Levin (2006)

Cynthia Rylant by Alice B. McGinty (2004)

E. B. White by Deb Aronson (2005)

E. L. Konigsburg by Renee Ambrosek (2006)

Gary Paulsen by Sarah L. Thomson (2003)

Gary Soto by Tamra Orr (2005)

J. D. Salinger by Michael A. Sommers (2006)

J. K. Rowling by William Compson (2003)

James Lincoln Collier by Liz Sonneborn (2006)

Jane Yolen by Susanna Daniel (2003)

Jerry Spinelli by David Seidman (2004)

Judy Blume by Cee Telford (2004)

Karen Cushman by Susanna Daniel (2006)

Karen Hesse by Nzingha Clarke (2006)

Katherine Paterson by Alice B. McGinty (2005)

Laurence Yep by Katherine Lawrence (2004)

Lois Duncan by Amy Sterling Casil (2005)

Lois Lowry by Susanna Daniel (2003)

Louis Sachar by Meg Greene (2003)

Lynne Reid Banks by Sherri Liberman (2006)

M. E. Kerr by Albert Spring (2006)

Madeleine L'Engle by Aaron Rosenberg (2006)

Mildred Taylor by Gillian Houghton (2005)

Paul Zindel by Susanna Daniel (2004)

Paula Fox by Susanna Daniel (2004)

Richard Peck by Michael A. Sommers (2003)

Robert Cormier by Sarah L. Thomson (2003)

S. E. Hinton by Antoine Wilson (2003)

Scott O'Dell by Simone Payment (2006)

Sharon Creech by Alice B. McGinty (2006)

Sid Fleischman by Jeri Freedman (2004)

Virginia Hamilton by Deborah Marinelli (2003)

Walter Dean Myers by Karen Burshtein (2004)

Will Hobbs by Paula Johanson (2006)

Scarecrow Studies in Young Adult Literature

Aidan Chambers: Master Literary Choreographer by Betty Greenway (2006)

Angela Johnson: Poetic Prose by KaaVonia Hinton (2006)

Ann Rinaldi: Historian and Storyteller by Jeanne M. McGlinn (2000)

Caroline Cooney: Faith and Fiction by Pamela Sissi Carroll (2001)

David Almond: Memory and Magic by Don Latham (2006)

Graham Salisbury: Island Boy by David Macinnis Gill (2005)

Jacqueline Woodson: The Real Thing by Lois Thomas Stover (2003)

Janet McDonald: The Original Project Girl by Catherine Ross-Stroud (2008)

Continued

Box 10.12   Young Adult Author Biographies   *Continued*

Karen Hesse by Rosemary Oliphant-Ingham (2005)

Norma Fox Mazer: A Writer's World by Arthea J. S. Reed (2000)

Orson Scott Card: Writer of the Terrible Choice by Edith S. Tyson (2003)

Sarah Dessen: From Burritos to Box Office by Wendy J. Glenn (2004)

Sharon Creech: The Words We Choose to Say by Mary Ann Tighe (2006)

Virginia Euwer Wolff: Capturing the Music of Young Voices by Suzanne Elizabeth Reid (2003)

What's So Scary about R. L. Stine? by Patrick Jones (1998)

Teen Reads: Student Companions to Young Adult Literature by Greenwood Publishing

Gary Paulsen by Jim Blasingame (2007)

Joan Bauer by Alleen Pace Nilsen (2007)

Sharon Creech by Pamela Sissi Carroll (2007)

Tamora Pierce by Bonnie Kunzel and Susan Fichtelberg (2007)

Walter Dean Myers by Myrna Dee Marler (2005)

Young Adult Author Series by Twayne Publishers

Presenting Avi by Susan P. Bloom and Cathryn M. Mercier (1997)

Presenting Cynthia Voigt by Suzanne Elizabeth Reed (1995)

Presenting Harry Mazer by Arthea J. S. Reed (1996)

Presenting Kathryn Lasky by Joanne Brown (1998)

Presenting Laurence Yep by Dianne Johnson-Feelings (1995)

Presenting Lynn Hall by Susan Stan (1996)

Presenting M. E. Kerr by Alleen Pace Nilsen (1997)

Presenting Madeleine L'Engle by Donald R. Hettinga (1993)

Presenting Mildred D. Taylor by Chris Crowe (1999)

Presenting Norma Fox Mazer by Sally Holmes Holtze (1987)

Presenting Paula Danziger by Kathleen Krull (1995)

Presenting Phyllis Reynolds Naylor by Lois Thomas Stover (1997)

Dozens of biographies and autobiographies have been written about individuals living through war atrocities. *Anne Frank: The Diary of a Young Girl* (1952) is one of the most frequently taught in high school. War biographies/autobiographies about World War II are most common in young adult literature (e.g., *The Upstairs Room* by Johanna Reiss, 1972; *The Lost Childhood: A World War II Memoir* by Yehuda Nir, 2002), but voices of other war survivors are becoming more prominent. In *Zlata's Diary* (1994) Zlata Filipovic describes her life as a preadolescent growing up during wartime in Sarajevo. Much like Anne Frank, Zlata chronicles her daily life and describes the horrors of war as seen by a young girl. In *Red Scarf Girl: A Memoir of the Cultural Revolution* (1997), Ji-li Jiang describes her life growing up during the Chinese Cultural Revolution—a tumultuous period in Chinese history in which Mao Zedong enlisted high school and college students (Red Guards) in an effort to break ties with pre-Communist China. *Thura's Diary* (2004) is a timely work about 19-year-old Thura al-Windawi, a young woman living in Baghdad prior to the first U.S. bombings. Through Thura's eyes, the reader witnesses the Baghdad bombings and efforts to reconstruct the city. Valerie Zenatti's *When I Was a Soldier* (2005) provides a unique point of view: Zenatti records two years of her life as a young woman serving in the Israeli army. For youth growing up in Israel, serving in the military is a rite of passage. See Box 10.13 for additional war autobiographies, biographies, diaries, and memoirs.

The *slave narrative,* an autobiographical form, developed during the 18th and 19th centuries when abolitionists began speaking out against slavery. Two of the best known are *Incidents in the Life of a Slave Girl* (1861) by Harriet Jacobs and Booker T. Washington's *Up from Slavery* (1901). Over the years, thousands of slaves and former slaves have given accounts of their experiences. Though not originally written for young adults, these narratives are common readings in middle schools and high schools and add a human element to sterile textbook accounts of slavery. They also laid the foundation for slave narratives (and historical fiction) written specifically for teens. *To Be a Slave* (1968) by Julius Lester is a well-known young adult classic. Box 10.14 features additional works.

Picture books are a popular format for biographies, and many are suitable for supplemental reading, mini-lessons, and for introducing

---

Box 10.13   Young Adult War Autobiographies, Biographies, Diaries, and Memoirs

Born on the Fourth of July by Ron Kovic. New York: McGraw-Hill, 1976.

Hello, America by Livia Bitton-Jackson. New York: Simon & Schuster, 2005.

In My Hands: Memories of a Holocaust Rescuer by Irene Opdyke (with Jennifer Armstrong). New York: Knopf/Random House, 2005.

Little Green: Growing Up During the Chinese Cultural Revolution by Chun Yu. New York: Simon & Schuster, 2005.

The Lost Childhood: A World War II Memoir by Yehuda Nir. New York: Scholastic, 2002.

No Pretty Pictures: A Child of War by Anita Lobel. New York: Greenwillow, 1998.

Red-tail Angels: The Story of the Tuskegee Airmen of World War II by Patricia C. McKissack and Fredrick L. McKissack. New York: Walker, 1995.

The Road from Home: The Story of an Armenian Girl by David Kherdian. New York: HarperCollins, 1979.

A Rumor of War by Philip Caputo. New York: Holt, Rinehart & Winston, 1977.

Snow Falling in Spring by Moying Li. New York: Farrar, Straus & Giroux, 2008.

Thura's Diary: My Life in Wartime Iraq by Thura al-Windawi. Trans. Robin Bray. New York: Viking/Penguin, 2004.

Upon the Head of the Goat: A Childhood in Hungary, 1939–1944 by Aranka Siegal. New York: Farrar, Straus & Giroux, 1981.

The Upstairs Room by Johanna Reiss. New York: Crowell, 1972.

We Are Witnesses: Five Diaries of Teenagers Who Died in the Holocaust edited by Jacob Boas. New York: Henry Holt, 1995.

Zlata's Diary: A Child's Life in Wartime Sarejevo by Zlata Filipovic. Trans. Christina Pribichevich-Zoric. New York: Viking/Penguin, 1994.

Box 10.14   Slave Narratives

Bound for the North Star by Dennis Brindell Fradin. New York: Clarion, 2001.

Days of Jubilee: The End of Slavery in the United States by Patricia C. McKissack and Fredrick L. McKissack. New York: Scholastic, 2003.

Freedom River by Doreen Rappaport. New York: Jump at the Sun/Hyperion, 2000.

Freedom Roads: Searching for the Underground Railroad by Joyce Hansen and Gary McGowan. Illus. James Ransome. Chicago: Cricket, 2003.

Get on Board: The Story of the Underground Railroad by Jim Haskins. New York: Scholastic, 1993.

Growing Up in Slavery: Stories of Young Slaves as Told by Themselves edited by Yuval Taylor.

Illus. Kathleen Judge. Chicago: Chicago Review Press, 2005.

Many Thousand Gone: African Americans from Slavery to Freedom by Virginia Hamilton. Illus. Leo Dillon and Diane Dillon. New York: Knopf/Random House, 1993.

No More!: Stories and Songs of Slave Resistance by Doreen Rappaport. Illus. Shane Evans. Cambridge, MA: Candlewick Press, 2002.

Rebels against Slavery, American Slave Revolts by Patricia C. McKissack and Fredrick L. McKissack. New York: Scholastic, 1996.

Struggle against Slavery: A History in Documents by David Waldstreicher. Oxford, NY: Oxford University Press, 2002.

---

new units in middle school and secondary classrooms. Sharon Darrow's *Through the Tempests Dark and Wild: A Story of Mary Shelley, Creator of Frankenstein* (2003), though somewhat fictionalized, traces the early years of Mary Shelley and makes a wonderful supplement to a unit on her work from the Romantic era. For the science classroom *John Muir: America's First Environmentalist* (2006) by Kathryn Lasky is a good addition to a unit on the environment. Box 10.15 features a sampling of additional biographical picture books.

Graphic novels (discussed in Chapter 12) are becoming a respected addition to young adult literature. *To Dance: A Ballerina's Graphic Novel* (2006), a Robert F. Sibert Honor book, by Siena Cherson Siegel is an autobiographical account of Siena Siegel's life as a dancer. From her early years running along the beach in Puerto Rico to performing with the New York City Ballet, Siena conveys the level of determination and the steadfast work ethic required of professional dancers.

We need only consider the popularity of reality TV shows such as *My Super Sweet 16, Survivor,* and *American Idol* to recognize the human fascination with real people's lives. Whether writing about Hollywood celebrities or history makers, young adult authors have over the years satisfied the teen craving for *real* stories about *real* people. Biographies, autobiographies, and memoirs remain constants in young adult literature. The next section addresses how young adult nonfiction literature can be used to teach summarizing skills.

Box 10.15   Notable Picture Book Biographies

America's Champion Swimmer: Gertrude Ederle by David A. Adler. Illus. Terry Widener. San Diego: Harcourt, 2000.

Emily Dickinson's Letters to the World by Jeanette Winter. New York: Foster/Farrar, Straus & Giroux, 2002.

Handel, Who Knew What He Liked by M. T. Anderson. Illus. Kevin Hawkes. Cambridge, MA: Candlewick Press, 2001.

Harvesting Hope: The Story of Cesar Chavez by Kathleen Krull. Illus. Yuyi Morales. San Diego: Harcourt, 2003.

Heroes for Civil Rights by David A. Adler. Illus. Bill Farnsworth. New York: Holiday House, 2008.

Leonardo, Beautiful Dreamer by Robert Byrd. New York: Dutton/Penguin, 2003.

Lou Gehrig: The Luckiest Man by David A. Adler. Illus. Terry Widener. San Diego: Harcourt, 1997.

The Man Who Made Time Travel by Kathryn Lasky. Illus. Kevin Hawkes. New York: HarperCollins, 2003.

Roberto Clemente: Pride of the Pittsburgh Pirates by Jonah Winter. Illus. Raúl Colón. New York: Atheneum/Simon & Schuster, 2005.

Satchel Paige by Lesa Cline-Ransome. Illus. James E. Ransome. New York: Simon & Schuster, 2000.

A Voice of Her Own: The Story of Phillis Wheatley, Slave Poet by Kathryn Lasky. Illus. Paul Lee. Cambridge, MA: Candlewick Press, 2003.

Walt Whitman: Words for America by Barbara Kerley. Illus. Brian Selznick. New York: Scholastic, 2004.

When Marian Sang: The True Recital of Marian Anderson: The Voice of a Century by Pam Muñoz Ryan. Illus. Brian Selznick. New York: Scholastic, 2002.

Teaching Text Structure with YA Nonfiction

Whether fiction or nonfiction, all texts have external and internal text structure. *External structure* is the overall text layout and design. Does the book have chapters, subheadings, visuals? Does it include an index? If so, what kind and how many? What about a table of contents or appendixes? How is the information organized on the page? Are there charts, diagrams, photos, maps, a glossary?

By the time teens reach high school, we assume they know how to use resource books, including their textbooks. Unfortunately, not all do. Students who struggle with nonfiction may not understand how books are organized. Just as a kindergartener who has limited exposure to books may not know the front from the back, the top from the bottom, a teen reader may confuse the table of contents with the index. Which is in the front? Which in back? Many aren't aware of multiple indexes (e.g., name and subject indexes) or aren't familiar with the various coding techniques that help readers locate information effectively (e.g., an italicized number beside a term in an index usually suggests a visual on the page; a bold number generally indicates a definition).

Explicit instruction in external text structure can aid students in locating, understanding, and managing information more efficiently.

A good explicit strategy for familiarizing students with external structure is *survey reading*. Common purposes of survey reading are to overview the material, establish the purpose for reading, assess difficulty of the text, and estimate the amount of time needed to complete the reading, but survey reading can also be used to help students understand the overall structure of a text. Table 10.2 contains a survey reading technique (SRT) developed for Barbara Rogasky's *Smoke and Ashes: The Story of the Holocaust* (2002). You may have students complete the questionnaire individually, or you may work through the questions orally in whole group. You may also use the model to design your own survey reading activity for another book. The activity is a simple process, and it is helpful for students unfamiliar with book structure:

Survey reading is a valuable procedure for drawing student's attention to a book's overall structure. Because the structure of subject matter textbooks is more complex than most young adult nonfiction, teachers can also use this type of strategy to help make textbooks more reader-friendly.

Internal structure is how text within a chapter, article, or paragraph is organized. Text may be either *narrative* or *expository*.[3] Narrative text is the primary text mode students encounter in the early grades; it is an account

Table 10.2

Survey Reading with *Smoke and Ashes*

1. What can you tell about the book from its front cover? From the back?
2. Is there useful information on the inside of the dust cover flap? If so, what information does it provide about the book?
3. Does this book have chapters? If so, how many and do they have subheadings?
4. Does it have a table of contents?
5. What kind of index does this book have? A general index, subject and/or author?
6. Look up *Hitler Youth* in the index. Why are pages 14 and 26 italicized?
7. Does this book contain a glossary or a list of key terms? If so, where is it located, and how is it helpful?
8. Survey the book for the following and circle all that you find: maps, archival photos, captions, timelines, graphs, tables, endnotes, footnotes, side notes.
9. Does the book contain a bibliography or list of additional resources? If so, where is it located?
10. What is the copyright of this book? (This is important so students can assess whether the information is up-to-date.)

---

[3]These categories are debated by discourse theorists who argue narrative may include expository, expository may contain narrative; nonetheless, they are useful categories in that they help us identify distinct modes of writing.

of events, and teens manage it well. It typically contains characters, themes, plots, and events and dialogue. Expository text informs the reader through explanation and is more difficult. It requires an understanding of several complex text patterns (i.e., description, sequence, comparison and contrast, cause and effect, and problem and solution). These five patterns are discussed next. Common signal words (see Table 10.3) aid in identifying relationships within the text, and easy-to-use graphic organizers help students develop an understanding of textual patterns. Samples are taken from young adult nonfiction.

Table 10.3

Signal Structures and/or Text Glue

If the text contains these . . .	You can probably expect to find these . . .
1. Question	1. An answer
2. A colon	2. A list, or explanatory phrase/sentence
3. A headline/subtitle	3. Information about the headline/subtitle
4. Therefore Because Since Consequently As a result This led to Nevertheless Thus As a result	4. Problem, results or conclusions, cause and effect
5. That is (i.e.) In other words Consists of Is equal to Means Are called	5. A definition
6. For example (e.g.) For instance (i.e.) Such as Is like Including To illustrate Most important Beside In front of Behind To begin with Also	6. Description/example(s)

Continued

T a b l e 1 0 . 3 *Continued*	
If the text contains these . . .	**You can probably expect to find these . . .**
7. Similarly In the same way Just like Just as Likewise In comparison Also	7. A comparison (how things are the same)
8. In contrast On the other hand However Whereas But Yet While Although	8. A contrast (how things are different)
9. First Second Next Finally (On) date Not long after Before After When Then	9. A sequence
10. Two causes Three reasons Two points The effect	10. A cause and effect pattern. An explanation about the causes, reasons, or points identified by the signal structure.

Source: Adapted from Schoenbach, Greenleaf, Cziko, and Hurwitz (1999).

Description

The description pattern is the most common organization pattern and the one with which students have the most experience. It is easily found in both narrative and expository writing. Descriptive writing involves explaining information about a person, a topic, a place, an event, a concept, or an idea. Details might include traits, facts, features, and characteristics. Descriptive writing lends itself easily to visualization. Read the following descriptive paragraph, visualize what you're reading, and examine the details in the bubble map in Figure 10.1.

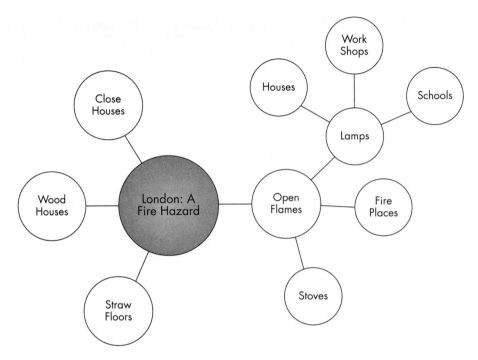

Figure 10.1   *Bubble Map*

In 1666 London was a bustling, crowded city of more than 500,000 people. Houses and other buildings were built very close together and were made from wood. People used dry straw to cover their floors just as people use carpets and rugs in modern times. Open flames were everywhere. They burned in oil lamps that lit houses, workshops, and schools. They crackled in fireplaces and stoves for cooking food and heating buildings. (Woods & Woods, 2007, p. 12)

Sequence or Time Order

Sequencing patterns involve ordering events, facts, and ideas. Some may have plenty of time order clues. Time reference in others may be inferred. Either way, a steady progression of events, facts, and/or ideas is apparent. Read the following paragraph and complete the flowchart in Figure 10.2. (You won't use the entire chart.)

In 1931 Japan invaded Manchuria, a northeastern province of China. The United States and many other nations denounced the invasion. In 1934 Japan withdrew from an international peacekeeping association called the League of Nations and scrapped an international treaty limiting the size of its navy. In 1937 Japan launched a major attack on China. (Goldstein, 2006, p. 31)

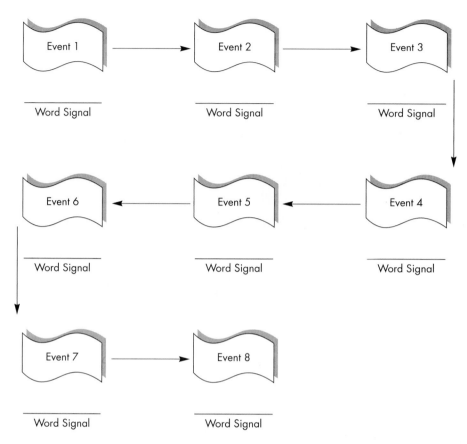

Figure 10.2   *Sequencing Flowchart*

Comparison and Contrast

Though a common organizational pattern, comparison and contrast is difficult to learn. (Most students struggle with transitional words when writing this text pattern.) There are two basic structures. The first, and easiest, is the block-by-block method. The first paragraph, for instance, describes one concept/person being compared; the second paragraph describes the second. The two are joined by a transitional phrase/sentence. The more difficult pattern is point-by-point. The writer describes one point about X, then compares/contrasts that same point with Y, and so forth. Point-by-point comparing/contrasting requires more skill. Writers must use more signal words, ensure smooth transitions, and make sure they balance details between X and Y. Read the following paragraph from Connie Goldsmith's nonfiction science book, *Influenza* (2007). What kind of comparison/contrast does she use? How would the information fit into the Venn diagram in Figure 10.3? Note that the modified Venn diagram has a place for *signal*

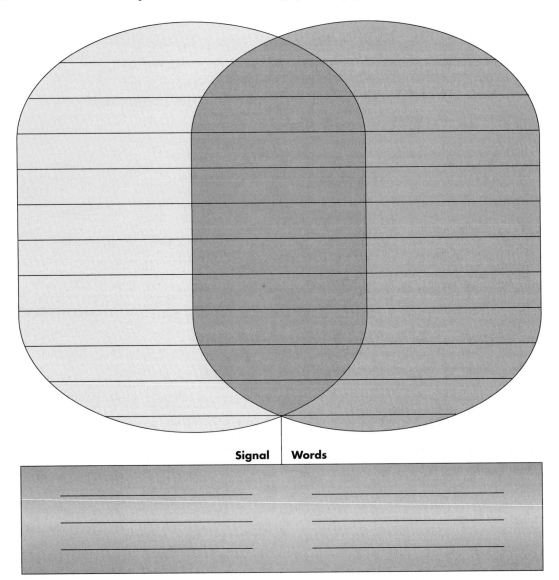

Figure 10.3   *Modified Venn Diagram*

words. Students need repeated exposure to words that connect and move text forward.

> Viruses are between twenty and one hundred times smaller than bacteria and can only be seen through an electron microscope. Viruses are so tiny that millions of them could fit inside the period at the end of this sentence. . . . Viruses are also much simpler than bacteria. They are inert bundles of genetic material in search of a host. (Goldsmith, 2007a, p. 13)

Cause and Effect

Cause and effect relationships are even more difficult. They involve explaining how events, facts, or ideas happen because of *other* events, facts, or ideas. This structure is difficult because one cause can have several effects, several causes may have one effect, and so forth. How could the following concepts fit in the graphic organizer in Figure 10.4?

> Ice can chisel its way through a rock, causing it to shatter. Water seeps into cracks in the rock, and then it freezes when the temperature drops. As it freezes, it expands and makes the crack bigger. When the ice thaws, even more water can penetrate the rock, expanding the crack further. (Hynes, 2006, p. 23)

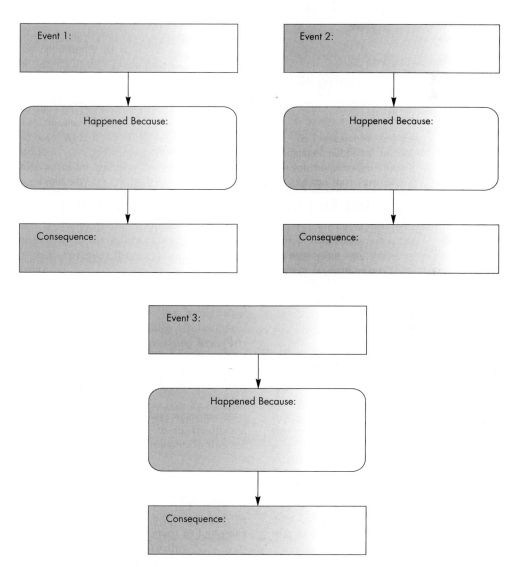

Figure 10.4   *Cause and Effect Mapping*

Problem-Solution

The problem-solution pattern involves identifying or describing a problem, then explaining how that problem is resolved. What steps or measures are taken to develop a solution? In *Superbugs Strike Back* (2007b), Goldsmith describes the development of penicillin during World War II and the fear researchers had that the penicillin would be lost during transportation. Read the following paragraph and complete the graphic organizer in Figure 10.5. Identify the problem, the three steps that are taken, and the solution.

> The Oxford team worried that the penicillin would be lost if the Germans shot down the plane carrying the two men. As a precaution, Florey and Heatley smeared the inside of their coats with mold spores. They wore some of the clothing and left some in Britain, where Chain stayed on to run the research. Mold spores can live for years, even in the lining of a jacket. No matter what happened on the dangerous flight, Florey knew the vital work could continue. (Goldsmith, 2007b, p. 31)

Generally speaking, expository structures are more difficult due to their complex patterns. It's important to remember that text difficulty can be affected by other factors: sentence structure, elaboration, vocabulary, coherence, clarity, and the reader's prior knowledge and interest.

Teaching Summarizing with YA Nonfiction

A summary is the bare essentials of a larger text. It is the gist, the key points worth remembering. Unlike paraphrasing, which is simply *restating* a text using different words, usually for clarity, summarizing is stripping away extraneous verbiage and unneeded examples to find core meaning. It is a

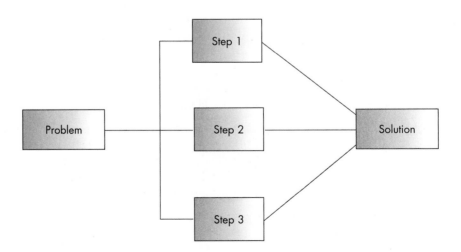

Figure 10.5 *Problem-Solution Map*

complex activity that takes years to develop and requires readers to discern between important details and irrelevant, though possibly interesting, details. It assumes skill in paraphrasing and identifying main ideas and supporting information. It also requires an understanding of text structure.

Summarizing is an essential comprehension tool. It improves comprehension, increases retention, and is a metacognitive tool that helps readers monitor their understanding of material—if you can't "sum it up," you don't get it. Summarizing enables readers to determine the importance of information. As students move through high school and enter college, they are repeatedly asked to summarize information, to break larger texts into smaller, more succinct portions. Their ability to extrapolate key information from increasingly complex and lengthy texts greatly influences their academic success.

Students who need practice in summarizing are easy to identify: they either write too much or too little. They may copy sentences or passages word for word, or they may *frontload* their summary; that is, if you ask for a three-page summary of a 15-page textbook chapter, two of the three pages may be about the first three chapters. More immature readers may choose information they find interesting as opposed to relevant concepts; they may also decide a detail is important based on the complexity of the sentence or passage—if they don't understand it, it must be important!

Students generally know that summarizing means choosing the most important information from a text and presenting it in a shorter text, but even good readers/writers struggle with *how much* information to include and *what* details are most important. Less able readers have the additional burden of not being able to identify main ideas and supporting sentences. Though crucial to academic achievement, summarizing is no doubt one of the most difficult strategies to grasp, and teaching it is equally challenging. Brown and Day (1983) identify the following rules for teaching summarizing:

1. Delete trivial or unimportant information.
2. Delete redundant information.
3. Categorize information.
4. Identify and use the author's main ideas.
5. Create your own main ideas if they are not stated.

Teachers must continually model summarizing strategies and provide students with ample practice. Be aware as you read through the following strategies that students will need repeated practice in summarizing. One or two "how-to summarize" lessons will achieve frustration, not proficiency. Here are 12 tips to remember when teaching summarizing:

1. Draw students' attention to summaries they encounter in their reading.
2. Teach them not to copy.
3. Remind them good summaries seldom include examples.

4.   Draw their attention to titles, illustrations, headings/subheadings, and topic sentences.
5.   Begin with short readings and short summaries.
6.   Teach summarizing from narrative texts first. Expository texts require a more complex understanding of text structure and textual clues.
7.   Stress the importance of polished summaries. Revision is essential.
8.   Have them critique and talk about their summaries with peers.
9.   Model the process of writing summaries.
10. Provide ample guided and independent practice.
11. Teach text structures and textual clues.
12. Use graphic organizers to organize important information prior to writing.

Words That Move Text

Students readily predict content from titles, subtitles, and story clues, but few receive practice or instruction in making predictions using text structure. Students who understand signal structures, predictors, and the "glue" that holds text together are better note takers and, in turn, better summarizers. To give students practice identifying word signals, teachers need to help them become familiar with signal structures: punctuation marks, words, and phrases that guide readers through text.

Give students a list similar to that found in Table 10.3 and several paragraphs containing some of the signal structures. Ask students to determine the text structure, then talk about what kind of information the structure signals. You might, for instance, give them a passage like this one taken from Barbara Rogasky's *Smoke and Ashes: The Story of the Holocaust* (2002).

> There were probably _three major reasons_ why the Germans set up the ghettos, began the mass murders and later established most of the concentration camps and all of the death camps in Poland and Eastern Europe.
>   _First_, obviously, because nearly all of Europe's Jews were there—five million of them.
>   _Second_, the land area was vast. Aside from the major cities, many lightly populated forested miles separated communities from one another. By today's standards, communications among them were simple and primitive. All this allowed the Nazis some element of surprise. Their intended victims were less likely to resist if they did not know what was coming. It also permitted some secrecy. The Germans wanted to hide what they were doing from the attention of the rest of the world. In this they were not quite successful, as later chapters will show.
>   _Third_, Eastern Europe had a history of anti-Semitism, of which the Germans were well aware. There had been large-scale pogroms as recently as twenty years earlier. Individual anti-Semitic incidents occurred often. The Nazis planned to take as much advantage of this as they could. (pp. 30–31)

Note the underlined phrase in the opening sentence. Ask students to explain what key information they should look for as they read the rest of the passage. Students may want to go through the passage and tell you the three points, but you want them to explain *how* they know what to look for. That is, get them to explain the signal clue and what it told them to expect. Have them underline or highlight that information, then write a brief summary that contains those three key points. Some students may simply want to copy word for word. A good technique for preventing them from doing so is to have them write an initial summary containing the three key points (some will copy; some won't) and then revise their summary, reducing it to one sentence that captures the essence of the passage. Experiment with writing your own sentence containing the gist of the three highlighted points.

Punctuation also helps readers identify important information. Many students don't know, for example, to "read over" most information set off in parentheses or by commas. Most adolescents will know that a series or list generally will follow a colon, but few will recognize that a sentence following a colon can explain the preceding sentence. Note the role the colon plays in the following two passages:

> As Benjamin Franklin calmly observed, Grenville's plan was simply bad economics: The more the colonists spent on taxes, the less money they would have to buy goods shipped from England. (Aronson, 2005, p. 77)

> The series especially packed them in every Saturday. Each episode had a cliffhanger ending: The hero seemed hopelessly cornered by evildoers or trapped by an avalanched, a stampeded, a tidal wave, or some other catastrophe. (Freedman, 2005, p. 84)

Once struggling readers understand the role punctuation plays in text structure, they become stronger readers and are better prepared to identify key information and can, therefore, write better summaries. When working with signal clues, remember to start small. Teach a few at a time.

"Meaty Words": Key Words and Phrases

Explaining to students that summaries include essential information, key words, and phrases isn't sufficient. They already know that. They need to see a proficient summarizer at work. They need especially to see how a good summarizer collapses ideas into smaller units. Place a passage on an overhead and ask students to identify essential words/phrases—meaty words—that explain the gist of the passage. Meaty words are mostly nouns and verbs. A student-teacher example might resemble the following:

> Throughout history, <u>religious fervor</u> has often <u>inspired</u> the <u>creation</u> of <u>huge buildings.</u> Some examples are the <u>Mayan pyramids</u> in Mexico, <u>Hindu temples</u> in India, or the great <u>cathedrals of medieval Europe.</u> <u>Neither these buildings</u> nor the massive <u>buildings of ancient Egypt</u> have been <u>called skyscrapers,</u> but they do have <u>one thing in common</u> with the nineteenth- and twentieth-century tall buildings we know as <u>skyscrapers.</u> It is the power of <u>the human ego.</u> Johnson explained it as a desire, *fueled*

> *by personal power,* to <u>reach</u> for a <u>"dominant height."</u> An <u>enormous tomb,</u> <u>a huge lighthouse, colossal houses of worship, and modern office towers</u> <u>all require the ambitious drive of kings, high priests, popes, or business</u> <u>executives.</u> These are the personalities needed to inspire and supervise huge construction projects. (Severance, 2000, p. 10)

Note the last sentence in the passage. It is a clincher sentence and adds no new information to the paragraph. Note, too, the expression "fueled by personal power." Most phrases and clauses set off by commas can be dismissed when summarizing. Here is a summary based on the underlined words/phrases written by a student who knows how to "collapse" ideas. The idea is to use the key words and as few additional words as possible. Compare the passage with the underlined words in the original.

> Religious fervor has inspired the creation of huge buildings such as the Mayan pyramids, the Hindu temples and European cathedrals. While these aren't called skyscrapers, they do have one thing in common with *modern buildings.* They were constructed by the *human* desire to reach a "dominant height."

Without giving the same level of detail, the student captured the gist of the passage. Note, for example, the use of the word *human* instead of the words *kings, high priests, popes,* or *business executives.* This word choice illustrates the student's ability to collapse these words into smaller units. What ideas did the student collapse with the phrase *modern buildings*?

Graphic Organizers

Graphic organizers are visual text representations. They help readers comprehend and manage key textual information. Teachers and researchers have developed a host of organizers over the years: flowcharts, spider and bubble maps, Venn diagrams, fishbone diagrams, character and concept maps, word maps, two- and three-column tables, time lines, tree diagrams, and more. They are terrific instructional tools for aiding students in identifying main ideas and supporting information, for organizing thoughts, and for helping students determine how much to write. By googling *graphic organizers* and *graphic organizer makers,* you can download and create a wealth of organizational charts. (SmartDraw is an easy-to-use graphic software as are Inspiration and Kidspiration.) You can help students who either write too much or not enough to manage information with graphic organizers. You might, for instance, have students develop a time line after reading a biography. Students then use the time line as the basis for their written summaries. It's a good idea to give students struggling with "how much to write" to include some perimeters to help them identify how many major accomplishments they need to include; otherwise some will write to infinity; others will write little. The graphic organizer in Figure 10.6 made with SmartDraw (www.smartdraw.com) illustrates an alternative to the traditional time line. Such a graphic organizer helps students manage information by outlining key points before they begin writing. Using

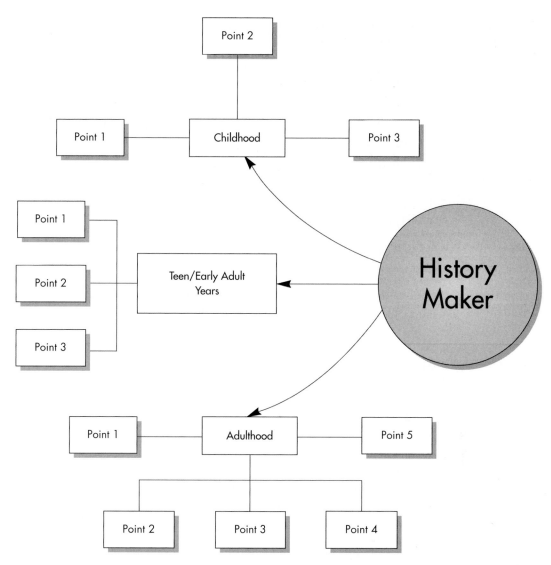

Figure 10.6   *Graphic Organizer*

such an organizational tool can help students balance their summaries and avoid telling every detail about the first 10 years of an individual's life, for example, then skipping the last decade. Teachers can develop graphic organizers, or students can use software such as SmartDraw individually as an organizational tool.

Guided Reading Procedure

Introduced by Manzo (1975), the guided reading procedure (GRP) requires that students read a text closely, then see how much they can recall. This procedure works well to help students develop summarizing skills. The procedure is as follows:

1. Choose a reading assignment (approximately 7 to 10 minutes).
2. Prepare students to read it (tell them you'll be asking them to recall information later).
3. Have students read silently.
4. When they finish, have them close their books and brainstorm as many details as they can remember. List the information randomly on the board as they recall it.
5. After they've recalled all they can, tell them you're going to write a summary together.
6. Begin working with them to organize the information on the board. Talk with them as you work about any details that can be deleted.
7. Once the information is grouped, you may write a paragraph together, or they may write them individually.

A variation of this activity would be to have students take notes as you or a peer reads aloud and then write a summary based on their notes. Good selections for read-alouds can be found in Chapter 9.

Summary Analysis by a Peer

Schoenbach, Greenleaf, Cziko, and Hurwitz (1999) found that students become more conscious of the steps involved in summarizing when they analyze summaries written by peers. The procedure is as follows:

1. Students read and summarize a text for homework.
2. In class, students draw a line under their summaries and trade with a partner.
3. Students respond to the following questions on their partner's paper:
   If you hadn't read the text yourself, would you understand what it was about from this summary? Why or why not?
   Is there anything important that should be added to this summary? What is it?
   Is there anything unimportant that could be left out of the summary? What is it?
4. Students return papers, read peer comments, and revise accordingly. (p. 89)

Polishing Summaries

Traditionally students receive little practice rewriting summaries. Summaries are like any other form of writing; they reflect process. First writings can sound awkward and may include vague or approximate language, erroneous details, and/or insignificant pieces of information. They also tend to be wordy and include an overabundance of dead and useless words (e.g., unnecessary prepositions, adjectives, and adverbs). They will also show more evidence of copying. When students revise summaries, they reduce the amount of copying, collapse more ideas, and eliminate some awkward structures.

Though a common class assignment in all content areas, summarizing is seldom explicitly taught. Students need frequent and repeated practice summarizing and critiquing summaries by others. The better students become at summarizing, the better readers and note takers they will be. Strategies such as the ones just discussed can aid students in developing this complex, essential skill.

Final Thoughts

Ironically, students encounter mostly fiction and narrative text structures in English language arts classes. They interact with their reading by analyzing character development, conflict, literary elements, setting, rising action, climax, denouement, and so forth. This type of experience with text doesn't prepare students to recognize, understand, or re-create more difficult text patterns encountered in other subjects. As English language arts teachers, we should include a fair amount of nonfiction in our curriculum, providing models for the kinds of writing we ask them to do and models for other kinds of real-world reading and writing. Explicit instruction in the text patterns described in this chapter and the signal words related to them will aid students in comprehension and will help students improve their writing. Remember, though, students will need repeated practice.

Professional Resources

Bamford, R. A., & Kristo, J. (2004). *Nonfiction in focus.* New York: Scholastic.

Blevins, W., & Boynton, A. (2003). *Teaching students to read nonfiction: Grades 4 and up.* New York: Scholastic.

Blevins, W., & Boynton, A. (2004). *Nonfiction passages with graphic organizers for independent practice: Grades 4 and up.* New York: Scholastic.

Camp, D. (2006). *Pairing fiction and nonfiction.* New York: Scholastic.

Daniels, H., & Zemelman, S. (2004). *Subjects matter: Every teacher's guide to content-area reading.* Portsmouth, NH: Heinemann.

Dymock, S., & Nicholson, T. (2007). *Teaching text structures: A key to nonfiction reading success.* New York: Scholastic.

Hamilton, N. (2005). *Uncovering the secrets of magazine writing: A step-by-step guide to writing creative nonfiction for print and Internet publication.* Boston: Allyn & Bacon.

Harvey, S. (1998). *Nonfiction matters: Reading, writing, and researching in Grades 3–8.* Portland, ME: Stenhouse.

Harvey, S., & Goudvis, A. (2007). *Toolkit texts: Grades 6–7: Short nonfiction for guided and independent practice.* Portsmouth, NH: Heinemann.

Hayes, D. A. (1989). Helping students GRASP the knack of writing summaries. *Journal of Reading, 33*(2), 96–101.

Hoyt, L. (2002). *Make it real: Strategies for success with informational texts.* Portsmouth, NH: Heinemann.

Hoyt, L., Mooney, M., & Parkes, B. (2003). *Exploring informational texts: From theory to practice.* Portsmouth, NH: Heinemann.

Irvin, J., Buehl, D. R., & Radcliffe, B. J. (2007). The demands of text. In *Strategies to enhance literacy and learning in middle school content area classrooms* (3rd ed., pp. 74–97). Boston: Allyn & Bacon.

Jenkins, C. B., & White, D. (2007). *Nonfiction: Author studies in the elementary classroom.* Portsmouth, NH: Heinemann.

Kissner, E. (2006). *Summarizing, paraphrasing, and retelling.* Portsmouth, NH: Heinemann.

Moore, D. (2007). *The truth of the matter: Art and craft in creative nonfiction.* New York: Longman.

Nguyen, B., & Shreve, P. (2005). *Contemporary creative nonfiction: I and eye.* New York: Longman.

Pike, K., & Mumper, J. (2004). *Making nonfiction and other informational texts come alive: A practical approach to reading, writing, and using nonfiction and other informational texts across the curriculum.* Boston: Allyn & Bacon.

Portalupi, J., & Fletcher, R. (2001). *Nonfiction craft lessons: Teaching information writing K–8.* Portland, ME: Stenhouse.

Robb, L. (2004). *Nonfiction writing: From the inside out.* New York: Scholastic.

Root, R., & Steinberg, M. (2007). *The fourth genre: Contemporary writers of/on creative nonfiction.* New York: Longman.

Stead, T. (2005). *Reality checks.* Portland, ME: Stenhouse.

ONLINE

Bio: www.biography.com

Bio4kids: www.biography.com/bio4kids/index.jsp

The Biography Channel: www.thebiography channel.co.uk/about_us.htm

Creative Nonfiction: www.creativenonfiction.org/index.htm

Emints National Center: www.emints.org/ethemes/resources/S00000287.shtml

Infoplease: www.infoplease.com/people.html

The National Review: www.nationalreview.com

Nonfiction Writers Blog: www.schoollibraryjournal.com/blog

On Writing Nonfiction for Children: www.falcon.jmu.edu/ramseyil/nonfictcriteria.htm

Oxford Dictionary of National Biography: www.oxforddnb.com

References

Abrahamson, R. F., & Carter, B. (1991). Nonfiction: The missing piece in the middle. *English Journal, 80*(1), 52–58.

Al-Windawi, T. (2004). *Thura's diary: My life in wartime Iraq.* Trans. Robin Bray. New York: Viking/Penguin, 2004.

Anne Frank: The diary of a young girl. (1952). New York: Doubleday.

Applegate, D. (2006). *The most famous man in America: The biography of Henry Ward Beecher.* New York: Doubleday/Random House.

Aronson, M. (1998). *Art attack: A brief cultural history of the avant-garde.* Boston: Houghton Mifflin.

Aronson, M. (2000). *Sir Walter Ralegh and the quest for El Dorado.* Boston: Houghton Mifflin.

Aronson, M. (2001). *Exploding the myths: The truth about teenagers and reading.* Lanham, MD: Scarecrow Press.

Aronson, M. (2003a). *Beyond the pale: New essays for a new era.* Lanham, MD: Scarecrow Press.

Aronson, M. (2003b). *Witch-hunt: Mysteries of the Salem witch trials.* New York: Simon & Schuster.

Aronson, M. (2004). *John Winthrop, Oliver Cromwell, and the Land of Promise.* Boston: Houghton Mifflin.

Aronson, M. (2005). *The real revolution: The global story of American independence.* New York: Clarion.

Aronson, M. (2007a). *Race: A history beyond black and white.* New York: Simon & Schuster.

Aronson, M. (2007b). *Up Close: Robert F. Kennedy.* New York: Penguin.

Aronson, M. (with John Glenn). (2007c). *The world made new: Why the age of exploration happened and how it changed the world.* New York: Random House.

Aronson, M., & Campbell, P. (2008). *War is . . . soldiers, survivors, and storytellers talk about war.* Cambridge, MA: Candlewick Press.

Bartoletti, S. C. (1996). *Growing up in coal country.* Boston: Houghton Mifflin.

Bartoletti, S. C. (1999a). *Kids on strike!* Boston: Houghton Mifflin.

Bartoletti, S. C. (1999b). *No man's land.* New York: Scholastic.

Bartoletti, S. C. (2000). *A coal miner's bride: The diary of Annetka Kaminski.* New York: Scholastic.

Bartoletti, S. C. (2001a). *Black potatoes: The story of the great Irish famine, 1845–1850.* Boston: Houghton Mifflin.

Bartoletti, S. C. (2001b). *The Christmas promise.* New York: Hyperion.

Bartoletti, S. C. (2004). *The flag maker.* Boston: Houghton Mifflin.

Bartoletti, S. C. (2005). *Hitler Youth: Growing up in Hitler's shadow.* New York: Scholastic.

Bartoletti, S. C. (2008). *The boy who dared.* New York: Scholastic.

Brown, A. L., & Day, J. D. (1983). Macrorules for summarizing texts: The development of expertise. *Journal of Verbal Learning and Verbal Behavior, 22*(1), 1–14.

Canfield, J., Hansen, M. V., Meyer, S. H., & Meyer, J. (2007). *Chicken soup for the teen soul.* Deerfield Beach, FL: Health Communications.

Capote, T. (1965). *In cold blood: A true account of a multiple murder and its consequences.* New York: Random House.

Carlson, R. (2000). *Don't sweat the small stuff for teens.* New York: Hyperion.

Crutcher, C. (2003). *King of the mild frontier: An ill-advised autobiography.* New York: Greenwillow/HarperCollins.

Darrow, S. (2003). *Through the tempests dark and wild: A story of Mary Shelley, creator of Frankenstein.* Illus. Angela Barrett. Cambridge, MA: Candlewick Press.

Daugherty, J. (1939). *Daniel Boone.* New York: Viking.

Filipovic, Z. (1994). *Zlata's diary: A child's life in wartime Sarejevo.* Trans. Christina Pribichevich-Zoric. New York: Viking/Penguin, 1994.

Foster, G. (1952). *Birthdays of freedom.* New York: Scribner.

Freedman, R. (1987). *Lincoln: A photobiography.* New York: Clarion.

Freedman, R. (2005). *Children of the Great Depression.* New York: Clarion.

Frey, J. (2003). *A million little pieces.* New York: Random House.

Fritz, J. (1989). *The great little Madison.* New York: Putnam/Penguin.

Goldsmith, C. (2007a). *Influenza: The next pandemic?* Minneapolis, MN: Lerner.

Goldsmith, C. (2007b). *Superbugs strike back.* Minneapolis, MN: Lerner.

Goldstein, M. J. (2006). *Japanese in America.* Minneapolis, MN: Lerner.

Gore, A. (2006). *An inconvenient truth: The planetary emergency of global warming and what we can do about it.* Emmaus, PA: Rodale.

Gore, A. (2007). *An inconvenient truth: The crisis of global warming.* New York: Viking/Penguin.

Herr, M. (1977). *Dispatches.* New York: Knopf/Random House.

Hynes, M. (2006). *Rocks and fossils.* Boston: Kingfisher.

Jacobs, H. A. (2001). *Incidents in the life of a slave girl.* New York: Penguin. (Original work published 1861)

Jiang, J. (1997). *Red scarf girl: A memoir of the Cultural Revolution.* New York: HarperCollins.

Johnson, G. W. (1959). *America is born: A history for Peter.* New York: Morrow.

Johnson, G. W. (1960a). *America grows up: A history for Peter.* New York: Morrow.

Johnson, G. W. (1960b). *America moves on: A history for Peter.* New York: Morrow.

Judson, C. I. (1950). *Abraham Lincoln, friend of the people.* Chicago: Wilcox and Follett.

Judson, C. I. (1953). *Theodore Roosevelt, fighting patriot.* Chicago: Wilcox and Follett.

Lach, W. (2005).*Vincent's colors: Words and pictures by Vincent van Gogh.* San Francisco: Chronicle Books.

Lasky, K. (2006). *John Muir: America's first environmentalist.* Illus. Stan Fellows. Cambridge, MA: Candlewick Press.

Lester, J. (1968). *To be a slave.* New York: Dial/Penguin.

Lyman, P., & Varian, H. (2003). *How much information?* Retrieved May 25, 2007, from http://www2.sims.berkeley.edu/research/projects/how-much-info-2003

Manzo, A. (1975). Guided reading procedure. *Journal of Reading, 18,* 287–291.

Matthews, J. (2006). *Pirates.* New York: Atheneum/Simon & Schuster.

Matthews, J. (2007). *Pirates most wanted: Thirteen of the most bloodthirsty pirates ever to sail the high seas.* New York: Atheneum/Simon & Schuster.

McCullough. D. G. (1992). *Truman.* New York: Simon & Schuster.

McCullough, D. G. (2001). *John Adams.* New York: Simon & Schuster.

Meigs, C. (1933). *Invincible Louisa: The story of the author of* Little Women. Boston: Little, Brown.

Meltzer, M. (2003). *Edgar Allan Poe.* Minneapolis, MN: Lerner.

Meltzer, M. (2005). *Emily Dickinson.* Minneapolis, MN: Lerner

Meltzer, M. (2006). *Nathaniel Hawthorne.* Minneapolis, MN: Lerner.

Meltzer, M. (2007). *Henry David Thoreau.* Minneapolis, MN: Lerner.

Montgomery, S., & Bishop, S. (1999). *The snake scientist.* Boston: Houghton Miffin.

Moore, J. G. (1968). *The many ways of seeing: An introduction to the pleasures of art.* Cleveland: World Publishing.

Murphy, J. (1990). *The boys' war: Confederate and union soldiers talk about the Civil War.* Boston: Houghton Mifflin.

Murphy, J. (1992). *The Long road to Gettysburg.* Boston: Houghton Mifflin.

Murphy, J. (1993). *Across America on an emigrant train.* New York: Clarion.

Murphy, J. (1995). *The great fire.* New York: Scholastic.

Murphy, J. (1996). *A Young patriot: The American Revolution as experienced by one boy.* Boston: Houghton Mifflin.

Murphy, J. (1998). *Gone a-whaling: The lure of the sea and the hunt for the great whale.* New York: Clarion.

Murphy, J. (2000a). *Blizzard! The storm that changed America.* New York: Scholastic.

Murphy, J. (2000b). *Pick & shovel poet: The journeys of Pascal D'Angelo.* Boston: Houghton Mifflin.

Murphy, J. (2003a). *An American plague: The true and terrifying story of the Yellow Fever Epidemic of 1793.* New York: Clarion.

Murphy, J. (2003b). *Inside the Alamo.* New York: Random House.

Murphy, J. (2007). *The real Benedict Arnold.* New York: Clarion.

Myers, W. D. (1993). *Malcolm X: By any means necessary.* New York: Scholastic.

Nir, Y. (2002). *The lost childhood: A World War II memoir.* New York: Scholastic.

Partridge, E. (2005). *John Lennon: All I want is the truth.* New York: Viking/Penguin.

Paulsen, G. (2001). *Caught by the sea: My life on boats.* New York: Bantam Doubleday Dell.

Reiss, J. (1972).*The upstairs room.* New York: Crowell.

Roach, M. (2005). *Spook: Science tackles the afterlife.* New York: W. W. Norton.

Rogasky, B. (2002). *Smoke and ashes: The story of the Holocaust.* New York: Holiday House.

Rosenblatt, L. (1978). *The reader, the text, the poem: The transactional theory of the literary work.* Carbondale: Southern Illinois UP.

Schoenbacuh, R., Greenleaf, C., Cziko, C., & Hurwitz, L. (1999). *Reading for understanding: A guide to improving reading in middle and high school classrooms.* San Francisco: Jossey-Bass.

Seeger, E. (1934). *Pageant of Chinese history.* New York: Longman, Green.

Severance, J. (2000). *Skyscrapers.* New York: Holiday House.

Shippen, K. (1945) *New found world.* New York: Viking.

Shippen, K. (1954). *Men, microscopes, and living things.* New York: Viking.

Siegel, S. C. (2006). *To dance: A ballerina's graphic novel.* Illus. Mark Siegel. New York: Simon & Schuster.

Snicket, L. (2002). *Lemony Snicket: The unauthorized autobiography.* New York: HarperCollins.

Sullivan, E. (2001, January). Some teens prefer the real thing: The case for young adult nonfiction. *English Journal, 90*(3), 43.

Thimmesh, C. (2006). *Team moon: How 400,000 people landed* Apollo 11 *on the moon.* Boston: Houghton Mifflin.

van Loon, H. W. (1921). *The story of mankind.* New York: Boni & Liveright.

Washington, B. T. (1998). *Up from slavery.* New York: Doubleday. (Original work published 1901)

Wolfe, T., & Johnson, E. W. (Eds.). (1973). *The new journalism.* London: Pan Books.

Woods, M., & Woods, M. B. (2007). *Fires.* Minneapolis, MN: Lerner.

Worthy, J., Moorman, M., & Turner, M. (1999). What Johnny likes to read is hard to find in school. *Reading Research Quarterly, 34*(1), 12–27.

Zenatti, V. (2005). *When I was a soldier.* Trans. Adriana Hunter. New York: Bloomsbury.

The Classical Canon and Young Adult Literature

Reading Skill: Synthesizing

Introduction

By the time you read this chapter you will have digested and discussed a wide array of young adult titles, and you've probably had some discussions about the classics and the apparent dichotomy between the two. This chapter is grounded in the premise that the two should not be viewed in opposition. Part of the dichotomy arises because the two are taught separately in teacher preparation programs, and part lies in the reality that schools are commonly structured so honors students read classical texts while at-risk students read young adult literature.[1] Another divisive factor is teacher knowledge and attitude.

Young adult literature, as you will see, can spark interest in the classics and vice versa. Although it's clear that young adult literature is more accessible, that doesn't warrant denying the classics to struggling readers. The classics shouldn't be reserved for exceptional students, and young adult literature shouldn't be reserved for at-risk readers. When we create that dichotomy, we send an elitist message about the classics and an inferior message about young adult literature—and we fail our students.

The term *canon* originally referred to the books of the Bible believed to be authentic and authoritative. Over time it extended to secular works in an effort to distinguish and identify certain writers as literary authorities (e.g., Shakespeare, Chaucer, Milton, Austen, Dickens, and Dante). Whether we've read their works or not, we recognize their names. We begin gaining familiarity with them in prose retellings and simplified texts in childhood, in viewing TV programs and movies, and by visiting libraries and bookstores, and we continue our relationship throughout our school and college years.

Over the last several decades, challenges to the European white male perspective have expanded the canon. Langston Hughes and James Baldwin, for example, have added a long-neglected black male perspective, and the Brontë sisters, Jane Austen, Anne Bradstreet, and Emily Dickinson have contributed female voices. Young adult literature, once "outside" the classical canon, is the camel's nose under the tent; enduring works by Robert Cormier, Robert Lipsyte, Judy Blume, Paul Zindel, Walter Dean Myers, Chris Crutcher, and others challenge the traditional boundaries.[2]

---

[1]Throughout this text I've melded those boundaries slightly. I resisted the urge to blend them more for one reason: you are familiar with the classics. My main purpose with the literature in this text is to introduce you to an unfamiliar genre. It is my hope that in the classroom you blur these boundaries even further.
[2]See Connie Zitlow's list of young adult classics in Chapter 3.

Although redefining the canon is an important conversation, that's not the direction of this chapter. The purpose here is to examine methods for integrating the classical canon and young adult literature and to illustrate ways young adult literature has been influenced by classical writers and has borrowed themes and motifs from fairy tale and folklore traditions.

Pairing Young Adult Literature with the Classics

Many teachers are familiar with young adult literature, would like to use it more, but feel pressured to teach the traditional canon. They fear test scores will drop; colleagues, including the department chair, will disapprove; and some aren't totally convinced it's quality literature—using it in the classroom is more about *fun* reading, giving students a break, than *real* learning. Young adult literature can be used to teach the same skills, however. One way to integrate it into the traditional curriculum is by pairing it with the classics by theme; that is, teachers develop units around themes in which students read a traditional classic *and* a young adult title and make intertextual (text-to-text) connections.

For instance, George Orwell's *1984* (1949) and Lois Lowry's *The Giver* (1993) would work well together. Both are dystopias and speak to the doom of humankind. Control mechanisms such as electronic devices that monitor human behavior appear in both works; so does language manipulation. Orwell's characters are forbidden to think. Those who do commit thought-crime. For characters in *The Giver,* thinking is unnecessary: all decisions, from what one eats to when children receive bicycles, are made for them. Characters in both stories are led to believe they live in a utopia. Language manipulation erodes truth and distorts reality. Characters in both worlds believe living conditions are the best ever. More common threads exist.

In a paired unit, students read the titles back to back, beginning with *The Giver,* the more reader-friendly text. They discuss emerging themes (e.g., language manipulation, complacency, totalitarianism, truth versus untruth, conformity) as they read. Once they begin reading *1984,* they respond to questions and activities that encourage them to make text-to-text connections. This structure works well, for the teacher can introduce abstract concepts (e.g., totalitarianism) with a reader-friendly book. By the time students encounter the same concept in Orwell's book, they have gained some prior knowledge, which can make his book easier.

It's not always possible to teach two novels per unit, but you can also blend genres. You might pair classical poetry with a young adult novel, the common theme being sense of place. The young adult novel might provide a feel for the time period in which classical poetry was written. For example, Veronica Bennett's *Angelmonster* (2006) might be paired with English romantic poetry.

Joan Kaywell

Joan Kaywell's four-book series, *Adolescent Literature as a Complement to the Classics* (1993–2000), illustrates dozens of classical and young adult pairings and provides activities and methodologies for teaching both. Although many of the original series pairings are dated,[3] the concept itself adds validity to both the canon and young adult literature by exposing students to a wider array of writing styles and text structures and requiring that students make text-to-text connections—a higher-order skill. In Table 11.1, Joan Kaywell suggests several new pairings with 25 classical texts.

Table 11.1

Young Adult Literature and the Classics by Joan Kaywell

Classic	YA Novel	Common Themes/Topics
To Kill a Mockingbird by Harper Lee	*Monster* by Walter Dean Myers	Trial: Guilty before Innocent
Lord of the Flies by William Golding	*The Clique* by Lisi Harrison	Use and Abuse of Power
The Diary of a Young Girl by Anne Frank	*Anne Frank and Me* by Cherie Bennett and Jeff Gottesfeld	Holocaust: Other Children's Experiences
The Adventures of Huckleberry Finn by Mark Twain	*The Watsons Go to Birmingham–1963* by Christopher Paul Curtis	Prejudice
Their Eyes Were Watching God by Zora Neale Hurston	*Copper Sun* by Sharon Draper	Making One's Identity
The Red Badge of Courage by Stephen Crane	*The River between Us* by Richard Peck	The Civil War
The Awakening by Kate Chopin	*Define Normal* by Julie Anne Peters	Discovering One's Identity
The Miracle Worker by William Gibson	*Accidents of Nature* by Harriet McBryde Johnson	Overcoming Disabilities
Fahrenheit 451 by Ray Bradbury	*Feed* by M. T. Anderson	Exploring the Future
Dracula by Bram Stoker	*Twilight* by Stephenie Meyer	Vampires
The Hunchback of Notre Dame by Victor Hugo	*Endgame* by Nancy Garden *Hunchback* by Randall Wright	Outcasts
Doctor Faustus by Christopher Marlowe	*Under the Baseball Moon* by John Ritter	Selling One's Soul to the Devil
A Separate Peace by John Knowles	*Black and White* by Paul Volponi	Friendship and Betrayal
The Crucible Acts by Arthur Miller	*The Minister's Daughter* by Julie Hearn *Harmless* by Dana Reinhardt	Salem Witch-Hunts/Mass Hysteria
A Lesson before Dying by Ernest J. Gaines	*Mississippi Trial, 1955* by Chris Crowe	Racism, Justice

Continued

---

[3]While this chapter was being written, the four-volume series was being updated and revised into two larger volumes: one for middle school, the other for high school.

T a b l e 11.1 *Continued*		
Robinson Crusoe by Daniel Defoe	*Wild Man Island* by Will Hobbs	Survival
Things Fall Apart by Chinua Achebe	*Last Child* by Michael Spooner	When Views Clash
Narrative of the Life of Frederick Douglass written by himself	*Letters from a Slave Boy: The Story of Joseph Jacobs* by Mary E. Lyons	Perspectives on What It's Like Being a Slave
A Farewell to Arms by Ernest Hemingway	*Postcards from No Man's Land* by Aidan Chambers	War and Love
Moby Dick by Herman Melville	*Voyage of Ice: Chronicles of Courage* by Michele Torrey	Whaling
The Scarlet Letter by Nathaniel Hawthorne	*Sandpiper* by Ellen Wittlinger	Sexual Behavior Alienation
The Call of the Wild by Jack London	*Jason's Gold* by Will Hobbs	Gold Rush Survival
The Catcher and the Rye by J. D. Salinger	*America* by E. R. Frank	Mental Illness Rebellion
Jane Eyre by Charlotte Brontë	*Set in Stone* by Linda Newbery	Gothic Setting Orphans
The Grapes of Wrath by John Steinbeck	*Poor Is Just a Starting Place* by Leslie J. Wyatt	The Great Depression
Pride and Prejudice by Jane Austen	*Cassandra's Sister: Growing Up Jane Austen* by Veronica Bennett	Women in 19th-Century Society Social Roles

Fracturing the Classical Canon

Young adult literature is clearly influenced by the traditional canon. Writers have added unique twists to classical texts: They've altered points of view, inserted well-known characters (and authors) into different story lines, borrowed heavily from theme, setting, style, and plot, and sometimes retold stories in different formats. Such texts can be wonderful complements or alternatives to original texts.

Walter Dean Myers's *Street Love* (2006), for instance, is a modern *Romeo and Juliet* story told in inner-city street hip-hop language. Damien (Romeo) and Junice (Juliet) come from different social realms: Damien has been accepted by Brown University; Junice lives in a drug-dealing family. The pair struggle with family and social obstacles. Note the soliloquy-like style, Shakespearean "feel," and complex metaphor of the following passage delivered by Damien. He is standing alone on a street corner; Junice has just walked away.

> *I have never felt so alone*
> *Cogito ergo sum; I think, therefore I am*
> *Dead thoughts in a dead language*
> *What good is thinking? What good is I am*

If I am is not something larger
Than I could ever be alone?
The thinking, the furrowed brow
Had always been, until this time
A comfort.
To this very moment every
Red horizon produced a new day
Every cloud its cleansing shower
The sun never stopped its
Brilliant arcing across my blue skies
What strange land have I entered
Where tsunami questions roar and crash the soul
And the gravity of the blood moon pulls no
Answers from the brooding tide?
What is there to think about
To weigh carefully
That Junice and Melissa enter
Some benigh level of Hell
And what if Hell is not so Hellish
As it won't be once I put it
Beyond my sight, into the cool
Regions of intellect. If Hell
Is not so Hellish once out of
My mind, what will life be,
When I am out of Junice?
Comfortable? Without a doubt.
Carefully planned? To the last letter.
Life will resume, the too-familiar
Curtain rises once again, but
I've forgotten all my lines.
More important than what happens
To me, for the first time
In my life more important than
What happens to me, is what will happen
To Junice?
Can I shut my eyes, seal my ears
Not know what she stutters through
Her tears
That every distance
From love is too far? That every
Battering of the heart is impossible
To heal, and that a lifetime
Of shielding the wounds
Is too high a price to pay?
Junice has laid down her dreams
For the world to see
While I still clutch mine to my bosom
And whine my prayers to God
Who wants more
Of me than I can bring to Heaven's door. (pp. 99–101)

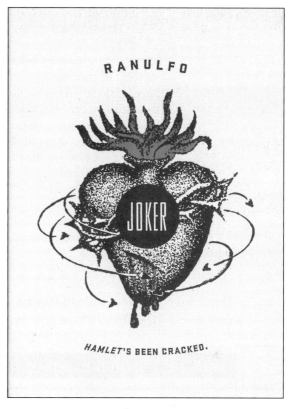

Used by permission
of HarperCollins
Publishers.

Shakespeare's influence on young adult literature is considerable. Ranulfo's *Joker: Hamlet's Been Cracked* (2006) is a modern retelling of *Hamlet.* After the death of his best friend, 17-year-old Matt questions his beliefs and his parents' broken relationship. Julius Lester (1995) has produced the best prose retelling of *Othello,* the tragic love story about Desdemona, daughter of a Venetian senator, and Othello, a noble moor. Virtually every Shakespearean play has been retold in picture-book format, and there are many wonderful renditions.

The Bard himself appears repeatedly in young adult literature, sometimes making cameo appearances, other times playing heftier roles. In Gary Blackwood's *The Shakespeare Stealer* (1998), a young orphan is ordered by his master, a competing theatre owner, to steal Shakepeare's script for *Hamlet.* Widge infiltrates the Globe Theatre intending to obey his master, but he ends up joining Shakespeare's acting troupe. Blackwood's story is rich in period detail, shady characters, and humor. Two sequels follow Widge's experiences as a member of Shakespeare's entourage: *Shakespeare's Scribe* (2000) and *Shakespeare's Spy* (2003). Michael Ortiz introduces readers to the Bard through journal writings of 13-year-old Susanna, Shakespeare's oldest daughter, in *Swan Town* (2006). Ortiz places Susanna in London, where she provides a unique perspective on the Bard's life and the Elizabethan era. Numerous books featuring Shakespeare or spin-offs to his work abound. Some examples are listed in Box 11.1.

 Box 11.1   Shakespeare in Young Adult Literature

Aldabra, or, The Tortoise Who Loved Shakespeare by Silvana Gandolfi. Trans. Lynne Sharon Schwartz. New York: Levine/Scholastic, 2004.

Elisa spends time in Italy with her grandmother, a retired Shakespearean actress, who is always willing to act out Shakespearean scenes with her. All is well until Elisa's grandmother starts talking about transforming into something nonhuman.

Ariel by Grace Tiffany. New York: HarperCollins, 2005.

Tiffany, a Shakespeare expert, tells the back story of Shakespeare's *The Tempest.* The story spans centuries, beginning with Ariel's birth.

Book of Air and Shadows by Michael Gruber. New York: HarperCollins, 2007.

Hints of an unknown autographed Shakespeare manuscript appear in encoded messages in old letters.

Two men journey to England in search of the priceless document. Reminiscent of Dan Brown's *The Da Vinci Code* (2003).

Caught in the Act by Peter Moore. New York: Viking/Penguin, 2005.

Ethan struggles with being the perfect student, perfect son. He falls for Lydia, a "goth" girl, who tries out, alongside Ethan, for a role in the school play *Macbeth.* Parallels exist between Macbeth's "tragic flaw" and Ethan's own weakness—his dishonesty.

Dating Hamlet: Ophelia's Story by Lisa Fiedler. New York: Henry Holt, 2002.

A story from Ophelia's viewpoint. She describes her reactions when she learns the truth about her father and expresses her feelings for Hamlet.

Continued

Box 11.1   Shakespeare in Young Adult Literature *Continued*

***The Devil and His Boy* by Anthony Horowitz. New York: Philomel/Penguin, 2000.**

Being chased by a criminal, Tom Falconer ends up in London, where he must fend for himself. He sees a Shakespearean play and joins, with some encouragement, an acting troupe scheduled to perform for the queen. Things heat up when Tom learns he is involved in a conspiracy to murder the queen. Rich in period detail.

***Enter Three Witches* by Caroline B. Cooney. New York: Scholastic, 2007.**

A behind-the-scenes perspective on the tragedy that befalls Lord Macbeth and Lady Macbeth. Told from the viewpoint of minor characters (and a few invented ones).

***Jason and the Bard* by Kate Gilmore. Boston: Houghton Mifflin, 1993.**

Jason spends the summer working at a Shakespeare festival. He gets a chance to act, make new friends, and fall in love.

***King of Shadows* by Susan Cooper. New York: McElderry/Simon & Schuster, 1999.**

Nat is performing in London (in a replica of the Globe) in an all-boy acting company. He is transported back in time and performs in the original theatre under the Bard himself.

***Loving Will Shakespeare* by Carolyn Meyer. Orlando, FL: Harcourt, 2006.**

A carefully researched historical novel about Anne Hathaway, a farmer's daughter, and her romance with Will Shakespeare, a much younger man.

***Ophelia* by Lisa M. Klein. New York: Bloomsbury, 2006.**

Ophelia is center stage in this reimagining of *Hamlet*. Klein tells the story of a beautiful girl, a lady-in-waiting to the queen, who falls in love with Prince Hamlet. When tragedy strikes, Ophelia must choose between her own life and her love for Hamlet.

***The Playmaker* by J. B. Cheaney. New York: Knopf/Random House, 2000.**

Fourteen-year-old Richard heads to London after his mother's death to build a new life and maybe find his father. He takes a position with a troupe performing Shakespeare's plays, the Lord Chamberlain's Men, and learns he is a talented actor. Fans may enjoy *The True Prince* (2002).

***Pretty Things* by Sarra Manning. New York: Dutton/Penguin, 2005.**

Four teenagers navigate love affairs during a production of *The Taming of the Shrew*.

***Romeo's Ex: Rosaline's Story* by Lisa Fiedler. New York: Henry Holt, 2006.**

Romeo and Juliet told from Juliet's cousin's point of view (15-year-old Rosalind). Great play on words and good use of original text.

***Romiette and Julio* by Sharon M. Draper. New York: Atheneum/Simon & Schuster, 1999.**

A reinvention of *Romeo and Juliet* minus the tragic ending. Julio Montague and his parents move to Cincinnati, where he meets Romiette Cappelle in a chatroom.

***Shakespeare Bats Cleanup* by Ron Koertge. Cambridge, MA: Candlewick Press, 2003.**

A star baseball player and Shakespeare lover, sidelined because of mono, begins writing poetry. Written in verse.

***Shakespeare's Daughter* by Peter W. Hassinger. New York: HarperCollins, 2004.**

Susanna Shakespeare is restless in her small town of Stratford-upon-Avon. Yearning to be a professional singer and pursue her own dreams, she sets out for

Continued

Box 11.1   Shakespeare in Young Adult Literature   *Continued*

London after the death of her brother, where she falls in love with Thomas Cole.

Shakespeare's Secret by Elise Broach. New York: Henry Holt, 2005.

Hero (a character in *Much Ado About Nothing*) has a Shakespearean scholar for a father and has moved into a new home. Hero learns a 17-carat diamond is hidden in the house. Clues leading to the discovery suggest the owner may be related to Shakespeare. Hero is involved in a school incident and, as her namesake, she must suffer until her name is cleared.

Spanking Shakespeare by Jake Wizner. New York: Random House, 2007.

A rip-roaring book about a young boy whose parents named him Shakespeare Shapiro. Shakespeare is a social misfit; his younger brother is cool. Shakespeare plans to have the last laugh with an end-of-term writing project.

The Two Loves of Will Shakespeare by Laurie Lawlor. New York: Holiday House, 2006.

Depicts young Will Shakespeare as a flamboyant young womanizer and prankster. The author mentions the basis of her story: Shakespeare applied for a marriage license to two women only two days apart. Both, however, had the first name Anne.

Undine by Penni Russon. New York: Greenwillow/HarperCollins, 2006.

Undine and Trout are best friends. Undine, believing her father dead, hears a mysterious voice telling her he is alive. Trout, a Shakespeare lover, makes a connection between words spoken by the voice and *The Tempest*.

When the Bough Breaks by Anna Myers. New York: Walker, 2000.

Myers melds the lives of four women across time: Shakespeare's Ophelia and Portia and two modern-day namesakes.

A Winter Night's Dream by Andrew Matthews. New York: Delacorte/Random House, 2004.

Casey falls in love with Dean, and Stewart falls for Lucy. After a series of occurrences, Casey and Stewart hook up. A loose retelling of *A Midsummer Night's Dream*.

Other famous writers appear in young adult literature. Victoria Bennett explores the life of *Frankenstein* author Mary Wollstonecraft Godwin Shelley and her stormy relationship with Percy Bysshe Shelley in *Angelmonster* (2006). Mary was born to progressive-thinking parents. Accustomed to intellectual conversations with poets, novelists, and philosophers, Mary (at age 16) fell in love with like-minded Percy Shelley, a married man and expectant father, notorious and denigrated during his time for his open marriage beliefs. The two eloped. After Harriet, Shelley's first wife, committed suicide, the two married; but their marriage was far from serene. The couple battled financial difficulties, struggled with severed family relationships, and Mary had to contend with Shelley's extramarital relationships (e.g., his former wife *and* Mary's half-sister). Mary's life was a series of tragedies. She lived through the death of her own mother at an early age, that of her own children, and the death of her husband—Shelley drowned at sea. Though Mary's emotional state is mostly fictionalized (it would have to be), Bennett narrates the ups and downs of the couple's life with accuracy and flair. *Angelmonster,* a slim volume and a quick read, is a superb complement to a unit on *Frankenstein* (1818) or the English romantic movement. Bennett re-creates Jane Austen's childhood in *Cassandra's Sister* (2007), giving readers a glimpse into the social world of Austen's youth.

Stephanie Hemphill creates a fictionalized portrait of Sylvia Plath in *Your Own, Sylvia: A Verse Portrait of Sylvia Plath* (2007). She structures her account of Plath's life around her writings and nonfiction sources. Poems are told from viewpoints of friends and family and are prefaced with an explanation. Hemphill details Plath's childhood, her young adult and college years, her first suicide attempt, for which she was hospitalized, and her relationship with Ted Hughes. Many of the poems mimic Plath's style (e.g., form, imagery, tone, and language). Hemphill's work makes an excellent companion to *The Bell Jar* (1963), a semi-autobiography detailing the protagonist's descent into profound depression.

Setting, atmosphere, and character find common ground in the classics and in young adult literature. One of the most noted settings in all literature is that shaped by Charles Dickens, creator of such immortalized characters as Ebenezer Scrooge, Fagin, Oliver Twist, and Miss Havishman. His portrait of the diseased, destitute, and filthy streets and slums of Victorian England and shady characters living there serve as social commentary on poverty and social stratification of Victorian England.[4] Dozens of young adult authors, whether writing realistic fiction or fantasy, have emulated his descriptions of the Victorian era. Livi Michael's *The Whispering Road* (2005), for instance, bears close resemblance to *Oliver Twist* (Dickens 1838). Two impoverished orphan siblings escape from the cruel hands of an abusive master in Manchester, England, and embark on a dangerous journey in search of their mother. Along the way, they encounter both ruffians and kindness, individuals who help them and others who wish them harm. Though laced with magical realism, Michael's work adds to the growing body of literature that speaks authentically to the plight of orphans in Victorian England and the ganglike manner in which they lived.

Avi's *The Traitor's Gate* (2007) is a twist on *David Copperfield* (1849–1850), considered the closest autobiographical account of Dickens's life. The central character in *The Traitor's Gate* (John Huffam) is fashioned after young Charles Dickens (birth name—Charles *John Huffman* Dickens). Like Dickens's father, a clerk by trade, the protagonist's father is sent to debtor's prison. Young John Huffman must figure out why his family is being spied upon by Inspector Copperfield and find a way to free his father. Part history, part social commentary, part mystery and suspense, Avi's work returns readers to the era Dickens immortalized.

---

[4]Oliver Twist's plea, "Please, sir, I want some more" made an enormous impact on readers in Victorian London, for it drew attention to poverty, homeless children, and the brutality children faced in orphanages.

Of course, where would we be without the fearless Sherlock Holmes? Created by Sir Arthur Conan Doyle toward the end of the Victorian era, the British detective is a long-standing literary archetype. Both adult and young adult authors have patterned protagonist sleuths after the infamous crime stopper. Nancy Springer's *Enola Holmes Mysteries* (2006) for younger readers features Sherlock's younger sister, Enola, as a relentless crime solver. Abandoned by her mother, she disguises herself from Sherlock for fear he will force her to attend a boarding school and sets out to solve her own crimes. For older readers, Laurie R. King's *Mary Russell Mystery* series (1994) features Mary Russell as Sherlock's trainee, junior partner, and later wife. Eleanor Updale's *Montmorency* series (2005, 2006, 2007), set during the Victorian era and featuring a villain turned Holmes-like detective, appeals to older readers as well. Additional young adult novels that play off Doyle's memorable character are included in Box 11.2.

Box 11.2   Young Adult Literature and Sherlock Holmes

Baker Street Detectives series (The Mystery of the Yellow Hands #1) by Jake Thoene and Luke Thoene. Carol Stream, IL: Tyndale, 2006.

Children are being kidnapped in London, and three friends (Danny, Duff, and Peachy), members of the Baker Street Brigade, aid Holmes in the investigation. When a friend of the trio is kidnapped, the team works harder to solve the case.

The Barker Street Regulars: A Dog Lover's Mystery by Susan Conant. New York: Bantam/Random House, 1998.

Dog lover and admirer of Sherlock Holmes, Holly Winter sets out, accompanied by her two malamutes, to solve the murder of an elderly friend who lives in a retirement home.

Conned Again, Watson!: Cautionary Tales of Logic, Math, and Probability by Colin Bruce. New York: Perseus, 2001.

A collection of funny short stories told in Sherlock Holmes fashion that illustrate the importance of understanding mathematics. Holmes uses his understanding of statistics, probability, and more to solve cases.

The Curious Incident of the Dog in the Night-time by Mark Haddon. New York: Doubleday/Random House, 2003.

Fifteen-year-old Christopher is mathematically gifted, but autistic. When a neighbor's dog is murdered, he wants to solve the crime and draws upon his favorite literary character, Sherlock Holmes, for help. Funny and poignant. Hailed as one of the best books of the year for exceptional literary merit.

Double Trouble Squared by Kathryn Lasky. San Diego: Harcourt, 1991.

A set of twins, Liberty and July, have telepathic powers. When their father's work moves them to London, the sisters connect with the ghost of Sherlock Holmes's twin brother. They uncover a lost manuscript belonging to Sir Arthur Conan Doyle.

Down the Rabbit Hole: An Echo Falls Mystery by Peter Abrahams. New York: Geringer/HarperCollins, 2005.

Thirteen-year-old Ingrid Levin-Hill is a Sherlock Holmes fan and sets out to solve a murder case in Echo Falls, her hometown. Does the new director of the town play, *Alice in Wonderland,* have anything to do with the murder?

Continued

Box 11.2   Young Adult Literature and Sherlock Holmes   *Continued*

Enola Holmes Mystery series *(The Case of the Missing Marquess #1)* by Nancy Springer. New York: Philomel/Penguin, 2006.

When the young sister of Sherlock Holmes discovers her mother is missing, she sets out on her own to find her. Disguised as a widow, Enola dodges villains and murders and becomes caught up in the kidnapping of the young Marquess of Basilwether. Holmes fans will enjoy the sequels, *The Case of the Left-handed Lady* (2007), *The Case of the Bizarre Bouquets* (2008a), and *The Case of the Peculiar Pink Fan* (2008b).

The Fall of the Amazing Zalindas by Tracy Mack and Michael Citrin. New York: Orchard/Scholastic, 2006.

A new series focusing on the street orphans who aided Holmes in solving his cases. In this volume, Wiggins, Stitch, Rohan, Pilar, and others take center stage in unraveling the mysterious deaths of three tightrope performers. Terrific period detail.

Mary Russell Mystery series *(The Beekeeper's Apprentice #1)* by Laurie R. King. New York: Bantam/Random House, 1994.

Mary Russell meets the retired Sherlock Holmes who is instantly fascinated by an intellect that rivals his own. In early series Mary is his apprentice; later she becomes his wife and partner. A fabulous series for older teens.

Montmorency series *(Montmorency: Thief, Liar, Gentleman? #1)* by Eleanor Updale. New York: Orchard/Scholastic, 2004.

The first installment begins with a thief falling through a roof and being badly injured while running from the police. A young doctor repairs his broken body; he is released from prison and lives a double life as thief and respectable gentleman. Later volumes place him in the role of spy/detective. Set in Victorian London. Fans will enjoy the sequels: *Montmorency on the Rocks* (2005), *Montmorency and the Assassins* (2006), and *Montmorency's Revenge* (2007).

The Raven League: Sherlock Holmes Is Missing by Alex Simmons and Bill McCay. New York: Razorbill/Sleuth/Penguin, 2006.

Archie Wiggins is kicked out of the Baker Street Irregulars, the gang of kids who aid Holmes in solving cases. When Holmes himself goes missing, Wiggins suspects the Irregulars and sets out to find the missing detective. For early teens.

Samurai Mystery series *(The Ghost in the Tokaido Inn #1)* by Dorothy Hoobler and Thomas Hoobler. New York: Philomel/Penguin, 1999.

Seikei dreams of being a samurai. When a valuable jewel is stolen, Seikei sets out to solve the crime and joins a group of kabuki actors. Set in 18th-century Japan. This series is often called a Japanese Sherlock Holmes mystery series.

Another well-liked time period young adult authors explore is that of the legendary King Arthur. Popularized by Sir Thomas Malory's *Le Morte d'Arthur* (1485), King Arthur, his Knights of the Round Table, and their ladies frequent the pages of innumerable young adult fantasy titles. T. A. Barron is an undeniable force in Arthurian legends for young adults. His two series, *The Lost Years of Merlin* (1996) and *The Great Tree of Avalon Trilogy* (2004), have earned critical acclaim and delve into innumerable legends. Meg Cabot's *Avalon High* (2006) is a quirky, modern-day twist on King Arthur.

Illustration copyright 2004 by Scholastic, Inc.
Used by permission.

Sixteen-year-old Ellie, new kid in town, lives with parents who are medieval scholars. Coincidentally, Ellie's new math teacher, Mr. Morton, belongs to a clandestine organization that believes King Arthur is destined to return. The math teacher insists Ellie and her classmates are reincarnations of Arthurian legends: the Lady of the Lake, Guinevere, and Lancelot. Bizarre events ensue and climax to a possible tragedy. Cabot weaves pieces of Tennyson's classic, "The Lady of Shalott" (1842), throughout the story, and readers familiar with the poem will read the story deeper. Those who dismiss Cabot as a breezy "chick lit" writer may want to read this title. Additional texts with Arthurian themes can be found in Box 11.3.

Young adult texts with mythological themes abound, and many are quite well written. Michael Cadnum, a talented young adult writer who delves into an array of genres (e.g., problem novel, fantasy, myth, and history), has penned several excellent books about classic legends based on Ovid's *Metamorphoses* (ca. AD 8), an ancient work grounded in Greek and Roman mythology that describes the creation of the world. *Starfall* (2004b) is a prose retelling of young Phaeton, son of Apollo, and his disastrous attempt to drive the Chariot of the Sun. *Nightsong* (2006) relates the tragic love story

Box 11.3   Arthurian Folklore, Myths, and Legends in Young Adult Literature

***The Book of Mordred* by Vivian Vande Velde. Boston: Houghton Mifflin, 2005.**

Merlin has disappeared, and the Knights of the Round Table are separating into factions. King Arthur struggles to hold his men together.

***The Dragon's Son* by Sarah L. Thomson. New York: Orchard/Scholastic, 2001.**

Thomson's retelling is based on medieval Welsh tales and is unique in that King Arthur's story is told through the eyes of minor characters (e.g., Gwenhwyfar's younger sister).

***The Extraordinary Adventures of Alfred Kropp* by Rick Yancey. New York: Bloomsbury, 2005.**

Kropp's uncle concocts a get-rich scheme: steal Excalibur, King Arthur's legendary sword. When Kropp accidentally delivers the sword to the wrong person, an evil man, he sets out to correct his mistake. Hilarious read.

Continued

Box 11.3   Arthurian Folklore, Myths, and Legends in Young Adult Literature   *Continued*

***Grail Prince* by Nancy McKenzie. New York: Del Rey/Random House, 2003.**

King Arthur is dead and only one great knight remains: Lancelot, who has forsaken Britain. Lancelot's son (Galahad) fights to keep Arthur's wishes alive: find the treasures of an ancient king. Galahad is haunted by his father's betrayal of King Arthur.

***Grail Quest* series (*The Camelot Spell #1*) by Laura Anne Gilman. New York: HarperCollins, 2006.**

When every adult in King Arthur's castle falls under a sleeping spell, three youth seek out Merlin, but find he is imprisoned in ice. Merlin provides clues and a magic map, and the three set out on a journey that will lift the spell.

***I Am Morgan le Fay: A Tale from Camelot* by Nancy Springer. New York: Philomel/ Penguin, 2001.**

Morgan's magical childhood ends when King Pendragon kidnaps her mother and murders her father. After Pendragon dies, Morgan uses her power and magic to change the course of history.

***Knight Life* by Peter David. New York: Ace/Penguin, 2002.**

A unique twist on the Arthurian legend set in modern times. King Arthur (Arthur Penn) is called upon by Merlin to lead the United States out of turmoil. With no throne, King Arthur runs for mayor of New York City. In *One Knight Only* (2003) Arthur has climbed the political ladder to the presidency. Humor abounds.

***Lady Ilena: Way of the Warrior* by Patricia Malone. New York: Delacorte/ Random House, 2005.**

Lady Ilena awaits her future husband, Durant, a Knight of the Round Table who is aiding King Arthur during a time of unrest. When Lady Ilena refuses a marriage proposal in the absence of Durant, she ignites a bloody battle. Ilena waivers under attack

and is banished from her people until she can prove herself worthy.

***The Last Grail Keeper* by Pamela Smith Hill. New York: Holiday House, 2001.**

The Holy Grail is uncovered in an archaeological dig, and Felicity and her mother (a professor of Arthurian literature) become linked across time with King Arthur. Felicity is the last Grail Keeper and must return it to King Arthur's time.

***The Legend of Lady Ilena* by Patricia Malone. New York: Delacorte/Random House, 2002.**

Ilean, daughter of Moren and Grenna, has grown up in the Vale of Enfert unaware that Dun Alyn is her true home. On his dying bed her father tells her to go to Dun Alyn and find Ryamen. Ilena takes the treacherous journey alone. Her warrior skills are tested along the way.

***Prince of Dreams* by Nancy McKenzie. New York: Del Rey/Random House, 2004.**

Years after the end of Camelot, the legends of Arthur, Lancelot, and Guinevere remain. Tristan, Prince of Lyonesse, dreams of restoring Camelot.

***Song of the Sparrow* by Lisa Ann Sandell. New York: Scholastic, 2007.**

Sixteen-year-old Elaine lives with her father in King Arthur's camp. Elaine's sole companion is Morgan, Arthur's sister. Elaine is in love with Lancelot, but when Gwynivere arrives in camp, Elaine must confront her jealous feelings and deal with her rival. Makes for an interesting exploration of feminist theory.

***Sword of the Rightful King: A Novel of King Arthur* by Jane Yolen. San Diego: Harcourt, 2003.**

King Arthur plans to prove he is the rightful king by pulling a sword from a stone, but someone beats him to the sword.

of Orpheus, the musician-poet, and Princess Eurydice. Both are fabulous renditions and can add immeasurably to a class study of Ovid's *Metamorphoses*. In the author box Cadnum addresses a theme in *Nightsong:* the manner in which the ancients disposed of unwanted children. Box 11.4 identifies a wide selection of young adult novels with mythological themes.

While classical Greek and Roman mythologies abound and make excellent primary and secondary sources of study, young adult literature features a diverse range of mythologies. Laurence Yep has written Chinese myths; Joseph Bruchac has written Native American myths; and Suzanne Fisher Staples has written Hindu myths. When incorporated into a traditional Roman and Greek mythology unit, these mythologies add a range of diverse perspectives.

On Writing *Nightsong*   by Michael Cadnum

At the beginning of my novel *Nightsong*, Orpheus discovers an abandoned infant. He takes pity on this baby and rescues her from a pack of wild dogs.

I did not discover such a rescue in any existing literature, ancient or modern. I imagined the event on my own, following in the tradition of lyricists and fabulists who have given voice and life to the immortals. I endowed the famous poet with a brave and hopeful character, and I also gave Orpheus what turned out to be a naive faith in the power of mercy. I also had to imagine this traveling poet to be someone who was not afraid to disrupt fate. The newborn's parents had abandoned the baby to her fortune after all, and in taking the infant into his arms Orpheus is telling the baby: I am your destiny.

Orpheus goes on to believe that he and his poetry can placate the domain of unending darkness, and even more—that song can rescue his bride from the Underworld. And as I continued to discover the adventure and distress of this novel, I felt how much like us, as writers and readers, this legendary poet has always been.

Orpheus's story is a journey. He travels with the kind of confidence we recognize in ourselves. He believes in life. And we who share his faith are shaken by his failure, and mourn with him when he discovers the ultimate limits of his gifts.

This is why the ending of this novel—which I likewise created without any ancient example as a

guide—has such deep personal meaning for me. When our faith in life is crushed, we have little left but song.

Copyright Michael Cadnum, 2008

Other works by Cadnum include *Calling Home* (1991), *Breaking the Fall* (1992), *Taking It* (1995), *Zero at the Bone* (1996), *Edge* (1997), *Heat* (1998a), *Rundown* (1999), *The Book of the Lion* (2001a), *Raven of the Waves* (2001b), *The Leopard Sword* (2002b), *Daughter of the Wind* (2003a), *Ship of Fire* (2003b), *Blood Gold* (2004a), *The Dragon Throne* (2005), and *The King's Arrow* (2008).

Box 11.4   Roman and Greek Mythology in Young Adult Novels

Corydon and the Island of Monsters by Tobias Druitt. New York: Knopf/Random House, 2006.

Corydon is driven from his village, captured, and displayed as a monster because he looks like a freak. Medusa, the Minotaur, the Sphinx, and other classical creatures are displayed alongside Corydon. Corydon and the beasts escape, go in separate directions in search of peace, but must reunite when an army, intent on murder, begins hunting them. Depicts the classic struggle between Greek monsters and gods.

Cupid: A Tale of Love and Desire by Julius Lester. Orlando, FL: Harcourt, 2007.

A fun twist to the classic Cupid. The god of love falls in love himself, and life for Cupid gets confusing.

The Foretelling by Alice Hoffman. New York: Little, Brown, 2005.

Rain is an Amazon female warrior living during a tumultuous and violent time. She is her people's future leader and must have no empathy toward the enemy (men). Can she resist a kind young man?

God of the Golden Fleece by Fred Saberhagen. New York: Forge/Tor, 2001.

Proteus, brain damaged from fighting a giant, can barely remember that he was sent to help Jason and the Argonauts. Proteus has superhuman strength, never grows tired, and can see what others cannot.

Goddess of Yesterday: A Tale of Troy by Caroline B. Cooney. New York: Delacorte/Random House, 2002.

Anaxandra was taken from her Aegean Island home as a child. She becomes a servant to Helen and Paris as they journey toward Troy.

Going Under by Kathe Koja. New York: Farrar, Straus & Giroux, 2006.

Hillary and Ivan are close siblings. When Hillary's close friend commits suicide, their relationship becomes strained. Based on the myths of Persephone and Narcissus.

The Great God Pan by Donna Jo Napoli. New York: Lamb/HarperCollins, 2003.

A retelling of the Greek myth about Pan, both god and goat, who roams the countryside playing melodies on his flute.

Inside the Walls of Troy: A Novel of the Women Who Lived the Trojan War by Clemence McLaren. New York: Simon Pulse/Simon & Schuster, 1996.

The events of the Trojan War are told through the eyes of Helen of Troy and Cassandra, sister of Paris, who can predict the future.

Ithaka by Adèle Geras. Orlando, FL: Harcourt, 2006.

The Trojan War has ended and Penelope awaits the return of Odysseus. Suitors vie for Penelope's hand in marriage so they might control the kingdom. Told through the eyes of Klymene, a young girl who longs for the attention of young Telemachus.

The Moon Riders by Theresa Tomlinson. New York: EOS/HarperCollins, 2006.

Myrina has trained for 13 years to be a moon rider. On the day she joins a tribe of fearless female warriors, a stowaway (Cassandra of Troy) is found among the group. Cassandra has prophetic visions, and the warriors learn they must join forces in the Trojan War.

Continued

Box 11.4   Roman and Greek Mythology in Young Adult Novels   *Continued*

Nobody's Princess by Esther Friesner. New York: Random House, 2007.

Helen of Sparta is a beautiful princess, and yet she wants more out of life. A fresh look at the young girl who becomes Helen of Troy.

The Orpheus Obsession by Dakota Lane. New York: HarperCollins, 2005.

A modern-day story about a 16-year-old from a troubled home who becomes obsessed with a rock star (Orpheus). Anooshka (Eurydice) descends into the underworld.

Quicksilver by Stephanie Spinner. New York: Knopf/Random House, 2005.

A reinvented story about Hermes, Prince of Thieves and son of Zeus, and friend to Pegasus. Hermes fulfills his father's wishes, travels through Hades, and practices the art of trickery, deception, and thievery.

Quiver by Stephanie Spinner. New York: Knopf/Random House, 2002.

A retelling of the myth of Atalanta, the female warrior who could run faster than any man in Greece. Atalanta's skills anger her father, and he demands she marry and produce an heir. Atalanta promises to marry the first man who can beat her in a foot race. Those who lose, die.

The Roman Mysteries series *(Thieves of Ostia #1)* by Caroline Lawrence. New Milford, CT: Roaring Brook Press, 2003.

A mystery series that provides period history of ancient Rome and the gods and goddesses they believed in.

Sirena by Donna Jo Napoli. New York: Scholastic, 1998.

Napoli brings to life the tragic love story between a mortal and a mermaid. Sirena falls in love with a human (Philoctetes) she rescues from the sea. Philoctetes must return home to fight the Trojan War, leaving his love behind.

Troy by Adèle Geras. San Diego: Harcourt, 2001.

Describes a city under siege from the viewpoint of the women who tended the wounded and fed the soldiers, and gods and goddesses bored with the war.

Waiting for Odysseus by Clemence McLaren. New York: Atheneum/Simon & Schuster, 2000.

Odysseus's epic journey is told through the eyes of Penelope, his wife; Circe, the sorceress; Odysseus's nanny, Eurycleia; and the goddess Athena. All women who loved him.

Fractured classic. Prose retelling. Borrowed character. Young adult literature is forever indebted to the great past masters. As you continue to explore young adult literature and its connection with the classics, don't be discouraged by the abundance of poorly written retellings and watered-down texts. Alongside beautifully illustrated picture books of classics such as Bruce Coville's prose retellings of Shakespeare's plays, you will find inferior texts. The same holds true for graphic novel renditions of classics. This chapter highlights some of the best works available today. You won't necessarily find the best on bookstore shelves, or in the education marketing materials that fill your mailbox. As a young adult literature expert, you will have the research skills to find them. Titles in Box 11.5 are a good starting point.

Box 11.5   Classical Spin-Offs, Fractured Classics, and Archetypes

***Angelmonster* by Veronica Bennett. Cambridge, MA: Candlewick Press, 2006.**

Bennett's tale reinvents the life of Mary Goodwin, author of *Frankenstein* (Shelley 1818), and her love affair with Percy Shelley. Bennett details their flight to Europe with Mary's half-sister, their hardscrabble lifestyle, and unconventional friendships with other poets. Mary is disowned by her father; She is a target of gossip and a victim of one tragedy after another.

***Bloodline* by Kate Cary. New York: Razorbill-Penguin, 2005.**

A continuation of Bram Stoker's *Dracula* (1897). Years have passed since Dracula's death. Nineteen-year-old John Shaw, a World War I soldier returning home from battle, has bizarre nightmares about Quincey Harker, his former commander. Shaw dismisses the nightmares as war drama until Harker arrives in England and begins seducing John's sister.

***Clay* by David Almond. New York: Delacorte/Random House, 2006.**

At the encouragement of Father O'Mahoney, Davie and his best friend, Geordie, befriend a new boy, Stephen Rose. Stephen is a gifted sculptor and can bring sculptures to life. Working together, the two sculpt and bring to life, Clay. What monster have they released into the world? A modern retelling of *Frankenstein* (Shelley 1818).

***Cyrano* by Geraldine McCaughrean. Orlando, FL: Harcourt, 2006.**

A prose retelling of Edmond Rostand's *Cyrano de Bergerac* (1897), the play about a heroic solider with an unusually long nose. When Cyrano falls for Roxane, he searches for a way to express his feelings for her.

***The Death Collector* by Justin Richards. New York: Bloomsbury, 2006.**

Three teens are pursued by Augustus Lorimore, a sinister character who brings the dead alive and creates half human, half robotic creatures. Vicotorian setting with Dickensian-like characters and atmosphere. A *Frankenstein* (Shelley 1818) spin-off.

***Downriver* by Will Hobbs. New York: Atheneum/Simon & Schuster, 1991.**

A group of teens on a hiking trip abandon their wilderness survival team, taking with them the team's boats. They explore white waters of the Grand Canyon and unknown caves. No one foresees the frightening changes that take place in Troy, the group leader. Intertextual connections with *Lord of the Flies* (Golding, 1954).

***Enthusiasm* by Polly Shulman. New York: Penguin, 2006.**

Ashleigh is seduced by the characters in Austen's *Pride and Prejudice* (1813). She and her friend, Julie, begin imitating the novel's heroines in dress and mannerisms and begin searching for true love. There's only one Mr. Darcy.

***Fire-Us* trilogy *(The Kindling #1)* by Jennifer Armstrong and Nancy Butcher. New York: HarperCollins, 2002.**

A virus has wiped out the adult population, and a group of Florida teens bands together to survive in a world with no electricity and abandoned houses, factories, and cars. A new kid shows up and invites them on a road trip to Washington, D. C. Reminiscent of William Golding's *Lord of the Flies* (1954).

***First Impressions* by Marilyn Sachs. New Milford, CT: Roaring Brook Press 2006.**

Alicia reread's *Pride and Prejudice* (Austen, 1813) at the request of her English teacher who gave her a C+ on a paper about the novel. On her second reading, Alicia realizes her first impressions were ungrounded. Austen mysteriously appears to Alicia as she rereads, and Alicia gains insight into the characters, Austen, and her own life.

Continued

Box 11.5　Classical Spin-Offs, Fractured Classics, and Archetypes　*Continued*

***Freak the Mighty* by Rodman Philbrick. New York: Blue Sky/Scholastic, 1993.**

Max is learning disabled and his new friend, Freak, has a physical birth defect. Max is big and "dumb," and Freak is tiny, but smart. Together they battle bullies, including Max's belligerent father. Strong parallels with Steinbeck's *Of Mice and Men* (1937).

***Jake, Reinvented* by Gordon Korman. New York: Hyperion, 2003.**

Reinvents F. Scott Fitzgerald's *The Great Gatsby* (1925). Rick Paradis, the story narrator, becomes friends with Jake Garrett (Jay Gatsby), star football player for Fitzgerald High and popular party host. Jake's parties become more frequent and elaborate as he attempts to get close to Didi (Daisy Buchanan). Rick discovers the true character of his classmates, including Jake.

***Just Ella* by Margaret Peterson Haddix. New York: Simon & Schuster, 1999.**

Ella is a working-class girl and is chosen to marry the prince. As Ella becomes acquainted with the royal family and they attempt to mold her into a princess, she learns her marriage may not have a happily-ever-after ending. A continuation of the *Cinderella* story.

***The Looking Glass Wars* by Frank Beddor. New York: Dial/Penguin, 2006.**

A reimagining of Lewis Carroll's *Alice's Adventures in Wonderland* (1865). Alyss Hart, the heiress to Wonderland, is chased away by her Aunt Redd. She escapes to London through the Pool of Tears and joins a band of street urchins. She is taken to an orphanage and later adopted by the Liddells. The Reverend Dodgson (Lewis Carroll) seems to believe her story, only she is devastated when his book alters the truth.

***Marly's Ghost: A Remix of Charles Dickens's A Christmas Carol* by David Levithan. Illus. Brian Selznick. New York: Dial/Penguin, 2006.**

Ben is dealing with the death of his girlfriend, Marly, who comes back to haunt him on Valentine's Day. She takes him on a journey through Valentine's Days past, present, and future, and he is forced to confront his pain and realize how he has been dishonoring Marly's memory. A twist on Dickens's *A Christmas Carol* (1843).

***Mary Wolf* by Cynthia D. Grant. New York: Atheneum/Simon & Schuster, 1995.**

Reminiscent of Steinbeck's *The Grapes of Wrath* (1939), this story follows 16-year-old Mary and her family as they travel aimlessly around the country. They live desperate street lives.

***Mr. and Mrs. Darcy Mystery* series (*Pride and Prescience #1*) by Carrie Bebris. New York: Forge/Tor, 2004.**

This series continues the adventures of Jane Austen's fictional characters from *Pride and Prejudice* (1813). Sequels include *Suspense and Sensibility* (2005) and *North by Northanger* (2006).

***Scribbler of Dreams* by Mary E. Pearson. San Diego: Harcourt, 2001.**

Seventeen-year-old Kaitlin falls in love with Bram Crutchfield despite a long-standing family feud. Kaitlin hides her identity from the Crutchfields, but one lie leads to another, and Kaitlin ends up entangled in a complex relationship. A modern-day *Romeo and Juliet* or *Hatfield and McCoy* story.

***The Sea of Trolls* by Nancy Farmer: New York: Atheneum/Simon & Schuster, 2004.**

Set in the North Sea in the late eighth century, a Saxon youth (Jack) and his sister are captured by marauding Northmen and trolls. Some common threads with *Beowulf*. The Saga continues in *The Land of the Silver Apples* (2007).

***Storm Thief* by Chris Wooding. New York: Orchard/Scholastic, 2006.**

Reminiscent of Coleridge's *The Rime of the Ancient Mariner*. This fantasy begins with an enthralling scene: A migrating bird has lost its flock in strong storms; disoriented, it struggles to find a place to land.

Continued

Box 11.5   Classical Spin-Offs, Fractured Classics, and Archetypes   *Continued*

***Switched* by Jessica Wollman. New York: Delacorte/Random House, 2007.**

Laura Mellon is tired of cleaning houses for college money, and Willa Pogue is tired of the demands placed on her as an heiress. When Laura takes a job as Willa's maid, the two realize they are identical look-alikes and trade places. A reinvention of Twain's *The Prince and the Pauper* (1881).

***The Young Man and the Sea* by Rodman Philbrick. New York: Blue Sky/Scholastic, 2004.**

After Skiff's mother dies, his fisherman father is too depressed to work. Skiff knows he can't take care of himself and his father with his meager lobster traps, so he takes to the sea in search of bluefin tuna. A retelling of Hemingway's *The Old Man and the Sea* (1952).

Classic Fairy Tales and Folklore

Fairy tales are rooted in oral tradition, so their histories are difficult to trace. They have several distinct characteristics. First, time is unspecified, but the stories take place "long, long ago." The traditional fairy tale begins with the familiar phrase, *Once upon a time* and contains motifs such as castles, moats, knights, and princesses, clues that suggest settings either around or prior to medieval times. Fairy tales also feature stock or flat characters such as beautiful princesses, evil queens, and gallant princes. Their behaviors are predictable, and other than a physical change (prince turns into a frog) the characters remain stagnant. There are also two social classes: the rich and the poor. The protagonist is most often a girl who is estranged from her family: she gets lost, captured, runs away, and so forth. Fairy tales contain magic, good and bad witches, and magical wands, cauldrons, and enchantments. The theme, as in most fantasy, is good against evil. In the fairy tale, however, good generally prevails, leading to a happily-ever-after ending. In the Western tradition there are three major fairy tale collections: Charles Perrault's *Stories or Tales of Olden Times* (1697), the Brothers Grimm's *Household Tales* (1812–1822), and Hans Christian Andersen's *Fairy Tales* (1835).

Classic fairy tales (and folklore) have long been influential in the development of fantasy literature for all ages. Writers have altered points of view (Jon Scieszka's

Reprinted by permission of Penguin Young Readers Group © 2005.

The True Story of the 3 Little Pigs, 1989), applied feminist theory (Teresa Bateman's *The Princesses Have a Ball,* 2002), blended fairy tales (Michael Gruber's *The Witch's Boy,* 2005), replaced human characters with animals (Janet Perlman's *The Penguin and the Pea,* 2004), added depth to flat characters (Neal Shusterman's *Red Rider's Hood,* 2005), and situated stories in different times, primarily modern day (Alex Flinn's *Beastly,* 2007). The list of quirky twists is endless.

Perhaps the most borrowed story line is that of Cinderella. Literally hundreds of Cinderella stories exist throughout the world (see Box 11.6), and the story line appears in stories for all ages. In the young adult novel the Cinderella motif appears in Gail Carson Levine's Newbery Honor book *Ella Enchanted* (1997). At birth, Ella was cursed with obedience by a foolish fairy— she can't refuse a command. After her mother's death, her father remarries, and Ella acquires a wicked stepmother and evil stepsisters. Unlike Cinderella, however, who is saved by a prince, Ella saves herself. Like the classic Cinderella, Levine's story takes place in a fantastical world. Mavis Jukes's *Cinderella 2000* (1999), however, situates Cinderella in the modern world. Fourteen-year-old Ashley hopes to spend New Year's Eve at a country club party; however, her stepmother and spiteful stepsisters jeopardize her evening.

Box 11.6   Cinderella Tales in Picture-Book Format

Adelita: A Mexican Cinderella Story by Tomie dePaola. New York: Penguin, 2002.

Ashpet: An Appalachian Tale by Joanne Compton. Illus. Kenn Compton. New York: Holiday House, 1994.

Bigfoot Cinderrrrella by Tony Johnston. Illus. James Warhola. New York: Penguin, 1998.

Bubba the Cowboy Prince: A Fractured Texas Tale by Helen Ketteman. Illus. James Warhola. New York: Scholastic, 1997.

Cendrillon: A Caribbean Cinderella by Robert D. San Souci. Illus. Brian Pinkney. New York: Simon & Schuster, 1998.

Chickerella by Mary Jane Auch and Herm Auch. New York: Holiday House, 2005.

Cinder Edna by Ellen B. Jackson. Illus. Kevin O'Malley. New York: HarperCollins, 1994.

Cinder-Elly by Frances Minters. Illus. G. Brian Karas. New York: Viking/Penguin, 1994.

Cinderella Penguin, or, The Little Glass Flipper by Janet Perlman. Tonawanda, NY: Kids Can Press, 1992.

Cinderella Skeleton by Robert D. San Souci. Illus. David Catrow. Orlando, FL: Harcourt, 2000.

Cinderhazel: The Cinderella of Halloween by Deborah Nourse Lattimore. New York: Scholastic, 1997.

Cinderlily: A Floral Fairy Tale by David Ellwand and Christine Tagg. Cambridge, MA: Candlewick Press, 2003.

Cindy Ellen: A Wild Western Cinderella by Susan Lowell. Illus. Jane Manning. New York: HarperCollins, 2000.

Dinorella: A Prehistoric Fairy Tale by Pamela Duncan Edwards. Illus. Henry Cole. New York: Hyperion, 1997.

Domitila: A Cinderella Tale from the Mexican Tradition by Jewell Reinhart Coburn. Illus. Connie McLennan. Walnut Creek, CA: Shen's Books, 2000.

The Egyptian Cinderella by Shirley Climo. Illus. Ruth Heller. New York: HarperCollins, 1989.

Continued

Box 11.6   Cinderella Tales in Picture-Book Format   *Continued*

Ella's Big Chance: A Jazz-Age Cinderella by Shirley Hughes. New York: Simon & Schuster, 2005.

The Golden Sandal: A Middle Eastern Cinderella Story by Rebecca Hickox. Illus. Will Hillenbrand. New York: Holiday House, 1998.

The Golden Slipper: A Vietnamese Legend by Darrell Lum. Illus. Makiko Nagano. New York: Troll, 1994.

I Was a Rat! by Philip Pullman. Illus. Kevin Hawkes. New York: Knopf/Random House, 2000.

The Irish Cinderlad by Shirley Climo. Illus. Loretta Krupinski. New York: HarperCollins, 1996.

The Korean Cinderella by Shirley Climo. Illus. Ruth Heller. New York: HarperCollins, 1996.

Little Firefly: An Algonquian Legend by Terri Cohlene. Illus. Charles Reasoner. Vero Beach, FL: Rourke, 1990.

Mufaro's Beautiful Daughters: An African Tale by John Steptoe. New York: HarperCollins, 1987.

The Persian Cinderella by Shirley Climo. Illus. Robert Florczak. New York: HarperCollins, 1999.

Princess Furball by Charlotte Huck. Illus. Anita Lobel. New York: Greenwillow/HarperCollins, 1989.

The Rough-face Girl by Rafe Martin. Illus. David Shannon. New York: Penguin, 1992.

Rufferella by Vanessa Gill-Brown and Mandy Stanley. New York: Scholastic, 2001.

The Salmon Princess: An Alaska Cinderella Story by Mindy Dwyer. Seattle, WA: Sasquatch, 2004.

Sidney Rella and the Glass Sneaker by Bernice Myers. Boston: Houghton Mifflin, 1995.

Smoky Mountain Rose: An Appalachian Cinderella by Alan Schroeder. Illus. Brad Sneed. New York: Dial/Penguin, 1997.

Sootface: An Ojibwa Cinderella Story by Robert D. San Souci. Illus. Daniel San Souci. New York: Delacorte/Random House, 1994.

Trollerella by Karen M. Stegman-Bourgeois. Illus. Ethan Long. New York: Holiday House, 2006.

The Turkey Girl: A Zuni Cinderella Story by Penny Pollock. Illus. Ed Young. New York: Little, Brown, 1986.

Yeh-Shen: A Cinderella Story from China by Ai-Ling Louie. Illus. Ed Young. New York: Penguin, 1982.

Writers, too, sometimes cleverly blend fairy tales. Neal Shusterman's *Darkfusion* series is an outstanding example of blended fairy tale and myth. In *Dread Locks* (2005a) 15-year-old Parker Baer learns he has new neighbors; the next day he finds a strange girl with spirals of long golden hair sleeping in his bed—an obvious take on *Goldilocks and the Three Bears*. But the story gets better: Tara (Goldilocks) never removes her dark glasses and lives in a house alone with stone statues. As Parker's friends and family meet Tara, they turn gray and lethargic, and the reader begins noticing a snakelike quality to Tara's locks—Medusa. Two other titles in this series include *Red Rider's Hood* (2005b) and *Duckling Ugly* (2006). All three, as the series title suggests, are creepy, but fun twists to the classic tales.

Part of the appeal of blended fairy tales (and myths) is figuring out the fairy tale (and myth and folklore) motifs. Michael Gruber's *The Witch's Boy* (2005) is a complex reworking of numerous fairy tales (e.g., *Little Red Riding Hood, Rumpelstiltskin, Hansel and Gretel, Goldilocks and the Three Bears*). Readers well-versed in childhood classics will be fascinated by the manner in which he weaves dozens of fairy tale motifs throughout a story about an orphaned

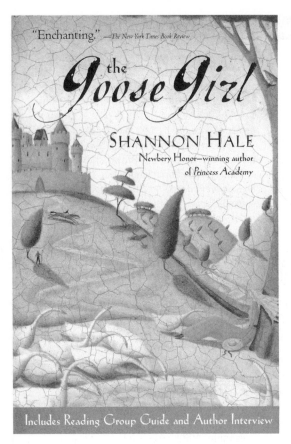

"Enchanting." —*The New York Times Book Review*

the
Goose Girl

SHANNON HALE

Newbery Honor—winning author
of *Princess Academy*

Includes Reading Group Guide and Author Interview

Reprinted by permission of Bloomsbury USA.

boy named Lump. An interesting question such blended tales raise is how individuals with no knowledge of classic fairy tales read the story. What do they take from it? *The Witch's Boy* is a superb title for exploring that question.

Fairy tales unfortunately "get little respect" in the high school curriculum. There's a belief that students are too old for them and should be reading more "serious" pieces of literature. Yet adults are mesmerized by fairy tales (and other fantasy). Gregory Maguire's *Wicked: The Life and Times of the Wicked Witch of the West* (1995) is a national bestseller and the source for the long-running Broadway musical, *Wicked. Harry Potter* (Rowling, 1997), though not a true fairy tale, illustrates adults' infatuation with magical worlds: thousands of adults, many dressed as Potter characters, waited in long lines for each new release. Movies, too, illustrate adult infatuation. The mixed live-action and animated film *Enchanted* (2007), about a banished fairy tale princess who finds herself in modern-day Manhattan, targeted an adult audience.

Fairy tales are more than just fun reads. They can offer social commentary (e.g., on gender roles), and they're wonderful writing models. They're especially terrific for teaching point of view, flat and round characters, and humor. They're also good sources for teaching setting and imagery. In the author box, Shannon Hale, author of the award-winning *The Goose Girl* (2003), discusses her own misguided beliefs about quality literature and the experience that led to her writing *The Goose Girl*.

Reading with Pleasure   by Shannon Hale

The truth is, I used to be a literary snob. I'm glad to get that off my chest.

As a child, my favorite books had been fantasy, and fairy tales were even better. Then starting in high school, I eschewed such books as frivolous. For years, I believed that only the "classics" had merit. You should know upfront that my high school English teachers and college professors were extraordinary, almost superhuman, and hands-down created my favorite classes. But based on the books we read in class, I came to believed that as a

responsible, intellectual adult the only worthwhile books:

- Show that characters may start out with potential but in the end almost everyone suffers and ends miserably (e.g., of Shakespeare, we only read the tragedies).
- Must be difficult and sometimes painful to read, and the more archaic and less accessible the language, the better for you.

Continued

Reading with Pleasure   *Continued*

- Are realistic fiction (unless hundreds of years old, like the *Odyssey*). Mystery, science fiction, fantasy, romance, picture books, graphic novels, adventure, horror, teen angst, fairy tales . . . anything that has a "genre" is inherently bad.

I really truly believed this. It was an unquestioned fact for all of high school and college. In grad school we exchanged "classics" for "literary fiction" (reading books by actual living authors felt so naughty!), but the same bullet points still applied. I barely even noticed how depressing the entire world seemed. After all, death, bad endings, hopelessness, despair, powerlessness—that was just *realism*.

Then I had one of them there Joycian epiphanies: I was 25 years old and I could not remember the last time I had stayed up late into the night reading because I couldn't bear to put the book down. The thought shocked me. Wasn't I a reader first and foremost? When had reading ceased to be a pleasure and turned into a duty? Couldn't there be books that had wonderful writing and were as good for you as broccoli and yet still keep you enthralled with story and characters?

So I started to write *The Goose Girl*. My goal was to please my adult self that had high expectations of writing and literary worth yet also please that internal reader part of me that was still somewhere between the ages of 10 and 16—that golden age when reading was still a flashlight-under-the-bedspread-gasp-aloud-can't-stop-turning-pages kind of fun. Thirty drafts and four years later, *The Goose Girl* was published as a young adult fantasy. Young adult?! The genre hadn't even existed when I was in high school. And should I be ashamed? Surely writing *fantasy*—and writing for *children* no less—was as far from the esteemed realistic fiction of the classics as one could get. Then I began to read all I could in the genre and had my proverbial socks knocked off again and again. Wowzers. It seemed I had fallen asleep somewhere over Steinbeck

and woken up in the Wonderland of young adult literature.

I envy the students of today. They get the chance to read books worth their salt that also thrill and please. It delights me to see that alongside the classics students are studying some books that allow a new bullet list:

- Adventure
- Humor
- Characters with hidden talents, with potential for real power
- Seemingly impossible things becoming possible
- An ending with real hope

To some, that may add up to "fantasy." Call me crazy, but that sounds more like the world I live in than many of the books I read in high school. Now, whenever I get the chance, I indulge in a little fairy tale fantasy reading late into the night. But I shamelessly call it realism.

Sequels to *The Goose Girl* include *Enna Burning* (2004) and *River Secrets* (2006). Other titles include *Princess Academy* (2005), *Book of a Thousand Days* (2007b), and *Austenland* (2007a).

Folktales grow out of a population's oral tradition. Folklorists believe in the possibility of the legend. For instance, many historians don't discount the possibility of a King Arthur, though lore about him has become more fantastical with time. The same is true for Robin Hood. Michael Cadnum has penned the most sophisticated young adult Robin Hood stories. *In a Dark*

Wood (1998b) depicts Robin Hood, his followers, and Sherwood Forest from Sheriff Nottingham's point of view.[5] *Forbidden Forest: The Story of Little John and Robin Hood* (2002) focuses on Little John, his flight, after killing a man, from the Sheriff, and how Robin Hood earned his loyalty. Cadnum's attention to medieval history is rich, accurate, and detailed and is an excellent alternative to Howard Pyle's classic, *The Merry Adventures of Robin Hood* (1883). Though Pyle's work is enduring, readers aren't always aware that he altered the legends for a younger audience.[6] Writing for young people, he paid little attention to historical accuracy. Also, in the original legend, "Robin Hood and the Bishop of Hereford," Robin Hood steals "all" from a traveler; Pyle has the traveler keep a third. In another original legend, "Robin Hood's Progress to Nottingham," Robin Hood kills 14 men. Pyle has the men threaten him and Robin Hood kills only one. Pyle's romanticized portrayal of Robin Hood is characteristic of early literature that sought to protect children from harm. The Robin Hood of the original legends wasn't a romantic hero. Cadnum presents a more plausible portrait. Nancy Springer's *Tales of Rowan Hood* series (2001) offers additional reading for those who can't get enough of Sherwood Forest and for those who enjoy a feminist twist to folklore. This series features Robin Hood's bold daughter and her band who live in Sherwood Forest.

Whether fairy tale or folklore, young adult literature abounds with retold and reinvented classic tales. They're good resources for examining culture and literary elements (e.g., point of view, character, and setting). They're especially good for discussing feminist theory. Boxes 11.7 and 11.8 present examples of fractured classics in picture-book format and those reinvented in young adult novels. The author box features a piece by Donna J. Napoli on an Irish fairy tale. Napoli's work, complex retellings, illustrates how fairy tales are good resources for cultural studies.

 Box 11.7   Fractured Fairy Tales, Fables, and Folklore in Picture-Book Format

The Frog Prince	*The Dog Prince: An Original Fairy Tale* by Lauren Mills (2001)
	A Frog Prince by Alix Berenzy (1989)
	The Frog Prince Continued by Jon Scieszka (1991)
	The Frog Principal by Stephanie Calmenson (2001)
	Pondlarker by Fred Gwynne (1990)
The Gingerbread Man	*Arnie the Doughnut* by Laurie Keller (2003)
	Bad Boys Get Cookie! by Margie Palatini (2006)
	Burger Boy by Alan Durant (2006)
	Ginger Bear by Mini Grey (2007)
	The Great Pancake Escape by Paul Many (2002)

Continued

---

[5]*In a Dark Wood* is a National Book Award finalist.
[6]Pyle's classic is a compilation of ballads and legends. He ordered them in such a way as to create a novel.

Box 11.7   Fractured Fairy Tales, Fables, and Folklore in Picture-Book Format   *Continued*

	The Matzo Ball Boy by Lisa Shulman (2005)
	The Runaway Latkes by Leslie Kimmelman (2000)
	The Runaway Rice Cake by Ying Chang Compestine (2001)
	Stop That Pickle! by Peter Armour (1993)
The Golden Goose	*The Little Golden Lamb* by Ellin Greene (2000)
Goldilocks and the Three Bears	*Beware of the Bears!* by Alan MacDonald (1998)
	Deep in the Forest by Brinton Turkle (1976)
	Dusty Locks and the Three Bears by Susan Lowell (2001)
	Goldilocks and the Three Martians by Stu Smith (2004)
	Goldilocks Returns by Lisa Campbell Ernst (2000)
	Santa and the Three Bears by Dominic Catalano (2000)
	Somebody and the Three Blairs by Marilyn Tolhurst (1991)
	Tackylocks and the Three Bears by Helen Lester (2002)
	The Three Snow Bears by Jan Brett (2007)
Hansel and Gretel	*Hansel and Diesel* by David Gordon (2006)
Henny Penny	*Chicken Little* by Steven Kellogg (1985)
	Earthquack! By Margie Palatini (2002)
Jack and the Beanstalk	*The Giant and the Beanstalk* by Diane Stanley (2004)
	Jack and the Giant: A Story Full of Beans by Jim Harris (1997)
	Jim and the Beanstalk by Raymond Briggs (1997)
	Kate and the Beanstalk by Mary Pope Osborne (2000)
	Look Out, Jack! The Giant Is Back! by Tom Birdseye (2001)
	McBroom and the Beanstalk by Sid Fleischman (1978)
The Little Red Hen	*Gator Gumbo: A Spicy-hot Tale* by Candace Fleming (2004)
	The Little Red Hen Makes a Pizza by Philemon Sturges (1999)
	Martha Moth Makes Socks by Cambria Evans (2006)
	Mr. Wolf's Pancakes by Jan Fearnley (2001)
	"Not Now!" Said the Cow by Joanne Oppenheim (1989)
Little Red Riding Hood	*Carmine: A Little More Red* by Melissa Sweet (2005)
	Little Red: A Frizzingly Good Yarn by Lynn Roberts (2005)
	Little Red Cowboy Hat by Susan Lowell (1997)
	Little Red Ink Drinker by Eric Sanvoisin (2002)
	Lon Po Po: A Red-Riding Hood Story from China by Ed Young (1989)
	Petite Rouge: A Cajun Red Riding Hood by Mike Artell (2001)
	The Wolf's Story: What Really Happened to Little Red Riding Hood by Toby Forward (2005)
The Boy Who Cried Wolf	*Never Cry Woof!: A Dog-u-drama* by Jane Wattenberg (2005)
	The Wolf Who Cried Boy by Bob Hartman (2002)
	Wolf! Wolf! by John Rocco (2007)
The Princess and the Pea	*The Cowboy and the Black-eyed Pea* by Tony Johnston (1992)
	The Penguin and the Pea by Janet Perlman (2004)
	The Very Smart Pea and the Princess-to-be by Mini Grey (2003)

Continued

Box 11.7   Fractured Fairy Tales, Fables, and Folklore in Picture-Book Format   *Continued*

Rapunzel

Falling for Rapunzel by Leah Wilcox (2003)
Princess Alopecia by Yaacov Peterseil (1999)
Rapunzel: A Groovy Fairy Tale by Lynn Roberts (2003)
Sugar Cane: A Caribbean Rapunzel by Patricia Storace (2007)

Rip Van Winkle

Rip Van Winkle's Return by Eric A. Kimmel (2007)

Rumpelstiltskin

Multiplying Menace: The Revenge of Rumpelstiltskin by Pam Calvert (2006)
Rumpelstiltskin's Daughter by Diane Stanley (1997)

Sleeping Beauty

Princess, Princess by Penny Dale (2003)
Sleeping Boy by Sonia Craddock (1999)
Sleepless Beauty by Frances Minters (1996)

Three Billy Goats Gruff

Oh, Look! by Patricia Polacco (2004)
The Three Armadillies Tuff by Jackie Mims Hopkins (2002)
Three Cool Kids by Rebecca Emberley (1995)
The Three Silly Billies by Margie Palatini (2005)
The Three Silly Girls Grubb by John Hassett and Ann Hassett (2002)
The Toll-bridge Troll by Patricia Rae Wolff (1995)

The Three Little Pigs

Alaska's Three Pigs by Arlene Laverde (2000)
My Lucky Day by Keiko Kasza (2003)
Pig, Pigger, Piggest by Rick Walton (1997)
Three Little Javelinas by Susan Lowell (2003)
The Three Little Pigs and the Fox by William H. Hooks (1998)
The Three Little Rigs by David Gordon (2005)
The Three Little Wolves and the Big Bad Pig by Eugene Trivizas (1993)
The Three Pigs by David Wiesner (2001)
The True Story of the 3 Little Pigs by Jon Scieszka (1989)
Where's the Big Bad Wolf? by Eileen Christelow (2002)

The Tortoise and the Hare

Hare and Tortoise Race to the Moon by Oliver J. Corwin (2002)

Twelve Dancing Princesses

The Princesses Have a Ball by Teresa Bateman (2002)

The Ugly Duckling

The Ugly Truckling by David Gordon (2004)

Combination of Tales

Bad Boys by Margie Palatini (2003)
Fairytale News by Colin Hawkins and Jacqui Hawkins (2004)
The Gold Miner's Daughter: A Melodramatic Fairy Tale by
    Jackie Mims Hopkins (2006)
The Jolly Postman by Janet Ahlberg and Allen Ahlberg (1986)
The Magician's Boy by Susan Cooper (2005)
Once Upon a Time, the End: Asleep in 60 Seconds by Geoffrey Kloske and Barry
    Blitt (2005)
The Stinky Cheese Man and Other Fairly Stupid Tales by Jon Scieszka (1992)
Who Is It? by Sally Grindley (2000)
With Love, Little Red Hen by Alma Flor Ada (2001)
Yo, Hungry Wolf! by David Vozar (1993)

Box 11.8   Young Adult Novel Fractured Fairy Tales

Beastly by Alex Flinn. New York: HarperCollins, 2007.

A modern-day version of *Beauty and the Beast* set in New York City. Flinn's version depicts both characters as victims of bad parenting who find each other.

Beauty: A Retelling of the Story of Beauty and the Beast by Robin McKinley. New York: Harper & Row, 1978.

McKinley reinvents the well-known classic, adding character depth and rich language. She returns to the classic in *Rose Daughter* (1997).

Briar Rose by Jane Yolen. New York: Tor, 1995.

Rebecca remembers her grandmother's *Sleeping Beauty* story about Briar Rose. After her grandmother's death, Rebecca embarks on a journey that takes her to Europe, where she explores the possibility that her grandmother might actually have been Briar Rose. A unique blending of *Sleeping Beauty* and the Holocaust.

Birdwing by Rafe Martin. New York: Levine/Scholastic, 2005.

A continuation of the Brothers Grimm tale, *The Six Swans*. Six brothers are turned into swans. Their sister manages to turn them back into humans, but one brother (Ardwin) keeps a swan's wing. The open sky beckons Ardwin. Is he boy or bird?

Confessions of an Ugly Stepsister by Gregory Maguire. New York: HarperCollins, 1999.

A complex retelling of *Cinderella* set in 17th-century Holland. Maguire tells the story from an ugly stepsister's point of view, thus raising questions about the cost of beauty and the value placed on physical appearance. Can beauty be an affliction?

Coraline by Neil Gaiman. New York: HarperCollins, 2002.

When Coraline's father tells her to count the doors and windows in her new home, Coraline comes upon a mysterious locked door. She finds the door key and steps into another world—an exact replica of her current life; however, these parents give her everything she wants. When Coraline attempts to return home, the Other Mother won't let her go. Intertextual connections with *Alice in Wonderland*.

Daughter of the Forest by Juliet Marillier. New York: Tor, 2000.

A wicked stepmother turns six brothers into swans. To reclaim her brothers' lives, Sorcha sets out on a treacherous and frightening journey. A retelling of the Celtic myth.

The Decoding of Lana Morris by Laura McNeal and Tom McNeal. New York: Knopf/Random House, 2007.

Sixteen-year-old Lana yearns for a better life. Her foster mother dislikes her, and Lana is forced to care for her younger siblings. When Lana by chance enters a mysterious shop, she learns she can have the power to alter her life. A *Cinderella* retelling.

The Door in the Hedge by Robin McKinley. New York: Greenwillow/HarperCollins, 1981.

Four stories make up this young adult classic. Two are retellings of *The Twelve Princesses* and *The Princess and the Frog*.

East by Edith Pattou. Orlando, FL: Harcourt, 2003.

A retelling of the classic, *East of the Sun, West of the Moon*. A young woman (Rose) travels on the back of an enchanted great white bear to a distant land, hoping her journey will heal her ailing family and bring prosperity.

Fairest by Gail Carson Levine. New York: HarperCollins, 2006.

A reimagining of *Snow White* that raises questions about perceptions of beauty. Fifteen-year-old Aza is so unattractive her parents keep her hidden. Aza

Continued

Box 11.8   Young Adult Novel Fractured Fairy Tales   *Continued*

has two talents: a miraculous singing voice and the ability to "throw" her voice—giving the illusion that someone else is singing. When circumstances place Aza in the royal court, she gains access to a magical mirror that will make her the fairest in the land.

Into the Woods by Lyn Gardner. Illus. Mini Grey. New York: Fickling/Random House, 2007.

The three Eden sisters live with their parents in a dilapidated mansion. When their parents are killed in an accident, the three run to the woods, where they have multiple adventures. Elements of numerous fairy tales abound: *The Pied Piper, The Snow Queen, Hansel and Gretel,* and *Rapunzel.* Wonderful, complex read.

Keturah and Lord Death by Martine Leavitt. Asheville, NC: Front Street, 2006.

Keturah becomes lost in the forest, loses strength, and almost dies. Death is a young lord. She escapes Death temporarily but must find her true love within 24 hours. Elements of *The Arabian Nights*.

Leaping Beauty: And Other Animal Fairy Tales by Gregory Maguire. Illus. Chris L. Demarest. New York: HarperCollins, 2004.

A collection of silly retellings: Three chickens outwit Goldifx. Cinder-Elephant loses her slipper. A hornet casts a sleeping spell on Beauty (a tadpole). Three little penguins build houses. There's more. Hilarious and wonderfully done.

Mira, Mirror by Mette Ivie Harrison. New York: Viking/Penguin, 2004.

Mira is apprenticed to a witch. Another apprentice tricks Mira and changes her into a magic mirror. Mira must use her skills as a magic mirror to release herself from the enchantment. Elements of *Snow White*.

Mirror Mirror by Gregory Maguire. New York: HarperCollins, 2003.

A dark retelling of *Snow White* set in Italy. Lurcrezia (evil stepmother) is jealous of Bianca's beauty and

orders her death. Rich in medieval Italy detail. A clever and elaborate retelling.

Once Upon a Time series (*The Storyteller's Daughter #1*) by various authors. New York: Simon & Schuster, 2002.

A complete series of retellings in novel form based on some of the most familiar classics: *The Arabian Nights, Sleeping Beauty, Snow White, The Little Mermaid, Little Red Riding Hood, The Magic Flute, Beauty and the Beast, Twelve Dancing Princesses, Rapunzel, The Frog Prince, Cinderella,* and *The White and the Black Bride*.

The Outlaws of Sherwood by Robin McKinley. New York: Greenwood/HarperCollins, 1988.

A retelling of *Robin Hood*. The character of Robin Hood is more fully developed. Includes an afterword discussing differences with previous versions.

The Phoenix Dance by Dia Calhoun. New York: Farrar, Straus & Giroux, 2005.

Twelve dancing princesses wore their shoes out one night dancing. When the queen blames the royal shoemaker, his apprentice (Phoenix Dance) sets out to solve the mystery. A multilayered story.

The Princess and the Pauper by Kate Brian. Simon & Schuster, 2003.

Twain's classic told with a female twist. When a real princess (Carina) meets an average high school girl (Julia), the two exchange places. Carina sets out for a concert, and Julia heads for an embassy ball. Light, witty, and makes for good discussion on wealth, materialism, and appearance.

The Pull of the Ocean by Jean-Claude Mourlevat. Trans. Y. Maudet. New York. Delacorte/Random House, 2006.

A modern adaptation of *Tom Thumb*. Seven brothers, awakened by the youngest, leave their home one rainy night fearing for their lives. They journey toward the ocean.

Continued

Box 11.8   Young Adult Novel Fractured Fairy Tales   *Continued*

The Rose and the Beast: Fairy Tales Retold by Francesca Lia Block. New York: HarperCollins, 2000.

Modern retellings in lyrical language of nine classics. Sleeping Beauty, Snow White, and Rose Red take control of their unfortunate situations (e.g., Snow White escapes the poisoned apple). Female characters are courageous and strong.

Son of a Witch by Gregory Maguire. New York: HarperCollins, 2005.

A continuation of *The Wizard of Oz.* Written a decade after his bestseller *Wicked,* this is the story of a young boy, Liir, found beaten and unconscious after Elphaba melted away. He is nursed back to health by Candle, and mysterious questions surround him. Is he the witch's son? Can he perform magic?

Spindle's End by Robin McKinley. New York: Putnam, 2000.

Rosie grows up in a village and has no idea she has been separated from her royal family in an effort to protect her from an evil curse. The truth comes to light. A rich restructuring of *Sleeping Beauty*.

Tales of the Frog Prince series (*The Frog Princess #1*) by E. D. Baker. New York: Bloomsbury, 2002.

Princess Emeralda (Emma) kisses a frog and is transformed into one. Together the "prince" and "princess" set out on a quest that will return them to human form. A twist on the classic *The Frog Prince*.

Wish Riders by Patrick Jennings. New York: Hyperion, 2006.

Fifteen-year-old Dusty is forced to work in a logging camp after the death of her parents. She and others escape on magical horses and are sheltered by an eccentric old woman. Fearing she is a witch, they flee. Elements of *Hansel and Gretel, Cinderella,* and more.

On Writing *Hush: An Irish Princess' Tale*   by Donna Jo Napoli

Since *Hush* is based on a tale unfamiliar to most American readers, let me give an overview. The main character of *Hush*, Melkorka, is a minor character in one of the Icelandic sagas—*The Laxdaela Saga*—which tell the tales of the Vikings who settled in Iceland. This particular saga tells of events in the late 800s and after. At one point in the saga, the Viking chieftain Hoskuld buys a woman from a Russian slave dealer when he visits the Norse country, and he brings her home to Iceland. The woman doesn't speak, although she isn't deaf. Hoskuld fathers a son with her (he already has a family—so she remains with slave status), and one day, when the child's a toddler, Hoskuld overhears the woman singing in a strange language. When he confronts Melkorka, she admits she was an Irish princess. That's the information she gives—that's what I started with.

Continued

On Writing *Hush: An Irish Princess' Tale*   *Continued*

Melkorka fascinated me for two reasons. First, her history has to have been remarkable, but she doesn't yield a single detail. That's a gold mine to a writer—I was free to make up that history. Second, she steadfastly maintains muteness through her ordeal. I am a linguist by training, so I study the ways people do and don't use language in communication. For a person to voluntarily give up their ability to produce language, oh my, that takes tremendous willpower, for it means giving up the ability to be understood in that wide range of ways that language allows. The instant I found out Melkorka was mute by choice I had no choice of my own; I needed to write her story.

I began my work on *Hush* the same way I begin any book: by trying to understand the world the story takes place in. I read books about the period of Viking invasions of Ireland (800 to 1000). My reading was catholic: economics, political history, flora and fauna, geography, religion, folk literature, whatever. I read about slavery in the middle ages, and about Russian slave dealers in particular. I visited Ireland—libraries and museums and excavation sites, of course, but I also tried as much as possible to see the skies and trees and birds Melkorka would have seen. I looked at illustrated manuscripts of the type Melkorka would have known. I listened to Irish music, ate Irish food, read Irish books (in English), danced Irish jigs. Basically, I did whatever I could to steep myself in any culture accessible to me that

might hark back to culture Melkorka might have been part of. I went to a town in the very north of Norway and took a postal boat down the coast, all the way to Bergen, stopping in the various fjords—with an excursion at Trondheim, with its museums and Viking artifacts.

All this could seem surprising to you. After all, who cares if a novel has historical accuracy? But to me research is crucial. We are all, to varying extents, products of the times and places in which we live. That doesn't mean that we are all alike today—how absurd. But I believe that two Americans, for example, who have never met each other, would find a lot more in common if we plopped them down in a room together than would either of them with an Irish or Norse person from 900. What we consider to be problems and the possible solutions we imagine to those problems would be drastically different. What we consider funny, sad, shocking, sexy, frightening, and on and on might differ in surprising ways. So if I am to make my reader understand the motives behind my characters' actions, I need to help my reader understand the world my characters inhabit to whatever extent possible given my own limitations.

Copyright Donna Jo Napoli, 2008

Other fairy tale and myth titles include *The Magic Circle* (1993), *Zel* (1996), *Sirena* (1998), *Crazy Jack* (1999a), *Spinners* (1999b), *Beast* (2000), *Breath* (2003a), *The Great God Pan* (2003b), and *Bound* (2004).

Teaching Synthesizing with Fractured Fairy Tales and the Classics

My son learned the difference between a cow and a horse when he was three. One Sunday I took him for a drive in the country, and the hillsides were dotted with farm animals. Our conversation went something like this:

"Cow!" he said, pointing toward the hillside.
"No, that's a horse. See its mane? That long hair on its neck?"
"Horsie? Not cow?"
"Yes, horsie. You ride horses. Over there's a cow. How do cows go?"
"Mooooo . . ."

He had seen pictures of cows and horses, but this was the first time he had seen them for real. He had partial definitions of both animals (e.g., both are big; they walk on four legs; they are found in fields; maybe they are similar in color). However, he didn't have enough prior knowledge or experience with them to tell them apart. To arrive at deeper understandings of both, he linked old information with new (e.g., possibly the horse had a mane, and you ride horses). He altered his schema. He did so by pulling together pieces of information and deleting others to come up with something new— a deeper understanding of horse and cow.

Whether reading a text or reading the world, the ability to piece together bits of information is an essential comprehension skill. Synthesizing, however, can be difficult for young adults, especially when they are confronted with challenging reading and writing assignments. For instance, when writing reports, which ideas do they choose? How do they combine them? The results are sometimes disjointed collections of statements, some of which are copied word for word; others are altered only slightly from the original. The ability to synthesize is related to the ability to summarize (see Chapter 10). A good summarizer can combine key ideas into new, concise thoughts.

Blended fairy tales and myths are superb genres for practicing synthesizing skills, primarily because examining the merging of plotlines, characters, and motifs is more engaging, and in some ways more tangible, than traditional approaches to synthesizing (e.g., taking notes on note cards, then writing paragraphs). Studying blended fairy tales and myths can also aid students in understanding *allusion*—a literary term we often talk about but don't explain well. To identify a traditional tale, students must be able to make implicit references (allusions) to other texts. Below are several ideas for using blended fairy tales and myths to teach synthesizing. I've also included ideas for teaching synthesizing with plays and prose retellings. The activities require that students make implicit references and text-to-text connections.

Unpack the Story

If you want to know how something fits together, take it apart. Students can learn a great deal about synthesizing by "breaking apart" a blended fairy tale. Choose a blended fairy tale or mythic young adult novel (e.g., Neal Shusterman's *Dread Locks,* 2005a). Identify the traditional tales within the story. For example, *Dread Locks* is a play on *Goldilocks and the Three Bears* and *Medusa.* Introduce the two tales to the class through read-alouds. In most cases you will be able to use picture books; in other cases you may need to provide a short text. Don't make the assumption that all your students know traditional tales. Schools are increasingly diverse; even students who know a particular tale may know a different version. Discuss the tales, then have them read *Dread Locks.* After reading the book, have students examine scenes in which the author makes allusions to classics. You might have them complete an allusion chart like the one in Table 11.2, then discuss their findings in class or make notes in a journal. Limit the number of points they should identify so the assignment doesn't become laborious.

T a b l e   1 1 . 2

Fairy Tale Allusions in *Dread Locks*, (2005) by Neal Shusterman

List an implicit reference to a classic fairy tale in the first column. Then explain the connection with the original text in the appropriate column.

Dread Locks (Provide Page Numbers)	*Goldilocks and the Three Bears*	*Medusa*
(p. 16) Parker finds Tara, a new neighbor, asleep in his bed.	The three bears find Goldilocks asleep in Baby Bear's bed.	
(pp. 16 & 20) Shusterman emphasizes Tara's golden curls: ". . . long, lopping curls—bright golden twists of hair tumbling . . ."	Same hair as Goldilocks.	
(p. 27) Tara calls Parker "Baby Baer." Baer is his last name.	An obvious allusion to Baby Bear.	
(p. 29) Parker visits Tara's house and struggles to get out of the "deep, comfortable chair."	Goldilocks tries out all three chairs owned by the bears and settles on Baby Bear's.	
(p. 31) Parker eats ice cream from a "little silver bowl."	Goldilocks samples porridge and eats Baby Bear's bowlful.	
(p. 46) Tara makes numerous references to Greek culture (e.g., Crete).		Medusa is a Greek female god.
(p. 41) Tara wears sunglasses and refuses to remove them. -and- (p. 59) Stone and statue motifs abound.		Those who gazed upon Medusa were turned to stone.
(p. 99) References to how Tara looks at people: "It [why she doesn't remove her sunglasses] has to do with the way I look at people. I see very deeply when I look at people. Very few have the strength to look back."		Medusa's power to turn people to stone.
(p. 101) "The others who tried to be my friends over the years were always too cold, or their tempers were too hot. But you, Baby Baer—you're just right."	A play on words from Goldilocks.	

Continued

T a b l e 1 1 . 2 *Continued*		
(p. 103) Tara takes Parker to her basement where she shows him dozens of stone statues with amazing lifelike detail.		Representative of the people Medusa turned to stone.
(p. 106) Parker destroys the statues out of anger with a bat. Afterward his hair is heavy with chalk dust: "I reached up to find I now had a full head of twisting curls, and every one of them writhed ever so slowly, like the tentacles of a sea anemone."		An allusion to Medusa's snake hair.
(p. 117) Those around Tara begin changing. Their skin turns gray and they become lethargic.		A suggestion that Tara has the same effect on people as Medusa.
(p. 162) Parker, aware he's changing, tricks Tara into meeting his gaze.		Medusa dies at the hands of Perseus. He kills her by looking at her through a mirror and cutting off her head.

Story Bookmarks

You may also create double-sided bookmarks from stock paper. On one side students list motifs from one classic tale (e.g., *Goldilocks and the Three Bears*), and on the other they list motifs from a classic (e.g., *Medusa*). If more than two tales or myths are evident, you may split each side of the card to allow for more. This activity draws student attention to blended motifs and requires that students make implicit references to classical texts. Have students share their cards in small group discussion once they are full.

Blending Plots, Characters, and Motifs

Students can practice synthesis by writing their own blended fairy tales. Students may write a short story, a manuscript for a blended fairy tale picture, a poem, or even a single scene in which they blend at least two traditional tales. To aid students in creating a blended tale, share with them several classic tales—this is a good place for picture books. You may also create a graphic organizer that helps them structure their ideas. You might, for instance, have them complete a character map that describes what a new character will look like or what he/she will do—a combination of two classic characters—such as the one in Figure 11.1. You might also have students develop an outline, either visually or with text of a plotline that utilizes elements from two tales. Unless your students are strong writers, you may want to limit them to two

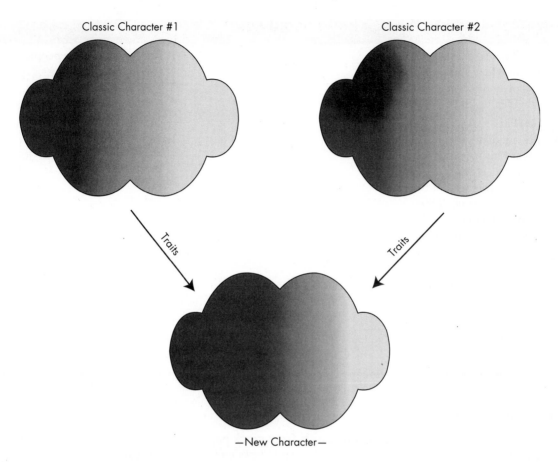

Classic Character #1

Classic Character #2

Traits

Traits

—New Character—

Figure 11.1   *Blended Character Map*

tales. Too much information can be overwhelming. They'll feel like they've walked into a wallpaper store with no idea what they want to purchase. Finally, they may need to do additional research on their traditional tales to provide a stronger knowledge base for their writing.

Key Concept Synthesis: Picture Books and Shakespeare

As we read, we synthesize key pieces of information. Less important pieces of information fall along the wayside. Most students struggle with synthesizing because they have difficulty identifying key concepts. The denser the text, the harder the task. Picture-book retellings of Shakespeare's plays can provide students with practice in identifying key concepts. After a unit study of *Hamlet*, for instance, you might read aloud Bruce Coville's (2004) picture-book retelling. Working as a class, make a list of the key events in Coville's version. Then make a second list of key concepts from the original play that are missing in the retelling. Discuss why Coville may have made the omissions.

Teaching Synthesis through Prose Retellings

Converting a play into a prose retelling isn't easy. Writers have to identify key points and combine them into a sensible new whole. After reading a classical play, have students convert the play to a picture book or short story. Begin by placing students in small groups and having them brainstorm, then list, the essential elements of the play. Students then compose individual retellings. Brainstorming and listing the key elements are essential steps. They help students focus on important details. Skipping this step can make the activity meaningless.

Final Thoughts

Some advocates of the classics believe young adult literature is too easy to read and offers little intellectual challenge. Rather than dismissing either genre, we need to take into account our goals (and objectives) in using books prior to selecting them and make choices accordingly. Are we wanting to teach students to navigate difficult texts? Are we hoping to select a piece that sparks good conversation and thought about humanity and the world in which we live? Are we wanting to expose students to good writing? Teach literary elements? Examine intertextuality? All of these? In defending the classics Carol Jago (2000) argues,

> I worry in our determination to provide students with literature they can
> "relate to" we sometimes end up teaching works that students actually
> don't need much help with at the expense of teaching classics that they
> most certainly do need assistance negotiating. (pp. 2–3)

Jago's argument is valid. If we don't introduce challenging words in context, we can't support vocabulary development. If we only teach novels with simplistic sentence structures and basic concepts, we limit how much we move students forward as readers. We can't improve reading or thinking skills if the text is too easy. The classics, no doubt, are a good source for teaching students to navigate complex sentence structures and for exploring complex issues. They can also be excellent texts for teaching vocabulary and the changing nature of the English language.

However, teaching literature is about more than teaching reading. It's about exploring what it means to be human. It's about teaching good story and creative writing, and a text need not be difficult to read (and I would argue should not be) for teaching those things. While the classics might be more difficult to navigate, and we can't argue they have much to teach us about history and humanity, young adult literature is a more manageable tool for teaching writing.

The point to remember is *balance*. We should teach students to navigate difficult texts, but we shouldn't always choose literature for that purpose. If we focus solely on helping students navigate difficult texts, students don't have enough cognitive resources, energy, or motivation to appreciate the story. They lose interest. They give up. We also send the message "reading is difficult." And it shouldn't always be. As adults, we don't make reading selections based on how the text(s) will improve our reading skills,[7] and we shouldn't choose books for students based on that one goal. Whether classic or young adult novel, we need focused goals that both challenge *and* encourage young adults. We need to remember, too, that the text is only one factor in learning. *How* we teach a text, whether classic or young adult novel, is by far more important than *what* we choose to teach.

Professional Resources

Bermel, A. (2004). *Shakespeare at the moment: Playing the comedies.* Portsmouth, NH: Heinemann.

Blau, S. (2003). *The literature workshop: Teaching texts and their readers.* Portsmouth, NH: Heinemann.

Bottigheimer, R. B. (2002). Misperceived perceptions: Perrault's fairy tales and English children's literature. *Children's Literature, 30,* 1–20.

Bowman, C., & Pieters, B. (2002). Shakespeare, our contemporary: Using technology to teach the Bard. *English Journal, 92*(1), 88–93.

Bowman, P. B., & Carpenter, M. (2004). "Oh, that's just folklore": Valuing the ordinary as an extraordinary teaching tool. *Language Arts, 81*(5), 385–396.

Bucolo, J. (2007). The Bard in the bathroom: Literary analysis, filmmaking, and Shakespeare. *English Journal, 96*(6), 50–55.

Buss, K., & Karnowski, L. (2000). *Reading and writing literary genres.* Newark, DE: IRA.

Gallo, D. R. (2001). How classics create an alliterate society. *English Journal, 90*(3), 33–39.

Glasser, J. E. (1994). Finding Ithaca: The *Odyssey* personalized. *English Journal, 83*(2), 66–69.

Gruner, E. R. (2003). Saving "Cinderella": History and story in *Ashpet* and *Ever After. Children's Literature, 31,* 142–156.

Hanlon, T. L. (1998). "To sleep, perchance to dream": Sleeping beauties and wide-awake plain Janes in the stories of Jane Yolen. *Children's Literature, 26,* 140–168.

Heitman, J. (2007). *Fairy tales in the library and language arts classroom for Grades 3–6.* Columbus, OH: Linworth.

Hertz, S. K., & Gallo, D. R. (2005). *From Hinton to Hamlet: Building bridges between young adult literature and the classics.* Columbus, OH: Greenwood.

House, J. (1992). The modern quest: Teaching myths and folktales. *English Journal, 81*(1), 72–74.

Isaac, M. L. (2000). *Heirs to Shakespeare.* Portsmouth, NH: Heinemann.

Jago, C. (2004). *Classics in the classroom.* Portsmouth, NH: Heinemann.

Kendall, S. (1990). Teaching mythology: Not the same old thing. *English Journal, 79*(4), 29–32.

Mello, R. (2001). Cinderella meets Ulysses. *Language Arts, 78*(6), 548–555.

Metzger, M. J. (2004). *Shakespeare with fear: Teaching for understanding.* Portsmouth, NH: Heinemann.

Milburn, M. (2002). Selling Shakespeare. *English Journal, 92*(1), 74–79.

Paquette, M. (2007). Sex and violence: Words at play in the Shakespeare classroom. *English Journal, 96*(3), 40–45.

Polette, N. (2005). *Teaching thinking skills with fairy tales and fantasy.* Portsmouth, NH: Libraries Unlimited.

Reese, D. (2007). Proceed with caution: Using Native American folktales in the classroom. *Language Arts, 84*(3), 245–257.

Ressler, P. (2005). Challenging normative sexual and gender identity beliefs through Romeo and Juliet. *English Journal, 95*(1), 52–57.

Robbins, B. (2005). Using *The Original* approach to teach Shakespeare. *English Journal, 95*(1), 65–68.

---

[7]An exception, of course, is an adult learning to read. All of us do choose some texts to deepen our knowledge base.

Stillman, P. R. (1985). *Introduction to myth* (2nd ed.). Portsmouth, NH: Heinemann.

Toepfer, M. M., & Haas, K. H. (2003). Imaginative departures with two Shakespearean plays. *English Journal, 92*(5), 30–34.

Weltsek, G. (2005). Using process drama to deconstruct *A Midsummer Night's Dream. English Journal, 95*(1), 75–81.

ONLINE

Absolute Shakespeare: www.absoluteshakespeare .com

The American Society of Jane Austen Scholars: www.facstaff.uww.edu/hipchene/JAusten/ home.htm

Classic Fairy Tales: www.webtech.kennesaw.edu/ jcheek3/fairytales.htm

The Complete Works of William Shakespeare: www.shakespeare.mit.edu/works.html

The Dickens Fellowship: www.dickensfellowship .org/Weblinks.htm

Edsitement—National Endowment for the Humanities: www.edsitement.neh.gov

Education World: www.educationworld.com/ a_lesson/lesson/lesson011.shtml

Electronic Literature Foundation: www.theplays.org

Electronic Shakespeare: www.wfu.edu/~tedforrl/ shakespeare

Electronic Text Center: www.etext.virginia.edu/ shakespeare

Exploring Shakespeare: www.rsc.org.uk/ exploringshakespeare/default.htm

Fairy Tale Unit: www.tooter4kids.com/classroom/ FairyTaleUnit.htm

Folger Shakespeare Library: www.folger.edu/ academic/sq/menu.htm

Grimm Fairy Tales: www.grimmfairytales.com/ en/main

In Search of Shakespeare: www.pbs.org/ shakespeare/educators

Jane Austen Society of North America: www.jasna.org

Myth*Ing Links: www.mythinglinks.org/ reference~teachers.html

Mythweb: www.mythweb.com/index.html

National Geographic's Grimm Fairy Tales: www.nationalgeographic.com/grimm/ index2.html

Oxford School Shakespeare: www.oup.co.uk/ oxed/secondary/teachingshakespeare

Scholastic's Myths, Folktales, & Fairy Tales: www.teacher.scholastic.com/writewit/mff/

Shakes Sphere: www.cummingsstudyguides.net/ xShakeSph.html#top

Shakespeare Birthplace Trust: www.shakespeare .org.uk/about_content2.htm

The Shakespeare Fellowship: www.shakespearefellowship.org

Shakespeare in Education: www.shakespeare .palomar.edu/educational.htm

Shakespeare Online: www.shakespeare-online.com

Shakespeare Resource Center: www.bardweb.net

Sherlock Holmes International: www .sherlock-holmes.org/english.htm#major

Sherlockian.Net: www.sherlockian.net

Social-studies.ca: www.social-studies.ca/index.html

Teacher Oz's Kingdom of History: www.teacheroz.com/index.htm

Teaching Heart: www.teachingheart.net/f.html

Victorian Web: www.victorianweb.org

Web English Teacher: www.webenglishteacher .com/classmyth.html

William Shakespeare's Complete Works: www.jollyroger.com/shakespeare

References

Achebe, C. (1958). *Things fall apart.* London: Heinemann.

Ada, A. F. (2001). *With love, little red hen.* Illus. Leslie Tryon. New York: Atheneum/Simon & Schuster.

Ahlberg, J., & Ahlberg, A. (1986). *The jolly postman.* New York: Little, Brown.

Anderson, M. T. (2002). *Feed.* Cambridge, MA: Candlewick Press.

Armour, P. (1993). *Stop that pickle!* Illus. Andrew Shachat. Boston: Houghton Mifflin.

Artell, M. (2001). *Petite Rouge: A cajun red riding hood.* Illus. Jim Harris. New York: Dial/ Penguin.

Austen, J. (2002). *Pride and prejudice.* New York: Penguin. (Original work published 1813)

Avi. (2007). *The traitor's gate.* New York: Atheneum/Simon & Schuster.

Barron, T. A. (1996). *The lost years of Merlin* series (*The lost years of Merlin* #1). New York: Penguin.

Barron, T. A. (2004). *The great tree of Avalon trilogy* (*Child of the dark prophecy* #1). New York: Philomel/Penguin.

Bateman, T. (2002). *The princesses have a ball.* Illus. Lynne Cravath. Morton Grove, IL: Whitman & Co.

Bebris, C. (2005). *Suspense and sensibility.* New York: Forge/Tor.

Bebris, C. (2006). *North by Northanger.* New York: Forge/Tor.

Bennett, C., & Gottesfeld, J. (2001). *Anne Frank and me.* New York: Penguin/Putnam.

Bennett, V. (2006). *Angelmonster.* Cambridge, MA: Candlewick Press.

Bennett, V. (2007). *Cassandra's sister: Growing up Jane Austen.* Cambridge, MA: Candlewick Press.

Berenzy, A. (1989). *A frog prince.* New York: Henry Holt.

Birdseye, T. (2001). *Look out, Jack! The giant is back!* Illus. Will Hillenbrand. New York: Holiday House.

Blackwood, G. (2000). *Shakespeare's scribe.* New York: Dutton/Penguin.

Blackwood, G. (2003). *Shakespeare's spy.* New York: Dutton/Penguin.

Blackwood, G. L. (1998). *The Shakespeare stealer.* New York: Dutton/Penguin.

Bradbury, R. (1953). *Fahrenheit 451.* Illus. Joe Mugnaini. New York: Ballantine.

Brett, J. (2007). *The three snow bears.* New York: Penguin.

Briggs, R. (1997). *Jim and the beanstalk.* New York: Putnam.

Brontë, C. (1995). *Jane Eyre.* New York: Penguin. (Original work published 1847)

Brown, D. (2003). *The Da Vinci code.* New York: Doubleday/Random House.

Cabot, M. (2006). *Avalon High.* New York: HarperCollins.

Cadnum, M. (1991). *Calling home.* New York: Viking/Penguin.

Cadnum, M. (1992). *Breaking the fall.* New York: Viking/Penguin.

Cadnum, M. (1995). *Taking it.* New York: Viking/Penguin.

Cadnum, M. (1996). *Zero at the bone.* New York: Viking/Penguin.

Cadnum, M. (1997). *Edge.* New York: Viking/Penguin.

Cadnum, M. (1998a). *Heat.* New York: Viking/Penguin.

Cadnum, M. (1998b). *In a dark wood.* New York: Orchard/Scholastic.

Cadnum, M. (1999). *Rundown.* New York: Viking/Penguin.

Cadnum, M. (2001a). *The book of the lion.* New York: Viking/Penguin.

Cadnum, M. (2001b). *Raven of the waves.* New York: Orchard/Scholastic.

Cadnum, M. (2002a). *Forbidden forest: The story of Little John and Robin Hood.* New York: Scholastic.

Cadnum, M. (2002b). *The leopard sword.* New York: Viking/Penguin.

Cadnum, M. (2003a). *Daughter of the wind.* New York: Orchard/Scholastic.

Cadnum, M. (2003b). *Ship of fire.* New York: Viking/Penguin.

Cadnum, M. (2004a). *Blood gold.* New York: Viking/Penguin.

Cadnum, M. (2004b). *Starfall: Phaeton and the Chariot of the Sun.* New York: Orchard/Scholastic.

Cadnum, M. (2005). *The dragon throne.* New York: Viking/Penguin.

Cadnum, M. (2006). *Nightsong: The legend of Orpheus and Eurydice.* New York: Orchard/Scholastic.

Cadnum, M. (2008). *The king's arrow.* New York: Penguin.

Calmenson, S. (2001). *The frog principal.* Illus. Denise Brunkus. New York: Scholastic.

Calvert, P. (2006). *Multiplying menace: The revenge of Rumpelstiltskin.* Illus. Wayne Geehan. Watertown, MA: Charlesbridge.

Carroll, L. (2005). *Alice in Wonderland.* New York: Sterling. (Original work published 1865)

Catalano, D. (2000). *Santa and the three bears.* Honesdale, PA: Boyds Mills Press.

Chambers, A. (2002). *Postcards from no man's land.* New York: Penguin.

Cheaney, J. B. (2002). *The true prince.* New York: Knopf/Random House.

Chopin, K. (1982). *The awakening.* New York: HarperCollins. (Original work published 1899)

Christelow, E. (2002). *Where's the big bad wolf?* New York: Clarion.

Compestine, Y. C. (2001). *The runaway rice cake.* Illus. Tungwai Chau. New York: Simon & Schuster.

Cooper, S. (2005). *The magician's boy.* Illus. Serena Riglietti. New York: McElderry/Simon & Schuster.

Corwin, O. J. (2002). *Hare and tortoise race to the moon.* New York: Harry N. Abrams.

Coville, B. (2004). *William Shakespeare's Hamlet.* New York: Dial/Penguin.

Craddock, S. (1999). *Sleeping boy.* Illus. Leonid Gore. New York: Atheneum/Simon & Schuster.

Crane, S. (1895). *The red badge of courage.* New York: Appleton.

Crowe, C. (2002). *Mississippi trial, 1955.* New York: Dial/Penguin.

Curtis, C. P. (1995). *The Watsons go to Birmingham—1963.* New York: Delacorte/Random House.

Dale, P. (2003). *Princess, princess.* Cambridge, MA: Candlewick Press.

David, P. (2003). *One knight only.* New York: Ace/Penguin.

Defoe, D. (1995). *Robinson Crusoe.* New York: Penguin. (Original work published 1719)

Dickens, C. (1990). *A Christmas carol.* New York: Tor. (Original work published 1843)

Dickens, C. (2003). *Oliver Twist.* New York: Penguin. (Original work published 1838)

Dickens, C. (2005). *David Copperfield.* New York: Penguin. (Original work published 1849–1850)

Douglass, F. (2005). *Narrative of the life of Frederick Douglass.* New York: Penguin. (Original work published 1845)

Draper, S. (2006). *Copper sun.* New York: Simon & Schuster.

Durant, A. (2006). *Burger boy.* Illus. Mei Matsuoka. New York: Clarion.

Emberley, R. (1995). *Three cool kids.* New York: Little, Brown.

Ernst, L. C. (2000). *Goldilocks returns.* New York: Simon & Schuster.

Evans, C. (2006). *Martha Moth makes socks.* Boston: Houghton Mifflin.

Farmer, N. (2007). *The land of the silver apples.* New York: Atheneum/Simon & Schuster.

Fearnley, J. (2001). *Mr. Wolf's pancakes.* Wilton, CT: Tiger Tales.

Fitzgerald, F. S. (1925). *The great Gatsby.* New York: Scribner.

Fleischman, S. (1978). *McBroom and the beanstalk.* Illus. Walter Lorraine. New York: Little, Brown.

Fleming, C. (2004). *Gator gumbo: A spicy-hot tale.* Illus. Sally Anne Lambert. New York: Farrar, Straus & Giroux.

Flinn, A. (2007). *Beastly.* New York: HarperCollins.

Forward, T. (2005). *The wolf's story: What really happened to Little Red Riding Hood.* Illus. Izhar Cohen. Cambridge, MA: Candlewick Press.

Frank, A. (1952). *The diary of a young girl.* Garden City, NY: Doubleday.

Frank, E. R. (2002). *America.* New York: Simon & Schuster.

Gaines, E. J. (1994). *A lesson before dying.* New York: Vintage.

Garden, N. (2006). *Endgame.* Orlando, FL: Harcourt.

Gibson, W. (2008). *The miracle worker.* New York: Simon & Schuster. (First performed 1959)

Golding, W. (1954). *Lord of the flies.* London: Faber & Faber.

Gordon, D. (2004). *The ugly truckling.* New York: Geringer/HarperCollins.

Gordon, D. (2005). *The three little rigs.* New York: Geringer/HarperCollins.

Gordon, D. (2006). *Hansel and Diesel.* New York: Geringer/HarperCollins.

Greene, E. (2000). *The little golden lamb.* Illus. Rosanne Litzinger. New York: Clarion.

Grey, M. (2003). *The very smart pea and the princess-to-be.* New York: Knopf/Random House.

Grey, M. (2007). *Ginger bear.* New York: Knopf/Random House.

Grindley, S. (2000). *Who is it?* Illus. Rosalind Beardshaw. Atlanta: Peachtree.

Gruber, M. (2005). *The witch's boy.* New York: HarperCollins.

Gwynne, F. (1990). *Pondlarker.* New York: Simon & Schuster.

Hale, S. (2003). *The goose girl.* New York: Bloomsbury.

Hale, S. (2004). *Enna burning.* New York: Bloomsbury.

Hale, S. (2005). *Princess Academy.* New York: Bloomsbury.

Hale, S. (2006). *River secrets.* New York: Bloomsbury.

Hale, S. (2007a). *Austenland.* New York: Bloomsbury.

Hale, S. (2007b). *Book of a thousand days*. New York: Bloomsbury.

Harris, J. (1997). *Jack and the giant: A story full of beans*. Flagstaff, AZ: Northland.

Harrison. L. (2004). *The clique*. New York: Little, Brown.

Hartman, B. (2002). *The wolf who cried boy*. Illus. Tim Raglin. New York: Penguin.

Hassett, J., & Hassett, A. (2002). *The three silly girls grubb*. Boston: Houghton Mifflin.

Hawkins, C., & Hawkins, J. (2004). *Fairytale news*. Cambridge, MA: Candlewick Press.

Hawthorne, N. (1999). *The scarlett letter*. New York: Penguin. (Original work published 1850)

Hearn, J. (2005). *The minister's daughter*. New York: Simon & Schuster.

Hemingway, E. (1940). *A farewell to arms*. New York: Scribner.

Hemingway, E. (1952). *The old man and the sea*. New York: Scribner.

Hemphill, S. (2007). *Your own, Sylvia: A verse portrait of Sylvia Plath*. New York: Random House.

Hobbs, W. (1999). *Jason's gold*. New York: HarperCollins.

Hobbs, W. (2002). *Wild man island*. New York: HarperCollins.

Hooks, W. H. (1998). *The three little pigs and the fox*. Illus. S. D. Schindler. New York: Simon & Schuster.

Hopkins, J. (2002). *The three armadillies tuff*. Illus. S. G. Brooks. Atlanta: Peachtree.

Hopkins, J. M. (2006). *The gold miner's daughter: A melodramatic fairy tale*. Illus. Jon Goodell. Atlanta: Peachtree.

Hugo, V. (1981). *The hunchback of Notre Dame*. New York: Bantam. (Original work published 1831)

Hurston, Z. N. (1937). *Their eyes were watching God*. Philadelphia, PA: Lippincott.

Jago, C. (2000). *With rigor for all: Teaching classics to contemporary students*. Portsmouth, NH: Heinemann.

Johnson, H. M. (2006). *Accidents of nature*. New York: Henry Holt.

Johnston, T. (1992). *The cowboy and the black-eyed pea*. Illus. Warren Ludwig. New York: Penguin.

Jukes, M. (1999). *Cinderella 2000*. New York: Delacorte/Random House.

Kasza, K. (2003). *My lucky day*. New York: Putnam.

Kaywell, J. F. (1993–2000). *Adolescent literature as a complement to the classics*. Vols. 1–4. Norwood, MA: Christopher-Gordon.

Keller, L. (2003). *Arnie the doughnut*. New York: Henry Holt.

Kellogg, S. (1985). *Chicken Little*. New York: HarperCollins.

Kimmel, E. A. (2007). *Rip Van Winkle's return*. Illus. Leonard Everett Fisher. New York: Farrar, Straus & Giroux.

Kimmelman, L. (2000). *The runaway latkes*. Illus. Paul Yalowitz. Morton Grove, IL: Albert Whitman.

King, L. R. (1994). *Mary Russell mysteries (The beekeeper's apprentice #1)*. New York: St. Martin's Press.

Kloske, G., & Blitt, B. (2005). *Once upon a time, the end: Asleep in 60 seconds*. New York: Atheneum/Simon & Schuster.

Knowles, J. (1959). *A separate peace*. London: Secker & Warburg.

Laverde, A. (2000). *Alaska's three pigs*. Illus. Mindy Dwyer. Seattle, WA: Sasquatch.

Lee, H. (1960). *To kill a mockingbird*. Philadelphia, PA: Lippincott.

Lester, H. (2002). *Tackylocks and the three bears*. Illus. Lynn Munsinger. Boston: Houghton Mifflin.

Lester, J. (1995). *Othello*. New York: Scholastic.

Levine, G. C. (1997). *Ella enchanted*. New York: HarperCollins.

London, J. (2001). *The call of the wild*. New York: Scholastic. (Original work published 1903)

Lowell, S. (1997). *Little red cowboy hat*. Illus. Randy Cecil. New York: Henry Holt.

Lowell, S. (2001). *Dusty Locks and the three bears*. Illus. Randy Cecil. New York: Henry Holt.

Lowell, S. (2003). *Three little javelinas*. Illus. Jim Harris. Flagstaff, AZ: Northland.

Lowry, L. (1993). *The giver*. Boston: Houghton Mifflin.

Lyons, M. E. (2007). *Letters from a slave boy: The story of Joseph Jacobs*. New York: Simon & Schuster.

MacDonald, A. (1998). *Beware of the bears!* Illus. Gwyneth Williamson. Waukesha, WI: Little Tiger.

Maguire, G. (1995). *Wicked: The life and times of the wicked witch of the west*. Illus. Douglas Smith. New York: HarperCollins.

Many, P. (2002). *The great pancake escape.* Illus. Scott Goto. New York: Walker.

Marlowe, C. (2001). *Doctor Faustus.* New York: Penguin. (Original work published 1604)

McKinley, R. (1997). *Rose daughter.* New York: Greenwillow/HarperCollins.

Melville, H. (2001). *Moby-Dick.* New York: Penguin. (Original work published 1851)

Meyer, S. (2005). *Twilight.* New York: Little, Brown.

Michael, L. (2005). *The whispering road.* New York: Penguin.

Miller, A. (1976). *The crucible* New York: Penguin.

Mills, L. (2001). *The dog prince: An original fairy tale.* Illus. Lauren Mills & Dennis Nolan. New York: Little, Brown.

Minters, F. (1996). *Sleepless beauty.* Illus. G. Brian Karas. New York: Viking/Penguin.

Myers, W. D. (1999). *Monster.* New York: HarperCollins.

Myers, W. D. (2006). *Street love.* New York: HarperCollins.

Napoli, D. J. (1993). *The magic circle.* New York: Penguin.

Napoli, D. J. (1996). *Zel.* New York: Penguin.

Napoli, D. J. (1998). *Sirena.* New York: Scholastic.

Napoli, D. J. (1999a). *Crazy Jack.* New York: Bantam Doubleday Dell/Random House.

Napoli, D. J. (1999b). *Spinners.* New York: Penguin.

Napoli, D. J. (2000). *Beast.* New York: Simon & Schuster.

Napoli, D. J. (2003a). *Breath.* New York: Simon & Schuster.

Napoli, D. J. (2003b). *The great god Pan.* New York: Random House.

Napoli, D. J. (2004). *Bound.* New York: Simon & Schuster.

Napoli, D. J. (2007). *Hush: An Irish princess' tale.* New York: Simon & Schuster.

Newbery, L. (2006). *Set in stone.* New York: Random House.

Oppenheim, J. (1989).*"Not now!" Said the cow.* Illus. Chris Demarest. New York: Bantam/Random House.

Ortiz, M. J. (2006). *Swan town: The secret journal of Susanna Shakespeare.* New York: HarperCollins.

Orwell, G. (1949). *Nineteen eighty-four.* New York: Harcourt.

Osborne, M. P. (2000). *Kate and the beanstalk.* Illus. Giselle Potter. New York: Simon & Schuster.

Ovid. (2004). *Metamorphoses.* New York: Penguin. (Originally published ca. AD 8).

Palatini, M. (2002). *Earthquack!* Illus. Barry Moser. New York: Simon & Schuster.

Palatini, M. (2003). *Bad boys.* Illus. Henry Cole. New York: Tegen/HarperCollins.

Palatini, M. (2005). *The three silly billies.* Illus. Barry Moser. New York: Simon & Schuster.

Palatini, M. (2006). *Bad boys get Cookie!* Illus. Henry Cole. New York: Tegen/HarperCollins.

Peck, R. (2003). *The river between us.* New York: Dial/Penguin.

Perlman, J. (2004). *The penguin and the pea.* Tonawanda, NY: Kids Can Press.

Peters, J. A. (2000). *Define normal.* New York: Little, Brown.

Peterseil, Y. (1999). *Princess Alopeica.* Illus. Avi Katz. New York: Pitspopany.

Plath, S. (1998). *The bell jar.* New York: Knopf/Random House. (Original work published 1963)

Polacco, P. (2004). *Oh, look!* New York: Philomel/Penguin.

Pyle, H. (2006). *The merry adventures of Robin Hood.* (Original work published 1883)

Ranulfo. (2006). *Joker: Hamlet's been cracked.* New York: HarperCollins.

Reinhardt, D. (2007). *Harmless.* New York: Lamb/Random House.

Ritter, J. (2006). *Under the baseball moon.* New York: Penguin.

Roberts, L. (2003). *Rapunzel: A groovy fairy tale.* Illus. David Roberts. New York: Harry N. Abrams.

Roberts, L. (2005). *Little Red: A frizzingly good yarn.* Illus. David Roberts. New York: Harry N. Abrams.

Rocco, J. (2007). *Wolf! wolf!* New York: Hyperion.

Rostand, E. (2003). *Cyrano de Bergerac.* New York: Penguin. (Original work published 1897)

Rowling, J. K. (1997). *Harry Potter and the sorcerer's stone.* New York: Scholastic.

Salinger, J. D. (1951). *The catcher in the rye.* New York: Little, Brown.

Sanvoisin, E. (2002). *Little red ink drinker.* Illus. Martin Matje. New York: Delacorte/Random House.

Scieszka, J. (1989). *The true story of the 3 little pigs.* Illus. Lane Smith. New York: Viking/Penguin.

Scieszka, J. (1991). *The frog prince continued.* Illus. Steve Johnson. New York: Viking/Penguin.

Scieszka, J. (1992). *The stinky cheese man and other fairly stupid tales.* Illus. Lane Smith. New York: Viking/Penguin.

Shelley, M. (2003). *Frankenstein.* New York: Penguin. (Original work published 1818)

Shulman, L. (2005). *The matzo ball boy.* Illus. Rosanne Litzinger. New York: Dutton/Penguin.

Shusterman, N. (2005a). *Dread locks.* New York: Dutton/Penguin.

Shusterman, N. (2005b). *Red rider's hood.* New York: Dutton/Penguin.

Shusterman, N. (2006). *Duckling ugly.* New York: Dutton/Penguin.

Smith, S. (2004). *Goldilocks and the three martians.* Illus. Michael Garland. New York: Penguin.

Spooner, M. (2005). *Last child.* New York: Henry Holt.

Springer, N. (2001). *Tales of Rowan Hood* series (*Rowan Hood: Outlaw girl of Sherwood Forest* #1). New York: Philomel/Penguin.

Springer, N. (2006). *Enola Holmes mysteries* (*The case of the missing marquess* #1). New York: Philomel/Penguin.

Springer, N. (2007). *The case of the left-handed lady.* New York: Philomel/Penguin.

Springer, N. (2008a). *The case of the bizarre bouquets.* New York: Philomel/Penguin.

Springer, N. (2008b). *The case of the peculiar pink fan.* New York: Philomel/Penguin.

Stanley, D. (1997). *Rumpelstiltskin's daughter.* New York: Morrow/HarperCollins.

Stanley, D. (2004). *The giant and the beanstalk.* New York: HarperCollins.

Steinbeck, J. (1939). *The grapes of wrath.* New York: Viking/Penguin.

Steinbeck, J. (2002). *Of mice and men.* New York: Penguin. (Original work published 1937)

Stoker, B. (2003). *Dracula.* New York: Penguin. (Original work published 1897)

Storace, P. (2007). *Sugar cane: A Caribbean Rapunzel.* Illus. Raúl Colón. New York: Hyperion.

Sturges, P. (1999). *The Little Red Hen makes a pizza.* Illus. Amy Walrod. New York: Penguin.

Sweet, M. (2005). *Carmine: A little more red.* Boston: Houghton Mifflin.

Tolhurst, M. (1991). *Somebody and the three Blairs.* Illus. Simone Abel. New York: Orchard/Scholastic.

Torrey, M. (2004). *Voyage of ice: Chronicles of courage.* New York: Knopf/Random House.

Trivizas, E. (1993). *The three little wolves and the big bad pig.* Illus. Helen Oxenbury. New York: Simon & Schuster.

Turkle, B. (1976). *Deep in the forest.* New York: Dutton/Penguin.

Twain, M. (1984). *The adventures of Huckleberry Finn.* London: Chatto & Windus.

Twain, M. (1996). *The prince and the pauper.* New York: Penguin. (Original work published 1881)

Updale, E. (2005). *Montmorency on the rocks: Doctor, aristocrat, murderer?* New York: Orchard/Scholastic.

Updale, E. (2006). *Montmorency and the assassins.* New York: Orchard/Scholastic.

Updale, E. (2007). *Montmorency's revenge.* New York: Orchard/Scholastic.

Volponi, P. (2005). *Black and white.* New York: Penguin.

Vozar, D. (1993). *Yo, hungry wolf!* Illus. Betsy Lewin. New York: Random House.

Walton, R. (1997). *Pig, pigger, piggest.* Illus. Jimmy Holder. Salt Lake City: Gibbs-Smith.

Wattenberg, J. (2005) *Never cry woof!: A dog-u-rama.* New York: Scholastic.

Wiesner, D. (2001). *The three pigs.* New York: Clarion.

Wilcox, L. (2003). *Falling for Rapunzel.* Illus. Lydia Monks. New York: Penguin.

Wittlinger, E. (2005). *Sandpiper.* New York: Simon & Schuster.

Wolff, P. R. (1995). *The toll-bridge troll.* Illus. Kimberly Bulcken Root. San Diego: Harcourt.

Wright, R. (2004). *Hunchback.* New York: Henry Holt.

Wyatt, L. J. (2005). *Poor is just a starting place.* New York: Holiday House.

Young, E. (1989). *Lon Po Po: A Red-Riding Hood story from China.* New York: Penguin.

The Popular Culture Influence

By Faith H. Wallace

Introduction

In the late 1990s, I was teaching eighth-grade English language arts in suburban New Jersey at the height of the *Buffy the Vampire Slayer* sensation (the high school teenager who saved the world from vampires and demons). The show had an almost cult-following, and a spin-off, *Angel,* was in production. My eighth graders were obsessed with Buffy and had, what seemed, their own language to talk about this shared experience: words like *shipper* and *fanfic.* Students gathered Wednesday mornings in my classrooms to talk about each episode: Was it good, was the story line consistent, were relationships working, could predictions be made about Buffy's future?

Students did more than talk; they read and wrote all things Buffy related. They read behind-the-scenes accounts, episode scripts, actor interviews, companion books, and novelizations. They even knew which authors deeply understood Buffy's world and specifically chose books by them.[1] Students wrote *fanfiction.* That is, they crafted their *own* Buffy stories and posted them to Buffy fan sites for others to read, critique, and discuss. Buffy wasn't the only popular culture phenomenon that engaged them. While students were reading and writing about Buffy, they were also immersed in *The X-Files, Angel, Titanic,* and other television and movie phenomena.

To say popular culture texts influenced these students is an understatement. All students, regardless of ability, were engaged in reading and writing about Buffy and other popular culture phenomena. While what's "in" may change with teenagers, the influential power and attraction of popular culture remain constant. This chapter introduces teachers to this dynamic and ever-changing genre, highlighting various text types (e.g., novelizations, companion books, fanfiction, graphic novels, and interactive texts). In addition, I illustrate ways popular culture has influenced young adult literature and provide a wealth of resources and references for finding relevant selections.

What Is Popular Culture?

Morrell (2004) explores the roots of popular culture in *Linking Literacy and Popular Culture: Finding Connections for Lifelong Learning,* explaining that early concepts of popular culture came from critical theorists and included any tools (e.g., news, commercials, brochures) used to control people's perceptions and information. These early theorists, German Jews, were exiled from Nazi Germany as a result of popular culture being conceived as propaganda. Later theorists saw popular culture more broadly: as a reflection of the cultural climate. In other words, whatever

---

[1]Nancy Holder was an overall favorite and continues to write about Buffy and Angel to this day, despite the end of the series in 2003.

is popular (e.g., movies, televisions, news, fashion) can be used to examine cultural beliefs and attitudes.

For example, for some time an unstated belief existed that black characters always died in action movies. In the 2001 science fiction action comedy *Evolution,* the character played by actor Orlando Jones jokingly says, "I've seen this movie, the black dude dies first" (Reitman, 2001). In the action, horror film *Deep Blue Sea* (1999), L. L. Cool J., the popular hip-hop artist, played the character Preacher who at one point says, "Ooh, I'm done! Brothers never make it out of situations like this! Not ever!" (Harlin, 1999). Interestingly, both characters survive, suggesting a change in society's beliefs about black male roles. Morrell notes, though, that regardless of message, how we see people and interpret messages reflects our own values and perceptions. That is, a person and message don't have value until we assign value.

Alvermann, Moon, and Hagood (1999) note that popular culture is "our consumption of cultural phenomena" such as television shows, movies, music, and video games (p. 3). Moreover, popular culture is our *engagement* or *interaction* with cultural phenomena; that is, how we communicate—make meaning, interpret, and share—within peer and work groups. Communicating with others often includes discussing current trends, whether we're considering a television reality show (e.g., *American Idol*) or the latest in gaming technology (e.g., XBox 360). Even box office bombs make for engaging conversation—remember *Waterworld* (1995) or *Catwoman* (2004)? Rarely is culture isolated; instead, cultural phenomena mirror life experiences. For instance, in 2006 both *V for Vendetta* and *United 93* hit box offices, both movies were about terrorism: one a futuristic science fiction adventure, the other a drama based on the September 11, 2001, terrorist attack.

What is popular within cultural phenomena does change, so allusions to popular culture can convey time and place. Everyday conversations do so all the time. Imagine a conversation where people are talking about television medical programs, including *House* (2004–   ), *St. Elsewhere* (1982–1988), and *MASH* (1972–1983). Each of these speaks to time and place. Those remembering *MASH* recall a time of war. *St. Elsewhere* took television to the edge, showing the first medical AIDS case. *House,* a new generation of medical dramas, capitalizes on current events and controversy (e.g., a Hurricane Katrina patient or a baseball player using steroids).

Morrell (2004) explains, "whether they are the producers or consumers, popular culture plays a central role in dictating how youth define themselves in relation to the larger world as well as framing their practices (i.e., dress, speech, or recreational activities) within that larger world" (p. 39). That is, young adults use cultural phenomena as a way to identify with peer groups, inspire creativity and action, and develop personal interests. Thus, marketing industries heavily target young adults through television, movies, music, and fashion. When young adults accept particular cultural phenomena as popular (e.g., a new musical group or fashion trend), a spending frenzy ensues in which young adults purchase any- and everything related to this new phenomena. For instance, Potter-related merchandising has expanded exponentially because of demand. Fans can purchase Bertie Botts Every Flavor Beans,[2] the famous Potter glasses, a DVD game, trading cards, and more.

Entire networks target young adults almost exclusively. The first was MTV, beginning in 1981, which has become a powerhouse in marketing music, fashion, and merchandise to young adults. The WB television network, originating in the mid-90s, targets a teen audience with shows like *7th Heaven, One Tree Hill,* and *Smallville.* Hollywood filmmakers also target a young audience: three top-grossing movies in 2005 were *Harry Potter and the Goblet of Fire, The Chronicles of Narnia,* and the *Charlie and the Chocolate Factory* remake. With emphasis on the young adult audience, it isn't surprising that young adults have their own award shows. MTV started the MTV Movie Awards in 1992 and reconceptualized award categories with Best On-Screen Duo, Best Kiss, and Best Villain. In 1999 *Seventeen* magazine began the Teen Choice Awards for television, movies, and music.[3] The 2007 Teen Choice Awards boasted winners such as Choice TV Breakout America Ferrera; Choice Hissy Fit, *Knocked Up;* and Choice TV Show Comedy, *The Office.*

The Quality Debate—In and Out of School Literacies

Popular culture is a young adult reality; teens immerse themselves in conversations based on their popular culture interests, giving them an "identity kit" in the sense that they have a way of speaking, thinking, acting, dressing, and participating that enables them to belong to a group—to recognize others and be recognized. Questions arise, however, regarding the role of popular culture in the classroom. How can popular culture texts be validated in schools? How do popular culture texts reshape or extend our understanding of literacy and that of our students? Popular culture texts can include, but are not limited to, television, film, music, comics, trading cards, and game texts. Often these texts are interconnected: "A hyperlink in a hypertext about a musical band can lead an Internet user to a video clip of the band's performance—a visual text—and the user later goes back to the original hypertext to read the rest of the text" (Xu, Perkins, & Zunich, 2005, p. 5). Popular culture texts, such as these and others, are generally not defined as young adult reading. New popular culture subgenres (e.g., novelizations, gaming manuals) rarely make reading lists, are usually considered unacceptable school reading, and often are unknown to adults. But is there a double standard regarding what "counts" as school reading? Morrell (2004) explains this beautifully:

> I hear many teachers dismiss genres of popular culture as violent, vulgar, or oppressive while they have no problem teaching classical texts like *Macbeth, Hamlet, The Sun Also Rises, The Great Gatsby,* and so on, texts that feature killing, adultery, fornication, excessive drinking, and racist and

---

[2]Bertie Botts Every Flavor Beans are the jellybeans of Harry Potter's world, and they do come in every flavor including pepper, sardine, and vomit.
[3]These awards were taken over by *Teen People* magazine in 2003.

> sexist language. I believe that teachers insist on these texts because they are powerful narratives of the awesome, yet flawed human condition. We do not necessarily celebrate the viewpoints and language that the authors use at all times, but we do celebrate the power of the narrative. (p. 119)

If we examine popular culture texts, we find stories that mirror life experiences, provide escape outlets, and present commentaries on societal issues. Likewise, we find underdeveloped plotlines, stereotypical characters, and contrived resolutions (true of any genre). Popular culture texts should be read in conjunction with canonical texts instead of being dismissed, for they are a reality of the young adult experience. Used in this way, teachers can encourage a discussion of the similarities and differences of life experiences across time and place and can use texts to initiate the critical examination of quality writing. The blanket negative view of popular culture texts sends a judgmental message to teens about their life experiences and creates the notion of two separate and unequal literacies: school literacy and out-of-school literacy.

When literacy is segregated in such a way, the school culture recognizes "a narrow band of literate enactments, sanctioned topics, and texts in print media" (King & O'Brien, 2002, p. 41). Literacy segregation exists across the nation in schools that teach traditional literacies to the exclusion of popular culture, that succumb to book challenges, and that buy into scripted reading programs. These schools marginalize readers and limit their access to meaningful print experiences. Perhaps more disturbing is the exclusion of out-of-school literacies even within the young adult literature field:

> The proliferation of studies on fiction define young adult literature as a discipline grounded completely in novels, in direct contrast to the public definition of young adult literature that typically includes all the materials young adults read. If the profession wants others to recognize the variety in the field, then its research should reflect the diversity with more critical articles on poetry, essays, drama, expository prose, and biography. (Poe, Samuels, & Carter, 1995, pp. 47–48)

Poe and colleagues note a more inclusive young adult literature definition is necessary, one that extends to popular culture texts.

Students engage in out-of-school literacies for several reasons, but two issues are important in discussing what engages them: what young adults like to read is often not accepted as school literacy (Gopalakrishnan & Ulanoff, 2005; Worthy, Moorman, & Turner, 1999), and many young adults find school materials and/or activities inaccessible (Alvermann & Heron, 2001; Black, 2005). When young adults face this dilemma, they are at risk for becoming struggling readers. Alvermann (2001) notes that the struggling reader label may be leveled at "some adolescents who for a number of reasons have turned their backs on a version of literacy called school literacy" in that schools "promote certain normative ways of reading texts," as well as what texts count as reading (p. 679). For many students, out-of-school literacies are the only avenue for *real* reading, writing, and communicating in which they are not judged, labeled, or marginalized.

Out-of-school literacy is often as complex and rigorous as in-school literacy. Young adults read widely both narrative and exposition. They read critical reviews and analyses of television shows, movies, music, and gaming. These readings can vary in complexity, purpose, message, and audience from critical reviews by a cultural elite to stream-of-consciousness blogs. Further, much young adult reading takes place electronically, exposing teens to local, regional, national, and international perspectives. In addition to researching and reading popular culture, young adults also compose, question, and debate through blogs, fanfiction, petitions, and essays.

In a media literacy case study, Alvermann found that out-of-school literacy provided a completely different perspective on the reading behaviors and capabilities of struggling readers. In one instance, Alvermann (2001) describes a struggling ninth-grade reader disengaged in a media literacy program. Numerous attempts to engage this young man in dialogue went unanswered until he started playing *Pokémon* video games and was given the accompanying gaming manual. Alvermann notes the student then engaged in electronic conversations with the researchers in which he was the more experienced other, forming what Frank Smith (1973, 1994) calls a literacy club. The student used the gaming manual in strategic ways: learning something and trying it out, searching for specific information, and moving ahead in the game. The more he read, the more he noted discoveries about language. For instance, he found interesting spelling patterns in characters' names.

A word of caution, though: When teachers attempt to situate popular culture texts alongside more traditional texts, they can strip away reading pleasure. Teens don't read popular culture texts to engage in theoretical debates, take tests, or write essays. They read for the enjoyment of the experience, to discuss how texts are meaningful to *them*, and to be inspired creatively. As teachers, we have to step beyond our comfort zone to understand teens' enjoyment of popular culture texts. We need to find a delicate balance between recognizing the pleasures and lure of popular culture texts and supporting students' critical media literacy. When we find that balance, students will merge what they learn about critical media literacy with their passion for popular culture texts and become more empowered and discerning readers. The books I discuss in the remaining sections are a starting place to encourage conversations about the role of popular culture in the classroom.

Popular Culture as a Grounding Force

If young adults use popular culture as a way to define themselves, then it makes sense that young adult literature uses popular culture as a grounding force—whether to situate plotlines within time and place or to provide characterization. For example, the main character in *My Cup Runneth Over: The Life of Angelica Cookson Potts* (Whytock, 2003) uses references to Jamie Oliver, television's *The Naked Chef*,[4] to ground her affinity with food and cooking and her aspirations of becoming a famous chef. Jamie Oliver becomes a constant reference throughout the book and a source of comfort for Angelica when she struggles with her love of cooking and eating (Angelica's story continues in *My Saucy Stuffed Ravioli* (Whytock, 2004). Where Angelica dreams about Jamie Oliver, Stacy Friedman and her friends in *You Are So Not Invited to My Bat Mitzvah!* (Rosenbloom, 2005) use myriad references to current fashion trends and music to situate their lives as they deal with young love and friendship. For example, the girls consider Reese Witherspoon's fashion prowess, dance to Ashlee Simpson's music, and reference *American Idol* auditions (a comparison to Stacy's nonsinging talents). Young adult literature may also show the humorous side of popular culture obsessions, such as the novel *Britney Spears Is a Three-Headed Alien!* (Gilden, 2001). In this spoof on teenage obsession with popular music, aliens who want to use Britney's popularity to take over the world abduct the famous Britney Spears. Two teen characters, obsessed with Britney, attempt to save Britney and the world, and, of course, meet their idol in the process. Gilden also uses *The X-Files* and other popular culture references to ground this Hollywood and popular culture spoof.

Obsession with Hollywood is part of being a young adult: the glitz and glamour is a seductive lure. Logically, young adult literature capitalizes on popular culture trends, basing entire series within Hollywood. Boasting more than 15 books, *The Cheetah Girls* (Gregory, 1999) follows several high school students on their quest to start a successful all-girl hip-hop musical group. Harris (2005) notes, "Part of the appeal of the 'Cheetah Girls' series is its sense of style and the suggestion of a global youth culture linking fashion, music, and friendship with a dollop of social consciousness that is often race or color and class based" (p. 219). *The Cheetah Girls* series might appear timid compared with other hot series steeped in glamour and style such as *Gossip Girls* (von Ziegesar, 2002). This bold series follows privileged Manhattan high school students through backstabbing, drug use, alcohol, sex, celebrity spotting, movie-making, and shopping.

As young adults watch peers propelled to superstar status, some marketing their own fashion, makeup, and fragrances, is it a wonder that the dream of becoming rich and famous flourishes among teens? A recent article in *Girl's Life* (Mulcahy & Bokram, 2005) explores young adult girls' fascination with glitz and glamour and the link to celebrities (e.g., Hilary Duff, Mary-Kate and Ashley Olsen, Paris Hilton, and Brittney Gastineau). The article suggests such fascination with riches can lead young adults to think money is power, and it doesn't matter whom you hurt. As such, the glitz and glamour of the rich and famous and the dream of living the Hollywood life thrives in young adult literature—some portraying the dark side of this glamorous lifestyle. Titles in Box 12.1 illustrate what is currently available to teens.

---

[4]Jamie Oliver is a host of *The Naked Chef* on the Food Network cable channel.

Box 12.1   Glitz, Glamour, and Hollywood in Young Adult Literature

***But I Don't Want to Be a Movie Star* by Margaret Pinder. New York: Dutton/ Penguin, 2006.**

Much to her dismay, Kat Shaw spends a summer with her drama-queen grandmother, Noni. Kat deplores Noni's self-indulgent lifestyle, but things change when Kat must impersonate Noni in order to land an important career-changing role. With the help of Noni's staff, Kat is transformed and learns something about Noni's life and herself at the same time.

***Confessions of a Hollywood Star* by Dyan Sheldon. Cambridge, MA, Candlewick Press, 2005.**

Before heading off to study theater in New York, Lola discovers a major movie will be filmed in her New Jersey hometown. She tells everyone she'll be in the movie, but she must convince the director to cast her. Lola's single-mindedness painfully borders stalking, and she alienates those who care for her. In the end she learns a lesson about pursuing dreams.

***Confessions of a Teen Nanny* by Victoria Ashton. New York, HarperCollins, 2005.**

The lure of money and material possessions cloud Adrienne's judgment as she works as a nanny to New York's rich and famous Warner family. Carmen, the older Warner daughter, buys Adrienne's friendship with clothing and adventures as a ruse to steal her boyfriend. The tension between Adrienne and Carmen heat up in the sequel, *Rich Girls* (2006), as Adrienne is employed by the Warners to break up Carmen and Brian, Adrienne's old boyfriend.

***Confessions of an Almost Movie Star* by Mary Kennedy. New York, Penguin, 2005.**

When a movie is filmed at a private school in New England, mystery and romance ensue as Jessie lands a film role and Tracy is given backstage passes. Does Hollywood heartthrob, Shane, really have an interest in Jessie? Why are Tracy's photographs stolen?

The sequel, *Tales of a Hollywood Gossip Queen* (2006), follows Jessie and Tracy to Hollywood on their next adventure.

***Crystal* by Walter Dean Myers. New York: Viking/Penguin, 1987.**

Crystal Brown is an aspiring model, but the demands of being a teenage model force Crystal to reconcile fame and fortune with integrity. When a fellow model commits suicide, Crystal makes a difficult decision about her modeling careeer.

***Face Value* by Catherine Johnson. New York: Walker, 2006.**

Lauren Bogle has been discovered as a model, and although Lauren seems ready to join the fashion world, her guardian, Vanessa, is cautious. Once a model, Lauren's mother spiraled out of control with drugs, prostitution, and died. Can Lauren be spared the same fate?

***Fame, Glory, and Other Things on My To Do List* by Janette Rallison. New York, Walker, 2005.**

Jessica plans to make it as an actress in Hollywood, so when a new boy, Jordan, shows up at school with a famous Hollywood director for a father, Jessica sees this as her chance. If Jordan's father could only see her in the *West Side Story* school production, Jessica is sure stardom will be hers. But Jessica's lust for fame causes her to betray Jordan, and *West Side Story* becomes more comedy than tragedy.

***Gangsta Rap* by Benjamin Zephaniah. New York: Bloomsbury, 2004.**

Ray, Prem, and Tyrone have been thrown out of school and have little respect for anyone or anything not related to music, particularly hip-hop. When the boys enroll in a school with a music program, everything changes, and their band suddenly launches into stardom.

Continued

Box 12.1   Glitz, Glamour, and Hollywood in Young Adult Literature   *Continued*

How My Private, Personal Journal Became a Bestseller by Julia DeVillers New York: Dutton/Penguin, 2004.

As unpopular Jamie traverses the landmines of high school, she creates an alter-ego, superhero, IS, in a series of journaled stories. As IS battles the Populors, Jamie inadvertently submits a story as an assignment, and a chain of events begins, sending Jamie into the spotlight with a bestselling book. How will Jamie handle this sudden fame? Can she stay true to herself and her reasons for creating IS?

Introducing Vivien Leigh Reid: Daughter of the Diva by Yvonne Collins and Sandy Rideout. New York: St. Martin's Griffin, 2005.

Vivien reluctantly spends the summer in Ireland with the mother who left her to become a movie star. She finds herself on the set of a movie with a bit part, bonding with the mother she hardly knows.

Jimi & Me by Jaime Adoff. New York: Jump/Hyperion, 2005.

Keith must deal with his biracial identity, his music producer father's murder, his affinity for Jimi Hendrix, and a half-brother he never knew in this moving story told through verse.

Lights, Camera, Disaster! by Gordon Korman, New York: Scholastic, 2004.

When a movie is filmed at MacDonald Hall, Bruno and Boots do everything possible to acquire a part. When they fail, they try to sabotage the movie, but a heartfelt conversation with the movie's teen star, Jordie, helps Bruno and Boots understand a different side of Hollywood. Part of the *MacDonald Hall* series.

My Life Starring Mum by Chloë Rayban. New York: Bloomsbury, 2006.

When rock star sensation Khandi demands her daughter Hollywood (Holly) Bliss leave boarding school to live with her, Hollywood's life unravels. Khandi doesn't understand that Holly much prefers her ordinary life studying for exams. When Khandi decides to undergo an image overhaul, Holly is thrust in the middle of the publicity. Can she make her mother understand?

So Super Stylish by Rose Wilkins, New York: Dial/Penguin, 2006.

Octavia Clairbrook-Cleeve wants to live a normal life, but the paparazzi pursuing her mother keep interfering. Amidst bad press surrounding her mother's whirlwind romance and young adult pressures, Octavia struggles with her own identity. In the end, Octavia learns through the love of her family, friends, and boyfriend that others and stereotypes do not define her.

Son of the Mob 2: Hollywood Hustle by Gordon Korman. New York: Hyperion, 2004.

In this sequel to *Son of the Mob* (2002), Vince tries to escape his mobster family life by attending a California film school. Vince doesn't know his father plans on using Vince to gain information about a congressman causing trouble for the mafia. Adventures begin as his "family" members turn up in California.

Summer on Wheels by Gary Soto. New York: Scholastic, 1995.

In this sequel to *Crazy Weekend* (1994), two friends take an action-packed six-day bike ride during their summer vacation. Along the way, the boys end up in a commercial and sing backup on a hip-hop CD.

Teen Idol by Meg Cabot. New York: HarperCollins, 2004.

Researching a new movie role, Luke Striker disguises himself as an ordinary high school student. Jen Greenley, high school advice columnist, is charged with showing Luke around and keeping his identity a secret, even from her best friend, a Luke Striker fan. Can she keep a secret even when Luke asks Jen for a date?

Continued

Box 12.1   Glitz, Glamour, and Hollywood in Young Adult Literature   *Continued*

***Theodora Twist* by Melissa Senate. New York: Delacorte/Random House, 2006.**

Theodora Twist, Hollywood teen, needs a publicity overhaul. She participates in a reality show meant to showcase how she cleans up her act with a host family, the Stewarts. Emily, a seemingly average teen, becomes Theodora's roommate. Who will be more affected by this arrangement?

***Tribute to Another Dead Rock Star* by Randy Powell. New York: Sunburst/Farrar, Straus & Giroux, 1999.**

Gary is confused when he attends a tribute concert for his deceased rock-star mother. Her reckless life is the center of Gary's confusion; he meets his half-brother who is mentally disabled and stepfamily in search of a family to call his own.

***True Confessions of a Hollywood Starlet* by Lola Douglas. New York: Razorbill/Penguin, 2005.**

At 16, Morgan Carter has already succumbed to the Hollywood lifestyle—drugs and alcohol. In an attempt to salvage her life, she enrolls in a midwestern high school as a "normal" teenager. What begins as a plan to jumpstart her failing career becomes a real transforming experience.

Popular Culture Texts

Popular culture texts are an important aspect of young adult lives. As teachers, we owe students an understanding of these texts, and we need to encourage their consumption in meaningful, but engaging, ways. In the following sections, I define and examine various popular culture subgenres but offer the following cautions. First, popular culture can be thought of as trends: What's "in" with young adults today may not be "in" tomorrow. Similarly, teens vary tremendously in what they enjoy, so popular culture texts will never be a one-size-fits-all match. In this chapter, I explore what is available and provide resources for finding relevant texts. Teachers play a primary role in determining appropriateness based on student interest and maturity.

Adaptations

Often, movies are made from great literary works. In 2005, *Pride & Prejudice* opened in box offices, turning this Jane Austen classic into a more accessible medium for romance fans. For three consecutive years (2001, 2002, and 2003) *The Lord of the Rings* dominated the box office, capturing several prestigious awards, including an Academy Award for Best Picture. According to the Mid-Continent Public Library,[5] more than 1,200 books, short stories, and plays have become movies since 1980. Movie adaptations generate

---

[5]Their complete list of movie adaptations can be found at www.mcpl.lib.mo.us/readers/movies/.

tremendous book sales. *USA Today* reported that *The Lord of the Rings* book sales boomed as a result of the movies, selling an additional 14 million copies, "almost half as much as the entire preceding 36 years" (Seiler, 2003). Movie releases are also marketing tools, and new book editions are released with movie-related cover art (e.g., Peter Jackson's remake of *The Lord of the Rings*). Movie-related cover art can be seen in young adult literature made into movies from classics such as *Charlie and the Chocolate Factory* (Dahl, 2005) to suspense thrillers such as *I Know What You Did Last Summer* (Duncan, 1999). Alice Hoffman's (2001) magical tale of friendship and romance, *Aquamarine*, was released in 2006, and a new paperback featuring cover art from the movie accompanied it. More young adult novels are finding their way into box offices—for better or worse—which translates into higher profits and more options for teens.

Young Adult Novels Turned into Movies

In 2007 the world was once again enveloped in J. K. Rowling's magic in the fifth installment of Harry Potter, *The Order of the Phoenix.* Like the first four movies, *Phoenix* was a top box office grosser.[6] Potter's success paved the way for other adaptations. With 13 adventures in Lemony Snicket's *A Series of Unfortunate Events* (1999), the movie adaptation covering the first three books featured such acting legends as Jim Carey, Catherine O'Hara, and Meryl Streep. The epic adventure *Eragon* (2003), penned by teenage author Christopher Paolini, is the first book in *The Inheritance Trilogy* and follows the adventures of Eragon and his dragon companion Saphira as they battle dark forces. The Book Sense Book of the Year Award[7] named *Eragon* the best in children's literature in 2004. It isn't surprising then that *Eragon* was adapted for the big screen with Jeremy Irons and John Malkovich playing leading roles.

Movie adaptations of young adult novels cut across every genre and style from *Holes* (Sachar, 1999) to *Sisterhood of the Traveling Pants* (Brashares, 2001) to *Mean Girls,* an adaptation of *Queen Bees and Wannabees* (Wiseman, 2002), a nonfiction work. Story adaptations are inevitable, and educators often frown upon them. However, they provide an opportunity to reflect on different interpretations, what works in adaptations, and what adaptations reveal about society. Teachers could, for instance, use movie adaptations to encourage students to watch movies critically, thinking about the effects of lighting, music, and storytelling angles. Instead, most teachers use movies and television shows as fillers for shortened days, the day before a holiday, and after standardized testing. Movies should be used purposefully, evaluated for specific adaptive elements, and be used as teaching tools rather than as time fillers.

---

[6]All five movies were in the top 10 grossing movies of the year, respectively.
[7]Formerly known as the ABBY Award, winners are selected by independent booksellers across the country (www.bookweb.org/).

Novelizations

With so many literary works finding new audiences in movie theaters, it makes sense to create books from movies as well. *Novelizations* are just that—novels created from another medium (e.g., television, movies, games). In novelizations, the story stays close to the original, but because the reader cannot rely on visual text in a book, novelizations add description, thoughts, and background. Mel Gilden (n.d.), author of television show novelizations such as *Beverly Hills 90210*,[8] says writing novelizations requires writers to move story snippets around to create coherence, handle a sometimes shifting point of view, and create smoother transitions In some cases, writers are given restrictions on how much they can alter or revise dialogue. Some writers see a difference between scripted and prose dialogue, saying script writing is succinct and relies on actors' skills to deliver. Other writers add explanations and background to explain irrational or unexplained transitions and actions. Still others emphasize original storytelling tone (Goldberg & Collins, 2006b). With so many restrictions, some novelizations hit and some miss; thus, they should not be blindly judged as lacking literary quality.

Novelizations have been created from a variety of televisions shows and movies (e.g., *Star Trek, Sabrina the Teenage Witch, Batman Begins,* and *Finding Nemo*). Even renowned young adult author Garth Nix once penned a novelization, *The Calusari* (1997), for the television show *The X-Files*. Movies are especially popular for novelizing (e.g., *Shrek* and *Shrek 2, Spider-Man* and *Spider-Man 2*[9]). The *Spider-Man 2* novelization provided more details about Peter Parker's (a.k.a. Spider-Man) struggles and added interaction with Mary Jane, Peter's love interest.

Movie novelizations such as *Shrek, Elf,* and *Finding Nemo* are marketed for all ages. In fact, *Finding Nemo* is available in multiple formats from picture book to novel to junior novel. Furthermore, novelizations are as diverse as movies, ranging from more adult romantic thrillers like *Mr. and Mrs. Smith* (winner of several Teen Choice Awards in 2005) to more young adult romantic comedies like *13 Going on 30* and comic book-turned-fantasy adventures like *Batman Begins.*

Gaming, like movies and television shows, is an impressive market for novelizations, ranging from adult action adventure and shooting games to adolescent games like *Pokemon*. Games are also adapted into movies and novelized (e.g., *Resident Evil* games in 2002 and 2004). Game novelizations require that authors understand the game and the rules of the gaming universe. Author Lynn Abbey says writing gaming novelizations is like playing a miniature golf game; the author must weave an entertaining story around a variety of specific obstacles (Silver, 2002). This "weaving" can make writing gaming novelizations tricky because, unlike movies and

---

[8]See Gilden's Web site for more details about writing novelizations: www.melgilden.com/melpage4.html.
[9]*Spider-Man* and *Spider-Man 2* novelizations are also available as e-books.

television shows, games don't follow scripts. Alan Dean Foster, long-time novelization writer, explains:

> Game novelizations are several orders of magnitude harder to do than film novelizations. Game "characters" usually aren't. They're simply ciphers provided to move the game along. Also, when doing a game novelization, you can't really stray much from the plot. But you can't really follow it too closely, either, or you'll end up giving away the details of the game. Then you've written a game manual, and not a novel. It's a real juggling act. (Cuciz, n.d.)

Despite difficulties, gaming novelizations do have a fan base. Fans are fickle, though, and often greet novelizations with mixed reviews as some readers want what Dietz calls a "regurgitation of the game" and others want the author to "enhance the game experience by developing the main characters more fully, to take advantage of intervals between action sequences, to provide back story, insert interesting sub-plots and open up parallel stories" (Dietz, 2006, p. 3). This "something more" moves the novelization beyond simply retelling the story to *novelized extensions.*

Novelized Extensions

Novelizations are exciting to read, especially after viewing a favorite movie, because the story lives on. However, an even more appealing form of novelization abounds to read, enjoy, and critique: *novelized extensions,* sometimes called tie-ins. Where novelizations move the same story to a different format, novelized extensions are *original* works based on a story world (e.g., *One Tree Hill, Alias,* or *24*). These original works create new stories using the *canon*— the actual copyrighted story line including characters, relationships, and back story of a particular story world. Novelized extensions can be likened to unaired television episodes or movie sequels. For example, *Smallville: City* (Grayson, 2004) is a novelized extension for the television show *Smallville.* In this novel, Clark Kent and Lex Luther are embroiled in a series of dangerous adventures in Metropolis. The story is based on the *Smallville* canon but was not a show episode.

Creativity abounds in novelized extensions because the writer is not restricted in the same ways as movie and television show screenwriters, particularly with budget constraints. In fact, the hit science fiction space drama *Farscape* was cancelled after the fourth season because of a demanding special effects budget for battle scenes and creature features. In the three novelized extensions, though, special effects are only limited by authors' imaginations. Further, movies and television (even gaming) generally focus storytelling on main characters. Novelized extensions are not limited in this way, and authors can write from different character perspectives. For example, *Alias: The Pursuit* (Skurnick, 2003) is a novelized extension for the hit television drama *Alias;* instead of telling a Sydney Bristow story, *Alias: The Pursuit* follows Michael Vaughn (Sydney's handler) on his own adventure. Novelized extensions are also not time limited—stories can take place before or after the time period of the original work. *Mortal Kombat* is an action-packed game turned into a movie and novelized, but a novelized extension, *Mortal Kombat* (Rovin, 1992), tells back stories of the characters prior to the gaming story line. This novelized extension is rich in Chinese legend and mythology.

Novelized extensions have unlimited boundaries, taking stories to new times and places, exploring perspectives of supporting characters, and experimenting with different formats. Nancy Holder, long-time novelization writer, addresses this creative side of novelized extensions:

> We tie-in writers have a vaster field of emotional depth and range to
> explore in print: just as there are occasional one-off episodes in TV
> series—the funny episode, the death of a character episode—so, too,
> are there arcs spanning several episodes, seasons, and even whole
> series. Because of the richness of many movie universes, the same is also
> true. Thus we have opportunities to do funny novels, capers, quests,
> short stories, novellas, and trilogies (to name a few of the forms I have
> used for tie-ins) that other authors don't. In addition, because most
> readers already know the characters and their universe, we have more
> real estate—more actual text space—to explore other things. I find it
> tremendously freeing to write tie-in work, rather than the converse.
> (Goldberg & Collins, 2006a, p. 3)

This creativity makes for a complex and captivating reading experience. Writers must consider *all* aspects of the story canon; fans of a story world pick up *any* inconsistency or potential plot change. As such, reading novelized extensions can encourage good strategic reading habits. That is, readers can be encouraged to use their story world prior knowledge to make inferences, connections, and to question the author. Readers can also look deeply at event sequencing between the book and show (or movie) and make inferences and connections. For example, a television show still running new episodes might interfere with the story line in a particular book, or the book may take place *between, before,* or *after* aired episodes. Case in point, a new novelized extension of *Buffy the Vampire Slayer* (Holder, 2006) was released in 2006, yet the series ended in 2003. Therefore, readers must consider their entire collection of prior knowledge to make sense of the text and situate what they are reading within the larger story world. (Nancy Holder talks more about the complexity of writing novelized extensions in the author box.) Finally, with so many authors writing novelized extensions, readers should be encouraged to consider voice and point of view and critique novelized extensions. In this way, readers can transition to more critical aspects of reading while still enjoying the experience. Novelizations and novelized extensions hold promise for balancing reading with popular culture, encouraging students to engage in strategic reading (e.g., inferring, connecting, and questioning), and evaluating writing quality.

The question becomes how do teachers, students, and fans find these texts. One excellent place to explore new releases is the International Association of Media Tie-In Writers Web site. Official Web sites for movies and televisions shows are also extremely helpful. At the official *Dragon Ball-Z* Web site, a link for merchandise includes graphic novels and adventure books, games, and DVDs. Unofficial Web sites, or fan-based sites, can also provide book information. Of course, searching a book warehouse such as Amazon.com or Barnes and Noble online is also productive. Remember, though, if the movie, television show, or game title is common (e.g., *Friends*), unrelated titles may appear in the search results so review them carefully.

Novelizations and Extensions from an Author's Point of View   by Nancy Holder

As a tie-in writer, I serve at least two masters—the licensee and the licensor. Once my editor likes a proposal I have sent, she takes it to the license holder for approval. In the case of *Buffy*, the copyright owner is Twentieth-Century Fox, and my proposals are vetted through the merchandising department. The publishing company cannot go forward until they/we have approval, which may rest on a proposal rewrite, or my agreement to make certain changes during the writing of the project.

I also have to figure out (with approval) where in a series to "freeze" my story. In New York–style print publishing, it takes about five to nine months from delivery of a manuscript to publication. So the show continues while my books stay behind. More than once on *Buffy* I could not divulge something I knew because it hadn't happened on the show yet. Occasionally, as shows evolve, the producers take them in a direction that is different than when my project is okayed, so books and shows diverge.

A show's fans tend to take exception to this "error" as ignorance on the part of the tie-in author. Likewise, if a book differs from their own show interpretation, they will feel the tie-in author has let them down. "Jacked-in" fans can interact with producers and tie-in writers, to the extent that we give them "shoutouts"—mentioning their names or their fan groups, for example—and taking their criticisms and wishes into account when crafting new stories. This has occasionally resulted in a breaking of the "fourth wall" of television, where authors acknowledge the show as a show as well as a representational reality. So influential fans can sometimes constitute my third set of masters.

In *Buffy*'s case, the first "extension" I wrote (with Christopher Golden) was aimed at young adults. Simon and Schuster realized teenagers would read longer, more complex *Buffy* novels, so the young adult line was dropped. However, many bookstores still shelve the *Buffy* material in the young adult sections. In most other "universes" I've written for, the demographics of my e-mail with fans mirror the intended readership—tweens and early YA for *Sabrina the Teenage Witch*, for instance.

The bottom line is tie-in authors have a few extra considerations to juggle when they're working . . . but I like to tell people it's one of the few jobs where you not only get paid to watch TV, but you can also deduct cable costs as a business expense.

Some recent titles by Nancy Holder include *Spirited* (2004), *Buffy the Vampire Slayer: Carnival of Souls* (2006a), *Pretty Little Devils* (2006b), *Daughter of the Shadows* (2007a), and *The Rose Bride* (2007b).

Fanfiction

Novelizations and novelized extensions are obviously popular with young adults, regardless of quality. While researching, I found more than 20 novelizations or novelized extensions for the hit family television drama *7th Heaven,* more than 15 for *Smallville,* the television show about Superman as a teenager, and more than 25 for the family comedy (television show and movie) *Lizzie McGuire.* Perhaps the appetite for such works stems from our own imaginations: what happened between episodes, what happened during the season break, what happened after the movie ended, and so on? It isn't surprising, then, that *fanfiction* (fanfic or fic, for short) is popular. Think of fanfiction as a novelized extension written by fans, including young adults. Fans use their knowledge of a particular story world (e.g., television, movies, gaming) as the basis for their own creations. Topics for fanfiction are as varied as our own musings: Was Captain Kirk ever jealous of Spock? After Saturday detention was over, did *The Breakfast Club* gang remain friends? While Hermione was dancing with Victor Krum at the Yule Ball, what did they talk about?

McCardle (2003) traces fanfiction back to *Star Trek* (1966–1969), when fans wrote short stories based on fanzine series (magazines for fans by fans) With Internet accessibility and the preponderance of self-published fan sites, fanfiction is flourishing. Fanfiction.net is an impressive hub for fanfiction activity, boasting fanfiction in categories such as Anime, Comic, Game, Movie, and TV Show. In the TV show category, there are too many titles to count; they are organized alphabetically and list the number of uploaded fanfiction pieces in parenthesis. Titles include everything from *Gilmore Girls* (8,520) to *Xena: Warrior Princess* (1,250) to *Friends* (2,952). Other categories show the same variety: the cartoon *Fairly Odd Parents* (650), the popular video game *EverQuest* (265), and the comic book and movie *X-Men* (6,967).

The beauty of fanfiction is that it isn't limited to movies, television, and games. Literature, both adult and young adult, provides many fanfiction outlets. On Fanfiction.net, *Harry Potter* has an unbelievable 235,700 pieces uploaded. *The Lord of the Rings* has an impressive 38,150 postings. Even Shakespeare has over 700! In addition, entire Web sites are devoted to fanfiction of popular books. Harry Potter Fanfiction claims to be the oldest and best site for Harry-related fanfiction with more than 22,000 stories of varying length, style, and topic. Other Potter sites create actual communities with houses and classrooms such as Fiction Alley. The widely regarded Mugglenet encourages critical discussions and has a section devoted to Harry Potter fanfiction.

Other young adult favorites have fanfiction followings on large database sites such as Fanfiction.net and on smaller fan sites, official author, and book Web sites. Meg Cabot's book club Web site features book discussions, including the bestselling *Princess Diaries* series. Lemony Snicket's *A Series of Unfortunate Events* (1999), 13 tales of the Bauldelaire orphans trying to find a home, has an incredible fan base. At The Quiet World fans can discuss

Snicket's adventures, read the lastest book and movie news and, of course, read, write, and discuss fanfiction. Anime Web Turnpike is a forum for everything anime,[10] including news updates and fanfiction.

Fanfiction writers, like those of novelized extensions, are only limited by imagination and have created entire fanfiction subgenres, including *crossovers, slash,* and *AU* (alternative universe). In crossovers, characters from different movies, televisions shows, games, or books interact in a given story line (think of students at the X-Men mutant academy attending Potter's Hogwarts). Slash fanfiction introduces romantic story lines with same-gender characters (*Buffy the Vampire Slayer* slash fanfiction sometimes includes relationships between Buffy and her friend Willow). Alternative universe fanfiction creates major changes to canon such as having central characters die or changing the time line of established events (imagine a story where Anakin Skywalker dies before becoming Darth Vader).

Young adults use fanfiction language when talking about popular culture. They may, for example, use such words as *spoiler* or *shipper.* Spoilers give away details fans might not already know (such as characters dying or guest appearances). Many fans were furious when Internet postings revealed Dumbledore's death in the sixth Harry Potter book only days (maybe hours) after its release. Fanfiction generally warns readers if stories contain spoilers. The term *shipper* originates from the word *relationship.* Fans who wish for certain character pairings such as Harry/Hermione or Mulder/Scully are called shippers. Confused yet? There is an entire glossary of terms for fanfiction, organized alphabetically at the Fanfiction Glossary Web site.

Fanfiction is perhaps most intriguing to teachers because it most closely creates a real writing network for young adults. Fanfiction is meant to be shared, revised, and published and provides a natural authoring cycle for young writers (Short, Harste, & Burke, 1996), even second language learners (Black, 2005). Fans can post fanfiction to Web sites or discussion groups for feedback and revise accordingly. In fact, a search for fanfiction on yahoo groups, a popular discussion group database, yielded more than 5,000 groups, but writers can search for fanfiction discussion groups based on specific titles such as *Artemis Fowl, Animorphs,* or *Charlie and the Chocolate Factory.* When fans do post their fanfiction to a database site such as the aforementioned Fanfiction.net, stories are rated on content (e.g., suitable for children, for mature audiences only) and categories by genre (e.g., romance, mystery). A more sophisticated site allows users to sort stories by character, length, and date published (uploaded). Database reviews are also encouraged, but *flaming,* leaving an extremely negative review without strong justification, is frowned upon in most fanfiction communities.

When you started reading this section, I bet you questioned whether this was for real. It is. And awards prove it. Sometimes specific franchises have their own awards, but there are also general fanfiction awards, which are nominated, read, and voted on by fans. For example, there is a Harry

---

[10]The term *anime* refers to Japanese animation.

Potter fanfiction award with specific categories ranging from fanfiction about specific characters to challenges to relationships. Categories are also rated (e.g., G, PG, PG-13, R). The popular science fiction television series *Stargate SG-1* has more global fan awards featuring everything from original artwork to fanfiction. Not to be outdone, the anime cartoon *Sailor Moon* has its own fanfiction awards, including various genres—with *songfic* as a category, where song lyrics are the medium for telling the story. Imagine supporting students' fanfiction talent by nominating their masterpieces for fanfiction awards!

Companion Books

Part of the success of an adaptation, novelized extension, or even fanfiction is getting the facts right. Writers, professional or amateur, must be well versed in the particular story line canon because fans quickly point out authors' mistakes. For example, Movie Mistakes is a forum for pointing out movie and television blunders. A quick search for movies such as *Star Wars Episode III* and televisions shows such as *Friends* lists mistakes posted by fans ranging from over 150 (*Star Wars*) to over 700 (*Friends*). No wonder so many companion books are available for various movies, televisions shows, and books. *Companion books* accompany or enhance the viewing or reading experience and are written in different styles (e.g., spoofs, critical essays) and in all formats (e.g., dictionaries, questions and answers). Some common companion books are *episode* or *movie guides, background enhancers,* and *fact finders.*

Episode and Movie Guides

Episode guides map out episodes for given seasons, providing specific information about the content, writing, plotlines, and behind-the-scene details. Many televisions shows have episode guides, official and unofficial, including young adult favorites *Dawson's Creek, Smallville,* and *Lizzie McGuire. Charmed,* a show about three powerful sisters battling demons, has a companion book, *The Power of Three* (Gallagher & Ruditis, 2004), which follows the show through four seasons. Other television favorites not specifically geared toward young adults but popular with them nonetheless have episode guides including *Alias, The Simpsons,* and *24.*

Movie guides provide information about the script (sometimes including the script), movie photography, and cast and crew interviews. Movie guides are available for all movie genres (e.g., the fantasy epic *The Chronicles of Narnia, Batman Begins,* and the animated film *Madagascar*). *The Sisterhood of the Traveling Pants: The Official Scrapbook* (Ephron & Chandler, 2005) includes highlights from *The Sisterhood of the Traveling Pants* movie adaptation (Brashares, 2001), with movie trivia, background on the actors, and movie production details. To determine whether movies or television shows have episode or movie guides, go to the official Web site and look for merchandise. Some fan sites also provide a comprehensive listing of available merchandise.

Background Enhancers

Other companion books function as *background enhancers* for the story line; that is, the companion book provides detailed information about the culture, occupations, races, or events in a particular story world. Background enhancers are popular with all mediums (e.g., movies such as *The Lord of the Rings,* television shows such as *Alias*), but many such companion books are available for young adult series books, especially fantasy series in which there are races, cultures, or events specific to the series. *The Artemis Fowl Files* (Colfer, 2004) is an interesting companion book because it provides background enhancers on the races of The Lower Elements (e.g., elves, dwarfs, sprites, and pixies) and schematics for specific technology used by the characters, and it also includes activities (e.g., word searches and crossword puzzles) and two short stories featuring characters from previous *Artemis Fowl* books.

Similar companion books are available for *The Spiderwick Chronicles* (2003), the five-part story of the Grace children as they learn about the faerie world. *The Notebook for Fantastical Observations* (DiTerlizzi & Black, 2005) is part background enhancer, part journal. DiTerlizzi and Black provide details about various races in the books—brownies, dragons, dwarves, and trolls—and include a journal for readers to log their own experiences within the faerie world. Magic, mystery, legend, and animal races are the backdrop for the successful *Redwall* (1986) fantasy series (over 10 books) by Brian Jacques. Many background enhancing companion books are available to accompany the *Redwall* series, including books specific to the different Redwall tribes. For example, *The Tribes of Redwall: Otters* (Jacques, 2002) details everything a fan needs to know about this valiant race: their domain, enemies, and weapons. Quizzes, recipes, and a pullout poster are also included in the companion book. A similar companion book is available for the Badgers and the Redwall villains and heroes.

These background enhancers tend to accompany series books, particularly fantasy adventures. But other young adult literature subgenres have background enhancers too. For example, the popular series, *The Princess Diaries,* about a young girl who learns she is actually a princess and heir to the thrown of Genovia, has two companion books outlining the intricacies of being a princess. *Princess Lessons* (Cabot, 2003) features guest authors (characters from the books) giving beauty and etiquette tips to help readers become princesses too. *Holes* (Sachar, 1999) is the young adult novel about Stanley Yelnat's experiences at juvenile detention camp and the secret plot of the warden. The companion book to *Holes, Stanley Yelnat's Survival Guide to Camp Green Lake* (Sachar, 2003), provides anecdotal advice on surviving Camp Green Lake. The spy adventure series about teen spy Alex Rider also has a companion book, *Alex Rider: The Gadgets* (Horowitz, 2005a), detailing Rider's spy technology like the infrared goggle and bulletproof ski suit. Due to the popularity of such companion books, I predict more background enhancers will be published for young adult series in the future.

Fact Finders

Other companion books take the fictional world of movies, television shows, or book series and fact find; that is, they provide links to literary legends, scientific principles, and historical elements, strengthening a reader's understanding of the story world. These fact finder books are great links to content area instruction. *The Sorcerer's Companion: A Guide to the Magical World of Harry Potter* (Kronzek & Kronzek, 2001) considers "the wealth of real mythology, folklore, and history that shimmers just beneath the surface" of the *Harry Potter* series (p. xiii). Organized alphabetically by topic, the book tackles the origins of ghouls, hinkypunks, and tea-leaf reading, and readers discover why Professor Sprout insists students wear earmuffs when working with the mandrake plants (p. 159). *The Sorcerer's Companion* clarifies comings and goings in the wizarding world and explains the significance of names, places, and facts throughout the series. Many fact finding companion books exist for the *Harry Potter* series, some outlined in *Expanding Your Harry Potter Library* (Wallace, 2005).

His *Dark Materials* (Pullman, 1995, 1997, 2000), an epic fantasy told in parallel worlds, tackles tough issues: the afterlife, organized religion, and identity. Readers journey with young adults Lyra and Will as they experience life, death, and sacrifice. The companion book, *The Magical Worlds of Philip Pullman: A Treasure of Fascinating Facts* (Colbert, 2006), identifies Pullman's influence for *His Dark Materials:* John Milton's *Paradise Lost* (p. 5). Throughout Colbert's fact finding book are plays on language (e.g., *alethia* is Latin for *truth,* which is part of the Alethiometer, a device Lyra uses to see the past, present, and future), allusions to literature (e.g., a letter by John Keats), and the role of mythologies (e.g., origins of harpies and differences between harpies and Erinyes). Interestingly, Colbert has a similar book for other fantasy epics such as *The Chronicles of Narnia* (Colbert, 2005), *The Lord of the Rings* (Colbert, 2002), and *Harry Potter* (Colbert, 2001).

Fact finder companion books obviously need facts to find, so the more complex the story, the better. A series of unofficial fact finding companions guided *The X-Files* fans through conspiracies, mysteries, and strange events from the show. For example, one *X-Files* episode dealt with a series of lightning-related deaths in a small town. *The Unofficial X-Files Companion II* (Genge, 1996) explores the fascination with lightning and strange, unexplained lightning events, linking the information to the episode whenever possible. Fact finding companion books naturally link to content area instruction. For example, young adults might explore mythology in the English language arts class or study natural phenomenon in science class. More popular culture links to content areas are listed in Box 12.2.

Other Companion Books

Many other types of companion books exist. Would you believe cookbook companion books are available for *The Sopranos* (Rucker & Scicolene, 2002) and for television cops Columbo and Andy Sipowcz (Garner, Beck, & Clark, 1997)? The *Redwall* series has its own cookbook (Jacques, 2005). Author Brian

Box 12.2   Popular Culture and Content Area Learning

Civilization created by Sid Meier, Microprose, 1991.

In this computer game, players build empires during historical time periods, taking into consideration other civilizations, government, economy, and exploration. Players have to contend with actual world leaders and historical events. The success of *Civilization* produced *Civilization II, III,* and *IV.* Some game criticism includes the generic way the story world handles difficult historical events such as slavery and trivializes (or leaves out) actual civilizations.

CSI: Crime Scene Investigation created by Anthony E. Zuiker, CBS.

This is a drama chronicling the work of forensic scientists who use cutting-edge science to solve crimes in Las Vegas. The elite CSI teams, using a variety of scientific gadgets, analyze evidence most people would never see and criminals never know they left.

Good Eats created by Alton Brown. Produced by Deanna Brown, The Food Network.

Mixing nutrition, science, math, and culture, *Good Eats* is not just another cooking show. Each episode, while entertaining, provides educational information in unique ways. In one episode about carrots, Brown re-creates the human eye in a round barbeque, complete with styrofoam rods and cones to explain how beta-carotene impacts the eye.

Mythbuster produced by John Luscombe, Judith Plavnik, and Peter Rees, The Discovery Channel.

Special-effects experts Adam Savage and Jamie Hyneman use science and math to unravel the strangest of urban legends, often re-creating, demonstrating, or

designing their own science experiments. Savage and Hyneman take on legends such as surviving a gunshot under water, the secret weapon of the Confederate Army, Robin Hood's archery prowess, and surviving a 33,000 fall without a parachute.

Naked Science produced by Robert Strange, National Geographic Channel.

Using animation, special effects, and computer simulations, scientists answer topical questions such as when will killer asteroids hit the earth, how are landslides triggered, and how can we predict tsunamis? The official Web site has episode synopses and quizzes.

Numb3rs produced by Cheryl Heuton and Nicolas Falacci, CBS.

In this police drama, the FBI employs Charlie Epps, a mathematical professor (and genius), to assist in crime fighting. Charlie solves difficult cases using math and science knowledge, often using specific equations or algorithms. Previous episodes have included prey-predator patterns, gambling equations, and sound wave movements.

The Science of Superheroes by Lois Gresh and Robert Weinberg. Hoboken, NJ: Wiley, 2002.

This book examines superheroes whose powers have scientific origins (e.g., Superman, the Flash, and the Incredible Hulk) and studies their abilities and what is scientifically possible.

Stargate SG-1 produced by Robert C. Cooper, Brad Wright, Joseph Mallozzi, and Paul Mullie, The SciFi Channel.

This science fiction drama uses ancient Egyptian mythology, the science of black holes, and more to

Continued

Box 12.2   Popular Culture and Content Area Learning   *Continued*

tell stories of scientists and soldiers traveling across the universe and interacting with a variety of alien races. Everything from natural phenomenon to viruses to new technologies is part of the ongoing story line in this long-running series.

Stepping through the Stargate: Science, Archaeology and the Military in Stargate SG-1 edited by P. N. Elrod and Roxanne Conrad. Dallas, TX: Benbella Books, 2004.

This companion book to *Stargate SG-1* explores and evaluates the Stargate story world. Authors discuss the effectiveness of an alien weapon, the staff weapon (including speculations of how the weapon works), the science of *spacetime* (focusing on wormholes), and the role of archaeology in the series.

Threshold produced by Brannon Braga, CBS.

Although this suspense drama lasted only one season, the main plot (and pilot episode) offers great links to science and mathematics. The plot revolves around an alien probe making contact with Earth in the mid-Atlantic ocean. Strangely, the probe is a four-dimensional object occupying three-dimensional space. Further, the probe creates an intricate fractal pattern wherever the signal is received and has the ability to alter human DNA.

Top Secret: A Handbook of Codes, Ciphers, and Secret Writing by Paul B. Janeczko. Cambridge, MA: Candlewick Press, 2004.

With the success (and controversy) of *The Da Vinci Code,* codes and code breaking are finding new popularity. This book includes information on codes, ciphers, unsolved mysteries, and famous code makers (and breakers).

The Truth Behind a Series of Unfortunate Events: Eyeballs, Leeches, Hypnotism, and Orphans—Exploring Lemony Snicket's World by Lois H. Gresh. New York: St. Martin's Griffin, 2004.

Gresh uses history, science, and literature to give readers new insight into the popular series. Topics include how to make Violet's inventions, background on orphans and orphanages (including famous orphans like Grammy Award winner, Faith Hill), and a lesson on reptiles (with a listing of the world's most deadly snakes). Gresh devotes a chapter to Snicket's word choice, discussing words such as *quagmire, aphorism,* and *bromidrosiphobia.*

Tycoon Games

There are several tycoon games including *Roller Coaster Tycoon* by Atari (1999), *Zoo Tycoon* by Microsoft (2000), and *Airport Tycoon* by Global Star Software (2002). In these simulation games, the player is in charge of building and maintaining property (e.g., a theme park, zoo, or airport). Challenges include dealing with finances, loans, and advertising, while ensuring customer safety and satisfaction and maintaining upkeep of the property.

Unsolved History directed by Dan Levitt, Robbin Shahani, and Pascal Franchot, The Discovery Channel.

This series takes a scientific approach to historical events, using forensic evidence, artifacts, interviews, and reenactments to understand frequently asked historical questions. Episodes tackle what really happened at the Alamo, did Hitler commit suicide, and was Princess Diana's death an accident. Episodes and box sets are available for purchase on DVD through The Discovery Channel store.

Jacques explains in the foreword, "In my stories, the food has as much a part of the saga as the battle, the quest, the poems, the riddles, and the songs." Cookbooks, like activity books such as the *Survivor* themed *Mad Libs* (Price & Stern, 2004) or the quiz book *So You Think You Know Harry Potter* (Gifford, 2002), bring a more interactive approach to favorite story worlds. Of course, auto/biographies continue to be available for all celebrities. Perhaps the most intriguing are ones like *Lemony Snicket: The Unauthorized Autobiography* (Snicket, 2002). In this laugh-out-loud unauthorized autobiography, readers are embroiled in the ongoing mystery of just who is Lemony Snicket and is he dead—clues, codes, letters, and newspaper articles fill the book's pages. Finally, companion books can be quite complex with critical essays tackling issues such as philosophy and social status (e.g., *Finding Serenity: Anti-heroes, Lost Shepherds and Space Hookers in Joss Whedon's Firefly*, Espenson, 2004).

With so much Internet activity, Web site guides aid in navigating myriad fan-based sites (e.g., *James Bond, Pokémon*). Fan-based sites provide meaningful discussion forums, and fan voices are finding their way into companion books, as is the case with *The Plot Thickens . . . Harry Potter Investigated by Fans for Fans* (Waters, 2004). Topics include musings about the significance of Harry's scar, the problems with the time-turner, and the truth about Percy's allegiances. Fan-based companion books are an exciting turn for fans, particularly young adults, as their opinions are respected and validated.

Gaming Texts

We've come a long way since Atari and Intelevision in the 1980s, haven't we? Gaming systems are faster, sharper, and more complex—it seems as if games don't actually end with winners or losers anymore; players keep advancing to more difficult levels. Further, the rise of Internet gaming allows gamers to play and communicate with fellow gamers around the world. Gaming is extremely popular with young adults in our digital age, although some researchers note gaming may be marketed more for boys and may negatively portray girls and women (Dietz, 1998) and, as such, has a larger male audience (Agosto, 2004). Despite the problems, gaming provides rich contexts for exploring literacy: gamers draw information from multiple sources, almost like research; create their own gaming texts or companions; use gaming manuals and fan sites in strategic ways; and learn and analyze gaming language (Gee, 2003). Gaming literacy extends beyond print literacy to include visual literacy and spatial relationships. Further, game literacy is highly dependent on prior knowledge of the game universe.

Games provide context for various adaptations and texts. For example, games have been made into movies (*Teenage Mutant Ninja Turtles,* 1990, and *Super Mario Bros,* 1993). Novelizations and novelized extensions exist for many games such as *Pokémon, Dragonball Z,* and *Everquest.* Novelized extensions may be a way to engage more girls in gaming literacy as research indicates girls are more interested in exploring game characters' lives than in winning (Agosto, 2004). Therefore, gaming fanfiction might be another valuable resource. Fanfiction.net has gaming fanfiction ranging from *Sonic the Hedgehog* to *Zelda*. Gaming companion books are usually gaming manuals or strategy guides, which include background information and tips for advancing through the game. Gamers use these texts strategically as they question game elements and find themselves in new situations. Gaming manuals or strategy guides can be found for numerous games such as *The Sims,* in which players create neighborhoods of people and activities, and *Final Fantasy,* a fantasy adventure game with monsters, kingdoms, and magic.

Gaming, from board games to virtual reality games, is a stronghold in the lives of young adults; naturally, young adult literature reflects this phenomenon. *Brainboy and the Deathmaster* (Seidler, 2003) follows orphaned young adults who have two things in common: superior intelligence and mastery of a series of video games. The gaming network creator has a sinister plan for these orphans as they work around the clock to conquer time. In *Heir Apparent* (Velde, 2002), teenager Giannine indulges in a technologically advanced virtual reality role-playing game. When game protestors damage the computer, Giannine learns she must actually win to survive. Box 12.3 includes some of my favorite young adult literature novels with gaming plots. Notice that some push technological boundaries as gaming continues to become technologically complex.

Box 12.3   Gaming Plots in Young Adult Literature

The Amulet of Komondor by Adam Osterweil. Asheville, NC: Front Street, 2003.

Middle school friends Joe and Katie are thrilled to find a CD-ROM version of their favorite role-playing card game, *DragonSteel.* Unbeknownst to them, the CD is a portal to the *DragonSteel* world. There, Joe and Katie must work through the game, finding jeweled amulet pieces in order to save the kingdom.

The Game of Sunken Places by M. T. Anderson. New York: Scholastic, 2004.

While visiting Gregory's eccentric Uncle Max, Gregory and friend Brian begin playing an enchanted role-playing board game and soon find they are actually living the game. While fighting trolls and ogres, the boys learn the game rules and their competitors' identities.

Head Games by Mariah Fredericks. New York: Atheneum/Simon & Schuster, 2005.

Judith has an easier time assuming computer game personas then being herself, maybe because her best friend doesn't acknowledge her existence anymore, and her father lives thousands of miles away. An unexpected game ally becomes a real-life friend and teaches Judith self-acceptance.

Keeper of the Kingdom by H. J. Ralles. Dallas, TX: Top Publications, 2001.

Matt begins playing a new computer game, *Keeper of the Kingdom,* has barely read the rules, and is mysteriously sucked inside the computer into a futuristic world. The Kingdom is embroiled in a war between humans, computers, and machines. Matt encounters

Continued

Box 12.3   Gaming Plots in Young Adult Literature   *Continued*

technological gadgets, secret doorways, and force fields as he tries to save his life and return to his own time.

Leo@fergusrules.com by Arne Tangherlini. Wellfleet, MA: Leapfrog Press, 1999.

A troubled teen dismissed from many schools, Leonora (Leo) is sent to live with her grandmother in the Philippines. There, she immerses herself in a role-playing computer game where she takes on an alternative persona. When an online friend disappears, Leo sets out to find him, all the way to a computer-generated hell.

Locked Inside by Nancy Werlin. New York: Delacorte/Random House, 2000.

Marnie Skyedottier plays a fantasy role-playing computer game in which she can be cool and confident, a transformation from the failing high school student hated by peers. When kidnapped and locked in a dungeon, Marnie must use role-playing skills to escape real-life danger. What does the kidnapping have to do with Marnie's deceased mother, a famous singer and writer?

Missing Abby by Lee Weatherly. New York: Fickling Random House, 2004.

Abby and Emma suffer torment by their peers because of their fascination with fantasy role-playing games. Emma sheds this identity at a new school with new friends, but when Abby disappears, Emma reenters Abby's Goth world and role-plays to find her. Could the role-playing game have something to do with Abby's disappearance?

The Night Room by E. M. Goldman. New York: Puffin/Penguin, 1995.

The Night Room is a high school reunion story for a technological age. Several teens experiment with a virtual reality computer program, showing their 10th high school reunion. At first, the program works according to plan, but then a computer hacker rewrites the program so it will kill one student.

Only You Can Save Mankind by Terry Pratchett. New York: HarperCollins, 1992.

Johnny begins playing a computer game when suddenly the alien he is supposed to kill surrenders and asks for safe passage. Johnny finds himself helping the aliens, but as other gamers attempt to play, they find empty screens. Can Johnny really save the aliens? First book in a trilogy.

User Unfriendly by Vivian Vande Velde. Orlando, FL: Magic Carpet/Harcourt, 1991.

Arvin Rizalli, his mother, and friends hook into an advanced computer role-playing game, only to find no game master. Somehow the computer controls the game, and the game becomes increasingly dangerous. Could a real illness threaten Arvin's mother? The teens race to finish the game to save her life.

Virtual World by Chris Westwood. New York: Viking, 1997.

A new virtual reality game, *Silicon Valley* is all the rage, but players seem to be disappearing. When Jack Norris gets his hands on a copy, he suspects something is wrong. The gaming is too realistic, blurring the lines between reality and the game, but the truth about the game is far more sinister.

Wizards of the Game by David Lubar. New York: Philomel/Penguin, 2003.

Eighth grader Mercer Dickensen is an avid *Wizards of Warrior* player, a fantasy role-playing game. When the game comes under scrutiny for using magic, Mercer finds himself an unlikely ally to real-life wizards.

Magazines and Zines

With its debut in 1944, *Seventeen* magazine lay the groundwork for one of the most successful magazine genres, teen magazines, and remains the most popular in circulation today. As a response to the Echo Boomers,[11] scores of magazines specifically targeting teens have entered the market, while some have folded (e.g., *Teen*), and newsstand copies have experienced drops in sales due to online magazines (e.g., *YM*), teen magazines and their online companions continue to play a pivotal role in teens' lives. Sporting magazines for boys, spin-offs (crossovers) from women's titles for girls (e.g., *Cosmogirl* and *Cosmo, Teen Vogue* and *Vogue*), online companion magazines, and zines[12] have established a new direction for teen readers and the publishing world (Henry Kaiser Family Foundation, 2004). Teen magazines cover any topic imaginable—everything from fashion, beauty, and finance to celebrity news, cars, and crafts. The content, design, and readability of these magazines appeal to teens, for they address salient teen issues.

Adolescent girls gravitate toward magazines with a pervasive emphasis on beauty, fashion, and celebrities, and many adults worry about the messages these magazines convey. Researchers (Kaplan & Cole, 2003; Labre & Walsh-Childers, 2003) suggest that these magazines send unrealistic and sometimes unhealthy messages to young girls about their femininity. A recent study analyzed the beauty content of online magazines and found three major themes: "Beauty is a requirement, beauty is achieved through products, and I can help you find the right products" (Labre & Walsh-Childers, 2003, p. 387). It is true that these magazines convey ideas of perfection and beauty, but articles from these magazines can be used to discuss our obsessions with appearance. Magazines countering these images also exist. *Teen Voices* challenges girls to see beyond makeup and clothes and includes topical articles (e.g., women in hip-hop music) and tough issues (e.g., same-sex marriage, individuality, and sports). With a similar message, the zine *Shameless* is marketed for teens who "get it"— that is, they know life goes beyond fashion, makeup, and dieting. Similar to *Shameless,* the zine *Gurl* looks realistically at issues that matter to young adult girls. With articles about body image and health and original stories and poetry, this zine has something for every teen girl. These magazines offer a refreshing alternative to magazines that create unrealistic standards for young adults.

Teen magazines have traditionally targeted female readers with beauty, fashion, relationship, and celebrity themes, but boys are targeted more with sports, adventure, technology, and exploration—science and history themes.

---

[11]Offspring of the Baby Boomers, known also as *Generation Y* or *Millennials,* they make up almost one-third of the U.S. population and play a key role in the economy. Ranging from elementary age children to recent college graduates, the money they spend excludes such things as medication and mortgages. They are the first generation to grow up with computers, cell phones, and sophisticated gaming systems (Fager, 2005).
[12]Zines, online magazines, can follow in the footsteps of mainstream magazines such as *Thrasher* and *Teen* but can also be written by teens such as *Smart Girl* and *Teen Ink.*

Sports Illustrated is a mainstay for adolescent boys, and while the "swimsuit issue" may be the most popular with boys (understandably so), each monthly issue is loaded with well-written, informative, and often hysterically funny articles. For example, Rick Reilly's articles (always the last page) are perfect for teaching voice and tone and for moving students beyond the five-paragraph essay.

Boy's Life (by Boy Scouts of America) includes articles and columns on outdoor adventures, sports, technology, and history. It also includes short stories written by such young adult authors as Walter Dean Myers (see *Plane Crazy* in the May 2006 issue). *Wasted Youth* and *Rolling Stone,* popular music magazines with boys, print interviews and news updates about today's musical artists. Boys are also drawn to car magazines (*Hot Rod* and *Motor Trend*), and history and social studies lovers enjoy magazines like *National Geographic, Smithsonian, World War II,* and the *Civil War Times.* These latter journals make great additions to content area classrooms.

The New York Times (in conjunction with Scholastic) has a teen-friendly news magazine, *New York Times Upfront,* focusing on current events for the 9th- through 12th-grade classrooms[13] Features from a recent issue included articles on globalization, citizenship, and interpreting the constitution. *Newsweek* (in conjunction with Weekly Reader) also has a teen crossover: *Teen Newsweek.* This magazine, targeting a middle grades audience, deals with national and international issues. The focus on the January 2006 issue started with the question "Does President George W. Bush have the power to allow spying on U.S. citizens?" *BrainEvent.com* is a teen news zine that encourages teens to examine world events, share their thoughts, and be inspired toward action. Topical news articles include cloning controversies, civil liberty debates, and a discussion regarding teen camera sites. These news magazines offer young adults an accessible way to become involved in current events.

Teachers and parents might be surprised to know that some magazines are devoted to specific movies, televisions shows, music, and gaming. Titan Magazines publishes magazines for televisions shows like *24, Battlestar Galactica,* and *Lost.* The *Stargate SG-1* magazine commonly includes interviews with new characters, news about the show and spin-off *Stargate: Atlantis,* and a journal from show scientist Dr. McKay. Gaming magazines are also quite popular and are devoted to the best gaming has to offer (e.g., *PC Gamer* and *Play*). Gaming zines are also well-liked. *Game Spot* focuses on all gaming needs, regardless of the gaming system; it includes game reviews, news reports, downloads, and strategy guides.

Magazines are a great source of information for young adults in the content areas because articles are well researched, engaging, and relatively short. Including magazines as a content area supplemental text isn't difficult, for magazines exist for any topic imaginable. For example, *ChemMatters,*

---

[13]Sample issues and teacher's guides are available at the Web site http://teacher.scholastic.com/products/classmags/upfront.htm.

published through the American Chemistry Society, focuses on chemistry in everyday life and targets high school chemistry courses. The magazine offers a teacher's guide with additional article information, experiments, and activities. Past articles investigated the chemistry of golf balls, cat litter, and liquid crystals. Each issue of *Plays: The Drama Magazine for Young People* contains 8 to 10 plays arranged by age-level appropriateness (elementary through high school). With enough scripts to have several small groups perform different plays, this magazine provides authentic material for Reader's Theater. Included are classic adaptations (e.g., Edgar Allan Poe) and student work. The October 2005 issue included the winner of the California Student Playwriting Contest, High School Division.

Magazines are a mainstay of American culture; they cover a variety of topics from fashion and photography to cars and crafts. Articles are informative, engaging, and short enough to finish in one sitting. Color, graphics, advertisements, and more fill magazine pages, making the reading experience also a viewing experience, in some ways mimicking digital texts—texts that Echo Boomers demand. If taken seriously and used effectively in the classroom, magazines can turn at-risk students on to reading. More magazines for content area classrooms can be found in Box 12.4.

baby boomer children

Box 12.4   Magazines for the Content Areas

AIM: American's Intercultural Magazine. Published by AIM Publication Association.

http://aimmagazine.org/articles.htm
Focusing on eliminating racism, this magazine includes articles, fiction, and poetry. Recent articles have dealt with interracial marriage and the devastating effects of Katrina.

Argo World

www.agclassroom.org/textversion/teen/agro/index.htm
This zine is for secondary teachers and their students. *Argo World* covers integrated science, biology, Earth systems, technology, social studies, and family and consumer science. Each topic has news articles, classroom activities, and grant opportunities.

Calliope. Published by Carus Publishing.

www.cricketmag.com/ProductDetail.asp?pid=14

Calliope focuses on world history, covering a wide range of topics (e.g., the impact of the Black Death, life during the fall of Rome). The magazine aims to show teens that history is amazing.

Choices. Published by Scholastic.

http://teacher.scholastic.com/products/classmags/choices.htm
Targeting middle and high school students, *Choices* covers topics in family and consumer science, life science, health, and home economics. Articles showcase real families and situations that support teens as they deal with life's challenges.

Cicada. Published by Carus Publishing.

www.cricketmag.com/ProductDetail.asp?pid=11
This magazine presents stories and poetry specific to adolescents, and some authors are teens. *Cicada* encourages teens to write and has an online writing forum for teens, *The Slam*.

Continued

Box 12.4   Magazines for the Content Areas   *Continued*

Cobblestone. Published by Carus Publishing.

www.cobblestonepub.com/magazine/COB
Cobblestone focuses on history. Lively articles and detailed graphics provide motivation for studying history. Themes have included rediscovering Jamestown, Ulysses S. Grant, and Henry Ford and the Model T.

Dig. Published by Carus Publishing.

www.cricketmag.com/ProductDetail
.asp?pid=13&type
Archaeology is the subject of *Dig* magazine. *Dig* readers learn about ancient cultures and how archaeologists uncovered information. Science experiments and projects are also included.

Faces. Published by Carus Publishing.

www.cobblestonepub.com/magazine/FAC
Readers learn about other cultures and traditions, promoting appreciation for diversity. In addition to articles, the magazine includes detailed photographs, maps, folktales, and time lines.

Muse. Published by Carus Publishing.

www.cricketmag.com/ProductDetail
.asp?pid=12&type
With a wide range of topics (from anthropology to zoology), *Muse* covers almost all content areas, calling itself a "guidebook for intellectual exploration" and encouraging young adults to question.

Odyssey. Published by Carus Publishing.

www.cobblestonepub.com/magazine/ODY
Topics range from space to technology to mathematics and links content to everyday life. For example, a past issue included an examination of extreme sports (e.g., snowboarding, race car driving).

Scholastic Math. Published by Scholastic.

http://teacher.scholastic.com/products/
classmags/math.htm
Using real-life situations to talk about mathematics, *Scholastic Math* motivates middle school readers to solve problems and think about real-life mathematics. Every issue contains a wide array of topics: math and sports, careers involving mathematics, and the history of mathematics.

Science World. Published by Scholastic.

http://teacher.scholastic.com/products/
classmags/scienceworld.htm
Includes hands-on experiments, news reports on scientific activity around the world, and articles linked to national science standards, *Science World* is an excellent source of reading in middle and high school science classrooms. Topics include life science, Earth and space science, physical science, chemistry, and technology.

Skipping Stones.

www.skippingstones.org
This nonprofit magazine for teens focuses on multiculturalism. The official Web site explains the magazine: "encourages cooperation, creativity and celebration of cultural and environmental richness. It provides a playful forum for sharing ideas and experiences among children from different lands and backgrounds."

YES Mag. Published by Peter Piper Publishing.

www.yesmag.bc.ca
YES Mag is a Canadian publication for teens interested in exploring science, technology, engineering, and mathematics. Issues include hands-on experiments, news articles, and environmental updates.

Z.

http://zmagsite.zmag.org/curTOC.htm
This zine focuses on injustice and civil liberties. A recent issue featured articles on immigration, tension between Iran and the United States, and abortion and gay rights. Sections include commentary, features, activism, and culture.

Going Graphic: Comic Books, Manga, and Graphic Novels

The graphic medium has always been popular with young adults, and this popularity continues into adulthood. Just look at the interest in *V for Vendetta* (Moore, 1988) with a recent movie adaptation. Comic books, perhaps the most widely known graphic medium, date back to the 1930s. The first superhero comic book (featuring Superman) appeared in 1938 (Gresh & Weinberg, 2002), and Superman comic books continue to be published featuring new story lines.[14] Talk about a popular series. Comic books may be best known for the superhero story, but the comic book is a format, not a genre, meaning comic book content covers all topics: everyday life, humor, detective stories, and even science fiction and fantasy. Furthermore, the content of comics should not be trivialized as material can explore tough topics from any aspect of reality: war, terrorism, politics, crime, and disaster. For example, the comic book *9-11: Artists Respond,* Vol. 1 (Dark Horse Comics, 2002) "is a good example of a comic book being used as a powerful tool for documenting and portraying tragedies, triumphs, and human spirits" (Xu et al., 2005, p. 107).

Sometimes used as a synonym for comic books, *mangas* are Japanese comic books featuring Japanese characters and animations. Like American comic books, mangas are a format, and experts say manga story lines are more complex than those of their American counterparts and focus more on developing story lines then on graphics (Lent, 2004). Furthermore, mangas are mainstream reading material in Japan: "About 40 percent of all published materials in highly literate and well-read Japan are manga, and about a dozen manga magazines each have a circulation of one million or more, the most popular claiming 6.2 million readers—and that's weekly" (p. 38). With such tremendous interest in Japan, it is no surprise that manga has found intense popularity in the United States.

Some manga currently available include *Antique Bakery* (Yoshinaga, 2005), a humorous look at culinary arts and relationships, *Bleach* (Kubo, 2004), a teen battles ghosts and demons, and *Dragon Voice* (Mishiyama, 2004), a teen pursues a dancing career. Online networks make finding manga easy: the Advanced Media Network Anime has an entire section for manga, and Anipike.com covers all things related to anime and manga. *Beckett Anime & Manga,* a monthly magazine published by Beckett Media LP, includes news updates, reviews, contests, and fan art. Box 12.5 provides manga titles spanning a range of genres.

Graphic Novels

Comic books have given rise to another format: graphic novels. Simply stated, a *graphic novel* is a novel told through the graphic, comic book style.

---

[14]New editions to famous DC Comics such as *Batman, Justice League,* and *Superman* can be found at www.dccomics.com/comics/. New editions to famous Marvel Comics such as *Spider-Man, Fantastic Four,* and *X-Men* can be found at www.marvel.com/comics/. There are currently six different comic series for *Spider-Man* and four for *Fantastic Four.*

Box 12.5   Manga

Confidential Confessions: Volume 1 by Reiko Momochi. Los Angeles, CA: Tokyopop, 2003.

This problem novel series focuses on tough issues facing teens such as suicide, abandonment, and body image. Six volumes make up this series.

Eerie Queerie by Shuri Shiozu. Los Angeles, CA: Tokyopop, 2004.

High school student Mitsuo communicates with ghosts. His classmates make fun of him, especially when he channels the ghosts of teenage girls, but he is determined to control this gift.

Full Moon Wo Sagashite: Volume 1 by Arina Tanemura. San Francisco, CA: Viz Media, 2001.

Mitsuki longs to fulfill a promise to become a famous singer, but obstacles such as throat cancer and an overprotective grandmother stand in her way. Can her death gods jumpstart her career?

GALS! Volume 1 by Mihona Fujii. New York: CMX/DC Comics, 2005.

These high school girls are obsessed with fashion and boys, and they have a code detailing how to get what they want.

Godchild: Volume 1 by Kaori Yuki. San Francisco, CA: Viz Media, 2006.

In this mystery series, Lord Cain Hargreaves solves strange cases set in 19th-century London. An unknown enemy of Hargreaves is a connection to his cases.

Gunslinger Girl: Volume 1 by Yu Aida. Houston, TX: ADV Manga, 2003.

In this science fiction adventure, young adult girls are turned into government assassins, trained to stop at nothing to protect their handlers. How much of their identity must they forfeit in the process?

Here Is Greenwood: Volume 1 by Yukie Nasu. San Francisco, CA: Viz Media, 2004.

When Kazuya loses the girl of his dreams to his brother, his friends in Ryokuto Academy try everything to cheer him up.

Iron Wok Jan: Volume 1 by Shinji Saijyo. Fremont, CA: ComicsOne, 2002.

Jan Akiyama sets out to fulfill his dream of being a master chef but is challenged by an equally talented young girl.

The Kindachi Case Files: The Opera House Murders by Yozaburo Kanari. Los Angeles, CA: Tokyopop, 2003.

When a series of strange events take place during a school production of *The Phantom of the Opera,* an unlikely student becomes a detective.

Loveless: Volume 1 by Yun Kouga. Los Angeles, CA: Tokyopop, 2006.

In this complex series, Konga weaves a story about friendship, love, and loss as Ritsuka desperately tries to unravel the mystery of his brother's murder. As Ritsuka digs deeper, he becomes embroiled in a warlike fantasy game.

Dresang (1999) calls graphic novels "literary comic book[s]" (p. 23), saying graphic novels are more sophisticated comic books, often dealing with difficult issues, and marketed for young adults. For example, the renown *Maus: A Survivor's Tale: My Father Bleeds History*[15] (Spiegelman, 1986) and *Maus II: A Survivor's Tale: And Here My Troubles Began* (Spiegelman, 1991)

---

[15]In 1992 this graphic novel won a Pulitzer Prize Special Award.

are powerful graphic novels, both dealing with concentration camp experiences and told through the perspectives of mice. Gene Luen Yang's *American Born Chinese* (2006), a graphic novel about the struggles of Chinese Americans, won the coveted 2007 Michael L. Printz Award. Classics are also adapted for the graphic novel format as a way to interest young adults, including *Frankenstein* (Reed, 2005), *Black Beauty* (Brigman & Richardson, 2005), and *Macbeth* (Cover, 2005). Further, graphic novels target adolescent girls with strong female characters and story lines. For instance, the graphic novel series *Witch* (Alfonsi, 2005) follows five friends with extraordinary powers, *Queen Bee* (Clugston, 2005) deals with middle school popularity struggles, and *Girl Stories* (Weinstein, 2006) is a hilarious coming-of-age story about Lauren, a teen struggling with identity issues. Moreover, the term *graphic novel* can also represent a series of comics compiled in one volume. For instance, *Runaways* (Vaughan, 2006) follows a group of teens as they discover their parents are not superheroes, but supervillains. *Runaways* was originally a comic book series, and all individual comics are anthologized here.

Reprinted by permission of Roaring Book Press and First Second Press © 2006.

Again, graphic novels are a format, not a genre, and thus come in all genres: comedy, fantasy, historical fiction, realistic fiction, and mystery (see Box 12.6). Due to the popularity of graphic novels, it isn't hard to find the right book for students. The American Library Association Web site has a page for Great Graphic Novels for Teens. In addition, No Flying, No Tights is a Web site devoted to reviewing graphic novels for young adults. Further, the Harvey Awards are specific to comic books and graphic mediums and go back as far as 1988.

Interactive Texts

With so much emphasis on graphic mediums, exploring the changing landscape of interactive texts is critical. Today's young adults, having grown up in the Internet world, are comfortable with nonlinear approaches to text experiences, moving forward and back within and around texts, and interacting with texts in new and different ways, sometimes creating their own texts as discussed with fanfiction and zines. Of course, interactive texts are not a new phenomenon. Bantam Books began publishing the *Choose Your Own Adventure* book series in the 1970s. In this series, readers determine the story line outcome by choosing their own paths. These books can be read time and again as readers make different plot choices, changing the story's

Box 12.6   Graphic Novels

***A.L.I.E.E.E.N.* by Lewis Trondheim. New York: First Second/Roaring Brook Press, 2006.**

In this wordless graphic novel, alien creatures take on human characteristics. Their adventures showcase universal stories of youth.

***The Baby-Sitters Club: Kristy's Great Idea* by Ann Martin and Raina Telgemeier. New York: Scholastic, 2006.**

Following in true *Baby-Sitter's Club* style, this adaptation follows the girls as they find adventures while growing up.

***Bone: Out From Boneville* by Jeff Smith. New York: Graphix/Scholastic, 2005.**

The Bone cousins are embroiled in hilarious adventures involving rats, dragons, and bugs. Mystery surrounds a hooded figure who wants Phoney Bone's soul in this comic book series turned graphic novel.

***Castle Waiting: The Lucky Road* by Linda Medley. Portland, OR: Olio Press, 2002.**

In this whimsical, fairy tale graphic novel, Medley plays on familiar themes and characteristics of classic fairy tales. First book in the *Castle Waiting* series.

***From Hell* by Alan Moore. Portland, OR: Top Shelf Productions, 2004.**

In this crime fiction graphic novel, Moore recounts the Jack the Ripper mystery in Victorian London, but the story takes an interesting twist on Jack the Ripper's identity.

***The Lost Colony* by Grady Klein. New York: First Second/Roaring Brook Press, 2006.**

In this story set in the 19th century, citizens on an unknown island find riches. In trying to conceal their find from the outside world, readers glimpse the true nature of the citizens. Provides powerful commentary about prejudice.

***Marvel 1602* by Neil Gaiman and Andy Kubert. New York: Marvel Comics, 2005.**

Famous superheroes such as Charles Xavier (*X-Men*) and Peter Parker (*Spider-Man*) continue to fight for good and evil—this time during the Elizabethan period.

***Pedro and Me: Friendship, Loss, and What I Learned* by Judd Winick. New York: Henry Holt, 2000.**

This memoir of *The Real World* teenagers, Pedro Zamora and Judd Winick, focuses on Pedro's battle with AIDS and how he affected Judd's life.

***The Tale of One Bad Rat* by Bryan Talbot. Milwavkie, OR: Dark Horse Comics, 1995.**

Runaway Helen Potter looks for solace from an abused street life in England. Throughout the journey, Helen reconnects with the Beatrix Potter tales. An inspirational survival story.

***Vampire Loves* by Joann Sfar. New York: First Second/Roaring Brook Press, 2006.**

This graphic novel follows the adventures of Ferdinand, a vampire looking for romance. He is careful to use only one tooth to bite his (willing) victims so as not to cause permanent damage and become addicted to their blood.

outcome. The success of this series sparked multiple reprints,[16] as well as specific adventure series, including one based on R. L. Stine's *Goosebumps* and another based on the *Star Wars* franchise. New titles in which readers choose the story path are constantly being developed. In fact, J. E. Bright publishes a series of "you decide" books called *Follow Your Heart* where readers (mostly middle and high school girls) make decisions about friendship and romance. The first in the series, *Follow Your Heart: Your Best Friend's Boyfriend* (Bright, 2006), asks readers to handle situations in which they develop instantaneous crushes on their best friend's boyfriend.

Other popular interactive texts include whodunits or five-minute mysteries. A case is presented and readers use their own deductive skills to solve it. For example, *Crime Files: Four-Minute Forensic Mysteries* (Brown, 2006) is the CSI-like book of mini-mysteries challenging readers to ponder evidence at strange crime scenes to solve cases. Solutions are provided at the end of each mystery, but the fun is in trying to solve the crime alone. *Clue Mysteries: 15 Whodunits to Solve in Minutes* (Cameron, 2003) brings the popular board game to life as readers try to solve short mysteries involving all game elements. Again, solutions are provided at the end of each mystery.

The interactive element is becoming more intriguing in informational texts. For example, *Egyptology* (Sands, Harris, Ward, & Andrew, 2004) isn't an ordinary informational text examining the ancient Egyptian culture. In this replica of an Egyptologist's journal (Miss Emily Sands), everything from sketches to postcards to maps seems authentic—letters come out of envelopes, postcards are fastened so the reader can view both sides, folded maps open, and fastened compartments hold cloth and game pieces. Written as a journal, the text contains information about ancient Egypt and the itinerary, thoughts, and experiences of Miss Sands. Drawings, sketches, photographs, and other visual elements accompany journal entries; thus, the text does not follow a typical text format of columns or sections. Candlewick Press offers similar interactive informational texts with *Dragonology* (Drake & Steer, 2003), *Wizardology* (Gilbert, Howe, Tomic, & Ward, 2005), and *Pirateology* (Steer, Lubber, Gilbert, & Ward, 2006). In similar fashion, the Penguin Group published *Fairyopolis: A Flower Fairies Journal* (Barker, 2005) detailing Cicely Mary Barker's research into all things related to flower fairies. The journal follows Cicely's activities and discoveries into the flower fairie world, starting with mysterious footprints (included in the text) and ending with a small compartment filled with fairy dust. These interactive informational texts are especially valuable when linked with content area learning, such as *Lewis and Clark on the Trail of Discovery: The Journey That Shaped America* (Gragg, 2003), marketed as a museum in a book.

---

[16]*The Cave of Time* (Packard), which was first published in 1979, was reprinted several times, most recently in 1996.

Digital Texts

In the digital age, texts are evolving to include more digital qualities: nonlinear paths and a juxtaposition of text and pictures (Dresang, 1999). In narrative texts, authors infuse "re-creations" of multimedia within the text to tell stories. For example, Kate Klise uses letters, notes, newspapers, drawings, bulletin boards, and more to tell the stories in the *Regarding the . . .* series. In *Regarding the Trees* (Klise, 2005), Principal Russ decides it's time to clean up the Geyser Creek Middle School campus, including removing trees, some over 100 years old. Hilarity ensues when the new Italian school chef and the local café owner plan a cook-off, a sixth-grade student moves into the weeping willow in protest of the tree removal, and the entire town becomes embroiled in a gender war. Such texts mirror digital hypertext elements familiar to young adults.

Texts are also adding digital accompaniments. At the least, books and authors have their own Web sites, some more interactive than others. Jerry Spinelli, author of books such as *Maniac Magee, The Library Card* (1990) and *Stargirl* (2000), has an official Web site containing links for frequently asked questions, book lists, and games. Laurie Halse Anderson's official Web site includes a journal (with photography) and information about her books (including *Speak,* 1999, and *Fever, 1793,* 2000).

Everworld (1999), by K. A. Applegate, is a 12-part series about high school students caught in a strange adventure involving ancient mythologies. The accompanying Web site provides series details, the characters and various species, and a chapter of the last book. *Warriors: The New Prophecy* fantasy series (2005) by Erin Hunter follows wild forest cat clans that work together to save themselves and their beloved forest from a terrible foe. The accompanying Web site includes information about the cat characters and clans, an interactive map of the forest, biographical information about the author, and games (including a way to be assigned your own warrior cat name and clan). These Web sites are similar to the companion books previously discussed.

CDs now accompany some books. *Magyk* (Sage, 2005), first book in the *Septemus Heap* series, filled with infants switched at birth, dark forces, magic, and mystery, is accompanied by a CD that contains book and author information, a game, and trivia based on the story line. The CD links to a Web site containing the same information. Early copies of *Inkspell* (2005), Cornelia Funke's sequel to *Inkheart* (2003), a story in which book characters come to life, came with a CD on which Funke reads selected chapters.[17] *Plastic Angel* (Nields, 2005) is the coming-of-age story of two unlikely teen friends—a musician and a model—and how, together, they learn about friendship, parent relationships, and choices as they write music together. Author Nerissa Nields is one part of the sister duo that makes the folk band The Nields.

---

[17]This is now available on Scholastic's Web site: www.scholastic.com/corneliafunke/index.htm.

Not surprisingly, the book comes with a CD featuring two songs from the book.[18]

The digital age affords authors and publishers more creative text opportunities. Digital texts can continue or enhance story lines. For example, Anthony Horowitz's horror series *The Gatekeepers* tells the story of ancient evils, a government plot, and five special teens (Horowitz, 2005b, 2006). The official *Gatekeepers* Web site is complete with articles, evidence, and case files pertaining to the books. Television is branching out to include accompanying digital texts to enhance the viewing experience. In addition to the episode guide and character backgrounds, the official site of the hit television show *24,* the homeland security thriller, includes a link called "Research" where pertinent information about episodes appears as a U.S. Department of Homeland Security research file. For example, clean air technology is discussed on the research link for a season five episode. Official Web sites for books, movies, television shows, or games are good starting points for researching digital texts. Unofficial fan sites might also have digital texts.

resources

Digital texts do not necessarily have to be "official" companion texts for story worlds. With Internet accessibility, fan sites, and discussion groups, role playing is expanding exponentially. Early role-playing games (e.g., *Dungeons and Dragons*) combined storytelling with game playing. Players were given a character to develop based on game parameters similar to a "choose your own path" book (see previous discussion). Role-playing board and computer games provide an outlet for players to create complex story lines while interacting with peers. There aren't always winners or losers in role-playing games; rather, players work together to create a cohesive story with goals, conflicts, and resolutions. Like *Dungeons and Dragons,* many official role-playing games exist such as the fantasy game *The Elder Scrolls* by Bethesda Software for PC or *World of Warcraft* by Vivendi Universal.

Role-playing games aren't relegated to official games, though. Movies, television shows, and books create their own role-playing Internet games—not unlike an interactive form of fanfiction. Players gather over the Internet (through Web sites and discussion boards) to role-play scenarios based on favorite story worlds and characters. Players write their role-playing actions and thoughts, and the game is often restricted to real time. Plot advances can only come from equal participation from all players. Role-playing in favorite story lines is popular with young adults: a search for *Harry Potter* role-playing game discussion boards on Yahoo Groups yielded 464 different groups, *Spider-Man* had 28, *The Princess Diaries* had 4, and a variety of role-playing groups for televisions shows on the WB network (e.g., *Supernatural, One Tree Hill*) had 25. This interactive approach to fanfiction becomes more

---

[18]An interesting side note is that The Nields are a favorite band of the characters in *Heart on My Sleeve* (Wittlinger, 2004).

complex when multiple writers are involved and action or plot sequences unfold as the game is played.

Looking to the Future

Whether reading young adult literature with gaming plots, favorite television show novelized extensions, or graphic novels about superheroes, young adults relish popular culture texts. As teachers, we should capitalize on this intrinsic motivation to encourage students to read widely. Once we understand student interest, we have an avenue to connect students with other young adult literature. For example, students who watch the television show *Alias* and read the novelized extensions and companion books might be interested in the young adult spy series *Alex Rider* by Anthony Horowitz (2001). On the other hand, if students prefer gaming to reading, introducing a young adult novel with a gaming plot might provide enough connection to spark reading interest.

The popular culture genre is a dynamic, ever-changing world driven largely by fans. With such a large fan base, what does the future hold for popular culture texts? As technology continues to advance, so, too, will communication opportunities. Therefore, popular culture texts can potentially take on an infinite number of styles, formats, and structures. As I consider what is currently available, I wonder if the following will ever come to pass: young adult literature with wireless web connections in the actual text; young adult literature with gaming plots in which readers can play the game they are reading; or virtual reality literature, in which readers can watch or participate in the story. Regardless of advances, this chapter introduces teachers to what is available now and how to find those texts.

Activity: Interest Inventory

Popular culture texts can be overwhelming, especially to those not yet introduced to this dynamic world. Because popular culture is ever changing, it is important to know how to find appropriate materials. Further, our tastes (and that of students) regarding popular culture are as varied as our tastes in food, cars, or home decor. This activity will give you an opportunity to familiarize yourself with popular culture texts while learning the interests of three to five young adults.

Start by giving an interest inventory to your group. Interest inventories are brief surveys about students' general (or specific) interests. Questions can include favorite hobbies, books, television shows, music, movies, and actors/actresses. Inventories can be streamlined for your students, or you can use ready-made inventories (Harp, 2000; Rhodes & Shanklin, 1993). For this activity, create questions (about five to eight) that focus on book, television, movie, and gaming interests. For example, you might ask: What are your all-time favorite movies? If you could watch only one television show, what would it be? Who is your favorite author?

Once you have administered your inventory, look for trends in the results. What do your students seem to like? Are there commonalities? Does a particular genre draw the most attention? Next, focus on two to three popular results (e.g., a television show, movie, game, book). Using information provided in this chapter and the Internet, determine what popular culture texts can be found for your selections (e.g., novelizations, novelized extensions, fanfiction, companion books, magazines or zines, games). What other interesting texts did you find during your search: comic books, graphic novels, and/or activity books? What new text forms did you find during your search?

Share your findings with your group of young adults by showing them book reviews, doing a book talk, or visiting a Web site. Listen to what they have to say about your selections: Do they show interest in reading any of the materials? Did they know such texts were available to them? Which selections were hits and misses? Answers may surprise you.

Professional Resources

Behen, L. D. (2006). *Using pop culture to teach information literacy: Methods to engage a new generation.* Portsmouth, NH: Libraries Unlimited.

Carter, J. B. (2007). *Building literacy connections with graphic novels: Page by page, panel by panel.* Urbana, IL: NCTE.

Cary, S. (2004). *Going graphic: Comics at work in the multilingual classroom.* Portsmouth, NH: Heinemann.

Evans, J. (2005). *Literacy moves on: Popular culture, new technologies, and critical literacy in the elementary classroom.* Portsmouth, NH: Heinemann.

Freedman, K. (2003). *Teaching visual culture: Curriculum, aesthetics, and the social life of art.* New York: Teachers College Press.

Jenkins, H. (Ed.). (2002). *Hop on pop: The politics and pleasures of popular culture.* Durham, NC: Duke University Press.

Jenkins, H. (Ed.). (2006). *Fans, bloggers, and gamers: Media consumers in a digital age.* New York: New York University.

Newkirk, T. (2002). *Misreading masculinity: Boys, literacy, and popular culture.* Portsmouth, NH: Heinemann.

Petracca, M. F., & Sorapure, M. (2006). *Common culture: Reading and writing about American popular culture* (2nd ed.). New York: Prentice Hall.

Sternheimer, K. (2003). *It's not the media: The truth about pop culture's influence on children.* Boulder, CO: Westview Press.

Williams, B. T. (2002). *Tuned in: Television and the teaching of writing.* Portsmouth, NH: Heinemann.

ONLINE

Advanced Media Network Anime: http://anime.advancedmn.com/index.php

American Library Association: www.ala.org

Anime Web Turnpike: www.anipike.com

Anipike.com: www.anipike.com

ChemMatters (magazine): www.chemistry.org/portal/a/c/s/1/home.html

Dragon Ball-Z: www.dragonballz.com

Everworld: http://scholastic.com/everworld

Fanfiction Glossary: www.subreality.com/glossary/terms.htm#A

Fanfiction.net: www.fanfiction.net

Fiction Alley: www.fictionalley.org

Gatekeepers: www.scholastic.com/gatekeepers

Gurl (zine): www.gurl.com

Harry Potter Fanfiction: www
.harrypotterfanfiction.com

Harry Potter Fanfiction Awards: http://
multifaceted.creative-musing.com/main.htm

Harvey Awards: www.harveyawards.org

International Association of Media Tie-In Writers:
www.iamtw.org

Jerry Spinelli (Web site): www.jerryspinelli.com

Laura Halse Anderson (Web site):
www.writerlady.com

Meg Cabot's Book Club: www.megcabotbookclub
.com

Movie Mistakes: www.moviemistakes.com

Mugglenet: www.mugglenet.com

New Prophecy Warriors: www.warriorcats.com/
content.html

No Flying, No Tights: www.noflyingnotights.com

Plays: The Drama Magazine for Young People:
www.playsmag.com

Sailor Moon Awards: http://awards.smfanfiction
.net/rules.html

Shameless (zine): www.shamelessmag.com

Stargate SG-1 Awards: www.sg1-awards.com

The Quiet World: http://thequietworld.com

24 (TV show): www.fox.com/24

References

Agosto, D. (2004). Girls and gaming: A summary of the research with implications for practice. *Teacher Librarian, 31*(3), 8–14.

Alvermann, D. E. (2001). Reading adolescents' reading identities: Looking back to see ahead. *Journal of Adolescent and Adult Literacy, 44,* 676–690.

Alvermann, D. E., & Heron, A. H. (2001). Literacy identity work: Playing to learn with popular media. *Journal of Adolescent and Adult Literacy, 45*(2), 118–122.

Alvermann, D. E., Moon, J. S., & Hagood, M. C. (1999). *Popular culture in the classroom: Teaching and researching critical media literacy.* Newark, DE: International Reading Association.

Anderson, L. H. (1999). *Speak.* New York: Farrar, Straus & Giroux.

Anderson, L. H. (2000). *Fever 1793.* New York: Simon & Schuster.

Applegate, K. A. (1999). *Everworld* series (*Search for Senna* #1). New York: Scholastic.

Ashton, V. (2006). *Confessions of a teen nanny: Rich girls.* New York: HarperCollins.

Barker, C. M. (2005). *Fairyopolis: A flower fairies journal.* New York: Fredrick Warne & Company/Penguin.

Black, R. W. (2005). Access and affiliation: The literacy and composition practices of English-language learners in an online fanfiction community. *Journal of Adolescent and Adult Literacy, 49*(2), 118–128.

Brashares, A. (2001). *The sisterhood of the traveling pants.* New York: Random House.

Bright, J. E. (2006). *Follow your heart: Your best friend's boyfriend.* New York: Scholastic.

Brigman, J., & Richardson, R. (2005). *Black Beauty.* New York: Puffin Graphics/Penguin.

Brown, J. (2006). *Crime files: Four-minute forensic mysteries.* New York: Scholastic.

Bussert, L. (2005). Comic books and graphic novels: Digital resources for an evolving form of art and literature. *College and Research Libraries, 66*(2), 103–106, 113.

Cabot, M. (2003). *Princess lessons.* New York: HarperCollins.

Cameron, V. (2003). *Clue mysteries: 15 whodunits to solve in minutes.* Philadelphia, PA: Running Press.

Campbell, K. (2001, September 13). Teens read, and advertisers see a green light. *The Christian Science Monitor,* p. 16.

Clugston, C. (2005). *Queen bee.* New York: Graphix/Scholastic.

Colbert, D. (2001). *The magical worlds of Harry Potter: A treasury of myths, legends, and fascinating facts.* Wrightsville Beach, NC: Lumina Press LLC.

Colbert, D. (2002). *The magical worlds of the Lord of the Rings: The amazing myths, legends, and facts behind the masterpiece.* New York: Berkley Books.

Colbert, D. (2005). *The magical worlds of Narnia: A treasury of myths, legends, and fascinating facts.* New York: Berkley Books.

Colbert, D. (2006). *The magical worlds of Philip Pullman: A treasury of fascinating facts.* New York: Berkley Books.

Colfer, E. (2004). *The Artemis Fowl files.* New York: Miramax.

Cover, A. B. (2005). *Macbeth.* New York: Puffin/Penguin.

Cuciz, D. (n.d.). *Interview with Alan Dean Foster.* Retrieved March 22, 2006, from http://archive.gamespy.com/legacy/interviews/afoster_a.shtm

Dahl, R. (2005). *Charlie and the chocolate factory.* New York: Knopf/Random House.

Dietz, T. L. (1998). An examination of violence and gender role portrayals in video games: Implications for gender socialization and aggressive behavior. *Sex Roles, 38,* 425–442.

Dietz, W. C. (2006). *How to novelize a game.* Retrieved March 2, 2006, from http://www.iamtw.org/art_novelizegame.html

DiTerlizzi, T., & Black, H. (2003). *The Spiderwick chronicles (The field guide #1).* New York: Simon & Schuster.

DiTerlizzi, T., & Black, H. (2005). *Notebook for fantastical observations.* New York: Simon & Schuster.

Drake, E., & Steer, D. (2003). *Dragonology: The complete book of dragons.* Cambridge, MA: Candlewick Press.

Dresang, E. T. (1999). *Radical change: Books for youth in a digital age.* New York: H. W. Wilson.

Duncan, L. (1999). *I know what you did last summer.* New York: Bantam Doubleday/Random House.

Ephron, D., & Chandler, E. (2005). *The sisterhood of the traveling pants: The official scrapbook.* New York: Delacorte/Random House.

Espenson, J. (Ed.). (2004). *Finding serenity: Anti-heroes, lost shepherds and space hookers in Joss Whedon's Firefly.* Dallas, TX: BenBella Books.

Fager, J. (Executive Producer). (2005, September 4). The echo boomers. *60 minutes* [Television broadcast]. New York: CBS News.

Funke, C. (2003). *Inkheart.* New York: Chicken House/Scholastic.

Funke, C. (2005). *Inkspell.* New York: Chicken House/Scholastic.

Gallagher, D. G., & Ruditis, P. (2004). *The power of three (charmed).* New York: Simon Spotlight Entertainment/Simon & Schuster.

Garner, G., Beck, K., & Clark, J. (1997). *The cop cookbook: Arresting recipes from the world's favorite cops, good guys, and private eyes.* Nashville, TN: Rutledge Hill Press.

Gee, J. P. (2003). *What video games have to teach us about learning and literacy.* Hampshire, England: Palgrave/Macmillan.

Genge, N. E. (1996). *The unofficial X-files companion II.* New York: Avon/HarperCollins.

Gifford, C. (2002). *So you think you know Harry Potter.* London: Hodder & Stoughton Ltd.

Gilbert, A. Y., Howe, J., Tomic, T., & Ward, H. (2005). *Wizardology: The book of the secrets of Merlin.* Cambridge, MA: Candlewick Press.

Gilden, M. (n.d.). *Are novelizations the scum of literature?* Retrieved March 2, 2006, from http://www.melgilden.com/Sampletext/EssaNovl.html

Gilden, M. (2001). *Britney Spears is a three-headed alien!* New York: ibooks/Simon & Schuster.

Goldberg, L., & Collins, M. A. (2006a). *Are tie-in writers hacks?* Retrieved March 2, 2006, from http://www.iamtw.org/art_are.html

Goldberg, L., & Collins, M. A. (2006b). *Writing a novelization.* Retrieved March 2, 2006, from http://www.iamtw.org/art_novelization.html

Gopalakrishnan, A., & Ulanoff, S. (2005). Resilient divas and incredible escapades: What a pilot survey of adolescent girls' reading preferences revealed. *SIGNAL Journal, 28*(1), 20–24.

Gragg, R. (2003). *Lewis and Clark on the trail of discovery: The journey that shaped America.* Nashville, TN: Rutledge Hill Press/Thomas Nelson.

Grayson, D. (2004). *Smallville: City.* New York: Aspect/DC Comics.

Gregory, D. (1999). *Wishing on a star.* New York: Jump at the Sun/Hyperion.

Gresh, L., & Weinberg, R. (2002). *The science of superheroes.* Hoboken, NJ: Wiley.

Harlin, R. (Writer). (1999). *Deep blue sea.* B. Berman (Producer). USA: Warner Bros.

Harp, B. (2000). *The handbook of literacy assessment and evaluation.* Norwood, MA: Christopher-Gordon.

Harris, V. J. (2005). The Cheetah Girls series: Multiracial identity, pop culture, and consumerism. In D. L. Henderson & J. P. May (Eds.), *Exploring culturally diverse literature for children and adolescents: Learning to listen in new ways* (pp. 216–228). Boston: Pearson.

Henry J. Kaiser Family Foundation. (2004, Fall). *Key Facts: Tweens, teens and magazines.* Retrieved May 24, 2006, from http://www.kff.org/entmedia/upload/Tweens-Teens-and-Magazines-Fact sheet.pdf

Hoffman, A. (2001). *Aquamarine.* New York: Scholastic.

Holder, N. (2004). *Spirited.* New York: Simon & Schuster.

Holder, N. (2006a). *Buffy the vampire slayer: Carnival of souls.* New York: Simon & Schuster.

Holder, N. (2006b). *Pretty little devils.* New York: Penguin.

Holder, N. (2007). *The rose bride: A retelling of the white bride and the black bride.* New York: Simon & Schuster.

Horowitz, A. (2001). *Alex Rider* series (*Stormbreaker* #1). New York: Philomel/Penguin.

Horowitz, A. (2005a). *Alex Rider: The gadgets.* New York: Penguin.

Horowitz, A. (2005b). *Raven's gate.* New York: Scholastic.

Horowitz, A. (2006). *Evil star.* New York: Scholastic.

Hunter, E. (2005). *Warriors: The new prophecy* series (*Midnight* #1). New York: HarperCollins.

Jacques, B. (1986). *Redwall: The legend begins.* New York: Firebird/Penguin.

Jacques, B. (2002). *The tribes of Redwall: Otters.* New York: Random House.

Jacques, B. (2005). *The Redwall cookbook.* New York: Philomel/Penguin.

Kaplan, E. B., & Cole, L. (2003). "I want to read stuff on boys": White, latina, and black girls reading *Seventeen* magazine and encountering adolescence. *Adolescence, 38*(149), 141–159.

Kennedy, M. (2006). *Tales of a Hollywood gossip queen.* New York: Berkley/Penguin.

King, J. R., & O'Brien, D. G. (2002). Adolescents' multiliteracies and their teachers' needs to know: Toward a digital detente In D. E. Alvermann (Ed.), *Adolescents and literacies in a digital world* (pp. 40–50). New York: Peter Lang.

Klise, K. (2005). *Regarding the trees.* Orlando, FL: Gulliver Books/Harcourt.

Korman, G. (2002). *Son of the mob.* New York: Hyperion.

Kronzek, A. Z., & Kronzek, E. (2001). *The sorcerer's companion: A guide to the magical world of Harry Potter.* New York: Broadway Books.

Kubo, T. (2004). *Bleach.* San Francisco, CA: Viz Media.

Labre, M. P., & Walsh-Childers, K. (2003). Friendly advice? Beauty messages in Web sites of teen magazines. *Mass Communication & Society, 6*(4), 379–396.

Lent, J. A. (2004). Far out and mundane: The mammoth world of manga. *Phi Kappa Phi Forum, 84*(3), 38–41.

McCardle, M. (2003). *Fan fiction, fandom and fanfare: What's all the fuss.* Boston: Boston University.

Mishiyama, Y. (2004). *Dragon voice.* Los Angeles, CA: Tokyopop.

Moore, A. (1988). *V for vendetta.* New York: DC Comics.

Morrell, E. (2004). *Linking literacy and popular culture: Finding connections for lifelong learning.* Norwood, MA: Christopher-Gordon.

Mulcahy, L., & Bokram, K. (2005). Rich girls: Louis Vuitton bags, mega-bucks sweet 16's and major bling aren't just for the Hilton sisters these days. Why girls everywhere suddenly want to live large. *Girl's Life.*

Nields, N. (2005). *Plastic angels.* New York: Orchard/Scholastic.

Nix, G. (1997). *The calusari.* New York: HarperTrophy/HarperCollins.

Packard, E. (1979). *Choose your own adventure: The cave of time.* New York: Bantam/Random House.

Paolini, C. (2003). *Eragon.* New York: Knopf/Random House.

Poe, E., Samuels, B. G., & Carter, B. (1995). Past perspectives and future directions: An interim analysis of twenty-five years of research on young adult literature. *The ALAN Review, 22*(2), 46–50.

Price, R., & Stern, L. (2004). *Mad libs: Survivor.* New York: Price Stern Sloan/Penguin.

Pullman, P. (1995). *His dark materials: The golden compass.* New York: Ballantine/Random House.

Pullman, P. (1997). *His dark materials: The subtle knife.* New York: Ballantine/Random House.

Pullman, P. (2000). *His dark materials: The amber spyglass.* New York: Ballantine/Random House.

Reed, G. (2005). *Frankenstein.* New York: Puffin Graphics/Penguin.

Reitman, I. (Writer). (2001). *Evolution.* J. Apple (Producer). United States: DreamWorks Distribution LLC.

Rhodes, L. K., & Shanklin, N. L. (1993). *Windows into literacy: Assessing learners K–8.* Portsmouth, NH: Heinemann.

Rosenbloom, F. (2005). *You are so not invited to my bat mitzvah.* New York: Hyperion.

Rovin, J. (1992). *Mortal kombat.* New York: Boulevard Books.

Rucker, A., & Scicolene, M. (2002). *The Sopranos family cookbook: As compiled by Artie Bucco.* New York: Warner Books/Little, Brown.

Sachar, L. (1999). *Holes.* New York: Farrar, Straus & Giroux.

Sachar, L. (2003). *Stanley Yelnats' survival guide to Camp Green Lake.* London: Bloomsbury.

Sage, A. (2005). *Magyk.* New York: Tegen/HarperCollins.

Sands, E., Harris, N., Ward, H., & Andrew, I. (2004). *Egyptology.* Cambridge, MA: Candlewick Press.

Seidler, T. (2003). *Brainboy and the deathmaster.* New York: Geringer/HarperCollins.

Seiler, A. (2003, December 16). 'rings' comes full circle. Retrieved February 27, 2006, from http://www.usatoday.com/life/movies/news/2003-12-12-lotr-main_x.htm

Short, K. G., Harste, J. C., & Burke, C. (1996). *Creating classrooms for authors and inquirers* (2nd ed.). Portsmouth, NH: Heinemann.

Silver, S. H. (2002). *A conversation with Lynn Abbey.* Retrieved March 22, 2006, from http://www.sfsite.com/11a/la139.htm

Skurnick, L. (2003). *Alias: The pursuit.* New York: Bantam/Random House.

Smith, F. (1994). *Understanding reading: A psycholinguistic analysis of reading and learning to read* (5th ed.). Hillsdale, NJ: Erlbaum.

Smith, F. (Ed.). (1973). *Psycholinguistics and reading.* New York: Holt, Rinehart and Winston.

Snicket, L. (1999). *A series of unfortunate events: The bad beginning.* New York: Scholastic.

Snicket, L. (2002). *Lemony Snicket: The unauthorized autobiography.* New York: HarperCollins.

Soto, G. (1994). *Crazy weekend.* New York: Scholastic.

Spiegelman, A. (1986). *Maus: A survivor's tale: My father bleeds.* New York: Pantheon/Random House.

Spiegelman, A. (1991). *Maus II: A survivor's tale: And here my troubles began.* New York: Pantheon/Random House.

Spinelli, J. (1990). *Maniac Magee.* New York: Little, Brown.

Spinelli, J. (1997). *The library card.* New York: Scholastic.

Spinelli, J. (2000). *Stargirl.* Knopf/Random House.

Steer, D. A., Lubber, W. C., Gilbert, A. Y., & Ward, H. (2006). *Pirateology: The pirate hunter's companion.* Cambridge, MA: Candlewick Press.

Vaughan, B. K. (2006). *Runaways, volume 1.* New York: Marvel Comics.

Velde, V. V. (2002). *Heir apparent.* Orlando, FL: Magic Carpet Books/Harcourt.

VOA Ziegesar, C. (2002). *Gossip girl.* New York: Little, Brown.

Wallace, F. H. (2005). Expanding your Harry Potter library. *Georgia Journal of Reading, 28*(2), 8–10.

Waters, G. (Ed.). (2004). *The plot thickens . . . Harry Potter investigated by fans for fans.* Niles, IL: Wizarding World Press.

Weinstein, L. R. (2006). *Girl stories*. New York: Henry Holt.

Whytock, C. (2003). *My cup runneth over: The life of Angelica Cookson Potts*. New York: Simon Pulse/Simon & Schuster.

Whytock, C. (2004). *My saucy stuffed ravioli: The life of Angelica Cookson Potts*. New York: Simon & Schuster.

Wiseman, R. (2002). *Queen bees and wannabees*. London: Piatkus.

Wittlinger, E. (2004). *Heart on my sleeve*. New York: Simon & Schuster.

Worthy, J., Moorman, M., & Turner, M. (1999). What Johnny likes to read is hard to find in school. *Reading Research Quarterly, 34*, 12–27.

Xu, S. H., Perkins, R. S., & Zunich, L. O. (2005). *Trading cards to comic strips: Popular culture texts and literacy learning in Grades K–8*. Newark, DE: International Reading Association.

Yang, G. L. (2006). *American born Chinese*. New York: First Second/Roaring Brook Press.

Yoshinaga, F. (2005). *Antique bakery*. Gardena, CA: Digital Manga.

C H A P T E R   **1 3**

YA Literature and Writing

Motivating Young Writers in the Real World

By James Blasingame

Introduction

Maria[1] has been writing all night; in fact, she has been pounding on her computer keyboard as fast as her fingers could go ever since she bolted down the dinner of warmed-up leftovers set out by her stepfather when her mother was called back to the hospital for a patient emergency. It's now 12:00 a.m., and she is no closer to finishing her homework for English class than she was when she sat down at the computer five hours ago. A half-written essay on "Fitzgerald's characterization of the protagonist in *The Great Gatsby*" and a set of grammar and usage pages (11th-grade level = orange book) await her attention, but she will probably finish one during lunch tomorrow and the other in the car on the way to school. What she is writing right now is just too appealing to abandon.

Maria (online persona/name: Bella in Baltimore) is online and sharing her thoughts and feelings about *Eclipse,* the latest book in the *Twilight* series from Stephenie Meyer, with her peers around the world. These books are about Bella (Isabella Marie Swan), a teenager from Phoenix, Arizona, who has gone to Forks, Washington, to spend time with her divorced father. Bella has a lab partner named Edward. Edward is a vampire. Bella and Edward are in love.

Maria is also in love with Edward, the vampire character, or maybe with Jacob, another young and handsome character from the first book, who turns out to be a werewolf in the second book. More than this, Maria is in love with reading, and even more than that, Maria is in love with talking about the books and about how they make her feel. Opportunities to talk face-to-face with others who are also *Twilight* aficionados are available once or twice a week at school, but the opportunity to talk online with others who are in love with Edward (or maybe Jacob) is always there, 24 hours a day. Specifically, Maria turns to Twilight Lexicon, a fansite (short for online fan Web site) where aficionados of Stephenie Meyer come for information and to interact. There are 120 fansites all over the world (and in eight languages) listed on the official Web site of the author of the *Twilight* series. (More on fansites in Box 13.1.)

On this particular evening Maria, aka Bella in Baltimore, has been writing back and forth with a group of *Twilight* readers on a message board hosted on the Twilight Lexicon fansite. The message board section Maria is participating in is called Sparkling in the Sun, a reference to the fact that the vampires in the *Twilight* series avoid public appearance in sunlight because their skin

---

[1]Maria is a fictitious construction. A-S-H-L-E-Y and all the information about online fansites and message boards are completely factual.

Stephenie Meyer's *Twilight* series, a national bestseller, appeals to both teens and adults.

Box 13.1   A Few Popular Fansites and the Books That Inspired Them

A fansite is a Web site created and maintained by fans of an actor, author, movie, book, video game, band, or any other element of pop culture. A fansite revolves around its subject and provides tangential resources that may be of interest to fans. This information may include such things as biographies of authors or actors, photographs, maps of real or fictitious places, and news of recent or upcoming events. Fansites are generally not the creation of the copyright holder of a book or movie and so are generally labeled "unofficial." Official Web sites of authors or actors sometimes have links to fansites of which they approve.

A fansite is a social phenomenon in that it is the construction of a large group with a shared interest. The actual Web site is often created by a core of people who are both fans of the site's subject and also knowledgeable about Web technology. Much of what appears on the site, however, is created by anonymous fans (identifying themselves as individuals by some sort of Web moniker, such as "JT in NYC") who participate in online discussions on various topics, called "discussion threads" or "fanfiction," which consist of stories and sequels written by fans but based on the original characters and plots that inspired the fansite. A fan of Harry Potter, for example, might participate in discussions about Hermione's intellectual and emotional maturation compared to her male classmates, or write a short story that takes place at Hogwarts and has any or all of J. K. Rowling's characters or even new additional characters beyond what Rowling imagined. A few popular fansites are described here.

Twilight Lexicon (*Twilight,* by Stephenie Meyer) at www.twilightlexicon.com/

Continued

Box 13.1   A Few Popular Fansites and the Books That Inspired Them   *Continued*

There are 120 fansites from all over the world and in eight languages listed on the official Stephenie Meyer Web site. One of the most complex and most commonly frequented by fans is Twilight Lexicon. Twilight Lexicon has sections on vampire mythology, character biographies, chapter discussion, places in the book, werewolf mythology, a biography of Stephenie Meyer, information about, the production (especially casting) of a movie based on the first book, news of the author's book tours, merchandise, and a discussion forum for fans.

Mugglenet.com (*Harry Potter,* by J. K. Rowling) at www.mugglenet.com

This may very well be the most complex fansite on the Internet, just as J. K. Rowling's story of a boy in England who discovers he is actually a powerful wizard is the most popular story in the world today. It includes biographies of the people who founded and maintain the Web site (most of whom are teenagers) and a long list of content offerings, including the following: job openings (to help run the fansite), links to other Harry Potter Web sites, competitions, "Wall of Shame" (a collection of negative e-mails about the Harry Potter books and movies), e-newsletter, photo gallery, MuggleShop (Harry Potter merchandise), MuggleCast (for downloading Harry Potter related podcasts), Advertise on MuggleNet, detailed information about the most recent (and final) book *Deathly Hallows,* letters to the editor (submitted online), "The Book Trolley" (other books recommended by fans), "Official Forums" (discussion boards) with various themes and a chat room with strict guidelines, detailed information about each movie (cast members and their biographies, for example), and fanfiction (an online literary publication where fans can submit their own Harry Potter stories).

The Secret Hour (*The Midnighters #1: The Secret Hour,* by Scott Westerfeld) at www.geocities.com/thesecrethour/bixby.html

The first in Scott Westerfeld's series of books about a group of teenagers, all born at the stroke of midnight, who have magical powers, including the ability to inhabit a 25th hour of the day not available to others. This Web site includes a section where enthusiasts may submit their art, stories, essays, or other creations centered on the book, a movie casting call where fans can suggest the best actors and actresses to play the various characters if a movie is made, Bixby blog (a blog for narratives and pictures about the real Bixby, Oklahoma, where the novel takes place), a set of downloadable icons and posters for use by the media, a personality inventory instrument intended to reveal which character a fan is most like, individual Web pages for each of the major characters (Dess, Jonathan, Melissa, Jessica, and Rex) with fictional biographies, quotations from them, and discussion forums for fans.

Shur' Tugal (*Eragon,* by Christopher Paolini) at www.shurtugal.com/

Eragon is the story of a fantasy world in which a teenage farm boy, named Eragon, discovers he is a Dragon Rider when his family farm is destroyed by the evil minions of a ruthless overlord. Riding a beautiful sapphire dragon, Eragon seeks to restore justice and order in his world. This fansite includes sections for downloading podcasts (taped programs that can be played on an Apple iPod), a fanfiction page for submitting fan written spin-offs from the book, a chat room, galleries of photos and artwork, information and pictures from the movie made of *Eragon,* a calendar of the author's appearances, a fan of the week, and a list of related links.

sparkles iridescently (but they don't die), betraying their true identities. The discussion topic is listed as "Discussion on the various characters throughout the books." One of the discussion topics reads "Which character do you relate to the most?" A perusal of the postings reveals that 53 percent of the discussion participants from around the world (471 people) have identified the series' heroine, Bella, as the character to whom they most relate. A-S-H-L-E-Y, from Canton, Ohio, explains:

> Its all bella! And its nothing like having a few common interests here and thereand looking alike. I see my world through bella's eyes. And thats the biggest reason why i love this book is because i have such a connection! I feel alot like Bella.

[A-S-H-L-E-Y goes on to quote from *Twilight*, pages 9 and 10].

> Bella says:
> "Maybe the truth was that I didn't relate well to people, period. Even my mother, who I was closer to than anyone else on the planet, was never in harmony with me, never exactly on the same page. Sometimes I wondered if I was seeing the same things through my eyes that the rest of the world was seeing through theirs. Maybe there was a glitch in my brain."

If it weren't for the mistakes in conventions—a convention of its own in online writing, the switch at this point in the posting from Bella's thoughts to A-S-H-L-E-Y's thoughts would be almost unnoticeable:

> I feel so out of place sometimes in this world that i feel soO alone and as if im the only one here. I have to sit down and run things through my head to see if there actully happening and if people see and feel what i feel.
> Im a big thinker and spend alot of time pondering of life and how things work and what people think and stuff like that! I love to talk about stuff soO send me a messege if you wan't more!
> But about bella . . . I feel such a connection . . . as if she is me and i am her!
> *(posted April 26, 2006, retrieved September 15, 2007, from*
> *www.twilightlexicon.com/forum/viewtopic.php?t=246)*

At this point it is nearly impossible to ignore that in the current standards-driven, No Child Left Behind environment, A-S-H-L-E-Y's posting (albeit without editing for conventions) seems to be right on target for meeting many of the most common writing standards and benchmarks used by state departments of education across the country. The federally funded Compendium of Content Standards and Benchmarks for K–12 Education, created by the Mid-continent Research for Education and Learning (2007, also known as the Mid-continent Regional Educational Laboratory), is a template for states as they create their own standards. Standard 1, Level IV (Grades 9–12), Benchmark 12, for Language Arts, Writing, Literary Style and Techniques States:

Language Arts
  Standard 1. Uses the general skills and strategies of the writing process

  Benchmark 12. Writes in response to literature (e.g., suggests an interpretation; recognizes possible ambiguities, nuances, and complexities in a text; interprets passages of a novel in terms of their significance to the novel as a whole; focuses on the theme of a literary work; explains concepts found in literary works; examines literature from several critical perspectives; understands author's stylistic devices and effects created; analyzes use of imagery and language)

Meanwhile, poor Jay Gatsby (aka James Gatz) languishes on the seat of the family SUV in the hospital parking lot where Maria left her *Great Gatsby* book after her mother drove her home from school.

The intrinsic motivation real teenagers like A-S-H-L-E-Y obviously feel to write genuinely and from the heart about their favorite characters and passages from young adult literature begs the question: Are the books in the *Twilight* series, or even young adult books in general, quality literature worth applying skills of literary analysis, or are they just juvenile pulp fiction with little redeeming social or literary value? Patty Campbell is editor of Scarecrow Press (which specializes in young adult literature) and winner of the American Library Association's Grolier Award for distinguished service to young adults and reading and the ALAN Award for service to the adolescent literature community from the Assembly on Literature of the National Council of Teachers of English. In her review of *Twilight*, Campbell (n.d.) states: "The precision and delicacy of Meyer's writing lifts this wonderful novel beyond the limitations of the horror genre to a place among the best of YA fiction."

Campbell, who is also a past president of the National Council of Teachers of English Assembly on Literature for Adolescents, provides her definition of exactly what young adult literature is:

> The central theme of most YA literature is becoming an adult, finding the answer to "Who am I and what am I going to do about it?" No matter what events are going on in the book, accomplishing that task is really what the book is about, and in the climactic moment the resolution of the external conflict is linked to a realization for the protagonist that helps shape an adult identity. (Campbell, 2000, p. 486)

For the young readers writing to each other online through the Twilight Lexicon fansite, "Who am I?" seems to be a final question in a set of questions that begins with discussing the characters and situations in the books but ends with the readers' discovering truths about themselves. Writing pedagogists acknowledge this type of writing as high-level cognitive activity. In his quintessential survey of writing pedagogy, *Teaching Writing as Reflective Practice*, George Hillocks (1995) places various types of writing along a continuum on which writing of a low cognitive level involves acts of summary, just "reiterat[ing]" what they [students] had found in some other source," the most common type of writing that Britton, Burgess, Martin, Mcleod, and Rosen (1975) found in most English schools (p. 9). Hillocks (1995) goes on to describe the writing at the other end of the continuum (higher-level writing) as writing he believes must include "meaning making" and that may be the result of acts of inquiry and discovery, sometimes including subsets as rigorous as "observation, interpretation, imagining, hypothesizing, testing, evaluating and so forth" along the path to making meaning (p. 13).

Hillocks (1995) also cites research about student engagement and what have been called "flow experiences" (p. 20). He revisits the work of Csikszentmihalyi and Larson (1984) and Csikszentmihalyi, Rathunde, and Whalen (1993), in which students were found to successfully engage in "difficult and challenging activities in athletics, art and academics" under certain circumstances to the point of such high concentration that they were oblivious to their surroundings (p. 20). According to Hillocks (1995), these circumstances included such things as enjoyment, interest, and immediate feedback (p. 20). Hillocks emphasizes Csikszentmihalyi and colleagues' highlighting of the contrast between video/computer games, which would seem to provide the required circumstances, and most classrooms, which would seem to be passive learning environments where actual participation, interest, and feedback are infrequent (pp. 20–21). Young people love activities in which they get to participate actively, activities that deal with their lives (directly or indirectly), and activities that provide immediate audience or peer response or feedback.

Harnessing Motivation to Think, Feel, and Write

The popularity of Stephenie Meyer's *Twilight* series (2005) teen vampire books has a lot to do with how easily young readers can identify with the characters, especially with the protagonist, Bella, whom the author puts into situations through which the reader can vicariously experience romance, excitement, and even danger. This is exactly what makes writing about their personal connections in online discussions so appealing to young readers too. It's about them, it's about their feelings, it's about what they think about the characters and stories—their reactions to the exciting and dangerous situations they experience vicariously—and the feedback is immediate. No wonder teenagers can spend hours online writing back and forth with people they only know by screen names (such as A-S-H-L-E-Y). These are "flow experiences" for them, coming at a time when their biggest inquiry in life is "Who am I?"

It is for this very reason—its propensity for helping teens answer the question, "Who am I?"—that young adult literature is the perfect catalyst for combining the developmental needs of adolescents with the experience of writing. In fact, writing will enhance their understanding of their reading and help them process it at the same time that just the right book can help young readers improve their writing skills. As experienced English language arts teachers know, reading and writing are two sides of the same coin. Students can extend their reading experience through writing and make even deeper meaning of what they read. Meaningful experiences with reading and writing are what our classrooms should be all about, and young adult literature is the perfect text for meaning-making among adolescents. Each young reader brings a different set of life experiences to the reading of a given text and will arrive at different interpretations, interpretations that can help that reader understand his or her own life. This interaction with text must be encouraged, facilitated, and nurtured. Louise Rosenblatt (1956), credited as the founder of reader-response theory and an advocate for a transactional view of reading, emphasized the teacher's role in helping students engage with their reading, saying "Above all, students need to be helped to have personally satisfying and personally meaningful transactions with literature"

(p. 66). Rosenblatt and other reader-response theorists believe that young readers should learn how to make their own meaning of their reading rather than being forced to memorize a meaning dictated by a literary scholar, a teaching approach that may actually be counterproductive to improving students' literacy. (See Box 13.2 for additional information on reader-response theory.) As unique individuals, young readers need not only freedom to arrive at their own understandings of an author's text but also effective means for expressing this individual meaning or understanding.

Box 13.2   Incorporating Reader-Response Theory in Teaching Writing

Reader-response theory gives us a starting point for the use of young adult literature in teaching writing. This theory holds that readers should be free to make their own meaning of a text, and I contend that writing is the ultimate and final vehicle for young readers to make that meaning after they have processed the reading through thinking, discussing, rethinking, and taking writing through the various steps in the process.

Louise Rosenblatt is easily credited with inventing the very concept of reader-response. Her seminal work, *Literature as Exploration,* first appeared in 1938, and is now in its fifth edition (Rosenblatt, 1995). *The Reader, the Text, the Poem: The Transactional Theory of the Literary Work,* also an important work, is most recently reprinted by Southern Illinois University Press (Rosenblatt, 1994). Rosenblatt continued to attend conferences and give talks about reader-response right up through her 100th birthday tribute at the 2004 National Council of Teachers of English Convention in Indianapolis, Indiana, three months before her death.

Rosenblatt rejected the idea (begun by the New Critics and still used by many high school English teachers) that a text (book, poem, whatever the written document) has one universal (true) meaning and that this meaning resides within the text itself, independent of the author's intention or the author's cultural bias or the reader's interpretation. According to Rosenblatt, a reader is required and that reader participates in a "transaction" with the writer's text in which the meaning is arrived at. Rosenblatt's theory is also called transactional theory because it is in the transaction between the reader and the text that meaning is made.

Robert Probst further emphasized that literature should be experienced *by* the reader and not analyzed *for* the reader. In his influential work *Adolescent Literature: Response and Analysis* (1984), Probst says,

> When literature is *read,* rather than worked upon, it draws into events and invites us to reflect upon our perceptions of them. . . . Literature . . . allows us both to experience and to reflect upon experience, and thus invites the self indulgence of those who seek to understand themselves and the world around them. (p. 4)

If, as George Hillocks (1995) proposes, writing at a high cognitive level involves "meaning making" from the writer's interaction with life experiences (p. 13), then young readers should be facilitated in incorporating the writing process into making their own meaning of their reading as reader-response requires.

"Meaningful transactions," as Rosenblatt (1995) calls them, can come about through the students' writing about their reading, but just as Rosenblatt suggested that the meaning doesn't happen until the text and reader come together, so also much of the meaning a young writer can make does not happen until pen is put to paper (or fingers to keyboard). Meaning-making is not only the province of Rosenblatt and reader-response theorists, but, as previously mentioned, is also the measure of writing used by George Hillocks (1995), who prizes acts of writing most in which we "begin with a question, search our memories for what we already know about this, compare our new observations to that prior knowledge" (pp. 102–103) and go on to form hypotheses, which we test in our imaginations, initially. Ultimately, Hillocks points out, the writer must formulate an interpretation of any new information, as well as discrepancies between old information and new, warranting a powerful act of imagination, enabling the writer to arrive at an idea he or she has never held before (p. 105).

Ideally, then, as adolescents read and write, they will, as Hillocks says, interpret new information, compare their interpretations to old information, and arrive at new ideas. Young adult literature provides the perfect fodder for this because it is most often about what they find most interesting: their own lives, the very dilemmas that teen writers or their peers are facing on an almost daily basis (or glamorous allegories for those dilemmas). Although she is not specifically referring to writing, Katherine Paterson, winner of the National Book Award and the Newbery Medal, makes this case very strongly:

> That's what books do for you. They give you practice doing difficult things in life. In a way, they prepare you for things that you are going to have to face or someone you know and care about is going through. They sort of help you know how it feels—though not exactly. It is the remove that gives you a deep pleasure rather than a total pain. (Scholastic, Inc., 2005. p. 1)

To make the most of the opportunity provided for real, meaningful writing by using young adult literature in the classroom, three knowledge bases are helpful: (1) a strong understanding of adolescent developmental psychology, (2) knowledge of best practice in writing instruction, and (3) a broad knowledge of what's available in young adult literature and how to find and evaluate its usefulness.

The Intersection between Adolescence and Writing

Adolescence is not just an intermediate placeholder between the stages of childhood and adulthood when young people learn a corresponding set of intermediate academic skills. Emotional and intellectual growth occur at dizzying speeds at this age, and formative events are happening in rapid-fire succession. Personalities are developing, values and beliefs are forming, and emotions are running very close to the surface, as any veteran middle grades teacher will attest to. It is perhaps the most complicated developmental time of life in the human experience, and understanding this time in order to work with it (rather than against it) is crucial to planning and implementing effective curriculum and instructional strategies (see Box 13.3). Teaching writing to adolescents will be most effective, as well as most beneficial to young learners, when their emotional, moral, and psychological development are taken into consideration and even harnessed as motivating forces to inspire their writing.

Box 13.3   A Few Resources on Adolescent Psychological Development

Adams, G. R., & Berzonsky, M. B. (EDs.). (2003). *Blackwell handbook of adolescence.* Malden, MA: Blackwell.

Body Image and Health Task Force. (1994). The Ohio State University. Retrieved December 6, 2007, from http://ohioline .osu.edu/hyg-fact/5000/5238.html

Carnegie Council on Adolescent Development. (1995). *Great transitions: Preparing adolescents for a new century.* New York: Carnegie.

Csikszentmihalyi, M., & Larson, R. (1984). *Being adolescent: Conflict and growth in the teenage years.* New York: Basic Books.

Erikson, E. H. (1964). *Insight and responsibility.* New York: W. W. Norton.

Erikson, E. H. (1968). *Identity: Youth and crisis.* New York: W. W. Norton.

Freedman, R. J. (1984). Reflections on beauty as it relates to health in adolescent females. *Women and Health, 9*(2/3), 29–45.

Kohlberg, L. (1981). *Essays on moral development.* San Francisco: Harper & Row.

Kohlberg, L. (1984). *The psychology of moral development: The nature and validity of moral stages.* San Francisco: Harper & Row.

Mazzarella, S. R. (Ed.). (2005). *Girl wide web; girls, the Internet, and the negotiation of identity.* New York: Peter Lang.

Moshman, D. (2005). *Adolescent psychological development: Rationality, morality, and identity.* Mahwah, NJ: Erlbaum.

Pajares, F., & Urdan, T. (2006). *Self-efficacy beliefs of adolescents.* Greenwich, CT: Information Age.

Piaget, J., & Inhelder, B. (1969). *The psychology of the child.* New York: Basic Books.

Pressley, M., & McCormick, C. B. (2007). *Child and adolescent development for educators.* New York: Guilford Press.

Stringer, S. A. (1997). *Conflict and connection: The psychology of young adult literature.* Portsmouth, NH: Boynton/Cook.

Sylvester, R., (2007). *The adolescent brain: Reaching for autonomy.* Thousand Oaks, CA: Corwin Press.

It may be true that many young writers do not dance with joy when they hear the words "writing assignment" at school, but under the right circumstances, even outside of school, they often choose to write and will write with enthusiasm and enjoyment. The writing must be an authentic form of communication for them, however, meaning that it must serve their purposes or meet their needs rather than meet the objectives of a curriculum they may find meaningless. Young people do have something to say to the world and a powerful urge to say it, whether it is expressing an opinion about popular culture in an online book review, concert recap, or video game evaluation, or defining and describing themselves to their peers in an online social networking site such as MySpace or Facebook. Students frequenty write in these genres and write with a feverish passion. Flow experiences with writing happen naturally outside of school all the time.

Less than one month after the release date of J. K. Rowling's seventh bestselling novel about the boy wizard, *Harry Potter and the Deathly Hallows (2007),* 2,178 reviews had been posted on amazon.com. All of these were not written by adolescents, but given that *Publishers Weekly* judges the appropriate reading audience age of this book to be between 9 and 12 years, it is reasonable to assume that the majority were. Not only did readers submit thousands of reviews, but these reviews themselves elicit comments, which are posted on amazon.com and attached to the appropriate review. The reading and writing connection couldn't be stronger than in this situation where writers read, then write, then read what someone else has written in response, and write again in reply to that person.

For this tech-savvy generation, the Internet is often an environment in which they choose to read and write, including the contributions they make to Wikipedia, an online, interactive encyclopedia to which anyone may submit an article, make an addition, or edit an inaccuracy. Wikipedia began in 2001 and by 2006 was "generating more traffic daily than MSNBC. com and the online versions of the *Times* and the *Wall Street Journal* combined" (Schiff, 2006, p. 1). Although Wikipedia founder Jimmy Wales balked at the suggestion by *New York Times* writer Jonathan Dee that a majority of the people among the "6.8 million registered users worldwide" who were contributing to the material on Wikipedia were not adults (Dee, 2007, pp. 1–2), anecdotal evidence suggests that young writers are indeed large contributors as in the case of the entry featured on the Wikipedia front page after an alleged terrorist attack on Fort Dix was filed and edited on May 8, 2007:

> Matthew Gruen—expanded and corrected . . . ultimately shaping it into a respectable, balanced and even footnoted 50-line account of that day's major development in the war on terror. By the time he was done, "2007 Fort Dix Attack Plot" was featured on Wikipedia's front page. Finally, around midnight, Gruen left a note on the site saying, "Off to bed," and the next morning he went back to his junior year of high school. (p. 1)

According to Dee, Gruen was 16 years old at the time.

Further evidence that adolescents will write when appropriate motivation exists is their creation and updating of personal blogs (blog is a portmanteau of "web" and "log").

> Of the world's approximately 38 million "blogs," or self-published Web pages, 52.8 percent belong to those age 19 or younger, according to survey data from the Perseus Co., a maker of Web-surveying software. By year's end, the firm expects the total number of blogs on the Web to reach 53.4 million. (MacDonald, 2005, p. 1)

A variation on blogging, MySpace, is also growing, according to *USA Today* columnist on Internet trends, Janet Kornblum (2005):

> The booming *MySpace,* a hybrid site that allows people to post their personal interests, write blogs, put up video and set up ways to communicate with their friends. That site has exploded to 34 million users in just two years—and is dominated by 14- to 34-year-olds. (p. 1)

According to Kornblum, teens use blogs "to do what they once did through personal diaries, phone conversations, and hangout sessions: cementing friendships with classmates, seeking new friends, venting, testing social limits, getting support, and getting all emo ("highly emotional" in blog-speak)" (p. 1).

Writing book reviews for amazon.com, creating and editing entries on Wikipedia, blogging, and using social networking Web sites are typical free-time activities that illustrate how earnestly young adults will use writing as a means for expressing themselves when the medium and the writing act meet their needs. These needs might be separated into two categories: (1) the *emotional, psychological,* and *social needs* of the individual writer—the needs that will drive that person to write; and (2) the *writing needs* of that individual—the situations and provisions that will best facilitate that person in the act of writing well.

Understanding this first set of needs is crucial to the thoughtful planning of a successful writing curriculum for teens because this understanding will enable teachers to develop writing activities that match those needs. These needs walk hand in hand with emotional and moral growth. In terms of moral development, adolescents make the transition from childhood to adulthood as they form consciences that operate and change their operations as they mature. According to noted developmental psychologist Lawrence Kohlberg (1981), as the individual moves through life, moral development, or conscience formation, advances through stages in which the motivation for moral decisions evolves from very simple, immediate concerns, such as punishment or personal benefit, to abstract or deferred benefit to humanity. Reading and writing tasks that deal with this moral development, especially when the topic is a complicated moral dilemma, hit adolescents where they live. In the complicated world in which they live, they are being asked to make moral choices often, if not constantly. The psychological pressure this places them under is not something to be underestimated or minimized, but rather should be acknowledged and accommodated through learning activities that will help them to process their developing beliefs and values in a safe environment that will not punish them for making the wrong, or the right, choices.

Just as Kohlberg arrived at stages of moral development, noted developmental psychologist Erik Erickson (1968) arrived at eight stages of social development, which he named according to sets of tensions between two polar opposite states of psychological development that he believed most human beings experience. The stage that is most relevant for anyone working with adolescents is Stage 5, which Erickson called "Identity vs. Role Confusion" and assigned to approximately ages 12 to 18. According to Erickson, who viewed this as the most important stage, this is when children ask the question "Who am I?" He coined the phrase identity crisis in referring to this stage. The individual attempts to determine personal beliefs, values, and roles in life such as gender roles and occupational roles. The successful resolution of each of the previous developmental conflicts affects the teenager's success in resolving this identity crisis stage. Here again, as with Kohlberg's theories, the importance of young people successfully answering the questions posed in Erickson's Stage 5 should not be underestimated, and learning activities that provide them with a safe means for doing so are crucial.

Sharon Stringer, Youngstown State University professor of psychology, applies Kohlberg and Erickson as rationale for the use of Robert Cormier's acclaimed novels *The Chocolate War* (1974), *Beyond the Chocolate War* (1985), *The Bumblebee Flies Anyway* (1983), *After the First Death* (1979), *I Am the Cheese* (1977), *and Tunes for Bears to Dance To* (1992) in which protagonists face a multitude of problems that reflect the very crises that Kohlberg and Erickson describe:

> Research indicates that self esteem decreases during early adolescence, particularly for young women (Atwater, 1992). Adolescents' idealism coincides with their enhanced sense of uniqueness, self consciousness, and critical thinking. Combined with the increase in family conflict during early adolescence, these changes heighten adolescents' need for peer approval. Conformity to the peer group peaks at approximately twelve to fourteen years of age (Steinberg, 1993). (Stringer, 1994, p. 27)

A Philosophy for Teaching Writing

In his work *Assessing Writers* (2005), Carl Anderson addresses the first group of needs—emotional, psychological, and social needs—when he sets the goal of teaching students to become "lifelong writers" (p. 15). Anderson explains that in order for young people to become lifelong writers, we must help them understand that writing can fulfill various purposes in their lives, and he gives examples of purposes for which a young writer might choose to put pencil to paper (or fingers to keyboard): "He might write to make sense of life's experiences. She might write to teach others about her passions. He might write to try to correct an injustice" (p. 16).

Anderson further describes the nature of a lifelong writer as someone who "understands that writing is an act of communication and thus writes for real audiences" (p. 16). Adolescents are searching for the tools to give them some sense of power over their world, power to make the world stop and listen to what they have to say, power to figure out what it is they have to say, and power to make some sense out of life. Writing can be that tool, and writing instruction can benefit immensely from harnessing the young writer's need to find avenues for self-expression, for voicing opinions and feelings, and for making meaning of the chaos that is teenage life.

Understanding the second set of needs, the writing needs of the individual writer, is also paramount for success because this informs how the teacher goes about setting up a classroom that will make the students' writing experiences successful ones. Ralph Fletcher, author of *What a Writer Needs* (1993), addresses the second group of needs, the writing needs of the individual, on his Web site, listing some of these needs and conditions as time to write, personal choice of what to write about, interpersonal interaction, response from an audience, and a payoff of some kind (Fletcher, n.d., p. 1).

Not only do Hillocks, Fletcher, and Anderson's tenets dovetail perfectly with what is known about adolescent developmental psychology, but anecdotal evidence of engaged young writers also provides further support.

Think of A-S-H-L-E-Y, the young woman writing in the online discussion on the fansite Twilight Lexicon about her identification with Bella, the protagonist in Stephenie Meyer's novel, *Twilight* (2005). Her writing is surely, as Anderson (2005) says, an attempt to make sense of her life, as well as a means for telling "others about her passions" (p. 16). As she writes about the parallels and similarities between her own personality and Bella's, she seems to be discovering things about herself, addressing some layer of the question "Who am I?" when she writes, "Im a big thinker and spend alot of time pondering of life and how things work and what people think and stuff like that!" This self-appraisal seems to fit Hillocks's (1995) requirement that authentic, high-cognitive level writing include inquiry, discovery, and meaning-making. It also fits Hillocks's acknowledgment that immediate feedback is crucial to motivation as found by Csikszentmihalyi et al. (1993); in fact, in this case the feedback is directly invited by the writer, who says, "I love to talk about stuff soO send me a messege if you wan't more!" This surely fulfills Anderson's (2005) requirement that writing be an act of communication with a real audience, and also Fletcher's (1993) call for choice, interpersonal interaction, and the payoff of an audience response.

Returning to the idea of a reading to writing connection, teachers can best help students grow as writers by providing them with experiences in which they not only make meaning of their reading but also make meaning in their own lives. Writing can serve as the perfect tool for this task provided the process includes inquiry, discovery, and meaning-making. The best books for facilitating this process will be those that provide young readers and writers with the material to make meaning in their own lives as they relate to their reading.

Young Adult Literature, Adolescence, and Best Practices for Teaching Writing

The best books for writing springboards are those that speak most directly to the students' life experience and provide fertile text for inquiry, discovery, and meaning-making. The topics of these best books are likely to reflect the dilemmas and obstacles that are hallmarks of adolescent development or reflect the diverse realities that young people face. As dark as his books often are, Robert Cormier, for example, seems to speak directly to the life experience of a great number of teenagers, and his popularity is astounding. *The Chocolate War* (1974), perhaps Cormier's most famous work, is the story of a Jerry Renault, a high school student who finds himself pinned between personal choices of conformity (in the form of a submission to school authority figures and student bullies) or independence (which comes with a high price). Jerry's dilemma and choices resonate deeply with young people, and as readers they quickly engage with the book and identify with him. Jerry chooses to make hard choices and accept the consequences when he "Dare[s] to Disturb the Universe," as the poster in his room says. Hundreds of thousands of young readers have vicariously experienced Jerry's dilemma, his choices, and the brutal consequences since the book came out in 1974, safely weighing the pros and cons of Jerry's decision and perhaps judging for themselves what they would have done and what they may do in similar situations in their own future. A longtime friend of Robert Cormier, Dr. John H. Bushman, Professor Emeritus from the University of Kansas, brings the topic of interacting with young adult literature back to the need of young readers to make meaning not just of their reading but also of their own lives:

> The themes that this emerging genre offers are realistic to the conflicts and struggles that young adults face as they develop their sense of identity, place in the world, and their sense of what is right and wrong. Reading and sharing how other teenagers face conflicts can open avenues and alternatives to methods of dealing with their own problems. Reading about other teenagers can help make sense of their own lives. (Bushman, 2000)

In their article "Moral Choices: Building a Bridge between YA Literature and Life," Bushman and co-author Shelly McNerny (2004) suggest categorizing young adult literature into "four main areas of [what Kohlberg called] adolescent moral reasoning: identity exploration, relationships with adults, relationships with peers, and the idea of social responsibility" (pp. 62–63). These categories work well for identifying books that provide good springboards for writing, although modification of the categories to (1) family relationships: traditional, nontraditional, functional, dysfunctional, or otherwise; (2) peer relationships; (3) relationships with and within society; and (4) search for self will make the identification even simpler. This becomes a useful framework for evaluating books for use in the writing classroom. The titles of books that fit well in these categories are too numerous to list, but a few proven ones in each category are provided in Box 13.4.

Box 13.4   Books That Explore Areas of Adolescent Moral Reasoning

Family Relationships

Armageddon Summer by Bruce Coville and Jane Yolen. Orlando, FL: Harcourt, 1998.

Chinese Handcuffs by Chris Crutcher. New York: Greenwillow Books, 1989.

Dark Sons by Nikki Grimes. New York: Jump at the Sun, 2005.

The First Part Last by Angela Johnson. New York: Simon & Schuster, 2003.

Heaven by Angela Johnson. New York: Simon & Schuster, 1998.

The Lone Ranger and Tonto Fistfight in Heaven by Sherman Alexie. New York: Atlantic Monthly Press, 1993.

Lord of the Deep by Graham Salisbury. New York: Delacorte, 2001.

Margaux with an X by Ron Koertge. New York: Candlewick Press, 2004.

Miracle's Boys by Jacqueline Woodson. New York: Putnam, 2000.

My Own True Name by Pat Mora. Houston, TX: Arte Publico, 2000.

Peer Relationships

The Bully by Paul Langan. West Berlin, NJ: Townsend Press, 2002.

Godless by Pete Hautman. New York: Simon & Schuster, 2004.

Continued

Box 13.4   Books That Explore Areas of Adolescent Moral Reasoning   *Continued*

The Gospel According to Larry by Janet Tashjian. New York: Holt, 2001.

Let Sleeping Freshmen Lie by David Lubar. New York: Dutton, 2005

Running Loose by Chris Crutcher. New York: Greenwillow Books, 1983.

The Sisterhood of the Traveling Pants by Ann Brashares. New York: Delacorte, 2001.

Someone to Love Me by Anne Schraff. West Berlin, NJ: Townsend Press, 2002.

Speak by Laurie Halse Anderson. New York: Farrar, Straus and Giroux, 1999.

Twists and Turns by Janet McDonald. New York: Farrar, Straus and Giroux, 2003.

Weedflower by Cynthia Kadohata. New York: Atheneum, 2006.

Relationships with and within Society

47 by Walter Mosley. New York: Little Brown, 2005.

Buried Onions by Gary Soto. Orlando, FL: Harcourt, 1997.

California Blue by David Klass. New York: Scholastic, 1994.

Feed by M.T. Anderson. New York: Candlewick Press, 2002.

Habibi by Naomi Shihab Nye. New York: Simon Pulse, 1999.

The Land by Mildred D. Taylor. New York: Phyllis Fogelman Books, 2001.

Mississippi Trial, 1955 by Chris Crowe. New York: Phyllis Fogelman Books, 2002.

Number the Stars by Lois Lowry. Boston: Houghton Mifflin, 1989.

Rain Is Not My Indian Name by Cynthia Leitich Smith. New York: HarperCollins, 2001.

The Watsons Go to Birmingham–1963 by Christopher Paul Curtis. New York: Delacorte/ Random House, 1995.

Search for Self

The Absolutely True Diary of a Part-Time Indian by Sherman Alexie. New York: Little Brown, 2007.

Always Running: La Vida Loca: Gang Days in L.A. by Luis Rodriguez. Willimantic, CT: Curbstone, 1993.

Beneath the Armor of an Athlete: Real Strength on the Wrestling Mat by Lisa Whitsett. Ferre Haute, IN: Wish, 2002.

Bud, Not Buddy by Christopher Paul Curtis. New York: Delacorte, 1999.

Catalyst by Laurie Halse Anderson. New York: Viking, 2000.

Forged by Fire by Sharon Draper. New York: Atheneum, 1997.

Hole in My Life by Jack Gantos. New York: Farrar, Straus and Giroux, 2002.

The Island by Gary Paulsen. New York: Orchard, 1988.

Rules of the Road by Joan Bauer. New York: Putnam, 1998.

Sweetblood by Pete Hautman. New York: Simon & Schuster, 2003.

How does the teacher best move the students from reading to writing? First of all, it is important to take what Applebee, Langer, Nystrand, and Gamorin (2003) describe as a "dialogic approach" to interacting with literature, which is in direct contrast to what Applebee et al. call an "IRE" approach, in which the teacher asks a question about the book, the student answers the question, and the teacher judges the student's answer (p. 693). In the dialogic approach the students work with their own ideas and interact with each other as they read, write, and discuss and "make predictions, summarize, link texts with one another and with background knowledge,

Discussing good books taps into curiosity and provides opportunities for students to develop writing ideas.

generate and answer text-related questions, and interrelate reading, writing and discussion" (p. 693). This would seem to fulfill Hillocks's (1995) insistence on meaning-making, especially given that this approach is not centered on the teacher's ideas about the literature at all but comes from the students' ideas in reader-response fashion. The results of Applebee et al.'s (2003) study of 974 students in 19 schools strongly suggest that students will build their literacy skills most significantly with this approach, but it also fulfills previously mentioned characteristics from Ralph Fletcher (1993) for response and payoff (the reactions of classmates in discussion and response to peer's written literary response) and Csikszentmihalyi et al.'s (1993) call for flow experiences with immediate feedback.

As students begin to write, a writing workshop approach can help them enter and engage in the writing process. Although there is no one, established, set process for all writers, generally writers engage in similar steps at various points in their efforts. Models of the writing process are best not perceived as lockstep required moments in the production of text but rather as identifiable moments of progression that may provide points for discussion if a writer needs help. The writing process is generally recursive, which is to say that writers begin at various points in the process and return to various points to begin moving forward again and again. A writer may write a sentence, read it back, reconsider certain words or phrases and revise them, finish out a paragraph, read it back, reconsider certain words, phrases, or sentences and revise them or even scrap them for a new attempt if the entirety did not seem to be meeting the writer's goals. This circular repetition is what is meant by recursive. A basic model of the writing process includes, in some form or other and most probably in a recursive sequence, (1) prewriting, (2) drafting, (3) responding, (4) revising, (5) editing, and sometimes (6) publishing.

Generating ideas, part of prewriting, is always the starting point for the writing process and often a difficult one. One method for doing this with adolescent readers is use of the reading log, sometimes called a reading-response journal. This is often just a spiral notebook in which the reader writes responses to his or her reading each day. Without effective guidance, however, this can regress to low cognitive effort that amounts to little more than summary, with hardly any depth of meaning-making at all. Seventh- and eighth-grade teacher Linda Berger (1996) suggests that "the inspiring slogan 'You Make the Meaning' [a declaration of literary independence she had posted around her classroom] was totally useless . . . if they did not know *how*" (p. 381). Upon first implementing response journals, Linda found that the majority of her students were just summarizing the reading as if to prove they had done the assignment. In collaboration, Berger and her students arrived at four basic questions:

What do you notice?
What do you question?
What do you feel?
What do you relate to? (p. 381)

Each question had five or six subquestions or prompts in case further help was needed. Berger was delighted with the results as they played out in the new journal entries: "As I reviewed the journals, I could see that my students no longer treaded water on the surface of the novels. They were diving deeply into books and uncovering meaning" (p. 382).

Another way of generating ideas for writing, especially when the reading is deep and has a grand array of possible topics is a class activity often called silent discussion (Bigelow, Childs, Treick O'Neill, n.d.). *Silent discussion* has many variations, but basically it involves choosing five or six provocative quotations from a book students are all reading or have just finished reading and writing each quotation in the center of one of a large piece of butcher paper (three to four feet long). placed on tables spread out around the classroom. Students work in five or six groups, one group for each table containing a paper with a quote. Each person equipped with a colored marker and a black or blue pen. Each group has a leader who takes the group through the activity. As this activity begins, each group reads the quotation at their table and discusses it to the degree necessary so that everyone understands where it came from in the story and what it means. Then each person uses his or her colored marker to write a response to the quotation. (The big piece of butcher paper and the table make it possible for everyone in the group to do this at once.) The response might be agreement with the quotation and an explanation of why, or disagreement and an explanation of why. It could be a connection to real-life today or any other response that occurs to the student. After about five minutes or whenever students seem to be ready, the teacher signals and each group rotates to the next table and repeats the process until every group has been to every table.

The next time around, as students begin at one table, they switch to their blue or black pens. They read as many of the responses to the quotation as they have time for before choosing one especially interesting response and responding to it (in an appropriate tone). Again, every five minutes or so, the teacher signals and groups rotate to the next table until they have visited every table again.

When the groups have made the two complete circuits and every banner now has a quotation, colored responses to the quotation, and blue or black responses to the response, the groups all stop. They choose one especially interesting colored response and all the blue or black responses that were written to it. Then each group presents the butcher paper at their table as they tape it for display to the wall. They read the quotation to the class and explain where it came from in the book and what it means. Then they read the responses they chose and explain why they chose them. The colorful butcher paper posters can stay up on the wall for a few days as the teacher sees fit.

Silent discussion generates any number of potential writing topics. Students are generating their own ideas, and they are also reading the ideas of their peers, any one of which might also provide an engaging topic to write about—ideas students hadn't previously considered but that make sense to them.

Once students have done some sort of prewriting activity and arrived at ideas for their writing, they need to consider their audience and purpose. To whom are they writing and what do they hope to accomplish? Again, as Ralph Fletcher (1993) holds, personal choice should hold sway, here (p. 1). Thinking back to A-S-H-L-E-Y at the beginning of the chapter and her posting about her favorite character in the novel *Twilight,* we can see that the more closely the writer cares about her audience, the more invested she is in articulating her thoughts and feelings accurately. When at all possible, young readers should be allowed to choose their audience and encouraged to pick an authentic one, not just the teacher, or as some students are prone to answer when asked who they're writing for, "everyone." Carl Anderson's (2005) examples of purpose bear considering once more at this point too, as he envisions a young writer who "might write to make sense of life's experiences. She might write to teach others about her passions. He might write to try to correct an injustice" (p. 16). "To go in my writing portfolio" is not an authentic purpose, by the way.

Arriving at a topic, an audience, and a purpose are three prewriting decisions that should precede drafting. Another prewriting decision is genre, also sometimes called mode or application. Considering the audience and the purpose, the writer arrives at the specific genre that will best fit his or her intentions. It might be a letter, a personal narrative, a literary response essay, a review, or a persuasive essay. One approach for making prewriting decisions is known by the acronym RAFTS. The brainchild of Nancy

Vandeventer, who was a junior high English teacher in Bozeman, Montana, when she came up with this idea in 1978, RAFTS guides writers through the following choices:

R = Role: What is my role as the writer? Who am I ?
A = Audience: To whom am I writing? Should I write formally? Informally?
F = Format: Which format should I use while writing?
T = Topic: What is the topic? Is it sufficiently focused?
S = Strong Verb: What am I trying to do in this piece of writing?

A student using a writing workshop approach such as the one espoused by Nancie Atwell (1987) in her quintessential work on the middle school writing workshop could use the RAFTS. method to arrive at the specifics of a paper based on her own choices.

Let's construct a RAFTS-generated paper for such a hypothetical student. Going back to Anderson's (2005) tenet that lifelong writers write with a purpose in mind, we could use one of his hypothetical purposes for our young writer: "She might write to teach others about her passions" (p. 16). And going back to the Twilight Lexicon, we might consider A-S-H-L-E-Y's passion for the book *Twilight* and for the character with whom she most identifies, Bella. Our young writer's RAFTS might look something like this:

Role: A book critic for a major newspaper
Audience: Other young women who have read *Twilight*
Format: A newspaper book review
Topic: Characterization in *Twilight*, particularly of Bella
Strong Verb: "Convince" peers that Stephenie Meyer has created a protagonist who is so much like a real teenager that real teenagers will fall right into the story as if it were happening to them.

Lessons on newspaper writing would obviously be of benefit here, and the writer might even need some education on what the conventions of a newspaper are if she is not accustomed to reading them. Regardless of what format fits best with the young writer's audience and purpose, a writing workshop approach based in process requires that drafting of the RAFTS piece, or any other sort of paper, be followed by peer responding. Here, again, harnessing the adolescent's developmental needs comes into play. The first step for the responder is to react to *what* the writer has to say and not to *how* it was said.

The tendency for peer responders may be to immediately respond to conventions, such as spelling, grammar and usage, syntax mistakes, and so on, but such tendencies are counterproductive. Studies show that young writers accustomed to having their work judged for correctness first, before content, are likely to produce text inferior in complexity to what they are truly capable of in their efforts to escape error. These writers have been found to avoid writing anything they aren't certain of, thus refraining from taking risks or using complex constructions or stretching for unfamiliar words for fear of criticism. Sondra Perl (1979) observed that responding to conventions too early resulted in "a concern for correct form that actually inhibited the development of ideas" (p. 324). Patrick Hartwell (1985) cites his own research with Bentley as well as that of Michael Rose, who found, for example, that students often avoided using the word "because" because [pun intended] they weren't sure how to punctuate a subordinate clause. Fellow writing researchers Linda Flower and John Hayes (1981) also found that when students' work is judged too soon for correctness "the writer must devote conscious attention to demands such as spelling and grammar, [with the result that] the task of translating can interfere with the more global process of planning what one wants to say" (p. 372).

Obviously, peer responding should not be about conventions but rather about responding to what the writer has to say. One method for this is called PQP, or Praise, Question, Polish (Lyons, 1981, p. 42). A variation on this is PQS, or Praise, Question, Suggest. In this responding model, the peer reader begins by telling the writer what he or she especially likes about the piece, including what it has to say and some of the techniques used to say it, such as word choice used for sensory imagery or figurative language used to convey emotion. The second act for the responder is to ask questions that arose during the reading of the paper. This questioning should have the effect of letting the writer know two things: (1) what questions he or she failed to anticipate on the part of the reader, indicating what aspects of the paper are unclear or need more development, and (2) what parts of the paper the reader finds most interesting and wants to know more about, again signaling what parts need more details or more development. The Suggest mode comes in last, at which point the peer responder suggests places or aspects of the paper that don't seem to accomplish what they might if the writing were stronger. The suggestions might propose the nature of the weakness and the general strategy for revision but never suggest what the specific change should be. In other words, a responder might say, "This part where you walk through the food court at the mall would be better if you used words that appeal to the senses, especially smell. What did you smell?" but not, "This part where you walk by Panda Express in the mall would be better if you wrote, 'the tart fragrance of hot and sour soup tickled my nostrils.'"

The next step in the writing process is revision, and here it is important to make the young writer understand that this is her or his paper, not their peers'. Suggestions for revision by peers should be taken under consideration, but ultimately, it is the writer's choice as to whether or not to take the suggestions. The important thing for the writer to do here is to consider what the reader seemed to get from the paper and compare that to what the writer intended. Depending on how well the two match up, mild or radical revision may be needed. Revision may include such acts as adding more to the piece, deleting parts that don't make a contribution or lead the reader off on an irrelevant tangent, reordering parts of the piece to arrive at a better sequence, further developing parts that don't have enough information to satisfy the reader or to move the piece along, or sometimes even taking one small part of a piece (realizing that this is the message the writer really wants to convey) and building a new paper around that piece.

Editing is the step that is often conflated with revision. Revision consists of making major changes in the paper, but editing is the act or proofreading for errors in conventions. One effective method for this is peer editing groups. In this technique a writing group or three to five participants take turns reading each other's papers and looking for mistakes. Self-editing is difficult because writers tend to read what they meant to write rather than what is actually on the paper. Peers, however, know only what is actually on the paper, not what was in the writer's mind when she wrote it. In this technique the group edits one paper at a time. One person, not the writer, but a peer, reads the paper aloud while the others follows along on their copies of the same paper.

The final step of publishing occurs only when a piece of writing will be made public. Perhaps it is going into a collection of works, perhaps it is being submitted to a literary magazine, perhaps it is being sent to the local newspaper for consideration for the editorial/opinion page, or perhaps it is being sent to someone as in the case of a business or personal letter. These are only a few examples of how a piece of writing becomes public and so requires the final step of preparing for publication. A student submitting a book review to a magazine that publishes book reviews needs to know what format requirements the publisher has and meet them or the piece might not receive any consideration at all. A-S-H-L-E-Y might want to submit her piece on *Twilight,* for example. Requirements could easily consist of a word limit (no more than 2,000 words), a font requirement (12-point font in courier), spacing and margin requirements (double-spacing, and margins of 1.25 on the left and 1 inch on the right), and rules about headers, footers, and page numbers (as in, none). Let's not even consider the phrase "camera ready." Students may not often use the publishing step in the writing process, but when they do take a step toward publishing their writing, their level of concern is often raised, which is likely also to raise the quality of their work as they progress through the other steps.

Final Thoughts

Although writing is one of the most complex of human endeavors, with the proper motivation adolescents will write. They will write a lot, and they will write well when the writing task matches their personal needs and the opportunity is made available to them. Young adult literature is the perfect vehicle for helping students negotiate their adolescence, make meaning of their lives, and intersect with the world. Writing about young adult literature is the perfect means, along with discussion, to allow students to consider their lives, consider the world as portrayed in their reading, and to negotiate some sort of truth. As they mature and become the people they will be as adults, their experience with the world can be broadened geometrically by reading. And as they read, their ability to process their own life experiences can be enhanced immensely by their writing.

Professional Resources

Anderson, C. (2000). *How's it going? A practical guide to conferring with student writers.* Portsmouth, NH: Heinemann. (Grades 3–8)

Anderson, C. (2005). *Assessing writers.* Portsmouth, NH: Heinemann. (Grades 4–8)

Angelillo, J. (2005). *Making revision matter.* New York: Scholastic. (Grades 3–6)

Angelillo, J. (2005). *Writing to the prompt: When students don't have a choice.* (Grades 3–8)

Baines, L., & Kunkel, A. (2002). *Teaching adolescents to write: The unsubtle art of naked teaching.* Boston: Allyn & Bacon.

Blasingame, J., & Bushman, J. H. (2005). *Teaching writing in middle and secondary schools.* Upper Saddle River, NJ: Pearson.

Burke, J. (2003). *Writing reminders: Tools, tips, and techniques.* Portsmouth, NH: Heinemann.

Carty, M. (2005). *Exploring writing in the content areas: Teaching and supporting learners in any subject.* Portsmouth, NH: Heinemann.

Cole, A. D. (2006). *Right answer writing: An all-in-one resource to help students craft better responses.* Portsmouth, NH: Heinemann. (Grades 4–12)

Cruz, M. C. (2004). *Independent writing: One teacher—thirty-two needs, topics, and plans.* Portsmouth, NH: Heinemann. (Grades 3–6)

Culham, R. (2003). *6 + 1 traits of writing: The complete guide.* New York: Scholastic. (Grades 3–12)

Daniels, H. (2007). *Content-area writing: Every teacher's guide.* Portsmouth, NH: Heinemann. (Grades 6–12)

Dean, D. (2006). *Strategic writing: The writing process and beyond in the secondary English classroom.* Urbana, IL: NCTE.

Dixon, C. J. (2007). *Lesson plans for teaching writing.* Urbana, IL: NCTE.

Fletcher, R. (1993). *What a writer needs.* Portsmouth, NH: Heinemann. (Grades K–12)

Fletcher, R. (2006). *Boy writers: Reclaiming their voices.* Portland, ME: Stenhouse. (Grades K–12)

Frost, H. (2001). *When I whisper, nobody listens.* Portsmouth, NH: Heinemann. (Grades 6–12)

Gallagher, K. (2006). *Teaching adolescent writers.* Portland, ME: Stenhouse.

Gere, A. R., Christenbury, L., & Sassi, K. (2005). *Writing on demand.* Portsmouth, NH: Heinemann. (Grades 7–10)

Gillis, C. (1997). *Writing outside the lines.* Portsmouth, NH: Boynton Cook. (Grades 6–12)

Gilmore, B. (2007). *"Is it done yet?": Teaching adolescents the art of revision.* Portsmouth, NH: Heinemann.

Gunnery, S. (2007). *A powerful structure that supports writers and promotes peer interaction.* Portland, ME: Stenhouse.

Hillocks, G., Jr. (2006). *Narrative writing: Learning a new model for teaching.* Portsmouth, NH: Heinemann.

Holbrook, S. (2005). *Practical poetry: A nonstandard approach to meeting content area standards.* Portsmouth, NH: Heinemann. (Grades 3–8)

Kashatus, W. (2002). *Past, present, and personal: Teaching writing in U.S. history.* Portsmouth, NH: Heinemann. (Grades 6–12)

King, S. (2000). *On writing.* New York: Simon & Schuster.

Kirby, D., & Kirby, D. L. (2007). *New directions in teaching memoir: A studio workshop approach.* Portsmouth, NH: Heinemann.

Kirby, D., Liner, T., & Kirby, D. L. (2003). *Inside out: Strategies for teaching writing* (3rd ed.). Portsmouth, NH: Heinemann.

Macrorie, K. (1968). *Writing to be read* (3rd ed.). Portsmouth, NH: Boynton/Cook.

Mahoney, J. (2002). *Power and portfolios: Best practices for high school classrooms.* Portsmouth, NH: Heinemann. (Grades 7–12)

Mermelstein, L. (2007). *Don't forget to share: The last crucial step in the writing workshop.* Portsmouth, NH: Heinemann. (Grades K–5)

Nelson, G. L. (2004). *Writing and being: Taking back our lives through the power of language.* Middle Island, NY: New World Press. (Grades 6–12)

Newkirk, T., & Kent, R. (Eds.). (2007). *Teaching the neglected "R": Rethinking writing instruction in secondary classrooms.* Portsmouth, NH: Heinemann.

Oczkus, L. (2007). *Guided writing: Practical lessons, powerful results.* Portsmouth, NH: Heinemann. (Grades 2–6)

Painter, K. (2006). *Living and teaching the writing workshop.* Portsmouth, NH: Heinemann. (Grades 4–8)

Ray, K. W. (2004). *About the authors.* Portsmouth, NH: Heinemann. (Grades K–2)

Robb, L. (2004). *Teaching nonfiction: Writing from the inside out.* New York: Scholastic. (Grades 3–10)

Rog, L. J., & Kropp, P. (2004). *The write genre: Classroom activities and mini-lessons that promote writing with clarity, style, and brilliance.* Portland, ME: Stenhouse.

Romano, T. (1995). *Writing with passion.* Portsmouth, NH: Boynton/Cook. (Grades 6–12)

Romano, T. (2004). *Crafting authentic voice.* Portsmouth, NH: Heinemann.

Samway, K. D. (2006). *When English language learners write.* Portsmouth, NH: Heinemann. (Grades K–8)

Sipe, R. B. (2006). *Purposeful writing: Genre study in the secondary writing workshop.* Portsmouth, NH: Heinemann. (Grades 6–12)

Spandel, V. (2005). *Creating writers.* Boston: Pearson Allyn & Bacon. (Grades 6–12)

Strong, W. (2001). *Coaching writing: The power of guided practice.* Portsmouth, NH: Heinemann. (Grades 6–10)

Strong, W. J. (2005). *Write for insight: Empowering content learning, Grades 6–12.* Boston: Allyn & Bacon.

Ward, C. C. (2006). *How writers grow.* Portsmouth, NH: Heinemann.

Willis, M. S. (1993). *Deep revision.* New York: Teachers and Writers Collaborative.

Zemelman, S., Daniels, H., & Steineke, N. (2007). *Content-area writing: Every teacher's guide.* Portsmouth, NH: Heinemann.

ONLINE

The ALAN Review: http://scholar.lib.vt.edu/ejournals/ALAN/

American Library Association's Young Adult Library Services Association: www.ala.org/ala/yalsa/yalsa.cfm

Arizona State University: www.asu.edu/clas/english/englished/yalit/webquest.htm

Assembly on Literature for Adolescents of the National Council of Teachers of English: www.alan-ya.org

Internet School Library Media Center: http://falcon.jmu.edu/~ramseyil/biochildhome.htm

Journal of Adolescent and Adult Literacy: www.reading.org/publications/journals/jaal/index.html

Kay E. Vandergrift, PhD, Rutgers University: www.scils.rutgers.edu/~kvander/YoungAdult/index.html

Ralph Fletcher: www.ralph.fletcher.com

SIGNAL Journal: www.kennesaw.edu/english/education/signal/PreviousIssues/

6 Plus 1 Writing from the Heartland Area Education Association, Johnston, Iowa: www.aea11.k12.ia.us/curriculum/6_traits/home.html

6 Plus 1 Writing from the Northwest Regional Educational Laboratory, Portland, Oregon: www.nwrel.org/assessment/department.php?d=1

Teri Lesesne, PhD, Sam Houston State University: www.shsu.edu/~lis_tsl/

Writing Resources from the Kent School District, Kent, Washington: www.kent.k12.wa.us/curriculum/writing/index.html

References

Anderson, C. (2005). *Assessing writing.* Portsmouth, NH: Heinemann.

Applebee, A. N., Langer, J. A., Nystrand, M., & Gamoran, A. (2003). Discussion-based approaches to developing understanding: Classroom instruction and student performance in middle and high school English. *American Educational Research Journal, 40*(3), 685–730.

Atwell, N. (1987). *In the middle: Writing, reading, and learning with adolescents.* Upper Montclair, NJ: Boynton/Cook.

Berger, L. (1996). Reader response journals: You make the meaning . . . and how. *Journal of Adolescent and Adult Literacy, 39*(5), 380–385.

Bigelow, B., Childs, S., & Treick O'Neill, J. (n.d.). Silent discussion of *Fahrenheit 9/11.* Retrieved November 5, 2007, from http://www.michaelmoore.com/books-films/fahrenheit911/teachersguide/index.php?section=7

Britton, J. N., Burgess, T., Martin, N., McLeod, A., & Rosen, H. (1975). *The development of writing abilities (11–18).* London: Macmillan.

Bushman, J. H. (2000, November 21). *Adolescent literature and moral development.* Presentation at the ALAN Workshop, National Council of Teachers of English Convention, Milwaukee, WI.

Bushman, J. H., & McNerny, S. (2004). Moral choices: Building a bridge between YA literature and life. *The ALAN Review, 32*(1), 61–67.

Campbell, P. (2000) Sand in the oyster. *The Horn Book Magazine, 77,* 483–487

Campbell, P. (n.d.). *Amazon editorial review.* Retrieved July 14, 2008, from http://www.amazon.com/Twilight-Saga-Book-1/dp/product-description/0316015849

Cormier, R. (1974). *The chocolate war.* New York: Pantheon Books.

Cormier, R. (1977). *I am the cheese.* New York: Knopf/Random House.

Cormier, R. (1979). *After the first death.* New York: Pantheon Books.

Cormier, R. (1983). *The bumblebee flies anyway.* New York: Pantheon Books.

Cormier, R. (1985). *Beyond the chocolate war.* New York: Knopf/Random House.

Cormier, R. (1992). *Tunes for bears to dance to.* New York: Delacorte/Random House.

Csikszentmihalyi, M., & Larson, R. (1984). *Being adolescent: Conflict and growth in the teenage years.* New York: Basic Books.

Csikszentmihalyi, M., Rathunde, K., & Whalen, S. (1993). *Talented teenagers: The roots of success and failure.* Cambridge, England: Cambridge University Press.

Curtis, C. P. (1995). *The Watsons go to Birmingham–1963.* New York: Delacorte/Random House.

Dee, J. (2007, July). All the news that's fit to print. *New York Times Magazine.* Retrieved September 2, 2007, from http://www.nytimes.com/2007/07/01/magazine/01WIKIPEDIA-t.html?ex=1188273600&en=bff44fcb229322c4&ei=5070

Erikson, E. H. (1968). *Identity: Youth and crisis.* New York: W. W. Norton.

Fletcher, R. (1993). *What a writer needs.* Portsmouth, NH: Heinemann.

Fletcher, R. (n.d.). *Tips for writing teachers.* Retrieved July 15, 2008, from http://www.ralphfletcher.com

Flower, L., & Hayes, J. R. (1981). A cognitive process theory of writing. *College Communication and Communication, 32*(4), 365–387.

Hartwell, P. (1985). Grammar, grammars, and the teaching of grammar. *College English, 47*(2), 105–127.

Hillocks, G. (1995). *Teaching writing as reflective practice.* New York: Teachers College Press.

Kohlberg, L. (1981). *The philosophy of moral development.* San Francisco: Harper & Row.

Kornblum, J. (2005). Teens wear their hearts on their blog. *USA Today.* Retrieved August 31, 2007, from http://www.usatoday.com/tech/news/techinnovations/2005-10-30-teen-blogs_x.htm

Lyons, B. (1981). The PQP method of teaching writing. *English Journal, 70*(3), 42–43.

MacDonald, J. G. (2005) Teens: It's a diary. Adults: It's unsafe. *Christian Science Monitor.* Retrieved August 31, 2007, from http://www.csmonitor.com/2005/0525/p11s02-lifp.html

Meyer, S. (2005). *Twilight* series (*Twilight* #1). New York: Little, Brown.

Mid-continent Research for Education and Learning. (2007). A compendium of content standards and benchmarks for K–12 education. In *Mid-continent Research for Education and Learning.* Retrieved September 15, 2007, from http://www.mcrel.org/compendium/topicsDetail.asp?topicsID=267&subjectID=7

Perl, S. (1979). The composing process of unskilled college writers. *Research in the Teaching of English, 13*(4), 317–336.

Probst, R. (1984). *Adolescent literature: Response and analysis.* Columbus, OH: Merrill.

Rosenblatt, L. (1938). *Literature as exploration.* New York: Appleton-Century.

Rosenblatt, L. (1956). The acid test for literature teaching. *English Journal, 45*(2), 66–74.

Rosenblatt, L. (1994). *The reader, the text, the poem: The transactional theory of the literary work.* Carbondale: Southern Illinois University Press.

Rosenblatt, L. (1995). *Literature as exploration.* New York: MLA.

Rowling, J. K. (2007). *Harry Potter and the deathly hallows.* New York: Scholastic.

Scholastic, Inc. (2005). Katherine Paterson's biography. *Scholastic Authors and Books.* Retrieved December 10, 2006, from http://www2.scholastic.com/browse/contributor.jsp?id=3555&FullBreadCrumb=%3Ca+href%3D%22javascript%3Ahistory.go%28-1%29%22%3EHome%3C%2Fa%3E

Schiff, S. (2006). *Know it all: Can Wikipedia conquer expertise?* Retrieved August 31, 2007, from http://www.newyorker.com/archive/2006/07/31/060731fa_fact

Stringer, S. (1994). The psychological changes of adolescence: A test of character. *The ALAN Review, 22*(1), 27–29.

Appendix A
Planning Successful Author Visits

By Pam. B. Cole

When I first heard about the field trip, I just thought it was going to be like any other. I imagined sitting in an uncomfortable chair bored and annoyed, wearily listening to a nagging author telling us about stuff we already knew. But of course, I was fortunately mistaken. It was really quite interesting. I really enjoyed the poetry writing contest (NOT because my partner and I won 2nd place! But it helps!) I was wondering if there were any conventions held for high school students.

Sincerely,
Camisha (8th grader)

Preferring to talk on the phone, play video games, and simply "hang out," Camisha was a nonreader until she met Will Hobbs. When her teacher developed a unit around Will Hobbs's work and informed the class they would have an opportunity to meet Mr. Hobbs and participate in a number of activities and competitive games based on his books, Camisha's attitude changed.

As English/language arts teachers and parents, we continually search for motivational strategies that will foster a love of reading in nonreaders like Camisha. In today's world, reading competes with other forms of entertainment, as well as with other literacy acts: television, movies, the Internet, e-mail and instant messaging, cell phones and text messaging, and so forth. How, we often conjecture, can

we help students prioritize and value reading when their lives are filled with other stimulating, often "addictive" activities? Like Camisha's teacher, many teachers are finding answers in author visits that engage students in meaningful activities, reflection, and interaction. While author visits are certainly no panacea, well-organized events—like the one Camisha attended—can ignite and invigorate a group of nonreaders.

Organizing a first-rate experience, however, takes advanced, detailed planning and a tremendous amount of collaboration. Numerous schedules and conflicts have to be considered and resolved, students have to be prepared, books purchased, space allocated, activities organized, authors must be secured, and travel plans arranged. To aid in creating a smooth, inspiring event, ideas that encourage meaningful interactions between students and authors and that improve the overall quality of the author's stay follow.

Students and Questions

Ask authors for advice on preparing for an author visit and most will say students need to have read their books. While teachers may be excited that students have a chance to meet a "real" writer, authors, though generally courteous, have little to offer students unfamiliar with their stories—authors *talk* about their writing; they are not *teachers* of writing. If students have not read their stories, conversations are one-sided. Teachers become frustrated and/or embarrassed because students have little interest in what the speaker has to say, or they ask

Reprinted with permission from *Florida Education Leadership Journal,* Vol. 4, No. 2, Spring 2004, pp. 46–49.

silly, meaningless questions. Such visits do little, if anything, to encourage students to read and write. With this said, authors should not be invited into classrooms where students have not read their work.

In addition, the kinds of questions students ask are indicative of how prepared they are. Students who are not well prepared may ask irrelevant and/or inappropriate personal questions: "How much money do you make?" "Are you married?" "What kind of car do you drive?" "Do you know J. K. Rowling?" Most kids know these questions irritate and embarrass adults, so if teachers address the inappropriateness of personal questions first, they can clear the way for authors to respond to better questions. Some inappropriate questions, incidentally, can be worded in an acceptable manner. "How much money do you make?" can be rephrased as "Can I make a living as a writer?" Well-phrased questions lead to better exchanges between students and authors.

Cautioning students not to ask personal questions and helping them word questions appropriately are measures that will improve question/answer sessions. However, students need opportunities to discuss, research, and explore their thoughts about an author's work prior to the author's appearance in order to develop thoughtful questions. If not given this time and encouraged to delve deeper into the literature and into their own reflections about the author's work, students will most likely ask ordinary questions that authors have answered repeatedly—ones that appear on Web sites, in biographies and research sources, and so forth. Well-prepared students will already be familiar with answers to basic questions and will have spent time reflecting on more unique and challenging ones. Authors repeatedly respond to questions like "Where do you get your ideas?" A student expecting a complete answer to that question is in for a long day. A better question would be "How much of that story is real?" This latter question is more focused and suggests the student is more involved in the author's

work and has a legitimate reason for posing the question.

When authors encounter students who have developed insightful questions about their writing, they enjoy the verbal exchange and find the experience invigorating. In these situations, authors leave sessions with new writing ideas, added reasons to write, and are more than willing to return again.

Setting

The old saying "You can lead a horse to water, but you can't make him drink" need not be true when preparing students for author visits. Experiences have shown me environment plays an important role in students' attitudes and behaviors. Cafeterias are perhaps the worst place because of acoustics; classrooms are generally too "familiar." Off-campus locations tend to work best. Interestingly, students who pay a small fee to ride a charter bus as opposed to regular buses seem more psyched. The charter bus elevates the experience—makes it a big deal, something to brag about. When students participate in an author visit on a college/university campus, for example, they seem to take the event more seriously. Moreover, when they know they are not the only school participating, they feel an obligation or challenge to "perform" or "show up" the other schools. For this reason, teachers and librarians can do well by developing partnerships throughout their district and region. (Partnerships can pay off financially as well.)

Writing the Author

One piece of advice I give teachers is *never* require a student or class to write an author (whether the author is visiting or not) or send individual thank-you notes for a visit. When teachers require students to correspond with authors, they burden authors and misuse their time: imagine the time it takes to open every envelope and respond to each in separate letters; imagine the number of students authors visit each year and/or talk with on the Internet or via snail mail; imagine getting up each day to write, only to find a stack of required letters, many of which begin something like "My teacher says we have to write an author. I chose you…."; finally, imagine responding to thirty or more "form" letters from the same class (even if they are sent in one envelope) in which each student asks the author to recommend a book or asks the author to name his/her favorite book. When teachers require classes to write authors, they lessen the likelihood that students will receive meaningful responses; the best students can hope for is a stock answer. While an author may be a "real" audience, using an author for a writing assignment is an unproductive, unfair demand.

Moreover, students who are required to correspond are not engaged in the writing and can find answers to common questions from Web sites and other research sources. Students who choose to write an author on their own, however, generally have more to say. Most have found a meaningful connection with the author's work and want to tell the author how the story affected them. Many identify closely with a character and want the author to know the story is about them, the story "saved their lives," or the story helped them understand they were not alone and so on.

When students feel this engaged and have personal desires to write authors, they should be encouraged to do so. They should use e-mail when possible; e-mail is faster and cheaper. (Many fans do not provide SASEs.) Many authors give their e-mail addresses freely and often post them on their Web sites, hoping e-mail will lessen the paper deluge. However, if e-mail is not possible, students should be encouraged to include a SASE with their letter, which saves the author time and expense.

I am not suggesting authors do not enjoy hearing from students. They do, that is, when kids *choose* to write. Kids are why they write. Authors have connections with them that many adults have lost. As teachers, however, we can help authors hear "real" questions by encouraging students to write authors only when they have legitimate questions or ideas they wish to share. We can also improve the likelihood that students will receive responses if we help eliminate meaningless correspondence, for authors will have more time to respond to serious inquiries. Serious letters can shape a writer's thinking for future stories; likewise, when students receive answers from carefully thought-out questions, authors sometimes provide information that helps students better understand their lives and world.

The Speaker's Itinerary

I once heard a librarian say she always gets "the most out of an author" when she plans an author appearance. While hosts may want to share authors with as many as possible and are excited about opportunities to spend time with favorite authors, being center stage takes tremendous physical and emotional energy. Like everyone, authors need breathing space; therefore, itineraries should be planned so authors have adequate down time to return to their rooms or elsewhere where they are not smothered. Authors who have breakfast with a group, then spend an entire day in a school, followed by dinner and a reading session have heavy agendas. While some authors will contract for the number of sessions per day (three should be the maximum), others do not and can be overused by the overly enthusiastic, well-intentioned host.

It is a good idea to consider all scheduling issues and space allocation problems well ahead of the author's visit. Careful planning can ensure that more students are able to hear and interact with an author and that any last minute glitches are ironed out. (When making decisions about how many students will hear the author, less is sometimes more.) Authors can be placed in uncomfortable positions if they are asked after arrival, or shortly before their arrival, if they mind speaking again because the auditorium is not large enough, the room is being used for another event, and so forth.

While most authors are gracious and accommo- dating, scheduling and space issues should be carefully considered prior to the author's visit and alternative solutions found. Jam-packed scheduling is inconsiderate and suggests care- less planning on the host's/school's part.

In addition, it is important to share a detailed itinerary not just with the author but also with administration and everyone involved in the event well in advance. Administrators and all personnel concerned should be made aware of the schedule and the importance of adhering to it. Closer to the date of the event, the host should touch base with everyone— doing so prevents confusion and ensures that everyone clearly understands what to expect. It is helpful, too, to have one individual contact- ing the author. Authors do numerous engage- ments; the more people involved, the greater the chance of miscommunication.

While it is important to consider the author's time, it is equally important to pay close attention to transportation and transitions between events. I've always feared leaving an author hanging somewhere—in airports, hotels, schools, conference centers, in traffic jams, and so forth—and not having enough time to get him/her from one event to the next. Likewise, I have been apprehensive about providing the author with complete contact information. I always write out a detailed itinerary, one that explains clearly who is responsible for seeing that the speaker gets from one event to the next, then follow up with e-mails to make sure everyone involved remembers his/her role.

While authors can resolve some of their own transportation and itinerary issues, they have little, if any, control over who spends time with them. Deciding who will trans- port authors from one event to the next and who will have meals with authors can be dif- ficult. Usually, a host has an abundance of help—fans are eager for individual time with favorite writers and will readily volunteer. Regrettably, not everyone has good social skills: some are star-struck; others are overly confident and want to impress the writer with

their knowledge of literature; some talk exces- sively and are too dominating; others are too quiet, and so forth. Two intolerable person- alities are those who declare author "own- ership"—who claim to have discovered the author, know his/her work better than anyone else, and know him/her personally as a friend (unbeknownst to the author). There are those, too, who are infatuated and can embarrass the author, host, and school. While coordina- tors should not exclude individuals with poor social skills from engaging with authors, coor- dinators should plan itineraries keeping these personalities in mind.

Clear and concise program information can also help visits run smoothly. A follow- up shortly before events to make sure authors received everything they need or have not misplaced or forgotten any necessary details is crucial. Following up with all information in one e-mail, or regular letter, is essential since programs are prepared piecemeal—making it likely that the author receives information bit by bit. Also, if a coordinator does not follow up, authors can mistakenly double book them- selves or forget the event. It pays to remember that while authors may personally commit themselves to an engagement, agents, publi- cists, and others book them as well.

Arranging accommodations may seem easy, but most everyone who travels has encountered at one time or the other problems with reservations and rooms. While it might be "cool" to have an author as a personal guest under such circumstances, authors might con- sider such arrangements uncomfortable. Many authors, too, travel with laptops so they can write and check e-mail while on the road. Although some authors may specifically request rooms with Internet access, most do not—many sim- ply don't think to request a room with Internet capabilities and a desk where they can work. Accommodations suited for business travel- ers (rooms with faxes, large desks, and Inter- net access) are better bets than luxury bed and breakfasts and resorts, which usually lack these capabilities. Accommodations located near restaurants and shopping areas are also better than isolated accommodations because authors can easily find food when they are alone or walk to a store if they need an extra shirt, socks, and so on. Since many authors are either coming from a previous event or headed toward another one, they sometimes need to pick up personal items. While most hosts will arrange for respectable lodging, these additional considerations can improve an author's stay.

Gifts

All hosts want to show an author how much they appreciate the visit, and many show gratefulness in the form of parting gifts. Keep in mind as you choose gifts that authors are carrying luggage and have little room for extras, particularly bulky gifts such as sweatshirts or gift baskets (yes, authors do receive gift baskets and they get left behind in hotels). Also, think creatively—authors have more caps, T-shirts, and mugs with school logos than they know what to do with it. Avoid loading up the author with useless items such as school yearbooks and student work. Small items such as unique writing instruments and flash drives are great bets.

Final Thoughts

We live in an era in which teens have multiple interests and place little value on personal reading. Teachers can do well to take advantage of as many opportunities as possible for engaging students in authentic reading experiences, among which, of course, is the chance to interact with an author students have studied. If a visit is carefully planned, the event can be a memorable experience for students, teachers, and authors; some students will discover a love of reading and become lifelong readers. Through carefully orchestrated student-author interactions, students can learn that literature truly teaches us about our lives and the world in which we live.

Appendix B
Awards

The ALAN Award

This award is presented annually by the Assembly on Literature for Adolescents of the National Council of Teachers of English (ALAN). Winners are selected for distinguished contributions to the field of young adult literature. Therefore, nonwriters (teachers, librarians, etc.) have won.

2007 Teri Lesesne
2006 Virginia Monseau and Marc Aronson
2005 Jerry Spinelli
2004 Jacqueline Woodson
2003 Norma Fox Mazer and Harry Mazer
2002 Paul Zindel
2001 Patty Campbell
2000 M. E. Kerr
1999 Robert Lipsyte
1998 S. E. Hinton
1997 Mildred D. Taylor
1996 Bill Morris
1995 Robert C. Small Jr.
1994 Walter Dean Myers
1993 Chris Crutcher
1992 Don Gallo
1991 Gary Paulsen
1990 Richard Peck
1989 Cynthia Voigt
1988 Ted Hipple
1987 Katherine Paterson and Alleen Pace Nilsen
1986 Madeleine L'Engle
1985 Sue Ellen Bridgers
1984 Louise Rosenblatt
1983 Ken Donelson
1982 Robert Cormier
1981 Sheila Schwartz
1980 Dwight Burton
1979 Gerri LaRocque
1978 Mary Sucher
1977 Marguerite Archer
1976 Margaret McElderry and M. Jerry Weiss
1975 Margaret Edwards
1974 Stephen Judy and G. Robert Carlsen

The ALEX Awards

The ALEX Awards, named after librarian Margaret "Alex"ander Edwards, honor the top 10 adult books for teenagers published during a calendar year. The awards are cosponsored by the Young Adult Library Services Association (YALSA) and *Booklist* magazine.

2008 *American Shaolin: Flying Kicks, Buddhist Monks, and the Legend of Iron Crotch: An Odyssey in the New China* by Matthew Polly
Bad Monkeys by Matt Ruff
Essex County Volume 1: Tales from the Farm by Jeff Lemire
Genghis: Birth of an Empire by Conn Iggulden
The God of Animals by Aryn Kyle
Long Way Gone: Memoirs of a Boy Soldier by Ishmael Beah
Mister Pip by Lloyd Jones
The Name of the Wind by Patrick Rothfuss
The Night Birds by Thomas Maltman
The Spellman File by Lisa Lutz

2007 *The Book of Lost Things* by John Connolly
The Whistling Season by Ivan Doig

Eagle Blue by Michael D'Orso
Water Elephants by Sara Gruen
Floor of the Sky by Pamela Carter Joern
Color of the Sea by John Hamamura
The Blind Side: Evolution of a Game by Michael Lewis
Black Swan Green by David Mitchell
The World Made Straight by Ron Rash
The Thirteenth Tale by Diane Setterfield

2006 *Midnight at the Dragon Café* by Judy Fong Bates
Upstate by Kalisha Buckhanon
Anansi Boys by Neil Gaiman
As Simple As Snow by Gregory Galloway
Never Let Me Go by Kazuo Ishiguro
Gil's All Fright Diner by A. Lee Martinez
The Necessary Beggar by Susan Palwick
My Jim by Nancy Rawles
Jesus Land: A Memoir by Julia Scheeres
The Glass Castle: A Memoir by Jeannette Walls

2005 *Candyfreak* by Steve Almond
Swimming to Antarctica by Lynn Cox
Donorboy by Brendan Halpin
Shadow Divers by Robert Kurson
Work of Wolves by Kent Meyers
Truth & Beauty: A Friendship by Ann Patchett
My Sister's Keeper by Jodi Picoult
Thinner Than Thou by Kit Reed
Project X by Jim Shepard
Rats by Robert Sullivan

Andre Norton Award for Young Adult Science Fiction and Fantasy

Named after the prolific science fiction and fantasy author Andre Norton, this new award is given annually to one young adult title that denotes excellence in the field of young adult science fiction and fantasy.

2007 Winner: *Magic or Madness* by Justine Larbalestier

Honor Titles: *Devilish* by Maureen Johnson
The King of Attolia by Megan Whalen Turner
Midnighters 2: Touching Darkness by Scott Westerfeld
Peeps by Scott Westerfeld
Life As We Knew It by Susan Beth Pfeffer

2006 Winner: *Valiant: A Modern Tale of Faerie* by Holly Black
Honor Titles: *The Amethyst Road* by Louise Spiegler
Siberia by Ann Halam
Stormwitch by Susan Vaught

The Caldecott Medal

Named in honor of a 19th-century English illustrator, Randolph Caldecott, this award is announced annually by the American Library Association and is given to the artist of the most distinguished American picture book for children. Many of these beautiful texts are appropriate for teens. The first award was given in 1938. Honor books can be found on ALA's Web site: www.ala.org

2008 *The Invention of Hugo Cabret* illustrated and written by Brian Selznick
2007 *Flotsam* illustrated and written by David Wiesner
2006 *The Hello, Goodbye Window* illustrated by Norton Juster and written by Chris Raschka
2005 *Kitten's First Full Moon* illustrated and written by Kevin Henkes
2004 *The Man Who Walked Between the Towers* illustrated and written by Mordicai Gerstein
2003 *My Friend Rabbit* illustrated and written by Eric Rohmann
2002 *The Three Pigs* illustrated and written by David Wiesner
2001 *So You Want to Be President?* illustrated by David Small and written by Judith St. George

2000 *Joseph Had a Little Overcoat* illustrated and written by Simms Taback

1999 *Snowflake Bentley* illustrated by Mary Azarian and written by Jacqueline Briggs Martin

1998 *Rapunzel* illustrated and retold by Paul O. Zelinsky

1997 *Golem* illustrated and written by David Wisniewski

1996 *Officer Buckle and Gloria* illustrated and written by Peggy Rathmann

1995 *Smoky Night* illustrated by David Diaz and written by Eve Bunting

1994 *Grandfather's Journey* illustrated and written by Allen Say

1993 *Mirette on the High Wire* illustrated and written by Emily Arnold McCully

1992 *Tuesday* illustrated and written by David Wiesner

1991 *Black and White* illustrated and written by David Macaulay

1990 *Lon Po Po: A Red-Riding Hood Story from China* illustrated and written by Ed Young

1989 *Song and Dance Man* illustrated by Stephen Gammell and written by Karen Ackerman

1988 *Owl Moon* illustrated by John Schoenherr and written by Jane Yolen

1987 *Hey, Al* illustrated by Richard Egielski and written by Arthur Yorinks

1986 *The Polar Express* illustrated and written by Chris Van Allsburg

1985 *Saint George and the Dragon* illustrated by Trina Schart Hyman and retold by Margaret Hodges

1984 *The Glorious Flight: Across the Channel with Louis Blériot* illustrated and written by Alice Provensen and Marti Provensen

1983 *Shadow* illustrated and written by Marcia Brown

1982 *Jumanji* illustrated and written by Chris Van Allsburg

1981 *Fables* illustrated and written by Arnold Lobel

1980 *Ox-Cart Man* illustrated by Barbara Cooney and written by Donald Hall

1979 *The Girl Who Loved Wild Horses* illustrated and written by Paul Goble

1978 *Noah's Ark* illustrated and written by Peter Spier

1977 *Ashanti to Zulu: African Traditions* illustrated by Leo Dillon and Diane Dillon and written by Margaret Musgrove

1976 *Why Mosquitoes Buzz in People's Ears: A West African Tale* illustrated by Leo Dillon and Diane Dillon and written by Verna Aardema

1975 *Arrow to the Sun: A Pueblo Indian Tale* illustrated and written by Gerald McDermott

1974 *Duffy and the Devil* illustrated and written by Harve Zemach and Margot Zemach

1973 *The Funny Little Woman* illustrated by Blair Lent and retold by Arlene Mosel

1972 *One Fine Day* illustrated and written by Nonny Hogrogian

1971 *A Story, a Story: An African Tale* illustrated and retold by Gail E. Haley

1970 *Sylvester and the Magic Pebble* illustrated and written by William Steig

1969 *The Fool of the World and the Flying Ship: A Russian Tale* illustrated by Uri Shulevitz and retold by Arthur Ransome

1968 *Drummer Hoff* illustrated by Ed Emberley and adapted by Barbara Emberley

1967 *Sam, Bangs, and Moonshine* illustrated and written by Evaline Ness

1966 *Always Room for One More* illustrated by Nonny Hogrogian and written by Sorche Nic Leodhas

1965 *May I Bring a Friend?* illustrated by Beni Montresor and written by Beatrice Schenk de Regniers

1964 *Where the Wild Things Are* illustrated and written by Maurice Sendak

1963   *The Snowy Day* illustrated and written by Ezra Jack Keats

1962   *Once a Mouse* illustrated and written by Marcia Brown

1961   *Baboushka and the Three Kings* illustrated by Nicolas Sidjakov and written by Ruth Robbins

1960   *Nine Days to Christmas: A Story of Mexico* illustrated by Aurora Labastida and written by Marie Hall Ets

1959   *Chanticleer and the Fox* illustrated and adapted by Barbara Cooney

1958   *Time of Wonder* illustrated and written by Robert McCloskey

1957   *A Tree Is Nice* illustrated by Marc Simont and written by Janice May Udry

1956   *Frog Went A-Courtin'* illustrated by Feodor Rojankovsky and written by John Langstaff

1955   *Cinderella, or the Little Glass Slipper* illustrated and written by Marcia Brown

1954   *Madeline's Rescue* illustrated and written by Ludwig Bemelmans

1953   *The Biggest Bear* illustrated and written by Lynd Ward

1952   *Finders Keepers* illustrated by Nicholas Mordvinoff and written by William Lipkind

1951   *The Egg Tree* illustrated and written by Katherine Milhous

1950   *Song of the Swallows* illustrated and written by Leo Politi

1949   *The Big Snow* illustrated and written by Berta Hader and Elmer Hader

1948   *White Snow, Bright Snow* illustrated by Roger Duvoisin and written by Alvin Tresselt

1947   *The Little Island* illustrated by Leonard Weisgard and written by Golden MacDonald

1946   *The Rooster Crows: A Book of American Rhymes and Jingles* illustrated and written by Maud Petersham and Miska Petersham

1945   *Prayer for a Child* illustrated by Elizabeth Orton Jones and written by Rachel Field

1944   *Many Moons* illustrated by Louis Slobodkin and written by James Thurber

1943   *The Little House* illustrated and written by Virginia Lee Burton

1942   *Make Way for Ducklings* illustrated and written by Robert McCloskey

1941   *They Were Strong and Good* illustrated and written by Robert Lawson

1940   *Abraham Lincoln* illustrated and written by Ingri Parin d'Aulaire and Edgar Parin d'Aulaire

1939   *Mei Li* illustrated and written by Thomas Handforth

1938   *Animals of the Bible* illustrated by Dorothy P. Lathrop and text selected by Helen Dean Fish

Coretta Scott King Award

Given to African American authors and illustrators for outstanding inspirational and educational contributions, the Coretta Scott King Book Award titles promote understanding and appreciation of the culture of all peoples and their contribution to the realization of the American dream. The award is designed to commemorate the life and works of Dr. Martin Luther King Jr. and to honor Mrs. Coretta Scott King for her courage and determination to continue the work for peace and world brotherhood. Honor books can be found on the ALA Web site: www.ala.org

2008   *Elijah of Buxton* by Christopher Paul Curtis

2007   *Copper Sun* by Sharon M. Draper

2006   *Day of Tears: A Novel in Dialogue* by Julius Lester

2005   *Remember: The Journey to School Integration* by Toni Morrison

2004   *The First Part Last* by Angela Johnson

2003   *Bronx Masquerade* by Nikki Grimes

2002   *The Land* by Mildred D. Taylor
2001   *Miracle's Boys* by Jacqueline Woodson
2000   *Bud, Not Buddy* by Christopher Paul Curtis
1999   *Heaven* by Angela Johnson
1998   *Forged by Fire* by Sharon M. Draper
1997   *Slam!* by Walter Dean Myers
1996   *Her Stories* by Virginia Hamilton, illustrated by Leo Dillon and Diane Dillon
1995   *Christmas in the Big House, Christmas in the Quarters* by Patricia C. McKissack and Frederick L. McKissack
1994   *Toning the Sweep* by Angela Johnson
1993   *The Dark Thirty: Southern Tales of the Supernatural* by Patricia A. McKissack
1992   *Now Is Your Time! The African-American Struggle for Freedom* by Walter Dean Myers
1991   *The Road to Memphis* by Mildred D. Taylor
1990   *A Long Hard Journey: The Story of the Pullman Porter* by Patricia C. McKissack and Frederick L. McKissack
1989   *Fallen Angels* by Walter Dean Myers
1988   *The Friendship* by Mildred D. Taylor
1987   *Justin and the Best Biscuits in the World* by Mildred Pitts Walter
1986   *The People Could Fly: American Black Folktales* by Virginia Hamilton, illustrated by Leo Dillon and Diane Dillion
1985   *Motown and Didi* by Walter Dean Myers
1984   *Everett Anderson's Good-bye* by Lucille Clifton, illustrated by Ann Grifalconi
1983   *Sweet Whispers, Brother Rush* by Virginia Hamilton
1982   *Let the Circle Be Unbroken* by Mildred D. Taylor
1981   *This Life* by Sidney Poitier
1980   *The Young Landlords* by Walter Dean Myers
1979   *Escape to Freedom: A Play about Young Frederick Douglass* by Ossie Davis
1978   *Africa Dream* by Eloise Greenfield, illustrated by Carole Byard

1977   *The Story of Stevie Wonder* by James Haskins
1976   *Duey's Tale* by Pearl Bailey
1975   *The Legend of Africania* by Dorothy Robinson, illustrated by Herbert Temple
1974   *Ray Charles* by Sharon Bell Mathis, illustrated by George Ford
1973   *I Never Had It Made: The Autobiography of Jackie Robinson* as told to Alfred Duckett
1972   *17 Black Artists* by Elton C. Fax
1971   *Black Troubador: Langston Hughes* by Charlemae Rollins
1970   *Martin Luther King, Jr: Man of Peace* by Lillie Patterson

Edgar Award for Best Young Adult Mystery

Named after the American writer Edgar Allan Poe, the Edgar Award is awarded for best young adult mystery published during a calendar year. It is sponsored by the Mystery Writers of America.

2007   Winner: *Buried* by Robin Merrow MacCready
        Honor Titles: *The Road of the Dead* by Kevin Brooks
        The Christopher Killer by Alane Ferguson
        Crunch Time by Mariah Fredericks
        The Night My Sister Went Missing by Carol Plum-Ucci

2006   Winner: *Last Shot: A Final Four Mystery* by John Feinstein
        Honor Titles: *Down the Rabbit Hole* by Peter Abrahams
        Quid Pro Quo by Vicki Grant
        Young Bond, Book One: Silverfin by Charlie Higson
        Spy Goddess, Book One: Live and Let Shop by Michael P. Spradlin

2005   Winner: *In Darkness, Death* by Dorothy Hoobler and Thomas Hoobler

Honor Titles: *Story Time* by Edward Bloor
Jude by Kate Morgenroth
The Book of Dead Days by Marcus Sedgwick
Missing Abby by Lee Weatherly

2004   Winner: *Acceleration* by Graham McNamee
Honor Titles: *Death and the Arrow* by Chris Priestly
Feast of Fools by Bridget Crowley
The Last Treasure by Janet S. Anderson
Uncovering Sadie's Secrets by Libby Sternberg

International Reading Association's Young Adult Book Award

Delivered first in 1975, this award is given for the best title in several categories. The categories range from books for primary readers to titles for young adults. Below are winners for the last 20 years. IRA began honoring a nonfiction young adult title in 1995. Additional titles for all grade levels can be found on the IRA Web site: www.reading.org

2007   *Leonardo's Shadow: Or, My Astonishing Life as Leonardo da Vinci's Servant* by Christopher Grey—Fiction
The Poet Slave of Cuba: A Biography of Juan Francisco Manzano by Margarita Engle, illustrated by Sean Qualls—Nonfiction

2006   *Black and White* by Paul Volponi—Fiction
JAZZ ABZ: An A to Z Collection of Jazz Portraits by Wynton Marsalis, illustrated by Paul Rogers—Nonfiction

2005   *Emako Blue* by Brenda Woods—Fiction
The Burn Journals by Brent Runyon—Nonfiction

2004   *Buddha Boy* by Kathe Koja—Fiction
At the End of Words: A Daughter's Memoir by Miriam Stone—Nonfiction

2003   *Mississippi Trial, 1955* by Chris Crowe—Fiction
Headin' for Better Times: The Arts of the Great Depression by Duane Damon—Nonfiction

2002   *A Step from Heaven* by An Na—Fiction
Meltdown: A Race Against Nuclear Disaster at Three Mile Island by Wilborn Hampton—Nonfiction

2001   *Jake's Orphan* by Peggy Brooke—Fiction
Girls Think of Everything by Catherine Thimmesh, illustrated by Melissa Sweet—Fiction

2000   *Bud, Not Buddy* by Christopher Paul Curtis—Fiction
Eleanor's Story: An American Girl in Hitler's Germany by Eleanor Ramrath Garner—Nonfiction

1999   *Choosing Up Sides* by John H. Ritter—Fiction
First in the Field: Baseball Hero Jackie Robinson by Derek T. Dingle—Nonfiction

1998   *Moving Mama to Town* by Ronder Thomas Young—Fiction
Just What the Doctor Ordered: The History of American Medicine by Brandon Marie Miller—Nonfiction

1997   *Don't You Dare Read This, Mrs. Dunphrey* by Margaret Peterson Haddix—Fiction
The Brooklyn Bridge by Elizabeth Mann—Nonfiction

1996   *The King's Shadow* by Elizabeth Alder—Fiction
The Case of the Mummified Pigs and Other Mysteries in Nature by Susan E. Quinlan—Nonfiction

1995   *Spite Fences* by Trudy Krisher—Fiction
Stranded at Plimoth Plantation 1626 by Gary Bowen—Nonfiction

1994   *Behind the Secret Window* by Nelly S. Toll—Fiction

1993 *Letters from Rifka* by Karen Hesse—Fiction

1992 *Rescue Josh McGuire* by Ben Mikaelsen—Fiction

1991 *Under the Hawthorn Tree: Children of the Famine* by Marita Conlon-McKenna—Fiction

1990 *Children of the River* by Linda Crew—Fiction

1989 *Probably Still Nick Swansen* by Virginia Euwer Wolff—Fiction

1988 *The Ruby in the Smoke* by Philip Pullman—Fiction

John Newbery Medal

The John Newbery Medal has traditionally been recognized as the most prestigious and longest running children's book award and is awarded by the American Library Association. Over the years, ALA realized literature for older teens was being marginalized and developed the Michael L. Printz Award as a result. Today, the Newbery Medal recognizes primarily upper elementary and middle school books, and the Michael L. Printz Award honors stories for older teens. Crossovers do occur. Honor books can be found on the ALA Web site: www.ala.org

2008 *Good Masters! Sweet Ladies! Voices from a Medieval Village* by Laura Amy Schlitz
2007 *The Higher Power of Lucky* by Susan Patron
2006 *Criss Cross* by Lynne Rae Perkins
2005 *Kira-Kira* by Cynthia Kadohata
2004 *The Tale of Despereaux: Being the Story of a Mouse, a Princess, Some Soup, and a Spool of Thread* by Kate DiCamillo
2003 *Crispin: The Cross of Lead* by Avi
2002 *A Single Shard* by Linda Sue Park
2001 *A Year Down Yonder* by Richard Peck
2000 *Bud, Not Buddy* by Christopher Paul Curtis

1999 *Holes* by Louis Sachar
1998 *Out of the Dust* by Karen Hesse
1997 *The View from Saturday* by E. L. Konigsburg
1996 *The Midwife's Apprentice* by Karen Cushman
1995 *Walk Two Moons* by Sharon Creech
1994 *The Giver* by Lois Lowry
1993 *Missing May* by Cynthia Rylant
1992 *Shiloh* by Phyllis Reynolds Naylor
1991 *Maniac Magee* by Jerry Spinelli
1990 *Number the Stars* by Lois Lowry
1989 *Joyful Noise: Poems for Two Voices* by Paul Fleischman
1988 *Lincoln: A Photobiography* by Russell Freedman
1987 *The Whipping Boy* by Sid Fleischman
1986 *Sarah, Plain and Tall* by Patricia MacLachlan
1985 *The Hero and the Crown* by Robin McKinley
1984 *Dear Mr. Henshaw* by Beverly Cleary
1983 *Dicey's Song* by Cynthia Voigt
1982 *A Visit to William Blake's Inn: Poems for Innocent and Experienced Travelers* by Nancy Willard
1981 *Jacob Have I Loved* by Katherine Paterson
1980 *A Gathering of Days: A New England Girl's Journal, 1830–1832* by Joan W. Blos
1979 *The Westing Game* by Ellen Raskin
1978 *Bridge to Terabithia* by Katherine Paterson
1977 *Roll of Thunder, Hear My Cry* by Mildred D. Taylor
1976 *The Grey King* by Susan Cooper
1975 *M. C. Higgins, the Great* by Virginia Hamilton
1974 *The Slave Dancer* by Paula Fox
1973 *Julie of the Wolves* by Jean Craighead George
1972 *Mrs. Frisby and the Rats of NIMH* by Robert C. O'Brien
1971 *Summer of the Swans* by Betsy Byars
1970 *Sounder* by William H. Armstrong

1969	*The High King* by Lloyd Alexander
1968	*From the Mixed-Up Files of Mrs. Basil E. Frankweiler* by E. L. Konigsburg
1967	*Up a Road Slowly* by Irene Hunt
1966	*I, Juan de Pareja* by Elizabeth Borton de Trevino
1965	*Shadow of a Bull* by Maia Wojciechowska
1964	*It's Like This, Cat* by Emily Neville
1963	*A Wrinkle in Time* by Madeleine L'Engle
1962	*The Bronze Bow* by Elizabeth George Speare
1961	*Island of the Blue Dolphins* by Scott O'Dell
1960	*Onion John* by Joseph Krumgold
1959	*The Witch of Blackbird Pond* by Elizabeth George Speare
1958	*Rifles for Watie* by Harold Keith
1957	*Miracles on Maple Hill* by Virginia Sorensen
1956	*Carry On, Mr. Bowditch* by Jean Lee Latham
1955	*The Wheel on the School* by Meindert DeJong
1954	*. . . And Now Miguel* by Joseph Krumgold
1953	*Secret of the Andes* by Ann Nolan Clark
1952	*Ginger Pye* by Eleanor Estes
1951	*Amos Fortune, Free Man* by Elizabeth Yates
1950	*The Door in the Wall* by Marguerite de Angeli
1949	*King of the Wind* by Marguerite Henry
1948	*The Twenty-One Balloons* by William Pène du Bois
1947	*Miss Hickory* by Carolyn Sherwin Bailey
1946	*Strawberry Girl* by Lois Lenski
1945	*Rabbit Hill* by Robert Lawson
1944	*Johnny Tremain* by Esther Forbes
1943	*Adam of the Road* by Elizabeth Janet Gray
1942	*The Matchlock Gun* by Walter Edmonds
1941	*Call It Courage* by Armstrong Sperry
1940	*Daniel Boone* by James Daugherty
1939	*Thimble Summer* by Elizabeth Enright
1938	*The White Stag* by Kate Seredy
1937	*Roller Skates* by Ruth Sawyer
1936	*Caddie Woodlawn* by Carol Ryrie Brink
1935	*Dobry* by Monica Shannon
1934	*Invincible Louisa: The Story of the Author of Little Women* by Cornelia Meigs
1933	*Young Fu of the Upper Yangtze* by Elizabeth Lewis
1932	*Waterless Mountain* by Laura Adams Armer
1931	*The Cat Who Went to Heaven* by Elizabeth Coatsworth
1930	*Hitty, Her First Hundred Years* by Rachel Field
1929	*The Trumpeter of Krakow* by Eric P. Kelly
1928	*Gay Neck, the Story of a Pigeon* by Dhan Gopal Mukerji
1927	*Smoky, the Cowhorse* by Will James
1926	*Shen of the Sea* by Arthur Bowie Chrisman
1925	*Tales from Silver Lands* by Charles Finger
1924	*The Dark Frigate* by Charles Hawes
1923	*The Voyages of Doctor Dolittle* by Hugh Lofting
1922	*The Story of Mankind* by Hendrik Willem van Loon

Margaret A. Edwards Award

Presented by the American Library Association, the Margaret A. Edwards Award is a lifetime achievement award that honors an author's contributions to the field of young adult literature. It is awarded to an author whose work helps adolescents develop an awareness of themselves and an understanding of their relationships and roles in society and the world. The award is sponsored by *School Library Journal*, and an in-depth interview is published in the June issue of the journal. Established in 1988, the award honors the late Margaret Alexander Edwards, librarian for the Enoch Pratt Free Library in Baltimore.

2008	Orson Scott Card
2007	Lois Lowry
2006	Jacqueline Woodson
2005	Francesca Lia Block
2004	Ursula K. Le Guin

2003   Nancy Garden
2002   Paul Zindel
2001   Robert Lipsyte
2000   Chris Crutcher
1999   Anne McCaffrey
1998   Madeline L'Engle
1997   Gary Paulsen
1996   Judy Blume
1995   Cynthia Voigt
1994   Walter Dean Myers
1993   M. E. Kerr
1992   Lois Duncan
1991   Robert Cormier
1990   Richard Peck
1989   No award given
1988   S. E. Hinton

Michael L. Printz Award

Established in 1999, this award is presented by the American Library Association and sponsored by *Booklist*. It is awarded for literary excellence and named after Michael Printz, a Topeka, Kansas, librarian and long-standing member of the Young Adult Library Services Association (YALSA/ALA).

2008   Winner: *The White Darkness* by Geraldine McCaughrean
Honor Titles: *Dreamquake: Book Two of the Dreamhunter Duet* by Elizabeth Knox
One Whole and Perfect Day by Judith Clarke
Repossessed by A. M. Jenkins
Your Own, Sylvia: A Verse Portrait of Sylvia Plath by Stephanie Hemphill

2007   Winner: *American Born Chinese* by Gene Luen Yang
Honor Titles: *The Astonishing Life of Octavian Nothing* by M. T. Anderson
An Abundance of Katherines by John Green
Surrender by Sonya Hartnett
The Book Thief by Markus Zusak

2006   Winner: *Looking for Alaska* by John Green

Honor Titles: *Black Juice* by Margo Lanagan
I Am the Messenger by Markus Zusak
John Lennon: All I Want Is the Truth by Elizabeth Partridge
A Wreath for Emmett Till by Marilyn Nelson

2005   Winner: *The Way I Live Now* by Meg Rosoff
Honor Titles: *Airborn* by Kenneth Oppel
Lizzie Bright and the Buckminster Boy by Gary D. Schmidt
Chandra's Secrets by Allan Stratton

2004   Winner: *The First Part Last* by Angela Johnson
Honor Titles: *A Northern Light* by Jennifer Donnelly
Keesha's House by Helen Frost
Fat Kid Rules the World by K. L. Going
The Earth, My Butt and Other Big Round Things by Carolyn Mackler

2003   Winner: *Postcards from No Man's Land* by Aidan Chambers
Honor Titles: *The House of the Scorpion* by Nancy Farmer
My Heartbeat by Garret Freymann-Weyr
Hole in My Life by Jack Gantos

2002   Winner: *A Step from Heaven* by An Na
Honor Titles: *The Ropemaker* by Peter Dickinson
Heart to Heart: New Poems Inspired by 20th Century Art edited by Jan Greenberg
Freewill by Chris Lynch
True Believer by Virginia Euwer Wolff

2001   Winner: *Kit's Wilderness* by David Almond
Honor Titles: *Many Stones* by Carolyn Coman
The Body of Christopher Creed by Carol Plum-Ucci
Angus, Thongs, and Full-frontal Snogging by Louise Rennison
Stuck in Neutral by Terry Trueman

2000   Winner: *Monster* by Walter Dean
       Myers
       Honor Titles: *Skellig* by David
       Almond
       Speak by Laurie Halse Anderson
       Hard Love by Ellen Wittlinger

Mildred L. Batchelder Award

This award is given annually to an American publisher for the most outstanding book originally published in a foreign language and translated into English. Recent winners are listed here. The complete list can be found on the ALA Web site: www.ala.org

2008   Winner: VIZ Media, for *Brave Story*,
       written by Miyuki Miyabe and
       translated from the Japanese by
       Alexander O. Smith
       Honor Titles: Milkweed Editions, for
       The Cat: Or, How I Lost Eternity, written
       by Jutta Richter, illustrated by Rotraut
       Susanne Berner, and translated from
       the German by Anna Brailovsky
       Phaidon Press, for *Nicholas and the
       Gang*, written by René Goscinny,
       illustrated by Jean-Jacques Sempé,
       and translated from the French by
       Anthea Bell

2007   Winner: Delacorte Press, for *The Pull
       of the Ocean*, written by Jean-Claude
       Mourlevat and translated from the
       French by Y. Maudet
       Honor Titles: Delacorte Press, for *The
       Killer's Tears*, written by Anne-Laure
       Bondoux and translated from the
       French by Y. Maudet
       Hyperion/Miramax, for *The Last
       Dragon*, written by Silvana De Mari and
       translated from the Italian by Shaun
       Whiteside

2006   Winner: Arthur A. Levine Books, for *An
       Innocent Soldier*, written by Josef Holub
       and translated from the German by
       Michael Hofmann

Honor Titles: Phaidon Press Limited,
for *Nicholas*, written by René Goscinny,
illustrated by Jean-Jacques Sempé,
and translated from the French by
Anthea Bell
Bloomsbury Children's Books, for
When I Was a Soldier, written by Valérie
Zenatti and translated from the French
by Adriana Hunter

2005   Winner: Delacorte Press/Random
       House Children's Books, for *The
       Shadows of Ghadames*, written by Joëlle
       Stolz and translated from the French
       by Catherine Temerson
       Honor Titles: Farrar, Straus and Giroux,
       for *The Crow-Girl: The Children of Crow
       Cove*, written by Bodil Bredsdorff and
       translated from the Danish by Faith
       Ingwersen
       Richard Jackson Books/Simon &
       Schuster's Atheneum division, for
       Daniel Half Human and the Good Nazi,
       written by David Chotjewitz and
       translated from the German by Doris
       Orgel

2004   Winner: Walter Lorraine Books/
       Houghton Mifflin Company, for *Run,
       Boy, Run*, written by Uri Orlev and
       translated from the Hebrew by Hillel
       Halkin
       Honor Title: Chronicle Books, for *The
       Man Who Went to the Far Side of the
       Moon: The Story of Apollo 11 Astronaut
       Michael Collins*, written by Bea Uusma
       Schyffert and translated from the
       Swedish by Emi Guner

2003   Winner: The Chicken House/
       Scholastic Publishing, for *The Thief
       Lord*, written byCornelia Funke and
       translated from the German by Oliver
       Latsch
       Honor Title: David R. Godine, for
       Henrietta and the Golden Eggs, written by
       Hanna Johansen, illustrated by Käthi

Bhend, and translated from the German by John Barrett

2002 Winner: Cricket Books/Carus Publishing, for *How I Became an American,* written by Karin Gündisch and translated from the German by James Skofield
Honor Title: Viking Press, for *A Book of Coupons,* written by Susie Morgenstern, illustrated by Serge Bloch, and translated from the French by Gill Rosner

2001 Winner: Arthur A. Levine/Scholastic Press, for *Samir and Yonatan,* written by Daniella Carmi and translated from the Hebrew by Yael Lotan
Honor Title: David R. Godine, for *Ultimate Game,* written by Christian Lehmann and translated from the French by William Rodarmor

2000 Winner: Walker and Company, for *The Baboon King,* written by Anton Quintana and translated from the Dutch by John Nieuwenhuizen
Honor Titles: Farrar, Straus and Giroux, for *Collector of Moments,* written by Quint Buchholz and translated from the German by Peter F. Neumeyer
R&S Books, for *Vendela in Venice,* written by Christina Björk, illustrated by Inga-Karin Eriksson, and translated from the Swedish by Patricia Crampton
Front Street, for *Asphalt Angels,* written by Ineke Holtwijk and translated from the Dutch by Wanda Boeke

Mythopoeic Fantasy Award

This award is given by the Mythopoeic Society, an organization devoted to the study and enjoyment of fantasy literature. The organization recognizes both adult and children's/young adult books annually for excellence in the fantasy/myth genre. Additional information

can be found at its Web site: http://mythsoc.org/awardwinners.html

2007 Winner: *Corbenic* by Catherine Fisher
Honor Titles: *Spirits That Walk in Shadow* by Nina Kiriki Hoffman
The Pinhoe Egg by Diana Wynne Jones
Keturah and Lord Death by Martine Leavitt
Wintersmith by Terry Pratchett

2006 Winner: *The Bartimaeus Trilogy* (consisting of *The Amulet of Samarkand, The Golem's Eye,* and *Ptolemy's Gate*) by Jonathan Stroud
Honor Titles: *Valiant: A Modern Tale of Faerie* by Holly Black
Wizards at War by Diane Duane
By These Ten Bones by Clare B. Dunkle

2005 Winner: *A Hat Full of Sky* by Terry Pratchett
Honor Titles: *Arthur Trilogy* (consisting of *The Seeing Stone, At the Crossing Places,* and *King of the Middle March*) by Kevin Crossley-Holland
The Sea of Trolls by Nancy Farmer
Wise Child Trilogy (consisting of *Wise Child, Juniper,* and *Colman*) by Monica Furlong
The Abhorsen Trilogy (consisting of *Sabriel, Lirael: Daughter of the Clayr,* and *Abhorsen*) by Garth Nix

2004 Winner: *The Hollow Kingdom* by Clare B. Dunkle
Honor Titles: *The Tale of Despereaux* by Kate DiCamillo
Inkheart by Cornelia Funke
The Goose Girl by Shannon Hale
The Wee Free Men by Terry Pratchett

2003 Winner: *Summerland* by Michael Chabon
Honor Titles: *Tithe: A Modern Faerie Tale* by Holly Black
The House of the Scorpion by Nancy Farmer

Coraline by Neil Gaiman
Heir Apparent by Vivian Vande Velde

2002   Winner: *The Ropemaker* by Peter Dickinson
Honor Titles: *The Wizard's Dilemma* by Diane Duane
Island of the Aunts by Eva Ibbotson
The Two Princesses of Bamarre by Gail Carson Levine

2001   Winner: *Aria of the Sea* by Dia Calhoun
Honor Titles: *Night Flying* by Rita Murphy
Beast by Donna Jo Napoli
Growing Wings by Laurel Winter
Boots and the Seven Leaguers by Jane Yolen

2000   Winner: *The Folk Keeper* by Franny Billingsley
Honor Titles: *Skellig* by David Almond
The Circle of Magic series by Tamora Pierce
Harry Potter and the Prisoner of Azkaban by J. K. Rowling
Kingdom series by Cynthia Voigt

1999   Winner: *Dark Lord of Derkholm* by Diana Wynne Jones
Honor Titles: *The Heavenward Path* by Kara Dalkey
Ella Enchanted by Gail Carson Levine
The Squire's Tale by Gerald Morris
Harry Potter and the Sorcerer's Stone by J. K. Rowling

1998   Winner: *Young Merlin Trilogy* (consisting of *Passager, Hobby,* and *Merlin*) by Jane Yolen
Honor Titles: *The Boggart and the Monster* by Susan Cooper
A Dark Horn Blowing by Dahlov Ipcar
Rose Daughter by Robin McKinley

1997   Winner: *The Wood Wife* by Terri Windling
Honor Titles: *One for the Morning Glory* by John Barnes
Winter Rose by Patricia A. McKillip

Fair Peril by Nancy Springer
The Book of the Long Sun by Gene Wolfe

1996   Winner: *The Crown of Dalemark* by Diana Wynne Jones
Honor Titles: *The Boggart* by Susan Cooper
Falcon's Egg by Luli Gray
Wren's War by Sherwood Smith
The Mennyms by Sylvia Waugh

1995   Winner: *Owl in Love* by Patrice Kindl
Honor Titles: *The Princess and the Lord of Night* by Emma Bull, illustrated by Susan Gaber
Switching Well by Peni R. Griffin
A Knot in the Grain and Other Stories by Robin McKinley
Good Griselle by Jane Yolen

1994   Winner: *The Kingdom of Kevin Malone* by Suzy McKee Chamas
Honor Titles: *The Mystery of the Cupboard* by Lynne Reid Banks
The Giver by Lois Lowry
Nevernever by Will Shetterly
Calling on Dragons by Patricia C. Wrede

1993   Winner: *Knight's Wyrd* by Debra Doyle and James D. Macdonald
Honor Titles: *The Ancient One* by T. A. Barron
Jennifer Murdley's Toad by Bruce Coville
Hobkin by Peni R. Griffin
Fish Soup by Ursula Le Guin

1992   Winner: *Haroun and the Sea of Stories* by Salman Rushdie
Honor Titles: *Jeremy Thatcher, Dragon Hatcher* by Bruce Coville
Castle in the Air by Diana Wynne Jones
Elsewhere by Will Shetterly
Song of the Gargoyle by Zilpha Keatley Snyder

The Pura Belpré Award

This biennial award is presented to a Latino/Latina writer whose work best portrays and celebrates the Latino culture. Illustrator awards and additional honor books can be found on the ALA Web site: www.ala.org

2008 Narrative Winner: *The Poet Slave of Cuba: A Biography of Juan Francisco Manzano* written by Margarita Engle and illustrated by Sean Qualls
Honor Titles: *Frida: ¡Viva la Vida! Long Live Life!* written by Carmen T. Bernier-Grand
Martina the Beautiful Cockroach: A Cuban Folktale written by Carmen Agra Deedy and illustrated by Michael Austin
Los Gatos Black on Halloween written by Marisa Montes and illustrated by Yuyi Morales
Illustration Winner: *Los Gatos Black on Halloween* illustrated by Yuyi Morales and written by Marisa Montes
Honor Titles: *My Name Is Gabito: The Life of Gabriel García Márquez/Me Llamo Gabito: La Vida de Gabriel García Márquez* illustrated by Raul Colón and written by Monica Brown
My Colors, My World/Mis Colores, Mi Mundo illustrated and written by Maya Christina González

2006 Narrative Winner: *The Tequila Worm* written by Viola Canales
Honor Titles: *César: ¡Sí, Se Puede! Yes, We Can!* written by Carmen T. Bernier-Grand and illustrated by David Diaz
Doña Flor: A Tall Tale about a Giant Woman with a Great Big Heart written by Pat Mora and illustrated by Raul Colón
Becoming Naomi León written by Pam Muñoz Ryan
Illustration Winner: *Doña Flor: A Tall Tale about a Giant Woman with a Great Big Heart* illustrated by Raul Colón and written by Pat Mora
Honor Titles: *Arrorró, Mi Niño: Latino Lullabies and Gentle Games* illustrated and selected by Lulu Delacre
César: ¡Sí, Se Puede! Yes, We Can! illustrated by David Diaz and written by Carmen T. Bernier-Grand

My Name Is Celia/ Me Llamo Celia: The Life of Celia Cruz/ La Vida de Celia Cruz illustrated by Rafael López and written by Monica Brown

2004 Narrative Winner: *Before We Were Free* written by Julia Álvarez
Honor Titles: *Cuba 15* written by Nancy Osa
My Diary from Here to There/Mi Diario de Aquí Hasta Allá written by Amada Irma Pérez
Illustration Winner: *Just a Minute: A Trickster Tale and Counting Book* illustrated and written by Yuyi Morales
Honor Titles: *First Day in Grapes* illustrated by Robert Casilla and written by L. King Pérez
The Pot That Juan Built illustrated by David Diaz and written by Nancy Andrews-Goebel
Harvesting Hope: The Story of Cesar Chavez illustrated by Yuyi Morales and written by Kathleen Krull

2002 Narrative Winner: *Esperanza Rising* written by Pam Muñoz Ryan
Honor Titles: *Breaking Through* written by Francisco Jiménez
Iguanas in the Snow written by Francisco X. Alarcón and illustrated by Maya Christina González
Illustration Winner: *Chato and the Party Animals* illustrated by Susan Guevara and written by Gary Soto
Honor Title: *Juan Bobo Goes to Work* illustrated by Joe Cepeda and retold by Marisa Montes

2000 Narrative Winner: *Under the Royal Palms: A Childhood in Cuba* written by Alma Flor Ada
Honor Titles: *From the Bellybutton of the Moon and Other Summer Poems/Del Ombligo de la Luna y Otro Poemas de Verano* written by Francisco X. Alarcón and illustrated by Maya Christina González

Laughing Out Loud, I Fly: Poems in English and Spanish written by Juan Felipe Herrera and illustrated by Karen Barbour
Illustration Winner: *Magic Windows* illustrated and written by Carmen Lomas Garza
Honor Titles: *Barrio: José's Neighborhood* illustrated and written by George Ancona
The Secret Star illustrated by Felipe Dávalos and written by Joseph Slate
Mama and Papa Have a Store illustrated and written by Amelia Lau Carling

1998   Narrative Winners: *Parrot in the Oven: Mi Vida* written by Victor Martinez
Honor Titles: *Laughing Tomatoes and Other Spring Poems/Jitomates Risueños y otros poemas de primavera* written by Francisco Alarcón and illustrated by Maya Christina González
Spirits of the High Mesa written by Floyd Martinez
Illustration Winner: *Snapshots from the Wedding* illustrated by Stephanie Garcia and written by Gary Soto
Honor Titles: *In My Family/En Mi Familia* illustrated by Carmen Lomas Garza
The Golden Flower: A Taino Myth from Puerto Rico illustrated by Enrique O. Sánchez and written by Nina Jaffe
Gathering the Sun: An Alphabet in Spanish and English illustrated by Simón Silva and written by Alma Flor Ada. English translation by Rosa Zubizarreta

1996   Narrative Winner: *An Island Like You: Stories of the Barrio* written by Judith Ortiz Cofer
Honor Titles: *The Bossy Gallito/El Gallo de Bodas: A Traditional Cuban Folktale* retold by Lucía González and illustrated by Lulu Delacre
Baseball in April, and Other Stories written by Gary Soto

Illustration Winner: *Chato's Kitchen* illustrated by Susan Guevara and written by Gary Soto
Honor Titles: *Pablo Remembers: The Fiesta of the Day of the Dead* illustrated and written by George Ancona
The Bossy Gallito/El Gallo de Bodas: A Traditional Cuban Folktale illustrated by Lulu Delacre and retold by Lucía González
Family Pictures/Cuadros de Familia illustrated and written by Carmen Lomas Garza

Robert F. Sibert Informational Book Award

This award is named in honor of Robert F. Sibert, long-time president of Bound to Stay Bound Books, Inc. Established in 2001 with support from Bound to Stay Books, the award is presented annually to the author of the most distinguished informational book published in the preceding year.

2008   Winner: *The Wall: Growing Up Behind the Iron Curtain* by Peter Sís
Honor Titles: *Lightship* by Brian Floca
Spiders by Nic Bishop

2007   Winner: *Team Moon: How 400,000 People Landed* Apollo 11 *on the Moon* by Catherine Thimmesh
Honor Titles: *Freedom Riders: John Lewis and Jim Zwerg on the Front Lines of the Civil Rights Movement* by Ann Bausum
Quest for the Tree Kangaroo: An Expedition to the Cloud Forest of New Guinea by Sy Montgomery
To Dance: A Ballerina's Graphic Novel by Siena Cherson Siegel

2006   Winner: *Secrets of a Civil War Submarine: Solving the Mysteries of the H. L. Hunley* by Sally M. Walker
Honor Title: *Hitler Youth: Growing Up in Hitler's Shadow* by Susan Campbell Bartoletti

2005   Winner: *The Voice That Challenged a Nation: Marian Anderson and the Struggle for Equal Rights* by Russell Freedman
Honor Titles: *Walt Whitman: Words for America* by Barbara Kerley
The Tarantula Scientist by Sy Montgomery
Sequoyah: The Cherokee Man Who Gave His People Writing by James Rumford

2004   Winner: *An American Plague: The True and Terrifying Story of the Yellow Fever Epidemic of 1793* by Jim Murphy
Honor Title: *I Face the Wind* by Vicki Cobb

2003   Winner: *The Life and Death of Adolf Hitler* by James Cross Giblin
Honor Title: *Six Days in October: The Stock Market Crash of 1929* by Karen Blumenthal
Hole in My Life by Jack Gantos
Action Jackson by Jan Greenberg
When Marian Sang: The True Recital of Marian Anderson by Pam Muñoz Ryan

2002   Winner: *Black Potatoes: The Story of the Great Irish Famine, 1845–1850* by Susan Campbell Bartoletti
Honor Titles: *Surviving Hitler: A Boy in the Nazi Death Camps* by Andrea Warren
Vincent van Gogh by Jan Greenberg and Sandra Jordan
Brooklyn Bridge by Lynn Curlee

2001   Winner: *Sir Walter Ralegh and the Quest for El Dorado* by Marc Aronson
Honor Titles: *The Longitude Prize* by Joan Dash
Blizzard! The Storm That Changed America by Jim Murphy
My Season with Penguins: An Antarctic Journal by Sophie Webb
Pedro and Me: Friendship, Loss, and What I Learned by Judd Winick

Schneider Family Book Award

This award, established in 2004, is given annually in three categories to the book that best portrays some aspect of living with a disability. The disability may be physical or mental.

2008   *Kami and the Yaks* by Andrea Stenn Stryer. Illus. Bert Dodson—Young Children
Reaching for Sun by Tracie Vaughn Zimmer—Middle School
Hurt Go Happy by Ginny Rorby—Teen

2007   *The Deaf Musicians* by Pete Seeger and Paul DuBois. Illus. R. Gregory Christine—Young Children
Rules by Cynthia Lord—Middle School
Small Steps by Louis Sachar—Teen

2006   *Dad, Jackie, and Me* by Myron Uhlberg. Illus. Colin Bootman—Young Children
Tending to Grace by Kimberly Newton Fusco—Middle School
Under the Wolf, Under the Dog by Adam Rapp—Teen

2005   *My Pal Victor/Mi amigo, Victor* by Diane Gonzaels Bertrand. Illus. Robert L. Sweetland—Young Children
Becoming Naomi León by Pam Muñoz Ryan—Middle School
My Thirteenth Winter: A Memoir by Samantha Abeel—Teen

2004   *Looking Out for Sarah* by Glenna Lang—Young Children
A Mango-Shaped Space by Wendy Mass—Middle School
Things Not Seen by Andrew Clements—Teen

Scott O'Dell Award for Historical Fiction

This award, named after Scott O'Dell, a noted young adult historical fiction novelist, is given annually to the best contribution in the field of historical fiction.

2008   *Elijah of Buxton* by Christopher Paul Curtis
2007   *The Green Glass Sea* by Ellen Klages
2006   *The Game of Silence* by Louise Erdich

2005   *Worth* by A. LaFaye
2004   *The River Between Us* by Richard Peck
2003   *Trouble Don't Last* by Shelley Pearsall
2002   *The Land* by Mildred D. Taylor
2001   *The Art of Keeping Cool* by Janet Taylor Lisle
2000   *Two Suns in the Sky* by Miriam Bat-Ami
1999   *Forty Acres and Maybe a Mule* by Harriette Gillem Robinet
1998   *Out of the Dust* by Karen Hesse
1997   *Jip, His Story* by Katherine Paterson
1996   *The Bomb* by Theodore Taylor
1995   *Under the Blood-Red Sun* by Graham Salisbury
1994   *Bull Run* by Paul Fleischman
1993   *Morning Girl* by Michael Dorris
1992   *Stepping on the Cracks* by Mary Downing Hahn
1991   *A Time of Troubles* by Pieter Van Raven
1990   *Shades of Grey* by Carolyn Reeder
1989   *The Honorable Prison* by Lyll Becerra de Jenkins
1988   *Charley Skedaddle* by Patricia Beatty
1987   *Streams to the River, River to the Sea* by Scott O'Dell
1986   *Sarah, Plain and Tall* by Patricia MacLachlan
1985   *The Fighting Ground* by Avi
1984   *The Sign of the Beaver* by Elizabeth George Speare

Top Ten Great Graphic Novels for Teens, 2008

The graphic novel is one of the fastest growing genres in young adult literature. The American Library Association has begun developing a list of the top 10 titles each year. These titles were published in 2007 and winners were announced in January 2008.

1. *Laika* by Nick Abadzis
2. *Re-Gifters* by Mike Carey, Sonny Liew, and Marc Hempel
3. *The Magical Life of Long Tack Sam* by Ann Marie Fleming
4. *Blue Beetle: Shell Shocked* and *Blue Beetle Road Trip* by Keith Giffen
5. *King of Thorn*, vols. 1–2 by Yuji Iwahara
6. *Sidescrollers* by Matthew Loux
7. *After School Nightmare*, vols. 1–5 by Setona Mizushiro
8. *Emma*, vols. 1–5 by Kaoru Mori
9. *The Wall: Growing Up Behind the Iron Curtain* by Peter Sís
10. *The Arrival* by Shaun Tan

ALA Outstanding Books for the College Bound

History

Columbus in the Americas by William Least Heat-Moon
A Distant Mirror: The Calamitous 14th Century by Barbara Tuchman
The Dream: Martin Luther King, Jr. and the Speech That Inspired a Nation by Drew D. Hansen
The Endurance: Shackleton's Legendary Antarctic Expedition by Caroline Alexander
The Farming of Bones by Edwidge Danticat
First They Killed My Father: A Daughter of Cambodia Remembers by Loung Ung
Founding Brothers: The Revolutionary Generation by Joseph J. Ellis
Give Me My Father's Body: The Life of Minik, the New York Eskimo by Kenn Harper
Indian Givers: How the Indians of the Americas Transformed the World by Jack Weatherford
Jefferson's Children: The Story of One American Family by Shannon Lanier
John Adams by David McCullough
Krakatoa: The Day the World Exploded: August 27, 1883 by Simon Winchester
Lindbergh by A. Scott Berg
The Modern Mind: An Intellectual History of the 20th Century by Peter Watson
Poets of World War II edited by Harvey Shapiro
The Sagas of Icelanders: A Selection edited by Jane Smiley

Six Wives: The Queens of Henry VIII by David Starkey

Smoke and Ashes: The Story of the Holocaust by Barbara Rogasky

Stone Heart: A Novel of Sacajawea by Diane Glancy

Terror of the Spanish Main, Sir Henry Morgan and His Buccaneers by Albert Marrin

Triangle: The Fire That Changed America by David Von Drehle

Troy by Adele Geras

Understanding September 11, Answering Questions about the Attacks on America by Mitch Frank

War Letters: Extraordinary Correspondence from American Wars edited by Andrew Carroll

Witch-Hunt: Mysteries of the Salem Witch Trials by Marc Aronson

Science and Technology

Atom: An Odyssey from the Big Bang to Life on Earth . . . and Beyond by Lawrence Krauss

The Demon in the Freezer: A True Story by Richard Preston

Dinner at the New Gene Café: How Genetic Engineering Is Changing What We Eat, How We Live, and the Global Politics of Food by Bill Lambrecht

Dr. Tatiana's Sex Advice to All Creation: The Definitive Guide to the Evolutionary Biology of Sex by Olivia Judson

El Niño: Unlocking the Secrets of the Master Weather-Maker by Madeline Nash

Eureka! Scientific Breakthroughs That Changed the World by Leslie Alan Horvitz

The Golden Ratio: The Story of Phi, the World's Most Astonishing Number by Mario Livio

Great Projects: The Epic Story of the Building of America from the Taming of the Mississippi to the Invention of the Internet by James Tobin

Hydrogen: The Essential Element by John S. Rigden

In Code: A Mathematical Journey by Sarah Flannery

Insect Lives: Stories of Mystery and Romance from a Hidden World edited by Erich Hoyt and Ted Schultz

Inventing Modern America: From the Microwave to the Mouse by David Brown

Last Breath: Cautionary Tales from the Limits of Human Endurance by Peter Stark

The Little Ice Age: How Climate Made History, 1300–1850 by Brian Fagan

Longitude: The True Story of a Lone Genius Who Solved the Greatest Scientific Problem of His Time by Dava Sobel

Madness: A Brief History by Roy Porter

The Number Devil: A Mathematical Adventure by Hans Enzensberger

Primal Teen: What the New Discoveries about the Teenage Brain Tell Us about Our Kids by Barbara Strauch

Promised the Moon: The Untold Story of the First Women in the Space Race by Stephanie Nolan

The Sand-Reckoner by Gillian Bradshaw

The Seven Daughters of Eve: The Science That Reveals Our Genetic Ancestry by Bryan Sykes

A Short History of Nearly Everything by Bill Bryson

Stiff: The Curious Lives of Human Cadavers by Mary Roach

The Universe in a Nutshell by Steven Hawking

What Do You Care What Other People Think?: Further Adventures of a Curious Character by Richard Feynman

Social Sciences

An American Insurrection: James Meredith and The Battle of Oxford, Mississippi, 1962 by William Doyle

And Still We Rise: The Trials and Triumps of Twelve Gifted Inner-City High School Students by Miles Corwin

Barefoot Heart: Stories of a Migrant Child by Elva Trevino Hart

Crossing Over: A Mexican Family on the Migrant Trail by Ruben Marinez

The Curious Incident of the Dog in the Night-Time by Mark Haddon

Damned Lies and Statistics: Untangling Numbers from the Media, Politicians, and Activists by Joel Best

Guns, Germs and Steel: The Fates of Human Societies by Jared Diamond

Geeks: How Two Lost Boys Rode the Internet Out of Idaho by Jon Katz

The Kite Runner by Khaled Hosseini

Light at the Edge of the World: A Journey through the Realm of Vanishing Cultures by Wade Davis

The Middle of Everywhere: The World's Refugees Come to Our Town by Mary Pipher

My Forbidden Face: Growing Up under the Taliban A Young Woman's Story by Latifa

Newjack, Guarding Sing Sing by Ted Conover

Nickel and Dimed: On (Not) Getting by in America by Barbara Ehrenreich

Speak Truth to Power: Human Rights Defenders Who Are Changing Our World by Kerry Kennedy Cuomo

True Notebooks by Mark Salzman

Tuesdays with Morrie: An Old Man, A Young Man, and Life's Greatest Lesson by Mitch Albom

Why Terrorism Works: Understanding the Threat, Responding to the Challenge by Alan M. Dershowitz

Caramelo by Sandra Cisneros

Chinese Cinderella: The True Story of an Unwanted Daughter by Adeline Mah

Feed by M. T. Anderson

Fires in the Mirror: Crown Heights, Brooklyn and Other Identities by Anna Deavere Smith

Forgotten Fire by Adam Bagdasarian

Go and Come Back by Joan Abelove

The Golden Compass by Philip Pullman

A Gracious Plenty by Sheri Reynolds

How to Read Literature Like a Professor: A Lively and Entertaining Guide to Reading between the Lines by Thomas C. Foster

In the Time of Butterflies by Julia Alvarez

Life Is Funny by E. R. Frank

Lucky: A Memoir by Alice Sebold

Me and Orson Welles by Robert Kaplow

Monster by Walter Dean Myers

My Heartbeat by Garrett Freymann-Weyr

Persepolis: The Story of a Childhood by Marjane Satrapi

Postcards from No Man's Land by Aidan Chambers

Push by Sapphire

A Rose That Grew from Concrete by Tupac Shakur

Speak by Laurie Halse Anderson

19 Varieties of Gazelle: Poems of the Middle East by Naomi Shihab Nye

Woe Is I: The Grammarphobe's Guide to Better English in Plain English by Patricia T. O'Connor

Literature and Language Arts

Bastard out of Carolina by Dorothy Allison

The Bean Trees by Barbara Kingsolver

Bird by Bird: Some Instructions on Writing and Life by Anne Lamott

Appendix C

Picture Books for the Classroom

English Language Arts

13 Monsters Who Should Be Avoided by Kevin Shortsleeve. Illus. Michael Austin. Atlanta: Peachtree, 1998.

All the Places to Love by Patricia MacLachlan. Illus. Mike Wimmer. New York: HarperCollins, 1994.

Anthony and the Girls by Ole Könnecke. Trans. Nancy Seitz. New York: Farrar, Straus & Giroux, 2006. (humor/gender roles)

Appalachia: The Voices of Sleeping Birds by Cynthia Rylant. Illus. Barry Moser. Orlando, FL: Harcourt, 1991.

Belinda by Pamela Allen. New York: Viking/Penguin, 1992. (humor)

Big Chickens by Leslie Helakoski. Illus. Henry Cole. New York: Dutton/Penguin, 2006. (humor)

A Chair for My Mother by Vera B. Williams. New York: Greenwillow/HarperCollins, 1982.

Cherish Today: A Celebration of Life's Moments by Kristina Evans. Illus. Bryan Collier. New York: Jump at the Sun/Hyperion, 2007.

A Child's Calendar by John Updike. Illus. Trina Schart Hyman. New York: Holiday House, 1999.

Christmas Day in the Morning by Pearl S. Buck. Illus. Mark Buehner. New York: HarperCollins, 2002.

Cowboy and Octopus by Jon Scieszka. Illus. Lane Smith. New York: Viking/Penguin, 2007. (humor)

Dark Sparkle Tea and Other Bedtime Poems by Tim Myers. Illus. Kelley Cunningham. Honesdale, PA: Wordsong/Boyds Mills Press, 2006.

Dear Deer: A Book of Homophones by Gene Barretta. New York: Henry Holt, 2007.

The Dirty Cowboy by Amy Timberlake. Illus. Adam Rex. New York: Farrar, Straus & Giroux, 2003. (humor)

Fly Away Home by Eve Bunting. Illus. Ronald Himler. New York: Clarion, 1991.

Four Hens and a Rooster by Lena Landström. Illus. Olof Landström. Trans. Joan Sandin. New York: R & S Books, 2005. (feminism)

Gawain and the Green Knight by Mark Shannon. Illus. David Shannon. New York: Putnam/Penguin, 1994.

Girls A to Z by Eve Bunting. Illus. Suzanne Bloom. Honesdale, PA: Boyds Mills Press, 2002. (gender roles)

The Giving Tree by Shel Silverstein. New York: HarperCollins, 1964.

Henry Hikes to Fitchburg by D. B. Johnson. Boston: Houghton Mifflin, 2000. (Henry David Thoreau)

The Hero Beowulf by Eric A. Kimmel. Illus. Leonard Everett Fisher. New York: Farrar, Straus & Giroux, 2005.

How Much Can a Bare Bear Bear?: What Are Homonyms and Homophones? by Brian P. Cleary. Illus. Brian Gable. Minneapolis, MN: Millbrook Press, 2005.

I Walk at Night by Lois Duncan. Illus. Steve Johnson and Lou Fancher. New York: Puffin/Penguin, 2000. (poetry)

I'll Always Love You by Hans Wilhelm. New York: Crown, 1985.

Imagine a Night by Sarah L. Thomson. Illus. Rob Gonsalves. New York: Atheneum/Simon & Schuster, 2003. (poetry)

The Incredible Book Eating Boy by Oliver Jeffers. New York: Philomel/Penguin, 2007. (humor)

Ivan the Terrier by Peter Catalanotto. New York: Atheneum/Simon & Schuster, 2007. (humor)

John Henry by Julius Lester. Illus. Jerry Pinkney. New York: Scholastic, 1994. (personification and hyperbole)

A Kick in the Head: An Everyday Guide to Poetic Forms edited by Paul Janeczko. Illus. Chris Raschka. Cambridge, MA: Candlewick Press, 2005.

Kitten's First Full Moon by Kevin Henkes. New York: Greenwillow/HarperCollins, 2004. (poetry)

Late for School by Mike Reiss. Illus. Michael Austin. Atlanta: Peachtree, 2003. (poetry)

The Little Red Hen: An Old Story by Margot Zemach. New York: Farrar, Straus & Giroux, 1983.

Long Night Moon by Cynthia Rylant. Illus. Mark Siegel. New York: Simon & Schuster, 2004. (poetry)

Me I Am! by Jack Prelutsky. Illus. Christine Davenier. New York: Farrar, Straus & Giroux, 2007. (poetry)

Meet Wild Boars by Meg Rosoff. Illus. Sophie Blackall. New York: Henry Holt, 2005. (humor)

Miss Crandall's School for Young Ladies and Little Misses of Color by Elizabeth Alexander and Marilyn Nelson. Illus. Floyd Cooper. Honesdale, PA: Wordsong/Boyds Mills Press, 2007. (poetry)

Mom and Dad Are Palindromes: A Dilemma for Words by Mark Shulman. Illus. Adam McCauley. San Francisco: Chronicle Books, 2006.

The Moon by Robert Louis Stevenson. Illus. Tracey Campbell Pearson. New York: Farrar, Straus & Giroux, 2006.

My Feet Are Laughing by Lissette Norman. Illus. Frank Morrison. New York: Farrar, Straus & Giroux, 2006.

No Moon, No Milk! by Chris Babcock. Illus. Mark Teague. New York: Crown, 1993. (humor)

Old Mr. Mackle Hackle by Gunnar Madsen. Illus. Irana Shepherd. New York: Little, Brown, 2005. (poetry)

Once upon a Tomb: Gravely Humorous Verses by J. Patrick Lewis. Illus. Simon Bartram. Cambridge, MA: Candlewick Press, 2006. (poetry/dark humor)

Owl Moon by Jane Yolen. Illus. John Schoenherr. New York: Philomel/Penguin, 1987.

Pass It On: African-American Poetry for Children edited by Wade Hudson. Illus. Floyd Cooper. New York: Scholastic, 1993.

Paul Revere's Ride by Henry Wadsworth Longfellow. Illus. Monica Vachula. Honesdale, PA: Boyds Mills Press, 2003.

Pitch and Throw, Grasp and Know: What Is a Synonym? by Brian P. Cleary. Illus. Brian Gable. Minneapolis, MN: Carolrhoda Books, 2005.

The Prince Won't Go to Bed! by Dayle Ann Dodds. Illus. Kyrsten Brooker. New York: Farrar, Straus & Giroux, 2007. (poetry)

Punctuation Takes a Vacation by Robin Pulver. Illus. Lynn Rowe Reed. New York: Holiday House, 2003.

The Relatives Came by Cynthia Rylant. Illus. Stephen Gammell. New York: Scholastic,1993.

Sister Tricksters: Rollicking Tales of Clever Females by Robert D. San Souci. Illus. Daniel San Souci. Little Rock, AK: August House, 2006.

Stopping by Woods on a Snowy Evening by Robert Frost. Illus. Susan Jeffers. New York: Dutton/Penguin, 2001.

Suddenly Alligator: An Adverbial Tale by Rick Walton. Illus. Jim Bradshaw. Salt Lake City: Gibbs Smith, 2004.

The Sunshine Home by Eve Bunting. Illus. Diane deGroat. New York: Clarion, 1994.

Sweet, Sweet Memory by Jacqueline Woodson. Illus. Floyd Cooper. Jump at the Sun/ Hyperion, 2007.

Two Bad Ants by Chris Van Allsburg. Boston: Houghton Mifflin, 1988. (metaphor/simile)

Two Sticks by Orel Protopopescu. Illus. Anne Wilsdorf. New York: Farrar, Straus & Giroux, 2007.

Vatos by Luis Alberto Urrea. Photographs by José Galvez. El Paso, TX: Cinco Puntos Press, 2000. (poetry)

When I Am Old with You by Angela Johnson. Illus. David Soman. New York: Orchard/Scholastic, 1993.

William Shakespeare's Hamlet by Bruce Coville. Illus. Leonid Gore. New York: Dial/ Penguin, 2004.

William Shakespeare's Romeo & Juliet by Bruce Coville. Illus. Dennis Nolan. New York: Dial/Penguin, 1999.

William Shakespeare's The Winter's Tale by Bruce Coville. Illus. LeUyen Pham. New York: Dial/Penguin, 2007.

Wonderful Words: Poems about Reading, Writing, Speaking, and Listening edited by Lee Bennett Hopkins. Illus. Karen Barbour. New York: Simon & Schuster, 2004. (poetry)

Mathematics

100 Days of School by Trudy Harris. Illus. Beth Griffis Johnson. Minneapolis, MN: Millbrook Press, 1999.

The Adventures of Penrose the Mathematical Cat by Theoni Pappas. San Carlos, CA: Wide World, 1997.

Alice in Pastaland: A Math Adventure by Alexandra Wright. Illus. Reagan Word. Watertown, MA: Charlesbridge, 1997.

Anno's Mysterious Multiplying Jar by Masaichiro Anno and Mitsumasa Anno. New York: Philomel/Penguin, 1983.

Beanstalk: The Measure of a Giant: A Math Adventure by Ann McCallum. Illus. James Balkovek. Watertown, MA: Charlesbridge, 2006.

The Best of Times: Math Strategies That Multiply by Greg Tang. Illus. Harry Briggs. New York: Scholastic, 2002.

Big Is Big (and Little, Little): A Book of Contrasts by J. Patrick Lewis. Illus. Bob Barner. New York: Holiday House, 2007.

Cheetah Math: Learning about Division from Baby Cheetahs by Ann Whitehead Nagda. New York: Henry Holt, 2007.

Cut Down to Size at High Noon: A Math Adventure by Scott Sundby. Illus. Wayne Geehan. Watertown, MA: Charlesbridge, 2000.

Divide and Ride by Stuart J. Murphy. Illus. George Ulrich. New York: HarperCollins, 1997.

The Doorbell Rang by Pat Hutchins. New York: Greenwillow/HarperCollins, 1986.

The Dot and the Line: A Romance in Lower Mathematics by Norton Juster. San Francisco, CA: Chronicle Books, 2001. (Original work published 1963)

Equal Shmequal: A Math Adventure by Virginia L. Kroll. Illus. Philomena O'Neill. Watertown, MA: Charlesbridge, 2005.

Fractals, Googols and Other Mathematical Tales by Theoni Pappas. San Carlos, CA: Wide World, 1993.

Fraction Fun by David A. Adler. Illus. Nancy Tobin. New York: Holiday House, 1996.

Grandpa Gazillion's Number Yard by Laurie Keller. New York: Henry Holt, 2005.

The Grapes of Math: Mind-Stretching Math Riddles by Greg Tang. Illus. Harry Briggs. New York: Scholastic, 2001.

Greedy Apostrophe: A Cautionary Tale by Jan Carr. Illus. Ethan Long. New York: Holiday House, 2007.

The Greedy Triangle by Marilyn Burns. Illus. Gordon Silveria. New York: Scholastic, 1994.

How Big Is Big? by Stephen Strauss. Illus. The Fernandes 4. Brookfield, CT: Millbrook Press, 1999.

How Much Is a Million? by David M. Schwartz. Illus. Steven Kellogg. New York: HarperCollins, 1985.

Incredible Comparisons by Russell Ash. New York: DK, 1996.

The King's Chessboard by David Birch. Illus. Devis Grebu. New York: Dial/Penguin, 1988.

The King's Commissioners by Aileen Friedman. Illus. Susan Guevara. New York: Scholastic, 1994.

The Librarian Who Measured the Earth by Kathryn Lasky. Illus. Kevin Hawkes. New York: Little, Brown, 1994.

Math Appeal by Greg Tang. Illus. Harry Briggs. New York: Scholastic, 2003.

Math Curse by Jon Scieszka. Illus. Lane Smith. New York: Viking/Penguin, 1995.

Math Fables: Lessons That Count by Greg Tang. Illus. Heather Cahoon. New York: Scholastic, 2004.

Math Fables Too: Making Science Count by Greg Tang. Illus. Taia Morley. New York: Scholastic, 2007.

Math for All Seasons: Mind-Stretching Math Riddles by Greg Tang. Illus. Harry Briggs. New York: Scholastic, 2002.

Math Potatoes: More Mind-Stretching Brain Food by Greg Tang. Illus. Harry Briggs. New York: Scholastic, 2005.

Math Talk: Mathematical Ideas in Poems for Two Voices by Theoni Pappas. San Carlos, CA: Wide World, 1991.

Math-terpieces by Greg Tang. Illus. Greg Paprocki. New York: Scholastic, 2003.

Mathematickles! by Betsy Franco. Illus. Steven Salerno. New York: McElderry/Simon & Schuster, 2003.

A Million Fish . . . More or Less by Patricia McKissack. Illus. Dena Schutzer. New York: Knopf/Random House, 1992.

The Monster Who Did My Math by Danny Schnitzlein. Illus. Bill Mayer. Atlanta: Peachtree, 2007.

Multiplying Menace: The Revenge of Rumpelstiltskin: A Math Adventure by Pam Calvert. Illus. Wayne Geehan. Watertown, MA: Charlesbridge, 2006.

Mummy Math: An Adventure in Geometry by Cindy Neuschwander. Illus. Bryan Langdo. New York: Henry Holt, 2005.

On Beyond a Million: An Amazing Math Journey by David M. Schwartz. Illus. Paul Meisel. New York: Random House, 1999.

Once Upon a Dime: A Math Adventure by Nancy Kelly Allen. Illus. Adam Doyle. Watertown, MA: Charlesbridge, 1999.

One Grain of Rice: A Mathematical Folk Tale by Demi. New York: Scholastic, 1997.

Patterns in Peru: An Adventure in Patterning by Cindy Neuschwander. Illus. Bryan Langdo. New York: Henry Holt, 2007.

A Place for Zero: A Math Adventure by Angeline Sparagna Lopresti. Illus. Phyllis Hornung, Watertown, MA, Charlesbridge, 2003.

Rabbits Rabbits Everywhere: A Fibonacci Tale by Ann McCallum. Illus. Gideon Kendall. Watertown, MA: Charlesbridge, 2007.

The Rajah's Rice: A Mathematical Folk Tale by David Barry. Illus. Donna Perrone. New York: Scientific American Books, 1994.

Shapes, Shapes, Shapes by Tana Hoban. New York: Greenwillow/HarperCollins, 1986.

Sir Cumference and the Dragon of Pi: A Math Adventure by Cindy Neuschwander. Illus. Wayne Geehan. Watertown, MA: Charlesbridge, 2004.

Sir Cumference and the First Round Table: A Math Adventure by Cindy Neuschwander. Illus. Wane Geehan. Watertown, MA: Charlesbridge, 1997.

Sir Cumference and the Great Knight of Angleland: A Math Adventure by Cindy Neuschwander. Illus. Wayne Geehan. Watertown, MA: Charlesbridge, 2001.

Sir Cumference and the Isle of Immeter: A Math Adventure by Cindy Neuschwander.

Illus. Wayne Geehan. Watertown, MA: Charlesbridge, 2006.

Sir Cumference and the Sword in the Cone: A Math Adventure by Cindy Neuschwander. Illus. Wayne Geehan. Watertown, MA: Charlesbridge, 2003.

Sold! A Mothematics Adventure by Nathan Zimelman. Illus. Bryan Barnard. Watertown, MA: Charlesbridge, 2000.

Spaghetti and Meatballs for All: A Mathematical Story by Marilyn Burns. Illus. Debbie Tilley. New York: Scholastic, 1997.

Stacks of Trouble by Martha F. Brenner. Illus. Liza Woodruff. New York: Kane Press, 2000.

Too Many Pumpkins by Linda White. Illus. Megan Lloyd. New York: Holiday House, 1996.

Twizzlers Percentages Book by Jerry Pallotta. Illus. Rob Bolster. New York: Scholastic, 2001.

Twizzlers Shapes and Patterns by Jerry Pallotta. Illus. Rob Bolster. New York: Scholastic, 2002.

Two of Everything: A Chinese Folktale by Lily Toy Hong. Morton Gove, IL: A. Whitman, 1993.

Weighing the Elephant by Ting-xing Ye. Illus. Suzane Langlois. Toronto: Annick, 1998.

What's Your Angle, Pythagoras? A Math Adventure by Julie Ellis. Illus. Phyllis Hornung. Watertown, MA: Charlesbridge, 2004.

The Wishing Club: A Story about Fractions by Donna Jo Napoli. Illus. Anna Currey. New York: Henry Holt, 2007.

Science

Amazon Diary by Hudson Talbott and Mark Greenberg. New York: Putnam/ Penguin, 1996.

And Still the Turtle Watched by Sheila MacGill-Callahan. Illus. Barry Moser. New York: Dial/Penguin, 1991.

And Then There Was One: The Mysteries of Extinction by Margery Facklam. Illus. Pamela Johnson. San Francisco: Sierra Club Books, 1990.

Arrowhawk by Lola M. Schaefer. Illus. Gabi Swiatkowska. New York: Henry Holt, 2004.

At Home in the Rain Forest by Diane Willow. Illus. Laura Jacques. Watertown, MA: Charlesbridge, 1991.

Beyond the Sea of Ice: The Voyages of Henry Hudson by Joan E. Goodman. Illus. Fernando Rangel. New York: Mikaya Press, 1999.

Big Alaska: Journey across America's Most Amazing State by Debbie S. Miller. Illus. Jon Van Zyle. New York: Walker/ Bloomsbury, 2006.

Bodies from the Ash: Life and Death in Ancient Pompeii by James M. Deem. Boston: Houghton Mifflin, 2005.

Bones: Our Skeletal System by Seymour Simon. New York: HarperCollins, 1998.

The Brain: Our Nervous System by Seymour Simon. New York: HarperCollins, 1997.

Butterfly Eyes and Other Secrets of the Meadow by Joyce Sidman. Illus. Beth Krommes. Boston: Houghton Mifflin, 2006.

Close to the Wind: The Beaufort Scale by Peter Malone. New York: Putnam, 2007.

Cloudy with a Chance of Meatballs by Judi Barrett. Illus. Ron Barrett. Atheneum/ Simon & Schuster, 1978.

Comets, Meteors, and Asteroids by Seymour Simon. New York: HarperCollins, 1994.

Dancers in the Garden by Joanne Ryder. Illus. Judith Lopez. San Francisco: Sierra Club Books, 1992.

The Dandelion Seed by Joseph Anthony. Illus. Cris Arbo. Nevada City, CA: Dawn, 1997.

Dear Mr. Blueberry by Simon James. New York: McElderry/Simon & Schuster, 1991.

Dear Rebecca, Winter Is Here by Jean Craighead George. Illus. Loretta Krupinski. New York: HarperCollins, 1993.

The Desert Is Theirs by Byrd Baylor. Illus. Peter Parnall. New York: Atheneum/Simon & Schuster, 1975.

Desert Voices by Byrd Baylor. Illus. Peter Parnall. New York: Atheneum/Simon & Schuster, 1981.

Destination: Space by Seymour Simon. New York: Smithsonian, 2006.

A Drop around the World by Barbara Shaw McKinney. Illus. Michael S. Maydak. Nevada City, CA: Dawn, 1998.

Earthdance by Joanne Ryder. Illus. Norman Gorbaty. New York: Henry Holt, 1996.

Everglades by Jean Craighead George. Illus. Wendell Minor. New York: HarperCollins, 1995.

Feathered Dinosaurs of China by Gregory Wenzel. Watertown, MA: Charlesbridge, 2004.

Flute's Journey: The Life of a Wood Thrush by Lynne Cherry. San Diego: Harcourt, 1997.

Following the Coast by Jim Arnosky. New York: HarperCollins, 2004.

Galaxies by Seymour Simon. New York: Morrow Junior Books, 1988.

A Garden of Whales by Maggie Steincrohn Davis. Illus. Jennifer Barrett O'Connell. Charlotte, VT: Camden House, 1993.

The Goodnight Circle by Carolyn Lesser. Illus. Lorinda B. Cauley. San Diego: Harcourt, 1984.

The Great Kapok Tree: A Tale of the Amazon Rain Forest by Lynne Cherry. San Diego: Harcourt, 1990.

The Heart of the Wood by Marguerite Davol. Illus. Sheila Hamanaka. New York: Simon & Schuster, 2002.

Here Is the Tropical Rain Forest by Madeleine Dunphy. Illus. Michael Rothman. Berkeley, CA: Web of Life Children's Books, 2006.

How Do You Lift a Lion? by Robert E. Wells. Morton Grove, IL: A. Whitman, 1996.

Hurricane by David Wiesner. New York: Clarion, 1990.

Hurricanes by Seymour Simon. New York: Smithsonian, 2007.

Ice Bear: In the Steps of the Polar Bear by Nicola Davies. Illus. Gary Blythe. Cambridge, MA: Candlewick Press, 2005.

Jack's Garden by Henry Cole. New York: Greenwillow/HarperCollins, 1995.

Just a Dream by Chris Van Allsburg. Boston: Houghton Mifflin, 1990.

Leaves by David Ezra Stein. New York: Putnam/Penguin, 2007.

Letting Swift River Go by Jane Yolen. Illus. Barbara Cooney. New York: Little, Brown, 1992.

Lifetimes by David L. Rice. Illus. Michael S. Maydak. Nevada City, CA: Dawn, 1997.

Lizard in the Sun by Joanne Ryder. Illus. Michael Rothman. New York: Morrow/HarperCollins, 1990.

The Lorax by Dr. Seuss. New York: Random House, 1971.

Lungs: Your Respiratory System by Seymour Simon. New York: Smithsonian, 2007.

The Man Who Made Time Travel by Kathryn Lasky. Illus. Kevin Henkes. New York: Farrar, Straus & Giroux, 2003.

Marvelous Mattie: How Margaret E. Knight Became an Inventor by Emily Arnold McCully. New York: Farrar, Straus & Giroux, 2006.

Morning, Noon, and Night by Jean Craighead George. Illus. Wendell Minor. New York: HarperCollins, 1999.

A Mother's Journey by Sandra Markle. Illus. Alan Marks. Watertown, MA: Charlesbridge, 2005.

Muscles: Our Muscular System by Seymour Simon. New York: HarperCollins, 1998.

My Father's Hands by Joanne Ryder. Illus. Mark Graham. New York: HarperCollins, 1994.

The New Way Things Work by David Macaulay. Boston: Houghton Mifflin, 1998.

Oh, Rats! The Story of Rats and People by Albert Marrin. Illus. C. B. Mordan. New York: Dutton/Penguin, 2006.

Once There Was a Tree by Natalia Romanova. Illus. Gennady Spirin. New York: Dial/ Penguin, 1985.

The Pebble in My Pocket: A History of Our Earth by Meredith Hooper. Illus. Christopher Coady. New York: Viking/Penguin, 1996.

Penguins by Seymour Simon. New York: Smithsonian, 2007.

Places of Power by Michael DeMunn. Illus. Noah Buchanan. Nevada City, CA: Dawn, 1997.

Prince William by Gloria Rand. Illus. Ted Rand. New York: Henry Holt, 1992.

A River Ran Wild: An Environmental History by Lynne Cherry. San Diego: Harcourt, 1992.

Shape Me a Rhyme: Nature's Forms in Poetry by Jane Yolen. Photographs by Jason Stemple. Honesdale, PA: Wordsong/ Boyds Mills Press, 2007.

Science Verse by Jon Scieszka. Illus. Lane Smith. New York: Viking/Penguin, 2004.

Sierra by Diane Siebert. Illus. Wendell Minor. New York: HarpeCollins, 1991.

The Snowflake: A Water Cycle Story by Neil Waldman. Brookfield, CT: Millbrook Press, 2003.

Snowflake Bentley by Jacqueline Briggs Martin. Illus. Mary Azarian. Boston: Houghton Mifflin, 1998.

Somewhere Today by Bert Kitchen. Cambridge, MA: Candlewick Press, 1992.

Spiders by Seymour Simon. New York: HarperCollins, 2003.

Starry Messenger: Galileo Galilei by Peter Sís. New York: Farrar, Straus & Giroux, 1996.

Stellaluna by Janell Cannon. Orlando, FL: Harcourt, 1993.

Surtsey: The Newest Place on Earth by Kathryn Lasky. Illus. Christopher Knight. New York: Hyperion, 1992.

Thirteen Moons on Turtle's Back: A Native American Year of Moons by Joseph Bruchac and Jonathan London. Illus. Thomas Locker. New York: Philomel/ Penguin, 1992.

This Is Our Earth by Laura Lee Benson. Illus. John Carrozza. Watertown, MA: Charlesbridge, 1997.

The Tree in the Ancient Forest by Carol Reed-Jones. Illus. Christopher Canyon. Nevada City, CA: Dawn, 1995.

The Tree of Life. Charles Darwin by Peter Sís. New York: Farrar, Straus & Giroux, 2003.

A Wasp Is Not a Bee by Marilyn Singer. Illus. Patrick O'Brien. New York: Henry Holt, 1995.

Water Dance by Thomas Locker. San Diego, CA: Harcourt, 1997.

Welcome to the Sea of Sand by Jane Yolen. Illus. Laura Regan. New York: Putnam/ Penguin, 1996.

When I Heard the Learn'd Astronomer by Walt Whitman. Illus. Loren Long. New York: Simon & Schuster, 2004.

Where Once There Was a Wood by Denis Fleming. New York: Henry Holt, 1996.

Where the Forest Meets the Sea by Jeannie Baker. New York: Greenwillow/ HarperCollins, 1987.

A Woodland Counting Book by Claudia McGehee. Iowa City: University of Iowa Press, 2006.

Social Studies
American History

A Is for America by Devin Scillian. Illus. Pam Carroll. Chelsea, MI: Sleeping Bear Press, 2001.

Ain't Nobody a Stranger to Me by Ann Grifalconi. Illus. Jerry Pinkney. New York: Jump at the Sun/Hyperion, 2007.

Anne Hutchinson's Way by Jeannine Atkins. Illus. Michael Dooling. New York: Farrar, Straus & Giroux, 2007.

Anno's Journey by Mitsumasa Anno. New York: Philomel/Penguin, 1981.

Arrow to the Sun: A Pueblo Indian Tale by Gerald McDermott. New York: Viking/Penguin, 2004. (Original work published 1974)

At Ellis Island: A History in Many Voices by Louise Peacock. Illus. Walter Lyon Krudop. New York: Atheneum/Simon & Schuster, 2007.

Baseball Saved Us by Ken Mochizuki. Illus. Dom Lee. New York: Lee & Low, 1993.

Beardream by Will Hobbs. Illus. Jill Kastner. New York: Atheneum/Simon & Schuster, 1997.

Beyond the Great Mountains by Ed Young. San Francisco: Chronicle Books, 2005.

Blues Journey by Walter Dean Myers. Illus. Christopher Myers. New York: Holiday House, 2003.

Boom Town by Sonia Levitin. Illus. Cat Bowman Smith. New York: Orchard/Scholastic, 1998.

Brother Eagle, Sister Sky by Chief Seattle. Illus. Susan Jeffers. New York: Dial/Penguin, 1991.

Conestoga Wagons by Richard Ammon. Illus. Bill Farnsworth. New York: Holiday House, 2000.

Dakota Dugout by Ann Warren Turner. Illus. Ronald Himler. New York: Macmillan, 1985.

Dandelions by Eve Bunting. Illus. Greg Shed. Orlando, FL: Harcourt, 1995.

A Day That Changed America: The Alamo by Shelley Tanaka. Illus. David Craig. New York: Hyperion, 2003.

A Day That Changed America: Gettysburg by Shelley Tanaka. Illus. David Craig. New York: Hyperion, 2003.

Down the Colorado: John Wesley Powell, the One-Armed Explorer by Deborah Kogan Ray. New York: Farrar, Straus & Giroux, 2007.

Drylongso by Virginia Hamilton. Illus. Jerry Pinkney. Orlando, FL: Harcourt, 1992.

Earthquake by Milly Lee. Illus. Yangsook Choi. New York: Farrar, Straus & Giroux, 2001.

The Escape of Oney Judge: Martha Washington's Slave Finds Freedom by Emily Arnold McCully. New York: Farrar, Straus & Giroux, 2007.

Four Feet, Two Sandals by Karen Lynn Williams & Khadra Mohammed. Illus. Doug Chayka. Grand Rapids, MI: Eerdmans Books.

Freedom Ship by Doreen Rappaport. Illus. Curtis James. New York: Hyperion, 2006.

From Slave Ship to Freedom Road by Julius Lester. Illus. Rod Brown. New York: Dial/Penguin, 1998.

Goin' Someplace Special by Patricia C. McKissack. Illus. Jerry Pinkney. New York: Atheneum/Simon & Schuster, 2001.

Grandfather's Journey by Allen Say. Boston: Houghton Mifflin, 1993.

In Coal Country by Judith Hendershot. Illus. Thomas B. Allen. New York: Knopf/Random House, 1987.

Jazz by Walter Dean Myers. Illus. Christopher Myers. New York: Holiday House, 2006.

Landed by Milly Lee. Illus. Yangsook Choi. New York: Farrar, Straus & Giroux, 2006.

Liberty by Lynn Curlee. New York: Atheneum/Simon & Schuster, 2000.

The Man Who Walked between the Towers by Mordicai Gerstein. Brookfield, CT: Roaring Brook Press, 2003.

The Middle Passage: White Ships/Black Cargo by Tom Feelings. New York: Dial/Penguin 1995.

Mississippi Morning by Ruth Vander Zee. Illus. Floyd Cooper. Grand Rapids, MI: Eerdmans Books, 2004.

Monsoon by Uma Krishnaswami. Illus. Jamel Akib. New York: Farrar, Straus & Giroux, 2003.

The Old African by Julius Lester. Illus. Jerry Pinkney. New York: Dial/Penguin, 2005.

One Thousand Tracings: Healing the Wounds of World War II by Lita Judge. New York: Hyperion, 2007.

The Other Side by Jacqueline Woodson. Illus. E. B. Lewis. New York: Putnam, 2001.

Patrol: An American Soldier in Vietnam by Walter Dean Myers. Illus. Ann Grifalconi. New York: HarperCollins, 2002.

Pennies in a Jar by Dori Chaconas. Illus. Ted Lewin. Atlanta: Peachtree, 2007.

Pink and Say by Patricia Polacco. New York: Philomel/Penguin, 1994.

Playing to Win: The Story of Althea Gibson by Karen Deans. Illus. Elbrite Brown. New York: Holiday House, 2007.

Sacagawea by Liselotte Erdrich. Illus. Julie Buffalohead. Minneapolis, MN: Carolrhoda Books, 2003.

Seeing the Elephant: A Story of the Civil War by Pat Hughes. Illus. Ken Stark. New York: Farrar, Straus & Giroux, 2007.

The Silk Route: 7,000 Miles of History by John S. Major. Illus. Stephen Fieser. New York: HarperCollins, 1995.

Smoky Night by Eve Bunting. Illus. David Diaz. Orlando, FL: Harcourt, 1994.

So You Want to Be President? by Judith St. George. Illus. David Small. New York: Philomel/Penguin, 2000.

The Star-spangled Banner by Amy Winstead. Illus. Bob Dacey and Debra Bandelin. Nashville, TN: Ideals Children's Books, 2003.

The Story of Ruby Bridges by Robert Coles. Illus. George Ford. New York: Scholastic, 1995.

Sweet Land of Liberty by Deborah Hopkinson. Illus. Leonard Jenkins. Atlanta: Peachtree, 2007.

Tattered Sails by Verla Kay. Illus. Dan Andreasen. New York: Putnam/Penguin, 2001.

Uptown by Collier Bryan. New York: Henry Holt, 2000.

The Wall by Eve Bunting. Illus. Ronald Himler. New York: Clarion, 1990.

We Are One: The Story of Bayard Rustin by Larry Dane Brimner. Honesdale, PA: Calkins Creek/Boyds Mills Press, 2007.

Yonder Mountain: A Cherokee Legend by Kay T. Bannon. Illus. Kristina Rodanas. New York: Marshall Cavendish, 2002.

Global Perspectives

Brothers in Hope: The Story of the Lost Boys of Sudan by Mary Williams. Illus. R. Gregory Christie. New York: Lee & Low, 2005.

The Day the Stones Walked: A Tale of Easter Island by T. A. Barron. Illus. William Low. New York: Philomel/Penguin, 2007.

The First Music by Dylan Pritchett. Illus. Erin Bennett Banks. Atlanta: LittleFolk/August House, 2006.

Good Yontif: A Picture Book of the Jewish Year by Rose Blue. Illus. Lynne Feldman. Brookfield, CT: Millbrook Press, 1997.

Hidden in Sand by Margaret Hodges. Illus. Paul Birling. New York: Scribner, 1994.

Long-Long's New Year by Catherine Gower. Illus. He Zhihong. Boston: Tuttle, 1995.

My Dadima Wears a Sari by Kashmira Sheth. Illus. Yoshiko Jaeggi. Atlanta: Peachtree, 2007.

Niño's Mask by Jeanette Winter. New York: Dial/Penguin, 2003.

One Day We Had to Run! by Sybella Wilkes. Brookfield, CT: Millbrook Press, 1994.

Ramadan by Suhaib Hamid Ghazi. Illus. Omar Rayyan. New York: Holiday House, 1996.

The Secret Seder by Doreen Rappaport. Illus. Emily Arnold McCully. New York: Hyperion, 2003.

The Seven Wonders of the Ancient World by Lynn
    Curlee. New York: Atheneum/Simon &
    Schuster, 2002.
Sitti's Secret by Naomi Shihab Nye. Illus.
    Nancy Carpenter. New York: Aladdin/
    Simon & Schuster, 1997.
Taj Mahal by Caroline Arnold and Madeleine
    Comora. Illus. Rahal Bhaghan.
    Minneapolis, MN: Carolrhoda Books,
    2007.
The Wall: Growing Up Behind the Iron Curtain by
    Peter Sís. New York: Farrar, Straus &
    Giroux, 2007.
*Where in the World? Around the Globe in 13 Works
    of Art* by Bob Raczka. Minneapolis, MN:
    Millbrook Press, 2007.
Whoever You Are by Mem Fox. Illus. Leslie
    Staub. San Diego: Harcourt, 1997.
*The Yellow Star: The Legend of King Christian
    X of Denmark* by Carmen Agra
    Deedy. Illus. Henri Sorensen. Atlanta:
    Peachtree, 2000.

Fairy Tale, Folklore, and Myth

*Agatha's Feather Bed: Not Just Another Wild
    Goose Story* by Carmen Agra Deedy.
    Illus. Laura L. Seeley. Atlanta:
    Peachtree, 1991.
The Bearskinner: A Tale of the Brothers Grimm by
    Laura Amy Schlitz. Illus. Max Grafe.
    Cambridge, MA: Candlewick Press,
    2007.
The Bossy Gallito retold by Lucía M. González.
    Illus. Lulu Delacre. New York:
    Scholastic, 1994.
Dear Peter Rabbit by Alma Flor Ada. Illus.
    Leslie Tryon. New York: Atheneum/
    Simon & Schuster, 1994.
The Enchanted Wood by Ruth Sanderson. New
    York: Little, Brown, 1991.
The Farmer in the Dell by John O'Brien.
    Honesdale, PA: Boyds Mills Press,
    2000.
The Frog Prince Continued by Jon Scieszka.
    Illus. Steve Johnson. New York: Puffin,
    1991.

The Frog Prince or Iron Henry by Jacob Grimm
    and Wilhelm Grimm. Trans. Naomi
    Lewis. Illus. Binette Schroeder. New
    York: North-South Books, 1989.
Froggy Went A-Courtin' by Kevin O'Malley.
    New York: Stewart, Tabori, & Chang,
    1992.
Go to Sleep, Gecko: A Balinese Folktale by
    Margaret Read MacDonald. Illus
    Geraldo Valério. Little Rock, AK:
    LittleFolk/August House, 2006.
*The Gold Miner's Daughter: A Melodramatic
    Fairy Tale* by Jackie Mims Hopkins.
    Illus. Jon Goodell. Atlanta, Peachtree,
    2006.
Goldilocks by Janice Russell. Honesdale, PA:
    Boyds Mills Press, 1997.
*The Great Smelly, Slobbery, Small-Tooth Dog:
    A Folktale from Great Britain* retold by
    Margaret Read MacDonald. Illus. Julie
    Paschkis. Atlanta: LittleFolk/August
    House, 2007.
The Greedy Man in the Moon by Rick Rossiter.
    Illus. Dick Smolinski. St. Petersburg,
    FL: Riverbank Press, 1994.
Hans Christina Andersen's Fairy Tales by Lisbeth
    Zwerger. Trans. Anthea Bell. New
    York: Penguin, 1991.
Hans Christian Andersen's Thumbelina by
    Lauren Mills. New York: Little, Brown,
    2005.
Hansel and Gretel by Will Moses. New York:
    Philomel/Penguin, 2006.
Heckedy Peg by Audrey Wood. Illus. Don
    Wood. Orlando, FL: Harcourt, 1987.
The Impudent Rooster by Sabina I. Răscol.
    Illus. Holly Berry. New York: Dutton/
    Penguin, 2004.
Iron Hans: A Grimms' Fairy Tale by Stephen
    Mitchell. Illus. Matt Tavares. Cambridge,
    MA: Candlewick Press, 2007.
It Could Always Be Worse: A Yiddish Folk Tale
    by Margot Zemach. New York: Farrar,
    Straus & Giroux, 1976.
Johnny Appleseed: The Story of a Legend by Will
    Moses. New York: Puffin/Penguin,
    2001.

The King's Equal by Katherine Paterson. Illus. Vladimir Vagin. New York: HarperCollins, 1992.

Light by Jane Breskin Zalben. New York: Dutton/Penguin, 2007.

The Little Ant by David Novak. Illus. David Drotleff. St. Petersburg, FL: Riverbank Press, 1994.

The Little Match Girl by Christine San José. Illus. Kestutis Kasparavicius. Honesdale, PA: Boyds Mills Press, 2002.

The Little Match Girl by Hans Christian Anderson. Illus. Rachel Isadora. New York: Putnam, 1987.

The Little Red Hen by Barry Downard. New York: Simon & Schuster, 2004.

The Little Red Hen: An Old Fable retold by Heather Forest. Illus. Susan Gaber. Little Rock, AK: LittleFolk/August House, 2006.

The Loathsome Dragon retold by David Wiesner & Kim Kahng. New York: Clarion, 2005.

Mabela the Clever by Margaret Read MacDonald. Illus. Tim Coffey. Morton Grove, IL: Albert Whitman.

Mary Was a Little Lamb by Gloria Rand. Illus. Ted Rand. New York: Henry Holt, 2004.

The McElderry Book of Grimms' Fairy Tales by Saviour Pirotta & Emma Chichester Clark. New York: McElderry/Simon & Schuster, 2006.

Mufaro's Beautiful Daughters: An African Tale by John Steptoe: New York: Amistad/HarperCollins, 1987.

Over the Hills and Far Away retold by Chris Conover. New York: Farrar, Straus & Giroux, 2004.

Pájaro Verde by Joe Hayes. Illus. Antonio Castro. El Paso, TX: Cinco Puntos Press, 2002.

Red Butterfly: How a Princess Smuggled the Secret of Silk Out of China by Deborah Noyes. Illus. Sophie Blackall. Cambridge, MA: Candlewick Press, 2007.

Rip Van Winkle by Washington Irving. Illus. John Howe. New York: Little, Brown, 1988.

Rip Van Winkle's Return by Eric A. Kimmel. Illus. Leonard Everett Fisher. New York: Farrar, Straus & Giroux, 2007.

She'll Be Comin' 'Round the Mountain by Philemon Sturges. Illus. Ashley Wolff. New York: Little, Brown, 2004.

Sleeping Beauty by Christine San José. Illus. Dominic Catalano. Honesdale, PA: Boyds Mills Press, 1997.

The Stinky Cheese Man and Other Fairly Stupid Tales by Jon Scieszka. Illus. Lane Smith. New York: Viking/Penguin, 1992.

Strega Nona by Tomie dePaola. Englewood Cliffs, NJ: Prentice-Hall, 1975.

Sugar Cane: A Caribbean Rapunzel by Patricia Storace. Illus. Raul Colón. New York: Jump at the Sun/Hyperion, 2007.

The Three Armadillies Tuff by Jackie Mims Hopkins. Illus. S. G. Brooks. Atlanta: Peachtree, 2002.

The Three Pigs by David Wiesner. New York: Clarion, 2001.

The Three Snow Bears by Jan Brett. New York: Putnam/Penguin, 2007.

The True Story of the 3 Little Pigs! by Jon Scieszka. Illus. Lane Smith. New York: Scholastic, 1989.

The Twelve Dancing Princesses by Rachel Isadora. New York: Putnam/Penguin, 2007.

What's the Time, Grandma Wolf? by Ken Brown. Atlanta: Peachtree, 2001.

When Turtle Grew Feathers by Tim Tingle. Illus. Stacey Schuett. Atlanta: LittleFolk/August House, 2007.

Wolf! Wolf! by John Rocco. New York: Hyperion, 2007.

Zomo the Rabbit: A Trickster Tale from West Africa by Gerald McDermott. San Diego: Harcourt, 1992.

Appendix D
YA Literature for Content Area Reading

YA Literature for the Art Classroom

The Art of Keeping Cool by Janet Taylor Lisle. New York: Atheneum/Simon & Schuster, 2000.

The Astonishing Adventures of Fanboy and Goth Girl by Barry Lyga. Boston: Houghton Mifflin, 2006.

Better Than Running at Night by Hillary Frank. Boston: Houghton Mifflin, 2002.

The Blue Mirror by Kathe Koja. New York: Farrar, Straus & Giroux, 2004.

Dante's Daughter by Kimberley Heuston. Asheville, NC: Front Street, 2003.

The Day My Mother Left by James Prosek. New York: Simon & Schuster, 2007.

The Decoding of Lana Morris by Laura McNeal and Tom McNeal. New York: Knopf/Random House, 2007.

Drawing Lessons by Tracy Mack. New York: Scholastic, 2000.

Drawing the Ocean by Carolyn MacCullough. New Milford, CT: Roaring Brook Press, 2006.

Fair Has Nothing to Do with It by Cynthia Cotten. New York: Farrar, Straus & Giroux, 2007.

Girl with a Pearl Earring by Tracy Chevalier. New York: Dutton/Penguin, 2000.

Harley, Like a Person by Cat Bauer. Delray Beach, FL: Winslow Press, 2000.

Harley's Ninth by Cat Bauer. New York: Knopf/Random House, 2007.

How to Get Suspended and Influence People by Adam Selzer. New York: Delacorte/Random House, 2007.

I Am Rembrandt's Daughter by Lynn Cullen. New York: Bloomsbury, 2007.

Leonardo's Shadow: Or, My Astonishing Life as Leonardo da Vinci's Servant by Christopher Grey. New York: Atheneum/Simon & Schuster, 2006.

Love & SK8 by Nancy Krulik. New York: Simon Pulse/Simon & Schuster, 2004.

Paint by Magic by Kathryn Reiss. San Diego: Harcourt, 2002.

The Passion of Artemisia by Susan Vreeland. New York: Viking/Penguin, 2002.

Pieces of Georgia: A Novel by Jen Bryant. New York: Knopf/Random House, 2006.

Portraits: Of Flowers and Shadows by Anna Kirwan. New York: Scholastic, 2005.

Primavera by Mary Jane Beaufrand. New York: Little, Brown, 2007.

River Boy by Tim Bowler. New York: McElderry/Simon & Schuster, 2000.

Seeing Emily by Joyce Lee Wong. New York: Amulet/Harry N. Abrams, 2005.

Shark Girl by Kelly Bingham. Cambridge, MA: Candlewick Press, 2007.

Silk Umbrellas by Carolyn Marsden. Cambridge, MA: Candlewick Press, 2004.

Simon Says by Elaine Marie Alphin. San Diego: Harcourt, 2002.

Trash by Sharon Darrow. Cambridge, MA: Candlewick Press, 2006.

Trick of the Eye by Dennis Haseley. New York: Dial/Penguin, 2004.

The Wish House by Celia Rees. Cambridge, MA: Candlewick Press, 2006.

YA Literature for the Drama/Acting Classroom

Accidental Love by Gary Soto. Orlando, FL: Harcourt, 2006.

Act I, Act II, Act Normal by Martha Weston. New Milford, CT: Roaring Brook Press, 2003.

The Actual Real Reality of Jennifer James by Gillian Shields. New York: HarperCollins, 2006.

Birdland by Tracy Mack. New York: Scholastic, 2003.

Caught in the Act by Peter Moore. New York: Viking/Penguin, 2005.

Circle the Soul Softly by Davida Wills Hurwin. New York: HarperCollins, 2006.

Confessions of a Hollywood Star by Dyan Sheldon. Cambridge, MA: Candlewick Press, 2006.

Cyrano by Geraldine McCaughrean. Orlando, FL: Harcourt, 2006.

The Devil and His Boy by Anthony Horowtiz. New York: Philomel/Penguin, 2000.

Do-over by Rachel Vail. New York: HarperTrophy/HarperCollins, 2005.

Dramarama by E. Lockhart. New York: Hyperion, 2006.

Enter Three Witches: A Story of Macbeth by Caroline B. Cooney. New York: Scholastic, 2007.

Fame, Glory, and Other Things on My To Do List by Janette Rallison. New York: Walker, 2005.

Far from Normal by Kate Klise. New York: Scholastic, 2006.

Far Traveler by Rebecca Tingle. New York: Putnam, 2005.

A Heart Divided by Cherie Bennett and Jeff Gottesfeld. New York: Delacorte/Random House, 2004.

The Hollywood Sisters: Backstage Pass by Mary Wilcox. New York: Delacorte/Random House, 2006.

Horror at the Haunted House by Peg Kehret. New York: Puffin/Penguin, 2002.

Leap of Faith by Kimberly Brubaker Bradley. New York: Dial/Penguin, 2007.

Never Mind the Goldbergs by Matthue Roth. New York: PUSH/Scholastic, 2005.

Penelope Bailey Takes the Stage by Susanna Reich. Tarrytown, NY: Marshall Cavendish, 2006.

The Playmaker by J. B. Cheaney. New York: Knopf/Random House, 2000.

Pretty Things by Sarra Manning. New York: Dutton/Penguin, 2005.

Replay by Sharon Creech. New York: Cotler/HarperCollins, 2005.

Ruby Parker Hits the Small Time by Rowan Coleman. New York: HarperTempest/HarperCollins, 2007.

The Rules for Hearts: A Family Drama by Sara Ryan. New York: Viking/Penguin, 2007.

The Secret of the Rose by Sarah L. Thomson. New York: Greenwillow/HarperCollins, 2006.

Secrets of My Hollywood Life: A Novel by Jen Calonita. New York: Little, Brown, 2006.

The Shakespeare Stealer by Gary Blackwood. New York: Dutton/Penguin, 1998.

Shakespeare's Scribe by Gary Blackwood. New York: Dutton/Penguin, 2000.

Shakespeare's Spy by Gary Blackwood. New York: Dutton/Penguin, 2003.

Starring Miss Darlene by Amy Schwartz. New Milford, CT: Roaring Brook Press, 2007.

Talk by Kathe Koja. New York: Farrar, Straus & Giroux, 2005.

This Must Be Love by Tui T. Sutherland. New York: HarperCollins, 2004.

YA Literature for the Mathematics Classroom

All of the Above by Shelley Pearsall. New York: Little, Brown, 2006.

An Abundance of Katherines by John Green. New York: Dutton/Penguin, 2006.

Archer's Quest by Linda Sue Park. New York: Clarion, 2006.

Blue Noon by Scott Westerfeld. New York: EOS/HarperCollins, 2005.

Chasing Vermeer by Blue Balliett. Illus. Brett Helquist. New York: Scholastic Press.

Chicks with Sticks: It's a Purl Thing by Elizabeth Lenhard. New York: Dutton/Penguin, 2005.

The Curious Incident of the Dog in the Night-Time by Mark Haddon. New York: Doubleday, 2003.

Do the Math: Secrets, Lies, and Algebra by Wendy Lichtman. New York: Greenwillow/HarperCollins, 2007.

Evil Genius by Catherine Jinks. Orlando, FL: Harcourt, 2007.

Gregor and the Code of Claw by Suzanne Collins. New York: Scholastic, 2007.

Hannah, Divided by Adele Griffin. New York: Hyperion, 2002.

A Higher Geometry by Sharelle Byars Moranville. New York: Henry Holt, 2006.

Lawn Boy by Gary Paulsen. New York: Lamb/Random House, 2007.

The Lemonade War by Jacqueline Davies. Boston: Houghton Mifflin, 2007.

Magic or Madness by Justine Larbalestier. New York: Razorbill/Penguin, 2005.

Number 8 by Anna Fienberg. New York: Walker, 2007.

The Puzzling World of Winston Breen: The Secret in the Box by Eric Berlin. New York: Putnam/Penguin, 2007.

The Quantum July by Ron King. New York: Delacorte/Random House, 2007.

Spy X: The Code by Peter Lerangis. New York: Scholastic, 2004.

Sticks by Joan Bauer. New York: Putnam, 2002.

The Toothpaste Millionaire by Jean Merrill. Boston: Houghton Mifflin, 2006.

Travis and Freddy's Adventures in Vegas by Henry Johnson and Paul Hoppe. New York: Dutton/Penguin, 2006.

The Voyage of Patience Goodspeed by Heather Vogel Frederick. New York: Simon & Schuster, 2002.

World Team by Tim Vyner. Brookfield, CT: Roaring Brook Press, 2002.

The Wright 3 by Blue Balliett. Illus. Brett Helquist. New York: Scholastic, 2006.

Zimmerman's Algorithm by S. Andrew Swann. New York: Daw Books, 2000.

YA Literature for the Science Classroom

Alosha by Christopher Pike. New York: Tor, 2004.

Angel Isle by Peter Dickinson. New York: Lamb/Random House, 2007.

Born Again by Kelly Kerney. Orlando, FL: Harcourt, 2006.

Charlie's Raven by Jean Craighead George. New York: Dutton/Penguin, 2004.

Clone by Malcolm Rose. New York: Scholastic, 2002.

The Cloud Chamber by Joyce Maynard. New York: Atheneum/Simon & Schuster, 2005.

Cryptid Hunters by Roland Smith. New York: Hyperion, 2005.

Dante's Equation by Jane Jensen. New York: Ballantine/Random House, 2003.

The Dark Clone by Carol Matas. New York: Scholastic, 2005.

Darkwing by Kenneth Oppel. New York: EOS/HarperCollins, 2007.

Dusk by Susan Gates. New York: Puffin/Penguin, 2004.

Elephant Run by Roland Smith. New York: Hyperion, 2007.

Evolution, Me, and Other Freaks of Nature by Robin Brande. New York: Knopf/Random House, 2007.

Flash Point by Sneed B. Collard III. Atlanta: Peachtree, 2006.

Flush by Carl Hiaasen. New York: Knopf/Random House, 2005.

Flux by Beth Goobie. Victoria, BC: Orca, 2004.

Genesis Alpha by Rune Michaels. New York: Atheneum/Simon & Schuster, 2007.

Go Big or Go Home by Will Hobbs. New York: HarperCollins, 2008.

Green Boy by Susan Cooper. New York: McElderry/Simon & Schuster, 2002.

The House of the Scorpion by Nancy Farmer. New York: Atheneum/Simon & Schuster, 2002.

Initiation by Virginia Frances Schwartz. Markham, ON: Fitzhenry & Whiteside, 2003.

The Killing Sea by Richard Lewis. New York: Simon & Schuster, 2007.

The King in the Window by Adam Gopnik. New York: Hyperion, 2005.

Kissing the Bee by Kathe Koja. New York: Farrar, Straus & Giroux, 2007.

The Last Universe by William Sleator. New York: Amulet/Harry N. Abrams, 2005.

Little Fur: The Legend Begins by Isobelle Carmody. New York: Random House, 2006.

Maximum Ride. School's Out—Forever by James Patterson. New York: Little, Brown, 2006.

Monkey Town: A Story of the Scopes Trial by Ronald Kidd. New York: Simon & Schuster, 2006.

Peak by Roland Smith. Orlando, FL: Harcourt, 2007.

Peeps: A Novel by Scott Westerfeld. New York: Razorbill/Penguin, 2005.

Probability Moon by Nancy Kress. New York. Tor, 2000.

Ringside, 1925: Views from the Scopes Trial by Jen Bryant. New York: Knopf/Random House, 2008.

Sand Dollar Summer by Kimberly K. Jones. New York: McElderry/Simon & Schuster, 2006.

The Secret under My Skin by Janet McNaughton. New York. EOS/HarperCollins, 2005.

Sex Kittens and Horn Dawgs Fall in Love by Maryrose Wood. New York: Delacorte/Random House, 2006.

Sharp North by Patrick Cave. New York: Atheneum/Simon & Schuster, 2006.

Siberia: A Novel by Ann Halam. New York: Lamb/Random House, 2005.

Snatched by Pete Hautman and Mary Logue. New York: Putnam/Penguin, 2006.

Spirit Walker by Michelle Paver. New York: Tegen/Harper Collins, 2006.

Taking Wing by Nancy Price Graff. New York: Clarion, 2005.

Taylor Five by Ann Halam. New York: Lamb/Random House, 2004.

They Came from Below by Blake Nelson. New York: Tor, 2007.

Thunder from the Sea by Joan Hiatt Harlow. New York: McElderry/Simon & Schuster, 2004.

The Tree-sitter: A Novel by Suzanne Matson. New York: Norton, 2006.

Tribes by Arthur Slade. New York: Lamb/Random House, 2002.

YA Literature for the Music Classroom

6X: The Uncensored Confessions by Nina Malkin. New York: Scholastic, 2005.

Amalee by Dar Williams. New York: Scholastic, 2004.

Autobiography of My Dead Brother by Walter Dean Myers. Illus. Christopher Myers. New York: HarperTempest/HarperCollins, 2005.

Befiddled by Pedro de Alcantara. New York: Delacorte/Random House, 2005.

Beige by Cecil Castellucci. Cambridge, MA: Candlewick Press, 2007.

The Big Nothing by Adrian Fogelin. Atlanta: Peachtree, 2004.

Big Slick by Eric Luper. New York: Farrar, Straus & Giroux, 2007.

The Black Canary by Jane Louise Curry. New York: McElderry/Simon & Schuster, 2005.

Blind Faith by Ellen Wittlinger. New York: Simon & Schuster, 2006.

Born Blue by Han Nolan. Orlando, FL: Harcourt, 2001.

Born to Rock by Gordon Korman. New York: Hyperion, 2006.

Broken Song by Kathryn Lasky. New York: Viking/Penguin, 2005.

Candy by Kevin Brooks. New York: Scholastic, 2005.

Celeste's Journey: A Novel by Eleanora Tate. New York: Little, Brown, 2007.

Come Sing, Jimmy Jo by Katherine Paterson. New York: Dutton/Penguin, 2005.

Criss Cross by Lynne Rae Perkins. New York: Greenwillow/HarperCollins, 2005.

A Crooked Kind of Perfect by Linda Urban. Orlando, FL: Harcourt, 2007.

Define Normal: A Novel by Julie Anne Peters. New York: Little, Brown, 2000.

Disappearing Act by Sid Fleischman. New York: Greenwillow/HarperCollins, 2003.

Diva by Alex Flinn. New York: Harper Tempest/HarperCollins, 2006.

Emako Blue by Brenda Woods. New York: Putnam, 2004.

Fairest by Gail Carson Levine. New York: HarperCollins, 2006.

Fat Kid Rules the World by K. L. Going. New York: Putnam, 2003.

Fiddle Fever by Sharon Arms Doucet. New York: Clarion, 2000.

Firmament by Tim Bowler. New York: Simon & Schuster, 2004.

Fly on the Wall: How One Girl Was Everything by E. Lockhart. New York: Delacorte/Random House, 2006.

For Freedom: The Story of a French Spy by Kimberly Brubaker Bradley. New York: Delacorte/Random House, 2003.

Gathering Blue by Lois Lowry. Boston: Houghton Mifflin, 2000.

Gentle's Holler: A Novel by Kerry Madden. New York: Viking/Penguin, 2005.

Get Real by Betty Hicks. New Milford, CT: Roaring Brook Press, 2006.

Give Me Liberty by L. M. Elliott. New York: Tegen/HarperCollins, 2006.

Good Enough by Paula Yoo. New York: HarperCollins, 2008.

Guitar Girl by Sarra Manning. New York: Dutton/Penguin, 2004.

Hannah Waters and the Daughter of Johann Sebastian Bach by Barbara Nickel. Toronto, ON: Penguin Canada, 2005.

Harlem Hustle by Janet McDonald. New York: Foster/Farrar, Straus & Giroux, 2006.

Harlem Summer by Walter Dean Myers. New York: Scholastic, 2007.

In the Cards: Fame by Mariah Fredericks. New York: Atheneum/Simon & Schuster, 2008.

Jimi and Me by Jaime Adoff. New York: Jump at the Sun/Hyperion, 2005.

Just Listen. A Novel by Sarah Dessen. New York: Viking/Penguin, 2006.

Kat Got Your Tongue by Lee Weatherly. New York: Fickling/Random House, 2007.

The Last Days: A Novel by Scott Westerfeld. New York: Razorbill/Penguin, 2007.

LBD: Live and Fabulous by Grace Dent. New York: Putnam, 2005.

Lemonade Mouth by Mark Peter Hughes. New York: Delacorte/Random House, 2007.

Lucky Stars by Lucy Frank. New York: Atheneum/Simon & Schuster, 2005.

The Midnight Train Home by Erika Tamar. New York: Knopf/Random House, 2000.

Misfits, Inc. No. 5. The Protester's Song by Mark Delaney. Atlanta: Peachtree, 2001.

Mismatch: A Novel by Lensey Namioka. New York: Delacorte/Random House, 2006.

Mountain Solo by Jeanette Ingold. Orlando, FL: Harcourt, 2003.

My Life Starring Mum by Chloë Rayban. New York: Bloomsbury, 2006.

My Not-So-Terrible Time at Hippie Hotel by Rosemary Graham. New York: Viking/Penguin, 2003.

Nailed by Patrick Jones. New York: Walker, 2006.

Nick and Norah's Infinite Playlist by Rachel Cohn and David Levithan. New York: Knopf/Random House, 2006.

November Blues by Sharon Draper. New York: Atheneum/Simon & Schuster, 2007.

The Orpheus Obsession by Dakota Lane. New York: HarperCollins, 2005.

Paganini's Blanket by D. Dina Friedman. New York: Farrar, Straus & Giroux, 2006.

Pay the Piper by Jane Yolen and Adam Stemple. New York: Starscape/Tor, 2005.

Pepperland by Mark Delaney. Atlanta: Peachtree, 2004.

Play to the Angel by Maurine F. Dahlberg. New York: Farrar, Straus & Giroux, 2000.

Plastic Angel by Nerissa Nields. New York: Orchard/Scholastic, 2005.

Plastic Fantastic by Simon Cheshire. New York: Delacorte/Random House, 2005.

Pop Princess by Rachel Cohn. New York: Simon & Schuster, 2004.

The Queen's Soprano by Carol Dines. Orlando, FL: Harcourt, 2006.

Resurrection Blues by Mike Tanner. Toronto, ON: Annick Press, 2005.

The Return of Death Eric by Sam Llewellyn. New York: Walker, 2006.

Ricochet by Julie Gonzalez. New York: Delacorte/Random House, 2007.

The Rising Star of Rusty Nail by Lesley M. M. Blume. New York: Knopf/Random House, 2007.

Rock Star Superstar by Blake Nelson. New York: Viking/Penguin, 2004.

Rockbuster by Gloria Skurzynski. New York: Atheneum/Simon & Schuster, 2001.

Safe by Susan Shaw. New York: Dutton/Penguin, 2007.

Second Fiddle: Or How to Tell a Blackbird from a Sausage by Siobhán Parkinson. New Milford, CT: Roaring Brook Press, 2007.

Shadows on the Sea by Joan Hiatt Harlow. New York: McElderry/Simon & Schuster, 2003.

Shanghai Shadows by Lois Ruby. New York: Holiday House, 2006.

Singer in the Snow by Louise Marley. New York: Viking/Penguin, 2005.

The Singer of All Songs by Kate Constable. New York: Levine/Scholastic, 2004.

Singer of Souls by Adam Stemple. New York: Tor, 2005.

Sisterland by Linda Newbery. New York: Fickling/Random House, 2004.

Sky by Roderick Townley. New York: Atheneum/Simon & Schuster, 2004.

Sweet By and By by Patricia Hermes. New York: HarperCollins, 2002.

Tadpole by Ruth White. New York: Farrar, Straus & Giroux, 2003.

Things Hoped For by Andrew Clements. New York: Philomel/Penguin, 2006.

This Lullaby: A Novel by Sarah Dessen. New York: Viking/Penguin, 2002.

Tithe: A Modern Faerie Tale by Holly Black. New York: Simon & Schuster, 2002.

Torn by Stefan Petrucha and Thomas Pendleton. New York: HarperTeen/HarperCollins, 2007.

Troll Bridge: A Rock 'n' Roll Fairy Tale by Jane Yolen and Adam Stemple. New York: Starscape/Tor, 2006.

Under the Baseball Moon by John H. Ritter. New York: Philomel/Penguin, 2006.

Vandal by Michael Simmons. New Milford, CT: Roaring Brook Press, 2006.

Waiting for Normal by Leslie Connor. New York: Tegen/HarperCollins, 2008.

When the Black Girl Sings by Bil Wright. New York: Simon & Schuster, 2007.

Where in the World by Simon French. Atlanta: Peachtree, 2003.

Yellow Bird, Black Spider by Dosh Archer and Mike Archer. New York: Bloomsbury, 2004.

Wild Roses by Deb Caletti. New York: Simon & Schuster, 2005.

Appendix E
Literary Terms Glossary[*]

allegory
A story in verse or prose that can be read and interpreted at several levels; thus, it is related to the fable and the parable. Characters and events stand for abstract principles and ideas.

alliteration
A play upon words where beginning consonants or stressed syllables are repeated in prose or verse (e.g., Sally sells seashells . . .).

allusion
An indirect or implicit reference to another work of literature, art, event, or person to which the reader is likely to be familiar.

antagonist
The character in opposition to the protagonist in literary works of drama or fiction.

apostrophe
A figure of speech in which a person (either living or absent), a thing, idea, or place is addressed, as in Walt Whitman's "O, Captain! My Captain."

archetype
A model, considered a prototype, from which other similar things are patterned. S. E. Hinton's *The Outsiders*, Robert Cormier's *The Chocolate War*, and Robert Lipsyte's *The Contender* can be considered prototypes of the young adult problem novel.

assonance
The repetition of similar vowel sounds, usually close together, that achieve a particular effect.

autobiography
A biography of a person's life written by that person. The autobiography covers an individual's entire life span, whereas a memoir may focus on a particular time (e.g., a president may pen a memoir of his time in office).

ballad
A poem, usually of folk origin, that tells a story in song and was originally accompanied by dance. Contains stanzas and usually has a recurrent refrain.

biography
A biography of a person's life written by another person.

black humor
Humor that makes fun of serious topics such as death, murder, war, illnesses, and terrorism.

blank verse
Poetry that consists of unrhymed lines that are usually in iambic pentameter.

caesura
A pause in a line of poetry, either for natural rhythm or designated by punctuation.

characterization
A physical, emotional, and social description of a character in a text or on stage. Readers learn about characters through the character's words, words of other characters, and the author's narrative.

climax
The height of intensity in a story or play. Once the intensity, or crisis, is reached, a resolution, or ending, follows.

---

[*]Compiled by Daisy Burress.

closet drama
A play written for reading rather than performing. Also refers to plays that were intended to be performed but seldom are.

comic relief
Comic episodes or interludes, mainly in tragedy, used purposefully to lessen tension and build upon the tragic element by contrast.

concrete poetry
Poetry that conveys meaning through graphic alignment of letters, words, or symbols. Text is arranged in shapes and images that in some way explain or define the poem. Also known as pattern poetry.

conflict
The tension in a story or situation between and among characters and/or forces.

consonance
The repetition of consonant sounds before or after vowels (e.g., black, block).

courtly love
A relationship between a knight or courtier and a noblewoman who is usually married. The knight or courtier feigns indifference to protect her honor.

cyberpunk
A literary term denoting a subgenre of science fiction. Usually set in the near future, the story depends on technology and cultural references. Characters live in a world where no one is ordinary.

dénouement
The final events or events following the climax that resolve the plot.

dime novel
Melodramatic romance or adventure novels that were popular between 1860 and 1895. They were usually in paperback and cheap.

dramatic monologue
A speaker reveals his or her inner thoughts about a critical situation in a verse composition addressed to an imaginary audience.

dystopia
An imaginary place where the condition of life is dreadful and individuals are deprived, oppressed, and/or terrorized.

epic
An extended narrative poem on a grand scale celebrating praiseworthy acts of legendary warriors and heroes. Epics generally incorporate myths, legends, folklore, and history.

epistolary novel
A novel written in the form of letters.

fable
A short narrative, usually with animals personifying humans, that addresses a moral.

fairy tale
A work of literature dramatizing fortunes and misfortunes of legendary heroes and heroines, with a happily-ever-after ending. Fairy tales are part of the oral tradition.

farce
A work of drama with exaggerated action, highly improbable plots, unrealistic characters, and situations that often creates a humorous effect.

feminist criticism
Interpretative and descriptive efforts to show women's experiences as portrayed in literary works.

figurative language
Use of figurative speech such as metaphors, similes, or alliterations.

flashback
A scene or event inserted in a story that describes previous happenings for the purpose of clarifying or giving reason for a particular episode.

flat and round characters
A flat character remains the same throughout the story (e.g., Sleeping Beauty); a round character changes as the story develops.

folio
A book or manuscript made by folding a sheet of paper to form two or four pages.

folk tale
A story that originated in part from oral tradition.

foreshadowing
Suggestions or hints in a narrative that prepare the reader for events that follow.

free verse
A literary work that has no specific meter or line length and is read with natural speech rhythms.

futuristic
A literary work, events, or ideas that express a vision of the future.

gothic novel/fiction
A literary work descended from romance novels set in medieval times that depicts scenes of terror and horror; popular during the 18th and 19th centuries. Popular settings included dark castles, mansions, and dungeons.

haiku
A Japanese lyric verse of three unrhymed lines of five, seven, and five syllables. Haikus traditionally invoked an aspect of nature.

historical novel
A fictional narrative reconstructed creatively from historical events or times, sometimes including both historical and fictional characters.

hyperbole
A figure of speech exaggerated especially for effect of meaning, such as "This book weighs a ton."

imagery
The use of figurative language incorporated in a literary work to aid the reader in forming mental pictures of story elements. Figurative language may represent actions, feelings, objects, or ideas.

intertextuality
Authors borrow text and interweave the borrowed material and/or ideas into their work. A writer might incorporate borrowed ideas, themes, plots, text structure, and characters, for example.

limerick
A light, witty, senseless verse, sometimes bawdy. It usually consists of five anapestic rhyming lines (aabba).

magical realism
A genre in which magical elements appear in an otherwise realistic or "normal" setting.

metaphor
Figurative language in literary works in which one thing is described in terms of another (e.g., "a sea of troubles").

motif
A recurring or dominant theme in literary works that may be a character, image, or a verbal pattern.

myth
Myths concern the origins of the world and how the creatures in it came to exist. Mythical beings are generally sacred gods and heroes. Myths take place before recorded history.

new criticism
Criticism of literary works in which evaluative emphasis is placed more on the text than on the personality of the writer and historical aspects of the work.

new historicism
A historical method that considers the basis of a literary work to be a result of time, place, and circumstances.

nonfiction novel
A literary form established with Truman Capote's *In Cold Blood* in which a true account (nonfiction) is presented with fictional techniques.

novel-in-verse/verse novel
A novel that utilizes poetic elements. Common forms include free verse and blank verse. It may or may not be divided into chapters and may include sections of prose.

onomatopoeia
The formation of words such as *dong, crackle, moo, pop, whizz, whoosh,* and *zoom* that mimic the sound associated with the object or motion.

parody
An artistic work that imitates another work for an amusing effect.

personification
Inanimate objects or abstractions possessing human qualities.

pillow book
A commonplace book, probably originated in Japan, consisting of a compilation of notes, jotting, and writings, such as is found in extended diaries or journals.

plot
The plan, scheme, or pattern of events in a play, poem, or work of fiction.

poetic license
Liberty taken by writers to distort or twist the nature or meaning of language, or events, to acquire a desired form.

point of view
The narrator or character's perspective in a literary work, movie, or art form.

protagonist
The principal character, human or nonhuman, in a play or literary work.

reader-response theory
An approach to literature that emphasizes the reader's role in creating the meaning and experience of a literary work.

realism
The depiction of people, subjects, and events as they appear in everyday life.

roman noir
Originally used in France to describe the gothic novel. Today it is associated with a sensational form of the thriller genre characterized by violence and criminal behavior.

romanticism
A period of elevated emphasis on human sensibility and feelings and the human relationship with nature.

satire
A literary work in which human vice or folly is attacked through irony, derision, or wit.

sestet
A six-line stanza of varying meter and rhyme.

simile
A figure of speech in which one thing is likened to another. Likenesses are marked by the words *like, as, than,* or *resembles.*

slapstick
A vociferous form of comedy marked by physical action, buffoonery, and rough practical jokes.

sonnet
A 14-line verse form, usually in iambic pentameter, with one of many conventional rhyme patterns.

stream of consciousness
A literary technique that presents thoughts and feelings of a character as they develop.

thriller
A tense, exciting, suspenseful fiction novel, story, play, or movie that moves swiftly.

tone
An expression of attitude, especially toward the audience, reflected in a writer's work.

tour de force
A literary term expressing an outstanding accomplishment of a writer's skill and mastery of a work.

tragic flaw
A defect in the character of a leading actor or actress in a tragedy that leads to his or her ruin or destruction.

utopia
A perfect world, particularly in terms of social, political, and moral views.

verbal irony
Saying what one does not mean. Writers often use irony to create humor or for rhetorical effect.

vernacular
Language used in one's native country or locality.

voice
A unique manner of expression of the writer of a work. described by many writers as "personality."

Credits

Page 2 Courtesy of Tim Keating (top); 4 Courtesy of Lois Lowry; 5 Courtesy of Giselle Benatar; 6 Compliments Gettysburg College; 7 Courtesy of Constance Myers, 10 Courtesy of Beth Gwinn; 11 Courtesy of John Bauer; 11 Courtesy of Joyce Tenneson; 12 Courtesy of Joe Hobbs; 14 Courtesy of Bill Hitz; 16 Courtesy of Jim Lundquist; 17 Courtesy of Michael Nye; 17 Courtesy of Greg Harring; 19 Courtesy of Bronwyn Rennix; 22 Courtesy of Meredith French; 22 (bottom) Courtesy of Joanna Breitstien; 23 Courtesy of Jean Thesman; 25 Courtesy of Barbara Smith-Baker; 33 BananaStock/PictureQuest; 74 Courtesy of the NCAC; 104 Courtesy of Kelly Hall; 119 Courtesy of Kevin Brooks; 128 Courtesy of Alex Flinn; 139 Courtesy of Pete Hautman; 174 Courtesy of Sam Jackson; 178 Courtesy of Deb Caletti; 185 Courtesy of R. Gonzalez; 190 Jerry Bauer; 209 Courtesy of Carol Pierce; 210 Courtesy of Sara Krulwich; 243 Courtesy of Bart Ehrenberg; 252 Courtesy of Graham Salisbury; 256 Courtesy of Christopher Curtis; 262 Courtesy of Ruth White; 266 Courtesy of Will Hobbs; 298 Courtesy of Geoffrey Reiss; 300 Courtesy of Tom Strychacz; 305 Courtesy of Lois Duncan; 307 Courtesy of Joseph Steinmetz; 313

© 2006 Olivia Gatti; 316 Courtesy of Christopher Golden; 318 Courtesy of Tom Lascher; 327 Courtesy of Dan Cutrona; 349 Courtesy William Sleator; 356 Courtesy of Sonia Levitin; 359 Courtesy of James DeVita; 367 Courtesy of Suzanne Collins; 374 Courtesy of Adam Stemple; 375 Courtesy of Jane Yolen; 404 Courtesy of Carolyn Soto; 407 Courtesy of Karen Remy; 409 Courtesy of Steven Lubar; 422 Courtesy J. Patrick Lewis; 423 Courtesy of Ava Tramer; 429 Courtesy Helen Frost; 430 Courtesy of James D. Gabbard; 440 Courtesy of Aaron Levy; 469 Courtesy of Susan Bartoletti; 471 Courtesy of Jim Murphy; 474 Courtesy of Marina Budhos; 485(a) Courtesy of Jack Gantos; 514 Courtesy of Joan Kaywell; 526 Courtesy of Dave Thomas; 535 Courtesy of Shannon Hale; 541 Courtesy of Barry Furrow; 568 Courtesy of Beth Gwinn; 598 BananaStock/PictureQuest

Photos on the following pages are courtesy of Pam Cole: *iv, 2, 6, 7, 9, 10, 13* (top), *14* (top and bottom), *20, 21, 24, 27, 37, 40, 49, 51, 66, 99, 100, 108, 170, 180, 188, 194, 208, 251, 258* (top and bottom), *297, 319, 350, 366, 402, 420, 444, 485, 612*

Index